William Collins' dream of knowledge for all began with the publication of his first book in 1819. A self-educated mill worker, he not only enriched millions of lives, but also founded a flourising publishing house. Today, staying true to this spirit, Collins books are packed with inspiration, innovation, and practical expertise. They place you at the centre of a world of possibility and give you exactly what you need to explore it.

Language is the key to this exploration, and at the heart of Collins Dictionaries is language as it is really used. New words, phrases, and meanings spring up every day, and all of them are captured and analysed by the Collins Word Web. Constantly updated, and with over 2.5 billion entries, this living language resource is unique to our dictionaries.

Words are tools for life. And a Collins Dictionary makes them work for you.

Collins. Do more.

Collins Spanish Dictionary

HarperCollins Publishers
Westerhill Road
Bishopbriggs
Glasgow
G64 2QT
Great Britain

First Edition 2006

Reprint 10 9 8 7 6 5 4 3

ISBN 978-0-00-720887-6

www.collinslanguage.com

A catalogue record for this book is available from the British Library

Typeset by Wordcraft, Glasgow

Printed in Italy by Rotolito Lombarda S.p.A.

MANAGING EDITOR
Michela Clari

EDITORS
José Martin Galera
Wendy Lee
José María Ruiz Vaca
Cordelia Lilly

EDITORIAL COORDINATION
Maree Airlie
Joyce Littlejohn
Marianne Noble

SERIES EDITOR
Lorna Knight

Acknowledgements
We would like to thank those authors and publishers who kindly gave permission for copyright material to be used in the Collins Word Web. We would also like to thank Times Newspapers Ltd for providing valuable data.

ÍNDICE

CONTENTS

INTRODUCCIÓN

Estamos muy satisfechos de que hayas decidido comprar este diccionario y esperamos que lo disfrutes y que te sirva de gran ayuda ya sea en el colegio, en el trabajo, en tus vacaciones o en casa.

Esta introducción pretende darte algunas indicaciones para ayurdarte a sacar el mayor provecho de este diccionario; no sólo de su extenso vocabulario, sino de toda la información que te proporciona cada entrada. Esta te ayudará a leer y comprender – y también a comunicarte y a expresarte – en inglés moderno. Este diccionario comienza con una lista de abreviaturas utilizadas en el texto y con una ilustración de los sonidos representados por los símbolos fonéticos.

EL MANEJO DE TU DICCIONARIO

La amplia información que te ofrece este diccionario aparece presentada en distintas tipografías, con caracteres de diversos tamaños y con distintos símbolos, abreviaturas y paréntesis. Los apartados siguientes explican las reglas y símbolos utilizados.

ENTRADAS

Las palabras que consultas en el diccionario – las entradas – aparecen ordenades alfabéticamente y en color para una identificación más rápida. La palabra que aparece en la parte superior de cada página es la primera entrada (si aparece en la página izquierda) y la última entrada (si aparece en la página derecha) de la página en cuestión. La información sobre el uso o la forma de determinadas entradas aparece entre paréntesis, detrás de la transcripción fonética, y generalmente en forma abreviada y en cursiva

(p. ej.: (*fam*), (*Com*)). En algunos casos se ha considerado oportuno agrupar palabras de una misma familia (**nación, nacionalismo; accept, acceptance**) bajo una misma entrada que aparece en color.

Las expresiones de uso corriente en las que aparece una entrada se dan en negrita (p. ej.: **hurry:** [...] **to be in a ~**).

SÍMBOLOS FONÉTICOS

La transcripción fonética de cada entrada inglesa (que indica su pronunciación) aparece entre corchetes, inmediatamente después de la entrada (p. ej. **knife** [naif]). En las páginas xv-xviii encontrarás una lista de los símbolos fonéticos utilizados en este diccionario.

TRADUCCIONES

Las traducciones de las entradas aparecen en caracteres normales, y en los casos en los que existen significados o usos diferentes, éstos aparecen separados mediante un punto y coma. A menudo encontrarás también otras palabras en cursiva y entre paréntesis antes de las traducciones. Estas sugieren contextos en los que la entrada podría aparecer (p. ej.: **alto** (*persona*) o (*sonido*)) o proporcionan sinónimos (p. ej.: **mismo** (*semejante*)).

PALABRAS CLAVE

Particular relevancia reciben ciertas palabras inglesas y españolas que han sido consideradas palabras 'clave' en cada lengua. Estas pueden, por ejemplo, ser de utilización muy corriente o tener distintos usos (**de, haber; get, that**). La combinación de triángulos y números te permitirá distinguir las diferentes categorías gramaticales y los diferentes significados. Las indicaciones en cursiva y entre paréntesis proporcionan además importante información adicional.

FALSOS AMIGOS

Las palabras que se prestan a confusión al traducir han sido identificadas. En tales entradas existen unas notas que te ayudaran a evitar errores.

INFORMACIÓN GRAMATICAL

Las categorías gramaticales aparecen en forma abreviada y en cursiva después de la transcripción fonética de cada entrada (*vt, adv, conj*). También se indican la forma femenina y los plurales irregulares de los sustantivos del inglés (**child, -ren**).

INTRODUCTION

We are delighted that you have decided to buy this Spanish dictionary and hope you will enjoy and benefit from using it at school, at home, on holiday or at work.

This introduction gives you a few tips on how to get the most out of your dictionary – not simply from its comprehensive wordlist but also from the information provided in each entry. This will help you to read and understand modern Spanish, as well as communicate and express yourself in the language. This dictionary begins by listing the abbreviations used in the text and illustrating the sounds shown by the phonetic symbols.

USING YOUR DICTIONARY

A wealth of information is presented in the dictionary, using various typefaces, sizes of type, symbols, abbreviations and brackets. The various conventions and symbols used are explained in the following sections.

HEADWORDS

The words you look up in a dictionary – 'headwords' – are listed alphabetically. They are printed in **colour** for rapid identification. The headwords appearing at the top of each page indicate the first (if it appears on a left-hand page) and last word (if it appears on a right-hand page) dealt with on the page in question.

Information about the usage or form of certain headwords is given in brackets after the phonetic spelling. This usually appears in abbreviated form and in italics (e.g. (*fam*), (*Com*)).

Where appropriate, words related to headwords are grouped in the same entry (**nación, nacionalismo; accept, acceptance**) and are also in colour. Common expressions in which the headword appears are shown in a different bold roman type (e.g. **cola:** [...] **hacer ~**).

PHONETIC SPELLINGS

The phonetic spelling of each headword (indicating its pronunciation) is given in square brackets immediately after the headword (e.g. **cohete** [koˈete]). A list of these symbols is given on pages xv-xviii.

TRANSLATIONS

Headword translations are given in ordinary type and, where more than one meaning or usage exists, these are separated by a semi-colon. You will often find other words in italics in brackets before the translations. These offer suggested contexts in which the headword might appear (e.g. **fare** (*on trains, buses*) or provide synonyms (e.g. **litter** (*rubbish*) o (*young animals*)). The gender of the Spanish translation also appears in italics immediately following the key element of the translation, except where this is a regular masculine singular noun ending in 'o', or a regular feminine noun ending in 'a'.

KEY WORDS

Special status is given to certain Spanish and English words which are considered as 'key' words in each language. They may, for example, occur very frequently or have several types of usage (e.g. **de, haber; get, that**). A combination of triangles and numbers helps you to distinguish different parts of speech and different meanings. Further helpful information is provided in brackets and italics.

FALSE FRIENDS

Words which can be easily confused have been identified in the dictionary. Notes at such entries will help you to avoid these common translation pitfalls.

GRAMMATICAL INFORMATION

Parts of speech are given in abbreviated form in italics after the phonetic spellings of headwords (e.g. *vt*, *adv*, *conj*). Genders of Spanish nouns are indicated as follows: *nm* for a masculine and *nf* for a feminine noun. Feminine and irregular plural forms of nouns are also shown (**irlandés, esa; luz** (*pl* **luces**)).

ABREVIATURAS		ABBREVIATIONS
abreviatura	*ab(b)r*	abbreviation
adjetivo, locución adjetiva	*adj*	adjective, adjectival phrase
administración	*Admin*	administration
adverbio, locución adverbial	*adv*	adverb, adverbial phrase
agricultura	*Agr*	agriculture
anatomía	*Anat*	anatomy
Argentina	*Arg*	Argentina
arquitectura	*Arq, Arch*	architecture
el automóvil	*Aut(o)*	the motor car and motoring
aviación, viajes aéreos	*Aviac, Aviat*	flying, air travel
biología	*Bio(l)*	biology
botánica, flores	*Bot*	botany
inglés británico	BRIT	British English
Centroamérica	CAM	Central America
química	*Chem*	chemistry
comercio, finanzas, banca	*Com(m)*	commerce, finance, banking
informática	*Comput*	computing
conjunción	*conj*	conjunction
construcción	*Constr*	building
compuesto	*cpd*	compound element
Cono Sur	CS	Southern Cone
cocina	*Culin*	cookery
economía	*Econ*	economics
eletricidad, electrónica	*Elec*	electricity, electronics
enseñanza, sistema escolar y universitario	*Escol*	schooling, schools and universities
España	ESP	Spain
especialmente	*esp*	especially
exclamación, interjección	*excl*	exclamation, interjection
femenino	*f*	feminine
lengua familiar (! vulgar)	*fam(!)*	colloquial usage (! particularly offensive)
ferrocarril	*Ferro*	railways
uso figurado	*fig*	figurative use
fotografía	*Foto*	photography
(verbo inglés) del cual la partícula es inseparable	*fus*	(phrasal verb) where the particle is inseparable
generalmente	*gen*	generally
geografía, geología	*Geo*	geography, geology
geometría	*Geom*	geometry

ABREVIATURAS		ABBREVIATIONS
historia	*Hist*	history
uso familiar (! vulgar)	*inf(!)*	colloquial usage (! particularly offensive)
infinitivo	*infin*	infinitive
informática	*Inform*	computing
invariable	*inv*	invariable
irregular	*irreg*	irregular
lo jurídico	*Jur*	law
América Latina	*LAM*	Latin America
gramática, lingüística	*Ling*	grammar, linguistics
masculino	*m*	masculine
matemáticas	*Mat(h)*	mathematics
masculino/femenino	*m/f*	masculine/feminine
medicina	*Med*	medicine
México	*MÉX, MEX*	Mexico
lo militar, ejército	*Mil*	military matters
música	*Mús, Mus*	music
substantivo, nombre	*n*	noun
navegación, náutica	*Náut, Naut*	sailing, navigation
sustantivo numérico	*num*	numeral noun
complemento	*obj*	(grammatical) object
	o.s.	oneself
peyorativo	*pey, pej*	derogatory, pejorative
fotografía	*Phot*	photography
fisiología	*Physiol*	physiology
plural	*pl*	plural
política	*Pol*	politics
participio de pasado	*pp*	past participle
preposición	*prep*	preposition
pronombre	*pron*	pronoun
psicología, psiquiatría	*Psico, Psych*	psychology, psychiatry
tiempo pasado	*pt*	past tense
química	*Quím*	chemistry
ferrocarril	*Rail*	railways
religión	*Rel*	religion
Río de la Plata	*RPL*	River Plate
	sb	somebody
Cono Sur	*SC*	Southern Cone
enseñanza, sistema escolar y universitario	*Scol*	schooling, schools and universities
singular	*sg*	singular
España	*SP*	Spain
	sth	something

ABREVIATURAS		ABBREVIATIONS
sujeto	*su(b)j*	(grammatical) subject
subjuntivo	*subjun*	subjunctive
tauromaquia	*Taur*	bullfighting
también	*tb*	also
técnica, tecnología	*Tec(h)*	technical term, technology
telecomunicaciones	*Telec, Tel*	telecommunications
imprenta, tipografía	*Tip, Typ*	typography, printing
televisión	*TV*	television
universidad	*Univ*	university
inglés norteamericano	*US*	American English
verbo	*vb*	verb
verbo intransitivo	*vi*	intransitive verb
verbo pronominal	*vr*	reflexive verb
verbo transitivo	*vt*	transitive verb
zoología	*Zool*	zoology
marca registrada	®	registered trademark
indica un equivalente cultural	≈	introduces a cultural equivalent

SPANISH PRONUNCIATION

VOWELS

a	[a]	pata	not as long as *a* in far. When followed by a consonant in the same syllable (i.e. in a closed syllable), as in *a*mante, the *a* is short, as in bat
e	[e]	me	like *e* in they. In a closed syllable, as in gente, the *e* is short as in pet
i	[i]	pino	as in mean or machine
o	[o]	lo	as in local. In a closed syllable, as in control, the *o* is short as in cot
u	[u]	lunes	as in rule. It is silent after q, and in *gue*, *gui*, unless marked *güe*, *güi* e.g. antig*ü*edad, when it is pronounced like *w* in wolf

SEMIVOWELS

i, y	[j]	bien hielo yunta	pronounced like *y* in yes
u	[w]	huevo fuento antig*ü*edad	unstressed *u* between consonant and vowel is pronounced like *w* in well. See notes on *u* above.

DIPHTHONGS

ai, ay	[ai]	baile	as *i* in ride
au	[au]	auto	as *ou* in shout
ei, ey	[ei]	buey	as *ey* in grey
eu	[eu]	deuda	both elements pronounced independently [e] + [u]
oi, oy	[oi]	hoy	as *oy* in toy

CONSONANTS

b	[b,β]	boda bomba labor	see notes on *v* below
c	[k]	caja	*c* before *a*, *o*, *u* is pronounced as in cat
ce, ci	[θe,θi]	cero cielo	*c* before *e* or *i* is pronounced as in thin
ch	[tʃ]	chiste	*ch* is pronounced as *ch* in chair
d	[d,ð]	danés ciudad	at the beginning of a phrase or after *l* or *n*, *d* is pronounced as in English. In any other position it is pronounced like *th* in the

g	[g, ɣ]	gafas paga	*g* before *a*, *o* or *u* is pronounced as in *g*ap, if at the beginning of a phrase or after *n*. In other positions the sound is softened
ge, gi	[xe, xi]	gente girar	*g* before *e* or *i* is pronounced similar to *ch* in Scottish lo*ch*
h		haber	*h* is always silent in Spanish
j	[x]	jugar	*j* is pronounced similar to *ch* in Scottish lo*ch*
ll	[ʎ]	talle	*ll* is pronounced like the *y* in *y*et or the *lli* in mil*li*on
ñ	[ʃ]	niño	*ñ* is pronounced like the *ni* in o*ni*on
q	[k]	que	*q* is pronounced as *k* in *k*ing
r, rr	[r, rr]	quitar garra	*r* is always pronounced in Spanish, unlike the silent *r* in dance*r*. *rr* is trilled, like a Scottish *r*
s	[s]	quizás isla	*s* is usually pronounced as in pa*ss*, but before *b*, *d*, *g*, *l*, *m* or *n* it is pronounced as in ro*s*e
v	[b, β]	vía	*v* is pronounced something like *b*. At the beginning of a phrase or after *m* or *n* it is pronounced as *b* in *b*oy. In any other position the sound is softened
z	[θ]	tenaz	*z* is pronounced as *th* in *th*in

f, k, l, m, n, p, t and x are pronounced as in English.

STRESS

The rules of stress in Spanish are as follows:

(a) when a word ends in a vowel or in *n* or *s*, the second last syllable is stressed:
pa*ta*ta, pa*ta*tas; *co*me, *co*men

(b) when a word ends in a consonant other than *n* or *s*, the stress falls on the last syllable:
pa*red*, ha*blar*

(c) when the rules set out in (a) and (b) are not applied, an acute accent appears over the stressed vowel:
co*mún*, geogra*fí*a, in*glés*

In the phonetic transcription, the symbol [ˈ] precedes the syllable on which the stress falls.

LA PRONUNCIACIÓN INGLESA

VOCALES

	Ejemplo inglés	*Explicación*
[ɑː]	father	Entre *a* de padre y *o* de noche
[ʌ]	but, come	*a* muy breve
[æ]	man, cat	Con los labios en la posición de *e* en pena y luego se pronuncia el sonido *a* parecido a la *a* de carro
[ə]	father, ago	Vocal neutra parecida a una *e* u *o* casi muda
[əː]	bird, heard	Entre *e* abierta y *o* cerrada, sonido alargado
[ɛ]	get, bed	Como en perro
[ɪ]	it, big	Más breve que en *si*
[iː]	tea, see	Como en fino
[ɔ]	hot, wash	Como en torre
[ɔː]	saw, all	Como en por
[u]	put, book	Sonido breve, más cerrado que burro
[uː]	too, you	Sonido largo, como en *uno*

DIPTONGOS

	Ejemplo inglés	*Explicación*
[aɪ]	fly, high	Como en fr*ai*le
[au]	how, house	Como en p*au*sa
[ɛə]	there, bear	Casi como en v*ea*, pero el sonido *a* se mezcla con el indistinto [ə]
[eɪ]	day, obey	*e* cerrada seguida por una *i* débil
[ɪə]	here, hear	Como en man*ía*, mezclándose el sonido *a* con el indistinto [ə]
[əu]	go, note	[ə] seguido por una breve *u*
[ɔɪ]	boy, oil	Como en v*oy*
[uə]	poor, sure	*u* bastante larga más el sonido indistinto [ə]

CONSONANTES

	Ejemplo inglés	*Explicación*
[b]	**b**ig, lo**bb**y	Como en tum*b*an
[d]	men**d**e**d**	Como en con*d*e, an*d*ar
[g]	**g**o, **g**et, bi**g**	Como en *g*rande, *g*ol
[dʒ]	**g**in, **j**u**dg**e	Como en la *ll* andaluza y en Generalitat (*catalán*)
[ŋ]	si**ng**	Como en ví*n*culo
[h]	**h**ouse, **h**e	Como la jota hispanoamericana
[j]	**y**oung, **y**es	Como en *y*a
[k]	**c**ome, mo**ck**	Como en *c*aña, Es*c*ocia
[r]	**r**ed, t**r**ead	Se pronuncia con la punta de la lengua hacia atrás y sin hacerla vibrar
[s]	**s**and, ye**s**	Como en ca*s*a, *s*esión
[z]	ro**s**e, **z**ebra	Como en de*s*de, mi*s*mo
[ʃ]	**sh**e, ma**ch**ine	Como en *ch*ambre (*francés*), roxo (*portugués*)
[tʃ]	**ch**in, ri**ch**	Como en *ch*ocolate
[v]	**v**alley	Como *f*, pero se retiran los dientes superiores vibrándolos contra el labio inferior
[w]	**w**ater, **wh**ich	Como la *u* de h*u*evo, p*u*ede
[ʒ]	vi**s**ion	Como en *j*ournal (*francés*)
[θ]	**th**ink, my**th**	Como en re*c*eta, *z*apato
[ð]	**th**is, **th**e	Como en habla*d*o, verda*d*

f, l, m, n, p, t y x iguales que en español.

El signo [*] indica que la r final escrita apenas se pronuncia en inglés británico cuando la palabra siguiente empieza con vocal.
El signo [ˈ] indica la sílaba acentuada.

LOS NÚMEROS		NUMBERS
un, uno(a)	1	one
dos	2	two
tres	3	three
cuatro	4	four
cinco	5	five
seis	6	six
siete	7	seven
ocho	8	eight
nueve	9	nine
diez	10	ten
once	11	eleven
doce	12	twelve
trece	13	thirteen
catorce	14	fourteen
quince	15	fifteen
dieciséis	16	sixteen
diecisiete	17	seventeen
dieciocho	18	eighteen
diecinueve	19	nineteen
veinte	20	twenty
veintiuno	21	twenty-one
veintidós	22	twenty-two
treinta	30	thirty
cuarenta	40	forty
cincuenta	50	fifty
sesenta	60	sixty
setenta	70	seventy
ochenta	80	eighty
noventa	90	ninety
cien, ciento	100	a hundred, one hundred
ciento uno(a)	101	a hundred and one
doscientos(as)	200	two hundred
trescientos(as)	300	three hundred
cuatrocientos(as)	400	four hundred
quiniento(as)	500	five hundred
seiscientos(as)	600	six hundred
setecientos(as)	700	seven hundred
ochocientos(as)	800	eight hundred
novecientos(as)	900	nine hundred
mil	1000	a thousand
cinco mil	5000	five thousand
un millón	1000000	a million

LOS NÚMEROS	NUMBERS
primer, primero(a), 1°, 1er, (1^{a}, 1^{era})	first, 1st
segundo(a), 2° (2^{a})	second, 2nd
tercer, tercero(a), 3° (3^{a})	third, 3rd
cuarto(a), 4° (4^{a})	fourth, 4th
quinto(a), 5° (5^{a})	fifth, 5th
sexto(a), 6° (6^{a})	sixth, 6th
séptimo(a)	seventh
octavo(a)	eighth
noveno(a)	ninth
décimo(a)	tenth
undécimo(a)	eleventh
duodécimo(a)	twelfth
decimotercio(a)	thirteenth
decimocuarto(a)	fourteenth
decimoquinto(a)	fifteenth
decimosexto(a)	sixteenth
decimoséptimo(a)	seventeenth
decimoctavo(a)	eighteenth
decimonoveno(a)	nineteenth
vigésimo(a)	twentieth
trigésimo(a)	thirtieth
centésimo(a)	hundredth
milésimo(a)	thousandth

NÚMEROS QUEBRADOS ETC	FRACTIONS ETC
un medio	a half
un tercio	a third
un cuarto	a quarter
un quinto	a fifth
cero coma cinco, 0,5	(nought) point five, 0.5
tres coma cuatro, 3,4	three point four, 3.4
diez por cien(to)	ten per cent
cien por cien	a hundred per cent

EJEMPLOS	EXAMPLES
va a llegar el 7 (de mayo)	he's arriving on the 7th (of May)
vive en el número 7	he lives at number 7
el capítulo/la página 7	chapter/page 7
llegó séptimo	he came in 7th

N.B. In Spanish the ordinal numbers from 1 to 10 are commonly used; from 11 to 20 rather less; above 21 they are rarely written and almost never heard in speech.

LA HORA	**THE TIME**
¿qué hora es?	*what time is it?*
es/son	*it's o it is*
medianoche, las doce (de la noche)	midnight, twelve p.m.
la una (de la madrugada)	one o'clock (in the morning), one (a.m.)
la una y cinco	five past one
la una y diez	ten past one
la una y cuarto *or* quince	a quarter past one, one fifteen
la una y veinticinco	twenty-five past one, one twenty-five
la una y media *or* treinta	half-past one, one thirty
las dos menos veinticinco, la una treinta y cinco	twenty-five to two, one thirty-five
las dos menos veinte, la una cuarenta	twenty to two, one forty
las dos menos cuarto, la una cuarenta y cinco	a quarter to two, one forty-five
las dos menos diez, la una cincuenta	ten to two, one fifty
mediodía, las doce (de la tarde)	twelve o'clock, midday, noon
la una (de la tarde)	one o'clock (in the afternoon), one (p.m.)
las siete (de la tarde)	seven o'clock (in the evening), seven (p.m.)
¿a qué hora?	*(at) what time?*
a medianoche	at midnight
a las siete	at seven o'clock
en veinte minutos	in twenty minutes
hace quince minutos	fifteen minutes ago

VERBOS IRREGULARES EN INGLÉS

PRESENTE	PASADO	PARTICIPIO
arise	arose	arisen
awake	awoke	awoken
be (am, is, are; being)	was, were	been
bear	bore	born(e)
beat	beat	beaten
become	became	become
begin	began	begun
bend	bent	bent
bet	bet, betted	bet, betted
bid (*at auction, cards*)	bid	bid
bid (*say*)	bade	bidden
bind	bound	bound
bite	bit	bitten
bleed	bled	bled
blow	blew	blown
break	broke	broken
breed	bred	bred
bring	brought	brought
build	built	built
burn	burnt, burned	burnt, burned
burst	burst	burst
buy	bought	bought
can	could	(been able)
cast	cast	cast
catch	caught	caught
choose	chose	chosen
cling	clung	clung
come	came	come
cost (*be valued at*)	cost	cost
cost (*work out price of*)	costed	costed
creep	crept	crept
cut	cut	cut
deal	dealt	dealt
dig	dug	dug
do (does)	did	done
draw	drew	drawn
dream	dreamed, dreamt	dreamed, dreamt
drink	drank	drunk
drive	drove	driven
dwell	dwelt	dwelt
eat	ate	eaten
fall	fell	fallen
feed	fed	fed
feel	felt	felt
fight	fought	fought
find	found	found
flee	fled	fled
fling	flung	flung
fly	flew	flown
forbid	forbad(e)	forbidden
forecast	forecast	forecast
forget	forgot	forgotten
forgive	forgave	forgiven
forsake	forsook	forsaken
freeze	froze	frozen
get	got	got, (*US*) gotten
give	gave	given
go (goes)	went	gone
grind	ground	ground
grow	grew	grown
hang	hung	hung
hang (*suspend*) (execute)	hanged	hanged
have	had	had
hear	heard	heard
hide	hid	hidden
hit	hit	hit
hold	held	held
hurt	hurt	hurt
keep	kept	kept
kneel	knelt, kneeled	knelt, kneeled
know	knew	known
lay	laid	laid
lead	led	led
lean	leant,	leant,

PRESENTE	PASADO	PARTICIPIO	PRESENTE	PASADO	PARTICIPIO
	leaned	leaned	**shine**	shone	shone
leap	leapt,	leapt,	**shoot**	shot	shot
	leaped	leaped	**show**	showed	shown
learn	learnt,	learnt,	**shrink**	shrank	shrunk
	learned	learned	**shut**	shut	shut
leave	left	left	**sing**	sang	sung
lend	lent	lent	**sink**	sank	sunk
let	let	let	**sit**	sat	sat
lie (lying)	lay	lain	**slay**	slew	slain
light	lit,	lit,	**sleep**	slept	slept
	lighted	lighted	**slide**	slid	slid
lose	lost	lost	**sling**	slung	slung
make	made	made	**slit**	slit	slit
may	might	–	**smell**	smelt,	smelt,
mean	meant	meant		smelled	smelled
meet	met	met	**sow**	sowed	sown,
mistake	mistook	mistaken			sowed
mow	mowed	mown,	**speak**	spoke	spoken
		mowed	**speed**	sped,	sped,
must	(had to)	(had to)		speeded	speeded
pay	paid	paid	**spell**	spelt,	spelt,
put	put	put		spelled	spelled
quit	quit,	quit,	**spend**	spent	spent
	quitted	quitted	**spill**	spilt,	spilt,
read	read	read		spilled	spilled
rid	rid	rid	**spin**	spun	spun
ride	rode	ridden	**spit**	spat	spat
ring	rang	rung	**spoil**	spoiled,	spoiled,
rise	rose	risen		spoilt	spoilt
run	ran	run	**spread**	spread	spread
saw	sawed	sawed,	**spring**	sprang	sprung
		sawn	**stand**	stood	stood
say	said	said	**steal**	stole	stolen
see	saw	seen	**stick**	stuck	stuck
seek	sought	sought	**sting**	stung	stung
sell	sold	sold	**stink**	stank	stunk
send	sent	sent	**stride**	strode	stridden
set	set	set	**strike**	struck	struck
sew	sewed	sewn	**strive**	strove	striven
shake	shook	shaken	**swear**	swore	sworn
shear	sheared	shorn,	**sweep**	swept	swept
		sheared	**swell**	swelled	swollen,
shed	shed	shed			swelled

PRESENTE	PASADO	PARTICIPIO	PRESENTE	PASADO	PARTICIPIO
swim	swam	swum	**wear**	wore	worn
swing	swung	swung	**weave** (*on loom*)	wove	woven
take	took	taken			
teach	taught	taught	**weave** (*wind*)	weaved	weaved
tear	tore	torn	**wed**	wedded, wed	wedded, wed
tell	told	told			
think	thought	thought	**weep**	wept	wept
throw	threw	thrown	**win**	won	won
thrust	thrust	thrust	**wind**	wound	wound
tread	trod	trodden	**wring**	wrung	wrung
wake	woke, waked	woken, waked	**write**	wrote	written

PALABRA CLAVE

a [a] (*a + el = al*) *prep* **1** (*dirección*) to; **fueron a Madrid/Grecia** they went to Madrid/Greece; **me voy a casa** I'm going home
2 (*distancia*): **está a 15 km de aquí** it's 15 kms from here
3 (*posición*): **estar a la mesa** to be at table; **al lado de** next to, beside; *V tb* **puerta**
4 (*tiempo*): **a las 10/a medianoche** at 10/midnight; **a la mañana siguiente** the following morning; **a los pocos días** after a few days; **estamos a 9 de julio** it's the ninth of July; **a los 24 años** at the age of 24; **al año/a la semana** a year/week later
5 (*manera*): **a la francesa** the French way; **a caballo** on horseback; **a oscuras** in the dark
6 (*medio, instrumento*): **a lápiz** in pencil; **a mano** by hand; **cocina a gas** gas stove
7 (*razón*): **a 30 céntimos el kilo** at 30 cents a kilo; **a más de 50 km/h** at more than 50 kms per hour
8 (*dativo*): **se lo di a él** I gave it to him; **vi al policía** I saw the policeman; **se lo compré a él** I bought it from him
9 (*tras ciertos verbos*): **voy a verle** I'm going to see him; **empezó a trabajar** he started working *o* to work
10 (*+ infin*): **al verlo, lo reconocí inmediatamente** when I saw him I recognized him at once; **el camino a recorrer** the distance we *etc* have to travel; **¡a callar!** keep quiet!; **¡a comer!** let's eat!

abad, esa [a'βað, 'ðesa] *nm/f* abbot/abbess; **abadía** *nf* abbey

abajo [a'βaxo] *adv* (*situación*) (down) below, underneath; (*en edificio*) downstairs; (*dirección*) down, downwards; **el piso de ~** the downstairs flat; **la parte de ~** the lower part; **¡~ el gobierno!** down with the government!; **cuesta/río ~** downhill/downstream; **de arriba ~** from top to bottom; **el ~ firmante** the undersigned; **más ~** lower *o* further down

abalanzarse [aβalan'θarse] *vr*: **~ sobre** *o* **contra** to throw o.s. at

abanderado, -a [aβande'raðo] *nm/f* (*portaestandarte*) standard bearer; (*de un movimiento*) champion, leader; (*MÉX: linier*) linesman, assistant referee

abandonado, -a [aβando'naðo, a] *adj* derelict; (*desatendido*) abandoned; (*desierto*) deserted; (*descuidado*) neglected

abandonar [aβando'nar] *vt* to leave; (*persona*) to abandon, desert; (*cosa*) to abandon, leave behind; (*descuidar*) to neglect; (*renunciar a*) to give up; (*Inform*) to quit; **abandonarse** *vr*: **~se a** to abandon o.s. to; **abandono** *nm* (*acto*) desertion, abandonment; (*estado*) abandon, neglect; (*renuncia*) withdrawal, retirement; **ganar por**

abandono to win by default
abanico [aβa'niko] *nm* fan; (*Náut*) derrick
abarcar [aβar'kar] *vt* to include, embrace; (*LAM*: *acaparar*) to monopolize
abarrotado, -a [aβarro'taðo, a] *adj* packed
abarrotar [aβarro'tar] *vt* (*local, estadio, teatro*) to fill, pack
abarrotero, -a [aβarro'tero, a] (*MÉX*) *nm/f* grocer; **abarrotes** (*MÉX*) *nmpl* groceries; **tienda de abarrotes** (*MÉX, CAM*) grocery store
abastecer [aβaste'θer] *vt*: **~ (de)** to supply (with); **abastecimiento** *nm* supply
abasto [a'βasto] *nm* supply; **no dar ~ a** to be unable to cope with
abatible [aβa'tiβle] *adj*: **asiento ~** tip-up seat; (*Auto*) reclining seat
abatido, -a [aβa'tiðo, a] *adj* dejected, downcast
abatir [aβa'tir] *vt* (*muro*) to demolish; (*pájaro*) to shoot *o* bring down; (*fig*) to depress
abdicar [aβði'kar] *vi* to abdicate
abdomen [aβ'ðomen] *nm* abdomen; **abdominales** *nmpl* (*tb*: **ejercicios abdominales**) sit-ups
abecedario [aβeθe'ðarjo] *nm* alphabet
abedul [aβe'ðul] *nm* birch
abeja [a'βexa] *nf* bee
abejorro [aβe'xorro] *nm* bumblebee
abertura [aβer'tura] *nf* = **apertura**
abeto [a'βeto] *nm* fir
abierto, -a [a'βjerto, a] *pp de* **abrir** ▷ *adj* open
abismal [aβis'mal] *adj* (*fig*) vast, enormous
abismo [a'βismo] *nm* abyss
ablandar [aβlan'dar] *vt* to soften; **ablandarse** *vr* to get softer
abocado, -a [aβo'kaðo, a] *adj* (*vino*) smooth, pleasant
abochornar [aβotʃor'nar] *vt* to embarrass
abofetear [aβofete'ar] *vt* to slap (in the face)
abogado, -a [aβo'ɣaðo, a] *nm/f* lawyer; (*notario*) solicitor; (*en tribunal*) barrister (*BRIT*), attorney (*US*); **abogado defensor** defence lawyer *o* (*US*) attorney
abogar [aβo'ɣar] *vi*: **~ por** to plead for; (*fig*) to advocate
abolir [aβo'lir] *vt* to abolish; (*cancelar*) to cancel
abolladura [aβoʎa'ðura] *nf* dent
abollar [aβo'ʎar] *vt* to dent
abombarse [aβom'barse] (*LAM*) *vr* to go bad
abominable [aβomi'naβle] *adj* abominable
abonado, -a [aβo'naðo, a] *adj* (*deuda*) paid(-up) ▷ *nm/f* subscriber
abonar [aβo'nar] *vt* (*deuda*) to settle; (*terreno*) to fertilize; (*idea*) to endorse; **abonarse** *vr* to subscribe; **abono** *nm* payment; fertilizer; subscription
abordar [aβor'ðar] *vt* (*barco*) to board; (*asunto*) to broach
aborigen [aβo'rixen] *nmf* aborigine
aborrecer [aβorre'θer] *vt* to hate, loathe
abortar [aβor'tar] *vi* (*malparir*) to have a miscarriage; (*deliberadamente*) to have an abortion; **aborto** *nm* miscarriage; abortion
abovedado, -a [aβoβe'ðaðo, a] *adj* vaulted, domed
abrasar [aβra'sar] *vt* to burn (up); (*Agr*) to dry up, parch
abrazar [aβra'θar] *vt* to embrace, hug
abrazo [a'βraθo] *nm* embrace, hug; **un ~** (*en carta*) with best wishes
abrebotellas [aβreβo'teʎas] *nm inv* bottle opener
abrecartas [aβre'kartas] *nm inv* letter opener
abrelatas [aβre'latas] *nm inv* tin (*BRIT*) *o* can opener
abreviatura [aβreβja'tura] *nf* abbreviation
abridor [aβri'ðor] *nm* bottle opener;

(*de latas*) tin (BRIT) *o* can opener
abrigador, a [aβriɣa'ðor, a] (MÉX) *adj* warm
abrigar [aβri'ɣar] *vt* (*proteger*) to shelter; (*ropa*) to keep warm; (*fig*) to cherish
abrigo [a'βriɣo] *nm* (*prenda*) coat, overcoat; (*lugar protegido*) shelter
abril [a'βril] *nm* April
abrillantador [aβriʎanta'ðor] *nm* polish
abrillantar [aβriʎan'tar] *vt* to polish
abrir [a'βrir] *vt* to open (up) ▷ *vi* to open; **abrirse** *vr* to open (up); (*extenderse*) to open out; (*cielo*) to clear; **~se paso** to find *o* force a way through
abrochar [aβro'tʃar] *vt* (*con botones*) to button (up); (*zapato, con broche*) to do up
abrupto, -a [a'βrupto, a] *adj* abrupt; (*empinado*) steep
absoluto, -a [aβso'luto, a] *adj* absolute; **en ~** *adv* not at all
absolver [aβsol'βer] *vt* to absolve; (*Jur*) to pardon; (*: acusado*) to acquit
absorbente [aβsor'βente] *adj* absorbent; (*interesante*) absorbing
absorber [aβsor'βer] *vt* to absorb; (*embeber*) to soak up
absorción [aβsor'θjon] *nf* absorption; (*Com*) takeover
abstemio, -a [aβs'temjo, a] *adj* teetotal
abstención [aβsten'θjon] *nf* abstention
abstenerse [aβste'nerse] *vr*: **~ (de)** to abstain *o* refrain (from)
abstinencia [aβsti'nenθja] *nf* abstinence; (*ayuno*) fasting
abstracto, -a [aβ'strakto, a] *adj* abstract
abstraer [aβstra'er] *vt* to abstract; **abstraerse** *vr* to be *o* become absorbed
abstraído, -a [aβstra'iðo, a] *adj* absent-minded
absuelto [aβ'swelto] *pp de* **absolver**
absurdo, -a [aβ'surðo, a] *adj* absurd
abuchear [aβutʃe'ar] *vt* to boo
abuelo, -a [a'βwelo, a] *nm/f* grandfather(-mother); **abuelos** *nmpl* grandparents
abultado, -a [aβul'taðo, a] *adj* bulky
abultar [aβul'tar] *vi* to be bulky
abundancia [aβun'danθja] *nf*: **una ~ de** plenty of; **abundante** *adj* abundant, plentiful
abundar [aβun'dar] *vi* to abound, be plentiful
aburrido, -a [aβu'rriðo, a] *adj* (*hastiado*) bored; (*que aburre*) boring; **aburrimiento** *nm* boredom, tedium
aburrir [aβu'rrir] *vt* to bore; **aburrirse** *vr* to be bored, get bored
abusado, -a [aβu'saðo, a] (MÉX: *fam*) *adj* (*astuto*) sharp, cunning ▷ *excl*: **¡~!** (*inv*) look out!, careful!
abusar [aβu'sar] *vi* to go too far; **~ de** to abuse
abusivo, -a [aβu'siβo, a] *adj* (*precio*) exorbitant
abuso [a'βuso] *nm* abuse
acá [a'ka] *adv* (*lugar*) here
acabado, -a [aka'βaðo, a] *adj* finished, complete; (*perfecto*) perfect; (*agotado*) worn out; (*fig*) masterly ▷ *nm* finish
acabar [aka'βar] *vt* (*llevar a su fin*) to finish, complete; (*consumir*) to use up; (*rematar*) to finish off ▷ *vi* to finish, end; **acabarse** *vr* to finish, stop; (*terminarse*) to be over; (*agotarse*) to run out; **~ con** to put an end to; **~ de llegar** to have just arrived; **~ por hacer** to end (up) by doing; **¡se acabó!** it's all over!; (*¡basta!*) that's enough!
acabóse [aka'βose] *nm*: **esto es el ~** this is the last straw
academia [aka'ðemja] *nf* academy; **academia de idiomas** language school; **académico, -a** *adj* academic
acalorado, -a [akalo'raðo, a] *adj* (*discusión*) heated
acampar [akam'par] *vi* to camp
acantilado [akanti'laðo] *nm* cliff
acaparar [akapa'rar] *vt* to

monopolize; (*acumular*) to hoard
acariciar [akari'θjar] *vt* to caress; (*esperanza*) to cherish
acarrear [akarre'ar] *vt* to transport; (*fig*) to cause, result in
acaso [a'kaso] *adv* perhaps, maybe; **(por) si ~** (just) in case
acatar [aka'tar] *vt* to respect; (*ley*) obey
acatarrarse [akata'rrarse] *vr* to catch a cold
acceder [akθe'ðer] *vi*: **~ a** (*petición etc*) to agree to; (*tener acceso a*) to have access to; (*Inform*) to access
accesible [akθe'siβle] *adj* accessible
acceso [ak'θeso] *nm* access, entry; (*camino*) access, approach; (*Med*) attack, fit
accesorio, -a [akθe'sorjo, a] *adj, nm* accessory
accidentado, -a [akθiðen'taðo, a] *adj* uneven; (*montañoso*) hilly; (*azaroso*) eventful ▷ *nm/f* accident victim
accidental [akθiðen'tal] *adj* accidental
accidente [akθi'ðente] *nm* accident; **accidentes** *nmpl* (*de terreno*) unevenness *sg*; **accidente laboral** *o* **de trabajo/de tráfico** industrial/road *o* traffic accident
acción [ak'θjon] *nf* action; (*acto*) action, act; (*Com*) share; (*Jur*) action, lawsuit; **accionar** *vt* to work, operate; (*Inform*) to drive
accionista [akθjo'nista] *nmf* shareholder, stockholder
acebo [a'θeβo] *nm* holly; (*árbol*) holly tree
acechar [aθe'tʃar] *vt* to spy on; (*aguardar*) to lie in wait for; **acecho** *nm*: **estar al acecho (de)** to lie in wait (for)
aceite [a'θeite] *nm* oil; **aceite de girasol/oliva** olive/sunflower oil; **aceitera** *nf* oilcan; **aceitoso, -a** *adj* oily
aceituna [aθei'tuna] *nf* olive; **aceituna rellena** stuffed olive
acelerador [aθelera'ðor] *nm* accelerator
acelerar [aθele'rar] *vt* to accelerate
acelga [a'θelɣa] *nf* chard, beet
acento [a'θento] *nm* accent; (*acentuación*) stress
acentuar [aθen'twar] *vt* to accent; to stress; (*fig*) to accentuate
acepción [aθep'θjon] *nf* meaning
aceptable [aθep'taβle] *adj* acceptable
aceptación [aθepta'θjon] *nf* acceptance; (*aprobación*) approval
aceptar [aθep'tar] *vt* to accept; (*aprobar*) to approve; **~ hacer algo** to agree to do sth
acequia [a'θekja] *nf* irrigation ditch
acera [a'θera] *nf* pavement (BRIT), sidewalk (US)
acerca [a'θerka]: **~ de** *prep* about, concerning
acercar [aθer'kar] *vt* to bring *o* move nearer; **acercarse** *vr* to approach, come near
acero [a'θero] *nm* steel
acérrimo, -a [a'θerrimo, a] *adj* (*partidario*) staunch; (*enemigo*) bitter
acertado, -a [aθer'taðo, a] *adj* correct; (*apropiado*) apt; (*sensato*) sensible
acertar [aθer'tar] *vt* (*blanco*) to hit; (*solución*) to get right; (*adivinar*) to guess ▷ *vi* to get it right, be right; **~ a** to manage to; **~ con** to happen *o* hit on
acertijo [aθer'tixo] *nm* riddle, puzzle
achacar [atʃa'kar] *vt* to attribute
achacoso, -a [atʃa'koso, a] *adj* sickly
achicar [atʃi'kar] *vt* to reduce; (*Náut*) to bale out
achicharrar [atʃitʃa'rrar] *vt* to scorch, burn
achichincle [atʃi'tʃinkle] (MÉX: *fam*) *nmf* minion
achicoria [atʃi'korja] *nf* chicory
achuras [a'tʃuras] (RPL) *nfpl* offal *sg*
acicate [aθi'kate] *nm* spur

acidez [aθi'ðeθ] *nf* acidity
ácido, -a ['aθiðo, a] *adj* sour, acid ▷ *nm* acid
acierto *etc* [a'θjerto] *vb V* **acertar** ▷ *nm* success; (*buen paso*) wise move; (*solución*) solution; (*habilidad*) skill, ability
acitronar [aθitro'nar] (MÉX: *fam*) *vt* to brown
aclamar [akla'mar] *vt* to acclaim; (*aplaudir*) to applaud
aclaración [aklara'θjon] *nf* clarification, explanation
aclarar [akla'rar] *vt* to clarify, explain; (*ropa*) to rinse ▷ *vi* to clear up; **aclararse** *vr* (*explicarse*) to understand; **~se la garganta** to clear one's throat
aclimatación [aklimata'θjon] *nf* acclimatization
aclimatar [aklima'tar] *vt* to acclimatize; **aclimatarse** *vr* to become acclimatized
acné [ak'ne] *nm* acne
acobardar [akoβar'ðar] *vt* to intimidate
acogedor, a [akoxe'ðor, a] *adj* welcoming; (*hospitalario*) hospitable
acoger [ako'xer] *vt* to welcome; (*abrigar*) to shelter
acogida [ako'xiða] *nf* reception; refuge
acomedido, -a [akome'ðiðo, a] (MÉX) *adj* helpful, obliging
acometer [akome'ter] *vt* to attack; (*emprender*) to undertake; **acometida** *nf* attack, assault
acomodado, -a [akomo'ðaðo, a] *adj* (*persona*) well-to-do
acomodador, a [akomoða'ðor, a] *nm/f* usher(ette)
acomodar [akomo'ðar] *vt* to adjust; (*alojar*) to accommodate; **acomodarse** *vr* to conform; (*instalarse*) to install o.s.; (*adaptarse*): **~se (a)** to adapt (to)
acompañar [akompa'ɲar] *vt* to accompany; (*documentos*) to enclose
acondicionar [akondiθjo'nar] *vt* to arrange, prepare; (*pelo*) to condition
aconsejar [akonse'xar] *vt* to advise, counsel; **~ a algn hacer** *o* **que haga algo** to advise sb to do sth
acontecer [akonte'θer] *vi* to happen, occur; **acontecimiento** *nm* event
acopio [a'kopjo] *nm* store, stock
acoplar [ako'plar] *vt* to fit; (*Elec*) to connect; (*vagones*) to couple
acorazado, -a [akora'θaðo, a] *adj* armour-plated, armoured ▷ *nm* battleship
acordar [akor'ðar] *vt* (*resolver*) to agree, resolve; (*recordar*) to remind; **acordarse** *vr* to agree; **~ hacer algo** to agree to do sth; **~se (de algo)** to remember (sth); **acorde** *adj* (*Mús*) harmonious; **acorde con** (*medidas etc*) in keeping with ▷ *nm* chord
acordeón [akorðe'on] *nm* accordion
acordonado, -a [akorðo'naðo, a] *adj* (*calle*) cordoned-off
acorralar [akorra'lar] *vt* to round up, corral
acortar [akor'tar] *vt* to shorten; (*duración*) to cut short; (*cantidad*) to reduce; **acortarse** *vr* to become shorter
acosar [ako'sar] *vt* to pursue relentlessly; (*fig*) to hound, pester; **acoso** *nm* harassment; **acoso sexual** sexual harassment
acostar [akos'tar] *vt* (*en cama*) to put to bed; (*en suelo*) to lay down; **acostarse** *vr* to go to bed; to lie down; **~se con algn** to sleep with sb
acostumbrado, -a [akostum'braðo, a] *adj* usual; **~ a** used to
acostumbrar [akostum'brar] *vt*: **~ a algn a algo** to get sb used to sth ▷ *vi*: **~ (a) hacer** to be in the habit of doing; **acostumbrarse** *vr*: **~se a** to get used to
acotación [akota'θjon] *nf* marginal note; (*Geo*) elevation mark; (*de límite*) boundary mark; (*Teatro*) stage direction
acotamiento [akota'mjento] (MÉX)

nm hard shoulder (*BRIT*), berm (*US*)
acre ['akre] *adj* (*olor*) acrid; (*fig*) biting ▷ *nm* acre
acreditar [akreði'tar] *vt* (*garantizar*) to vouch for, guarantee; (*autorizar*) to authorize; (*dar prueba de*) to prove; (*Com: abonar*) to credit; (*embajador*) to accredit
acreedor, a [akree'ðor, a] *nm/f* creditor
acribillar [akriβi'ʎar] *vt*: **~ a balazos** to riddle with bullets
acróbata [a'kroβata] *nmf* acrobat
acta ['akta] *nf* certificate; (*de comisión*) minutes *pl*, record; **acta de matrimonio/nacimiento** (*MÉX*) marriage/birth certificate; **acta notarial** affidavit
actitud [akti'tuð] *nf* attitude; (*postura*) posture
activar [akti'βar] *vt* to activate; (*acelerar*) to speed up
actividad [aktiβi'ðað] *nf* activity
activo, -a [ak'tiβo, a] *adj* active; (*vivo*) lively ▷ *nm* (*Com*) assets *pl*
acto ['akto] *nm* act, action; (*ceremonia*) ceremony; (*Teatro*) act; **en el ~** immediately
actor [ak'tor] *nm* actor; (*Jur*) plaintiff ▷ *adj*: **parte ~a** prosecution
actriz [ak'triθ] *nf* actress
actuación [aktwa'θjon] *nf* action; (*comportamiento*) conduct, behaviour; (*Jur*) proceedings *pl*; (*desempeño*) performance
actual [ak'twal] *adj* present(-day), current

> No confundir **actual** con la palabra inglesa *actual*.

actualidad *nf* present; **actualidades** *nfpl* (*noticias*) news *sg*; **en la actualidad** at present; (*hoy día*) nowadays; **actualizar** [aktwali'θar] *vt* to update, modernize; **actualmente** [aktwal'mente] *adv* at present; (*hoy día*) nowadays

> No confundir **actualmente** con la palabra inglesa *actually*.

actuar [ak'twar] *vi* (*obrar*) to work, operate; (*actor*) to act, perform ▷ *vt* to work, operate; **~ de** to act as
acuarela [akwa'rela] *nf* watercolour
acuario [a'kwarjo] *nm* aquarium; (*Astrología*): **A~** Aquarius
acuático, -a [a'kwatiko, a] *adj* aquatic
acudir [aku'ðir] *vi* (*asistir*) to attend; (*ir*) to go; **~ a** (*fig*) to turn to; **~ a una cita** to keep an appointment; **~ en ayuda de** to go to the aid of
acuerdo *etc* [a'kwerðo] *vb V* **acordar** ▷ *nm* agreement; **¡de ~!** agreed!; **de ~ con** (*persona*) in agreement with; (*acción, documento*) in accordance with; **estar de ~** to be agreed, agree
acumular [akumu'lar] *vt* to accumulate, collect
acuñar [aku'ɲar] *vt* (*moneda*) to mint; (*frase*) to coin
acupuntura [akupun'tura] *nf* acupuncture
acurrucarse [akurru'karse] *vr* to crouch; (*ovillarse*) to curl up
acusación [akusa'θjon] *nf* accusation
acusar [aku'sar] *vt* to accuse; (*revelar*) to reveal; (*denunciar*) to denounce
acuse [a'kuse] *nm*: **~ de recibo** acknowledgement of receipt
acústica [a'kustika] *nf* acoustics *pl*
acústico, -a [a'kustiko, a] *adj* acoustic
adaptación [aðapta'θjon] *nf* adaptation
adaptador [aðapta'ðor] *nm* (*Elec*) adapter, adaptor; **adaptador universal** universal adapter *o* adaptor
adaptar [aðap'tar] *vt* to adapt; (*acomodar*) to fit
adecuado, -a [aðe'kwaðo, a] *adj* (*apto*) suitable; (*oportuno*) appropriate
a. de J.C. *abr* (= *antes de Jesucristo*) B.C.
adelantado, -a [aðelan'taðo, a] *adj* advanced; (*reloj*) fast; **pagar por ~** to pay in advance
adelantamiento [aðelanta'mjento]

nm (*Auto*) overtaking

adelantar [aðelan'tar] *vt* to move forward; (*avanzar*) to advance; (*acelerar*) to speed up; (*Auto*) to overtake ▷ *vi* to go forward, advance; **adelantarse** *vr* to go forward, advance

adelante [aðe'lante] *adv* forward(s), ahead ▷ *excl* come in!; **de hoy en ~** from now on; **más ~** later on; (*más allá*) further on

adelanto [aðe'lanto] *nm* advance; (*mejora*) improvement; (*progreso*) progress

adelgazar [aðelɣa'θar] *vt* to thin (down) ▷ *vi* to get thin; (*con régimen*) to slim down, lose weight

ademán [aðe'man] *nm* gesture; **ademanes** *nmpl* manners

además [aðe'mas] *adv* besides; (*por otra parte*) moreover; (*también*) also; **~ de** besides, in addition to

adentrarse [aðen'trarse] *vr*: **~ en** to go into, get inside; (*penetrar*) to penetrate (into)

adentro [a'ðentro] *adv* inside, in; **mar ~** out at sea; **tierra ~** inland

adepto, -a [a'ðepto, a] *nm/f* supporter

aderezar [aðere'θar] *vt* (*ensalada*) to dress; (*comida*) to season; **aderezo** *nm* dressing; seasoning

adeudar [aðeu'ðar] *vt* to owe

adherirse [aðe'rirse] *vr*: **~ a** to adhere to; (*partido*) to join

adhesión [aðe'sjon] *nf* adhesion; (*fig*) adherence

adicción [aðik'θjon] *nf* addiction

adición [aði'θjon] *nf* addition

adicto, -a [a'ðikto, a] *adj*: **~ a** addicted to; (*dedicado*) devoted to ▷ *nm/f* supporter, follower; (*toxicómano*) addict

adiestrar [aðjes'trar] *vt* to train, teach; (*conducir*) to guide, lead

adinerado, -a [aðine'raðo, a] *adj* wealthy

adiós [a'ðjos] *excl* (*para despedirse*) goodbye!, cheerio!; (*al pasar*) hello!

aditivo [aði'tiβo] *nm* additive

adivinanza [aðiβi'nanθa] *nf* riddle

adivinar [aðiβi'nar] *vt* to prophesy; (*conjeturar*) to guess; **adivino, -a** *nm/f* fortune-teller

adj *abr* (= *adjunto*) encl

adjetivo [aðxe'tiβo] *nm* adjective

adjudicar [aðxuði'kar] *vt* to award; **adjudicarse** *vr*: **~se algo** to appropriate sth

adjuntar [aðxun'tar] *vt* to attach, enclose; **adjunto, -a** *adj* attached, enclosed ▷ *nm/f* assistant

administración [aðministra'θjon] *nf* administration; (*dirección*) management; **administrador, a** *nm/f* administrator, manager(ess)

administrar [aðminis'trar] *vt* to administer; **administrativo, -a** *adj* administrative

admirable [aðmi'raβle] *adj* admirable

admiración [aðmira'θjon] *nf* admiration; (*asombro*) wonder; (*Ling*) exclamation mark

admirar [aðmi'rar] *vt* to admire; (*extrañar*) to surprise

admisible [aðmi'siβle] *adj* admissible

admisión [aðmi'sjon] *nf* admission; (*reconocimiento*) acceptance

admitir [aðmi'tir] *vt* to admit; (*aceptar*) to accept

adobar [aðo'βar] *vt* (*Culin*) to season

adobe [a'ðoβe] *nm* adobe, sun-dried brick

adolecer [aðole'θer] *vi*: **~ de** to suffer from

adolescente [aðoles'θente] *nmf* adolescent, teenager

adonde [a'ðonðe] *conj* (to) where

adónde [a'ðonde] *adv* = **dónde**

adopción [aðop'θjon] *nf* adoption

adoptar [aðop'tar] *vt* to adopt

adoptivo, -a [aðop'tiβo, a] *adj* (*padres*) adoptive; (*hijo*) adopted

adoquín [aðo'kin] *nm* paving stone

adorar [aðo'rar] *vt* to adore

adornar [aðor'nar] *vt* to adorn
adorno [a'ðorno] *nm* ornament; (*decoración*) decoration
adosado, -a [aðo'saðo, a] *adj*: **casa adosada** semi-detached house
adosar [aðo'sar] (*MÉX*) *vt* (*adjuntar*) to attach, enclose (*with a letter*)
adquiero *etc vb V* **adquirir**
adquirir [aðki'rir] *vt* to acquire, obtain
adquisición [aðkisi'θjon] *nf* acquisition
adrede [a'ðreðe] *adv* on purpose
ADSL *nm abr* broadband
aduana [a'ðwana] *nf* customs *pl*
aduanero, -a [aðwa'nero, a] *adj* customs *cpd* ▷ *nm/f* customs officer
adueñarse [aðwe'ɲarse] *vr*: **~ de** to take possession of
adular [aðu'lar] *vt* to flatter
adulterar [aðulte'rar] *vt* to adulterate
adulterio [aðul'terjo] *nm* adultery
adúltero, -a [a'ðultero, a] *adj* adulterous ▷ *nm/f* adulterer/ adulteress
adulto, -a [a'ðulto, a] *adj, nm/f* adult
adverbio [að'βerβjo] *nm* adverb
adversario, -a [aðβer'sarjo, a] *nm/f* adversary
adversidad [aðβersi'ðað] *nf* adversity; (*contratiempo*) setback
adverso, -a [að'βerso, a] *adj* adverse
advertencia [aðβer'tenθja] *nf* warning; (*prefacio*) preface, foreword
advertir [aðβer'tir] *vt* to notice; (*avisar*): **~ a algn de** to warn sb about *o* of
Adviento [að'βjento] *nm* Advent
advierto *etc vb V* **advertir**
aéreo, -a [a'ereo, a] *adj* aerial
aerobic [ae'roβik] *nm* aerobics *sg*; **aerobics** (*MÉX*) *nmpl* aerobics *sg*
aeromozo, -a [aero'moθo, a] (*LAM*) *nm/f* air steward(ess)
aeronáutica [aero'nautika] *nf* aeronautics *sg*
aeronave [aero'naβe] *nm* spaceship
aeroplano [aero'plano] *nm* aeroplane
aeropuerto [aero'pwerto] *nm* airport
aerosol [aero'sol] *nm* aerosol
afamado, -a [afa'maðo, a] *adj* famous
afán [a'fan] *nm* hard work; (*deseo*) desire
afanador, a [afana'ðor, a] (*MÉX*) *nm/f* (*de limpieza*) cleaner
afanar [afa'nar] *vt* to harass; (*fam*) to pinch
afear [afe'ar] *vt* to disfigure
afección [afek'θjon] *nf* (*Med*) disease
afectado, -a [afek'taðo, a] *adj* affected
afectar [afek'tar] *vt* to affect
afectísimo, -a [afek'tisimo, a] *adj* affectionate; **suyo ~** yours truly
afectivo, -a [afek'tiβo, a] *adj* (*problema etc*) emotional
afecto [a'fekto] *nm* affection; **tenerle ~ a algn** to be fond of sb
afectuoso, -a [afek'twoso, a] *adj* affectionate
afeitar [afei'tar] *vt* to shave; **afeitarse** *vr* to shave
afeminado, -a [afemi'naðo, a] *adj* effeminate
Afganistán [afɣanis'tan] *nm* Afghanistan
afianzar [afjan'θar] *vt* to strengthen; to secure; **afianzarse** *vr* to become established
afiche [a'fitʃe] (*RPL*) *nm* poster
afición [afi'θjon] *nf* fondness, liking; **la ~** the fans *pl*; **pinto por ~** I paint as a hobby; **aficionado, -a** *adj* keen, enthusiastic; (*no profesional*) amateur ▷ *nm/f* enthusiast, fan; amateur; **ser aficionado a algo** to be very keen on *o* fond of sth
aficionar [afiθjo'nar] *vt*: **~ a algn a algo** to make sb like sth; **aficionarse** *vr*: **~se a algo** to grow fond of sth
afilado, -a [afi'laðo, a] *adj* sharp
afilar [afi'lar] *vt* to sharpen

afiliarse [afi'ljarse] *vr* to affiliate
afín [a'fin] *adj* (*parecido*) similar; (*conexo*) related
afinar [afi'nar] *vt* (*Tec*) to refine; (*Mús*) to tune ▷ *vi* (*tocar*) to play in tune; (*cantar*) to sing in tune
afincarse [afin'karse] *vr* to settle
afinidad [afini'ðað] *nf* affinity; (*parentesco*) relationship; **por ~** by marriage
afirmación [afirma'θjon] *nf* affirmation
afirmar [afir'mar] *vt* to affirm, state; **afirmativo, -a** *adj* affirmative
afligir [afli'xir] *vt* to afflict; (*apenar*) to distress
aflojar [aflo'xar] *vt* to slacken; (*desatar*) to loosen, undo; (*relajar*) to relax ▷ *vi* to drop; (*bajar*) to go down; **aflojarse** *vr* to relax
afluente [aflu'ente] *adj* flowing ▷ *nm* tributary
afmo, -a *abr* (= *afectísimo(a) suyo(a)*) Yours
afónico, -a [a'foniko, a] *adj*: **estar ~** to have a sore throat; to have lost one's voice
aforo [a'foro] *nm* (*de teatro etc*) capacity
afortunado, -a [afortu'naðo, a] *adj* fortunate, lucky
África ['afrika] *nf* Africa; **África del Sur** South Africa; **africano, -a** *adj, nm/f* African
afrontar [afron'tar] *vt* to confront; (*poner cara a cara*) to bring face to face
afrutado, -a [afru'taðo, a] *adj* fruity
after ['after] (*pl* **~s**) *nm* after-hours club; **afterhours** [after'aurs] *nm inv* = **after**
afuera [a'fwera] *adv* out, outside; **afueras** *nfpl* outskirts
agachar [aɣa'tʃar] *vt* to bend, bow; **agacharse** *vr* to stoop, bend
agalla [a'ɣaʎa] *nf* (*Zool*) gill; **tener ~s** (*fam*) to have guts
agarradera [aɣarra'ðera] (*MÉX*) *nf* handle
agarrado, -a [aɣa'rraðo, a] *adj* mean, stingy
agarrar [aɣa'rrar] *vt* to grasp, grab; (*LAM*: *tomar*) to take, catch; (*recoger*) to pick up ▷ *vi* (*planta*) to take root; **agarrarse** *vr* to hold on (tightly)
agencia [a'xenθja] *nf* agency; **agencia de viajes** travel agency; **agencia inmobiliaria** estate (*BRIT*) *o* real estate (*US*) agent's (office)
agenciarse [axen'θjarse] *vr* to obtain, procure
agenda [a'xenda] *nf* diary; **~ electronica** PDA

> No confundir **agenda** con la palabra inglesa *agenda*.

agente [a'xente] *nmf* agent; (*tb*: **~ de policía**) policeman/policewoman; **agente de seguros** insurance agent; **agente de tránsito** (*MÉX*) traffic cop; **agente inmobiliario** estate agent (*BRIT*), realtor (*US*)
ágil ['axil] *adj* agile, nimble; **agilidad** *nf* agility, nimbleness
agilizar [axili'θar] *vt* (*trámites*) to speed up
agiotista [axjo'tista] (*MÉX*) *nmf* (*usurero*) usurer
agitación [axita'θjon] *nf* (*de mano etc*) shaking, waving; (*de líquido etc*) stirring; (*fig*) agitation
agitado, -a [axi'aðo, a] *adj* hectic; (*viaje*) bumpy
agitar [axi'tar] *vt* to wave, shake; (*líquido*) to stir; (*fig*) to stir up, excite; **agitarse** *vr* to get excited; (*inquietarse*) to get worried *o* upset
aglomeración [aɣlomera'θjon] *nf* agglomeration; **aglomeración de gente/tráfico** mass of people/traffic jam
agnóstico, -a [aɣ'nostiko, a] *adj, nm/f* agnostic
agobiar [aɣo'βjar] *vt* to weigh down; (*oprimir*) to oppress; (*cargar*) to burden
agolparse [aɣol'parse] *vr* to crowd together
agonía [aɣo'nia] *nf* death throes *pl*;

(*fig*) agony, anguish
agonizante [aɣoni'θante] *adj* dying
agonizar [aɣoni'θar] *vi* to be dying
agosto [a'ɣosto] *nm* August
agotado, -a [aɣo'taðo, a] *adj* (*persona*) exhausted; (*libros*) out of print; (*acabado*) finished; (*Com*) sold out; **agotador, a** [aɣota'ðor, a] *adj* exhausting
agotamiento [aɣota'mjento] *nm* exhaustion
agotar [aɣo'tar] *vt* to exhaust; (*consumir*) to drain; (*recursos*) to use up, deplete; **agotarse** *vr* to be exhausted; (*acabarse*) to run out; (*libro*) to go out of print
agraciado, -a [aɣra'θjaðo, a] *adj* (*atractivo*) attractive; (*en sorteo etc*) lucky
agradable [aɣra'ðaβle] *adj* pleasant, nice
agradar [aɣra'ðar] *vt*: **él me agrada** I like him
agradecer [aɣraðe'θer] *vt* to thank; (*favor etc*) to be grateful for; **agradecido, -a** *adj* grateful; **¡muy agradecido!** thanks a lot!; **agradecimiento** *nm* thanks *pl*; gratitude
agradezco *etc vb V* **agradecer**
agrado [a'ɣraðo] *nm*: **ser de tu** *etc* **~** to be to your *etc* liking
agrandar [aɣran'dar] *vt* to enlarge; (*fig*) to exaggerate; **agrandarse** *vr* to get bigger
agrario, -a [a'ɣrarjo, a] *adj* agrarian, land *cpd*; (*política*) agricultural, farming
agravante [aɣra'βante] *adj* aggravating ▷ *nm*: **con el ~ de que ...** with the further difficulty that ...
agravar [aɣra'βar] *vt* (*pesar sobre*) to make heavier; (*irritar*) to aggravate; **agravarse** *vr* to worsen, get worse
agraviar [aɣra'βjar] *vt* to offend; (*ser injusto con*) to wrong
agredir [aɣre'ðir] *vt* to attack
agregado, -a [aɣre'ɣaðo, a] *nm/f*: **A~** ≈ teacher (*who is not head of department*) ▷ *nm* aggregate; (*persona*) attaché
agregar [aɣre'ɣar] *vt* to gather; (*añadir*) to add; (*persona*) to appoint
agresión [aɣre'sjon] *nf* aggression
agresivo, -a [aɣre'siβo, a] *adj* aggressive
agriar [a'ɣrjar] *vt* to (turn) sour
agrícola [a'ɣrikola] *adj* farming *cpd*, agricultural
agricultor, a [aɣrikul'tor, a] *nm/f* farmer
agricultura [aɣrikul'tura] *nf* agriculture, farming
agridulce [aɣri'ðulθe] *adj* bittersweet; (*Culin*) sweet and sour
agrietarse [aɣrje'tarse] *vr* to crack; (*piel*) to chap
agrio, -a ['aɣrjo, a] *adj* bitter
agrupación [aɣrupa'θjon] *nf* group; (*acto*) grouping
agrupar [aɣru'par] *vt* to group
agua ['aɣwa] *nf* water; (*Náut*) wake; (*Arq*) slope of a roof; **aguas** *nfpl* (*de piedra*) water *sg*, sparkle *sg*; (*Med*) water *sg*, urine *sg*; (*Náut*) waters; **agua bendita/destilada/potable** holy/distilled/drinking water; **agua caliente** hot water; **agua corriente** running water; **agua de colonia** eau de cologne; **agua mineral (con/sin gas)** (sparkling/still) mineral water; **agua oxigenada** hydrogen peroxide; **aguas abajo/arriba** downstream/upstream; **aguas jurisdiccionales** territorial waters
aguacate [aɣwa'kate] *nm* avocado (pear)
aguacero [aɣwa'θero] *nm* (heavy) shower, downpour
aguado, -a [a'ɣwaðo, a] *adj* watery, watered down
aguafiestas [aɣwa'fjestas] *nmf inv* spoilsport, killjoy
aguamiel [aɣwa'mjel] (MÉX) *nf* fermented maguey *o* agave juice
aguanieve [aɣwa'njeβe] *nf* sleet
aguantar [aɣwan'tar] *vt* to bear, put up with; (*sostener*) to hold up ▷ *vi* to

last; **aguantarse** *vr* to restrain o.s.; **aguante** *nm* (*paciencia*) patience; (*resistencia*) endurance

aguar [a'ɣwar] *vt* to water down

aguardar [aɣwar'ðar] *vt* to wait for

aguardiente [aɣwar'ðjente] *nm* brandy, liquor

aguarrás [aɣwa'rras] *nm* turpentine

aguaviva [aɣwa'biβa] (RPL) *nf* jellyfish

agudeza [aɣu'ðeθa] *nf* sharpness; (*ingenio*) wit

agudo, -a [a'ɣuðo, a] *adj* sharp; (*voz*) high-pitched, piercing; (*dolor, enfermedad*) acute

agüero [a'ɣwero] *nm*: **buen/mal ~** good/bad omen

aguijón [aɣi'xon] *nm* sting; (*fig*) spur

águila ['aɣila] *nf* eagle; (*fig*) genius

aguileño, -a [aɣi'leɲo, a] *adj* (*nariz*) aquiline; (*rostro*) sharp-featured

aguinaldo [aɣi'naldo] *nm* Christmas box

aguja [a'ɣuxa] *nf* needle; (*de reloj*) hand; (*Arq*) spire; (*Tec*) firing-pin; **agujas** *nfpl* (*Zool*) ribs; (*Ferro*) points

agujerear [aɣuxere'ar] *vt* to make holes in

agujero [aɣu'xero] *nm* hole

agujetas [aɣu'xetas] *nfpl* stitch *sg*; (*rigidez*) stiffness *sg*

ahí [a'i] *adv* there; **de ~ que** so that, with the result that; **~ llega** here he comes; **por ~** that way; (*allá*) over there; **200 o por ~** 200 or so

ahijado, -a [ai'xaðo, a] *nm/f* godson/daughter

ahogar [ao'ɣar] *vt* to drown; (*asfixiar*) to suffocate, smother; (*fuego*) to put out; **ahogarse** *vr* (*en el agua*) to drown; (*por asfixia*) to suffocate

ahogo [a'oɣo] *nm* breathlessness; (*fig*) financial difficulty

ahondar [aon'dar] *vt* to deepen, make deeper; (*fig*) to study thoroughly ▷ *vi*: **~ en** to study thoroughly

ahora [a'ora] *adv* now; (*hace poco*) a moment ago, just now; (*dentro de poco*) in a moment; **~ voy** I'm coming; **~ mismo** right now; **~ bien** now then; **por ~** for the present

ahorcar [aor'kar] *vt* to hang

ahorita [ao'rita] (*fam*) *adv* (LAM: *en este momento*) right now; (MÉX: *hace poco*) just now; (: *dentro de poco*) in a minute

ahorrar [ao'rrar] *vt* (*dinero*) to save; (*esfuerzos*) to save, avoid; **ahorro** *nm* (*acto*) saving; **ahorros** *nmpl* (*dinero*) savings

ahuecar [awe'kar] *vt* to hollow (out); (*voz*) to deepen; **ahuecarse** *vr* to give o.s. airs

ahumar [au'mar] *vt* to smoke, cure; (*llenar de humo*) to fill with smoke ▷ *vi* to smoke; **ahumarse** *vr* to fill with smoke

ahuyentar [aujen'tar] *vt* to drive off, frighten off; (*fig*) to dispel

aire ['aire] *nm* air; (*viento*) wind; (*corriente*) draught; (*Mús*) tune; **al ~ libre** in the open air; **aire acondicionado** air conditioning; **airear** *vt* to air; **airearse** *vr* (*persona*) to go out for a breath of fresh air; **airoso, -a** *adj* windy; draughty; (*fig*) graceful

aislado, -a [ais'laðo, a] *adj* isolated; (*incomunicado*) cut-off; (*Elec*) insulated

aislar [ais'lar] *vt* to isolate; (*Elec*) to insulate

ajardinado, -a [axarði'naðo, a] *adj* landscaped

ajedrez [axe'ðreθ] *nm* chess

ajeno, -a [a'xeno, a] *adj* (*que pertenece a otro*) somebody else's; **~ a** foreign to

ajetreado, -a [axetre'aðo, a] *adj* busy

ajetreo [axe'treo] *nm* bustle

ají [a'xi] (CS) *nm* chil(l)i, red pepper; (*salsa*) chil(l)i sauce

ajillo [a'xiʎo] *nm*: **gambas al ~** garlic prawns

ajo ['axo] *nm* garlic

ajuar [a'xwar] *nm* household

furnishings *pl*; (*de novia*) trousseau; (*de niño*) layette

ajustado, -a [axus'taðo, a] *adj* (*tornillo*) tight; (*cálculo*) right; (*ropa*) tight(-fitting); (*resultado*) close

ajustar [axus'tar] *vt* (*adaptar*) to adjust; (*encajar*) to fit; (*Tec*) to engage; (*Imprenta*) to make up; (*apretar*) to tighten; (*concertar*) to agree (on); (*reconciliar*) to reconcile; (*cuentas, deudas*) to settle ▷ *vi* to fit; **ajustarse** *vr*: **~se a** (*precio etc*) to be in keeping with, fit in with; **~ las cuentas a algn** to get even with sb

ajuste [a'xuste] *nm* adjustment; (*Costura*) fitting; (*acuerdo*) compromise; (*de cuenta*) settlement

al [al] = **a + el**; *V* **a**

ala ['ala] *nf* wing; (*de sombrero*) brim; winger; **ala delta** *nf* hang-glider

alabanza [ala'βanθa] *nf* praise

alabar [ala'βar] *vt* to praise

alacena [ala'θena] *nf* kitchen cupboard (BRIT) *o* closet (US)

alacrán [ala'kran] *nm* scorpion

alambrada [alam'braða] *nf* wire fence; (*red*) wire netting

alambre [a'lambre] *nm* wire; **alambre de púas** barbed wire

alameda [ala'meða] *nf* (*plantío*) poplar grove; (*lugar de paseo*) avenue, boulevard

álamo ['alamo] *nm* poplar

alarde [a'larðe] *nm* show, display; **hacer ~ de** to boast of

alargador [alarɣa'ðor] *nm* (*Elec*) extension lead

alargar [alar'ɣar] *vt* to lengthen, extend; (*paso*) to hasten; (*brazo*) to stretch out; (*cuerda*) to pay out; (*conversación*) to spin out; **alargarse** *vr* to get longer

alarma [a'larma] *nf* alarm; **alarma de incendios** fire alarm; **alarmar** *vt* to alarm; **alarmarse** to get alarmed; **alarmante** [alar'mante] *adj* alarming

alba ['alβa] *nf* dawn

albahaca [al'βaka] *nf* basil

Albania [al'βanja] *nf* Albania

albañil [alβa'ɲil] *nm* bricklayer; (*cantero*) mason

albarán [alβa'ran] *nm* (*Com*) delivery note, invoice

albaricoque [alβari'koke] *nm* apricot

albedrío [alβe'ðrio] *nm*: **libre ~** free will

alberca [al'βerka] *nf* reservoir; (MÉX: *piscina*) swimming pool

albergar [alβer'ɣar] *vt* to shelter

albergue *etc* [al'βerɣe] *vb V* **albergar** ▷ *nm* shelter, refuge; **albergue juvenil** youth hostel

albóndiga [al'βondiɣa] *nf* meatball

albornoz [alβor'noθ] *nm* (*de los árabes*) burnous; (*para el baño*) bathrobe

alborotar [alβoro'tar] *vi* to make a row ▷ *vt* to agitate, stir up; **alborotarse** *vr* to get excited; (*mar*) to get rough; **alboroto** *nm* row, uproar

álbum ['alβum] (*pl* **~s, ~es**) *nm* album; **álbum de recortes** scrapbook

albur [al'βur] (MÉX) *nm* (*juego de palabras*) pun; (*doble sentido*) double entendre

alcachofa [alka'tʃofa] *nf* artichoke

alcalde, -esa [al'kalde, esa] *nm/f* mayor(ess)

alcaldía [alkal'dia] *nf* mayoralty; (*lugar*) mayor's office

alcance *etc* [al'kanθe] *vb V* **alcanzar** ▷ *nm* reach; (*Com*) adverse balance; **al ~ de algn** available to sb

alcancía [alkan'θia] (LAM) *nf* (*para ahorrar*) money box; (*para colectas*) collection box

alcantarilla [alkanta'riʎa] *nf* (*de aguas cloacales*) sewer; (*en la calle*) gutter

alcanzar [alkan'θar] *vt* (*algo: con la mano, el pie*) to reach; (*alguien: en el camino etc*) to catch up (with); (*autobús*) to catch; (*bala*) to hit, strike ▷ *vi* (*ser suficiente*) to be enough; **~ a hacer** to manage to do

alcaparra [alka'parra] *nf* caper
alcayata [alka'jata] *nf* hook
alcázar [al'kaθar] *nm* fortress; (*Náut*) quarter-deck
alcoba [al'koβa] *nf* bedroom
alcohol [al'kol] *nm* alcohol; **alcohol metílico** methylated spirits *pl* (BRIT), wood alcohol (US); **alcohólico, -a** *adj, nm/f* alcoholic; **alcoholímetro** [alko'limetro] *nm* Breathalyser® (BRIT), drunkometer (US); **alcoholismo** [alko'lismo] *nm* alcoholism
alcornoque [alkor'noke] *nm* cork tree; (*fam*) idiot
aldea [al'dea] *nf* village; **aldeano, -a** *adj* village *cpd* ▷ *nm/f* villager
aleación [alea'θjon] *nf* alloy
aleatorio, -a [alea'torjo, a] *adj* random
aleccionar [alekθjo'nar] *vt* to instruct; (*adiestrar*) to train
alegar [ale'ɣar] *vt* to claim; (*Jur*) to plead ▷ *vi* (LAM: *discutir*) to argue
alegoría [aleɣo'ria] *nf* allegory
alegrar [ale'ɣrar] *vt* (*causar alegría*) to cheer (up); (*fuego*) to poke; (*fiesta*) to liven up; **alegrarse** *vr* (*fam*) to get merry *o* tight; **~se de** to be glad about
alegre [a'leɣre] *adj* happy, cheerful; (*fam*) merry, tight; (*chiste*) risqué, blue; **alegría** *nf* happiness; merriment
alejar [ale'xar] *vt* to remove; (*fig*) to estrange; **alejarse** *vr* to move away
alemán, -ana [ale'man, ana] *adj, nm/f* German ▷ *nm* (*Ling*) German
Alemania [ale'manja] *nf* Germany
alentador, a [alenta'ðor, a] *adj* encouraging
alentar [alen'tar] *vt* to encourage
alergia [a'lerxja] *nf* allergy
alero [a'lero] *nm* (*de tejado*) eaves *pl*; (*guardabarros*) mudguard
alerta [a'lerta] *adj, nm* alert
aleta [a'leta] *nf* (*de pez*) fin; (*ala*) wing; (*de foca, Deporte*) flipper; (*Auto*) mudguard
aletear [alete'ar] *vi* to flutter
alevín [ale'βin] *nm* fry, young fish
alevosía [aleβo'sia] *nf* treachery
alfabeto [alfa'βeto] *nm* alphabet
alfalfa [al'falfa] *nf* alfalfa, lucerne
alfarería [alfare'ria] *nf* pottery; (*tienda*) pottery shop; **alfarero, -a** *nm/f* potter
alféizar [al'feiθar] *nm* window-sill
alférez [al'fereθ] *nm* (*Mil*) second lieutenant; (*Náut*) ensign
alfil [al'fil] *nm* (*Ajedrez*) bishop
alfiler [alfi'ler] *nm* pin; (*broche*) clip
alfombra [al'fombra] *nf* carpet; (*más pequeña*) rug; **alfombrilla** *nf* rug, mat; (*Inform*) mouse mat *o* pad
alforja [al'forxa] *nf* saddlebag
algas ['alɣas] *nfpl* seaweed
álgebra ['alxeβra] *nf* algebra
algo ['alɣo] *pron* something; anything ▷ *adv* somewhat, rather; **¿~ más?** anything else?; (*en tienda*) is that all?; **por ~ será** there must be some reason for it
algodón [alɣo'ðon] *nm* cotton; (*planta*) cotton plant; **algodón de azúcar** candy floss (BRIT), cotton candy (US); **algodón hidrófilo** cotton wool (BRIT), absorbent cotton (US)
alguien ['alɣjen] *pron* someone, somebody; (*en frases interrogativas*) anyone, anybody
alguno, -a [al'ɣuno, a] *adj* (*delante de nm*): **algún** some; (*después de n*): **no tiene talento ~** he has no talent, he doesn't have any talent ▷ *pron* (*alguien*) someone, somebody; **algún que otro libro** some book or other; **algún día iré** I'll go one *o* some day; **sin interés ~** without the slightest interest; **~ que otro** an occasional one; **~s piensan** some (people) think
alhaja [a'laxa] *nf* jewel; (*tesoro*) precious object, treasure
alhelí [ale'li] *nm* wallflower, stock
aliado, -a [a'ljaðo, a] *adj* allied
alianza [a'ljanθa] *nf* alliance; (*anillo*) wedding ring
aliar [a'ljar] *vt* to ally; **aliarse** *vr* to form an alliance

alias ['aljas] *adv* alias
alicatado [alika'taðo] (ESP) *nm* tiling
alicates [ali'kates] *nmpl* pliers
aliciente [ali'θjente] *nm* incentive; (*atracción*) attraction
alienación [aljena'θjon] *nf* alienation
aliento [a'ljento] *nm* breath; (*respiración*) breathing; **sin ~** breathless
aligerar [alixe'rar] *vt* to lighten; (*reducir*) to shorten; (*aliviar*) to alleviate; (*mitigar*) to ease; (*paso*) to quicken
alijo [a'lixo] *nm* consignment
alimaña [ali'maɲa] *nf* pest
alimentación [alimenta'θjon] *nf* (*comida*) food; (*acción*) feeding; (*tienda*) grocer's (shop)
alimentar [alimen'tar] *vt* to feed; (*nutrir*) to nourish; **alimentarse** *vr* to feed
alimenticio, -a [alimen'tiθjo, a] *adj* food *cpd*; (*nutritivo*) nourishing, nutritious
alimento [ali'mento] *nm* food; (*nutrición*) nourishment
alineación [alinea'θjon] *nf* alignment; (*Deporte*) line-up
alinear [aline'ar] *vt* to align; (*Deporte*) to select, pick
aliñar [ali'ɲar] *vt* (*Culin*) to season; **aliño** *nm* (*Culin*) dressing
alioli [ali'oli] *nm* garlic mayonnaise
alisar [ali'sar] *vt* to smooth
alistarse [alis'tarse] *vr* to enlist; (*inscribirse*) to enrol
aliviar [ali'βjar] *vt* (*carga*) to lighten; (*persona*) to relieve; (*dolor*) to relieve, alleviate
alivio [a'liβjo] *nm* alleviation, relief
aljibe [al'xiβe] *nm* cistern
allá [a'ʎa] *adv* (*lugar*) there; (*por ahí*) over there; (*tiempo*) then; **~ abajo** down there; **más ~** further on; **más ~ de** beyond; **¡~ tú!** that's your problem!; **¡~ voy!** I'm coming!
allanamiento [aʎana'mjento] *nm* (LAM: *de policía*) raid; **allanamiento de morada** burglary
allanar [aʎa'nar] *vt* to flatten, level (out); (*igualar*) to smooth (out); (*fig*) to subdue; (*Jur*) to burgle, break into
allegado, -a [aʎe'ɣaðo, a] *adj* near, close ▷ *nm/f* relation
allí [a'ʎi] *adv* there; **~ mismo** right there; **por ~** over there; (*por ese camino*) that way
alma ['alma] *nf* soul; (*persona*) person
almacén [alma'θen] *nm* (*depósito*) warehouse, store; (*Mil*) magazine; (CS: *de comestibles*) grocer's (shop); **grandes almacenes** department store *sg*; **almacenaje** *nm* storage
almacenar [almaθe'nar] *vt* to store, put in storage; (*proveerse*) to stock up with
almanaque [alma'nake] *nm* almanac
almeja [al'mexa] *nf* clam
almendra [al'mendra] *nf* almond; **almendro** *nm* almond tree
almíbar [al'miβar] *nm* syrup
almidón [almi'ðon] *nm* starch
almirante [almi'rante] *nm* admiral
almohada [almo'aða] *nf* pillow; (*funda*) pillowcase; **almohadilla** *nf* cushion; (*para alfileres*) pincushion; (*Tec*) pad
almohadón [almoa'ðon] *nm* large pillow; bolster
almorranas [almo'rranas] *nfpl* piles, haemorrhoids
almorzar [almor'θar] *vt*: **~ una tortilla** to have an omelette for lunch ▷ *vi* to (have) lunch
almuerzo *etc* [al'mwerθo] *vb V* **almorzar** ▷ *nm* lunch
alocado, -a [alo'kaðo, a] *adj* crazy
alojamiento [aloxa'mjento] *nm* lodging(s) *pl*; (*viviendas*) housing
alojar [alo'xar] *vt* to lodge; **alojarse** *vr* to lodge, stay
alondra [a'londra] *nf* lark, skylark
alpargata [alpar'ɣata] *nf* rope-soled sandal, espadrille
Alpes ['alpes] *nmpl*: **los ~** the Alps

alpinismo [alpi'nismo] *nm* mountaineering, climbing; **alpinista** *nmf* mountaineer, climber
alpiste [al'piste] *nm* birdseed
alquilar [alki'lar] *vt* (*propietario: inmuebles*) to let, rent (out); (: *coche*) to hire out; (: *TV*) to rent (out); (*alquilador: inmuebles, TV*) to rent; (: *coche*) to hire; **"se alquila casa"** "house to let (BRIT) *o* for rent (US)"
alquiler [alki'ler] *nm* renting; letting; hiring; (*arriendo*) rent; hire charge; **de ~** for hire; **alquiler de automóviles** *o* **coches** car hire
alquimia [al'kimja] *nf* alchemy
alquitrán [alki'tran] *nm* tar
alrededor [alreðe'ðor] *adv* around, about; **~ de** around, about; **mirar a su ~** to look (round) about one; **alrededores** *nmpl* surroundings
alta ['alta] *nf* (certificate of) discharge
altar [al'tar] *nm* altar
altavoz [alta'βoθ] *nm* loudspeaker; (*amplificador*) amplifier
alteración [altera'θjon] *nf* alteration; (*alboroto*) disturbance
alterar [alte'rar] *vt* to alter; to disturb; **alterarse** *vr* (*persona*) to get upset
altercado [alter'kaðo] *nm* argument
alternar [alter'nar] *vt* to alternate ▷ *vi* to alternate; (*turnar*) to take turns; **alternarse** *vr* to alternate; to take turns; **~ con** to mix with; **alternativa** *nf* alternative; (*elección*) choice; **alternativo, -a** *adj* alternative; (*alterno*) alternating; **alterno, -a** *adj* alternate; (*Elec*) alternating
Alteza [al'teθa] *nf* (*tratamiento*) Highness
altibajos [alti'βaxos] *nmpl* ups and downs
altiplano [alti'plano] *nm* = **altiplanicie**
altisonante [altiso'nante] *adj* high-flown, high-sounding
altitud [alti'tuð] *nf* height; (*Aviac, Geo*) altitude
altivo, -a [al'tiβo, a] *adj* haughty, arrogant
alto, -a ['alto, a] *adj* high; (*persona*) tall; (*sonido*) high, sharp; (*noble*) high, lofty ▷ *nm* halt; (*Mús*) alto; (*Geo*) hill ▷ *adv* (*de sitio*) high; (*de sonido*) loud, loudly ▷ *excl* halt!; **la pared tiene 2 metros de ~** the wall is 2 metres high; **en alta mar** on the high seas; **en voz alta** in a loud voice; **las altas horas de la noche** the small *o* wee hours; **en lo ~ de** at the top of; **pasar por ~** to overlook; **altoparlante** [altopar'lante] (LAM) *nm* loudspeaker
altura [al'tura] *nf* height; (*Náut*) depth; (*Geo*) latitude; **la pared tiene 1.80 de ~** the wall is 1 metre 80cm high; **a estas ~s** at this stage; **a estas ~s del año** at this time of the year
alubia [a'luβja] *nf* bean
alucinación [aluθina'θjon] *nf* hallucination
alucinar [aluθi'nar] *vi* to hallucinate ▷ *vt* to deceive; (*fascinar*) to fascinate
alud [a'luð] *nm* avalanche; (*fig*) flood
aludir [alu'ðir] *vi*: **~ a** to allude to; **darse por aludido** to take the hint
alumbrado [alum'braðo] *nm* lighting
alumbrar [alum'brar] *vt* to light (up) ▷ *vi* (*Med*) to give birth
aluminio [alu'minjo] *nm* aluminium (BRIT), aluminum (US)
alumno, -a [a'lumno, a] *nm/f* pupil, student
alusión [alu'sjon] *nf* allusion
alusivo, -a [alu'siβo, a] *adj* allusive
aluvión [alu'βjon] *nm* alluvium; (*fig*) flood
alverja [al'βerxa] (LAM) *nf* pea
alza ['alθa] *nf* rise; (*Mil*) sight
alzamiento [alθa'mjento] *nm* (*rebelión*) rising
alzar [al'θar] *vt* to lift (up); (*precio, muro*) to raise; (*cuello de abrigo*) to turn up; (*Agr*) to gather in; (*Imprenta*) to gather; **alzarse** *vr* to get up,

rise; (*rebelarse*) to revolt; (*Com*) to go fraudulently bankrupt; (*Jur*) to appeal

ama ['ama] *nf* lady of the house; (*dueña*) owner; (*institutriz*) governess; (*madre adoptiva*) foster mother; **ama de casa** housewife; **ama de llaves** housekeeper

amabilidad [amaβili'ðað] *nf* kindness; (*simpatía*) niceness; **amable** *adj* kind; nice; **es usted muy amable** that's very kind of you

amaestrado, -a [amaes'traðo, a] *adj* (*animal: en circo etc*) performing

amaestrar [amaes'trar] *vt* to train

amago [a'maɣo] *nm* threat; (*gesto*) threatening gesture; (*Med*) symptom

amainar [amai'nar] *vi* (*viento*) to die down

amamantar [amaman'tar] *vt* to suckle, nurse

amanecer [amane'θer] *vi* to dawn ▷ *nm* dawn; **~ afiebrado** to wake up with a fever

amanerado, -a [amane'raðo, a] *adj* affected

amante [a'mante] *adj*: **~ de** fond of ▷ *nmf* lover

amapola [ama'pola] *nf* poppy

amar [a'mar] *vt* to love

amargado, -a [amar'ɣaðo, a] *adj* bitter

amargar [amar'ɣar] *vt* to make bitter; (*fig*) to embitter; **amargarse** *vr* to become embittered

amargo, -a [a'marɣo, a] *adj* bitter

amarillento, -a [amari'ʎento, a] *adj* yellowish; (*tez*) sallow; **amarillo, -a** *adj, nm* yellow

amarrado, -a [ama'rraðo, a] (MÉX: *fam*) *adj* mean, stingy

amarrar [ama'rrar] *vt* to moor; (*sujetar*) to tie up

amarras [a'marras] *nfpl*: **soltar ~** to set sail

amasar [ama'sar] *vt* (*masa*) to knead; (*mezclar*) to mix, prepare; (*confeccionar*) to concoct

amateur [ama'ter] *nmf* amateur

amazona [ama'θona] *nf* horsewoman; **Amazonas** *nm*: **el Amazonas** the Amazon

ámbar ['ambar] *nm* amber

ambición [ambi'θjon] *nf* ambition; **ambicionar** *vt* to aspire to; **ambicioso, -a** *adj* ambitious

ambidextro, -a [ambi'ðekstro, a] *adj* ambidextrous

ambientación [ambjenta'θjon] *nf* (*Cine, Teatro etc*) setting; (*Radio*) sound effects

ambiente [am'bjente] *nm* atmosphere; (*medio*) environment

ambigüedad [ambiɣwe'ðað] *nf* ambiguity; **ambiguo, -a** *adj* ambiguous

ámbito ['ambito] *nm* (*campo*) field; (*fig*) scope

ambos, -as ['ambos, as] *adj pl, pron pl* both

ambulancia [ambu'lanθja] *nf* ambulance

ambulante [ambu'lante] *adj* travelling *cpd*, itinerant

ambulatorio [ambula'torio] *nm* state health-service clinic

amén [a'men] *excl* amen; **~ de** besides

amenaza [ame'naθa] *nf* threat; **amenazar** [amena'θar] *vt* to threaten ▷ *vi*: **amenazar con hacer** to threaten to do

ameno, -a [a'meno, a] *adj* pleasant

América [a'merika] *nf* America; **América Central/Latina** Central/ Latin America; **América del Norte/del Sur** North/South America; **americana** *nf* coat, jacket; *V tb* **americano**; **americano, -a** *adj, nm/f* American

ametralladora [ametraʎa'ðora] *nf* machine gun

amigable [ami'ɣaβle] *adj* friendly

amígdala [a'miɣðala] *nf* tonsil; **amigdalitis** *nf* tonsillitis

amigo, -a [a'miɣo, a] *adj* friendly ▷ *nm/f* friend; (*amante*) lover; **ser ~ de algo** to be fond of sth; **ser muy ~s** to be

close friends
aminorar [amino'rar] *vt* to diminish; (*reducir*) to reduce; **~ la marcha** to slow down
amistad [amis'tað] *nf* friendship; **amistades** *nfpl* (*amigos*) friends; **amistoso, -a** *adj* friendly
amnesia [am'nesja] *nf* amnesia
amnistía [amnis'tia] *nf* amnesty
amo ['amo] *nm* owner; (*jefe*) boss
amolar [amo'lar] (MÉX: *fam*) *vt* to ruin, damage
amoldar [amol'dar] *vt* to mould; (*adaptar*) to adapt
amonestación [amonesta'θjon] *nf* warning; **amonestaciones** *nfpl* (*Rel*) marriage banns
amonestar [amones'tar] *vt* to warn; (*Rel*) to publish the banns of
amontonar [amonto'nar] *vt* to collect, pile up; **amontonarse** *vr* to crowd together; (*acumularse*) to pile up
amor [a'mor] *nm* love; (*amante*) lover; **hacer el ~** to make love; **amor propio** self-respect
amoratado, -a [amora'taðo, a] *adj* purple
amordazar [amorða'θar] *vt* to muzzle; (*fig*) to gag
amorfo, -a [a'morfo, a] *adj* amorphous, shapeless
amoroso, -a [amo'roso, a] *adj* affectionate, loving
amortiguador [amortigwa'ðor] *nm* shock absorber; (*parachoques*) bumper; **amortiguadores** *nmpl* (*Auto*) suspension *sg*
amortiguar [amorti'ɣwar] *vt* to deaden; (*ruido*) to muffle; (*color*) to soften
amotinar [amoti'nar] *vt* to stir up, incite (to riot); **amotinarse** *vr* to mutiny
amparar [ampa'rar] *vt* to protect; **ampararse** *vr* to seek protection; (*de la lluvia etc*) to shelter; **amparo** *nm* help, protection; **al amparo de** under the protection of
amperio [am'perjo] *nm* ampère, amp
ampliación [amplja'θjon] *nf* enlargement; (*extensión*) extension
ampliar [am'pljar] *vt* to enlarge; to extend
amplificador [amplifika'ðor] *nm* amplifier
amplificar [amplifi'kar] *vt* to amplify
amplio, -a ['ampljo, a] *adj* spacious; (*de falda etc*) full; (*extenso*) extensive; (*ancho*) wide; **amplitud** *nf* spaciousness; extent; (*fig*) amplitude
ampolla [am'poʎa] *nf* blister; (*Med*) ampoule
amputar [ampu'tar] *vt* to cut off, amputate
amueblar [amwe'βlar] *vt* to furnish
anales [a'nales] *nmpl* annals
analfabetismo [analfaβe'tismo] *nm* illiteracy; **analfabeto, -a** *adj, nm/f* illiterate
analgésico [anal'xesiko] *nm* painkiller, analgesic
análisis [a'nalisis] *nm inv* analysis
analista [ana'lista] *nmf* (*gen*) analyst
analizar [anali'θar] *vt* to analyse
analógico, -a [ana'loxiko, a] *adj* (*Inform*) analog; (*reloj*) analogue (BRIT), analog (US)
análogo, -a [a'naloɣo, a] *adj* analogous, similar
ananá [ana'na] (RPL) *nm* pineapple
anarquía [anar'kia] *nf* anarchy; **anarquista** *nmf* anarchist
anatomía [anato'mia] *nf* anatomy
anca ['anka] *nf* rump, haunch; **ancas** *nfpl* (*fam*) behind *sg*
ancho, -a ['antʃo, a] *adj* wide; (*falda*) full; (*fig*) liberal ▷ *nm* width; (*Ferro*) gauge; **ponerse ~** to get conceited; **estar a sus anchas** to be at one's ease
anchoa [an'tʃoa] *nf* anchovy
anchura [an'tʃura] *nf* width; (*extensión*) wideness
anciano, -a [an'θjano, a] *adj* old, aged ▷ *nm/f* old man/woman; elder
ancla ['ankla] *nf* anchor

Andalucía [andalu'θia] *nf* Andalusia; **andaluz, -a** *adj, nm/f* Andalusian
andamio [an'damjo] *nm* scaffold(ing)
andar [an'dar] *vt* to go, cover, travel ▷ *vi* to go, walk, travel; (*funcionar*) to go, work; (*estar*) to be ▷ *nm* walk, gait, pace; **andarse** *vr* to go away; **~ a pie/a caballo/en bicicleta** to go on foot/on horseback/by bicycle; **~ haciendo algo** to be doing sth; **¡anda!** (*sorpresa*) go on!; **anda por** *o* **en los 40** he's about 40
andén [an'den] *nm* (*Ferro*) platform; (*Náut*) quayside; (CAM: *de la calle*) pavement (BRIT), sidewalk (US)
Andes ['andes] *nmpl*: **los ~** the Andes
andinismo [andi'nismo] (LAM) *nm* mountaineering, climbing
Andorra [an'dorra] *nf* Andorra
andrajoso, -a [andra'xoso, a] *adj* ragged
anduve *etc vb V* **andar**
anécdota [a'nekðota] *nf* anecdote, story
anegar [ane'ɣar] *vt* to flood; (*ahogar*) to drown
anemia [a'nemja] *nf* anaemia
anestesia [anes'tesja] *nf* (*sustancia*) anaesthetic; (*proceso*) anaesthesia; **anestesia general/local** general/ local anaesthetic
anexar [anek'sar] *vt* to annex; (*documento*) to attach; **anexión** *nf* annexation; **anexo, -a** *adj* attached ▷ *nm* annexe
anfibio, -a [an'fiβjo, a] *adj* amphibious ▷ *nm* amphibian
anfiteatro [anfite'atro] *nm* amphitheatre; (*Teatro*) dress circle
anfitrión, -ona [anfi'trjon, ona] *nm/f* host(ess)
ánfora ['anfora] *nf* (*cántaro*) amphora; (MÉX *Pol*) ballot box
ángel ['anxel] *nm* angel; **ángel de la guarda** guardian angel
angina [an'xina] *nf* (*Med*) inflammation of the throat; **tener ~s** to have tonsillitis; **angina de pecho** angina
anglicano, -a [angli'kano, a] *adj, nm/f* Anglican
anglosajón, -ona [anglosa'xon, ona] *adj* Anglo-Saxon
anguila [an'gila] *nf* eel
angula [an'gula] *nf* elver, baby eel
ángulo ['angulo] *nm* angle; (*esquina*) corner; (*curva*) bend
angustia [an'gustja] *nf* anguish
anhelar [ane'lar] *vt* to be eager for; (*desear*) to long for, desire ▷ *vi* to pant, gasp; **anhelo** *nm* eagerness; desire
anidar [ani'ðar] *vi* to nest
anillo [a'niʎo] *nm* ring; **anillo de boda/compromiso** wedding/ engagement ring
animación [anima'θjon] *nf* liveliness; (*vitalidad*) life; (*actividad*) activity; bustle
animado, -a [ani'maðo, a] *adj* lively; (*vivaz*) animated; **animador, a** *nm/f* (*TV*) host(ess), compère; (*Deporte*) cheerleader
animal [ani'mal] *adj* animal; (*fig*) stupid ▷ *nm* animal; (*fig*) fool; (*bestia*) brute
animar [ani'mar] *vt* (*Bio*) to animate, give life to; (*fig*) to liven up, brighten up, cheer up; (*estimular*) to stimulate; **animarse** *vr* to cheer up; to feel encouraged; (*decidirse*) to make up one's mind
ánimo ['animo] *nm* (*alma*) soul; (*mente*) mind; (*valentía*) courage ▷ *excl* cheer up!
animoso, -a [ani'moso, a] *adj* brave; (*vivo*) lively
aniquilar [aniki'lar] *vt* to annihilate, destroy
anís [a'nis] *nm* aniseed; (*licor*) anisette
aniversario [aniβer'sarjo] *nm* anniversary
anoche [a'notʃe] *adv* last night; **antes de ~** the night before last

anochecer [anotʃe'θer] *vi* to get dark ▷ *nm* nightfall, dark; **al ~** at nightfall

anodino, -a [ano'ðino, a] *adj* dull, anodyne

anomalía [anoma'lia] *nf* anomaly

anonadado, -a [anona'ðaðo, a] *adj*: **estar ~** to be overwhelmed *o* amazed

anonimato [anoni'mato] *nm* anonymity

anónimo, -a [a'nonimo, a] *adj* anonymous; (*Com*) limited ▷ *nm* (*carta anónima*) anonymous letter; (: *maliciosa*) poison-pen letter

anormal [anor'mal] *adj* abnormal

anotación [anota'θjon] *nf* note; annotation

anotar [ano'tar] *vt* to note down; (*comentar*) to annotate

ansia ['ansja] *nf* anxiety; (*añoranza*) yearning; **ansiar** *vt* to long for

ansiedad [ansje'ðað] *nf* anxiety

ansioso, -a [an'sjoso, a] *adj* anxious; (*anhelante*) eager; **~ de** *o* **por algo** greedy for sth

antaño [an'taɲo] *adv* long ago, formerly

Antártico [an'tartiko] *nm*: **el ~** the Antarctic

ante ['ante] *prep* before, in the presence of; (*problema etc*) faced with ▷ *nm* (*piel*) suede; **~ todo** above all

anteanoche [antea'notʃe] *adv* the night before last

anteayer [antea'jer] *adv* the day before yesterday

antebrazo [ante'βraθo] *nm* forearm

antecedente [anteθe'ðente] *adj* previous ▷ *nm* antecedent; **antecedentes** *nmpl* (*historial*) record *sg*; **antecedentes penales** criminal record

anteceder [anteθe'ðer] *vt* to precede, go before

antecesor, a [anteθe'sor, a] *nm/f* predecessor

antelación [antela'θjon] *nf*: **con ~** in advance

antemano [ante'mano]: **de ~** *adv* beforehand, in advance

antena [an'tena] *nf* antenna; (*de televisión etc*) aerial; **antena parabólica** satellite dish

antenoche [ante'notʃe] (LAM) *adv* the night before last

anteojo [ante'oxo] *nm* eyeglass; **anteojos** *nmpl* (LAM: *gafas*) glasses, spectacles

antepasados [antepa'saðos] *nmpl* ancestors

anteponer [antepo'ner] *vt* to place in front; (*fig*) to prefer

anterior [ante'rjor] *adj* preceding, previous; **anterioridad** *nf*: **con anterioridad a** prior to, before

antes ['antes] *adv* (*con prioridad*) before ▷ *prep*: **~ de** before ▷ *conj*: **~ de ir/de que te vayas** before going/ before you go; **~ bien** (but) rather; **dos días ~** two days before *o* previously; **no quiso venir ~** she didn't want to come any earlier; **tomo el avión ~ que el barco** I take the plane rather than the boat; **~ de** *o* **que nada** (*en el tiempo*) first of all; (*indicando preferencia*) above all; **~ que yo** before me; **lo ~ posible** as soon as possible; **cuanto ~ mejor** the sooner the better

antibalas [anti'βalas] *adj inv*: **chaleco ~** bullet-proof jacket

antibiótico [anti'βjotiko] *nm* antibiotic

anticaspa [anti'kaspa] *adj inv* anti-dandruff *cpd*

anticipación [antiθipa'θjon] *nf* anticipation; **con 10 minutos de ~** 10 minutes early

anticipado, -a [antiθi'paðo, a] *adj* (*pago*) advance; **por ~** in advance

anticipar [antiθi'par] *vt* to anticipate; (*adelantar*) to bring forward; (*Com*) to advance; **anticiparse** *vr*: **~se a su época** to be ahead of one's time

anticipo [anti'θipo] *nm* (*Com*) advance

anticonceptivo, -a [antikonθep'tiβo, a] *adj, nm* contraceptive
anticongelante [antikonxe'lante] *nm* antifreeze
anticuado, -a [anti'kwaðo, a] *adj* out-of-date, old-fashioned; (*desusado*) obsolete
anticuario [anti'kwarjo] *nm* antique dealer
anticuerpo [anti'kwerpo] *nm* (*Med*) antibody
antidepresivo [antiðepre'siβo] *nm* antidepressant
antidóping [anti'dopin] *adj inv*: **control ~** drugs test
antídoto [an'tiðoto] *nm* antidote
antiestético, -a [anties'tetiko, a] *adj* unsightly
antifaz [anti'faθ] *nm* mask; (*velo*) veil
antiglobalización [antigloβaliθa'θjon] *nf* anti-globalization; **antiglobalizador, a** *adj* anti-globalization *cpd*
antiguamente [antiɣwa'mente] *adv* formerly; (*hace mucho tiempo*) long ago
antigüedad [antiɣwe'ðað] *nf* antiquity; (*artículo*) antique; (*rango*) seniority
antiguo, -a [an'tiɣwo, a] *adj* old, ancient; (*que fue*) former
Antillas [an'tiʎas] *nfpl*: **las ~** the West Indies
antílope [an'tilope] *nm* antelope
antinatural [antinatu'ral] *adj* unnatural
antipatía [antipa'tia] *nf* antipathy, dislike; **antipático, -a** *adj* disagreeable, unpleasant
antirrobo [anti'rroβo] *adj inv* (*alarma etc*) anti-theft
antisemita [antise'mita] *adj* anti-Semitic ▷*nmf* anti-Semite
antiséptico, -a [anti'septiko, a] *adj* antiseptic ▷*nm* antiseptic
antivirus [anti'birus] *nm inv* (*Comput*) antivirus program
antojarse [anto'xarse] *vr* (*desear*): **se me antoja comprarlo** I have a mind to buy it; (*pensar*): **se me antoja que ...** I have a feeling that ...
antojitos [anto'xitos] (*MÉX*) *nmpl* snacks, nibbles
antojo [an'toxo] *nm* caprice, whim; (*rosa*) birthmark; (*lunar*) mole
antología [antolo'xia] *nf* anthology
antorcha [an'tortʃa] *nf* torch
antro ['antro] *nm* cavern
antropología [antropolo'xia] *nf* anthropology
anual [a'nwal] *adj* annual
anuario [a'nwarjo] *nm* yearbook
anulación [anula'θjon] *nf* annulment; (*cancelación*) cancellation
anular [anu'lar] *vt* (*contrato*) to annul, cancel; (*ley*) to revoke, repeal; (*suscripción*) to cancel ▷*nm* ring finger
anunciar [anun'θjar] *vt* to announce; (*proclamar*) to proclaim; (*Com*) to advertise
anuncio [a'nunθjo] *nm* announcement; (*señal*) sign; (*Com*) advertisement; (*cartel*) poster
anzuelo [an'θwelo] *nm* hook; (*para pescar*) fish hook
añadidura [aɲaði'ðura] *nf* addition, extra; **por ~** besides, in addition
añadir [aɲa'ðir] *vt* to add
añejo, -a [a'ɲexo, a] *adj* old; (*vino*) mellow
añicos [a'ɲikos] *nmpl*: **hacer ~** to smash, shatter
año ['aɲo] *nm* year; **¡Feliz A~ Nuevo!** Happy New Year!; **tener 15 ~s** to be 15 (years old); **los ~s 90** the nineties; **el ~ que viene** next year; **año bisiesto/ escolar/fiscal/sabático** leap/school/ tax/sabbatical year
añoranza [aɲo'ranθa] *nf* nostalgia; (*anhelo*) longing
apa ['apa] (*MÉX*) *excl* goodness me!, good gracious!
apabullar [apaβu'ʎar] *vt* to crush, squash
apacible [apa'θiβle] *adj* gentle, mild

apaciguar [apaθi'ɣwar] *vt* to pacify, calm (down)
apadrinar [apaðri'nar] *vt* to sponsor, support; (*Rel*) to be godfather to
apagado, -a [apa'ɣaðo, a] *adj* (*volcán*) extinct; (*color*) dull; (*voz*) quiet; (*sonido*) muted, muffled; (*persona: apático*) listless; **estar ~** (*fuego, luz*) to be out; (*Radio, TV etc*) to be off
apagar [apa'ɣar] *vt* to put out; (*Elec, Radio, TV*) to turn off; (*sonido*) to silence, muffle; (*sed*) to quench
apagón [apa'ɣon] *nm* blackout; power cut
apalabrar [apala'βrar] *vt* to agree to; (*contratar*) to engage
apalear [apale'ar] *vt* to beat, thrash
apantallar [apanta'ʎar] (*MÉX*) *vt* to impress
apañar [apa'ɲar] *vt* to pick up; (*asir*) to take hold of, grasp; (*reparar*) to mend, patch up; **apañarse** *vr* to manage, get along
apapachar [apapa'tʃar] (*MÉX: fam*) *vt* to cuddle, hug
aparador [apara'ðor] *nm* sideboard; (*MÉX: escaparate*) shop window
aparato [apa'rato] *nm* apparatus; (*máquina*) machine; (*doméstico*) appliance; (*boato*) ostentation; **aparato digestivo** (*Anat*) digestive system; **aparatoso, -a** *adj* showy, ostentatious
aparcamiento [aparka'mjento] *nm* car park (*BRIT*), parking lot (*US*)
aparcar [apar'kar] *vt, vi* to park
aparear [apare'ar] *vt* (*objetos*) to pair, match; (*animales*) to mate; **aparearse** *vr* to make a pair; to mate
aparecer [apare'θer] *vi* to appear; **aparecerse** *vr* to appear
aparejador, a [aparexa'ðor, a] *nm/f* (*Arq*) master builder
aparejo [apa'rexo] *nm* harness; rigging; (*de poleas*) block and tackle
aparentar [aparen'tar] *vt* (*edad*) to look; (*fingir*): **~ tristeza** to pretend to be sad
aparente [apa'rente] *adj* apparent; (*adecuado*) suitable
aparezco *etc vb V* **aparecer**
aparición [apari'θjon] *nf* appearance; (*de libro*) publication; (*espectro*) apparition
apariencia [apa'rjenθja] *nf* (outward) appearance; **en ~** outwardly, seemingly
apartado, -a [apar'taðo, a] *adj* separate; (*lejano*) remote ▷ *nm* (*tipográfico*) paragraph; **apartado de correos** (*ESP*) post office box; **apartado postal** (*LAM*) post office box
apartamento [aparta'mento] *nm* apartment, flat (*BRIT*)
apartar [apar'tar] *vt* to separate; (*quitar*) to remove; **apartarse** *vr* to separate, part; (*irse*) to move away; to keep away
aparte [a'parte] *adv* (*separadamente*) separately; (*además*) besides ▷ *nm* aside; (*tipográfico*) new paragraph
aparthotel [aparto'tel] *nm* serviced apartments
apasionado, -a [apasjo'naðo, a] *adj* passionate
apasionar [apasjo'nar] *vt* to excite; **le apasiona el fútbol** she's crazy about football; **apasionarse** *vr* to get excited
apatía [apa'tia] *nf* apathy
apático, -a [a'patiko, a] *adj* apathetic
Apdo *abr* (*= Apartado (de Correos)*) PO Box
apeadero [apea'ðero] *nm* halt, stop, stopping place
apearse [ape'arse] *vr* (*jinete*) to dismount; (*bajarse*) to get down *o* out; (*Auto, Ferro*) to get off *o* out
apechugar [apetʃu'ɣar] *vr*: **~ con algo** to face up to sth
apegarse [ape'ɣarse] *vr*: **~ a** to become attached to; **apego** *nm* attachment, devotion
apelar [ape'lar] *vi* to appeal; **~ a** (*fig*) to resort to

apellidar [apeʎi'ðar] *vt* to call, name; **apellidarse** *vr*: **se apellida Pérez** her (sur)name's Pérez
apellido [ape'ʎiðo] *nm* surname
apenar [ape'nar] *vt* to grieve, trouble; (LAM: *avergonzar*) to embarrass; **apenarse** *vr* to grieve; (LAM: *avergonzarse*) to be embarrassed
apenas [a'penas] *adv* scarcely, hardly ▷ *conj* as soon as, no sooner
apéndice [a'pendiθe] *nm* appendix; **apendicitis** *nf* appendicitis
aperitivo [aperi'tiβo] *nm* (*bebida*) aperitif; (*comida*) appetizer
apertura [aper'tura] *nf* opening; (*Pol*) liberalization
apestar [apes'tar] *vt* to infect ▷ *vi*: **~ (a)** to stink (of)
apetecer [apete'θer] *vt*: **¿te apetece un café?** do you fancy a (cup of) coffee?; **apetecible** *adj* desirable; (*comida*) appetizing
apetito [ape'tito] *nm* appetite; **apetitoso, -a** *adj* appetizing; (*fig*) tempting
apiadarse [apja'ðarse] *vr*: **~ de** to take pity on
ápice ['apiθe] *nm* whit, iota
apilar [api'lar] *vt* to pile *o* heap up
apiñarse [api'ɲarse] *vr* to crowd *o* press together
apio ['apjo] *nm* celery
apisonadora [apisona'ðora] *nf* steamroller
aplacar [apla'kar] *vt* to placate
aplastante [aplas'tante] *adj* overwhelming; (*lógica*) compelling
aplastar [aplas'tar] *vt* to squash (flat); (*fig*) to crush
aplaudir [aplau'ðir] *vt* to applaud
aplauso [a'plauso] *nm* applause; (*fig*) approval, acclaim
aplazamiento [aplaθa'mjento] *nm* postponement
aplazar [apla'θar] *vt* to postpone, defer
aplicación [aplika'θjon] *nf* application; (*esfuerzo*) effort
aplicado, -a [apli'kaðo, a] *adj* diligent, hard-working
aplicar [apli'kar] *vt* (*ejecutar*) to apply; **aplicarse** *vr* to apply o.s.
aplique *etc* [a'plike] *vb V* **aplicar** ▷ *nm* wall light
aplomo [a'plomo] *nm* aplomb, self-assurance
apodar [apo'ðar] *vt* to nickname
apoderado [apoðe'raðo] *nm* agent, representative
apoderarse [apoðe'rarse] *vr*: **~ de** to take possession of
apodo [a'poðo] *nm* nickname
apogeo [apo'xeo] *nm* peak, summit
apoquinar [apoki'nar] (*fam*) *vt* to fork out, cough up
aporrear [aporre'ar] *vt* to beat (up)
aportar [apor'tar] *vt* to contribute ▷ *vi* to reach port; **aportarse** *vr* (LAM: *llegar*) to arrive, come
aposta [a'posta] *adv* deliberately, on purpose
apostar [apos'tar] *vt* to bet, stake; (*tropas etc*) to station, post ▷ *vi* to bet
apóstol [a'postol] *nm* apostle
apóstrofo [a'postrofo] *nm* apostrophe
apoyar [apo'jar] *vt* to lean, rest; (*fig*) to support, back; **apoyarse** *vr*: **~se en** to lean on; **apoyo** *nm* (*gen*) support; backing, help
apreciable [apre'θjaβle] *adj* considerable; (*fig*) esteemed
apreciar [apre'θjar] *vt* to evaluate, assess; (*Com*) to appreciate, value; (*persona*) to respect; (*tamaño*) to gauge, assess; (*detalles*) to notice
aprecio [a'preθjo] *nm* valuation, estimate; (*fig*) appreciation
aprehender [apreen'der] *vt* to apprehend, detain
apremio [a'premjo] *nm* urgency
aprender [apren'der] *vt, vi* to learn; **~ algo de memoria** to learn sth (off) by heart
aprendiz, a [apren'diθ, a] *nm/f* apprentice; (*principiante*) learner;

aprendizaje *nm* apprenticeship
aprensión [apren'sjon] *nm* apprehension, fear; **aprensivo, -a** *adj* apprehensive
apresar [apre'sar] *vt* to seize; (*capturar*) to capture
apresurado, -a [apresu'raðo, a] *adj* hurried, hasty
apresurar [apresu'rar] *vt* to hurry, accelerate; **apresurarse** *vr* to hurry, make haste
apretado, -a [apre'taðo, a] *adj* tight; (*escritura*) cramped
apretar [apre'tar] *vt* to squeeze; (*Tec*) to tighten; (*presionar*) to press together, pack ▷ *vi* to be too tight
apretón [apre'ton] *nm* squeeze; **apretón de manos** handshake
aprieto [a'prjeto] *nm* squeeze; (*dificultad*) difficulty; **estar en un ~** to be in a fix
aprisa [a'prisa] *adv* quickly, hurriedly
aprisionar [aprisjo'nar] *vt* to imprison
aprobación [aproβa'θjon] *nf* approval
aprobar [apro'βar] *vt* to approve (of); (*examen, materia*) to pass ▷ *vi* to pass
apropiado, -a [apro'pjaðo, a] *adj* suitable
apropiarse [apro'pjarse] *vr*: **~ de** to appropriate
aprovechado, -a [aproβe'tʃaðo, a] *adj* industrious, hard-working; (*económico*) thrifty; (*pey*) unscrupulous
aprovechar [aproβe'tʃar] *vt* to use; (*explotar*) to exploit; (*experiencia*) to profit from; (*oferta, oportunidad*) to take advantage of ▷ *vi* to progress, improve; **aprovecharse** *vr*: **~se de** to make use of; to take advantage of; **¡que aproveche!** enjoy your meal!
aproximación [aproksima'θjon] *nf* approximation; (*de lotería*) consolation prize
aproximar [aproksi'mar] *vt* to bring nearer; **aproximarse** *vr* to come near, approach
apruebo *etc vb V* **aprobar**
aptitud [apti'tuð] *nf* aptitude
apto, -a ['apto, a] *adj* suitable
apuesta [a'pwesta] *nf* bet, wager
apuesto, -a [a'pwesto, a] *adj* neat, elegant
apuntar [apun'tar] *vt* (*con arma*) to aim at; (*con dedo*) to point at *o* to; (*anotar*) to note (down); (*Teatro*) to prompt; **apuntarse** *vr* (*Deporte: tanto, victoria*) to score; (*Escol*) to enrol

No confundir **apuntar** con la palabra inglesa *appoint*.

apunte [a'punte] *nm* note
apuñalar [apuɲa'lar] *vt* to stab
apurado, -a [apu'raðo, a] *adj* needy; (*difícil*) difficult; (*peligroso*) dangerous; (LAM: *con prisa*) hurried, rushed
apurar [apu'rar] *vt* (*agotar*) to drain; (*recursos*) to use up; (*molestar*) to annoy; **apurarse** *vr* (*preocuparse*) to worry; (LAM: *darse prisa*) to hurry
apuro [a'puro] *nm* (*aprieto*) fix, jam; (*escasez*) want, hardship; (*vergüenza*) embarrassment; (LAM: *prisa*) haste, urgency
aquejado, -a [ake'xaðo, a] *adj*: **~ de** (*Med*) afflicted by
aquel, aquella [a'kel, a'keʎa] *adj* that; **~los(as)** those
aquél, aquélla [a'kel, a'keʎa] *pron* that (one); **~los(as)** those (ones)
aquello [a'keʎo] *pron* that, that business
aquí [a'ki] *adv* (*lugar*) here; (*tiempo*) now; **~ arriba** up here; **~ mismo** right here; **~ yace** here lies; **de ~ a siete días** a week from now
ara ['ara] *nf*: **en ~s de** for the sake of
árabe ['araβe] *adj, nmf* Arab ▷ *nm* (*Ling*) Arabic
Arabia [a'raβja] *nf* Arabia; **Arabia Saudí** *o* **Saudita** Saudi Arabia
arado [a'raðo] *nm* plough
Aragón [ara'ɣon] *nm* Aragon; **aragonés, -esa** *adj, nm/f* Aragonese
arancel [aran'θel] *nm* tariff, duty
arandela [aran'dela] *nf* (*Tec*) washer

araña [a'raɲa] *nf* (*Zool*) spider; (*lámpara*) chandelier
arañar [ara'ɲar] *vt* to scratch
arañazo [ara'ɲaθo] *nm* scratch
arbitrar [arβi'trar] *vt* to arbitrate in; (*Deporte*) to referee ▷ *vi* to arbitrate
arbitrario, -a [arβi'trarjo, a] *adj* arbitrary
árbitro ['arβitro] *nm* arbitrator; (*Deporte*) referee; (*Tenis*) umpire
árbol ['arβol] *nm* (*Bot*) tree; (*Náut*) mast; (*Tec*) axle, shaft; **árbol de Navidad** Christmas tree
arboleda [arβo'leða] *nf* grove, plantation
arbusto [ar'βusto] *nm* bush, shrub
arca ['arka] *nf* chest, box
arcada [ar'kaða] *nf* arcade; (*de puente*) arch, span; **arcadas** *nfpl* (*náuseas*) retching *sg*
arcaico, -a [ar'kaiko, a] *adj* archaic
arce ['arθe] *nm* maple tree
arcén [ar'θen] *nm* (*de autopista*) hard shoulder; (*de carretera*) verge
archipiélago [artʃi'pjelaɣo] *nm* archipelago
archivador [artʃiβa'ðor] *nm* filing cabinet
archivar [artʃi'βar] *vt* to file (away); **archivo** *nm* file, archive(s) *pl*; **archivo adjunto** (*Inform*) attachment; **archivo de seguridad** (*Inform*) backup file
arcilla [ar'θiʎa] *nf* clay
arco ['arko] *nm* arch; (*Mat*) arc; (*Mil, Mús*) bow; **arco iris** rainbow
arder [ar'ðer] *vi* to burn; **estar que arde** (*persona*) to fume
ardid [ar'ðið] *nm* ploy, trick
ardiente [ar'ðjente] *adj* burning, ardent
ardilla [ar'ðiʎa] *nf* squirrel
ardor [ar'ðor] *nm* (*calor*) heat; (*fig*) ardour; **ardor de estómago** heartburn
arduo, -a ['arðwo, a] *adj* arduous
área ['area] *nf* area; (*Deporte*) penalty area
arena [a'rena] *nf* sand; (*de una lucha*) arena; **arenas movedizas** quicksand *sg*; **arenal** [are'nal] *nm* (*terreno arenoso*) sandy spot
arenisca [are'niska] *nf* sandstone; (*cascajo*) grit
arenoso, -a [are'noso, a] *adj* sandy
arenque [a'renke] *nm* herring
arete [a'rete] (*MÉX*) *nm* earring
Argel [ar'xel] *n* Algiers; **Argelia** *nf* Algeria; **argelino, -a** *adj, nm/f* Algerian
Argentina [arxen'tina] *nf* (*tb*: **la ~**) Argentina
argentino, -a [arxen'tino, a] *adj* Argentinian; (*de plata*) silvery ▷ *nm/f* Argentinian
argolla [ar'ɣoʎa] *nf* (large) ring
argot [ar'ɣo] (*pl* **~s**) *nm* slang
argucia [ar'ɣuθja] *nf* subtlety, sophistry
argumentar [arɣumen'tar] *vt, vi* to argue
argumento [arɣu'mento] *nm* argument; (*razonamiento*) reasoning; (*de novela etc*) plot; (*Cine, TV*) storyline
aria ['arja] *nf* aria
aridez [ari'ðeθ] *nf* aridity, dryness
árido, -a ['ariðo, a] *adj* arid, dry
Aries ['arjes] *nm* Aries
arisco, -a [a'risko, a] *adj* surly; (*insociable*) unsociable
aristócrata [aris'tokrata] *nmf* aristocrat
arma ['arma] *nf* arm; **armas** *nfpl* arms; **arma blanca** blade, knife; **arma de doble filo** double-edged sword; **arma de fuego** firearm; **armas de destrucción masiva** weapons of mass destruction
armada [ar'maða] *nf* armada; (*flota*) fleet
armadillo [arma'ðiʎo] *nm* armadillo
armado, -a [ar'maðo, a] *adj* armed; (*Tec*) reinforced
armadura [arma'ðura] *nf* (*Mil*) armour; (*Tec*) framework; (*Zool*) skeleton; (*Física*) armature
armamento [arma'mento] *nm* armament; (*Náut*) fitting-out

armar [ar'mar] *vt* (*soldado*) to arm; (*máquina*) to assemble; (*navío*) to fit out; **~la, ~ un lío** to start a row, kick up a fuss
armario [ar'marjo] *nm* wardrobe; (*de cocina, baño*) cupboard; **armario empotrado** built-in cupboard
armatoste [arma'toste] *nm* (*mueble*) monstrosity; (*máquina*) contraption
armazón [arma'θon] *nf o m* body, chassis; (*de mueble etc*) frame; (*Arq*) skeleton
armiño [ar'miɲo] *nm* stoat; (*piel*) ermine
armisticio [armis'tiθjo] *nm* armistice
armonía [armo'nia] *nf* harmony
armónica [ar'monika] *nf* harmonica
armonizar [armoni'θar] *vt* to harmonize; (*diferencias*) to reconcile
aro ['aro] *nm* ring; (*tejo*) quoit; (cs: *pendiente*) earring
aroma [a'roma] *nm* aroma, scent; **aromaterapia** *n* aromatherapy; **aromático, -a** [aro'matiko, a] *adj* aromatic
arpa ['arpa] *nf* harp
arpía [ar'pia] *nf* shrew
arpón [ar'pon] *nm* harpoon
arqueología [arkeolo'xia] *nf* archaeology; **arqueólogo, -a** *nm/f* archaeologist
arquetipo [arke'tipo] *nm* archetype
arquitecto [arki'tekto] *nm* architect; **arquitectura** *nf* architecture
arrabal [arra'βal] *nm* poor suburb, slum; **arrabales** *nmpl* (*afueras*) outskirts
arraigar [arrai'ɣar] *vt* to establish ▷ *vi* to take root
arrancar [arran'kar] *vt* (*sacar*) to extract, pull out; (*arrebatar*) to snatch (away); (*Inform*) to boot; (*fig*) to extract ▷ *vi* (*Auto, máquina*) to start; (*ponerse en marcha*) to get going; **~ de** to stem from
arranque *etc* [a'rranke] *vb V* **arrancar** ▷ *nm* sudden start; (*Auto*) start; (*fig*) fit, outburst
arrasar [arra'sar] *vt* (*aplanar*) to level, flatten; (*destruir*) to demolish
arrastrar [arras'trar] *vt* to drag (along); (*fig*) to drag down, degrade; (*agua, viento*) to carry away ▷ *vi* to drag, trail on the ground; **arrastrarse** *vr* to crawl; (*fig*) to grovel; **llevar algo arrastrado** to drag sth along
arrear [arre'ar] *vt* to drive on, urge on ▷ *vi* to hurry along
arrebatar [arreβa'tar] *vt* to snatch (away), seize; (*fig*) to captivate
arrebato [arre'βato] *nm* fit of rage, fury; (*éxtasis*) rapture
arrecife [arre'θife] *nm* reef
arreglado, -a [arre'ɣlaðo, a] *adj* (*ordenado*) neat, orderly; (*moderado*) moderate, reasonable
arreglar [arre'ɣlar] *vt* (*poner orden*) to tidy up; (*algo roto*) to fix, repair; (*problema*) to solve; **arreglarse** *vr* to reach an understanding; **arreglárselas** (*fam*) to get by, manage
arreglo [a'rreɣlo] *nm* settlement; (*orden*) order; (*acuerdo*) agreement; (*Mús*) arrangement, setting
arremangar [arreman'gar] *vt* to roll up, turn up; **arremangarse** *vr* to roll up one's sleeves
arremeter [arreme'ter] *vi*: **~ contra** to attack, rush at
arrendamiento [arrenda'mjento] *nm* letting; (*alquilar*) hiring; (*contrato*) lease; (*alquiler*) rent; **arrendar** *vt* to let, lease; to rent; **arrendatario, -a** *nm/f* tenant
arreos [a'rreos] *nmpl* (*de caballo*) harness *sg*, trappings
arrepentimiento [arrepenti'mjento] *nm* regret, repentance
arrepentirse [arrepen'tirse] *vr* to repent; **~ de** to regret
arresto [a'rresto] *nm* arrest; (*Mil*) detention; (*audacia*) boldness, daring; **arresto domiciliario** house arrest
arriar [a'rrjar] *vt* (*velas*) to haul down;

(*bandera*) to lower, strike; (*cable*) to pay out

PALABRA CLAVE

arriba [a'rriβa] *adv* **1** (*posición*) above; **desde arriba** from above; **arriba de todo** at the very top, right on top; **Juan está arriba** Juan is upstairs; **lo arriba mencionado** the aforementioned
2 (*dirección*): **calle arriba** up the street
3 de arriba abajo from top to bottom; **mirar a algn de arriba abajo** to look sb up and down
4 para arriba: de 5000 euros para arriba from 5000 euros up(wards)
▷ *adj*: **de arriba: el piso de arriba** the upstairs (BRIT) flat *o* apartment; **la parte de arriba** the top *o* upper part
▷ *prep*: **arriba de** (LAM: *por encima de*) above; **arriba de 200 dólares** more than 200 dollars
▷ *excl*: **¡arriba!** up!; **¡manos arriba!** hands up!; **¡arriba España!** long live Spain!

arribar [arri'βar] *vi* to put into port; (*llegar*) to arrive
arriendo *etc* [a'rrjendo] *vb V* **arrendar** ▷ *nm* = **arrendamiento**
arriesgado, -a [arrjes'ɣaðo, a] *adj* (*peligroso*) risky; (*audaz*) bold, daring
arriesgar [arrjes'ɣar] *vt* to risk; (*poner en peligro*) to endanger; **arriesgarse** *vr* to take a risk
arrimar [arri'mar] *vt* (*acercar*) to bring close; (*poner de lado*) to set aside; **arrimarse** *vr* to come close *o* closer; **~se a** to lean on
arrinconar [arrinko'nar] *vt* (*colocar*) to put in a corner; (*enemigo*) to corner; (*fig*) to put on one side; (*abandonar*) to push aside
arroba [a'rroβa] *nf* (*Internet*) at (sign)
arrodillarse [arroði'ʎarse] *vr* to kneel (down)
arrogante [arro'ɣante] *adj* arrogant
arrojar [arro'xar] *vt* to throw, hurl; (*humo*) to emit, give out; (*Com*) to yield, produce; **arrojarse** *vr* to throw *o* hurl o.s.
arrojo [a'rroxo] *nm* daring
arrollador, a [arroʎa'ðor, a] *adj* overwhelming
arrollar [arro'ʎar] *vt* (*Auto etc*) to run over, knock down; (*Deporte*) to crush
arropar [arro'par] *vt* to cover, wrap up; **arroparse** *vr* to wrap o.s. up
arroyo [a'rrojo] *nm* stream; (*de la calle*) gutter
arroz [a'rroθ] *nm* rice; **arroz con leche** rice pudding
arruga [a'rruɣa] *nf* (*de cara*) wrinkle; (*de vestido*) crease; **arrugar** [arru'ɣar] *vt* to wrinkle; to crease; **arrugarse** *vr* to get creased
arruinar [arrwi'nar] *vt* to ruin, wreck; **arruinarse** *vr* to be ruined, go bankrupt
arsenal [arse'nal] *nm* naval dockyard; (*Mil*) arsenal
arte ['arte] (*gen m en sg y siempre f en pl*) *nm* art; (*maña*) skill, guile; **artes** *nfpl* (*bellas artes*) arts
artefacto [arte'fakto] *nm* appliance
arteria [ar'terja] *nf* artery
artesanía [artesa'nia] *nf* craftsmanship; (*artículos*) handicrafts *pl*; **artesano, -a** *nm/f* artisan, craftsman(-woman)
ártico, -a ['artiko, a] *adj* Arctic ▷ *nm*: **el Á~** the Arctic
articulación [artikula'θjon] *nf* articulation; (*Med, Tec*) joint
artículo [ar'tikulo] *nm* article; (*cosa*) thing, article; **artículos** *nmpl* (*Com*) goods; **artículos de escritorio** stationery
artífice [ar'tifiθe] *nmf* (*fig*) architect
artificial [artifi'θjal] *adj* artificial
artillería [artiʎe'ria] *nf* artillery
artilugio [arti'luxjo] *nm* gadget
artimaña [arti'maɲa] *nf* trap, snare; (*astucia*) cunning
artista [ar'tista] *nmf* (*pintor*) artist,

painter; (*Teatro*) artist, artiste; **artista de cine** film actor/actress; **artístico, -a** *adj* artistic
artritis [ar'tritis] *nf* arthritis
arveja [ar'βexa] (LAM) *nf* pea
arzobispo [arθo'βispo] *nm* archbishop
as [as] *nm* ace
asa ['asa] *nf* handle; (*fig*) lever
asado [a'saðo] *nm* roast (meat); (LAM: *barbacoa*) barbecue

ASADO

Traditional Latin American barbecues, especially in the River Plate area, are celebrated in the open air around a large grill which is used to grill mainly beef and various kinds of spicy pork sausage. They are usually very common during the summer and can go on for several days. The head cook is nearly always a man.

asador [asa'ðor] *nm* spit
asadura [asa'ðura] *nf* entrails *pl*, offal
asalariado, -a [asala'rjaðo, a] *adj* paid, salaried ▷ *nm/f* wage earner
asaltar [asal'tar] *vt* to attack, assault; (*fig*) to assail; **asalto** *nm* attack, assault; (*Deporte*) round
asamblea [asam'blea] *nf* assembly; (*reunión*) meeting
asar [a'sar] *vt* to roast
ascendencia [asθen'denθja] *nf* ancestry; (LAM: *influencia*) ascendancy; **de ~ francesa** of French origin
ascender [asθen'der] *vi* (*subir*) to ascend, rise; (*ser promovido*) to gain promotion ▷ *vt* to promote; **~ a** to amount to; **ascendiente** *nm* influence ▷ *nmf* ancestor
ascensión [asθen'sjon] *nf* ascent; (*Rel*): **la A~** the Ascension
ascenso [as'θenso] *nm* ascent; (*promoción*) promotion
ascensor [asθen'sor] *nm* lift (BRIT), elevator (US)
asco ['asko] *nm*: **¡qué ~!** how revolting *o* disgusting; **el ajo me da ~** I hate *o* loathe garlic; **estar hecho un ~** to be filthy
ascua ['askwa] *nf* ember
aseado, -a [ase'aðo, a] *adj* clean; (*arreglado*) tidy; (*pulcro*) smart
asear [ase'ar] *vt* to clean, wash; to tidy (up)
asediar [ase'ðjar] *vt* (*Mil*) to besiege, lay siege to; (*fig*) to chase, pester; **asedio** *nm* siege; (*Com*) run
asegurado, -a [aseɣu'raðo, a] *adj* insured
asegurador, a [aseɣura'ðor, a] *nm/f* insurer
asegurar [aseɣu'rar] *vt* (*consolidar*) to secure, fasten; (*dar garantía de*) to guarantee; (*preservar*) to safeguard; (*afirmar, dar por cierto*) to assure, affirm; (*tranquilizar*) to reassure; (*tomar un seguro*) to insure; **asegurarse** *vr* to assure o.s., make sure
asemejarse [aseme'xarse] *vr* to be alike; **~ a** to be like, resemble
asentado, -a [asen'taðo, a] *adj* established, settled
asentar [asen'tar] *vt* (*sentar*) to seat, sit down; (*poner*) to place, establish; (*alisar*) to level, smooth down *o* out; (*anotar*) to note down ▷ *vi* to be suitable, suit
asentir [asen'tir] *vi* to assent, agree; **~ con la cabeza** to nod (one's head)
aseo [a'seo] *nm* cleanliness; **aseos** *nmpl* (*servicios*) toilet *sg* (BRIT), cloakroom *sg* (BRIT), restroom *sg* (US)
aséptico, -a [a'septiko, a] *adj* germ-free, free from infection
asequible [ase'kiβle] *adj* (*precio*) reasonable; (*meta*) attainable; (*persona*) approachable
asesinar [asesi'nar] *vt* to murder; (*Pol*) to assassinate; **asesinato** *nm* murder; assassination
asesino, -a [ase'sino, a] *nm/f*

murderer, killer; (*Pol*) assassin

asesor, a [ase'sor, a] *nm/f* adviser, consultant; **asesorar** [aseso'rar] *vt* (*Jur*) to advise, give legal advice to; (*Com*) to act as consultant to; **asesorarse** *vr*: **asesorarse con** *o* **de** to take advice from, consult; **asesoría** *nf* (*cargo*) consultancy; (*oficina*) consultant's office

asestar [ases'tar] *vt* (*golpe*) to deal, strike

asfalto [as'falto] *nm* asphalt

asfixia [as'fiksja] *nf* asphyxia, suffocation; **asfixiar** [asfik'sjar] *vt* to asphyxiate, suffocate; **asfixiarse** *vr* to be asphyxiated, suffocate

así [a'si] *adv* (*de esta manera*) in this way, like this, thus; (*aunque*) although; (*tan pronto como*) as soon as; **~ que** so; **~ como** as well as; **~ y todo** even so; **¿no es ~?** isn't it?, didn't you? *etc*; **~ de grande** this big

Asia ['asja] *nf* Asia; **asiático, -a** *adj*, *nm/f* Asian, Asiatic

asiduo, -a [a'siðwo, a] *adj* assiduous; (*frecuente*) frequent ▷ *nm/f* regular (customer)

asiento [a'sjento] *nm* (*mueble*) seat, chair; (*de coche, en tribunal etc*) seat; (*localidad*) seat, place; (*fundamento*) site; **asiento delantero/trasero** front/back seat

asignación [asiɣna'θjon] *nf* (*atribución*) assignment; (*reparto*) allocation; (*sueldo*) salary; **asignación (semanal)** pocket money

asignar [asiɣ'nar] *vt* to assign, allocate

asignatura [asiɣna'tura] *nf* subject; course

asilo [a'silo] *nm* (*refugio*) asylum, refuge; (*establecimiento*) home, institution; **asilo político** political asylum

asimilar [asimi'lar] *vt* to assimilate

asimismo [asi'mismo] *adv* in the same way, likewise

asistencia [asis'tenθja] *nf* audience; (*Med*) attendance; (*ayuda*) assistance; **asistencia en carretera** roadside assistance; **asistente** *nmf* assistant; **los asistentes** those present; **asistente social** social worker

asistido, -a [asis'tiðo, a] *adj*: **~ por ordenador** computer-assisted

asistir [asis'tir] *vt* to assist, help ▷ *vi*: **~ a** to attend, be present at

asma ['asma] *nf* asthma

asno ['asno] *nm* donkey; (*fig*) ass

asociación [asoθja'θjon] *nf* association; (*Com*) partnership; **asociado, -a** *adj* associate ▷ *nm/f* associate; (*Com*) partner

asociar [aso'θjar] *vt* to associate

asomar [aso'mar] *vt* to show, stick out ▷ *vi* to appear; **asomarse** *vr* to appear, show up; **~ la cabeza por la ventana** to put one's head out of the window

asombrar [asom'brar] *vt* to amaze, astonish; **asombrarse** *vr* (*sorprenderse*) to be amazed; (*asustarse*) to get a fright; **asombro** *nm* amazement, astonishment; (*susto*) fright; **asombroso, -a** *adj* astonishing, amazing

asomo [a'somo] *nm* hint, sign

aspa ['aspa] *nf* (*cruz*) cross; (*de molino*) sail; **en ~** X-shaped

aspaviento [aspa'βjento] *nm* exaggerated display of feeling; (*fam*) fuss

aspecto [as'pekto] *nm* (*apariencia*) look, appearance; (*fig*) aspect

áspero, -a ['aspero, a] *adj* rough; bitter; sour; harsh

aspersión [asper'sjon] *nf* sprinkling

aspiración [aspira'θjon] *nf* breath, inhalation; (*Mús*) short pause; **aspiraciones** *nfpl* (*ambiciones*) aspirations

aspirador [aspira'ðor] *nm* = **aspiradora**

aspiradora [aspira'ðora] *nf* vacuum cleaner, Hoover®

aspirante [aspi'rante] *nmf*

(*candidato*) candidate; (*Deporte*) contender
aspirar [aspi'rar] *vt* to breathe in ▷ *vi*: **~ a** to aspire to
aspirina [aspi'rina] *nf* aspirin
asqueroso, -a [aske'roso, a] *adj* disgusting, sickening
asta ['asta] *nf* lance; (*arpón*) spear; (*mango*) shaft, handle; (*Zool*) horn; **a media ~** at half mast
asterisco [aste'risko] *nm* asterisk
astilla [as'tiʎa] *nf* splinter; (*pedacito*) chip; **astillas** *nfpl* (*leña*) firewood *sg*
astillero [asti'ʎero] *nm* shipyard
astro ['astro] *nm* star
astrología [astrolo'xia] *nf* astrology; **astrólogo, -a** *nm/f* astrologer
astronauta [astro'nauta] *nmf* astronaut
astronomía [astrono'mia] *nf* astronomy
astucia [as'tuθja] *nf* astuteness; (*ardid*) clever trick
asturiano, -a [astu'rjano, a] *adj, nm/f* Asturian
astuto, -a [as'tuto, a] *adj* astute; (*taimado*) cunning
asumir [asu'mir] *vt* to assume
asunción [asun'θjon] *nf* assumption; (*Rel*): **A~** Assumption
asunto [a'sunto] *nm* (*tema*) matter, subject; (*negocio*) business
asustar [asus'tar] *vt* to frighten; **asustarse** *vr* to be (*o* become) frightened
atacar [ata'kar] *vt* to attack
atadura [ata'ðura] *nf* bond, tie
atajar [ata'xar] *vt* (*enfermedad, mal*) to stop ▷ *vi* (*persona*) to take a short cut
atajo [a'taxo] *nm* short cut
atañer [ata'ɲer] *vi*: **~ a** to concern
ataque *etc* [a'take] *vb V* **atacar** ▷ *nm* attack; **ataque cardíaco** heart attack
atar [a'tar] *vt* to tie, tie up
atarantado, -a [ataran'taðo, a] (MÉX) *adj* (*aturdido*) dazed
atardecer [atarðe'θer] *vi* to get dark ▷ *nm* evening; (*crepúsculo*) dusk
atareado, -a [atare'aðo, a] *adj* busy
atascar [atas'kar] *vt* to clog up; (*obstruir*) to jam; (*fig*) to hinder; **atascarse** *vr* to stall; (*cañería*) to get blocked up; **atasco** *nm* obstruction; (*Auto*) traffic jam
ataúd [ata'uð] *nm* coffin
ataviar [ata'βjar] *vt* to deck, array
atemorizar [atemori'θar] *vt* to frighten, scare
Atenas [a'tenas] *n* Athens
atención [aten'θjon] *nf* attention; (*bondad*) kindness ▷ *excl* (be) careful!, look out!
atender [aten'der] *vt* to attend to, look after; (*Tel*) to answer ▷ *vi* to pay attention
atenerse [ate'nerse] *vr*: **~ a** to abide by, adhere to
atentado [aten'taðo] *nm* crime, illegal act; (*asalto*) assault; (*tb*: **~ terrorista**) terrorist attack; **~ contra la vida de algn** attempt on sb's life; **atentado suicida** suicide bombing
atentamente [atenta'mente] *adv*: **Le saluda ~** Yours faithfully
atentar [aten'tar] *vi*: **~ a** *o* **contra** to commit an outrage against
atento, -a [a'tento, a] *adj* attentive, observant; (*cortés*) polite, thoughtful; **estar ~ a** (*explicación*) to pay attention to
atenuar [ate'nwar] *vt* (*disminuir*) to lessen, minimize
ateo, -a [a'teo, a] *adj* atheistic ▷ *nm/f* atheist
aterrador, a [aterra'ðor, a] *adj* frightening
aterrizaje [aterri'θaxe] *nm* landing; **aterrizaje forzoso** emergency *o* forced landing
aterrizar [aterri'θar] *vi* to land
aterrorizar [aterrori'θar] *vt* to terrify
atesorar [ateso'rar] *vt* to hoard
atestar [ates'tar] *vt* to pack, stuff; (*Jur*) to attest, testify to
atestiguar [atesti'ɣwar] *vt* to testify

to, bear witness to
atiborrar [atiβo'rrar] *vt* to fill, stuff; **atiborrarse** *vr* to stuff o.s.
ático ['atiko] *nm* (*desván*) attic; (*apartamento*) penthouse
atinado, -a [ati'naðo, a] *adj* (*sensato*) wise; (*correcto*) right, correct
atinar [ati'nar] *vi* (*al disparar*): **~ al blanco** to hit the target; (*fig*) to be right
atizar [ati'θar] *vt* to poke; (*horno etc*) to stoke; (*fig*) to stir up, rouse
atlántico, -a [at'lantiko, a] *adj* Atlantic ▷ *nm*: **el (océano) A~** the Atlantic (Ocean)
atlas ['atlas] *nm inv* atlas
atleta [at'leta] *nm* athlete; **atlético, -a** *adj* athletic; **atletismo** *nm* athletics *sg*
atmósfera [at'mosfera] *nf* atmosphere
atolladero [atoʎa'ðero] *nm* (*fig*) jam, fix
atómico, -a [a'tomiko, a] *adj* atomic
átomo ['atomo] *nm* atom
atónito, -a [a'tonito, a] *adj* astonished, amazed
atontado, -a [aton'taðo, a] *adj* stunned; (*bobo*) silly, daft
atormentar [atormen'tar] *vt* to torture; (*molestar*) to torment; (*acosar*) to plague, harass
atornillar [atorni'ʎar] *vt* to screw on *o* down
atosigar [atosi'ɣar] *vt* to harass, pester
atracador, a [atraka'ðor, a] *nm/f* robber
atracar [atra'kar] *vt* (*Náut*) to moor; (*robar*) to hold up, rob ▷ *vi* to moor; **atracarse** *vr*: **~se (de)** to stuff o.s. (with)
atracción [atrak'θjon] *nf* attraction
atraco [a'trako] *nm* holdup, robbery
atracón [atra'kon] *nm*: **darse** *o* **pegarse un ~ (de)** (*fam*) to stuff o.s. (with)
atractivo, -a [atrak'tiβo, a] *adj* attractive ▷ *nm* appeal
atraer [atra'er] *vt* to attract
atragantarse [atraɣan'tarse] *vr*: **~ (con)** to choke (on); **se me ha atragantado el chico** I can't stand the boy
atrancar [atran'kar] *vt* (*puerta*) to bar, bolt
atrapar [atra'par] *vt* to trap; (*resfriado etc*) to catch
atrás [a'tras] *adv* (*movimiento*) back(-wards); (*lugar*) behind; (*tiempo*) previously; **ir hacia ~** to go back(wards), to go to the rear; **estar ~** to be behind *o* at the back
atrasado, -a [atra'saðo, a] *adj* slow; (*pago*) overdue, late; (*país*) backward
atrasar [atra'sar] *vi* to be slow; **atrasarse** *vr* to remain behind; (*tren*) to be *o* run late; **atraso** *nm* slowness; lateness, delay; (*de país*) backwardness; **atrasos** *nmpl* (*Com*) arrears
atravesar [atraβe'sar] *vt* (*cruzar*) to cross (over); (*traspasar*) to pierce; to go through; (*poner al través*) to lay *o* put across; **atravesarse** *vr* to come in between; (*intervenir*) to interfere
atravieso *etc vb V* **atravesar**
atreverse [atre'βerse] *vr* to dare; (*insolentarse*) to be insolent; **atrevido, -a** *adj* daring; insolent; **atrevimiento** *nm* daring; insolence
atribución [atriβu'θjon] *nf* attribution; **atribuciones** *nfpl* (*Pol*) powers; (*Admin*) responsibilities
atribuir [atriβu'ir] *vt* to attribute; (*funciones*) to confer
atributo [atri'βuto] *nm* attribute
atril [a'tril] *nm* (*para libro*) lectern; (*Mús*) music stand
atropellar [atrope'ʎar] *vt* (*derribar*) to knock over *o* down; (*empujar*) to push (aside); (*Auto*) to run over, run down; (*agraviar*) to insult; **atropello** *nm* (*Auto*) accident; (*empujón*) push; (*agravio*) wrong; (*atrocidad*) outrage
atroz [a'troθ] *adj* atrocious, awful
ATS *nmf abr* (= *Ayudante Técnico*

Sanitario) nurse
atuendo [a'twendo] *nm* attire
atún [a'tun] *nm* tuna
aturdir [atur'ðir] *vt* to stun; (*de ruido*) to deafen; (*fig*) to dumbfound, bewilder
audacia [au'ðaθja] *nf* boldness, audacity; **audaz** *adj* bold, audacious
audición [auði'θjon] *nf* hearing; (*Teatro*) audition
audiencia [au'ðjenθja] *nf* audience; (*Jur: tribunal*) court
audífono [au'ðifono] *nm* (*para sordos*) hearing aid
auditor [auði'tor] *nm* (*Jur*) judge advocate; (*Com*) auditor
auditorio [auði'torjo] *nm* audience; (*sala*) auditorium
auge ['auxe] *nm* boom; (*clímax*) climax
augurar [auɣu'rar] *vt* to predict; (*presagiar*) to portend
augurio [au'ɣurjo] *nm* omen
aula ['aula] *nf* classroom; (*en universidad etc*) lecture room
aullar [au'ʎar] *vi* to howl, yell
aullido [au'ʎiðo] *nm* howl, yell
aumentar [aumen'tar] *vt* to increase; (*precios*) to put up; (*producción*) to step up; (*con microscopio, anteojos*) to magnify ▷ *vi* to increase, be on the increase; **aumentarse** *vr* to increase, be on the increase; **aumento** *nm* increase; rise
aun [a'un] *adv* even; **~ así** even so; **~ más** even *o* yet more
aún [a'un] *adv*: **~ está aquí** he's still here; **~ no lo sabemos** we don't know yet; **¿no ha venido ~?** hasn't she come yet?
aunque [a'unke] *conj* though, although, even though
aúpa [a'upa] *excl* come on!
auricular [auriku'lar] *nm* (*Tel*) receiver; **auriculares** *nmpl* (*cascos*) headphones
aurora [au'rora] *nf* dawn
ausencia [au'senθja] *nf* absence
ausentarse [ausen'tarse] *vr* to go away; (*por poco tiempo*) to go out
ausente [au'sente] *adj* absent
austero, -a [aus'tero, a] *adj* austere
austral [aus'tral] *adj* southern ▷ *nm monetary unit of Argentina*
Australia [aus'tralja] *nf* Australia; **australiano, -a** *adj, nm/f* Australian
Austria ['austrja] *nf* Austria; **austríaco, -a** *adj, nm/f* Austrian
auténtico, -a [au'tentiko, a] *adj* authentic
auto ['auto] *nm* (*Jur*) edict, decree; (*: orden*) writ; (*Auto*) car; **autos** *nmpl* (*Jur*) proceedings; (*: acta*) court record *sg*
autoadhesivo [autoaðe'siβo] *adj* self-adhesive; (*sobre*) self-sealing
autobiografía [autoβjoɣra'fia] *nf* autobiography
autobomba [auto'bomba] (RPL) *nm* fire engine
autobronceador [autoβronθea'ðor] *adj* self-tanning
autobús [auto'βus] *nm* bus; **autobús de línea** long-distance coach
autocar [auto'kar] *nm* coach (BRIT), (passenger) bus (US)
autóctono, -a [au'toktono, a] *adj* native, indigenous
autodefensa [autoðe'fensa] *nf* self-defence
autodidacta [autoði'ðakta] *adj* self-taught
autoescuela [autoes'kwela] (ESP) *nf* driving school
autógrafo [au'toɣrafo] *nm* autograph
autómata [au'tomata] *nm* automaton
automático, -a [auto'matiko, a] *adj* automatic ▷ *nm* press stud
automóvil [auto'moβil] *nm* (motor) car (BRIT), automobile (US); **automovilismo** *nm* (*actividad*) motoring; (*Deporte*) motor racing; **automovilista** *nmf* motorist, driver
autonomía [autono'mia] *nf* autonomy; **autónomo, -a** (ESP), **autonómico, -a** (ESP) *adj* (*Pol*)

autonomous
autopista [auto'pista] *nf* motorway (BRIT), freeway (US); **autopista de cuota** (ESP) *o* **peaje** (MÉX) toll (BRIT) *o* turnpike (US) road
autopsia [au'topsja] *nf* autopsy, postmortem
autor, a [au'tor, a] *nm/f* author
autoridad [autori'ðað] *nf* authority; **autoritario, -a** *adj* authoritarian
autorización [autoriθa'θjon] *nf* authorization; **autorizado, -a** *adj* authorized; (*aprobado*) approved
autorizar [autori'θar] *vt* to authorize; (*aprobar*) to approve
autoservicio [autoser'βiθjo] *nm* (*tienda*) self-service shop (BRIT) *o* store (US); (*restaurante*) self-service restaurant
autostop [auto'stop] *nm* hitch-hiking; **hacer ~** to hitch-hike; **autostopista** *nmf* hitch-hiker
autovía [auto'βia] *nf* ≈ A-road (BRIT), dual carriageway (BRIT), ≈ state highway (US)
auxiliar [auksi'ljar] *vt* to help ▷ *nmf* assistant; **auxilio** *nm* assistance, help; **primeros auxilios** first aid *sg*
Av *abr* (= *Avenida*) Av(e)
aval [a'βal] *nm* guarantee; (*persona*) guarantor
avalancha [aβa'lantʃa] *nf* avalanche
avance [a'βanθe] *nm* advance; (*pago*) advance payment; (*Cine*) trailer
avanzar [aβan'θar] *vt, vi* to advance
avaricia [aβa'riθja] *nf* avarice, greed; **avaricioso, -a** *adj* avaricious, greedy
avaro, -a [a'βaro, a] *adj* miserly, mean ▷ *nm/f* miser
Avda *abr* (= *Avenida*) Av(e)
AVE ['aβe] *nm abr* (= *Alta Velocidad Española*) ≈ bullet train
ave ['aβe] *nf* bird; **ave de rapiña** bird of prey
avecinarse [aβeθi'narse] *vr* (*tormenta*: *fig*) to be on the way
avellana [aβe'ʎana] *nf* hazelnut; **avellano** *nm* hazel tree
avemaría [aβema'ria] *nm* Hail Mary, Ave Maria
avena [a'βena] *nf* oats *pl*
avenida [aβe'niða] *nf* (*calle*) avenue
aventajar [aβenta'xar] *vt* (*sobrepasar*) to surpass, outstrip
aventón [aβen'ton] (MÉX: *fam*) *nm* ride; **dar ~ a algn** to give sb a ride
aventura [aβen'tura] *nf* adventure; **aventurero, -a** *adj* adventurous
avergonzar [aβerɣon'θar] *vt* to shame; (*desconcertar*) to embarrass; **avergonzarse** *vr* to be ashamed; to be embarrassed
avería [aβe'ria] *nf* (*Tec*) breakdown, fault
averiado, -a [aβe'rjaðo, a] *adj* broken down; **"~"** "out of order"
averiguar [aβeri'ɣwar] *vt* to investigate; (*descubrir*) to find out, ascertain
avestruz [aβes'truθ] *nm* ostrich
aviación [aβja'θjon] *nf* aviation; (*fuerzas aéreas*) air force
aviador, a [aβja'ðor, a] *nm/f* aviator, airman(-woman)
ávido, -a ['aβiðo, a] *adj* avid, eager
avinagrado, -a [aβina'ɣraðo, a] *adj* sour, acid
avión [a'βjon] *nm* aeroplane; (*ave*) martin; **avión de reacción** jet (plane)
avioneta [aβjo'neta] *nf* light aircraft
avisar [aβi'sar] *vt* (*advertir*) to warn, notify; (*informar*) to tell; (*aconsejar*) to advise, counsel; **aviso** *nm* warning; (*noticia*) notice
avispa [a'βispa] *nf* wasp
avispado, -a [aβis'paðo, a] *adj* sharp, clever
avivar [aβi'βar] *vt* to strengthen, intensify
axila [ak'sila] *nf* armpit
ay [ai] *excl* (*dolor*) ow!, ouch!; (*aflicción*) oh!, oh dear!; **¡~ de mi!** poor me!
ayer [a'jer] *adv, nm* yesterday; **antes de ~** the day before yesterday; **~ mismo** only yesterday
ayote [a'jote] (CAM) *nm* pumpkin

ayuda [a'juða] *nf* help, assistance ▷ *nm* page; **ayudante** *nmf* assistant, helper; (*Escol*) assistant; (*Mil*) adjutant
ayudar [aju'ðar] *vt* to help, assist
ayunar [aju'nar] *vi* to fast; **ayunas** *nfpl*: **estar en ayunas** to be fasting; **ayuno** *nm* fast; fasting
ayuntamiento [ajunta'mjento] *nm* (*consejo*) town (*o* city) council; (*edificio*) town (*o* city) hall
azafata [aθa'fata] *nf* air stewardess
azafrán [aθa'fran] *nm* saffron
azahar [aθa'ar] *nm* orange/lemon blossom
azar [a'θar] *nm* (*casualidad*) chance, fate; (*desgracia*) misfortune, accident; **por ~** by chance; **al ~** at random
Azores [a'θores]. *nfpl*: **las ~** the Azores
azotar [aθo'tar] *vt* to whip, beat; (*pegar*) to spank; **azote** *nm* (*látigo*) whip; (*latigazo*) lash, stroke; (*en las nalgas*) spank; (*calamidad*) calamity
azotea [aθo'tea] *nf* (flat) roof
azteca [aθ'teka] *adj, nmf* Aztec
azúcar [a'θukar] *nm* sugar; **azucarado, -a** *adj* sugary, sweet
azucarero, -a [aθuka'rero, a] *adj* sugar *cpd* ▷ *nm* sugar bowl
azucena [aθu'θena] *nf* white lily
azufre [a'θufre] *nm* sulphur
azul [a'θul] *adj, nm* blue; **azul celeste/marino** sky/navy blue
azulejo [aθu'lexo] *nm* tile
azuzar [aθu'θar] *vt* to incite, egg on

B.A. *abr* (= *Buenos Aires*) B.A.
baba ['baβa] *nf* spittle, saliva; **babear** *vi* to drool, slaver
babero [ba'βero] *nm* bib
babor [ba'βor] *nm* port (side)
babosada [baβo'saða] (MÉX, CAM: *fam*) *nf* drivel; **baboso, -a** [ba'βoso, a] (LAM: *fam*) *adj* silly
baca ['baka] *nf* (*Auto*) luggage *o* roof rack
bacalao [baka'lao] *nm* cod(fish)
bache ['batʃe] *nm* pothole, rut; (*fig*) bad patch
bachillerato [batʃiʎe'rato] *nm higher secondary school course*
bacinica [baθi'nika] (LAM) *nf* potty
bacteria [bak'terja] *nf* bacterium, germ
Bahama [ba'ama]: **las (Islas) ~** *nfpl* the Bahamas
bahía [ba'ia] *nf* bay
bailar [bai'lar] *vt, vi* to dance; **bailarín, -ina** *nm/f* (ballet) dancer; **baile** *nm* dance; (*formal*) ball
baja ['baxa] *nf* drop, fall; (*Mil*)

casualty; **dar de ~** (*soldado*) to discharge; (*empleado*) to dismiss
bajada [ba'xaða] *nf* descent; (*camino*) slope; (*de aguas*) ebb
bajar [ba'xar] *vi* to go down, come down; (*temperatura, precios*) to drop, fall ▷ *vt* (*cabeza*) to bow; (*escalera*) to go down, come down; (*precio, voz*) to lower; (*llevar abajo*) to take down; **bajarse** *vr* (*de coche*) to get out; (*de autobús, tren*) to get off; **~ de** (*coche*) to get out of; (*autobús, tren*) to get off; **~se algo de Internet** to download sth from the Internet
bajío [ba'xio] (LAM) *nm* lowlands *pl*
bajo, -a ['baxo] *adj* (*mueble, número, precio*) low; (*piso*) ground; (*de estatura*) small, short; (*color*) pale; (*sonido*) faint, soft, low; (*voz: en tono*) deep; (*metal*) base; (*humilde*) low, humble ▷ *adv* (*hablar*) softly, quietly; (*volar*) low ▷ *prep* under, below, underneath ▷ *nm* (*Mús*) bass; **~ la lluvia** in the rain
bajón [ba'xon] *nm* fall, drop
bakalao [baka'lao] (ESP: *fam*) *nm* rave (music)
bala ['bala] *nf* bullet
balacear [balaθe'ar] (MÉX, CAM) *vt* to shoot
balance [ba'lanθe] *nm* (*Com*) balance; (*: libro*) balance sheet; (*: cuenta general*) stocktaking
balancear [balanθe'ar] *vt* to balance ▷ *vi* to swing (to and fro); (*vacilar*) to hesitate; **balancearse** *vr* to swing (to and fro), to hesitate
balanza [ba'lanθa] *nf* scales *pl*, balance; **balanza comercial** balance of trade; **balanza de pagos** balance of payments
balaustrada [balaus'traða] *nf* balustrade; (*pasamanos*) banisters *pl*
balazo [ba'laθo] *nm* (*golpe*) shot; (*herida*) bullet wound
balbucear [balβuθe'ar] *vi, vt* to stammer, stutter
balcón [bal'kon] *nm* balcony
balde ['balde] *nm* bucket, pail; **de ~** (for) free, for nothing; **en ~** in vain
baldosa [bal'dosa] *nf* (*azulejo*) floor tile; (*grande*) flagstone; **baldosín** *nm* (small) tile
Baleares [bale'ares] *nfpl*: **las (Islas) ~** the Balearic Islands
balero [ba'lero] (LAM) *nm* (*juguete*) cup-and-ball toy
baliza [ba'liθa] *nf* (*Aviac*) beacon; (*Náut*) buoy
ballena [ba'ʎena] *nf* whale
ballet [ba'le] (*pl* **~s**) *nm* ballet
balneario [balne'arjo] *nm* spa; (CS: *en la costa*) seaside resort
balón [ba'lon] *nm* ball
baloncesto [balon'θesto] *nm* basketball
balonmano [balon'mano] *nm* handball
balsa ['balsa] *nf* raft; (*Bot*) balsa wood
bálsamo ['balsamo] *nm* balsam, balm
baluarte [ba'lwarte] *nm* bastion, bulwark
bambú [bam'bu] *nm* bamboo
banana [ba'nana] (LAM) *nf* banana; **banano** *nm* (LAM: *árbol*) banana tree; (CAM: *fruta*) banana
banca ['banka] *nf* (*Com*) banking
bancario, -a [ban'karjo, a] *adj* banking *cpd*, bank *cpd*
bancarrota [banka'rrota] *nf* bankruptcy; **hacer ~** to go bankrupt
banco ['banko] *nm* bench; (*Escol*) desk; (*Com*) bank; (*Geo*) stratum; **banco de arena** sandbank; **banco de crédito** credit bank; **banco de datos** databank
banda ['banda] *nf* band; (*pandilla*) gang; (*Náut*) side, edge; **banda ancha** broadband; **banda sonora** soundtrack
bandada [ban'daða] *nf* (*de pájaros*) flock; (*de peces*) shoal
bandazo [ban'daθo] *nm*: **dar ~s** to sway from side to side
bandeja [ban'dexa] *nf* tray
bandera [ban'dera] *nf* flag
banderilla [bande'riʎa] *nf* banderilla
bandido [ban'diðo] *nm* bandit

bando ['bando] *nm* (*edicto*) edict, proclamation; (*facción*) faction; **bandos** *nmpl* (*Rel*) banns

bandolera [bando'lera] *nf*: **llevar en ~** to wear across one's chest

banquero [ban'kero] *nm* banker

banqueta [ban'keta] *nf* stool; (MÉX: *en calle*) pavement (BRIT), sidewalk (US)

banquete [ban'kete] *nm* banquet; (*para convidados*) formal dinner; **banquete de boda(s)** wedding reception

banquillo [ban'kiʎo] *nm* (*Jur*) dock, prisoner's bench; (*banco*) bench; (*para los pies*) footstool

banquina [ban'kina] (RPL) *nf* hard shoulder (BRIT), berm (US)

bañadera [baɲa'ðera] (RPL) *nf* bathtub

bañador [baɲa'ðor] (ESP) *nm* swimming costume (BRIT), bathing suit (US)

bañar [ba'ɲar] *vt* to bath, bathe; (*objeto*) to dip; (*de barniz*) to coat; **bañarse** *vr* (*en el mar*) to bathe, swim; (*en la bañera*) to have a bath

bañera [ba'ɲera] (ESP) *nf* bath(tub)

bañero, -a [ba'ɲero, a] (CS) *nm/f* lifeguard

bañista [ba'ɲista] *nmf* bather

baño ['baɲo] *nm* (*en bañera*) bath; (*en río*) dip, swim; (*cuarto*) bathroom; (*bañera*) bath(tub); (*capa*) coating; **darse** *o* **tomar un ~** (*en bañera*) to have *o* take a bath; (*en mar, piscina*) to have a swim; **baño María** bain-marie

bar [bar] *nm* bar

barahúnda [bara'unda] *nf* uproar, hubbub

baraja [ba'raxa] *nf* pack (of cards); **barajar** *vt* (*naipes*) to shuffle; (*fig*) to jumble up

baranda [ba'randa] *nf* = **barandilla**

barandilla [baran'diʎa] *nf* rail, railing

barata [ba'rata] (MÉX) *nf* (bargain) sale

baratillo [bara'tiʎo] *nm* (*tienda*) junkshop; (*subasta*) bargain sale; (*conjunto de cosas*) secondhand goods *pl*

barato, -a [ba'rato, a] *adj* cheap ▷ *adv* cheap, cheaply

barba ['barβa] *nf* (*mentón*) chin; (*pelo*) beard

barbacoa [barβa'koa] *nf* (*parrilla*) barbecue; (*carne*) barbecued meat

barbaridad [barβari'ðað] *nf* barbarity; (*acto*) barbarism; (*atrocidad*) outrage; **una ~** (*fam*) loads; **¡qué ~!** (*fam*) how awful!

barbarie [bar'βarje] *nf* barbarism, savagery; (*crueldad*) barbarity

bárbaro, -a ['barβaro, a] *adj* barbarous, cruel; (*grosero*) rough, uncouth ▷ *nm/f* barbarian ▷ *adv*: **lo pasamos ~** (*fam*) we had a great time; **¡qué ~!** (*fam*) how marvellous!; **un éxito ~** (*fam*) a terrific success; **es un tipo ~** (*fam*) he's a great bloke

barbero [bar'βero] *nm* barber, hairdresser

barbilla [bar'βiʎa] *nf* chin, tip of the chin

barbudo, -a [bar'βuðo, a] *adj* bearded

barca ['barka] *nf* (small) boat; **barcaza** *nf* barge

Barcelona [barθe'lona] *n* Barcelona

barco ['barko] *nm* boat; (*grande*) ship; **barco de carga/pesca** cargo/fishing boat; **barco de vela** sailing ship

barda ['barða] (MÉX) *nf* (*de madera*) fence

baremo [ba'remo] *nm* (*Mat: fig*) scale

barítono [ba'ritono] *nm* baritone

barman ['barman] *nm* barman

barniz [bar'niθ] *nm* varnish; (*en loza*) glaze; (*fig*) veneer; **barnizar** *vt* to varnish; (*loza*) to glaze

barómetro [ba'rometro] *nm* barometer

barquillo [bar'kiʎo] *nm* cone, cornet

barra ['barra] *nf* bar, rod; (*de un bar, café*) bar; (*de pan*) French stick; (*palanca*) lever; **barra de labios** lipstick; **barra**

libre free bar

barraca [ba'rraka] *nf* hut, cabin

barranco [ba'rranko] *nm* ravine; (*fig*) difficulty

barrena [ba'rrena] *nf* drill

barrer [ba'rrer] *vt* to sweep; (*quitar*) to sweep away

barrera [ba'rrera] *nf* barrier

barriada [ba'rrjaða] *nf* quarter, district

barricada [barri'kaða] *nf* barricade

barrida [ba'rriða] *nf* sweep, sweeping

barriga [ba'rriɣa] *nf* belly; (*panza*) paunch; **barrigón, -ona** *adj* potbellied; **barrigudo, -a** *adj* potbellied

barril [ba'rril] *nm* barrel, cask

barrio ['barrjo] *nm* (*vecindad*) area, neighborhood (*US*); (*en afueras*) suburb; **barrio chino** (*ESP*) red-light district

barro ['barro] *nm* (*lodo*) mud; (*objetos*) earthenware; (*Med*) pimple

barroco, -a [ba'rroko, a] *adj, nm* baroque

barrote [ba'rrote] *nm* (*de ventana*) bar

bartola [bar'tola] *nf*: **tirarse** *o* **tumbarse a la ~** to take it easy, be lazy

bártulos ['bartulos] *nmpl* things, belongings

barullo [ba'ruʎo] *nm* row, uproar

basar [ba'sar] *vt* to base; **basarse** *vr*: **~se en** to be based on

báscula ['baskula] *nf* (platform) scales

base ['base] *nf* base; **a ~ de** on the basis of; (*mediante*) by means of; **base de datos** (*Inform*) database

básico, -a ['basiko, a] *adj* basic

basílica [ba'silika] *nf* basilica

básquetbol ['basketbol] (*LAM*) *nm* basketball

PALABRA CLAVE

bastante [bas'tante] *adj* **1** (*suficiente*) enough; **bastante dinero** enough *o* sufficient money; **bastantes libros** enough books

2 (*valor intensivo*): **bastante gente** quite a lot of people; **tener bastante calor** to be rather hot

▷ *adv*: **bastante bueno/malo** quite good/rather bad; **bastante rico** pretty rich; **(lo) bastante inteligente (como) para hacer algo** clever enough *o* sufficiently clever to do sth

bastar [bas'tar] *vi* to be enough *o* sufficient; **bastarse** *vr* to be self-sufficient; **~ para** to be enough to; **¡basta!** (that's) enough!

bastardo, -a [bas'tarðo, a] *adj, nm/f* bastard

bastidor [basti'ðor] *nm* frame; (*de coche*) chassis; (*Teatro*) wing; **entre ~es** (*fig*) behind the scenes

basto, -a ['basto, a] *adj* coarse, rough; **bastos** *nmpl* (*Naipes*) ≈ clubs

bastón [bas'ton] *nm* stick, staff; (*para pasear*) walking stick

bastoncillo [baston'θiʎo] *nm* cotton bud

basura [ba'sura] *nf* rubbish (*BRIT*), garbage (*US*) ▷ *adj*: **comida/televisión ~** junk food/TV

basurero [basu'rero] *nm* (*hombre*) dustman (*BRIT*), garbage man (*US*); (*lugar*) dump; (*cubo*) (rubbish) bin (*BRIT*), trash can (*US*)

bata ['bata] *nf* (*gen*) dressing gown; (*cubretodo*) smock, overall; (*Med, Tec etc*) lab(oratory) coat

batalla [ba'taʎa] *nf* battle; **de ~** (*fig*) for everyday use; **batalla campal** pitched battle

batallón [bata'ʎon] *nm* battalion

batata [ba'tata] *nf* sweet potato

batería [bate'ria] *nf* battery; (*Mús*) drums; **batería de cocina** kitchen utensils

batido, -a [ba'tiðo, a] *adj* (*camino*) beaten, well-trodden ▷ *nm* (*Culin*: *de leche*) milk shake

batidora [bati'ðora] *nf* beater, mixer; **batidora eléctrica** food mixer, blender

batir [ba'tir] *vt* to beat, strike; (*vencer*) to beat, defeat; (*revolver*) to beat, mix; **batirse** *vr* to fight; **~ palmas** to applaud
batuta [ba'tuta] *nf* baton; **llevar la ~** (*fig*) to be the boss, be in charge
baúl [ba'ul] *nm* trunk; (*Auto*) boot (BRIT), trunk (US)
bautismo [bau'tismo] *nm* baptism, christening
bautizar [bauti'θar] *vt* to baptize, christen; (*fam: diluir*) to water down; **bautizo** *nm* baptism, christening
bayeta [ba'jeta] *nf* floorcloth
baza ['baθa] *nf* trick; **meter ~** to butt in
bazar [ba'θar] *nm* bazaar
bazofia [ba'θofja] *nf* trash
be [be] *nf name of the letter B*; **be chica/grande** (MÉX) V/B; **be larga** (LAM) B
beato, -a [be'ato, a] *adj* blessed; (*piadoso*) pious
bebé [be'βe] (*pl* **~s**) *nm* baby
bebedero [beβe'ðero, a] (MÉX, CS) *nm* drinking fountain
bebedor, a [beβe'ðor, a] *adj* hard-drinking
beber [be'βer] *vt, vi* to drink
bebida [be'βiða] *nf* drink; **bebido, -a** *adj* drunk
beca ['beka] *nf* grant, scholarship; **becario, -a** [be'karjo, a] *nm/f* scholarship holder, grant holder
bedel [be'ðel] *nm* (*Escol*) janitor; (*Univ*) porter
béisbol ['beisβol] *nm* baseball
Belén [be'len] *nm* Bethlehem; **belén** *nm* (*de Navidad*) nativity scene, crib
belga ['belɣa] *adj, nmf* Belgian
Bélgica ['belxika] *nf* Belgium
bélico, -a ['beliko, a] *adj* (*actitud*) warlike
belleza [be'ʎeθa] *nf* beauty
bello, -a ['beʎo, a] *adj* beautiful, lovely; **Bellas Artes** Fine Art
bellota [be'ʎota] *nf* acorn
bemol [be'mol] *nm* (*Mús*) flat; **esto tiene ~es** (*fam*) this is a tough one
bencina [ben'θina] *nf* (*Quím*) benzine
bendecir [bende'θir] *vt* to bless
bendición [bendi'θjon] *nf* blessing
bendito, -a [ben'dito, a] *pp de* **bendecir** ▷ *adj* holy; (*afortunado*) lucky; (*feliz*) happy; (*sencillo*) simple ▷ *nm/f* simple soul
beneficencia [benefi'θenθja] *nf* charity
beneficiario, -a [benefi'θjarjo, a] *nm/f* beneficiary
beneficio [bene'fiθjo] *nm* (*bien*) benefit, advantage; (*ganancia*) profit, gain; **a ~ de algn** in aid of sb; **beneficioso, -a** *adj* beneficial
benéfico, -a [be'nefiko, a] *adj* charitable
beneplácito [bene'plaθito] *nm* approval, consent
benévolo, -a [be'neβolo, a] *adj* benevolent, kind
benigno, -a [be'niɣno, a] *adj* kind; (*suave*) mild; (*Med: tumor*) benign, non-malignant
berberecho [berβe'retʃo] *nm* (*Zool, Culin*) cockle
berenjena [beren'xena] *nf* aubergine (BRIT), eggplant (US)
Berlín [ber'lin] *n* Berlin
berlinesa [berli'nesa] (RPL) *nf* doughnut, donut (US)
bermudas [ber'muðas] *nfpl* Bermuda shorts
berrido [be'rriðo] *nm* bellow(ing)
berrinche [be'rrintʃe] (*fam*) *nm* temper, tantrum
berro ['berro] *nm* watercress
berza ['berθa] *nf* cabbage
besamel [besa'mel] *nf* (*Culin*) white sauce, bechamel sauce
besar [be'sar] *vt* to kiss; (*fig: tocar*) to graze; **besarse** *vr* to kiss (one another); **beso** *nm* kiss
bestia ['bestja] *nf* beast, animal; (*fig*) idiot; **bestia de carga** beast of burden; **bestial** [bes'tjal] *adj* bestial; (*fam*) terrific; **bestialidad** *nf* bestiality; (*fam*) stupidity

besugo [be'suɣo] *nm* sea bream; (*fam*) idiot
besuquear [besuke'ar] *vt* to cover with kisses; **besuquearse** *vr* to kiss and cuddle
betabel [beta'bel] (*MÉX*) *nm* beetroot (*BRIT*), beet (*US*)
betún [be'tun] *nm* shoe polish; (*Quím*) bitumen
biberón [biβe'ron] *nm* feeding bottle
Biblia ['biβlja] *nf* Bible
bibliografía [biβljoɣra'fia] *nf* bibliography
biblioteca [biβljo'teka] *nf* library; (*mueble*) bookshelves; **biblioteca de consulta** reference library; **bibliotecario, -a** *nm/f* librarian
bicarbonato [bikarβo'nato] *nm* bicarbonate
bicho ['bitʃo] *nm* (*animal*) small animal; (*sabandija*) bug, insect; (*Taur*) bull
bici ['biθi] (*fam*) *nf* bike
bicicleta [biθi'kleta] *nf* bicycle, cycle; **ir en ~** to cycle
bidé [bi'ðe] (*pl* **~s**) *nm* bidet
bidón [bi'ðon] *nm* (*de aceite*) drum; (*de gasolina*) can

PALABRA CLAVE

bien [bjen] *nm* **1** (*bienestar*) good; **te lo digo por tu bien** I'm telling you for your own good; **el bien y el mal** good and evil
2 (*posesión*): **bienes** goods; **bienes de consumo** consumer goods; **bienes inmuebles** *o* **raíces/bienes muebles** real estate *sg*/personal property *sg*
▷ *adv* **1** (*de manera satisfactoria, correcta etc*) well; **trabaja/come bien** she works/eats well; **contestó bien** he answered correctly; **me siento bien** I feel fine; **no me siento bien** I don't feel very well; **se está bien aquí** it's nice here
2 (*frases*): **hiciste bien en llamarme** you were right to call me
3 (*valor intensivo*) very; **un cuarto bien caliente** a nice warm room; **bien se ve que ...** it's quite clear that ...
4 estar bien: estoy muy bien aquí I feel very happy here; **está bien que vengan** it's all right for them to come; **¡está bien! lo haré** oh all right, I'll do it
5 (*de buena gana*): **yo bien que iría pero ...** I'd gladly go but ...
▷ *excl*: **¡bien!** (*aprobación*) O.K.!; **¡muy bien!** well done! ▷ *adj inv* (*matiz despectivo*): **gente bien** posh people
▷ *conj* **1 bien ... bien: bien en coche bien en tren** either by car or by train
2 (*LAM*): **no bien: no bien llegue te llamaré** as soon as I arrive I'll call you
3 si bien even though; *V tb* **más**

bienal [bje'nal] *adj* biennial
bienestar [bjenes'tar] *nm* well-being, welfare
bienvenida [bjembe'niða] *nf* welcome; **dar la ~ a algn** to welcome sb
bienvenido [bjembe'niðo] *excl* welcome!
bife ['bife] (*CS*) *nm* steak
bifurcación [bifurka'θjon] *nf* fork
bígamo, -a ['biɣamo, a] *adj* bigamous ▷ *nm/f* bigamist
bigote [bi'ɣote] *nm* moustache; **bigotudo, -a** *adj* with a big moustache
bikini [bi'kini] *nm* bikini; (*Culin*) toasted ham and cheese sandwich
bilingüe [bi'lingwe] *adj* bilingual
billar [bi'ʎar] *nm* billiards *sg*; **billares** *nmpl* (*lugar*) billiard hall; (*sala de juegos*) amusement arcade; **billar americano** pool
billete [bi'ʎete] *nm* ticket; (*de banco*) (bank)note (*BRIT*), bill (*US*); (*carta*) note; **~ de 20 libras** £20 note; **billete de ida y vuelta** return (*BRIT*) *o* round-trip (*US*) ticket; **billete sencillo** *o* **de ida** single (*BRIT*) *o* one-way (*US*) ticket; **billete electrónico** e-ticket
billetera [biʎe'tera] *nf* wallet

billón [bi'ʎon] *nm* billion
bimensual [bimen'swal] *adj* twice monthly
bingo ['bingo] *nm* bingo
biodegradable [bioðeɣra'ðaβle] *adj* biodegradable
biografía [bjoɣra'fia] *nf* biography
biología [bjolo'xia] *nf* biology; **biológico, -a** *adj* biological; (*cultivo, producto*) organic; **biólogo, -a** *nm/f* biologist
biombo ['bjombo] *nm* (folding) screen
bioterrorismo [bjoterro'rismo] *nm* bioterrorism
biquini [bi'kini] *nm o* (*RPL*) *f* bikini
birlar [bir'lar] (*fam*) *vt* to pinch
Birmania [bir'manja] *nf* Burma
birome [bi'rome] (*RPL*) *nf* ballpoint (pen)
birria ['birrja] *nf*: **ser una ~** (*película, libro*) to be rubbish
bis [bis] *excl* encore!
bisabuelo, -a [bisa'βwelo, a] *nm/f* great-grandfather(-mother)
bisagra [bi'saɣra] *nf* hinge
bisiesto [bi'sjesto] *adj*: **año ~** leap year
bisnieto, -a [bis'njeto, a] *nm/f* great-grandson/daughter
bisonte [bi'sonte] *nm* bison
bisté [bis'te] *nm* = **bistec**
bistec [bis'tek] *nm* steak
bisturí [bistu'ri] *nm* scalpel
bisutería [bisute'ria] *nf* imitation *o* costume jewellery
bit [bit] *nm* (*Inform*) bit
bizco, -a ['biθko, a] *adj* cross-eyed
bizcocho [biθ'kotʃo] *nm* (*Culin*) sponge cake
blanca ['blanka] *nf* (*Mús*) minim; **estar sin ~** (*ESP*: *fam*) to be broke; *V tb* **blanco**
blanco, -a ['blanko, a] *adj* white ▷ *nm/f* white man/woman, white ▷ *nm* (*color*) white; (*en texto*) blank; (*Mil, fig*) target; **en ~** blank; **noche en ~** sleepless night
blandir [blan'dir] *vt* to brandish
blando, -a ['blando, a] *adj* soft; (*tierno*) tender, gentle; (*carácter*) mild; (*fam*) cowardly
blanqueador [blankea'ðor] (*MÉX*) *nm* bleach
blanquear [blanke'ar] *vt* to whiten; (*fachada*) to whitewash; (*paño*) to bleach ▷ *vi* to turn white
blanquillo [blan'kiʎo] (*MÉX, CAM*) *nm* egg
blasfemar [blasfe'mar] *vi* to blaspheme, curse
bledo ['bleðo] *nm*: **me importa un ~** I couldn't care less
blindado, -a [blin'daðo, a] *adj* (*Mil*) armour-plated; (*antibala*) bullet-proof; **coche** (*ESP*) *o* **carro** (*LAM*) **~** armoured car
bloc [blok] (*pl* **~s**) *nm* writing pad
blof [blof] (*MÉX*) *nm* bluff; **blofear** (*MÉX*) *vi* to bluff
blog [bloɣ] (*pl* **~s**) *nm* blog
bloque ['bloke] *nm* block; (*Pol*) bloc
bloquear [bloke'ar] *vt* to blockade; **bloqueo** *nm* blockade; (*Com*) freezing, blocking; **bloqueo mental** mental block
blusa ['blusa] *nf* blouse
bobada [bo'βaða] *nf* foolish action; foolish statement; **decir ~s** to talk nonsense
bobina [bo'βina] *nf* (*Tec*) bobbin; (*Foto*) spool; (*Elec*) coil
bobo, -a ['boβo, a] *adj* (*tonto*) daft, silly; (*cándido*) naôve ▷ *nm/f* fool, idiot ▷ *nm* (*Teatro*) clown, funny man
boca ['boka] *nf* mouth; (*de crustáceo*) pincer; (*de cañón*) muzzle; (*entrada*) mouth, entrance; **bocas** *nfpl* (*de río*) mouth *sg*; **~ abajo/arriba** face down/up; **se me hace la ~ agua** my mouth is watering; **boca de incendios** hydrant; **boca del estómago** pit of the stomach; **boca de metro** underground (*BRIT*) *o* subway (*US*) entrance
bocacalle [boka'kaʎe] *nf* (entrance to a) street; **la primera ~** the first

turning *o* street

bocadillo [boka'ðiʎo] *nm* sandwich

bocado [bo'kaðo] *nm* mouthful, bite; (*de caballo*) bridle

bocajarro [boka'xarro]: **a ~** *adv* (*disparar*) point-blank

bocanada [boka'naða] *nf* (*de vino*) mouthful, swallow; (*de aire*) gust, puff

bocata [bo'kata] (*fam*) *nm* sandwich

bocazas [bo'kaθas] (*fam*) *nm inv* bigmouth

boceto [bo'θeto] *nm* sketch, outline

bochorno [bo'tʃorno] *nm* (*vergüenza*) embarrassment; (*calor*): **hace ~** it's very muggy

bocina [bo'θina] *nf* (*Mús*) trumpet; (*Auto*) horn; (*para hablar*) megaphone

boda ['boða] *nf* (*tb*: **~s**) wedding, marriage; (*fiesta*) wedding reception; **bodas de oro/plata** golden/silver wedding *sg*

bodega [bo'ðeɣa] *nf* (*de vino*) (wine) cellar; (*depósito*) storeroom; (*de barco*) hold

bodegón [boðe'ɣon] *nm* (*Arte*) still life

bofetada [bofe'taða] *nf* slap (in the face)

boga ['boɣa] *nf*: **en ~** (*fig*) in vogue

Bogotá [boɣo'ta] *n* Bogotá

bohemio, -a [bo'emjo, a] *adj, nm/f* Bohemian

bohío [bo'io] (CAM) *nm* shack, hut

boicot [boi'kot] (*pl* **~s**) *nm* boycott; **boicotear** *vt* to boycott

bóiler ['boiler] (MÉX) *nm* boiler

boina ['boina] *nf* beret

bola ['bola] *nf* ball; (*canica*) marble; (*Naipes*) (grand) slam; (*betún*) shoe polish; (*mentira*) tale, story; **bolas** *nfpl* (LAM: *caza*) bolas *sg*; **bola de billar** billiard ball; **bola de nieve** snowball

boleadoras [bolea'ðoras] *nfpl* bolas *sg*

bolear [bole'ar] (MÉX) *vt* (*zapatos*) to polish, shine

bolera [bo'lera] *nf* skittle *o* bowling alley

bolero, -a (MÉX) [bo'lero] *nm/f* (*limpiabotas*) shoeshine boy/girl

boleta [bo'leta] (LAM) *nf* (*de rifa*) ticket; (CS: *recibo*) receipt; **boleta de calificaciones** (MÉX) report card

boletería [bolete'ria] (LAM) *nf* ticket office

boletín [bole'tin] *nm* bulletin; (*periódico*) journal, review; **boletín de noticias** news bulletin

boleto [bo'leto] *nm* (LAM) ticket; **boleto de ida y vuelta** (LAM) round trip ticket; **boleto electrónico** (LAM) e-ticket; **boleto redondo** (MÉX) round trip ticket

boli ['boli] (*fam*) *nm* Biro®

bolígrafo [bo'liɣrafo] *nm* ball-point pen, Biro®

bolilla [bo'liʎa] (RPL) *nf* topic

bolillo [bo'liʎo] (MÉX) *nm* (bread) roll

bolita [bo'lita] (CS) *nf* marble

bolívar [bo'liβar] *nm monetary unit of Venezuela*

Bolivia [bo'liβja] *nf* Bolivia; **boliviano, -a** *adj, nm/f* Bolivian

bollería [boʎe'ria] *nf* cakes *pl* and pastries *pl*

bollo ['boʎo] *nm* (*pan*) roll; (*bulto*) bump, lump; (*abolladura*) dent

bolo ['bolo] *nm* skittle; (*píldora*) (large) pill; **(juego de) bolos** *nmpl* skittles *sg*

bolsa ['bolsa] *nf* (*para llevar algo*) bag; (MÉX, CAM: *bolsillo*) pocket; (MÉX: *de mujer*) handbag; (*Anat*) cavity, sac; (*Com*) stock exchange; (*Minería*) pocket; **de ~** pocket *cpd*; **bolsa de agua caliente** hot water bottle; **bolsa de aire** air pocket; **bolsa de dormir** (MÉX, RPL) sleeping bag; **bolsa de la compra** shopping bag; **bolsa de papel/plástico** paper/ plastic bag

bolsear [bolse'ar] (MÉX, CAM) *vt*: **~ a algn** to pick sb's pocket

bolsillo [bol'siʎo] *nm* pocket; (*cartera*) purse; **de ~** pocket(-size)

bolso ['bolso] *nm* (*bolsa*) bag; (*de mujer*) handbag

bomba ['bomba] *nf* (*Mil*) bomb; (*Tec*)

pump ▷ *adj* (*fam*): **noticia ~** bombshell ▷ *adv* (*fam*): **pasarlo ~** to have a great time; **bomba atómica/de efecto retardado/de humo** atomic/time/ smoke bomb

bombacha [bom'batʃa] (RPL) *nf* panties *pl*

bombardear [bombarðe'ar] *vt* to bombard; (*Mil*) to bomb; **bombardeo** *nm* bombardment; bombing

bombazo [bom'baθo] (MÉX) *nm* (*explosión*) explosion; (*fam*: *notición*) bombshell; (: *éxito*) smash hit

bombear [bombe'ar] *vt* (*agua*) to pump (out *o* up)

bombero [bom'bero] *nm* fireman

bombilla [bom'biʎa] (ESP) *nf* (light) bulb

bombita [bom'bita] (RPL) *nf* (light) bulb

bombo ['bombo] *nm* (*Mús*) bass drum; (*Tec*) drum

bombón [bom'bon] *nm* chocolate; (MÉX: *de caramelo*) marshmallow

bombona [bom'bona] (ESP) *nf* (*de butano, oxígeno*) cylinder

bonachón, -ona [bona'tʃon, ona] *adj* good-natured, easy-going

bonanza [bo'nanθa] *nf* (*Náut*) fair weather; (*fig*) bonanza; (*Minería*) rich pocket *o* vein

bondad [bon'dað] *nf* goodness, kindness; **tenga la ~ de** (please) be good enough to

bonito, -a [bo'nito, a] *adj* pretty; (*agradable*) nice ▷ *nm* (*atún*) tuna (fish)

bono ['bono] *nm* voucher; (*Finanzas*) bond

bonobús [bono'βus] (ESP) *nm* bus pass

bonoloto [bono'loto] *nf* *state-run weekly lottery*

boquerón [boke'ron] *nm* (*pez*) (kind of) anchovy; (*agujero*) large hole

boquete [bo'kete] *nm* gap, hole

boquiabierto, -a [bokia'βjerto, a] *adj*: **quedarse ~** to be amazed *o* flabbergasted

boquilla [bo'kiʎa] *nf* (*para riego*) nozzle; (*para cigarro*) cigarette holder; (*Mús*) mouthpiece

borbotón [borβo'ton] *nm*: **salir a borbotones** to gush out

borda ['borða] *nf* (*Náut*) (ship's) rail; **tirar algo/caerse por la ~** to throw sth/fall overboard

bordado [bor'ðaðo] *nm* embroidery

bordar [bor'ðar] *vt* to embroider

borde ['borðe] *nm* edge, border; (*de camino etc*) side; (*en la costura*) hem; **al ~ de** (*fig*) on the verge *o* brink of; **ser ~** (ESP: *fam*) to be rude; **bordear** *vt* to border

bordillo [bor'ðiʎo] *nm* kerb (BRIT), curb (US)

bordo ['borðo] *nm* (*Náut*) side; **a ~** on board

borlote [bor'lote] (MÉX) *nm* row, uproar

borrachera [borra'tʃera] *nf* (*ebriedad*) drunkenness; (*orgía*) spree, binge

borracho, -a [bo'rratʃo, a] *adj* drunk ▷ *nm/f* (*habitual*) drunkard, drunk; (*temporal*) drunk, drunk man/woman

borrador [borra'ðor] *nm* (*escritura*) first draft, rough sketch; (*goma*) rubber (BRIT), eraser

borrar [bo'rrar] *vt* to erase, rub out

borrasca [bo'rraska] *nf* storm

borrego, -a [bo'rreɣo, a] *nm/f* (*Zool*: *joven*) (yearling) lamb; (*adulto*) sheep ▷ *nm* (MÉX: *fam*) false rumour

borrico, -a [bo'rriko, a] *nm/f* donkey/she-donkey; (*fig*) stupid man/woman

borrón [bo'rron] *nm* (*mancha*) stain

borroso, -a [bo'rroso, a] *adj* vague, unclear; (*escritura*) illegible

bosque ['boske] *nm* wood; (*grande*) forest

bostezar [boste'θar] *vi* to yawn; **bostezo** *nm* yawn

bota ['bota] *nf* (*calzado*) boot; (*para vino*) leather wine bottle; **botas de agua** *o* **goma** Wellingtons

botana [bo'tana] (MÉX) *nf* snack,

appetizer

botánica [bo'tanika] *nf* (*ciencia*) botany; *V tb* **botánico**

botánico, -a [bo'taniko, a] *adj* botanical ▷ *nm/f* botanist

botar [bo'tar] *vt* to throw, hurl; (*Náut*) to launch; (*LAM*: *echar*) to throw out ▷ *vi* (*ESP*: *saltar*) to bounce

bote ['bote] *nm* (*salto*) bounce; (*golpe*) thrust; (*ESP*: *envase*) tin, can; (*embarcación*) boat; (*MÉX*, *CAM*: *pey*: *cárcel*) jail; **de ~ en ~** packed, jammed full; **bote de la basura** (*MÉX*) dustbin (*BRIT*), trashcan (*US*); **bote salvavidas** lifeboat

botella [bo'teʎa] *nf* bottle; **botellín** *nm* small bottle; **botellón** *nm* (*ESP*: *fam*) outdoor drinking session

botijo [bo'tixo] *nm* (earthenware) jug

botín [bo'tin] *nm* (*calzado*) half boot; (*polaina*) spat; (*Mil*) booty

botiquín [boti'kin] *nm* (*armario*) medicine cabinet; (*portátil*) first-aid kit

botón [bo'ton] *nm* button; (*Bot*) bud

botones [bo'tones] *nm inv* bellboy (*BRIT*), bellhop (*US*)

bóveda ['boβeða] *nf* (*Arq*) vault

boxeador [boksea'ðor] *nm* boxer

boxeo [bok'seo] *nm* boxing

boya ['boja] *nf* (*Náut*) buoy; (*de caña*) float

boyante [bo'jante] *adj* prosperous

bozal [bo'θal] *nm* (*para caballos*) halter; (*de perro*) muzzle

bragas ['braɣas] *nfpl* (*de mujer*) panties, knickers (*BRIT*)

bragueta [bra'ɣeta] *nf* fly, flies *pl*

braille [breil] *nm* braille

brasa ['brasa] *nf* live *o* hot coal

brasero [bra'sero] *nm* brazier

brasier [bra'sjer] (*MÉX*) *nm* bra

Brasil [bra'sil] *nm* (*tb*: **el ~**) Brazil; **brasileño, -a** *adj*, *nm/f* Brazilian

brassier [bra'sjer] (*MÉX*) *nm V* **brasier**

bravo, -a ['braβo, a] *adj* (*valiente*) brave; (*feroz*) ferocious; (*salvaje*) wild; (*mar etc*) rough, stormy ▷ *excl* bravo!; **bravura** *nf* bravery; ferocity

braza ['braθa] *nf* fathom; **nadar a ~** to swim breast-stroke

brazalete [braθa'lete] *nm* (*pulsera*) bracelet; (*banda*) armband

brazo ['braθo] *nm* arm; (*Zool*) foreleg; (*Bot*) limb, branch; **luchar a ~ partido** to fight hand-to-hand; **ir cogidos del ~** to walk arm in arm

brebaje [bre'βaxe] *nm* potion

brecha ['bretʃa] *nf* (*hoyo, vacío*) gap, opening; (*Mil, fig*) breach

brega ['breɣa] *nf* (*lucha*) struggle; (*trabajo*) hard work

breva ['breβa] *nf* early fig

breve ['breβe] *adj* short, brief ▷ *nf* (*Mús*) breve; **en ~** (*pronto*) shortly, before long; **brevedad** *nf* brevity, shortness

bribón, -ona [bri'βon, ona] *adj* idle, lazy ▷ *nm/f* (*pícaro*) rascal, rogue

bricolaje [briko'laxe] *nm* do-it-yourself, DIY

brida ['briða] *nf* bridle, rein; (*Tec*) clamp

bridge [britʃ] *nm* bridge

brigada [bri'ɣaða] *nf* (*unidad*) brigade; (*de trabajadores*) squad, gang ▷ *nm* ≈ staff-sergeant, sergeant-major

brillante [bri'ʎante] *adj* brilliant ▷ *nm* diamond

brillar [bri'ʎar] *vi* to shine; (*joyas*) to sparkle

brillo ['briʎo] *nm* shine; (*brillantez*) brilliance; (*fig*) splendour; **sacar ~ a** to polish

brincar [brin'kar] *vi* to skip about, hop about, jump about

brinco ['brinko] *nm* jump, leap

brindar [brin'dar] *vi*: **~ a** *o* **por** to drink (a toast) to ▷ *vt* to offer, present

brindis ['brindis] *nm inv* toast

brío ['brio] *nm* spirit, dash

brisa ['brisa] *nf* breeze

británico, -a [bri'taniko, a] *adj* British ▷ *nm/f* Briton, British person

brizna ['briθna] *nf* (*de hierba, paja*) blade; (*de tabaco*) leaf

broca ['broka] *nf* (*Tec*) drill, bit
brocha ['brotʃa] *nf* (large) paintbrush; **brocha de afeitar** shaving brush
broche ['brotʃe] *nm* brooch
broma ['broma] *nf* joke; **de** *o* **en ~** in fun, as a joke; **broma pesada** practical joke; **bromear** *vi* to joke
bromista [bro'mista] *adj* fond of joking ▷ *nmf* joker, wag
bronca ['bronka] *nf* row; **echar una ~ a algn** to tick sb off
bronce ['bronθe] *nm* bronze; **bronceado, -a** *adj* bronze; (*por el sol*) tanned ▷ *nm* (sun)tan; (*Tec*) bronzing
bronceador [bronθea'ðor] *nm* suntan lotion
broncearse [bronθe'arse] *vr* to get a suntan
bronquio ['bronkjo] *nm* (*Anat*) bronchial tube
bronquitis [bron'kitis] *nf inv* bronchitis
brotar [bro'tar] *vi* (*Bot*) to sprout; (*aguas*) to gush (forth); (*Med*) to break out
brote ['brote] *nm* (*Bot*) shoot; (*Med, fig*) outbreak
bruces ['bruθes]: **de bruces** *adv*: **caer** *o* **dar de ~** to fall headlong, fall flat
bruja ['bruxa] *nf* witch; **brujería** *nf* witchcraft
brujo ['bruxo] *nm* wizard, magician
brújula ['bruxula] *nf* compass
bruma ['bruma] *nf* mist
brusco, -a ['brusko, a] *adj* (*súbito*) sudden; (*áspero*) brusque
Bruselas [bru'selas] *n* Brussels
brutal [bru'tal] *adj* brutal; **brutalidad** [brutali'ðað] *nf* brutality
bruto, -a ['bruto, a] *adj* (*idiota*) stupid; (*bestial*) brutish; (*peso*) gross; **en ~** raw, unworked
Bs.As. *abr* (= *Buenos Aires*) B.A.
bucal [bu'kal] *adj* oral; **por vía ~** orally
bucear [buθe'ar] *vi* to dive ▷ *vt* to explore; **buceo** *nm* diving
bucle ['bukle] *nm* curl
budismo [bu'ðismo] *nm* Buddhism
buen [bwen] *adj m V* **bueno**
buenamente [bwena'mente] *adv* (*fácilmente*) easily; (*voluntariamente*) willingly
buenaventura [bwenaβen'tura] *nf* (*suerte*) good luck; (*adivinación*) fortune
buenmozo [bwen'moθo] (*MÉX*) *adj* handsome

PALABRA CLAVE

bueno, -a ['bweno, a] (*antes de nmsg:* **buen**) *adj* **1** (*excelente etc*) good; **es un libro bueno, es un buen libro** it's a good book; **hace bueno, hace buen tiempo** the weather is fine, it is fine; **el bueno de Paco** good old Paco; **fue muy bueno conmigo** he was very nice *o* kind to me
2 (*apropiado*): **ser bueno para** to be good for; **creo que vamos por buen camino** I think we're on the right track
3 (*irónico*): **le di un buen rapapolvo** I gave him a good *o* real ticking off; **¡buen conductor estás hecho!** some *o* a fine driver you are!; **¡estaría bueno que ...!** a fine thing it would be if ...!
4 (*atractivo, sabroso*): **está bueno este bizcocho** this sponge is delicious; **Carmen está muy buena** Carmen is gorgeous
5 (*saludos*): **¡buen día!, ¡buenos días!** (good) morning!; **¡buenas (tardes)!** (good) afternoon!; (*más tarde*) (good) evening!; **¡buenas noches!** good night!
6 (*otras locuciones*): **estar de buenas** to be in a good mood; **por las buenas o por las malas** by hook or by crook; **de buenas a primeras** all of a sudden
▷ *excl*: **¡bueno!** all right!; **bueno, ¿y qué?** well, so what?

Buenos Aires [bweno'saires] *nm* Buenos Aires
buey [bwei] *nm* ox
búfalo ['bufalo] *nm* buffalo

bufanda [bu'fanda] *nf* scarf
bufete [bu'fete] *nm* (*despacho de abogado*) lawyer's office
bufón [bu'fon] *nm* clown
buhardilla [buar'ðiʎa] *nf* attic
búho ['buo] *nm* owl; (*fig*) hermit, recluse
buitre ['bwitre] *nm* vulture
bujía [bu'xia] *nf* (*vela*) candle; (*Elec*) candle (power); (*Auto*) spark plug
bula ['bula] *nf* (papal) bull
bulbo ['bulβo] *nm* bulb
bulevar [bule'βar] *nm* boulevard
Bulgaria [bul'ɣarja] *nf* Bulgaria; **búlgaro, -a** *adj, nm/f* Bulgarian
bulla ['buʎa] *nf* (*ruido*) uproar; (*de gente*) crowd
bullicio [bu'ʎiθjo] *nm* (*ruido*) uproar; (*movimiento*) bustle
bulto ['bulto] *nm* (*paquete*) package; (*fardo*) bundle; (*tamaño*) size, bulkiness; (*Med*) swelling, lump; (*silueta*) vague shape
buñuelo [bu'ɲwelo] *nm* ≈ doughnut (BRIT), ≈ donut (US); (*fruta de sartén*) fritter
buque ['buke] *nm* ship, vessel; **buque de guerra** warship
burbuja [bur'βuxa] *nf* bubble
burdel [bur'ðel] *nm* brothel
burgués, -esa [bur'ɣes, esa] *adj* middle-class, bourgeois; **burguesía** *nf* middle class, bourgeoisie
burla ['burla] *nf* (*mofa*) gibe; (*broma*) joke; (*engaño*) trick; **burlar** [bur'lar] *vt* (*engañar*) to deceive ▷ *vi* to joke; **burlarse** *vr* to joke; **burlarse de** to make fun of
burlón, -ona [bur'lon, ona] *adj* mocking
buró [bu'ro] (MÉX) *nm* bedside table
burocracia [buro'kraθja] *nf* civil service
burrada [bu'rraða] *nf*: **decir** *o* **soltar ~s** to talk nonsense; **hacer ~s** to act stupid; **una ~** (ESP: *mucho*) a (hell of a) lot
burro, -a ['burro, a] *nm/f* donkey/ she-donkey; (*fig*) ass, idiot
bursátil [bur'satil] *adj* stock-exchange *cpd*
bus [bus] *nm* bus
busca ['buska] *nf* search, hunt ▷ *nm* (*Tel*) bleeper; **en ~ de** in search of
buscador [buska'ðor] *nm* (*Internet*) search engine
buscar [bus'kar] *vt* to look for, search for, seek ▷ *vi* to look, search, seek; **se busca secretaria** secretary wanted
busque *etc vb V* **buscar**
búsqueda ['buskeða] *nf* = **busca**
busto ['busto] *nm* (*Anat, Arte*) bust
butaca [bu'taka] *nf* armchair; (*de cine, teatro*) stall, seat
butano [bu'tano] *nm* butane (gas)
buzo ['buθo] *nm* diver
buzón [bu'θon] *nm* (*en puerta*) letter box; (*en calle*) pillar box

C. *abr* (= *centígrado*) C; (*compañía*) Co.
C/ *abr* (= *calle*) St
cabal [ka'βal] *adj* (*exacto*) exact; (*correcto*) right, proper; (*acabado*) finished, complete; **cabales** *nmpl*: **no está en sus cabales** she isn't in her right mind
cábalas ['kaβalas] *nfpl*: **hacer ~** to guess
cabalgar [kaβal'ɣar] *vt, vi* to ride
cabalgata [kaβal'ɣata] *nf* procession
caballa [ka'βaʎa] *nf* mackerel
caballería [kaβaʎe'ria] *nf* mount; (*Mil*) cavalry
caballero [kaβa'ʎero] *nm* gentleman; (*de la orden de caballería*) knight; (*trato directo*) sir
caballete [kaβa'ʎete] *nm* (*Arte*) easel; (*Tec*) trestle
caballito [kaβa'ʎito] *nm* (*caballo pequeño*) small horse, pony; **caballitos** *nmpl* (*en verbena*) roundabout, merry-go-round
caballo [ka'βaʎo] *nm* horse; (*Ajedrez*) knight; (*Naipes*) queen; **ir en ~** to ride; **caballo de carreras** racehorse; **caballo de fuerza** *o* **vapor** horsepower
cabaña [ka'βaɲa] *nf* (*casita*) hut, cabin
cabecear [kaβeθe'ar] *vt, vi* to nod
cabecera [kaβe'θera] *nf* head; (*Imprenta*) headline
cabecilla [kaβe'θiʎa] *nm* ringleader
cabellera [kaβe'ʎera] *nf* (head of) hair; (*de cometa*) tail
cabello [ka'βeʎo] *nm* (*tb*: **~s**) hair; **cabello de ángel** *confectionery and pastry filling made of pumpkin and syrup*
caber [ka'βer] *vi* (*entrar*) to fit, go; **caben 3 más** there's room for 3 more
cabestrillo [kaβes'triʎo] *nm* sling
cabeza [ka'βeθa] *nf* head; (*Pol*) chief, leader; **cabeza de ajo** bulb of garlic; **cabeza de familia** head of the household; **cabeza rapada** skinhead; **cabezada** *nf* (*golpe*) butt; **dar cabezadas** to nod off; **cabezón, -ona** *adj* (*vino*) heady; (*fam*: *persona*) pig-headed
cabida [ka'βiða] *nf* space
cabina [ka'βina] *nf* cabin; (*de avión*) cockpit; (*de camión*) cab; **cabina telefónica** telephone (BRIT) box *o* booth
cabizbajo, -a [kaβiθ'βaxo, a] *adj* crestfallen, dejected
cable ['kaβle] *nm* cable
cabo ['kaβo] *nm* (*de objeto*) end, extremity; (*Mil*) corporal; (*Náut*) rope, cable; (*Geo*) cape; **al ~ de 3 días** after 3 days; **llevar a ~** to carry out
cabra ['kaβra] *nf* goat
cabré *etc vb V* **caber**
cabrear [kaβre'ar] (*fam*) *vt* to bug; **cabrearse** *vr* (*enfadarse*) to fly off the handle
cabrito [ka'βrito] *nm* kid
cabrón [ka'βron] *nm* cuckold; (*fam!*) bastard (*!*)
caca ['kaka] (*fam*) *nf* pooh
cacahuete [kaka'wete] (ESP) *nm* peanut

cacao [ka'kao] *nm* cocoa; (*Bot*) cacao
cacarear [kakare'ar] *vi* (*persona*) to boast; (*gallina*) to crow
cacería [kaθe'ria] *nf* hunt
cacarizo, -a [kaka'riθo, a] (MÉX) *adj* pockmarked
cacerola [kaθe'rola] *nf* pan, saucepan
cachalote [katʃa'lote] *nm* (*Zool*) sperm whale
cacharro [ka'tʃarro] *nm* earthenware pot; **cacharros** *nmpl* pots and pans
cachear [katʃe'ar] *vt* to search, frisk
cachemir [katʃe'mir] *nm* cashmere
cachetada [katʃe'taða] (LAM: *fam*) *nf* (*bofetada*) slap
cachete [ka'tʃete] *nm* (*Anat*) cheek; (ESP: *bofetada*) slap (in the face)
cachivache [katʃi'βatʃe] *nm* (*trasto*) piece of junk; **cachivaches** *nmpl* junk *sg*
cacho ['katʃo] *nm* (small) bit; (LAM: *cuerno*) horn
cachondeo [katʃon'deo] (ESP: *fam*) *nm* farce, joke
cachondo, -a [ka'tʃondo, a] *adj* (*Zool*) on heat; (*fam*: *sexualmente*) randy; (: *gracioso*) funny
cachorro, -a [ka'tʃorro, a] *nm/f* (*perro*) pup, puppy; (*león*) cub
cachucha [ka'tʃuka] (MÉX: *fam*) *nf* cap
cacique [ka'θike] *nm* chief, local ruler; (*Pol*) local party boss
cactus ['kaktus] *nm inv* cactus
cada ['kaða] *adj inv* each; (*antes de número*) every; **~ día** each day, every day; **~ dos días** every other day; **~ uno/a** each one, every one; **~ vez más/menos** more and more/less and less; **~ vez que ...** whenever, every time (that) ...; **uno de ~ diez** one out of every ten
cadáver [ka'ðaβer] *nm* (dead) body, corpse
cadena [ka'ðena] *nf* chain; (*TV*) channel; **trabajo en ~** assembly line work; **cadena montañosa** mountain range; **cadena perpetua** (*Jur*) life imprisonment
cadera [ka'ðera] *nf* hip
cadete [ka'ðete] *nm* cadet
caducar [kaðu'kar] *vi* to expire; **caduco, -a** *adj* expired; (*persona*) very old
caer [ka'er] *vi* to fall (down); **caerse** *vr* to fall (down); **me cae bien/mal** I get on well with him/I can't stand him; **~ en la cuenta** to realize; **dejar ~** to drop; **su cumpleaños cae en viernes** her birthday falls on a Friday
café [ka'fe] (*pl* **~s**) *nm* (*bebida, planta*) coffee; (*lugar*) café ▷ *adj* (MÉX: *color*) brown, tan; **café con leche** white coffee; **café negro** (LAM) black coffee; **café solo** (ESP) black coffee
cafetera [kafe'tera] *nf* coffee pot
cafetería [kafete'ria] *nf* (*gen*) café
cafetero, -a [kafe'tero, a] *adj* coffee *cpd*; **ser muy ~** to be a coffee addict
cafishio [ka'fiʃjo] (CS) *nm* pimp
cagar [ka'ɣar] (*fam!*) *vt* to bungle, mess up ▷ *vi* to have a shit (*!*)
caída [ka'iða] *nf* fall; (*declive*) slope; (*disminución*) fall, drop
caído, -a [ka'iðo, a] *adj* drooping
caiga *etc vb V* **caer**
caimán [kai'man] *nm* alligator
caja ['kaxa] *nf* box; (*para reloj*) case; (*de ascensor*) shaft; (*Com*) cashbox; (*donde se hacen los pagos*) cashdesk; (: *en supermercado*) checkout, till; **caja de ahorros** savings bank; **caja de cambios** gearbox; **caja de fusibles** fuse box; **caja fuerte** *o* **de caudales** safe, strongbox
cajero, -a [ka'xero, a] *nm/f* cashier; **cajero automático** cash dispenser
cajetilla [kaxe'tiʎa] *nf* (*de cigarrillos*) packet
cajón [ka'xon] *nm* big box; (*de mueble*) drawer
cajuela (MÉX) *nf* (*Auto*) boot (BRIT), trunk (US)
cal [kal] *nf* lime
cala ['kala] *nf* (*Geo*) cove, inlet; (*de barco*) hold

calabacín [kalaβa'θin] *nm* (*Bot*) baby marrow; (: *más pequeño*) courgette (*BRIT*), zucchini (*US*)
calabacita [kalaβa'θita] (*MÉX*) *nf* courgette (*BRIT*), zucchini (*US*)
calabaza [kala'βaθa] *nf* (*Bot*) pumpkin
calabozo [kala'βoθo] *nm* (*cárcel*) prison; (*celda*) cell
calada [ka'laða] (*ESP*) *nf* (*de cigarrillo*) puff
calado, -a [ka'laðo, a] *adj* (*prenda*) lace *cpd* ▷ *nm* (*Náut*) draught
calamar [kala'mar] *nm* squid *no pl*
calambre [ka'lambre] *nm* (*Elec*) shock
calar [ka'lar] *vt* to soak, drench; (*penetrar*) to pierce, penetrate; (*comprender*) to see through; (*vela*) to lower; **calarse** *vr* (*Auto*) to stall; **~se las gafas** to stick one's glasses on
calavera [kala'βera] *nf* skull
calcar [kal'kar] *vt* (*reproducir*) to trace; (*imitar*) to copy
calcetín [kalθe'tin] *nm* sock
calcio ['kalθjo] *nm* calcium
calcomanía [kalkoma'nia] *nf* transfer
calculador, a [kalkula'ðor, a] *adj* (*persona*) calculating; **calculadora** [kalkula'ðora] *nf* calculator
calcular [kalku'lar] *vt* (*Mat*) to calculate, compute; **~ que ...** to reckon that ...
caldera [kal'dera] *nf* boiler
calderilla [kalde'riʎa] *nf* (*moneda*) small change
caldo ['kaldo] *nm* stock; (*consomé*) consommé
calefacción [kalefak'θjon] *nf* heating; **calefacción central** central heating
calefón [kale'fon] (*RPL*) *nm* boiler
calendario [kalen'darjo] *nm* calendar
calentador [kalenta'ðor] *nm* heater
calentamiento [kalenta'mjento] *nm* (*Deporte*) warm-up; **calentamiento global** global warming
calentar [kalen'tar] *vt* to heat (up); **calentarse** *vr* to heat up, warm up; (*fig: discusión etc*) to get heated
calentón [kalen'ton] (*RPL: fam*) *adj* (*sexualmente*) horny, randy (*BRIT*)
calentura [kalen'tura] *nf* (*Med*) fever, (high) temperature
calesita [kale'sita] (*RPL*) *nf* merry-go-round, carousel
calibre [ka'liβre] *nm* (*de cañón*) calibre, bore; (*diámetro*) diameter; (*fig*) calibre
calidad [kali'ðað] *nf* quality; **de ~** quality *cpd*; **en ~ de** in the capacity of, as
cálido, -a ['kaliðo, a] *adj* hot; (*fig*) warm
caliente *etc* [ka'ljente] *vb V* **calentar** ▷ *adj* hot; (*fig*) fiery; (*disputa*) heated; (*fam: cachondo*) randy
calificación [kalifika'θjon] *nf* qualification; (*de alumno*) grade, mark
calificado, -a [kalifi'kaðo, a] (*LAM*) *adj* (*competente*) qualified; (*obrero*) skilled
calificar [kalifi'kar] *vt* to qualify; (*alumno*) to grade, mark; **~ de** to describe as
calima [ka'lima] *nf* (*cerca del mar*) mist
cáliz ['kaliθ] *nm* chalice
caliza [ka'liθa] *nf* limestone
callado, -a [ka'ʎaðo, a] *adj* quiet
callar [ka'ʎar] *vt* (*asunto delicado*) to keep quiet about, say nothing about; (*persona, opinión*) to silence ▷ *vi* to keep quiet, be silent; **callarse** *vr* to keep quiet, be silent; **¡cállate!** be quiet!, shut up!
calle ['kaʎe] *nf* street; (*Deporte*) lane; **~ arriba/abajo** up/down the street; **calle de sentido único** one-way street; **calle mayor** (*ESP*) high (*BRIT*) *o* main (*US*) street; **calle peatonal** pedestrianized *o* pedestrian street; **calle principal** (*LAM*) high (*BRIT*) *o* main

(*US*) street; **callejear** *vi* to wander (about) the streets; **callejero, -a** *adj* street *cpd* ▷ *nm* street map; **callejón** *nm* alley, passage; **callejón sin salida** cul-de-sac; **callejuela** *nf* side-street, alley

callista [ka'ʎista] *nmf* chiropodist

callo ['kaʎo] *nm* callus; (*en el pie*) corn; **callos** *nmpl* (*Culin*) tripe *sg*

calma ['kalma] *nf* calm

calmante [kal'mante] *nm* sedative, tranquillizer

calmar [kal'mar] *vt* to calm, calm down ▷ *vi* (*tempestad*) to abate; (*mente etc*) to become calm

calor [ka'lor] *nm* heat; (*agradable*) warmth; **hace ~** it's hot; **tener ~** to be hot

caloría [kalo'ria] *nf* calorie

calumnia [ka'lumnja] *nf* calumny, slander

caluroso, -a [kalu'roso, a] *adj* hot; (*sin exceso*) warm; (*fig*) enthusiastic

calva ['kalβa] *nf* bald patch; (*en bosque*) clearing

calvario [kal'βarjo] *nm* stations *pl* of the cross

calvicie [kal'βiθje] *nf* baldness

calvo, -a ['kalβo, a] *adj* bald; (*terreno*) bare, barren; (*tejido*) threadbare

calza ['kalθa] *nf* wedge, chock

calzada [kal'θaða] *nf* roadway, highway

calzado, -a [kal'θaðo, a] *adj* shod ▷ *nm* footwear

calzador [kalθa'ðor] *nm* shoehorn

calzar [kal'θar] *vt* (*zapatos etc*) to wear; (*mueble*) to put a wedge under; **calzarse** *vr*: **~se los zapatos** to put on one's shoes; **¿qué (número) calza?** what size do you take?

calzón [kal'θon] *nm* (*ESP*: *pantalón corto*) shorts; (*LAM*: *ropa interior*: *de hombre*) underpants, pants (*BRIT*), shorts (*US*); (: *de mujer*) panties, knickers (*BRIT*)

calzoncillos [kalθon'θiʎos] *nmpl* underpants

cama ['kama] *nf* bed; **hacer la ~** to make the bed; **cama individual/de matrimonio** single/double bed

camaleón [kamale'on] *nm* chameleon

cámara ['kamara] *nf* chamber; (*habitación*) room; (*sala*) hall; (*Cine*) cine camera; (*fotográfica*) camera; **cámara de aire** (*ESP*) inner tube; **cámara de comercio** chamber of commerce; **cámara de gas** gas chamber; **cámara digital** digital camera; **cámara frigorífica** cold-storage room

camarada [kama'raða] *nmf* comrade, companion

camarera [kama'rera] *nf* (*en restaurante*) waitress; (*en casa, hotel*) maid

camarero [kama'rero] *nm* waiter

camarógrafo, -a [kama'rografo, a] (*LAM*) *nm/f* cameraman/camerawoman

camarón [kama'ron] *nm* shrimp

camarote [kama'rote] *nm* cabin

cambiable [kam'bjaβle] *adj* (*variable*) changeable, variable; (*intercambiable*) interchangeable

cambiante [kam'bjante] *adj* variable

cambiar [kam'bjar] *vt* to change; (*dinero*) to exchange ▷ *vi* to change; **cambiarse** *vr* (*mudarse*) to move; (*de ropa*) to change; **~ de idea** *u* **opinión** to change one's mind; **~se de ropa** to change (one's clothes)

cambio ['kambjo] *nm* change; (*trueque*) exchange; (*Com*) rate of exchange; (*oficina*) bureau de change; (*dinero menudo*) small change; **a ~ de** in return *o* exchange for; **en ~** on the other hand; (*en lugar de*) instead; **cambio climático** climate change; **cambio de divisas** foreign exchange; **cambio de marchas** *o* **velocidades** gear lever

camelar [kame'lar] *vt* to sweet-talk

camello [ka'meʎo] *nm* camel; (*fam*: *traficante*) pusher

camerino [kame'rino] *nm* dressing

room

camilla [ka'miʎa] *nf* (*Med*) stretcher

caminar [kami'nar] *vi* (*marchar*) to walk, go ▷ *vt* (*recorrer*) to cover, travel

caminata [kami'nata] *nf* long walk; (*por el campo*) hike

camino [ka'mino] *nm* way, road; (*sendero*) track; **a medio ~** halfway (there); **en el ~** on the way, en route; **~ de** on the way to; **Camino de Santiago** Way of St James; **camino particular** private road

CAMINO DE SANTIAGO

The **Camino de Santiago** is a medieval pilgrim route stretching from the Pyrenees to Santiago de Compostela in north-west Spain, where tradition has it the body of the Apostle James is buried. Nowadays it is a popular tourist route as well as a religious one.

camión [ka'mjon] *nm* lorry (BRIT), truck (US); (MÉX: *autobús*) bus; **camión cisterna** tanker; **camión de la basura** dustcart, refuse lorry; **camión de mudanzas** removal (BRIT) *o* moving (US) van; **camionero, -a** *nm/f* lorry *o* truck driver

camioneta [kamjo'neta] *nf* van, light truck

camisa [ka'misa] *nf* shirt; (*Bot*) skin; **camisa de fuerza** straitjacket

camiseta [kami'seta] *nf* (*prenda*) tee-shirt; (*ropa interior*) vest; (*de deportista*) top

camisón [kami'son] *nm* nightdress, nightgown

camorra [ka'morra] *nf*: **buscar ~** to look for trouble

camote [ka'mote] *nm* (MÉX, CS: *batata*) sweet potato, yam; (MÉX: *bulbo*) tuber, bulb; (CS: *fam*: *enamoramiento*) crush

campamento [kampa'mento] *nm* camp

campana [kam'pana] *nf* bell; **campanada** *nf* peal; **campanario** *nm* belfry

campanilla [kampa'niʎa] *nf* small bell

campaña [kam'paɲa] *nf* (*Mil, Pol*) campaign; **campaña electoral** election campaign

campechano, -a [kampe'tʃano, a] *adj* (*franco*) open

campeón, -ona [kampe'on, ona] *nm/f* champion; **campeonato** *nm* championship

cámper ['kamper] (LAM) *nm o f* caravan (BRIT), trailer (US)

campera [kam'pera] (RPL) *nf* anorak

campesino, -a [kampe'sino, a] *adj* country *cpd*, rural; (*gente*) peasant *cpd* ▷ *nm/f* countryman/woman; (*agricultor*) farmer

campestre [kam'pestre] *adj* country *cpd*, rural

camping ['kampin] (*pl* **~s**) *nm* camping; (*lugar*) campsite; **ir** *o* **estar de ~** to go camping

campo ['kampo] *nm* (*fuera de la ciudad*) country, countryside; (*Agr, Elec*) field; (*de fútbol*) pitch; (*de golf*) course; (*Mil*) camp; **campo de batalla** battlefield; **campo de concentración** concentration camp; **campo de deportes** sports ground, playing field; **campo visual** field of vision, visual field

camuflaje [kamu'flaxe] *nm* camouflage

cana ['kana] *nf* white *o* grey hair; **tener ~s** to be going grey

Canadá [kana'ða] *nm* Canada; **canadiense** *adj, nmf* Canadian ▷ *nf* fur-lined jacket

canal [ka'nal] *nm* canal; (*Geo*) channel, strait; (*de televisión*) channel; (*de tejado*) gutter; **canal de Panamá** Panama Canal

canaleta [kana'leta] (LAM) *nf* (*de tejado*) gutter

canalizar [kanali'θar] *vt* to channel

canalla [ka'naʎa] *nf* rabble, mob ▷*nm* swine
canapé [kana'pe] (*pl* **~s**) *nm* sofa, settee; (*Culin*) canapé
Canarias [ka'narjas] *nfpl* (*tb*: **las Islas ~**) the Canary Islands, the Canaries
canario, -a [ka'narjo, a] *adj, nm/f* (native) of the Canary Isles ▷*nm* (*Zool*) canary
canasta [ka'nasta] *nf* (round) basket
canasto [ka'nasto] *nm* large basket
cancela [kan'θela] *nf* gate
cancelación [kanθela'θjon] *nf* cancellation
cancelar [kanθe'lar] *vt* to cancel; (*una deuda*) to write off
cáncer ['kanθer] *nm* (*Med*) cancer; **C~** (*Astrología*) Cancer
cancha ['kantʃa] *nf* (*de baloncesto*) court; (LAM: *campo*) pitch; **cancha de tenis** (LAM) tennis court
canciller [kanθi'ʎer] *nm* chancellor
canción [kan'θjon] *nf* song; **canción de cuna** lullaby
candado [kan'daðo] *nm* padlock
candente [kan'dente] *adj* red-hot; (*fig*: *tema*) burning
candidato, -a [kandi'ðato, a] *nm/f* candidate
cándido, -a ['kandiðo, a] *adj* simple; naive

> No confundir **cándido** con la palabra inglesa *candid*.

candil [kan'dil] *nm* oil lamp; **candilejas** *nfpl* (*Teatro*) footlights
canela [ka'nela] *nf* cinnamon
canelones [kane'lones] *nmpl* cannelloni
cangrejo [kan'grexo] *nm* crab
canguro [kan'guro] *nm* kangaroo; **hacer de ~** to babysit
caníbal [ka'niβal] *adj, nmf* cannibal
canica [ka'nika] *nf* marble
canijo, -a [ka'nixo, a] *adj* frail, sickly
canilla [ka'niʎa] (RPL) *nf* tap (BRIT), faucet (US)
canjear [kanxe'ar] *vt* to exchange
canoa [ka'noa] *nf* canoe
canon ['kanon] *nm* canon; (*pensión*) rent; (*Com*) tax
canonizar [kanoni'θar] *vt* to canonize
canoso, -a [ka'noso, a] *adj* grey-haired
cansado, -a [kan'saðo, a] *adj* tired, weary; (*tedioso*) tedious, boring
cansancio [kan'sanθjo] *nm* tiredness, fatigue
cansar [kan'sar] *vt* (*fatigar*) to tire, tire out; (*aburrir*) to bore; (*fastidiar*) to bother; **cansarse** *vr* to tire, get tired; (*aburrirse*) to get bored
cantábrico, -a [kan'taβriko, a] *adj* Cantabrian
cantante [kan'tante] *adj* singing ▷*nmf* singer
cantar [kan'tar] *vt* to sing ▷*vi* to sing; (*insecto*) to chirp ▷*nm* (*acción*) singing; (*canción*) song; (*poema*) poem
cántaro ['kantaro] *nm* pitcher, jug; **llover a ~s** to rain cats and dogs
cante ['kante] *nm* (*Mús*) *Andalusian folk song*; **cante jondo** flamenco singing
cantera [kan'tera] *nf* quarry
cantero [kan'tero] (RPL) *nm* (*arriate*) border
cantidad [kanti'ðað] *nf* quantity, amount; **~ de** lots of
cantimplora [kantim'plora] *nf* (*frasco*) water bottle, canteen
cantina [kan'tina] *nf* canteen; (*de estación*) buffet; (LAM: *bar*) bar
cantinero, -a [kanti'nero, a] (MÉX) *nm/f* barman/barmaid, bartender (US)
canto ['kanto] *nm* singing; (*canción*) song; (*borde*) edge, rim; (*de cuchillo*) back; **canto rodado** boulder
cantor, a [kan'tor, a] *nm/f* singer
canturrear [kanturre'ar] *vi* to sing softly
canuto [ka'nuto] *nm* (*tubo*) small tube; (*fam*: *droga*) joint
caña ['kaɲa] *nf* (*Bot*: *tallo*) stem, stalk; (*carrizo*) reed; (*vaso*) tumbler; (*de cerveza*)

glass of beer; (*Anat*) shinbone; **caña de azúcar** sugar cane; **caña de pescar** fishing rod
cañada [ka'ɲaða] *nf* (*entre dos montañas*) gully, ravine; (*camino*) cattle track
cáñamo ['kaɲamo] *nm* hemp
cañería [kaɲe'ria] *nf* (*tubo*) pipe
caño ['kaɲo] *nm* (*tubo*) tube, pipe; (*de albañal*) sewer; (*Mús*) pipe; (*de fuente*) jet
cañón [ka'ɲon] *nm* (*Mil*) cannon; (*de fusil*) barrel; (*Geo*) canyon, gorge
caoba [ka'oβa] *nf* mahogany
caos ['kaos] *nm* chaos
capa ['kapa] *nf* cloak, cape; (*Geo*) layer, stratum; **capa de ozono** ozone layer
capacidad [kapaθi'ðað] *nf* (*medida*) capacity; (*aptitud*) capacity, ability
caparazón [kapara'θon] *nm* shell
capataz [kapa'taθ] *nm* foreman
capaz [ka'paθ] *adj* able, capable; (*amplio*) capacious, roomy
capellán [kape'ʎan] *nm* chaplain; (*sacerdote*) priest
capicúa [kapi'kua] *adj inv* (*número, fecha*) reversible
capilla [ka'piʎa] *nf* chapel
capital [kapi'tal] *adj* capital ▷ *nm* (*Com*) capital ▷ *nf* (*ciudad*) capital; **capital social** share *o* authorized capital
capitalismo [kapita'lismo] *nm* capitalism; **capitalista** *adj, nmf* capitalist
capitán [kapi'tan] *nm* captain
capítulo [ka'pitulo] *nm* chapter
capó [ka'po] *nm* (*Auto*) bonnet
capón [ka'pon] *nm* (*gallo*) capon
capota [ka'pota] *nf* (*de mujer*) bonnet; (*Auto*) hood (BRIT), top (US)
capote [ka'pote] *nm* (*abrigo: de militar*) greatcoat; (*de torero*) cloak
capricho [ka'pritʃo] *nm* whim, caprice; **caprichoso, -a** *adj* capricious
Capricornio [kapri'kornjo] *nm* Capricorn
cápsula ['kapsula] *nf* capsule
captar [kap'tar] *vt* (*comprender*) to understand; (*Radio*) to pick up; (*atención, apoyo*) to attract
captura [kap'tura] *nf* capture; (*Jur*) arrest; **capturar** *vt* to capture; to arrest
capucha [ka'putʃa] *nf* hood, cowl
capuchón [kapu'tʃon] (ESP) *nm* (*de bolígrafo*) cap
capullo [ka'puʎo] *nm* (*Bot*) bud; (*Zool*) cocoon; (*fam*) idiot
caqui ['kaki] *nm* khaki
cara ['kara] *nf* (*Anat: de moneda*) face; (*de disco*) side; (*descaro*) boldness; **~ a** facing; **de ~** opposite, facing; **dar la ~** to face the consequences; **¿~ o cruz?** heads or tails?; **¡qué ~ (más dura)!** what a nerve!
Caracas [ka'rakas] *n* Caracas
caracol [kara'kol] *nm* (*Zool*) snail; (*concha*) (sea) shell
carácter [ka'rakter] (*pl* **caracteres**) *nm* character; **tener buen/mal ~** to be good natured/bad tempered
característica [karakte'ristika] *nf* characteristic
característico, -a [karakte'ristiko, a] *adj* characteristic
caracterizar [karakteri'θar] *vt* to characterize, typify
caradura [kara'ðura] *nmf*: **es un ~** he's got a nerve
carajillo [kara'xiʎo] *nm* *coffee with a dash of brandy*
carajo [ka'raxo] (*fam!*) *nm*: **¡~!** shit! (!)
caramba [ka'ramba] *excl* good gracious!
caramelo [kara'melo] *nm* (*dulce*) sweet; (*azúcar fundida*) caramel
caravana [kara'βana] *nf* caravan; (*fig*) group; (*Auto*) tailback
carbón [kar'βon] *nm* coal; **papel ~** carbon paper
carbono [kar'βono] *nm* carbon
carburador [karβura'ðor] *nm* carburettor
carburante [karβu'rante] *nm* (*para motor*) fuel
carcajada [karka'xaða] *nf* (loud)

laugh, guffaw

cárcel ['karθel] *nf* prison, jail; (*Tec*) clamp

carcoma [kar'koma] *nf* woodworm

cardar [kar'ðar] *vt* (*pelo*) to backcomb

cardenal [karðe'nal] *nm* (*Rel*) cardinal; (*Med*) bruise

cardíaco, -a [kar'ðiako, a] *adj* cardiac, heart *cpd*

cardinal [karði'nal] *adj* cardinal

cardo ['karðo] *nm* thistle

carecer [kare'θer] *vi*: **~ de** to lack, be in need of

carencia [ka'renθja] *nf* lack; (*escasez*) shortage; (*Med*) deficiency

careta [ka'reta] *nf* mask

carga ['karɣa] *nf* (*peso, Elec*) load; (*de barco*) cargo, freight; (*Mil*) charge; (*responsabilidad*) duty, obligation

cargado, -a [kar'ɣaðo, a] *adj* loaded; (*Elec*) live; (*café, té*) strong; (*cielo*) overcast

cargamento [karɣa'mento] *nm* (*acción*) loading; (*mercancías*) load, cargo

cargar [kar'ɣar] *vt* (*barco, arma*) to load; (*Elec*) to charge; (*Com: algo en cuenta*) to charge; (*Inform*) to load ▷ *vi* (*Mil*) to charge; (*Auto*) to load (up); **~ con** to pick up, carry away; (*peso: fig*) to shoulder, bear; **cargarse** *vr* (*fam: estropear*) to break; (*: matar*) to bump off

cargo ['karɣo] *nm* (*puesto*) post, office; (*responsabilidad*) duty, obligation; (*Jur*) charge; **hacerse ~ de** to take charge of *o* responsibility for

carguero [kar'ɣero] *nm* freighter, cargo boat; (*avión*) freight plane

Caribe [ka'riβe] *nm*: **el ~** the Caribbean; **del ~** Caribbean; **caribeño, -a** [kari'βeɲo, a] *adj* Caribbean

caricatura [karika'tura] *nf* caricature

caricia [ka'riθja] *nf* caress

caridad [kari'ðað] *nf* charity

caries ['karjes] *nf inv* tooth decay

cariño [ka'riɲo] *nm* affection, love; (*caricia*) caress; (*en carta*) love ...; **tener ~ a** to be fond of; **cariñoso, -a** *adj* affectionate

carisma [ka'risma] *nm* charisma

caritativo, -a [karita'tiβo, a] *adj* charitable

cariz [ka'riθ] *nm*: **tener** *o* **tomar buen/mal ~** to look good/bad

carmín [kar'min] *nm* lipstick

carnal [kar'nal] *adj* carnal; **primo ~** first cousin

carnaval [karna'βal] *nm* carnival

CARNAVAL

Carnaval is the traditional period of fun, feasting and partying which takes place in the three days before the start of Lent ("Cuaresma"). Although in decline during the Franco years the carnival has grown in popularity recently in Spain. Cádiz and Tenerife are particularly well-known for their flamboyant celebrations with fancy-dress parties, parades and firework displays being the order of the day.

carne ['karne] *nf* flesh; (*Culin*) meat; **se me pone la ~ de gallina sólo verlo** I get the creeps just seeing it; **carne de cerdo/cordero/ternera/vaca** pork/lamb/veal/beef; **carne de gallina** (*fig*) gooseflesh; **carne molida** (LAM) mince (BRIT), ground meat (US); **carne picada** (ESP, RPL) mince (BRIT), ground meat (US)

carné [kar'ne] (ESP) (*pl* **~s**) *nm*: **~ de conducir** driving licence (BRIT), driver's license (US); **~ de identidad** identity card; **~ de socio** membership card

carnero [kar'nero] *nm* sheep, ram; (*carne*) mutton

carnet [kar'ne] (ESP) (*pl* **~s**) *nm* = **carné**

carnicería [karniθe'ria] *nf* butcher's (shop); (*fig: matanza*) carnage,

slaughter
carnicero, -a [karni'θero, a] *adj* carnivorous ▷ *nm/f* butcher; (*carnívoro*) carnivore
carnívoro, -a [kar'niβoro, a] *adj* carnivorous
caro, -a ['karo, a] *adj* dear; (*Com*) dear, expensive ▷ *adv* dear, dearly
carpa ['karpa] *nf* (*pez*) carp; (*de circo*) big top; (LAM: *tienda de campaña*) tent
carpeta [kar'peta] *nf* folder, file; **carpeta de anillas** ring binder
carpintería [karpinte'ria] *nf* carpentry, joinery; **carpintero** *nm* carpenter
carraspear [karraspe'ar] *vi* to clear one's throat
carraspera [karras'pera] *nf* hoarseness
carrera [ka'rrera] *nf* (*acción*) run(ning); (*espacio recorrido*) run; (*competición*) race; (*trayecto*) course; (*profesión*) career; (*licenciatura*) degree; **a la ~** at (full) speed; **carrera de obstáculos** (*Deporte*) steeplechase
carrete [ka'rrete] *nm* reel, spool; (*Tec*) coil
carretera [karre'tera] *nf* (main) road, highway; **carretera de circunvalación** ring road; **carretera nacional** ≈ A road (BRIT), ≈ state highway (US)
carretilla [karre'tiʎa] *nf* trolley; (*Agr*) (wheel)barrow
carril [ka'rril] *nm* furrow; (*de autopista*) lane; (*Ferro*) rail; **carril-bici** cycle lane
carrito [ka'rrito] *nm* trolley
carro ['karro] *nm* cart, wagon; (*Mil*) tank; (LAM: *coche*) car; **carro patrulla** (LAM) patrol *o* panda (BRIT) car
carrocería [karroθe'ria] *nf* bodywork, coachwork
carroña [ka'rroɲa] *nf* carrion *no pl*
carroza [ka'rroθa] *nf* (*carruaje*) coach
carrusel [karru'sel] *nm* merry-go-round, roundabout
carta ['karta] *nf* letter; (*Culin*) menu; (*naipe*) card; (*mapa*) map; (*Jur*) document; **carta certificada/urgente** registered/special-delivery letter
cartabón [karta'βon] *nm* set square
cartel [kar'tel] *nm* (*anuncio*) poster, placard; (*Escol*) wall chart; (*Com*) cartel; **cartelera** *nf* hoarding, billboard; (*en periódico etc*) entertainments guide; **"en cartelera"** "showing"
cartera [kar'tera] *nf* (*de bolsillo*) wallet; (*de colegial, cobrador*) satchel; (*de señora*) handbag; (*para documentos*) briefcase; (*Com*) portfolio; **ocupa la ~ de Agricultura** she is Minister of Agriculture
carterista [karte'rista] *nmf* pickpocket
cartero [kar'tero] *nm* postman
cartilla [kar'tiʎa] *nf* primer, first reading book; **cartilla de ahorros** savings book
cartón [kar'ton] *nm* cardboard; **cartón piedra** papier-mâché
cartucho [kar'tutʃo] *nm* (*Mil*) cartridge
cartulina [kartu'lina] *nf* card
casa ['kasa] *nf* house; (*hogar*) home; (*Com*) firm, company; **en ~** at home; **casa consistorial** town hall; **casa de campo** country house; **casa de huéspedes** boarding house; **casa de socorro** first aid post; **casa rodante** (CS) caravan (BRIT), trailer (US)
casado, -a [ka'saðo, a] *adj* married ▷ *nm/f* married man/woman
casar [ka'sar] *vt* to marry; (*Jur*) to quash, annul; **casarse** *vr* to marry, get married
cascabel [kaska'βel] *nm* (small) bell
cascada [kas'kaða] *nf* waterfall
cascanueces [kaska'nweθes] *nm inv* nutcrackers *pl*
cascar [kas'kar] *vt* to crack, split, break (open); **cascarse** *vr* to crack, split, break (open)
cáscara ['kaskara] *nf* (*de huevo, fruta seca*) shell; (*de fruta*) skin; (*de limón*) peel
casco ['kasko] *nm* (*de bombero,*

soldado) helmet; (*Náut: de barco*) hull; (*Zool: de caballo*) hoof; (*botella*) empty bottle; (*de ciudad*): **el ~ antiguo** the old part; **el ~ urbano** the town centre; **los ~s azules** the UN peace-keeping force, the blue berets

cascote [kas'kote] *nm* rubble

caserío [kase'rio] (ESP) *nm* farmhouse; (*casa*) country mansion

casero, -a [ka'sero, a] *adj* (*pan etc*) home-made ▷*nm/f* (*propietario*) landlord/lady; **ser muy ~** to be home-loving; **"comida casera"** "home cooking"

caseta [ka'seta] *nf* hut; (*para bañista*) cubicle; (*de feria*) stall

casete [ka'sete] *nm o f* cassette

casi ['kasi] *adv* almost, nearly; **~ nada** hardly anything; **~ nunca** hardly ever, almost never; **~ te caes** you almost fell

casilla [ka'siʎa] *nf* (*casita*) hut, cabin; (*Ajedrez*) square; (*para cartas*) pigeonhole; **casilla de correo** (CS) P.O. Box; **casillero** *nm* (*para cartas*) pigeonholes *pl*

casino [ka'sino] *nm* club; (*de juego*) casino

caso ['kaso] *nm* case; **en ~ de** in case of; **en ~ de que ...** in case ...; **el ~ es que ...** the fact is that ...; **en ese/todo ~** in that/any case; **hacer ~ a** to pay attention to; **venir al ~** to be relevant

caspa ['kasp̄a] *nf* dandruff

cassette [ka'sete] *nm o f* = **casete**

castaña [kas'taɲa] *nf* chestnut

castaño, -a [kas'taɲo, a] *adj* chestnut(-coloured), brown ▷*nm* chestnut tree

castañuelas [kasta'ɲwelas] *nfpl* castanets

castellano, -a [kaste'ʎano, a] *adj, nm/f* Castilian ▷*nm* (*Ling*) Castilian, Spanish

castigar [kasti'ɣar] *vt* to punish; (*Deporte*) to penalize; **castigo** *nm* punishment; (*Deporte*) penalty

Castilla [kas'tiʎa] *nf* Castille

castillo [kas'tiʎo] *nm* castle

castizo, -a [kas'tiθo, a] *adj* (*Ling*) pure

casto, -a ['kasto, a] *adj* chaste, pure

castor [kas'tor] *nm* beaver

castrar [kas'trar] *vt* to castrate

casual [ka'swal] *adj* chance, accidental

> No confundir **casual** con la palabra inglesa *casual*.

casualidad *nf* chance, accident; (*combinación de circunstancias*) coincidence; **da la casualidad de que ...** it (just) so happens that ...; **¡qué casualidad!** what a coincidence!

cataclismo [kata'klismo] *nm* cataclysm

catador, a [kata'ðor, a] *nm/f* wine taster

catalán, -ana [kata'lan, ana] *adj, nm/f* Catalan ▷*nm* (*Ling*) Catalan

catalizador [kataliθa'ðor] *nm* catalyst; (*Auto*) catalytic convertor

catalogar [katalo'ɣar] *vt* to catalogue; **~ a algn (de)** (*fig*) to categorize sb (as)

catálogo [ka'taloɣo] *nm* catalogue

Cataluña [kata'luɲa] *nf* Catalonia

catar [ka'tar] *vt* to taste, sample

catarata [kata'rata] *nf* (*Geo*) waterfall; (*Med*) cataract

catarro [ka'tarro] *nm* catarrh; (*constipado*) cold

catástrofe [ka'tastrofe] *nf* catastrophe

catear [kate'ar] (*fam*) *vt* (*examen, alumno*) to fail

cátedra ['kateðra] *nf* (*Univ*) chair, professorship

catedral [kate'ðral] *nf* cathedral

catedrático, -a [kate'ðratiko, a] *nm/f* professor

categoría [kateɣo'ria] *nf* category; (*rango*) rank, standing; (*calidad*) quality; **de ~** (*hotel*) top-class

cateto, -a ['kateto, a] (ESP: *pey*) *nm/f* peasant

catolicismo [katoli'θismo] *nm* Catholicism

católico, -a [ka'toliko, a] *adj, nm/f* Catholic
catorce [ka'torθe] *num* fourteen
cauce ['kauθe] *nm* (*de río*) riverbed; (*fig*) channel
caucho ['kautʃo] (ESP) *nm* rubber
caudal [kau'ðal] *nm* (*de río*) volume, flow; (*fortuna*) wealth; (*abundancia*) abundance
caudillo [kau'ðiʎo] *nm* leader, chief
causa ['kausa] *nf* cause; (*razón*) reason; (*Jur*) lawsuit, case; **a ~ de** because of; **causar** [kau'sar] *vt* to cause
cautela [kau'tela] *nf* caution, cautiousness; **cauteloso, -a** *adj* cautious, wary
cautivar [kauti'βar] *vt* to capture; (*atraer*) to captivate
cautiverio [kauti'βerjo] *nm* captivity
cautividad [kautiβi'ðað] *nf* = **cautiverio**
cautivo, -a [kau'tiβo, a] *adj, nm/f* captive
cauto, -a ['kauto, a] *adj* cautious, careful
cava ['kaβa] *nm champagne-type wine*
cavar [ka'βar] *vt* to dig
caverna [ka'βerna] *nf* cave, cavern
cavidad [kaβi'ðað] *nf* cavity
cavilar [kaβi'lar] *vt* to ponder
cayendo *etc vb V* **caer**
caza ['kaθa] *nf* (*acción: gen*) hunting; (*: con fusil*) shooting; (*una caza*) hunt, chase; (*de animales*) game ▷ *nm* (*Aviac*) fighter; **ir de ~** to go hunting; **caza mayor** game hunting; **cazador, a** [kaθa'ðor, a] *nm/f* hunter; **cazadora** *nf* jacket; **cazar** [ka'θar] *vt* to hunt; (*perseguir*) to chase; (*prender*) to catch
cazo ['kaθo] *nm* saucepan
cazuela [ka'θwela] *nf* (*vasija*) pan; (*guisado*) casserole
CD *nm abr* (= *compact disc*) CD
CD-ROM [θeðe'rom] *nm abr* CD-ROM
CE *nf abr* (= *Comunidad Europea*) EC
cebada [θe'βaða] *nf* barley
cebar [θe'βar] *vt* (*animal*) to fatten (up); (*anzuelo*) to bait; (*Mil, Tec*) to prime
cebo ['θeβo] *nm* (*para animales*) feed, food; (*para peces, fig*) bait; (*de arma*) charge
cebolla [θe'βoʎa] *nf* onion; **cebolleta** *nf* spring onion
cebra ['θeβra] *nf* zebra
cecear [θeθe'ar] *vi* to lisp
ceder [θe'ðer] *vt* to hand over, give up, part with ▷ *vi* (*renunciar*) to give in, yield; (*disminuir*) to diminish, decline; (*romperse*) to give way
cedro ['θeðro] *nm* cedar
cédula ['θeðula] *nf* certificate, document; **cédula de identidad** (LAM) identity card; **cédula electoral** (LAM) ballot
cegar [θe'ɣar] *vt* to blind; (*tubería etc*) to block up, stop up ▷ *vi* to go blind; **cegarse** *vr*: **~se (de)** to be blinded (by)
ceguera [θe'ɣera] *nf* blindness
ceja ['θexa] *nf* eyebrow
cejar [θe'xar] *vi* (*fig*) to back down
celador, a [θela'ðor, a] *nm/f* (*de edificio*) watchman; (*de museo etc*) attendant
celda ['θelda] *nf* cell
celebración [θeleβra'θjon] *nf* celebration
celebrar [θele'βrar] *vt* to celebrate; (*alabar*) to praise ▷ *vi* to be glad; **celebrarse** *vr* to occur, take place
célebre ['θelebre] *adj* famous
celebridad [θeleβri'ðað] *nf* fame; (*persona*) celebrity
celeste [θe'leste] *adj* (*azul*) sky-blue
celestial [θeles'tjal] *adj* celestial, heavenly
celo¹ ['θelo] *nm* zeal; (*Rel*) fervour; (*Zool*): **en ~** on heat; **celos** *nmpl* jealousy *sg*; **dar ~s a algn** to make sb jealous; **tener ~s** to be jealous
celo²® ['θelo] *nm* Sellotape®
celofán [θelo'fan] *nm* cellophane
celoso, -a [θe'loso, a] *adj* jealous; (*trabajador*) zealous
celta ['θelta] *adj* Celtic ▷ *nmf* Celt

célula ['θelula] *nf* cell
celulitis [θelu'litis] *nf* cellulite
cementerio [θemen'terjo] *nm* cemetery, graveyard
cemento [θe'mento] *nm* cement; (*hormigón*) concrete; (LAM: *cola*) glue
cena ['θena] *nf* evening meal, dinner; **cenar** [θe'nar] *vt* to have for dinner ▷ *vi* to have dinner
cenicero [θeni'θero] *nm* ashtray
ceniza [θe'niθa] *nf* ash, ashes *pl*
censo ['θenso] *nm* census; **censo electoral** electoral roll
censura [θen'sura] *nf* (*Pol*) censorship; **censurar** [θensu'rar] *vt* (*idea*) to censure; (*cortar: película*) to censor
centella [θen'teʎa] *nf* spark
centenar [θente'nar] *nm* hundred
centenario, -a [θente'narjo, a] *adj* centenary; hundred-year-old ▷ *nm* centenary
centeno [θen'teno] *nm* (*Bot*) rye
centésimo, -a [θen'tesimo, a] *adj* hundredth
centígrado [θen'tiɣraðo] *adj* centigrade
centímetro [θen'timetro] *nm* centimetre (BRIT), centimeter (US)
céntimo ['θentimo] *nm* cent
centinela [θenti'nela] *nm* sentry, guard
centollo [θen'toʎo] *nm* spider crab
central [θen'tral] *adj* central ▷ *nf* head office; (*Tec*) plant; (*Tel*) exchange; **central eléctrica** power station; **central nuclear** nuclear power station; **central telefónica** telephone exchange
centralita [θentra'lita] *nf* switchboard
centralizar [θentrali'θar] *vt* to centralize
centrar [θen'trar] *vt* to centre
céntrico, -a ['θentriko, a] *adj* central
centrifugar [θentrifu'ɣar] *vt* to spin-dry
centro ['θentro] *nm* centre; **centro comercial** shopping centre; **centro de atención al cliente** call centre; **centro de salud** health centre; **centro escolar** school; **centro juvenil** youth club; **centro turístico** (*lugar muy visitado*) tourist centre; **centro urbano** urban area, city
centroamericano, -a [θentroameri'kano, a] *adj, nm/f* Central American
ceñido, -a [θe'ɲiðo, a] *adj* (*chaqueta, pantalón*) tight(-fitting)
ceñir [θe'ɲir] *vt* (*rodear*) to encircle, surround; (*ajustar*) to fit (tightly)
ceño ['θeɲo] *nm* frown, scowl; **fruncir el ~** to frown, knit one's brow
cepillar [θepi'ʎar] *vt* to brush; (*madera*) to plane (down)
cepillo [θe'piʎo] *nm* brush; (*para madera*) plane; **cepillo de dientes** toothbrush
cera ['θera] *nf* wax
cerámica [θe'ramika] *nf* pottery; (*arte*) ceramics
cerca ['θerka] *nf* fence ▷ *adv* near, nearby, close; **~ de** near, close to
cercanías [θerka'nias] *nfpl* (*afueras*) outskirts, suburbs
cercano, -a [θer'kano, a] *adj* close, near
cercar [θer'kar] *vt* to fence in; (*rodear*) to surround
cerco ['θerko] *nm* (*Agr*) enclosure; (LAM: *valla*) fence; (*Mil*) siege
cerdo, -a ['θerðo, a] *nm/f* pig/sow
cereal [θere'al] *nm* cereal; **cereales** *nmpl* cereals, grain *sg*
cerebro [θe'reβro] *nm* brain; (*fig*) brains *pl*
ceremonia [θere'monja] *nf* ceremony; **ceremonioso, -a** *adj* ceremonious
cereza [θe'reθa] *nf* cherry
cerilla [θe'riʎa] *nf* (*fósforo*) match
cerillo [θe'riʎo] (MÉX) *nm* match
cero ['θero] *nm* nothing, zero
cerquillo [θer'kiʎo] (CAM, RPL) *nm*

fringe (BRIT), bangs *pl* (US)
cerrado, -a [θe'rraðo, a] *adj* closed, shut; (*con llave*) locked; (*tiempo*) cloudy, overcast; (*curva*) sharp; (*acento*) thick, broad
cerradura [θerra'ðura] *nf* (*acción*) closing; (*mecanismo*) lock
cerrajero [θerra'xero] *nm* locksmith
cerrar [θe'rrar] *vt* to close, shut; (*paso, carretera*) to close; (*grifo*) to turn off; (*cuenta, negocio*) to close ▷ *vi* to close, shut; (*noche*) to come down; **cerrarse** *vr* to close, shut; **~ con llave** to lock; **~ un trato** to strike a bargain
cerro ['θerro] *nm* hill
cerrojo [θe'rroxo] *nm* (*herramienta*) bolt; (*de puerta*) latch
certamen [θer'tamen] *nm* competition, contest
certero, -a [θer'tero, a] *adj* (*gen*) accurate
certeza [θer'teθa] *nf* certainty
certidumbre [θerti'ðumβre] *nf* = **certeza**
certificado, -a [θertifi'kaðo, a] *adj* (*carta, paquete*) registered; (*aprobado*) certified ▷ *nm* certificate; **certificado médico** medical certificate
certificar [θertifi'kar] *vt* (*asegurar, atestar*) to certify
cervatillo [θerβa'tiʎo] *nm* fawn
cervecería [θerβeθe'ria] *nf* (*fábrica*) brewery; (*bar*) public house, pub
cerveza [θer'βeθa] *nf* beer
cesar [θe'sar] *vi* to cease, stop ▷ *vt* (*funcionario*) to remove from office
cesárea [θe'sarea] *nf* (*Med*) Caesarean operation *o* section
cese ['θese] *nm* (*de trabajo*) dismissal; (*de pago*) suspension
césped ['θespeð] *nm* grass, lawn
cesta ['θesta] *nf* basket
cesto ['θesto] *nm* (large) basket, hamper
cfr *abr* (= *confróntese*) cf.
chabacano, -a [tʃaβa'kano, a] *adj* vulgar, coarse
chabola [tʃa'βola] (ESP) *nf* shack; **barrio de chabolas** shanty town
chacal [tʃa'kal] *nm* jackal
chacha ['tʃatʃa] (*fam*) *nf* maid
cháchara ['tʃatʃara] *nf* chatter; **estar de ~** to chatter away
chacra ['tʃakra] (CS) *nf* smallholding
chafa ['tʃafa] (MÉX: *fam*) *adj* useless, dud
chafar [tʃa'far] *vt* (*aplastar*) to crush; (*plan etc*) to ruin
chal [tʃal] *nm* shawl
chalado, -a [tʃa'lado, a] (*fam*) *adj* crazy
chalé [tʃa'le] (*pl* **~s**) *nm* villa, ≈ detached house
chaleco [tʃa'leko] *nm* waistcoat, vest (US); **chaleco de seguridad** (*Aut*) reflective safety vest; **chaleco salvavidas** life jacket
chalet [tʃa'le] (*pl* **~s**) *nm* = **chalé**
chamaco, -a (MÉX) [tʃa'mako, a] *nm/f* (*niño*) kid
chambear [tʃambe'ar] (MÉX: *fam*) *vi* to earn one's living
champán [tʃam'pan] *nm* champagne
champiñón [tʃampi'ɲon] *nm* mushroom
champú [tʃam'pu] (*pl* **~es, ~s**) *nm* shampoo
chamuscar [tʃamus'kar] *vt* to scorch, sear, singe
chance ['tʃanθe] (LAM) *nm* chance
chancho, -a ['tʃantʃo, a] (LAM) *nm/f* pig
chanchullo [tʃan'tʃuʎo] (*fam*) *nm* fiddle
chandal [tʃan'dal] *nm* tracksuit
chantaje [tʃan'taxe] *nm* blackmail
chapa ['tʃapa] *nf* (*de metal*) plate, sheet; (*de madera*) board, panel; (RPL *Auto*) number (BRIT) *o* license (US) plate; **chapado, -a** *adj*: **chapado en oro** gold-plated
chaparrón [tʃapa'rron] *nm* downpour, cloudburst
chaperón [tʃape'ron] (MÉX) *nm*: **hacer de ~** to play gooseberry;

chaperona (*LAM*) *nf*: **hacer de chaperona** to play gooseberry
chapopote [tʃapo'pote] (*MÉX*) *nm* tar
chapulín [tʃapu'lin] (*MÉX, CAM*) *nm* grasshopper
chapurrear [tʃapurre'ar] *vt* (*idioma*) to speak badly
chapuza [tʃa'puθa] *nf* botched job
chapuzón [tʃapu'θon] *nm*: **darse un ~** to go for a dip
chaqueta [tʃa'keta] *nf* jacket
chaquetón [tʃake'ton] *nm* long jacket
charca ['tʃarka] *nf* pond, pool
charco ['tʃarko] *nm* pool, puddle
charcutería [tʃarkute'ria] *nf* (*tienda*) *shop selling chiefly pork meat products*; (*productos*) cooked pork meats *pl*
charla ['tʃarla] *nf* talk, chat; (*conferencia*) lecture; **charlar** [tʃar'lar] *vi* to talk, chat; **charlatán, -ana** [tʃarla'tan, ana] *nm/f* (*hablador*) chatterbox; (*estafador*) trickster
charol [tʃa'rol] *nm* varnish; (*cuero*) patent leather
charola [tʃa'rola] (*MÉX*) *nf* tray
charro ['tʃarro, a] (*MÉX*) *nm* typical Mexican
chasco ['tʃasko] *nm* (*desengaño*) disappointment
chasis ['tʃasis] *nm inv* chassis
chasquido [tʃas'kiðo] *nm* crack; click
chat [tʃat] *nm* (*Internet*) chat room
chatarra [tʃa'tarra] *nf* scrap (metal)
chatear [tʃate'ar] *vi* (*Internet*) to chat
chato, -a ['tʃato, a] *adj* flat; (*nariz*) snub
chaucha ['tʃautʃa] (*RPL*) *nf* runner (*BRIT*) *o* pole (*US*) bean
chaval, a [tʃa'βal, a] (*ESP*) *nm/f* kid, lad/lass
chavo, -a ['tʃaβo] (*MÉX*: *fam*) *nm/f* guy/girl
checar [tʃe'kar] (*MÉX*) *vt*: **~ tarjeta** (*al entrar*) to clock in *o* on; (: *al salir*) to clock off *o* out
checo, -a ['tʃeko, a] *adj, nm/f* Czech ▷ *nm* (*Ling*) Czech
checoslovaco, -a [tʃekoslo'βako, a] *adj, nm/f* Czech, Czechoslovak
Checoslovaquia [tʃekoslo'βakja] *nf* (*Hist*) Czechoslovakia
cheque ['tʃeke] *nm* cheque (*BRIT*), check (*US*); **cobrar un ~** to cash a cheque; **cheque al portador** cheque payable to bearer; **cheque de viaje** traveller's cheque (*BRIT*), traveler's check (*US*); **cheque en blanco** blank cheque
chequeo [tʃe'keo] *nm* (*Med*) check-up; (*Auto*) service
chequera [tʃe'kera] (*LAM*) *nf* chequebook (*BRIT*), checkbook (*US*)
chévere ['tʃeβere] (*LAM*: *fam*) *adj* great
chícharo ['tʃitʃaro] (*MÉX, CAM*) *nm* pea
chichón [tʃi'tʃon] *nm* bump, lump
chicle ['tʃikle] *nm* chewing gum
chico, -a ['tʃiko, a] *adj* small, little ▷ *nm/f* (*niño*) child; (*muchacho*) boy/girl
chiflado, -a [tʃi'flaðo, a] *adj* crazy
chiflar [tʃi'flar] *vt* to hiss, boo
chilango, -a [tʃi'lango, a] (*MÉX*) *adj* of *o* from Mexico City
Chile ['tʃile] *nm* Chile; **chileno, -a** *adj, nm/f* Chilean
chile ['tʃile] *nm* chilli pepper
chillar [tʃi'ʎar] *vi* (*persona*) to yell, scream; (*animal salvaje*) to howl; (*cerdo*) to squeal
chillido [tʃi'ʎiðo] *nm* (*de persona*) yell, scream; (*de animal*) howl
chimenea [tʃime'nea] *nf* chimney; (*hogar*) fireplace
China ['tʃina] *nf* (*tb*: **la ~**) China
chinche ['tʃintʃe] *nf* (*insecto*) (bed)bug; (*Tec*) drawing pin (*BRIT*), thumbtack (*US*) ▷ *nmf* nuisance, pest
chincheta [tʃin'tʃeta] *nf* drawing pin (*BRIT*), thumbtack (*US*)
chingada [tʃin'gaða] (*MÉX*: *fam!*) *nf*: **hijo de la ~** bastard
chino, -a ['tʃino, a] *adj, nm/f* Chinese ▷ *nm* (*Ling*) Chinese
chipirón [tʃipi'ron] *nm* (*Zool, Culin*)

squid
Chipre ['tʃipre] *nf* Cyprus; **chipriota** *adj, nmf* Cypriot
chiquillo, -a [tʃi'kiʎo, a] *nm/f* (*fam*) kid
chirimoya [tʃiri'moja] *nf* custard apple
chiringuito [tʃirin'ɣito] *nm* small open-air bar
chiripa [tʃi'ripa] *nf* fluke
chirriar [tʃi'rrjar] *vi* to creak, squeak
chirrido [tʃi'rriðo] *nm* creak(ing), squeak(ing)
chisme ['tʃisme] *nm* (*habladurías*) piece of gossip; (*fam: objeto*) thingummyjig
chismoso, -a [tʃis'moso, a] *adj* gossiping ▷ *nm/f* gossip
chispa ['tʃispa] *nf* spark; (*fig*) sparkle; (*ingenio*) wit; (*fam*) drunkenness
chispear [tʃispe'ar] *vi* (*lloviznar*) to drizzle
chiste ['tʃiste] *nm* joke, funny story
chistoso, -a [tʃis'toso, a] *adj* funny, amusing
chivo, -a ['tʃiβo, a] *nm/f* (billy-/nanny-)goat; **chivo expiatorio** scapegoat
chocante [tʃo'kante] *adj* startling; (*extraño*) odd; (*ofensivo*) shocking
chocar [tʃo'kar] *vi* (*coches etc*) to collide, crash ▷ *vt* to shock; (*sorprender*) to startle; **~ con** to collide with; (*fig*) to run into, run up against; **¡chócala!** (*fam*) put it there!
chochear [tʃotʃe'ar] *vi* to be senile
chocho, -a ['tʃotʃo, a] *adj* doddering, senile; (*fig*) soft, doting
choclo ['tʃoklo] (CS) *nm* (*grano*) sweet corn; (*mazorca*) corn on the cob
chocolate [tʃoko'late] *adj, nm* chocolate; **chocolatina** *nf* chocolate
chofer [tʃo'fer] *nm* = **chófer**
chófer ['tʃofer] *nm* driver
chollo ['tʃoʎo] (ESP: *fam*) *nm* bargain, snip
choque *etc* ['tʃoke] *vb V* **chocar** ▷ *nm* (*impacto*) impact; (*golpe*) jolt; (*Auto*) crash; (*fig*) conflict; **choque frontal** head-on collision
chorizo [tʃo'riθo] *nm* *hard pork sausage*, (type of) salami
chorrada [tʃo'rraða] (ESP: *fam*) *nf*: **¡es una ~!** that's crap! (!); **decir ~s** to talk crap (!)
chorrear [tʃorre'ar] *vi* to gush (out), spout (out); (*gotear*) to drip, trickle
chorro ['tʃorro] *nm* jet; (*fig*) stream
choza ['tʃoθa] *nf* hut, shack
chubasco [tʃu'βasko] *nm* squall
chubasquero [tʃuβas'kero] *nm* lightweight raincoat
chuchería [tʃutʃe'ria] *nf* trinket
chuleta [tʃu'leta] *nf* chop, cutlet
chulo ['tʃulo] *nm* (*de prostituta*) pimp
chupaleta [tʃupa'leta] (MÉX) *nf* lollipop
chupar [tʃu'par] *vt* to suck; (*absorber*) to absorb; **chuparse** *vr* to grow thin
chupete [tʃu'pete] (ESP, CS) *nm* dummy (BRIT), pacifier (US)
chupetín [tʃupe'tin] (RPL) *nf* lollipop
chupito [tʃu'pito] (*fam*) *nm* shot
chupón [tʃu'pon] *nm* (*piruleta*) lollipop; (LAM: *chupete*) dummy (BRIT), pacifier (US)
churro ['tʃurro] *nm* (type of) fritter
chusma ['tʃusma] *nf* rabble, mob
chutar [tʃu'tar] *vi* to shoot (at goal)
Cía *abr* (= *compañía*) Co.
cianuro [θja'nuro] *nm* cyanide
cibercafé [θiβerka'fe] *nm* cybercafé
cibernauta [θiβer'nauta] *nmf* web surfer, Internet user
ciberterrorista [θiβerterro'rista] *nmf* cyberterrorist
cicatriz [θika'triθ] *nf* scar; **cicatrizarse** *vr* to heal (up), form a scar
ciclismo [θi'klismo] *nm* cycling
ciclista [θi'klista] *adj* cycle *cpd* ▷ *nmf* cyclist
ciclo ['θiklo] *nm* cycle; **cicloturismo** *nm* touring by bicycle
ciclón [θi'klon] *nm* cyclone
ciego, -a ['θjeɣo, a] *adj* blind ▷ *nm/f*

blind man/woman

cielo ['θjelo] *nm* sky; (*Rel*) heaven; **¡~s!** good heavens!

ciempiés [θjem'pjes] *nm inv* centipede

cien [θjen] *num V* **ciento**

ciencia ['θjenθja] *nf* science; **ciencias** *nfpl* (*Escol*) science *sg*; **ciencia-ficción** *nf* science fiction

científico, -a [θjen'tifiko, a] *adj* scientific ▷ *nm/f* scientist

ciento ['θjento] *num* hundred; **pagar al 10 por ~** to pay at 10 per cent; *V tb* **cien**

cierre *etc* ['θjerre] *vb V* **cerrar** ▷ *nm* closing, shutting; (*con llave*) locking; (LAM: *cremallera*) zip (fastener)

cierro *etc vb V* **cerrar**

cierto, -a ['θjerto, a] *adj* sure, certain; (*un tal*) a certain; (*correcto*) right, correct; **por ~** by the way; **~ hombre** a certain man; **ciertas personas** certain *o* some people; **sí, es ~** yes, that's correct

ciervo ['θjerβo] *nm* deer; (*macho*) stag

cifra ['θifra] *nf* number; (*secreta*) code; **cifrar** [θi'frar] *vt* to code, write in code

cigala [θi'ɣala] *nf* Norway lobster

cigarra [θi'ɣarra] *nf* cicada

cigarrillo [θiɣa'rriʎo] *nm* cigarette

cigarro [θi'ɣarro] *nm* cigarette; (*puro*) cigar

cigüeña [θi'ɣweɲa] *nf* stork

cilíndrico, -a [θi'lindriko, a] *adj* cylindrical

cilindro [θi'lindro] *nm* cylinder

cima ['θima] *nf* (*de montaña*) top, peak; (*de árbol*) top; (*fig*) height

cimentar [θimen'tar] *vt* to lay the foundations of; (*fig: fundar*) to found

cimiento [θi'mjento] *nm* foundation

cincel [θin'θel] *nm* chisel

cinco ['θinko] *num* five

cincuenta [θin'kwenta] *num* fifty

cine ['θine] *nm* cinema; **cinematográfico, -a** [θinemato'ɣrafiko, a] *adj* cine-, film *cpd*

cínico, -a ['θiniko, a] *adj* cynical ▷ *nm/f* cynic

cinismo [θi'nismo] *nm* cynicism

cinta ['θinta] *nf* band, strip; (*de tela*) ribbon; (*película*) reel; (*de máquina de escribir*) ribbon; **cinta adhesiva/aislante** sticky/insulating tape; **cinta de vídeo** videotape; **cinta magnetofónica** tape; **cinta métrica** tape measure

cintura [θin'tura] *nf* waist

cinturón [θintu'ron] *nm* belt; **cinturón de seguridad** safety belt

ciprés [θi'pres] *nm* cypress (tree)

circo ['θirko] *nm* circus

circuito [θir'kwito] *nm* circuit

circulación [θirkula'θjon] *nf* circulation; (*Auto*) traffic

circular [θirku'lar] *adj, nf* circular ▷ *vi, vt* to circulate ▷ *vi* (*Auto*) to drive; **"circule por la derecha"** "keep (to the) right"

círculo ['θirkulo] *nm* circle; **círculo vicioso** vicious circle

circunferencia [θirkunfe'renθja] *nf* circumference

circunstancia [θirkuns'tanθja] *nf* circumstance

cirio ['θirjo] *nm* (wax) candle

ciruela [θi'rwela] *nf* plum; **ciruela pasa** prune

cirugía [θiru'xia] *nf* surgery; **cirugía estética** *o* **plástica** plastic surgery

cirujano [θiru'xano] *nm* surgeon

cisne ['θisne] *nm* swan

cisterna [θis'terna] *nf* cistern, tank

cita ['θita] *nf* appointment, meeting; (*de novios*) date; (*referencia*) quotation

citación [θita'θjon] *nf* (*Jur*) summons *sg*

citar [θi'tar] *vt* (*gen*) to make an appointment with; (*Jur*) to summons; (*un autor, texto*) to quote; **citarse** *vr*: **se ~on en el cine** they arranged to meet at the cinema

cítricos ['θitrikos] *nmpl* citrus fruit(s)

ciudad [θju'ðað] *nf* town; (*más

grande) city; **ciudadano, -a** *nm/f* citizen

cívico, -a ['θiβiko, a] *adj* civic

civil [θi'βil] *adj* civil ▷ *nm* (*guardia*) policeman; **civilización** [θiβiliθa'θjon] *nf* civilization; **civilizar** [θiβili'θar] *vt* to civilize

cizaña [θi'θaɲa] *nf* (*fig*) discord

cl. *abr* (= *centilitro*) cl.

clamor [kla'mor] *nm* clamour, protest

clandestino, -a [klandes'tino, a] *adj* clandestine; (*Pol*) underground

clara ['klara] *nf* (*de huevo*) egg white

claraboya [klara'βoja] *nf* skylight

clarear [klare'ar] *vi* (*el día*) to dawn; (*el cielo*) to clear up, brighten up; **clarearse** *vr* to be transparent

claridad [klari'ðað] *nf* (*de día*) brightness; (*de estilo*) clarity

clarificar [klarifi'kar] *vt* to clarify

clarinete [klari'nete] *nm* clarinet

claro, -a ['klaro, a] *adj* clear; (*luminoso*) bright; (*color*) light; (*evidente*) clear, evident; (*poco espeso*) thin ▷ *nm* (*en bosque*) clearing ▷ *adv* clearly ▷ *excl*: **¡~ que sí!** of course!; **¡~ que no!** of course not!

clase ['klase] *nf* class; **dar ~(s)** to teach; **clase alta/media/obrera** upper/middle/working class; **clases particulares** private lessons *o* tuition *sg*

clásico, -a ['klasiko, a] *adj* classical

clasificación [klasifika'θjon] *nf* classification; (*Deporte*) league (table)

clasificar [klasifi'kar] *vt* to classify

claustro ['klaustro] *nm* cloister

cláusula ['klausula] *nf* clause

clausura [klau'sura] *nf* closing, closure

clavar [kla'βar] *vt* (*clavo*) to hammer in; (*cuchillo*) to stick, thrust

clave ['klaβe] *nf* key; (*Mús*) clef; **clave de acceso** password; **clave lada** (MÉX) dialling (BRIT) *o* area (US) code

clavel [kla'βel] *nm* carnation

clavícula [kla'βikula] *nf* collar bone

clavija [kla'βixa] *nf* peg, dowel, pin; (*Elec*) plug

clavo ['klaβo] *nm* (*de metal*) nail; (*Bot*) clove

claxon ['klakson] (*pl* **~s**) *nm* horn

clérigo ['klerixo] *nm* priest

clero ['klero] *nm* clergy

clicar [kli'kar] *vi* (*Internet*) to click; **~ en el icono** to click on an icon; **~ dos veces** to double-click

cliché [kli'tʃe] *nm* cliché; (*Foto*) negative

cliente, -a ['kljente, a] *nm/f* client, customer; **clientela** [kljen'tela] *nf* clientele, customers *pl*

clima ['klima] *nm* climate; **climatizado, -a** [klimati'θaðo, a] *adj* air-conditioned

clímax ['klimaks] *nm inv* climax

clínica ['klinika] *nf* clinic; (*particular*) private hospital

clip [klip] (*pl* **~s**) *nm* paper clip

clítoris ['klitoris] *nm inv* (*Anat*) clitoris

cloaca [klo'aka] *nf* sewer

clonar [klo'nar] *vt* to clone

cloro ['kloro] *nm* chlorine

clóset ['kloset] (MÉX) *nm* cupboard

club [klub] (*pl* **~s** *o* **~es**) *nm* club; **club nocturno** night club

cm *abr* (= *centímetro, centímetros*) cm

coágulo [ko'axulo] *nm* clot

coalición [koali'θjon] *nf* coalition

coartada [koar'taða] *nf* alibi

coartar [koar'tar] *vt* to limit, restrict

coba ['koβa] *nf*: **dar ~ a algn** (*adular*) to suck up to sb

cobarde [ko'βarðe] *adj* cowardly ▷ *nm* coward; **cobardía** *nf* cowardice

cobaya [ko'βaja] *nf* guinea pig

cobertizo [koβer'tiθo] *nm* shelter

cobertura [koβer'tura] *nf* cover; **aquí no hay ~** (*Tel*) I can't get a signal

cobija [ko'βixa] (LAM) *nf* blanket; **cobijar** [koβi'xar] *vt* (*cubrir*) to cover; (*proteger*) to shelter; **cobijo** *nm* shelter

cobra ['koβra] *nf* cobra

cobrador, a [koβra'ðor, a] *nm/f* (*de*

autobús) conductor/conductress; (*de impuestos, gas*) collector
cobrar [ko'βrar] *vt* (*cheque*) to cash; (*sueldo*) to collect, draw; (*objeto*) to recover; (*precio*) to charge; (*deuda*) to collect ▷*vi* to be paid; **cóbrese al entregar** cash on delivery; **¿me cobra, por favor?** how much do I owe you?, can I have the bill, please?
cobre ['koβre] *nm* copper; **cobres** *nmpl* (*Mús*) brass instruments
cobro ['koβro] *nm* (*de cheque*) cashing; **presentar al ~** to cash
cocaína [koka'ina] *nf* cocaine
cocción [kok'θjon] *nf* (*Culin*) cooking; (*en agua*) boiling
cocer [ko'θer] *vt, vi* to cook; (*en agua*) to boil; (*en horno*) to bake
coche ['kotʃe] *nm* (*Auto*) car (BRIT), automobile (US); (*de tren, de caballos*) coach, carriage; (*para niños*) pram (BRIT), baby carriage (US); **ir en ~** to drive; **coche celular** police van; **coche de bomberos** fire engine; **coche de carreras** racing car; **coche fúnebre** hearse; **coche-cama** (*pl* **coches-cama**) *nm* (*Ferro*) sleeping car, sleeper
cochera [ko'tʃera] *nf* garage; (*de autobuses, trenes*) depot
coche restaurante (*pl* **coches restaurante**) *nm* (*Ferro*) dining car, diner
cochinillo [kotʃi'niʎo] *nm* (*Culin*) suckling pig, sucking pig
cochino, -a [ko'tʃino, a] *adj* filthy, dirty ▷*nm/f* pig
cocido [ko'θiðo] *nm* stew
cocina [ko'θina] *nf* kitchen; (*aparato*) cooker, stove; (*acto*) cookery; **cocina eléctrica/de gas** electric/gas cooker; **cocina francesa** French cuisine; **cocinar** *vt, vi* to cook
cocinero, -a [koθi'nero, a] *nm/f* cook
coco ['koko] *nm* coconut
cocodrilo [koko'ðrilo] *nm* crocodile
cocotero [koko'tero] *nm* coconut palm
cóctel ['koktel] *nm* cocktail; **cóctel molotov** petrol bomb, Molotov cocktail
codazo [ko'ðaθo] *nm*: **dar un ~ a algn** to nudge sb
codicia [ko'ðiθja] *nf* greed; **codiciar** *vt* to covet
código ['koðiɣo] *nm* code; **código civil** common law; **código de barras** bar code; **código de circulación** highway code; **código de la zona** (LAM) dialling (BRIT) *o* area (US) code; **código postal** postcode
codillo [ko'ðiʎo] *nm* (*Zool*) knee; (*Tec*) elbow (joint)
codo ['koðo] *nm* (*Anat, de tubo*) elbow; (*Zool*) knee
codorniz [koðor'niθ] *nf* quail
coexistir [koe(k)sis'tir] *vi* to coexist
cofradía [kofra'ðia] *nf* brotherhood, fraternity
cofre ['kofre] *nm* (*de joyas*) case; (*de dinero*) chest
coger [ko'xer] (ESP) *vt* to take (hold of); (*objeto caído*) to pick up; (*frutas*) to pick, harvest; (*resfriado, ladrón, pelota*) to catch ▷*vi*: **~ por el buen camino** to take the right road; **cogerse** *vr* (*el dedo*) to catch; **~se a algo** to get hold of sth
cogollo [ko'ɣoʎo] *nm* (*de lechuga*) heart
cogote [ko'ɣote] *nm* back *o* nape of the neck
cohabitar [koaβi'tar] *vi* to live together, cohabit
coherente [koe'rente] *adj* coherent
cohesión [koe'sjon] *nm* cohesion
cohete [ko'ete] *nm* rocket
cohibido, -a [koi'βiðo, a] *adj* (*Psico*) inhibited; (*tímido*) shy
coincidencia [koinθi'ðenθja] *nf* coincidence
coincidir [koinθi'ðir] *vi* (*en idea*) to coincide, agree; (*en lugar*) to coincide
coito ['koito] *nm* intercourse, coitus
coja *etc vb V* **coger**
cojear [koxe'ar] *vi* (*persona*) to limp,

hobble; (*mueble*) to wobble, rock
cojera [ko'xera] *nf* limp
cojín [ko'xin] *nm* cushion
cojo, -a etc ['koxo, a] *vb V* **coger** ▷ *adj* (*que no puede andar*) lame, crippled; (*mueble*) wobbly ▷ *nm/f* lame person, cripple
cojón [ko'xon] (*fam!*) *nm*: **¡cojones!** shit! (!); **cojonudo, -a** (*fam*) *adj* great, fantastic
col [kol] *nf* cabbage; **coles de Bruselas** Brussels sprouts
cola ['kola] *nf* tail; (*de gente*) queue; (*lugar*) end, last place; (*para pegar*) glue, gum; **hacer ~** to queue (up)
colaborador, a [kolaβora'ðor, a] *nm/f* collaborator
colaborar [kolaβo'rar] *vi* to collaborate
colada [ko'laða] (ESP) *nf*: **hacer la ~** to do the washing
colador [kola'ðor] *nm* (*para líquidos*) strainer; (*para verduras etc*) colander
colapso [ko'lapso] *nm* collapse
colar [ko'lar] *vt* (*líquido*) to strain off; (*metal*) to cast ▷ *vi* to ooze, seep (through); **colarse** *vr* to jump the queue; **~se en** to get into without paying; (*fiesta*) to gatecrash
colcha ['koltʃa] *nf* bedspread
colchón [kol'tʃon] *nm* mattress; **colchón inflable** air bed *o* mattress
colchoneta [koltʃo'neta] *nf* (*en gimnasio*) mat; (*de playa*) air bed
colección [kolek'θjon] *nf* collection; **coleccionar** *vt* to collect; **coleccionista** *nmf* collector
colecta [ko'lekta] *nf* collection
colectivo, -a [kolek'tiβo, a] *adj* collective, joint ▷ *nm* (ARG: *autobús*) (small) bus
colega [ko'leɣa] *nmf* colleague; (ESP: *amigo*) mate
colegial, a [kole'xjal, a] *nm/f* schoolboy(-girl)
colegio [ko'lexjo] *nm* college; (*escuela*) school; (*de abogados etc*) association; **colegio electoral** polling station; **colegio mayor** (ESP) hall of residence

COLEGIO

A **colegio** is normally a private primary or secondary school. In the state system it means a primary school although these are also called **escuelas**. State secondary schools are called **institutos**.

cólera ['kolera] *nf* (*ira*) anger; (*Med*) cholera
colesterol [koleste'rol] *nm* cholesterol
coleta [ko'leta] *nf* pigtail
colgante [kol'ɣante] *adj* hanging ▷ *nm* (*joya*) pendant
colgar [kol'ɣar] *vt* to hang (up); (*ropa*) to hang out ▷ *vi* to hang; (*Tel*) to hang up
cólico ['koliko] *nm* colic
coliflor [koli'flor] *nf* cauliflower
colilla [ko'liʎa] *nf* cigarette end, butt
colina [ko'lina] *nf* hill
colisión [koli'sjon] *nf* collision; **colisión frontal** head-on crash
collar [ko'ʎar] *nm* necklace; (*de perro*) collar
colmar [kol'mar] *vt* to fill to the brim; (*fig*) to fulfil, realize
colmena [kol'mena] *nf* beehive
colmillo [kol'miʎo] *nm* (*diente*) eye tooth; (*de elefante*) tusk; (*de perro*) fang
colmo ['kolmo] *nm*: **¡es el ~!** it's the limit!
colocación [koloka'θjon] *nf* (*acto*) placing; (*empleo*) job, position
colocar [kolo'kar] *vt* to place, put, position; (*dinero*) to invest; (*poner en empleo*) to find a job for; **colocarse** *vr* to get a job
Colombia [ko'lombja] *nf* Colombia; **colombiano, -a** *adj, nm/f* Colombian
colonia [ko'lonja] *nf* colony; (*agua de colonia*) cologne; (MÉX: *de casas*)

residential area; **colonia proletaria** (*MÉX*) shantytown
colonización [koloniθa'θjon] *nf* colonization; **colonizador, a** [koloniθa'ðor, a] *adj* colonizing ▷ *nm/f* colonist, settler
colonizar [koloni'θar] *vt* to colonize
coloquio [ko'lokjo] *nm* conversation; (*congreso*) conference
color [ko'lor] *nm* colour
colorado, -a [kolo'raðo, a] *adj* (*rojo*) red; (*MÉX*: *chiste*) smutty, rude
colorante [kolo'rante] *nm* colouring
colorear [kolore'ar] *vt* to colour
colorete [kolo'rete] *nm* blusher
colorido [kolo'riðo] *nm* colouring
columna [ko'lumna] *nf* column; (*pilar*) pillar; (*apoyo*) support; (*tb*: **~ vertebral**) spine, spinal column; (*fig*) backbone
columpiar [kolum'pjar] *vt* to swing; **columpiarse** *vr* to swing; **columpio** *nm* swing
coma ['koma] *nf* comma ▷ *nm* (*Med*) coma
comadre [ko'maðre] *nf* (*madrina*) godmother; (*chismosa*) gossip; **comadrona** *nf* midwife
comal [ko'mal] (*MÉX, CAM*) *nm* griddle
comandante [koman'dante] *nm* commandant
comarca [ko'marka] *nf* region
comba ['komba] (*ESP*) *nf* (*cuerda*) skipping rope; **saltar a la ~** to skip
combate [kom'bate] *nm* fight
combatir [komba'tir] *vt* to fight, combat
combinación [kombina'θjon] *nf* combination; (*Quím*) compound; (*prenda*) slip
combinar [kombi'nar] *vt* to combine
combustible [kombus'tiβle] *nm* fuel
comedia [ko'meðja] *nf* comedy; (*Teatro*) play, drama; **comediante** [kome'ðjante] *nmf* (comic) actor/actress
comedido, -a [kome'ðiðo, a] *adj* moderate
comedor, a [kome'ðor, a] *nm* (*habitación*) dining room; (*cantina*) canteen
comensal [komen'sal] *nmf* fellow guest (*o* diner)
comentar [komen'tar] *vt* to comment on; **comentario** [komen'tarjo] *nm* comment, remark; (*literario*) commentary; **comentarios** *nmpl* (*chismes*) gossip *sg*; **comentarista** [komenta'rista] *nmf* commentator
comenzar [komen'θar] *vt, vi* to begin, start; **~ a hacer algo** to begin *o* start doing sth
comer [ko'mer] *vt* to eat; (*Damas, Ajedrez*) to take, capture ▷ *vi* to eat; (*ESP, MÉX*: *almorzar*) to have lunch; **comerse** *vr* to eat up
comercial [komer'θjal] *adj* commercial; (*relativo al negocio*) business *cpd*; **comercializar** *vt* (*producto*) to market; (*pey*) to commercialize
comerciante [komer'θjante] *nmf* trader, merchant
comerciar [komer'θjar] *vi* to trade, do business
comercio [ko'merθjo] *nm* commerce, trade; (*tienda*) shop, store; (*negocio*) business; (*fig*) dealings *pl*; **comercio electrónico** e-commerce; **comercio exterior/interior** foreign/domestic trade
comestible [komes'tiβle] *adj* eatable, edible; **comestibles** *nmpl* food *sg*, foodstuffs
cometa [ko'meta] *nm* comet ▷ *nf* kite
cometer [kome'ter] *vt* to commit
cometido [kome'tiðo] *nm* task, assignment
cómic ['komik] *nm* comic
comicios [ko'miθjos] *nmpl* elections
cómico, -a ['komiko, a] *adj* comic(al) ▷ *nm/f* comedian

comida [ko'miða] *nf* (*alimento*) food; (*almuerzo, cena*) meal; (*de mediodía*) lunch; **comida basura** junk food; **comida chatarra** (*MÉX*) junk food
comidilla [komi'ðiʎa] *nf*: **ser la ~ del barrio** *o* **pueblo** to be the talk of the town
comienzo *etc* [ko'mjenθo] *vb V* **comenzar** ▷ *nm* beginning, start
comillas [ko'miʎas] *nfpl* quotation marks
comilona [komi'lona] (*fam*) *nf* blow-out
comino [ko'mino] *nm*: **(no) me importa un ~** I don't give a damn
comisaría [komisa'ria] *nf* (*de policía*) police station; (*Mil*) commissariat
comisario [komi'sarjo] *nm* (*Mil etc*) commissary; (*Pol*) commissar
comisión [komi'sjon] *nf* commission; **Comisiones Obreras** (*ESP*) Communist trade union
comité [komi'te] (*pl* **~s**) *nm* committee
comitiva [komi'tiβa] *nf* retinue
como ['komo] *adv* as; (*tal* **~**) like; (*aproximadamente*) about, approximately ▷ *conj* (*ya que, puesto que*) as, since; **¡~ no!** of course!; **~ no lo haga hoy** unless he does it today; **~ si** as if; **es tan alto ~ ancho** it is as high as it is wide
cómo ['komo] *adv* how?, why? ▷ *excl* what?, I beg your pardon? ▷ *nm*: **el ~ y el porqué** the whys and wherefores
cómoda ['komoða] *nf* chest of drawers
comodidad [komoði'ðað] *nf* comfort
comodín [komo'ðin] *nm* joker
cómodo, -a ['komoðo, a] *adj* comfortable; (*práctico, de fácil uso*) convenient
compact [kom'pakt] (*pl* **~s**) *nm* (*tb*: **~ disc**) compact disk player
compacto, -a [kom'pakto, a] *adj* compact
compadecer [kompaðe'θer] *vt* to pity, be sorry for; **compadecerse** *vr*: **~se de** to pity, be *o* feel sorry for
compadre [kom'paðre] *nm* (*padrino*) godfather; (*amigo*) friend, pal
compañero, -a [kompa'ɲero, a] *nm/f* companion; (*novio*) boy/girlfriend; **compañero de clase** classmate
compañía [kompa'ɲia] *nf* company; **hacer ~ a algn** to keep sb company
comparación [kompara'θjon] *nf* comparison; **en ~ con** in comparison with
comparar [kompa'rar] *vt* to compare
comparecer [kompare'θer] *vi* to appear (in court)
comparsa [kom'parsa] *nmf* (*Teatro*) extra
compartimiento [komparti'mjento] *nm* (*Ferro*) compartment
compartir [kompar'tir] *vt* to share; (*dinero, comida etc*) to divide (up), share (out)
compás [kom'pas] *nm* (*Mús*) beat, rhythm; (*Mat*) compasses *pl*; (*Náut etc*) compass
compasión [kompa'sjon] *nf* compassion, pity
compasivo, -a [kompa'siβo, a] *adj* compassionate
compatible [kompa'tiβle] *adj* compatible
compatriota [kompa'trjota] *nmf* compatriot, fellow countryman/woman
compenetrarse [kompene'trarse] *vr* to be in tune
compensación [kompensa'θjon] *nf* compensation
compensar [kompen'sar] *vt* to compensate
competencia [kompe'tenθja] *nf* (*incumbencia*) domain, field; (*Jur, habilidad*) competence; (*rivalidad*) competition
competente [kompe'tente] *adj*

competent
competición [kompeti'θjon] *nf* competition
competir [kompe'tir] *vi* to compete
compinche [kom'pintʃe] (LAM) *nmf* mate, buddy (US)
complacer [kompla'θer] *vt* to please; **complacerse** *vr* to be pleased
complaciente [kompla'θjente] *adj* kind, obliging, helpful
complejo, -a [kom'plexo, a] *adj, nm* complex
complementario, -a [komplemen'tarjo, a] *adj* complementary
completar [komple'tar] *vt* to complete
completo, -a [kom'pleto, a] *adj* complete; (*perfecto*) perfect; (*lleno*) full ▷ *nm* full complement
complicado, -a [kompli'kaðo, a] *adj* complicated; **estar ~ en** to be mixed up in
cómplice ['kompliθe] *nmf* accomplice
complot [kom'plo(t)] (*pl* **~s**) *nm* plot
componer [kompo'ner] *vt* (*Mús, Literatura, Imprenta*) to compose; (*algo roto*) to mend, repair; (*arreglar*) to arrange; **componerse** *vr*: **~se de** to consist of
comportamiento [komporta'mjento] *nm* behaviour, conduct
comportarse [kompor'tarse] *vr* to behave
composición [komposi'θjon] *nf* composition
compositor, a [komposi'tor, a] *nm/f* composer
compostura [kompos'tura] *nf* (*actitud*) composure
compra ['kompra] *nf* purchase; **hacer la ~** to do the shopping; **ir de ~s** to go shopping; **comprador, a** *nm/f* buyer, purchaser; **comprar** [kom'prar] *vt* to buy, purchase
comprender [kompren'der] *vt* to understand; (*incluir*) to comprise, include
comprensión [kompren'sjon] *nf* understanding; **comprensivo, -a** *adj* (*actitud*) understanding
compresa [kom'presa] *nf* (*para mujer*) sanitary towel (BRIT) *o* napkin (US)
comprimido, -a [kompri'miðo, a] *adj* compressed ▷ *nm* (*Med*) pill, tablet
comprimir [kompri'mir] *vt* to compress; (*Internet*) to zip
comprobante [kompro'βante] *nm* proof; (*Com*) voucher; **comprobante de compra** proof of purchase
comprobar [kompro'βar] *vt* to check; (*probar*) to prove; (*Tec*) to check, test
comprometer [komprome'ter] *vt* to compromise; (*poner en peligro*) to endanger; **comprometerse** *vr* (*involucrarse*) to get involved
compromiso [kompro'miso] *nm* (*obligación*) obligation; (*cometido*) commitment; (*convenio*) agreement; (*apuro*) awkward situation
compuesto, -a [kom'pwesto, a] *adj*: **~ de** composed of, made up of ▷ *nm* compound
computadora [komputa'ðora] (LAM) *nf* computer; **computadora central** mainframe (computer); **computadora personal** personal computer
cómputo ['komputo] *nm* calculation
comulgar [komul'ɣar] *vi* to receive communion
común [ko'mun] *adj* common ▷ *nm*: **el ~** the community
comunicación [komunika'θjon] *nf* communication; (*informe*) report
comunicado [komuni'kado] *nm* announcement; **comunicado de prensa** press release
comunicar [komuni'kar] *vt, vi* to communicate; **comunicarse** *vr* to communicate; **está comunicando** (*Tel*) the line's engaged (BRIT) *o*

busy (US); **comunicativo, -a** *adj* communicative
comunidad [komuni'ðað] *nf* community; **comunidad autónoma** (ESP) autonomous region; **Comunidad (Económica) Europea** European (Economic) Community; **comunidad de vecinos** residents' association
comunión [komu'njon] *nf* communion
comunismo [komu'nismo] *nm* communism; **comunista** *adj, nmf* communist

PALABRA CLAVE

con [kon] *prep* 1 (*medio, compañía*) with; **comer con cuchara** to eat with a spoon; **pasear con algn** to go for a walk with sb
2 (*a pesar de*): **con todo, merece nuestros respetos** all the same, he deserves our respect
3 (*para con*): **es muy bueno para con los niños** he's very good with (the) children
4 (+ *infin*): **con llegar a las seis estará bien** if you come by six it will be fine
▷ *conj*: **con que: será suficiente con que le escribas** it will be sufficient if you write to her

concebir [konθe'βir] *vt, vi* to conceive
conceder [konθe'ðer] *vt* to concede
concejal, a [konθe'xal, a] *nm/f* town councillor
concentración [konθentra'θjon] *nf* concentration
concentrar [konθen'trar] *vt* to concentrate; **concentrarse** *vr* to concentrate
concepto [kon'θepto] *nm* concept
concernir [konθer'nir] *vi* to concern; **en lo que concierne a ...** as far as ... is concerned; **en lo que a mí concierne** as far as I'm concerned
concertar [konθer'tar] *vt* (*Mús*) to harmonize; (*acordar: precio*) to agree; (*: tratado*) to conclude; (*trato*) to arrange, fix up; (*combinar: esfuerzos*) to coordinate ▷ *vi* to harmonize, be in tune
concesión [konθe'sjon] *nf* concession
concesionario [konθesjo'narjo] *nm* (licensed) dealer, agent
concha ['kontʃa] *nf* shell
conciencia [kon'θjenθja] *nf* conscience; **tomar ~ de** to become aware of; **tener la ~ tranquila** to have a clear conscience
concienciar [konθjen'θjar] *vt* to make aware; **concienciarse** *vr* to become aware
concienzudo, -a [konθjen'θuðo, a] *adj* conscientious
concierto *etc* [kon'θjerto] *vb V* **concertar** ▷ *nm* concert; (*obra*) concerto
conciliar [konθi'ljar] *vt* to reconcile; **~ el sueño** to get to sleep
concilio [kon'θiljo] *nm* council
conciso, -a [kon'θiso, a] *adj* concise
concluir [konklu'ir] *vt, vi* to conclude; **concluirse** *vr* to conclude
conclusión [konklu'sjon] *nf* conclusion
concordar [konkor'ðar] *vt* to reconcile ▷ *vi* to agree, tally
concordia [kon'korðja] *nf* harmony
concretar [konkre'tar] *vt* to make concrete, make more specific; **concretarse** *vr* to become more definite
concreto, -a [kon'kreto, a] *adj, nm* (LAM: *hormigón*) concrete; **en ~** (*en resumen*) to sum up; (*específicamente*) specifically; **no hay nada en ~** there's nothing definite
concurrido, -a [konku'rriðo, a] *adj* (*calle*) busy; (*local, reunión*) crowded
concursante [konkur'sante] *nmf* competitor
concurso [kon'kurso] *nm* (*de público*) crowd; (*Escol, Deporte, competencia*)

competition; (*ayuda*) help, cooperation

condal [kon'dal] *adj*: **la Ciudad C~** Barcelona

conde ['konde] *nm* count

condecoración [kondekora'θjon] *nf* (*Mil*) medal

condena [kon'dena] *nf* sentence; **condenación** [kondena'θjon] *nf* condemnation; (*Rel*) damnation; **condenar** [konde'nar] *vt* to condemn; (*Jur*) to convict; **condenarse** *vr* (*Rel*) to be damned

condesa [kon'desa] *nf* countess

condición [kondi'θjon] *nf* condition; **a ~ de que ...** on condition that ...; **condicional** *adj* conditional

condimento [kondi'mento] *nm* seasoning

condominio [kondo'minjo] (LAM) *nm* condominium

condón [kon'don] *nm* condom

conducir [kondu'θir] *vt* to take, convey; (*Auto*) to drive ▷ *vi* to drive; (*fig*) to lead; **conducirse** *vr* to behave

conducta [kon'dukta] *nf* conduct, behaviour

conducto [kon'dukto] *nm* pipe, tube; (*fig*) channel

conductor, a [konduk'tor, a] *adj* leading, guiding ▷ *nm* (*Física*) conductor; (*de vehículo*) driver

conduje *etc vb V* **conducir**

conduzco *etc vb V* **conducir**

conectado, -a [konek'taðo, a] *adj* (*Inform*) on-line

conectar [konek'tar] *vt* to connect (up); (*enchufar*) plug in

conejillo [kone'xiʎo] *nm*: **~ de Indias** guinea pig

conejo [ko'nexo] *nm* rabbit

conexión [konek'sjon] *nf* connection

confección [confe(k)'θjon] *nf* preparation; (*industria*) clothing industry

confeccionar [konfekθjo'nar] *vt* to make (up)

conferencia [konfe'renθja] *nf* conference; (*lección*) lecture; (ESP *Tel*) call; **conferencia de prensa** press conference

conferir [konfe'rir] *vt* to award

confesar [konfe'sar] *vt* to confess, admit

confesión [konfe'sjon] *nf* confession

confesionario [konfesjo'narjo] *nm* confessional

confeti [kon'feti] *nm* confetti

confiado, -a [kon'fjaðo, a] *adj* (*crédulo*) trusting; (*seguro*) confident

confianza [kon'fjanθa] *nf* trust; (*seguridad*) confidence; (*familiaridad*) intimacy, familiarity

confiar [kon'fjar] *vt* to entrust ▷ *vi* to trust; **~ en algn** to trust sb; **~ en que ...** to hope that ...

confidencial [konfiðen'θjal] *adj* confidential

confidente [konfi'ðente] *nmf* confidant/e; (*policial*) informer

configurar [konfiɣu'rar] *vt* to shape, form

confín [kon'fin] *nm* limit; **confines** *nmpl* confines, limits

confirmar [konfir'mar] *vt* to confirm

confiscar [konfis'kar] *vt* to confiscate

confite [kon'fite] *nm* sweet (BRIT), candy (US); **confitería** [konfite'ria] *nf* (*tienda*) confectioner's (shop)

confitura [konfi'tura] *nf* jam

conflictivo, -a [konflik'tiβo, a] *adj* (*asunto, propuesta*) controversial; (*país, situación*) troubled

conflicto [kon'flikto] *nm* conflict; (*fig*) clash

confluir [kon'flwir] *vi* (*ríos*) to meet; (*gente*) to gather

conformar [konfor'mar] *vt* to shape, fashion ▷ *vi* to agree; **conformarse** *vr* to conform; (*resignarse*) to resign o.s.; **~se con algo** to be happy with sth

conforme [kon'forme] *adj*

(*correspondiente*): **~ con** in line with; (*de acuerdo*): **estar ~s (con algo)** to be in agreement (with sth) ▷ *adv* as ▷ *excl* agreed! ▷ *prep*: **~ a** in accordance with; **quedarse ~ (con algo)** to be satisfied (with sth)

confortable [konfor'taβle] *adj* comfortable

confortar [konfor'tar] *vt* to comfort

confrontar [konfron'tar] *vt* to confront; (*dos personas*) to bring face to face; (*cotejar*) to compare

confundir [konfun'dir] *vt* (*equivocar*) to mistake, confuse; (*turbar*) to confuse; **confundirse** *vr* (*turbarse*) to get confused; (*equivocarse*) to make a mistake; (*mezclarse*) to mix

confusión [konfu'sjon] *nf* confusion

confuso, -a [kon'fuso, a] *adj* confused

congelado, -a [konxe'laðo, a] *adj* frozen; **congelados** *nmpl* frozen food(s); **congelador** *nm* (*aparato*) freezer, deep freeze

congelar [konxe'lar] *vt* to freeze; **congelarse** *vr* (*sangre, grasa*) to congeal

congeniar [konxe'njar] *vi* to get on (BRIT) *o* along (US) well

congestión [konxes'tjon] *nf* congestion

congestionar [konxestjo'nar] *vt* to congest

congraciarse [kongra'θjarse] *vr* to ingratiate o.s.

congratular [kongratu'lar] *vt* to congratulate

congregar [kongre'ɣar] *vt* to gather together; **congregarse** *vr* to gather together

congresista [kongre'sista] *nmf* delegate, congressman/woman

congreso [kon'greso] *nm* congress

conjetura [konxe'tura] *nf* guess; **conjeturar** *vt* to guess

conjugar [konxu'ɣar] *vt* to combine, fit together; (*Ling*) to conjugate

conjunción [konxun'θjon] *nf* conjunction

conjunto, -a [kon'xunto, a] *adj* joint, united ▷ *nm* whole; (*Mús*) band; **en ~** as a whole

conmemoración [konmemora'θjon] *nf* commemoration

conmemorar [konmemo'rar] *vt* to commemorate

conmigo [kon'miɣo] *pron* with me

conmoción [konmo'θjon] *nf* shock; (*fig*) upheaval; **conmoción cerebral** (*Med*) concussion

conmovedor, a [konmoβe'ðor, a] *adj* touching, moving; (*emocionante*) exciting

conmover [konmo'βer] *vt* to shake, disturb; (*fig*) to move

conmutador [konmuta'ðor] *nm* switch; (LAM: *centralita*) switchboard; (: *central*) telephone exchange

cono ['kono] *nm* cone; **Cono Sur** Southern Cone

conocedor, a [konoθe'ðor, a] *adj* expert, knowledgeable ▷ *nm/f* expert

conocer [kono'θer] *vt* to know; (*por primera vez*) to meet, get to know; (*entender*) to know about; (*reconocer*) to recognize; **conocerse** *vr* (*una persona*) to know o.s.; (*dos personas*) to (get to) know each other; **~ a algn de vista** to know sb by sight

conocido, -a [kono'θiðo, a] *adj* (well-)known ▷ *nm/f* acquaintance

conocimiento [konoθi'mjento] *nm* knowledge; (*Med*) consciousness; **conocimientos** *nmpl* (*saber*) knowledge *sg*

conozco *etc vb V* **conocer**

conque ['konke] *conj* and so, so then

conquista [kon'kista] *nf* conquest; **conquistador, a** *adj* conquering ▷ *nm* conqueror; **conquistar** [konkis'tar] *vt* to conquer

consagrar [konsa'ɣrar] *vt* (*Rel*) to consecrate; (*fig*) to devote

consciente [kons'θjente] *adj* conscious

consecución [konseku'θjon] *nf* acquisition; (*de fin*) attainment
consecuencia [konse'kwenθja] *nf* consequence, outcome; (*coherencia*) consistency
consecuente [konse'kwente] *adj* consistent
consecutivo, -a [konseku'tiβo, a] *adj* consecutive
conseguir [konse'ɣir] *vt* to get, obtain; (*objetivo*) to attain
consejero, -a [konse'xero, a] *nm/f* adviser, consultant; (*Pol*) councillor
consejo [kon'sexo] *nm* advice; (*Pol*) council; **consejo de administración** (*Com*) board of directors; **consejo de guerra** court martial; **consejo de ministros** cabinet meeting
consenso [kon'senso] *nm* consensus
consentimiento [konsenti'mjento] *nm* consent
consentir [konsen'tir] *vt* (*permitir, tolerar*) to consent to; (*mimar*) to pamper, spoil; (*aguantar*) to put up with ▷ *vi* to agree, consent; **~ que algn haga algo** to allow sb to do sth
conserje [kon'serxe] *nm* caretaker; (*portero*) porter
conservación [konserβa'θjon] *nf* conservation; (*de alimentos, vida*) preservation
conservador, a [konserβa'ðor, a] *adj* (*Pol*) conservative ▷ *nm/f* conservative
conservante [konser'βante] *nm* preservative
conservar [konser'βar] *vt* to conserve, keep; (*alimentos, vida*) to preserve; **conservarse** *vr* to survive
conservas [kon'serβas] *nfpl* canned food(s) *pl*
conservatorio [konserβa'torjo] *nm* (*Mús*) conservatoire, conservatory
considerable [konsiðe'raβle] *adj* considerable
consideración [konsiðera'θjon] *nf* consideration; (*estimación*) respect
considerado, -a [konsiðe'raðo, a] *adj* (*atento*) considerate; (*respetado*) respected
considerar [konsiðe'rar] *vt* to consider
consigna [kon'siɣna] *nf* (*orden*) order, instruction; (*para equipajes*) left-luggage office
consigo *etc* [kon'siɣo] *vb V* **conseguir** ▷ *pron* (*m*) with him; (*f*) with her; (*Vd*) with you; (*reflexivo*) with o.s.
consiguiendo *etc vb V* **conseguir**
consiguiente [konsi'ɣjente] *adj* consequent; **por ~** and so, therefore, consequently
consistente [konsis'tente] *adj* consistent; (*sólido*) solid, firm; (*válido*) sound
consistir [konsis'tir] *vi*: **~ en** (*componerse de*) to consist of
consola [kon'sola] *nf* (*mueble*) console table; (*de videojuegos*) console
consolación [konsola'θjon] *nf* consolation
consolar [konso'lar] *vt* to console
consolidar [konsoli'ðar] *vt* to consolidate
consomé [konso'me] (*pl* **~s**) *nm* consommé, clear soup
consonante [konso'nante] *adj* consonant, harmonious ▷ *nf* consonant
consorcio [kon'sorθjo] *nm* consortium
conspiración [konspira'θjon] *nf* conspiracy
conspirar [konspi'rar] *vi* to conspire
constancia [kon'stanθja] *nf* constancy; **dejar ~ de** to put on record
constante [kons'tante] *adj, nf* constant
constar [kons'tar] *vi* (*evidenciarse*) to be clear *o* evident; **~ de** to consist of
constipado, -a [konsti'paðo, a] *adj*: **estar ~** to have a cold ▷ *nm* cold

No confundir **constipado** con la palabra inglesa *constipated*.

constitución [konstitu'θjon] *nf* constitution

constituir [konstitu'ir] *vt* (*formar, componer*) to constitute, make up; (*fundar, erigir, ordenar*) to constitute, establish

construcción [konstruk'θjon] *nf* construction, building

constructor, a [konstruk'tor, a] *nm/f* builder

construir [konstru'ir] *vt* to build, construct

construyendo *etc vb V* **construir**

consuelo [kon'swelo] *nm* consolation, solace

cónsul ['konsul] *nm* consul; **consulado** *nm* consulate

consulta [kon'sulta] *nf* consultation; (*Med*): **horas de ~** surgery hours; **consultar** [konsul'tar] *vt* to consult; **consultar algo con algn** to discuss sth with sb; **consultorio** [konsul'torjo] *nm* (*Med*) surgery

consumición [konsumi'θjon] *nf* consumption; (*bebida*) drink; (*comida*) food; **consumición mínima** cover charge

consumidor, a [konsumi'ðor, a] *nm/f* consumer

consumir [konsu'mir] *vt* to consume; **consumirse** *vr* to be consumed; (*persona*) to waste away

consumismo [konsu'mismo] *nm* consumerism

consumo [kon'sumo] *nm* consumption

contabilidad [kontaβili'ðað] *nf* accounting, book-keeping; (*profesión*) accountancy; **contable** *nmf* accountant

contacto [kon'takto] *nm* contact; (*Auto*) ignition; **estar/ponerse en ~ con algn** to be/to get in touch with sb

contado, -a [kon'taðo, a] *adj*: **~s** (*escasos*) numbered, scarce, few ▷ *nm*: **pagar al ~** to pay (in) cash

contador [konta'ðor] *nm* (ESP: *aparato*) meter ▷ *nmf* (LAM *Com*) accountant

contagiar [konta'xjar] *vt* (*enfermedad*) to pass on, transmit; (*persona*) to infect; **contagiarse** *vr* to become infected

contagio [kon'taxjo] *nm* infection; **contagioso, -a** *adj* infectious; (*fig*) catching

contaminación [kontamina'θjon] *nf* contamination; (*polución*) pollution

contaminar [kontami'nar] *vt* to contaminate; (*aire, agua*) to pollute

contante [kon'tante] *adj*: **dinero ~ (y sonante)** cash

contar [kon'tar] *vt* (*páginas, dinero*) to count; (*anécdota, chiste etc*) to tell ▷ *vi* to count; **~ con** to rely on, count on

contemplar [kontem'plar] *vt* to contemplate; (*mirar*) to look at

contemporáneo, -a [kontempo'raneo, a] *adj, nm/f* contemporary

contenedor [kontene'ðor] *nm* container

contener [konte'ner] *vt* to contain, hold; (*retener*) to hold back, contain; **contenerse** *vr* to control *o* restrain o.s.

contenido, -a [konte'niðo, a] *adj* (*moderado*) restrained; (*risa etc*) suppressed ▷ *nm* contents *pl*, content

contentar [konten'tar] *vt* (*satisfacer*) to satisfy; (*complacer*) to please; **contentarse** *vr* to be satisfied

contento, -a [kon'tento, a] *adj* (*alegre*) pleased; (*feliz*) happy

contestación [kontesta'θjon] *nf* answer, reply

contestador [kontesta'ðor] *nm* (*tb*: **~ automático**) answering machine

contestar [kontes'tar] *vt* to answer, reply; (*Jur*) to corroborate, confirm

> No confundir **contestar** con la palabra inglesa *contest*.

contexto [kon'te(k)sto] *nm* context

contigo [kon'tiɣo] *pron* with you

contiguo, -a [kon'tiɣwo, a] *adj* adjacent, adjoining
continente [konti'nente] *adj, nm* continent
continuación [kontinwa'θjon] *nf* continuation; **a ~** then, next
continuar [konti'nwar] *vt* to continue, go on with ▷*vi* to continue, go on; **~ hablando** to continue talking *o* to talk
continuidad [kontinwi'ðað] *nf* continuity
continuo, -a [kon'tinwo, a] *adj* (*sin interrupción*) continuous; (*acción perseverante*) continual
contorno [kon'torno] *nm* outline; (*Geo*) contour; **contornos** *nmpl* neighbourhood *sg*, surrounding area *sg*
contra ['kontra] *prep, adv* against ▷*nm inv* con ▷*nf*: **la C~** (*de Nicaragua*) the Contras *pl*
contraataque [kontraa'take] *nm* counter-attack
contrabajo [kontra'βaxo] *nm* double bass
contrabandista [kontraβan'dista] *nmf* smuggler
contrabando [kontra'βando] *nm* (*acción*) smuggling; (*mercancías*) contraband
contracción [kontrak'θjon] *nf* contraction
contracorriente [kontrako'rrjente] *nf* cross-current
contradecir [kontraðe'θir] *vt* to contradict
contradicción [kontraðik'θjon] *nf* contradiction
contradictorio, -a [kontraðik'torjo, a] *adj* contradictory
contraer [kontra'er] *vt* to contract; (*limitar*) to restrict; **contraerse** *vr* to contract; (*limitarse*) to limit o.s.
contraluz [kontra'luθ] *nm* view against the light
contrapartida [kontrapar'tiða] *nf*: **como ~ (de)** in return (for)
contrapelo [kontra'pelo]: **a ~** *adv* the wrong way
contrapeso [kontra'peso] *nm* counterweight
contraportada [kontrapor'taða] *nf* (*de revista*) back cover
contraproducente [kontraproðu'θente] *adj* counterproductive
contrario, -a [kon'trarjo, a] *adj* contrary; (*persona*) opposed; (*sentido, lado*) opposite ▷*nm/f* enemy, adversary; (*Deporte*) opponent; **al** *o* **por el ~** on the contrary; **de lo ~** otherwise
contrarreloj [kontrarre'lo] *nf* (*tb*: **prueba ~**) time trial
contrarrestar [kontrarres'tar] *vt* to counteract
contrasentido [kontrasen'tiðo] *nm* (*contradicción*) contradiction
contraseña [kontra'seɲa] *nf* (*Inform*) password
contrastar [kontras'tar] *vt, vi* to contrast
contraste [kon'traste] *nm* contrast
contratar [kontra'tar] *vt* *firmar un acuerdo para*, to contract for; (*empleados, obreros*) to hire, engage
contratiempo [kontra'tjempo] *nm* setback
contratista [kontra'tista] *nmf* contractor
contrato [kon'trato] *nm* contract
contraventana [kontraβen'tana] *nf* shutter
contribución [kontriβu'θjon] *nf* (*municipal etc*) tax; (*ayuda*) contribution
contribuir [kontriβu'ir] *vt, vi* to contribute; (*Com*) to pay (in taxes)
contribuyente [kontriβu'jente] *nmf* (*Com*) taxpayer; (*que ayuda*) contributor
contrincante [kontrin'kante] *nmf* opponent
control [kon'trol] *nm* control; (*inspección*) inspection, check; **control de pasaportes** passport inspection; **controlador, a** *nm/f* controller; **controlador aéreo** air-traffic controller; **controlar** [kontro'lar] *vt*

to control; (*inspeccionar*) to inspect, check
contundente [kontun'dente] *adj* (*instrumento*) blunt; (*argumento, derrota*) overwhelming
contusión [kontu'sjon] *nf* bruise
convalecencia [kombale'θenθja] *nf* convalescence
convalecer [kombale'θer] *vi* to convalesce, get better
convalidar [kombali'ðar] *vt* (*título*) to recognize
convencer [komben'θer] *vt* to convince; **~ a algn (de** *o* **para hacer algo)** to persuade sb (to do sth)
convención [komben'θjon] *nf* convention
conveniente [kombe'njente] *adj* suitable; (*útil*) useful
convenio [kom'benjo] *nm* agreement, treaty
convenir [kombe'nir] *vi* (*estar de acuerdo*) to agree; (*venir bien*) to suit, be suitable

No confundir **convenir** con la palabra inglesa *convene*.

convento [kom'bento] *nm* convent
convenza *etc vb V* **convencer**
convergir [komber'xir] *vi* = **converger**
conversación [kombersa'θjon] *nf* conversation
conversar [komber'sar] *vi* to talk, converse
conversión [komber'sjon] *nf* conversion
convertir [komber'tir] *vt* to convert
convidar [kombi'ðar] *vt* to invite; **~ a algn a una cerveza** to buy sb a beer
convincente [kombin'θente] *adj* convincing
convite [kom'bite] *nm* invitation; (*banquete*) banquet
convivencia [kombi'βenθja] *nf* coexistence, living together
convivir [kombi'βir] *vi* to live together
convocar [kombo'kar] *vt* to summon, call (together)
convocatoria [komboka'torja] *nf* (*de oposiciones, elecciones*) notice; (*de huelga*) call
cónyuge ['konjuxe] *nmf* spouse
coñac [ko'ɲa(k)] (*pl* **~s**) *nm* cognac, brandy
coño ['koɲo] (*fam!*) *excl* (*enfado*) shit! (!); (*sorpresa*) bloody hell! (!)
cool [kul] *adj* (*fam*) cool
cooperación [koopera'θjon] *nf* cooperation
cooperar [koope'rar] *vi* to cooperate
cooperativa [koopera'tiβa] *nf* cooperative
coordinadora [koorðina'ðora] *nf* (*comité*) coordinating committee
coordinar [koorði'nar] *vt* to coordinate
copa ['kopa] *nf* cup; (*vaso*) glass; (*bebida*): **tomar una ~** (to have a) drink; (*de árbol*) top; (*de sombrero*) crown; **copas** *nfpl* (*Naipes*) ≈ hearts
copia ['kopja] *nf* copy; **copia de respaldo** *o* **seguridad** (*Inform*) back-up copy; **copiar** *vt* to copy
copla ['kopla] *nf* verse; (*canción*) (popular) song
copo ['kopo] *nm*: **~ de nieve** snowflake; **~s de maíz** cornflakes
coqueta [ko'keta] *adj* flirtatious, coquettish; **coquetear** *vi* to flirt
coraje [ko'raxe] *nm* courage; (*ánimo*) spirit; (*ira*) anger
coral [ko'ral] *adj* choral ▷ *nf* (*Mús*) choir ▷ *nm* (*Zool*) coral
coraza [ko'raθa] *nf* (*armadura*) armour; (*blindaje*) armour-plating
corazón [kora'θon] *nm* heart
corazonada [koraθo'naða] *nf* impulse; (*presentimiento*) hunch
corbata [kor'βata] *nf* tie
corchete [kor'tʃete] *nm* catch, clasp
corcho ['kortʃo] *nm* cork; (*Pesca*) float
cordel [kor'ðel] *nm* cord, line
cordero [kor'ðero] *nm* lamb
cordial [kor'ðjal] *adj* cordial

cordillera [korði'ʎera] *nf* range (of mountains)
Córdoba ['korðoβa] *n* Cordova
cordón [kor'ðon] *nm* (*cuerda*) cord, string; (*de zapatos*) lace; (*Mil etc*) cordon; **cordón umbilical** umbilical cord
cordura [kor'ðura] *nf*: **con ~** (*obrar, hablar*) sensibly
corneta [kor'neta] *nf* bugle
cornisa [kor'nisa] *nf* (*Arq*) cornice
coro ['koro] *nm* chorus; (*conjunto de cantores*) choir
corona [ko'rona] *nf* crown; (*de flores*) garland
coronel [koro'nel] *nm* colonel
coronilla [koro'niʎa] *nf* (*Anat*) crown (of the head)
corporal [korpo'ral] *adj* corporal, bodily
corpulento, -a [korpu'lento, a] *adj* (*persona*) heavily-built
corral [ko'rral] *nm* farmyard
correa [ko'rrea] *nf* strap; (*cinturón*) belt; (*de perro*) lead, leash; **correa del ventilador** (*Auto*) fan belt
corrección [korrek'θjon] *nf* correction; (*reprensión*) rebuke; **correccional** *nm* reformatory
correcto, -a [ko'rrekto, a] *adj* correct; (*persona*) well-mannered
corredizo, -a [korre'ðiθo, a] *adj* (*puerta etc*) sliding
corredor, a [korre'ðor, a] *nm* (*pasillo*) corridor; (*balcón corrido*) gallery; (*Com*) agent, broker ▷ *nm/f* (*Deporte*) runner
corregir [korre'xir] *vt* (*error*) to correct; **corregirse** *vr* to reform
correo [ko'rreo] *nm* post, mail; (*persona*) courier; **Correos** *nmpl* (ESP) Post Office *sg*; **correo aéreo** airmail; **correo basura** (*Inform*) spam; **correo electrónico** e-mail, electronic mail; **correo web** webmail
correr [ko'rrer] *vt* to run; (*cortinas*) to draw; (*cerrojo*) to shoot ▷ *vi* to run; (*líquido*) to run, flow; **correrse** *vr* to slide, move; (*colores*) to run
correspondencia [korrespon'denθja] *nf* correspondence; (*Ferro*) connection
corresponder [korrespon'der] *vi* to correspond; (*convenir*) to be suitable; (*pertenecer*) to belong; (*concernir*) to concern; **corresponderse** *vr* (*por escrito*) to correspond; (*amarse*) to love one another
correspondiente [korrespon'djente] *adj* corresponding
corresponsal [korrespon'sal] *nmf* correspondent
corrida [ko'rriða] *nf* (*de toros*) bullfight
corrido, -a [ko'rriðo, a] *adj* (*avergonzado*) abashed; **un kilo ~** a good kilo
corriente [ko'rrjente] *adj* (*agua*) running; (*dinero etc*) current; (*común*) ordinary, normal ▷ *nf* current ▷ *nm* current month; **estar al ~ de** to be informed about; **corriente eléctrica** electric current
corrija *etc vb V* **corregir**
corro ['korro] *nm* ring, circle (of people)
corromper [korrom'per] *vt* (*madera*) to rot; (*fig*) to corrupt
corrosivo, -a [korro'siβo, a] *adj* corrosive
corrupción [korrup'θjon] *nf* rot, decay; (*fig*) corruption
corsé [kor'se] *nm* corset
cortacésped [korta'θespeð] *nm* lawn mower
cortado, -a [kor'taðo, a] *adj* (*gen*) cut; (*leche*) sour; (*tímido*) shy; (*avergonzado*) embarrassed ▷ *nm* coffee (with a little milk)
cortafuegos [korta'fweɣos] *nm inv* (*en el bosque*) firebreak, fire lane (US); (*Internet*) firewall
cortar [kor'tar] *vt* to cut; (*suministro*) to cut off; (*un pasaje*) to cut out ▷ *vi* to cut; **cortarse** *vr* (*avergonzarse*) to become embarrassed; (*leche*) to turn, curdle; **~se el pelo** to have one's hair cut

cortauñas [korta'uɲas] *nm inv* nail clippers *pl*
corte ['korte] *nm* cut, cutting; (*de tela*) piece, length ▷ *nf*: **las C~s** the Spanish Parliament; **corte de luz** power cut; **corte y confección** dressmaking
cortejo [kor'texo] *nm* entourage; **cortejo fúnebre** funeral procession
cortés [kor'tes] *adj* courteous, polite
cortesía [korte'sia] *nf* courtesy
corteza [kor'teθa] *nf* (*de árbol*) bark; (*de pan*) crust
cortijo [kor'tixo] (ESP) *nm* farm, farmhouse
cortina [kor'tina] *nf* curtain
corto, -a ['korto, a] *adj* (*breve*) short; (*tímido*) bashful; **~ de luces** not very bright; **~ de vista** short-sighted; **estar ~ de fondos** to be short of funds; **cortocircuito** *nm* short circuit; **cortometraje** *nm* (*Cine*) short
cosa ['kosa] *nf* thing; **~ de** about; **eso es ~ mía** that's my business
coscorrón [kosko'rron] *nm* bump on the head
cosecha [ko'setʃa] *nf* (*Agr*) harvest; (*de vino*) vintage; **cosechar** [kose'tʃar] *vt* to harvest, gather (in)
coser [ko'ser] *vt* to sew
cosmético, -a [kos'metiko, a] *adj, nm* cosmetic
cosquillas [kos'kiʎas] *nfpl*: **hacer ~** to tickle; **tener ~** to be ticklish
costa ['kosta] *nf* (*Geo*) coast; **a toda ~** at all costs; **Costa Brava** Costa Brava; **Costa Cantábrica** Cantabrian Coast; **Costa del Sol** Costa del Sol
costado [kos'taðo] *nm* side
costanera [kosta'nera] (CS) *nf* promenade, sea front
costar [kos'tar] *vt* (*valer*) to cost; **me cuesta hablarle** I find it hard to talk to him
Costa Rica [kosta'rika] *nf* Costa Rica; **costarricense** *adj, nmf* Costa Rican; **costarriqueño, -a** *adj, nm/f* Costa Rican
coste ['koste] *nm* = **costo**
costear [koste'ar] *vt* to pay for
costero, -a [kos'tero, a] *adj* (*pueblecito, camino*) coastal
costilla [kos'tiʎa] *nf* rib; (*Culin*) cutlet
costo ['kosto] *nm* cost, price; **costo de (la) vida** cost of living; **costoso, -a** *adj* costly, expensive
costra ['kostra] *nf* (*corteza*) crust; (*Med*) scab
costumbre [kos'tumbre] *nf* custom, habit
costura [kos'tura] *nf* sewing, needlework; (*zurcido*) seam
costurera [kostu'rera] *nf* dressmaker
costurero [kostu'rero] *nm* sewing box *o* case
cotidiano, -a [koti'ðjano, a] *adj* daily, day to day
cotilla [ko'tiʎa] (ESP: *fam*) *nmf* gossip; **cotillear** (ESP) *vi* to gossip; **cotilleo** (ESP) *nm* gossip(ing)
cotizar [koti'θar] *vt* (*Com*) to quote, price; **cotizarse** *vr*: **~se a** to sell at, fetch; (*Bolsa*) to stand at, be quoted at
coto ['koto] *nm* (*terreno cercado*) enclosure; (*de caza*) reserve
cotorra [ko'torra] *nf* parrot
coyote [ko'jote] *nm* coyote, prairie wolf
coz [koθ] *nf* kick
crack [krak] *nm* (*droga*) crack
cráneo ['kraneo] *nm* skull, cranium
cráter ['krater] *nm* crater
crayón [kra'jon] (MÉX, RPL) *nm* crayon, chalk
creación [krea'θjon] *nf* creation
creador, a [krea'ðor, a] *adj* creative ▷ *nm/f* creator
crear [kre'ar] *vt* to create, make
crecer [kre'θer] *vi* to grow; (*precio*) to rise
creces ['kreθes]: **con ~** *adv* amply, fully
crecido, -a [kre'θiðo, a] *adj* (*persona, planta*) full-grown; (*cantidad*) large
crecimiento [kreθi'mjento] *nm* growth; (*aumento*) increase
credencial [kreðen'θjal] *nf*

(*LAM*: *tarjeta*) card; **credenciales** *nfpl* credentials; **credencial de socio** (*LAM*) membership card

crédito ['kreðito] *nm* credit

credo ['kreðo] *nm* creed

creencia [kre'enθja] *nf* belief

creer [kre'er] *vt, vi* to think, believe; **creerse** *vr* to believe o.s. (to be); **~ en** to believe in; **creo que sí/no** I think/don't think so; **¡ya lo creo!** I should think so!

creído, -a [kre'iðo, a] *adj* (*engreído*) conceited

crema ['krema] *nf* cream; **crema batida** (*LAM*) whipped cream; **crema pastelera** (confectioner's) custard

cremallera [krema'ʎera] *nf* zip (fastener)

crepe ['krepe] (*ESP*) *nf* pancake

cresta ['kresta] *nf* (*Geo, Zool*) crest

creyendo *etc vb V* **creer**

creyente [kre'jente] *nmf* believer

creyó *etc vb V* **creer**

crezco *etc vb V* **crecer**

cría *etc* ['kria] *vb V* **criar** ▷ *nf* (*de animales*) rearing, breeding; (*animal*) young; *V tb* **crío**

criadero [kria'ðero] *nm* (*Zool*) breeding place

criado, -a [kri'aðo, a] *nm* servant ▷ *nf* servant, maid

criador [kria'ðor] *nm* breeder

crianza [kri'anθa] *nf* rearing, breeding; (*fig*) breeding

criar [kri'ar] *vt* (*educar*) to bring up; (*producir*) to grow, produce; (*animales*) to breed

criatura [kria'tura] *nf* creature; (*niño*) baby, (small) child

cribar [kri'βar] *vt* to sieve

crimen ['krimen] *nm* crime

criminal [krimi'nal] *adj, nmf* criminal

crines ['krines] *nfpl* mane

crío, -a ['krio, a] (*fam*) *nm/f* (*niño*) kid

crisis ['krisis] *nf inv* crisis; **crisis nerviosa** nervous breakdown

crismas ['krismas] (*ESP*) *nm inv* Christmas card

cristal [kris'tal] *nm* crystal; (*de ventana*) glass, pane; (*lente*) lens; **cristalino, -a** *adj* crystalline; (*fig*) clear ▷ *nm* lens (of the eye)

cristianismo [kristja'nismo] *nm* Christianity

cristiano, -a [kris'tjano, a] *adj, nm/f* Christian

Cristo ['kristo] *nm* Christ; (*crucifijo*) crucifix

criterio [kri'terjo] *nm* criterion; (*juicio*) judgement

crítica ['kritika] *nf* criticism; *V tb* **crítico**

criticar [kriti'kar] *vt* to criticize

crítico, -a ['kritiko, a] *adj* critical ▷ *nm/f* critic

Croacia [kro'aθja] *nf* Croatia

cromo ['kromo] *nm* chrome

crónica ['kronika] *nf* chronicle, account

crónico, -a ['kroniko, a] *adj* chronic

cronómetro [kro'nometro] *nm* stopwatch

croqueta [kro'keta] *nf* croquette

cruce *etc* ['kruθe] *vb V* **cruzar** ▷ *nm* (*para peatones*) crossing; (*de carreteras*) crossroads

crucero [kru'θero] *nm* (*viaje*) cruise

crucificar [kruθifi'kar] *vt* to crucify

crucifijo [kruθi'fixo] *nm* crucifix

crucigrama [kruθi'ɣrama] *nm* crossword (puzzle)

cruda ['kruða] (*MÉX, CAM*: *fam*) *nf* hangover

crudo, -a ['kruðo, a] *adj* raw; (*no maduro*) unripe; (*petróleo*) crude; (*rudo, cruel*) cruel ▷ *nm* crude (oil)

cruel [krwel] *adj* cruel; **crueldad** *nf* cruelty

crujiente [kru'xjente] *adj* (*galleta etc*) crunchy

crujir [kru'xir] *vi* (*madera etc*) to creak; (*dedos*) to crack; (*dientes*) to grind; (*nieve, arena*) to crunch

cruz [kruθ] *nf* cross; (*de moneda*) tails *sg*; **cruz gamada** swastika

cruzada [kru'θaða] *nf* crusade

cruzado, -a [kru'θaðo, a] *adj* crossed ▷ *nm* crusader
cruzar [kru'θar] *vt* to cross; **cruzarse** *vr* (*líneas etc*) to cross; (*personas*) to pass each other
Cruz Roja *nf* Red Cross
cuaderno [kwa'ðerno] *nm* notebook; (*de escuela*) exercise book; (*Náut*) logbook
cuadra ['kwaðra] *nf* (*caballeriza*) stable; (LAM: *entre calles*) block
cuadrado, -a [kwa'ðraðo, a] *adj* square ▷ *nm* (*Mat*) square
cuadrar [kwa'ðrar] *vt* to square ▷ *vi*: **~ con** to square with, tally with; **cuadrarse** *vr* (*soldado*) to stand to attention
cuadrilátero [kwaðri'latero] *nm* (*Deporte*) boxing ring; (*Geom*) quadrilateral
cuadrilla [kwa'ðriʎa] *nf* party, group
cuadro ['kwaðro] *nm* square; (*Arte*) painting; (*Teatro*) scene; (*diagrama*) chart; (*Deporte, Med*) team; **tela a ~s** checked (BRIT) *o* chequered (US) material
cuajar [kwa'xar] *vt* (*leche*) to curdle; (*sangre*) to congeal; (*Culin*) to set; **cuajarse** *vr* to curdle; to congeal; to set; (*llenarse*) to fill up
cuajo ['kwaxo] *nm*: **de ~** (*arrancar*) by the roots; (*cortar*) completely
cual [kwal] *adv* like, as ▷ *pron*: **el** *etc* **~** which; (*persona sujeto*) who; (: *objeto*) whom ▷ *adj* such as; **cada ~** each one; **déjalo tal ~** leave it just as it is
cuál [kwal] *pron interr* which (one)
cualesquier, a [kwales'kjer(a)] *pl de* **cualquier(a)**
cualidad [kwali'ðað] *nf* quality
cualquier [kwal'kjer] *adj V* **cualquiera**
cualquiera [kwal'kjera] (*pl* **cualesquiera**) *adj* (*delante de nm y f* **cualquier**) any ▷ *pron* anybody; **un coche ~ servirá** any car will do; **no es un hombre ~** he isn't just anybody; **cualquier día/libro** any day/book; **eso ~ lo sabe hacer** anybody can do that; **es un ~** he's a nobody
cuando ['kwando] *adv* when; (*aún si*) if, even if ▷ *conj* (*puesto que*) since ▷ *prep*: **yo, ~ niño ...** when I was a child ...; **~ no sea así** even if it is not so; **~ más** at (the) most; **~ menos** at least; **~ no** if not, otherwise; **de ~ en ~** from time to time
cuándo ['kwando] *adv* when; **¿desde ~?** since when?
cuantía [kwan'tia] *nf* extent

PALABRA CLAVE

cuanto, -a ['kwanto, a] *adj* **1** (*todo*): **tiene todo cuanto desea** he's got everything he wants; **le daremos cuantos ejemplares necesite** we'll give him as many copies as *o* all the copies he needs; **cuantos hombres la ven** all the men who see her

2 unos cuantos: había unos cuantos periodistas there were a few journalists

3 (*+ más*): **cuanto más vino bebes peor te sentirás** the more wine you drink the worse you'll feel

▷ *pron*: **tiene cuanto desea** he has everything he wants; **tome cuanto/cuantos quiera** take as much/many as you want

▷ *adv*: **en cuanto: en cuanto profesor** as a teacher; **en cuanto a mí** as for me; *V tb* **antes**

▷ *conj* **1 cuanto más gana menos gasta** the more he earns the less he spends; **cuanto más joven más confiado** the younger you are the more trusting you are

2 en cuanto: en cuanto llegue/llegué as soon as I arrive/arrived

cuánto, -a ['kwanto, a] *adj* (*exclamación*) what a lot of; (*interr*: *sg*) how much?; (: *pl*) how many? ▷ *pron, adv* how; (: *interr*: *sg*) how much?; (: *pl*) how many?; **¡cuánta gente!** what a lot of people!; **¿~ cuesta?** how much does it cost?; **¿a ~s estamos?** what's the date?

cuarenta [kwa'renta] *num* forty

cuarentena [kwaren'tena] *nf* quarantine

cuaresma [kwa'resma] *nf* Lent

cuarta ['kwarta] *nf* (*Mat*) quarter, fourth; (*palmo*) span

cuartel [kwar'tel] *nm* (*Mil*) barracks *pl*; **cuartel de bomberos** (RPL) fire station; **cuartel general** headquarters *pl*

cuarteto [kwar'teto] *nm* quartet

cuarto, -a ['kwarto, a] *adj* fourth ▷*nm* (*Mat*) quarter, fourth; (*habitación*) room; **cuarto de baño** bathroom; **cuarto de estar** living room; **cuarto de hora** quarter (of an) hour; **cuarto de kilo** quarter kilo; **cuartos de final** quarter finals

cuatro ['kwatro] *num* four

Cuba ['kuβa] *nf* Cuba

cuba ['kuβa] *nf* cask, barrel

cubano, -a [ku'βano, a] *adj, nm/f* Cuban

cubata [ku'βata] *nm* (*fam*) large drink (*of rum and coke etc*)

cubeta [ku'βeta] (ESP, MÉX) *nf* (*balde*) bucket, tub

cúbico, -a ['kuβiko, a] *adj* cubic

cubierta [ku'βjerta] *nf* cover, covering; (*neumático*) tyre; (*Náut*) deck

cubierto, -a [ku'βjerto, a] *pp de* **cubrir** ▷*adj* covered ▷*nm* cover; (*lugar en la mesa*) place; **cubiertos** *nmpl* cutlery *sg*; **a ~** under cover

cubilete [kuβi'lete] *nm* (*en juegos*) cup

cubito [ku'βito] *nm* (*tb*: **~ de hielo**) ice-cube

cubo ['kuβo] *nm* (*Mat*) cube; (ESP: *balde*) bucket, tub; (*Tec*) drum; **cubo de (la) basura** dustbin (BRIT), trash can (US)

cubrir [ku'βrir] *vt* to cover; **cubrirse** *vr* (*cielo*) to become overcast

cucaracha [kuka'ratʃa] *nf* cockroach

cuchara [ku'tʃara] *nf* spoon; (*Tec*) scoop; **cucharada** *nf* spoonful; **cucharadita** *nf* teaspoonful

cucharilla [kutʃa'riʎa] *nf* teaspoon

cucharón [kutʃa'ron] *nm* ladle

cuchilla [ku'tʃiʎa] *nf* (large) knife; (*de arma blanca*) blade; **cuchilla de afeitar** razor blade

cuchillo [ku'tʃiʎo] *nm* knife

cuchitril [kutʃi'tril] *nm* hovel

cuclillas [ku'kliʎas] *nfpl*: **en ~** squatting

cuco, -a ['kuko, a] *adj* pretty; (*astuto*) sharp ▷*nm* cuckoo

cucurucho [kuku'rutʃo] *nm* cornet

cueca ['kweka] *nf Chilean national dance*

cuello ['kweʎo] *nm* (*Anat*) neck; (*de vestido, camisa*) collar

cuenca ['kwenka] *nf* (*Anat*) eye socket; (*Geo*) bowl, deep valley

cuenco ['kwenko] *nm* bowl

cuenta *etc* ['kwenta] *vb V* **contar** ▷*nf* (*cálculo*) count, counting; (*en café, restaurante*) bill (BRIT), check (US); (*Com*) account; (*de collar*) bead; **a fin de ~s** in the end; **caer en la ~** to catch on; **darse ~ de** to realize; **tener en ~** to bear in mind; **echar ~s** to take stock; **cuenta atrás** countdown; **cuenta corriente/de ahorros** current/savings account; **cuenta de correo (electrónica)** (*Inform*) email account; **cuentakilómetros** *nm inv* ≈ milometer; (*de velocidad*) speedometer

cuento *etc* ['kwento] *vb V* **contar** ▷*nm* story; **cuento chino** tall story; **cuento de hadas** a fairy tale

cuerda ['kwerða] *nf* rope; (*fina*) string; (*de reloj*) spring; **dar ~ a un reloj** to wind up a clock; **cuerda floja** tightrope; **cuerdas vocales** vocal cords

cuerdo, -a ['kwerðo, a] *adj* sane; (*prudente*) wise, sensible

cuerno ['kwerno] *nm* horn

cuero ['kwero] *nm* leather; **en ~s** stark naked; **cuero cabelludo** scalp

cuerpo ['kwerpo] *nm* body

cuervo ['kwerβo] *nm* crow
cuesta *etc* ['kwesta] *vb V* **costar** ▷ *nf* slope; (*en camino etc*) hill; **~ arriba/abajo** uphill/downhill; **a ~s** on one's back
cueste *etc vb V* **costar**
cuestión [kwes'tjon] *nf* matter, question, issue
cuete ['kwete] *adj* (*MÉX*: *fam*) drunk ▷ *nm* (*LAM*: *cohete*) rocket; (*MÉX*, *RPL*: *fam*: *embriaguez*) drunkenness; (*MÉX*: *Culin*) steak
cueva ['kweβa] *nf* cave
cuidado [kwi'ðaðo] *nm* care, carefulness; (*preocupación*) care, worry ▷ *excl* careful!, look out!; **eso me tiene sin ~** I'm not worried about that
cuidadoso, -a [kwiða'ðoso, a] *adj* careful; (*preocupado*) anxious
cuidar [kwi'ðar] *vt* (*Med*) to care for; (*ocuparse de*) to take care of, look after ▷ *vi*: **~ de** to take care of, look after; **cuidarse** *vr* to look after o.s.; **~se de hacer algo** to take care to do sth
culata [ku'lata] *nf* (*de fusil*) butt
culebra [ku'leβra] *nf* snake
culebrón [kule'βron] (*fam*) *nm* (*TV*) soap(-opera)
culo ['kulo] *nm* bottom, backside; (*de vaso, botella*) bottom
culpa ['kulpa] *nf* fault; (*Jur*) guilt; **por ~ de** because of; **echar la ~ a algn** to blame sb for sth; **tener la ~ (de)** to be to blame (for); **culpable** *adj* guilty ▷ *nmf* culprit; **culpar** [kul'par] *vt* to blame; (*acusar*) to accuse
cultivar [kulti'βar] *vt* to cultivate
cultivo [kul'tiβo] *nm* (*acto*) cultivation; (*plantas*) crop
culto, -a ['kulto, a] *adj* (*que tiene cultura*) cultured, educated ▷ *nm* (*homenaje*) worship; (*religión*) cult
cultura [kul'tura] *nf* culture
culturismo [kultu'rismo] *nm* body-building
cumbia ['kumbja] *nf popular Colombian dance*
cumbre ['kumbre] *nf* summit, top
cumpleaños [kumple'aɲos] *nm inv* birthday
cumplido, -a [kum'pliðo, a] *adj* (*abundante*) plentiful; (*cortés*) courteous ▷ *nm* compliment; **visita de ~** courtesy call
cumplidor, a [kumpli'ðor, a] *adj* reliable
cumplimiento [kumpli'mjento] *nm* (*de un deber*) fulfilment; (*acabamiento*) completion
cumplir [kum'plir] *vt* (*orden*) to carry out, obey; (*promesa*) to carry out, fulfil; (*condena*) to serve ▷ *vi*: **~ con** (*deber*) to carry out, fulfil; **cumplirse** *vr* (*plazo*) to expire; **hoy cumple dieciocho años** he is eighteen today
cuna ['kuna] *nf* cradle, cot
cundir [kun'dir] *vi* (*noticia, rumor, pánico*) to spread; (*rendir*) to go a long way
cuneta [ku'neta] *nf* ditch
cuña ['kuɲa] *nf* wedge
cuñado, -a [ku'ɲaðo, a] *nm/f* brother-/sister-in-law
cuota ['kwota] *nf* (*parte proporcional*) share; (*cotización*) fee, dues *pl*
cupe *etc vb V* **caber**
cupiera *etc vb V* **caber**
cupo ['kupo] *vb V* **caber** ▷ *nm* quota
cupón [ku'pon] *nm* coupon
cúpula ['kupula] *nf* dome
cura ['kura] *nf* (*curación*) cure; (*método curativo*) treatment ▷ *nm* priest
curación [kura'θjon] *nf* cure; (*acción*) curing
curandero, -a [kuran'dero, a] *nm/f* quack
curar [ku'rar] *vt* (*Med*: *herida*) to treat, dress; (: *enfermo*) to cure; (*Culin*) to cure, salt; (*cuero*) to tan; **curarse** *vr* to get well, recover
curiosear [kurjose'ar] *vt* to glance at, look over ▷ *vi* to look round, wander round; (*explorar*) to poke about
curiosidad [kurjosi'ðað] *nf* curiosity
curioso, -a [ku'rjoso, a] *adj* curious ▷ *nm/f* bystander, onlooker

curita [ku'rita] (*LAM*) *nf* (sticking) plaster (*BRIT*), Bandaid® (*US*)
currante [ku'rrante] (*ESP*: *fam*) *nmf* worker
currar [ku'rrar] (*ESP*: *fam*) *vi* to work
currículo [ku'rrikulo] = **curriculum**
curriculum [ku'rrikulum] *nm* curriculum vitae
cursi ['kursi] (*fam*) *adj* affected
cursillo [kur'siʎo] *nm* short course
cursiva [kur'siβa] *nf* italics *pl*
curso ['kurso] *nm* course; **en ~** (*año*) current; (*proceso*) going on, under way
cursor [kur'sor] *nm* (*Inform*) cursor
curul [ku'rul] (*MÉX*) *nm* (*escaño*) seat
curva ['kurβa] *nf* curve, bend
custodia [kus'toðja] *nf* safekeeping; custody
cutis ['kutis] *nm inv* skin, complexion
cutre ['kutre] (*ESP*: *fam*) *adj* (*lugar*) grotty
cuyo, -a ['kujo, a] *pron* (*de quien*) whose; (*de que*) whose, of which; **en ~ caso** in which case
C.V. *abr* (= *caballos de vapor*) H.P.

D. *abr* (= *Don*) Esq
dado, -a ['daðo, a] *pp de* **dar** ▷ *nm* die; **dados** *nmpl* dice; **~ que** given that
daltónico, -a [dal'toniko, a] *adj* colour-blind
dama ['dama] *nf* (*gen*) lady; (*Ajedrez*) queen; **damas** *nfpl* (*juego*) draughts *sg*; **dama de honor** bridesmaid
damasco [da'masko] (*RPL*) *nm* apricot
danés, -esa [da'nes, esa] *adj* Danish ▷ *nm/f* Dane
dañar [da'ɲar] *vt* (*objeto*) to damage; (*persona*) to hurt; **dañarse** *vr* (*objeto*) to get damaged
dañino, -a [da'ɲino, a] *adj* harmful
daño ['daɲo] *nm* (*objeto*) damage; (*persona*) harm, injury; **~s y perjuicios** (*Jur*) damages; **hacer ~ a** to damage; (*persona*) to hurt, injure; **hacerse ~** to hurt o.s.

PALABRA CLAVE

dar [dar] *vt* **1** (*gen*) to give; (*obra de*

teatro) to put on; (*film*) to show; (*fiesta*) to hold; **dar algo a algn** to give sb sth *o* sth to sb; **dar de beber a algn** to give sb a drink
2 (*producir: intereses*) to yield; (*fruta*) to produce
3 (*locuciones + n*): **da gusto escucharle** it's a pleasure to listen to him; *V tb* **paseo**
4 (*+ n: = perífrasis de verbo*): **me da asco** it sickens me
5 (*considerar*): **dar algo por descontado/entendido** to take sth for granted/as read; **dar algo por concluido** to consider sth finished
6 (*hora*): **el reloj dio las 6** the clock struck 6 (o'clock)
7: **me da lo mismo** it's all the same to me; *V tb* **igual, más**
▷ *vi* **1** **dar con: dimos con él dos horas más tarde** we came across him two hours later; **al final di con la solución** I eventually came up with the answer
2: **dar en** (*blanco, suelo*) to hit; **el sol me da en la cara** the sun is shining (right) on my face
3: **dar de sí** (*zapatos etc*) to stretch, give
darse *vr* **1**: **darse por vencido** to give up
2 (*ocurrir*): **se han dado muchos casos** there have been a lot of cases
3: **darse a: se ha dado a la bebida** he's taken to drinking
4: **se me dan bien/mal las ciencias** I'm good/bad at science
5: **dárselas de: se las da de experto** he fancies himself *o* poses as an expert

dardo ['darðo] *nm* dart
dátil ['datil] *nm* date
dato ['dato] *nm* fact, piece of information; **datos personales** personal details
dcha. *abr* (*= derecha*) r.h.
d. de C. *abr* (*= después de Cristo*) A.D.

PALABRA CLAVE

de [de] (*de + el = del*) *prep* **1** (*posesión*) of; **la casa de Isabel/mis padres** Isabel's/my parents' house; **es de ellos** it's theirs
2 (*origen, distancia, con números*) from; **soy de Gijón** I'm from Gijón; **de 8 a 20** from 8 to 20; **salir del cine** to go out of *o* leave the cinema; **de 2 en 2** 2 by 2, 2 at a time
3 (*valor descriptivo*): **una copa de vino** a glass of wine; **la mesa de la cocina** the kitchen table; **un billete de 10 euros** a 10 euro note; **un niño de tres años** a three-year-old (child); **una máquina de coser** a sewing machine; **ir vestido de gris** to be dressed in grey; **la niña del vestido azul** the girl in the blue dress; **trabaja de profesora** she works as a teacher; **de lado** sideways; **de atrás/delante** rear/front
4 (*hora, tiempo*): **a las 8 de la mañana** at 8 o'clock in the morning; **de día/noche** by day/night; **de hoy en ocho días** a week from now; **de niño era gordo** as a child he was fat
5 (*comparaciones*): **más/menos de cien personas** more/less than a hundred people; **el más caro de la tienda** the most expensive in the shop; **menos/más de lo pensado** less/more than expected
6 (*causa*): **del calor** from the heat
7 (*tema*) about; **clases de inglés** English classes; **¿sabes algo de él?** do you know anything about him?; **un libro de física** a physics book
8 (*adj + de + infin*): **fácil de entender** easy to understand
9 (*oraciones pasivas*): **fue respetado de todos** he was loved by all
10 (*condicional + infin*) if; **de ser posible** if possible; **de no terminarlo hoy** if I *etc* don't finish it today

dé [de] *vb V* **dar**

debajo [de'βaxo] *adv* underneath; **~ de** below, under; **por ~ de** beneath

debate [de'βate] *nm* debate; **debatir** *vt* to debate

deber [de'βer] *nm* duty ▷ *vt* to owe ▷ *vi*: **debe (de)** it must, it should; **deberes** *nmpl* (*Escol*) homework; **deberse** *vr*: **~se a** to be owing *o* due to; **debo hacerlo** I must do it; **debe de ir** he should go

debido, -a [de'βiðo, a] *adj* proper, just; **~ a** due to, because of

débil ['deβil] *adj* (*persona, carácter*) weak; (*luz*) dim; **debilidad** *nf* weakness; dimness

debilitar [deβili'tar] *vt* to weaken; **debilitarse** *vr* to grow weak

débito ['deβito] *nm* debit; **débito bancario** (LAM) direct debit (BRIT) *o* billing (US)

debutar [deβu'tar] *vi* to make one's debut

década ['dekaða] *nf* decade

decadencia [deka'ðenθja] *nf* (*estado*) decadence; (*proceso*) decline, decay

decaído, -a [deka'iðo, a] *adj*: **estar ~** (*abatido*) to be down

decano, -a [de'kano, a] *nm/f* (*de universidad etc*) dean

decena [de'θena] *nf*: **una ~** ten (or so)

decente [de'θente] *adj* decent

decepción [deθep'θjon] *nf* disappointment

> No confundir **decepción** con la palabra inglesa *deception*.

decepcionar [deθepθjo'nar] *vt* to disappoint

decidir [deθi'ðir] *vt, vi* to decide; **decidirse** *vr*: **~se a** to make up one's mind to

décimo, -a ['deθimo, a] *adj* tenth ▷ *nm* tenth

decir [de'θir] *vt* to say; (*contar*) to tell; (*hablar*) to speak ▷ *nm* saying; **decirse** *vr*: **se dice que** it is said that; **es ~** that is (to say); **~ para sí** to say to o.s.; **querer ~** to mean; **¡dígame!** (*Tel*) hello!; (*en tienda*) can I help you?

decisión [deθi'sjon] *nf* (*resolución*) decision; (*firmeza*) decisiveness

decisivo, -a [deθi'siβo, a] *adj* decisive

declaración [deklara'θjon] *nf* (*manifestación*) statement; (*de amor*) declaration; **declaración fiscal** *o* **de la renta** income-tax return

declarar [dekla'rar] *vt* to declare ▷ *vi* to declare; (*Jur*) to testify; **declararse** *vr* to propose

decoración [dekora'θjon] *nf* decoration

decorado [deko'raðo] *nm* (*Cine, Teatro*) scenery, set

decorar [deko'rar] *vt* to decorate; **decorativo, -a** *adj* ornamental, decorative

decreto [de'kreto] *nm* decree

dedal [de'ðal] *nm* thimble

dedicación [deðika'θjon] *nf* dedication

dedicar [deði'kar] *vt* (*libro*) to dedicate; (*tiempo, dinero*) to devote; (*palabras: decir, consagrar*) to dedicate, devote; **dedicatoria** *nf* (*de libro*) dedication

dedo ['deðo] *nm* finger; **hacer ~** (*fam*) to hitch (a lift); **dedo anular** ring finger; **dedo corazón** middle finger; **dedo (del pie)** toe; **dedo gordo** (*de la mano*) thumb; (*del pie*) big toe; **dedo índice** index finger; **dedo meñique** little finger; **dedo pulgar** thumb

deducción [deðuk'θjon] *nf* deduction

deducir [deðu'θir] *vt* (*concluir*) to deduce, infer; (*Com*) to deduct

defecto [de'fekto] *nm* defect, flaw; **defectuoso, -a** *adj* defective, faulty

defender [defen'der] *vt* to defend; **defenderse** *vr* (*desenvolverse*) to get by

defensa [de'fensa] *nf* defence ▷ *nm* (*Deporte*) defender, back; **defensivo, -a** *adj* defensive; **a la defensiva** on the defensive

defensor, a [defen'sor, a] *adj* defending ▷ *nm/f* (*abogado defensor*) defending counsel; (*protector*) protector
deficiencia [defi'θjenθja] *nf* deficiency
deficiente [defi'θjente] *adj* (*defectuoso*) defective; **~ en** lacking *o* deficient in; **ser un ~ mental** to be mentally handicapped
déficit ['defiθit] (*pl* **~s**) *nm* deficit
definición [defini'θjon] *nf* definition
definir [defi'nir] *vt* (*determinar*) to determine, establish; (*decidir*) to define; (*aclarar*) to clarify; **definitivo, -a** *adj* definitive; **en definitiva** definitively; (*en resumen*) in short
deformación [deforma'θjon] *nf* (*alteración*) deformation; (*Radio etc*) distortion
deformar [defor'mar] *vt* (*gen*) to deform; **deformarse** *vr* to become deformed; **deforme** *adj* (*informe*) deformed; (*feo*) ugly; (*malhecho*) misshapen
defraudar [defrau'ðar] *vt* (*decepcionar*) to disappoint; (*estafar*) to defraud
defunción [defun'θjon] *nf* death, demise
degenerar [dexene'rar] *vi* to degenerate
degradar [deɣra'ðar] *vt* to debase, degrade; **degradarse** *vr* to demean o.s.
degustación [deɣusta'θjon] *nf* sampling, tasting
dejar [de'xar] *vt* to leave; (*permitir*) to allow, let; (*abandonar*) to abandon, forsake; (*beneficios*) to produce, yield ▷ *vi*: **~ de** (*parar*) to stop; (*no hacer*) to fail to; **~ a un lado** to leave *o* set aside; **~ entrar/salir** to let in/out; **~ pasar** to let through
del [del] (=**de** + **el**) *V* **de**
delantal [delan'tal] *nm* apron
delante [de'lante] *adv* in front; (*enfrente*) opposite; (*adelante*) ahead; **~ de** in front of, before
delantera [delan'tera] *nf* (*de vestido, casa etc*) front part; (*Deporte*) forward line; **llevar la ~ (a algn)** to be ahead (of sb)
delantero, -a [delan'tero, a] *adj* front ▷ *nm* (*Deporte*) forward, striker
delatar [dela'tar] *vt* to inform on *o* against, betray; **delator, a** *nm/f* informer
delegación [deleɣa'θjon] *nf* (*acción, delegados*) delegation; (*Com: oficina*) office, branch; **delegación de policía** (*MÉX*) police station
delegado, -a [dele'ɣaðo, a] *nm/f* delegate; (*Com*) agent
delegar [dele'ɣar] *vt* to delegate
deletrear [deletre'ar] *vt* to spell (out)
delfín [del'fin] *nm* dolphin
delgado, -a [del'ɣaðo, a] *adj* thin; (*persona*) slim, thin; (*tela etc*) light, delicate
deliberar [deliβe'rar] *vt* to debate, discuss
delicadeza [delika'ðeθa] *nf* (*gen*) delicacy; (*refinamiento, sutileza*) refinement
delicado, -a [deli'kaðo, a] *adj* (*gen*) delicate; (*sensible*) sensitive; (*quisquilloso*) touchy
delicia [de'liθja] *nf* delight
delicioso, -a [deli'θjoso, a] *adj* (*gracioso*) delightful; (*exquisito*) delicious
delimitar [delimi'tar] *vt* (*función, responsabilidades*) to define
delincuencia [delin'kwenθja] *nf* delinquency; **delincuente** *nmf* delinquent; (*criminal*) criminal
delineante [deline'ante] *nmf* draughtsman/woman
delirante [deli'rante] *adj* delirious
delirar [deli'rar] *vi* to be delirious, rave
delirio [de'lirjo] *nm* (*Med*) delirium; (*palabras insensatas*) ravings *pl*
delito [de'lito] *nm* (*gen*) crime;

(*infracción*) offence

delta ['delta] *nm* delta

demacrado, -a [dema'krado, a] *adj*: **estar ~** to look pale and drawn, be wasted away

demanda [de'manda] *nf* (*pedido, Com*) demand; (*petición*) request; (*Jur*) action, lawsuit; **demandar** [deman'dar] *vt* (*gen*) to demand; (*Jur*) to sue, file a lawsuit against

demás [de'mas] *adj*: **los ~ niños** the other *o* remaining children ▷ *pron*: **los/ las ~** the others, the rest (of them); **lo ~** the rest (of it)

demasía [dema'sia] *nf* (*exceso*) excess, surplus; **comer en ~** to eat to excess

demasiado, -a [dema'sjaðo, a] *adj*: **~ vino** too much wine ▷ *adv* (*antes de adj, adv*) too; **~s libros** too many books; **¡esto es ~!** that's the limit!; **hace ~ calor** it's too hot; **~ despacio** too slowly; **~s** too many

demencia [de'menθja] *nf* (*locura*) madness

democracia [demo'kraθja] *nf* democracy

demócrata [de'mokrata] *nmf* democrat; **democrático, -a** *adj* democratic

demoler [demo'ler] *vt* to demolish; **demolición** *nf* demolition

demonio [de'monjo] *nm* devil, demon; **¡~s!** hell!, damn!; **¿cómo ~s?** how the hell?

demora [de'mora] *nf* delay

demos ['demos] *vb V* **dar**

demostración [demostra'θjon] *nf* (*Mat*) proof; (*de afecto*) show, display

demostrar [demos'trar] *vt* (*probar*) to prove; (*mostrar*) to show; (*manifestar*) to demonstrate

den [den] *vb V* **dar**

denegar [dene'ɣar] *vt* (*rechazar*) to refuse; (*Jur*) to reject

denominación [denomina'θjon] *nf* (*acto*) naming; **Denominación de Origen** *see note*

DENOMINACIÓN DE ORIGEN

The **Denominación de Origen**, abbreviated to **D.O.**, is a prestigious classification awarded to food products such as wines, cheeses, sausages and hams which meet the stringent quality and production standards of the designated region. **D.O.** labels serve as a guarantee of quality.

densidad [densi'ðað] *nf* density; (*fig*) thickness

denso, -a ['denso, a] *adj* dense; (*espeso, pastoso*) thick; (*fig*) heavy

dentadura [denta'ðura] *nf* (set of) teeth *pl*; **dentadura postiza** false teeth *pl*

dentera [den'tera] *nf* (*grima*): **dar ~ a algn** to set sb's teeth on edge

dentífrico, -a [den'tifriko, a] *adj* dental ▷ *nm* toothpaste

dentista [den'tista] *nmf* dentist

dentro ['dentro] *adv* inside ▷ *prep*: **~ de** in, inside, within; **por ~** (on the) inside; **mirar por ~** to look inside; **~ de tres meses** within three months

denuncia [de'nunθja] *nf* (*delación*) denunciation; (*acusación*) accusation; (*de accidente*) report; **denunciar** *vt* to report; (*delatar*) to inform on *o* against

departamento [departa'mento] *nm* *sección administrativa*, department, section; (*LAM*: *apartamento*) flat (*BRIT*), apartment

depender [depen'der] *vi*: **~ de** to depend on; **depende** it (all) depends

dependienta [depen'djenta] *nf* saleswoman, shop assistant

dependiente [depen'djente] *adj* dependent ▷ *nm* salesman, shop assistant

depilar [depi'lar] *vt* (*con cera*) to wax; (*cejas*) to pluck

deportar [depor'tar] *vt* to deport

deporte [de'porte] *nm* sport; **hacer ~** to play sports; **deportista** *adj* sports *cpd* ▷ *nmf* sportsman/woman; **deportivo, -a** *adj* (*club, periódico*) sports *cpd* ▷ *nm* sports car
depositar [deposi'tar] *vt* (*dinero*) to deposit; (*mercancías*) to put away, store; **depositarse** *vr* to settle
depósito [de'posito] *nm* (*gen*) deposit; (*almacén*) warehouse, store; (*de agua, gasolina etc*) tank; **depósito de cadáveres** mortuary
depredador, a [depreða'ðor, a] *adj* predatory ▷ *nm* predator
depresión [depre'sjon] *nf* depression; **depresión nerviosa** nervous breakdown
deprimido, -a [depri'miðo, a] *adj* depressed
deprimir [depri'mir] *vt* to depress; **deprimirse** *vr* (*persona*) to become depressed
deprisa [de'prisa] *adv* quickly, hurriedly
depurar [depu'rar] *vt* to purify; (*purgar*) to purge
derecha [de'retʃa] *nf* right(-hand) side; (*Pol*) right; **a la ~** (*estar*) on the right; (*torcer etc*) (to the) right
derecho, -a [de'retʃo, a] *adj* right, right-hand ▷ *nm* (*privilegio*) right; (*lado*) right(-hand) side; (*leyes*) law ▷ *adv* straight, directly; **derechos** *nmpl* (*de aduana*) duty *sg*; (*de autor*) royalties; **tener ~ a** to have a right to; **derechos de autor** royalties
deriva [de'riβa] *nf*: **ir** *o* **estar a la ~** to drift, be adrift
derivado [deri'βaðo] *nm* (*Com*) by-product
derivar [deri'βar] *vt* to derive; (*desviar*) to direct ▷ *vi* to derive, be derived; (*Náut*) to drift; **derivarse** *vr* to derive, be derived; to drift
derramamiento [derrama'mjento] *nm* (*dispersión*) spilling; **derramamiento de sangre** bloodshed
derramar [derra'mar] *vt* to spill; (*verter*) to pour out; (*esparcir*) to scatter; **derramarse** *vr* to pour out
derrame [de'rrame] *nm* (*de líquido*) spilling; (*de sangre*) shedding; (*de tubo etc*) overflow; (*pérdida*) leakage; **derrame cerebral** brain haemorrhage
derredor [derre'ðor] *adv*: **al** *o* **en ~ de** around, about
derretir [derre'tir] *vt* (*gen*) to melt; (*nieve*) to thaw; **derretirse** *vr* to melt
derribar [derri'βar] *vt* to knock down; (*construcción*) to demolish; (*persona, gobierno, político*) to bring down
derrocar [derro'kar] *vt* (*gobierno*) to bring down, overthrow
derrochar [derro'tʃar] *vt* to squander; **derroche** *nm* (*despilfarro*) waste, squandering
derrota [de'rrota] *nf* (*Náut*) course; (*Mil, Deporte etc*) defeat, rout; **derrotar** *vt* (*gen*) to defeat; **derrotero** *nm* (*rumbo*) course
derrumbar [derrum'bar] *vt* (*edificio*) to knock down; **derrumbarse** *vr* to collapse
des *etc vb V* **dar**
desabrochar [desaβro'tʃar] *vt* (*botónes, broches*) to undo, unfasten; **desabrocharse** *vr* (*ropa etc*) to come undone
desacato [desa'kato] *nm* (*falta de respeto*) disrespect; (*Jur*) contempt
desacertado, -a [desaθer'taðo, a] *adj* (*equivocado*) mistaken; (*inoportuno*) unwise
desacierto [desa'θjerto] *nm* mistake, error
desaconsejar [desakonse'xar] *vt* to advise against
desacreditar [desakreði'tar] *vt* (*desprestigiar*) to discredit, bring into disrepute; (*denigrar*) to run down
desacuerdo [desa'kwerðo] *nm* disagreement, discord
desafiar [desa'fjar] *vt* (*retar*) to challenge; (*enfrentarse a*) to defy
desafilado, -a [desafi'laðo, a]

adj blunt
desafinado, -a [desafi'naðo, a] *adj*: **estar ~** to be out of tune
desafinar [desafi'nar] *vi* (*al cantar*) to be *o* go out of tune
desafío *etc* [desa'fio] *vb* V **desafiar** ▷ *nm* (*reto*) challenge; (*combate*) duel; (*resistencia*) defiance
desafortunado, -a [desafortu'naðo, a] *adj* (*desgraciado*) unfortunate, unlucky
desagradable [desaɣra'ðaβle] *adj* (*fastidioso, enojoso*) unpleasant; (*irritante*) disagreeable
desagradar [desaɣra'ðar] *vi* (*disgustar*) to displease; (*molestar*) to bother
desagradecido, -a [desaɣraðe'θiðo, a] *adj* ungrateful
desagrado [desa'ɣraðo] *nm* (*disgusto*) displeasure; (*contrariedad*) dissatisfaction
desagüe [des'aɣwe] *nm* (*de un líquido*) drainage; (*cañería*) drainpipe; (*salida*) outlet, drain
desahogar [desao'ɣar] *vt* (*aliviar*) to ease, relieve; (*ira*) to vent; **desahogarse** *vr* (*relajarse*) to relax; (*desfogarse*) to let off steam
desahogo [desa'oɣo] *nm* (*alivio*) relief; (*comodidad*) comfort, ease
desahuciar [desau'θjar] *vt* (*enfermo*) to give up hope for; (*inquilino*) to evict
desairar [desai'rar] *vt* (*menospreciar*) to slight, snub
desalentador, a [desalenta'ðor, a] *adj* discouraging
desaliño [desa'liɲo] *nm* slovenliness
desalmado, -a [desal'maðo, a] *adj* (*cruel*) cruel, heartless
desalojar [desalo'xar] *vt* (*expulsar, echar*) to eject; (*abandonar*) to move out of ▷ *vi* to move out
desamor [desa'mor] *nm* (*frialdad*) indifference; (*odio*) dislike
desamparado, -a [desampa'raðo, a] *adj* (*persona*) helpless; (*lugar: expuesto*) exposed; (*desierto*) deserted
desangrar [desan'grar] *vt* to bleed; (*fig: persona*) to bleed dry; **desangrarse** *vr* to lose a lot of blood
desanimado, -a [desani'maðo, a] *adj* (*persona*) downhearted; (*espectáculo, fiesta*) dull
desanimar [desani'mar] *vt* (*desalentar*) to discourage; (*deprimir*) to depress; **desanimarse** *vr* to lose heart
desapacible [desapa'θiβle] *adj* (*gen*) unpleasant
desaparecer [desapare'θer] *vi* (*gen*) to disappear; (*el sol, el luz*) to vanish; **desaparecido, -a** *adj* missing; **desaparición** *nf* disappearance
desapercibido, -a [desaperθi'βiðo, a] *adj* (*desprevenido*) unprepared; **pasar ~** to go unnoticed
desaprensivo, -a [desapren'siβo, a] *adj* unscrupulous
desaprobar [desapro'βar] *vt* (*reprobar*) to disapprove of; (*condenar*) to condemn; (*no consentir*) to reject
desaprovechado, -a [desaproβe'tʃaðo, a] *adj* (*oportunidad, tiempo*) wasted; (*estudiante*) slack
desaprovechar [desaproβe'tʃar] *vt* to waste
desarmador [desarma'ðor] (*MÉX*) *nm* screwdriver
desarmar [desar'mar] *vt* (*Mil, fig*) to disarm; (*Tec*) to take apart, dismantle; **desarme** *nm* disarmament
desarraigar [desarrai'ɣar] *vt* to uproot; **desarraigo** *nm* uprooting
desarreglar [desarre'ɣlar] *vt* (*desordenar*) to disarrange; (*trastocar*) to upset, disturb
desarrollar [desarro'ʎar] *vt* (*gen*) to develop; **desarrollarse** *vr* to develop; (*ocurrir*) to take place; (*Foto*) to develop; **desarrollo** *nm* development
desarticular [desartiku'lar] *vt* (*hueso*) to dislocate; (*objeto*) to take apart; (*fig*) to break up
desasosegar [desasose'ɣar] *vt* (*inquietar*) to disturb, make uneasy

desasosiego *etc* [desaso'sjeɣo] *vb V* **desasosegar** ▷ *nm* (*intranquilidad*) uneasiness, restlessness; (*ansiedad*) anxiety

desastre [de'sastre] *nm* disaster; **desastroso, -a** *adj* disastrous

desatar [desa'tar] *vt* (*nudo*) to untie; (*paquete*) to undo; (*separar*) to detach; **desatarse** *vr* (*zapatos*) to come untied; (*tormenta*) to break

desatascar [desatas'kar] *vt* (*cañería*) to unblock, clear

desatender [desaten'der] *vt no prestar atención a*, to disregard; (*abandonar*) to neglect

desatino [desa'tino] *nm* (*idiotez*) foolishness, folly; (*error*) blunder

desatornillar [desatorni'ʎar] *vt* to unscrew

desatrancar [desatran'kar] *vt* (*puerta*) to unbolt; (*cañería*) to clear, unblock

desautorizado, -a [desautori'θaðo, a] *adj* unauthorized

desautorizar [desautori'θar] *vt* (*oficial*) to deprive of authority; (*informe*) to deny

desayunar [desaju'nar] *vi* to have breakfast ▷ *vt* to have for breakfast; **desayuno** *nm* breakfast

desazón [desa'θon] *nf* anxiety

desbarajuste [desβara'xuste] *nm* confusion, disorder

desbaratar [desβara'tar] *vt* (*deshacer, destruir*) to ruin

desbloquear [desβloke'ar] *vt* (*negociaciónes, tráfico*) to get going again; (*Com: cuenta*) to unfreeze

desbordar [desβor'ðar] *vt* (*sobrepasar*) to go beyond; (*exceder*) to exceed; **desbordarse** *vr* (*río*) to overflow; (*entusiasmo*) to erupt

descabellado, -a [deskaβe'ʎaðo, a] *adj* (*disparatado*) wild, crazy

descafeinado, -a [deskafei'naðo, a] *adj* decaffeinated ▷ *nm* decaffeinated coffee

descalabro [deska'laβro] *nm* blow; (*desgracia*) misfortune

descalificar [deskalifi'kar] *vt* to disqualify; (*desacreditar*) to discredit

descalzar [deskal'θar] *vt* (*zapato*) to take off; **descalzo, -a** *adj* barefoot(ed)

descambiar [deskam'bjar] *vt* to exchange

descaminado, -a [deskami'naðo, a] *adj* (*equivocado*) on the wrong road; (*fig*) misguided

descampado [deskam'paðo] *nm* open space

descansado, -a [deskan'saðo, a] *adj* (*gen*) rested; (*que tranquiliza*) restful

descansar [deskan'sar] *vt* (*gen*) to rest ▷ *vi* to rest, have a rest; (*echarse*) to lie down

descansillo [deskan'siʎo] *nm* (*de escalera*) landing

descanso [des'kanso] *nm* (*reposo*) rest; (*alivio*) relief; (*pausa*) break; (*Deporte*) interval, half time

descapotable [deskapo'taβle] *nm* (*tb*: **coche ~**) convertible

descarado, -a [deska'raðo, a] *adj* shameless; (*insolente*) cheeky

descarga [des'karɣa] *nf* (*Arq, Elec, Mil*) discharge; (*Náut*) unloading; **descargar** [deskar'ɣar] *vt* to unload; (*golpe*) to let fly; **descargarse** *vr* to unburden o.s.; **descargarse algo de Internet** to download sth from the Internet

descaro [des'karo] *nm* nerve

descarriar [deska'rrjar] *vt* (*descaminar*) to misdirect; (*fig*) to lead astray; **descarriarse** *vr* (*perderse*) to lose one's way; (*separarse*) to stray; (*pervertirse*) to err, go astray

descarrilamiento [deskarrila'mjento] *nm* (*de tren*) derailment

descarrilar [deskarri'lar] *vi* to be derailed

descartar [deskar'tar] *vt* (*rechazar*) to reject; (*eliminar*) to rule out; **descartarse** *vr* (*Naipes*) to discard; **~se de** to shirk

descendencia [desθen'denθja] *nf* (*origen*) origin, descent; (*hijos*) offspring

descender [desθen'der] *vt* (*bajar: escalera*) to go down ▷ *vi* to descend; (*temperatura, nivel*) to fall, drop; **~ de** to be descended from

descendiente [desθen'djente] *nmf* descendant

descenso [des'θenso] *nm* descent; (*de temperatura*) drop

descifrar [desθi'frar] *vt* to decipher; (*mensaje*) to decode

descolgar [deskol'ɣar] *vt* (*bajar*) to take down; (*teléfono*) to pick up; **descolgarse** *vr* to let o.s. down

descolorido, -a [deskolo'riðo, a] *adj* faded; (*pálido*) pale

descompasado, -a [deskompa'saðo, a] *adj* (*sin proporción*) out of all proportion; (*excesivo*) excessive

descomponer [deskompo'ner] *vt* (*desordenar*) to disarrange, disturb; (*Tec*) to put out of order; (*dividir*) to break down (into parts); (*fig*) to provoke; **descomponerse** *vr* (*corromperse*) to rot, decompose; (*LAM Tec*) to break down

descomposición [deskomposi'θjon] *nf* (*de un objeto*) breakdown; (*de fruta etc*) decomposition; **descomposición de vientre** (*ESP*) stomach upset, diarrhoea

descompostura [deskompos'tura] *nf* (*MÉX: avería*) breakdown, fault; (*LAM: diarrea*) diarrhoea

descomprimir [deskompri'mir] (*Internet*) to unzip

descompuesto, -a [deskom'pwesto, a] *adj* (*corrompido*) decomposed; (*roto*) broken

desconcertado, -a [deskonθer'taðo, a] *adj* disconcerted, bewildered

desconcertar [deskonθer'tar] *vt* (*confundir*) to baffle; (*incomodar*) to upset, put out; **desconcertarse** *vr* (*turbarse*) to be upset

desconchado, -a [deskon'tʃaðo, a] *adj* (*pintura*) peeling

desconcierto *etc* [deskon'θjerto] *vb V* **desconcertar** ▷ *nm* (*gen*) disorder; (*desorientación*) uncertainty; (*inquietud*) uneasiness

desconectar [deskonek'tar] *vt* to disconnect

desconfianza [deskon'fjanθa] *nf* distrust

desconfiar [deskon'fjar] *vi* to be distrustful; **~ de** to distrust, suspect

descongelar [deskonxe'lar] *vt* to defrost; (*Com, Pol*) to unfreeze

descongestionar [deskonxestjo'nar] *vt* (*cabeza, tráfico*) to clear

desconocer [deskono'θer] *vt* (*ignorar*) not to know, be ignorant of

desconocido, -a [deskono'θiðo, a] *adj* unknown ▷ *nm/f* stranger

desconocimiento [deskonoθi'mjento] *nm falta de conocimientos*, ignorance

desconsiderado, -a [deskonsiðe'raðo, a] *adj* inconsiderate; (*insensible*) thoughtless

desconsuelo *etc* [deskon'swelo] *vb V* **desconsolar** ▷ *nm* (*tristeza*) distress; (*desesperación*) despair

descontado, -a [deskon'taðo, a] *adj*: **dar por ~ (que)** to take (it) for granted (that)

descontar [deskon'tar] *vt* (*deducir*) to take away, deduct; (*rebajar*) to discount

descontento, -a [deskon'tento, a] *adj* dissatisfied ▷ *nm* dissatisfaction, discontent

descorchar [deskor'tʃar] *vt* to uncork

descorrer [desko'rrer] *vt* (*cortinas, cerrojo*) to draw back

descortés [deskor'tes] *adj* (*mal educado*) discourteous; (*grosero*) rude

descoser [desko'ser] *vt* to unstitch; **descoserse** *vr* to come apart (at the seams)

descosido, -a [desko'siðo, a] *adj* (*Costura*) unstitched

descreído, -a [deskre'iðo, a] *adj* (*incrédulo*) incredulous; (*falto de fe*) unbelieving

descremado, -a [deskre'maðo, a] *adj* skimmed

describir [deskri'βir] *vt* to describe; **descripción** [deskrip'θjon] *nf* description

descrito [des'krito] *pp de* **describir**

descuartizar [deskwarti'θar] *vt* (*animal*) to cut up

descubierto, -a [desku'βjerto, a] *pp de* **descubrir** ▷ *adj* uncovered, bare; (*persona*) bareheaded ▷ *nm* (*bancario*) overdraft; **al ~** in the open

descubrimiento [deskuβri'mjento] *nm* (*hallazgo*) discovery; (*revelación*) revelation

descubrir [desku'βrir] *vt* to discover, find; (*inaugurar*) to unveil; (*vislumbrar*) to detect; (*revelar*) to reveal, show; (*destapar*) to uncover; **descubrirse** *vr* to reveal o.s.; (*quitarse sombrero*) to take off one's hat; (*confesar*) to confess

descuento *etc* [des'kwento] *vb V* **descontar** ▷ *nm* discount

descuidado, -a [deskwi'ðaðo, a] *adj* (*sin cuidado*) careless; (*desordenado*) untidy; (*olvidadizo*) forgetful; (*dejado*) neglected; (*desprevenido*) unprepared

descuidar [deskwi'ðar] *vt* (*dejar*) to neglect; (*olvidar*) to overlook; **descuidarse** *vr* (*distraerse*) to be careless; (*abandonarse*) to let o.s. go; (*desprevenirse*) to drop one's guard; **¡descuida!** don't worry!; **descuido** *nm* (*dejadez*) carelessness; (*olvido*) negligence

PALABRA CLAVE

desde ['desðe] *prep* **1** (*lugar*) from; **desde Burgos hasta mi casa hay 30 km** it's 30 km from Burgos to my house
2 (*posición*): **hablaba desde el balcón** she was speaking from the balcony
3 (*tiempo*: + *adv*, *n*): **desde ahora** from now on; **desde la boda** since the wedding; **desde niño** since I *etc* was a child; **desde 3 años atrás** since 3 years ago
4 (*tiempo*: + *vb*, *fecha*) since; for; **nos conocemos desde 1992/desde hace 20 años** we've known each other since 1992/for 20 years; **no le veo desde 1997/desde hace 5 años** I haven't seen him since 1997/for 5 years
5 (*gama*): **desde los más lujosos hasta los más económicos** from the most luxurious to the most reasonably priced
6: **desde luego (que no)** of course (not)
▷ *conj*: **desde que: desde que recuerdo** for as long as I can remember; **desde que llegó no ha salido** he hasn't been out since he arrived

desdén [des'ðen] *nm* scorn

desdeñar [desðe'ɲar] *vt* (*despreciar*) to scorn

desdicha [des'ðitʃa] *nf* (*desgracia*) misfortune; (*infelicidad*) unhappiness; **desdichado, -a** *adj* (*sin suerte*) unlucky; (*infeliz*) unhappy

desear [dese'ar] *vt* to want, desire, wish for

desechar [dese'tʃar] *vt* (*basura*) to throw out *o* away; (*ideas*) to reject, discard; **desechos** *nmpl* rubbish *sg*, waste *sg*

desembalar [desemba'lar] *vt* to unpack

desembarazar [desembara'θar] *vt* (*desocupar*) to clear; (*desenredar*) to free; **desembarazarse** *vr*: **~se de** to free o.s. of, get rid of

desembarcar [desembar'kar] *vt* (*mercancías etc*) to unload ▷ *vi* to disembark

desembocadura [desemboka'ðura] *nf* (*de río*) mouth; (*de calle*) opening

desembocar [desembo'kar] *vi* (*río*) to flow into; (*fig*) to result in
desembolso [desem'bolso] *nm* payment
desembrollar [desembro'ʎar] *vt* (*madeja*) to unravel; (*asunto, malentendido*) to sort out
desemejanza [deseme'xanθa] *nf* dissimilarity
desempaquetar [desempake'tar] *vt* (*regalo*) to unwrap; (*mercancía*) to unpack
desempate [desem'pate] *nm* (*Fútbol*) replay, play-off; (*Tenis*) tie-break(er)
desempeñar [desempe'ɲar] *vt* (*cargo*) to hold; (*papel*) to perform; (*lo empeñado*) to redeem; **~ un papel** (*fig*) to play (a role)
desempleado, -a [desemple'aðo, a] *nm/f* unemployed person; **desempleo** *nm* unemployment
desencadenar [desenkaðe'nar] *vt* to unchain; (*ira*) to unleash; **desencadenarse** *vr* to break loose; (*tormenta*) to burst; (*guerra*) to break out
desencajar [desenka'xar] *vt* (*hueso*) to dislocate; (*mecanismo, pieza*) to disconnect, disengage
desencanto [desen'kanto] *nm* disillusionment
desenchufar [desentʃu'far] *vt* to unplug
desenfadado, -a [desenfa'ðaðo, a] *adj* (*desenvuelto*) uninhibited; (*descarado*) forward; **desenfado** *nm* (*libertad*) freedom; (*comportamiento*) free and easy manner; (*descaro*) forwardness
desenfocado, -a [desenfo'kaðo, a] *adj* (*Foto*) out of focus
desenfreno [desen'freno] *nm* wildness; (*de las pasiones*) lack of self-control
desenganchar [desengan'tʃar] *vt* (*gen*) to unhook; (*Ferro*) to uncouple
desengañar [desenga'ɲar] *vt* to disillusion; **desengañarse** *vr* to become disillusioned; **desengaño** *nm* disillusionment; (*decepción*) disappointment
desenlace [desen'laθe] *nm* outcome
desenmascarar [desenmaska'rar] *vt* to unmask
desenredar [desenre'ðar] *vt* (*pelo*) to untangle; (*problema*) to sort out
desenroscar [desenros'kar] *vt* to unscrew
desentenderse [desenten'derse] *vr*: **~ de** to pretend not to know about; (*apartarse*) to have nothing to do with
desenterrar [desente'rrar] *vt* to exhume; (*tesoro, fig*) to unearth, dig up
desentonar [desento'nar] *vi* (*Mús*) to sing (*o* play) out of tune; (*color*) to clash
desentrañar [desentra'ɲar] *vt* (*misterio*) to unravel
desenvoltura [desenβol'tura] *nf* ease
desenvolver [desenβol'βer] *vt* (*paquete*) to unwrap; (*fig*) to develop; **desenvolverse** *vr* (*desarrollarse*) to unfold, develop; (*arreglárselas*) to cope
deseo [de'seo] *nm* desire, wish; **deseoso, -a** *adj*: **estar deseoso de** to be anxious to
desequilibrado, -a [desekili'βraðo, a] *adj* unbalanced
desertar [deser'tar] *vi* to desert
desértico, -a [de'sertiko, a] *adj* desert *cpd*
desesperación [desespera'θjon] *nf* (*impaciencia*) desperation, despair; (*irritación*) fury
desesperar [desespe'rar] *vt* to drive to despair; (*exasperar*) to drive to distraction ▷ *vi*: **~ de** to despair of; **desesperarse** *vr* to despair, lose hope
desestabilizar [desestaβili'θar] *vt* to destabilize
desestimar [desesti'mar] *vt* (*menospreciar*) to have a low opinion of; (*rechazar*) to reject
desfachatez [desfatʃa'teθ] *nf* (*insolencia*) impudence; (*descaro*) rudeness

desfalco [des'falko] *nm* embezzlement
desfallecer [desfaʎe'θer] *vi* (*perder las fuerzas*) to become weak; (*desvanecerse*) to faint
desfasado, -a [desfa'saðo, a] *adj* (*anticuado*) old-fashioned; **desfase** *nm* (*diferencia*) gap
desfavorable [desfaβo'raβle] *adj* unfavourable
desfigurar [desfiɣu'rar] *vt* (*cara*) to disfigure; (*cuerpo*) to deform
desfiladero [desfila'ðero] *nm* gorge
desfilar [desfi'lar] *vi* to parade; **desfile** *nm* procession; **desfile de modelos** fashion show
desgana [des'ɣana] *nf* (*falta de apetito*) loss of appetite; (*apatía*) unwillingness; **desganado, -a** *adj*: **estar desganado** (*sin apetito*) to have no appetite; (*sin entusiasmo*) to have lost interest
desgarrar [desɣa'rrar] *vt* to tear (up); (*fig*) to shatter; **desgarro** *nm* (*en tela*) tear; (*aflicción*) grief
desgastar [desɣas'tar] *vt* (*deteriorar*) to wear away *o* down; (*estropear*) to spoil; **desgastarse** *vr* to get worn out; **desgaste** *nm* wear (and tear)
desglosar [desɣlo'sar] *vt* (*factura*) to break down
desgracia [des'ɣraθja] *nf* misfortune; (*accidente*) accident; (*vergüenza*) disgrace; (*contratiempo*) setback; **por ~** unfortunately; **desgraciado, -a** [desɣra'θjaðo, a] *adj* (*sin suerte*) unlucky, unfortunate; (*miserable*) wretched; (*infeliz*) miserable
desgravar [desɣra'βar] *vt* (*impuestos*) to reduce the tax *o* duty on
desguace [des'ɣwaθe] (ESP) *nm* junkyard
deshabitado, -a [desaβi'taðo, a] *adj* uninhabited
deshacer [desa'θer] *vt* (*casa*) to break up; (*Tec*) to take apart; (*enemigo*) to defeat; (*diluir*) to melt; (*contrato*) to break; (*intriga*) to solve; **deshacerse** *vr* (*disolverse*) to melt; (*despedazarse*) to come apart *o* undone; **~se de** to get rid of; **~se en lágrimas** to burst into tears
deshecho, -a [des'etʃo, a] *adj* undone; (*roto*) smashed; (*persona*): **estar ~** to be shattered
desheredar [desere'ðar] *vt* to disinherit
deshidratar [desiðra'tar] *vt* to dehydrate
deshielo [des'jelo] *nm* thaw
deshonesto, -a [deso'nesto, a] *adj* indecent
deshonra [des'onra] *nf* (*deshonor*) dishonour; (*vergüenza*) shame
deshora [des'ora]: **a ~** *adv* at the wrong time
deshuesadero [deswesa'ðero] (MÉX) *nm* junkyard
deshuesar [deswe'sar] *vt* (*carne*) to bone; (*fruta*) to stone
desierto, -a [de'sjerto, a] *adj* (*casa, calle, negocio*) deserted ▷ *nm* desert
designar [desiɣ'nar] *vt* (*nombrar*) to designate; (*indicar*) to fix
desigual [desi'ɣwal] *adj* (*terreno*) uneven; (*lucha etc*) unequal
desilusión [desilu'sjon] *nf* disillusionment; (*decepción*) disappointment; **desilusionar** *vt* to disillusion; to disappoint; **desilusionarse** *vr* to become disillusioned
desinfectar [desinfek'tar] *vt* to disinfect
desinflar [desin'flar] *vt* to deflate
desintegración [desinteɣra'θjon] *nf* disintegration
desinterés [desinte'res] *nm* (*desgana*) lack of interest; (*altruismo*) unselfishness
desintoxicarse [desintoksi'karse] *vr* (*drogadicto*) to undergo detoxification
desistir [desis'tir] *vi* (*renunciar*) to stop, desist
desleal [desle'al] *adj* (*infiel*) disloyal; (*Com: competencia*) unfair; **deslealtad**

nf disloyalty
desligar [desli'ɣar] *vt* (*desatar*) to untie, undo; (*separar*) to separate; **desligarse** *vr* (*de un compromiso*) to extricate o.s.
desliz [des'liθ] *nm* (*fig*) lapse; **deslizar** *vt* to slip, slide
deslumbrar [deslum'brar] *vt* to dazzle
desmadrarse [desma'ðrarse] (*fam*) *vr* (*descontrolarse*) to run wild; (*divertirse*) to let one's hair down; **desmadre** (*fam*) *nm* (*desorganización*) chaos; (*jaleo*) commotion
desmán [des'man] *nm* (*exceso*) outrage; (*abuso de poder*) abuse
desmantelar [desmante'lar] *vt* (*deshacer*) to dismantle; (*casa*) to strip
desmaquillador [desmakiʎa'ðor] *nm* make-up remover
desmayar [desma'jar] *vi* to lose heart; **desmayarse** *vr* (*Med*) to faint; **desmayo** *nm* (*Med: acto*) faint; (*: estado*) unconsciousness
desmemoriado, -a [desmemo'rjado, a] *adj* forgetful
desmentir [desmen'tir] *vt* (*contradecir*) to contradict; (*refutar*) to deny
desmenuzar [desmenu'θar] *vt* (*deshacer*) to crumble; (*carne*) to chop; (*examinar*) to examine closely
desmesurado, -a [desmesu'raðo, a] *adj* disproportionate
desmontable [desmon'taβle] *adj* (*que se quita: pieza*) detachable; (*plegable*) collapsible, folding
desmontar [desmon'tar] *vt* (*deshacer*) to dismantle; (*tierra*) to level ▷ *vi* to dismount
desmoralizar [desmorali'θar] *vt* to demoralize
desmoronar [desmoro'nar] *vt* to wear away, erode; **desmoronarse** *vr* (*edificio, dique*) to collapse; (*economía*) to decline
desnatado, -a [desna'taðo, a] *adj* skimmed
desnivel [desni'βel] *nm* (*de terreno*) unevenness
desnudar [desnu'ðar] *vt* (*desvestir*) to undress; (*despojar*) to strip; **desnudarse** *vr* (*desvestirse*) to get undressed; **desnudo, -a** *adj* naked ▷ *nm/f* nude; **desnudo de** devoid *o* bereft of
desnutrición [desnutri'θjon] *nf* malnutrition; **desnutrido, -a** *adj* undernourished
desobedecer [desoβeðe'θer] *vt, vi* to disobey; **desobediencia** *nf* disobedience
desocupado, -a [desoku'paðo, a] *adj* at leisure; (*desempleado*) unemployed; (*deshabitado*) empty, vacant
desodorante [desoðo'rante] *nm* deodorant
desolación [desola'θjon] *nf* (*de lugar*) desolation; (*fig*) grief
desolar [deso'lar] *vt* to ruin, lay waste
desorbitado, -a [desorβi'taðo, a] *adj* (*excesivo: ambición*) boundless; (*deseos*) excessive; (*: precio*) exorbitant
desorden [des'orðen] *nm* confusion; (*político*) disorder, unrest
desorganización [desorɣaniθa'θjon] *nf* (*de persona*) disorganization; (*en empresa, oficina*) disorder, chaos
desorientar [desorjen'tar] *vt* (*extraviar*) to mislead; (*confundir, desconcertar*) to confuse; **desorientarse** *vr* (*perderse*) to lose one's way
despabilado, -a [despaβi'laðo, a] *adj* (*despierto*) wide-awake; (*fig*) alert, sharp
despachar [despa'tʃar] *vt* (*negocio*) to do, complete; (*enviar*) to send, dispatch; (*vender*) to sell, deal in; (*billete*) to issue; (*mandar ir*) to send away
despacho [des'patʃo] *nm* (*oficina*) office; (*de paquetes*) dispatch; (*venta*) sale; (*comunicación*) message
despacio [des'paθjo] *adv* slowly
desparpajo [despar'paxo] *nm* self-

confidence; (*pey*) nerve
desparramar [desparra'mar] *vt* (*esparcir*) to scatter; (*líquido*) to spill
despecho [des'petʃo] *nm* spite
despectivo, -a [despek'tiβo, a] *adj* (*despreciativo*) derogatory; (*Ling*) pejorative
despedida [despe'ðiða] *nf* (*adiós*) farewell; (*de obrero*) sacking
despedir [despe'ðir] *vt* (*visita*) to see off, show out; (*empleado*) to dismiss; (*inquilino*) to evict; (*objeto*) to hurl; (*olor etc*) to give out *o* off; **despedirse** *vr*: **~se de** to say goodbye to
despegar [despe'ɣar] *vt* to unstick ▷ *vi* (*avión*) to take off; **despegarse** *vr* to come loose, come unstuck; **despego** *nm* detachment
despegue *etc* [des'peɣe] *vb V* **despegar** ▷ *nm* takeoff
despeinado, -a [despei'naðo, a] *adj* dishevelled, unkempt
despejado, -a [despe'xaðo, a] *adj* (*lugar*) clear, free; (*cielo*) clear; (*persona*) wide-awake, bright
despejar [despe'xar] *vt* (*gen*) to clear; (*misterio*) to clear up ▷ *vi* (*el tiempo*) to clear; **despejarse** *vr* (*tiempo, cielo*) to clear (up); (*misterio*) to become clearer; (*cabeza*) to clear
despensa [des'pensa] *nf* larder
despeñarse [despe'ɲarse] *vr* to hurl o.s. down; (*coche*) to tumble over
desperdicio [desper'ðiθjo] *nm* (*despilfarro*) squandering; **desperdicios** *nmpl* (*basura*) rubbish *sg* (BRIT), garbage *sg* (US); (*residuos*) waste *sg*
desperezarse [despere'θarse] *vr* to stretch
desperfecto [desper'fekto] *nm* (*deterioro*) slight damage; (*defecto*) flaw, imperfection
despertador [desperta'ðor] *nm* alarm clock
despertar [desper'tar] *nm* awakening ▷ *vt* (*persona*) to wake up; (*recuerdos*) to revive; (*sentimiento*) to arouse ▷ *vi* to awaken, wake up; **despertarse** *vr* to awaken, wake up
despido *etc* [des'piðo] *vb V* **despedir** ▷ *nm* dismissal, sacking
despierto, -a etc [des'pjerto, a] *vb V* **despertar** ▷ *adj* awake; (*fig*) sharp, alert
despilfarro [despil'farro] *nm* (*derroche*) squandering; (*lujo desmedido*) extravagance
despistar [despis'tar] *vt* to throw off the track *o* scent; (*confundir*) to mislead, confuse; **despistarse** *vr* to take the wrong road; (*confundirse*) to become confused
despiste [des'piste] *nm* absent-mindedness; **un ~** a mistake *o* slip
desplazamiento [desplaθa'mjento] *nm* displacement
desplazar [despla'θar] *vt* to move; (*Náut*) to displace; (*Inform*) to scroll; (*fig*) to oust; **desplazarse** *vr* (*persona*) to travel
desplegar [desple'ɣar] *vt* (*tela, papel*) to unfold, open out; (*bandera*) to unfurl; **despliegue** *etc* [des'pleɣe] *vb V* **desplegar** ▷ *nm* display
desplomarse [desplo'marse] *vr* (*edificio, gobierno, persona*) to collapse
desplumar [desplu'mar] *vt* (*ave*) to pluck; (*fam: estafar*) to fleece
despoblado, -a [despo'βlaðo, a] *adj* (*sin habitantes*) uninhabited
despojar [despo'xar] *vt* (*alguien: de sus bienes*) to divest of, deprive of; (*casa*) to strip, leave bare; (*alguien: de su cargo*) to strip of
despojo [des'poxo] *nm* (*acto*) plundering; (*objetos*) plunder, loot; **despojos** *nmpl* (*de ave, res*) offal *sg*
desposado, -a [despo'saðo, a] *adj, nm/f* newly-wed
despreciar [despre'θjar] *vt* (*desdeñar*) to despise, scorn; (*afrentar*) to slight; **desprecio** *nm* scorn, contempt; slight
desprender [despren'der] *vt* (*broche*) to unfasten; (*olor*) to give off; **desprenderse** *vr* (*botón: caerse*) to fall off; (*broche*) to come unfastened; (*olor,

perfume) to be given off; **~se de algo que ...** to draw from sth that ...

desprendimiento [desprendi'mjento] *nm* (*gen*) loosening; (*generosidad*) disinterestedness; (*de tierra, rocas*) landslide; **desprendimiento de retina** detachment of the retina

despreocupado, -a [despreoku'paðo, a] *adj* (*sin preocupación*) unworried, nonchalant; (*negligente*) careless

despreocuparse [despreoku'parse] *vr* not to worry; **~ de** to have no interest in

desprestigiar [despresti'xjar] *vt* (*criticar*) to run down; (*desacreditar*) to discredit

desprevenido, -a [despreβe'niðo, a] *adj* (*no preparado*) unprepared, unready

desproporcionado, -a [desproporθjo'naðo, a] *adj* disproportionate, out of proportion

desprovisto, -a [despro'βisto, a] *adj*: **~ de** devoid of

después [des'pwes] *adv* afterwards, later; (*próximo paso*) next; **~ de comer** after lunch; **un año ~** a year later; **~ se debatió el tema** next the matter was discussed; **~ de corregido el texto** after the text had been corrected; **~ de todo** after all

desquiciado, -a [deski'θjaðo, a] *adj* deranged

destacar [desta'kar] *vt* to emphasize, point up; (*Mil*) to detach, detail ▷ *vi* (*resaltarse*) to stand out; (*persona*) to be outstanding *o* exceptional; **destacarse** *vr* to stand out; to be outstanding *o* exceptional

destajo [des'taxo] *nm*: **trabajar a ~** to do piecework

destapar [desta'par] *vt* (*botella*) to open; (*cacerola*) to take the lid off; (*descubrir*) to uncover; **destaparse** *vr* (*revelarse*) to reveal one's true character

destartalado, -a [destarta'laðo, a] *adj* (*desordenado*) untidy; (*ruinoso*) tumbledown

destello [des'teʎo] *nm* (*de estrella*) twinkle; (*de faro*) signal light

destemplado, -a [destem'plaðo, a] *adj* (*Mús*) out of tune; (*voz*) harsh; (*Med*) out of sorts; (*tiempo*) unpleasant, nasty

desteñir [deste'ɲir] *vt* to fade ▷ *vi* to fade; **desteñirse** *vr* to fade; **esta tela no destiñe** this fabric will not run

desternillarse [desterni'ʎarse] *vr*: **~ de risa** to split one's sides laughing

desterrar [deste'rrar] *vt* (*exiliar*) to exile; (*fig*) to banish, dismiss

destiempo [des'tjempo]: **a ~** *adv* out of turn

destierro *etc* [des'tjerro] *vb V* **desterrar** ▷ *nm* exile

destilar [desti'lar] *vt* to distil; **destilería** *nf* distillery

destinar [desti'nar] *vt* (*funcionario*) to appoint, assign; (*fondos*): **~ (a)** to set aside (for)

destinatario, -a [destina'tarjo, a] *nm/f* addressee

destino [des'tino] *nm* (*suerte*) destiny; (*de avión, viajero*) destination; **con ~ a Londres** (*barco*) (bound) for London; (*avión, carta*) to London

destituir [destitu'ir] *vt* to dismiss

destornillador [destorniʎa'ðor] *nm* screwdriver

destornillar [destorni'ʎar] *vt* (*tornillo*) to unscrew; **destornillarse** *vr* to unscrew

destreza [des'treθa] *nf* (*habilidad*) skill; (*maña*) dexterity

destrozar [destro'θar] *vt* (*romper*) to smash, break (up); (*estropear*) to ruin; (*nervios*) to shatter

destrozo [des'troθo] *nm* (*acción*) destruction; (*desastre*) smashing; **destrozos** *nmpl* (*pedazos*) pieces; (*daños*) havoc *sg*

destrucción [destruk'θjon] *nf* destruction

destruir [destru'ir] *vt* to destroy

desuso [des'uso] *nm* disuse; **caer en**

~ to become obsolete
desvalijar [desvali'xar] *vt* (*persona*) to rob; (*casa, tienda*) to burgle; (*coche*) to break into
desván [des'βan] *nm* attic
desvanecer [desβane'θer] *vt* (*disipar*) to dispel; (*borrar*) to blur; **desvanecerse** *vr* (*humo etc*) to vanish, disappear; (*color*) to fade; (*recuerdo, sonido*) to fade away; (*Med*) to pass out; (*duda*) to be dispelled
desvariar [desβa'rjar] *vi* (*enfermo*) to be delirious
desvelar [desβe'lar] *vt* to keep awake; **desvelarse** *vr* (*no poder dormir*) to stay awake; (*preocuparse*) to be vigilant *o* watchful
desventaja [desβen'taxa] *nf* disadvantage
desvergonzado, -a [desβerɣon'θaðo, a] *adj* shameless
desvestir [desβes'tir] *vt* to undress; **desvestirse** *vr* to undress
desviación [desβja'θjon] *nf* deviation; (*Auto*) diversion, detour
desviar [des'βjar] *vt* to turn aside; (*río*) to alter the course of; (*navío*) to divert, re-route; (*conversación*) to sidetrack; **desviarse** *vr* (*apartarse del camino*) to turn aside; (: *barco*) to go off course
desvío *etc* [des'βio] *vb V* **desviar** ▷ *nm* (*desviación*) detour, diversion; (*fig*) indifference
desvivirse [desβi'βirse] *vr*: **~ por** (*anhelar*) to long for, crave for; (*hacer lo posible por*) to do one's utmost for
detallar [deta'ʎar] *vt* to detail
detalle [de'taʎe] *nm* detail; (*gesto*) gesture, token; **al ~** in detail; (*Com*) retail
detallista [deta'ʎista] *nmf* (*Com*) retailer
detective [detek'tiβe] *nmf* detective; **detective privado** private detective
detener [dete'ner] *vt* (*gen*) to stop; (*Jur*) to arrest; (*objeto*) to keep; **detenerse** *vr* to stop; (*demorarse*): **~se en** to delay over, linger over
detenidamente [deteniða'mente] *adv* (*minuciosamente*) carefully; (*extensamente*) at great length
detenido, -a [dete'niðo, a] *adj* (*arrestado*) under arrest ▷ *nm/f* person under arrest, prisoner
detenimiento [deteni'mjento] *nm*: **con ~** thoroughly; (*observar, considerar*) carefully
detergente [deter'xente] *nm* detergent
deteriorar [deterjo'rar] *vt* to spoil, damage; **deteriorarse** *vr* to deteriorate; **deterioro** *nm* deterioration
determinación [determina'θjon] *nf* (*empeño*) determination; (*decisión*) decision; **determinado, -a** *adj* specific
determinar [determi'nar] *vt* (*plazo*) to fix; (*precio*) to settle; **determinarse** *vr* to decide
detestar [detes'tar] *vt* to detest
detractor, a [detrak'tor, a] *nm/f* slanderer, libeller
detrás [de'tras] *adv* (*tb*: **por ~**) behind; (*atrás*) at the back; **~ de** behind
detrimento [detri'mento] *nm*: **en ~ de** to the detriment of
deuda ['deuða] *nf* debt; **deuda exterior/pública** foreign/national debt
devaluación [deβalwa'θjon] *nf* devaluation
devastar [deβas'tar] *vt* (*destruir*) to devastate
deveras [de'βeras] (*MÉX*) *nf inv*: **un amigo de (a) ~** a true *o* real friend
devoción [deβo'θjon] *nf* devotion
devolución [deβolu'θjon] *nf* (*reenvío*) return, sending back; (*reembolso*) repayment; (*Jur*) devolution
devolver [deβol'βer] *vt* to return; (*lo extraviado, lo prestado*) to give back; (*carta al correo*) to send back; (*Com*) to repay, refund ▷ *vi* (*vomitar*) to be sick
devorar [deβo'rar] *vt* to devour

devoto, -a [de'βoto, a] *adj* devout ▷ *nm/f* admirer
devuelto *pp de* **devolver**
devuelva *etc vb V* **devolver**
di *etc vb V* **dar; decir**
día ['dia] *nm* day; **¿qué ~ es?** what's the date?; **estar/poner al ~** to be/keep up to date; **el ~ de hoy/de mañana** today/tomorrow; **al ~ siguiente** (on) the following day; **vivir al ~** to live from hand to mouth; **de ~** by day, in daylight; **en pleno ~** in full daylight; **Día de la Independencia** Independence Day; **Día de los Muertos** (*MÉX*) All Souls' Day; **Día de Reyes** Epiphany; **día feriado** (*LAM*) holiday; **día festivo** (*ESP*) holiday; **día lectivo** teaching day; **día libre** day off
diabetes [dja'βetes] *nf* diabetes
diablo ['djaβlo] *nm* devil; **diablura** *nf* prank
diadema [dja'ðema] *nf* tiara
diafragma [dja'fraɣma] *nm* diaphragm
diagnóstico [diaɣ'nostiko] *nm* = **diagnosis**
diagonal [djaɣo'nal] *adj* diagonal
diagrama [dja'ɣrama] *nm* diagram
dial [djal] *nm* dial
dialecto [dja'lekto] *nm* dialect
dialogar [djalo'ɣar] *vi*: **~ con** (*Pol*) to hold talks with
diálogo ['djaloɣo] *nm* dialogue
diamante [dja'mante] *nm* diamond
diana ['djana] *nf* (*Mil*) reveille; (*de blanco*) centre, bull's-eye
diapositiva [djaposi'tiβa] *nf* (*Foto*) slide, transparency
diario, -a ['djarjo, a] *adj* daily ▷ *nm* newspaper; **a ~** daily; **de ~** everyday
diarrea [dja'rrea] *nf* diarrhoea
dibujar [diβu'xar] *vt* to draw, sketch; **dibujo** *nm* drawing; **dibujos animados** cartoons
diccionario [dikθjo'narjo] *nm* dictionary
dice *etc vb V* **decir**
dicho, -a ['ditʃo, a] *pp de* **decir** ▷ *adj*: **en ~s países** in the aforementioned countries ▷ *nm* saying
dichoso, -a [di'tʃoso, a] *adj* happy
diciembre [di'θjembre] *nm* December
dictado [dik'taðo] *nm* dictation
dictador [dikta'ðor] *nm* dictator; **dictadura** *nf* dictatorship
dictar [dik'tar] *vt* (*carta*) to dictate; (*Jur: sentencia*) to pronounce; (*decreto*) to issue; (*LAM: clase*) to give
didáctico, -a [di'ðaktiko, a] *adj* educational
diecinueve [djeθi'nweβe] *num* nineteen
dieciocho [djeθi'otʃo] *num* eighteen
dieciséis [djeθi'seis] *num* sixteen
diecisiete [djeθi'sjete] *num* seventeen
diente ['djente] *nm* (*Anat, Tec*) tooth; (*Zool*) fang; (*: de elefante*) tusk; (*de ajo*) clove
diera *etc vb V* **dar**
diesel ['disel] *adj*: **motor ~** diesel engine
diestro, -a ['djestro, a] *adj* (*derecho*) right; (*hábil*) skilful
dieta ['djeta] *nf* diet; **estar a ~** to be on a diet
diez [djeθ] *num* ten
diferencia [dife'renθja] *nf* difference; **a ~ de** unlike; **diferenciar** *vt* to differentiate between ▷ *vi* to differ; **diferenciarse** *vr* to differ, be different; (*distinguirse*) to distinguish o.s.
diferente [dife'rente] *adj* different
diferido [dife'riðo] *nm*: **en ~** (*TV etc*) recorded
difícil [di'fiθil] *adj* difficult
dificultad [difikul'tað] *nf* difficulty; (*problema*) trouble
dificultar [difikul'tar] *vt* (*complicar*) to complicate, make difficult; (*estorbar*) to obstruct
difundir [difun'dir] *vt* (*calor, luz*) to diffuse; (*Radio, TV*) to broadcast; **~**

una noticia to spread a piece of news; **difundirse** *vr* to spread (out)
difunto, -a [di'funto, a] *adj* dead, deceased ▷ *nm/f* deceased (person)
difusión [difu'sjon] *nf* (*Radio, TV*) broadcasting
diga *etc vb V* **decir**
digerir [dixe'rir] *vt* to digest; (*fig*) to absorb; **digestión** *nf* digestion; **digestivo, -a** *adj* digestive
digital [dixi'tal] *adj* digital
dignarse [diɣ'narse] *vr* to deign to
dignidad [diɣni'ðað] *nf* dignity
digno, -a ['diɣno, a] *adj* worthy
digo *etc vb V* **decir**
dije *etc vb V* **decir**
dilatar [dila'tar] *vt* (*cuerpo*) to dilate; (*prolongar*) to prolong
dilema [di'lema] *nm* dilemma
diluir [dilu'ir] *vt* to dilute
diluvio [di'luβjo] *nm* deluge, flood
dimensión [dimen'sjon] *nf* dimension
diminuto, -a [dimi'nuto, a] *adj* tiny, diminutive
dimitir [dimi'tir] *vi* to resign
dimos *vb V* **dar**
Dinamarca [dina'marka] *nf* Denmark
dinámico, -a [di'namiko, a] *adj* dynamic
dinamita [dina'mita] *nf* dynamite
dínamo ['dinamo] *nf* dynamo
dineral [dine'ral] *nm* large sum of money, fortune
dinero [di'nero] *nm* money; **dinero en efectivo** *o* **metálico** cash; **dinero suelto** (loose) change
dio *vb V* **dar**
dios [djos] *nm* god; **¡D~ mío!** (oh,) my God!; **¡por D~!** for heaven's sake!; **diosa** ['djosa] *nf* goddess
diploma [di'ploma] *nm* diploma
diplomacia [diplo'maθja] *nf* diplomacy; (*fig*) tact
diplomado, -a [diplo'maðo, a] *adj* qualified
diplomático, -a [diplo'matiko, a] *adj* diplomatic ▷ *nm/f* diplomat
diputación [diputa'θjon] *nf* (*tb*: **~ provincial**) ≈ county council
diputado, -a [dipu'taðo, a] *nm/f* delegate; (*Pol*) ≈ member of parliament (BRIT) ≈ representative (US)
dique ['dike] *nm* dyke
diré *etc vb V* **decir**
dirección [direk'θjon] *nf* direction; (*señas*) address; (*Auto*) steering; (*gerencia*) management; (*Pol*) leadership; **dirección única/ prohibida** one-way street/no entry
direccional [direkθjo'nal] (MÉX) *nf* (*Auto*) indicator
directa [di'rekta] *nf* (*Auto*) top gear
directiva [direk'tiβa] *nf* (*tb*: **junta ~**) board of directors
directo, -a [di'rekto, a] *adj* direct; (*Radio, TV*) live; **transmitir en ~** to broadcast live
director, a [direk'tor, a] *adj* leading ▷ *nm/f* director; (*Escol*) head(teacher) (BRIT), principal (US); (*gerente*) manager/ess; (*Prensa*) editor; **director de cine** film director; **director general** managing director
directorio [direk'torjo] (MÉX) *nm* (*telefónico*) phone book
dirigente [diri'xente] *nmf* (*Pol*) leader
dirigir [diri'xir] *vt* to direct; (*carta*) to address; (*obra de teatro, film*) to direct; (*Mús*) to conduct; (*negocio*) to manage; **dirigirse** *vr*: **~se a** to go towards, make one's way towards; (*hablar con*) to speak to
dirija *etc vb V* **dirigir**
disciplina [disθi'plina] *nf* discipline
discípulo, -a [dis'θipulo, a] *nm/f* disciple
Discman® ['diskman] *nm* Discman®
disco ['disko] *nm* disc; (*Deporte*) discus; (*Tel*) dial; (*Auto*: *semáforo*) light; (*Mús*) record; **disco compacto/de larga duración** compact disc/long-playing record; **disco de freno** brake

disc; **disco flexible/duro** *o* **rígido** (*Inform*) floppy/hard disk

disconforme [diskon'forme] *adj* differing; **estar ~ (con)** to be in disagreement (with)

discordia [dis'korðja] *nf* discord

discoteca [disko'teka] *nf* disco(theque)

discreción [diskre'θjon] *nf* discretion; (*reserva*) prudence; **comer a ~** to eat as much as one wishes

discreto, -a [dis'kreto, a] *adj* discreet

discriminación [diskrimina'θjon] *nf* discrimination

disculpa [dis'kulpa] *nf* excuse; (*pedir perdón*) apology; **pedir ~s a/por** to apologize to/for; **disculpar** *vt* to excuse, pardon; **disculparse** *vr* to excuse o.s.; to apologize

discurso [dis'kurso] *nm* speech

discusión [disku'sjon] *nf* (*diálogo*) discussion; (*riña*) argument

discutir [disku'tir] *vt* (*debatir*) to discuss; (*pelear*) to argue about; (*contradecir*) to argue against ▷ *vi* (*debatir*) to discuss; (*pelearse*) to argue

disecar [dise'kar] *vt* (*conservar: animal*) to stuff; (*: planta*) to dry

diseñar [dise'ɲar] *vt, vi* to design

diseño [di'seɲo] *nm* design

disfraz [dis'fraθ] *nm* (*máscara*) disguise; (*excusa*) pretext; **disfrazar** *vt* to disguise; **disfrazarse** *vr*: **disfrazarse de** to disguise o.s. as

disfrutar [disfru'tar] *vt* to enjoy ▷ *vi* to enjoy o.s.; **~ de** to enjoy, possess

disgustar [disɣus'tar] *vt* (*no gustar*) to displease; (*contrariar, enojar*) to annoy, upset; **disgustarse** *vr* (*enfadarse*) to get upset; (*dos personas*) to fall out

> No confundir **disgustar** con la palabra inglesa *disgust*.

disgusto [dis'ɣusto] *nm* (*contrariedad*) annoyance; (*tristeza*) grief; (*riña*) quarrel

disimular [disimu'lar] *vt* (*ocultar*) to hide, conceal ▷ *vi* to dissemble

dislocarse [dislo'karse] *vr* (*articulación*) to sprain, dislocate

disminución [disminu'θjon] *nf* decrease, reduction

disminuido, -a [disminu'iðo, a] *nm/f*: **~ mental/físico** mentally/physically handicapped person

disminuir [disminu'ir] *vt* to decrease, diminish

disolver [disol'βer] *vt* (*gen*) to dissolve; **disolverse** *vr* to dissolve; (*Com*) to go into liquidation

dispar [dis'par] *adj* different

disparar [dispa'rar] *vt, vi* to shoot, fire

disparate [dispa'rate] *nm* (*tontería*) foolish remark; (*error*) blunder; **decir ~s** to talk nonsense

disparo [dis'paro] *nm* shot

dispersar [disper'sar] *vt* to disperse; **dispersarse** *vr* to scatter

disponer [dispo'ner] *vt* (*arreglar*) to arrange; (*ordenar*) to put in order; (*preparar*) to prepare, get ready ▷ *vi*: **~ de** to have, own; **disponerse** *vr*: **~se a** *o* **para hacer** to prepare to do

disponible [dispo'niβle] *adj* available

disposición [disposi'θjon] *nf* arrangement, disposition; (*voluntad*) willingness; (*Inform*) layout; **a su ~** at your service

dispositivo [disposi'tiβo] *nm* device, mechanism

dispuesto, -a [dis'pwesto, a] *pp de* **disponer** ▷ *adj* (*arreglado*) arranged; (*preparado*) disposed

disputar [dispu'tar] *vt* (*carrera*) to compete in

disquete [dis'kete] *nm* floppy disk, diskette

distancia [dis'tanθja] *nf* distance; **distanciar** [distan'θjar] *vt* to space out; **distanciarse** *vr* to become estranged; **distante** [dis'tante] *adj* distant

diste *vb V* **dar**

disteis *vb V* **dar**

distinción [distin'θjon] *nf* distinction; (*elegancia*) elegance; (*honor*) honour
distinguido, -a [distin'giðo, a] *adj* distinguished
distinguir [distin'gir] *vt* to distinguish; (*escoger*) to single out; **distinguirse** *vr* to be distinguished
distintivo [distin'tiβo] *nm* badge; (*fig*) characteristic
distinto, -a [dis'tinto, a] *adj* different; (*claro*) clear
distracción [distrak'θjon] *nf* distraction; (*pasatiempo*) hobby, pastime; (*olvido*) absent-mindedness, distraction
distraer [distra'er] *vt* (*atención*) to distract; (*divertir*) to amuse; (*fondos*) to embezzle; **distraerse** *vr* (*entretenerse*) to amuse o.s.; (*perder la concentración*) to allow one's attention to wander
distraído, -a [distra'iðo, a] *adj* (*gen*) absent-minded; (*entretenido*) amusing
distribuidor, a [distriβui'ðor, a] *nm/f* distributor; **distribuidora** *nf* (*Com*) dealer, agent; (*Cine*) distributor
distribuir [distriβu'ir] *vt* to distribute
distrito [dis'trito] *nm* (*sector, territorio*) region; (*barrio*) district; **Distrito Federal** (MÉX) Federal District; **distrito postal** postal district
disturbio [dis'turβjo] *nm* disturbance; (*desorden*) riot
disuadir [diswa'ðir] *vt* to dissuade
disuelto [di'swelto] *pp de* **disolver**
DIU *nm abr* (= *dispositivo intrauterino*) IUD
diurno, -a ['djurno, a] *adj* day *cpd*
divagar [diβa'ɣar] *vi* (*desviarse*) to digress
diván [di'βan] *nm* divan
diversidad [diβersi'ðað] *nf* diversity, variety
diversión [diβer'sjon] *nf* (*gen*) entertainment; (*actividad*) hobby, pastime
diverso, -a [di'βerso, a] *adj* diverse; **~s libros** several books; **diversos** *nmpl* sundries
divertido, -a [diβer'tiðo, a] *adj* (*chiste*) amusing; (*fiesta etc*) enjoyable
divertir [diβer'tir] *vt* (*entretener, recrear*) to amuse; **divertirse** *vr* (*pasarlo bien*) to have a good time; (*distraerse*) to amuse o.s.
dividendos [diβi'ðendos] *nmpl* (*Com*) dividends
dividir [diβi'ðir] *vt* (*gen*) to divide; (*distribuir*) to distribute, share out
divierta *etc vb V* **divertir**
divino, -a [di'βino, a] *adj* divine
divirtiendo *etc vb V* **divertir**
divisa [di'βisa] *nf* (*emblema*) emblem, badge; **divisas** *nfpl* foreign exchange *sg*
divisar [diβi'sar] *vt* to make out, distinguish
división [diβi'sjon] *nf* (*gen*) division; (*de partido*) split; (*de país*) partition
divorciar [diβor'θjar] *vt* to divorce; **divorciarse** *vr* to get divorced; **divorcio** *nm* divorce
divulgar [diβul'ɣar] *vt* (*ideas*) to spread; (*secreto*) to divulge
DNI (ESP) *nm abr* (= *Documento Nacional de Identidad*) *national identity card*

DNI

The **Documento Nacional de Identidad** is a Spanish ID card which must be carried at all times and produced on request for the police. It contains the holder's photo, fingerprints and personal details. It is also known as the **DNI** or "carnet de identidad".

Dña. *abr* (= *doña*) Mrs
do [do] *nm* (*Mús*) do, C
dobladillo [doβla'ðiʎo] *nm* (*de vestido*) hem; (*de pantalón: vuelta*) turn-up (BRIT), cuff (US)
doblar [do'βlar] *vt* to double; (*papel*) to fold; (*caño*) to bend; (*la esquina*) to

turn, go round; (*film*) to dub ▷ *vi* to turn; (*campana*) to toll; **doblarse** *vr* (*plegarse*) to fold (up), crease; (*encorvarse*) to bend; **~ a la derecha/ izquierda** to turn right/left

doble ['doβle] *adj* double; (*de dos aspectos*) dual; (*fig*) two-faced ▷ *nm* double ▷ *nmf* (*Teatro*) double, stand-in; **dobles** *nmpl* (*Deporte*) doubles *sg*; **con ~ sentido** with a double meaning

doce ['doθe] *num* twelve; **docena** *nf* dozen

docente [do'θente] *adj*: **centro/ personal ~** teaching establishment/ staff

dócil ['doθil] *adj* (*pasivo*) docile; (*obediente*) obedient

doctor, a [dok'tor, a] *nm/f* doctor

doctorado [dokto'raðo] *nm* doctorate

doctrina [dok'trina] *nf* doctrine, teaching

documentación [dokumenta'θjon] *nf* documentation, papers *pl*

documental [dokumen'tal] *adj, nm* documentary

documento [doku'mento] *nm* (*certificado*) document; **documento adjunto** (*Inform*) attachment; **documento nacional de identidad** identity card

dólar ['dolar] *nm* dollar

doler [do'ler] *vt, vi* to hurt; (*fig*) to grieve; **dolerse** *vr* (*de su situación*) to grieve, feel sorry; (*de las desgracias ajenas*) to sympathize; **me duele el brazo** my arm hurts

dolor [do'lor] *nm* pain; (*fig*) grief, sorrow; **dolor de cabeza/estómago/ muelas** headache/stomachache/ toothache

domar [do'mar] *vt* to tame

domesticar [domesti'kar] *vt* = **domar**

doméstico, -a [do'mestiko, a] *adj* (*vida, servicio*) home; (*tareas*) household; (*animal*) tame, pet

domicilio [domi'θiljo] *nm* home; **servicio a ~** home delivery service; **sin ~ fijo** of no fixed abode; **domicilio particular** private residence

dominante [domi'nante] *adj* dominant; (*persona*) domineering

dominar [domi'nar] *vt* (*gen*) to dominate; (*idiomas*) to be fluent in ▷ *vi* to dominate, prevail

domingo [do'mingo] *nm* Sunday; **Domingo de Ramos/Resurrección** Palm/Easter Sunday

dominio [do'minjo] *nm* (*tierras*) domain; (*autoridad*) power, authority; (*de las pasiones*) grip, hold; (*de idiomas*) command

don [don] *nm* (*talento*) gift; **~ Juan Gómez** Mr Juan Gómez, Juan Gómez Esq (BRIT)

DON/DOÑA

The term **don/doña** often abbreviated to **D./Dña** is placed before the first name as a mark of respect to an older or more senior person – eg Don Diego, Doña Inés. Although becoming rarer in Spain it is still used with names and surnames on official documents and formal correspondence – eg "Sr. D. Pedro Rodríguez Hernández", "Sra. Dña. Inés Rodríguez Hernández".

dona ['dona] (MÉX) *nf* doughnut, donut (US)

donar [do'nar] *vt* to donate

donativo [dona'tiβo] *nm* donation

donde ['donde] *adv* where ▷ *prep*: **el coche está allí ~ el farol** the car is over there by the lamppost *o* where the lamppost is; **en ~** where, in which

dónde ['donde] *adv* where?; **¿a ~ vas?** where are you going (to)?; **¿de ~ vienes?** where have you been?; **¿por ~?** where?, whereabouts?

dondequiera [donde'kjera] *adv* anywhere; **por ~** everywhere, all over

the place ▷ *conj*: **~ que** wherever
donut® [do'nut] (*ESP*) *nm* doughnut, donut (*US*)
doña ['doɲa] *nf*: **~ Alicia** Alicia; **~ Victoria Benito** Mrs Victoria Benito
dorado, -a [do'raðo, a] *adj* (*color*) golden; (*Tec*) gilt
dormir [dor'mir] *vt*: **~ la siesta** to have an afternoon nap ▷ *vi* to sleep; **dormirse** *vr* to fall asleep
dormitorio [dormi'torjo] *nm* bedroom
dorsal [dor'sal] *nm* (*Deporte*) number
dorso ['dorso] *nm* (*de mano*) back; (*de hoja*) other side
dos [dos] *num* two
dosis ['dosis] *nf inv* dose, dosage
dotado, -a [do'taðo, a] *adj* gifted; **~ de** endowed with
dotar [do'tar] *vt* to endow; **dote** *nf* dowry; **dotes** *nfpl* (*talentos*) gifts
doy [doj] *vb V* **dar**
drama ['drama] *nm* drama; **dramaturgo** [drama'turɣo] *nm* dramatist, playwright
drástico, -a ['drastiko, a] *adj* drastic
drenaje [dre'naxe] *nm* drainage
droga ['droɣa] *nf* drug; **drogadicto, -a** [droɣa'ðikto, a] *nm/f* drug addict
droguería [droɣe'ria] *nf* hardware shop (*BRIT*) *o* store (*US*)
ducha ['dutʃa] *nf* (*baño*) shower; (*Med*) douche; **ducharse** *vr* to take a shower
duda ['duða] *nf* doubt; **no cabe ~** there is no doubt about it; **dudar** *vt, vi* to doubt; **dudoso, -a** [du'ðoso, a] *adj* (*incierto*) hesitant; (*sospechoso*) doubtful
duela *etc vb V* **doler**
duelo ['dwelo] *vb V* **doler** ▷ *nm* (*combate*) duel; (*luto*) mourning
duende ['dwende] *nm* imp, goblin
dueño, -a ['dweɲo, a] *nm/f* (*propietario*) owner; (*de pensión, taberna*) landlord/lady; (*empresario*) employer
duermo *etc vb V* **dormir**
dulce ['dulθe] *adj* sweet ▷ *adv* gently, softly ▷ *nm* sweet
dulcería [dulθe'ria] (*LAM*) *nf* confectioner's (shop)
dulzura [dul'θura] *nf* sweetness; (*ternura*) gentleness
dúo ['duo] *nm* duet
duplicar [dupli'kar] *vt* (*hacer el doble de*) to duplicate
duque ['duke] *nm* duke; **duquesa** *nf* duchess
duración [dura'θjon] *nf* (*de película, disco etc*) length; (*de pila etc*) life; (*curso: de acontecimientos etc*) duration
duradero, -a [dura'ðero, a] *adj* (*tela etc*) hard-wearing; (*fe, paz*) lasting
durante [du'rante] *prep* during
durar [du'rar] *vi* to last; (*recuerdo*) to remain
durazno [du'raθno] (*LAM*) *nm* (*fruta*) peach; (*árbol*) peach tree
durex ['dureks] (*MÉX, ARG*) *nm* (*tira adhesiva*) Sellotape® (*BRIT*), Scotch tape® (*US*)
dureza [du'reθa] *nf* (*calidad*) hardness
duro, -a ['duro, a] *adj* hard; (*carácter*) tough ▷ *adv* hard ▷ *nm* (*moneda*) five-peseta coin *o* piece
DVD *nm abr* (= *disco de vídeo digital*) DVD

E *abr* (= *este*) E
e [e] *conj* and
ébano ['eβano] *nm* ebony
ebrio, -a ['eβrjo, a] *adj* drunk
ebullición [eβuʎi'θjon] *nf* boiling
echar [e'tʃar] *vt* to throw; (*agua, vino*) to pour (out); (*empleado: despedir*) to fire, sack; (*hojas*) to sprout; (*cartas*) to post; (*humo*) to emit, give out ▷ *vi*: **~ a correr** to run off; **echarse** *vr* to lie down; **~ llave a** to lock (up); **~ abajo** (*gobierno*) to overthrow; (*edificio*) to demolish; **~ mano a** to lay hands on; **~ una mano a algn** (*ayudar*) to give sb a hand; **~ de menos** to miss; **~se atrás** (*fig*) to back out
eclesiástico, -a [ekle'sjastiko, a] *adj* ecclesiastical
eco ['eko] *nm* echo; **tener ~** to catch on
ecología [ekolo'ɣia] *nf* ecology; **ecológico, -a** *adj* (*producto, método*) environmentally-friendly; (*agricultura*) organic; **ecologista** *adj* ecological, environmental ▷ *nmf* environmentalist
economía [ekono'mia] *nf* (*sistema*) economy; (*carrera*) economics
económico, -a [eko'nomiko, a] *adj* (*barato*) cheap, economical; (*ahorrativo*) thrifty; (*Com: año etc*) financial; (*: situación*) economic
economista [ekono'mista] *nmf* economist
Ecuador [ekwa'ðor] *nm* Ecuador; **ecuador** *nm* (*Geo*) equator
ecuatoriano, -a [ekwato'rjano, a] *adj, nm/f* Ecuadorian
ecuestre [e'kwestre] *adj* equestrian
edad [e'ðað] *nf* age; **¿qué ~ tienes?** how old are you?; **tiene ocho años de ~** he's eight (years old); **de ~ mediana/avanzada** middle-aged/advanced in years; **la E~ Media** the Middle Ages
edición [eði'θjon] *nf* (*acto*) publication; (*ejemplar*) edition
edificar [edifi'kar] *vt, vi* to build
edificio [eði'fiθjo] *nm* building; (*fig*) edifice, structure
Edimburgo [eðim'burɣo] *nm* Edinburgh
editar [eði'tar] *vt* (*publicar*) to publish; (*preparar textos*) to edit
editor, a [eði'tor, a] *nm/f* (*que publica*) publisher; (*redactor*) editor ▷ *adj* publishing *cpd*; **editorial** *adj* editorial ▷ *nm* leading article, editorial; **casa editorial** publisher
edredón [eðre'ðon] *nm* duvet
educación [eðuka'θjon] *nf* education; (*crianza*) upbringing; (*modales*) (good) manners *pl*
educado, -a [eðu'kaðo, a] *adj*: **bien/mal ~** well/badly behaved
educar [eðu'kar] *vt* to educate; (*criar*) to bring up; (*voz*) to train
EE. UU. *nmpl abr* (= *Estados Unidos*) US(A)
efectivamente [efectiβa'mente] *adv* (*como respuesta*) exactly, precisely; (*verdaderamente*) really; (*de hecho*) in fact
efectivo, -a [efek'tiβo, a] *adj* effective; (*real*) actual, real ▷ *nm*: **pagar**

en ~ to pay (in) cash; **hacer ~ un cheque** to cash a cheque

efecto [e'fekto] *nm* effect, result; **efectos** *nmpl* (*efectos personales*) effects; (*bienes*) goods; (*Com*) assets; **en ~** in fact; (*respuesta*) exactly, indeed; **efecto invernadero** greenhouse effect; **efectos especiales/ secundarios/sonoros** special/side/ sound effects

efectuar [efek'twar] *vt* to carry out; (*viaje*) to make

eficacia [efi'kaθja] *nf* (*de persona*) efficiency; (*de medicamento etc*) effectiveness

eficaz [efi'kaθ] *adj* (*persona*) efficient; (*acción*) effective

eficiente [efi'θjente] *adj* efficient

egipcio, -a [e'xipθjo, a] *adj, nm/f* Egyptian

Egipto [e'xipto] *nm* Egypt

egoísmo [eɣo'ismo] *nm* egoism

egoísta [eɣo'ista] *adj* egoistical, selfish ▷ *nmf* egoist

Eire ['eire] *nm* Eire

ej. *abr* (= *ejemplo*) eg

eje ['exe] *nm* (*Geo, Mat*) axis; (*de rueda*) axle; (*de máquina*) shaft, spindle

ejecución [exeku'θjon] *nf* execution; (*cumplimiento*) fulfilment; (*Mús*) performance; (*Jur*: *embargo de deudor*) attachment

ejecutar [exeku'tar] *vt* to execute, carry out; (*matar*) to execute; (*cumplir*) to fulfil; (*Mús*) to perform; (*Jur*: *embargar*) to attach, distrain (on)

ejecutivo, -a [exeku'tiβo, a] *adj* executive; **el (poder) ~** the executive (power)

ejemplar [exem'plar] *adj* exemplary ▷ *nm* example; (*Zool*) specimen; (*de libro*) copy; (*de periódico*) number, issue

ejemplo [e'xemplo] *nm* example; **por ~** for example

ejercer [exer'θer] *vt* to exercise; (*influencia*) to exert; (*un oficio*) to practise ▷ *vi* (*practicar*): **~ (de)** to practise (as)

ejercicio [exer'θiθjo] *nm* exercise; (*período*) tenure; **hacer ~** to take exercise; **ejercicio comercial** financial year

ejército [e'xerθito] *nm* army; **entrar en el ~** to join the army, join up; **ejército del aire/de tierra** Air Force/Army

ejote [e'xote] (*MÉX*) *nm* green bean

○ **PALABRA CLAVE**

el [el] (*f* **la**, *pl* **los, las,** *neutro* **lo**) *art def* **1** the; **el libro/la mesa/los estudiantes** the book/table/students
2 (*con n abstracto: no se traduce*): **el amor/la juventud** love/youth
3 (*posesión: se traduce a menudo por adj posesivo*): **romperse el brazo** to break one's arm; **levantó la mano** he put his hand up; **se puso el sombrero** she put her hat on
4 (*valor descriptivo*): **tener la boca grande/los ojos azules** to have a big mouth/blue eyes
5 (*con días*) on; **me iré el viernes** I'll leave on Friday; **los domingos suelo ir a nadar** on Sundays I generally go swimming
6 (*lo +adj*): **lo difícil/caro** what is difficult/expensive; (*cuán*): **no se da cuenta de lo pesado que es** he doesn't realise how boring he is
▷ *pron demos* **1**: **mi libro y el de usted** my book and yours; **las de Pepe son mejores** Pepe's are better; **no la(s) blanca(s) sino la(s) gris(es)** not the white one(s) but the grey one(s)
2: **lo de: lo de ayer** what happened yesterday; **lo de las facturas** that business about the invoices
▷ *pron relativo* **1** (*indef*): **el que: el (los) que quiera(n) que se vaya(n)** anyone who wants to can leave; **llévese el que más le guste** take the one you like best
2 (*def*): **el que: el que compré ayer** the one I bought yesterday; **los que se van** those who leave

3: **lo que: lo que pienso yo/más me gusta** what I think/like most
▷ *conj*: **el que: el que lo diga** the fact that he says so; **el que sea tan vago me molesta** his being so lazy bothers me
▷ *excl*: **¡el susto que me diste!** what a fright you gave me!
▷ *pron personal* **1** (*persona*: *m*) him; (: *f*) her; (: *pl*) them; **lo/las veo** I can see him/them
2 (*animal, cosa*: *sg*) it; (: *pl*) them; **lo** (*o* **la) veo** I can see it; **los** (*o* **las) veo** I can see them
3 (*como sustituto de frase*): **lo: no lo sabía** I didn't know; **ya lo entiendo** I understand now

él [el] *pron* (*persona*) he; (*cosa*) it; (*después de prep*: *persona*) him; (: *cosa*) it; **de ~** his
elaborar [elaβo'rar] *vt* (*producto*) to make, manufacture; (*preparar*) to prepare; (*madera, metal etc*) to work; (*proyecto etc*) to work on *o* out
elástico, -a [e'lastiko, a] *adj* elastic; (*flexible*) flexible ▷ *nm* elastic; (*un elástico*) elastic band
elección [elek'θjon] *nf* election; (*selección*) choice, selection; **elecciones generales** general election *sg*
electorado [elekto'raðo] *nm* electorate, voters *pl*
electricidad [elektriθi'ðað] *nf* electricity
electricista [elektri'θista] *nmf* electrician
eléctrico, -a [e'lektriko, a] *adj* electric
electro... [elektro] *prefijo* electro...; **electrocardiograma** *nm* electrocardiogram; **electrocutar** *vt* to electrocute; **electrodo** *nm* electrode; **electrodomésticos** *nmpl* (electrical) household appliances
electrónica [elek'tronika] *nf* electronics *sg*
electrónico, -a [elek'troniko, a] *adj* electronic
elefante [ele'fante] *nm* elephant
elegancia [ele'ɣanθja] *nf* elegance, grace; (*estilo*) stylishness
elegante [ele'ɣante] *adj* elegant, graceful; (*estiloso*) stylish, fashionable
elegir [ele'xir] *vt* (*escoger*) to choose, select; (*optar*) to opt for; (*presidente*) to elect
elemental [elemen'tal] *adj* (*claro, obvio*) elementary; (*fundamental*) elemental, fundamental
elemento [ele'mento] *nm* element; (*fig*) ingredient; **elementos** *nmpl* elements, rudiments
elevación [eleβa'θjon] *nf* elevation; (*acto*) raising, lifting; (*de precios*) rise; (*Geo etc*) height, altitude
elevar [ele'βar] *vt* to raise, lift (up); (*precio*) to put up; **elevarse** *vr* (*edificio*) to rise; (*precios*) to go up
eligiendo *etc vb V* **elegir**
elija *etc vb V* **elegir**
eliminar [elimi'nar] *vt* to eliminate, remove
eliminatoria [elimina'torja] *nf* heat, preliminary (round)
élite ['elite] *nf* elite
ella ['eʎa] *pron* (*persona*) she; (*cosa*) it; (*después de prep*: *persona*) her; (: *cosa*) it; **de ~** hers
ellas ['eʎas] *pron* (*personas y cosas*) they; (*después de prep*) them; **de ~** theirs
ello ['eʎo] *pron* it
ellos ['eʎos] *pron* they; (*después de prep*) them; **de ~** theirs
elogiar [elo'xjar] *vt* to praise; **elogio** *nm* praise
elote [e'lote] (*MÉX*) *nm* corn on the cob
eludir [elu'ðir] *vt* to avoid
email [i'mel] *nm* email; (*dirección*) email address; **mandar un ~ a algn** to email sb, send sb an email
embajada [emba'xaða] *nf* embassy
embajador, a [embaxa'ðor, a] *nm/f* ambassador/ambassadress
embalar [emba'lar] *vt* to parcel, wrap (up); **embalarse** *vr* to go fast

embalse [em'balse] *nm* (*presa*) dam; (*lago*) reservoir

embarazada [embara'θaða] *adj* pregnant ▷ *nf* pregnant woman

No confundir **embarazada** con la palabra inglesa *embarrassed*.

embarazo [emba'raθo] *nm* (*de mujer*) pregnancy; (*impedimento*) obstacle, obstruction; (*timidez*) embarrassment; **embarazoso, -a** *adj* awkward, embarrassing

embarcación [embarka'θjon] *nf* (*barco*) boat, craft; (*acto*) embarkation, boarding

embarcadero [embarka'ðero] *nm* pier, landing stage

embarcar [embar'kar] *vt* (*cargamento*) to ship, stow; (*persona*) to embark, put on board; **embarcarse** *vr* to embark, go on board

embargar [embar'ɣar] *vt* (*Jur*) to seize, impound

embargo [em'barɣo] *nm* (*Jur*) seizure; (*Com, Pol*) embargo

embargue *etc vb V* **embargar**

embarque *etc* [em'barke] *vb V* **embarcar** ▷ *nm* shipment, loading

embellecer [embeʎe'θer] *vt* to embellish, beautify

embestida [embes'tiða] *nf* attack, onslaught; (*carga*) charge

embestir [embes'tir] *vt* to attack, assault; to charge, attack ▷ *vi* to attack

emblema [em'blema] *nm* emblem

embobado, -a [embo'βaðo, a] *adj* (*atontado*) stunned, bewildered

embolia [em'bolja] *nf* (*Med*) clot

émbolo ['embolo] *nm* (*Auto*) piston

emborrachar [emborra'tʃar] *vt* to make drunk, intoxicate; **emborracharse** *vr* to get drunk

emboscada [embos'kaða] *nf* ambush

embotar [embo'tar] *vt* to blunt, dull

embotellamiento [emboteʎa'mjento] *nm* (*Auto*) traffic jam

embotellar [embote'ʎar] *vt* to bottle

embrague [em'braɣe] *nm* (*tb*: **pedal de ~**) clutch

embrión [em'brjon] *nm* embryo

embrollo [em'broʎo] *nm* (*enredo*) muddle, confusion; (*aprieto*) fix, jam

embrujado, -a [embru'xado, a] *adj* bewitched; **casa embrujada** haunted house

embrutecer [embrute'θer] *vt* (*atontar*) to stupefy

embudo [em'buðo] *nm* funnel

embuste [em'buste] *nm* (*mentira*) lie; **embustero, -a** *adj* lying, deceitful ▷ *nm/f* (*mentiroso*) liar

embutido [embu'tiðo] *nm* (*Culin*) sausage; (*Tec*) inlay

emergencia [emer'xenθja] *nf* emergency; (*surgimiento*) emergence

emerger [emer'ɣer] *vi* to emerge, appear

emigración [emiɣra'θjon] *nf* emigration; (*de pájaros*) migration

emigrar [emi'ɣrar] *vi* (*personas*) to emigrate; (*pájaros*) to migrate

eminente [emi'nente] *adj* eminent, distinguished; (*elevado*) high

emisión [emi'sjon] *nf* (*acto*) emission; (*Com etc*) issue; (*Radio, TV*: *acto*) broadcasting; (: *programa*) broadcast, programme (BRIT), program (US)

emisora [emi'sora] *nf* radio *o* broadcasting station

emitir [emi'tir] *vt* (*olor etc*) to emit, give off; (*moneda etc*) to issue; (*opinión*) to express; (*Radio*) to broadcast

emoción [emo'θjon] *nf* emotion; (*excitación*) excitement; (*sentimiento*) feeling

emocionante [emoθjo'nante] *adj* (*excitante*) exciting, thrilling

emocionar [emoθjo'nar] *vt* (*excitar*) to excite, thrill; (*conmover*) to move, touch; (*impresionar*) to impress

emoticón [emoti'kon], **emoticono** [emoti'kono] *nm* smiley

emotivo, -a [emo'tiβo, a] *adj* emotional

empacho [em'patʃo] *nm* (*Med*) indigestion; (*fig*) embarrassment

empalagoso, -a [empala'ɣoso, a] *adj* cloying; (*fig*) tiresome

empalmar [empal'mar] *vt* to join, connect ▷ *vi* (*dos caminos*) to meet, join; **empalme** *nm* joint, connection; junction; (*de trenes*) connection

empanada [empa'naða] *nf* pie, pasty

empañarse [empa'ɲarse] *vr* (*cristales etc*) to steam up

empapar [empa'par] *vt* (*mojar*) to soak, saturate; (*absorber*) to soak up, absorb; **empaparse** *vr*: **~se de** to soak up

empapelar [empape'lar] *vt* (*paredes*) to paper

empaquetar [empake'tar] *vt* to pack, parcel up

empastar [empas'tar] *vt* (*embadurnar*) to paste; (*diente*) to fill

empaste [em'paste] *nm* (*de diente*) filling

empatar [empa'tar] *vi* to draw, tie; **~on a dos** they drew two-all; **empate** *nm* draw, tie

empecé *etc vb V* **empezar**

empedernido, -a [empeðer'niðo, a] *adj* hard, heartless; (*fumador*) inveterate

empeine [em'peine] *nm* (*de pie, zapato*) instep

empeñado, -a [empe'ɲaðo, a] *adj* (*persona*) determined; (*objeto*) pawned

empeñar [empe'ɲar] *vt* (*objeto*) to pawn, pledge; (*persona*) to compel; **empeñarse** *vr* (*endeudarse*) to get into debt; **~se en** to be set on, be determined to

empeño [em'peɲo] *nm* (*determinación, insistencia*) determination, insistence; **casa de ~s** pawnshop

empeorar [empeo'rar] *vt* to make worse, worsen ▷ *vi* to get worse, deteriorate

empezar [empe'θar] *vt, vi* to begin, start

empiece *etc vb V* **empezar**

empiezo *etc vb V* **empezar**

emplasto [em'plasto] *nm* (*Med*) plaster

emplazar [empla'θar] *vt* (*ubicar*) to site, place, locate; (*Jur*) to summons; (*convocar*) to summon

empleado, -a [emple'aðo, a] *nm/f* (*gen*) employee; (*de banco etc*) clerk

emplear [emple'ar] *vt* (*usar*) to use, employ; (*dar trabajo a*) to employ; **emplearse** *vr* (*conseguir trabajo*) to be employed; (*ocuparse*) to occupy o.s.

empleo [em'pleo] *nm* (*puesto*) job; (*puestos: colectivamente*) employment; (*uso*) use, employment

empollar [empo'ʎar] (ESP: *fam*) *vt, vi* to swot (up); **empollón, -ona** (ESP: *fam*) *nm/f* swot

emporio [em'porjo] (LAM) *nm* (*gran almacén*) department store

empotrado, -a [empo'traðo, a] *adj* (*armario etc*) built-in

emprender [empren'der] *vt* (*empezar*) to begin, embark on; (*acometer*) to tackle, take on

empresa [em'presa] *nf* (*de espíritu etc*) enterprise; (*Com*) company, firm; **empresariales** *nfpl* business studies; **empresario, -a** *nm/f* (*Com*) businessman(-woman)

empujar [empu'xar] *vt* to push, shove

empujón [empu'xon] *nm* push, shove

empuñar [empu'ɲar] *vt* (*asir*) to grasp, take (firm) hold of

○ PALABRA CLAVE

en [en] *prep* **1** (*posición*) in; (*: sobre*) on; **está en el cajón** it's in the drawer; **en Argentina/La Paz** in Argentina/La Paz; **en la oficina/el colegio** at the office/school; **está en el suelo/quinto piso** it's on the floor/the fifth floor

2 (*dirección*) into; **entró en el aula** she

went into the classroom; **meter algo en el bolso** to put sth into one's bag
3 (*tiempo*) in; on; **en 1605/3 semanas/ invierno** in 1605/3 weeks/winter; **en (el mes de) enero** in (the month of) January; **en aquella ocasión/época** on that occasion/at that time
4 (*precio*) for; **lo vendió en 20 dólares** he sold it for 20 dollars
5 (*diferencia*) by; **reducir/aumentar en una tercera parte/un 20 por ciento** to reduce/increase by a third/20 per cent
6 (*manera*): **en avión/autobús** by plane/bus; **escrito en inglés** written in English
7 (*después de vb que indica gastar etc*) on; **han cobrado demasiado en dietas** they've charged too much to expenses; **se le va la mitad del sueldo en comida** he spends half his salary on food
8 (*tema, ocupación*): **experto en la materia** expert on the subject; **trabaja en la construcción** he works in the building industry
9 (*adj + en + infin*): **lento en reaccionar** slow to react

enaguas [e'naɣwas] *nfpl* petticoat *sg*, underskirt *sg*
enajenación [enaxena'θjon] *nf* (*Psico*: *tb*: **~ mental**) mental derangement
enamorado, -a [enamo'raðo, a] *adj* in love ▷ *nm/f* lover; **estar ~ (de)** to be in love (with)
enamorar [enamo'rar] *vt* to win the love of; **enamorarse** *vr*: **~se de algn** to fall in love with sb
enano, -a [e'nano, a] *adj* tiny ▷ *nm/f* dwarf
encabezamiento [enkaβeθa'mjento] *nm* (*de carta*) heading; (*de periódico*) headline
encabezar [enkaβe'θar] *vt* (*movimiento, revolución*) to lead, head; (*lista*) to head, be at the top of; (*carta*) to put a heading to
encadenar [enkaðe'nar] *vt* to chain (together); (*poner grilletes a*) to shackle
encajar [enka'xar] *vt* (*ajustar*): **~ (en)** to fit (into); (*fam*: *golpe*) to take ▷ *vi* to fit (well); (*fig*: *corresponder a*) to match
encaje [en'kaxe] *nm* (*labor*) lace
encallar [enka'ʎar] *vi* (*Náut*) to run aground
encaminar [enkami'nar] *vt* to direct, send
encantado, -a [enkan'taðo, a] *adj* (*hechizado*) bewitched; (*muy contento*) delighted; **¡~!** how do you do, pleased to meet you
encantador, a [enkanta'ðor, a] *adj* charming, lovely ▷ *nm/f* magician, enchanter/enchantress
encantar [enkan'tar] *vt* (*agradar*) to charm, delight; (*hechizar*) to bewitch, cast a spell on; **me encanta eso** I love that; **encanto** *nm* (*hechizo*) spell, charm; (*fig*) charm, delight
encarcelar [enkarθe'lar] *vt* to imprison, jail
encarecer [enkare'θer] *vt* to put up the price of; **encarecerse** *vr* to get dearer
encargado, -a [enkar'ɣaðo, a] *adj* in charge ▷ *nm/f* agent, representative; (*responsable*) person in charge
encargar [enkar'ɣar] *vt* to entrust; (*recomendar*) to urge, recommend; **encargarse** *vr*: **~se de** to look after, take charge of; **~ algo a algn** to put sb in charge of sth; **~ a algn que haga algo** to ask sb to do sth
encargo [en'karɣo] *nm* (*tarea*) assignment, job; (*responsabilidad*) responsibility; (*Com*) order
encariñarse [enkari'ɲarse] *vr*: **~ con** to grow fond of, get attached to
encarnación [enkarna'θjon] *nf* incarnation, embodiment
encarrilar [enkarri'lar] *vt* (*tren*) to put back on the rails; (*fig*) to correct, put on the right track

encasillar [enkasi'ʎar] *vt* (*fig*) to pigeonhole; (*actor*) to typecast
encendedor [enθende'ðor] *nm* lighter
encender [enθen'der] *vt* (*con fuego*) to light; (*luz, radio*) to put on, switch on; (*avivar: pasión*) to inflame; **encenderse** *vr* to catch fire; (*excitarse*) to get excited; (*de cólera*) to flare up; (*el rostro*) to blush
encendido [enθen'diðo] *nm* (*Auto*) ignition
encerado [enθe'raðo] *nm* (*Escol*) blackboard
encerrar [enθe'rrar] *vt* (*confinar*) to shut in, shut up; (*comprender, incluir*) to include, contain
encharcado, -a [entʃar'kaðo, a] *adj* (*terreno*) flooded
encharcarse [entʃar'karse] *vr* to get flooded
enchufado, -a [entʃu'faðo, a] (*fam*) *nm/f* well-connected person
enchufar [entʃu'far] *vt* (*Elec*) to plug in; (*Tec*) to connect, fit together; **enchufe** *nm* (*Elec: clavija*) plug; (*: toma*) socket; (*do dos tubos*) joint, connection; (*fam: influencia*) contact, connection; (*: puesto*) cushy job
encía [en'θia] *nf* gum
encienda *etc vb V* **encender**
encierro *etc* [en'θjerro] *vb V* **encerrar** ▷ *nm* shutting in, shutting up; (*calabozo*) prison
encima [en'θima] *adv* (*sobre*) above, over; (*además*) besides; **~ de** (*en*) on, on top of; (*sobre*) above, over; (*además de*) besides, on top of; **por ~ de** over; **¿llevas dinero ~?** have you (got) any money on you?; **se me vino ~** it took me by surprise
encina [en'θina] *nf* holm oak
encinta [en'θinta] *adj* pregnant
enclenque [en'klenke] *adj* weak, sickly
encoger [enko'xer] *vt* to shrink, contract; **encogerse** *vr* to shrink, contract; (*fig*) to cringe; **~se de hombros** to shrug one's shoulders
encomendar [enkomen'dar] *vt* to entrust, commend; **encomendarse** *vr*: **~se a** to put one's trust in
encomienda *etc* [enko'mjenda] *vb V* **encomendar** ▷ *nf* (*encargo*) charge, commission; (*elogio*) tribute; **encomienda postal** (LAM) package
encontrar [enkon'trar] *vt* (*hallar*) to find; (*inesperadamente*) to meet, run into; **encontrarse** *vr* to meet (each other); (*situarse*) to be (situated); **~se con** to meet; **~se bien (de salud)** to feel well
encrucijada [enkruθi'xaða] *nf* crossroads *sg*
encuadernación [enkwaðerna'θjon] *nf* binding
encuadrar [enkwa'ðrar] *vt* (*retrato*) to frame; (*ajustar*) to fit, insert; (*contener*) to contain
encubrir [enku'βrir] *vt* (*ocultar*) to hide, conceal; (*criminal*) to harbour, shelter
encuentro *etc* [en'kwentro] *vb V* **encontrar** ▷ *nm* (*de personas*) meeting; (*Auto etc*) collision, crash; (*Deporte*) match, game; (*Mil*) encounter
encuerado, -a (MÉX) [enkwe'raðo, a] *adj* nude, naked
encuesta [en'kwesta] *nf* inquiry, investigation; (*sondeo*) (public) opinion poll
encumbrar [enkum'brar] *vt* (*persona*) to exalt
endeble [en'deβle] *adj* (*persona*) weak; (*argumento, excusa, persona*) weak
endemoniado, -a [endemo'njaðo, a] *adj* possessed (of the devil); (*travieso*) devilish
enderezar [endere'θar] *vt* (*poner derecho*) to straighten (out); (*: verticalmente*) to set upright; (*situación*) to straighten *o* sort out; (*dirigir*) to direct; **enderezarse** *vr* (*persona sentada*) to straighten up
endeudarse [endeu'ðarse] *vr* to get into debt

endiablado, -a [endja'βlaðo, a] *adj* devilish, diabolical; (*travieso*) mischievous

endilgar [endil'ɣar] (*fam*) *vt*: **~le algo a algn** to lumber sb with sth

endiñar [endi'ɲar] (*ESP*: *fam*) *vt* (*boféton*) to land, belt

endosar [endo'sar] *vt* (*cheque etc*) to endorse

endulzar [endul'θar] *vt* to sweeten; (*suavizar*) to soften

endurecer [endure'θer] *vt* to harden; **endurecerse** *vr* to harden, grow hard

enema [e'nema] *nm* (*Med*) enema

enemigo, -a [ene'miɣo, a] *adj* enemy, hostile ▷ *nm/f* enemy

enemistad [enemis'tað] *nf* enmity

enemistar [enemis'tar] *vt* to make enemies of, cause a rift between; **enemistarse** *vr* to become enemies; (*amigos*) to fall out

energía [ener'xia] *nf* (*vigor*) energy, drive; (*empuje*) push; (*Tec, Elec*) energy, power; **energía eólica** wind power; **energía solar** solar energy *o* power

enérgico, -a [e'nerxiko, a] *adj* (*gen*) energetic; (*voz, modales*) forceful

energúmeno, -a [ener'ɣumeno, a] (*fam*) *nm/f* (*fig*) madman(-woman)

enero [e'nero] *nm* January

enfadado, -a [enfa'ðaðo, a] *adj* angry, annoyed

enfadar [enfa'ðar] *vt* to anger, annoy; **enfadarse** *vr* to get angry *o* annoyed

enfado [en'faðo] *nm* (*enojo*) anger, annoyance; (*disgusto*) trouble, bother

énfasis ['enfasis] *nm* emphasis, stress

enfático, -a [en'fatiko, a] *adj* emphatic

enfermar [enfer'mar] *vt* to make ill ▷ *vi* to fall ill, be taken ill

enfermedad [enferme'ðað] *nf* illness; **enfermedad venérea** venereal disease

enfermera [enfer'mera] *nf* nurse

enfermería [enferme'ria] *nf* infirmary; (*de colegio etc*) sick bay

enfermero [enfer'mero] *nm* (male) nurse

enfermizo, -a [enfer'miθo, a] *adj* (*persona*) sickly, unhealthy; (*fig*) unhealthy

enfermo, -a [en'fermo, a] *adj* ill, sick ▷ *nm/f* invalid, sick person; (*en hospital*) patient; **caer** *o* **ponerse ~** to fall ill

enfocar [enfo'kar] *vt* (*foto etc*) to focus; (*problema etc*) to approach

enfoque *etc* [en'foke] *vb V* **enfocar** ▷ *nm* focus

enfrentar [enfren'tar] *vt* (*peligro*) to face (up to), confront; (*oponer*) to bring face to face; **enfrentarse** *vr* (*dos personas*) to face *o* confront each other; (*Deporte*: *dos equipos*) to meet; **~se a** *o* **con** to face up to, confront

enfrente [en'frente] *adv* opposite; **la casa de ~** the house opposite, the house across the street; **~ de** opposite, facing

enfriamiento [enfria'mjento] *nm* chilling, refrigeration; (*Med*) cold, chill

enfriar [enfri'ar] *vt* (*alimentos*) to cool, chill; (*algo caliente*) to cool down; **enfriarse** *vr* to cool down; (*Med*) to catch a chill; (*amistad*) to cool

enfurecer [enfure'θer] *vt* to enrage, madden; **enfurecerse** *vr* to become furious, fly into a rage; (*mar*) to get rough

enganchar [engan'tʃar] *vt* to hook; (*dos vagones*) to hitch up; (*Tec*) to couple, connect; (*Mil*) to recruit; **engancharse** *vr* (*Mil*) to enlist, join up

enganche [en'gantʃe] *nm* hook; (*ESP Tec*) coupling, connection; (*acto*) hooking (up); (*Mil*) recruitment, enlistment; (*MÉX*: *depósito*) deposit

engañar [enga'ɲar] *vt* to deceive; (*estafar*) to cheat, swindle; **engañarse** *vr* (*equivocarse*) to be wrong; (*disimular la verdad*) to deceive o.s.

engaño [en'gaɲo] *nm* deceit;

(*estafa*) trick, swindle; (*error*) mistake, misunderstanding; (*ilusión*) delusion; **engañoso, -a** *adj* (*tramposo*) crooked; (*mentiroso*) dishonest, deceitful; (*aspecto*) deceptive; (*consejo*) misleading

engatusar [engatu'sar] (*fam*) *vt* to coax

engendro [en'xendro] *nm* (*Bio*) foetus; (*fig*) monstrosity

englobar [englo'βar] *vt* to include, comprise

engordar [engor'ðar] *vt* to fatten ▷*vi* to get fat, put on weight

engorroso, -a [engo'rroso, a] *adj* bothersome, trying

engranaje [engra'naxe] *nm* (*Auto*) gear

engrasar [engra'sar] *vt* (*Tec: poner grasa*) to grease; (*: lubricar*) to lubricate, oil; (*manchar*) to make greasy

engreído, -a [engre'iðo, a] *adj* vain, conceited

enhebrar [ene'βrar] *vt* to thread

enhorabuena [enora'βwena] *excl*: **¡~!** congratulations! ▷*nf*: **dar la ~ a** to congratulate

enigma [e'niɣma] *nm* enigma; (*problema*) puzzle; (*misterio*) mystery

enjambre [en'xambre] *nm* swarm

enjaular [enxau'lar] *vt* to (put in a) cage; (*fam*) to jail, lock up

enjuagar [enxwa'ɣar] *vt* (*ropa*) to rinse (out)

enjuague *etc* [en'xwaɣe] *vb V* **enjuagar** ▷*nm* (*Med*) mouthwash; (*de ropa*) rinse, rinsing

enlace [en'laθe] *nm* link, connection; (*relación*) relationship; (*tb*: **~ matrimonial**) marriage; (*de carretera, trenes*) connection; **enlace sindical** shop steward

enlatado, -a [enla'taðo, a] *adj* (*alimentos, productos*) tinned, canned

enlazar [enla'θar] *vt* (*unir con lazos*) to bind together; (*atar*) to tie; (*conectar*) to link, connect; (*LAM: caballo*) to lasso

enloquecer [enloke'θer] *vt* to drive mad ▷*vi* to go mad

enmarañar [enmara'ɲar] *vt* (*enredar*) to tangle (up), entangle; (*complicar*) to complicate; (*confundir*) to confuse

enmarcar [enmar'kar] *vt* (*cuadro*) to frame

enmascarar [enmaska'rar] *vt* to mask; **enmascararse** *vr* to put on a mask

enmendar [enmen'dar] *vt* to emend, correct; (*constitución etc*) to amend; (*comportamiento*) to reform; **enmendarse** *vr* to reform, mend one's ways; **enmienda** *nf* correction; amendment; reform

enmudecer [enmuðe'θer] *vi* (*perder el habla*) to fall silent; (*guardar silencio*) to remain silent

ennoblecer [ennoβle'θer] *vt* to ennoble

enojado, -a [eno'xaðo, a] (*LAM*) *adj* angry

enojar [eno'xar] *vt* (*encolerizar*) to anger; (*disgustar*) to annoy, upset; **enojarse** *vr* to get angry; to get annoyed

enojo [e'noxo] *nm* (*cólera*) anger; (*irritación*) annoyance

enorme [e'norme] *adj* enormous, huge; (*fig*) monstrous

enredadera [enreða'ðera] *nf* (*Bot*) creeper, climbing plant

enredar [enre'ðar] *vt* (*cables, hilos etc*) to tangle (up), entangle; (*situación*) to complicate, confuse; (*meter cizaña*) to sow discord among *o* between; (*implicar*) to embroil, implicate; **enredarse** *vr* to get entangled, get tangled (up); (*situación*) to get complicated; (*persona*) to get embroiled; (*LAM: fam*) to meddle

enredo [en'reðo] *nm* (*maraña*) tangle; (*confusión*) mix-up, confusion; (*intriga*) intrigue

enriquecer [enrike'θer] *vt* to make rich, enrich; **enriquecerse** *vr* to get rich

enrojecer [enroxe'θer] *vt* to redden ▷ *vi* (*persona*) to blush; **enrojecerse** *vr* to blush

enrollar [enro'ʎar] *vt* to roll (up), wind (up)

ensalada [ensa'laða] *nf* salad; **ensaladilla (rusa)** *nf* Russian salad

ensanchar [ensan'tʃar] *vt* (*hacer más ancho*) to widen; (*agrandar*) to enlarge, expand; (*Costura*) to let out; **ensancharse** *vr* to get wider, expand

ensayar [ensa'jar] *vt* to test, try (out); (*Teatro*) to rehearse

ensayo [en'sajo] *nm* test, trial; (*Quím*) experiment; (*Teatro*) rehearsal; (*Deporte*) try; (*Escol, Literatura*) essay

enseguida [ense'ɣiða] *adv* at once, right away

ensenada [ense'naða] *nf* inlet, cove

enseñanza [ense'ɲanθa] *nf* (*educación*) education; (*acción*) teaching; (*doctrina*) teaching, doctrine; **enseñanza (de) primaria/secundaria** elementary/secondary education

enseñar [ense'ɲar] *vt* (*educar*) to teach; (*mostrar, señalar*) to show

enseres [en'seres] *nmpl* belongings

ensuciar [ensu'θjar] *vt* (*manchar*) to dirty, soil; (*fig*) to defile; **ensuciarse** *vr* to get dirty; (*bebé*) to dirty one's nappy

entablar [enta'βlar] *vt* (*recubrir*) to board (up); (*Ajedrez, Damas*) to set up; (*conversación*) to strike up; (*Jur*) to file ▷ *vi* to draw

ente ['ente] *nm* (*organización*) body, organization; (*fam: persona*) odd character

entender [enten'der] *vt* (*comprender*) to understand; (*darse cuenta*) to realize ▷ *vi* to understand; (*creer*) to think, believe; **entenderse** *vr* (*comprenderse*) to be understood; (*ponerse de acuerdo*) to agree, reach an agreement; **~ de** to know all about; **~ algo de** to know a little about; **~ en** to deal with, have to do with; **~ mal** to misunderstand; **~se con algn** (*llevarse bien*) to get on *o* along with sb; **~se mal** (*dos personas*) to get on badly

entendido, -a [enten'diðo, a] *adj* (*comprendido*) understood; (*hábil*) skilled; (*inteligente*) knowledgeable ▷ *nm/f* (*experto*) expert ▷ *excl* agreed!; **entendimiento** *nm* (*comprensión*) understanding; (*inteligencia*) mind, intellect; (*juicio*) judgement

enterado, -a [ente'raðo, a] *adj* well-informed; **estar ~ de** to know about, be aware of

enteramente [entera'mente] *adv* entirely, completely

enterar [ente'rar] *vt* (*informar*) to inform, tell; **enterarse** *vr* to find out, get to know

enterito [ente'rito] (RPL) *nm* boiler suit (BRIT), overalls (US)

entero, -a [en'tero, a] *adj* (*total*) whole, entire; (*fig: honesto*) honest; (*: firme*) firm, resolute ▷ *nm* (*Com: punto*) point

enterrar [ente'rrar] *vt* to bury

entidad [enti'ðað] *nf* (*empresa*) firm, company; (*organismo*) body; (*sociedad*) society; (*Filosofía*) entity

entiendo *etc vb V* **entender**

entierro [en'tjerro] *nm* (*acción*) burial; (*funeral*) funeral

entonación [entona'θjon] *nf* (*Ling*) intonation

entonar [ento'nar] *vt* (*canción*) to intone; (*colores*) to tone; (*Med*) to tone up ▷ *vi* to be in tune

entonces [en'tonθes] *adv* then, at that time; **desde ~** since then; **en aquel ~** at that time; **(pues) ~** and so

entornar [entor'nar] *vt* (*puerta, ventana*) to half-close, leave ajar; (*los ojos*) to screw up

entorpecer [entorpe'θer] *vt* (*entendimiento*) to dull; (*impedir*) to obstruct, hinder; (*: tránsito*) to slow down, delay

entrada [en'traða] *nf* (*acción*) entry, access; (*sitio*) entrance, way in; (*Inform*) input; (*Com*) receipts *pl*, takings *pl*; (*Culin*) starter; (*Deporte*) innings *sg*;

(*Teatro*) house, audience; (*billete*) ticket; **~s y salidas** (*Com*) income and expenditure; **de ~** from the outset; **entrada de aire** (*Tec*) air intake *o* inlet

entrado, -a [en'traðo, a] *adj*: **~ en años** elderly; **una vez ~ el verano** in the summer(time), when summer comes

entramparse [entram'parse] *vr* to get into debt

entrante [en'trante] *adj* next, coming; **mes/año ~** next month/year; **entrantes** *nmpl* starters

entraña [en'traɲa] *nf* (*fig: centro*) heart, core; (*raíz*) root; **entrañas** *nfpl* (*Anat*) entrails; (*fig*) heart *sg*; **entrañable** *adj* close, intimate; **entrañar** *vt* to entail

entrar [en'trar] *vt* (*introducir*) to bring in; (*Inform*) to input ▷ *vi* (*meterse*) to go in, come in, enter; (*comenzar*): **~ diciendo** to begin by saying; **hacer ~** to show in; **me entró sed/sueño** I started to feel thirsty/sleepy; **no me entra** I can't get the hang of it

entre ['entre] *prep* (*dos*) between; (*más de dos*) among(st)

entreabrir [entrea'βrir] *vt* to half-open, open halfway

entrecejo [entre'θexo] *nm*: **fruncir el ~** to frown

entredicho [entre'ðitʃo] *nm* (*Jur*) injunction; **poner en ~** to cast doubt on; **estar en ~** to be in doubt

entrega [en'treɣa] *nf* (*de mercancías*) delivery; (*de novela etc*) instalment; **entregar** [entre'ɣar] *vt* (*dar*) to hand (over), deliver; **entregarse** *vr* (*rendirse*) to surrender, give in, submit; (*dedicarse*) to devote o.s.

entremeses [entre'meses] *nmpl* hors d'œuvres

entremeter [entreme'ter] *vt* to insert, put in; **entremeterse** *vr* to meddle, interfere; **entremetido, -a** *adj* meddling, interfering

entremezclar [entremeθ'klar] *vt* to intermingle; **entremezclarse** *vr* to intermingle

entrenador, a [entrena'ðor, a] *nm/f* trainer, coach

entrenarse [entre'narse] *vr* to train

entrepierna [entre'pjerna] *nf* crotch

entresuelo [entre'swelo] *nm* mezzanine

entretanto [entre'tanto] *adv* meanwhile, meantime

entretecho [entre'tetʃo] (*cs*) *nm* attic

entretejer [entrete'xer] *vt* to interweave

entretener [entrete'ner] *vt* (*divertir*) to entertain, amuse; (*detener*) to hold up, delay; **entretenerse** *vr* (*divertirse*) to amuse o.s.; (*retrasarse*) to delay, linger; **entretenido, -a** *adj* entertaining, amusing; **entretenimiento** *nm* entertainment, amusement

entrever [entre'βer] *vt* to glimpse, catch a glimpse of

entrevista [entre'βista] *nf* interview; **entrevistar** *vt* to interview; **entrevistarse** *vr* to have an interview

entristecer [entriste'θer] *vt* to sadden, grieve; **entristecerse** *vr* to grow sad

entrometerse [entrome'terse] *vr*: **~ (en)** to interfere (in *o* with)

entumecer [entume'θer] *vt* to numb, benumb; **entumecerse** *vr* (*por el frío*) to go *o* become numb

enturbiar [entur'βjar] *vt* (*el agua*) to make cloudy; (*fig*) to confuse; **enturbiarse** *vr* (*oscurecerse*) to become cloudy; (*fig*) to get confused, become obscure

entusiasmar [entusjas'mar] *vt* to excite, fill with enthusiasm; (*gustar mucho*) to delight; **entusiasmarse** *vr*: **~se con** *o* **por** to get enthusiastic *o* excited about

entusiasmo [entu'sjasmo] *nm* enthusiasm; (*excitación*) excitement

entusiasta [entu'sjasta] *adj* enthusiastic ▷ *nmf* enthusiast
enumerar [enume'rar] *vt* to enumerate
envainar [embai'nar] *vt* to sheathe
envalentonar [embalento'nar] *vt* to give courage to; **envalentonarse** *vr* (*pey: jactarse*) to boast, brag
envasar [emba'sar] *vt* (*empaquetar*) to pack, wrap; (*enfrascar*) to bottle; (*enlatar*) to can; (*embolsar*) to pocket
envase [em'base] *nm* (*en paquete*) packing, wrapping; (*en botella*) bottling; (*en lata*) canning; (*recipiente*) container; (*paquete*) package; (*botella*) bottle; (*lata*) tin (BRIT), can
envejecer [embexe'θer] *vt* to make old, age ▷ *vi* (*volverse viejo*) to grow old; (*parecer viejo*) to age
envenenar [embene'nar] *vt* to poison; (*fig*) to embitter
envergadura [emberɣa'ðura] *nf* (*fig*) scope, compass
enviar [em'bjar] *vt* to send; **~ un mensaje a algn** (*por movil*) to text sb, to send sb a text message
enviciarse [embi'θjarse] *vr*: **~ (con)** to get addicted (to)
envidia [em'biðja] *nf* envy; **tener ~ a** to envy, be jealous of; **envidiar** *vt* to envy
envío [em'bio] *nm* (*acción*) sending; (*de mercancías*) consignment; (*de dinero*) remittance
enviudar [embju'ðar] *vi* to be widowed
envoltura [embol'tura] *nf* (*cobertura*) cover; (*embalaje*) wrapper, wrapping; **envoltorio** *nm* package
envolver [embol'βer] *vt* to wrap (up); (*cubrir*) to cover; (*enemigo*) to surround; (*implicar*) to involve, implicate
envuelto [em'bwelto] *pp de* **envolver**
enyesar [enje'sar] *vt* (*pared*) to plaster; (*Med*) to put in plaster
enzarzarse [enθar'θarse] *vr*: **~ en** (*pelea*) to get mixed up in; (*disputa*) to get involved in
épica ['epika] *nf* epic
epidemia [epi'ðemja] *nf* epidemic
epilepsia [epi'lepsja] *nf* epilepsy
episodio [epi'soðjo] *nm* episode
época ['epoka] *nf* period, time; (*Hist*) age, epoch; **hacer ~** to be epoch-making
equilibrar [ekili'βrar] *vt* to balance; **equilibrio** *nm* balance, equilibrium; **mantener/perder el equilibrio** to keep/lose one's balance; **equilibrista** *nmf* (*funámbulo*) tightrope walker; (*acróbata*) acrobat
equipaje [eki'paxe] *nm* luggage; (*avíos*): **hacer el ~** to pack; **equipaje de mano** hand luggage
equipar [eki'par] *vt* (*proveer*) to equip
equipararse [ekipa'rarse] *vr*: **~ con** to be on a level with
equipo [e'kipo] *nm* (*conjunto de cosas*) equipment; (*Deporte*) team; (*de obreros*) shift
equis ['ekis] *nf inv* (the letter) X
equitación [ekita'θjon] *nf* horse riding
equivalente [ekiβa'lente] *adj, nm* equivalent
equivaler [ekiβa'ler] *vi* to be equivalent *o* equal
equivocación [ekiβoka'θjon] *nf* mistake, error
equivocado, -a [ekiβo'kaðo, a] *adj* wrong, mistaken
equivocarse [ekiβo'karse] *vr* to be wrong, make a mistake; **~ de camino** to take the wrong road
era ['era] *vb V* **ser** ▷ *nf* era, age
erais *vb V* **ser**
éramos *vb V* **ser**
eran *vb V* **ser**
eras *vb V* **ser**
erección [erek'θjon] *nf* erection
eres *vb V* **ser**
erigir [eri'xir] *vt* to erect, build; **erigirse** *vr*: **~se en** to set o.s. up as
erizo [e'riθo] *nm* (*Zool*) hedgehog; **erizo de mar** sea-urchin

ermita [er'mita] *nf* hermitage; **ermitaño, -a** [ermi'taɲo, a] *nm/f* hermit

erosión [ero'sjon] *nf* erosion

erosionar [erosjo'nar] *vt* to erode

erótico, -a [e'rotiko, a] *adj* erotic; **erotismo** *nm* eroticism

errante [e'rrante] *adj* wandering, errant

erróneo, -a [e'rroneo, a] *adj* (*equivocado*) wrong, mistaken

error [e'rror] *nm* error, mistake; (*Inform*) bug; **error de imprenta** misprint

eructar [eruk'tar] *vt* to belch, burp

erudito, -a [eru'ðito, a] *adj* erudite, learned

erupción [erup'θjon] *nf* eruption; (*Med*) rash

es *vb V* **ser**

esa ['esa] (*pl* **~s**) *adj demos V* **ese**

ésa ['esa] (*pl* **~s**) *pron V* **ése**

esbelto, -a [es'βelto, a] *adj* slim, slender

esbozo [es'βoθo] *nm* sketch, outline

escabeche [eska'βetʃe] *nm* brine; (*de aceitunas etc*) pickle; **en ~** pickled

escabullirse [eskaβu'ʎirse] *vr* to slip away, to clear out

escafandra [eska'fandra] *nf* (*buzo*) diving suit; (*escafandra espacial*) space suit

escala [es'kala] *nf* (*proporción, Mús*) scale; (*de mano*) ladder; (*Aviac*) stopover; **hacer ~ en** to stop *o* call in at

escalafón [eskala'fon] *nm* (*escala de salarios*) salary scale, wage scale

escalar [eska'lar] *vt* to climb, scale

escalera [eska'lera] *nf* stairs *pl*, staircase; (*escala*) ladder; (*Naipes*) run; **escalera de caracol** spiral staircase; **escalera de incendios** fire escape; **escalera mecánica** escalator

escalfar [eskal'far] *vt* (*huevos*) to poach

escalinata [eskali'nata] *nf* staircase

escalofriante [eskalo'frjante] *adj* chilling

escalofrío [eskalo'frio] *nm* (*Med*) chill; **escalofríos** *nmpl* (*fig*) shivers

escalón [eska'lon] *nm* step, stair; (*de escalera*) rung

escalope [eska'lope] *nm* (*Culin*) escalope

escama [es'kama] *nf* (*de pez, serpiente*) scale; (*de jabón*) flake; (*fig*) resentment

escampar [eskam'par] *vb impers* to stop raining

escandalizar [eskandali'θar] *vt* to scandalize, shock; **escandalizarse** *vr* to be shocked; (*ofenderse*) to be offended

escándalo [es'kandalo] *nm* scandal; (*alboroto, tumulto*) row, uproar; **escandaloso, -a** *adj* scandalous, shocking

escandinavo, -a [eskandi'naβo, a] *adj, nm/f* Scandinavian

escanear [eskane'ar] *vt* to scan

escaño [es'kaɲo] *nm* bench; (*Pol*) seat

escapar [eska'par] *vi* (*gen*) to escape, run away; (*Deporte*) to break away; **escaparse** *vr* to escape, get away; (*agua, gas*) to leak (out)

escaparate [eskapa'rate] *nm* shop window

escape [es'kape] *nm* (*de agua, gas*) leak; (*de motor*) exhaust

escarabajo [eskara'βaxo] *nm* beetle

escaramuza [eskara'muθa] *nf* skirmish

escarbar [eskar'βar] *vt* (*tierra*) to scratch

escarceos [eskar'θeos] *nmpl*: **en mis ~ con la política ...** in my dealings with politics ...; **escarceos amorosos** love affairs

escarcha [es'kartʃa] *nf* frost; **escarchado, -a** [eskar'tʃaðo, a] *adj* (*Culin: fruta*) crystallized

escarlatina [eskarla'tina] *nf* scarlet fever

escarmentar [eskarmen'tar] *vt* to punish severely ▷ *vi* to learn one's lesson

escarmiento *etc* [eskar'mjento] *vb* V **escarmentar** ▷ *nm* (*ejemplo*) lesson; (*castigo*) punishment
escarola [eska'rola] *nf* endive
escarpado, -a [eskar'paðo, a] *adj* (*pendiente*) sheer, steep; (*rocas*) craggy
escasear [eskase'ar] *vi* to be scarce
escasez [eska'seθ] *nf* (*falta*) shortage, scarcity; (*pobreza*) poverty
escaso, -a [es'kaso, a] *adj* (*poco*) scarce; (*raro*) rare; (*ralo*) thin, sparse; (*limitado*) limited
escatimar [eskati'mar] *vt* to skimp (on), be sparing with
escayola [eska'jola] *nf* plaster
escena [es'θena] *nf* scene; **escenario** [esθe'narjo] *nm* (*Teatro*) stage; (*Cine*) set; (*fig*) scene

No confundir **escenario** con la palabra inglesa *scenery*.

escenografía *nf* set design
escéptico, -a [es'θeptiko, a] *adj* sceptical ▷ *nm/f* sceptic
esclarecer [esklare'θer] *vt* (*misterio, problema*) to shed light on
esclavitud [esklaβi'tuð] *nf* slavery
esclavizar [esklaβi'θar] *vt* to enslave
esclavo, -a [es'klaβo, a] *nm/f* slave
escoba [es'koβa] *nf* broom; **escobilla** *nf* brush
escocer [esko'θer] *vi* to burn, sting; **escocerse** *vr* to chafe, get chafed
escocés, -esa [esko'θes, esa] *adj* Scottish ▷ *nm/f* Scotsman(-woman), Scot
Escocia [es'koθja] *nf* Scotland
escoger [esko'xer] *vt* to choose, pick, select; **escogido, -a** *adj* chosen, selected
escolar [esko'lar] *adj* school *cpd* ▷ *nmf* schoolboy(-girl), pupil
escollo [es'koʎo] *nm* (*obstáculo*) pitfall
escolta [es'kolta] *nf* escort; **escoltar** *vt* to escort
escombros [es'kombros] *nmpl* (*basura*) rubbish *sg*; (*restos*) debris *sg*
esconder [eskon'der] *vt* to hide, conceal; **esconderse** *vr* to hide; **escondidas** (LAM) *nfpl*: **a escondidas** secretly; **escondite** *nm* hiding place; (ESP: *juego*) hide-and-seek; **escondrijo** *nm* hiding place, hideout
escopeta [esko'peta] *nf* shotgun
escoria [es'korja] *nf* (*de alto horno*) slag; (*fig*) scum, dregs *pl*
Escorpio [es'korpjo] *nm* Scorpio
escorpión [eskor'pjon] *nm* scorpion
escotado, -a [esko'taðo, a] *adj* low-cut
escote [es'kote] *nm* (*de vestido*) low neck; **pagar a ~** to share the expenses
escotilla [esko'tiʎa] *nf* (*Náut*) hatch(way)
escozor [esko'θor] *nm* (*dolor*) sting(ing)
escribible [eskri'βiβle] *adj* writable
escribir [eskri'βir] *vt, vi* to write; **~ a máquina** to type; **¿cómo se escribe?** how do you spell it?
escrito, -a [es'krito, a] *pp de* **escribir** ▷ *nm* (*documento*) document; (*manuscrito*) text, manuscript; **por ~** in writing
escritor, a [eskri'tor, a] *nm/f* writer
escritorio [eskri'torjo] *nm* desk
escritura [eskri'tura] *nf* (*acción*) writing; (*caligrafía*) (hand)writing; (*Jur*: *documento*) deed
escrúpulo [es'krupulo] *nm* scruple; (*minuciosidad*) scrupulousness; **escrupuloso, -a** *adj* scrupulous
escrutinio [eskru'tinjo] *nm* (*examen atento*) scrutiny; (*Pol*: *recuento de votos*) count(ing)
escuadra [es'kwaðra] *nf* (*Mil etc*) squad; (*Náut*) squadron; (*flota*: *de coches etc*) fleet; **escuadrilla** *nf* (*de aviones*) squadron; (LAM: *de obreros*) gang
escuadrón [eskwa'ðron] *nm* squadron
escuálido, -a [es'kwaliðo, a] *adj* skinny, scraggy; (*sucio*) squalid
escuchar [esku'tʃar] *vt* to listen to ▷ *vi* to listen
escudo [es'kuðo] *nm* shield
escuela [es'kwela] *nf* school; **escuela**

de artes y oficios (ESP) ≈ technical college; **escuela de choferes** (LAM) driving school; **escuela de manejo** (MÉX) driving school

escueto, -a [es'kweto, a] *adj* plain; (*estilo*) simple

escuincle, -a [es'kwinkle, a] (MÉX: *fam*) *nm/f* kid

esculpir [eskul'pir] *vt* to sculpt; (*grabar*) to engrave; (*tallar*) to carve; **escultor, a** *nm/f* sculptor(-tress); **escultura** *nf* sculpture

escupidera [eskupi'ðera] *nf* spittoon

escupir [esku'pir] *vt, vi* to spit (out)

escurreplatos [eskurre'platos] (ESP) *nm inv* draining board (BRIT), drainboard (US)

escurridero [eskurri'ðero] (LAM) *nm* draining board (BRIT), drainboard (US)

escurridizo, -a [eskurri'ðiθo, a] *adj* slippery

escurridor [eskurri'ðor] *nm* colander

escurrir [esku'rrir] *vt* (*ropa*) to wring out; (*verduras, platos*) to drain ▷ *vi* (*líquidos*) to drip; **escurrirse** *vr* (*secarse*) to drain; (*resbalarse*) to slip, slide; (*escaparse*) to slip away

ese ['ese] (*f* **esa**, *pl* **esos, esas**) *adj demos* (*sg*) that; (*pl*) those

ése ['ese] (*f* **ésa**, *pl* **ésos, ésas**) *pron* (*sg*) that (one); (*pl*) those (ones); **~ ... éste ...** the former ... the latter ...; **no me vengas con ésas** don't give me any more of that nonsense

esencia [e'senθja] *nf* essence; **esencial** *adj* essential

esfera [es'fera] *nf* sphere; (*de reloj*) face; **esférico, -a** *adj* spherical

esforzarse [esfor'θarse] *vr* to exert o.s., make an effort

esfuerzo *etc* [es'fwerθo] *vb V* **esforzarse** ▷ *nm* effort

esfumarse [esfu'marse] *vr* (*apoyo, esperanzas*) to fade away

esgrima [es'ɣrima] *nf* fencing

esguince [es'ɣinθe] *nm* (*Med*) sprain

eslabón [esla'βon] *nm* link

eslip [ez'lip] *nm* pants *pl* (BRIT), briefs *pl*

eslovaco, -a [eslo'βako, a] *adj, nm/f* Slovak, Slovakian ▷ *nm* (*Ling*) Slovak, Slovakian

Eslovaquia [eslo'βakja] *nf* Slovakia

esmalte [es'malte] *nm* enamel; **esmalte de uñas** nail varnish *o* polish

esmeralda [esme'ralda] *nf* emerald

esmerarse [esme'rarse] *vr* (*aplicarse*) to take great pains, exercise great care; (*afanarse*) to work hard

esmero [es'mero] *nm* (great) care

esnob [es'nob] (*pl* **~s**) *adj* (*persona*) snobbish ▷ *nmf* snob

eso ['eso] *pron* that, that thing *o* matter; **~ de su coche** that business about his car; **~ de ir al cine** all that about going to the cinema; **a ~ de las cinco** at about five o'clock; **en ~** thereupon, at that point; **~ es** that's it; **¡~ sí que es vida!** now that is really living!; **por ~ te lo dije** that's why I told you; **y ~ que llovía** in spite of the fact it was raining

esos *adj demos V* **ese**

ésos *pron V* **ése**

espabilar *etc* [espaβi'lar] = **despabilar** **etc**

espacial [espa'θjal] *adj* (*del espacio*) space *cpd*

espaciar [espa'θjar] *vt* to space (out)

espacio [es'paθjo] *nm* space; (*Mús*) interval; (*Radio, TV*) programme (BRIT), program (US); **el ~** space; **espacio aéreo/exterior** air/outer space; **espacioso, -a** *adj* spacious, roomy

espada [es'paða] *nf* sword; **espadas** *nfpl* (*Naipes*) spades

espaguetis [espa'ɣetis] *nmpl* spaghetti *sg*

espalda [es'palda] *nf* (*gen*) back; **espaldas** *nfpl* (*hombros*) shoulders; **a ~s de algn** behind sb's back; **estar de ~s** to have one's back turned; **tenderse de ~s** to lie (down) on one's back; **volver la ~ a algn** to cold-shoulder sb

espantajo [espan'taxo] *nm* = **espantapájaros**
espantapájaros [espanta'paxaros] *nm inv* scarecrow
espantar [espan'tar] *vt* (*asustar*) to frighten, scare; (*ahuyentar*) to frighten off; (*asombrar*) to horrify, appal; **espantarse** *vr* to get frightened *o* scared; to be appalled
espanto [es'panto] *nm* (*susto*) fright; (*terror*) terror; (*asombro*) astonishment; **espantoso, -a** *adj* frightening; terrifying; astonishing
España [es'paɲa] *nf* Spain; **español, a** *adj* Spanish ▷ *nm/f* Spaniard ▷ *nm* (*Ling*) Spanish
esparadrapo [espara'ðrapo] *nm* (sticking) plaster (BRIT), adhesive tape (US)
esparcir [espar'θir] *vt* to spread; (*diseminar*) to scatter; **esparcirse** *vr* to spread (out), to scatter; (*divertirse*) to enjoy o.s.
espárrago [es'parraɣo] *nm* asparagus
esparto [es'parto] *nm* esparto (grass)
espasmo [es'pasmo] *nm* spasm
espátula [es'patula] *nf* spatula
especia [es'peθja] *nf* spice
especial [espe'θjal] *adj* special; **especialidad** *nf* speciality (BRIT), specialty (US)
especie [es'peθje] *nf* (*Bio*) species; (*clase*) kind, sort; **en ~** in kind
especificar [espeθifi'kar] *vt* to specify; **específico, -a** *adj* specific
espécimen [es'peθimen] (*pl* **especímenes**) *nm* specimen
espectáculo [espek'takulo] *nm* (*gen*) spectacle; (*Teatro etc*) show
espectador, a [espekta'ðor, a] *nm/f* spectator
especular [espeku'lar] *vt, vi* to speculate
espejismo [espe'xismo] *nm* mirage
espejo [es'pexo] *nm* mirror; **(espejo) retrovisor** rear-view mirror
espeluznante [espeluθ'nante] *adj* horrifying, hair-raising
espera [es'pera] *nf* (*pausa, intervalo*) wait; (*Jur: plazo*) respite; **en ~ de** waiting for; (*con expectativa*) expecting
esperanza [espe'ranθa] *nf* (*confianza*) hope; (*expectativa*) expectation; **hay pocas ~s de que venga** there is little prospect of his coming; **esperanza de vida** life expectancy
esperar [espe'rar] *vt* (*aguardar*) to wait for; (*tener expectativa de*) to expect; (*desear*) to hope for ▷ *vi* to wait; to expect; to hope; **hacer ~ a algn** to keep sb waiting; **~ un bebé** to be expecting (a baby)
esperma [es'perma] *nf* sperm
espeso, -a [es'peso, a] *adj* thick; **espesor** *nm* thickness
espía [es'pia] *nmf* spy; **espiar** *vt* (*observar*) to spy on
espiga [es'piɣa] *nf* (*Bot: de trigo etc*) ear
espigón [espi'ɣon] *nm* (*Bot*) ear; (*Náut*) breakwater
espina [es'pina] *nf* thorn; (*de pez*) bone; **espina dorsal** (*Anat*) spine
espinaca [espi'naka] *nf* spinach
espinazo [espi'naθo] *nm* spine, backbone
espinilla [espi'niʎa] *nf* (*Anat: tibia*) shin(bone); (*grano*) blackhead
espinoso, -a [espi'noso, a] *adj* (*planta*) thorny, prickly; (*asunto*) difficult
espionaje [espjo'naxe] *nm* spying, espionage
espiral [espi'ral] *adj, nf* spiral
espirar [espi'rar] *vt* to breathe out, exhale
espiritista [espiri'tista] *adj, nmf* spiritualist
espíritu [es'piritu] *nm* spirit; **Espíritu Santo** Holy Ghost *o* Spirit; **espiritual** *adj* spiritual
espléndido, -a [es'plendiðo, a] *adj* (*magnífico*) magnificent, splendid; (*generoso*) generous

esplendor [esplen'dor] *nm* splendour
espolvorear [espolβore'ar] *vt* to dust, sprinkle
esponja [es'ponxa] *nf* sponge; (*fig*) sponger; **esponjoso, -a** *adj* spongy
espontaneidad [espontanei'ðað] *nf* spontaneity; **espontáneo, -a** *adj* spontaneous
esposa [es'posa] *nf* wife; **esposas** *nfpl* handcuffs; **esposar** *vt* to handcuff
esposo [es'poso] *nm* husband
espray [es'prai] *nm* spray
espuela [es'pwela] *nf* spur
espuma [es'puma] *nf* foam; (*de cerveza*) froth, head; (*de jabón*) lather; **espuma de afeitar** shaving foam; **espumadera** *nf* (*utensilio*) skimmer; **espumoso, -a** *adj* frothy, foamy; (*vino*) sparkling
esqueleto [eske'leto] *nm* skeleton
esquema [es'kema] *nm* (*diagrama*) diagram; (*dibujo*) plan; (*Filosofía*) schema
esquí [es'ki] (*pl* **~s**) *nm* (*objeto*) ski; (*Deporte*) skiing; **esquí acuático** water-skiing; **esquiar** *vi* to ski
esquilar [eski'lar] *vt* to shear
esquimal [eski'mal] *adj, nmf* Eskimo
esquina [es'kina] *nf* corner; **esquinazo** [eski'naθo] *nm*: **dar esquinazo a algn** to give sb the slip
esquirol [eski'rol] (ESP) *nm* strikebreaker, scab
esquivar [eski'βar] *vt* to avoid
esta ['esta] *adj demos V* **este²**
está *vb V* **estar**
ésta *pron V* **éste**
estabilidad [estaβili'ðað] *nf* stability; **estable** *adj* stable
establecer [estaβle'θer] *vt* to establish; **establecerse** *vr* to establish o.s.; (*echar raíces*) to settle (down); **establecimiento** *nm* establishment
establo [es'taβlo] *nm* (*Agr*) stable
estaca [es'taka] *nf* stake, post; (*de tienda de campaña*) peg
estacada [esta'kaða] *nf* (*cerca*) fence, fencing; (*palenque*) stockade
estación [esta'θjon] *nf* station; (*del año*) season; **estación balnearia** seaside resort; **estación de autobuses** bus station; **estación de servicio** service station
estacionamiento [estaθjona'mjento] *nm* (*Auto*) parking; (*Mil*) stationing
estacionar [estaθjo'nar] *vt* (*Auto*) to park; (*Mil*) to station
estadía [esta'ðia] (LAM) *nf* stay
estadio [es'taðjo] *nm* (*fase*) stage, phase; (*Deporte*) stadium
estadista [esta'ðista] *nm* (*Pol*) statesman; (*Mat*) statistician
estadística [esta'ðistika] *nf* figure, statistic; (*ciencia*) statistics *sg*
estado [es'taðo] *nm* (*Pol: condición*) state; **estar en ~** to be pregnant; **estado civil** marital status; **estado de ánimo** state of mind; **estado de cuenta** bank statement; **estado de sitio** state of siege; **estado mayor** staff; **Estados Unidos** United States (of America)
estadounidense [estaðouni'ðense] *adj* United States *cpd*, American ▷ *nmf* American
estafa [es'tafa] *nf* swindle, trick; **estafar** *vt* to swindle, defraud
estáis *vb V* **estar**
estallar [esta'ʎar] *vi* to burst; (*bomba*) to explode, go off; (*epidemia, guerra, rebelión*) to break out; **~ en llanto** to burst into tears; **estallido** *nm* explosion; (*fig*) outbreak
estampa [es'tampa] *nf* print, engraving; **estampado, -a** [estam'paðo, a] *adj* printed ▷ *nm* (*impresión: acción*) printing; (*: efecto*) print; (*marca*) stamping
estampar [estam'par] *vt* (*imprimir*) to print; (*marcar*) to stamp; (*metal*) to engrave; (*poner sello en*) to stamp; (*fig*) to stamp, imprint

estampida [estam'piða] *nf* stampede
estampido [estam'piðo] *nm* bang, report
estampilla [estam'piʎa] (*LAM*) *nf* (postage) stamp
están *vb V* **estar**
estancado, -a [estan'kaðo, a] *adj* stagnant
estancar [estan'kar] *vt* (*aguas*) to hold up, hold back; (*Com*) to monopolize; (*fig*) to block, hold up; **estancarse** *vr* to stagnate
estancia [es'tanθja] *nf* (*ESP, MÉX*: *permanencia*) stay; (*sala*) room; (*RPL*: *de ganado*) farm, ranch; **estanciero** (*RPL*) *nm* farmer, rancher
estanco, -a [es'tanko, a] *adj* watertight ▷ *nm* tobacconist's (shop), cigar store (*US*)

ESTANCO

Cigarettes, tobacco, postage stamps and official forms are all sold under state monopoly in shops called **estancos**. Although tobacco products can also be bought in bars and quioscos they are generally more expensive.

estándar [es'tandar] *adj, nm* standard
estandarte [estan'darte] *nm* banner, standard
estanque [es'tanke] *nm* (*lago*) pool, pond; (*Agr*) reservoir
estanquero, -a [estan'kero, a] *nm/f* tobacconist
estante [es'tante] *nm* (*armario*) rack, stand; (*biblioteca*) bookcase; (*anaquel*) shelf; **estantería** *nf* shelving, shelves *pl*

PALABRA CLAVE

estar [es'tar] *vi* **1** (*posición*) to be; **está en la plaza** it's in the square; **¿está Juan?** is Juan in?; **estamos a 30 km de Junín** we're 30 kms from Junín
2 (+ *adj*: *estado*) to be; **estar enfermo** to be ill; **está muy elegante** he's looking very smart; **¿cómo estás?** how are you keeping?
3 (+ *gerundio*) to be; **estoy leyendo** I'm reading
4 (*uso pasivo*): **está condenado a muerte** he's been condemned to death; **está envasado en ...** it's packed in ...
5 (*con fechas*): **¿a cuántos estamos?** what's the date today?; **estamos a 5 de mayo** it's the 5th of May
6 (*locuciones*): **¿estamos?** (*¿de acuerdo?*) okay?; (*¿listo?*) ready?
7: **estar de: estar de vacaciones/viaje** to be on holiday/away *o* on a trip; **está de camarero** he's working as a waiter
8: **estar para: está para salir** he's about to leave; **no estoy para bromas** I'm not in the mood for jokes
9: **estar por** (*propuesta etc*) to be in favour of; (*persona etc*) to support, side with; **está por limpiar** it still has to be cleaned
10: **estar sin: estar sin dinero** to have no money; **está sin terminar** it isn't finished yet
estarse *vr*: **se estuvo en la cama toda la tarde** he stayed in bed all afternoon

estas ['estas] *adj demos V* **este²**
éstas *pron V* **éste**
estatal [esta'tal] *adj* state *cpd*
estático, -a [es'tatiko, a] *adj* static
estatua [es'tatwa] *nf* statue
estatura [esta'tura] *nf* stature, height
este¹ ['este] *nm* east
este² ['este] (*f* **esta**, *pl* **estos, estas**) *adj demos* (*sg*) this; (*pl*) these
esté *etc vb V* **estar**
éste ['este] (*f* **ésta**, *pl* **éstos, éstas**) *pron* (*sg*) this (one); (*pl*) these (ones);

ése ... ~ ... the former ... the latter ...
estén *etc vb V* **estar**
estepa [es'tepa] *nf* (*Geo*) steppe
estera [es'tera] *nf* mat(ting)
estéreo [es'tereo] *adj inv, nm* stereo; **estereotipo** *nm* stereotype
estéril [es'teril] *adj* sterile, barren; (*fig*) vain, futile; **esterilizar** *vt* to sterilize
esterlina [ester'lina] *adj*: **libra ~** pound sterling
estés *etc vb V* **estar**
estética [es'tetika] *nf* aesthetics *sg*
estético, -a [es'tetiko, a] *adj* aesthetic
estiércol [es'tjerkol] *nm* dung, manure
estigma [es'tiɣma] *nm* stigma
estilo [es'tilo] *nm* style; (*Tec*) stylus; (*Natación*) stroke; **algo por el ~** something along those lines
estima [es'tima] *nf* esteem, respect; **estimación** [estima'θjon] *nf* (*evaluación*) estimation; (*aprecio, afecto*) esteem, regard; **estimado, a** *adj* esteemed; **E~ señor** Dear Sir
estimar [esti'mar] *vt* (*evaluar*) to estimate; (*valorar*) to value; (*apreciar*) to esteem, respect; (*pensar, considerar*) to think, reckon
estimulante [estimu'lante] *adj* stimulating ▷ *nm* stimulant
estimular [estimu'lar] *vt* to stimulate; (*excitar*) to excite
estímulo [es'timulo] *nm* stimulus; (*ánimo*) encouragement
estirar [esti'rar] *vt* to stretch; (*dinero, suma etc*) to stretch out; **estirarse** *vr* to stretch
estirón [esti'ron] *nm* pull, tug; (*crecimiento*) spurt, sudden growth; **dar** *o* **pegar un ~** (*fam*: *niño*) to shoot up (*inf*)
estirpe [es'tirpe] *nf* stock, lineage
estival [esti'βal] *adj* summer *cpd*
esto ['esto] *pron* this, this thing *o* matter; **~ de la boda** this business about the wedding
Estocolmo [esto'kolmo] *nm* Stockholm
estofado [esto'faðo] *nm* stew
estómago [es'tomaɣo] *nm* stomach; **tener ~** to be thick-skinned
estorbar [estor'βar] *vt* to hinder, obstruct; (*molestar*) to bother, disturb ▷ *vi* to be in the way; **estorbo** *nm* (*molestia*) bother, nuisance; (*obstáculo*) hindrance, obstacle
estornudar [estornu'ðar] *vi* to sneeze
estos ['estos] *adj demos V* **este²**
éstos *pron V* **éste**
estoy *vb V* **estar**
estrado [es'traðo] *nm* platform
estrafalario, -a [estrafa'larjo, a] *adj* odd, eccentric
estrago [es'traɣo] *nm* ruin, destruction; **hacer ~s en** to wreak havoc among
estragón [estra'ɣon] *nm* tarragon
estrambótico, -a [estram'botiko, a] *adj* (*persona*) eccentric; (*peinado, ropa*) outlandish
estrangular [estrangu'lar] *vt* (*persona*) to strangle; (*Med*) to strangulate
estratagema [estrata'xema] *nf* (*Mil*) stratagem; (*astucia*) cunning
estrategia [estra'texja] *nf* strategy; **estratégico, -a** *adj* strategic
estrato [es'trato] *nm* stratum, layer
estrechar [estre'tʃar] *vt* (*reducir*) to narrow; (*Costura*) to take in; (*abrazar*) to hug, embrace; **estrecharse** *vr* (*reducirse*) to narrow, grow narrow; (*abrazarse*) to embrace; **~ la mano** to shake hands
estrechez [estre'tʃeθ] *nf* narrowness; (*de ropa*) tightness; **estrecheces** *nfpl* (*dificultades económicas*) financial difficulties
estrecho, -a [es'tretʃo, a] *adj* narrow; (*apretado*) tight; (*íntimo*) close, intimate; (*miserable*) mean ▷ *nm* strait; **~ de miras** narrow-minded
estrella [es'treʎa] *nf* star; **estrella de mar** (*Zool*) starfish; **estrella fugaz** shooting star

estrellar [estre'ʎar] *vt* (*hacer añicos*) to smash (to pieces); (*huevos*) to fry; **estrellarse** *vr* to smash; (*chocarse*) to crash; (*fracasar*) to fail

estremecer [estreme'θer] *vt* to shake; **estremecerse** *vr* to shake, tremble

estrenar [estre'nar] *vt* (*vestido*) to wear for the first time; (*casa*) to move into; (*película, obra de teatro*) to première; **estrenarse** *vr* (*persona*) to make one's début; **estreno** *nm* (*Cine etc*) première

estreñido, -a [estre'ɲiðo, a] *adj* constipated

estreñimiento [estreɲi'mjento] *nm* constipation

estrepitoso, -a [estrepi'toso, a] *adj* noisy; (*fiesta*) rowdy

estría [es'tria] *nf* groove

estribar [estri'βar] *vi*: **~ en** to lie on

estribillo [estri'βiʎo] *nm* (*Literatura*) refrain; (*Mús*) chorus

estribo [es'triβo] *nm* (*de jinete*) stirrup; (*de coche, tren*) step; (*de puente*) support; (*Geo*) spur; **perder los ~s** to fly off the handle

estribor [estri'βor] *nm* (*Náut*) starboard

estricto, -a [es'trikto, a] *adj* (*riguroso*) strict; (*severo*) severe

estridente [estri'ðente] *adj* (*color*) loud; (*voz*) raucous

estropajo [estro'paxo] *nm* scourer

estropear [estrope'ar] *vt* to spoil; (*dañar*) to damage; **estropearse** *vr* (*objeto*) to get damaged; (*persona, piel*) to be ruined

estructura [estruk'tura] *nf* structure

estrujar [estru'xar] *vt* (*apretar*) to squeeze; (*aplastar*) to crush; (*fig*) to drain, bleed

estuario [es'twarjo] *nm* estuary

estuche [es'tutʃe] *nm* box, case

estudiante [estu'ðjante] *nmf* student; **estudiantil** *adj* student *cpd*

estudiar [estu'ðjar] *vt* to study

estudio [es'tuðjo] *nm* study; (*Cine, Arte, Radio*) studio; **estudios** *nmpl* studies; (*erudición*) learning *sg*; **estudioso, -a** *adj* studious

estufa [es'tufa] *nf* heater, fire

estupefaciente [estupefa'θjente] *nm* drug, narcotic

estupefacto, -a [estupe'fakto, a] *adj* speechless, thunderstruck

estupendo, -a [estu'pendo, a] *adj* wonderful, terrific; (*fam*) great; **¡~!** that's great!, fantastic!

estupidez [estupi'ðeθ] *nf* (*torpeza*) stupidity; (*acto*) stupid thing (to do)

estúpido, -a [es'tupiðo, a] *adj* stupid, silly

estuve *etc vb V* **estar**

ETA ['eta] (ESP) *nf abr* (= *Euskadi ta Askatasuna*) ETA

etapa [e'tapa] *nf* (*de viaje*) stage; (*Deporte*) leg; (*parada*) stopping place; (*fase*) stage, phase

etarra [e'tarra] *nmf* member of ETA

etc. *abr* (= *etcétera*) etc

etcétera [et'θetera] *adv* etcetera

eternidad [eterni'ðað] *nf* eternity; **eterno, -a** *adj* eternal, everlasting

ética ['etika] *nf* ethics *pl*

ético, -a ['etiko, a] *adj* ethical

etiqueta [eti'keta] *nf* (*modales*) etiquette; (*rótulo*) label, tag

Eucaristía [eukaris'tia] *nf* Eucharist

euforia [eu'forja] *nf* euphoria

euro ['euro] *nm* (*moneda*) euro

eurodiputado, -a [eurodipu'taðo, a] *nm/f* Euro MP, MEP

Europa [eu'ropa] *nf* Europe; **europeo, -a** *adj, nm/f* European

Euskadi [eus'kaði] *nm* the Basque Country *o* Provinces *pl*

euskera [eus'kera] *nm* (*Ling*) Basque

evacuación [eβakwa'θjon] *nf* evacuation

evacuar [eβa'kwar] *vt* to evacuate

evadir [eβa'ðir] *vt* to evade, avoid; **evadirse** *vr* to escape

evaluar [eβa'lwar] *vt* to evaluate

evangelio [eβan'xeljo] *nm* gospel

evaporar [eβapo'rar] *vt* to evaporate; **evaporarse** *vr* to vanish
evasión [eβa'sjon] *nf* escape, flight; (*fig*) evasion; **evasión de capitales** flight of capital
evasiva [eβa'siβa] *nf* (*pretexto*) excuse
evento [e'βento] *nm* event
eventual [eβen'twal] *adj* possible, conditional (upon circumstances); (*trabajador*) casual, temporary

No confundir **eventual** con la palabra inglesa *eventual*.

evidencia [eβi'ðenθja] *nf* evidence, proof
evidente [eβi'ðente] *adj* obvious, clear, evident
evitar [eβi'tar] *vt* (*evadir*) to avoid; (*impedir*) to prevent; **~ hacer algo** to avoid doing sth
evocar [eβo'kar] *vt* to evoke, call forth
evolución [eβolu'θjon] *nf* (*desarrollo*) evolution, development; (*cambio*) change; (*Mil*) manoeuvre; **evolucionar** *vi* to evolve; to manoeuvre
ex [eks] *adj* ex-; **el ~ ministro** the former minister, the ex-minister
exactitud [eksakti'tuð] *nf* exactness; (*precisión*) accuracy; (*puntualidad*) punctuality; **exacto, -a** *adj* exact; accurate; punctual; **¡exacto!** exactly!
exageración [eksaxera'θjon] *nf* exaggeration
exagerar [eksaxe'rar] *vt, vi* to exaggerate
exaltar [eksal'tar] *vt* to exalt, glorify; **exaltarse** *vr* (*excitarse*) to get excited *o* worked up
examen [ek'samen] *nm* examination; **examen de conducir** driving test; **examen de ingreso** entrance examination
examinar [eksami'nar] *vt* to examine; **examinarse** *vr* to be examined, take an examination
excavadora [ekskaβa'ðora] *nf* excavator
excavar [ekska'βar] *vt* to excavate
excedencia [eksθe'ðenθja] *nf*: **estar en ~** to be on leave; **pedir** *o* **solicitar la ~** to ask for leave
excedente [eksθe'ðente] *adj, nm* excess, surplus
exceder [eksθe'ðer] *vt* to exceed, surpass; **excederse** *vr* (*extralimitarse*) to go too far
excelencia [eksθe'lenθja] *nf* excellence; **su E~** his Excellency; **excelente** *adj* excellent
excéntrico, -a [eks'θentriko, a] *adj, nm/f* eccentric
excepción [eksθep'θjon] *nf* exception; **a ~ de** with the exception of, except for; **excepcional** *adj* exceptional
excepto [eks'θepto] *adv* excepting, except (for)
exceptuar [eksθep'twar] *vt* to except, exclude
excesivo, -a [eksθe'siβo, a] *adj* excessive
exceso [eks'θeso] *nm* (*gen*) excess; (*Com*) surplus; **exceso de equipaje/peso** excess luggage/weight; **exceso de velocidad** speeding
excitado, -a [eksθi'taðo, a] *adj* excited; (*emociónes*) aroused
excitar [eksθi'tar] *vt* to excite; (*incitar*) to urge; **excitarse** *vr* to get excited
exclamación [eksklama'θjon] *nf* exclamation
exclamar [ekscla'mar] *vi* to exclaim
excluir [eksklu'ir] *vt* to exclude; (*dejar fuera*) to shut out; (*descartar*) to reject
exclusiva [eksklu'siβa] *nf* (*Prensa*) exclusive, scoop; (*Com*) sole right
exclusivo, -a [eksklu'siβo, a] *adj* exclusive; **derecho ~** sole *o* exclusive right
Excmo. *abr* = **excelentísmo**
excomulgar [ekskomul'ɣar] *vt* (*Rel*) to excommunicate
excomunión [ekskomu'njon] *nf* excommunication

excursión [ekskur'sjon] *nf* excursion, outing; **excursionista** *nmf* (*turista*) sightseer
excusa [eks'kusa] *nf* excuse; (*disculpa*) apology; **excusar** [eksku'sar] *vt* to excuse
exhaustivo, -a [eksaus'tiβo, a] *adj* (*análisis*) thorough; (*estudio*) exhaustive
exhausto, -a [ek'sausto, a] *adj* exhausted
exhibición [eksiβi'θjon] *nf* exhibition, display, show
exhibir [eksi'βir] *vt* to exhibit, display, show
exigencia [eksi'xenθja] *nf* demand, requirement; **exigente** *adj* demanding
exigir [eksi'xir] *vt* (*gen*) to demand, require; **~ el pago** to demand payment
exiliado, -a [eksi'ljaðo, a] *adj* exiled ▷ *nm/f* exile
exilio [ek'siljo] *nm* exile
eximir [eksi'mir] *vt* to exempt
existencia [eksis'tenθja] *nf* existence; **existencias** *nfpl* stock(s) *pl*
existir [eksis'tir] *vi* to exist, be
éxito ['eksito] *nm* (*triunfo*) success; (*Mús etc*) hit; **tener ~** to be successful

> No confundir **éxito** con la palabra inglesa *exit*.

exorbitante [eksorβi'tante] *adj* (*precio*) exorbitant; (*cantidad*) excessive
exótico, -a [ek'sotiko, a] *adj* exotic
expandir [ekspan'dir] *vt* to expand
expansión [ekspan'sjon] *nf* expansion
expansivo, -a [ekspan'siβo, a] *adj*: **onda expansiva** shock wave
expatriarse [ekspa'trjarse] *vr* to emigrate; (*Pol*) to go into exile
expectativa [ekspekta'tiβa] *nf* (*espera*) expectation; (*perspectiva*) prospect
expedición [ekspeði'θjon] *nf* (*excursión*) expedition
expediente [ekspe'ðjente] *nm* expedient; (*Jur: procedimento*) action, proceedings *pl*; (*: papeles*) dossier, file, record
expedir [ekspe'ðir] *vt* (*despachar*) to send, forward; (*pasaporte*) to issue
expensas [eks'pensas] *nfpl*: **a ~ de** at the expense of
experiencia [ekspe'rjenθja] *nf* experience
experimentado, -a [eksperimen'taðo, a] *adj* experienced
experimentar [eksperimen'tar] *vt* (*en laboratorio*) to experiment with; (*probar*) to test, try out; (*notar, observar*) to experience; (*deterioro, pérdida*) to suffer; **experimento** *nm* experiment
experto, -a [eks'perto, a] *adj* expert, skilled ▷ *nm/f* expert
expirar [ekspi'rar] *vi* to expire
explanada [eskpla'naða] *nf* (*llano*) plain
explayarse [ekspla'jarse] *vr* (*en discurso*) to speak at length; **~ con algn** to confide in sb
explicación [eksplika'θjon] *nf* explanation
explicar [ekspli'kar] *vt* to explain; **explicarse** *vr* to explain (o.s.)
explícito, -a [eks'pliθito, a] *adj* explicit
explique *etc vb V* **explicar**
explorador, a [eksplora'ðor, a] *nm/f* (*pionero*) explorer; (*Mil*) scout ▷ *nm* (*Med*) probe; (*Tec*) (radar) scanner
explorar [eksplo'rar] *vt* to explore; (*Med*) to probe; (*radar*) to scan
explosión [eksplo'sjon] *nf* explosion; **explosivo, -a** *adj* explosive
explotación [eksplota'θjon] *nf* exploitation; (*de planta etc*) running
explotar [eksplo'tar] *vt* to exploit to run, operate ▷ *vi* to explode
exponer [ekspo'ner] *vt* to expose; (*cuadro*) to display; (*vida*) to risk; (*idea*) to explain; **exponerse** *vr*: **~se a (hacer) algo** to run the risk of (doing) sth
exportación [eksporta'θjon] *nf* (*acción*) export; (*mercancías*) exports *pl*
exportar [ekspor'tar] *vt* to export

exposición [eksposi'θjon] *nf* (*gen*) exposure; (*de arte*) show, exhibition; (*explicación*) explanation; (*declaración*) account, statement

expresamente [ekspresa'mente] *adv* (*decir*) clearly; (*a propósito*) expressly

expresar [ekspre'sar] *vt* to express; **expresión** *nf* expression

expresivo, -a [ekspre'siβo, a] *adj* (*persona, gesto, palabras*) expressive; (*cariñoso*) affectionate

expreso, -a [eks'preso, a] *pp de* **expresar** ▷ *adj* (*explícito*) express; (*claro*) specific, clear; (*tren*) fast ▷ *adv*: **enviar ~** to send by express (delivery)

express [eks'pres] (LAM) *adv*: **enviar algo ~** to send sth special delivery

exprimidor [eksprimi'ðor] *nm* squeezer

exprimir [ekspri'mir] *vt* (*fruta*) to squeeze; (*zumo*) to squeeze out

expuesto, -a [eks'pwesto, a] *pp de* **exponer** ▷ *adj* exposed; (*cuadro etc*) on show, on display

expulsar [ekspul'sar] *vt* (*echar*) to eject, throw out; (*alumno*) to expel; (*despedir*) to sack, fire; (*Deporte*) to send off; **expulsión** *nf* expulsion; sending-off

exquisito, -a [ekski'sito, a] *adj* exquisite; (*comida*) delicious

éxtasis ['ekstasis] *nm* ecstasy

extender [eksten'der] *vt* to extend; (*los brazos*) to stretch out, hold out; (*mapa, tela*) to spread (out), open (out); (*mantequilla*) to spread; (*certificado*) to issue; (*cheque, recibo*) to make out; (*documento*) to draw up; **extenderse** *vr* (*gen*) to extend; (*persona: en el suelo*) to stretch out; (*epidemia*) to spread; **extendido, -a** *adj* (*abierto*) spread out, open; (*brazos*) outstretched; (*costumbre*) widespread

extensión [eksten'sjon] *nf* (*de terreno, mar*) expanse, stretch; (*de tiempo*) length, duration; (*Tel*) extension; **en toda la ~ de la palabra** in every sense of the word

extenso, -a [eks'tenso, a] *adj* extensive

exterior [ekste'rjor] *adj* (*de fuera*) external; (*afuera*) outside, exterior; (*apariencia*) outward; (*deuda, relaciónes*) foreign ▷ *nm* (*gen*) exterior, outside; (*aspecto*) outward appearance; (*Deporte*) wing(er); (*países extranjeros*) abroad; **en el ~** abroad; **al ~** outwardly, on the surface

exterminar [ekstermi'nar] *vt* to exterminate

externo, -a [eks'terno, a] *adj* (*exterior*) external, outside; (*superficial*) outward ▷ *nm/f* day pupil

extinguir [ekstin'gir] *vt* (*fuego*) to extinguish, put out; (*raza, población*) to wipe out; **extinguirse** *vr* (*fuego*) to go out; (*Bio*) to die out, become extinct

extintor [ekstin'tor] *nm* (fire) extinguisher

extirpar [ekstir'par] *vt* (*Med*) to remove (surgically)

extra ['ekstra] *adj inv* (*tiempo*) extra; (*chocolate, vino*) good-quality ▷ *nmf* extra ▷ *nm* extra; (*bono*) bonus

extracción [ekstrak'θjon] *nf* extraction; (*en lotería*) draw

extracto [eks'trakto] *nm* extract

extradición [ekstraði'θjon] *nf* extradition

extraer [ekstra'er] *vt* to extract, take out

extraescolar [ekstraesko'lar] *adj*: **actividad ~** extracurricular activity

extranjero, -a [ekstran'xero, a] *adj* foreign ▷ *nm/f* foreigner ▷ *nm* foreign countries *pl*; **en el ~** abroad

> No confundir **extranjero** con la palabra inglesa *stranger*.

extrañar [ekstra'ɲar] *vt* (*sorprender*) to find strange *o* odd; (*echar de menos*) to miss; **extrañarse** *vr* (*sorprenderse*) to be amazed, be surprised; **me extraña** I'm surprised

extraño, -a [eks'traɲo, a] *adj* (*extranjero*) foreign; (*raro, sorprendente*)

strange, odd
extraordinario, -a [ekstraorði'narjo, a] *adj* extraordinary; (*edición, número*) special ▷ *nm* (*de periódico*) special edition; **horas extraordinarias** overtime *sg*
extrarradio [ekstra'rraðjo] *nm* suburbs
extravagante [ekstraβa'ɣante] *adj* (*excéntrico*) eccentric; (*estrafalario*) outlandish
extraviado, -a [ekstra'βjaðo, a] *adj* lost, missing
extraviar [ekstra'βjar] *vt* (*persona: desorientar*) to mislead, misdirect; (*perder*) to lose, misplace; **extraviarse** *vr* to lose one's way, get lost
extremar [ekstre'mar] *vt* to carry to extremes
extremaunción [ekstremaun'θjon] *nf* extreme unction
extremidad [ekstremi'ðað] *nf* (*punta*) extremity; **extremidades** *nfpl* (*Anat*) extremities
extremo, -a [eks'tremo, a] *adj* extreme; (*último*) last ▷ *nm* end; (*límite, grado sumo*) extreme; **en último ~** as a last resort
extrovertido, -a [ekstroβer'tiðo, a] *adj, nm/f* extrovert
exuberante [eksuβe'rante] *adj* exuberant; (*fig*) luxuriant, lush
eyacular [ejaku'lar] *vt, vi* to ejaculate

o lose one's way, get lost
extremar [ekstre'mar] *vt* to carry to extremes
extremaunción [ekstremaun'θjon] *nf* extreme unction
extremidad [ekstremi'ðað] *nf* (*punta*) extremity; **extremidades** *nfpl* (*Anat*) extremities
extremo, -a [eks'tremo, a] *adj* extreme; (*último*) last ▷ *nm* end; (*límite, grado sumo*) extreme; **en último ~** as a last resort
extrovertido, -a [ekstroβer'tiðo, a]

adj, nm/f extrovert
exuberante [eksuβe'rante] *adj* exuberant; (*fig*) luxuriant, lush
eyacular [ejaku'lar] *vt, vi* to ejaculate

fa [fa] *nm* (*Mús*) fa, F
fabada [fa'βaða] *nf* bean and sausage stew
fábrica ['faβrika] *nf* factory; **marca de ~** trademark; **precio de ~** factory price

No confundir **fábrica** con la palabra inglesa *fabric*.

fabricación [faβrika'θjon] *nf* (*manufactura*) manufacture; (*producción*) production; **de ~ casera** home-made; **fabricación en serie** mass production
fabricante [faβri'kante] *nmf* manufacturer
fabricar [faβri'kar] *vt* (*manufacturar*) to manufacture, make; (*construir*) to build; (*cuento*) to fabricate, devise
fábula ['faβula] *nf* (*cuento*) fable; (*chisme*) rumour; (*mentira*) fib
fabuloso, -a [faβu'loso, a] *adj* (*oportunidad, tiempo*) fabulous, great
facción [fak'θjon] *nf* (*Pol*) faction; **facciones** *nfpl* (*de rostro*) features
faceta [fa'θeta] *nf* facet
facha ['fatʃa] (*fam*) *nf* (*aspecto*) look; (*cara*) face
fachada [fa'tʃaða] *nf* (*Arq*) façade, front
fácil ['faθil] *adj* (*simple*) easy; (*probable*) likely
facilidad [faθili'ðað] *nf* (*capacidad*) ease; (*sencillez*) simplicity; (*de palabra*) fluency; **facilidades** *nfpl* facilities; **facilidades de pago** credit facilities
facilitar [faθili'tar] *vt* (*hacer fácil*) to make easy; (*proporcionar*) to provide
factor [fak'tor] *nm* factor
factura [fak'tura] *nf* (*cuenta*) bill; **facturación** *nf* (*de equipaje*) check-in; **facturar** *vt* (*Com*) to invoice, charge for; (*equipaje*) to check in
facultad [fakul'tað] *nf* (*aptitud, Escol etc*) faculty; (*poder*) power
faena [fa'ena] *nf* (*trabajo*) work; (*quehacer*) task, job
faisán [fai'san] *nm* pheasant
faja ['faxa] *nf* (*para la cintura*) sash; (*de mujer*) corset; (*de tierra*) strip
fajo ['faxo] *nm* (*de papeles*) bundle; (*de billetes*) wad
falda ['falda] *nf* (*prenda de vestir*) skirt; **falda pantalón** culottes *pl*, split skirt
falla ['faʎa] *nf* (*defecto*) fault, flaw; **falla humana** (*LAM*) human error
fallar [fa'ʎar] *vt* (*Jur*) to pronounce sentence on ▷ *vi* (*memoria*) to fail; (*motor*) to miss
Fallas ['faʎas] *nfpl* *Valencian celebration of the feast of St Joseph*

FALLAS

In the week of 19 March (the feast of San José), Valencia honours its patron saint with a spectacular fiesta called **Las Fallas**. The **Fallas** are huge papier-mâché, cardboard and wooden sculptures which are built by competing teams throughout the year. They depict politicians and well-known public figures and are thrown onto bonfires and set alight once a jury has judged them – only the best sculpture escapes the flames.

fallecer [faʎe'θer] *vi* to pass away, die; **fallecimiento** *nm* decease, demise
fallido, -a [fa'ʎiðo, a] *adj* (*gen*) frustrated, unsuccessful
fallo ['faʎo] *nm* (*Jur*) verdict, ruling; (*fracaso*) failure; **fallo cardíaco** heart failure; **fallo humano** (ESP) human error
falsificar [falsifi'kar] *vt* (*firma etc*) to forge; (*moneda*) to counterfeit
falso, -a ['falso, a] *adj* false; (*documento, moneda etc*) fake; **en ~** falsely
falta ['falta] *nf* (*defecto*) fault, flaw; (*privación*) lack, want; (*ausencia*) absence; (*carencia*) shortage; (*equivocación*) mistake; (*Deporte*) foul; **echar en ~** to miss; **hacer ~ hacer algo** to be necessary to do sth; **me hace ~ una pluma** I need a pen; **falta de educación** bad manners *pl*; **falta de ortografía** spelling mistake
faltar [fal'tar] *vi* (*escasear*) to be lacking, be wanting; (*ausentarse*) to be absent, be missing; **faltan 2 horas para llegar** there are 2 hours to go till arrival; **~ al respeto a algn** to be disrespectful to sb; **¡no faltaba más!** (*no hay de qué*) don't mention it
fama ['fama] *nf* (*renombre*) fame; (*reputación*) reputation
familia [fa'milja] *nf* family; **familia numerosa** large family; **familia política** in-laws *pl*
familiar [fami'ljar] *adj* (*relativo a la familia*) family *cpd*; (*conocido, informal*) familiar ▷ *nm* relative, relation
famoso, -a [fa'moso, a] *adj* (*renombrado*) famous
fan [fan] (*pl* **~s**) *nmf* fan
fanático, -a [fa'natiko, a] *adj* fanatical ▷ *nm/f* fanatic; (*Cine, Deporte*) fan
fanfarrón, -ona [fanfa'rron, ona] *adj* boastful
fango ['fango] *nm* mud
fantasía [fanta'sia] *nf* fantasy, imagination; **joyas de ~** imitation jewellery *sg*
fantasma [fan'tasma] *nm* (*espectro*) ghost, apparition; (*fanfarrón*) show-off
fantástico, -a [fan'tastiko, a] *adj* fantastic
farmacéutico, -a [farma'θeutiko, a] *adj* pharmaceutical ▷ *nm/f* chemist (BRIT), pharmacist
farmacia [far'maθja] *nf* chemist's (shop) (BRIT), pharmacy; **farmacia de guardia** all-night chemist
fármaco ['farmako] *nm* drug
faro ['faro] *nm* (*Náut: torre*) lighthouse; (*Auto*) headlamp; **faros antiniebla** fog lamps; **faros delanteros/traseros** headlights/rear lights
farol [fa'rol] *nm* lantern, lamp
farola [fa'rola] *nf* street lamp (BRIT) *o* light (US)
farra ['farra] (LAM: *fam*) *nf* party; **ir de ~** to go on a binge
farsa ['farsa] *nf* (*gen*) farce
farsante [far'sante] *nmf* fraud, fake
fascículo [fas'θikulo] *nm* (*de revista*) part, instalment
fascinar [fasθi'nar] *vt* (*gen*) to fascinate
fascismo [fas'θismo] *nm* fascism; **fascista** *adj, nmf* fascist
fase ['fase] *nf* phase
fashion ['faʃon] *adj* (*fam*) trendy
fastidiar [fasti'ðjar] *vt* (*molestar*) to annoy, bother; (*estropear*) to spoil; **fastidiarse** *vr*: **¡que se fastidie!** (*fam*) he'll just have to put up with it!
fastidio [fas'tiðjo] *nm* (*molestia*) annoyance; **fastidioso, -a** *adj* (*molesto*) annoying
fatal [fa'tal] *adj* (*gen*) fatal; (*desgraciado*) ill-fated; (*fam: malo, pésimo*) awful; **fatalidad** *nf* (*destino*) fate; (*mala suerte*) misfortune

fatiga [fa'tiɣa] *nf* (*cansancio*) fatigue, weariness
fatigar [fati'ɣar] *vt* to tire, weary
fatigoso, -a [fati'ɣoso, a] *adj* (*cansador*) tiring
fauna ['fauna] *nf* fauna
favor [fa'βor] *nm* favour; **estar a ~ de** to be in favour of; **haga el ~ de ...** would you be so good as to ..., kindly ...; **por ~** please; **favorable** *adj* favourable
favorecer [faβore'θer] *vt* to favour; (*vestido etc*) to become, flatter; **este peinado le favorece** this hairstyle suits him
favorito, -a [faβo'rito, a] *adj, nm/f* favourite
fax [faks] *nm inv* fax; **mandar por ~** to fax
fe [fe] *nf* (*Rel*) faith; (*documento*) certificate; **actuar con buena/mala ~** to act in good/bad faith
febrero [fe'βrero] *nm* February
fecha ['fetʃa] *nf* date; **con ~ adelantada** postdated; **en ~ próxima** soon; **hasta la ~** to date, so far; **poner ~** to date; **fecha de caducidad** (*de producto alimenticio*) sell-by date; (*de contrato etc*) expiry date; **fecha de nacimiento** date of birth; **fecha límite** *o* **tope** deadline
fecundo, -a [fe'kundo, a] *adj* (*fértil*) fertile; (*fig*) prolific; (*productivo*) productive
federación [feðera'θjon] *nf* federation
felicidad [feliθi'ðað] *nf* happiness; **¡~es!** (*deseos*) best wishes, congratulations!; (*en cumpleaños*) happy birthday!
felicitación [feliθita'θjon] *nf* (*tarjeta*) greeting(s) card
felicitar [feliθi'tar] *vt* to congratulate
feliz [fe'liθ] *adj* happy
felpudo [fel'puðo] *nm* doormat
femenino, -a [feme'nino, a] *adj, nm* feminine
feminista [femi'nista] *adj, nmf* feminist
fenómeno [fe'nomeno] *nm* phenomenon; (*fig*) freak, accident ▷ *adj* great ▷ *excl* great!, marvellous!; **fenomenal** *adj* = **fenómeno**
feo, -a ['feo, a] *adj* (*gen*) ugly; (*desagradable*) bad, nasty
féretro ['feretro] *nm* (*ataúd*) coffin; (*sarcófago*) bier
feria ['ferja] *nf* (*gen*) fair; (*descanso*) holiday, rest day; (*MÉX*: *cambio*) small *o* loose change; (*CS*: *mercado*) village market
feriado [fe'rjaðo] (*LAM*) *nm* holiday
fermentar [fermen'tar] *vi* to ferment
feroz [fe'roθ] *adj* (*cruel*) cruel; (*salvaje*) fierce
férreo, -a ['ferreo, a] *adj* iron
ferretería [ferrete'ria] *nf* (*tienda*) ironmonger's (shop) (*BRIT*), hardware store (*US*)
ferrocarril [ferroka'rril] *nm* railway
ferroviario, -a [ferro'βjarjo, a] *adj* rail *cpd*
ferry ['ferri] (*pl* **~s** *o* **ferries**) *nm* ferry
fértil ['fertil] *adj* (*productivo*) fertile; (*rico*) rich; **fertilidad** *nf* (*gen*) fertility; (*productividad*) fruitfulness
fervor [fer'βor] *nm* fervour
festejar [feste'xar] *vt* (*celebrar*) to celebrate
festejo [fes'texo] *nm* celebration; **festejos** *nmpl* (*fiestas*) festivals
festín [fes'tin] *nm* feast, banquet
festival [festi'βal] *nm* festival
festividad [festiβi'ðað] *nf* festivity
festivo, -a [fes'tiβo, a] *adj* (*de fiesta*) festive; (*Cine, Literatura*) humorous; **día ~** holiday
feto ['feto] *nm* foetus
fiable ['fjaβle] *adj* (*persona*) trustworthy; (*máquina*) reliable
fiambre ['fjambre] *nm* cold meat
fiambrera [fjam'brera] *nf* (*para almuerzo*) lunch box
fianza ['fianθa] *nf* surety; (*Jur*): **libertad bajo ~** release on bail

fiar [fi'ar] *vt* (*salir garante de*) to guarantee; (*vender a crédito*) to sell on credit ▷ *vi* to trust; **fiarse** *vr* to trust (in), rely on; **~ a** (*secreto*) to confide (to); **~se de algn** to rely on sb
fibra ['fiβra] *nf* fibre; **fibra óptica** optical fibre
ficción [fik'θjon] *nf* fiction
ficha ['fitʃa] *nf* (*Tel*) token; (*en juegos*) counter, marker; (*tarjeta*) (index) card; **fichaje** *nm* (*Deporte*) signing; **fichar** *vt* (*archivar*) to file, index; (*Deporte*) to sign; **estar fichado** to have a record; **fichero** *nm* box file; (*Inform*) file
ficticio, -a [fik'tiθjo, a] *adj* (*imaginario*) fictitious; (*falso*) fabricated
fidelidad [fiðeli'ðað] *nf* (*lealtad*) fidelity, loyalty; **alta ~** high fidelity, hi-fi
fideos [fi'ðeos] *nmpl* noodles
fiebre ['fjeβre] *nf* (*Med*) fever; (*fig*) fever, excitement; **tener ~** to have a temperature; **fiebre aftosa** foot-and-mouth disease
fiel [fjel] *adj* (*leal*) faithful, loyal; (*fiable*) reliable; (*exacto*) accurate, faithful ▷ *nm*: **los ~es** the faithful
fieltro ['fjeltro] *nm* felt
fiera ['fjera] *nf* (*animal feroz*) wild animal *o* beast; (*fig*) dragon; *V tb* **fiero**
fiero, -a ['fjero, a] *adj* (*cruel*) cruel; (*feroz*) fierce; (*duro*) harsh
fierro ['fjerro] (LAM) *nm* (*hierro*) iron
fiesta ['fjesta] *nf* party; (*de pueblo*) festival; (*vacaciones*: *tb*: **~s**) holiday *sg*; **fiesta mayor** annual festival; **fiesta patria** (LAM) independence day

FIESTAS

Fiestas can be official public holidays or holidays set by each autonomous region, many of which coincide with religious festivals. There are also many **fiestas** all over Spain for a local patron saint or the Virgin Mary. These often last several days and can include religious processions, carnival parades, bullfights and dancing.

figura [fi'ɣura] *nf* (*gen*) figure; (*forma, imagen*) shape, form; (*Naipes*) face card
figurar [fiɣu'rar] *vt* (*representar*) to represent; (*fingir*) to figure ▷ *vi* to figure; **figurarse** *vr* (*imaginarse*) to imagine; (*suponer*) to suppose
fijador [fixa'ðor] *nm* (*Foto etc*) fixative; (*de pelo*) gel
fijar [fi'xar] *vt* (*gen*) to fix; (*estampilla*) to affix, stick (on); **fijarse** *vr*: **~se en** to notice
fijo, -a ['fixo, a] *adj* (*gen*) fixed; (*firme*) firm; (*permanente*) permanent ▷ *adv*: **mirar ~** to stare
fila ['fila] *nf* row; (*Mil*) rank; **ponerse en ~** to line up, get into line; **fila india** single file
filatelia [fila'telja] *nf* philately, stamp collecting
filete [fi'lete] *nm* (*de carne*) fillet steak; (*de pescado*) fillet
filiación [filja'θjon] *nf* (*Pol*) affiliation
filial [fi'ljal] *adj* filial ▷ *nf* subsidiary
Filipinas [fili'pinas] *nfpl*: **las (Islas) ~** the Philippines; **filipino, -a** *adj, nm/f* Philippine
filmar [fil'mar] *vt* to film, shoot
filo ['filo] *nm* (*gen*) edge; **sacar ~ a** to sharpen; **al ~ del mediodía** at about midday; **de doble ~** double-edged
filología [filolo'ɣia] *nf* philology; **filología inglesa** (*Univ*) English Studies
filón [fi'lon] *nm* (*Minería*) vein, lode; (*fig*) goldmine
filosofía [filoso'fia] *nf* philosophy; **filósofo, -a** *nm/f* philosopher
filtrar [fil'trar] *vt, vi* to filter, strain; **filtrarse** *vr* to filter; **filtro** *nm* (*Tec, utensilio*) filter
fin [fin] *nm* end; (*objetivo*) aim, purpose; **al ~ y al cabo** when all's said and done; **a ~ de** in order to; **por ~** finally; **en ~** in short; **fin de semana**

weekend
final [fi'nal] *adj* final ▷ *nm* end, conclusion ▷ *nf* final; **al ~** in the end; **a ~es de** at the end of; **finalidad** *nf* (*propósito*) purpose, intention; **finalista** *nmf* finalist; **finalizar** *vt* to end, finish; (*Inform*) to log out *o* off ▷ *vi* to end, come to an end
financiar [finan'θjar] *vt* to finance; **financiero, -a** *adj* financial ▷ *nm/f* financier
finca ['finka] *nf* (*casa de campo*) country house; (ESP: *bien inmueble*) property, land; (LAM: *granja*) farm
finde ['finde] *nm abr* (*fam: fin de semana*) weekend
fingir [fin'xir] *vt* (*simular*) to simulate, feign ▷ *vi* (*aparentar*) to pretend
finlandés, -esa [finlan'des, esa] *adj* Finnish ▷ *nm/f* Finn ▷ *nm* (*Ling*) Finnish
Finlandia [fin'landja] *nf* Finland
fino, -a ['fino, a] *adj* fine; (*delgado*) slender; (*de buenas maneras*) polite, refined; (*jerez*) fino, dry
firma ['firma] *nf* signature; (*Com*) firm, company
firmamento [firma'mento] *nm* firmament
firmar [fir'mar] *vt* to sign
firme ['firme] *adj* firm; (*estable*) stable; (*sólido*) solid; (*constante*) steady; (*decidido*) resolute ▷ *nm* road (surface); **firmeza** *nf* firmness; (*constancia*) steadiness; (*solidez*) solidity
fiscal [fis'kal] *adj* fiscal ▷ *nmf* public prosecutor; **año ~** tax *o* fiscal year
fisgonear [fisɣone'ar] *vt* to poke one's nose into ▷ *vi* to pry, spy
física ['fisika] *nf* physics *sg*; *V tb* **físico**
físico, -a ['fisiko, a] *adj* physical ▷ *nm* physique ▷ *nm/f* physicist
fisura [fi'sura] *nf* crack; (*Med*) fracture
flác(c)ido, -a ['fla(k)θiðo, a] *adj* flabby
flaco, -a ['flako, a] *adj* (*muy delgado*) skinny, thin; (*débil*) weak, feeble
flagrante [fla'ɣrante] *adj* flagrant
flama ['flama] (MÉX) *nf* flame; **flamable** (MÉX) *adj* flammable
flamante [fla'mante] (*fam*) *adj* brilliant; (*nuevo*) brand-new
flamenco, -a [fla'menko, a] *adj* (*de Flandes*) Flemish; (*baile, música*) flamenco ▷ *nm* (*baile, música*) flamenco; (*Zool*) flamingo
flamingo [fla'mingo] (MÉX) *nm* flamingo
flan [flan] *nm* creme caramel

> No confundir **flan** con la palabra inglesa *flan*.

flash [flaʃ] (*pl* **~** *o* **~es**) *nm* (*Foto*) flash
flauta ['flauta] *nf* (*Mús*) flute
flecha ['fletʃa] *nf* arrow
flechazo [fle'tʃaθo] *nm* love at first sight
fleco ['fleko] *nm* fringe
flema ['flema] *nm* phlegm
flequillo [fle'kiʎo] *nm* (*pelo*) fringe
flexible [flek'siβle] *adj* flexible
flexión [flek'sjon] *nf* press-up
flexo ['flekso] *nm* adjustable table-lamp
flirtear [flirte'ar] *vi* to flirt
flojera [flo'xera] (LAM: *fam*) *nf*: **me da ~** I can't be bothered
flojo, -a ['floxo, a] *adj* (*gen*) loose; (*sin fuerzas*) limp; (*débil*) weak
flor [flor] *nf* flower; **a ~ de** on the surface of; **flora** *nf* flora; **florecer** *vi* (*Bot*) to flower, bloom; (*fig*) to flourish; **florería** (LAM) *nf* florist's (shop); **florero** *nm* vase; **floristería** *nf* florist's (shop)
flota ['flota] *nf* fleet
flotador [flota'ðor] *nm* (*gen*) float; (*para nadar*) rubber ring
flotar [flo'tar] *vi* (*gen*) to float; **flote** *nm*: **a flote** afloat; **salir a flote** (*fig*) to get back on one's feet
fluidez [flui'ðeθ] *nf* fluidity; (*fig*) fluency
fluido, -a ['fluiðo, a] *adj, nm* fluid
fluir [flu'ir] *vi* to flow
flujo ['fluxo] *nm* flow; **flujo y reflujo** ebb and flow

flúor ['fluor] *nm* fluoride
fluorescente [flwores'θente] *adj* fluorescent ▷*nm* fluorescent light
fluvial [fluβi'al] *adj* (*navegación, cuenca*) fluvial, river *cpd*
fobia ['fobja] *nf* phobia; **fobia a las alturas** fear of heights
foca ['foka] *nf* seal
foco ['foko] *nm* focus; (*Elec*) floodlight; (*MÉX: bombilla*) (light) bulb
fofo, -a ['fofo, a] *adj* soft, spongy; (*carnes*) flabby
fogata [fo'ɣata] *nf* bonfire
fogón [fo'ɣon] *nm* (*de cocina*) ring, burner
folio ['foljo] *nm* folio, page
follaje [fo'ʎaxe] *nm* foliage
folleto [fo'ʎeto] *nm* (*Pol*) pamphlet
follón [fo'ʎon] (*ESP: fam*) *nm* (*lío*) mess; (*conmoción*) fuss; **armar un ~** to kick up a row
fomentar [fomen'tar] *vt* (*Med*) to foment
fonda ['fonda] *nf* inn
fondo ['fondo] *nm* (*de mar*) bottom; (*de coche, sala*) back; (*Arte etc*) background; (*reserva*) fund; **fondos** *nmpl* (*Com*) funds, resources; **una investigación a ~** a thorough investigation; **en el ~** at bottom, deep down
fonobuzón [fonoβu'θon] *nm* voice mail
fontanería [fontane'ria] *nf* plumbing; **fontanero, -a** *nm/f* plumber
footing ['futɪn] *nm* jogging; **hacer ~** to jog, go jogging
forastero, -a [foras'tero, a] *nm/f* stranger
forcejear [forθexe'ar] *vi* (*luchar*) to struggle
forense [fo'rense] *nmf* pathologist
forma ['forma] *nf* (*figura*) form, shape; (*Med*) fitness; (*método*) way, means; **las ~s** the conventions; **estar en ~** to be fit; **de ~ que ...** so that ...; **de todas ~s** in any case
formación [forma'θjon] *nf* (*gen*) formation; (*educación*) education; **formación profesional** vocational training
formal [for'mal] *adj* (*gen*) formal; (*fig: serio*) serious; (*: de fiar*) reliable; **formalidad** *nf* formality; seriousness; **formalizar** *vt* (*Jur*) to formalize; (*situación*) to put in order, regularize; **formalizarse** *vr* (*situación*) to be put in order, be regularized
formar [for'mar] *vt* (*componer*) to form, shape; (*constituir*) to make up, constitute; (*Escol*) to train, educate; **formarse** *vr* (*Escol*) to be trained, educated; (*cobrar forma*) to form, take form; (*desarrollarse*) to develop
formatear [formate'ar] *vt* to format
formato [for'mato] *nm* format
formidable [formi'ðaβle] *adj* (*temible*) formidable; (*estupendo*) tremendous
fórmula ['formula] *nf* formula
formulario [formu'larjo] *nm* form
fornido, -a [for'niðo, a] *adj* well-built
foro ['foro] *nm* (*Pol, Inform etc*) forum
forrar [fo'rrar] *vt* (*abrigo*) to line; (*libro*) to cover; **forro** *nm* (*de cuaderno*) cover; (*Costura*) lining; (*de sillón*) upholstery; **forro polar** fleece
fortalecer [fortale'θer] *vt* to strengthen
fortaleza [forta'leθa] *nf* (*Mil*) fortress, stronghold; (*fuerza*) strength; (*determinación*) resolution
fortuito, -a [for'twito, a] *adj* accidental
fortuna [for'tuna] *nf* (*suerte*) fortune, (good) luck; (*riqueza*) fortune, wealth
forzar [for'θar] *vt* (*puerta*) to force (open); (*compeler*) to compel
forzoso, -a [for'θoso, a] *adj* necessary
fosa ['fosa] *nf* (*sepultura*) grave; (*en tierra*) pit; **fosas nasales** nostrils
fósforo ['fosforo] *nm* (*Quím*) phosphorus; (*cerilla*) match

fósil ['fosil] *nm* fossil
foso ['foso] *nm* ditch; (*Teatro*) pit; (*Auto*) inspection pit
foto ['foto] *nf* photo, snap(shot); **sacar una ~** to take a photo *o* picture; **foto (de) carné** passport(-size) photo
fotocopia [foto'kopja] *nf* photocopy; **fotocopiadora** *nf* photocopier; **fotocopiar** *vt* to photocopy
fotografía [fotoɤra'fia] *nf* (*Arte*) photography; (*una fotografía*) photograph; **fotografiar** *vt* to photograph
fotógrafo, -a [fo'toɤrafo, a] *nm/f* photographer
fotomatón [fotoma'ton] *nm* photo booth
FP (ESP) *nf abr* (= *Formación Profesional*) *vocational courses for 14- to 18-year-olds*
fracasar [fraka'sar] *vi* (*gen*) to fail
fracaso [fra'kaso] *nm* failure
fracción [frak'θjon] *nf* fraction
fractura [frak'tura] *nf* fracture, break
fragancia [fra'ɤanθja] *nf* (*olor*) fragrance, perfume
frágil ['fraxil] *adj* (*débil*) fragile; (*Com*) breakable
fragmento [fraɤ'mento] *nm* (*pedazo*) fragment
fraile ['fraile] *nm* (*Rel*) friar; (: *monje*) monk
frambuesa [fram'bwesa] *nf* raspberry
francés, -esa [fran'θes, esa] *adj* French ▷ *nm/f* Frenchman(-woman) ▷ *nm* (*Ling*) French
Francia ['franθja] *nf* France
franco, -a ['franko, a] *adj* (*cándido*) frank, open; (*Com*: *exento*) free ▷ *nm* (*moneda*) franc
francotirador, a [frankotira'ðor, a] *nm/f* sniper
franela [fra'nela] *nf* flannel
franja ['franxa] *nf* fringe
franquear [franke'ar] *vt* (*camino*) to clear; (*carta, paquete postal*) to frank, stamp; (*obstáculo*) to overcome
franqueo [fran'keo] *nm* postage
franqueza [fran'keθa] *nf* (*candor*) frankness
frasco ['frasko] *nm* bottle, flask
frase ['frase] *nf* sentence; **frase hecha** set phrase; (*pey*) stock phrase
fraterno, -a [fra'terno, a] *adj* brotherly, fraternal
fraude ['frauðe] *nm* (*cualidad*) dishonesty; (*acto*) fraud
frazada [fra'saða] (LAM) *nf* blanket
frecuencia [fre'kwenθja] *nf* frequency; **con ~** frequently, often
frecuentar [frekwen'tar] *vt* to frequent
frecuente [fre'kwente] *adj* (*gen*) frequent
fregadero [freɤa'ðero] *nm* (kitchen) sink
fregar [fre'ɤar] *vt* (*frotar*) to scrub; (*platos*) to wash (up); (LAM: *fam*: *fastidiar*) to annoy; (: *malograr*) to screw up
fregona [fre'ɤona] *nf* mop
freír [fre'ir] *vt* to fry
frenar [fre'nar] *vt* to brake; (*fig*) to check
frenazo [fre'naθo] *nm*: **dar un ~** to brake sharply
frenesí [frene'si] *nm* frenzy
freno ['freno] *nm* (*Tec, Auto*) brake; (*de cabalgadura*) bit; (*fig*) check; **freno de mano** handbrake
frente ['frente] *nm* (*Arq, Pol*) front; (*de objeto*) front part ▷ *nf* forehead, brow; **~ a** in front of; (*en situación opuesta de*) opposite; **al ~ de** (*fig*) at the head of; **chocar de ~** to crash head-on; **hacer ~ a** to face up to
fresa ['fresa] (ESP) *nf* strawberry
fresco, -a ['fresko, a] *adj* (*nuevo*) fresh; (*frío*) cool; (*descarado*) cheeky ▷ *nm* (*aire*) fresh air; (*Arte*) fresco; (LAM: *jugo*) fruit drink ▷ *nm/f* (*fam*): **ser un ~** to have a nerve; **tomar el ~** to get some fresh air; **frescura** *nf* freshness; (*descaro*) cheek, nerve
frialdad [frial'dað] *nf* (*gen*) coldness; (*indiferencia*) indifference

frigidez [frixi'ðeθ] *nf* frigidity
frigorífico [friɣo'rifiko] *nm* refrigerator
frijol [fri'xol] *nm* kidney bean
frío, -a *etc* ['frio, a] *vb V* **freír** ▷ *adj* cold; (*indiferente*) indifferent ▷ *nm* cold; indifference; **hace ~** it's cold; **tener ~** to be cold
frito, -a ['frito, a] *adj* fried; **me trae ~ ese hombre** I'm sick and tired of that man; **fritos** *nmpl* fried food
frívolo, -a ['friβolo, a] *adj* frivolous
frontal [fron'tal] *adj* frontal; **choque ~** head-on collision
frontera [fron'tera] *nf* frontier; **fronterizo, -a** *adj* frontier *cpd*; (*contiguo*) bordering
frontón [fron'ton] *nm* (*Deporte*: *cancha*) pelota court; (*: juego*) pelota
frotar [fro'tar] *vt* to rub; **frotarse** *vr*: **~se las manos** to rub one's hands
fructífero, -a [fruk'tifero, a] *adj* fruitful
fruncir [frun'θir] *vt* to pucker; (*Costura*) to pleat; **~ el ceño** to knit one's brow
frustrar [frus'trar] *vt* to frustrate
fruta ['fruta] *nf* fruit; **frutería** *nf* fruit shop; **frutero, -a** *adj* fruit *cpd* ▷ *nm/f* fruiterer ▷ *nm* fruit bowl
frutilla [fru'tiʎa] (cs) *nf* strawberry
fruto ['fruto] *nm* fruit; (*fig*: *resultado*) result; (*: beneficio*) benefit; **frutos secos** nuts and dried fruit *pl*
fucsia ['fuksja] *nf* fuchsia
fue [fwe] *vb V* **ser; ir**
fuego ['fweɣo] *nm* (*gen*) fire; **a ~ lento** on a low heat; **¿tienes ~?** have you (got) a light?; **fuego amigo** friendly fire; **fuegos artificiales** fireworks
fuente ['fwente] *nf* fountain; (*manantial*: *fig*) spring; (*origen*) source; (*plato*) large dish
fuera *etc* ['fwera] *vb V* **ser; ir** ▷ *adv* out(side); (*en otra parte*) away; (*excepto, salvo*) except, save ▷ *prep*: **~ de** outside; (*fig*) besides; **~ de sí** beside o.s.; **por ~** (on the) outside
fuera-borda [fwera'βorða] *nm* speedboat
fuerte ['fwerte] *adj* strong; (*golpe*) hard; (*ruido*) loud; (*comida*) rich; (*lluvia*) heavy; (*dolor*) intense ▷ *adv* strongly; hard; loud(ly)
fuerza *etc* ['fwerθa] *vb V* **forzar** ▷ *nf* (*fortaleza*) strength; (*Tec, Elec*) power; (*coacción*) force; (*Mil, Pol*) force; **a ~ de** by dint of; **cobrar ~s** to recover one's strength; **tener ~s para** to have the strength to; **a la ~** forcibly, by force; **por ~** of necessity; **fuerza de voluntad** willpower; **fuerzas aéreas** air force *sg*; **fuerzas armadas** armed forces
fuga ['fuɣa] *nf* (*huida*) flight, escape; (*de gas etc*) leak
fugarse [fu'ɣarse] *vr* to flee, escape
fugaz [fu'ɣaθ] *adj* fleeting
fugitivo, a [fuxi'tiβo, a] *adj, nm/f* fugitive
fui [fwi] *vb V* **ser; ir**
fulano, -a [fu'lano, a] *nm/f* so-and-so, what's-his-name/what's-her-name
fulminante [fulmi'nante] *adj* (*fig*: *mirada*) fierce; (*Med*: *enfermedad, ataque*) sudden; (*fam*: *éxito, golpe*) sudden
fumador, a [fuma'ðor, a] *nm/f* smoker
fumar [fu'mar] *vt, vi* to smoke; **~ en pipa** to smoke a pipe
función [fun'θjon] *nf* function; (*en trabajo*) duties *pl*; (*espectáculo*) show; **entrar en funciones** to take up one's duties
funcionar [funθjo'nar] *vi* (*gen*) to function; (*máquina*) to work; **"no funciona"** "out of order"
funcionario, -a [funθjo'narjo, a] *nm/f* civil servant
funda ['funda] *nf* (*gen*) cover; (*de almohada*) pillowcase
fundación [funda'θjon] *nf* foundation
fundamental [fundamen'tal] *adj* fundamental, basic
fundamento [funda'mento] *nm*

(*base*) foundation

fundar [fun'dar] *vt* to found; **fundarse** *vr*: **~se en** to be founded on

fundición [fundi'θjon] *nf* fusing; (*fábrica*) foundry

fundir [fun'dir] *vt* (*gen*) to fuse; (*metal*) to smelt, melt down; (*nieve etc*) to melt; (*Com*) to merge; (*estatua*) to cast; **fundirse** *vr* (*colores etc*) to merge, blend; (*unirse*) to fuse together; (*Elec*: *fusible, lámpara etc*) to fuse, blow; (*nieve etc*) to melt

fúnebre ['funeβre] *adj* funeral *cpd*, funereal

funeral [fune'ral] *nm* funeral; **funeraria** *nf* undertaker's

funicular [funiku'lar] *nm* (*tren*) funicular; (*teleférico*) cable car

furgón [fur'ɣon] *nm* wagon; **furgoneta** *nf* (*Auto, Com*) (transit) van (BRIT), pick-up (truck) (US)

furia ['furja] *nf* (*ira*) fury; (*violencia*) violence; **furioso, -a** *adj* (*iracundo*) furious; (*violento*) violent

furtivo, -a [fur'tiβo, a] *adj* furtive ▷ *nm* poacher

fusible [fu'siβle] *nm* fuse

fusil [fu'sil] *nm* rifle; **fusilar** *vt* to shoot

fusión [fu'sjon] *nf* (*gen*) melting; (*unión*) fusion; (*Com*) merger

fútbol ['futβol] *nm* football (BRIT), soccer (US); **fútbol americano** American football (BRIT), football (US); **fútbol sala** indoor football (BRIT) *o* soccer (US); **futbolín** *nm* table football; **futbolista** *nmf* footballer

futuro, -a [fu'turo, a] *adj, nm* future

gabardina [gaβar'ðina] *nf* raincoat, gabardine

gabinete [gaβi'nete] *nm* (*Pol*) cabinet; (*estudio*) study; (*de abogados etc*) office

gachas ['gatʃas] *nfpl* porridge *sg*

gafas ['gafas] *nfpl* glasses; **gafas de sol** sunglasses

gafe ['gafe] (ESP) *nmf* jinx

gaita ['gaita] *nf* bagpipes *pl*

gajes ['gaxes] *nmpl*: **~ del oficio** occupational hazards

gajo ['gaxo] *nm* (*de naranja*) segment

gala ['gala] *nf* (*traje de etiqueta*) full dress; **galas** *nfpl* (*ropa*) finery *sg*; **estar de ~** to be in one's best clothes; **hacer ~ de** to display

galápago [ga'lapaɣo] *nm* (*Zool*) turtle

galardón [galar'ðon] *nm* award, prize

galaxia [ga'laksja] *nf* galaxy

galera [ga'lera] *nf* (*nave*) galley; (*carro*) wagon; (*Imprenta*) galley

galería [gale'ria] *nf* (*gen*) gallery;

(*balcón*) veranda(h); (*pasillo*) corridor; **galería comercial** shopping mall
Gales ['gales] *nm* (*tb*: **País de ~**) Wales; **galés, -esa** *adj* Welsh ▷*nm/f* Welshman(-woman) ▷*nm* (*Ling*) Welsh
galgo, -a ['galɣo, a] *nm/f* greyhound
gallego, -a [ga'ʎeɣo, a] *adj, nm/f* Galician
galleta [ga'ʎeta] *nf* biscuit (BRIT), cookie (US)
gallina [ga'ʎina] *nf* hen ▷*nmf* (*fam*: *cobarde*) chicken; **gallinero** *nm* henhouse; (*Teatro*) top gallery
gallo ['gaʎo] *nm* cock, rooster
galopar [galo'par] *vi* to gallop
gama ['gama] *nf* (*fig*) range
gamba ['gamba] *nf* prawn (BRIT), shrimp (US)
gamberro, -a [gam'berro, a] (ESP) *nm/f* hooligan, lout
gamuza [ga'muθa] *nf* chamois
gana ['gana] *nf* (*deseo*) desire, wish; (*apetito*) appetite; (*voluntad*) will; (*añoranza*) longing; **de buena ~** willingly; **de mala ~** reluctantly; **me da ~s de** I feel like, I want to; **no me da la ~** I don't feel like it; **tener ~s de** to feel like
ganadería [ganaðe'ria] *nf* (*ganado*) livestock; (*ganado vacuno*) cattle *pl*; (*cría, comercio*) cattle raising
ganadero, -a [gana'ðero, a] (ESP) *nm/f* (*hacendado*) rancher
ganado [ga'naðo] *nm* livestock; **ganado porcino** pigs *pl*
ganador, a [gana'ðor, a] *adj* winning ▷*nm/f* winner
ganancia [ga'nanθja] *nf* (*lo ganado*) gain; (*aumento*) increase; (*beneficio*) profit; **ganancias** *nfpl* (*ingresos*) earnings; (*beneficios*) profit *sg*, winnings
ganar [ga'nar] *vt* (*obtener*) to get, obtain; (*sacar ventaja*) to gain; (*salario etc*) to earn; (*Deporte, premio*) to win; (*derrotar a*) to beat; (*alcanzar*) to reach ▷*vi* (*Deporte*) to win; **ganarse** *vr*: **~se la vida** to earn one's living
ganchillo [gan'tʃiʎo] *nm* crochet
gancho ['gantʃo] *nm* (*gen*) hook; (*colgador*) hanger
gandul, a [gan'dul, a] *adj, nm/f* good-for-nothing, layabout
ganga ['ganga] *nf* bargain
gangrena [gan'grena] *nf* gangrene
ganso, -a ['ganso, a] *nm/f* (*Zool*) goose; (*fam*) idiot
ganzúa [gan'θua] *nf* skeleton key
garabato [gara'βato] *nm* (*escritura*) scrawl, scribble
garaje [ga'raxe] *nm* garage
garantía [garan'tia] *nf* guarantee
garantizar [garanti'θar] *vt* to guarantee
garbanzo [gar'βanθo] *nm* chickpea (BRIT), garbanzo (US)
garfio ['garfjo] *nm* grappling iron
garganta [gar'ɣanta] *nf* (*Anat*) throat; (*de botella*) neck; **gargantilla** *nf* necklace
gárgaras ['garɣaras] *nfpl*: **hacer ~** to gargle
gargarear [garɣare'ar] (LAM) *vi* to gargle
garita [ga'rita] *nf* cabin, hut; (*Mil*) sentry box
garra ['garra] *nf* (*de gato, Tec*) claw; (*de ave*) talon; (*fam*: *mano*) hand, paw
garrafa [ga'rrafa] *nf* carafe, decanter
garrapata [garra'pata] *nf* tick
gas [gas] *nm* gas; **gases lacrimógenos** tear gas *sg*
gasa ['gasa] *nf* gauze
gaseosa [gase'osa] *nf* lemonade
gaseoso, -a [gase'oso, a] *adj* gassy, fizzy
gasoil [ga'soil] *nm* diesel (oil)
gasóleo [ga'soleo] *nm* = **gasoil**
gasolina [gaso'lina] *nf* petrol (BRIT), gas(oline) (US); **gasolinera** *nf* petrol (BRIT) *o* gas (US) station
gastado, -a [gas'taðo, a] *adj* (*dinero*) spent; (*ropa*) worn out; (*usado*: *frase etc*) trite
gastar [gas'tar] *vt* (*dinero, tiempo*) to

spend; (*fuerzas*) to use up; (*desperdiciar*) to waste; (*llevar*) to wear; **gastarse** *vr* to wear out; (*estropearse*) to waste; **~ en** to spend on; **~ bromas** to crack jokes; **¿qué número gastas?** what size (shoe) do you take?

gasto ['gasto] *nm* (*desembolso*) expenditure, spending; (*consumo, uso*) use; **gastos** *nmpl* (*desembolsos*) expenses; (*cargos*) charges, costs

gastronomía [gastrono'mia] *nf* gastronomy

gatear [gate'ar] *vi* (*andar a gatas*) to go on all fours

gatillo [ga'tiʎo] *nm* (*de arma de fuego*) trigger; (*de dentista*) forceps

gato, -a ['gato, a] *nm/f* cat ▷ *nm* (*Tec*) jack; **andar a gatas** to go on all fours

gaucho ['gautʃo] *nm* gaucho

GAUCHO

Gauchos are the herdsmen or riders of the Southern Cone plains. Although popularly associated with Argentine folklore, **gauchos** belong equally to the cattle-raising areas of Southern Brazil and Uruguay. **Gauchos'** traditions and clothing reflect their mixed ancestry and cultural roots. Their baggy trousers are Arabic in origin, while the horse and guitar are inherited from the Spanish conquistadors; the poncho, maté and **boleadoras** (strips of leather weighted at either end with stones) form part of the Indian tradition.

gaviota [ga'βjota] *nf* seagull

gay [ge] *adj inv, nm* gay, homosexual

gazpacho [gaθ'patʃo] *nm* gazpacho

gel [xel] *nm*: **~ de baño/ducha** bath/shower gel

gelatina [xela'tina] *nf* jelly; (*polvos etc*) gelatine

gema ['xema] *nf* gem

gemelo, -a [xe'melo, a] *adj, nm/f* twin; **gemelos** *nmpl* (*de camisa*) cufflinks; (*prismáticos*) field glasses, binoculars

gemido [xe'miðo] *nm* (*quejido*) moan, groan; (*aullido*) howl

Géminis ['xeminis] *nm* Gemini

gemir [xe'mir] *vi* (*quejarse*) to moan, groan; (*aullar*) to howl

generación [xenera'θjon] *nf* generation

general [xene'ral] *adj* general ▷ *nm* general; **por lo** *o* **en ~** in general; **Generalitat** *nf Catalan parliament*; **generalizar** *vt* to generalize; **generalizarse** *vr* to become generalized, spread

generar [xene'rar] *vt* to generate

género ['xenero] *nm* (*clase*) kind, sort; (*tipo*) type; (*Bio*) genus; (*Ling*) gender; (*Com*) material; **género humano** human race

generosidad [xenerosi'ðað] *nf* generosity; **generoso, -a** *adj* generous

genial [xe'njal] *adj* inspired; (*idea*) brilliant; (*estupendo*) wonderful

genio ['xenjo] *nm* (*carácter*) nature, disposition; (*humor*) temper; (*facultad creadora*) genius; **de mal ~** bad-tempered

genital [xeni'tal] *adj* genital; **genitales** *nmpl* genitals

genoma [xe'noma] *nm* genome

gente ['xente] *nf* (*personas*) people *pl*; (*parientes*) relatives *pl*

gentil [xen'til] *adj* (*elegante*) graceful; (*encantador*) charming

No confundir **gentil** con la palabra inglesa *gentle*.

genuino, -a [xe'nwino, a] *adj* genuine

geografía [xeoɣra'fia] *nf* geography

geología [xeolo'xia] *nf* geology

geometría [xeome'tria] *nf* geometry

gerente [xe'rente] *nmf* (*supervisor*) manager; (*jefe*) director

geriatría [xeria'tria] *nf* (*Med*) geriatrics *sg*
germen ['xermen] *nm* germ
gesticular [xestiku'lar] *vi* to gesticulate; (*hacer muecas*) to grimace; **gesticulación** *nf* gesticulation; (*mueca*) grimace
gestión [xes'tjon] *nf* management; (*diligencia, acción*) negotiation
gesto ['xesto] *nm* (*mueca*) grimace; (*ademán*) gesture
Gibraltar [xiβral'tar] *nm* Gibraltar; **gibraltareño, -a** *adj, nm/f* Gibraltarian
gigante [xi'ɣante] *adj, nmf* giant; **gigantesco, -a** *adj* gigantic
gilipollas [xili'poʎas] (*fam*) *adj inv* daft ▷ *nmf inv* wally
gimnasia [xim'nasja] *nf* gymnastics *pl*; **gimnasio** *nm* gymnasium; **gimnasta** *nmf* gymnast
ginebra [xi'neβra] *nf* gin
ginecólogo, -a [xine'koloɣo, a] *nm/f* gynaecologist
gira ['xira] *nf* tour, trip
girar [xi'rar] *vt* (*dar la vuelta*) to turn (around); (*: rápidamente*) to spin; (*Com: giro postal*) to draw; (*: letra de cambio*) to issue ▷ *vi* to turn (round); (*rápido*) to spin
girasol [xira'sol] *nm* sunflower
giratorio, -a [xira'torjo, a] *adj* revolving
giro ['xiro] *nm* (*movimiento*) turn, revolution; (*Ling*) expression; (*Com*) draft; **giro bancario/postal** bank draft/money order
gis [xis] (MÉX) *nm* chalk
gitano, -a [xi'tano, a] *adj, nm/f* gypsy
glacial [gla'θjal] *adj* icy, freezing
glaciar [gla'θjar] *nm* glacier
glándula ['glandula] *nf* gland
global [glo'βal] *adj* global; **globalización** *nf* globalization
globo ['gloβo] *nm* (*esfera*) globe, sphere; (*aerostato, juguete*) balloon
glóbulo ['gloβulo] *nm* globule; (*Anat*) corpuscle
gloria ['glorja] *nf* glory
glorieta [glo'rjeta] *nf* (*de jardín*) bower, arbour; (*plazoleta*) roundabout (BRIT), traffic circle (US)
glorioso, -a [glo'rjoso, a] *adj* glorious
glotón, -ona [glo'ton, ona] *adj* gluttonous, greedy ▷ *nm/f* glutton
glucosa [glu'kosa] *nf* glucose
gobernador, a [goβerna'ðor, a] *adj* governing ▷ *nm/f* governor; **gobernante** *adj* governing
gobernar [goβer'nar] *vt* (*dirigir*) to guide, direct; (*Pol*) to rule, govern ▷ *vi* to govern; (*Náut*) to steer
gobierno *etc* [go'βjerno] *vb V* **gobernar** ▷ *nm* (*Pol*) government; (*dirección*) guidance, direction; (*Náut*) steering
goce *etc* ['goθe] *vb V* **gozar** ▷ *nm* enjoyment
gol [gol] *nm* goal
golf [golf] *nm* golf
golfa ['golfa] (*fam!*) *nf* (*mujer*) slut, whore
golfo, -a ['golfo, a] *nm* (*Geo*) gulf ▷ *nm/f* (*fam: niño*) urchin; (*gamberro*) lout
golondrina [golon'drina] *nf* swallow
golosina [golo'sina] *nf* (*dulce*) sweet; **goloso, -a** *adj* sweet-toothed
golpe ['golpe] *nm* blow; (*de puño*) punch; (*de mano*) smack; (*de remo*) stroke; (*fig: choque*) clash; **no dar ~** to be bone idle; **de un ~** with one blow; **de ~** suddenly; **golpe (de estado)** coup (d'état); **golpear** *vt, vi* to strike, knock; (*asestar*) to beat; (*de puño*) to punch; (*golpetear*) to tap
goma ['goma] *nf* (*caucho*) rubber; (*elástico*) elastic; (*una goma*) elastic band; **goma de borrar** eraser, rubber (BRIT); **goma espuma** foam rubber
gomina [go'mina] *nf* hair gel
gomita [go'mita] (RPL) *nf* rubber band

gordo, -a ['gorðo, a] *adj* (*gen*) fat; (*fam*) enormous; **el (premio) ~** (*en lotería*) first prize
gorila [go'rila] *nm* gorilla
gorra ['gorra] *nf* cap; (*de bebé*) bonnet; (*militar*) bearskin; **entrar de ~** (*fam*) to gatecrash; **ir de ~** to sponge
gorrión [go'rrjon] *nm* sparrow
gorro ['gorro] *nm* (*gen*) cap; (*de bebé, mujer*) bonnet
gorrón, -ona [go'rron, ona] *nm/f* scrounger; **gorronear** (*fam*) *vi* to scrounge
gota ['gota] *nf* (*gen*) drop; (*de sudor*) bead; (*Med*) gout; **gotear** *vi* to drip; (*lloviznar*) to drizzle; **gotera** *nf* leak
gozar [go'θar] *vi* to enjoy o.s.; **~ de** (*disfrutar*) to enjoy; (*poseer*) to possess
gr. *abr* (= *gramo, gramos*) g
grabación [graβa'θjon] *nf* recording
grabado [gra'βaðo] *nm* print, engraving
grabadora [graβa'ðora] *nf* tape-recorder; **grabadora de CD/DVD** CD/DVD writer
grabar [gra'βar] *vt* to engrave; (*discos, cintas*) to record
gracia ['graθja] *nf* (*encanto*) grace, gracefulness; (*humor*) humour, wit; **¡(muchas) ~s!** thanks (very much)!; **~s a** thanks to; **dar las ~s a algn por algo** to thank sb for sth; **tener ~** (*chiste etc*) to be funny; **no me hace ~** I am not keen; **gracioso, -a** *adj* (*divertido*) funny, amusing; (*cómico*) comical ▷ *nm/f* (*Teatro*) comic character
grada ['graða] *nf* (*de escalera*) step; (*de anfiteatro*) tier, row; **gradas** *nfpl* (*Deporte: de estadio*) terraces
grado ['graðo] *nm* degree; (*de aceite, vino*) grade; (*grada*) step; (*Mil*) rank; **de buen ~** willingly; **grado centígrado/ Fahrenheit** degree centigrade/ Fahrenheit
graduación [graðwa'θjon] *nf* (*del alcohol*) proof, strength; (*Escol*) graduation; (*Mil*) rank
gradual [gra'ðwal] *adj* gradual
graduar [gra'ðwar] *vt* (*gen*) to graduate; (*Mil*) to commission; **graduarse** *vr* to graduate; **~se la vista** to have one's eyes tested
gráfica ['grafika] *nf* graph
gráfico, -a ['grafiko, a] *adj* graphic ▷ *nm* diagram; **gráficos** *nmpl* (*Inform*) graphics
grajo ['graxo] *nm* rook
gramática [gra'matika] *nf* grammar
gramo ['gramo] *nm* gramme (BRIT), gram (US)
gran [gran] *adj V* **grande**
grana ['grana] *nf* (*color, tela*) scarlet
granada [gra'naða] *nf* pomegranate; (*Mil*) grenade
granate [gra'nate] *adj* deep red
Gran Bretaña [-bre'taɲa] *nf* Great Britain
grande ['grande] (*antes de nmsg* **gran**) *adj* (*de tamaño*) big, large; (*alto*) tall; (*distinguido*) great; (*impresionante*) grand ▷ *nm* grandee
granel [gra'nel]: **a ~** *adv* (*Com*) in bulk
granero [gra'nero] *nm* granary, barn
granito [gra'nito] *nm* (*Agr*) small grain; (*roca*) granite
granizado [grani'θaðo] *nm* iced drink
granizar [grani'θar] *vi* to hail; **granizo** *nm* hail
granja ['granxa] *nf* (*gen*) farm; **granjero, -a** *nm/f* farmer
grano ['grano] *nm* grain; (*semilla*) seed; (*de café*) bean; (*Med*) pimple, spot
granuja [gra'nuxa] *nmf* rogue; (*golfillo*) urchin
grapa ['grapa] *nf* staple; (*Tec*) clamp; **grapadora** *nf* stapler
grasa ['grasa] *nf* (*gen*) grease; (*de cocinar*) fat, lard; (*sebo*) suet; (*mugre*) filth; **grasiento, -a** *adj* greasy; (*de aceite*) oily; **graso, -a** *adj* (*leche, queso, carne*) fatty; (*pelo, piel*) greasy
gratinar [grati'nar] *vt* to cook au gratin
gratis ['gratis] *adv* free
grato, -a ['grato, a] *adj* (*agradable*)

pleasant, agreeable

gratuito, -a [gra'twito, a] *adj* (*gratis*) free; (*sin razón*) gratuitous

grave ['graβe] *adj* heavy; (*serio*) grave, serious; **gravedad** *nf* gravity

Grecia ['greθja] *nf* Greece

gremio ['gremjo] *nm* trade, industry

griego, -a ['grjeɣo, a] *adj, nm/f* Greek

grieta ['grjeta] *nf* crack

grifo ['grifo] (ESP) *nm* tap (BRIT), faucet (US)

grillo ['griʎo] *nm* (*Zool*) cricket

gripa ['gripa] (MÉX) *nf* flu, influenza

gripe ['gripe] *nf* flu, influenza; **gripe aviar** bird flu

gris [gris] *adj* (*color*) grey

gritar [gri'tar] *vt, vi* to shout, yell; **grito** *nm* shout, yell; (*de horror*) scream

grosella [gro'seʎa] *nf* (red)currant

grosero, -a [gro'sero, a] *adj* (*poco cortés*) rude, bad-mannered; (*ordinario*) vulgar, crude

grosor [gro'sor] *nm* thickness

grúa ['grua] *nf* (*Tec*) crane; (*de petróleo*) derrick

grueso, -a ['grweso, a] *adj* thick; (*persona*) stout ▷ *nm* bulk; **el ~ de** the bulk of

grulla ['gruʎa] *nf* crane

grumo ['grumo] *nm* clot, lump

gruñido [gru'ɲiðo] *nm* grunt; (*de persona*) grumble

gruñir [gru'ɲir] *vi* (*animal*) to growl; (*persona*) to grumble

grupo ['grupo] *nm* group; (*Tec*) unit, set; **grupo de presión** pressure group; **grupo sanguíneo** blood group

gruta ['gruta] *nf* grotto

guacho, -a ['gwatʃo, a] (CS) *nm/f* homeless child

guajolote [gwaxo'lote] (MÉX) *nm* turkey

guante ['gwante] *nm* glove; **guantes de goma** rubber gloves; **guantera** *nf* glove compartment

guapo, -a ['gwapo, a] *adj* good-looking, attractive; (*elegante*) smart

guarda ['gwarða] *nmf* (*persona*) guard, keeper ▷ *nf* (*acto*) guarding; (*custodia*) custody; **guarda jurado** (armed) security guard; **guardabarros** *nm inv* mudguard (BRIT), fender (US); **guardabosques** *nm inv* gamekeeper; **guardacostas** *nm inv* coastguard vessel ▷ *nmf* guardian, protector; **guardaespaldas** *nmf inv* bodyguard; **guardameta** *nmf* goalkeeper; **guardar** *vt* (*gen*) to keep; (*vigilar*) to guard, watch over; (*dinero: ahorrar*) to save; **guardarse** *vr* (*preservarse*) to protect o.s.; (*evitar*) to avoid; **guardar cama** to stay in bed; **guardarropa** *nm* (*armario*) wardrobe; (*en establecimiento público*) cloakroom

guardería [gwarðe'ria] *nf* nursery

guardia ['gwarðja] *nf* (*Mil*) guard; (*cuidado*) care, custody ▷ *nmf* guard; (*policía*) policeman(-woman); **estar de ~** to be on guard; **montar ~** to mount guard; **Guardia Civil** Civil Guard

guardián, -ana [gwar'ðjan, ana] *nm/f* (*gen*) guardian, keeper

guarida [gwa'riða] *nf* (*de animal*) den, lair; (*refugio*) refuge

guarnición [gwarni'θjon] *nf* (*de vestimenta*) trimming; (*de piedra*) mount; (*Culin*) garnish; (*arneses*) harness; (*Mil*) garrison

guarro, -a ['gwarro, a] *nm/f* pig

guasa ['gwasa] *nf* joke; **guasón, -ona** *adj* (*bromista*) joking ▷ *nm/f* wit; joker

Guatemala [gwate'mala] *nf* Guatemala

guay [gwai] (*fam*) *adj* super, great

güero, -a ['gwero, a] (MÉX) *adj* blond(e)

guerra ['gerra] *nf* war; **dar ~** to annoy; **guerra civil** civil war; **guerra fría** cold war; **guerrero, -a** *adj* fighting; (*carácter*) warlike ▷ *nm/f* warrior

guerrilla [ge'rriʎa] *nf* guerrilla warfare; (*tropas*) guerrilla band *o* group

guía *etc* ['gia] *vb V* **guiar** ▷ *nmf* (*persona*) guide; (*nf: libro*) guidebook; **guía telefónica** telephone directory;

guía turística tourist guide
guiar [gi'ar] *vt* to guide, direct; (*Auto*) to steer; **guiarse** *vr*: **~se por** to be guided by
guinda ['ginda] *nf* morello cherry
guindilla [gin'diʎa] *nf* chilli pepper
guiñar [gi'ɲar] *vt* to wink
guión [gi'on] *nm* (*Ling*) hyphen, dash; (*Cine*) script; **guionista** *nmf* scriptwriter
guiri ['giri] (*ESP*: *fam, pey*) *nmf* foreigner
guirnalda [gir'nalda] *nf* garland
guisado [gi'saðo] *nm* stew
guisante [gi'sante] *nm* pea
guisar [gi'sar] *vt, vi* to cook; **guiso** *nm* cooked dish
guitarra [gi'tarra] *nf* guitar
gula ['gula] *nf* gluttony, greed
gusano [gu'sano] *nm* worm; (*lombriz*) earthworm
gustar [gus'tar] *vt* to taste, sample ▷ *vi* to please, be pleasing; **~ de algo** to like *o* enjoy sth; **me gustan las uvas** I like grapes; **le gusta nadar** she likes *o* enjoys swimming
gusto ['gusto] *nm* (*sentido, sabor*) taste; (*placer*) pleasure; **tiene ~ a menta** it tastes of mint; **tener buen ~** to have good taste; **coger el** *o* **tomar ~ a algo** to take a liking to sth; **sentirse a ~** to feel at ease; **mucho ~ (en conocerle)** pleased to meet you; **el ~ es mío** the pleasure is mine; **con ~** willingly, gladly

ha *vb V* **haber**
haba ['aβa] *nf* bean
Habana [a'βana] *nf*: **la ~** Havana
habano [a'βano] *nm* Havana cigar
habéis *vb V* **haber**

PALABRA CLAVE

haber [a'βer] *vb aux* **1** (*tiempos compuestos*) to have; **había comido** I had eaten; **antes/después de haberlo visto** before seeing/after seeing *o* having seen it
2: **¡haberlo dicho antes!** you should have said so before!
3: **haber de: he de hacerlo** I have to do it; **ha de llegar mañana** it should arrive tomorrow
▷ *vb impers* **1** (*existencia*: *sg*) there is; (: *pl*) there are; **hay un hermano/dos hermanos** there is one brother/there are two brothers; **¿cuánto hay de aquí a Sucre?** how far is it from here to Sucre?
2 (*obligación*): **hay que hacer algo**

something must be done; **hay que apuntarlo para acordarse** you have to write it down to remember
3: **¡hay que ver!** well I never!
4: **¡no hay de** *o* **por** (*LAM*) **qué!** don't mention it!, not at all!
5: **¿qué hay?** (*¿qué pasa?*) what's up?, what's the matter?; (*¿qué tal?*) how's it going?
▷ *vt*: **he aquí unas sugerencias** here are some suggestions; **no hay cintas blancas pero sí las hay rojas** there aren't any white ribbons but there are some red ones
▷ *nm* (*en cuenta*) credit side; **haberes** *nmpl* assets; **¿cuánto tengo en el haber?** how much do I have in my account?; **tiene varias novelas en su haber** he has several novels to his credit
haberse *vr*: **habérselas con algn** to have it out with sb

habichuela [aβi'tʃwela] *nf* kidney bean
hábil ['aβil] *adj* (*listo*) clever, smart; (*capaz*) fit, capable; (*experto*) expert; **día ~** working day; **habilidad** *nf* skill, ability
habitación [aβita'θjon] *nf* (*cuarto*) room; (*Bio: morada*) habitat; **habitación doble** *o* **de matrimonio** double room; **habitación individual** *o* **sencilla** single room
habitante [aβi'tante] *nmf* inhabitant
habitar [aβi'tar] *vt* (*residir en*) to inhabit; (*ocupar*) to occupy ▷ *vi* to live
hábito ['aβito] *nm* habit
habitual [aβi'twal] *adj* usual
habituar [aβi'twar] *vt* to accustom; **habituarse** *vr*: **~se a** to get used to
habla ['aβla] *nf* (*capacidad de hablar*) speech; (*idioma*) language; (*dialecto*) dialect; **perder el ~** to become speechless; **de ~ francesa** French-speaking; **estar al ~** to be in contact; (*Tel*) to be on the line; **¡González al ~!** (*Tel*) González speaking!
hablador, a [aβla'ðor, a] *adj* talkative ▷ *nm/f* chatterbox
habladuría [aβlaðu'ria] *nf* rumour; **habladurías** *nfpl* gossip *sg*
hablante [a'βlante] *adj* speaking ▷ *nmf* speaker
hablar [a'βlar] *vt* to speak, talk ▷ *vi* to speak; **hablarse** *vr* to speak to each other; **~ con** to speak to; **~ de** to speak of *o* about; **¡ni ~!** it's out of the question!; **"se habla inglés"** "English spoken here"
habré *etc* [a'βre] *vb V* **haber**
hacendado [aθen'daðo] (*LAM*) *nm* rancher, farmer
hacendoso, -a [aθen'doso, a] *adj* industrious

PALABRA CLAVE

hacer [a'θer] *vt* **1** (*fabricar, producir*) to make; (*construir*) to build; **hacer una película/un ruido** to make a film/noise; **el guisado lo hice yo** I made *o* cooked the stew
2 (*ejecutar: trabajo etc*) to do; **hacer la colada** to do the washing; **hacer la comida** to do the cooking; **¿qué haces?** what are you doing?; **hacer el malo** *o* **el papel del malo** (*Teatro*) to play the villain
3 (*estudios, algunos deportes*) to do; **hacer español/económicas** to do *o* study Spanish/economics; **hacer yoga/gimnasia** to do yoga/go to gym
4 (*transformar, incidir en*): **esto lo hará más difícil** this will make it more difficult; **salir te hará sentir mejor** going out will make you feel better
5 (*cálculo*): **2 y 2 hacen 4** 2 and 2 make 4; **éste hace 100** this one makes 100
6 (+ *sub*): **esto hará que ganemos** this will make us win; **harás que no quiera venir** you'll stop him wanting to come
7 (*como sustituto de vb*) to do; **él bebió y yo hice lo mismo** he drank and I did likewise
8 **no hace más que criticar** all he does is criticize

▷ *vb semi-aux* (*directo*): **hacer** +*infin*: **les hice venir** I made *o* had them come; **hacer trabajar a los demás** to get others to work
▷ *vi* **1 haz como que no lo sabes** act as if you don't know
2 (*ser apropiado*): **si os hace** if it's alright with you
3 hacer de: hacer de Otelo to play Othello
▷ *vb impers* **1 hace calor/frío** it's hot/ cold; *V tb* **bueno, sol, tiempo**
2 (*tiempo*): **hace 3 años** 3 years ago; **hace un mes que voy/no voy** I've been going/I haven't been for a month
3 ¿cómo has hecho para llegar tan rápido? how did you manage to get here so quickly?
hacerse *vr* **1** (*volverse*) to become; **se hicieron amigos** they became friends
2 (*acostumbrarse*): **hacerse a** to get used to
3 se hace con huevos y leche it's made out of eggs and milk; **eso no se hace** that's not done
4 (*obtener*): **hacerse de** *o* **con algo** to get hold of sth
5 (*fingirse*): **hacerse el sueco** to turn a deaf ear

hacha ['atʃa] *nf* axe; (*antorcha*) torch
hachís [a'tʃis] *nm* hashish
hacia ['aθja] *prep* (*en dirección de*) towards; (*cerca de*) near; (*actitud*) towards; **~ adelante/atrás** forwards/backwards; **~ arriba/abajo** up(wards)/down(wards); **~ mediodía/ las cinco** about noon/five
hacienda [a'θjenda] *nf* (*propiedad*) property; (*finca*) farm; (LAM: *rancho*) ranch; **(Ministerio de) H~** Exchequer (BRIT), Treasury Department (US); **hacienda pública** public finance
hada ['aða] *nf* fairy
hago *etc vb V* **hacer**
Haití [ai'ti] *nm* Haiti
halagar [ala'ɣar] *vt* to flatter
halago [a'laɣo] *nm* flattery
halcón [al'kon] *nm* falcon, hawk
hallar [a'ʎar] *vt* (*gen*) to find; (*descubrir*) to discover; (*toparse con*) to run into; **hallarse** *vr* to be (situated)
halterofilia [altero'filja] *nf* weightlifting
hamaca [a'maka] *nf* hammock
hambre ['ambre] *nf* hunger; (*plaga*) famine; (*deseo*) longing; **tener ~** to be hungry; **¡me muero de ~!** I'm starving!; **hambriento, -a** *adj* hungry, starving
hamburguesa [ambur'ɣesa] *nf* hamburger; **hamburguesería** *nf* burger bar
han *vb V* **haber**
harapos [a'rapos] *nmpl* rags
haré *vb V* **hacer**
harina [a'rina] *nf* flour; **harina de maíz** cornflour (BRIT), cornstarch (US); **harina de trigo** wheat flour
hartar [ar'tar] *vt* to satiate, glut; (*fig*) to tire, sicken; **hartarse** *vr* (*de comida*) to fill o.s., gorge o.s.; (*cansarse*): **~se (de)** to get fed up (with); **harto, -a** *adj* (*lleno*) full; (*cansado*) fed up ▷ *adv* (*bastante*) enough; (*muy*) very; **estar harto de hacer algo/de algn** to be fed up of doing sth/with sb
has *vb V* **haber**
hasta ['asta] *adv* even ▷ *prep* (*alcanzando a*) as far as; up to; down to; (*de tiempo: a tal hora*) till, until; (*antes de*) before ▷ *conj*: **~ que ...** until; **~ luego/el sábado** see you soon/on Saturday; **~ ahora** (*al despedirse*) see you in a minute; **~ pronto** see you soon
hay *vb V* **haber**
Haya ['aja] *nf*: **la ~** The Hague
haya *etc* ['aja] *vb V* **haber** ▷ *nf* beech tree
haz [aθ] *vb V* **hacer** ▷ *nm* (*de luz*) beam
hazaña [a'θaɲa] *nf* feat, exploit
hazmerreír [aθmerre'ir] *nm inv* laughing stock
he *vb V* **haber**
hebilla [e'βiʎa] *nf* buckle, clasp
hebra ['eβra] *nf* thread; (*Bot: fibra*)

fibre, grain
hebreo, -a [e'βreo, a] *adj, nm/f* Hebrew ▷*nm* (*Ling*) Hebrew
hechizar [etʃi'θar] *vt* to cast a spell on, bewitch
hechizo [e'tʃiθo] *nm* witchcraft, magic; (*acto de magía*) spell, charm
hecho, -a ['etʃo, a] *pp de* **hacer** ▷*adj* (*carne*) done; (*Costura*) ready-to-wear ▷*nm* deed, act; (*dato*) fact; (*cuestión*) matter; (*suceso*) event ▷*excl* agreed!, done!; **de ~** in fact, as a matter of fact; **el ~ es que ...** the fact is that ...; **¡bien ~!** well done!
hechura [e'tʃura] *nf* (*forma*) form, shape; (*de persona*) build
hectárea [ek'tarea] *nf* hectare
helada [e'laða] *nf* frost
heladera [ela'ðera] (LAM) *nf* (*refrigerador*) refrigerator
helado, -a [e'laðo, a] *adj* frozen; (*glacial*) icy; (*fig*) chilly, cold ▷*nm* ice cream
helar [e'lar] *vt* to freeze, ice (up); (*dejar atónito*) to amaze; (*desalentar*) to discourage ▷*vi* to freeze; **helarse** *vr* to freeze
helecho [e'letʃo] *nm* fern
hélice ['eliθe] *nf* (*Tec*) propeller
helicóptero [eli'koptero] *nm* helicopter
hembra ['embra] *nf* (*Bot, Zool*) female; (*mujer*) woman; (*Tec*) nut
hemorragia [emo'rraxja] *nf* haemorrhage
hemorroides [emo'rroiðes] *nfpl* haemorrhoids, piles
hemos *vb V* **haber**
heno ['eno] *nm* hay
heredar [ere'ðar] *vt* to inherit; **heredero, -a** *nm/f* heir(ess)
hereje [e'rexe] *nmf* heretic
herencia [e'renθja] *nf* inheritance
herida [e'riða] *nf* wound, injury; *V tb* **herido**
herido, -a [e'riðo, a] *adj* injured, wounded ▷*nm/f* casualty
herir [e'rir] *vt* to wound, injure; (*fig*) to offend
hermanastro, -a [erma'nastro, a] *nm/f* stepbrother/sister
hermandad [erman'dað] *nf* brotherhood
hermano, -a [er'mano, a] *nm/f* brother/sister; **hermano**(-a) gemelo(-a), twin brother/sister; **hermano**(-a) político(-a), brother-in-law/sister-in-law
hermético, -a [er'metiko, a] *adj* hermetic; (*fig*) watertight
hermoso, -a [er'moso, a] *adj* beautiful, lovely; (*estupendo*) splendid; (*guapo*) handsome; **hermosura** *nf* beauty
hernia ['ernja] *nf* hernia; **hernia discal** slipped disc
héroe ['eroe] *nm* hero
heroína [ero'ina] *nf* (*mujer*) heroine; (*droga*) heroin
herradura [erra'ðura] *nf* horseshoe
herramienta [erra'mjenta] *nf* tool
herrero [e'rrero] *nm* blacksmith
hervidero [erβi'ðero] *nm* (*fig*) swarm; (*Pol etc*) hotbed
hervir [er'βir] *vi* to boil; (*burbujear*) to bubble; **~ a fuego lento** to simmer; **hervor** *nm* boiling; (*fig*) ardour, fervour
heterosexual [eterosek'swal] *adj* heterosexual
hice *etc vb V* **hacer**
hidratante [iðra'tante] *adj*: **crema ~** moisturizing cream, moisturizer; **hidratar** *vt* (*piel*) to moisturize; **hidrato** *nm* hydrate; **hidratos de carbono** carbohydrates
hidráulico, -a [i'ðrauliko, a] *adj* hydraulic
hidro... [iðro] *prefijo* hydro..., water-...; **hidroeléctrico, -a** *adj* hydroelectric; **hidrógeno** *nm* hydrogen
hiedra ['jeðra] *nf* ivy
hiel [jel] *nf* gall, bile; (*fig*) bitterness
hiela *etc vb V* **helar**
hielo ['jelo] *nm* (*gen*) ice; (*escarcha*)

frost; (*fig*) coldness, reserve
hiena ['jena] *nf* hyena
hierba ['jerβa] *nf* (*pasto*) grass; (*Culin, Med: planta*) herb; **mala ~** weed; (*fig*) evil influence; **hierbabuena** *nf* mint
hierro ['jerro] *nm* (*metal*) iron; (*objeto*) iron object
hígado ['iɣaðo] *nm* liver
higiene [i'xjene] *nf* hygiene; **higiénico, -a** *adj* hygienic
higo ['iɣo] *nm* fig; **higo seco** dried fig; **higuera** *nf* fig tree
hijastro, -a [i'xastro, a] *nm/f* stepson/daughter
hijo, -a ['ixo, a] *nm/f* son/daughter, child; **hijos** *nmpl* children, sons and daughters; **hijo adoptivo** adopted child; **hijo de papá/mamá** daddy's/mummy's boy; **hijo de puta** (*fam!*) bastard (*!*), son of a bitch (*!*); **hijo/a político/a** son-/daughter-in-law
hilera [i'lera] *nf* row, file
hilo ['ilo] *nm* thread; (*Bot*) fibre; (*metal*) wire; (*de agua*) trickle, thin stream
hilvanar [ilβa'nar] *vt* (*Costura*) to tack (BRIT), baste (US); (*fig*) to do hurriedly
himno ['imno] *nm* hymn; **himno nacional** national anthem
hincapié [inka'pje] *nm*: **hacer ~ en** to emphasize
hincar [in'kar] *vt* to drive (in), thrust (in)
hincha ['intʃa] (*fam*) *nmf* fan
hinchado, -a [in'tʃaðo, a] *adj* (*gen*) swollen; (*persona*) pompous
hinchar [in'tʃar] *vt* (*gen*) to swell; (*inflar*) to blow up, inflate; (*fig*) to exaggerate; **hincharse** *vr* (*inflarse*) to swell up; (*fam: de comer*) to stuff o.s.; **hinchazón** *nf* (*Med*) swelling; (*altivez*) arrogance
hinojo [i'noxo] *nm* fennel
hipermercado [ipermer'kado] *nm* hypermarket, superstore
hípico, -a ['ipiko, a] *adj* horse *cpd*
hipnotismo [ipno'tismo] *nm* hypnotism; **hipnotizar** *vt* to hypnotize
hipo ['ipo] *nm* hiccups *pl*
hipocresía [ipokre'sia] *nf* hypocrisy; **hipócrita** *adj* hypocritical ▷ *nmf* hypocrite
hipódromo [i'poðromo] *nm* racetrack
hipopótamo [ipo'potamo] *nm* hippopotamus
hipoteca [ipo'teka] *nf* mortgage
hipótesis [i'potesis] *nf inv* hypothesis
hispánico, -a [is'paniko, a] *adj* Hispanic
hispano, -a [is'pano, a] *adj* Hispanic, Spanish, Hispano- ▷ *nm/f* Spaniard; **Hispanoamérica** *nf* Latin America; **hispanoamericano, -a** *adj, nm/f* Latin American
histeria [is'terja] *nf* hysteria
historia [is'torja] *nf* history; (*cuento*) story, tale; **historias** *nfpl* (*chismes*) gossip *sg*; **dejarse de ~s** to come to the point; **pasar a la ~** to go down in history; **historiador, a** *nm/f* historian; **historial** *nm* (*profesional*) curriculum vitae, C.V.; (*Med*) case history; **histórico, -a** *adj* historical; (*memorable*) historic
historieta [isto'rjeta] *nf* tale, anecdote; (*dibujos*) comic strip
hito ['ito] *nm* (*fig*) landmark
hizo *vb V* **hacer**
hocico [o'θiko] *nm* snout
hockey ['xokei] *nm* hockey; **hockey sobre hielo/patines** ice/roller hockey
hogar [o'ɣar] *nm* fireplace, hearth; (*casa*) home; (*vida familiar*) home life; **hogareño, -a** *adj* home *cpd*; (*persona*) home-loving
hoguera [o'ɣera] *nf* (*gen*) bonfire
hoja ['oxa] *nf* (*gen*) leaf; (*de flor*) petal; (*de papel*) sheet; (*página*) page; **hoja de afeitar** (LAM) razor blade; **hoja electrónica** *o* **de cálculo** spreadsheet; **hoja informativa** leaflet, handout
hojalata [oxa'lata] *nf* tin(plate)
hojaldre [o'xaldre] *nm* (*Culin*) puff

pastry
hojear [oxe'ar] *vt* to leaf through, turn the pages of
hojuela [o'xwela] (*MÉX*) *nf* flake
hola ['ola] *excl* hello!
holá [o'la] (*RPL*) *excl* hello!
Holanda [o'landa] *nf* Holland; **holandés, -esa** *adj* Dutch ▷ *nm/f* Dutchman(-woman) ▷ *nm* (*Ling*) Dutch
holgado, -a [ol'ɣaðo, a] *adj* (*ropa*) loose, baggy; (*rico*) comfortable
holgar [ol'ɣar] *vi* (*descansar*) to rest; (*sobrar*) to be superfluous
holgazán, -ana [olɣa'θan, ana] *adj* idle, lazy ▷ *nm/f* loafer
hollín [o'ʎin] *nm* soot
hombre ['ombre] *nm* (*gen*) man; (*raza humana*): **el ~** man(kind) ▷ *excl*: **¡sí ~!** (*claro*) of course!; (*para énfasis*) man, old boy; **hombre de negocios** businessman; **hombre de pro** honest man; **hombre-rana** frogman
hombrera [om'brera] *nf* shoulder strap
hombro ['ombro] *nm* shoulder
homenaje [ome'naxe] *nm* (*gen*) homage; (*tributo*) tribute
homicida [omi'θiða] *adj* homicidal ▷ *nmf* murderer; **homicidio** *nm* murder, homicide
homologar [omolo'ðar] *vt* (*Com: productos, tamaños*) to standardize
homólogo, -a [o'moloɣo, a] *nm/f*: **su** *etc* **~** his *etc* counterpart *o* opposite number
homosexual [omosek'swal] *adj, nmf* homosexual
honda ['onda] (*CS*) *nf* catapult
hondo, -a ['ondo, a] *adj* deep; **lo ~** the depth(s) *pl*, the bottom; **hondonada** *nf* hollow, depression; (*cañón*) ravine
Honduras [on'duras] *nf* Honduras
hondureño, -a [ondu'reɲo, a] *adj, nm/f* Honduran
honestidad [onesti'ðað] *nf* purity, chastity; (*decencia*) decency; **honesto, -a** *adj* chaste; decent; honest; (*justo*) just
hongo ['ongo] *nm* (*Bot: gen*) fungus; (*: comestible*) mushroom; (*: venenoso*) toadstool
honor [o'nor] *nm* (*gen*) honour; **en ~ a la verdad** to be fair; **honorable** *adj* honourable
honorario, -a [ono'rarjo, a] *adj* honorary; **honorarios** *nmpl* fees
honra ['onra] *nf* (*gen*) honour; (*renombre*) good name; **honradez** *nf* honesty; (*de persona*) integrity; **honrado, -a** *adj* honest, upright; **honrar** [on'rar] *vt* to honour
hora ['ora] *nf* (*una hora*) hour; (*tiempo*) time; **¿qué ~ es?** what time is it?; **¿a qué ~?** at what time?; **media ~** half an hour; **a la ~ de recreo** at playtime; **a primera ~** first thing (in the morning); **a última ~** at the last moment; **a altas ~s** in the small hours; **¡a buena ~!** about time too!; **pedir ~** to make an appointment; **dar la ~** to strike the hour; **horas de oficina/trabajo** office/working hours; **horas de visita** visiting times; **horas extras** *o* **extraordinarias** overtime *sg*; **horas pico** (*LAM*) rush *o* peak hours; **horas punta** (*ESP*) rush hours
horario, -a [o'rarjo, a] *adj* hourly, hour *cpd* ▷ *nm* timetable; **horario comercial** business hours *pl*
horca ['orka] *nf* gallows *sg*
horcajadas [orka'xaðas]: **a ~** *adv* astride
horchata [or'tʃata] *nf* *cold drink made from tiger nuts and water*, tiger nut milk
horizontal [oriθon'tal] *adj* horizontal
horizonte [ori'θonte] *nm* horizon
horma ['orma] *nf* mould
hormiga [or'miɣa] *nf* ant; **hormigas** *nfpl* (*Med*) pins and needles
hormigón [ormi'ɣon] *nm* concrete; **hormigón armado/pretensado** reinforced/prestressed concrete;

hormigonera *nf* cement mixer
hormigueo [ormi'ɣeo] *nm* (*comezón*) itch
hormona [or'mona] *nf* hormone
hornillo [or'niʎo] *nm* (*cocina*) portable stove; **hornillo de gas** gas ring
horno ['orno] *nm* (*Culin*) oven; (*Tec*) furnace; **alto ~** blast furnace
horóscopo [o'roskopo] *nm* horoscope
horquilla [or'kiʎa] *nf* hairpin; (*Agr*) pitchfork
horrendo, -a [o'rrendo, a] *adj* horrendous, frightful
horrible [o'rriβle] *adj* horrible, dreadful
horripilante [orripi'lante] *adj* hair-raising, horrifying
horror [o'rror] *nm* horror, dread; (*atrocidad*) atrocity; **¡qué ~!** (*fam*) how awful!; **horrorizar** *vt* to horrify, frighten; **horrorizarse** *vr* to be horrified; **horroroso, -a** *adj* horrifying, ghastly
hortaliza [orta'liθa] *nf* vegetable
hortelano, -a [orte'lano, a] *nm/f* (market) gardener
hortera [or'tera] (*fam*) *adj* tacky
hospedar [ospe'ðar] *vt* to put up; **hospedarse** *vr* to stay, lodge
hospital [ospi'tal] *nm* hospital
hospitalario, -a [ospita'larjo, a] *adj* (*acogedor*) hospitable; **hospitalidad** *nf* hospitality
hostal [os'tal] *nm* small hotel
hostelería [ostele'ria] *nf* hotel business *o* trade
hostia ['ostja] *nf* (*Rel*) host, consecrated wafer; (*fam!*: *golpe*) whack, punch ▷ *excl* (*fam!*): **¡~(s)!** damn!
hostil [os'til] *adj* hostile
hotdog [ot'dog] (*LAM*) *nm* hot dog
hotel [o'tel] *nm* hotel; **hotelero, -a** *adj* hotel *cpd* ▷ *nm/f* hotelier

HOTEL

In Spain you can choose from the following categories of accommodation, in descending order of quality and price: **hotel** (from 5 stars to 1), **hostal**, **pensión**, **casa de huéspedes**, **fonda**. The State also runs luxury hotels called **paradores**, which are usually sited in places of particular historical interest and are often historic buildings themselves.

hoy [oi] *adv* (*este día*) today; (*la actualidad*) now(adays) ▷ *nm* present time; **~ (en) día** now(adays)
hoyo ['ojo] *nm* hole, pit
hoz [oθ] *nf* sickle
hube *etc vb V* **haber**
hucha ['utʃa] *nf* money box
hueco, -a ['weko, a] *adj* (*vacío*) hollow, empty; (*resonante*) booming ▷ *nm* hollow, cavity
huelga *etc* ['welɣa] *vb V* **holgar** ▷ *nf* strike; **declararse en ~** to go on strike, come out on strike; **huelga de hambre** hunger strike; **huelga general** general strike
huelguista [wel'ɣista] *nmf* striker
huella ['weʎa] *nf* (*pisada*) tread; (*marca del paso*) footprint, footstep; (*: de animal, máquina*) track; **huella dactilar** fingerprint
huelo *etc vb V* **oler**
huérfano, -a ['werfano, a] *adj* orphan(ed) ▷ *nm/f* orphan
huerta ['werta] *nf* market garden; (*en Murcia y Valencia*) irrigated region
huerto ['werto] *nm* kitchen garden; (*de árboles frutales*) orchard
hueso ['weso] *nm* (*Anat*) bone; (*de fruta*) stone
huésped ['wespeð] *nmf* guest
hueva ['weβa] *nf* roe
huevera [we'βera] *nf* eggcup
huevo ['weβo] *nm* egg; **huevo a la copa** (*CS*) soft-boiled egg; **huevo duro/escalfado** hard-boiled/poached egg; **huevo estrellado** (*LAM*) fried egg; **huevo frito** (*ESP*) fried egg; **huevo**

pasado por agua soft-boiled egg; **huevos revueltos** scrambled eggs; **huevo tibio** (MÉX) soft-boiled egg
huida [u'iða] *nf* escape, flight
huir [u'ir] *vi* (*escapar*) to flee, escape; (*evitar*) to avoid
hule ['ule] *nm* oilskin; (MÉX: *goma*) rubber
hulera [u'lera] (MÉX) *nf* catapult
humanidad [umani'ðað] *nf* (*género humano*) man(kind); (*cualidad*) humanity
humanitario, -a [umani'tarjo, a] *adj* humanitarian
humano, -a [u'mano, a] *adj* (*gen*) human; (*humanitario*) humane ▷ *nm* human; **ser ~** human being
humareda [uma'reða] *nf* cloud of smoke
humedad [ume'ðað] *nf* (*de clima*) humidity; (*de pared etc*) dampness; **a prueba de ~** damp-proof; **humedecer** *vt* to moisten, wet; **humedecerse** *vr* to get wet
húmedo, -a ['umeðo, a] *adj* (*mojado*) damp, wet; (*tiempo etc*) humid
humilde [u'milde] *adj* humble, modest
humillación [umiʎa'θjon] *nf* humiliation; **humillante** *adj* humiliating
humillar [umi'ʎar] *vt* to humiliate
humo ['umo] *nm* (*de fuego*) smoke; (*gas nocivo*) fumes *pl*; (*vapor*) steam, vapour; **humos** *nmpl* (*fig*) conceit *sg*
humor [u'mor] *nm* (*disposición*) mood, temper; (*lo que divierte*) humour; **de buen/mal ~** in a good/bad mood; **humorista** *nmf* comic; **humorístico, -a** *adj* funny, humorous
hundimiento [undi'mjento] *nm* (*gen*) sinking; (*colapso*) collapse
hundir [un'dir] *vt* to sink; (*edificio, plan*) to ruin, destroy; **hundirse** *vr* to sink, collapse
húngaro, -a ['ungaro, a] *adj, nm/f* Hungarian
Hungría [un'gria] *nf* Hungary
huracán [ura'kan] *nm* hurricane
huraño, -a [u'raɲo, a] *adj* (*antisocial*) unsociable
hurgar [ur'ɣar] *vt* to poke, jab; (*remover*) to stir (up); **hurgarse** *vr*: **~se (las narices)** to pick one's nose
hurón, -ona [u'ron, ona] *nm* (*Zool*) ferret
hurtadillas [urta'ðiʎas]: **a ~** *adv* stealthily, on the sly
hurtar [ur'tar] *vt* to steal; **hurto** *nm* theft, stealing
husmear [usme'ar] *vt* (*oler*) to sniff out, scent; (*fam*) to pry into
huyo *etc vb V* **huir**

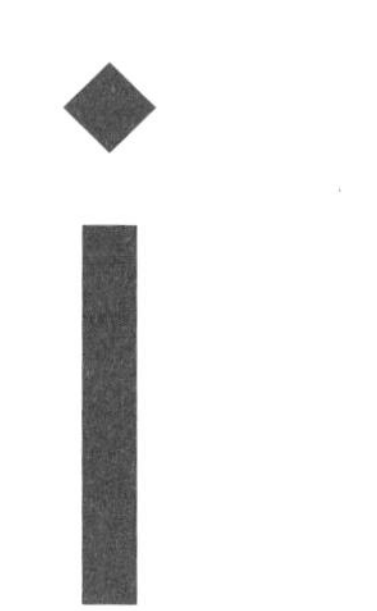

iba *etc vb V* **ir**
ibérico, -a [i'βeriko, a] *adj* Iberian
iberoamericano, -a [iβeroameri'kano, a] *adj, nm/f* Latin American
Ibiza [i'βiθa] *nf* Ibiza
iceberg [iθe'βer] *nm* iceberg
icono [i'kono] *nm* ikon, icon
ida ['iða] *nf* going, departure; **~ y vuelta** round trip, return
idea [i'ðea] *nf* idea; **no tengo la menor ~** I haven't a clue
ideal [iðe'al] *adj, nm* ideal; **idealista** *nmf* idealist; **idealizar** *vt* to idealize
ídem ['iðem] *pron* ditto
idéntico, -a [i'ðentiko, a] *adj* identical
identidad [iðenti'ðað] *nf* identity
identificación [iðentifika'θjon] *nf* identification
identificar [iðentifi'kar] *vt* to identify; **identificarse** *vr*: **~se con** to identify with
ideología [iðeolo'xia] *nf* ideology
idilio [i'ðiljo] *nm* love-affair
idioma [i'ðjoma] *nm* (*gen*) language
No confundir **idioma** con la palabra inglesa *idiom*.
idiota [i'ðjota] *adj* idiotic ▷ *nmf* idiot
ídolo ['iðolo] *nm* (*tb fig*) idol
idóneo, -a [i'ðoneo, a] *adj* suitable
iglesia [i'ɣlesja] *nf* church
ignorante [iɣno'rante] *adj* ignorant, uninformed ▷ *nmf* ignoramus
ignorar [iɣno'rar] *vt* not to know, be ignorant of; (*no hacer caso a*) to ignore
igual [i'ɣwal] *adj* (*gen*) equal; (*similar*) like, similar; (*mismo*) (the) same; (*constante*) constant; (*temperatura*) even ▷ *nmf* equal; **~ que** like, the same as; **me da** *o* **es ~** I don't care; **son ~es** they're the same; **al ~ que** (*prep, conj*) like, just like
igualar [iɣwa'lar] *vt* (*gen*) to equalize, make equal; (*allanar, nivelar*) to level (off), even (out); **igualarse** *vr* (*platos de balanza*) to balance out
igualdad [iɣwal'dað] *nf* equality; (*similaridad*) sameness; (*uniformidad*) uniformity
igualmente [iɣwal'mente] *adv* equally; (*también*) also, likewise ▷ *excl* the same to you!
ilegal [ile'ɣal] *adj* illegal
ilegítimo, -a [ile'xitimo, a] *adj* illegitimate
ileso, -a [i'leso, a] *adj* unhurt
ilimitado, -a [ilimi'taðo, a] *adj* unlimited
iluminación [ilumina'θjon] *nf* illumination; (*alumbrado*) lighting
iluminar [ilumi'nar] *vt* to illuminate, light (up); (*fig*) to enlighten
ilusión [ilu'sjon] *nf* illusion; (*quimera*) delusion; (*esperanza*) hope; **hacerse ilusiones** to build up one's hopes; **ilusionado, -a** *adj* excited; **ilusionar** *vi*: **le ilusiona ir de vacaciones** he's looking forward to going on holiday; **ilusionarse** *vr*: **ilusionarse (con)** to get excited (about)
iluso, -a [i'luso, a] *adj* easily deceived ▷ *nm/f* dreamer

ilustración [ilustra'θjon] *nf* illustration; (*saber*) learning, erudition; **la I~** the Enlightenment; **ilustrado, -a** *adj* illustrated; learned
ilustrar [ilus'trar] *vt* to illustrate; (*instruir*) to instruct; (*explicar*) to explain, make clear
ilustre [i'lustre] *adj* famous, illustrious
imagen [i'maxen] *nf* (*gen*) image; (*dibujo*) picture
imaginación [imaxina'θjon] *nf* imagination
imaginar [imaxi'nar] *vt* (*gen*) to imagine; (*idear*) to think up; (*suponer*) to suppose; **imaginarse** *vr* to imagine; **imaginario, -a** *adj* imaginary; **imaginativo, -a** *adj* imaginative
imán [i'man] *nm* magnet
imbécil [im'beθil] *nmf* imbecile, idiot
imitación [imita'θjon] *nf* imitation; **de ~** imitation *cpd*
imitar [imi'tar] *vt* to imitate; (*parodiar, remedar*) to mimic, ape
impaciente [impa'θjente] *adj* impatient; (*nervioso*) anxious
impacto [im'pakto] *nm* impact
impar [im'par] *adj* odd
imparcial [impar'θjal] *adj* impartial, fair
impecable [impe'kaβle] *adj* impeccable
impedimento [impeði'mento] *nm* impediment, obstacle
impedir [impe'ðir] *vt* (*obstruir*) to impede, obstruct; (*estorbar*) to prevent; **~ a algn hacer** *o* **que algn haga algo** to prevent sb (from) doing sth, stop sb doing sth
imperativo, -a [impera'tiβo, a] *adj* (*urgente, Ling*) imperative
imperdible [imper'ðiβle] *nm* safety pin
imperdonable [imperðo'naβle] *adj* unforgivable, inexcusable
imperfecto, -a [imper'fekto, a] *adj* imperfect
imperio [im'perjo] *nm* empire; (*autoridad*) rule, authority; (*fig*) pride, haughtiness
impermeable [imperme'aβle] *adj* waterproof ▷ *nm* raincoat, mac (BRIT)
impersonal [imperso'nal] *adj* impersonal
impertinente [imperti'nente] *adj* impertinent
ímpetu ['impetu] *nm* (*impulso*) impetus, impulse; (*impetuosidad*) impetuosity; (*violencia*) violence
implantar [implan'tar] *vt* to introduce
implemento [imple'mento] (LAM) *nm* tool, implement
implicar [impli'kar] *vt* to involve; (*entrañar*) to imply
implícito, -a [im'pliθito, a] *adj* (*tácito*) implicit; (*sobreentendido*) implied
imponente [impo'nente] *adj* (*impresionante*) impressive, imposing; (*solemne*) grand
imponer [impo'ner] *vt* (*gen*) to impose; (*exigir*) to exact; **imponerse** *vr* to assert o.s.; (*prevalecer*) to prevail; **imponible** *adj* (*Com*) taxable
impopular [impopu'lar] *adj* unpopular
importación [importa'θjon] *nf* (*acto*) importing; (*mercancías*) imports *pl*
importancia [impor'tanθja] *nf* importance; (*valor*) value, significance; (*extensión*) size, magnitude; **no tiene ~** it's nothing; **importante** *adj* important; valuable, significant
importar [impor'tar] *vt* (*del extranjero*) to import; (*costar*) to amount to ▷ *vi* to be important, matter; **me importa un rábano** I couldn't care less; **no importa** it doesn't matter; **¿le importa que fume?** do you mind if I smoke?
importe [im'porte] *nm* (*total*) amount; (*valor*) value
imposible [impo'siβle] *adj* (*gen*) impossible; (*insoportable*) unbearable,

intolerable

imposición [imposi'θjon] *nf* imposition; (*Com: impuesto*) tax; (*: inversión*) deposit

impostor, a [impos'tor, a] *nm/f* impostor

impotencia [impo'tenθja] *nf* impotence; **impotente** *adj* impotent

impreciso, -a [impre'θiso, a] *adj* imprecise, vague

impregnar [impreɣ'nar] *vt* to impregnate; **impregnarse** *vr* to become impregnated

imprenta [im'prenta] *nf* (*acto*) printing; (*aparato*) press; (*casa*) printer's; (*letra*) print

imprescindible [impresθin'diβle] *adj* essential, vital

impresión [impre'sjon] *nf* (*gen*) impression; (*Imprenta*) printing; (*edición*) edition; (*Foto*) print; (*marca*) imprint; **impresión digital** fingerprint

impresionante [impresjo'nante] *adj* impressive; (*tremendo*) tremendous; (*maravilloso*) great, marvellous

impresionar [impresjo'nar] *vt* (*conmover*) to move; (*afectar*) to impress, strike; (*película fotográfica*) to expose; **impresionarse** *vr* to be impressed; (*conmoverse*) to be moved

impreso, -a [im'preso, a] *pp de* **imprimir** ▷ *adj* printed; **impresos** *nmpl* printed matter; **impresora** *nf* printer

imprevisto, -a [impre'βisto, a] *adj* (*gen*) unforeseen; (*inesperado*) unexpected

imprimir [impri'mir] *vt* to imprint, impress, stamp; (*textos*) to print; (*Inform*) to output, print out

improbable [impro'βaβle] *adj* improbable; (*inverosímil*) unlikely

impropio, -a [im'propjo, a] *adj* improper

improvisado, -a [improβi'saðo, a] *adj* improvised

improvisar [improβi'sar] *vt* to improvise

improviso, -a [impro'βiso, a] *adj*: **de ~** unexpectedly, suddenly

imprudencia [impru'ðenθja] *nf* imprudence; (*indiscreción*) indiscretion; (*descuido*) carelessness; **imprudente** *adj* unwise, imprudent; (*indiscreto*) indiscreet

impuesto, -a [im'pwesto, a] *adj* imposed ▷ *nm* tax; **impuesto al valor agregado** *o* **añadido** (LAM) value added tax (BRIT) ≈ sales tax (US); **impuesto sobre el valor añadido** (ESP) value added tax (BRIT) ≈ sales tax (US)

impulsar [impul'sar] *vt* to drive; (*promover*) to promote, stimulate

impulsivo, -a [impul'siβo, a] *adj* impulsive; **impulso** *nm* impulse; (*fuerza, empuje*) thrust, drive; (*fig: sentimiento*) urge, impulse

impureza [impu'reθa] *nf* impurity; **impuro, -a** *adj* impure

inaccesible [inakθe'siβle] *adj* inaccessible

inaceptable [inaθep'taβle] *adj* unacceptable

inactivo, -a [inak'tiβo, a] *adj* inactive

inadecuado, -a [inaðe'kwaðo, a] *adj* (*insuficiente*) inadequate; (*inapto*) unsuitable

inadvertido, -a [inaðβer'tiðo, a] *adj* (*no visto*) unnoticed

inaguantable [inaɣwan'taβle] *adj* unbearable

inanimado, -a [inani'maðo, a] *adj* inanimate

inaudito, -a [inau'ðito, a] *adj* unheard-of

inauguración [inauɣura'θjon] *nf* inauguration; opening

inaugurar [inauɣu'rar] *vt* to inaugurate; (*exposición*) to open

inca ['inka] *nmf* Inca

incalculable [inkalku'laβle] *adj* incalculable

incandescente [inkandes'θente] *adj* incandescent

incansable [inkan'saβle] *adj*

tireless, untiring

incapacidad [inkapaθi'ðað] *nf* incapacity; (*incompetencia*) incompetence; **incapacidad física/mental** physical/mental disability

incapacitar [inkapaθi'tar] *vt* (*inhabilitar*) to incapacitate, render unfit; (*descalificar*) to disqualify

incapaz [inka'paθ] *adj* incapable

incautarse [inkau'tarse] *vr*: **~ de** to seize, confiscate

incauto, -a [in'kauto, a] *adj* (*imprudente*) incautious, unwary

incendiar [inθen'djar] *vt* to set fire to; (*fig*) to inflame; **incendiarse** *vr* to catch fire; **incendiario, -a** *adj* incendiary

incendio [in'θendjo] *nm* fire

incentivo [inθen'tiβo] *nm* incentive

incertidumbre [inθerti'ðumbre] *nf* (*inseguridad*) uncertainty; (*duda*) doubt

incesante [inθe'sante] *adj* incessant

incesto [in'θesto] *nm* incest

incidencia [inθi'ðenθja] *nf* (*Mat*) incidence

incidente [inθi'ðente] *nm* incident

incidir [inθi'ðir] *vi* (*influir*) to influence; (*afectar*) to affect

incienso [in'θjenso] *nm* incense

incierto, -a [in'θjerto, a] *adj* uncertain

incineración [inθinera'θjon] *nf* incineration; (*de cadáveres*) cremation

incinerar [inθine'rar] *vt* to burn; (*cadáveres*) to cremate

incisión [inθi'sjon] *nf* incision

incisivo, -a [inθi'siβo, a] *adj* sharp, cutting; (*fig*) incisive

incitar [inθi'tar] *vt* to incite, rouse

inclemencia [inkle'menθja] *nf* (*severidad*) harshness, severity; (*del tiempo*) inclemency

inclinación [inklina'θjon] *nf* (*gen*) inclination; (*de tierras*) slope, incline; (*de cabeza*) nod, bow; (*fig*) leaning, bent

inclinar [inkli'nar] *vt* to incline; (*cabeza*) to nod, bow ▷ *vi* to lean, slope; **inclinarse** *vr* to bow; (*encorvarse*) to stoop; **~se a** (*parecerse a*) to take after, resemble; **~se ante** to bow down to; **me inclino a pensar que ...** I'm inclined to think that ...

incluir [inklu'ir] *vt* to include; (*incorporar*) to incorporate; (*meter*) to enclose

inclusive [inklu'siβe] *adv* inclusive ▷ *prep* including

incluso [in'kluso] *adv* even

incógnita [in'koɣnita] *nf* (*Mat*) unknown quantity

incógnito [in'koɣnito] *nm*: **de ~** incognito

incoherente [inkoe'rente] *adj* incoherent

incoloro, -a [inko'loro, a] *adj* colourless

incomodar [inkomo'ðar] *vt* to inconvenience; (*molestar*) to bother, trouble; (*fastidiar*) to annoy

incomodidad [inkomoði'ðað] *nf* inconvenience; (*fastidio, enojo*) annoyance; (*de vivienda*) discomfort

incómodo, -a [in'komoðo, a] *adj* (*inconfortable*) uncomfortable; (*molesto*) annoying; (*inconveniente*) inconvenient

incomparable [inkompa'raβle] *adj* incomparable

incompatible [inkompa'tiβle] *adj* incompatible

incompetente [inkompe'tente] *adj* incompetent

incompleto, -a [inkom'pleto, a] *adj* incomplete, unfinished

incomprensible [inkompren'siβle] *adj* incomprehensible

incomunicado, -a [inkomuni'kaðo, a] *adj* (*aislado*) cut off, isolated; (*confinado*) in solitary confinement

incondicional [inkondiθjo'nal] *adj* unconditional; (*apoyo*) wholehearted; (*partidario*) staunch

inconfundible [inkonfun'diβle] *adj* unmistakable

incongruente [inkon'grwente] *adj* incongruous

inconsciente [inkons'θjente] *adj*

unconscious; thoughtless

inconsecuente [inkonse'kwente] *adj* inconsistent

inconstante [inkons'tante] *adj* inconstant

incontable [inkon'taβle] *adj* countless, innumerable

inconveniencia [inkombe'njenθja] *nf* unsuitability, inappropriateness; (*descortesía*) impoliteness; **inconveniente** *adj* unsuitable; impolite ▷ *nm* obstacle; (*desventaja*) disadvantage; **el inconveniente es que ...** the trouble is that ...

incordiar [inkor'ðjar] (*fam*) *vt* to bug, annoy

incorporar [inkorpo'rar] *vt* to incorporate; **incorporarse** *vr* to sit up; **~se a** to join

incorrecto, -a [inko'rrekto, a] *adj* (*gen*) incorrect, wrong; (*comportamiento*) bad-mannered

incorregible [inkorre'xiβle] *adj* incorrigible

incrédulo, -a [in'kreðulo, a] *adj* incredulous, unbelieving; sceptical

increíble [inkre'iβle] *adj* incredible

incremento [inkre'mento] *nm* increment; (*aumento*) rise, increase

increpar [inkre'par] *vt* to reprimand

incruento, -a [in'krwento, a] *adj* bloodless

incrustar [inkrus'tar] *vt* to incrust; (*piedras: en joya*) to inlay

incubar [inku'βar] *vt* to incubate

inculcar [inkul'kar] *vt* to inculcate

inculto, -a [in'kulto, a] *adj* (*persona*) uneducated; (*grosero*) uncouth ▷ *nm/f* ignoramus

incumplimiento [inkumpli'mjento] *nm* non-fulfilment; **incumplimiento de contrato** breach of contract

incurrir [inku'rrir] *vi*: **~ en** to incur; (*crimen*) to commit

indagar [inda'ɣar] *vt* to investigate; to search; (*averiguar*) to ascertain

indecente [inde'θente] *adj* indecent, improper; (*lascivo*) obscene

indeciso, -a [inde'θiso, a] *adj* (*por decidir*) undecided; (*vacilante*) hesitant

indefenso, -a [inde'fenso, a] *adj* defenceless

indefinido, -a [indefi'niðo, a] *adj* indefinite; (*vago*) vague, undefined

indemne [in'demne] *adj* (*objeto*) undamaged; (*persona*) unharmed, unhurt

indemnizar [indemni'θar] *vt* to indemnify; (*compensar*) to compensate

independencia [indepen'denθja] *nf* independence

independiente [indepen'djente] *adj* (*libre*) independent; (*autónomo*) self-sufficient

indeterminado, -a [indetermi'naðo, a] *adj* indefinite; (*desconocido*) indeterminate

India ['indja] *nf*: **la ~** India

indicación [indika'θjon] *nf* indication; (*señal*) sign; (*sugerencia*) suggestion, hint

indicado, -a [indi'kaðo, a] *adj* (*momento, método*) right; (*tratamiento*) appropriate; (*solución*) likely

indicador [indika'ðor] *nm* indicator; (*Tec*) gauge, meter

indicar [indi'kar] *vt* (*mostrar*) to indicate, show; (*termómetro etc*) to read, register; (*señalar*) to point to

índice ['indiθe] *nm* index; (*catálogo*) catalogue; (*Anat*) index finger, forefinger; **índice de materias** table of contents

indicio [in'diθjo] *nm* indication, sign; (*en pesquisa etc*) clue

indiferencia [indife'renθja] *nf* indifference; (*apatía*) apathy; **indiferente** *adj* indifferent

indígena [in'dixena] *adj* indigenous, native ▷ *nmf* native

indigestión [indixes'tjon] *nf* indigestion

indigesto, -a [indi'xesto, a] *adj* (*alimento*) indigestible; (*fig*) turgid

indignación [indiɣna'θjon] *nf*

indignation
indignar [indiɣ'nar] *vt* to anger, make indignant; **indignarse** *vr*: **~se por** to get indignant about
indigno, -a [in'diɣno, a] *adj* (*despreciable*) low, contemptible; (*inmerecido*) unworthy
indio, -a ['indjo, a] *adj, nm/f* Indian
indirecta [indi'rekta] *nf* insinuation, innuendo; (*sugerencia*) hint
indirecto, -a [indi'rekto, a] *adj* indirect
indiscreción [indiskre'θjon] *nf* (*imprudencia*) indiscretion; (*irreflexión*) tactlessness; (*acto*) gaffe, faux pas
indiscreto, -a [indis'kreto, a] *adj* indiscreet
indiscutible [indisku'tiβle] *adj* indisputable, unquestionable
indispensable [indispen'saβle] *adj* indispensable, essential
indispuesto, -a [indis'pwesto, a] *adj* (*enfermo*) unwell, indisposed
indistinto, -a [indis'tinto, a] *adj* indistinct; (*vago*) vague
individual [indiβi'ðwal] *adj* individual; (*habitación*) single ▷ *nm* (*Deporte*) singles *sg*
individuo, -a [indi'βiðwo, a] *adj, nm* individual
índole ['indole] *nf* (*naturaleza*) nature; (*clase*) sort, kind
inducir [indu'θir] *vt* to induce; (*inferir*) to infer; (*persuadir*) to persuade
indudable [indu'ðaβle] *adj* undoubted; (*incuestionable*) unquestionable
indultar [indul'tar] *vt* (*perdonar*) to pardon, reprieve; (*librar de pago*) to exempt; **indulto** *nm* pardon; exemption
industria [in'dustrja] *nf* industry; (*habilidad*) skill; **industrial** *adj* industrial ▷ *nm* industrialist
inédito, -a [in'eðito, a] *adj* (*texto*) unpublished; (*nuevo*) new
ineficaz [inefi'kaθ] *adj* (*inútil*) ineffective; (*ineficiente*) inefficient
ineludible [inelu'ðiβle] *adj* inescapable, unavoidable
ineptitud [inepti'tuð] *nf* ineptitude, incompetence; **inepto, -a** *adj* inept, incompetent
inequívoco, -a [ine'kiβoko, a] *adj* unequivocal; (*inconfundible*) unmistakable
inercia [in'erθja] *nf* inertia; (*pasividad*) passivity
inerte [in'erte] *adj* inert; (*inmóvil*) motionless
inesperado, -a [inespe'raðo, a] *adj* unexpected, unforeseen
inestable [ines'taβle] *adj* unstable
inevitable [ineβi'taβle] *adj* inevitable
inexacto, -a [inek'sakto, a] *adj* inaccurate; (*falso*) untrue
inexperto, -a [inek'sperto, a] *adj* (*novato*) inexperienced
infalible [infa'liβle] *adj* infallible; (*plan*) foolproof
infame [in'fame] *adj* infamous; (*horrible*) dreadful; **infamia** *nf* infamy; (*deshonra*) disgrace
infancia [in'fanθja] *nf* infancy, childhood
infantería [infante'ria] *nf* infantry
infantil [infan'til] *adj* (*pueril, aniñado*) infantile; (*cándido*) childlike; (*literatura, ropa etc*) children's
infarto [in'farto] *nm* (*tb*: **~ de miocardio**) heart attack
infatigable [infati'ɣaβle] *adj* tireless, untiring
infección [infek'θjon] *nf* infection; **infeccioso, -a** *adj* infectious
infectar [infek'tar] *vt* to infect; **infectarse** *vr* to become infected
infeliz [infe'liθ] *adj* unhappy, wretched ▷ *nmf* wretch
inferior [infe'rjor] *adj* inferior; (*situación*) lower ▷ *nmf* inferior, subordinate
inferir [infe'rir] *vt* (*deducir*) to infer, deduce; (*causar*) to cause
infidelidad [infiðeli'ðað] *nf* (*gen*)

infidelity, unfaithfulness

infiel [in'fjel] *adj* unfaithful, disloyal; (*erróneo*) inaccurate ▷ *nmf* infidel, unbeliever

infierno [in'fjerno] *nm* hell

infiltrarse [infil'trarse] *vr*: **~ en** to infiltrate in(to); (*persona*) to work one's way in(to)

ínfimo, -a ['infimo, a] *adj* (*más bajo*) lowest; (*despreciable*) vile, mean

infinidad [infini'ðað] *nf* infinity; (*abundancia*) great quantity

infinito, -a [infi'nito, a] *adj, nm* infinite

inflación [infla'θjon] *nf* (*hinchazón*) swelling; (*monetaria*) inflation; (*fig*) conceit

inflamable [infl'maβle] *adj* flammable

inflamar [infla'mar] *vt* (*Med: fig*) to inflame; **inflamarse** *vr* to catch fire; to become inflamed

inflar [in'flar] *vt* (*hinchar*) to inflate, blow up; (*fig*) to exaggerate; **inflarse** *vr* to swell (up); (*fig*) to get conceited

inflexible [inflek'siβle] *adj* inflexible; (*fig*) unbending

influencia [influ'enθja] *nf* influence

influir [influ'ir] *vt* to influence

influjo [in'fluxo] *nm* influence

influya *etc vb V* **influir**

influyente [influ'jente] *adj* influential

información [informa'θjon] *nf* information; (*noticias*) news *sg*; (*Jur*) inquiry; **I~** (*oficina*) Information Office; (*mostrador*) Information Desk; (*Tel*) Directory Enquiries

informal [infor'mal] *adj* (*gen*) informal

informar [infor'mar] *vt* (*gen*) to inform; (*revelar*) to reveal, make known ▷ *vi* (*Jur*) to plead; (*denunciar*) to inform; (*dar cuenta de*) to report on; **informarse** *vr* to find out; **~se de** to inquire into

informática [infor'matika] *nf* computer science, information technology

informe [in'forme] *adj* shapeless ▷ *nm* report

infracción [infrak'θjon] *nf* infraction, infringement

infravalorar [infrabalo'rar] *vt* to undervalue, underestimate

infringir [infrin'xir] *vt* to infringe, contravene

infundado, -a [infun'daðo, a] *adj* groundless, unfounded

infundir [infun'dir] *vt* to infuse, instil

infusión [infu'sjon] *nf* infusion; **infusión de manzanilla** camomile tea

ingeniería [inxenje'ria] *nf* engineering; **ingeniería genética** genetic engineering; **ingeniero, -a** *nm/f* engineer; **ingeniero civil** *o* **de caminos** civil engineer

ingenio [in'xenjo] *nm* (*talento*) talent; (*agudeza*) wit; (*habilidad*) ingenuity, inventiveness; **ingenio azucarero** (LAM) sugar refinery; **ingenioso, -a** [inxe'njoso, a] *adj* ingenious, clever; (*divertido*) witty; **ingenuo, -a** *adj* ingenuous

ingerir [inxe'rir] *vt* to ingest; (*tragar*) to swallow; (*consumir*) to consume

Inglaterra [ingla'terra] *nf* England

ingle ['ingle] *nf* groin

inglés, -esa [in'gles, esa] *adj* English ▷ *nm/f* Englishman(-woman) ▷ *nm* (*Ling*) English

ingrato, -a [in'grato, a] *adj* (*gen*) ungrateful

ingrediente [ingre'ðjente] *nm* ingredient

ingresar [ingre'sar] *vt* (*dinero*) to deposit ▷ *vi* to come in; **~ en el hospital** to go into hospital

ingreso [in'greso] *nm* (*entrada*) entry; (*en hospital etc*) admission; **ingresos** *nmpl* (*dinero*) income *sg*; (*Com*) takings *pl*

inhabitable [inaβi'taβle] *adj* uninhabitable

inhalar [ina'lar] *vt* to inhale

inhibir [ini'βir] *vt* to inhibit

inhóspito, -a [i'nospito, a] *adj* (*región, paisaje*) inhospitable
inhumano, -a [inu'mano, a] *adj* inhuman
inicial [ini'θjal] *adj, nf* initial
iniciar [ini'θjar] *vt* (*persona*) to initiate; (*empezar*) to begin, commence; (*conversación*) to start up
iniciativa [iniθja'tiβa] *nf* initiative; **iniciativa privada** private enterprise
ininterrumpido, -a [ininterrum'piðo, a] *adj* uninterrupted
injertar [inxer'tar] *vt* to graft; **injerto** *nm* graft
injuria [in'xurja] *nf* (*agravio, ofensa*) offence; (*insulto*) insult

> No confundir **injuria** con la palabra inglesa *injury*.

injusticia [inxus'tiθja] *nf* injustice
injusto, -a [in'xusto, a] *adj* unjust, unfair
inmadurez [inmaðu'reθ] *nf* immaturity
inmediaciones [inmeðja'θjones] *nfpl* neighbourhood *sg*, environs
inmediato, -a [inme'ðjato, a] *adj* immediate; (*contiguo*) adjoining; (*rápido*) prompt; (*próximo*) neighbouring, next; **de ~** immediately
inmejorable [inmexo'raβle] *adj* unsurpassable; (*precio*) unbeatable
inmenso, -a [in'menso, a] *adj* immense, huge
inmigración [inmiɣra'θjon] *nf* immigration
inmobiliaria [inmoβi'ljarja] *nf* estate agency
inmolar [inmo'lar] *vt* to immolate, sacrifice
inmoral [inmo'ral] *adj* immoral
inmortal [inmor'tal] *adj* immortal; **inmortalizar** *vt* to immortalize
inmóvil [in'moβil] *adj* immobile
inmueble [in'mweβle] *adj*: **bienes ~s** real estate, landed property ▷ *nm* property
inmundo, -a [in'mundo, a] *adj* filthy
inmune [in'mune] *adj*: **~ (a)** (*Med*) immune (to)
inmunidad [inmuni'ðað] *nf* immunity
inmutarse [inmu'tarse] *vr* to turn pale; **no se inmutó** he didn't turn a hair
innato, -a [in'nato, a] *adj* innate
innecesario, -a [inneθe'sarjo, a] *adj* unnecessary
innovación [innoβa'θjon] *nf* innovation
innovar [inno'βar] *vt* to introduce
inocencia [ino'θenθja] *nf* innocence
inocentada [inoθen'taða] *nf* practical joke
inocente [ino'θente] *adj* (*ingenuo*) naive, innocent; (*inculpable*) innocent; (*sin malicia*) harmless ▷ *nmf* simpleton; **el día de los (Santos) I~s** ≈ April Fools' Day

> **DÍA DE LOS (SANTOS) INOCENTES**
>
> The 28th December, el **día de los (Santos) Inocentes**, is when the Church commemorates the story of Herod's slaughter of the innocent children of Judaea. On this day Spaniards play **inocentadas** (practical jokes) on each other, much like our April Fool's Day pranks.

inodoro [ino'ðoro] *nm* toilet, lavatory (BRIT)
inofensivo, -a [inofen'siβo, a] *adj* inoffensive, harmless
inolvidable [inolβi'ðaβle] *adj* unforgettable
inoportuno, -a [inopor'tuno, a] *adj* untimely; (*molesto*) inconvenient
inoxidable [inoksi'ðaβle] *adj*: **acero ~** stainless steel
inquietar [inkje'tar] *vt* to worry, trouble; **inquietarse** *vr* to worry, get upset; **inquieto, -a** *adj* anxious,

worried; **inquietud** *nf* anxiety, worry
inquilino, -a [inki'lino, a] *nm/f* tenant
insaciable [insa'θjaβle] *adj* insatiable
inscribir [inskri'βir] *vt* to inscribe; **~ a algn en** (*lista*) to put sb on; (*censo*) to register sb on
inscripción [inskrip'θjon] *nf* inscription; (*Escol etc*) enrolment; (*en censo*) registration
insecticida [insekti'θiða] *nm* insecticide
insecto [in'sekto] *nm* insect
inseguridad [inseɣuri'ðað] *nf* insecurity; **inseguridad ciudadana** lack of safety in the streets
inseguro, -a [inse'ɣuro, a] *adj* insecure; (*inconstante*) unsteady; (*incierto*) uncertain
insensato, -a [insen'sato, a] *adj* foolish, stupid
insensible [insen'siβle] *adj* (*gen*) insensitive; (*movimiento*) imperceptible; (*sin sentido*) numb
insertar [inser'tar] *vt* to insert
inservible [inser'βiβle] *adj* useless
insignia [in'siɣnja] *nf* (*señal distintiva*) badge; (*estandarte*) flag
insignificante [insiɣnifi'kante] *adj* insignificant
insinuar [insi'nwar] *vt* to insinuate, imply
insípido, -a [in'sipiðo, a] *adj* insipid
insistir [insis'tir] *vi* to insist; **~ en algo** to insist on sth; (*enfatizar*) to stress sth
insolación [insola'θjon] *nf* (*Med*) sunstroke
insolente [inso'lente] *adj* insolent
insólito, -a [in'solito, a] *adj* unusual
insoluble [inso'luβle] *adj* insoluble
insomnio [in'somnjo] *nm* insomnia
insonorizado, -a [insonori'θaðo, a] *adj* (*cuarto etc*) soundproof
insoportable [insopor'taβle] *adj* unbearable
inspección [inspek'θjon] *nf* inspection, check; **inspeccionar** *vt* (*examinar*) to inspect, examine; (*controlar*) to check
inspector, a [inspek'tor, a] *nm/f* inspector
inspiración [inspira'θjon] *nf* inspiration
inspirar [inspi'rar] *vt* to inspire; (*Med*) to inhale; **inspirarse** *vr*: **~se en** to be inspired by
instalación [instala'θjon] *nf* (*equipo*) fittings *pl*, equipment; **instalación eléctrica** wiring
instalar [insta'lar] *vt* (*establecer*) to instal; (*erguir*) to set up, erect; **instalarse** *vr* to establish o.s.; (*en una vivienda*) to move into
instancia [ins'tanθja] *nf* (*Jur*) petition; (*ruego*) request; **en última ~** as a last resort
instantáneo, -a [instan'taneo, a] *adj* instantaneous; **café ~** instant coffee
instante [ins'tante] *nm* instant, moment; **al ~** right now
instar [ins'tar] *vt* to press, urge
instaurar [instau'rar] *vt* (*costumbre*) to establish; (*normas, sistema*) to bring in, introduce; (*gobierno*) to instal
instigar [insti'ɣar] *vt* to instigate
instinto [ins'tinto] *nm* instinct; **por ~** instinctively
institución [institu'θjon] *nf* institution, establishment
instituir [institu'ir] *vt* to establish; (*fundar*) to found; **instituto** *nm* (*gen*) institute; (ESP *Escol*) ≈ comprehensive (BRIT) *o* high (US) school
institutriz [institu'triθ] *nf* governess
instrucción [instruk'θjon] *nf* instruction
instruir [instru'ir] *vt* (*gen*) to instruct; (*enseñar*) to teach, educate
instrumento [instru'mento] *nm* (*gen*) instrument; (*herramienta*) tool, implement
insubordinarse [insuβorði'narse]

vr to rebel
insuficiente [insufi'θjente] *adj* (*gen*) insufficient; (*Escol*: *calificación*) unsatisfactory
insular [insu'lar] *adj* insular
insultar [insul'tar] *vt* to insult; **insulto** *nm* insult
insuperable [insupe'raβle] *adj* (*excelente*) unsurpassable; (*problema etc*) insurmountable
insurrección [insurrek'θjon] *nf* insurrection, rebellion
intachable [inta'tʃaβle] *adj* irreproachable
intacto, -a [in'takto, a] *adj* intact
integral [inte'ɣral] *adj* integral; (*completo*) complete; **pan ~** wholemeal (BRIT) *o* wholewheat (US) bread
integrar [inte'ɣrar] *vt* to make up, compose; (*Mat*: *fig*) to integrate
integridad [inteɣri'ðað] *nf* wholeness; (*carácter*) integrity; **íntegro, -a** *adj* whole, entire; (*honrado*) honest
intelectual [intelek'twal] *adj*, *nmf* intellectual
inteligencia [inteli'xenθja] *nf* intelligence; (*ingenio*) ability; **inteligente** *adj* intelligent
intemperie [intem'perje] *nf*: **a la ~** out in the open, exposed to the elements
intención [inten'θjon] *nf* (*gen*) intention, purpose; **con segundas intenciones** maliciously; **con ~** deliberately
intencionado, -a [intenθjo'naðo, a] *adj* deliberate; **mal ~** ill-disposed, hostile
intensidad [intensi'ðað] *nf* (*gen*) intensity; (*Elec*, *Tec*) strength; **llover con ~** to rain hard
intenso, -a [in'tenso, a] *adj* intense; (*sentimiento*) profound, deep
intentar [inten'tar] *vt* (*tratar*) to try, attempt; **intento** *nm* attempt
interactivo, -a [interak'tiβo, a] *adj* (*Inform*) interactive
intercalar [interka'lar] *vt* to insert
intercambio [inter'kambjo] *nm* exchange, swap
interceder [interθe'ðer] *vi* to intercede
interceptar [interθep'tar] *vt* to intercept
interés [inte'res] *nm* (*gen*) interest; (*parte*) share, part; (*pey*) self-interest; **intereses creados** vested interests
interesado, -a [intere'saðo, a] *adj* interested; (*prejuiciado*) prejudiced; (*pey*) mercenary, self-seeking
interesante [intere'sante] *adj* interesting
interesar [intere'sar] *vt*, *vi* to interest, be of interest to; **interesarse** *vr*: **~se en** *o* **por** to take an interest in
interferir [interfe'rir] *vt* to interfere with; (*Tel*) to jam ▷ *vi* to interfere
interfón [inter'fon] (MÉX) *nm* entry phone
interino, -a [inte'rino, a] *adj* temporary ▷ *nm/f* temporary holder of a post; (*Med*) locum; (*Escol*) supply teacher
interior [inte'rjor] *adj* inner, inside; (*Com*) domestic, internal ▷ *nm* interior, inside; (*fig*) soul, mind; **Ministerio del I~** ≈ Home Office (BRIT) ≈ Department of the Interior (US); **interiorista** (ESP) *nmf* interior designer
interjección [interxek'θjon] *nf* interjection
interlocutor, a [interloku'tor, a] *nm/f* speaker
intermedio, -a [inter'meðjo, a] *adj* intermediate ▷ *nm* interval
interminable [intermi'naβle] *adj* endless
intermitente [intermi'tente] *adj* intermittent ▷ *nm* (*Auto*) indicator
internacional [internaθjo'nal] *adj* international
internado [inter'naðo] *nm* boarding school
internar [inter'nar] *vt* to intern; (*en*

un manicomio) to commit; **internarse** *vr* (*penetrar*) to penetrate
internauta [inter'nauta] *nmf* web surfer, Internet user
Internet, internet [inter'net] *nm o f* Internet
interno, -a [in'terno, a] *adj* internal, interior; (*Pol etc*) domestic ▷ *nm/f* (*alumno*) boarder
interponer [interpo'ner] *vt* to interpose, put in; **interponerse** *vr* to intervene
interpretación [interpreta'θjon] *nf* interpretation
interpretar [interpre'tar] *vt* to interpret; (*Teatro, Mús*) to perform, play; **intérprete** *nmf* (*Ling*) interpreter, translator; (*Mús, Teatro*) performer, artist(e)
interrogación [interroɣa'θjon] *nf* interrogation; (*Ling*: *tb*: **signo de ~**) question mark
interrogar [interro'ɣar] *vt* to interrogate, question
interrumpir [interrum'pir] *vt* to interrupt
interrupción [interrup'θjon] *nf* interruption
interruptor [interrup'tor] *nm* (*Elec*) switch
intersección [intersek'θjon] *nf* intersection
interurbano, -a [interur'βano, a] *adj*: **llamada interurbana** long-distance call
intervalo [inter'βalo] *nm* interval; (*descanso*) break
intervenir [interβe'nir] *vt* (*controlar*) to control, supervise; (*Med*) to operate on ▷ *vi* (*participar*) to take part, participate; (*mediar*) to intervene
interventor, a [interβen'tor, a] *nm/f* inspector; (*Com*) auditor
intestino [intes'tino] *nm* (*Med*) intestine
intimar [inti'mar] *vi* to become friendly
intimidad [intimi'ðað] *nf* intimacy; (*familiaridad*) familiarity; (*vida privada*) private life; (*Jur*) privacy
íntimo, -a ['intimo, a] *adj* intimate
intolerable [intole'raβle] *adj* intolerable, unbearable
intoxicación [intoksika'θjon] *nf* poisoning; **intoxicación alimenticia** food poisoning
intranet [intra'net] *nf* intranet
intranquilo, -a [intran'kilo, a] *adj* worried
intransitable [intransi'taβle] *adj* impassable
intrépido, -a [in'trepiðo, a] *adj* intrepid
intriga [in'triɣa] *nf* intrigue; (*plan*) plot; **intrigar** *vt, vi* to intrigue
intrínseco, -a [in'trinseko, a] *adj* intrinsic
introducción [introðuk'θjon] *nf* introduction
introducir [introðu'θir] *vt* (*gen*) to introduce; (*moneda etc*) to insert; (*Inform*) to input, enter
intromisión [intromi'sjon] *nf* interference, meddling
introvertido, -a [introβer'tiðo, a] *adj, nm/f* introvert
intruso, -a [in'truso, a] *adj* intrusive ▷ *nm/f* intruder
intuición [intwi'θjon] *nf* intuition
inundación [inunda'θjon] *nf* flood(ing); **inundar** *vt* to flood; (*fig*) to swamp, inundate
inusitado, -a [inusi'taðo, a] *adj* unusual, rare
inútil [in'util] *adj* useless; (*esfuerzo*) vain, fruitless
inutilizar [inutili'θar] *vt* to make *o* render useless
invadir [imba'ðir] *vt* to invade
inválido, -a [im'baliðo, a] *adj* invalid ▷ *nm/f* invalid
invasión [imba'sjon] *nf* invasion
invasor, a [imba'sor, a] *adj* invading ▷ *nm/f* invader
invención [imben'θjon] *nf* invention
inventar [imben'tar] *vt* to invent

inventario [imben'tarjo] *nm* inventory
invento [im'bento] *nm* invention
inventor, a [imben'tor, a] *nm/f* inventor
invernadero [imberna'ðero] *nm* greenhouse
inverosímil [imbero'simil] *adj* implausible
inversión [imber'sjon] *nf* (*Com*) investment
inverso, -a [im'berso, a] *adj* inverse, opposite; **en el orden ~** in reverse order; **a la inversa** inversely, the other way round
inversor, a [imber'sor, a] *nm/f* (*Com*) investor
invertir [imber'tir] *vt* (*Com*) to invest; (*volcar*) to turn upside down; (*tiempo etc*) to spend
investigación [imbestiɣa'θjon] *nf* investigation; (*Escol*) research; **investigación y desarrollo** research and development
investigar [imbesti'ɣar] *vt* to investigate; (*Escol*) to do research into
invierno [im'bjerno] *nm* winter
invisible [imbi'siβle] *adj* invisible
invitado, -a [imbi'taðo, a] *nm/f* guest
invitar [imbi'tar] *vt* to invite; (*incitar*) to entice; (*pagar*) to buy, pay for
invocar [imbo'kar] *vt* to invoke, call on
involucrar [imbolu'krar] *vt*: **~ en** to involve in; **involucrarse** *vr* (*persona*): **~se en** to get mixed up in
involuntario, -a [imbolun'tarjo, a] *adj* (*movimiento, gesto*) involuntary; (*error*) unintentional
inyección [injek'θjon] *nf* injection
inyectar [injek'tar] *vt* to inject
iPod® ['ipoð] (*pl* **~s**) *nm* iPod®

PALABRA CLAVE

ir [ir] *vi* **1** to go; (*a pie*) to walk; (*viajar*) to travel; **ir caminando** to walk; **fui en tren** I went *o* travelled by train; **¡(ahora) voy!** (I'm just) coming!
2: **ir (a) por: ir (a) por el médico** to fetch the doctor
3 (*progresar: persona, cosa*) to go; **el trabajo va muy bien** work is going very well; **¿cómo te va?** how are things going?; **me va muy bien** I'm getting on very well; **le fue fatal** it went awfully badly for him
4 (*funcionar*): **el coche no va muy bien** the car isn't running very well
5: **te va estupendamente ese color** that colour suits you fantastically well
6 (*locuciones*): **¿vino? – ¡que va!** did he come? – of course not!; **vamos, no llores** come on, don't cry; **¡vaya coche!** what a car!, that's some car!
7: **no vaya a ser: tienes que correr, no vaya a ser que pierdas el tren** you'll have to run so as not to miss the train
8 (*+ pp*): **iba vestido muy bien** he was very well dressed
9: **ni me** *etc* **va ni me** *etc* **viene** I *etc* don't care
▷ *vb aux* **1 ir a: voy/iba a hacerlo hoy** I am/was going to do it today
2 (*+ gerundio*): **iba anocheciendo** it was getting dark; **todo se me iba aclarando** everything was gradually becoming clearer to me
3 (*+ pp: = pasivo*): **van vendidos 300 ejemplares** 300 copies have been sold so far
irse *vr* **1**: **¿por dónde se va al zoológico?** which is the way to the zoo?
2 (*marcharse*) to leave; **ya se habrán ido** they must already have left *o* gone

ira ['ira] *nf* anger, rage
Irak [i'rak] *nm* = **Iraq**
Irán [i'ran] *nm* Iran; **iraní** *adj, nmf* Iranian
Iraq [i'rak] *nm* Iraq; **iraquí** *adj, nmf* Iraqi

iris ['iris] *nm inv* (*tb*: **arco ~**) rainbow; (*Anat*) iris

Irlanda [ir'landa] *nf* Ireland; **irlandés, -esa** *adj* Irish ▷ *nm/f* Irishman(-woman); **los irlandeses** the Irish

ironía [iro'nia] *nf* irony; **irónico, -a** *adj* ironic(al)

IRPF *nm abr* (= *Impuesto sobre la Renta de las Personas Físicas*) (personal) income tax

irreal [irre'al] *adj* unreal

irregular [irreɣu'lar] *adj* (*gen*) irregular; (*situación*) abnormal

irremediable [irreme'ðjaβle] *adj* irremediable; (*vicio*) incurable

irreparable [irrepa'raβle] *adj* (*daños*) irreparable; (*pérdida*) irrecoverable

irrespetuoso, -a [irrespe'twoso, a] *adj* disrespectful

irresponsable [irrespon'saβle] *adj* irresponsible

irreversible [irreβer'sible] *adj* irreversible

irrigar [irri'ɣar] *vt* to irrigate

irrisorio, -a [irri'sorjo, a] *adj* derisory, ridiculous

irritar [irri'tar] *vt* to irritate, annoy

irrupción [irrup'θjon] *nf* irruption; (*invasión*) invasion

isla ['isla] *nf* island

Islam [is'lam] *nm* Islam; **las enseñanzas del ~** the teachings of Islam; **islámico, -a** *adj* Islamic

islandés, -esa [islan'des, esa] *adj* Icelandic ▷ *nm/f* Icelander

Islandia [is'landja] *nf* Iceland

isleño, -a [is'leɲo, a] *adj* island *cpd* ▷ *nm/f* islander

Israel [isra'el] *nm* Israel; **israelí** *adj, nmf* Israeli

istmo ['istmo] *nm* isthmus

Italia [i'talja] *nf* Italy; **italiano, -a** *adj, nm/f* Italian

itinerario [itine'rarjo] *nm* itinerary, route

ITV (ESP) *nf abr* (= *inspección técnica de vehículos*) roadworthiness test, ≈ MOT (BRIT)

IVA ['iβa] *nm abr* (= *impuesto sobre el valor añadido*) VAT

izar [i'θar] *vt* to hoist

izdo, -a *abr* (= *izquierdo, a*) l

izquierda [iθ'kjerda] *nf* left; (*Pol*) left (wing); **a la ~** (*estar*) on the left; (*torcer etc*) (to the) left

izquierdo, -a [iθ'kjerðo, a] *adj* left

jabalí [xaβa'li] *nm* wild boar
jabalina [xaβa'lina] *nf* javelin
jabón [xa'βon] *nm* soap
jaca ['xaka] *nf* pony
jacal [xa'kal] (*MÉX*) *nm* shack
jacinto [xa'θinto] *nm* hyacinth
jactarse [xak'tarse] *vr* to boast, brag
jadear [xaðe'ar] *vi* to pant, gasp for breath
jaguar [xa'ɣwar] *nm* jaguar
jaiba ['xaiβa] (*LAM*) *nf* crab
jalar [xa'lar] (*LAM*) *vt* to pull
jalea [xa'lea] *nf* jelly
jaleo [xa'leo] *nm* racket, uproar; **armar un ~** to kick up a racket
jalón [xa'lon] (*LAM*) *nm* tug
jamás [xa'mas] *adv* never
jamón [xa'mon] *nm* ham; **jamón dulce** *o* **de York** cooked ham; **jamón serrano** cured ham
Japón [xa'pon] *nm* Japan; **japonés, -esa** *adj, nm/f* Japanese ▷ *nm* (*Ling*) Japanese
jaque ['xake] *nm* (*Ajedrez*) check; **jaque mate** checkmate
jaqueca [xa'keka] *nf* (very bad) headache, migraine
jarabe [xa'raβe] *nm* syrup
jardín [xar'ðin] *nm* garden; **jardín infantil** *o* **de infancia** nursery (school); **jardinería** *nf* gardening; **jardinero, -a** *nm/f* gardener
jarra ['xarra] *nf* jar; (*jarro*) jug
jarro ['xarro] *nm* jug
jarrón [xa'rron] *nm* vase
jaula ['xaula] *nf* cage
jauría [xau'ria] *nf* pack of hounds
jazmín [xaθ'min] *nm* jasmine
J.C. *abr* (= *Jesucristo*) J.C.
jeans [jins, dʒins] (*LAM*) *nmpl* jeans, denims; **unos ~** a pair of jeans
jefatura [xefa'tura] *nf* (*tb*: **~ de policía**) police headquarters *sg*
jefe, -a ['xefe, a] *nm/f* (*gen*) chief, head; (*patrón*) boss; **jefe de cocina** chef; **jefe de estación** stationmaster; **jefe de Estado** head of state; **jefe de estudios** (*Escol*) director of studies; **jefe de gobierno** head of government
jengibre [xen'xiβre] *nm* ginger
jeque ['xeke] *nm* sheik
jerárquico, -a [xe'rarkiko, a] *adj* hierarchic(al)
jerez [xe'reθ] *nm* sherry
jerga ['xerɣa] *nf* jargon
jeringa [xe'ringa] *nf* syringe; (*LAM*: *molestia*) annoyance, bother; **jeringuilla** *nf* syringe
jeroglífico [xero'ɣlifiko] *nm* hieroglyphic
jersey [xer'sei] (*pl* **~s**) *nm* jersey, pullover, jumper
Jerusalén [xerusa'len] *n* Jerusalem
Jesucristo [xesu'kristo] *nm* Jesus Christ
jesuita [xe'swita] *adj, nm* Jesuit
Jesús [xe'sus] *nm* Jesus; **¡~!** good heavens!; (*al estornudar*) bless you!
jinete [xi'nete] *nmf* horseman(-woman), rider
jipijapa [xipi'xapa] (*LAM*) *nm* straw hat
jirafa [xi'rafa] *nf* giraffe

jirón [xi'ron] *nm* rag, shred
jitomate [xito'mate] (MÉX) *nm* tomato
joder [xo'ðer] (*fam!*) *vt, vi* to fuck (*!*)
jogging ['joɣin] (RPL) *nm* tracksuit (BRIT), sweat suit (US)
jornada [xor'naða] *nf* (*viaje de un día*) day's journey; (*camino o viaje entero*) journey; (*día de trabajo*) working day
jornal [xor'nal] *nm* (day's) wage; **jornalero** *nm* (day) labourer
joroba [xo'roβa] *nf* hump, hunched back; **jorobado, -a** *adj* hunchbacked ▷ *nm/f* hunchback
jota ['xota] *nf* (the letter) J; (*danza*) *Aragonese dance*; **no saber ni ~** to have no idea
joven ['xoβen] (*pl* **jóvenes**) *adj* young ▷ *nm* young man, youth ▷ *nf* young woman, girl
joya ['xoja] *nf* jewel, gem; (*fig: persona*) gem; **joyas de fantasía** costume *o* imitation jewellery; **joyería** *nf* (*joyas*) jewellery; (*tienda*) jeweller's (shop); **joyero** *nm* (*persona*) jeweller; (*caja*) jewel case
juanete [xwa'nete] *nm* (*del pie*) bunion
jubilación [xuβila'θjon] *nf* (*retiro*) retirement
jubilado, -a [xuβi'laðo, a] *adj* retired ▷ *nm/f* pensioner (BRIT), senior citizen
jubilar [xuβi'lar] *vt* to pension off, retire; (*fam*) to discard; **jubilarse** *vr* to retire
júbilo ['xuβilo] *nm* joy, rejoicing; **jubiloso, -a** *adj* jubilant
judía [xu'ðia] (ESP) *nf* (*Culin*) bean; **judía blanca/verde** haricot/French bean; *V tb* **judío**
judicial [xuði'θjal] *adj* judicial
judío, -a [xu'ðio, a] *adj* Jewish ▷ *nm/f* Jew(ess)
judo ['juðo] *nm* judo
juego *etc* ['xweɣo] *vb V* **jugar** ▷ *nm* (*gen*) play; (*pasatiempo, partido*) game; (*en casino*) gambling; (*conjunto*) set; **fuera de ~** (*Deporte: persona*) offside; (*: pelota*) out of play; **juego de palabras** pun, play on words; **Juegos Olímpicos** Olympic Games
juerga ['xwerɣa] (ESP: *fam*) *nf* binge; (*fiesta*) party; **ir de ~** to go out on a binge
jueves ['xweβes] *nm inv* Thursday
juez [xweθ] *nmf* judge; **juez de instrucción** examining magistrate; **juez de línea** linesman; **juez de salida** starter
jugada [xu'ɣaða] *nf* play; **buena ~** good move *o* shot *o* stroke *etc*
jugador, a [xuɣa'ðor, a] *nm/f* player; (*en casino*) gambler
jugar [xu'ɣar] *vt, vi* to play; (*en casino*) to gamble; (*apostar*) to bet; **~ al fútbol** to play football
juglar [xu'ɣlar] *nm* minstrel
jugo ['xuɣo] *nm* (*Bot*) juice; (*fig*) essence, substance; **jugo de naranja** (LAM) orange juice; **jugoso, -a** *adj* juicy; (*fig*) substantial, important
juguete [xu'ɣete] *nm* toy; **juguetear** *vi* to play; **juguetería** *nf* toyshop
juguetón, -ona [xuɣe'ton, ona] *adj* playful
juicio ['xwiθjo] *nm* judgement; (*razón*) sanity, reason; (*opinión*) opinion
julio ['xuljo] *nm* July
jumper ['dʒumper] (LAM) *nm* pinafore dress (BRIT), jumper (US)
junco ['xunko] *nm* rush, reed
jungla ['xungla] *nf* jungle
junio ['xunjo] *nm* June
junta ['xunta] *nf* (*asamblea*) meeting, assembly; (*comité, consejo*) council, committee; (*Com, Finanzas*) board; (*Tec*) joint; **junta directiva** board of directors
juntar [xun'tar] *vt* to join, unite; (*maquinaria*) to assemble, put together; (*dinero*) to collect; **juntarse** *vr* to join, meet; (*reunirse: personas*) to meet, assemble; (*arrimarse*) to approach, draw closer; **~se con algn** to join sb
junto, -a ['xunto, a] *adj* joined; (*unido*) united; (*anexo*) near, close;

(*contiguo, próximo*) next, adjacent ▷ *adv*: **todo ~** all at once; **~s** together; **~ a** near (to), next to; **~ con** (together) with

jurado [xu'raðo] *nm* (*Jur: individuo*) juror; (*: grupo*) jury; (*de concurso: grupo*) panel (of judges); (*: individuo*) member of a panel

juramento [xura'mento] *nm* oath; (*maldición*) oath, curse; **prestar ~** to take the oath; **tomar ~ a** to swear in, administer the oath to

jurar [xu'rar] *vt, vi* to swear; **~ en falso** to commit perjury; **tenérsela jurada a algn** to have it in for sb

jurídico, -a [xu'riðiko, a] *adj* legal

jurisdicción [xurisðik'θjon] *nf* (*poder, autoridad*) jurisdiction; (*territorio*) district

justamente [xusta'mente] *adv* justly, fairly; (*precisamente*) just, exactly

justicia [xus'tiθja] *nf* justice; (*equidad*) fairness, justice

justificación [xustifika'θjon] *nf* justification; **justificar** *vt* to justify

justo, -a ['xusto, a] *adj* (*equitativo*) just, fair, right; (*preciso*) exact, correct; (*ajustado*) tight ▷ *adv* (*precisamente*) exactly, precisely; (*LAM: apenas a tiempo*) just in time

juvenil [xuβe'nil] *adj* youthful

juventud [xuβen'tuð] *nf* (*adolescencia*) youth; (*jóvenes*) young people *pl*

juzgado [xuθ'ɣaðo] *nm* tribunal; (*Jur*) court

juzgar [xuθ'ɣar] *vt* to judge; **a ~ por ...** to judge by ..., judging by ...

kárate ['karate] *nm* karate

kg *abr* (= *kilogramo*) kg

kilo ['kilo] *nm* kilo; **kilogramo** *nm* kilogramme; **kilometraje** *nm* distance in kilometres ≈ mileage; **kilómetro** *nm* kilometre; **kilovatio** *nm* kilowatt

kiosco ['kjosko] *nm* = **quiosco**

kleenex® [kli'neks] *nm* paper handkerchief, tissue

Kosovo [ko'soβo] *nm* Kosovo

km *abr* (= *kilómetro*) km

kv *abr* (= *kilovatio*) kw

l *abr* (= *litro*) l

la [la] *art def* the ▷ *pron* her; (*Ud.*) you; (*cosa*) it ▷ *nm* (*Mús*) la; **~ del sombrero rojo** the girl in the red hat; *V tb* **el**

laberinto [laβe'rinto] *nm* labyrinth

labio ['laβjo] *nm* lip

labor [la'βor] *nf* labour; (*Agr*) farm work; (*tarea*) job, task; (*Costura*) needlework; **labores domésticas** *o* **del hogar** household chores; **laborable** *adj* (*Agr*) workable; **día laborable** working day; **laboral** *adj* (*accidente*) at work; (*jornada*) working

laboratorio [laβora'torjo] *nm* laboratory

laborista [laβo'rista] *adj*: **Partido L~** Labour Party

labrador, a [laβra'ðor, a] *adj* farming *cpd* ▷ *nm/f* farmer

labranza [la'βranθa] *nf* (*Agr*) cultivation

labrar [la'βrar] *vt* (*gen*) to work; (*madera etc*) to carve; (*fig*) to cause, bring about

laca ['laka] *nf* lacquer

lacio, -a ['laθjo, a] *adj* (*pelo*) straight

lacón [la'kon] *nm* shoulder of pork

lactancia [lak'tanθja] *nf* lactation

lácteo, -a ['lakteo, a] *adj*: **productos ~s** dairy products

ladear [laðe'ar] *vt* to tip, tilt ▷ *vi* to tilt; **ladearse** *vr* to lean

ladera [la'ðera] *nf* slope

lado ['laðo] *nm* (*gen*) side; (*fig*) protection; (*Mil*) flank; **al ~ de** beside; **poner de ~** to put on its side; **poner a un ~** to put aside; **por todos ~s** on all sides, all round (BRIT)

ladrar [la'ðrar] *vi* to bark; **ladrido** *nm* bark, barking

ladrillo [la'ðriʎo] *nm* (*gen*) brick; (*azulejo*) tile

ladrón, -ona [la'ðron, ona] *nm/f* thief

lagartija [laɣar'tixa] *nf* (*Zool*) (small) lizard

lagarto [la'ɣarto] *nm* (*Zool*) lizard

lago ['laɣo] *nm* lake

lágrima ['laɣrima] *nf* tear

laguna [la'ɣuna] *nf* (*lago*) lagoon; (*hueco*) gap

lamentable [lamen'taβle] *adj* lamentable, regrettable; (*miserable*) pitiful

lamentar [lamen'tar] *vt* (*sentir*) to regret; (*deplorar*) to lament; **lamentarse** *vr* to lament; **lo lamento mucho** I'm very sorry

lamer [la'mer] *vt* to lick

lámina ['lamina] *nf* (*plancha delgada*) sheet; (*para estampar, estampa*) plate

lámpara ['lampara] *nf* lamp; **lámpara de alcohol/gas** spirit/gas lamp; **lámpara de pie** standard lamp

lana ['lana] *nf* wool

lancha ['lantʃa] *nf* launch; **lancha motora** motorboat, speedboat

langosta [lan'gosta] *nf* (*crustáceo*) lobster; (: *de río*) crayfish; **langostino** *nm* Dublin Bay prawn

lanza ['lanθa] *nf* (*arma*) lance, spear

lanzamiento [lanθa'mjento] *nm* (*gen*) throwing; (*Náut, Com*) launch, launching; **lanzamiento de peso** putting the shot

lanzar [lan'θar] *vt* (*gen*) to throw; (*Deporte: pelota*) to bowl; (*Náut, Com*) to launch; (*Jur*) to evict; **lanzarse** *vr* to throw o.s.

lapa ['lapa] *nf* limpet

lapicero [lapi'θero] (CAM) *nm* (*bolígrafo*) ballpoint pen, Biro®

lápida ['lapiða] *nf* stone; **lápida mortuoria** headstone

lápiz ['lapiθ] *nm* pencil; **lápiz de color** coloured pencil; **lápiz de labios** lipstick; **lápiz de ojos** eyebrow pencil

largar [lar'ɣar] *vt* (*soltar*) to release; (*aflojar*) to loosen; (*lanzar*) to launch; (*fam*) to let fly; (*velas*) to unfurl; (LAM: *lanzar*) to throw; **largarse** *vr* (*fam*) to beat it; **~se a** (CS: *empezar*) to start to

largo, -a ['larɣo, a] *adj* (*longitud*) long; (*tiempo*) lengthy; (*fig*) generous ▷ *nm* length; (*Mús*) largo; **dos años ~s** two long years; **tiene 9 metros de ~** it is 9 metres long; **a la larga** in the long run; **a lo ~ de** along; (*tiempo*) all through, throughout

> No confundir **largo** con la palabra inglesa *large*.

largometraje *nm* feature film

laringe [la'rinxe] *nf* larynx; **laringitis** *nf* laryngitis

las [las] *art def* the ▷ *pron* them; **~ que cantan** the ones *o* women *o* girls who sing; *V tb* **el**

lasaña [la'saɲa] *nf* lasagne, lasagna

láser ['laser] *nm* laser

lástima ['lastima] *nf* (*pena*) pity; **dar ~** to be pitiful; **es una ~ que ...** it's a pity that ...; **¡qué ~!** what a pity!; **está hecha una ~** she looks pitiful

lastimar [lasti'mar] *vt* (*herir*) to wound; (*ofender*) to offend; **lastimarse** *vr* to hurt o.s.

lata ['lata] *nf* (*metal*) tin; (*caja*) tin (BRIT), can; (*fam*) nuisance; **en ~** tinned (BRIT), canned; **dar la ~** to be a nuisance

latente [la'tente] *adj* latent

lateral [late'ral] *adj* side *cpd*, lateral ▷ *nm* (*Teatro*) wings

latido [la'tiðo] *nm* (*de corazón*) beat

latifundio [lati'fundjo] *nm* large estate

latigazo [lati'ɣaθo] *nm* (*golpe*) lash; (*sonido*) crack

látigo ['latiɣo] *nm* whip

latín [la'tin] *nm* Latin

latino, -a [la'tino, a] *adj* Latin; **latinoamericano, -a** *adj, nm/f* Latin-American

latir [la'tir] *vi* (*corazón, pulso*) to beat

latitud [lati'tuð] *nf* (*Geo*) latitude

latón [la'ton] *nm* brass

laurel [lau'rel] *nm* (*Bot*) laurel; (*Culin*) bay

lava ['laβa] *nf* lava

lavabo [la'βaβo] *nm* (*pila*) washbasin; (*tb*: **~s**) toilet

lavado [la'βaðo] *nm* washing; (*de ropa*) laundry; (*Arte*) wash; **lavado de cerebro** brainwashing; **lavado en seco** dry-cleaning

lavadora [laβa'ðora] *nf* washing machine

lavanda [la'βanda] *nf* lavender

lavandería [laβande'ria] *nf* laundry; (*automática*) launderette

lavaplatos [laβa'platos] *nm inv* dishwasher

lavar [la'βar] *vt* to wash; (*borrar*) to wipe away; **lavarse** *vr* to wash o.s.; **~se las manos** to wash one's hands; **~se los dientes** to brush one's teeth; **~ y marcar** (*pelo*) to shampoo and set; **~ en seco** to dry-clean; **~ los platos** to wash the dishes

lavarropas [laβa'rropas] (RPL) *nm inv* washing machine

lavavajillas [laβaβa'xiʎas] *nm inv* dishwasher

laxante [lak'sante] *nm* laxative

lazarillo [laθa'riʎo] *nm* (*tb*: **perro ~**) guide dog

lazo ['laθo] *nm* knot; (*lazada*) bow; (*para animales*) lasso; (*trampa*) snare;

(*vínculo*) tie
le [le] *pron* (*directo*) him (*o* her); (*: usted*) you; (*indirecto*) to him (*o* her *o* it); (*: usted*) to you
leal [le'al] *adj* loyal; **lealtad** *nf* loyalty
lección [lek'θjon] *nf* lesson
leche ['letʃe] *nf* milk; **tiene mala ~** (*fam!*) he's a swine (*!*); **leche condensada** condensed milk; **leche desnatada** skimmed milk
lecho ['letʃo] *nm* (*cama: de río*) bed; (*Geo*) layer
lechón [le'tʃon] *nm* sucking (BRIT) *o* suckling (US) pig
lechoso, -a [le'tʃoso, a] *adj* milky
lechuga [le'tʃuɣa] *nf* lettuce
lechuza [le'tʃuθa] *nf* owl
lector, a [lek'tor, a] *nm/f* reader ▷ *nm*: **~ de discos compactos** CD player
lectura [lek'tura] *nf* reading
leer [le'er] *vt* to read
legado [le'ɣaðo] *nm* (*don*) bequest; (*herencia*) legacy; (*enviado*) legate
legajo [le'ɣaxo] *nm* file
legal [le'ɣal] *adj* (*gen*) legal; (*persona*) trustworthy; **legalizar** [leɣali'θar] *vt* to legalize; (*documento*) to authenticate
legaña [le'ɣaɲa] *nf* sleep (*in eyes*)
legión [le'xjon] *nf* legion; **legionario, -a** *adj* legionary ▷ *nm* legionnaire
legislación [lexisla'θjon] *nf* legislation
legislar [lexis'lar] *vi* to legislate
legislatura [lexisla'tura] *nf* (*Pol*) period of office
legítimo, -a [le'xitimo, a] *adj* (*genuino*) authentic; (*legal*) legitimate
legua ['leɣwa] *nf* league
legumbres [le'ɣumbres] *nfpl* pulses
leído, -a [le'iðo, a] *adj* well-read
lejanía [lexa'nia] *nf* distance; **lejano, -a** *adj* far-off; (*en el tiempo*) distant; (*fig*) remote
lejía [le'xia] *nf* bleach
lejos ['lexos] *adv* far, far away; **a lo ~** in the distance; **de** *o* **desde ~** from afar; **~ de** far from
lema ['lema] *nm* motto; (*Pol*) slogan
lencería [lenθe'ria] *nf* linen, drapery
lengua ['lengwa] *nf* tongue; (*Ling*) language; **morderse la ~** to hold one's tongue
lenguado [len'gwaðo] *nm* sole
lenguaje [len'gwaxe] *nm* language; **lenguaje de programación** program(m)ing language
lengüeta [len'gweta] *nf* (*Anat*) epiglottis; (*zapatos*) tongue; (*Mús*) reed
lente ['lente] *nf* lens; (*lupa*) magnifying glass; **lentes** *nfpl* lenses ▷ *nmpl* (LAM: *gafas*) glasses; **lentes bifocales/de sol** (LAM) bifocals/sunglasses; **lentes de contacto** contact lenses
lenteja [len'texa] *nf* lentil; **lentejuela** *nf* sequin
lentilla [len'tiʎa] *nf* contact lens
lentitud [lenti'tuð] *nf* slowness; **con ~** slowly
lento, -a ['lento, a] *adj* slow
leña ['leɲa] *nf* firewood; **leñador, a** *nm/f* woodcutter
leño ['leɲo] *nm* (*trozo de árbol*) log; (*madero*) timber; (*fig*) blockhead
Leo ['leo] *nm* Leo
león [le'on] *nm* lion; **león marino** sea lion
leopardo [leo'parðo] *nm* leopard
leotardos [leo'tarðos] *nmpl* tights
lepra ['lepra] *nf* leprosy; **leproso, -a** *nm/f* leper
les [les] *pron* (*directo*) them; (*: ustedes*) you; (*indirecto*) to them; (*: ustedes*) to you
lesbiana [les'βjana] *adj, nf* lesbian
lesión [le'sjon] *nf* wound, lesion; (*Deporte*) injury; **lesionado, -a** *adj* injured ▷ *nm/f* injured person
letal [le'tal] *adj* lethal
letanía [leta'nia] *nf* litany
letra ['letra] *nf* letter; (*escritura*) handwriting; (*Mús*) lyrics *pl*; **letra de cambio** bill of exchange; **letra de imprenta** print; **letrado, -a** *adj* learned ▷ *nm/f* lawyer; **letrero** *nm*

(*cartel*) sign; (*etiqueta*) label
letrina [le'trina] *nf* latrine
leucemia [leu'θemja] *nf* leukaemia
levadura [leβa'ðura] *nf* (*para el pan*) yeast; (*de cerveza*) brewer's yeast
levantar [leβan'tar] *vt* (*gen*) to raise; (*del suelo*) to pick up; (*hacia arriba*) to lift (up); (*plan*) to make, draw up; (*mesa*) to clear; (*campamento*) to strike; (*fig*) to cheer up, hearten; **levantarse** *vr* to get up; (*enderezarse*) to straighten up; (*rebelarse*) to rebel; **~ el ánimo** to cheer up
levante [le'βante] *nm* east coast; **el L~** *region of Spain extending from Castellón to Murcia*
levar [le'βar] *vt* to weigh
leve ['leβe] *adj* light; (*fig*) trivial
levita [le'βita] *nf* frock coat
léxico ['leksiko] *nm* (*vocabulario*) vocabulary
ley [lei] *nf* (*gen*) law; (*metal*) standard
leyenda [le'jenda] *nf* legend
leyó *etc vb V* **leer**
liar [li'ar] *vt* to tie (up); (*unir*) to bind; (*envolver*) to wrap (up); (*enredar*) to confuse; (*cigarrillo*) to roll; **liarse** *vr* (*fam*) to get involved; **~se a palos** to get involved in a fight
Líbano ['liβano] *nm*: **el ~** the Lebanon
libélula [li'βelula] *nf* dragonfly
liberación [liβera'θjon] *nf* liberation; (*de la cárcel*) release
liberal [liβe'ral] *adj, nmf* liberal
liberar [liβe'rar] *vt* to liberate
libertad [liβer'tað] *nf* liberty, freedom; **libertad bajo fianza** bail; **libertad bajo palabra** parole; **libertad condicional** probation; **libertad de culto/de prensa/de comercio** freedom of worship/of the press/of trade
libertar [liβer'tar] *vt* (*preso*) to set free; (*de una obligación*) to release; (*eximir*) to exempt
libertino, -a [liβer'tino, a] *adj* permissive ▷ *nm/f* permissive person
libra ['liβra] *nf* pound; **L~** (*Astrología*) Libra; **libra esterlina** pound sterling
libramiento [liβra'mjento] (*MÉX*) *nm* ring road (*BRIT*), beltway (*US*)
librar [li'βrar] *vt* (*de peligro*) to save; (*batalla*) to wage, fight; (*de impuestos*) to exempt; (*cheque*) to make out; (*Jur*) to exempt; **librarse** *vr*: **~se de** to escape from, free o.s. from
libre ['liβre] *adj* free; (*lugar*) unoccupied; (*asiento*) vacant; (*de deudas*) free of debts; **~ de impuestos** free of tax; **tiro ~** free kick; **los 100 metros ~s** the 100 metres free-style (race); **al aire ~** in the open air
librería [liβre'ria] *nf* (*tienda*) bookshop

> No confundir **librería** con la palabra inglesa *library*.

librero, -a *nm/f* bookseller
libreta [li'βreta] *nf* notebook
libro ['liβro] *nm* book; **libro de bolsillo** paperback; **libro de texto** textbook; **libro electrónico** e-book
Lic. *abr* = **licenciado, a**
licencia [li'θenθja] *nf* (*gen*) licence; (*permiso*) permission; **licencia de caza** game licence; **licencia por enfermedad** (*MÉX, RPL*) sick leave; **licenciado, -a** *adj* licensed ▷ *nm/f* graduate; **licenciar** *vt* (*empleado*) to dismiss; (*permitir*) to permit, allow; (*soldado*) to discharge; (*estudiante*) to confer a degree upon; **licenciarse** *vr*: **licenciarse en Derecho** to graduate in law
lícito, -a ['liθito, a] *adj* (*legal*) lawful; (*justo*) fair, just; (*permisible*) permissible
licor [li'kor] *nm* spirits *pl* (*BRIT*), liquor (*US*); (*de frutas etc*) liqueur
licuadora [likwa'ðora] *nf* blender
líder ['liðer] *nmf* leader; **liderato** *nm* leadership; **liderazgo** *nm* leadership
lidia ['liðja] *nf* bullfighting; (*una lidia*) bullfight; **toros de ~** fighting bulls; **lidiar** *vt, vi* to fight
liebre ['ljeβre] *nf* hare
lienzo ['ljenθo] *nm* linen; (*Arte*) canvas; (*Arq*) wall

liga ['liɣa] *nf* (*de medias*) garter, suspender; (LAM: *goma*) rubber band; (*confederación*) league
ligadura [liɣa'ðura] *nf* bond, tie; (*Med, Mús*) ligature
ligamento [liɣa'mento] *nm* ligament
ligar [li'ɣar] *vt* (*atar*) to tie; (*unir*) to join; (*Med*) to bind up; (*Mús*) to slur ▷ *vi* to mix, blend; (*fam*): **(él) liga mucho** he pulls a lot of women; **ligarse** *vr* to commit o.s.
ligero, -a [li'xero, a] *adj* (*de peso*) light; (*tela*) thin; (*rápido*) swift, quick; (*ágil*) agile, nimble; (*de importancia*) slight; (*de carácter*) flippant, superficial ▷ *adv*: **a la ligera** superficially
liguero [li'ɣero] *nm* suspender (BRIT) *o* garter (US) belt
lija ['lixa] *nf* (*Zool*) dogfish; (*tb*: **papel de ~**) sandpaper
lila ['lila] *nf* lilac
lima ['lima] *nf* file; (*Bot*) lime; **lima de uñas** nailfile; **limar** *vt* to file
limitación [limita'θjon] *nf* limitation, limit
limitar [limi'tar] *vt* to limit; (*reducir*) to reduce, cut down ▷ *vi*: **~ con** to border on; **limitarse** *vr*: **~se a** to limit o.s. to
límite ['limite] *nm* (*gen*) limit; (*fin*) end; (*frontera*) border; **límite de velocidad** speed limit
limítrofe [li'mitrofe] *adj* neighbouring
limón [li'mon] *nm* lemon ▷ *adj*: **amarillo ~** lemon-yellow; **limonada** *nf* lemonade
limosna [li'mosna] *nf* alms *pl*; **vivir de ~** to live on charity
limpiador [limpja'ðor] (MÉX) *nm* = **limpiaparabrisas**
limpiaparabrisas [limpjapara'βrisas] *nm inv* windscreen (BRIT) *o* windshield (US) wiper
limpiar [lim'pjar] *vt* to clean; (*con trapo*) to wipe; (*quitar*) to wipe away; (*zapatos*) to shine, polish; (*fig*) to clean up
limpieza [lim'pjeθa] *nf* (*estado*) cleanliness; (*acto*) cleaning; (*: de las calles*) cleansing; (*: de zapatos*) polishing; (*habilidad*) skill; (*fig: Policía*) clean-up; (*pureza*) purity; (*Mil*): **operación de ~** mopping-up operation; **limpieza en seco** dry cleaning
limpio, -a ['limpjo, a] *adj* clean; (*moralmente*) pure; (*Com*) clear, net; (*fam*) honest ▷ *adv*: **jugar ~** to play fair; **pasar a** (ESP) *o* **en** (LAM) **~** to make a clean copy of
lince ['linθe] *nm* lynx
linchar [lin'tʃar] *vt* to lynch
lindar [lin'dar] *vi* to adjoin; **~ con** to border on
lindo, -a ['lindo, a] *adj* pretty, lovely ▷ *adv*: **nos divertimos de lo ~** we had a marvellous time; **canta muy ~** (LAM) he sings beautifully
línea ['linea] *nf* (*gen*) line; **en ~** (*Inform*) on line; **línea aérea** airline; **línea de meta** goal line; (*en carrera*) finishing line; **línea discontinua** (*Auto*) broken line; **línea recta** straight line
lingote [lin'gote] *nm* ingot
lingüista [lin'gwista] *nmf* linguist; **lingüística** *nf* linguistics *sg*
lino ['lino] *nm* linen; (*Bot*) flax
linterna [lin'terna] *nf* torch (BRIT), flashlight (US)
lío ['lio] *nm* bundle; (*fam*) fuss; (*desorden*) muddle, mess; **armar un ~** to make a fuss
liquen ['liken] *nm* lichen
liquidación [likiða'θjon] *nf* liquidation; **venta de ~** clearance sale
liquidar [liki'ðar] *vt* (*mercancías*) to liquidate; (*deudas*) to pay off; (*empresa*) to wind up
líquido, -a ['likiðo, a] *adj* liquid; (*ganancia*) net ▷ *nm* liquid; **líquido imponible** net taxable income
lira ['lira] *nf* (*Mús*) lyre; (*moneda*) lira
lírico, -a ['liriko, a] *adj* lyrical

lirio ['lirjo] *nm* (*Bot*) iris
lirón [li'ron] *nm* (*Zool*) dormouse; (*fig*) sleepyhead
Lisboa [lis'βoa] *n* Lisbon
lisiar [li'sjar] *vt* to maim
liso, -a ['liso, a] *adj* (*terreno*) flat; (*cabello*) straight; (*superficie*) even; (*tela*) plain
lista ['lista] *nf* list; (*de alumnos*) school register; (*de libros*) catalogue; (*de platos*) menu; (*de precios*) price list; **pasar ~** to call the roll; **tela de ~s** striped material; **lista de espera** waiting list; **lista de precios** price list; **listín** *nm* (*tb*: **listín telefónico** *o* **de teléfonos**) telephone directory
listo, -a ['listo, a] *adj* (*perspicaz*) smart, clever; (*preparado*) ready
listón [lis'ton] *nm* (*de madera, metal*) strip
litera [li'tera] *nf* (*en barco, tren*) berth; (*en dormitorio*) bunk, bunk bed
literal [lite'ral] *adj* literal
literario, -a [lite'rarjo, a] *adj* literary
literato, -a [lite'rato, a] *adj* literary ▷ *nm/f* writer
literatura [litera'tura] *nf* literature
litigio [li'tixjo] *nm* (*Jur*) lawsuit; (*fig*): **en ~ con** in dispute with
litografía [litoɤra'fia] *nf* lithography; (*una litografía*) lithograph
litoral [lito'ral] *adj* coastal ▷ *nm* coast, seaboard
litro ['litro] *nm* litre
lívido, -a ['liβiðo, a] *adj* livid
llaga ['ʎaɤa] *nf* wound
llama ['ʎama] *nf* flame; (*Zool*) llama
llamada [ʎa'maða] *nf* call; **llamada a cobro revertido** reverse-charge (BRIT) *o* collect (US) call; **llamada al orden** call to order; **llamada de atención** warning; **llamada local** (LAM) local call; **llamada metropolitana** (ESP) local call; **llamada por cobrar** (MÉX) reverse-charge (BRIT) *o* collect (US) call
llamamiento [ʎama'mjento] *nm* call
llamar [ʎa'mar] *vt* to call; (*atención*) to attract ▷ *vi* (*por teléfono*) to telephone; (*a la puerta*) to knock (*o* ring); (*por señas*) to beckon; (*Mil*) to call up; **llamarse** *vr* to be called, be named; **¿cómo se llama (usted)?** what's your name?
llamativo, -a [ʎama'tiβo, a] *adj* showy; (*color*) loud
llano, -a ['ʎano, a] *adj* (*superficie*) flat; (*persona*) straightforward; (*estilo*) clear ▷ *nm* plain, flat ground
llanta ['ʎanta] *nf* (ESP) (wheel) rim; **llanta (de goma)** (LAM: *neumático*) tyre; (: *cámara*) inner (tube); **llanta de repuesto** (LAM) spare tyre
llanto ['ʎanto] *nm* weeping
llanura [ʎa'nura] *nf* plain
llave ['ʎaβe] *nf* key; (*del agua*) tap; (*Mecánica*) spanner; (*de la luz*) switch; (*Mús*) key; **echar la ~ a** to lock up; **llave de contacto** (ESP *Auto*) ignition key; **llave de encendido** (LAM *Auto*) ignition key; **llave de paso** stopcock; **llave inglesa** monkey wrench; **llave maestra** master key; **llavero** *nm* keyring
llegada [ʎe'ɤaða] *nf* arrival
llegar [ʎe'ɤar] *vi* to arrive; (*alcanzar*) to reach; (*bastar*) to be enough; **llegarse** *vr*: **~se a** to approach; **~ a** to manage to, succeed in; **~ a saber** to find out; **~ a ser** to become; **~ a las manos de** to come into the hands of
llenar [ʎe'nar] *vt* to fill; (*espacio*) to cover; (*formulario*) to fill in *o* up; (*fig*) to heap
lleno, -a ['ʎeno, a] *adj* full, filled; (*repleto*) full up ▷ *nm* (*Teatro*) full house; **dar de ~ contra un muro** to hit a wall head-on
llevadero, -a [ʎeβa'ðero, a] *adj* bearable, tolerable
llevar [ʎe'βar] *vt* to take; (*ropa*) to wear; (*cargar*) to carry; (*quitar*) to take away; (*en coche*) to drive; (*transportar*) to transport; (*traer*: *dinero*) to carry; (*conducir*) to lead; (*Mat*) to carry ▷ *vi* (*suj*: *camino etc*): **~ a** to lead to; **llevarse** *vr* to carry off, take away; **llevamos**

dos días aquí we have been here for two days; **él me lleva 2 años** he's 2 years older than me; **~ los libros** (*Com*) to keep the books; **~se bien** to get on well (together)

llorar [ʎo'rar] *vt, vi* to cry, weep; **~ de risa** to cry with laughter

llorón, -ona [ʎo'ron, ona] *adj* tearful ▷ *nm/f* cry-baby

lloroso, -a [ʎo'roso, a] *adj* (*gen*) weeping, tearful; (*triste*) sad, sorrowful

llover [ʎo'βer] *vi* to rain

llovizna [ʎo'βiθna] *nf* drizzle; **lloviznar** *vi* to drizzle

llueve *etc vb V* **llover**

lluvia ['ʎuβja] *nf* rain; **lluvia radioactiva** (radioactive) fallout; **lluvioso, -a** *adj* rainy

lo [lo] *art def*: **~ bel~** the beautiful, what is beautiful, that which is beautiful ▷ *pron* (*persona*) him; (*cosa*) it; **~ que sea** whatever; *V tb* **el**

loable [lo'aβle] *adj* praiseworthy

lobo ['loβo] *nm* wolf; **lobo de mar** (*fig*) sea dog

lóbulo ['loβulo] *nm* lobe

local [lo'kal] *adj* local ▷ *nm* place, site; (*oficinas*) premises *pl*; **localidad** *nf* (*barrio*) locality; (*lugar*) location; (*Teatro*) seat, ticket; **localizar** *vt* (*ubicar*) to locate, find; (*restringir*) to localize; (*situar*) to place

loción [lo'θjon] *nf* lotion

loco, -a ['loko, a] *adj* mad ▷ *nm/f* lunatic, mad person; **estar ~ con** *o* **por algo/por algn** to be mad about sth/sb

locomotora [lokomo'tora] *nf* engine, locomotive

locuaz [lo'kwaθ] *adj* loquacious

locución [loku'θjon] *nf* expression

locura [lo'kura] *nf* madness; (*acto*) crazy act

locutor, a [loku'tor, a] *nm/f* (*Radio*) announcer; (*comentarista*) commentator; (*TV*) newsreader

locutorio [loku'torjo] *nm* (*en telefónica*) telephone booth

lodo ['loðo] *nm* mud

lógica ['loxika] *nf* logic

lógico, -a ['loxiko, a] *adj* logical

login ['loxin] *nm* login

logística [lo'xistika] *nf* logistics *sg*

logotipo [loðo'tipo] *nm* logo

logrado, -a [lo'ðraðo, a] *adj* (*interpretación, reproducción*) polished, excellent

lograr [lo'ɣrar] *vt* to achieve; (*obtener*) to get, obtain; **~ hacer** to manage to do; **~ que algn venga** to manage to get sb to come

logro ['loɣro] *nm* achievement, success

lóker ['loker] (LAM) *nm* locker

loma ['loma] *nf* hillock (BRIT), small hill

lombriz [lom'briθ] *nf* worm

lomo ['lomo] *nm* (*de animal*) back; (*Culin: de cerdo*) pork loin; (*: de vaca*) rib steak; (*de libro*) spine

lona ['lona] *nf* canvas

loncha ['lontʃa] *nf* = **lonja**

lonchería [lontʃe'ria] (LAM) *nf* snack bar, diner (US)

Londres ['londres] *n* London

longaniza [longa'niθa] *nf* pork sausage

longitud [lonxi'tuð] *nf* length; (*Geo*) longitude; **tener 3 metros de ~** to be 3 metres long; **longitud de onda** wavelength

lonja ['lonxa] *nf* slice; (*de tocino*) rasher; **lonja de pescado** fish market

loro ['loro] *nm* parrot

los [los] *art def* the ▷ *pron* them; (*ustedes*) you; **mis libros y ~ tuyos** my books and yours; *V tb* **el**

losa ['losa] *nf* stone

lote ['lote] *nm* portion; (*Com*) lot

lotería [lote'ria] *nf* lottery; (*juego*) lotto

LOTERÍA

Millions of pounds are spent on lotteries each year in Spain, two of which are state-run: the

Lotería Primitiva and the **Lotería Nacional**, with money raised going directly to the government. One of the most famous lotteries is run by the wealthy and influential society for the blind, "la ONCE".

loza ['loθa] *nf* crockery
lubina [lu'βina] *nf* sea bass
lubricante [luβri'kante] *nm* lubricant
lubricar [luβri'kar] *vt* to lubricate
lucha ['lutʃa] *nf* fight, struggle; **lucha de clases** class struggle; **lucha libre** wrestling; **luchar** *vi* to fight
lúcido, -a ['luθido, a] *adj* (*persona*) lucid; (*mente*) logical; (*idea*) crystal-clear
luciérnaga [lu'θjernaɤa] *nf* glow-worm
lucir [lu'θir] *vt* to illuminate, light (up); (*ostentar*) to show off ▷ *vi* (*brillar*) to shine; **lucirse** *vr* (*irónico*) to make a fool of o.s.
lucro ['lukro] *nm* profit, gain
lúdico, -a ['ludiko, a] *adj* (*aspecto, actividad*) play *cpd*
luego ['lweɤo] *adv* (*después*) next; (*más tarde*) later, afterwards
lugar [lu'ɤar] *nm* place; (*sitio*) spot; **en primer ~** in the first place, firstly; **en ~ de** instead of; **hacer ~** to make room; **fuera de ~** out of place; **sin ~ a dudas** without doubt, undoubtedly; **dar ~ a** to give rise to; **tener ~** to take place; **yo en su ~** if I were him; **lugar común** commonplace
lúgubre ['luɤuβre] *adj* mournful
lujo ['luxo] *nm* luxury; (*fig*) profusion, abundance; **de ~** luxury *cpd*, de luxe; **lujoso, -a** *adj* luxurious
lujuria [lu'xurja] *nf* lust
lumbre ['lumbre] *nf* fire; (*para cigarrillo*) light
luminoso, -a [lumi'noso, a] *adj* luminous, shining
luna ['luna] *nf* moon; (*de un espejo*) glass; (*de gafas*) lens; (*fig*) crescent; **estar en la ~** to have one's head in the clouds; **luna de miel** honeymoon; **luna llena/nueva** full/new moon
lunar [lu'nar] *adj* lunar ▷ *nm* (*Anat*) mole; **tela de ~es** spotted material
lunes ['lunes] *nm inv* Monday
lupa ['lupa] *nf* magnifying glass
lustre ['lustre] *nm* polish; (*fig*) lustre; **dar ~ a** to polish
luto ['luto] *nm* mourning; **llevar el** *o* **vestirse de ~** to be in mourning
Luxemburgo [luksem'burɤo] *nm* Luxembourg
luz [luθ] (*pl* **luces**) *nf* light; **dar a ~ un niño** to give birth to a child; **sacar a la ~** to bring to light; **dar** *o* **encender** (ESP) *o* **prender** (LAM)**/apagar la ~** to switch the light on/off; **tener pocas luces** to be dim *o* stupid; **traje de luces** bullfighter's costume; **luces de tráfico** traffic lights; **luz de freno** brake light; **luz roja/verde** red/green light

m *abr* (= *metro*) m; (= *minuto*) m
macana [ma'kana] (*MÉX*) *nf* truncheon (*BRIT*), billy club (*US*)
macarrones [maka'rrones] *nmpl* macaroni *sg*
macedonia [maθe'ðonja] *nf* (*tb*: **~ de frutas**) fruit salad
maceta [ma'θeta] *nf* (*de flores*) pot of flowers; (*para plantas*) flowerpot
machacar [matʃa'kar] *vt* to crush, pound ▷ *vi* (*insistir*) to go on, keep on
machete [ma'tʃete] *nm* machete, (large) knife
machetear [matʃete'ar] (*MÉX*) *vt* to swot (*BRIT*), grind away (*US*)
machismo [ma'tʃismo] *nm* male chauvinism; **machista** *adj, nm* sexist
macho ['matʃo] *adj* male; (*fig*) virile ▷ *nm* male; (*fig*) he-man
macizo, -a [ma'θiθo, a] *adj* (*grande*) massive; (*fuerte, sólido*) solid ▷ *nm* mass, chunk
madeja [ma'ðexa] *nf* (*de lana*) skein, hank; (*de pelo*) mass, mop
madera [ma'ðera] *nf* wood; (*fig*) nature, character; **una ~** a piece of wood
madrastra [ma'ðrastra] *nf* stepmother
madre ['maðre] *adj* mother *cpd* ▷ *nf* mother; (*de vino etc*) dregs *pl*; **madre política/soltera** mother-in-law/ unmarried mother
Madrid [ma'ðrið] *n* Madrid
madriguera [maðri'ɣera] *nf* burrow
madrileño, -a [maðri'leɲo, a] *adj* of *o* from Madrid ▷ *nm/f* native of Madrid
madrina [ma'ðrina] *nf* godmother; (*Arq*) prop, shore; (*Tec*) brace; (*de boda*) bridesmaid
madrugada [maðru'ɣaða] *nf* early morning; (*alba*) dawn, daybreak
madrugador, a [maðruɣa'ðor, a] *adj* early-rising
madrugar [maðru'ɣar] *vi* to get up early; (*fig*) to get ahead
madurar [maðu'rar] *vt, vi* (*fruta*) to ripen; (*fig*) to mature; **madurez** *nf* ripeness; maturity; **maduro, -a** *adj* ripe; mature
maestra *nf* *V* **maestro**
maestría [maes'tria] *nf* mastery; (*habilidad*) skill, expertise
maestro, -a [ma'estro, a] *adj* masterly; (*principal*) main ▷ *nm/f* master/mistress; (*profesor*) teacher ▷ *nm* (*autoridad*) authority; (*Mús*) maestro; (*experto*) master; **maestro albañil** master mason
magdalena [maɣða'lena] *nf* fairy cake
magia ['maxja] *nf* magic; **mágico, -a** *adj* magic(al) ▷ *nm/f* magician
magisterio [maxis'terjo] *nm* (*enseñanza*) teaching; (*profesión*) teaching profession; (*maestros*) teachers *pl*
magistrado [maxis'traðo] *nm* magistrate
magistral [maxis'tral] *adj* magisterial; (*fig*) masterly
magnate [maɣ'nate] *nm* magnate, tycoon

magnético, -a [maɣ'netiko, a] *adj* magnetic
magnetofón [maɣneto'fon] *nm* tape recorder
magnetófono [maɣne'tofono] *nm* = **magnetofón**
magnífico, -a [maɣ'nifiko, a] *adj* splendid, magnificent
magnitud [maɣni'tuð] *nf* magnitude
mago, -a ['maɣo, a] *nm/f* magician; **los Reyes M~s** the Three Wise Men
magro, -a ['maɣro, a] *adj* (*carne*) lean
mahonesa [mao'nesa] *nf* mayonnaise
maître ['metre] *nm* head waiter
maíz [ma'iθ] *nm* maize (BRIT), corn (US); sweet corn
majestad [maxes'tað] *nf* majesty
majo, -a ['maxo, a] *adj* nice; (*guapo*) attractive, good-looking; (*elegante*) smart
mal [mal] *adv* badly; (*equivocadamente*) wrongly ▷ *adj* = **malo** ▷ *nm* evil; (*desgracia*) misfortune; (*daño*) harm, damage; (*Med*) illness; **~ que bien** rightly or wrongly; **ir de ~ en peor** to get worse and worse
malabarista [malaβa'rista] *nmf* juggler
malaria [ma'larja] *nf* malaria
malcriado, -a [mal'krjaðo, a] *adj* spoiled
maldad [mal'dað] *nf* evil, wickedness
maldecir [malde'θir] *vt* to curse
maldición [maldi'θjon] *nf* curse
maldito, -a [mal'dito, a] *adj* (*condenado*) damned; (*perverso*) wicked; **¡~ sea!** damn it!
malecón [male'kon] (LAM) *nm* sea front, promenade
maleducado, -a [maleðu'kaðo, a] *adj* bad-mannered, rude
malentendido [malenten'diðo] *nm* misunderstanding
malestar [males'tar] *nm* (*gen*) discomfort; (*fig*: *inquietud*) uneasiness; (*Pol*) unrest
maleta [ma'leta] *nf* case, suitcase; (*Auto*) boot (BRIT), trunk (US); **hacer las ~s** to pack; **maletero** *nm* (*Auto*) boot (BRIT), trunk (US); **maletín** *nm* small case, bag
maleza [ma'leθa] *nf* (*malas hierbas*) weeds *pl*; (*arbustos*) thicket
malgastar [malɣas'tar] *vt* (*tiempo, dinero*) to waste; (*salud*) to ruin
malhechor, a [male'tʃor, a] *nm/f* delinquent
malhumorado, -a [malumo'raðo, a] *adj* bad-tempered
malicia [ma'liθja] *nf* (*maldad*) wickedness; (*astucia*) slyness, guile; (*mala intención*) malice, spite; (*carácter travieso*) mischievousness
maligno, -a [ma'liɣno, a] *adj* evil; (*malévolo*) malicious; (*Med*) malignant
malla ['maʎa] *nf* mesh; (*de baño*) swimsuit; (*de ballet, gimnasia*) leotard; **mallas** *nfpl* tights; **malla de alambre** wire mesh
Mallorca [ma'ʎorka] *nf* Majorca
malo, -a ['malo, a] *adj* bad, false ▷ *nm/f* villain; **estar ~** to be ill
malograr [malo'ɣrar] *vt* to spoil; (*plan*) to upset; (*ocasión*) to waste
malparado, -a [malpa'raðo, a] *adj*: **salir ~** to come off badly
malpensado, -a [malpen'saðo, a] *adj* nasty
malteada [malte'aða] (LAM) *nf* milkshake
maltratar [maltra'tar] *vt* to ill-treat, mistreat
malvado, -a [mal'βaðo, a] *adj* evil, villainous
Malvinas [mal'βinas] *nfpl* (*tb*: **Islas ~**) Falklands, Falkland Islands
mama ['mama] *nf* (*de animal*) teat; (*de mujer*) breast
mamá [ma'ma] (*pl* **~s**) (*fam*) *nf* mum, mummy
mamar [ma'mar] *vt, vi* to suck
mamarracho [mama'rratʃo] *nm* sight, mess

mameluco [mameluko] (RPL) *nm* dungarees *pl* (BRIT), overalls *pl* (US)
mamífero [ma'mifero] *nm* mammal
mampara [mam'para] *nf* (*entre habitaciones*) partition; (*biombo*) screen
mampostería [mamposte'ria] *nf* masonry
manada [ma'naða] *nf* (*Zool*) herd; (*: de leones*) pride; (*: de lobos*) pack
manantial [manan'tjal] *nm* spring
mancha ['mantʃa] *nf* stain, mark; (*Zool*) patch; **manchar** *vt* (*gen*) to stain, mark; (*ensuciar*) to soil, dirty
manchego, -a [man'tʃeɣo, a] *adj* of *o* from La Mancha
manco, -a ['manko, a] *adj* (*de un brazo*) one-armed; (*de una mano*) one-handed; (*fig*) defective, faulty
mancuernas [man'kwernas] (MÉX) *nfpl* cufflinks
mandado [man'daðo] (LAM) *nm* errand
mandamiento [manda'mjento] *nm* (*orden*) order, command; (*Rel*) commandment
mandar [man'dar] *vt* (*ordenar*) to order; (*dirigir*) to lead, command; (*enviar*) to send; (*pedir*) to order, ask for ▷ *vi* to be in charge; (*pey*) to be bossy; **¿mande?** (MÉX: *¿cómo dice?*) pardon?, excuse me?; **~ hacer un traje** to have a suit made
mandarina [manda'rina] (ESP) *nf* tangerine, mandarin (orange)
mandato [man'dato] *nm* (*orden*) order; (*Pol: período*) term of office; (*: territorio*) mandate
mandíbula [man'diβula] *nf* jaw
mandil [man'dil] *nm* apron
mando ['mando] *nm* (*Mil*) command; (*de país*) rule; (*el primer lugar*) lead; (*Pol*) term of office; (*Tec*) control; **~ a la izquierda** left-hand drive; **mando a distancia** remote control
mandón, -ona [man'don, ona] *adj* bossy, domineering
manejar [mane'xar] *vt* to manage; (*máquina*) to work, operate; (*caballo etc*) to handle; (*casa*) to run, manage; (LAM: *coche*) to drive; **manejarse** *vr* (*comportarse*) to act, behave; (*arreglárselas*) to manage; **manejo** *nm* (*de bicicleta*) handling; (*de negocio*) management, running; (LAM *Auto*) driving; (*facilidad de trato*) ease, confidence; **manejos** *nmpl* (*intrigas*) intrigues
manera [ma'nera] *nf* way, manner, fashion; **maneras** *nfpl* (*modales*) manners; **su ~ de ser** the way he is; (*aire*) his manner; **de ninguna ~** no way, by no means; **de otra ~** otherwise; **de todas ~s** at any rate; **no hay ~ de persuadirle** there's no way of convincing him
manga ['manga] *nf* (*de camisa*) sleeve; (*de riego*) hose
mango ['mango] *nm* handle; (*Bot*) mango
manguera [man'gera] *nf* hose
maní [ma'ni] (LAM) *nm* peanut
manía [ma'nia] *nf* (*Med*) mania; (*fig: moda*) rage, craze; (*disgusto*) dislike; (*malicia*) spite; **coger ~ a algn** to take a dislike to sb; **tener ~ a algn** to dislike sb; **maníaco, -a** *adj* maniac(al) ▷ *nm/f* maniac
maniático, -a [ma'njatiko, a] *adj* maniac(al) ▷ *nm/f* maniac
manicomio [mani'komjo] *nm* mental hospital (BRIT), insane asylum (US)
manifestación [manifesta'θjon] *nf* (*declaración*) statement, declaration; (*de emoción*) show, display; (*Pol: desfile*) demonstration; (*: concentración*) mass meeting
manifestar [manifes'tar] *vt* to show, manifest; (*declarar*) to state, declare; **manifiesto, -a** *adj* clear, manifest ▷ *nm* manifesto
manillar [mani'ʎar] *nm* handlebars *pl*
maniobra [ma'njoβra] *nf* manoeuvre; **maniobras** *nfpl* (*Mil*) manoeuvres; **maniobrar** *vt* to manoeuvre

manipulación [manipula'θjon] *nf* manipulation
manipular [manipu'lar] *vt* to manipulate; (*manejar*) to handle
maniquí [mani'ki] *nm* dummy ▷ *nmf* model
manivela [mani'βela] *nf* crank
manjar [man'xar] *nm* (tasty) dish
mano ['mano] *nf* hand; (*Zool*) foot, paw; (*de pintura*) coat; (*serie*) lot, series; **a ~** by hand; **a ~ derecha/izquierda** on the right(-hand side)/left(-hand side); **de primera ~** (at) first hand; **de segunda ~** (at) second hand; **robo a ~ armada** armed robbery; **estrechar la ~ a algn** to shake sb's hand; **mano de obra** labour, manpower; **manos libres** *adj inv* (*teléfono, dispositivo*) hands-free ▷ *nm inv* hands-free kit
manojo [ma'noxo] *nm* handful, bunch; (*de llaves*) bunch
manopla [ma'nopla] *nf* mitten
manosear [manose'ar] *vt* (*tocar*) to handle, touch; (*desordenar*) to mess up, rumple; (*insistir en*) to overwork; (LAM: *acariciar*) to caress, fondle
manotazo [mano'taθo] *nm* slap, smack
mansalva [man'salβa]: **a ~** *adv* indiscriminately
mansión [man'sjon] *nf* mansion
manso, -a ['manso, a] *adj* gentle, mild; (*animal*) tame
manta ['manta] (ESP) *nf* blanket
manteca [man'teka] *nf* fat; (CS: *mantequilla*) butter; **manteca de cerdo** lard
mantecado [mante'kaðo] (ESP) *nm* *Christmas sweet made from flour, almonds and lard*
mantel [man'tel] *nm* tablecloth
mantendré *etc vb V* **mantener**
mantener [mante'ner] *vt* to support, maintain; (*alimentar*) to sustain; (*conservar*) to keep; (*Tec*) to maintain, service; **mantenerse** *vr* (*seguir de pie*) to be still standing; (*no ceder*) to hold one's ground; (*subsistir*) to sustain o.s., keep going; **mantenimiento** *nm* maintenance; sustenance; (*sustento*) support
mantequilla [mante'kiʎa] *nf* butter
mantilla [man'tiʎa] *nf* mantilla; **mantillas** *nfpl* (*de bebé*) baby clothes
manto ['manto] *nm* (*capa*) cloak; (*de ceremonia*) robe, gown
mantuve *etc vb V* **mantener**
manual [ma'nwal] *adj* manual ▷ *nm* manual, handbook
manuscrito, -a [manus'krito, a] *adj* handwritten ▷ *nm* manuscript
manutención [manuten'θjon] *nf* maintenance; (*sustento*) support
manzana [man'θana] *nf* apple; (*Arq*) block (of houses)
manzanilla [manθa'niʎa] *nf* (*planta*) camomile; (*infusión*) camomile tea
manzano [man'θano] *nm* apple tree
maña ['maɲa] *nf* (*gen*) skill, dexterity; (*pey*) guile; (*destreza*) trick, knack
mañana [ma'ɲana] *adv* tomorrow ▷ *nm* future ▷ *nf* morning; **de** *o* **por la ~** in the morning; **¡hasta ~!** see you tomorrow!; **~ por la ~** tomorrow morning
mapa ['mapa] *nm* map
maple ['maple] (LAM) *nm* maple
maqueta [ma'keta] *nf* (scale) model
maquiladora [makila'ðora] (MÉX) *nf* (*Com*) bonded assembly plant
maquillaje [maki'ʎaxe] *nm* make-up; (*acto*) making up
maquillar [maki'ʎar] *vt* to make up; **maquillarse** *vr* to put on (some) make-up
máquina ['makina] *nf* machine; (*de tren*) locomotive, engine; (*Foto*) camera; (*fig*) machinery; **escrito a ~** typewritten; **máquina de coser** sewing machine; **máquina de escribir** typewriter; **máquina fotográfica** camera
maquinaria [maki'narja] *nf* (*máquinas*) machinery; (*mecanismo*) mechanism, works *pl*
maquinilla [maki'niʎa] (ESP) *nf*

(*tb*: **~ de afeitar**) razor
maquinista [maki'nista] *nmf* (*de tren*) engine driver; (*Tec*) operator; (*Náut*) engineer
mar [mar] *nm o f* sea; **~ adentro** out at sea; **en alta ~** on the high seas; **la ~ de** (*fam*) lots of; **el Mar Negro/Báltico** the Black/Baltic Sea
maraña [ma'raɲa] *nf* (*maleza*) thicket; (*confusión*) tangle
maravilla [mara'βiʎa] *nf* marvel, wonder; (*Bot*) marigold; **maravillar** *vt* to astonish, amaze; **maravillarse** *vr* to be astonished, be amazed; **maravilloso, -a** *adj* wonderful, marvellous
marca ['marka] *nf* (*gen*) mark; (*sello*) stamp; (*Com*) make, brand; **de ~** excellent, outstanding; **marca de fábrica** trademark; **marca registrada** registered trademark
marcado, -a [mar'kaðo, a] *adj* marked, strong
marcador [marka'ðor] *nm* (*Deporte*) scoreboard; (*: persona*) scorer
marcapasos [marka'pasos] *nm inv* pacemaker
marcar [mar'kar] *vt* (*gen*) to mark; (*número de teléfono*) to dial; (*gol*) to score; (*números*) to record, keep a tally of; (*pelo*) to set ▷ *vi* (*Deporte*) to score; (*Tel*) to dial
marcha ['martʃa] *nf* march; (*Tec*) running, working; (*Auto*) gear; (*velocidad*) speed; (*fig*) progress; (*dirección*) course; **poner en ~** to put into gear; (*fig*) to set in motion, get going; **dar ~ atrás** to reverse, put into reverse; **estar en ~** to be under way, be in motion
marchar [mar'tʃar] *vi* (*ir*) to go; (*funcionar*) to work, go; **marcharse** *vr* to go (away), leave
marchitar [martʃi'tar] *vt* to wither, dry up; **marchitarse** *vr* (*Bot*) to wither; (*fig*) to fade away; **marchito, -a** *adj* withered, faded; (*fig*) in decline
marciano, -a [mar'θjano, a] *adj*, *nm/f* Martian
marco ['marko] *nm* frame; (*moneda*) mark; (*fig*) framework
marea [ma'rea] *nf* tide; **marea negra** oil slick
marear [mare'ar] *vt* (*fig*) to annoy, upset; (*Med*): **~ a algn** to make sb feel sick; **marearse** *vr* (*tener náuseas*) to feel sick; (*desvanecerse*) to feel faint; (*aturdirse*) to feel dizzy; (*fam: emborracharse*) to get tipsy
maremoto [mare'moto] *nm* tidal wave
mareo [ma'reo] *nm* (*náusea*) sick feeling; (*en viaje*) travel sickness; (*aturdimiento*) dizziness; (*fam: lata*) nuisance
marfil [mar'fil] *nm* ivory
margarina [marɣa'rina] *nf* margarine
margarita [marɣa'rita] *nf* (*Bot*) daisy; (*Tip*) daisywheel
margen ['marxen] *nm* (*borde*) edge, border; (*fig*) margin, space ▷ *nf* (*de río etc*) bank; **dar ~ para** to give an opportunity for; **mantenerse al ~** to keep out (of things)
marginar [marxi'nar] *vt* (*socialmente*) to marginalize, ostracize
mariachi [ma'rjatʃi] *nm* (*persona*) mariachi musician; (*grupo*) mariachi band

MARIACHI

Mariachi music is the musical style most characteristic of Mexico. From the state of Jalisco in the 19th century, this music spread rapidly throughout the country, until each region had its own particular style of the Mariachi "sound". A Mariachi band can be made up of several singers, up to eight violins, two trumpets, guitars, a "vihuela" (an old form of guitar), and a harp. The dance associated with this music is called the "zapateado".

marica [ma'rika] (*fam*) *nm* sissy
maricón [mari'kon] (*fam*) *nm* queer
marido [ma'riðo] *nm* husband
marihuana [mari'wana] *nf* marijuana, cannabis
marina [ma'rina] *nf* navy; **marina mercante** merchant navy
marinero, -a [mari'nero, a] *adj* sea *cpd* ▷ *nm* sailor, seaman
marino, -a [ma'rino, a] *adj* sea *cpd*, marine ▷ *nm* sailor
marioneta [marjo'neta] *nf* puppet
mariposa [mari'posa] *nf* butterfly
mariquita [mari'kita] *nf* ladybird (BRIT), ladybug (US)
marisco [ma'risko] (ESP) *nm* shellfish *inv*, seafood; **mariscos** (LAM) *nmpl* = **marisco**
marítimo, -a [ma'ritimo, a] *adj* sea *cpd*, maritime
mármol ['marmol] *nm* marble
marqués, -esa [mar'kes, esa] *nm/f* marquis/marchioness
marrón [ma'rron] *adj* brown
marroquí [marro'ki] *adj, nmf* Moroccan ▷ *nm* Morocco (leather)
Marruecos [ma'rrwekos] *nm* Morocco
martes ['martes] *nm inv* Tuesday; **~ y trece** ≈ Friday 13th

MARTES Y TRECE

According to Spanish superstition Tuesday is an unlucky day, even more so if it falls on the 13th of the month.

martillo [mar'tiʎo] *nm* hammer
mártir ['martir] *nmf* martyr; **martirio** *nm* martyrdom; (*fig*) torture, torment
marxismo [mark'sismo] *nm* Marxism
marzo ['marθo] *nm* March

PALABRA CLAVE

más [mas] *adj, adv* **1**: **más (que** *o* **de)** (*compar*) more (than), ...+ er (than); **más grande/inteligente** bigger/ more intelligent; **trabaja más (que yo)** he works more (than me); *V tb* **cada**
2 (*superl*): **el más** the most, ...+ est; **el más grande/inteligente (de)** the biggest/most intelligent (in)
3 (*negativo*): **no tengo más dinero** I haven't got any more money; **no viene más por aquí** he doesn't come round here any more
4 (*adicional*): **no le veo más solución que ...** I see no other solution than to ...; **¿quién más?** anybody else?
5 (+ *adj*: *valor intensivo*): **¡qué perro más sucio!** what a filthy dog!; **¡es más tonto!** he's so stupid!
6 (*locuciones*): **más o menos** more or less; **los más** most people; **es más** furthermore; **más bien** rather; **¡qué más da!** what does it matter!; *V tb* **no**
7: **por más: por más que te esfuerces** no matter how hard you try; **por más que quisiera ...** much as I should like to ...
8: **de más: veo que aquí estoy de más** I can see I'm not needed here; **tenemos uno de más** we've got one extra
▷ *prep*: **2 más 2 son 4** 2 and *o* plus 2 are 4
▷ *nm inv*: **este trabajo tiene sus más y sus menos** this job's got its good points and its bad points

mas [mas] *conj* but
masa ['masa] *nf* (*mezcla*) dough; (*volumen*) volume, mass; (*Física*) mass; **en ~** en masse; **las ~s** (*Pol*) the masses
masacre [ma'sakre] *nf* massacre
masaje [ma'saxe] *nm* massage
máscara ['maskara] *nf* mask; **máscara antigás/de oxígeno** gas/oxygen mask; **mascarilla** *nf* (*de*

belleza, Med) mask
masculino, -a [masku'lino, a] *adj* masculine; (*Bio*) male
masía [ma'sia] *nf* farmhouse
masivo, -a [ma'siβo, a] *adj* mass *cpd*
masoquista [maso'kista] *nmf* masochist
máster ['master] (*ESP*) *nm* master
masticar [masti'kar] *vt* to chew
mástil ['mastil] *nm* (*de navío*) mast; (*de guitarra*) neck
mastín [mas'tin] *nm* mastiff
masturbarse [mastur'βarse] *vr* to masturbate
mata ['mata] *nf* (*arbusto*) bush, shrub; (*de hierba*) tuft
matadero [mata'ðero] *nm* slaughterhouse, abattoir
matamoscas [mata'moskas] *nm inv* (*pala*) fly swat
matanza [ma'tanθa] *nf* slaughter
matar [ma'tar] *vt, vi* to kill; **matarse** *vr* (*suicidarse*) to kill o.s., commit suicide; (*morir*) to be *o* get killed; **~ el hambre** to stave off hunger
matasellos [mata'seʎos] *nm inv* postmark
mate ['mate] *adj* matt ▷ *nm* (*en ajedrez*) (check)mate; (*LAM*: *hierba*) maté; (: *vasija*) gourd
matemáticas [mate'matikas] *nfpl* mathematics; **matemático, -a** *adj* mathematical ▷ *nm/f* mathematician
materia [ma'terja] *nf* (*gen*) matter; (*Tec*) material; (*Escol*) subject; **en ~ de** on the subject of; **materia prima** raw material; **material** *adj* material ▷ *nm* material; (*Tec*) equipment; **materialista** *adj* materialist(ic); **materialmente** *adv* materially; (*fig*) absolutely
maternal [mater'nal] *adj* motherly, maternal
maternidad [materni'ðað] *nf* motherhood, maternity; **materno, -a** *adj* maternal; (*lengua*) mother *cpd*
matinal [mati'nal] *adj* morning *cpd*
matiz [ma'tiθ] *nm* shade; **matizar** *vt* (*variar*) to vary; (*Arte*) to blend; **matizar de** to tinge with
matón [ma'ton] *nm* bully
matorral [mato'rral] *nm* thicket
matrícula [ma'trikula] *nf* (*registro*) register; (*Auto*) registration number; (: *placa*) number plate; **matrícula de honor** (*Univ*) *top marks in a subject at university with the right to free registration the following year*; **matricular** *vt* to register, enrol
matrimonio [matri'monjo] *nm* (*pareja*) (married) couple; (*unión*) marriage
matriz [ma'triθ] *nf* (*Anat*) womb; (*Tec*) mould
matrona [ma'trona] *nf* (*persona de edad*) matron; (*comadrona*) midwife
matufia [ma'tufja] (*RPL*: *fam*) *nf* put-up job
maullar [mau'ʎar] *vi* to mew, miaow
maxilar [maksi'lar] *nm* jaw(bone)
máxima ['maksima] *nf* maxim
máximo, -a ['maksimo, a] *adj* maximum; (*más alto*) highest; (*más grande*) greatest ▷ *nm* maximum; **como ~** at most
mayo ['majo] *nm* May
mayonesa [majo'nesa] *nf* mayonnaise
mayor [ma'jor] *adj* main, chief; (*adulto*) adult; (*de edad avanzada*) elderly; (*Mús*) major; (*compar*: *de tamaño*) bigger; (: *de edad*) older; (*superl*: *de tamaño*) biggest; (: *de edad*) oldest ▷ *nm* (*adulto*) adult; **mayores** *nmpl* (*antepasados*) ancestors; **al por ~** wholesale; **mayor de edad** adult
mayoral [majo'ral] *nm* foreman
mayordomo [major'ðomo] *nm* butler
mayoría [majo'ria] *nf* majority, greater part
mayorista [majo'rista] *nmf* wholesaler
mayoritario, -a [majori'tarjo, a] *adj* majority *cpd*
mayúscula [ma'juskula] *nf* capital

letter
mazapán [maθa'pan] *nm* marzipan
mazo ['maθo] *nm* (*martillo*) mallet; (*de flores*) bunch; (*Deporte*) bat
me [me] *pron* (*directo*) me; (*indirecto*) (to) me; (*reflexivo*) (to) myself; **¡dá~lo!** give it to me!
mear [me'ar] (*fam*) *vi* to pee, piss (*!*)
mecánica [me'kanika] *nf* (*Escol*) mechanics *sg*; (*mecanismo*) mechanism; *V tb* **mecánico**
mecánico, -a [me'kaniko, a] *adj* mechanical ▷ *nm/f* mechanic
mecanismo [meka'nismo] *nm* mechanism; (*marcha*) gear
mecanografía [mekanoɣra'fia] *nf* typewriting; **mecanógrafo, -a** *nm/f* typist
mecate [me'kate] (*MÉX, CAM*) *nm* rope
mecedora [meθe'ðora] *nf* rocking chair
mecer [me'θer] *vt* (*cuna*) to rock; **mecerse** *vr* to rock; (*rama*) to sway
mecha ['metʃa] *nf* (*de vela*) wick; (*de bomba*) fuse
mechero [me'tʃero] *nm* (cigarette) lighter
mechón [me'tʃon] *nm* (*gen*) tuft; (*de pelo*) lock
medalla [me'ðaʎa] *nf* medal
media ['meðja] *nf* stocking; (*LAM: calcetín*) sock; (*promedio*) average
mediado, -a [me'ðjaðo, a] *adj* half-full; (*trabajo*) half-completed; **a ~s de** in the middle of, halfway through
mediano, -a [me'ðjano, a] *adj* (*regular*) medium, average; (*mediocre*) mediocre
medianoche [meðja'notʃe] *nf* midnight
mediante [me'ðjante] *adv* by (means of), through
mediar [me'ðjar] *vi* (*interceder*) to mediate, intervene
medicamento [meðika'mento] *nm* medicine, drug
medicina [meði'θina] *nf* medicine
médico, -a ['meðiko, a] *adj* medical ▷ *nm/f* doctor
medida [me'ðiða] *nf* measure; (*medición*) measurement; (*prudencia*) moderation, prudence; **en cierta/gran ~** up to a point/to a great extent; **un traje a la ~** a made-to-measure suit; **~ de cuello** collar size; **a ~ de** in proportion to; (*de acuerdo con*) in keeping with; **a ~ que** (*conforme*) as; **medidor** (*LAM*) *nm* meter
medio, -a ['meðjo, a] *adj* half (a); (*punto*) mid, middle; (*promedio*) average ▷ *adv* half ▷ *nm* (*centro*) middle, centre; (*promedio*) average; (*método*) means, way; (*ambiente*) environment; **medios** *nmpl* means, resources; **~ litro** half a litre; **las tres y media** half past three; **a ~ terminar** half finished; **pagar a medias** to share the cost; **medio ambiente** environment; **medio de transporte** means of transport; **Medio Oriente** Middle East; **medios de comunicación** media; **medioambiental** *adj* (*política, efectos*) environmental
mediocre [me'ðjokre] *adj* mediocre
mediodía [meðjo'ðia] *nm* midday, noon
medir [me'ðir] *vt, vi* (*gen*) to measure
meditar [meði'tar] *vt* to ponder, think over, meditate on; (*planear*) to think out
mediterráneo, -a [meðite'rraneo, a] *adj* Mediterranean ▷ *nm*: **el M~** the Mediterranean
médula ['meðula] *nf* (*Anat*) marrow; **médula espinal** spinal cord
medusa [me'ðusa] (*ESP*) *nf* jellyfish
megáfono [me'ɣafono] *nm* megaphone
megapíxel [meɣa'piksel] (*pl* **megapixels** *or* **~es**) *nm* megapixel
mejilla [me'xiʎa] *nf* cheek
mejillón [mexi'ʎon] *nm* mussel
mejor [me'xor] *adj, adv* (*compar*) better; (*superl*) best; **a lo ~** probably; (*quizá*) maybe; **~ dicho** rather; **tanto ~**

so much the better
mejora [me'xora] *nf* improvement; **mejorar** *vt* to improve, make better ▷ *vi* to improve, get better; **mejorarse** *vr* to improve, get better
melancólico, -a [melan'koliko, a] *adj* (*triste*) sad, melancholy; (*soñador*) dreamy
melena [me'lena] *nf* (*de persona*) long hair; (*Zool*) mane
mellizo, -a [me'ʎiθo, a] *adj, nm/f* twin
melocotón [meloko'ton] (ESP) *nm* peach
melodía [melo'ðia] *nf* melody, tune
melodrama [melo'ðrama] *nm* melodrama; **melodramático, -a** *adj* melodramatic
melón [me'lon] *nm* melon
membrete [mem'brete] *nm* letterhead
membrillo [mem'briʎo] *nm* quince; **(carne de) ~** quince jelly
memoria [me'morja] *nf* (*gen*) memory; **memorias** *nfpl* (*de autor*) memoirs; **memorizar** *vt* to memorize
menaje [me'naxe] *nm* (*tb*: **artículos de ~**) household items
mencionar [menθjo'nar] *vt* to mention
mendigo, -a [men'diɣo, a] *nm/f* beggar
menear [mene'ar] *vt* to move; **menearse** *vr* to shake; (*balancearse*) to sway; (*moverse*) to move; (*fig*) to get a move on
menestra [me'nestra] *nf* (*tb*: **~ de verduras**) vegetable stew
menopausia [meno'pausja] *nf* menopause
menor [me'nor] *adj* (*más pequeño*: *compar*) smaller; (: *superl*) smallest; (*más joven*: *compar*) younger; (: *superl*) youngest; (*Mús*) minor ▷ *nmf* (*joven*) young person, juvenile; **no tengo la ~ idea** I haven't the faintest idea; **al por ~** retail; **menor de edad** person under age
Menorca [me'norka] *nf* Minorca

PALABRA CLAVE

menos [menos] *adj* **1**: **menos (que** *o* **de)** (*compar*: *cantidad*) less (than); (: *número*) fewer (than); **con menos entusiasmo** with less enthusiasm; **menos gente** fewer people; *V tb* **cada**
2 (*superl*): **es el que menos culpa tiene** he is the least to blame
▷ *adv* **1** (*compar*): **menos (que** *o* **de)** less (than); **me gusta menos que el otro** I like it less than the other one
2 (*superl*): **es el menos listo (de su clase)** he's the least bright in his class; **de todas ellas es la que menos me agrada** out of all of them she's the one I like least
3 (*locuciones*): **no quiero verle y menos visitarle** I don't want to see him, let alone visit him; **tenemos siete de menos** we're seven short; **(por) lo menos** at (the very) least; **¡menos mal!** thank goodness!
▷ *prep* except; (*cifras*) minus; **todos menos él** everyone except (for) him; **5 menos 2** 5 minus 2
▷ *conj*: **a menos que: a menos que venga mañana** unless he comes tomorrow

menospreciar [menospre'θjar] *vt* to underrate, undervalue; (*despreciar*) to scorn, despise
mensaje [men'saxe] *nm* message; **enviar un ~ a algn** (*por móvil*) to text sb, send sb a text message; **mensaje de texto** text message; **mensajero, -a** *nm/f* messenger
menso, -a ['menso, a] (MÉX: *fam*) *adj* stupid
menstruación [menstrua'θjon] *nf* menstruation
mensual [men'swal] *adj* monthly; **100 euros ~es** 100 euros a month; **mensualidad** *nf* (*salario*) monthly

salary; (*Com*) monthly payment, monthly instalment
menta ['menta] *nf* mint
mental [men'tal] *adj* mental; **mentalidad** *nf* mentality; **mentalizar** *vt* (*sensibilizar*) to make aware; (*convencer*) to convince; (*padres*) to prepare (mentally); **mentalizarse** *vr* (*concienciarse*) to become aware; **mentalizarse (de)** to get used to the idea (of); **mentalizarse de que ...** (*convencerse*) to get it into one's head that ...
mente ['mente] *nf* mind
mentir [men'tir] *vi* to lie
mentira [men'tira] *nf* (*una mentira*) lie; (*acto*) lying; (*invención*) fiction; **parece mentira que ...** it seems incredible that ..., I can't believe that ...; **mentiroso, -a** [menti'roso, a] *adj* lying ▷ *nm/f* liar
menú [me'nu] (*pl* **~s**) *nm* menu; **menú del día** set menu; **menú turistico** tourist menu
menudencias [menu'ðenθjas] (LAM) *nfpl* giblets
menudo, -a [me'nuðo, a] *adj* (*pequeño*) small, tiny; (*sin importancia*) petty, insignificant; **¡~ negocio!** (*fam*) some deal!; **a ~** often, frequently
meñique [me'ɲike] *nm* little finger
mercadillo [merka'ðiʎo] (ESP) *nm* flea market
mercado [mer'kaðo] *nm* market; **mercado de pulgas** (LAM) flea market
mercancía [merkan'θia] *nf* commodity; **mercancías** *nfpl* goods, merchandise *sg*
mercenario, -a [merθe'narjo, a] *adj, nm* mercenary
mercería [merθe'ria] *nf* haberdashery (BRIT), notions *pl* (US); (*tienda*) haberdasher's (BRIT), notions store (US)
mercurio [mer'kurjo] *nm* mercury
merecer [mere'θer] *vt* to deserve, merit ▷ *vi* to be deserving, be worthy; **merece la pena** it's worthwhile; **merecido, -a** *adj* (well) deserved; **llevar su merecido** to get one's deserts
merendar [meren'dar] *vt* to have for tea ▷ *vi* to have tea; (*en el campo*) to have a picnic; **merendero** *nm* open-air cafe
merengue [me'renge] *nm* meringue
meridiano [meri'ðjano] *nm* (*Geo*) meridian
merienda [me'rjenda] *nf* (light) tea, afternoon snack; (*de campo*) picnic
mérito ['merito] *nm* merit; (*valor*) worth, value
merluza [mer'luθa] *nf* hake
mermelada [merme'laða] *nf* jam
mero, -a ['mero, a] *adj* mere; (MÉX, CAM: *fam*) very
merodear [meroðe'ar] *vi*: **~ por** to prowl about
mes [mes] *nm* month
mesa ['mesa] *nf* table; (*de trabajo*) desk; (*Geo*) plateau; **poner/quitar la ~** to lay/clear the table; **mesa electoral** *officials in charge of a polling station*; **mesa redonda** (*reunión*) round table; **mesero, -a** (LAM) *nm/f* waiter/ waitress
meseta [me'seta] *nf* (*Geo*) plateau, tableland
mesilla [me'siʎa] *nf* (*tb*: **~ de noche**) bedside table
mesón [me'son] *nm* inn
mestizo, -a [mes'tiθo, a] *adj* half-caste, of mixed race ▷ *nm/f* half-caste
meta ['meta] *nf* goal; (*de carrera*) finish
metabolismo [metaβo'lismo] *nm* metabolism
metáfora [me'tafora] *nf* metaphor
metal [me'tal] *nm* (*materia*) metal; (*Mús*) brass; **metálico, -a** *adj* metallic; (*de metal*) metal ▷ *nm* (*dinero contante*) cash
meteorología [meteorolo'xia] *nf* meteorology
meter [me'ter] *vt* (*colocar*) to put, place; (*introducir*) to put in, insert; (*involucrar*) to involve; (*causar*) to make,

cause; **meterse** *vr*: **~se en** to go into, enter; (*fig*) to interfere in, meddle in; **~se a** to start; **~se a escritor** to become a writer; **~se con uno** to provoke sb, pick a quarrel with sb

meticuloso, -a [metiku'loso, a] *adj* meticulous, thorough

metódico, -a [me'toðiko, a] *adj* methodical

método ['metoðo] *nm* method

metralleta [metra'ʎeta] *nf* sub-machine-gun

métrico, -a ['metriko, a] *adj* metric

metro ['metro] *nm* metre; (*tren*) underground (BRIT), subway (US)

metrosexual [metrosek'swal] *adj*, *nm* metrosexual

mexicano, -a [mexi'kano, a] *adj*, *nm/f* Mexican

México ['mexiko] *nm* Mexico; **Ciudad de ~** Mexico City

mezcla ['meθkla] *nf* mixture; **mezcladora** (MÉX) *nf* (*tb*: **mezcladora de cemento**) cement mixer; **mezclar** *vt* to mix (up); **mezclarse** *vr* to mix, mingle; **mezclarse en** to get mixed up in, get involved in

mezquino, -a [meθ'kino, a] *adj* mean

mezquita [meθ'kita] *nf* mosque

mg. *abr* (= *miligramo*) mg

mi [mi] *adj pos* my ▷ *nm* (*Mús*) E

mí [mi] *pron* me; myself

mía *pron V* **mío**

michelín [mitʃe'lin] (*fam*) *nm* (*de grasa*) spare tyre

microbio [mi'kroβjo] *nm* microbe

micrófono [mi'krofono] *nm* microphone

microondas [mikro'ondas] *nm inv* (*tb*: **horno ~**) microwave (oven)

microscopio [mikro'skopjo] *nm* microscope

miedo ['mjeðo] *nm* fear; (*nerviosismo*) apprehension, nervousness; **tener ~** to be afraid; **de ~** wonderful, marvellous; **hace un frío de ~** (*fam*) it's terribly cold; **miedoso, -a** *adj* fearful, timid

miel [mjel] *nf* honey

miembro ['mjembro] *nm* limb; (*socio*) member; **miembro viril** penis

mientras ['mjentras] *conj* while; (*duración*) as long as ▷ *adv* meanwhile; **~ tanto** meanwhile

miércoles ['mjerkoles] *nm inv* Wednesday

mierda ['mjerða] (*fam!*) *nf* shit (*!*)

miga ['miɣa] *nf* crumb; (*fig: meollo*) essence; **hacer buenas ~s** (*fam*) to get on well

mil [mil] *num* thousand; **dos ~ libras** two thousand pounds

milagro [mi'laɣro] *nm* miracle; **milagroso, -a** *adj* miraculous

milésima [mi'lesima] *nf* (*de segundo*) thousandth

mili ['mili] (ESP: *fam*) *nf*: **hacer la ~** to do one's military service

milímetro [mi'limetro] *nm* millimetre

militante [mili'tante] *adj* militant

militar [mili'tar] *adj* military ▷ *nmf* soldier ▷ *vi* (*Mil*) to serve; (*en un partido*) to be a member

milla ['miʎa] *nf* mile

millar [mi'ʎar] *nm* thousand

millón [mi'ʎon] *num* million; **millonario, -a** *nm/f* millionaire

milusos [mi'lusos] (MÉX) *nm inv* odd-job man

mimar [mi'mar] *vt* to spoil, pamper

mimbre ['mimbre] *nm* wicker

mímica ['mimika] *nf* (*para comunicarse*) sign language; (*imitación*) mimicry

mimo ['mimo] *nm* (*caricia*) caress; (*de niño*) spoiling; (*Teatro*) mime; (*: actor*) mime artist

mina ['mina] *nf* mine

mineral [mine'ral] *adj* mineral ▷ *nm* (*Geo*) mineral; (*mena*) ore

minero, -a [mi'nero, a] *adj* mining *cpd* ▷ *nm/f* miner

miniatura [minja'tura] *adj inv*, *nf* miniature

minidisco [mini'disko] *nm*

MiniDisc®
minifalda [mini'falda] *nf* miniskirt
mínimo, -a ['minimo, a] *adj, nm* minimum
minino, -a [mi'nino, a] (*fam*) *nm/f* puss, pussy
ministerio [minis'terjo] *nm* Ministry; **Ministerio de Hacienda/de Asuntos Exteriores** Treasury (BRIT), Treasury Department (US)/Foreign Office (BRIT), State Department (US)
ministro, -a [mi'nistro, a] *nm/f* minister
minoría [mino'ria] *nf* minority
minúscula [mi'nuskula] *nf* small letter
minúsculo, -a [mi'nuskulo, a] *adj* tiny, minute
minusválido, -a [minus'βaliðo, a] *adj* (physically) handicapped ▷ *nm/f* (physically) handicapped person
minuta [mi'nuta] *nf* (*de comida*) menu
minutero [minu'tero] *nm* minute hand
minuto [mi'nuto] *nm* minute
mío, -a ['mio, a] *pron*: **el ~/la mía** mine; **un amigo ~** a friend of mine; **lo ~** what is mine
miope [mi'ope] *adj* short-sighted
mira ['mira] *nf* (*de arma*) sight(s) (*pl*); (*fig*) aim, intention
mirada [mi'raða] *nf* look, glance; (*expresión*) look, expression; **clavar la ~ en** to stare at; **echar una ~ a** to glance at
mirado, -a [mi'raðo, a] *adj* (*sensato*) sensible; (*considerado*) considerate; **bien/mal ~** (*estimado*) well/not well thought of; **bien ~ ...** all things considered ...
mirador [mira'ðor] *nm* viewpoint, vantage point
mirar [mi'rar] *vt* to look at; (*observar*) to watch; (*considerar*) to consider, think over; (*vigilar, cuidar*) to watch, look after ▷ *vi* to look; (*Arq*) to face; **mirarse** *vr* (*dos personas*) to look at each other; **~ bien/mal** to think highly of/have a poor opinion of; **~se al espejo** to look at o.s. in the mirror
mirilla [mi'riʎa] *nf* spyhole, peephole
mirlo ['mirlo] *nm* blackbird
misa ['misa] *nf* mass
miserable [mise'raβle] *adj* (*avaro*) mean, stingy; (*nimio*) miserable, paltry; (*lugar*) squalid; (*fam*) vile, despicable ▷ *nmf* (*malvado*) rogue
miseria [mi'serja] *nf* (*pobreza*) poverty; (*tacañería*) meanness, stinginess; (*condiciones*) squalor; **una ~** a pittance
misericordia [miseri'korðja] *nf* (*compasión*) compassion, pity; (*piedad*) mercy
misil [mi'sil] *nm* missile
misión [mi'sjon] *nf* mission; **misionero, -a** *nm/f* missionary
mismo, -a ['mismo, a] *adj* (*semejante*) same; (*después de pron*) -self; (*para enfásis*) very ▷ *adv*: **aquí/hoy ~** right here/this very day; **ahora ~** right now ▷ *conj*: **lo ~ que** just like *o* as; **el ~ traje** the same suit; **en ese ~ momento** at that very moment; **vino el ~ ministro** the minister himself came; **yo ~ lo vi** I saw it myself; **lo ~** the same (thing); **da lo ~** it's all the same; **quedamos en las mismas** we're no further forward; **por lo ~** for the same reason
misterio [mis'terjo] *nm* mystery; **misterioso, -a** *adj* mysterious
mitad [mi'tað] *nf* (*medio*) half; (*centro*) middle; **a ~ de precio** (at) half-price; **en** *o* **a ~ del camino** halfway along the road; **cortar por la ~** to cut through the middle
mitin ['mitin] (*pl* **mítines**) *nm* meeting
mito ['mito] *nm* myth
mixto, -a ['miksto, a] *adj* mixed
ml. *abr* (= *mililitro*) ml
mm. *abr* (= *milímetro*) mm
mobiliario [moβi'ljarjo] *nm* furniture

mochila [mo'tʃila] *nf* rucksack (BRIT), back-pack
moco ['moko] *nm* mucus; **mocos** *nmpl* (*fam*) snot; **limpiarse los ~s de la nariz** (*fam*) to wipe one's nose
moda ['moða] *nf* fashion; (*estilo*) style; **a la** *o* **de ~** in fashion, fashionable; **pasado de ~** out of fashion
modales [mo'ðales] *nmpl* manners
modelar [moðe'lar] *vt* to model
modelo [mo'ðelo] *adj inv, nmf* model
módem ['moðem] *nm* (*Inform*) modem
moderado, -a [moðe'raðo, a] *adj* moderate
moderar [moðe'rar] *vt* to moderate; (*violencia*) to restrain, control; (*velocidad*) to reduce; **moderarse** *vr* to restrain o.s., control o.s.
modernizar [moðerni'θar] *vt* to modernize
moderno, -a [mo'ðerno, a] *adj* modern; (*actual*) present-day
modestia [mo'ðestja] *nf* modesty; **modesto, -a** *adj* modest
modificar [moðifi'kar] *vt* to modify
modisto, -a [mo'ðisto, a] *nm/f* (*diseñador*) couturier, designer; (*que confecciona*) dressmaker
modo ['moðo] *nm* way, manner; (*Mús*) mode; **modos** *nmpl* manners; **de ningún ~** in no way; **de todos ~s** at any rate; **modo de empleo** directions *pl* (for use)
mofarse [mo'farse] *vr*: **~ de** to mock, scoff at
mofle ['mofle] (MÉX, CAM) *nm* silencer (BRIT), muffler (US)
mogollón [moɣo'ʎon] (ESP: *fam*) *adv* a hell of a lot
moho ['moo] *nm* mould, mildew; (*en metal*) rust
mojar [mo'xar] *vt* to wet; (*humedecer*) to damp(en), moisten; (*calar*) to soak; **mojarse** *vr* to get wet
molcajete [molka'xete] (MÉX) *nm* mortar
molde ['molde] *nm* mould; (*Costura*) pattern; (*fig*) model; **moldeado** *nm* soft perm; **moldear** *vt* to mould
mole ['mole] *nf* mass, bulk; (*edificio*) pile
moler [mo'ler] *vt* to grind, crush
molestar [moles'tar] *vt* to bother; (*fastidiar*) to annoy; (*incomodar*) to inconvenience, put out ▷ *vi* to be a nuisance; **molestarse** *vr* to bother; (*incomodarse*) to go to trouble; (*ofenderse*) to take offence; **¿(no) te molesta si ...?** do you mind if ...?

> No confundir **molestar** con la palabra inglesa *molest*.

molestia [mo'lestja] *nf* bother, trouble; (*incomodidad*) inconvenience; (*Med*) discomfort; **es una ~** it's a nuisance; **molesto, -a** *adj* (*que fastidia*) annoying; (*incómodo*) inconvenient; (*inquieto*) uncomfortable, ill at ease; (*enfadado*) annoyed
molido, -a [mo'liðo, a] *adj*: **estar ~** (*fig*) to be exhausted *o* dead beat
molinillo [moli'niʎo] *nm* hand mill; **molinillo de café** coffee grinder
molino [mo'lino] *nm* (*edificio*) mill; (*máquina*) grinder
momentáneo, -a [momen'taneo, a] *adj* momentary
momento [mo'mento] *nm* moment; **de ~** at *o* for the moment
momia ['momja] *nf* mummy
monarca [mo'narka] *nmf* monarch, ruler; **monarquía** *nf* monarchy
monasterio [monas'terjo] *nm* monastery
mondar [mon'dar] *vt* to peel; **mondarse** *vr* (ESP): **~se de risa** (*fam*) to split one's sides laughing
mondongo [mon'dongo] (LAM) *nm* tripe
moneda [mo'neða] *nf* (*tipo de dinero*) currency, money; (*pieza*) coin; **una ~ de 2 euros** a 2 euro piece; **monedero** *nm* purse
monitor, a [moni'tor, a] *nm/f* instructor, coach ▷ *nm* (*TV*) set; (*Inform*) monitor

monja ['monxa] *nf* nun
monje ['monxe] *nm* monk
mono, -a ['mono, a] *adj* (*bonito*) lovely, pretty; (*gracioso*) nice, charming ▷ *nm/f* monkey, ape ▷ *nm* dungarees *pl*; (*overoles*) overalls *pl*
monopatín [monopa'tin] *nm* skateboard
monopolio [mono'poljo] *nm* monopoly; **monopolizar** *vt* to monopolize
monótono, -a [mo'notono, a] *adj* monotonous
monstruo ['monstrwo] *nm* monster ▷ *adj inv* fantastic; **monstruoso, -a** *adj* monstrous
montaje [mon'taxe] *nm* assembly; (*Teatro*) décor; (*Cine*) montage
montaña [mon'taɲa] *nf* (*monte*) mountain; (*sierra*) mountains *pl*, mountainous area; **montaña rusa** roller coaster; **montañero, -a** *nm/f* mountaineer; **montañismo** *nm* mountaineering
montar [mon'tar] *vt* (*subir a*) to mount, get on; (*Tec*) to assemble, put together; (*negocio*) to set up; (*arma*) to cock; (*colocar*) to lift on to; (*Culin*) to beat ▷ *vi* to mount, get on; (*sobresalir*) to overlap; **~ en bicicleta** to ride a bicycle; **~ en cólera** to get angry; **~ a caballo** to ride, go horseriding
monte ['monte] *nm* (*montaña*) mountain; (*bosque*) woodland; (*área sin cultivar*) wild area, wild country; **monte de piedad** pawnshop
montón [mon'ton] *nm* heap, pile; (*fig*): **un ~ de** heaps *o* lots of
monumento [monu'mento] *nm* monument
moño ['moɲo] *nm* bun
moqueta [mo'keta] *nf* fitted carpet
mora ['mora] *nf* blackberry; *V tb* **moro**
morado, -a [mo'raðo, a] *adj* purple, violet ▷ *nm* bruise
moral [mo'ral] *adj* moral ▷ *nf* (*ética*) ethics *pl*; (*moralidad*) morals *pl*, morality; (*ánimo*) morale
moraleja [mora'lexa] *nf* moral
morboso, -a [mor'βoso, a] *adj* morbid
morcilla [mor'θiʎa] *nf* blood sausage ≈ black pudding (BRIT)
mordaza [mor'ðaθa] *nf* (*para la boca*) gag; (*Tec*) clamp
morder [mor'ðer] *vt* to bite; (*fig: consumir*) to eat away, eat into; **mordisco** *nm* bite
moreno, -a [mo'reno, a] *adj* (*color*) (dark) brown; (*de tez*) dark; (*de pelo moreno*) dark-haired; (*negro*) black
morfina [mor'fina] *nf* morphine
moribundo, -a [mori'βundo, a] *adj* dying
morir [mo'rir] *vi* to die; (*fuego*) to die down; (*luz*) to go out; **morirse** *vr* to die; (*fig*) to be dying; **murió en un accidente** he was killed in an accident; **~se por algo** to be dying for sth
moro, -a ['moro, a] *adj* Moorish ▷ *nm/f* Moor
moroso, -a [mo'roso, a] *nm/f* bad debtor, defaulter
morraña [mo'rraɲa] (MÉX) *nf* (*cambio*) small *o* loose change
morro ['morro] *nm* (*Zool*) snout, nose; (*Auto, Aviac*) nose
morsa ['morsa] *nf* walrus
mortadela [morta'ðela] *nf* mortadella
mortal [mor'tal] *adj* mortal; (*golpe*) deadly; **mortalidad** *nf* mortality
mortero [mor'tero] *nm* mortar
mosca ['moska] *nf* fly
Moscú [mos'ku] *n* Moscow
mosquearse [moske'arse] (*fam*) *vr* (*enojarse*) to get cross; (*ofenderse*) to take offence
mosquitero [moski'tero] *nm* mosquito net
mosquito [mos'kito] *nm* mosquito
mostaza [mos'taθa] *nf* mustard
mosto ['mosto] *nm* (unfermented)

grape juice

mostrador [mostra'ðor] *nm* (*de tienda*) counter; (*de café*) bar

mostrar [mos'trar] *vt* to show; (*exhibir*) to display, exhibit; (*explicar*) to explain; **mostrarse** *vr*: **~se amable** to be kind; to prove to be kind; **no se muestra muy inteligente** he doesn't seem (to be) very intelligent

mota ['mota] *nf* speck, tiny piece; (*en diseño*) dot

mote ['mote] *nm* nickname

motín [mo'tin] *nm* (*del pueblo*) revolt, rising; (*del ejército*) mutiny

motivar [moti'βar] *vt* (*causar*) to cause, motivate; (*explicar*) to explain, justify; **motivo** *nm* motive, reason

moto ['moto] (*fam*) *nf* = **motocicleta**

motocicleta [motoθi'kleta] *nf* motorbike (BRIT), motorcycle

motoneta [moto'neta] (CS) *nf* scooter

motor [mo'tor] *nm* motor, engine; **motor a chorro** *o* **de reacción/de explosión** jet engine/internal combustion engine

motora [mo'tora] *nf* motorboat

movedizo, -a *adj V* **arena**

mover [mo'βer] *vt* to move; (*cabeza*) to shake; (*accionar*) to drive; (*fig*) to cause, provoke; **moverse** *vr* to move; (*fig*) to get a move on

móvil ['moβil] *adj* mobile; (*pieza de máquina*) moving; (*mueble*) movable ▷ *nm* (*motivo*) motive; (*teléfono*) mobile

movimiento [moβi'mjento] *nm* movement; (*Tec*) motion; (*actividad*) activity

mozo, -a ['moθo, a] *adj* (*joven*) young ▷ *nm/f* youth, young man/girl; (CS: *mesero*) waiter/waitress

MP3 *nm* MP3; **reproductor (de) ~** MP3 player

mucama [mu'kama] (RPL) *nf* maid

muchacho, -a [mu'tʃatʃo, a] *nm/f* (*niño*) boy/girl; (*criado*) servant; (*criada*) maid

muchedumbre [mutʃe'ðumbre] *nf* crowd

PALABRA CLAVE

mucho, -a ['mutʃo, a] *adj* **1** (*cantidad*) a lot of, much; (*número*) lots of, a lot of, many; **mucho dinero** a lot of money; **hace mucho calor** it's very hot; **muchas amigas** lots *o* a lot of friends

2 (*sg*: *grande*): **ésta es mucha casa para él** this house is much too big for him

▷ *pron*: **tengo mucho que hacer** I've got a lot to do; **muchos dicen que ...** a lot of people say that ...; *V tb* **tener**

▷ *adv* **1 me gusta mucho** I like it a lot; **lo siento mucho** I'm very sorry; **come mucho** he eats a lot; **¿te vas a quedar mucho?** are you going to be staying long?

2 (*respuesta*) very; **¿estás cansado? - ¡mucho!** are you tired? - very!

3 (*locuciones*): **como mucho** at (the) most; **con mucho: el mejor con mucho** by far the best; **ni mucho menos: no es rico ni mucho menos** he's far from being rich

4: **por mucho que: por mucho que le creas** no matter how *o* however much you believe her

muda ['muða] *nf* change of clothes

mudanza [mu'ðanθa] *nf* (*de casa*) move

mudar [mu'ðar] *vt* to change; (*Zool*) to shed ▷ *vi* to change; **mudarse** *vr* (*ropa*) to change; **~se de casa** to move house

mudo, -a ['muðo, a] *adj* dumb; (*callado, Cine*) silent

mueble ['mweβle] *nm* piece of furniture; **muebles** *nmpl* furniture *sg*

mueca ['mweka] *nf* face, grimace; **hacer ~s a** to make faces at

muela ['mwela] *nf* back tooth; **muela del juicio** wisdom tooth

muelle ['mweʎe] *nm* spring; (*Náut*) wharf; (*malecón*) pier
muero*etc vb V* **morir**
muerte ['mwerte] *nf* death; (*homicidio*) murder; **dar ~ a** to kill
muerto, -a ['mwerto, a] *pp de* **morir** ▷ *adj* dead ▷ *nm/f* dead man/woman; (*difunto*) deceased; (*cadáver*) corpse; **estar ~ de cansancio** to be dead tired; **Día de los Muertos** (*MÉX*) All Souls' Day

DÍA DE LOS MUERTOS

All Souls' Day (or "Day of the Dead") in Mexico coincides with All Saints' Day, which is celebrated in the Catholic countries of Latin America on November 1st and 2nd. All Souls' Day is actually a celebration which begins in the evening of October 31st and continues until November 2nd. It is a combination of the Catholic tradition of honouring the Christian saints and martyrs, and the ancient Mexican or Aztec traditions, in which death was not something sinister. For this reason all the dead are honoured by bringing offerings of food, flowers and candles to the cemetery.

muestra ['mwestra] *nf* (*señal*) indication, sign; (*demostración*) demonstration; (*prueba*) proof; (*estadística*) sample; (*modelo*) model, pattern; (*testimonio*) token
muestro*etc vb V* **mostrar**
muevo*etc vb V* **mover**
mugir [mu'xir] *vi* (*vaca*) to moo
mugre ['muɣre] *nf* dirt, filth
mujer [mu'xer] *nf* woman; (*esposa*) wife; **mujeriego** *nm* womanizer
mula ['mula] *nf* mule
muleta [mu'leta] *nf* (*para andar*) crutch; (*Taur*) *stick with red cape attached*
multa ['multa] *nf* fine; **poner una ~ a** to fine; **multar** *vt* to fine
multicines [multi'θines] *nmpl* multiscreen cinema *sg*
multinacional [multinaθjo'nal] *nf* multinational
múltiple ['multiple] *adj* multiple; (*pl*) many, numerous
multiplicar [multipli'kar] *vt* (*Mat*) to multiply; (*fig*) to increase; **multiplicarse** *vr* (*Bio*) to multiply; (*fig*) to be everywhere at once
multitud [multi'tuð] *nf* (*muchedumbre*) crowd; **~ de** lots of
mundial [mun'djal] *adj* world-wide, universal; (*guerra, récord*) world *cpd*
mundo ['mundo] *nm* world; **todo el ~** everybody; **tener ~** to be experienced, know one's way around
munición [muni'θjon] *nf* ammunition
municipal [muniθi'pal] *adj* municipal, local
municipio [muni'θipjo] *nm* (*ayuntamiento*) town council, corporation; (*territorio administrativo*) town, municipality
muñeca [mu'ɲeka] *nf* (*Anat*) wrist; (*juguete*) doll
muñeco [mu'ɲeko] *nm* (*figura*) figure; (*marioneta*) puppet; (*fig*) puppet, pawn
mural [mu'ral] *adj* mural, wall *cpd* ▷ *nm* mural
muralla [mu'raʎa] *nf* (city) wall(s) (*pl*)
murciélago [mur'θjelaɣo] *nm* bat
murmullo [mur'muʎo] *nm* murmur(ing); (*cuchicheo*) whispering
murmurar [murmu'rar] *vi* to murmur, whisper; (*cotillear*) to gossip
muro ['muro] *nm* wall
muscular [musku'lar] *adj* muscular
músculo ['muskulo] *nm* muscle
museo [mu'seo] *nm* museum; **museo de arte** art gallery
musgo ['musɣo] *nm* moss
música ['musika] *nf* music; *V tb* **músico**
músico, -a ['musiko, a] *adj* musical

▷ *nm/f* musician

muslo ['muslo] *nm* thigh

musulmán, -ana [musul'man, ana] *nm/f* Moslem

mutación [muta'θjon] *nf* (*Bio*) mutation; (*cambio*) (sudden) change

mutilar [muti'lar] *vt* to mutilate; (*a una persona*) to maim

mutuo, -a ['mutwo, a] *adj* mutual

muy [mwi] *adv* very; (*demasiado*) too; **M~ Señor mío** Dear Sir; **~ de noche** very late at night; **eso es ~ de él** that's just like him

N *abr* (= *norte*) N

nabo ['naβo] *nm* turnip

nacer [na'θer] *vi* to be born; (*de huevo*) to hatch; (*vegetal*) to sprout; (*río*) to rise; **nací en Barcelona** I was born in Barcelona; **nacido, -a** *adj* born; **recién nacido** newborn; **nacimiento** *nm* birth; (*de Navidad*) Nativity; (*de río*) source

nación [na'θjon] *nf* nation; **nacional** *adj* national; **nacionalismo** *nm* nationalism

nada ['naða] *pron* nothing ▷ *adv* not at all, in no way; **no decir ~** to say nothing, not to say anything; **~ más** nothing else; **de ~** don't mention it

nadador, a [naða'ðor, a] *nm/f* swimmer

nadar [na'ðar] *vi* to swim

nadie ['naðje] *pron* nobody, no-one; **~ habló** nobody spoke; **no había ~** there was nobody there, there wasn't anybody there

nado ['naðo] **a nado**: *adv*: **pasar a ~** to swim across

nafta ['nafta] (RPL) *nf* petrol (BRIT), gas (US)
naipe ['naipe] *nm* (playing) card; **naipes** *nmpl* cards
nalgas ['nalɣas] *nfpl* buttocks
nalguear [nalɣe'ar] (MÉX, CAM) *vt* to spank
nana ['nana] (ESP) *nf* lullaby
naranja [na'ranxa] *adj inv, nf* orange; **media ~** (*fam*) better half; **naranjada** *nf* orangeade; **naranjo** *nm* orange tree
narciso [nar'θiso] *nm* narcissus
narcótico, -a [nar'kotiko, a] *adj, nm* narcotic; **narcotizar** *vt* to drug; **narcotráfico** *nm* drug trafficking *o* running
nariz [na'riθ] *nf* nose; **nariz chata/ respingona** snub/turned-up nose
narración [narra'θjon] *nf* narration
narrar [na'rrar] *vt* to narrate, recount; **narrativa** *nf* narrative
nata ['nata] *nf* cream; **nata montada** whipped cream
natación [nata'θjon] *nf* swimming
natal [na'tal] *adj*: **ciudad ~** home town; **natalidad** *nf* birth rate
natillas [na'tiʎas] *nfpl* custard *sg*
nativo, -a [na'tiβo, a] *adj, nm/f* native
natural [natu'ral] *adj* natural; (*fruta etc*) fresh ▷ *nmf* native ▷ *nm* (*disposición*) nature
naturaleza [natura'leθa] *nf* nature; (*género*) nature, kind; **naturaleza muerta** still life
naturalmente [natural'mente] *adv* (*de modo natural*) in a natural way; **¡~!** of course!
naufragar [naufra'ɣar] *vi* to sink; **naufragio** *nm* shipwreck
nauseabundo, -a [nausea'βundo, a] *adj* nauseating, sickening
náuseas ['nauseas] *nfpl* nausea *sg*; **me da ~** it makes me feel sick
náutico, -a ['nautiko, a] *adj* nautical
navaja [na'βaxa] *nf* knife; (*de barbero, peluquero*) razor
naval [na'βal] *adj* naval
Navarra [na'βarra] *n* Navarre
nave ['naβe] *nf* (*barco*) ship, vessel; (*Arq*) nave; **nave espacial** spaceship; **nave industrial** factory premises *pl*
navegador [naβeɣa'ðor] *nm* (*Inform*) browser
navegante [naβe'ɣante] *nmf* navigator
navegar [naβe'ɣar] *vi* (*barco*) to sail; (*avión*) to fly; **~ por Internet** to surf the Net
Navidad [naβi'ðað] *nf* Christmas; **Navidades** *nfpl* Christmas time; **¡Feliz ~!** Merry Christmas!; **navideño, -a** *adj* Christmas *cpd*
nazca *etc vb V* **nacer**
nazi ['naθi] *adj, nmf* Nazi
NE *abr* (= *nor(d)este*) NE
neblina [ne'βlina] *nf* mist
necesario, -a [neθe'sarjo, a] *adj* necessary
neceser [neθe'ser] *nm* toilet bag; (*bolsa grande*) holdall
necesidad [neθesi'ðað] *nf* need; (*lo inevitable*) necessity; (*miseria*) poverty; **en caso de ~** in case of need *o* emergency; **hacer sus ~es** to relieve o.s.
necesitado, -a [neθesi'taðo, a] *adj* needy, poor; **~ de** in need of
necesitar [neθesi'tar] *vt* to need, require
necio, -a ['neθjo, a] *adj* foolish
nectarina [nekta'rina] *nf* nectarine
nefasto, -a [ne'fasto, a] *adj* ill-fated, unlucky
negación [neɣa'θjon] *nf* negation; (*rechazo*) refusal, denial
negar [ne'ɣar] *vt* (*renegar, rechazar*) to refuse; (*prohibir*) to refuse, deny; (*desmentir*) to deny; **negarse** *vr*: **~se a** to refuse to
negativa [neɣa'tiβa] *nf* negative; (*rechazo*) refusal, denial
negativo, -a [neɣa'tiβo, a] *adj, nm* negative

negociante [neɣo'θjante] *nmf* businessman/woman
negociar [neɣo'θjar] *vt, vi* to negotiate; **~ en** to deal *o* trade in
negocio [ne'ɣoθjo] *nm* (*Com*) business; (*asunto*) affair, business; (*operación comercial*) deal, transaction; (*lugar*) place of business; **los ~s** business *sg*; **hacer ~** to do business
negra ['neɣra] *nf* (*Mús*) crotchet; *V tb* **negro**
negro, -a ['neɣro, a] *adj* black; (*suerte*) awful ▷ *nm* black ▷ *nm/f* black man/woman
nene, -a ['nene, a] *nm/f* baby, small child
neón [ne'on] *nm*: **luces/lámpara de ~** neon lights/lamp
neoyorquino, -a [neojor'kino, a] *adj* (of) New York
nervio ['nerβjo] *nm* nerve; **nerviosismo** *nm* nervousness, nerves *pl*; **nervioso, -a** *adj* nervous
neto, -a ['neto, a] *adj* net
neumático, -a [neu'matiko, a] *adj* pneumatic ▷ *nm* (ESP) tyre (BRIT), tire (US); **neumático de recambio** spare tyre
neurólogo, -a [neu'roloɣo, a] *nm/f* neurologist
neurona [neu'rona] *nf* nerve cell
neutral [neu'tral] *adj* neutral; **neutralizar** *vt* to neutralize; (*contrarrestar*) to counteract
neutro, -a ['neutro, a] *adj* (*Bio, Ling*) neuter
neutrón [neu'tron] *nm* neutron
nevada [ne'βaða] *nf* snowstorm; (*caída de nieve*) snowfall
nevar [ne'βar] *vi* to snow
nevera [ne'βera] (ESP) *nf* refrigerator (BRIT), icebox (US)
nevería [neβe'ria] (MÉX) *nf* ice-cream parlour
nexo ['nekso] *nm* link, connection
ni [ni] *conj* nor, neither; (*tb*: **~ siquiera**) not ... even; **~ aunque que** not even if; **~ blanco ~ negro** neither white nor black
Nicaragua [nika'raɣwa] *nf* Nicaragua; **nicaragüense** *adj, nmf* Nicaraguan
nicho ['nitʃo] *nm* niche
nicotina [niko'tina] *nf* nicotine
nido ['niðo] *nm* nest
niebla ['njeβla] *nf* fog; (*neblina*) mist
niego *etc vb V* **negar**
nieto, -a ['njeto, a] *nm/f* grandson/daughter; **nietos** *nmpl* grandchildren
nieve *etc* ['njeβe] *vb V* **nevar** ▷ *nf* snow; (MÉX: *helado*) ice cream
NIF *nm abr* (= *Número de Identificación Fiscal*) *personal identification number used for financial and tax purposes*
ninfa ['ninfa] *nf* nymph
ningún *adj V* **ninguno**
ninguno, -a [nin'guno, a] (*adj* **ningún**) no *pron* (*nadie*) nobody; (*ni uno*) none, not one; (*ni uno ni otro*) neither; **de ninguna manera** by no means, not at all
niña ['niɲa] *nf* (*Anat*) pupil; *V tb* **niño**
niñera [ni'ɲera] *nf* nursemaid, nanny
niñez [ni'ɲeθ] *nf* childhood; (*infancia*) infancy
niño, -a ['niɲo, a] *adj* (*joven*) young; (*inmaduro*) immature ▷ *nm/f* child, boy/girl
nipón, -ona [ni'pon, ona] *adj, nm/f* Japanese
níquel ['nikel] *nm* nickel
níspero ['nispero] *nm* medlar
nítido, -a ['nitiðo, a] *adj* clear; sharp
nitrato [ni'trato] *nm* nitrate
nitrógeno [ni'troxeno] *nm* nitrogen
nivel [ni'βel] *nm* (*Geo*) level; (*norma*) level, standard; (*altura*) height; **nivel de aceite** oil level; **nivel de aire** spirit level; **nivel de vida** standard of living; **nivelar** *vt* to level out; (*fig*) to even up; (*Com*) to balance
no [no] *adv* no; not; (*con verbo*) not ▷ *excl* no!; **~ tengo nada** I don't have anything, I have nothing; **~ es el mío** it's not mine; **ahora ~** not now; **¿~ lo sabes?** don't you know?; **~ mucho** not

much; **~ bien termine, lo entregaré** as soon as I finish, I'll hand it over; **~ más: ayer ~ más** just yesterday; **¡pase ~ más!** come in!; **¡a que ~ lo sabes!** I bet you don't know!; **¡cómo ~!** of course!; **la ~ intervención** non-intervention

noble ['noβle] *adj, nmf* noble; **nobleza** *nf* nobility

noche ['notʃe] *nf* night, night-time; (*la tarde*) evening; **de ~, por la ~** at night; **es de ~** it's dark; **Noche de San Juan** *see note*

NOCHE DE SAN JUAN

The **Noche de San Juan** on the 24th June is a **fiesta** coinciding with the summer solstice and which has taken the place of other ancient pagan festivals. Traditionally fire plays a major part in these festivities with celebrations and dancing taking place around bonfires in towns and villages across the country.

nochebuena [notʃe'βwena] *nf* Christmas Eve

NOCHEBUENA

Traditional Christmas celebrations in Spanish-speaking countries mainly take place on the night of **Nochebuena**, Christmas Eve. Families gather together for a large meal and the more religiously inclined attend Midnight Mass. While presents are traditionally given by **los Reyes Magos** on the 6th January, more and more people are exchanging gifts on Christmas Eve.

nochevieja [notʃe'βjexa] *nf* New Year's Eve

nocivo, -a [no'θiβo, a] *adj* harmful

noctámbulo, -a [nok'tambulo, a] *nm/f* sleepwalker

nocturno, -a [nok'turno, a] *adj* (*de la noche*) nocturnal, night *cpd*; (*de la tarde*) evening *cpd* ▷ *nm* nocturne

nogal [no'ɣal] *nm* walnut tree

nómada ['nomaða] *adj* nomadic ▷ *nmf* nomad

nombrar [nom'brar] *vt* (*designar*) to name; (*mencionar*) to mention; (*dar puesto a*) to appoint

nombre ['nombre] *nm* name; (*sustantivo*) noun; **~ y apellidos** name in full; **poner ~ a** to call, name; **nombre común/propio** common/proper noun; **nombre de pila/de soltera** Christian/maiden name

nómina ['nomina] *nf* (*lista*) payroll; (*hoja*) payslip

nominal [nomi'nal] *adj* nominal

nominar [nomi'nar] *vt* to nominate

nominativo, -a [nomina'tiβo, a] *adj* (*Com*): **cheque ~ a X** cheque made out to X

nordeste [nor'ðeste] *adj* north-east, north-eastern, north-easterly ▷ *nm* north-east

nórdico, -a ['norðiko, a] *adj* Nordic

noreste [no'reste] *adj, nm* = **nordeste**

noria ['norja] *nf* (*Agr*) waterwheel; (*de carnaval*) big (BRIT) *o* Ferris (US) wheel

norma ['norma] *nf* rule (of thumb)

normal [nor'mal] *adj* (*corriente*) normal; (*habitual*) usual, natural; **normalizarse** *vr* to return to normal; **normalmente** *adv* normally

normativa [norma'tiβa] *nf* (set of) rules *pl*, regulations *pl*

noroeste [noro'este] *adj* north-west, north-western, north-westerly ▷ *nm* north-west

norte ['norte] *adj* north, northern, northerly ▷ *nm* north; (*fig*) guide

norteamericano, -a [norteameri'kano, a] *adj, nm/f* (North) American

Noruega [no'rweɣa] *nf* Norway

noruego, -a [no'rweɣo, a] *adj, nm/f* Norwegian

nos [nos] *pron* (*directo*) us; (*indirecto*) us; to us; for us; from us; (*reflexivo*) (to) ourselves; (*recíproco*) (to) each other; **~ levantamos a las 7** we get up at 7
nosotros, -as [no'sotros, as] *pron* (*sujeto*) we; (*después de prep*) us
nostalgia [nos'talxja] *nf* nostalgia
nota ['nota] *nf* note; (*Escol*) mark
notable [no'taβle] *adj* notable; (*Escol*) outstanding
notar [no'tar] *vt* to notice, note; **notarse** *vr* to be obvious; **se nota que ...** one observes that ...
notario [no'tarjo] *nm* notary
noticia [no'tiθja] *nf* (*información*) piece of news; **las ~s** the news *sg*; **tener ~s de algn** to hear from sb
No confundir **noticia** con la palabra inglesa *notice*.
noticiero [noti'θjero] (*LAM*) *nm* news bulletin
notificar [notifi'kar] *vt* to notify, inform
notorio, -a [no'torjo, a] *adj* (*público*) well-known; (*evidente*) obvious
novato, -a [no'βato, a] *adj* inexperienced ▷ *nm/f* beginner, novice
novecientos, -as [noβe'θjentos, as] *num* nine hundred
novedad [noβe'ðað] *nf* (*calidad de nuevo*) newness; (*noticia*) piece of news; (*cambio*) change, (new) development
novel [no'βel] *adj* new; (*inexperto*) inexperienced ▷ *nmf* beginner
novela [no'βela] *nf* novel
noveno, -a [no'βeno, a] *adj* ninth
noventa [no'βenta] *num* ninety
novia *nf V* **novio**
novicio, -a [no'βiθjo, a] *nm/f* novice
noviembre [no'βjembre] *nm* November
novillada [noβi'ʎaða] *nf* (*Taur*) *bullfight with young bulls*; **novillero** *nm* novice bullfighter; **novillo** *nm* young bull, bullock; **hacer novillos** (*fam*) to play truant
novio, -a ['noβjo, a] *nm/f* boyfriend/girlfriend; (*prometido*) fiancé/fiancée; (*recién casado*) bridegroom/bride; **los ~s** the newly-weds
nube ['nuβe] *nf* cloud
nublado, -a [nu'βlaðo, a] *adj* cloudy; **nublarse** *vr* to grow dark
nubosidad [nuβosi'ðað] *nf* cloudiness; **había mucha ~** it was very cloudy
nuca ['nuka] *nf* nape of the neck
nuclear [nukle'ar] *adj* nuclear
núcleo ['nukleo] *nm* (*centro*) core; (*Física*) nucleus; **núcleo urbano** city centre
nudillo [nu'ðiʎo] *nm* knuckle
nudista [nu'ðista] *adj* nudist
nudo ['nuðo] *nm* knot; (*de carreteras*) junction
nuera ['nwera] *nf* daughter-in-law
nuestro, -a ['nwestro, a] *adj pos* our ▷ *pron* ours; **~ padre** our father; **un amigo ~** a friend of ours; **es el ~** it's ours
Nueva York [-jɔrk] *n* New York
Nueva Zelanda [-θe'landa] *nf* New Zealand
nueve ['nweβe] *num* nine
nuevo, -a ['nweβo, a] *adj* (*gen*) new; **de ~** again
nuez [nweθ] *nf* walnut; (*Anat*) Adam's apple; **nuez moscada** nutmeg
nulo, -a ['nulo, a] *adj* (*inepto, torpe*) useless; (*inválido*) (null and) void; (*Deporte*) drawn, tied
núm. *abr* (= *número*) no.
numerar [nume'rar] *vt* to number
número ['numero] *nm* (*gen*) number; (*tamaño: de zapato*) size; (*ejemplar: de diario*) number, issue; **sin ~** numberless, unnumbered; **número atrasado** back number; **número de matrícula/teléfono** registration/telephone number; **número impar/par** odd/even number; **número romano** Roman numeral
numeroso, -a [nume'roso, a] *adj* numerous
nunca ['nunka] *adv* (*jamás*) never; **~**

lo pensé I never thought it; **no viene ~** he never comes; **~ más** never again; **más que ~** more than ever

nupcias ['nupθjas] *nfpl* wedding *sg*, nuptials

nutria ['nutrja] *nf* otter

nutrición [nutri'θjon] *nf* nutrition

nutrir [nu'trir] *vt* (*alimentar*) to nourish; (*dar de comer*) to feed; (*fig*) to strengthen; **nutritivo, -a** *adj* nourishing, nutritious

nylon [ni'lon] *nm* nylon

ñango, -a ['ɲango, a] (MÉX) *adj* puny

ñapa ['ɲapa] (LAM) *nf* extra

ñata ['ɲata] (LAM: *fam*) *nf* nose; *V tb* **ñato**

ñato, -a ['ɲato, a] (LAM) *adj* snub-nosed

ñoñería [ɲoɲe'ria] *nf* insipidness

ñoño, -a ['ɲoɲo, a] *adj* (*fam: tonto*) silly, stupid; (*soso*) insipid; (*persona*) spineless; (ESP: *película, novela*) sentimental

O *abr* (= *oeste*) W
o [o] *conj* or
oasis [o'asis] *nm inv* oasis
obcecarse [oβθe'karse] *vr* to get *o* become stubborn
obedecer [oβeðe'θer] *vt* to obey; **obediente** *adj* obedient
obertura [oβer'tura] *nf* overture
obeso, -a [o'βeso, a] *adj* obese
obispo [o'βispo] *nm* bishop
obituario [oβɪ'twarjo] (LAM) *nm* obituary
objetar [oβxe'tar] *vt, vi* to object
objetivo, -a [oβxe'tiβo, a] *adj, nm* objective
objeto [oβ'xeto] *nm* (*cosa*) object; (*fin*) aim
objetor, a [oβxe'tor, a] *nm/f* objector
obligación [oβliɤa'θjon] *nf* obligation; (*Com*) bond
obligar [oβli'ɤar] *vt* to force; **obligarse** *vr* to bind o.s.; **obligatorio, -a** *adj* compulsory, obligatory
oboe [o'βoe] *nm* oboe
obra ['oβra] *nf* work; (*Arq*) construction, building; (*Teatro*) play; **por ~ de** thanks to (the efforts of); **obra maestra** masterpiece; **obras públicas** public works; **obrar** *vt* to work; (*tener efecto*) to have an effect on ▷ *vi* to act, behave; (*tener efecto*) to have an effect; **la carta obra en su poder** the letter is in his/her possession
obrero, -a [o'βrero, a] *adj* (*clase*) working; (*movimiento*) labour *cpd* ▷ *nm/f* (*gen*) worker; (*sin oficio*) labourer
obsceno, -a [oβs'θeno, a] *adj* obscene
obscu... = **oscu...**
obsequiar [oβse'kjar] *vt* (*ofrecer*) to present with; (*agasajar*) to make a fuss of, lavish attention on; **obsequio** *nm* (*regalo*) gift; (*cortesía*) courtesy, attention
observación [oβserβa'θjon] *nf* observation; (*reflexión*) remark
observador, a [oβserβa'ðor, a] *nm/f* observer
observar [oβser'βar] *vt* to observe; (*anotar*) to notice; **observarse** *vr* to keep to, observe
obsesión [oβse'sjon] *nf* obsession; **obsesivo, -a** *adj* obsessive
obstáculo [oβs'takulo] *nm* obstacle; (*impedimento*) hindrance, drawback
obstante [oβs'tante]: **no ~** *adv* nevertheless
obstinado, -a [oβsti'naðo, a] *adj* obstinate, stubborn
obstinarse [oβsti'narse] *vr* to be obstinate; **~ en** to persist in
obstruir [oβstru'ir] *vt* to obstruct
obtener [oβte'ner] *vt* (*gen*) to obtain; (*premio*) to win
obturador [oβtura'ðor] *nm* (*Foto*) shutter
obvio, -a ['oββjo, a] *adj* obvious
oca ['oka] *nf* (*animal*) goose; (*juego*) ≈ snakes and ladders
ocasión [oka'sjon] *nf* (*oportunidad*) opportunity, chance; (*momento*) occasion, time; (*causa*) cause; **de ~**

secondhand; **ocasionar** *vt* to cause
ocaso [o'kaso] *nm* (*fig*) decline
occidente [okθi'ðente] *nm* west
OCDE *nf abr* (= *Organización de Cooperación y Desarrollo Económico*) OECD
océano [o'θeano] *nm* ocean; **Océano índico** Indian Ocean
ochenta [o'tʃenta] *num* eighty
ocho ['otʃo] *num* eight; **dentro de ~ días** within a week
ocio ['oθjo] *nm* (*tiempo*) leisure; (*pey*) idleness
octavilla [okta'viʎa] *nf* leaflet, pamphlet
octavo, -a [ok'taβo, a] *adj* eighth
octubre [ok'tuβre] *nm* October
oculista [oku'lista] *nmf* oculist
ocultar [okul'tar] *vt* (*esconder*) to hide; (*callar*) to conceal; **oculto, -a** *adj* hidden; (*fig*) secret
ocupación [okupa'θjon] *nf* occupation
ocupado, -a [oku'paðo, a] *adj* (*persona*) busy; (*plaza*) occupied, taken; (*teléfono*) engaged; **ocupar** *vt* (*gen*) to occupy; **ocuparse** *vr*: **ocuparse de** *o* **en** (*gen*) to concern o.s. with; (*cuidar*) to look after
ocurrencia [oku'rrenθja] *nf* (*idea*) bright idea
ocurrir [oku'rrir] *vi* to happen; **ocurrirse** *vr*: **se me ocurrió que ...** it occurred to me that ...
odiar [o'ðjar] *vt* to hate; **odio** *nm* hate, hatred; **odioso, -a** *adj* (*gen*) hateful; (*malo*) nasty
odontólogo, -a [oðon'toloɣo, a] *nm/f* dentist, dental surgeon
oeste [o'este] *nm* west; **una película del ~** a western
ofender [ofen'der] *vt* (*agraviar*) to offend; (*insultar*) to insult; **ofenderse** *vr* to take offence; **ofensa** *nf* offence; **ofensiva** *nf* offensive; **ofensivo, -a** *adj* offensive
oferta [o'ferta] *nf* offer; (*propuesta*) proposal; **la ~ y la demanda** supply and demand; **artículos en ~** goods on offer
oficial [ofi'θjal] *adj* official ▷ *nm* (*Mil*) officer
oficina [ofi'θina] *nf* office; **oficina de correos** post office; **oficina de información** information bureau; **oficina de turismo** tourist office; **oficinista** *nmf* clerk
oficio [o'fiθjo] *nm* (*profesión*) profession; (*puesto*) post; (*Rel*) service; **ser del ~** to be an old hand; **tener mucho ~** to have a lot of experience; **oficio de difuntos** funeral service
ofimática [ofi'matika] *nf* office automation
ofrecer [ofre'θer] *vt* (*dar*) to offer; (*proponer*) to propose; **ofrecerse** *vr* (*persona*) to offer o.s., volunteer; (*situación*) to present itself; **¿qué se le ofrece?, ¿se le ofrece algo?** what can I do for you?, can I get you anything?
ofrecimiento [ofreθi'mjento] *nm* offer
oftalmólogo, -a [oftal'moloɣo, a] *nm/f* ophthalmologist
oída [o'iða] *nf*: **de ~s** by hearsay
oído [o'iðo] *nm* (*Anat*) ear; (*sentido*) hearing
oigo *etc vb V* **oír**
oír [o'ir] *vt* (*gen*) to hear; (*atender a*) to listen to; **¡oiga!** listen!; **~ misa** to attend mass
OIT *nf abr* (= *Organización Internacional del Trabajo*) ILO
ojal [o'xal] *nm* buttonhole
ojalá [oxa'la] *excl* if only (it were so)!, some hope! ▷ *conj* if only ...!, would that ...!; **~ (que) venga hoy** I hope he comes today
ojeada [oxe'aða] *nf* glance
ojera [o'xera] *nf*: **tener ~s** to have bags under one's eyes
ojo ['oxo] *nm* eye; (*de puente*) span; (*de cerradura*) keyhole ▷ *excl* careful!; **tener ~ para** to have an eye for; **ojo de buey** porthole
okey ['okei] (LAM) *excl* O.K.

okupa [o'kupa] (ESP: *fam*) *nmf* squatter
ola ['ola] *nf* wave
olé [o'le] *excl* bravo!, olé!
oleada [ole'aða] *nf* big wave, swell; (*fig*) wave
oleaje [ole'axe] *nm* swell
óleo ['oleo] *nm* oil; **oleoducto** *nm* (oil) pipeline
oler [o'ler] *vt* (*gen*) to smell; (*inquirir*) to pry into; (*fig*: *sospechar*) to sniff out ▷ *vi* to smell; **~ a** to smell of
olfatear [olfate'ar] *vt* to smell; (*inquirir*) to pry into; **olfato** *nm* sense of smell
olimpiada [olim'piaða] *nf*: **las O~s** the Olympics; **olímpico, -a** [o'limpiko, a] *adj* Olympic
oliva [o'liβa] *nf* (*aceituna*) olive; **aceite de ~** olive oil; **olivo** *nm* olive tree
olla ['oʎa] *nf* pan; (*comida*) stew; **olla exprés** *o* **a presión** (ESP) pressure cooker; **olla podrida** *type of Spanish stew*
olmo ['olmo] *nm* elm (tree)
olor [o'lor] *nm* smell; **oloroso, -a** *adj* scented
olvidar [olβi'ðar] *vt* to forget; (*omitir*) to omit; **olvidarse** *vr* (*fig*) to forget o.s.; **se me olvidó** I forgot
olvido [ol'βiðo] *nm* oblivion; (*despiste*) forgetfulness
ombligo [om'bliɣo] *nm* navel
omelette [ome'lete] (LAM) *nf* omelet(te)
omisión [omi'sjon] *nf* (*abstención*) omission; (*descuido*) neglect
omiso, -a [o'miso, a] *adj*: **hacer caso ~ de** to ignore, pass over
omitir [omi'tir] *vt* to omit
omnipotente [omnipo'tente] *adj* omnipotent
omóplato [o'moplato] *nm* shoulder blade
OMS *nf abr* (= *Organización Mundial de la Salud*) WHO
once ['onθe] *num* eleven; **onces** (CS) *nfpl* tea break *sg*
onda ['onda] *nf* wave; **onda corta/larga/media** short/long/medium wave; **ondear** *vt, vi* to wave; (*tener ondas*) to be wavy; (*agua*) to ripple
ondulación [ondula'θjon] *nf* undulation; **ondulado, -a** *adj* wavy
ONG *nf abr* (= *organización no gubernamental*) NGO
ONU ['onu] *nf abr* (= *Organización de las Naciones Unidas*) UNO
opaco, -a [o'pako, a] *adj* opaque
opción [op'θjon] *nf* (*gen*) option; (*derecho*) right, option
OPEP ['opep] *nf abr* (= *Organización de Países Exportadores de Petróleo*) OPEC
ópera ['opera] *nf* opera; **ópera bufa** *o* **cómica** comic opera
operación [opera'θjon] *nf* (*gen*) operation; (*Com*) transaction, deal
operador, a [opera'ðor, a] *nm/f* operator; (*Cine*: *de proyección*) projectionist; (: *de rodaje*) cameraman
operar [ope'rar] *vt* (*producir*) to produce, bring about; (*Med*) to operate on ▷ *vi* (*Com*) to operate, deal; **operarse** *vr* to occur; (*Med*) to have an operation
opereta [ope'reta] *nf* operetta
opinar [opi'nar] *vt* to think ▷ *vi* to give one's opinion; **opinión** *nf* (*creencia*) belief; (*criterio*) opinion
opio ['opjo] *nm* opium
oponer [opo'ner] *vt* (*resistencia*) to put up, offer; **oponerse** *vr* (*objetar*) to object; (*estar frente a frente*) to be opposed; (*dos personas*) to oppose each other; **~ A a B** to set A against B; **me opongo a pensar que ...** I refuse to believe *o* think that ...
oportunidad [oportuni'ðað] *nf* (*ocasión*) opportunity; (*posibilidad*) chance
oportuno, -a [opor'tuno, a] *adj* (*en su tiempo*) opportune, timely; (*respuesta*) suitable; **en el momento ~** at the right moment
oposición [oposi'θjon] *nf* opposition; **oposiciones** *nfpl* (*Escol*)

public examinations
opositor, a [oposi'tor, a] *nm/f* (*adversario*) opponent; (*candidato*): **~ (a)** candidate (for)
opresión [opre'sjon] *nf* oppression; **opresor, a** *nm/f* oppressor
oprimir [opri'mir] *vt* to squeeze; (*fig*) to oppress
optar [op'tar] *vi* (*elegir*) to choose; **~ por** to opt for; **optativo, -a** *adj* optional
óptico, -a ['optiko, a] *adj* optic(al) ▷ *nm/f* optician; **óptica** *nf* optician's (shop); **desde esta óptica** from this point of view
optimismo [opti'mismo] *nm* optimism; **optimista** *nmf* optimist
opuesto, -a [o'pwesto, a] *adj* (*contrario*) opposite; (*antagónico*) opposing
oración [ora'θjon] *nf* (*Rel*) prayer; (*Ling*) sentence
orador, a [ora'ðor, a] *nm/f* (*conferenciante*) speaker, orator
oral [o'ral] *adj* oral
orangután [orangu'tan] *nm* orangutan
orar [o'rar] *vi* to pray
oratoria [ora'torja] *nf* oratory
órbita ['orβita] *nf* orbit
orden ['orðen] *nm* (*gen*) order ▷ *nf* (*gen*) order; (*Inform*) command; **en ~ de prioridad** in order of priority; **orden del día** agenda
ordenado, -a [orðe'naðo, a] *adj* (*metódico*) methodical; (*arreglado*) orderly
ordenador [orðena'ðor] *nm* computer; **ordenador central** mainframe computer
ordenar [orðe'nar] *vt* (*mandar*) to order; (*poner orden*) to put in order, arrange; **ordenarse** *vr* (*Rel*) to be ordained
ordeñar [orðe'ɲar] *vt* to milk
ordinario, -a [orði'narjo, a] *adj* (*común*) ordinary, usual; (*vulgar*) vulgar, common
orégano [o'reɣano] *nm* oregano
oreja [o'rexa] *nf* ear; (*Mecánica*) lug, flange
orfanato [orfa'nato] *nm* orphanage
orfebrería [orfeβre'ria] *nf* gold/silver work
orgánico, -a [or'ɣaniko, a] *adj* organic
organismo [orɣa'nismo] *nm* (*Bio*) organism; (*Pol*) organization
organización [orɣaniθa'θjon] *nf* organization; **organizar** *vt* to organize
órgano ['orɣano] *nm* organ
orgasmo [or'ɣasmo] *nm* orgasm
orgía [or'xia] *nf* orgy
orgullo [or'ɣuʎo] *nm* pride; **orgulloso, -a** *adj* (*gen*) proud; (*altanero*) haughty
orientación [orjenta'θjon] *nf* (*posición*) position; (*dirección*) direction
oriental [orjen'tal] *adj* eastern; (*del Extremo Oriente*) oriental
orientar [orjen'tar] *vt* (*situar*) to orientate; (*señalar*) to point; (*dirigir*) to direct; (*guiar*) to guide; **orientarse** *vr* to get one's bearings
oriente [o'rjente] *nm* east; **el O~ Medio** the Middle East; **el Próximo/Extremo O~** the Near/Far East
origen [o'rixen] *nm* origin
original [orixi'nal] *adj* (*nuevo*) original; (*extraño*) odd, strange; **originalidad** *nf* originality
originar [orixi'nar] *vt* to start, cause; **originarse** *vr* to originate; **originario, -a** *adj* original; **originario de** native of
orilla [o'riʎa] *nf* (*borde*) border; (*de río*) bank; (*de bosque, tela*) edge; (*de mar*) shore
orina [o'rina] *nf* urine; **orinal** *nm* (chamber) pot; **orinar** *vi* to urinate; **orinarse** *vr* to wet o.s.
oro ['oro] *nm* gold; **oros** *nmpl* (*Naipes*) hearts
orquesta [or'kesta] *nf* orchestra; **orquesta sinfónica** symphony orchestra

orquídea [or'kiðea] *nf* orchid
ortiga [or'tiɣa] *nf* nettle
ortodoxo, -a [orto'ðokso, a] *adj* orthodox
ortografía [ortoɣra'fia] *nf* spelling
ortopedia [orto'peðja] *nf* orthopaedics *sg*; **ortopédico, -a** *adj* orthopaedic
oruga [o'ruɣa] *nf* caterpillar
orzuelo [or'θwelo] *nm* stye
os [os] *pron* (*gen*) you; (*a vosotros*) to you
osa ['osa] *nf* (she-)bear; **Osa Mayor/ Menor** Great/Little Bear
osadía [osa'ðia] *nf* daring
osar [o'sar] *vi* to dare
oscilación [osθila'θjon] *nf* (*movimiento*) oscillation; (*fluctuación*) fluctuation
oscilar [osθi'lar] *vi* to oscillate; to fluctuate
oscurecer [oskure'θer] *vt* to darken ▷ *vi* to grow dark; **oscurecerse** *vr* to grow *o* get dark
oscuridad [oskuri'ðað] *nf* obscurity; (*tinieblas*) darkness
oscuro, -a [os'kuro, a] *adj* dark; (*fig*) obscure; **a oscuras** in the dark
óseo, -a ['oseo, a] *adj* bone *cpd*
oso ['oso] *nm* bear; **oso de peluche** teddy bear; **oso hormiguero** anteater
ostentar [osten'tar] *vt* (*gen*) to show; (*pey*) to flaunt, show off; (*poseer*) to have, possess
ostión [os'tjon] (*MÉX*) *nm* = **ostra**
ostra ['ostra] *nf* oyster
OTAN ['otan] *nf abr* (= *Organización del Tratado del Atlántico Norte*) NATO
otitis [o'titis] *nf* earache
otoñal [oto'ɲal] *adj* autumnal
otoño [o'toɲo] *nm* autumn
otorgar [otor'ɣar] *vt* (*conceder*) to concede; (*dar*) to grant
otorrino, -a [oto'rrino, a], **otorrinolaringólogo, -a** [otorrinolarin'goloɣo, a] *nm/f* ear, nose and throat specialist

PALABRA CLAVE

otro, -a ['otro, a] *adj* **1** (*distinto*: *sg*) another; (: *pl*) other; **con otros amigos** with other *o* different friends
2 (*adicional*): **tráigame otro café (más), por favor** can I have another coffee please; **otros diez días más** another ten days
▷ *pron* **1 el otro** the other one; **(los) otros** (the) others; **de otro** somebody else's; **que lo haga otro** let somebody else do it
2 (*recíproco*): **se odian (la) una a (la) otra** they hate one another *o* each other
3: **otro tanto: comer otro tanto** to eat the same *o* as much again; **recibió una decena de telegramas y otras tantas llamadas** he got about ten telegrams and as many calls

ovación [oβa'θjon] *nf* ovation
oval [o'βal] *adj* oval; **ovalado, -a** *adj* oval; **óvalo** *nm* oval
ovario [o'βario] *nm* ovary
oveja [o'βexa] *nf* sheep
overol [oβe'rol] (*LAM*) *nm* overalls *pl*
ovillo [o'βiʎo] *nm* (*de lana*) ball of wool
OVNI ['oβni] *nm abr* (= *objeto volante no identificado*) UFO
ovulación [oβula'θjon] *nf* ovulation; **óvulo** *nm* ovum
oxidación [oksiða'θjon] *nf* rusting
oxidar [oksi'ðar] *vt* to rust; **oxidarse** *vr* to go rusty
óxido ['oksiðo] *nm* oxide
oxigenado, -a [oksixe'naðo, a] *adj* (*Quím*) oxygenated; (*pelo*) bleached
oxígeno [ok'sixeno] *nm* oxygen
oyente [o'jente] *nmf* listener
oyes *etc vb V* **oír**
ozono [o'θono] *nm* ozone

P

pabellón [paβe'ʎon] *nm* bell tent; (*Arq*) pavilion; (*de hospital etc*) block, section; (*bandera*) flag
pacer [pa'θer] *vi* to graze
paciencia [pa'θjenθja] *nf* patience
paciente [pa'θjente] *adj, nmf* patient
pacificación [paθifika'θjon] *nf* pacification
pacífico, -a [pa'θifiko, a] *adj* (*persona*) peaceable; (*existencia*) peaceful; **el (Océano) P~** the Pacific (Ocean)
pacifista [paθi'fista] *nmf* pacifist
pacotilla [pako'tiʎa] *nf*: **de ~** (*actor, escritor*) third-rate
pactar [pak'tar] *vt* to agree to *o* on ▷ *vi* to come to an agreement
pacto ['pakto] *nm* (*tratado*) pact; (*acuerdo*) agreement
padecer [paðe'θer] *vt* (*sufrir*) to suffer; (*soportar*) to endure, put up with; **padecimiento** *nm* suffering
padrastro [pa'ðrastro] *nm* stepfather
padre ['paðre] *nm* father ▷ *adj* (*fam*): **un éxito ~** a tremendous success; **padres** *nmpl* parents; **padre político** father-in-law
padrino [pa'ðrino] *nm* (*Rel*) godfather; (*tb*: **~ de boda**) best man; (*fig*) sponsor, patron; **padrinos** *nmpl* godparents
padrón [pa'ðron] *nm* (*censo*) census, roll
padrote [pa'ðrote] (*MÉX*: *fam*) *nm* pimp
paella [pa'eʎa] *nf* paella, *dish of rice with meat, shellfish etc*
paga ['paɣa] *nf* (*pago*) payment; (*sueldo*) pay, wages *pl*
pagano, -a [pa'ɣano, a] *adj, nm/f* pagan, heathen
pagar [pa'ɣar] *vt* to pay; (*las compras, crimen*) to pay for; (*fig*: *favor*) to repay ▷ *vi* to pay; **~ al contado/a plazos** to pay (in) cash/in instalments
pagaré [paɣa're] *nm* I.O.U.
página ['paxina] *nf* page; **página de inicio** (*Inform*) home page; **página web** (*Inform*) web page
pago ['paɣo] *nm* (*dinero*) payment; **en ~ de** in return for; **pago anticipado/a cuenta/contra reembolso/en especie** advance payment/payment on account/cash on delivery/payment in kind
pág(s). *abr* (= *página(s)*) p(p).
pague *etc vb V* **pagar**
país [pa'is] *nm* (*gen*) country; (*región*) land; **los P~es Bajos** the Low Countries; **el P~ Vasco** the Basque Country
paisaje [pai'saxe] *nm* landscape, scenery
paisano, -a [pai'sano, a] *adj* of the same country ▷ *nm/f* (*compatriota*) fellow countryman/woman; **vestir de ~** (*soldado*) to be in civvies; (*guardia*) to be in plain clothes
paja ['paxa] *nf* straw; (*fig*) rubbish (*BRIT*), trash (*US*)
pajarita [paxa'rita] *nf* (*corbata*) bow tie

pájaro ['paxaro] *nm* bird; **pájaro carpintero** woodpecker
pajita [pa'xita] *nf* (drinking) straw
pala ['pala] *nf* spade, shovel; (*raqueta etc*) bat; (: *de tenis*) racquet; (*Culin*) slice; **pala mecánica** power shovel
palabra [pa'laβra] *nf* word; (*facultad*) (power of) speech; (*derecho de hablar*) right to speak; **tomar la ~** (*en mitin*) to take the floor
palabrota [pala'brota] *nf* swearword
palacio [pa'laθjo] *nm* palace; (*mansión*) mansion, large house; **palacio de justicia** courthouse; **palacio municipal** town *o* city hall
paladar [pala'ðar] *nm* palate; **paladear** *vt* to taste
palanca [pa'lanka] *nf* lever; (*fig*) pull, influence
palangana [palan'gana] *nf* washbasin
palco ['palko] *nm* box
Palestina [pales'tina] *nf* Palestine; **palestino, -a** *nm/f* Palestinian
paleta [pa'leta] *nf* (*de pintor*) palette; (*de albañil*) trowel; (*de ping-pong*) bat; (MÉX, CAM: *helado*) ice lolly (BRIT), Popsicle® (US)
palidecer [paliðe'θer] *vi* to turn pale; **palidez** *nf* paleness; **pálido, -a** *adj* pale
palillo [pa'liʎo] *nm* (*mondadientes*) toothpick; (*para comer*) chopstick
palito [pa'lito] (RPL) *nm* (*helado*) ice lolly (BRIT), Popsicle® (US)
paliza [pa'liθa] *nf* beating, thrashing
palma ['palma] *nf* (*Anat*) palm; (*árbol*) palm tree; **batir** *o* **dar ~s** to clap, applaud; **palmada** *nf* slap; **palmadas** *nfpl* clapping *sg*, applause *sg*
palmar [pal'mar] (*fam*) *vi* (*tb*: **~la**) to die, kick the bucket
palmear [palme'ar] *vi* to clap
palmera [pal'mera] *nf* (*Bot*) palm tree
palmo ['palmo] *nm* (*medida*) span; (*fig*) small amount; **~ a ~** inch by inch
palo ['palo] *nm* stick; (*poste*) post; (*de tienda de campaña*) pole; (*mango*) handle, shaft; (*golpe*) blow, hit; (*de golf*) club; (*de béisbol*) bat; (*Náut*) mast; (*Naipes*) suit
paloma [pa'loma] *nf* dove, pigeon
palomitas [palo'mitas] *nfpl* popcorn *sg*
palpar [pal'par] *vt* to touch, feel
palpitar [palpi'tar] *vi* to palpitate; (*latir*) to beat
palta ['palta] (CS) *nf* avocado
paludismo [palu'ðismo] *nm* malaria
pamela [pa'mela] *nf* picture hat, sun hat
pampa ['pampa] *nf* pampas, prairie
pan [pan] *nm* bread; (*una barra*) loaf; **pan integral** wholemeal (BRIT) *o* wholewheat (US) bread; **pan rallado** breadcrumbs *pl*; **pan tostado** (MÉX: *tostada*) toast
pana ['pana] *nf* corduroy
panadería [panaðe'ria] *nf* baker's (shop); **panadero, -a** *nm/f* baker
Panamá [pana'ma] *nm* Panama; **panameño, -a** *adj* Panamanian
pancarta [pan'karta] *nf* placard, banner
panceta [pan'θeta] (ESP, RPL) *nf* bacon
pancho ['pantʃo] (RPL) *nm* hot dog
pancito [pan'θito] *nm* (bread) roll
panda ['panda] *nm* (*Zool*) panda
pandereta [pande'reta] *nf* tambourine
pandilla [pan'diʎa] *nf* set, group; (*de criminales*) gang; (*pey*: *camarilla*) clique
panecillo [pane'θiʎo] (ESP) *nm* (bread) roll
panel [pa'nel] *nm* panel; **panel solar** solar panel
panfleto [pan'fleto] *nm* pamphlet
pánico ['paniko] *nm* panic
panorama [pano'rama] *nm* panorama; (*vista*) view
panqueque [pan'keke] (LAM) *nm* pancake
pantalla [pan'taʎa] *nf* (*de cine*) screen; (*de lámpara*) lampshade

pantalón [panta'lon] *nm* trousers; **pantalones** *nmpl* trousers; **pantalones cortes** shorts
pantano [pan'tano] *nm* (*ciénaga*) marsh, swamp; (*depósito: de agua*) reservoir; (*fig*) jam, difficulty
panteón [pante'on] *nm* (*monumento*) pantheon
pantera [pan'tera] *nf* panther
pantimedias [panti'meðjas] (*MÉX*) *nfpl* = **pantis**
pantis ['pantis] *nmpl* tights (*BRIT*), pantyhose (*US*)
pantomima [panto'mima] *nf* pantomime
pantorrilla [panto'rriʎa] *nf* calf (of the leg)
pants [pants] (*MÉX*) *nmpl* tracksuit (*BRIT*), sweat suit (*US*)
pantufla [pan'tufla] *nf* slipper
panty(s) ['panti(s)] *nm(pl)* tights (*BRIT*), pantyhose (*US*)
panza ['panθa] *nf* belly, paunch
pañal [pa'ɲal] *nm* nappy (*BRIT*), diaper (*US*); **pañales** *nmpl* (*fig*) early stages, infancy *sg*
paño ['paɲo] *nm* (*tela*) cloth; (*pedazo de tela*) (piece of) cloth; (*trapo*) duster, rag; **paños menores** underclothes
pañuelo [pa'ɲwelo] *nm* handkerchief, hanky; (*fam: para la cabeza*) (head)scarf
papa ['papa] *nm*: **el P~** the Pope ▷ *nf* (*LAM: patata*) potato; **papas fritas** (*LAM*) French fries, chips (*BRIT*); (*de bolsa*) crisps (*BRIT*), potato chips (*US*)
papá [pa'pa] (*fam*) *nm* dad(dy), pa (*US*)
papada [pa'paða] *nf* double chin
papagayo [papa'ɣajo] *nm* parrot
papalote [papa'lote] (*MÉX, CAM*) *nm* kite
papanatas [papa'natas] (*fam*) *nm inv* simpleton
papaya [pa'paja] *nf* papaya
papear [pape'ar] (*fam*) *vt, vi* to scoff
papel [pa'pel] *nm* paper; (*hoja de papel*) sheet of paper; (*Teatro: fig*) role; **papel de aluminio** aluminium (*BRIT*) *o* aluminum (*US*) foil; **papel de arroz/envolver/fumar** rice/wrapping/cigarette paper; **papel de estaño** *o* **plata** tinfoil; **papel de lija** sandpaper; **papel higiénico** toilet paper; **papel moneda** paper money; **papel secante** blotting paper
papeleo [pape'leo] *nm* red tape
papelera [pape'lera] *nf* wastepaper basket; (*en la calle*) litter bin; **papelera (de reciclaje)** (*Inform*) wastebasket
papelería [papele'ria] *nf* stationer's (shop)
papeleta [pape'leta] (*ESP*) *nf* (*Pol*) ballot paper
paperas [pa'peras] *nfpl* mumps *sg*
papilla [pa'piʎa] *nf* (*de bebé*) baby food
paquete [pa'kete] *nm* (*de cigarrillos etc*) packet; (*Correos etc*) parcel
par [par] *adj* (*igual*) like, equal; (*Mat*) even ▷ *nm* equal; (*de guantes*) pair; (*de veces*) couple; (*Pol*) peer; (*Golf, Com*) par; **abrir de ~ en ~** to open wide
para ['para] *prep* for; **no es ~ comer** it's not for eating; **decir ~ sí** to say to o.s.; **¿~ qué lo quieres?** what do you want it for?; **se casaron ~ separarse otra vez** they married only to separate again; **lo tendré ~ mañana** I'll have it (for) tomorrow; **ir ~ casa** to go home, head for home; **~ profesor es muy estúpido** he's very stupid for a teacher; **¿quién es usted ~ gritar así?** who are you to shout like that?; **tengo bastante ~ vivir** I have enough to live on; *V tb* **con**
parabién [para'βjen] *nm* congratulations *pl*
parábola [pa'raβola] *nf* parable; (*Mat*) parabola; **parabólica** *nf* (*tb*: **antena parábolica**) satellite dish
parabrisas [para'βrisas] *nm inv* windscreen (*BRIT*), windshield (*US*)
paracaídas [paraka'iðas] *nm inv* parachute; **paracaidista** *nmf* parachutist; (*Mil*) paratrooper
parachoques [para'tʃokes] *nm inv*

(*Auto*) bumper; (*Mecánica etc*) shock absorber

parada [pa'raða] *nf* stop; (*acto*) stopping; (*de industria*) shutdown, stoppage; (*lugar*) stopping place; **parada de autobús** bus stop; **parada de taxis** taxi stand *o* rank (BRIT)

paradero [para'ðero] *nm* stopping-place; (*situación*) whereabouts

parado, -a [pa'raðo, a] *adj* (*persona*) motionless, standing still; (*fábrica*) closed, at a standstill; (*coche*) stopped; (LAM: *de pie*) standing (up); (ESP: *sin empleo*) unemployed, idle

paradoja [para'ðoxa] *nf* paradox

parador [para'ðor] *nm* parador, state-run hotel

paragolpes [para'golpes] (RPL) *nm inv* (*Auto*) bumper, fender (US)

paraguas [pa'raɣwas] *nm inv* umbrella

Paraguay [para'ɣwai] *nm* Paraguay; **paraguayo, -a** *adj, nm/f* Paraguayan

paraíso [para'iso] *nm* paradise, heaven

paraje [pa'raxe] *nm* place, spot

paralelo, -a [para'lelo, a] *adj* parallel

parálisis [pa'ralisis] *nf inv* paralysis; **paralítico, -a** *adj, nm/f* paralytic

paralizar [parali'θar] *vt* to paralyse; **paralizarse** *vr* to become paralysed; (*fig*) to come to a standstill

páramo ['paramo] *nm* bleak plateau

paranoico, -a [para'noiko, a] *nm/f* paranoiac

parapente [para'pente] *nm* (*deporte*) paragliding; (*aparato*) paraglider

parapléjico, -a [para'plexiko, a] *adj, nm/f* paraplegic

parar [pa'rar] *vt* to stop; (*golpe*) to ward off ▷ *vi* to stop; **pararse** *vr* to stop; (LAM: *ponerse de pie*) to stand up; **ha parado de llover** it has stopped raining; **van a ir a ~ a comisaría** they're going to end up in the police station; **~se en** to pay attention to

pararrayos [para'rrajos] *nm inv* lightning conductor

parásito, -a [pa'rasito, a] *nm/f* parasite

parcela [par'θela] *nf* plot, piece of ground

parche ['partʃe] *nm* (*gen*) patch

parchís [par'tʃis] *nm* ludo

parcial [par'θjal] *adj* (*pago*) part-; (*eclipse*) partial; (*Jur*) prejudiced, biased; (*Pol*) partisan

parecer [pare'θer] *nm* (*opinión*) opinion, view; (*aspecto*) looks *pl* ▷ *vi* (*tener apariencia*) to seem, look; (*asemejarse*) to look *o* seem like; (*aparecer, llegar*) to appear; **parecerse** *vr* to look alike, resemble each other; **al ~** apparently; **según parece** evidently, apparently; **~se a** to look like, resemble; **me parece que** I think (that), it seems to me that

parecido, -a [pare'θiðo, a] *adj* similar ▷ *nm* similarity, likeness, resemblance; **bien ~** good-looking, nice-looking

pared [pa'reð] *nf* wall

pareja [pa'rexa] *nf* (*par*) pair; (*dos personas*) couple; (*otro: de un par*) other one (of a pair); (*persona*) partner

parentesco [paren'tesko] *nm* relationship

paréntesis [pa'rentesis] *nm inv* parenthesis; (*en escrito*) bracket

parezco *etc vb V* **parecer**

pariente [pa'rjente] *nmf* relative, relation

> No confundir **pariente** con la palabra inglesa *parent*.

parir [pa'rir] *vt* to give birth to ▷ *vi* (*mujer*) to give birth, have a baby

París [pa'ris] *n* Paris

parka ['parka] (LAM) *nf* anorak

parking ['parkin] *nm* car park (BRIT), parking lot (US)

parlamentar [parlamen'tar] *vi* to parley

parlamentario, -a [parlamen'tarjo, a] *adj* parliamentary ▷ *nm/f* member of parliament

parlamento [parla'mento] *nm* parliament
parlanchín, -ina [parlan'tʃin, ina] *adj* indiscreet ▷ *nm/f* chatterbox
parlar [par'lar] *vi* to chatter (away)
paro ['paro] *nm* (*huelga*) stoppage (of work), strike; (*ESP*: *desempleo*) unemployment; (: *subsidio*) unemployment benefit; **estar en ~** (*ESP*) to be unemployed; **paro cardíaco** cardiac arrest
parodia [pa'roðja] *nf* parody; **parodiar** *vt* to parody
parpadear [parpaðe'ar] *vi* (*ojos*) to blink; (*luz*) to flicker
párpado ['parpaðo] *nm* eyelid
parque ['parke] *nm* (*lugar verde*) park; (*MÉX*: *munición*) ammunition; **parque de atracciones** fairground; **parque de bomberos** (*ESP*) fire station; **parque infantil/temático/zoológico** playground/theme park/zoo
parqué [par'ke] *nm* parquet (flooring)
parquímetro [par'kimetro] *nm* parking meter
parra ['parra] *nf* (grape)vine
párrafo ['parrafo] *nm* paragraph; **echar un ~** (*fam*) to have a chat
parranda [pa'rranda] (*fam*) *nf* spree, binge
parrilla [pa'rriʎa] *nf* (*Culin*) grill; (*de coche*) grille; **(carne a la) ~** barbecue; **parrillada** *nf* barbecue
párroco ['parroko] *nm* parish priest
parroquia [pa'rrokja] *nf* parish; (*iglesia*) parish church; (*Com*) clientele, customers *pl*; **parroquiano, -a** *nm/f* parishioner; (*Com*) client, customer
parte ['parte] *nm* message; (*informe*) report ▷ *nf* part; (*lado, cara*) side; (*de reparto*) share; (*Jur*) party; **en alguna ~ de Europa** somewhere in Europe; **en** *o* **por todas ~s** everywhere; **en gran ~** to a large extent; **la mayor ~ de los españoles** most Spaniards; **de un tiempo a esta ~** for some time past; **de ~ de algn** on sb's behalf; **¿de ~ de quién?** (*Tel*) who is speaking?; **por ~ de** on the part of; **yo por mi ~** I for my part; **por otra ~** on the other hand; **dar ~** to inform; **tomar ~** to take part; **parte meteorológico** weather forecast *o* report
participación [partiθipa'θjon] *nf* (*acto*) participation, taking part; (*parte, Com*) share; (*de lotería*) shared prize; (*aviso*) notice, notification
participante [partiθi'pante] *nmf* participant
participar [partiθi'par] *vt* to notify, inform ▷ *vi* to take part, participate
partícipe [par'tiθipe] *nmf* participant
particular [partiku'lar] *adj* (*especial*) particular, special; (*individual, personal*) private, personal ▷ *nm* (*punto, asunto*) particular, point; (*individuo*) individual; **tiene coche ~** he has a car of his own
partida [par'tiða] *nf* (*salida*) departure; (*Com*) entry, item; (*juego*) game; (*grupo de personas*) band, group; **mala ~** dirty trick; **partida de nacimiento/matrimonio/defunción** (*ESP*) birth/marriage/death certificate
partidario, -a [parti'ðarjo, a] *adj* partisan ▷ *nm/f* supporter, follower
partido [par'tiðo] *nm* (*Pol*) party; (*Deporte*) game, match; **sacar ~ de** to profit *o* benefit from; **tomar ~** to take sides
partir [par'tir] *vt* (*dividir*) to split, divide; (*compartir, distribuir*) to share (out), distribute; (*romper*) to break open, split open; (*rebanada*) to cut (off) ▷ *vi* (*ponerse en camino*) to set off *o* out; (*comenzar*) to start (off *o* out); **partirse** *vr* to crack *o* split *o* break (in two *etc*); **a ~ de** (starting) from
partitura [parti'tura] *nf* (*Mús*) score
parto ['parto] *nm* birth; (*fig*) product, creation; **estar de ~** to be in labour
parvulario [parβu'larjo] (*ESP*) *nm* nursery school, kindergarten
pasa ['pasa] *nf* raisin; **pasa de Corinto** currant

pasacintas [pasa'θintas] (LAM) *nm* cassette player
pasada [pa'saða] *nf* passing, passage; **de ~** in passing, incidentally; **una mala ~** a dirty trick
pasadizo [pasa'ðiθo] *nm* (*pasillo*) passage, corridor; (*callejuela*) alley
pasado, -a [pa'saðo, a] *adj* past; (*malo: comida, fruta*) bad; (*muy cocido*) overdone; (*anticuado*) out of date ▷ *nm* past; **~ mañana** the day after tomorrow; **el mes ~** last month
pasador [pasa'ðor] *nm* (*cerrojo*) bolt; (*de pelo*) hair slide; (*horquilla*) grip
pasaje [pa'saxe] *nm* passage; (*pago de viaje*) fare; (*los pasajeros*) passengers *pl*; (*pasillo*) passageway
pasajero, -a [pasa'xero, a] *adj* passing; (*situación, estado*) temporary; (*amor, enfermedad*) brief ▷ *nm/f* passenger
pasamontañas [pasamon'taɲas] *nm inv* balaclava helmet
pasaporte [pasa'porte] *nm* passport
pasar [pa'sar] *vt* to pass; (*tiempo*) to spend; (*desgracias*) to suffer, endure; (*noticia*) to give, pass on; (*río*) to cross; (*barrera*) to pass through; (*falta*) to overlook, tolerate; (*contrincante*) to surpass, do better than; (*coche*) to overtake; (*Cine*) to show; (*enfermedad*) to give, infect with ▷ *vi* (*gen*) to pass; (*terminarse*) to be over; (*ocurrir*) to happen; **pasarse** *vr* (*flores*) to fade; (*comida*) to go bad *o* off; (*fig*) to overdo it, go too far; **~ de** to go beyond, exceed; **~ por** (LAM) to fetch; **~lo bien/mal** to have a good/bad time; **¡pase!** come in!; **hacer ~** to show in; **lo que pasa es que ...** the thing is ...; **~se al enemigo** to go over to the enemy; **se me pasó** I forgot; **no se le pasa nada** he misses nothing; **pase lo que pase** come what may; **¿qué pasa?** what's going on?, what's up?; **¿qué te pasa?** what's wrong?
pasarela [pasa'rela] *nf* footbridge; (*en barco*) gangway
pasatiempo [pasa'tjempo] *nm* pastime, hobby
Pascua ['paskwa] *nf* (*en Semana Santa*) Easter; **Pascuas** *nfpl* Christmas (time); **¡felices ~s!** Merry Christmas!
pase ['pase] *nm* pass; (*Cine*) performance, showing
pasear [pase'ar] *vt* to take for a walk; (*exhibir*) to parade, show off ▷ *vi* to walk, go for a walk; **pasearse** *vr* to walk, go for a walk; **~ en coche** to go for a drive; **paseo** *nm* (*avenida*) avenue; (*distancia corta*) walk, stroll; **dar un** *o* **ir de paseo** to go for a walk; **paseo marítimo** (ESP) promenade
pasillo [pa'siʎo] *nm* passage, corridor
pasión [pa'sjon] *nf* passion
pasivo, -a [pa'siβo, a] *adj* passive; (*inactivo*) inactive ▷ *nm* (*Com*) liabilities *pl*, debts *pl*
pasmoso, -a [pas'moso, a] *adj* amazing, astonishing
paso, -a ['paso, a] *adj* dried ▷ *nm* step; (*modo de andar*) walk; (*huella*) footprint; (*rapidez*) speed, pace, rate; (*camino accesible*) way through, passage; (*cruce*) crossing; (*pasaje*) passing, passage; (*Geo*) pass; (*estrecho*) strait; **a ese ~** (*fig*) at that rate; **salir al ~ de** *o* **a** to waylay; **estar de ~** to be passing through; **prohibido el ~** no entry; **ceda el ~** give way; **paso a nivel** (*Ferro*) level-crossing; **paso (de) cebra** (ESP) zebra crossing; **paso de peatones** pedestrian crossing; **paso elevado** flyover
pasota [pa'sota] (ESP: *fam*) *adj, nmf* ≈ dropout; **ser un ~** to be a bit of a dropout; (*ser indiferente*) not to care about anything
pasta ['pasta] *nf* paste; (*Culin: masa*) dough; (*: de bizcochos etc*) pastry; (*fam*) dough; **pastas** *nfpl* (*bizcochos*) pastries, small cakes; (*fideos, espaguetis etc*) pasta; **pasta dentífrica** *o* **de dientes** toothpaste
pastar [pas'tar] *vt, vi* to graze
pastel [pas'tel] *nm* (*dulce*) cake; (*Arte*)

pastel; **pastel de carne** meat pie; **pastelería** *nf* cake shop
pastilla [pas'tiʎa] *nf* (*de jabón, chocolate*) bar; (*píldora*) tablet, pill
pasto ['pasto] *nm* (*hierba*) grass; (*lugar*) pasture, field; **pastor, a** [pas'tor, a] *nm/f* shepherd/ess ▷ *nm* (*Rel*) clergyman, pastor; **pastor alemán** Alsatian
pata ['pata] *nf* (*pierna*) leg; (*pie*) foot; (*de muebles*) leg; **~s arriba** upside down; **metedura de ~** (*fam*) gaffe; **meter la ~** (*fam*) to put one's foot in it; **tener buena/mala ~** to be lucky/unlucky; **pata de cabra** (*Tec*) crowbar; **patada** *nf* kick; (*en el suelo*) stamp
patata [pa'tata] *nf* potato; **patatas fritas** chips, French fries; (*de bolsa*) crisps
paté [pa'te] *nm* pâté
patente [pa'tente] *adj* obvious, evident; (*Com*) patent ▷ *nf* patent
paternal [pater'nal] *adj* fatherly, paternal; **paterno, -a** *adj* paternal
patético, -a [pa'tetiko, a] *adj* pathetic, moving
patilla [pa'tiʎa] *nf* (*de gafas*) side(piece); **patillas** *nfpl* sideburns
patín [pa'tin] *nm* skate; (*de trineo*) runner; **patín de ruedas** roller skate; **patinaje** *nm* skating; **patinar** *vi* to skate; (*resbalarse*) to skid, slip; (*fam*) to slip up, blunder
patineta [pati'neta] *nf* (MÉX: *patinete*) scooter; (CS: *monopatín*) skateboard
patinete [pati'nete] *nm* scooter
patio ['patjo] *nm* (*de casa*) patio, courtyard; **patio de recreo** playground
pato ['pato] *nm* duck; **pagar el ~** (*fam*) to take the blame, carry the can
patoso, -a [pa'toso, a] (*fam*) *adj* clumsy
patotero [pato'tero] (CS) *nm* hooligan, lout
patraña [pa'traɲa] *nf* story, fib
patria ['patrja] *nf* native land, mother country
patrimonio [patri'monjo] *nm* inheritance; (*fig*) heritage
patriota [pa'trjota] *nmf* patriot
patrocinar [patroθi'nar] *vt* to sponsor
patrón, -ona [pa'tron, ona] *nm/f* (*jefe*) boss, chief, master(mistress); (*propietario*) landlord/lady; (*Rel*) patron saint ▷ *nm* (*Tec, Costura*) pattern
patronato [patro'nato] *nm* sponsorship; (*acto*) patronage; (*fundación benéfica*) trust, foundation
patrulla [pa'truʎa] *nf* patrol
pausa ['pausa] *nf* pause, break
pauta ['pauta] *nf* line, guide line
pava ['paβa] (RPL) *nf* kettle
pavimento [paβi'mento] *nm* (*de losa*) pavement, paving
pavo ['paβo] *nm* turkey; **pavo real** peacock
payaso, -a [pa'jaso, a] *nm/f* clown
payo, -a ['pajo, a] *nm/f* non-gipsy
paz [paθ] *nf* peace; (*tranquilidad*) peacefulness, tranquillity; **hacer las paces** to make peace; (*fig*) to make up; **¡déjame en ~!** leave me alone!
PC *nm* PC, personal computer
P.D. *abr* (= *posdata*) P.S., p.s.
peaje [pe'axe] *nm* toll
peatón [pea'ton] *nm* pedestrian; **peatonal** *adj* pedestrian
peca ['peka] *nf* freckle
pecado [pe'kaðo] *nm* sin; **pecador, a** *adj* sinful ▷ *nm/f* sinner
pecaminoso, -a [pekami'noso, a] *adj* sinful
pecar [pe'kar] *vi* (*Rel*) to sin; **peca de generoso** he is generous to a fault
pecera [pe'θera] *nf* fish tank; (*redonda*) goldfish bowl
pecho ['petʃo] *nm* (*Anat*) chest; (*de mujer*) breast; **dar el ~ a** to breast-feed; **tomar algo a ~** to take sth to heart
pechuga [pe'tʃuɣa] *nf* breast
peculiar [peku'ljar] *adj* special, peculiar; (*característico*) typical, characteristic
pedal [pe'ðal] *nm* pedal; **pedalear** *vi* to pedal

pedante [pe'ðante] *adj* pedantic ▷*nmf* pedant
pedazo [pe'ðaθo] *nm* piece, bit; **hacerse ~s** to smash, shatter
pediatra [pe'ðjatra] *nmf* paediatrician
pedido [pe'ðiðo] *nm* (*Com*) order; (*petición*) request
pedir [pe'ðir] *vt* to ask for, request; (*comida, Com: mandar*) to order; (*necesitar*) to need, demand, require ▷*vi* to ask; **me pidió que cerrara la puerta** he asked me to shut the door; **¿cuánto piden por el coche?** how much are they asking for the car?
pedo ['peðo] (*fam!*) *nm* fart
pega ['peɣa] *nf* snag; **poner ~s (a)** to complain (about)
pegadizo, -a [peɣa'ðiθo, a] *adj* (*Mús*) catchy
pegajoso, -a [peɣa'xoso, a] *adj* sticky, adhesive
pegamento [peɣa'mento] *nm* gum, glue
pegar [pe'ɣar] *vt* (*papel, sellos*) to stick (on); (*cartel*) to stick up; (*coser*) to sew (on); (*unir: partes*) to join, fix together; (*Comput*) to paste; (*Med*) to give, infect with; (*dar: golpe*) to give, deal ▷*vi* (*adherirse*) to stick, adhere; (*ir juntos: colores*) to match, go together; (*golpear*) to hit; (*quemar: el sol*) to strike hot, burn; **pegarse** *vr* (*gen*) to stick; (*dos personas*) to hit each other, fight; (*fam*): **~ un grito** to let out a yell; **~ un salto** to jump (with fright); **~ en** to touch; **~se un tiro** to shoot o.s.
pegatina [peɣa'tina] *nf* sticker
pegote [pe'ɣote] (*fam*) *nm* eyesore, sight
peinado [pei'naðo] *nm* hairstyle
peinar [pei'nar] *vt* to comb; (*hacer estilo*) to style; **peinarse** *vr* to comb one's hair
peine ['peine] *nm* comb; **peineta** *nf* ornamental comb
p.ej. *abr* (= *por ejemplo*) e.g.
Pekín [pe'kin] *n* Pekin(g)
pelado, -a [pe'laðo, a] *adj* (*fruta, patata etc*) peeled; (*cabeza*) shorn; (*campo, fig*) bare; (*fam: sin dinero*) broke
pelar [pe'lar] *vt* (*fruta, patatas etc*) to peel; (*cortar el pelo a*) to cut the hair of; (*quitar la piel: animal*) to skin; **pelarse** *vr* (*la piel*) to peel off; **voy a ~me** I'm going to get my hair cut
peldaño [pel'daɲo] *nm* step
pelea [pe'lea] *nf* (*lucha*) fight; (*discusión*) quarrel, row; **peleado, -a** [pele'aðo, a] *adj*: **estar peleado (con algn)** to have fallen out (with sb); **pelear** [pele'ar] *vi* to fight; **pelearse** *vr* to fight; (*reñirse*) to fall out, quarrel
pelela [pe'lela] (cs) *nf* potty
peletería [pelete'ria] *nf* furrier's, fur shop
pelícano [pe'likano] *nm* pelican
película [pe'likula] *nf* film; (*cobertura ligera*) thin covering; (*Foto: rollo*) roll *o* reel of film; **película de dibujos (animados)/del oeste** cartoon/ western
peligro [pe'liɣro] *nm* danger; (*riesgo*) risk; **correr ~ de** to run the risk of; **peligroso, -a** *adj* dangerous; risky
pelirrojo, -a [peli'rroxo, a] *adj* red-haired, red-headed ▷*nm/f* redhead
pellejo [pe'ʎexo] *nm* (*de animal*) skin, hide
pellizcar [peʎiθ'kar] *vt* to pinch, nip
pelma ['pelma] (ESP: *fam*) *nmf* pain (in the neck)
pelmazo [pel'maθo] (*fam*) *nm* = **pelma**
pelo ['pelo] *nm* (*cabellos*) hair; (*de barba, bigote*) whisker; (*de animal: pellejo*) hair, fur, coat; **venir al ~** to be exactly what one needs; **un hombre de ~ en pecho** a brave man; **por los ~s** by the skin of one's teeth; **no tener ~s en la lengua** to be outspoken, not to mince one's words; **con ~s y señales** in minute detail; **tomar el ~ a algn** to pull sb's leg
pelota [pe'lota] *nf* ball; **en ~** stark naked; **hacer la ~ (a algn)** (ESP: *fam*) to

creep (to sb); **pelota vasca** pelota
pelotón [pelo'ton] *nm* (*Mil*) squad, detachment
peluca [pe'luka] *nf* wig
peluche [pe'lutʃe] *nm*: **oso/muñeco de ~** teddy bear/soft toy
peludo, -a [pe'luðo, a] *adj* hairy, shaggy
peluquería [peluke'ria] *nf* hairdresser's; **peluquero, -a** *nm/f* hairdresser
pelusa [pe'lusa] *nf* (*Bot*) down; (*en tela*) fluff
pena ['pena] *nf* (*congoja*) grief, sadness; (*remordimiento*) regret; (*dificultad*) trouble; (*dolor*) pain; (*Jur*) sentence; **merecer** *o* **valer la ~** to be worthwhile; **a duras ~s** with great difficulty; **¡qué ~!** what a shame!; **pena capital** capital punishment; **pena de muerte** death penalty
penal [pe'nal] *adj* penal ▷ *nm* (*cárcel*) prison
penalidad [penali'ðað] *nf* (*problema, dificultad*) trouble, hardship; (*Jur*) penalty, punishment; **penalidades** *nfpl* trouble *sg*, hardship *sg*
penalti [pe'nalti] *nm* = **penalty**
penalty [pe'nalti] (*pl* **~s** *o* **penalties**) *nm* penalty (kick)
pendiente [pen'djente] *adj* pending, unsettled ▷ *nm* earring ▷ *nf* hill, slope
pene ['pene] *nm* penis
penetrante [pene'trante] *adj* (*herida*) deep; (*persona, arma*) sharp; (*sonido*) penetrating, piercing; (*mirada*) searching; (*viento, ironía*) biting
penetrar [pene'trar] *vt* to penetrate, pierce; (*entender*) to grasp ▷ *vi* to penetrate, go in; (*entrar*) to enter, go in; (*líquido*) to soak in; (*fig*) to pierce
penicilina [peniθi'lina] *nf* penicillin
península [pe'ninsula] *nf* peninsula; **peninsular** *adj* peninsular
penique [pe'nike] *nm* penny
penitencia [peni'tenθja] *nf* penance
penoso, -a [pe'noso, a] *adj* (*lamentable*) distressing; (*difícil*) arduous, difficult
pensador, a [pensa'ðor, a] *nm/f* thinker
pensamiento [pensa'mjento] *nm* thought; (*mente*) mind; (*idea*) idea
pensar [pen'sar] *vt* to think; (*considerar*) to think over, think out; (*proponerse*) to intend, plan; (*imaginarse*) to think up, invent ▷ *vi* to think; **~ en** to aim at, aspire to; **pensativo, -a** *adj* thoughtful, pensive
pensión [pen'sjòn] *nf* (*casa*) boarding *o* guest house; (*dinero*) pension; (*cama y comida*) board and lodging; **media ~** half-board; **pensión completa** full board; **pensionista** *nmf* (*jubilado*) (old-age) pensioner; (*huésped*) lodger
penúltimo, -a [pe'nultimo, a] *adj* penultimate, last but one
penumbra [pe'numbra] *nf* half-light
peña ['peɲa] *nf* (*roca*) rock; (*cuesta*) cliff, crag; (*grupo*) group, circle; (*LAM*: *club*) folk club
peñasco [pe'ɲasco] *nm* large rock, boulder
peñón [pe'ɲon] *nm* wall of rock; **el P~** the Rock (of Gibraltar)
peón [pe'on] *nm* labourer; (*LAM Agr*) farm labourer, farmhand; (*Ajedrez*) pawn
peonza [pe'onθa] *nf* spinning top
peor [pe'or] *adj* (*comparativo*) worse; (*superlativo*) worst ▷ *adv* worse; worst; **de mal en ~** from bad to worse
pepinillo [pepi'niʎo] *nm* gherkin
pepino [pe'pino] *nm* cucumber; **(no) me importa un ~** I don't care one bit
pepita [pe'pita] *nf* (*Bot*) pip; (*Minería*) nugget
pepito [pe'pito] (*ESP*) *nm* (*tb*: **~ de ternera**) steak sandwich
pequeño, -a [pe'keɲo, a] *adj* small, little
pera ['pera] *nf* pear; **peral** *nm* pear tree
percance [per'kanθe] *nm* setback, misfortune
percatarse [perka'tarse] *vr*: **~ de** to

notice, take note of
percebe [per'θeβe] *nm* barnacle
percepción [perθep'θjon] *nf* (*vista*) perception; (*idea*) notion, idea
percha ['pertʃa] *nf* (coat)hanger; (*ganchos*) coat hooks *pl*; (*de ave*) perch
percibir [perθi'βir] *vt* to perceive, notice; (*Com*) to earn, get
percusión [perku'sjon] *nf* percussion
perdedor, a [perðe'ðor, a] *adj* losing ▷ *nm/f* loser
perder [per'ðer] *vt* to lose; (*tiempo, palabras*) to waste; (*oportunidad*) to lose, miss; (*tren*) to miss ▷ *vi* to lose; **perderse** *vr* (*extraviarse*) to get lost; (*desaparecer*) to disappear, be lost to view; (*arruinarse*) to be ruined; **echar a ~** (*comida*) to spoil, ruin; (*oportunidad*) to waste
pérdida ['perðiða] *nf* loss; (*de tiempo*) waste; **pérdidas** *nfpl* (*Com*) losses
perdido, -a [per'ðiðo, a] *adj* lost
perdiz [per'ðiθ] *nf* partridge
perdón [per'ðon] *nm* (*disculpa*) pardon, forgiveness; (*clemencia*) mercy; **¡~!** sorry!, I beg your pardon!; **perdonar** *vt* to pardon, forgive; (*la vida*) to spare; (*excusar*) to exempt, excuse; **¡perdone (usted)!** sorry!, I beg your pardon!
perecedero, -a [pereθe'ðero, a] *adj* perishable
perecer [pere'θer] *vi* to perish, die
peregrinación [pereɣrina'θjon] *nf* (*Rel*) pilgrimage
peregrino, -a [pere'ɣrino, a] *adj* (*idea*) strange, absurd ▷ *nm/f* pilgrim
perejil [pere'xil] *nm* parsley
perenne [pe'renne] *adj* everlasting, perennial
pereza [pe'reθa] *nf* laziness, idleness; **perezoso, -a** *adj* lazy, idle
perfección [perfek'θjon] *nf* perfection; **perfeccionar** *vt* to perfect; (*mejorar*) to improve; (*acabar*) to complete, finish
perfecto, -a [per'fekto, a] *adj* perfect; (*total*) complete
perfil [per'fil] *nm* profile; (*contorno*) silhouette, outline; (*Arq*) (cross) section; **perfiles** *nmpl* features
perforación [perfora'θjon] *nf* perforation; (*con taladro*) drilling; **perforadora** *nf* punch
perforar [perfo'rar] *vt* to perforate; (*agujero*) to drill, bore; (*papel*) to punch a hole in ▷ *vi* to drill, bore
perfume [per'fume] *nm* perfume, scent
periferia [peri'ferja] *nf* periphery; (*de ciudad*) outskirts *pl*
periférico [peri'feriko] (LAM) *nm* ring road (BRIT), beltway (US)
perilla [pe'riʎa] *nf* (*barba*) goatee; (LAM: *de puerta*) doorknob, door handle
perímetro [pe'rimetro] *nm* perimeter
periódico, -a [pe'rjoðiko, a] *adj* periodic(al) ▷ *nm* newspaper
periodismo [perjo'ðismo] *nm* journalism; **periodista** *nmf* journalist
periodo [pe'rjoðo] *nm* period
período [pe'rioðo] *nm* = **periodo**
periquito [peri'kito] *nm* budgerigar, budgie
perito, -a [pe'rito, a] *adj* (*experto*) expert; (*diestro*) skilled, skilful ▷ *nm/f* expert; skilled worker; (*técnico*) technician
perjudicar [perxuði'kar] *vt* (*gen*) to damage, harm; **perjudicial** *adj* damaging, harmful; (*en detrimento*) detrimental; **perjuicio** *nm* damage, harm
perjurar [perxu'rar] *vi* to commit perjury
perla ['perla] *nf* pearl; **me viene de ~s** it suits me fine
permanecer [permane'θer] *vi* (*quedarse*) to stay, remain; (*seguir*) to continue to be
permanente [perma'nente] *adj* permanent, constant ▷ *nf* perm
permiso [per'miso] *nm* permission; (*licencia*) permit, licence; **con ~** excuse me; **estar de ~** (*Mil*) to be on leave;

permiso de conducir driving licence (BRIT), driver's license (US); **permiso por enfermedad** (LAM) sick leave
permitir [permi'tir] *vt* to permit, allow
pernera [per'nera] *nf* trouser leg
pero ['pero] *conj* but; (*aún*) yet ▷ *nm* (*defecto*) flaw, defect; (*reparo*) objection
perpendicular [perpendiku'lar] *adj* perpendicular
perpetuo, -a [per'petwo, a] *adj* perpetual
perplejo, -a [per'plexo, a] *adj* perplexed, bewildered
perra ['perra] *nf* (*Zool*) bitch; **estar sin una ~** (ESP: *fam*) to be flat broke
perrera [pe'rrera] *nf* kennel
perrito [pe'rrito] *nm* (*tb*: **~ caliente**) hot dog
perro ['perro] *nm* dog
persa ['persa] *adj, nmf* Persian
persecución [perseku'θjon] *nf* pursuit, chase; (*Rel, Pol*) persecution
perseguir [perse'ɣir] *vt* to pursue, hunt; (*cortejar*) to chase after; (*molestar*) to pester, annoy; (*Rel, Pol*) to persecute
persiana [per'sjana] *nf* (Venetian) blind
persistente [persis'tente] *adj* persistent
persistir [persis'tir] *vi* to persist
persona [per'sona] *nf* person; **persona mayor** elderly person
personaje [perso'naxe] *nm* important person, celebrity; (*Teatro etc*) character
personal [perso'nal] *adj* (*particular*) personal; (*para una persona*) single, for one person ▷ *nm* personnel, staff; **personalidad** *nf* personality
personarse [perso'narse] *vr* to appear in person
personificar [personifi'kar] *vt* to personify
perspectiva [perspek'tiβa] *nf* perspective; (*vista, panorama*) view, panorama; (*posibilidad futura*) outlook, prospect
persuadir [perswa'ðir] *vt* (*gen*) to persuade; (*convencer*) to convince; **persuadirse** *vr* to become convinced; **persuasión** *nf* persuasion
pertenecer [pertene'θer] *vi* to belong; (*fig*) to concern; **perteneciente** *adj*: **perteneciente a** belonging to; **pertenencia** *nf* ownership; **pertenencias** *nfpl* (*bienes*) possessions, property *sg*
pertenezca *etc vb V* **pertenecer**
pértiga ['pertiɣa] *nf*: **salto de ~** pole vault
pertinente [perti'nente] *adj* relevant, pertinent; (*apropiado*) appropriate; **~ a** concerning, relevant to
perturbación [perturβa'θjon] *nf* (*Pol*) disturbance; (*Med*) upset, disturbance
Perú [pe'ru] *nm* Peru; **peruano, -a** *adj, nm/f* Peruvian
perversión [perβer'sjon] *nf* perversion; **perverso, -a** *adj* perverse; (*depravado*) depraved
pervertido, -a [perβer'tiðo, a] *adj* perverted ▷ *nm/f* pervert
pervertir [perβer'tir] *vt* to pervert, corrupt
pesa ['pesa] *nf* weight; (*Deporte*) shot
pesadez [pesa'ðeθ] *nf* (*peso*) heaviness; (*lentitud*) slowness; (*aburrimiento*) tediousness
pesadilla [pesa'ðiʎa] *nf* nightmare, bad dream
pesado, -a [pe'saðo, a] *adj* heavy; (*lento*) slow; (*difícil, duro*) tough, hard; (*aburrido*) boring, tedious; (*tiempo*) sultry
pésame ['pesame] *nm* expression of condolence, message of sympathy; **dar el ~** to express one's condolences
pesar [pe'sar] *vt* to weigh ▷ *vi* to weigh; (*ser pesado*) to weigh a lot, be heavy; (*fig: opinión*) to carry weight; **no pesa mucho** it's not very heavy ▷ *nm* (*arrepentimiento*) regret; (*pena*) grief, sorrow; **a ~ de** *o* **pese a (que)** in spite

of, despite

pesca ['peska] *nf* (*acto*) fishing; (*lo pescado*) catch; **ir de ~** to go fishing

pescadería [peskaðe'ria] *nf* fish shop, fishmonger's (*BRIT*)

pescadilla [peska'ðiʎa] *nf* whiting

pescado [pes'kaðo] *nm* fish

pescador, a [peska'ðor, a] *nm/f* fisherman/woman

pescar [pes'kar] *vt* (*tomar*) to catch; (*intentar tomar*) to fish for; (*conseguir: trabajo*) to manage to get ▷ *vi* to fish, go fishing

pesebre [pe'seβre] *nm* manger

peseta [pe'seta] *nf* (*Hist*) peseta

pesimista [pesi'mista] *adj* pessimistic ▷ *nmf* pessimist

pésimo, -a ['pesimo, a] *adj* awful, dreadful

peso ['peso] *nm* weight; (*balanza*) scales *pl*; (*moneda*) peso; **vender al ~** to sell by weight; **peso bruto/neto** gross/net weight; **peso pesado/pluma** heavyweight/featherweight

pesquero, -a [pes'kero, a] *adj* fishing *cpd*

pestaña [pes'taɲa] *nf* (*Anat*) eyelash; (*borde*) rim

peste ['peste] *nf* plague; (*mal olor*) stink, stench

pesticida [pesti'θiða] *nm* pesticide

pestillo [pes'tiʎo] *nm* (*cerrojo*) bolt; (*picaporte*) door handle

petaca [pe'taka] *nf* (*de cigarros*) cigarette case; (*de pipa*) tobacco pouch; (*MÉX: maleta*) suitcase

pétalo ['petalo] *nm* petal

petardo [pe'tardo] *nm* firework, firecracker

petición [peti'θjon] *nf* (*pedido*) request, plea; (*memorial*) petition; (*Jur*) plea

peto ['peto] (*ESP*) *nm* dungarees *pl*, overalls *pl* (*US*)

petróleo [pe'troleo] *nm* oil, petroleum; **petrolero, -a** *adj* petroleum *cpd* ▷ *nm* (oil) tanker

peyorativo, -a [pejora'tiβo, a] *adj* pejorative

pez [peθ] *nm* fish; **pez espada** swordfish

pezón [pe'θon] *nm* teat, nipple

pezuña [pe'θuɲa] *nf* hoof

pianista [pja'nista] *nmf* pianist

piano ['pjano] *nm* piano

piar [pjar] *vi* to cheep

pibe, -a ['piβe, a] (*RPL*) *nm/f* boy/girl

picadero [pika'ðero] *nm* riding school

picadillo [pika'ðiʎo] *nm* mince, minced meat

picado, -a [pi'kaðo, a] *adj* pricked, punctured; (*Culin*) minced, chopped; (*mar*) choppy; (*diente*) bad; (*tabaco*) cut; (*enfadado*) cross

picador [pika'ðor] *nm* (*Taur*) picador; (*minero*) faceworker

picadura [pika'ðura] *nf* (*pinchazo*) puncture; (*de abeja*) sting; (*de mosquito*) bite; (*tabaco picado*) cut tobacco

picante [pi'kante] *adj* hot; (*comentario*) racy, spicy

picaporte [pika'porte] *nm* (*manija*) doorhandle; (*pestillo*) latch

picar [pi'kar] *vt* (*agujerear, perforar*) to prick, puncture; (*abeja*) to sting; (*mosquito, serpiente*) to bite; (*Culin*) to mince, chop; (*incitar*) to incite, goad; (*dañar, irritar*) to annoy, bother; (*quemar: lengua*) to burn, sting ▷ *vi* (*pez*) to bite, take the bait; (*sol*) to burn, scorch; (*abeja, Med*) to sting; (*mosquito*) to bite; **picarse** *vr* (*agriarse*) to turn sour, go off; (*ofenderse*) to take offence

picardía [pikar'ðia] *nf* villainy; (*astucia*) slyness, craftiness; (*una picardía*) dirty trick; (*palabra*) rude/bad word *o* expression

pícaro, -a ['pikaro, a] *adj* (*malicioso*) villainous; (*travieso*) mischievous ▷ *nm* (*astuto*) crafty sort; (*sinvergüenza*) rascal, scoundrel

pichi ['pitʃi] (*ESP*) *nm* pinafore dress (*BRIT*), jumper (*US*)

pichón [pi'tʃon] *nm* young pigeon

pico ['piko] *nm* (*de ave*) beak; (*punta*)

sharp point; (*Tec*) pick, pickaxe; (*Geo*) peak, summit; **y ~** and a bit; **las seis y ~** six and a bit

picor [pi'kor] *nm* itch

picoso, -a [pi'koso, a] (*MÉX*) *adj* (*comida*) hot

picudo, -a [pi'kuðo, a] *adj* pointed, with a point

pidió *etc vb V* **pedir**

pido *etc vb V* **pedir**

pie [pje] (*pl* **~s**) *nm* foot; (*fig*: *motivo*) motive, basis; (: *fundamento*) foothold; **ir a ~** to go on foot, walk; **estar de ~** to be standing (up); **ponerse de ~** to stand up; **de ~s a cabeza** from top to bottom; **al ~ de la letra** (*citar*) literally, verbatim; (*copiar*) exactly, word for word; **en ~ de guerra** on a war footing; **dar ~ a** to give cause for; **hacer ~** (*en el agua*) to touch (the) bottom

piedad [pje'ðað] *nf* (*lástima*) pity, compassion; (*clemencia*) mercy; (*devoción*) piety, devotion

piedra ['pjeðra] *nf* stone; (*roca*) rock; (*de mechero*) flint; (*Meteorología*) hailstone; **piedra preciosa** precious stone

piel [pjel] *nf* (*Anat*) skin; (*Zool*) skin, hide, fur; (*cuero*) leather; (*Bot*) skin, peel

pienso *etc vb V* **pensar**

pierdo *etc vb V* **perder**

pierna ['pjerna] *nf* leg

pieza ['pjeθa] *nf* piece; (*habitación*) room; **pieza de recambio** *o* **repuesto** spare (part)

pigmeo, -a [piɣ'meo, a] *adj, nm/f* pigmy

pijama [pi'xama] *nm* pyjamas *pl* (*BRIT*), pajamas *pl* (*US*)

pila ['pila] *nf* (*Elec*) battery; (*montón*) heap, pile; (*lavabo*) sink

píldora ['pildora] *nf* pill; **la ~ (anticonceptiva)** the (contraceptive) pill

pileta [pi'leta] (*RPL*) *nf* (*fregadero*) (kitchen) sink; (*piscina*) swimming pool

pillar [pi'ʎar] *vt* (*saquear*) to pillage, plunder; (*fam*: *coger*) to catch; (: *agarrar*) to grasp, seize; (: *entender*) to grasp, catch on to; **pillarse** *vr*: **~se un dedo con la puerta** to catch one's finger in the door

pillo, -a ['piʎo, a] *adj* villainous; (*astuto*) sly, crafty ▷ *nm/f* rascal, rogue, scoundrel

piloto [pi'loto] *nm* pilot; (*de aparato*) (pilot) light; (*Auto*: *luz*) tail *o* rear light; (: *conductor*) driver; **piloto automático** automatic pilot

pimentón [pimen'ton] *nm* paprika

pimienta [pi'mjenta] *nf* pepper

pimiento [pi'mjento] *nm* pepper, pimiento

pin [pin] (*pl* **~s**) *nm* badge

pinacoteca [pinako'teka] *nf* art gallery

pinar [pi'nar] *nm* pine forest (*BRIT*), pine grove (*US*)

pincel [pin'θel] *nm* paintbrush

pinchadiscos [pintʃa'ðiskos] (*ESP*) *nmf inv* disc-jockey, DJ

pinchar [pin'tʃar] *vt* (*perforar*) to prick, pierce; (*neumático*) to puncture; (*fig*) to prod; (*Inform*) to click

pinchazo [pin'tʃaθo] *nm* (*perforación*) prick; (*de neumático*) puncture; (*fig*) prod

pincho ['pintʃo] *nm* savoury (snack); **pincho de tortilla** small slice of omelette; **pincho moruno** shish kebab

ping-pong ['pin'pon] *nm* table tennis

pingüino [pin'gwino] *nm* penguin

pino ['pino] *nm* pine (tree)

pinta ['pinta] *nf* spot; (*de líquidos*) spot, drop; (*aspecto*) appearance, look(s) (*pl*); **pintado, -a** *adj* spotted; (*de colores*) colourful; **pintadas** *nfpl* graffiti *sg*

pintalabios [pinta'laβjos] (*ESP*) *nm inv* lipstick

pintar [pin'tar] *vt* to paint ▷ *vi* to paint; (*fam*) to count, be important; **pintarse** *vr* to put on make-up

pintor, a [pin'tor, a] *nm/f* painter

pintoresco, -a [pinto'resko, a] *adj* picturesque

pintura [pin'tura] *nf* painting; **pintura al óleo** oil painting
pinza ['pinθa] *nf* (*Zool*) claw; (*para colgar ropa*) clothes peg; (*Tec*) pincers *pl*; **pinzas** *nfpl* (*para depilar etc*) tweezers *pl*
piña ['piɲa] *nf* (*de pino*) pine cone; (*fruta*) pineapple; (*fig*) group
piñata [pi'ɲata] *nf* *container hung up at parties to be beaten with sticks until sweets or presents fall out*

PIÑATA

Piñata is a very popular party game in Mexico. The **piñata** itself is a hollow figure made of papier maché, or, traditionally, from adobe, in the shape of an object, a star, a person or an animal. It is filled with either sweets and toys, or fruit and yam beans. The game consists of hanging the **piñata** from the ceiling, and beating it with a stick, blindfolded, until it breaks and the presents fall out.

piñón [pi'ɲon] *nm* (*fruto*) pine nut; (*Tec*) pinion
pío, -a ['pio, a] *adj* (*devoto*) pious, devout; (*misericordioso*) merciful
piojo ['pjoxo] *nm* louse
pipa ['pipa] *nf* pipe; **pipas** *nfpl* (*Bot*) (edible) sunflower seeds
pipí [pi'pi] (*fam*) *nm*: **hacer ~** to have a wee(-wee) (BRIT), have to go (wee-wee) (US)
pique ['pike] *nm* (*resentimiento*) pique, resentment; (*rivalidad*) rivalry, competition; **irse a ~** to sink; (*esperanza, familia*) to be ruined
piqueta [pi'keta] *nf* pick(axe)
piquete [pi'kete] *nm* (*Mil*) squad, party; (*de obreros*) picket; (MÉX: *de insecto*) bite; **piquetear** (LAM) *vt* to picket
pirado, -a [pi'raðo, a] (*fam*) *adj* round the bend ▷ *nm/f* nutter
piragua [pi'raɣwa] *nf* canoe; **piragüismo** *nm* canoeing
pirámide [pi'ramiðe] *nf* pyramid
pirata [pi'rata] *adj, nmf* pirate; **pirata informático** hacker
Pirineo(s) [piri'neo(s)] *nm(pl)* Pyrenees *pl*
pirómano, -a [pi'romano, a] *nm/f* (*Med, Jur*) arsonist
piropo [pi'ropo] *nm* compliment, (piece of) flattery
pirueta [pi'rweta] *nf* pirouette
piruleta [piru'leta] (ESP) *nf* lollipop
pis [pis] (*fam*) *nm* pee, piss; **hacer ~** to have a pee; (*para niños*) to wee-wee
pisada [pi'saða] *nf* (*paso*) footstep; (*huella*) footprint
pisar [pi'sar] *vt* (*caminar sobre*) to walk on, tread on; (*apretar con el pie*) to press; (*fig*) to trample on, walk all over ▷ *vi* to tread, step, walk
piscina [pis'θina] *nf* swimming pool
Piscis ['pisθis] *nm* Pisces
piso ['piso] *nm* (*suelo, planta*) floor; (ESP: *apartamento*) flat (BRIT), apartment; **primer ~** (ESP) first floor; (LAM: *planta baja*) ground floor
pisotear [pisote'ar] *vt* to trample (on *o* underfoot)
pista ['pista] *nf* track, trail; (*indicio*) clue; **pista de aterrizaje** runway; **pista de baile** dance floor; **pista de hielo** ice rink; **pista de tenis** (ESP) tennis court
pistola [pis'tola] *nf* pistol; (*Tec*) spray-gun
pistón [pis'ton] *nm* (*Tec*) piston; (*Mús*) key
pitar [pi'tar] *vt* (*silbato*) to blow; (*rechiflar*) to whistle at, boo ▷ *vi* to whistle; (*Auto*) to sound *o* toot one's horn; (LAM: *fumar*) to smoke
pitillo [pi'tiʎo] *nm* cigarette
pito ['pito] *nm* whistle; (*de coche*) horn
pitón [pi'ton] *nm* (*Zool*) python
pitonisa [pito'nisa] *nf* fortune-teller
pitorreo [pito'rreo] *nm* joke; **estar de ~** to be joking
píxel ['piksel] (*pl* **pixels** *or* **~es**) *nm*

pixel

piyama [pi'jama] (LAM) *nm* pyjamas *pl* (BRIT), pajamas *pl* (US)

pizarra [pi'θarra] *nf* (*piedra*) slate; (ESP: *encerado*) blackboard; **pizarra blanca** whiteboard; **pizarra interactiva** interactive whiteboard

pizarrón [piθa'rron] (LAM) *nm* blackboard

pizca ['piθka] *nf* pinch, spot; (*fig*) spot, speck; **ni ~** not a bit

placa ['plaka] *nf* plate; (*distintivo*) badge, insignia; **placa de matrícula** (LAM) number plate

placard [pla'kar] (RPL) *nm* cupboard

placer [pla'θer] *nm* pleasure ▷ *vt* to please

plaga ['plaɣa] *nf* pest; (*Med*) plague; (*abundancia*) abundance

plagio ['plaxjo] *nm* plagiarism

plan [plan] *nm* (*esquema, proyecto*) plan; (*idea, intento*) idea, intention; **tener ~** (*fam*) to have a date; **tener un ~** (*fam*) to have an affair; **en ~ económico** (*fam*) on the cheap; **vamos en ~ de turismo** we're going as tourists; **si te pones en ese ~ ...** if that's your attitude ...

plana ['plana] *nf* sheet (of paper), page; (*Tec*) trowel; **en primera ~** on the front page

plancha ['plantʃa] *nf* (*para planchar*) iron; (*rótulo*) plate, sheet; (*Náut*) gangway; **a la ~** (*Culin*) grilled; **planchar** *vt* to iron ▷ *vi* to do the ironing

planear [plane'ar] *vt* to plan ▷ *vi* to glide

planeta [pla'neta] *nm* planet

plano, -a ['plano, a] *adj* flat, level, even ▷ *nm* (*Mat, Tec*) plane; (*Foto*) shot; (*Arq*) plan; (*Geo*) map; (*de ciudad*) map, street plan; **primer ~** close-up

planta ['planta] *nf* (*Bot, Tec*) plant; (*Anat*) sole of the foot, foot; (*piso*) floor; (LAM: *personal*) staff; **planta baja** ground floor

plantar [plan'tar] *vt* (*Bot*) to plant; (*levantar*) to erect, set up; **plantarse** *vr* to stand firm; **~ a algn en la calle** to throw sb out; **dejar plantado a algn** (*fam*) to stand sb up

plantear [plante'ar] *vt* (*problema*) to pose; (*dificultad*) to raise

plantilla [plan'tiʎa] *nf* (*de zapato*) insole; (ESP: *personal*) personnel; **ser de ~** (ESP) to be on the staff

plantón [plan'ton] *nm* (*Mil*) guard, sentry; (*fam*) long wait; **dar (un) ~ a algn** to stand sb up

plasta ['plasta] (ESP: *fam*) *adj inv* boring ▷ *nmf* bore

plástico, -a ['plastiko, a] *adj* plastic ▷ *nm* plastic

Plastilina® [plasti'lina] *nf* Plasticine®

plata ['plata] *nf* (*metal*) silver; (*cosas hechas de plata*) silverware; (CS: *dinero*) cash, dough

plataforma [plata'forma] *nf* platform; **plataforma de lanzamiento/perforación** launch(ing) pad/drilling rig

plátano ['platano] *nm* (*fruta*) banana; (*árbol*) plane tree; banana tree

platea [pla'tea] *nf* (*Teatro*) pit

plática ['platika] *nf* talk, chat; **platicar** *vi* to talk, chat

platillo [pla'tiʎo] *nm* saucer; **platillos** *nmpl* (*Mús*) cymbals; **platillo volante** flying saucer

platino [pla'tino] *nm* platinum; **platinos** *nmpl* (*Auto*) contact points

plato ['plato] *nm* plate, dish; (*parte de comida*) course; (*comida*) dish; **primer ~** first course; **plato combinado** set main course (*served on one plate*); **plato fuerte** main course

playa ['plaja] *nf* beach; (*costa*) seaside; **playa de estacionamiento** (CS) car park (BRIT), parking lot (US)

playera [pla'jera] *nf* (MÉX: *camiseta*) T-shirt; **playeras** *nfpl* (*zapatos*) canvas shoes

plaza ['plaθa] *nf* square; (*mercado*) market(place); (*sitio*) room, space; (*de* *vehículo*) seat, place; (*colocación*) post, job; **plaza de toros** bullring

plazo ['plaθo] *nm* (*lapso de tiempo*) time, period; (*fecha de vencimiento*) expiry date; (*pago parcial*) instalment; **a corto/largo ~** short-/long-term; **comprar algo a ~s** to buy sth on hire purchase (BRIT) *o* on time (US)

plazoleta [plaθo'leta] *nf* small square

plebeyo, -a [ple'βejo, a] *adj* plebeian; (*pey*) coarse, common

plegable [ple'ɣaβle] *adj* collapsible; (*silla*) folding

pleito ['pleito] *nm* (*Jur*) lawsuit, case; (*fig*) dispute, feud

plenitud [pleni'tuð] *nf* plenitude, fullness; (*abundancia*) abundance

pleno, -a ['pleno, a] *adj* full; (*completo*) complete ▷*nm* plenum; **en ~ día** in broad daylight; **en ~ verano** at the height of summer; **en plena cara** full in the face

pliego *etc* ['pljeɣo] *vb V* **plegar** ▷*nm* (*hoja*) sheet (of paper); (*carta*) sealed letter/document; **pliego de condiciones** details *pl*, specifications *pl*

pliegue *etc* ['pljeɣe] *vb V* **plegar** ▷*nm* fold, crease; (*de vestido*) pleat

plomería [plome'ria] (LAM) *nf* plumbing; **plomero** (LAM) *nm* plumber

plomo ['plomo] *nm* (*metal*) lead; (*Elec*) fuse; **sin ~** unleaded

pluma ['pluma] *nf* feather; (*para escribir*): **~ (estilográfica)** ink pen; **~ fuente** (LAM) fountain pen

plumero [plu'mero] *nm* (*para el polvo*) feather duster

plumón [plu'mon] *nm* (*de ave*) down

plural [plu'ral] *adj* plural

pluriempleo [pluriem'pleo] *nm* having more than one job

plus [plus] *nm* bonus

población [poβla'θjon] *nf* population; (*pueblo, ciudad*) town, city

poblado, -a [po'βlaðo, a] *adj* inhabited ▷*nm* (*aldea*) village; (*pueblo*) (small) town; **densamente ~** densely populated

poblador, a [poβla'ðor, a] *nm/f* settler, colonist

pobre ['poβre] *adj* poor ▷*nmf* poor person; **pobreza** *nf* poverty

pocilga [po'θilɣa] *nf* pigsty

PALABRA CLAVE

poco, -a ['poko, a] *adj* **1** (*sg*) little, not much; **poco tiempo** little *o* not much time; **de poco interés** of little interest, not very interesting; **poca cosa** not much

2 (*pl*) few, not many; **unos pocos** a few, some; **pocos niños comen lo que les conviene** few children eat what they should

▷*adv* **1** little, not much; **cuesta poco** it doesn't cost much

2 (*+ adj*: *negativo, antónimo*): **poco amable/inteligente** not very nice/ intelligent

3: **por poco me caigo** I almost fell

4: **a poco: a poco de haberse casado** shortly after getting married

5: **poco a poco** little by little

▷*nm* a little, a bit; **un poco triste/de dinero** a little sad/money

podar [po'ðar] *vt* to prune

PALABRA CLAVE

poder [po'ðer] *vi* **1** (*tener capacidad*) can, be able to; **no puedo hacerlo** I can't do it, I'm unable to do it

2 (*tener permiso*) can, may, be allowed to; **¿se puede?** may I (*o* we)?; **puedes irte ahora** you may go now; **no se puede fumar en este hospital** smoking is not allowed in this hospital

3 (*tener posibilidad*) may, might, could; **puede llegar mañana** he may *o* might arrive tomorrow; **pudiste haberte hecho daño** you might *o* could have

hurt yourself; **¡podías habérmelo dicho antes!** you might have told me before!
4: **puede ser** perhaps; **puede ser que lo sepa Tomás** Tomás may *o* might know
5: **¡no puedo más!** I've had enough!; **es tonto a más no poder** he's as stupid as they come
6: **poder con: no puedo con este crío** this kid's too much for me
▷ *nm* power; **detentar** *o* **ocupar** *o* **estar en el poder** to be in power; **poder adquisitivo/ejecutivo/legislativo** purchasing/executive/legislative power; **poder judicial** judiciary

poderoso, -a [poðeroso, a] *adj* (*político, país*) powerful
podio ['poðjo] *nm* (*Deporte*) podium
podium ['poðjum] = **podio**
podrido, -a [po'ðriðo, a] *adj* rotten, bad; (*fig*) rotten, corrupt
podrir [po'ðrir] = **pudrir**
poema [po'ema] *nm* poem
poesía [poe'sia] *nf* poetry
poeta [po'eta] *nmf* poet; **poético, -a** *adj* poetic(al)
poetisa [poe'tisa] *nf* (woman) poet
póker ['poker] *nm* poker
polaco, -a [po'lako, a] *adj* Polish ▷ *nm/f* Pole
polar [po'lar] *adj* polar
polea [po'lea] *nf* pulley
polémica [po'lemika] *nf* polemics *sg*; (*una polémica*) controversy, polemic
polen ['polen] *nm* pollen
policía [poli'θia] *nmf* policeman/woman ▷ *nf* police; **policíaco, -a** *adj* police *cpd*; **novela policíaca** detective story; **policial** *adj* police *cpd*
polideportivo [poliðepor'tiβo] *nm* sports centre *o* complex
polígono [po'liɣono] *nm* (*Mat*) polygon; **polígono industrial** (ESP) industrial estate
polilla [po'liʎa] *nf* moth
polio ['poljo] *nf* polio
política [po'litika] *nf* politics *sg*; (*económica, agraria etc*) policy; *V tb* **político**
político, -a [po'litiko, a] *adj* political; (*discreto*) tactful; (*de familia*) ...-in-law ▷ *nm/f* politician; **padre ~** father-in-law
póliza ['poliθa] *nf* certificate, voucher; (*impuesto*) tax stamp; **póliza de seguro(s)** insurance policy
polizón [poli'θon] *nm* stowaway
pollera [po'ʎera] (CS) *nf* skirt
pollo ['poʎo] *nm* chicken
polo ['polo] *nm* (*Geo, Elec*) pole; (*helado*) ice lolly (BRIT), Popsicle® (US); (*Deporte*) polo; (*suéter*) polo-neck; **polo Norte/Sur** North/South Pole
Polonia [po'lonja] *nf* Poland
poltrona [pol'trona] *nf* easy chair
polución [polu'θjon] *nf* pollution
polvera [pol'βera] *nf* powder compact
polvo ['polβo] *nm* dust; (*Quím, Culin, Med*) powder; **polvos** *nmpl* (*maquillaje*) powder *sg*; **en ~** powdered; **quitar el ~** to dust; **estar hecho ~** (*fam*) to be worn out *o* exhausted; **polvos de talco** talcum powder *sg*
pólvora ['polβora] *nf* gunpowder
polvoriento, -a [polβo'rjento, a] *adj* (*superficie*) dusty; (*sustancia*) powdery
pomada [po'maða] *nf* cream, ointment
pomelo [po'melo] *nm* grapefruit
pómez ['pomeθ] *nf*: **piedra ~** pumice stone
pomo ['pomo] *nm* doorknob
pompa ['pompa] *nf* (*burbuja*) bubble; (*bomba*) pump; (*esplendor*) pomp, splendour
pómulo ['pomulo] *nm* cheekbone
pon [pon] *vb V* **poner**
ponchadura [pontʃa'dura] (MÉX) *nf* puncture (BRIT), flat (US); **ponchar** (MÉX) *vt* (*llanta*) to puncture

ponche ['pontʃe] *nm* punch
poncho ['pontʃo] *nm* poncho
pondré *etc vb V* **poner**

PALABRA CLAVE

poner [po'ner] *vt* **1** (*colocar*) to put; (*telegrama*) to send; (*obra de teatro*) to put on; (*película*) to show; **ponlo más fuerte** turn it up; **¿qué ponen en el Excelsior?** what's on at the Excelsior?
2 (*tienda*) to open; (*instalar: gas etc*) to put in; (*radio, TV*) to switch *o* turn on
3 (*suponer*): **pongamos que ...** let's suppose that ...
4 (*contribuir*): **el gobierno ha puesto otro millón** the government has contributed another million
5 (*Tel*): **póngame con el Sr. López** can you put me through to Mr. López?
6: **poner de: le han puesto de director general** they've appointed him general manager
7 (+ *adj*) to make; **me estás poniendo nerviosa** you're making me nervous
8 (*dar nombre*): **al hijo le pusieron Diego** they called their son Diego
▷ *vi* (*gallina*) to lay
ponerse *vr* **1** (*colocarse*): **se puso a mi lado** he came and stood beside me; **tú ponte en esa silla** you go and sit on that chair
2 (*vestido, cosméticos*) to put on; **¿por qué no te pones el vestido nuevo?** why don't you put on *o* wear your new dress?
3 (+ *adj*) to turn; to get, become; **se puso muy serio** he got very serious; **después de lavarla la tela se puso azul** after washing it the material turned blue
4: **ponerse a: se puso a llorar** he started to cry; **tienes que ponerte a estudiar** you must get down to studying

pongo *etc vb V* **poner**

poniente [po'njente] *nm* (*occidente*) west; (*viento*) west wind
pontífice [pon'tifiθe] *nm* pope, pontiff
popa ['popa] *nf* stern
popote [po'pote] (*MÉX*) *nm* straw
popular [popu'lar] *adj* popular; (*cultura*) of the people, folk *cpd*; **popularidad** *nf* popularity

PALABRA CLAVE

por [por] *prep* **1** (*objetivo*) for; **luchar por la patria** to fight for one's country
2 (+ *infin*): **por no llegar tarde** so as not to arrive late; **por citar unos ejemplos** to give a few examples
3 (*causa*) out of, because of; **por escasez de fondos** through *o* for lack of funds
4 (*tiempo*): **por la mañana/noche** in the morning/at night; **se queda por una semana** she's staying (for) a week
5 (*lugar*): **pasar por Madrid** to pass through Madrid; **ir a Guayaquil por Quito** to go to Guayaquil via Quito; **caminar por la calle** to walk along the street; *V tb* **todo**
6 (*cambio, precio*): **te doy uno nuevo por el que tienes** I'll give you a new one (in return) for the one you've got
7 (*valor distributivo*): **6 euros por hora/cabeza** 6 euros an *o* per hour/a *o* per head
8 (*modo, medio*) by; **por correo/avión** by post/air; **entrar por la entrada principal** to go in through the main entrance
9: **10 por 10 son 100** 10 times 10 is 100
10 (*en lugar de*): **vino él por su jefe** he came instead of his boss
11: **por mí que revienten** as far as I'm concerned they can drop dead
12: **¿por qué?** why?; **¿por qué no?** why not?

porcelana [porθe'lana] *nf* porcelain;

(*china*) china
porcentaje [porθen'taxe] *nm* percentage
porción [por'θjon] *nf* (*parte*) portion, share; (*cantidad*) quantity, amount
porfiar [por'fjar] *vi* to persist, insist; (*disputar*) to argue stubbornly
pormenor [porme'nor] *nm* detail, particular
pornografía [pornoɣra'fia] *nf* pornography
poro ['poro] *nm* pore
pororó [poro'ro] (RPL) *nm* popcorn
poroso, -a [po'roso, a] *adj* porous
poroto [po'roto] (CS) *nm* bean
porque ['porke] *conj* (*a causa de*) because; (*ya que*) since; (*con el fin de*) so that, in order that
porqué [por'ke] *nm* reason, cause
porquería [porke'ria] *nf* (*suciedad*) filth, dirt; (*acción*) dirty trick; (*objeto*) small thing, trifle; (*fig*) rubbish
porra ['porra] (ESP) *nf* (*arma*) stick, club
porrazo [po'rraθo] *nm* blow, bump
porro ['porro] (*fam*) *nm* (*droga*) joint (*fam*)
porrón [po'rron] *nm glass wine jar with a long spout*
portaaviones [porta'(a)βjones] *nm inv* aircraft carrier
portada [por'taða] *nf* (*de revista*) cover
portador, a [porta'ðor, a] *nm/f* carrier, bearer; (*Com*) bearer, payee
portaequipajes [portaeki'paxes] *nm inv* (*Auto: maletero*) boot; (*: baca*) luggage rack
portafolio [porta'foljo] (LAM) *nm* briefcase
portal [por'tal] *nm* (*entrada*) vestibule, hall; (*portada*) porch, doorway; (*puerta de entrada*) main door; (*Internet*) portal; **portales** *nmpl* (LAM) arcade *sg*
portamaletas [portama'letas] *nm inv* (*Auto: maletero*) boot; (*: baca*) roof rack
portarse [por'tarse] *vr* to behave, conduct o.s.
portátil [por'tatil] *adj* portable
portavoz [porta'βoθ] *nmf* spokesman/woman
portazo [por'taθo] *nm*: **dar un ~** to slam the door
porte ['porte] *nm* (*Com*) transport; (*precio*) transport charges *pl*
portentoso, -a [porten'toso, a] *adj* marvellous, extraordinary
porteño, -a [por'teɲo, a] *adj* of *o* from Buenos Aires
portería [porte'ria] *nf* (*oficina*) porter's office; (*Deporte*) goal
portero, -a [por'tero, a] *nm/f* porter; (*conserje*) caretaker; (*ujier*) doorman; (*Deporte*) goalkeeper; **portero automático** (ESP) entry phone
pórtico ['portiko] *nm* (*patio*) portico, porch; (*fig*) gateway; (*arcada*) arcade
portorriqueño, -a [portorri'keɲo, a] *adj* Puerto Rican
Portugal [portu'ɣal] *nm* Portugal; **portugués, -esa** *adj, nm/f* Portuguese ▷ *nm* (*Ling*) Portuguese
porvenir [porβe'nir] *nm* future
pos [pos] *prep*: **en ~ de** after, in pursuit of
posaderas [posa'ðeras] *nfpl* backside *sg*, buttocks
posar [po'sar] *vt* (*en el suelo*) to lay down, put down; (*la mano*) to place, put gently ▷ *vi* (*modelo*) to sit, pose; **posarse** *vr* to settle; (*pájaro*) to perch; (*avión*) to land, come down
posavasos [posa'basos] *nm inv* coaster; (*para cerveza*) beermat
posdata [pos'ðata] *nf* postscript
pose ['pose] *nf* pose
poseedor, a [posee'ðor, a] *nm/f* owner, possessor; (*de récord, puesto*) holder
poseer [pose'er] *vt* to possess, own; (*ventaja*) to enjoy; (*récord, puesto*) to hold
posesivo, -a [pose'siβo, a] *adj* possessive

posibilidad [posiβili'ðað] *nf* possibility; (*oportunidad*) chance; **posibilitar** *vt* to make possible; (*hacer realizable*) to make feasible
posible [po'siβle] *adj* possible; (*realizable*) feasible; **de ser ~** if possible; **en lo ~** as far as possible
posición [posi'θjon] *nf* position; (*rango social*) status
positivo, -a [posi'tiβo, a] *adj* positive
poso ['poso] *nm* sediment; (*heces*) dregs *pl*
posponer [pospo'ner] *vt* (*relegar*) to put behind/below; (*aplazar*) to postpone
posta ['posta] *nf*: **a ~** deliberately, on purpose
postal [pos'tal] *adj* postal ▷ *nf* postcard
poste ['poste] *nm* (*de telégrafos etc*) post, pole; (*columna*) pillar
póster ['poster] (*pl* **~es, ~s**) *nm* poster
posterior [poste'rjor] *adj* back, rear; (*siguiente*) following, subsequent; (*más tarde*) later
postgrado [post'graðo] *nm* = **posgrado**
postizo, -a [pos'tiθo, a] *adj* false, artificial ▷ *nm* hairpiece
postre ['postre] *nm* sweet, dessert
póstumo, -a ['postumo, a] *adj* posthumous
postura [pos'tura] *nf* (*del cuerpo*) posture, position; (*fig*) attitude, position
potable [po'taβle] *adj* drinkable; **agua ~** drinking water
potaje [po'taxe] *nm* thick vegetable soup
potencia [po'tenθja] *nf* power; **potencial** [poten'θjal] *adj, nm* potential
potente [po'tente] *adj* powerful
potro, -a ['potro, a] *nm/f* (*Zool*) colt/filly ▷ *nm* (*de gimnasia*) vaulting horse
pozo ['poθo] *nm* well; (*de río*) deep pool; (*de mina*) shaft
PP (ESP) *nm abr* = **Partido Popular**
práctica ['praktika] *nf* practice; (*método*) method; (*arte, capacidad*) skill; **en la ~** in practice
practicable [prakti'kaβle] *adj* practicable; (*camino*) passable
practicante [prakti'kante] *nmf* (*Med: ayudante de doctor*) medical assistant; (*: enfermero*) nurse; (*quien practica algo*) practitioner ▷ *adj* practising
practicar [prakti'kar] *vt* to practise; (*Deporte*) to play; (*realizar*) to carry out, perform
práctico, -a ['praktiko, a] *adj* practical; (*instruído: persona*) skilled, expert
practique *etc vb V* **practicar**
pradera [pra'ðera] *nf* meadow; (*US etc*) prairie
prado ['praðo] *nm* (*campo*) meadow, field; (*pastizal*) pasture
Praga ['praɣa] *n* Prague
pragmático, -a [praɣ'matiko, a] *adj* pragmatic
precario, -a [pre'karjo, a] *adj* precarious
precaución [prekau'θjon] *nf* (*medida preventiva*) preventive measure, precaution; (*prudencia*) caution, wariness
precedente [preθe'ðente] *adj* preceding; (*anterior*) former ▷ *nm* precedent
preceder [preθe'ðer] *vt, vi* to precede, go before, come before
precepto [pre'θepto] *nm* precept
precinto [pre'θinto] *nm* (*tb*: **~ de garantía**) seal
precio ['preθjo] *nm* price; (*costo*) cost; (*valor*) value, worth; (*de viaje*) fare; **precio al contado/de coste/de oportunidad** cash/cost/bargain price; **precio al por menor** retail price; **precio de ocasión** bargain price; **precio de venta al público** retail price; **precio tope** top price
preciosidad [preθjosi'ðað] *nf* (*valor*)

(high) value, (great) worth; (*encanto*) charm; (*cosa bonita*) beautiful thing; **es una ~** it's lovely, it's really beautiful

precioso, -a [pre'θjoso, a] *adj* precious; (*de mucho valor*) valuable; (*fam*) lovely, beautiful

precipicio [preθi'piθjo] *nm* cliff, precipice; (*fig*) abyss

precipitación [preθipita'θjon] *nf* haste; (*lluvia*) rainfall

precipitado, -a [preθipi'taðo, a] *adj* (*conducta*) hasty, rash; (*salida*) hasty, sudden

precipitar [preθipi'tar] *vt* (*arrojar*) to hurl down, throw; (*apresurar*) to hasten; (*acelerar*) to speed up, accelerate; **precipitarse** *vr* to throw o.s.; (*apresurarse*) to rush; (*actuar sin pensar*) to act rashly

precisamente [preθisa'mente] *adv* precisely; (*exactamente*) precisely, exactly

precisar [preθi'sar] *vt* (*necesitar*) to need, require; (*fijar*) to determine exactly, fix; (*especificar*) to specify

precisión [preθi'sjon] *nf* (*exactitud*) precision

preciso, -a [pre'θiso, a] *adj* (*exacto*) precise; (*necesario*) necessary, essential

preconcebido, -a [prekonθe'βiðo, a] *adj* preconceived

precoz [pre'koθ] *adj* (*persona*) precocious; (*calvicie etc*) premature

predecir [preðe'θir] *vt* to predict, forecast

predestinado, -a [preðesti'naðo, a] *adj* predestined

predicar [preði'kar] *vt, vi* to preach

predicción [preðik'θjon] *nf* prediction

predilecto, -a [preði'lekto, a] *adj* favourite

predisposición [preðisposi'θjon] *nf* inclination; prejudice, bias

predominar [preðomi'nar] *vt* to dominate ▷ *vi* to predominate; (*prevalecer*) to prevail; **predominio** *nm* predominance; prevalence

preescolar [pre(e)sko'lar] *adj* preschool

prefabricado, -a [prefaβri'kaðo, a] *adj* prefabricated

prefacio [pre'faθjo] *nm* preface

preferencia [prefe'renθja] *nf* preference; **de ~** preferably, for preference

preferible [prefe'riβle] *adj* preferable

preferir [prefe'rir] *vt* to prefer

prefiero *etc vb V* **preferir**

prefijo [pre'fixo] *nm* (*Tel*) (dialling) code

pregunta [pre'ɣunta] *nf* question; **hacer una ~** to ask a question; **preguntas frecuentes** FAQs, frequently asked questions

preguntar [preɣun'tar] *vt* to ask; (*cuestionar*) to question ▷ *vi* to ask; **preguntarse** *vr* to wonder; **preguntar por algn** to ask for sb; **preguntón, -ona** [preɣun'ton, ona] *adj* inquisitive

prehistórico, -a [preis'toriko, a] *adj* prehistoric

prejuicio [pre'xwiθjo] *nm* (*acto*) prejudgement; (*idea preconcebida*) preconception; (*parcialidad*) prejudice, bias

preludio [pre'luðjo] *nm* prelude

prematuro, -a [prema'turo, a] *adj* premature

premeditar [premeði'tar] *vt* to premeditate

premiar [pre'mjar] *vt* to reward; (*en un concurso*) to give a prize to

premio ['premjo] *nm* reward; prize; (*Com*) premium

prenatal [prena'tal] *adj* antenatal, prenatal

prenda ['prenda] *nf* (*ropa*) garment, article of clothing; (*garantía*) pledge; **prendas** *nfpl* (*talentos*) talents, gifts

prender [pren'der] *vt* (*captar*) to catch, capture; (*detener*) to arrest; (*Costura*) to pin, attach; (*sujetar*) to fasten ▷ *vi* to catch; (*arraigar*) to take root; **prenderse** *vr* (*encenderse*) to catch fire

prendido, -a [pren'diðo, a] (LAM) *adj* (*luz etc*) on

prensa ['prensa] *nf* press; **la ~** the press

preñado, -a [pre'ɲaðo, a] *adj* pregnant; **~ de** pregnant with, full of

preocupación [preokupa'θjon] *nf* worry, concern; (*ansiedad*) anxiety

preocupado, -a [preoku'paðo, a] *adj* worried, concerned; (*ansioso*) anxious

preocupar [preoku'par] *vt* to worry; **preocuparse** *vr* to worry; **~se de algo** (*hacerse cargo*) to take care of sth

preparación [prepara'θjon] *nf* (*acto*) preparation; (*estado*) readiness; (*entrenamiento*) training

preparado, -a [prepa'raðo, a] *adj* (*dispuesto*) prepared; (*Culin*) ready (to serve) ▷ *nm* preparation

preparar [prepa'rar] *vt* (*disponer*) to prepare, get ready; (*Tec*: *tratar*) to prepare, process; (*entrenar*) to teach, train; **prepararse** *vr*: **~se a** *o* **para** to prepare to *o* for, get ready to *o* for; **preparativo, -a** *adj* preparatory, preliminary; **preparativos** *nmpl* preparations; **preparatoria** (MÉX) *nf* sixth-form college (BRIT), senior high school (US)

presa ['presa] *nf* (*cosa apresada*) catch; (*víctima*) victim; (*de animal*) prey; (*de agua*) dam

presagiar [presa'xjar] *vt* to presage, forebode; **presagio** *nm* omen

prescindir [presθin'dir] *vi*: **~ de** (*privarse de*) to do *o* go without; (*descartar*) to dispense with

prescribir [preskri'βir] *vt* to prescribe

presencia [pre'senθja] *nf* presence; **presenciar** *vt* to be present at; (*asistir a*) to attend; (*ver*) to see, witness

presentación [presenta'θjon] *nf* presentation; (*introducción*) introduction

presentador, a [presenta'ðor, a] *nm/f* presenter, compère

presentar [presen'tar] *vt* to present; (*ofrecer*) to offer; (*mostrar*) to show, display; (*a una persona*) to introduce; **presentarse** *vr* (*llegar inesperadamente*) to appear, turn up; (*ofrecerse*: *como candidato*) to run, stand; (*aparecer*) to show, appear; (*solicitar empleo*) to apply

presente [pre'sente] *adj* present ▷ *nm* present; **hacer ~** to state, declare; **tener ~** to remember, bear in mind

presentimiento [presenti'mjento] *nm* premonition, presentiment

presentir [presen'tir] *vt* to have a premonition of

preservación [preserβa'θjon] *nf* protection, preservation

preservar [preser'βar] *vt* to protect, preserve; **preservativo** *nm* sheath, condom

presidencia [presi'ðenθja] *nf* presidency; (*de comité*) chairmanship

presidente [presi'ðente] *nmf* president; (*de comité*) chairman/woman

presidir [presi'ðir] *vt* (*dirigir*) to preside at, preside over; (: *comité*) to take the chair at; (*dominar*) to dominate, rule ▷ *vi* to preside; to take the chair

presión [pre'sjon] *nf* pressure; **presión atmosférica** atmospheric *o* air pressure; **presionar** *vt* to press; (*fig*) to press, put pressure on ▷ *vi*: **presionar para** to press for

preso, -a ['preso, a] *nm/f* prisoner; **tomar** *o* **llevar ~ a algn** to arrest sb, take sb prisoner

prestación [presta'θjon] *nf* service; (*subsidio*) benefit; **prestaciones** *nfpl* (*Tec, Auto*) performance features

prestado, -a [pres'taðo, a] *adj* on loan; **pedir ~** to borrow

prestamista [presta'mista] *nmf* moneylender

préstamo ['prestamo] *nm* loan; **préstamo hipotecario** mortgage

prestar [pres'tar] *vt* to lend, loan;

(*atención*) to pay; (*ayuda*) to give

prestigio [pres'tixjo] *nm* prestige; **prestigioso, -a** *adj* (*honorable*) prestigious; (*famoso, renombrado*) renowned, famous

presumido, -a [presu'miðo, a] *adj* (*persona*) vain

presumir [presu'mir] *vt* to presume ▷ *vi* (*tener aires*) to be conceited; **presunto, -a** *adj* (*supuesto*) supposed, presumed; (*así llamado*) so-called; **presuntuoso, -a** *adj* conceited, presumptuous

presupuesto [presu'pwesto] *pp de* **presuponer** ▷ *nm* (*Finanzas*) budget; (*estimación*: *de costo*) estimate

pretencioso, -a [preten'θjoso, a] *adj* pretentious

pretender [preten'der] *vt* (*intentar*) to try to, seek to; (*reivindicar*) to claim; (*buscar*) to seek, try for; (*cortejar*) to woo, court; **~ que** to expect that

No confundir **pretender** con la palabra inglesa *pretend*.

pretendiente *nmf* (*amante*) suitor; (*al trono*) pretender; **pretensión** *nf* (*aspiración*) aspiration; (*reivindicación*) claim; (*orgullo*) pretension

pretexto [pre'teksto] *nm* pretext; (*excusa*) excuse

prevención [preβen'θjon] *nf* prevention; (*precaución*) precaution

prevenido, -a [preβe'niðo, a] *adj* prepared, ready; (*cauteloso*) cautious

prevenir [preβe'nir] *vt* (*impedir*) to prevent; (*predisponer*) to prejudice, bias; (*avisar*) to warn; (*preparar*) to prepare, get ready; **prevenirse** *vr* to get ready, prepare; **~se contra** to take precautions against; **preventivo, -a** *adj* preventive, precautionary

prever [pre'βer] *vt* to foresee

previo, -a ['preβjo, a] *adj* (*anterior*) previous; (*preliminar*) preliminary ▷ *prep*: **~ acuerdo de los otros** subject to the agreement of the others

previsión [preβi'sjon] *nf* (*perspicacia*) foresight; (*predicción*) forecast; **previsto, -a** *adj* anticipated, forecast

prima ['prima] *nf* (*Com*) bonus; (*de seguro*) premium; *V tb* **primo**

primario, -a [pri'marjo, a] *adj* primary

primavera [prima'βera] *nf* spring(-time)

primera [pri'mera] *nf* (*Auto*) first gear; (*Ferro*: *tb*: **~ clase**) first class; **de ~** (*fam*) first-class, first-rate

primero, -a [pri'mero, a] (*adj* **primer**) first; (*principal*) prime *adv* first; (*más bien*) sooner, rather; **primera plana** front page

primitivo, -a [primi'tiβo, a] *adj* primitive; (*original*) original

primo, -a ['primo, a] *adj* prime ▷ *nm/f* cousin; (*fam*) fool, idiot; **materias primas** raw materials; **primo hermano** first cousin

primogénito, -a [primo'xenito, a] *adj* first-born

primoroso, -a [primo'roso, a] *adj* exquisite, delicate

princesa [prin'θesa] *nf* princess

principal [prinθi'pal] *adj* principal, main ▷ *nm* (*jefe*) chief, principal

príncipe ['prinθipe] *nm* prince

principiante [prinθi'pjante] *nmf* beginner

principio [prin'θipjo] *nm* (*comienzo*) beginning, start; (*origen*) origin; (*primera etapa*) rudiment, basic idea; (*moral*) principle; **desde el ~** from the first; **en un ~** at first; **a ~s de** at the beginning of

pringue ['pringe] *nm* (*grasa*) grease, fat, dripping

prioridad [priori'ðað] *nf* priority

prisa ['prisa] *nf* (*apresuramiento*) hurry, haste; (*rapidez*) speed; (*urgencia*) (sense of) urgency; **a** *o* **de ~** quickly; **correr ~** to be urgent; **darse ~** to hurry up; **tener ~** to be in a hurry

prisión [pri'sjon] *nf* (*cárcel*) prison; (*período de cárcel*) imprisonment; **prisionero, -a** *nm/f* prisoner

prismáticos [pris'matikos] *nmpl*

binoculars
privado, -a [pri'βaðo, a] *adj* private
privar [pri'βar] *vt* to deprive; **privativo, -a** *adj* exclusive
privilegiar [priβile'xjar] *vt* to grant a privilege to; (*favorecer*) to favour
privilegio [priβi'lexjo] *nm* privilege; (*concesión*) concession
pro [pro] *nm o f* profit, advantage ▷ *prep*: **asociación ~ ciegos** association for the blind ▷ *prefijo*: **~ americano** pro-American; **en ~ de** on behalf of, for; **los ~s y los contras** the pros and cons
proa ['proa] *nf* bow, prow; **de ~** bow *cpd*, fore
probabilidad [proβaβili'ðað] *nf* probability, likelihood; (*oportunidad, posibilidad*) chance, prospect; **probable** *adj* probable, likely
probador [proβa'ðor] *nm* (*en tienda*) fitting room
probar [pro'βar] *vt* (*demostrar*) to prove; (*someter a prueba*) to test, try out; (*ropa*) to try on; (*comida*) to taste ▷ *vi* to try; **~se un traje** to try on a suit
probeta [pro'βeta] *nf* test tube
problema [pro'βlema] *nm* problem
procedente [proθe'ðente] *adj* (*razonable*) reasonable; (*conforme a derecho*) proper, fitting; **~ de** coming from, originating in
proceder [proθe'ðer] *vi* (*avanzar*) to proceed; (*actuar*) to act; (*ser correcto*) to be right (and proper), be fitting ▷ *nm* (*comportamiento*) behaviour, conduct; **~ de** to come from, originate in; **procedimiento** *nm* procedure; (*proceso*) process; (*método*) means *pl*, method
procesador [proθesa'ðor] *nm* processor; **procesador de textos** word processor
procesar [proθe'sar] *vt* to try, put on trial
procesión [proθe'sjon] *nf* procession
proceso [pro'θeso] *nm* process; (*Jur*) trial
proclamar [prokla'mar] *vt* to proclaim
procrear [prokre'ar] *vt, vi* to procreate
procurador, a [prokura'ðor, a] *nm/f* attorney
procurar [proku'rar] *vt* (*intentar*) to try, endeavour; (*conseguir*) to get, obtain; (*asegurar*) to secure; (*producir*) to produce
prodigio [pro'ðixjo] *nm* prodigy; (*milagro*) wonder, marvel; **prodigioso, -a** *adj* prodigious, marvellous
pródigo, -a ['proðiɣo, a] *adj*: **hijo ~** prodigal son
producción [proðuk'θjon] *nf* (*gen*) production; (*producto*) output; **producción en serie** mass production
producir [proðu'θir] *vt* to produce; (*causar*) to cause, bring about; **producirse** *vr* (*cambio*) to come about; (*accidente*) to take place; (*problema etc*) to arise; (*hacerse*) to be produced, be made; (*estallar*) to break out
productividad [proðuktiβi'ðað] *nf* productivity; **productivo, -a** *adj* productive; (*provechoso*) profitable
producto [pro'ðukto] *nm* product
productor, a [proðuk'tor, a] *adj* productive, producing ▷ *nm/f* producer
proeza [pro'eθa] *nf* exploit, feat
profano, -a [pro'fano, a] *adj* profane ▷ *nm/f* layman/woman
profecía [profe'θia] *nf* prophecy
profesión [profe'sjon] *nf* profession; (*en formulario*) occupation; **profesional** *adj* professional
profesor, a [profe'sor, a] *nm/f* teacher; **profesorado** *nm* teaching profession
profeta [pro'feta] *nmf* prophet
prófugo, -a ['profuɣo, a] *nm/f* fugitive; (*Mil: desertor*) deserter
profundidad [profundi'ðað] *nf* depth; **profundizar** *vi*: **profundizar en** to go deeply into; **profundo, -a** *adj* deep; (*misterio, pensador*) profound

progenitor [proxeni'tor] *nm* ancestor; **progenitores** *nmpl* (*padres*) parents
programa [pro'ɣrama] *nm* programme (BRIT), program (US); **programa de estudios** curriculum, syllabus; **programación** *nf* programming; **programador, a** *nm/f* programmer; **programar** *vt* to program
progresar [proɣre'sar] *vi* to progress, make progress; **progresista** *adj*, *nmf* progressive; **progresivo, -a** *adj* progressive; (*gradual*) gradual; (*continuo*) continuous; **progreso** *nm* progress
prohibición [proiβi'θjon] *nf* prohibition, ban
prohibir [proi'βir] *vt* to prohibit, ban, forbid; **prohibido** *o* **se prohibe fumar** no smoking; **"prohibido el paso"** "no entry"
prójimo, -a ['proximo, a] *nm/f* fellow man; (*vecino*) neighbour
prólogo ['proloɣo] *nm* prologue
prolongar [prolon'ɣar] *vt* to extend; (*reunión etc*) to prolong; (*calle, tubo*) to extend
promedio [pro'meðjo] *nm* average; (*de distancia*) middle, mid-point
promesa [pro'mesa] *nf* promise
prometer [prome'ter] *vt* to promise ▷ *vi* to show promise; **prometerse** *vr* (*novios*) to get engaged; **prometido, -a** *adj* promised; engaged ▷ *nm/f* fiancé/fiancée
prominente [promi'nente] *adj* prominent
promoción [promo'θjon] *nf* promotion
promotor [promo'tor] *nm* promoter; (*instigador*) instigator
promover [promo'βer] *vt* to promote; (*causar*) to cause; (*instigar*) to instigate, stir up
promulgar [promul'ɣar] *vt* to promulgate; (*anunciar*) to proclaim
pronombre [pro'nombre] *nm* pronoun
pronosticar [pronosti'kar] *vt* to predict, foretell, forecast; **pronóstico** *nm* prediction, forecast; **pronóstico del tiempo** weather forecast
pronto, -a ['pronto, a] *adj* (*rápido*) prompt, quick; (*preparado*) ready ▷ *adv* quickly, promptly; (*en seguida*) at once, right away; (*dentro de poco*) soon; (*temprano*) early ▷ *nm*: **tiene unos ~s muy malos** he gets ratty all of a sudden (*inf*); **de ~** suddenly; **por lo ~** meanwhile, for the present
pronunciación [pronunθja'θjon] *nf* pronunciation
pronunciar [pronun'θjar] *vt* to pronounce; (*discurso*) to make, deliver; **pronunciarse** *vr* to revolt, rebel; (*declararse*) to declare o.s.
propagación [propaɣa'θjon] *nf* propagation
propaganda [propa'ɣanda] *nf* (*Pol*) propaganda; (*Com*) advertising
propenso, -a [pro'penso, a] *adj* inclined to; **ser ~ a** to be inclined to, have a tendency to
propicio, -a [pro'piθjo, a] *adj* favourable, propitious
propiedad [propje'ðað] *nf* property; (*posesión*) possession, ownership; **propiedad particular** private property
propietario, -a [propje'tarjo, a] *nm/f* owner, proprietor
propina [pro'pina] *nf* tip
propio, -a ['propjo, a] *adj* own, of one's own; (*característico*) characteristic, typical; (*debido*) proper; (*mismo*) selfsame, very; **el ~ ministro** the minister himself; **¿tienes casa propia?** have you a house of your own?
proponer [propo'ner] *vt* to propose, put forward; (*problema*) to pose; **proponerse** *vr* to propose, intend
proporción [propor'θjon] *nf* proportion; (*Mat*) ratio; **proporciones** *nfpl* (*dimensiones*) dimensions; (*fig*) size *sg*; **proporcionado, -a** *adj* proportionate; (*regular*)

medium, middling; (*justo*) just right; **proporcionar** *vt* (*dar*) to give, supply, provide

proposición [proposi'θjon] *nf* proposition; (*propuesta*) proposal

propósito [pro'posito] *nm* purpose; (*intento*) aim, intention ▷ *adv*: **a ~** by the way, incidentally; (*a posta*) on purpose, deliberately; **a ~ de** about, with regard to

propuesta [pro'pwesta] *vb V* **proponer** ▷ *nf* proposal

propulsar [propul'sar] *vt* to drive, propel; (*fig*) to promote, encourage; **propulsión** *nf* propulsion; **propulsión a chorro** *o* **por reacción** jet propulsion

prórroga ['prorroɣa] *nf* extension; (*Jur*) stay; (*Com*) deferment; (*Deporte*) extra time; **prorrogar** *vt* (*período*) to extend; (*decisión*) to defer, postpone

prosa ['prosa] *nf* prose

proseguir [prose'ɣir] *vt* to continue, carry on ▷ *vi* to continue, go on

prospecto [pros'pekto] *nm* prospectus

prosperar [prospe'rar] *vi* to prosper, thrive, flourish; **prosperidad** *nf* prosperity; (*éxito*) success; **próspero, -a** *adj* prosperous, flourishing; (*que tiene éxito*) successful

prostíbulo [pros'tiβulo] *nm* brothel (BRIT), house of prostitution (US)

prostitución [prostitu'θjon] *nf* prostitution

prostituir [prosti'twir] *vt* to prostitute; **prostituirse** *vr* to prostitute o.s., become a prostitute

prostituta [prosti'tuta] *nf* prostitute

protagonista [protaɣo'nista] *nmf* protagonist

protección [protek'θjon] *nf* protection

protector, a [protek'tor, a] *adj* protective, protecting ▷ *nm/f* protector

proteger [prote'xer] *vt* to protect; **protegido, -a** *nm/f* protégé/protégée

proteína [prote'ina] *nf* protein

protesta [pro'testa] *nf* protest; (*declaración*) protestation

protestante [protes'tante] *adj* Protestant

protestar [protes'tar] *vt* to protest, declare ▷ *vi* to protest

protocolo [proto'kolo] *nm* protocol

prototipo [proto'tipo] *nm* prototype

provecho [pro'βetʃo] *nm* advantage, benefit; (*Finanzas*) profit; **¡buen ~!** bon appétit!; **en ~ de** to the benefit of; **sacar ~ de** to benefit from, profit by

provenir [proβe'nir] *vi*: **~ de** to come *o* stem from

proverbio [pro'βerβjo] *nm* proverb

providencia [proβi'ðenθja] *nf* providence

provincia [pro'βinθja] *nf* province

provisión [proβi'sjon] *nf* provision; (*abastecimiento*) provision, supply; (*medida*) measure, step

provisional [proβisjo'nal] *adj* provisional

provocar [proβo'kar] *vt* to provoke; (*alentar*) to tempt, invite; (*causar*) to bring about, lead to; (*promover*) to promote; (*estimular*) to rouse, stimulate; **¿te provoca un café?** (CAM) would you like a coffee?; **provocativo, -a** *adj* provocative

proxeneta [prokse'neta] *nm* pimp

próximamente [proksima'mente] *adv* shortly, soon

proximidad [proksimi'ðað] *nf* closeness, proximity; **próximo, -a** *adj* near, close; (*vecino*) neighbouring; (*siguiente*) next

proyectar [projek'tar] *vt* (*objeto*) to hurl, throw; (*luz*) to cast, shed; (*Cine*) to screen, show; (*planear*) to plan

proyectil [projek'til] *nm* projectile, missile

proyecto [pro'jekto] *nm* plan; (*estimación de costo*) detailed estimate

proyector [projek'tor] *nm* (*Cine*) projector

prudencia [pru'ðenθja] *nf* (*sabiduría*)

wisdom; (*cuidado*) care; **prudente** *adj* sensible, wise; (*conductor*) careful

prueba *etc* ['prweβa] *vb V* **probar** ▷ *nf* proof; (*ensayo*) test, trial; (*degustación*) tasting, sampling; (*de ropa*) fitting; **a ~** on trial; **a ~ de** proof against; **a ~ de agua/fuego** waterproof/fireproof; **someter a ~** to put to the test

psico... [siko] *prefijo* psycho...; **psicología** *nf* psychology; **psicológico, -a** *adj* psychological; **psicólogo, -a** *nm/f* psychologist; **psicópata** *nmf* psychopath; **psicosis** *nf inv* psychosis

psiquiatra [si'kjatra] *nmf* psychiatrist; **psiquiátrico, -a** *adj* psychiatric

PSOE [pe'soe] (ESP) *nm abr* = **Partido Socialista Obrero Español**

púa ['pua] *nf* (*Bot, Zool*) prickle, spine; (*para guitarra*) plectrum (BRIT), pick (US); **alambre de ~** barbed wire

pubertad [puβer'tað] *nf* puberty

publicación [puβlika'θjon] *nf* publication

publicar [puβli'kar] *vt* (*editar*) to publish; (*hacer público*) to publicize; (*divulgar*) to make public, divulge

publicidad [puβliθi'ðað] *nf* publicity; (*Com: propaganda*) advertising; **publicitario, -a** *adj* publicity *cpd*; advertising *cpd*

público, -a ['puβliko, a] *adj* public ▷ *nm* public; (*Teatro etc*) audience

puchero [pu'tʃero] *nm* (*Culin: guiso*) stew; (*: olla*) cooking pot; **hacer ~s** to pout

pucho ['putʃo] (CS: *fam*) *nm* cigarette, fag (BRIT)

pude *etc vb V* **poder**

pudiente [pu'ðjente] *adj* (*rico*) wealthy, well-to-do

pudiera *etc vb V* **poder**

pudor [pu'ðor] *nm* modesty

pudrir [pu'ðrir] *vt* to rot; **pudrirse** *vr* to rot, decay

pueblo ['pweβlo] *nm* people; (*nación*) nation; (*aldea*) village

puedo *etc vb V* **poder**

puente ['pwente] *nm* bridge; **hacer ~** (*fam*) *to take extra days off work between 2 public holidays*; to take a long weekend; **puente aéreo** shuttle service; **puente colgante** suspension bridge; **puente levadizo** drawbridge

HACER PUENTE

When a public holiday in Spain falls on a Tuesday or Thursday it is common practice for employers to make the Monday or Friday a holiday as well and to give everyone a four-day weekend. This is known as **hacer puente**. When a named public holiday such as the **Día de la Constitución** falls on a Tuesday or Thursday, people refer to the whole holiday period as e.g. the **puente de la Constitución**.

puerco, -a ['pwerko, a] *nm/f* pig/sow ▷ *adj* (*sucio*) dirty, filthy; (*obsceno*) disgusting; **puerco espín** porcupine

pueril [pwe'ril] *adj* childish

puerro ['pwerro] *nm* leek

puerta ['pwerta] *nf* door; (*de jardín*) gate; (*portal*) doorway; (*fig*) gateway; (*portería*) goal; **a la ~** at the door; **a ~ cerrada** behind closed doors; **puerta giratoria** revolving door

puerto ['pwerto] *nm* port; (*paso*) pass; (*fig*) haven, refuge

Puerto Rico [pwerto'riko] *nm* Puerto Rico; **puertorriqueño, -a** *adj, nm/f* Puerto Rican

pues [pwes] *adv* (*entonces*) then; (*bueno*) well, well then; (*así que*) so ▷ *conj* (*ya que*) since; **¡~ sí!** yes!, certainly!

puesta ['pwesta] *nf* (*apuesta*) bet, stake; **puesta al día** updating; **puesta a punto** fine tuning; **puesta de sol** sunset; **puesta en marcha** starting

puesto, -a ['pwesto, a] *pp de* **poner** ▷ *adj*: **tener algo ~** to have sth on, be wearing sth ▷ *nm* (*lugar, posición*) place; (*trabajo*) post, job; (*Com*) stall ▷ *conj*: **~ que** since, as

púgil ['puxil] *nm* boxer

pulga ['pulɣa] *nf* flea

pulgada [pul'ɣaða] *nf* inch

pulgar [pul'ɣar] *nm* thumb

pulir [pu'lir] *vt* to polish; (*alisar*) to smooth; (*fig*) to polish up, touch up

pulmón [pul'mon] *nm* lung; **pulmonía** *nf* pneumonia

pulpa ['pulpa] *nf* pulp; (*de fruta*) flesh, soft part

pulpería [pulpe'ria] (LAM) *nf* (*tienda*) small grocery store

púlpito ['pulpito] *nm* pulpit

pulpo ['pulpo] *nm* octopus

pulque ['pulke] *nm* pulque

PULQUE

Pulque is a thick, white, alcoholic drink which is very popular in Mexico. In ancient times it was considered sacred by the Aztecs. It is produced by fermenting the juice of the **maguey**, a Mexican cactus similar to the agave. It can be drunk by itself or mixed with fruit or vegetable juice.

pulsación [pulsa'θjon] *nf* beat; **pulsaciones** pulse rate

pulsar [pul'sar] *vt* (*tecla*) to touch, tap; (*Mús*) to play; (*botón*) to press, push ▷ *vi* to pulsate; (*latir*) to beat, throb

pulsera [pul'sera] *nf* bracelet

pulso ['pulso] *nm* (*Anat*) pulse; (*fuerza*) strength; (*firmeza*) steadiness, steady hand

pulverizador [pulβeriθa'ðor] *nm* spray, spray gun

pulverizar [pulβeri'θar] *vt* to pulverize; (*líquido*) to spray

puna ['puna] (CAM) *nf* mountain sickness

punta ['punta] *nf* point, tip; (*extremo*) end; (*fig*) touch, trace; **horas ~** peak *o* rush hours; **sacar ~ a** to sharpen

puntada [pun'taða] *nf* (*Costura*) stitch

puntal [pun'tal] *nm* prop, support

puntapié [punta'pje] *nm* kick

puntería [punte'ria] *nf* (*de arma*) aim, aiming; (*destreza*) marksmanship

puntero, -a [pun'tero, a] *adj* leading ▷ *nm* (*palo*) pointer

puntiagudo, -a [puntja'ɣuðo, a] *adj* sharp, pointed

puntilla [pun'tiʎa] *nf* (*encaje*) lace edging *o* trim; **(andar) de ~s** (to walk) on tiptoe

punto ['punto] *nm* (*gen*) point; (*señal diminuta*) spot, dot; (*Costura, Med*) stitch; (*lugar*) spot, place; (*momento*) point, moment; **a ~** ready; **estar a ~ de** to be on the point of *o* about to; **en ~** on the dot; **hasta cierto ~** to some extent; **hacer ~** (ESP: *tejer*) to knit; **dos ~s** (*Ling*) colon; **punto de interrogación** question mark; **punto de vista** point of view, viewpoint; **punto final** full stop (BRIT), period (US); **punto muerto** dead center; (*Auto*) neutral (gear); **punto y aparte** (*en dictado*) full stop, new paragraph; **punto y coma** semicolon

puntocom [punto'kom] *adj inv, nf inv* dotcom

puntuación [puntwa'θjon] *nf* punctuation; (*puntos: en examen*) mark(s) (*pl*); (*Deporte*) score

puntual [pun'twal] *adj* (*a tiempo*) punctual; (*exacto*) exact, accurate; **puntualidad** *nf* punctuality; exactness, accuracy

puntuar [pun'twar] *vi* (*Deporte*) to score, count

punzante [pun'θante] *adj* (*dolor*) shooting, sharp; (*herramienta*) sharp

puñado [pu'ɲaðo] *nm* handful

puñal [pu'ɲal] *nm* dagger; **puñalada** *nf* stab

puñetazo [puɲe'taθo] *nm* punch

puño ['puɲo] *nm* (*Anat*) fist; (*cantidad*) fistful, handful; (*Costura*) cuff; (*de* *herramienta*) handle

pupila [pu'pila] *nf* pupil

pupitre [pu'pitre] *nm* desk

puré [pu're] *nm* purée; (*sopa*) (thick) soup; **puré de papas** (*LAM*) mashed potatoes; **puré de patatas** (*ESP*) mashed potatoes

purga ['purɣa] *nf* purge; **purgante** *adj, nm* purgative

purgatorio [purɣa'torjo] *nm* purgatory

purificar [purifi'kar] *vt* to purify; (*refinar*) to refine

puritano, -a [puri'tano, a] *adj* (*actitud*) puritanical; (*iglesia, tradición*) puritan ▷*nm/f* puritan

puro, -a ['puro, a] *adj* pure; (*verdad*) simple, plain ▷*nm* cigar

púrpura ['purpura] *nf* purple

pus [pus] *nm* pus

puse *etc vb V* **poder**

pusiera *etc vb V* **poder**

puta ['puta] (*fam!*) *nf* whore, prostitute

putrefacción [putrefak'θjon] *nf* rotting, putrefaction

PVP *nm abr* (= *precio de venta al público*) RRP

pyme, PYME ['pime] *nf abr* (= *Pequeña y Mediana Empresa*) SME

PALABRA CLAVE

que [ke] *conj* **1** (*con oración subordinada: muchas veces no se traduce*) that; **dijo que vendría** he said (that) he would come; **espero que lo encuentres** I hope (that) you find it; *V tb* **el**

2 (*en oración independiente*): **¡que entre!** send him in; **¡que aproveche!** enjoy your meal!; **¡que se mejore tu padre!** I hope your father gets better

3 (*enfático*): **¿me quieres? – ¡que sí!** do you love me? – of course!

4 (*consecutivo: muchas veces no se traduce*) that; **es tan grande que no lo puedo levantar** it's so big (that) I can't lift it

5 (*comparaciones*) than; **yo que tú/él** if I were you/him; *V tb* **más, menos, mismo**

6 (*valor disyuntivo*): **que le guste o no** whether he likes it or not; **que venga o que no venga** whether he comes or not

7 (*porque*): **no puedo, que tengo que quedarme en casa** I can't, I've got to stay in
▷ *pron* 1 (*cosa*) that, which; (+ *prep*) which; **el sombrero que te compraste** the hat (that *o* which) you bought; **la cama en que dormí** the bed (that *o* which) I slept in
2 (*persona*: *suj*) that, who; (: *objeto*) that, whom; **el amigo que me acompañó al museo** the friend that *o* who went to the museum with me; **la chica que invité** the girl (that *o* whom) I invited

qué [ke] *adj* what?, which? ▷ *pron* what?; **¡~ divertido!** how funny!; **¿~ edad tienes?** how old are you?; **¿de ~ me hablas?** what are you saying to me?; **¿~ tal?** how are you?, how are things?; **¿~ hay (de nuevo)?** what's new?
quebrado, -a [ke'βraðo, a] *adj* (*roto*) broken ▷ *nm/f* bankrupt ▷ *nm* (*Mat*) fraction
quebrantar [keβran'tar] *vt* (*infringir*) to violate, transgress
quebrar [ke'βrar] *vt* to break, smash ▷ *vi* to go bankrupt
quedar [ke'ðar] *vi* to stay, remain; (*encontrarse*: *sitio*) to be; (*haber aún*) to remain, be left; **quedarse** *vr* to remain, stay (behind); **~se (con) algo** to keep sth; **~ en** (*acordar*) to agree on/to; **~ en nada** to come to nothing; **~ por hacer** to be still to be done; **~ ciego/mudo** to be left blind/dumb; **no te queda bien ese vestido** that dress doesn't suit you; **eso queda muy lejos** that's a long way (away); **quedamos a las seis** we agreed to meet at six
quedo, -a ['keðo, a] *adj* still ▷ *adv* softly, gently
quehacer [kea'θer] *nm* task, job; **quehaceres (domésticos)** *nmpl* household chores
queja ['kexa] *nf* complaint; **quejarse** *vr* (*enfermo*) to moan, groan; (*protestar*) to complain; **quejarse de que** to complain (about the fact) that;
quejido *nm* moan
quemado, -a [ke'maðo, a] *adj* burnt
quemadura [kema'ðura] *nf* burn, scald
quemar [ke'mar] *vt* to burn; (*fig*: *malgastar*) to burn up, squander ▷ *vi* to be burning hot; **quemarse** *vr* (*consumirse*) to burn (up); (*del sol*) to get sunburnt
quemarropa [kema'rropa]: **a ~** *adv* point-blank
quepo *etc vb V* **caber**
querella [ke'reʎa] *nf* (*Jur*) charge; (*disputa*) dispute

PALABRA CLAVE

querer [ke'rer] *vt* 1 (*desear*) to want; **quiero más dinero** I want more money; **quisiera** *o* **querría un té** I'd like a tea; **sin querer** unintentionally; **quiero ayudar/que vayas** I want to help/you to go
2 (*preguntas*: *para pedir algo*): **¿quiere abrir la ventana?** could you open the window?; **¿quieres echarme una mano?** can you give me a hand?
3 (*amar*) to love; (*tener cariño a*) to be fond of; **te quiero** I love you; **quiere mucho a sus hijos** he's very fond of his children
4 **le pedí que me dejara ir pero no quiso** I asked him to let me go but he refused

querido, -a [ke'riðo, a] *adj* dear ▷ *nm/f* darling; (*amante*) lover
queso ['keso] *nm* cheese; **queso crema** (LAM) cream cheese; **queso de untar** (ESP) cream cheese; **queso manchego** *sheep's milk cheese made in La Mancha*; **queso rallado** grated cheese
quicio ['kiθjo] *nm* hinge; **sacar a algn de ~** to get on sb's nerves
quiebra ['kjeβra] *nf* break, split; (*Com*) bankruptcy; (*Econ*) slump
quiebro ['kjeβro] *nm* (*del cuerpo*)

swerve

quien [kjen] *pron* who; **hay ~ piensa que** there are those who think that; **no hay ~ lo haga** no-one will do it

quién [kjen] *pron* who, whom; **¿~ es?** who's there?

quienquiera [kjen'kjera] (*pl* **quienesquiera**) *pron* whoever

quiero *etc vb V* **querer**

quieto, -a ['kjeto, a] *adj* still; (*carácter*) placid

No confundir **quieto** con la palabra inglesa *quiet*.

quietud *nf* stillness

quilate [ki'late] *nm* carat

químico, -a ['kimiko, a] *adj* chemical ▷ *nm/f* chemist ▷ *nf* chemistry

quincalla [kin'kaʎa] *nf* hardware, ironmongery (BRIT)

quince ['kinθe] *num* fifteen; **~ días** a fortnight; **quinceañero, -a** *nm/f* teenager; **quincena** *nf* fortnight; (*pago*) fortnightly pay; **quincenal** *adj* fortnightly

quiniela [ki'njela] *nf* football pools *pl*; **quinielas** *nfpl* (*impreso*) pools coupon *sg*

quinientos, -as [ki'njentos, as] *adj, num* five hundred

quinto, -a ['kinto, a] *adj* fifth ▷ *nf* country house; (*Mil*) call-up, draft

quiosco ['kjosko] *nm* (*de música*) bandstand; (*de periódicos*) news stand

quirófano [ki'rofano] *nm* operating theatre

quirúrgico, -a [ki'rurxiko, a] *adj* surgical

quise *etc vb V* **querer**

quisiera *etc vb V* **querer**

quisquilloso, -a [kiski'ʎoso, a] *adj* (*susceptible*) touchy; (*meticuloso*) pernickety

quiste ['kiste] *nm* cyst

quitaesmalte [kitaes'malte] *nm* nail-polish remover

quitamanchas [kita'mantʃas] *nm inv* stain remover

quitanieves [kita'njeβes] *nm inv* snowplough (BRIT), snowplow (US)

quitar [ki'tar] *vt* to remove, take away; (*ropa*) to take off; (*dolor*) to relieve; **¡quita de ahí!** get away!; **quitarse** *vr* to withdraw; (*ropa*) to take off; **se quitó el sombrero** he took off his hat

Quito ['kito] *n* Quito

quizá(s) [ki'θa(s)] *adv* perhaps, maybe

rábano ['raβano] *nm* radish; **me importa un ~** I don't give a damn
rabia ['raβja] *nf* (*Med*) rabies *sg*; (*ira*) fury, rage; **rabiar** *vi* to have rabies; to rage, be furious; **rabiar por algo** to long for sth
rabieta [ra'βjeta] *nf* tantrum, fit of temper
rabino [ra'βino] *nm* rabbi
rabioso, -a [ra'βjoso, a] *adj* rabid; (*fig*) furious
rabo ['raβo] *nm* tail
racha ['ratʃa] *nf* gust of wind; **buena/mala ~** spell of good/bad luck
racial [ra'θjal] *adj* racial, race *cpd*
racimo [ra'θimo] *nm* bunch
ración [ra'θjon] *nf* portion; **raciones** *nfpl* rations
racional [raθjo'nal] *adj* (*razonable*) reasonable; (*lógico*) rational
racionar [raθjo'nar] *vt* to ration (out)
racismo [ra'θismo] *nm* racism; **racista** *adj, nm* racist
radar [ra'ðar] *nm* radar
radiador [raðja'ðor] *nm* radiator
radiante [ra'ðjante] *adj* radiant
radical [raði'kal] *adj, nmf* radical
radicar [raði'kar] *vi*: **~ en** (*dificultad, problema*) to lie in; (*solución*) to consist in
radio ['raðjo] *nf* radio; (*aparato*) radio (set) ▷ *nm* (*Mat*) radius; (*Quím*) radium; **radioactividad** *nf* radioactivity; **radioactivo, -a** *adj* radioactive; **radiografía** *nf* X-ray; **radioterapia** *nf* radiotherapy; **radioyente** *nmf* listener
ráfaga ['rafaɣa] *nf* gust; (*de luz*) flash; (*de tiros*) burst
raíz [ra'iθ] *nf* root; **a ~ de** as a result of; **raíz cuadrada** square root
raja ['raxa] *nf* (*de melón etc*) slice; (*grieta*) crack; **rajar** *vt* to split; (*fam*) to slash; **rajarse** *vr* to split, crack; **rajarse de** to back out of
rajatabla [raxa'taβla]: **a ~** *adv* (*estrictamente*) strictly, to the letter
rallador [raʎa'ðor] *nm* grater
rallar [ra'ʎar] *vt* to grate
rama ['rama] *nf* branch; **ramaje** *nm* branches *pl*, foliage; **ramal** *nm* (*de cuerda*) strand; (*Ferro*) branch line (BRIT); (*Auto*) branch (road) (BRIT)
rambla ['rambla] *nf* (*avenida*) avenue
ramo ['ramo] *nm* branch; (*sección*) department, section
rampa ['rampa] *nf* ramp; **rampa de acceso** entrance ramp
rana ['rana] *nf* frog; **salto de ~** leapfrog
ranchero [ran'tʃero] (MÉX) *nm* (*hacendado*) rancher; smallholder
rancho ['rantʃo] *nm* (*grande*) ranch; (*pequeño*) small farm
rancio, -a ['ranθjo, a] *adj* (*comestibles*) rancid; (*vino*) aged, mellow; (*fig*) ancient
rango ['rango] *nm* rank, standing
ranura [ra'nura] *nf* groove; (*de teléfono etc*) slot
rapar [ra'par] *vt* to shave; (*los cabellos*) to crop
rapaz [ra'paθ] (*nf* **~a**) *nmf* young

boy/girl ▷ *adj* (*Zool*) predatory
rape ['rape] *nm* (*pez*) monkfish; **al ~** cropped
rapé [ra'pe] *nm* snuff
rapidez [rapi'ðeθ] *nf* speed, rapidity; **rápido, -a** *adj* fast, quick ▷ *adv* quickly ▷ *nm* (*Ferro*) express; **rápidos** *nmpl* rapids
rapiña [ra'piɲa] *nm* robbery; **ave de ~** bird of prey
raptar [rap'tar] *vt* to kidnap; **rapto** *nm* kidnapping; (*impulso*) sudden impulse; (*éxtasis*) ecstasy, rapture
raqueta [ra'keta] *nf* racquet
raquítico, -a [ra'kitiko, a] *adj* stunted; (*fig*) poor, inadequate
rareza [ra'reθa] *nf* rarity; (*fig*) eccentricity
raro, -a ['raro, a] *adj* (*poco común*) rare; (*extraño*) odd, strange; (*excepcional*) remarkable
ras [ras] *nm*: **a ~ de** level with; **a ~ de tierra** at ground level
rasar [ra'sar] *vt* (*igualar*) to level
rascacielos [raska'θjelos] *nm inv* skyscraper
rascar [ras'kar] *vt* (*con las uñas etc*) to scratch; (*raspar*) to scrape; **rascarse** *vr* to scratch (o.s.)
rasgar [ras'ɣar] *vt* to tear, rip (up)
rasgo ['rasɣo] *nm* (*con pluma*) stroke; **rasgos** *nmpl* (*facciones*) features, characteristics; **a grandes ~s** in outline, broadly
rasguño [ras'ɣuɲo] *nm* scratch
raso, -a ['raso, a] *adj* (*liso*) flat, level; (*a baja altura*) very low ▷ *nm* satin; **cielo ~** clear sky
raspadura [raspa'ðura] *nf* (*acto*) scrape, scraping; (*marca*) scratch; **raspaduras** *nfpl* (*de papel etc*) scrapings
raspar [ras'par] *vt* to scrape; (*arañar*) to scratch; (*limar*) to file
rastra ['rastra] *nf* (*Agr*) rake; **a ~s** by dragging; (*fig*) unwillingly
rastrear [rastre'ar] *vt* (*seguir*) to track
rastrero, -a [ras'trero, a] *adj* (*Bot*, *Zool*) creeping; (*fig*) despicable, mean
rastrillo [ras'triʎo] *nm* rake
rastro ['rastro] *nm* (*Agr*) rake; (*pista*) track, trail; (*vestigio*) trace; **el R~** (ESP) the Madrid fleamarket
rasurado [rasu'raðo] (MÉX) *nm* shaving; **rasuradora** [rasura'ðora] (MÉX) *nf* electric shaver; **rasurar** [rasu'rar] (MÉX) *vt* to shave; **rasurarse** *vr* to shave
rata ['rata] *nf* rat
ratear [rate'ar] *vt* (*robar*) to steal
ratero, -a [ra'tero, a] *adj* light-fingered ▷ *nm/f* (*carterista*) pickpocket; (*ladrón*) petty thief
rato ['rato] *nm* while, short time; **a ~s** from time to time; **hay para ~** there's still a long way to go; **al poco ~** soon afterwards; **pasar el ~** to kill time; **pasar un buen/mal ~** to have a good/rough time; **en mis ~s libres** in my spare time
ratón [ra'ton] *nm* mouse; **ratonera** *nf* mousetrap
raudal [rau'ðal] *nm* torrent; **a ~es** in abundance
raya ['raja] *nf* line; (*marca*) scratch; (*en tela*) stripe; (*de pelo*) parting; (*límite*) boundary; (*pez*) ray; (*puntuación*) dash; **a ~s** striped; **pasarse de la ~** to go too far; **tener a ~** to keep in check; **rayar** *vt* to line; to scratch; (*subrayar*) to underline ▷ *vi*: **rayar en** *o* **con** to border on
rayo ['rajo] *nm* (*del sol*) ray, beam; (*de luz*) shaft; (*en una tormenta*) (flash of) lightning; **rayos X** X-rays
raza ['raθa] *nf* race; **raza humana** human race
razón [ra'θon] *nf* reason; (*justicia*) right, justice; (*razonamiento*) reasoning; (*motivo*) reason, motive; (*Mat*) ratio; **a ~ de 10 cada día** at the rate of 10 a day; **en ~ de** with regard to; **dar ~ a algn** to agree that sb is right; **tener ~** to be right; **razón de ser** raison d'être; **razón directa/inversa** direct/inverse proportion; **razonable**

adj reasonable; (*justo, moderado*) fair; **razonamiento** *nm* (*juicio*) judg(e)ment; (*argumento*) reasoning; **razonar** *vt, vi* to reason, argue

re [re] *nm* (*Mús*) D

reacción [reak'θjon] *nf* reaction; **avión a ~** jet plane; **reacción en cadena** chain reaction; **reaccionar** *vi* to react

reacio, -a [re'aθjo, a] *adj* stubborn

reactivar [reakti'βar] *vt* to revitalize

reactor [reak'tor] *nm* reactor

real [re'al] *adj* real; (*del rey, fig*) royal

realidad [reali'ðað] *nf* reality, fact; (*verdad*) truth

realista [rea'lista] *nmf* realist

realización [realiθa'θjon] *nf* fulfilment

realizador, a [realiθa'ðor, a] *nm/f* film-maker

realizar [reali'θar] *vt* (*objetivo*) to achieve; (*plan*) to carry out; (*viaje*) to make, undertake; **realizarse** *vr* to come about, come true

realmente [real'mente] *adv* really, actually

realzar [real'θar] *vt* to enhance; (*acentuar*) to highlight

reanimar [reani'mar] *vt* to revive; (*alentar*) to encourage; **reanimarse** *vr* to revive

reanudar [reanu'ðar] *vt* (*renovar*) to renew; (*historia, viaje*) to resume

reaparición [reapari'θjon] *nf* reappearance

rearme [re'arme] *nm* rearmament

rebaja [re'βaxa] *nf* (*Com*) reduction; (*: descuento*) discount; **rebajas** *nfpl* (*Com*) sale; **rebajar** *vt* (*bajar*) to lower; (*reducir*) to reduce; (*disminuir*) to lessen; (*humillar*) to humble

rebanada [reβa'naða] *nf* slice

rebañar [reβa'ɲar] *vt* (*comida*) to scrape up; (*plato*) to scrape clean

rebaño [re'βaɲo] *nm* herd; (*de ovejas*) flock

rebatir [reβa'tir] *vt* to refute

rebeca [re'βeka] *nf* cardigan

rebelarse [reβe'larse] *vr* to rebel, revolt

rebelde [re'βelde] *adj* rebellious; (*niño*) unruly ▷ *nmf* rebel; **rebeldía** *nf* rebelliousness; (*desobediencia*) disobedience

rebelión [reβe'ljon] *nf* rebellion

reblandecer [reβlande'θer] *vt* to soften

rebobinar [reβoβi'nar] *vt* (*cinta, película de video*) to rewind

rebosante [reβo'sante] *adj* overflowing

rebosar [reβo'sar] *vi* (*líquido, recipiente*) to overflow; (*abundar*) to abound, be plentiful

rebotar [reβo'tar] *vt* to bounce; (*rechazar*) to repel ▷ *vi* (*pelota*) to bounce; (*bala*) to ricochet; **rebote** *nm* rebound; **de rebote** on the rebound

rebozado, -a [reβo'θaðo, a] *adj* fried in batter *o* breadcrumbs

rebozar [reβo'θar] *vt* to wrap up; (*Culin*) to fry in batter *o* breadcrumbs

rebuscado, -a [reβus'kaðo, a] *adj* (*amanerado*) affected; (*palabra*) recherché; (*idea*) far-fetched

rebuscar [reβus'kar] *vi*: **~ (en/por)** to search carefully (in/for)

recado [re'kaðo] *nm* (*mensaje*) message; (*encargo*) errand; **tomar un ~** (*Tel*) to take a message

recaer [reka'er] *vi* to relapse; **~ en** to fall to *o* on; (*criminal etc*) to fall back into, relapse into; **recaída** *nf* relapse

recalcar [rekal'kar] *vt* (*fig*) to stress, emphasize

recalentar [rekalen'tar] *vt* (*volver a calentar*) to reheat; (*calentar demasiado*) to overheat

recámara [re'kamara] (MÉX) *nf* bedroom

recambio [re'kambjo] *nm* spare; (*de pluma*) refill

recapacitar [rekapaθi'tar] *vi* to reflect

recargado, -a [rekar'ɣaðo, a] *adj* overloaded

recargar [rekar'ɣar] *vt* to overload; (*batería*) to recharge; **~ el saldo de** (*Tel*) to top up; **recargo** *nm* surcharge; (*aumento*) increase

recatado, -a [reka'taðo, a] *adj* (*modesto*) modest, demure; (*prudente*) cautious

recaudación [rekauða'θjon] *nf* (*acción*) collection; (*cantidad*) takings *pl*; (*en deporte*) gate; **recaudador, a** *nm/f* tax collector

recelar [reθe'lar] *vt*: **~ que ...** (*sospechar*) to suspect that ...; (*temer*) to fear that ... ▷ *vi*: **~ de** to distrust; **recelo** *nm* distrust, suspicion

recepción [reθep'θjon] *nf* reception; **recepcionista** *nmf* receptionist

receptor, a [reθep'tor, a] *nm/f* recipient ▷ *nm* (*Tel*) receiver

recesión [reθe'sjon] *nf* (*Com*) recession

receta [re'θeta] *nf* (*Culin*) recipe; (*Med*) prescription

> No confundir **receta** con la palabra inglesa *receipt*.

rechazar [retʃa'θar] *vt* to reject; (*oferta*) to turn down; (*ataque*) to repel

rechazo [re'tʃaθo] *nm* rejection

rechinar [retʃi'nar] *vi* to creak; (*dientes*) to grind

rechistar [retʃis'tar] *vi*: **sin ~** without a murmur

rechoncho, -a [re'tʃontʃo, a] (*fam*) *adj* thickset (BRIT), heavy-set (US)

rechupete [retʃu'pete]: **de ~** *adj* (*comida*) delicious, scrumptious

recibidor [reθiβi'ðor] *nm* entrance hall

recibimiento [reθiβi'mjento] *nm* reception, welcome

recibir [reθi'βir] *vt* to receive; (*dar la bienvenida*) to welcome ▷ *vi* to entertain; **recibo** *nm* receipt

reciclable [reθɪ'klaβle] *adj* recyclable

reciclar [reθi'klar] *vt* to recycle

recién [re'θjen] *adv* recently, newly; **los ~ casados** the newly-weds; **el ~ llegado** the newcomer; **el ~ nacido** the newborn child

reciente [re'θjente] *adj* recent; (*fresco*) fresh

recinto [re'θinto] *nm* enclosure; (*área*) area, place

recio, -a ['reθjo, a] *adj* strong, tough; (*voz*) loud ▷ *adv* hard, loud(ly)

recipiente [reθi'pjente] *nm* receptacle

recíproco, -a [re'θiproco, a] *adj* reciprocal

recital [reθi'tal] *nm* (*Mús*) recital; (*Literatura*) reading

recitar [reθi'tar] *vt* to recite

reclamación [reklama'θjon] *nf* claim, demand; (*queja*) complaint

reclamar [rekla'mar] *vt* to claim, demand ▷ *vi*: **~ contra** to complain about; **reclamo** *nm* (*anuncio*) advertisement; (*tentación*) attraction

reclinar [rekli'nar] *vt* to recline, lean; **reclinarse** *vr* to lean back

reclusión [reklu'sjon] *nf* (*prisión*) prison; (*refugio*) seclusion

recluta [re'kluta] *nmf* recruit ▷ *nf* recruitment; **reclutar** *vt* (*datos*) to collect; (*dinero*) to collect up; **reclutamiento** *nm* recruitment

recobrar [reko'βrar] *vt* (*salud*) to recover; (*rescatar*) to get back; **recobrarse** *vr* to recover

recodo [re'koðo] *nm* (*de río, camino*) bend

recogedor [rekoxe'ðor] *nm* dustpan

recoger [reko'xer] *vt* to collect; (*Agr*) to harvest; (*levantar*) to pick up; (*juntar*) to gather; (*pasar a buscar*) to come for, get; (*dar asilo*) to give shelter to; (*faldas*) to gather up; (*pelo*) to put up; **recogerse** *vr* (*retirarse*) to retire; **recogido, -a** *adj* (*lugar*) quiet, secluded; (*pequeño*) small ▷ *nf* (*Correos*) collection; (*Agr*) harvest

recolección [rekolek'θjon] *nf* (*Agr*) harvesting; (*colecta*) collection

recomendación [rekomenda'θjon] *nf* (*sugerencia*) suggestion, recommendation; (*referencia*) reference

recomendar [rekomen'dar] *vt* to suggest, recommend; (*confiar*) to entrust

recompensa [rekom'pensa] *nf* reward, recompense; **recompensar** *vt* to reward, recompense

reconciliación [rekonθilja'θjon] *nf* reconciliation

reconciliar [rekonθi'ljar] *vt* to reconcile; **reconciliarse** *vr* to become reconciled

recóndito, -a [re'kondito, a] *adj* (*lugar*) hidden, secret

reconocer [rekono'θer] *vt* to recognize; (*registrar*) to search; (*Med*) to examine; **reconocido, -a** *adj* recognized; (*agradecido*) grateful; **reconocimiento** *nm* recognition; search; examination; gratitude; (*confesión*) admission

reconquista [rekon'kista] *nf* reconquest; **la R~** the Reconquest (of Spain)

reconstituyente [rekonstitu'jente] *nm* tonic

reconstruir [rekonstru'ir] *vt* to reconstruct

reconversión [rekonβer'sjon] *nf* (*reestructuración*) restructuring; **reconversión industrial** industrial rationalization

recopilación [rekopila'θjon] *nf* (*resumen*) summary; (*compilación*) compilation; **recopilar** *vt* to compile

récord ['rekorð] (*pl* **~s**) *adj inv, nm* record

recordar [rekor'ðar] *vt* (*acordarse de*) to remember; (*acordar a otro*) to remind ▷ *vi* to remember

> No confundir **recordar** con la palabra inglesa *record*.

recorrer [reko'rrer] *vt* (*país*) to cross, travel through; (*distancia*) to cover; (*registrar*) to search; (*repasar*) to look over; **recorrido** *nm* run, journey; **tren de largo recorrido** main-line train

recortar [rekor'tar] *vt* to cut out; **recorte** *nm* (*acción, de prensa*) cutting; (*de telas, chapas*) trimming; **recorte presupuestario** budget cut

recostar [rekos'tar] *vt* to lean; **recostarse** *vr* to lie down

recoveco [reko'βeko] *nm* (*de camino, río etc*) bend; (*en casa*) cubby hole

recreación [rekrea'θjon] *nf* recreation

recrear [rekre'ar] *vt* (*entretener*) to entertain; (*volver a crear*) to recreate; **recreativo, -a** *adj* recreational; **recreo** *nm* recreation; (*Escol*) break, playtime

recriminar [rekrimi'nar] *vt* to reproach ▷ *vi* to recriminate; **recriminarse** *vr* to reproach each other

recrudecer [rekruðe'θer] *vt, vi* to worsen; **recrudecerse** *vr* to worsen

recta ['rekta] *nf* straight line

rectángulo, -a [rek'tangulo, a] *adj* rectangular ▷ *nm* rectangle

rectificar [rektifi'kar] *vt* to rectify; (*volverse recto*) to straighten ▷ *vi* to correct o.s.

rectitud [rekti'tuð] *nf* straightness

recto, -a ['rekto, a] *adj* straight; (*persona*) honest, upright; **siga todo ~** go straight on ▷ *nm* rectum

rector, a [rek'tor, a] *adj* governing

recuadro [re'kwaðro] *nm* box; (*Tip*) inset

recubrir [reku'βrir] *vt*: **~ (con)** (*pintura, crema*) to cover (with)

recuento [re'kwento] *nm* inventory; **hacer el ~ de** to count *o* reckon up

recuerdo [re'kwerðo] *nm* souvenir; **recuerdos** *nmpl* (*memorias*) memories; **¡~s a tu madre!** give my regards to your mother!

recular [reku'lar] *vi* to back down

recuperación [rekupera'θjon] *nf* recovery

recuperar [rekupe'rar] *vt* to recover; (*tiempo*) to make up; **recuperarse** *vr* to recuperate

recurrir [reku'rrir] *vi* (*Jur*) to appeal; **~ a** to resort to; (*persona*) to turn to;

recurso *nm* resort; (*medios*) means *pl*, resources *pl*; (*Jur*) appeal
red [reð] *nf* net, mesh; (*Ferro etc*) network; (*trampa*) trap; **la R~** (*Internet*) the Net
redacción [reðak'θjon] *nf* (*acción*) editing; (*personal*) editorial staff; (*Escol*) essay, composition
redactar [reðak'tar] *vt* to draw up, draft; (*periódico*) to edit
redactor, a [reðak'tor, a] *nm/f* editor
redada [re'ðaða] *nf* (*de policía*) raid, round-up
rededor [reðe'ðor] *nm*: **al** *o* **en ~** around, round about
redoblar [reðo'βlar] *vt* to redouble ▷ *vi* (*tambor*) to roll
redonda [re'ðonda] *nf*: **a la ~** around, round about
redondear [reðonde'ar] *vt* to round, round off
redondel [reðon'del] *nm* (*círculo*) circle; (*Taur*) bullring, arena
redondo, -a [re'ðondo, a] *adj* (*circular*) round; (*completo*) complete
reducción [reðuk'θjon] *nf* reduction
reducido, -a [reðu'θiðo, a] *adj* reduced; (*limitado*) limited; (*pequeño*) small
reducir [reðu'θir] *vt* to reduce; to limit; **reducirse** *vr* to diminish
redundancia [reðun'danθja] *nf* redundancy
reembolsar [re(e)mbol'sar] *vt* (*persona*) to reimburse; (*dinero*) to repay, pay back; (*depósito*) to refund; **reembolso** *nm* reimbursement; refund
reemplazar [re(e)mpla'θar] *vt* to replace; **reemplazo** *nm* replacement; **de reemplazo** (*Mil*) reserve
reencuentro [re(e)n'kwentro] *nm* reunion
reescribible [reeskri'βiβle] *adj* rewritable
refacción [refak'θjon] (*MÉX*) *nf* spare (part)
referencia [refe'renθja] *nf* reference; **con ~ a** with reference to
referéndum [refe'rendum] (*pl* **~s**) *nm* referendum
referente [refe'rente] *adj*: **~ a** concerning, relating to
réferi ['referi] (*LAM*) *nmf* referee
referir [refe'rir] *vt* (*contar*) to tell, recount; (*relacionar*) to refer, relate; **referirse** *vr*: **~se a** to refer to
refilón [refi'lon]: **de ~** *adv* obliquely
refinado, -a [refi'naðo, a] *adj* refined
refinar [refi'nar] *vt* to refine; **refinería** *nf* refinery
reflejar [refle'xar] *vt* to reflect; **reflejo, -a** *adj* reflected; (*movimiento*) reflex ▷ *nm* reflection; (*Anat*) reflex
reflexión [reflek'sjon] *nf* reflection; **reflexionar** *vt* to reflect on ▷ *vi* to reflect; (*detenerse*) to pause (to think)
reflexivo, -a [reflek'siβo, a] *adj* thoughtful; (*Ling*) reflexive
reforma [re'forma] *nf* reform; (*Arq etc*) repair; **reforma agraria** agrarian reform
reformar [refor'mar] *vt* to reform; (*modificar*) to change, alter; (*Arq*) to repair; **reformarse** *vr* to mend one's ways
reformatorio [reforma'torjo] *nm* reformatory
reforzar [refor'θar] *vt* to strengthen; (*Arq*) to reinforce; (*fig*) to encourage
refractario, -a [refrak'tarjo, a] *adj* (*Tec*) heat-resistant
refrán [re'fran] *nm* proverb, saying
refregar [refre'ɣar] *vt* to scrub
refrescante [refres'kante] *adj* refreshing, cooling
refrescar [refres'kar] *vt* to refresh ▷ *vi* to cool down; **refrescarse** *vr* to get cooler; (*tomar aire fresco*) to go out for a breath of fresh air; (*beber*) to have a drink
refresco [re'fresko] *nm* soft drink, cool drink; **"~s"** "refreshments"
refriega [re'frjeɣa] *nf* scuffle, brawl

refrigeración [refrixera'θjon] *nf* refrigeration; (*de sala*) air-conditioning
refrigerador [refrixera'ðor] *nm* refrigerator (BRIT), icebox (US)
refrigerar [refrixe'rar] *vt* to refrigerate; (*sala*) to air-condition
refuerzo [re'fwerθo] *nm* reinforcement; (*Tec*) support
refugiado, -a [refu'xjaðo, a] *nm/f* refugee
refugiarse [refu'xjarse] *vr* to take refuge, shelter
refugio [re'fuxjo] *nm* refuge; (*protección*) shelter
refunfuñar [refunfu'ɲar] *vi* to grunt, growl; (*quejarse*) to grumble
regadera [reɣa'ðera] *nf* watering can
regadío [rega'ðio] *nm* irrigated land
regalado, -a [reɣa'laðo, a] *adj* comfortable, luxurious; (*gratis*) free, for nothing
regalar [reɣa'lar] *vt* (*dar*) to give (as a present); (*entregar*) to give away; (*mimar*) to pamper, make a fuss of
regaliz [reɣa'liθ] *nm* liquorice
regalo [re'ɣalo] *nm* (*obsequio*) gift, present; (*gusto*) pleasure
regañadientes [reɣaɲa'ðjentes]: **a ~** *adv* reluctantly
regañar [reɣa'ɲar] *vt* to scold ▷ *vi* to grumble; **regañón, -ona** *adj* nagging
regar [re'ɣar] *vt* to water, irrigate; (*fig*) to scatter, sprinkle
regatear [reɣate'ar] *vt* (*Com*) to bargain over; (*escatimar*) to be mean with ▷ *vi* to bargain, haggle; (*Deporte*) to dribble; **regateo** *nm* bargaining; dribbling; (*del cuerpo*) swerve, dodge
regazo [re'ɣaθo] *nm* lap
regenerar [rexene'rar] *vt* to regenerate
régimen ['reximen] (*pl* **regímenes**) *nm* regime; (*Med*) diet
regimiento [rexi'mjento] *nm* regiment
regio, -a ['rexjo, a] *adj* royal, regal; (*fig: suntuoso*) splendid; (CS: *fam*) great, terrific
región [re'xjon] *nf* region
regir [re'xir] *vt* to govern, rule; (*dirigir*) to manage, run ▷ *vi* to apply, be in force
registrar [rexis'trar] *vt* (*buscar*) to search; (*: en cajón*) to look through; (*inspeccionar*) to inspect; (*anotar*) to register, record; (*Inform*) to log; **registrarse** *vr* to register; (*ocurrir*) to happen
registro [re'xistro] *nm* (*acto*) registration; (*Mús, libro*) register; (*inspección*) inspection, search; **registro civil** registry office
regla ['reɣla] *nf* (*ley*) rule, regulation; (*de medir*) ruler, rule; (*Med: período*) period; **en ~** in order
reglamentación [reɣlamenta'θjon] *nf* (*acto*) regulation; (*lista*) rules *pl*
reglamentar [reɣlamen'tar] *vt* to regulate; **reglamentario, -a** *adj* statutory; **reglamento** *nm* rules *pl*, regulations *pl*
regocijarse [reɣoθi'xarse] *vr* (*alegrarse*) to rejoice; **regocijo** *nm* joy, happiness
regrabadora [regraβa'ðora] *nf* rewriter; **regrabadora de DVD** DVD rewriter
regresar [reɣre'sar] *vi* to come back, go back, return; **regreso** *nm* return
reguero [re'ɣero] *nm* (*de sangre etc*) trickle; (*de humo*) trail
regulador [reɣula'ðor] *nm* regulator; (*de radio etc*) knob, control
regular [reɣu'lar] *adj* regular; (*normal*) normal, usual; (*común*) ordinary; (*organizado*) regular, orderly; (*mediano*) average; (*fam*) not bad, so-so ▷ *adv* so-so, alright ▷ *vt* (*controlar*) to control, regulate; (*Tec*) to adjust; **por lo ~** as a rule; **regularidad** *nf* regularity; **regularizar** *vt* to regularize
rehabilitación [reaβilita'θjon] *nf* rehabilitation; (*Arq*) restoration
rehabilitar [reaβili'tar] *vt* to rehabilitate; (*Arq*) to restore; (*reintegrar*) to reinstate

rehacer [rea'θer] *vt* (*reparar*) to mend, repair; (*volver a hacer*) to redo, repeat; **rehacerse** *vr* (*Med*) to recover
rehén [re'en] *nm* hostage
rehuir [reu'ir] *vt* to avoid, shun
rehusar [reu'sar] *vt, vi* to refuse
reina ['reina] *nf* queen; **reinado** *nm* reign
reinar [rei'nar] *vi* to reign
reincidir [reinθi'ðir] *vi* to relapse
reincorporarse [reinkorpo'rarse] *vr*: **~ a** to rejoin
reino ['reino] *nm* kingdom; **reino animal/vegetal** animal/plant kingdom; **el Reino Unido** the United Kingdom
reintegrar [reinte'ɣrar] *vt* (*reconstituir*) to reconstruct; (*persona*) to reinstate; (*dinero*) to refund, pay back; **reintegrarse** *vr*: **~se a** to return to
reír [re'ir] *vi* to laugh; **reírse** *vr* to laugh; **~se de** to laugh at
reiterar [reite'rar] *vt* to reiterate
reivindicación [reiβindika'θjon] *nf* (*demanda*) claim, demand; (*justificación*) vindication
reivindicar [reiβindi'kar] *vt* to claim
reja ['rexa] *nf* (*de ventana*) grille, bars *pl*; (*en la calle*) grating
rejilla [re'xiʎa] *nf* grating, grille; (*muebles*) wickerwork; (*de ventilación*) vent; (*de coche etc*) luggage rack
rejoneador [rexonea'ðor] *nm* mounted bullfighter
rejuvenecer [rexuβene'θer] *vt, vi* to rejuvenate
relación [rela'θjon] *nf* relation, relationship; (*Mat*) ratio; (*narración*) report; **con ~ a, en ~ con** in relation to; **relaciones públicas** public relations; **relacionar** *vt* to relate, connect; **relacionarse** *vr* to be connected, be linked
relajación [relaxa'θjon] *nf* relaxation
relajar [rela'xar] *vt* to relax; **relajarse** *vr* to relax
relamerse [rela'merse] *vr* to lick one's lips
relámpago [re'lampaɣo] *nm* flash of lightning; **visita ~** lightning visit
relatar [rela'tar] *vt* to tell, relate
relativo, -a [rela'tiβo, a] *adj* relative; **en lo ~ a** concerning
relato [re'lato] *nm* (*narración*) story, tale
relegar [rele'ɣar] *vt* to relegate
relevante [rele'βante] *adj* eminent, outstanding
relevar [rele'βar] *vt* (*sustituir*) to relieve; **relevarse** *vr* to relay; **~ a algn de un cargo** to relieve sb of his post
relevo [re'leβo] *nm* relief; **carrera de ~s** relay race
relieve [re'ljeβe] *nm* (*Arte, Tec*) relief; (*fig*) prominence, importance; **bajo ~** bas-relief
religión [reli'xjon] *nf* religion; **religioso, -a** *adj* religious ▷ *nm/f* monk/nun
relinchar [relin'tʃar] *vi* to neigh
reliquia [re'likja] *nf* relic; **reliquia de familia** heirloom
rellano [re'ʎano] *nm* (*Arq*) landing
rellenar [reʎe'nar] *vt* (*llenar*) to fill up; (*Culin*) to stuff; (*Costura*) to pad; **relleno, -a** *adj* full up; stuffed ▷ *nm* stuffing; (*de tapicería*) padding
reloj [re'lo(x)] *nm* clock; **poner el ~ (en hora)** to set one's watch (*o* the clock); **reloj (de pulsera)** wristwatch; **reloj despertador** alarm (clock); **reloj digital** digital watch; **relojero, -a** *nm/f* clockmaker; watchmaker
reluciente [relu'θjente] *adj* brilliant, shining
relucir [relu'θir] *vi* to shine; (*fig*) to excel
remachar [rema'tʃar] *vt* to rivet; (*fig*) to hammer home, drive home; **remache** *nm* rivet
remangar [reman'gar] *vt* to roll up
remanso [re'manso] *nm* pool
remar [re'mar] *vi* to row
rematado, -a [rema'taðo, a] *adj* complete, utter

rematar [rema'tar] *vt* to finish off; (*Com*) to sell off cheap ▷ *vi* to end, finish off; (*Deporte*) to shoot
remate [re'mate] *nm* end, finish; (*punta*) tip; (*Deporte*) shot; (*Arq*) top; **de** *o* **para ~** to crown it all (BRIT), to top it off
remedar [reme'ðar] *vt* to imitate
remediar [reme'ðjar] *vt* to remedy; (*subsanar*) to make good, repair; (*evitar*) to avoid
remedio [re'meðjo] *nm* remedy; (*alivio*) relief, help; (*Jur*) recourse, remedy; **poner ~ a** to correct, stop; **no tener más ~** to have no alternative; **¡qué ~!** there's no choice!; **sin ~** hopeless
remendar [remen'dar] *vt* to repair; (*con parche*) to patch
remiendo [re'mjendo] *nm* mend; (*con parche*) patch; (*cosido*) darn
remilgado, -a [remil'ɣaðo, a] *adj* prim; (*afectado*) affected
remiso, -a [re'miso, a] *adj* slack, slow
remite [re'mite] *nm* (*en sobre*) name and address of sender
remitir [remi'tir] *vt* to remit, send ▷ *vi* to slacken; (*en carta*): **remite: X** sender: X; **remitente** *nmf* sender
remo ['remo] *nm* (*de barco*) oar; (*Deporte*) rowing
remojar [remo'xar] *vt* to steep, soak; (*galleta etc*) to dip, dunk
remojo [re'moxo] *nm*: **dejar la ropa en ~** to leave clothes to soak
remolacha [remo'latʃa] *nf* beet, beetroot
remolcador [remolka'ðor] *nm* (*Náut*) tug; (*Auto*) breakdown lorry
remolcar [remol'kar] *vt* to tow
remolino [remo'lino] *nm* eddy; (*de agua*) whirlpool; (*de viento*) whirlwind; (*de gente*) crowd
remolque [re'molke] *nm* tow, towing; (*cuerda*) towrope; **llevar a ~** to tow
remontar [remon'tar] *vt* to mend; **remontarse** *vr* to soar; **~se a** (*Com*) to amount to; **~ el vuelo** to soar
remorder [remor'ðer] *vt* to distress, disturb; **~le la conciencia a algn** to have a guilty conscience; **remordimiento** *nm* remorse
remoto, -a [re'moto, a] *adj* remote
remover [remo'βer] *vt* to stir; (*tierra*) to turn over; (*objetos*) to move round
remuneración [remunera'θjon] *nf* remuneration
remunerar [remune'rar] *vt* to remunerate; (*premiar*) to reward
renacer [rena'θer] *vi* to be reborn; (*fig*) to revive; **renacimiento** *nm* rebirth; **el Renacimiento** the Renaissance
renacuajo [rena'kwaxo] *nm* (*Zool*) tadpole
renal [re'nal] *adj* renal, kidney *cpd*
rencilla [ren'θiʎa] *nf* quarrel
rencor [ren'kor] *nm* rancour, bitterness; **rencoroso, -a** *adj* spiteful
rendición [rendi'θjon] *nf* surrender
rendido, -a [ren'diðo, a] *adj* (*sumiso*) submissive; (*cansado*) worn-out, exhausted
rendija [ren'dixa] *nf* (*hendedura*) crack, cleft
rendimiento [rendi'mjento] *nm* (*producción*) output; (*Tec, Com*) efficiency
rendir [ren'dir] *vt* (*vencer*) to defeat; (*producir*) to produce; (*dar beneficio*) to yield; (*agotar*) to exhaust ▷ *vi* to pay; **rendirse** *vr* (*someterse*) to surrender; (*cansarse*) to wear o.s. out; **~ homenaje** *o* **culto a** to pay homage to
renegar [rene'ɣar] *vi* (*renunciar*) to renounce; (*blasfemar*) to blaspheme; (*quejarse*) to complain
RENFE ['renfe] *nf abr* (= *Red Nacional de los Ferrocarriles Españoles*)
renglón [ren'glon] *nm* (*línea*) line; (*Com*) item, article; **a ~ seguido** immediately after
renombre [re'nombre] *nm* renown
renovación [renoβa'θjon] *nf* (*de*

contrato) renewal; (*Arq*) renovation
renovar [reno'βar] *vt* to renew; (*Arq*) to renovate
renta ['renta] *nf* (*ingresos*) income; (*beneficio*) profit; (*alquiler*) rent; **renta vitalicia** annuity; **rentable** *adj* profitable
renuncia [re'nunθja] *nf* resignation; **renunciar** [renun'θjar] *vt* to renounce; (*tabaco, alcohol etc*): **renunciar a** to give up; (*oferta, oportunidad*) to turn down; (*puesto*) to resign ▷ *vi* to resign
reñido, -a [re'ɲiðo, a] *adj* (*batalla*) bitter, hard-fought; **estar ~ con algn** to be on bad terms with sb
reñir [re'ɲir] *vt* (*regañar*) to scold ▷ *vi* (*estar peleado*) to quarrel, fall out; (*combatir*) to fight
reo ['reo] *nmf* culprit, offender; (*acusado*) accused, defendant
reojo [re'oxo]: **de ~** *adv* out of the corner of one's eye
reparación [repara'θjon] *nf* (*acto*) mending, repairing; (*Tec*) repair; (*fig*) amends *pl*, reparation
reparar [repa'rar] *vt* to repair; (*fig*) to make amends for; (*observar*) to observe ▷ *vi*: **~ en** (*darse cuenta de*) to notice; (*prestar atención a*) to pay attention to
reparo [re'paro] *nm* (*advertencia*) observation; (*duda*) doubt; (*dificultad*) difficulty; **poner ~s (a)** to raise objections (to)
repartidor, a [reparti'ðor, a] *nm/f* distributor
repartir [repar'tir] *vt* to distribute, share out; (*Correos*) to deliver; **reparto** *nm* distribution; delivery; (*Teatro, Cine*) cast; (CAM: *urbanización*) housing estate (BRIT), real estate development (US)
repasar [repa'sar] *vt* (*Escol*) to revise; (*Mecánica*) to check, overhaul; (*Costura*) to mend; **repaso** *nm* revision; overhaul, checkup; mending
repecho [re'petʃo] *nm* steep incline
repelente [repe'lente] *adj* repellent, repulsive
repeler [repe'ler] *vt* to repel
repente [re'pente] *nm*: **de ~** suddenly
repentino, -a [repen'tino, a] *adj* sudden
repercusión [reperku'sjon] *nf* repercussion
repercutir [reperku'tir] *vi* (*objeto*) to rebound; (*sonido*) to echo; **~ en** (*fig*) to have repercussions on
repertorio [reper'torjo] *nm* list; (*Teatro*) repertoire
repetición [repeti'θjon] *nf* repetition
repetir [repe'tir] *vt* to repeat; (*plato*) to have a second helping of ▷ *vi* to repeat; (*sabor*) to come back; **repetirse** *vr* (*volver sobre un tema*) to repeat o.s.
repetitivo, -a [repeti'tiβo, a] *adj* repetitive, repetitious
repique [re'pike] *nm* pealing, ringing; **repiqueteo** *nm* pealing; (*de tambor*) drumming
repisa [re'pisa] *nf* ledge, shelf; (*de ventana*) windowsill; **la ~ de la chimenea** the mantelpiece
repito *etc vb V* **repetir**
replantearse [replante'arse] *vr*: **~ un problema** to reconsider a problem
repleto, -a [re'pleto, a] *adj* replete, full up
réplica ['replika] *nf* answer; (*Arte*) replica
replicar [repli'kar] *vi* to answer; (*objetar*) to argue, answer back
repliegue [re'pljeɣe] *nm* (*Mil*) withdrawal
repoblación [repoβla'θjon] *nf* repopulation; (*de río*) restocking; **repoblación forestal** reafforestation
repoblar [repo'βlar] *vt* to repopulate; (*con árboles*) to reafforest
repollito [repo'ʎito] (CS) *nm*: **~s de Bruselas** (Brussels) sprouts
repollo [re'poʎo] *nm* cabbage
reponer [repo'ner] *vt* to replace, put back; (*Teatro*) to revive; **reponerse** *vr* to recover; **~ que ...** to reply that ...
reportaje [repor'taxe] *nm* report,

article
reportero, -a [repor'tero, a] *nm/f* reporter
reposacabezas [reposaka'βeθas] *nm inv* headrest
reposar [repo'sar] *vi* to rest, repose
reposera [repo'sera] (*RPL*) *nf* deck chair
reposición [reposi'θjon] *nf* replacement; (*Cine*) remake
reposo [re'poso] *nm* rest
repostar [repos'tar] *vt* to replenish; (*Auto*) to fill up (with petrol (*BRIT*) *o* gasoline (*US*))
repostería [reposte'ria] *nf* confectioner's (shop)
represa [re'presa] *nf* dam; (*lago artificial*) lake, pool
represalia [repre'salja] *nf* reprisal
representación [representa'θjon] *nf* representation; (*Teatro*) performance; **representante** *nmf* representative; performer
representar [represen'tar] *vt* to represent; (*Teatro*) to perform; (*edad*) to look; **representarse** *vr* to imagine; **representativo, -a** *adj* representative
represión [repre'sjon] *nf* repression
reprimenda [repri'menda] *nf* reprimand, rebuke
reprimir [repri'mir] *vt* to repress
reprobar [repro'βar] *vt* to censure, reprove
reprochar [repro'tʃar] *vt* to reproach; **reproche** *nm* reproach
reproducción [reproðuk'θjon] *nf* reproduction
reproducir [reproðu'θir] *vt* to reproduce; **reproducirse** *vr* to breed; (*situación*) to recur
reproductor, a [reproðuk'tor, a] *adj* reproductive ▷ *nm* player; **reproductor de CD** CD player
reptil [rep'til] *nm* reptile
república [re'puβlika] *nf* republic; **República Dominicana** Dominican Republic; **republicano, -a** *adj, nm* republican
repudiar [repu'ðjar] *vt* to repudiate; (*fe*) to renounce
repuesto [re'pwesto] *nm* (*pieza de recambio*) spare (part); (*abastecimiento*) supply; **rueda de ~** spare wheel
repugnancia [repuɣ'nanθja] *nf* repugnance; **repugnante** *adj* repugnant, repulsive
repugnar [repuɣ'nar] *vt* to disgust
repulsa [re'pulsa] *nf* rebuff
repulsión [repul'sjon] *nf* repulsion, aversion; **repulsivo, -a** *adj* repulsive
reputación [reputa'θjon] *nf* reputation
requerir [reke'rir] *vt* (*pedir*) to ask, request; (*exigir*) to require; (*llamar*) to send for, summon
requesón [reke'son] *nm* cottage cheese
requete... [re'kete] *prefijo* extremely
réquiem ['rekjem] (*pl* **~s**) *nm* requiem
requisito [reki'sito] *nm* requirement, requisite
res [res] *nf* beast, animal
resaca [re'saka] *nf* (*de mar*) undertow, undercurrent; (*fam*) hangover
resaltar [resal'tar] *vi* to project, stick out; (*fig*) to stand out
resarcir [resar'θir] *vt* to compensate; **resarcirse** *vr* to make up for
resbaladero [resβala'ðero] (*MÉX*) *nm* slide
resbaladizo, -a [resβala'ðiθo, a] *adj* slippery
resbalar [resβa'lar] *vi* to slip, slide; (*fig*) to slip (up); **resbalarse** *vr* to slip, slide; to slip (up); **resbalón** *nm* (*acción*) slip
rescatar [reska'tar] *vt* (*salvar*) to save, rescue; (*objeto*) to get back, recover; (*cautivos*) to ransom
rescate [res'kate] *nm* rescue; (*de objeto*) recovery; **pagar un ~** to pay a ransom
rescindir [resθin'dir] *vt* to rescind
rescisión [resθi'sjon] *nf* cancellation
resecar [rese'kar] *vt* to dry

thoroughly; (*Med*) to cut out, remove; **resecarse** *vr* to dry up

reseco, -a [re'seko, a] *adj* very dry; (*fig*) skinny

resentido, -a [resen'tiðo, a] *adj* resentful

resentimiento [resenti'mjento] *nm* resentment, bitterness

resentirse [resen'tirse] *vr* (*debilitarse: persona*) to suffer; **~ de** (*consecuencias*) to feel the effects of; **~ de (*o* por) algo** to resent sth, be bitter about sth

reseña [re'seɲa] *nf* (*cuenta*) account; (*informe*) report; (*Literatura*) review

reseñar [rese'ɲar] *vt* to describe; (*Literatura*) to review

reserva [re'serβa] *nf* reserve; (*reservación*) reservation

reservado, -a [reser'βaðo, a] *adj* reserved; (*retraído*) cold, distant ▷ *nm* private room

reservar [reser'βar] *vt* (*guardar*) to keep; (*habitación, entrada*) to reserve; **reservarse** *vr* to save o.s.; (*callar*) to keep to o.s.

resfriado [resfri'aðo] *nm* cold; **resfriarse** *vr* to cool; (*Med*) to catch a cold

resguardar [resɣwar'ðar] *vt* to protect, shield; **resguardarse** *vr*: **~se de** to guard against; **resguardo** *nm* defence; (*vale*) voucher; (*recibo*) receipt, slip

residencia [resi'ðenθja] *nf* residence; **residencia de ancianos** residential home, old people's home; **residencia universitaria** hall of residence; **residencial** *nf* (*urbanización*) housing estate

residente [resi'ðente] *adj, nmf* resident

residir [resi'ðir] *vi* to reside, live; **~ en** to reside in, lie in

residuo [re'siðwo] *nm* residue

resignación [resiɣna'θjon] *nf* resignation; **resignarse** *vr*: **resignarse a *o* con** to resign o.s. to, be resigned to

resina [re'sina] *nf* resin

resistencia [resis'tenθja] *nf* (*dureza*) endurance, strength; (*oposición, Elec*) resistance; **resistente** *adj* strong, hardy; resistant

resistir [resis'tir] *vt* (*soportar*) to bear; (*oponerse a*) to resist, oppose; (*aguantar*) to put up with ▷ *vi* to resist; (*aguantar*) to last, endure; **resistirse** *vr*: **~se a** to refuse to, resist

resoluto, -a [reso'luto, a] *adj* resolute

resolver [resol'βer] *vt* to resolve; (*solucionar*) to solve, resolve; (*decidir*) to decide, settle; **resolverse** *vr* to make up one's mind

resonar [reso'nar] *vi* to ring, echo

resoplar [reso'plar] *vi* to snort; **resoplido** *nm* heavy breathing

resorte [re'sorte] *nm* spring; (*fig*) lever

resortera [resor'tera] (MÉX) *nf* catapult

respaldar [respal'dar] *vt* to back (up), support; **respaldarse** *vr* to lean back; **~se con *o* en** (*fig*) to take one's stand on; **respaldo** *nm* (*de sillón*) back; (*fig*) support, backing

respectivo, -a [respek'tiβo, a] *adj* respective; **en lo ~ a** with regard to

respecto [res'pekto] *nm*: **al ~** on this matter; **con ~ a, ~ de** with regard to, in relation to

respetable [respe'taβle] *adj* respectable

respetar [respe'tar] *vt* to respect; **respeto** *nm* respect; (*acatamiento*) deference; **respetos** *nmpl* respects; **respetuoso, -a** *adj* respectful

respingo [res'pingo] *nm* start, jump

respiración [respira'θjon] *nf* breathing; (*Med*) respiration; (*ventilación*) ventilation; **respiración asistida** artificial respiration (*by machine*)

respirar [respi'rar] *vi* to breathe; **respiratorio, -a** *adj* respiratory; **respiro** *nm* breathing; (*fig: descanso*) respite

resplandecer [resplande'θer] *vi* to shine; **resplandeciente** *adj* resplendent, shining; **resplandor** *nm* brilliance, brightness; (*de luz, fuego*) blaze

responder [respon'der] *vt* to answer ▷ *vi* to answer; (*fig*) to respond; (*pey*) to answer back; **~ de** *o* **por** to answer for; **respondón, -ona** *adj* cheeky

responsabilidad [responsaβili'ðað] *nf* responsibility

responsabilizarse [responsaβili'θarse] *vr* to make o.s. responsible, take charge

responsable [respon'saβle] *adj* responsible

respuesta [res'pwesta] *nf* answer, reply

resquebrajar [reskeβra'xar] *vt* to crack, split; **resquebrajarse** *vr* to crack, split

resquicio [res'kiθjo] *nm* chink; (*hendedura*) crack

resta ['resta] *nf* (*Mat*) remainder

restablecer [restaβle'θer] *vt* to re-establish, restore; **restablecerse** *vr* to recover

restante [res'tante] *adj* remaining; **lo ~** the remainder

restar [res'tar] *vt* (*Mat*) to subtract; (*fig*) to take away ▷ *vi* to remain, be left

restauración [restaura'θjon] *nf* restoration

restaurante [restau'rante] *nm* restaurant

restaurar [restau'rar] *vt* to restore

restituir [restitu'ir] *vt* (*devolver*) to return, give back; (*rehabilitar*) to restore

resto ['resto] *nm* (*residuo*) rest, remainder; (*apuesta*) stake; **restos** *nmpl* remains

restorán [resto'ran] *nm* (*Lam*) restaurant

restregar [restre'ɣar] *vt* to scrub, rub

restricción [restrik'θjon] *nf* restriction

restringir [restrin'xir] *vt* to restrict, limit

resucitar [resuθi'tar] *vt, vi* to resuscitate, revive

resuelto, -a [re'swelto, a] *pp de* **resolver** ▷ *adj* resolute, determined

resultado [resul'taðo] *nm* result; (*conclusión*) outcome; **resultante** *adj* resulting, resultant

resultar [resul'tar] *vi* (*ser*) to be; (*llegar a ser*) to turn out to be; (*salir bien*) to turn out well; (*Com*) to amount to; **~ de** to stem from; **me resulta difícil hacerlo** it's difficult for me to do it

resumen [re'sumen] (*pl* **resúmenes**) *nm* summary, résumé; **en ~** in short

resumir [resu'mir] *vt* to sum up; (*cortar*) to abridge, cut down; (*condensar*) to summarize

> No confundir **resumir** con la palabra inglesa *resume*.

resurgir [resur'xir] *vi* (*reaparecer*) to reappear

resurrección [resurre(k)'θjon] *nf* resurrection

retablo [re'taβlo] *nm* altarpiece

retaguardia [reta'ɣwarðja] *nf* rearguard

retahíla [reta'ila] *nf* series, string

retal [re'tal] *nm* remnant

retar [re'tar] *vt* to challenge; (*desafiar*) to defy, dare

retazo [re'taθo] *nm* snippet (BRIT), fragment

retención [reten'θjon] *nf* (*tráfico*) hold-up; **retención fiscal** deduction for tax purposes

retener [rete'ner] *vt* (*intereses*) to withhold

reticente [reti'θente] *adj* (*tono*) insinuating; (*postura*) reluctant; **ser ~ a hacer algo** to be reluctant *o* unwilling to do sth

retina [re'tina] *nf* retina

retintín [retin'tin] *nm* jangle, jingle

retirada [reti'raða] *nf* (*Mil, refugio*) retreat; (*de dinero*) withdrawal; (*de embajador*) recall; **retirado, -a** *adj* (*lugar*) remote; (*vida*) quiet; (*jubilado*)

retired
retirar [reti'rar] *vt* to withdraw; (*quitar*) to remove; (*jubilar*) to retire, pension off; **retirarse** *vr* to retreat, withdraw; to retire; (*acostarse*) to retire, go to bed; **retiro** *nm* retreat; retirement; (*pago*) pension
reto ['reto] *nm* dare, challenge
retocar [reto'kar] *vt* (*fotografía*) to touch up, retouch
retoño [re'toɲo] *nm* sprout, shoot; (*fig*) offspring, child
retoque [re'toke] *nm* retouching
retorcer [retor'θer] *vt* to twist; (*manos, lavado*) to wring; **retorcerse** *vr* to become twisted; (*mover el cuerpo*) to writhe
retorcido, -a [retor'θiðo, a] *adj* (*persona*) devious
retorcijón [retorθi'jon] (*LAM*) *nm* (*tb*: **~ de tripas**) stomach cramp
retórica [re'torika] *nf* rhetoric; (*pey*) affectedness
retorno [re'torno] *nm* return
retortijón [retorti'xon] (*ESP*) *nm* (*tb*: **~ de tripas**) stomach cramp
retozar [reto'θar] *vi* (*juguetear*) to frolic, romp; (*saltar*) to gambol
retracción [retrak'θjon] *nf* retraction
retraerse [retra'erse] *vr* to retreat, withdraw; **retraído, -a** *adj* shy, retiring; **retraimiento** *nm* retirement; (*timidez*) shyness
retransmisión [retransmi'sjon] *nf* repeat (broadcast)
retransmitir [retransmi'tir] *vt* (*mensaje*) to relay; (*TV etc*) to repeat, retransmit; (*: en vivo*) to broadcast live
retrasado, -a [retra'saðo, a] *adj* late; (*Med*) mentally retarded; (*país etc*) backward, underdeveloped
retrasar [retra'sar] *vt* (*demorar*) to postpone, put off; (*retardar*) to slow down ▷*vi* (*atrasarse*) to be late; (*reloj*) to be slow; (*producción*) to fall (off); (*quedarse atrás*) to lag behind; **retrasarse** *vr* to be late; to be slow; to fall (off); to lag behind
retraso [re'traso] *nm* (*demora*) delay; (*lentitud*) slowness; (*tardanza*) lateness; (*atraso*) backwardness; **retrasos** *nmpl* (*Finanzas*) arrears; **llegar con ~** to arrive late; **retraso mental** mental deficiency
retratar [retra'tar] *vt* (*Arte*) to paint the portrait of; (*fotografiar*) to photograph; (*fig*) to depict, describe; **retrato** *nm* portrait; (*fig*) likeness; **retrato-robot** (*ESP*) *nm* Identikit®
retrete [re'trete] *nm* toilet
retribuir [retri'βwir] *vt* (*recompensar*) to reward; (*pagar*) to pay
retro... ['retro] *prefijo* retro...
retroceder [retroθe'ðer] *vi* (*echarse atrás*) to move back(wards); (*fig*) to back down
retroceso [retro'θeso] *nm* backward movement; (*Med*) relapse; (*fig*) backing down
retrospectivo, -a [retrospek'tiβo, a] *adj* retrospective
retrovisor [retroβi'sor] *nm* (*tb*: **espejo ~**) rear-view mirror
retumbar [retum'bar] *vi* to echo, resound
reúma [re'uma], **reuma** ['reuma] *nm* rheumatism
reunión [reu'njon] *nf* (*asamblea*) meeting; (*fiesta*) party
reunir [reu'nir] *vt* (*juntar*) to reunite, join (together); (*recoger*) to gather (together); (*personas*) to get together; (*cualidades*) to combine; **reunirse** *vr* (*personas: en asamblea*) to meet, gather
revalidar [reβali'ðar] *vt* (*ratificar*) to confirm, ratify
revalorizar [reβalori'θar] *vt* to revalue, reassess
revancha [re'βantʃa] *nf* revenge
revelación [reβela'θjon] *nf* revelation
revelado [reβe'laðo] *nm* developing
revelar [reβe'lar] *vt* to reveal; (*Foto*) to develop
reventa [re'βenta] *nf* (*de*

·a concierto) touting
eβen'tar] *vt* to burst,

..ventón [reβen'ton] *nm* (*Auto*) blow-out (BRIT), flat (US)
reverencia [reβe'renθja] *nf* reverence; **reverenciar** *vt* to revere
reverendo, -a [reβe'rendo, a] *adj* reverend
reverente [reβe'rente] *adj* reverent
reversa [re'βersa] (MÉX, CAM) *nf* reverse (gear)
reversible [reβer'siβle] *adj* (*prenda*) reversible
reverso [re'βerso] *nm* back, other side; (*de moneda*) reverse
revertir [reβer'tir] *vi* to revert
revés [re'βes] *nm* back, wrong side; (*fig*) reverse, setback; (*Deporte*) backhand; **al ~** the wrong way round; (*de arriba abajo*) upside down; (*ropa*) inside out; **volver algo del ~** to turn sth round; (*ropa*) to turn sth inside out
revisar [reβi'sar] *vt* (*examinar*) to check; (*texto etc*) to revise; **revisión** *nf* revision; **revisión salarial** wage review
revisor, a [reβi'sor, a] *nm/f* inspector; (*Ferro*) ticket collector
revista [re'βista] *nf* magazine, review; (*Teatro*) revue; (*inspección*) inspection; **pasar ~ a** to review, inspect; **revista del corazón** *magazine featuring celebrity gossip and real-life romance stories*
revivir [reβi'βir] *vi* to revive
revolcarse [reβol'karse] *vr* to roll about
revoltijo [reβol'tixo] *nm* mess, jumble
revoltoso, -a [reβol'toso, a] *adj* (*travieso*) naughty, unruly
revolución [reβolu'θjon] *nf* revolution; **revolucionario, -a** *adj, nm/f* revolutionary
revolver [reβol'βer] *vt* (*desordenar*) to disturb, mess up; (*mover*) to move about ▷ *vi*: **~ en** to go through, rummage (about) in; **revolverse** *vr* (*volver contra*) to turn on *o* against
revólver [re'βolβer] *nm* revolver
revuelo [re'βwelo] *nm* fluttering; (*fig*) commotion
revuelta [re'βwelta] *nf* (*motín*) revolt; (*agitación*) commotion
revuelto, -a [re'βwelto, a] *pp de* **revolver** ▷ *adj* (*mezclado*) mixed-up, in disorder
rey [rei] *nm* king; **Día de R~es** Twelfth Night; **los R~es Magos** the Three Wise Men, the Magi

REYES MAGOS

On the night before the 6th January (the Epiphany), children go to bed expecting **los Reyes Magos** (the Three Wise Men) to bring them presents. Twelfth Night processions, known as **cabalgatas**, take place that evening when 3 people dressed as **los Reyes Magos** arrive in the town by land or sea to the delight of the children.

reyerta [re'jerta] *nf* quarrel, brawl
rezagado, -a [reθa'ɣaðo, a] *nm/f* straggler
rezar [re'θar] *vi* to pray; **~ con** (*fam*) to concern, have to do with; **rezo** *nm* prayer
rezumar [reθu'mar] *vt* to ooze
ría ['ria] *nf* estuary
riada [ri'aða] *nf* flood
ribera [ri'βera] *nf* (*de río*) bank; (*: área*) riverside
ribete [ri'βete] *nm* (*de vestido*) border; (*fig*) addition
ricino [ri'θino] *nm*: **aceite de ~** castor oil
rico, -a ['riko, a] *adj* rich; (*adinerado*) wealthy, rich; (*lujoso*) luxurious; (*comida*) delicious; (*niño*) lovely, cute ▷ *nm/f* rich person
ridiculez [riðiku'leθ] *nf* absurdity

ridiculizar [riðikuli'θar] *vt* to ridicule
ridículo, -a [ri'ðikulo, a] *adj* ridiculous; **hacer el ~** to make a fool of o.s.; **poner a algn en ~** to make a fool of sb
riego ['rjeɣo] *nm* (*aspersión*) watering; (*irrigación*) irrigation; **riego sanguíneo** blood flow *o* circulation
riel [rjel] *nm* rail
rienda ['rjenda] *nf* rein; **dar ~ suelta a** to give free rein to
riesgo ['rjesɣo] *nm* risk; **correr el ~ de** to run the risk of
rifa ['rifa] *nf* (*lotería*) raffle; **rifar** *vt* to raffle
rifle ['rifle] *nm* rifle
rigidez [rixi'ðeθ] *nf* rigidity, stiffness; (*fig*) strictness; **rígido, -a** *adj* rigid, stiff; strict, inflexible
rigor [ri'ɣor] *nm* strictness, rigour; (*inclemencia*) harshness; **de ~** de rigueur, essential; **riguroso, -a** *adj* rigorous; harsh; (*severo*) severe
rimar [ri'mar] *vi* to rhyme
rimbombante [rimbom'bante] *adj* pompous
rímel ['rimel] *nm* mascara
rímmel ['rimel] *nm* = **rímel**
rin [rin] (*MÉX*) *nm* (wheel) rim
rincón [rin'kon] *nm* corner (*inside*)
rinoceronte [rinoθe'ronte] *nm* rhinoceros
riña ['riɲa] *nf* (*disputa*) argument; (*pelea*) brawl
riñón [ri'ɲon] *nm* kidney
río *etc* ['rio] *vb V* **reír** ▷ *nm* river; (*fig*) torrent, stream; **río abajo/arriba** downstream/upstream; **Río de la Plata** River Plate
rioja [ri'oxa] *nm* (*vino*) rioja (wine)
rioplatense [riopla'tense] *adj* of *o* from the River Plate region
riqueza [ri'keθa] *nf* wealth, riches *pl*; (*cualidad*) richness
risa ['risa] *nf* laughter; (*una risa*) laugh; **¡qué ~!** what a laugh!
risco ['risko] *nm* crag, cliff
ristra ['ristra] *nf* string
risueño, -a [ri'sweɲo, a] *adj* (*sonriente*) smiling; (*contento*) cheerful
ritmo ['ritmo] *nm* rhythm; **a ~ lento** slowly; **trabajar a ~ lento** to go slow; **ritmo cardíaco** heart rate
rito ['rito] *nm* rite
ritual [ri'twal] *adj, nm* ritual
rival [ri'βal] *adj, nmf* rival; **rivalidad** *nf* rivalry; **rivalizar** *vi*: **rivalizar con** to rival, vie with
rizado, -a [ri'θaðo, a] *adj* curly ▷ *nm* curls *pl*
rizar [ri'θar] *vt* to curl; **rizarse** *vr* (*pelo*) to curl; (*agua*) to ripple; **rizo** *nm* curl; ripple
RNE *nf abr* = **Radio Nacional de España**
robar [ro'βar] *vt* to rob; (*objeto*) to steal; (*casa etc*) to break into; (*Naipes*) to draw
roble ['roβle] *nm* oak; **robledal** *nm* oakwood
robo ['roβo] *nm* robbery, theft
robot [ro'βot] *nm* robot; **robot (de cocina)** (*ESP*) food processor
robustecer [roβuste'θer] *vt* to strengthen
robusto, -a [ro'βusto, a] *adj* robust, strong
roca ['roka] *nf* rock
roce ['roθe] *nm* (*caricia*) brush; (*Tec*) friction; (*en la piel*) graze; **tener ~ con** to be in close contact with
rociar [ro'θjar] *vt* to spray
rocín [ro'θin] *nm* nag, hack
rocío [ro'θio] *nm* dew
rocola [ro'kola] (*LAM*) *nf* jukebox
rocoso, -a [ro'koso, a] *adj* rocky
rodaballo [roða'baʎo] *nm* turbot
rodaja [ro'ðaxa] *nf* slice
rodaje [ro'ðaxe] *nm* (*Cine*) shooting, filming; (*Auto*): **en ~** running in
rodar [ro'ðar] *vt* (*vehículo*) to wheel (along); (*escalera*) to roll down; (*viajar por*) to travel (over) ▷ *vi* to roll; (*coche*) to go, run; (*Cine*) to shoot, film
rodear [roðe'ar] *vt* to surround ▷ *vi*

to go round; **rodearse** *vr*: **~se de amigos** to surround o.s. with friends

rodeo [ro'ðeo] *nm* (*ruta indirecta*) detour; (*evasión*) evasion; (*Deporte*) rodeo; **hablar sin ~s** to come to the point, speak plainly

rodilla [ro'ðiʎa] *nf* knee; **de ~s** kneeling; **ponerse de ~s** to kneel (down)

rodillo [ro'ðiʎo] *nm* roller; (*Culin*) rolling-pin

roedor, a [roe'ðor, a] *adj* gnawing ▷ *nm* rodent

roer [ro'er] *vt* (*masticar*) to gnaw; (*corroer, fig*) to corrode

rogar [ro'ɣar] *vt, vi* (*pedir*) to ask for; (*suplicar*) to beg, plead; **se ruega no fumar** please do not smoke

rojizo, -a [ro'xiθo, a] *adj* reddish

rojo, -a ['roxo, a] *adj, nm* red; **al ~ vivo** red-hot

rol [rol] *nm* list, roll; (*papel*) role

rollito [ro'ʎito] *nm* (*tb*: **~ de primavera**) spring roll

rollizo, -a [ro'ʎiθo, a] *adj* (*objeto*) cylindrical; (*persona*) plump

rollo ['roʎo] *nm* roll; (*de cuerda*) coil; (*madera*) log; (ESP: *fam*) bore; **¡qué ~!** (ESP: *fam*) what a carry-on!

Roma ['roma] *n* Rome

romance [ro'manθe] *nm* (*amoroso*) romance; (*Literatura*) ballad

romano, -a [ro'mano, a] *adj, nm/f* Roman; **a la romana** in batter

romanticismo [romanti'θismo] *nm* romanticism

romántico, -a [ro'mantiko, a] *adj* romantic

rombo ['rombo] *nm* (*Geom*) rhombus

romería [rome'ria] *nf* (*Rel*) pilgrimage; (*excursión*) trip, outing

ROMERÍA

Originally a pilgrimage to a shrine or church to express devotion to the Virgin Mary or a local Saint, the **romería** has also become a rural festival which accompanies the pilgrimage. People come from all over to attend, bringing their own food and drink, and spend the day in celebration.

romero, -a [ro'mero, a] *nm/f* pilgrim ▷ *nm* rosemary

romo, -a ['romo, a] *adj* blunt; (*fig*) dull

rompecabezas [rompeka'βeθas] *nm inv* riddle, puzzle; (*juego*) jigsaw (puzzle)

rompehuelgas [rompe'welɣas] (LAM) *nm inv* strikebreaker, scab

rompeolas [rompe'olas] *nm inv* breakwater

romper [rom'per] *vt* to break; (*hacer pedazos*) to smash; (*papel, tela etc*) to tear, rip ▷ *vi* (*olas*) to break; (*sol, diente*) to break through; **romperse** *vr* to break; **~ un contrato** to break a contract; **~ a** (*empezar a*) to start (suddenly) to; **~ a llorar** to burst into tears; **~ con algn** to fall out with sb

ron [ron] *nm* rum

roncar [ron'kar] *vi* to snore

ronco, -a ['ronko, a] *adj* (*afónico*) hoarse; (*áspero*) raucous

ronda ['ronda] *nf* (*gen*) round; (*patrulla*) patrol; **rondar** *vt* to patrol ▷ *vi* to patrol; (*fig*) to prowl round

ronquido [ron'kiðo] *nm* snore, snoring

ronronear [ronrone'ar] *vi* to purr

roña ['roɲa] *nf* (*Veterinaria*) mange; (*mugre*) dirt, grime; (*óxido*) rust

roñoso, -a [ro'ɲoso, a] *adj* (*mugriento*) filthy; (*tacaño*) mean

ropa ['ropa] *nf* clothes *pl*, clothing; **ropa blanca** linen; **ropa de cama** bed linen; **ropa de color** coloureds *pl*; **ropa interior** underwear; **ropa sucia** dirty washing; **ropaje** *nm* gown, robes *pl*

ropero [ro'pero] *nm* linen cupboard; (*guardarropa*) wardrobe

rosa ['rosa] *adj* pink ▷ *nf* rose

rosado, -a [ro'saðo, a] *adj* pink

▷*nm* rosé

rosal [ro'sal] *nm* rosebush

rosario [ro'sarjo] *nm* (*Rel*) rosary; **rezar el ~** to say the rosary

rosca ['roska] *nf* (*de tornillo*) thread; (*de humo*) coil, spiral; (*pan, postre*) ring-shaped roll/pastry

rosetón [rose'ton] *nm* rosette; (*Arq*) rose window

rosquilla [ros'kiʎa] *nf* doughnut-shaped fritter

rostro ['rostro] *nm* (*cara*) face

rotativo, -a [rota'tiβo, a] *adj* rotary

roto, -a ['roto, a] *pp de* **romper** ▷*adj* broken

rotonda [ro'tonda] *nf* roundabout

rótula ['rotula] *nf* kneecap; (*Tec*) ball-and-socket joint

rotulador [rotula'ðor] *nm* felt-tip pen

rótulo ['rotulo] *nm* heading, title; label; (*letrero*) sign

rotundamente [rotunda'mente] *adv* (*negar*) flatly; (*responder, afirmar*) emphatically; **rotundo, -a** *adj* round; (*enfático*) emphatic

rotura [ro'tura] *nf* (*acto*) breaking; (*Med*) fracture

rozadura [roθa'ðura] *nf* abrasion, graze

rozar [ro'θar] *vt* (*frotar*) to rub; (*arañar*) to scratch; (*tocar ligeramente*) to shave, touch lightly; **rozarse** *vr* to rub (together); **~se con** (*fam*) to rub shoulders with

rte. *abr* (= *remite, remitente*) sender

RTVE *nf abr* = **Radiotelevisión Española**

rubí [ru'βi] *nm* ruby; (*de reloj*) jewel

rubio, -a ['ruβjo, a] *adj* fair-haired, blond(e) ▷*nm/f* blond/blonde; **tabaco ~** Virginia tobacco

rubor [ru'βor] *nm* (*sonrojo*) blush; (*timidez*) bashfulness; **ruborizarse** *vr* to blush

rúbrica ['ruβrika] *nf* (*de la firma*) flourish; **rubricar** *vt* (*firmar*) to sign with a flourish; (*concluir*) to sign and seal

rudimentario, -a [ruðimen'tarjo, a] *adj* rudimentary

rudo, -a ['ruðo, a] *adj* (*sin pulir*) unpolished; (*grosero*) coarse; (*violento*) violent; (*sencillo*) simple

rueda ['rweða] *nf* wheel; (*círculo*) ring, circle; (*rodaja*) slice, round; **rueda de auxilio** (RPL) spare tyre; **rueda delantera/trasera/de repuesto** front/back/spare wheel; **rueda de prensa** press conference; **rueda gigante** (LAM) big (BRIT) *o* Ferris (US) wheel

ruedo ['rweðo] *nm* (*círculo*) circle; (*Taur*) arena, bullring

ruego *etc* ['rweɣo] *vb V* **rogar** ▷*nm* request

rugby ['ruɣβi] *nm* rugby

rugido [ru'xiðo] *nm* roar

rugir [ru'xir] *vi* to roar

rugoso, -a [ru'ɣoso, a] *adj* (*arrugado*) wrinkled; (*áspero*) rough; (*desigual*) ridged

ruido ['rwiðo] *nm* noise; (*sonido*) sound; (*alboroto*) racket, row; (*escándalo*) commotion, rumpus; **ruidoso, -a** *adj* noisy, loud; (*fig*) sensational

ruin [rwin] *adj* contemptible, mean

ruina ['rwina] *nf* ruin; (*colapso*) collapse; (*de persona*) ruin, downfall

ruinoso, -a [rwi'noso, a] *adj* ruinous; (*destartalado*) dilapidated, tumbledown; (*Com*) disastrous

ruiseñor [rwise'ɲor] *nm* nightingale

rulero [ru'lero] (RPL) *nm* roller

ruleta [ru'leta] *nf* roulette

rulo ['rulo] *nm* (*para el pelo*) curler

Rumanía [ruma'nia] *nf* Rumania

rumba ['rumba] *nf* rumba

rumbo ['rumbo] *nm* (*ruta*) route, direction; (*ángulo de dirección*) course, bearing; (*fig*) course of events; **ir con ~ a** to be heading for

rumiante [ru'mjante] *nm* ruminant

rumiar [ru'mjar] *vt* to chew; (*fig*) to chew over ▷*vi* to chew the cud

rumor [ru'mor] *nm* (*ruido sordo*) low sound; (*murmuración*) murmur, buzz; **rumorearse** *vr*: **se rumorea que ...** it is rumoured that ...
rupestre [ru'pestre] *adj* rock *cpd*
ruptura [rup'tura] *nf* rupture
rural [ru'ral] *adj* rural
Rusia ['rusja] *nf* Russia; **ruso, -a** *adj, nm/f* Russian
rústico, -a ['rustiko, a] *adj* rustic; (*ordinario*) coarse, uncouth ▷ *nm/f* yokel
ruta ['ruta] *nf* route
rutina [ru'tina] *nf* routine

S *abr* (= *santo, a*) St; (= *sur*) S
s. *abr* (= *siglo*) C.; (= *siguiente*) foll
S.A. *abr* (= *Sociedad Anónima*) Ltd. (BRIT), Inc. (US)
sábado ['saβaðo] *nm* Saturday
sábana ['saβana] *nf* sheet
sabañón [saβa'ɲon] *nm* chilblain
saber [sa'βer] *vt* to know; (*llegar a conocer*) to find out, learn; (*tener capacidad de*) to know how to ▷ *vi*: **~ a** to taste of, taste like ▷ *nm* knowledge, learning; **a ~** namely; **¿sabes conducir/nadar?** can you drive/swim?; **¿sabes francés?** do you speak French?; **~ de memoria** to know by heart; **hacer ~ algo a algn** to inform sb of sth, let sb know sth
sabiduría [saβiðu'ria] *nf* (*conocimientos*) wisdom; (*instrucción*) learning
sabiendas [sa'βjendas]: **a ~** *adv* knowingly
sabio, -a ['saβjo,a] *adj* (*docto*) learned; (*prudente*) wise, sensible
sabor [sa'βor] *nm* taste, flavour;

saborear *vt* to taste, savour; (*fig*) to relish
sabotaje [saβo'taxe] *nm* sabotage
sabré *etc vb V* **saber**
sabroso, -a [sa'βroso, a] *adj* tasty; (*fig: fam*) racy, salty
sacacorchos [saka'kortʃos] *nm inv* corkscrew
sacapuntas [saka'puntas] *nm inv* pencil sharpener
sacar [sa'kar] *vt* to take out; (*fig: extraer*) to get (out); (*quitar*) to remove, get out; (*hacer salir*) to bring out; (*conclusión*) to draw; (*novela etc*) to publish, bring out; (*ropa*) to take off; (*obra*) to make; (*premio*) to receive; (*entradas*) to get; (*Tenis*) to serve; **~ adelante** (*niño*) to bring up; (*negocio*) to carry on, go on with; **~ a algn a bailar** to get sb up to dance; **~ una foto** to take a photo; **~ la lengua** to stick out one's tongue; **~ buenas/malas notas** to get good/bad marks
sacarina [saka'rina] *nf* saccharin(e)
sacerdote [saθer'ðote] *nm* priest
saciar [sa'θjar] *vt* (*hambre, sed*) to satisfy; **saciarse** *vr* (*de comida*) to get full up
saco ['sako] *nm* bag; (*grande*) sack; (*su contenido*) bagful; (*LAM: chaqueta*) jacket; **saco de dormir** sleeping bag
sacramento [sakra'mento] *nm* sacrament
sacrificar [sakrifi'kar] *vt* to sacrifice; **sacrificio** *nm* sacrifice
sacristía [sakris'tia] *nf* sacristy
sacudida [saku'ðiða] *nf* (*agitación*) shake, shaking; (*sacudimiento*) jolt, bump; **sacudida eléctrica** electric shock
sacudir [saku'ðir] *vt* to shake; (*golpear*) to hit
Sagitario [saxi'tarjo] *nm* Sagittarius
sagrado, -a [sa'ɣraðo, a] *adj* sacred, holy
Sáhara ['saara] *nm*: **el ~** the Sahara (desert)
sal [sal] *vb V* **salir** ▷ *nf* salt; **sales de baño** bath salts
sala ['sala] *nf* room; (*tb*: **~ de estar**) living room; (*Teatro*) house, auditorium; (*de hospital*) ward; **sala de espera** waiting room; **sala de estar** living room; **sala de fiestas** dance hall
salado, -a [sa'laðo, a] *adj* salty; (*fig*) witty, amusing; **agua salada** salt water
salar [sa'lar] *vt* to salt, add salt to
salario [sa'larjo] *nm* wage, pay
salchicha [sal'tʃitʃa] *nf* (pork) sausage; **salchichón** *nm* (salami-type) sausage
saldo ['saldo] *nm* (*pago*) settlement; (*de una cuenta*) balance; (*lo restante*) remnant(s) (*pl*), remainder; (*de móvil*) credit; **saldos** *nmpl* (*en tienda*) sale
saldré *etc vb V* **salir**
salero [sa'lero] *nm* salt cellar
salgo *etc vb V* **salir**
salida [sa'liða] *nf* (*puerta etc*) exit, way out; (*acto*) leaving, going out; (*de tren, Aviac*) departure; (*Tec*) output, production; (*fig*) way out; (*Com*) opening; (*Geo, válvula*) outlet; (*de gas*) leak; **calle sin ~** cul-de-sac; **salida de baño** (*RPL*) bathrobe; **salida de emergencia/incendios** emergency exit/fire escape

PALABRA CLAVE

salir [sa'lir] *vi* **1** (*partir: tb:* **salir de**) to leave; **Juan ha salido** Juan is out; **salió de la cocina** he came out of the kitchen
2 (*aparecer*) to appear; (*disco, libro*) to come out; **anoche salió en la tele** she appeared *o* was on TV last night; **salió en todos los periódicos** it was in all the papers
3 (*resultar*): **la muchacha nos salió muy trabajadora** the girl turned out to be a very hard worker; **la comida te ha salido exquisita** the food was delicious; **sale muy caro** it's very expensive

4: **salirle a uno algo: la entrevista que hice me salió bien/mal** the interview I did went *o* turned out well/badly
5: **salir adelante: no sé como haré para salir adelante** I don't know how I'll get by
salirse *vr* (*líquido*) to spill; (*animal*) to escape

saliva [sa'liβa] *nf* saliva
salmo ['salmo] *nm* psalm
salmón [sal'mon] *nm* salmon
salmonete [salmo'nete] *nm* red mullet
salón [sa'lon] *nm* (*de casa*) living room, lounge; (*muebles*) lounge suite; **salón de baile** dance hall; **salón de belleza** beauty parlour
salpicadera [salpika'ðera] (*MÉX*) *nf* mudguard (*BRIT*), fender (*US*)
salpicadero [salpika'ðero] *nm* (*Auto*) dashboard
salpicar [salpi'kar] *vt* (*rociar*) to sprinkle, spatter; (*esparcir*) to scatter
salpicón [salpi'kon] *nm* (*tb*: **~ de marisco**) seafood salad
salsa ['salsa] *nf* sauce; (*con carne asada*) gravy; (*fig*) spice
saltamontes [salta'montes] *nm inv* grasshopper
saltar [sal'tar] *vt* to jump (over), leap (over); (*dejar de lado*) to skip, miss out ▷ *vi* to jump, leap; (*pelota*) to bounce; (*al aire*) to fly up; (*quebrarse*) to break; (*al agua*) to dive; (*fig*) to explode, blow up
salto ['salto] *nm* jump, leap; (*al agua*) dive; **salto de agua** waterfall; **salto de altura/longitud** high/long jump
salud [sa'luð] *nf* health; **¡(a su) ~!** cheers!, good health!; **saludable** *adj* (*de buena salud*) healthy; (*provechoso*) good, beneficial
saludar [salu'ðar] *vt* to greet; (*Mil*) to salute; **saludo** *nm* greeting; **"saludos"** (*en carta*) "best wishes", "regards"
salvación [salβa'θjon] *nf* salvation; (*rescate*) rescue
salvado [sal'βaðo] *nm* bran
salvaje [sal'βaxe] *adj* wild; (*tribu*) savage
salvamanteles [salβaman'teles] *nm inv* table mat
salvamento [salβa'mento] *nm* rescue
salvapantallas [salβapan'taʎas] *nm inv* screen saver
salvar [sal'βar] *vt* (*rescatar*) to save, rescue; (*resolver*) to overcome, resolve; (*cubrir distancias*) to cover, travel; (*hacer excepción*) to except, exclude; (*barco*) to salvage
salvavidas [salβa'βiðas] *adj inv*: **bote/chaleco ~** lifeboat/life jacket
salvo, -a ['salβo, a] *adj* safe ▷ *adv* except (for), save; **a ~** out of danger; **~ que** unless
san [san] *adj* saint; **S~ Juan** St John
sanar [sa'nar] *vt* (*herida*) to heal; (*persona*) to cure ▷ *vi* (*persona*) to get well, recover; (*herida*) to heal
sanatorio [sana'torjo] *nm* sanatorium
sanción [san'θjon] *nf* sanction
sancochado, -a [sanko'tʃado, a] (*MÉX*) *adj* (*Culin*) underdone, rare
sandalia [san'dalja] *nf* sandal
sandía [san'dia] *nf* watermelon
sandwich ['sandwitʃ] (*pl* **~s, ~es**) *nm* sandwich
sanfermines [sanfer'mines] *nmpl* *festivities in celebration of San Fermín (Pamplona)*

SANFERMINES

The **Sanfermines** is a week-long festival in Pamplona made famous by Ernest Hemingway. From the 7th July, the feast of "San Fermín", crowds of mainly young people take to the streets drinking, singing and dancing. Early in the morning bulls are released along the narrow streets leading to the bullring, and young men risk serious injury to show their bravery by running out in front of them, a custom which is also typical of many Spanish villages.

sangrar [san'grar] *vt, vi* to bleed; **sangre** *nf* blood
sangría [san'gria] *nf* sangria, *sweetened drink of red wine with fruit*
sangriento, -a [san'grjento, a] *adj* bloody
sanguíneo, -a [san'gineo, a] *adj* blood *cpd*
sanidad [sani'ðað] *nf* (*tb*: **~ pública**) public health
San Isidro [sani'sidro] *nm* *patron saint of Madrid*

SAN ISIDRO

San Isidro is the patron saint of Madrid, and gives his name to the week-long festivities which take place around the 15th May. Originally an 18th-century trade fair, the **San Isidro** celebrations now include music, dance, a famous **romería**, theatre and bullfighting.

sanitario, -a [sani'tarjo, a] *adj* health *cpd*; **sanitarios** *nmpl* toilets (BRIT), washroom (US)
sano, -a ['sano, a] *adj* healthy; (*sin daños*) sound; (*comida*) wholesome; (*entero*) whole, intact; **~ y salvo** safe and sound
No confundir **sano** con la palabra inglesa *sane*.
Santiago [san'tjaɤo] *nm*: **~ (de Chile)** Santiago
santiamén [santja'men] *nm*: **en un ~** in no time at all
santidad [santi'ðað] *nf* holiness, sanctity
santiguarse [santi'ɤwarse] *vr* to make the sign of the cross
santo, -a ['santo, a] *adj* holy; (*fig*) wonderful, miraculous ▷ *nm/f* saint ▷ *nm* saint's day; **~ y seña** password
santuario [san'twarjo] *nm* sanctuary, shrine
sapo ['sapo] *nm* toad
saque ['sake] *nm* (*Tenis*) service, serve; (*Fútbol*) throw-in; **saque de esquina** corner (kick)
saquear [sake'ar] *vt* (*Mil*) to sack; (*robar*) to loot, plunder; (*fig*) to ransack
sarampión [saram'pjon] *nm* measles *sg*
sarcástico, -a [sar'kastiko, a] *adj* sarcastic
sardina [sar'ðina] *nf* sardine
sargento [sar'xento] *nm* sergeant
sarmiento [sar'mjento] *nm* (*Bot*) vine shoot
sarna ['sarna] *nf* itch; (*Med*) scabies
sarpullido [sarpu'ʎiðo] *nm* (*Med*) rash
sarro ['sarro] *nm* (*en dientes*) tartar, plaque
sartén [sar'ten] *nf* frying pan
sastre ['sastre] *nm* tailor; **sastrería** *nf* (*arte*) tailoring; (*tienda*) tailor's (shop)
Satanás [sata'nas] *nm* Satan
satélite [sa'telite] *nm* satellite
sátira ['satira] *nf* satire
satisfacción [satisfak'θjon] *nf* satisfaction
satisfacer [satisfa'θer] *vt* to satisfy; (*gastos*) to meet; (*pérdida*) to make good; **satisfacerse** *vr* to satisfy o.s., be satisfied; (*vengarse*) to take revenge; **satisfecho, -a** *adj* satisfied; (*contento*) content(ed), happy; (*tb*: **satisfecho de sí mismo**) self-satisfied, smug
saturar [satu'rar] *vt* to saturate; **saturarse** *vr* (*mercado, aeropuerto*) to reach saturation point
sauce ['sauθe] *nm* willow; **sauce llorón** weeping willow
sauna ['sauna] *nf* sauna
savia ['saβja] *nf* sap
saxofón [sakso'fon] *nm* saxophone

sazonar [saθo'nar] *vt* to ripen; (*Culin*) to flavour, season
scooter [e'skuter] (ESP) *nf* scooter
Scotch® [skotʃ] (LAM) *nm* Sellotape® (BRIT), Scotch tape® (US)
SE *abr* (= *sudeste*) SE

PALABRA CLAVE

se [se] *pron* **1** (*reflexivo*: *sg*: *m*) himself; (: *f*) herself; (: *pl*) themselves; (: *cosa*) itself; (: *de Vd*) yourself; (: *de Vds*) yourselves; **se está preparando** she's preparing herself
2 (*con complemento indirecto*) to him; to her; to them; to it; to you; **a usted se lo dije ayer** I told you yesterday; **se compró un sombrero** he bought himself a hat; **se rompió la pierna** he broke his leg
3 (*uso recíproco*) each other, one another; **se miraron (el uno al otro)** they looked at each other *o* one another
4 (*en oraciones pasivas*): **se han vendido muchos libros** a lot of books have been sold
5 (*impers*): **se dice que ...** people say that ..., it is said that ...; **allí se come muy bien** the food there is very good, you can eat very well there

sé *etc* [se] *vb V* **saber; ser**
sea *etc vb V* **ser**
sebo ['seβo] *nm* fat, grease
secador [seka'ðor] *nm*: **~ de pelo** hair-dryer
secadora [seka'ðora] *nf* tumble dryer
secar [se'kar] *vt* to dry; **secarse** *vr* to dry (off); (*río, planta*) to dry up
sección [sek'θjon] *nf* section
seco, -a ['seko, a] *adj* dry; (*carácter*) cold; (*respuesta*) sharp, curt; **parar en ~** to stop dead; **decir algo a secas** to say sth curtly
secretaría [sekreta'ria] *nf* secretariat
secretario, -a [sekre'tarjo, a] *nm/f* secretary
secreto, -a [se'kreto, a] *adj* secret; (*persona*) secretive ▷ *nm* secret; (*calidad*) secrecy
secta ['sekta] *nf* sect
sector [sek'tor] *nm* sector
secuela [se'kwela] *nf* consequence
secuencia [se'kwenθja] *nf* sequence
secuestrar [sekwes'trar] *vt* to kidnap; (*bienes*) to seize, confiscate; **secuestro** *nm* kidnapping; seizure, confiscation
secundario, -a [sekun'darjo, a] *adj* secondary
sed [seð] *nf* thirst; **tener ~** to be thirsty
seda ['seða] *nf* silk
sedal [se'ðal] *nm* fishing line
sedán [se'ðan] (LAM) *nm* saloon (BRIT), sedan (US)
sedante [se'ðante] *nm* sedative
sede ['seðe] *nf* (*de gobierno*) seat; (*de compañía*) headquarters *pl*; **Santa S~** Holy See
sedentario, -a [seðen'tario, a] *adj* sedentary
sediento, -a [se'ðjento, a] *adj* thirsty
sedimento [seði'mento] *nm* sediment
seducción [seðuk'θjon] *nf* seduction
seducir [seðu'θir] *vt* to seduce; (*cautivar*) to charm, fascinate; (*atraer*) to attract; **seductor, a** *adj* seductive; charming, fascinating; attractive ▷ *nm/f* seducer
segar [se'ɣar] *vt* (*mies*) to reap, cut; (*hierba*) to mow, cut
seglar [se'ɣlar] *adj* secular, lay
seguida [se'ɣiða] *nf*: **en ~** at once, right away
seguido, -a [se'ɣiðo, a] *adj* (*continuo*) continuous, unbroken; (*recto*) straight ▷ *adv* (*directo*) straight (on); (*después*) after; (LAM: *a menudo*) often; **~s** consecutive, successive; **5 días ~s** 5 days running, 5 days in a row
seguir [se'ɣir] *vt* to follow; (*venir*

después) to follow on, come after; (*proseguir*) to continue; (*perseguir*) to chase, pursue ▷ *vi* (*gen*) to follow; (*continuar*) to continue, carry *o* go on; **seguirse** *vr* to follow; **sigo sin comprender** I still don't understand; **sigue lloviendo** it's still raining

según [se'ɣun] *prep* according to ▷ *adv*: **¿irás? – ~** are you going? – it all depends ▷ *conj* as; **~ caminamos** while we walk

segundo, -a [se'ɣundo, a] *adj* second ▷ *nm* second ▷ *nf* second meaning; **de segunda mano** second-hand; **segunda (clase)** second class; **segunda (marcha)** (*Auto*) second (gear)

seguramente [seɣura'mente] *adv* surely; (*con certeza*) for sure, with certainty

seguridad [seɣuri'ðað] *nf* safety; (*del estado, de casa etc*) security; (*certidumbre*) certainty; (*confianza*) confidence; (*estabilidad*) stability; **seguridad social** social security

seguro, -a [se'ɣuro, a] *adj* (*cierto*) sure, certain; (*fiel*) trustworthy; (*libre de peligro*) safe; (*bien defendido, firme*) secure ▷ *adv* for sure, certainly ▷ *nm* (*Com*) insurance; **seguro contra terceros/a todo riesgo** third party/ comprehensive insurance; **seguros sociales** social security *sg*

seis [seis] *num* six

seísmo [se'ismo] *nm* tremor, earthquake

selección [selek'θjon] *nf* selection; **seleccionar** *vt* to pick, choose, select

selectividad [selektiβi'ðað] (ESP) *nf* university entrance examination

selecto, -a [se'lekto, a] *adj* select, choice; (*escogido*) selected

sellar [se'ʎar] *vt* (*documento oficial*) to seal; (*pasaporte, visado*) to stamp

sello ['seʎo] *nm* stamp; (*precinto*) seal

selva ['selβa] *nf* (*bosque*) forest, woods *pl*; (*jungla*) jungle

semáforo [se'maforo] *nm* (*Auto*) traffic lights *pl*; (*Ferro*) signal

semana [se'mana] *nf* week; **entre ~** during the week; **Semana Santa** Holy Week; **semanal** *adj* weekly; **semanario** *nm* weekly magazine

SEMANA SANTA

In Spain celebrations for **Semana Santa** (Holy Week) are often spectacular. "Viernes Santo", "Sábado Santo" and "Domingo de Resurrección" (Good Friday, Holy Saturday, Easter Sunday) are all national public holidays, with additional days being given as local holidays. There are fabulous **procesiones** all over the country, with members of "cofradías" (brotherhoods) dressing in hooded robes and parading their "pasos" (religious floats and sculptures) through the streets. Seville has the most famous Holy Week processions.

sembrar [sem'brar] *vt* to sow; (*objetos*) to sprinkle, scatter about; (*noticias etc*) to spread

semejante [seme'xante] *adj* (*parecido*) similar ▷ *nm* fellow man, fellow creature; **~s** alike, similar; **nunca hizo cosa ~** he never did any such thing; **semejanza** *nf* similarity, resemblance

semejar [seme'xar] *vi* to seem like, resemble; **semejarse** *vr* to look alike, be similar

semen ['semen] *nm* semen

semestral [semes'tral] *adj* half-yearly, bi-annual

semicírculo [semi'θirkulo] *nm* semicircle

semidesnatado, -a [semiðesna'taðo, a] *adj* semi-skimmed

semifinal [semifi'nal] *nf* semifinal

semilla [se'miʎa] *nf* seed

seminario [semi'narjo] *nm* (*Rel*) seminary; (*Escol*) seminar
sémola ['semola] *nf* semolina
senado [se'naðo] *nm* senate; **senador, a** *nm/f* senator
sencillez [senθi'ʎeθ] *nf* simplicity; (*de persona*) naturalness; **sencillo, -a** *adj* simple; natural, unaffected
senda ['senda] *nf* path, track
senderismo [sende'rismo] *nm* hiking
sendero [sen'dero] *nm* path, track
sendos, -as ['sendos, as] *adj pl*: **les dio ~ golpes** he hit both of them
senil [se'nil] *adj* senile
seno ['seno] *nm* (*Anat*) bosom, bust; (*fig*) bosom; **~s** breasts
sensación [sensa'θjon] *nf* sensation; (*sentido*) sense; (*sentimiento*) feeling; **sensacional** *adj* sensational
sensato, -a [sen'sato, a] *adj* sensible
sensible [sen'sible] *adj* sensitive; (*apreciable*) perceptible, appreciable; (*pérdida*) considerable

No confundir **sensible** con la palabra inglesa *sensible*.

sensiblero, -a *adj* sentimental
sensitivo, -a [sensi'tiβo, a] *adj* sense *cpd*
sensorial [senso'rjal] *adj* sensory
sensual [sen'swal] *adj* sensual
sentada [sen'taða] *nf* sitting; (*protesta*) sit-in
sentado, -a [sen'taðo, a] *adj*: **estar ~** to sit, be sitting (down); **dar por ~** to take for granted, assume
sentar [sen'tar] *vt* to sit, seat; (*fig*) to establish ▷ *vi* (*vestido*) to suit; (*alimento*): **~ bien/mal a** to agree/ disagree with; **sentarse** *vr* (*persona*) to sit, sit down; (*los depósitos*) to settle
sentencia [sen'tenθja] *nf* (*máxima*) maxim, saying; (*Jur*) sentence; **sentenciar** *vt* to sentence
sentido, -a [sen'tiðo, a] *adj* (*pérdida*) regrettable; (*carácter*) sensitive ▷ *nm* sense; (*sentimiento*) feeling; (*significado*) sense, meaning; (*dirección*) direction; **mi más ~ pésame** my deepest sympathy; **tener ~** to make sense; **sentido común** common sense; **sentido del humor** sense of humour; **sentido único** one-way (street)
sentimental [sentimen'tal] *adj* sentimental; **vida ~** love life
sentimiento [senti'mjento] *nm* feeling
sentir [sen'tir] *vt* to feel; (*percibir*) to perceive, sense; (*lamentar*) to regret, be sorry for ▷ *vi* (*tener la sensación*) to feel; (*lamentarse*) to feel sorry ▷ *nm* opinion, judgement; **~se bien/mal** to feel well/ill; **lo siento** I'm sorry
seña ['seɲa] *nf* sign; (*Mil*) password; **señas** *nfpl* (*dirección*) address *sg*; **señas personales** personal description *sg*
señal [se'ɲal] *nf* sign; (*síntoma*) symptom; (*Ferro, Tel*) signal; (*marca*) mark; (*Com*) deposit; **en ~ de** as a token *o* sign of; **señalar** *vt* to mark; (*indicar*) to point out, indicate
señor [se'ɲor] *nm* (*hombre*) man; (*caballero*) gentleman; (*dueño*) owner, master; (*trato: antes de nombre propio*) Mr; (*: hablando directamente*) sir; **muy ~ mío** Dear Sir; **el ~ alcalde/presidente** the mayor/president
señora [se'ɲora] *nf* (*dama*) lady; (*trato: antes de nombre propio*) Mrs; (*: hablando directamente*) madam; (*esposa*) wife; **Nuestra S~** Our Lady
señorita [seɲo'rita] *nf* (*con nombre y/o apellido*) Miss; (*mujer joven*) young lady
señorito [seɲo'rito] *nm* young gentleman; (*pey*) rich kid
sepa *etc vb V* **saber**
separación [separa'θjon] *nf* separation; (*división*) division; (*hueco*) gap
separar [sepa'rar] *vt* to separate; (*dividir*) to divide; **separarse** *vr* (*parte*) to come away; (*partes*) to come apart; (*persona*) to leave, go away; (*matrimonio*) to separate; **separatismo** *nm* separatism

sepia ['sepja] *nf* cuttlefish
septentrional [septentrjo'nal] *adj* northern
septiembre [sep'tjembre] *nm* September
séptimo, -a ['septimo, a] *adj, nm* seventh
sepulcral [sepul'kral] *adj* (*fig: silencio, atmósfera*) deadly; **sepulcro** *nm* tomb, grave
sepultar [sepul'tar] *vt* to bury; **sepultura** *nf* (*acto*) burial; (*tumba*) grave, tomb
sequía [se'kia] *nf* drought
séquito ['sekito] *nm* (*de rey etc*) retinue; (*seguidores*) followers *pl*

PALABRA CLAVE

ser [ser] *vi* **1** (*descripción*) to be; **es médica/muy alta** she's a doctor/very tall; **la familia es de Cuzco** his (*o* her *etc*) family is from Cuzco; **soy Ana** (*Tel*) Ana speaking *o* here
2 (*propiedad*): **es de Joaquín** it's Joaquín's, it belongs to Joaquín
3 (*horas, fechas, números*): **es la una** it's one o'clock; **son las seis y media** it's half-past six; **es el 1 de junio** it's the first of June; **somos/son seis** there are six of us/them
4 (*en oraciones pasivas*): **ha sido descubierto ya** it's already been discovered
5: **es de esperar que ...** it is to be hoped *o* I *etc* hope that ...
6 (*locuciones con sub*): **o sea** that is to say; **sea él sea su hermana** either him or his sister
7: **a no ser por él ...** but for him ...
8: **a no ser que: a no ser que tenga uno ya** unless he's got one already
▷ *nm* being; **ser humano** human being

sereno, -a [se'reno, a] *adj* (*persona*) calm, unruffled; (*el tiempo*) fine, settled; (*ambiente*) calm, peaceful ▷ *nm* night watchman
serial [ser'jal] *nm* serial
serie ['serje] *nf* series; (*cadena*) sequence, succession; **fuera de ~** out of order; (*fig*) special, out of the ordinary; **fabricación en ~** mass production
seriedad [serje'ðað] *nf* seriousness; (*formalidad*) reliability; **serio, -a** *adj* serious; reliable, dependable; grave, serious; **en serio** *adv* seriously
serigrafía [seriɣra'fia] *nf* silk-screen printing
sermón [ser'mon] *nm* (*Rel*) sermon
seropositivo, -a [seroposi'tiβo] *adj* HIV positive
serpentear [serpente'ar] *vi* to wriggle; (*camino, río*) to wind, snake
serpentina [serpen'tina] *nf* streamer
serpiente [ser'pjente] *nf* snake; **serpiente de cascabel** rattlesnake
serranía [serra'nia] *nf* mountainous area
serrar [se'rrar] *vt* = **aserrar**
serrín [se'rrin] *nm* sawdust
serrucho [se'rrutʃo] *nm* saw
service ['serβis] (RPL) *nm* (*Auto*) service
servicio [ser'βiθjo] *nm* service; (LAM *Auto*) service; **servicios** *nmpl* (ESP) toilet(s); **servicio incluido** service charge included; **servicio militar** military service
servidumbre [serβi'ðumbre] *nf* (*sujeción*) servitude; (*criados*) servants *pl*, staff
servil [ser'βil] *adj* servile
servilleta [serβi'ʎeta] *nf* serviette, napkin
servir [ser'βir] *vt* to serve ▷ *vi* to serve; (*tener utilidad*) to be of use, be useful; **servirse** *vr* to serve *o* help o.s.; **~se de algo** to make use of sth, use sth; **sírvase pasar** please come in
sesenta [se'senta] *num* sixty
sesión [se'sjon] *nf* (*Pol*) session, sitting; (*Cine*) showing

seso ['seso] *nm* brain; **sesudo, -a** *adj* sensible, wise
seta ['seta] *nf* mushroom; **seta venenosa** toadstool
setecientos, -as [sete'θjentos, as] *adj, num* seven hundred
setenta [se'tenta] *num* seventy
seto ['seto] *nm* hedge
severo, -a [se'βero, a] *adj* severe
Sevilla [se'βiʎa] *n* Seville; **sevillano, -a** *adj* of *o* from Seville ▷ *nm/f* native *o* inhabitant of Seville
sexo ['sekso] *nm* sex
sexto, -a ['seksto, a] *adj, nm* sixth
sexual [sek'swal] *adj* sexual; **vida ~** sex life
si [si] *conj* if ▷ *nm* (*Mús*) B; **me pregunto ~ ...** I wonder if *o* whether ...
sí [si] *adv* yes ▷ *nm* consent ▷ *pron* (*uso impersonal*) oneself; (*sg*: *m*) himself; (: *f*) herself; (: *de cosa*) itself; (*de usted*) yourself; (*pl*) themselves; (*de ustedes*) yourselves; (*recíproco*) each other; **él no quiere pero yo ~** he doesn't want to but I do; **ella ~ vendrá** she will certainly come, she is sure to come; **claro que ~** of course; **creo que ~** I think so
siamés, -esa [sja'mes, esa] *adj, nm/f* Siamese
SIDA ['siðа] *nm abr* (= *Síndrome de Inmunodeficiencia Adquirida*) AIDS
siderúrgico, -a [siðe'rurxico, a] *adj* iron and steel *cpd*
sidra ['siðra] *nf* cider
siembra ['sjembra] *nf* sowing
siempre ['sjempre] *adv* always; (*todo el tiempo*) all the time; **~ que** (*cada vez*) whenever; (*dado que*) provided that; **como ~** as usual; **para ~** for ever
sien [sjen] *nf* temple
siento *etc* ['sjento] *vb V* **sentar; sentir**
sierra ['sjerra] *nf* (*Tec*) saw; (*cadena de montañas*) mountain range
siervo, -a ['sjerβo, a] *nm/f* slave
siesta ['sjesta] *nf* siesta, nap; **echar la ~** to have an afternoon nap *o* a siesta
siete ['sjete] *num* seven
sifón [si'fon] *nm* syphon
sigla ['siɤla] *nf* abbreviation; acronym
siglo ['siɤlo] *nm* century; (*fig*) age
significado [siɤnifi'kaðo] *nm* (*de palabra etc*) meaning
significar [siɤnifi'kar] *vt* to mean, signify; (*notificar*) to make known, express
signo ['siɤno] *nm* sign; **signo de admiración** *o* **exclamación** exclamation mark; **signo de interrogación** question mark
sigo *etc vb V* **seguir**
siguiente [si'ɤjente] *adj* next, following
siguió *etc vb V* **seguir**
sílaba ['silaβa] *nf* syllable
silbar [sil'βar] *vt, vi* to whistle; **silbato** *nm* whistle; **silbido** *nm* whistle, whistling
silenciador [silenθja'ðor] *nm* silencer
silenciar [silen'θjar] *vt* (*persona*) to silence; (*escándalo*) to hush up; **silencio** *nm* silence, quiet; **silencioso, -a** *adj* silent, quiet
silla ['siʎa] *nf* (*asiento*) chair; (*tb*: **~ de montar**) saddle; **silla de ruedas** wheelchair
sillón [si'ʎon] *nm* armchair, easy chair
silueta [si'lweta] *nf* silhouette; (*de edificio*) outline; (*figura*) figure
silvestre [sil'βestre] *adj* wild
simbólico, -a [sim'boliko, a] *adj* symbolic(al)
simbolizar [simboli'θar] *vt* to symbolize
símbolo ['simbolo] *nm* symbol
similar [simi'lar] *adj* similar
simio ['simjo] *nm* ape
simpatía [simpa'tia] *nf* liking; (*afecto*) affection; (*amabilidad*) kindness; **simpático, -a** *adj* nice, pleasant; kind

> No confundir **simpático** con la palabra inglesa *sympathetic*.

simpatizante [simpati'θante] *nmf* sympathizer

simpatizar [simpati'θar] *vi*: **~ con** to get on well with

simple ['simple] *adj* simple; (*elemental*) simple, easy; (*mero*) mere; (*puro*) pure, sheer ▷ *nmf* simpleton; **simpleza** *nf* simpleness; (*necedad*) silly thing; **simplificar** *vt* to simplify

simposio [sim'posjo] *nm* symposium

simular [simu'lar] *vt* to simulate

simultáneo, -a [simul'taneo, a] *adj* simultaneous

sin [sin] *prep* without; **la ropa está ~ lavar** the clothes are unwashed; **~ que** without; **~ embargo** however, still

sinagoga [sina'ɣoɣa] *nf* synagogue

sinceridad [sinθeri'ðað] *nf* sincerity; **sincero, -a** *adj* sincere

sincronizar [sinkroni'θar] *vt* to synchronize

sindical [sindi'kal] *adj* union *cpd*, trade-union *cpd*; **sindicalista** *adj*, *nmf* trade unionist

sindicato [sindi'kato] *nm* (*de trabajadores*) trade(s) union; (*de negociantes*) syndicate

síndrome ['sinðrome] *nm* (*Med*) syndrome; **síndrome de abstinencia** (*Med*) withdrawal symptoms; **síndrome de de la clase turista** (*Med*) economy-class syndrome

sinfín [sin'fin] *nm*: **un ~ de** a great many, no end of

sinfonía [sinfo'nia] *nf* symphony

singular [singu'lar] *adj* singular; (*fig*) outstanding, exceptional; (*raro*) peculiar, odd

siniestro, -a [si'njestro, a] *adj* sinister ▷ *nm* (*accidente*) accident

sinnúmero [sin'numero] *nm* = **sinfín**

sino ['sino] *nm* fate, destiny ▷ *conj* (*pero*) but; (*salvo*) except, save

sinónimo, -a [si'nonimo, a] *adj* synonymous ▷ *nm* synonym

síntesis ['sintesis] *nf* synthesis; **sintético, -a** *adj* synthetic

sintió *vb V* **sentir**

síntoma ['sintoma] *nm* symptom

sintonía [sinto'nia] *nf* (*Radio, Mús: de programa*) tuning; **sintonizar** *vt* (*Radio: emisora*) to tune (in)

sinvergüenza [simber'ɣwenθa] *nmf* rogue, scoundrel; **¡es un ~!** he's got a nerve!

siquiera [si'kjera] *conj* even if, even though ▷ *adv* at least; **ni ~** not even

Siria ['sirja] *nf* Syria

sirviente, -a [sir'βjente, a] *nm/f* servant

sirvo *etc vb V* **servir**

sistema [sis'tema] *nm* system; (*método*) method; **sistema educativo** education system; **sistemático, -a** *adj* systematic

SISTEMA EDUCATIVO

The reform of the Spanish **sistema educativo** (education system) begun in the early 90s has replaced the courses **EGB**, **BUP** and **COU** with the following: "Primaria" a compulsory 6 years; "Secundaria" a compulsory 4 years and "Bachillerato" an optional 2-year secondary school course, essential for those wishing to go on to higher education.

sitiar [si'tjar] *vt* to besiege, lay siege to

sitio ['sitjo] *nm* (*lugar*) place; (*espacio*) room, space; (*Mil*) siege; **sitio de taxis** (*MÉX: parada*) taxi stand *o* rank (*BRIT*); **sitio web** (*Inform*) website

situación [sitwa'θjon] *nf* situation, position; (*estatus*) position, standing

situado, -a [situ'aðo] *adj* situated, placed

situar [si'twar] *vt* to place, put; (*edificio*) to locate, situate

slip [slip] *nm* pants *pl*, briefs *pl*

smoking ['smokin, es'mokin] (*pl* **~s**) *nm* dinner jacket (*BRIT*), tuxedo (*US*)

No confundir **smoking** con la palabra inglesa *smoking*.

SMS *nm* (*mensaje*) text message, SMS message
snob [es'nob] = **esnob**
SO *abr* (= *suroeste*) SW
sobaco [so'βako] *nm* armpit
sobar [so'βar] *vt* (*ropa*) to rumple; (*comida*) to play around with
soberanía [soβera'nia] *nf* sovereignty; **soberano, -a** *adj* sovereign; (*fig*) supreme ▷ *nm/f* sovereign
soberbia [so'βerβja] *nf* pride; haughtiness, arrogance; magnificence
soberbio, -a [so'βerβjo, a] *adj* (*orgulloso*) proud; (*altivo*) arrogant; (*estupendo*) magnificent, superb
sobornar [soβor'nar] *vt* to bribe; **soborno** *nm* bribe
sobra ['soβra] *nf* excess, surplus; **sobras** *nfpl* left-overs, scraps; **de ~** surplus, extra; **tengo de ~** I've more than enough; **sobrado, -a** *adj* (*más que suficiente*) more than enough; (*superfluo*) excessive; **sobrante** *adj* remaining, extra ▷ *nm* surplus, remainder
sobrar [so'βrar] *vt* to exceed, surpass ▷ *vi* (*tener de más*) to be more than enough; (*quedar*) to remain, be left (over)
sobrasada [soβra'saða] *nf* *pork sausage spread*
sobre ['soβre] *prep* (*gen*) on; (*encima*) on (top of); (*por encima de, arriba de*) over, above; (*más que*) more than; (*además*) in addition to, besides; (*alrededor de*) about ▷ *nm* envelope; **~ todo** above all
sobrecama [soβre'kama] *nf* bedspread
sobrecargar [soβrekar'ɣar] *vt* (*camión*) to overload; (*Com*) to surcharge
sobredosis [soβre'ðosis] *nf inv* overdose
sobreentender [soβre(e)nten'der] *vt* to deduce, infer; **sobreentenderse** *vr*: **se sobreentiende que ...** it is implied that ...
sobrehumano, -a [soβreu'mano, a] *adj* superhuman
sobrellevar [soβreʎe'βar] *vt* to bear, endure
sobremesa [soβre'mesa] *nf*: **durante la ~** after dinner
sobrenatural [soβrenatu'ral] *adj* supernatural
sobrenombre [soβre'nombre] *nm* nickname
sobrepasar [soβrepa'sar] *vt* to exceed, surpass
sobreponerse [soβrepo'nerse] *vr*: **~ a** to overcome
sobresaliente [soβresa'ljente] *adj* outstanding, excellent
sobresalir [soβresa'lir] *vi* to project, jut out; (*fig*) to stand out, excel
sobresaltar [soβresal'tar] *vt* (*asustar*) to scare, frighten; (*sobrecoger*) to startle; **sobresalto** *nm* (*movimiento*) start; (*susto*) scare; (*turbación*) sudden shock
sobretodo [soβre'toðo] *nm* overcoat
sobrevenir [soβreβe'nir] *vi* (*ocurrir*) to happen (unexpectedly); (*resultar*) to follow, ensue
sobrevivir [soβreβi'βir] *vi* to survive
sobrevolar [soβreβo'lar] *vt* to fly over
sobriedad [soβrje'ðað] *nf* sobriety, soberness; (*moderación*) moderation, restraint
sobrino, -a [so'βrino, a] *nm/f* nephew/niece
sobrio, -a ['soβrjo, a] *adj* sober; (*moderado*) moderate, restrained
socarrón, -ona [soka'rron, ona] *adj* (*sarcástico*) sarcastic, ironic(al)
socavón [soka'βon] *nm* (*hoyo*) hole
sociable [so'θjaβle] *adj* (*persona*) sociable, friendly; (*animal*) social
social [so'θjal] *adj* social; (*Com*) company *cpd*
socialdemócrata [soθjalde'mokrata] *nmf* social democrat

socialista [soθja'lista] *adj, nm* socialist
socializar [soθjali'θar] *vt* to socialize
sociedad [soθje'ðað] *nf* society; (*Com*) company; **sociedad anónima** limited company; **sociedad de consumo** consumer society
socio, -a ['soθjo, a] *nm/f* (*miembro*) member; (*Com*) partner
sociología [soθjolo'xia] *nf* sociology; **sociólogo, -a** *nm/f* sociologist
socorrer [soko'rrer] *vt* to help; **socorrista** *nmf* first aider; (*en piscina, playa*) lifeguard; **socorro** *nm* (*ayuda*) help, aid; (*Mil*) relief; **¡socorro!** help!
soda ['soða] *nf* (*sosa*) soda; (*bebida*) soda (water)
sofá [so'fa] (*pl* **~s**) *nm* sofa, settee; **sofá-cama** *nm* studio couch; sofa bed
sofocar [sofo'kar] *vt* to suffocate; (*apagar*) to smother, put out; **sofocarse** *vr* to suffocate; (*fig*) to blush, feel embarrassed; **sofoco** *nm* suffocation; embarrassment
sofreír [sofre'ir] *vt* (*Culin*) to fry lightly
soga ['soɣa] *nf* rope
sois *etc vb V* **ser**
soja ['soxa] *nf* soya
sol [sol] *nm* sun; (*luz*) sunshine, sunlight; (*Mús*) G; **hace ~** it's sunny
solamente [sola'mente] *adv* only, just
solapa [so'lapa] *nf* (*de chaqueta*) lapel; (*de libro*) jacket
solapado, -a [sola'paðo, a] *adj* (*intenciónes*) underhand; (*gestos, movimiento*) sly
solar [so'lar] *adj* solar, sun *cpd*
soldado [sol'daðo] *nm* soldier; **soldado raso** private
soldador [solda'ðor] *nm* soldering iron; (*persona*) welder
soldar [sol'dar] *vt* to solder, weld
soleado, -a [sole'aðo, a] *adj* sunny
soledad [sole'ðað] *nf* solitude; (*estado infeliz*) loneliness
solemne [so'lemne] *adj* solemn
soler [so'ler] *vi* to be in the habit of, be accustomed to; **suele salir a las ocho** she usually goes out at eight o'clock
solfeo [sol'feo] *nm* solfa
solicitar [soliθi'tar] *vt* (*permiso*) to ask for, seek; (*puesto*) to apply for; (*votos*) to canvass for; (*atención*) to attract
solícito, -a [so'liθito, a] *adj* (*diligente*) diligent; (*cuidadoso*) careful; **solicitud** *nf* (*calidad*) great care; (*petición*) request; (*a un puesto*) application
solidaridad [soliðari'ðað] *nf* solidarity; **solidario, -a** *adj* (*participación*) joint, common; (*compromiso*) mutually binding
sólido, -a ['soliðo, a] *adj* solid
soliloquio [soli'lokjo] *nm* soliloquy
solista [so'lista] *nmf* soloist
solitario, -a [soli'tarjo, a] *adj* (*persona*) lonely, solitary; (*lugar*) lonely, desolate ▷ *nm/f* (*recluso*) recluse; (*en la sociedad*) loner ▷ *nm* solitaire
sollozar [soʎo'θar] *vi* to sob; **sollozo** *nm* sob
solo, -a ['solo, a] *adj* (*único*) single, sole; (*sin compañía*) alone; (*solitario*) lonely; **hay una sola dificultad** there is just one difficulty; **a solas** alone, by oneself
sólo ['solo] *adv* only, just
solomillo [solo'miʎo] *nm* sirloin
soltar [sol'tar] *vt* (*dejar ir*) to let go of; (*desprender*) to unfasten, loosen; (*librar*) to release, set free; (*risa etc*) to let out
soltero, -a [sol'tero, a] *adj* single, unmarried ▷ *nm/f* bachelor/single woman; **solterón, -ona** *nm/f* old bachelor/spinster
soltura [sol'tura] *nf* looseness, slackness; (*de los miembros*) agility, ease of movement; (*en el hablar*) fluency, ease
soluble [so'luβle] *adj* (*Quím*) soluble; (*problema*) solvable; **~ en agua** soluble in water
solución [solu'θjon] *nf* solution; **solucionar** *vt* (*problema*) to solve;

(*asunto*) to settle, resolve
solventar [solβen'tar] *vt* (*pagar*) to settle, pay; (*resolver*) to resolve; **solvente** *adj* (*Econ*: *empresa, persona*) solvent
sombra ['sombra] *nf* shadow; (*como protección*) shade; **sombras** *nfpl* (*oscuridad*) darkness *sg*, shadows; **tener buena/mala ~** to be lucky/unlucky
sombrero [som'brero] *nm* hat
sombrilla [som'briʎa] *nf* parasol, sunshade
sombrío, -a [som'brio, a] *adj* (*oscuro*) dark; (*triste*) sombre, sad; (*persona*) gloomy
someter [some'ter] *vt* (*país*) to conquer; (*persona*) to subject to one's will; (*informe*) to present, submit; **someterse** *vr* to give in, yield, submit; **~ a** to subject to
somier [so'mjer] (*pl* **~s**) *n* spring mattress
somnífero [som'nifero] *nm* sleeping pill
somos *vb V* **ser**
son [son] *vb V* **ser** ▷ *nm* sound
sonaja [so'naxa] (*MÉX*) *nf* = **sonajero**
sonajero [sona'xero] *nm* (baby's) rattle
sonambulismo [sonambu'lismo] *nm* sleepwalking; **sonámbulo, -a** *nm/f* sleepwalker
sonar [so'nar] *vt* to ring ▷ *vi* to sound; (*hacer ruido*) to make a noise; (*pronunciarse*) to be sounded, be pronounced; (*ser conocido*) to sound familiar; (*campana*) to ring; (*reloj*) to strike, chime; **sonarse** *vr*: **~se (las narices)** to blow one's nose; **me suena ese nombre** that name rings a bell
sonda ['sonda] *nf* (*Náut*) sounding; (*Tec*) bore, drill; (*Med*) probe
sondear [sonde'ar] *vt* to sound; to bore (into), drill; to probe, sound; (*fig*) to sound out; **sondeo** *nm* sounding; boring, drilling; (*fig*) poll, enquiry
sonido [so'niðo] *nm* sound
sonoro, -a [so'noro, a] *adj* sonorous; (*resonante*) loud, resonant
sonreír [sonre'ir] *vi* to smile; **sonreírse** *vr* to smile; **sonriente** *adj* smiling; **sonrisa** *nf* smile
sonrojarse [sonro'xarse] *vr* to blush, go red; **sonrojo** *nm* blush
soñador, a [soɲa'ðor, a] *nm/f* dreamer
soñar [so'ɲar] *vt, vi* to dream; **~ con** to dream about *o* of
soñoliento, -a [soɲo'ljento, a] *adj* sleepy, drowsy
sopa ['sopa] *nf* soup
soplar [so'plar] *vt* (*polvo*) to blow away, blow off; (*inflar*) to blow up; (*vela*) to blow out ▷ *vi* to blow; **soplo** *nm* blow, puff; (*de viento*) puff, gust
soplón, -ona [so'plon, ona] (*fam*) *nm/f* (*niño*) telltale; (*de policía*) grass (*fam*)
soporífero [sopo'rifero] *nm* sleeping pill
soportable [sopor'taβle] *adj* bearable
soportar [sopor'tar] *vt* to bear, carry; (*fig*) to bear, put up with

No confundir **soportar** con la palabra inglesa *support*.

soporte *nm* support; (*fig*) pillar, support
soprano [so'prano] *nf* soprano
sorber [sor'βer] *vt* (*chupar*) to sip; (*absorber*) to soak up, absorb
sorbete [sor'βete] *nm* iced fruit drink
sorbo ['sorβo] *nm* (*trago*: *grande*) gulp, swallow; (: *pequeño*) sip
sordera [sor'ðera] *nf* deafness
sórdido, -a ['sorðiðo, a] *adj* dirty, squalid
sordo, -a ['sorðo, a] *adj* (*persona*) deaf ▷ *nm/f* deaf person; **sordomudo, -a** *adj* deaf and dumb
sorna ['sorna] *nf* sarcastic tone
soroche [so'rotʃe] (*CAM*) *nm* mountain sickness
sorprendente [sorpren'dente] *adj* surprising
sorprender [sorpren'der] *vt* to

surprise; **sorpresa** *nf* surprise
sortear [sorte'ar] *vt* to draw lots for; (*rifar*) to raffle; (*dificultad*) to avoid; **sorteo** *nm* (*en lotería*) draw; (*rifa*) raffle
sortija [sor'tixa] *nf* ring; (*rizo*) ringlet, curl
sosegado, -a [sose'ɣaðo, a] *adj* quiet, calm
sosiego [so'sjeɣo] *nm* quiet(ness), calm(ness)
soso, -a ['soso, a] *adj* (*Culin*) tasteless; (*aburrido*) dull, uninteresting
sospecha [sos'petʃa] *nf* suspicion; **sospechar** *vt* to suspect; **sospechoso, -a** *adj* suspicious; (*testimonio, opinión*) suspect ▷ *nm/f* suspect
sostén [sos'ten] *nm* (*apoyo*) support; (*sujetador*) bra; (*alimentación*) sustenance, food
sostener [soste'ner] *vt* to support; (*mantener*) to keep up, maintain; (*alimentar*) to sustain, keep going; **sostenerse** *vr* to support o.s.; (*seguir*) to continue, remain; **sostenido, -a** *adj* continuous, sustained; (*prolongado*) prolonged
sotana [so'tana] *nf* (*Rel*) cassock
sótano ['sotano] *nm* basement
soy [soi] *vb V* **ser**
soya ['soja] (LAM) *nf* soya (BRIT), soy (US)
Sr. *abr* (= *Señor*) Mr
Sra. *abr* (= *Señora*) Mrs
Sres. *abr* (= *Señores*) Messrs
Srta. *abr* (= *Señorita*) Miss
Sta. *abr* (= *Santa*) St
Sto. *abr* (= *Santo*) St
su [su] *pron* (*de él*) his; (*de ella*) her; (*de una cosa*) its; (*de ellos, ellas*) their; (*de usted, ustedes*) your
suave ['swaβe] *adj* gentle; (*superficie*) smooth; (*trabajo*) easy; (*música, voz*) soft, sweet; **suavidad** *nf* gentleness; smoothness; softness, sweetness; **suavizante** *nm* (*de ropa*) softener; (*del pelo*) conditioner; **suavizar** *vt* to soften; (*quitar la aspereza*) to smooth (out)
subasta [su'βasta] *nf* auction; **subastar** *vt* to auction (off)
subcampeón, -ona [suβkampe'on, ona] *nm/f* runner-up
subconsciente [suβkon'sθjente] *adj, nm* subconscious
subdesarrollado, -a [suβðesarro'ʎaðo, a] *adj* underdeveloped
subdesarrollo [suβðesa'rroʎo] *nm* underdevelopment
subdirector, a [suβðirek'tor, a] *nm/f* assistant director
súbdito, -a ['suβðito, a] *nm/f* subject
subestimar [suβesti'mar] *vt* to underestimate, underrate
subida [su'βiða] *nf* (*de montaña etc*) ascent, climb; (*de precio*) rise, increase; (*pendiente*) slope, hill
subir [su'βir] *vt* (*objeto*) to raise, lift up; (*cuesta, calle*) to go up; (*colina, montaña*) to climb; (*precio*) to raise, put up ▷ *vi* to go up, come up; (*a un coche*) to get in; (*a un autobús, tren o avión*) to get on, board; (*precio*) to rise, go up; (*río, marea*) to rise; **subirse** *vr* to get up, climb
súbito, -a ['suβito, a] *adj* (*repentino*) sudden; (*imprevisto*) unexpected
subjetivo, -a [suβxe'tiβo, a] *adj* subjective
sublevar [suβle'βar] *vt* to rouse to revolt; **sublevarse** *vr* to revolt, rise
sublime [su'βlime] *adj* sublime
submarinismo [suβmari'nismo] *nm* scuba diving
submarino, -a [suβma'rino, a] *adj* underwater ▷ *nm* submarine
subnormal [suβnor'mal] *adj* subnormal ▷ *nmf* subnormal person
subordinado, -a [suβorði'naðo, a] *adj, nm/f* subordinate
subrayar [suβra'jar] *vt* to underline
subsanar [suβsa'nar] *vt* to rectify
subsidio [suβ'siðjo] *nm* (*ayuda*) aid, financial help; (*subvención*) subsidy,

grant; (*de enfermedad, paro etc*) benefit, allowance

subsistencia [suβsis'tenθja] *nf* subsistence

subsistir [suβsis'tir] *vi* to subsist; (*sobrevivir*) to survive, endure

subte ['suβte] (RPL) *nm* underground (BRIT), subway (US)

subterráneo, -a [suβte'rraneo, a] *adj* underground, subterranean ▷ *nm* underpass, underground passage

subtítulo [suβ'titulo] *nm* (*Cine*) subtitle

suburbio [su'βurβjo] *nm* (*barrio*) slum quarter

subvención [suββen'θjon] *nf* (*Econ*) subsidy, grant; **subvencionar** *vt* to subsidize

sucedáneo, -a [suθe'ðaneo, a] *adj* substitute ▷ *nm* substitute (food)

suceder [suθe'ðer] *vt, vi* to happen; (*seguir*) to succeed, follow; **lo que sucede es que ...** the fact is that ...; **sucesión** *nf* succession; (*serie*) sequence, series

sucesivamente [suθesiβa'mente] *adv*: **y así ~** and so on

sucesivo, -a [suθe'siβo, a] *adj* successive, following; **en lo ~** in future, from now on

suceso [su'θeso] *nm* (*hecho*) event, happening; (*incidente*) incident

No confundir **suceso** con la palabra inglesa *success*.

suciedad [suθje'ðað] *nf* (*estado*) dirtiness; (*mugre*) dirt, filth

sucio, -a ['suθjo, a] *adj* dirty

suculento, -a [suku'lento, a] *adj* succulent

sucumbir [sukum'bir] *vi* to succumb

sucursal [sukur'sal] *nf* branch (office)

sudadera [suða'ðera] *nf* sweatshirt

Sudáfrica [suð'afrika] *nf* South Africa

Sudamérica [suða'merika] *nf* South America; **sudamericano, -a** *adj, nm/f* South American

sudar [su'ðar] *vt, vi* to sweat

sudeste [su'ðeste] *nm* south-east

sudoeste [suðo'este] *nm* south-west

sudor [su'ðor] *nm* sweat; **sudoroso, -a** *adj* sweaty, sweating

Suecia ['sweθja] *nf* Sweden; **sueco, -a** *adj* Swedish ▷ *nm/f* Swede

suegro, -a ['sweɣro, a] *nm/f* father-/mother-in-law

suela ['swela] *nf* sole

sueldo ['sweldo] *nm* pay, wage(s) (*pl*)

suele *etc vb V* **soler**

suelo ['swelo] *nm* (*tierra*) ground; (*de casa*) floor

suelto, -a ['swelto, a] *adj* loose; (*libre*) free; (*separado*) detached; (*ágil*) quick, agile ▷ *nm* (loose) change, small change

sueñito [swe'ɲito] (LAM) *nm* nap

sueño *etc* ['sweɲo] *vb V* **soñar** ▷ *nm* sleep; (*somnolencia*) sleepiness, drowsiness; (*lo soñado, fig*) dream; **tener ~** to be sleepy

suero ['swero] *nm* (*Med*) serum; (*de leche*) whey

suerte ['swerte] *nf* (*fortuna*) luck; (*azar*) chance; (*destino*) fate, destiny; (*especie*) sort, kind; **tener ~** to be lucky

suéter ['sweter] *nm* sweater

suficiente [sufi'θjente] *adj* enough, sufficient ▷ *nm* (*Escol*) pass

sufragio [su'fraxjo] *nm* (*voto*) vote; (*derecho de voto*) suffrage

sufrido, -a [su'friðo, a] *adj* (*persona*) tough; (*paciente*) long-suffering, patient

sufrimiento [sufri'mjento] *nm* (*dolor*) suffering

sufrir [su'frir] *vt* (*padecer*) to suffer; (*soportar*) to bear, put up with; (*apoyar*) to hold up, support ▷ *vi* to suffer

sugerencia [suxe'renθja] *nf* suggestion

sugerir [suxe'rir] *vt* to suggest; (*sutilmente*) to hint

sugestión [suxes'tjon] *nf* suggestion; (*sutil*) hint; **sugestionar** *vt* to influence

sugestivo, -a [suxes'tiβo, a] *adj* stimulating; (*fascinante*) fascinating
suicida [sui'θiða] *adj* suicidal ▷ *nmf* suicidal person; (*muerto*) suicide, person who has committed suicide; **suicidarse** *vr* to commit suicide, kill o.s.; **suicidio** *nm* suicide
Suiza ['swiθa] *nf* Switzerland; **suizo, -a** *adj, nm/f* Swiss
sujeción [suxe'θjon] *nf* subjection
sujetador [suxeta'ðor] *nm* (*sostén*) bra
sujetar [suxe'tar] *vt* (*fijar*) to fasten; (*detener*) to hold down; **sujetarse** *vr* to subject o.s.; **sujeto, -a** *adj* fastened, secure ▷ *nm* subject; (*individuo*) individual; **sujeto a** subject to
suma ['suma] *nf* (*cantidad*) total, sum; (*de dinero*) sum; (*acto*) adding (up), addition; **en ~** in short
sumamente [suma'mente] *adv* extremely, exceedingly
sumar [su'mar] *vt* to add (up) ▷ *vi* to add up
sumergir [sumer'xir] *vt* to submerge; (*hundir*) to sink
suministrar [sumini'strar] *vt* to supply, provide; **suministro** *nm* supply; (*acto*) supplying, providing
sumir [su'mir] *vt* to sink, submerge; (*fig*) to plunge
sumiso, -a [su'miso, a] *adj* submissive, docile
sumo, -a ['sumo, a] *adj* great, extreme; (*autoridad*) highest, supreme
suntuoso, -a [sun'twoso, a] *adj* sumptuous, magnificent
supe *etc vb V* **saber**
super... [super] *prefijo* super..., over...
superbueno, -a [super'bweno, a] *adj* great, fantastic
súper ['super] *nf* (*gasolina*) four-star (petrol)
superar [supe'rar] *vt* (*sobreponerse a*) to overcome; (*rebasar*) to surpass, do better than; (*pasar*) to go beyond; **superarse** *vr* to excel o.s.
superficial [superfi'θjal] *adj* superficial; (*medida*) surface *cpd*, of the surface
superficie [super'fiθje] *nf* surface; (*área*) area
superfluo, -a [su'perflwo, a] *adj* superfluous
superior [supe'rjor] *adj* (*piso, clase*) upper; (*temperatura, número, nivel*) higher; (*mejor: calidad, producto*) superior, better ▷ *nmf* superior; **superioridad** *nf* superiority
supermercado [supermer'kaðo] *nm* supermarket
superponer [superpo'ner] *vt* to superimpose
superstición [supersti'θjon] *nf* superstition; **supersticioso, -a** *adj* superstitious
supervisar [superβi'sar] *vt* to supervise
supervivencia [superβi'βenθja] *nf* survival
superviviente [superβi'βjente] *adj* surviving
supiera *etc vb V* **saber**
suplantar [suplan'tar] *vt* to supplant
suplemento [suple'mento] *nm* supplement
suplente [su'plente] *adj, nm* substitute
supletorio, -a [suple'torjo, a] *adj* supplementary ▷ *nm* supplement; **teléfono ~** extension
súplica ['suplika] *nf* request; (*Jur*) petition
suplicar [supli'kar] *vt* (*cosa*) to beg (for), plead for; (*persona*) to beg, plead with
suplicio [su'pliθjo] *nm* torture
suplir [su'plir] *vt* (*compensar*) to make good, make up for; (*reemplazar*) to replace, substitute ▷ *vi*: **~ a** to take the place of, substitute for
supo *etc vb V* **saber**
suponer [supo'ner] *vt* to suppose; **suposición** *nf* supposition
suprimir [supri'mir] *vt* to suppress;

(*derecho, costumbre*) to abolish; (*palabra etc*) to delete; (*restricción*) to cancel, lift

supuesto, -a [su'pwesto, a] *pp de* **suponer** ▷ *adj* (*hipotético*) supposed ▷ *nm* assumption, hypothesis; **~ que** since; **por ~** of course

sur [sur] *nm* south

surcar [sur'kar] *vt* to plough; **surco** *nm* (*en metal, disco*) groove; (*Agr*) furrow

surgir [sur'xir] *vi* to arise, emerge; (*dificultad*) to come up, crop up

suroeste [suro'este] *nm* south-west

surtido, -a [sur'tiðo, a] *adj* mixed, assorted ▷ *nm* (*selección*) selection, assortment; (*abastecimiento*) supply, stock; **surtidor** *nm* (*tb*: **surtidor de gasolina**) petrol pump (BRIT), gas pump (US)

surtir [sur'tir] *vt* to supply, provide ▷ *vi* to spout, spurt

susceptible [susθep'tiβle] *adj* susceptible; (*sensible*) sensitive; **~ de** capable of

suscitar [susθi'tar] *vt* to cause, provoke; (*interés, sospechas*) to arouse

suscribir [suskri'βir] *vt* (*firmar*) to sign; (*respaldar*) to subscribe to, endorse; **suscribirse** *vr* to subscribe; **suscripción** *nf* subscription

susodicho, -a [suso'ðitʃo, a] *adj* above-mentioned

suspender [suspen'der] *vt* (*objeto*) to hang (up), suspend; (*trabajo*) to stop, suspend; (*Escol*) to fail; (*interrumpir*) to adjourn; (*atrasar*) to postpone

suspense [sus'pense] (ESP) *nm* suspense; **película/novela de ~** thriller

suspensión [suspen'sjon] *nf* suspension; (*fig*) stoppage, suspension

suspenso, -a [sus'penso, a] *adj* hanging, suspended; (ESP *Escol*) failed ▷ *nm* (ESP *Escol*) fail; **película** *o* **novela de ~** (LAM) thriller; **quedar** *o* **estar en ~** to be pending

suspicaz [suspi'kaθ] *adj* suspicious, distrustful

suspirar [suspi'rar] *vi* to sigh; **suspiro** *nm* sigh

sustancia [sus'tanθja] *nf* substance

sustento [sus'tento] *nm* support; (*alimento*) sustenance, food

sustituir [sustitu'ir] *vt* to substitute, replace; **sustituto, -a** *nm/f* substitute, replacement

susto ['susto] *nm* fright, scare

sustraer [sustra'er] *vt* to remove, take away; (*Mat*) to subtract

susurrar [susu'rrar] *vi* to whisper; **susurro** *nm* whisper

sutil [su'til] *adj* (*aroma, diferencia*) subtle; (*tenue*) thin; (*inteligencia, persona*) sharp

suyo, -a ['sujo, a] (*con artículo o después del verbo* **ser**) *adj* (*de él*) his; (*de ella*) hers; (*de ellos, ellas*) theirs; (*de Ud, Uds*) yours; **un amigo ~** a friend of his (*o* hers *o* theirs *o* yours)

Tabacalera [taβaka'lera] *nf Spanish state tobacco monopoly*
tabaco [ta'βako] *nm* tobacco; (*ESP*: *fam*) cigarettes *pl*
tabaquería [tabake'ria] (*LAM*) *nf* tobacconist's (shop) (*BRIT*), smoke shop (*US*); **tabaquero, -a** (*LAM*) *nm/f* tobacconist
taberna [ta'βerna] *nf* bar, pub (*BRIT*)
tabique [ta'βike] *nm* partition (wall)
tabla ['taβla] *nf* (*de madera*) plank; (*estante*) shelf; (*de vestido*) pleat; (*Arte*) panel; **tablas** *nfpl*: **estar** *o* **quedar en ~s** to draw; **tablado** *nm* (*plataforma*) platform; (*Teatro*) stage
tablao [ta'βlao] *nm* (*tb*: **~ flamenco**) flamenco show
tablero [ta'βlero] *nm* (*de madera*) plank, board; (*de ajedrez, damas*) board; **tablero de mandos** (*LAM Auto*) dashboard
tableta [ta'βleta] *nf* (*Med*) tablet; (*de chocolate*) bar
tablón [ta'βlon] *nm* (*de suelo*) plank; (*de techo*) beam; **tablón de anuncios** notice (*BRIT*) *o* bulletin (*US*) board
tabú [ta'βu] *nm* taboo
taburete [taβu'rete] *nm* stool
tacaño, -a [ta'kaɲo, a] *adj* mean
tacha ['tatʃa] *nf* flaw; (*Tec*) stud; **tachar** *vt* (*borrar*) to cross out; **tachar de** to accuse of
tacho ['tatʃo] (*CS*) *nm* (*balde*) bucket; **tacho de la basura** rubbish bin (*BRIT*), trash can (*US*)
taco ['tako] *nm* (*Billar*) cue; (*de billetes*) book; (*CS*: *de zapato*) heel; (*tarugo*) peg; (*palabrota*) swear word
tacón [ta'kon] *nm* heel; **de ~ alto** high-heeled
táctica ['taktika] *nf* tactics *pl*
táctico, -a ['taktiko, a] *adj* tactical
tacto ['takto] *nm* touch; (*fig*) tact
tajada [ta'xaða] *nf* slice
tajante [ta'xante] *adj* sharp
tajo ['taxo] *nm* (*corte*) cut; (*Geo*) cleft
tal [tal] *adj* such ▷ *pron* (*persona*) someone, such a one; (*cosa*) something, such a thing ▷ *adv*: **~ como** (*igual*) just as ▷ *conj*: **con ~ de que** provided that; **~ cual** (*como es*) just as it is; **~ vez** perhaps; **~ como** such as; **~ para cual** (*dos iguales*) two of a kind; **¿qué ~?** how are things?; **¿qué ~ te gusta?** how do you like it?
taladrar [tala'ðrar] *vt* to drill; **taladro** *nm* drill
talante [ta'lante] *nm* (*humor*) mood; (*voluntad*) will, willingness
talar [ta'lar] *vt* to fell, cut down; (*devastar*) to devastate
talco ['talko] *nm* (*polvos*) talcum powder
talento [ta'lento] *nm* talent; (*capacidad*) ability
TALGO ['talɣo] (*ESP*) *nm abr* (*= tren articulado ligero Goicoechea-Oriol*) ≈ HST (*BRIT*)
talismán [talis'man] *nm* talisman
talla ['taʎa] *nf* (*estatura, fig, Med*) height, stature; (*palo*) measuring rod; (*Arte*) carving; (*medida*) size
tallar [ta'ʎar] *vt* (*madera*) to carve;

(*metal etc*) to engrave; (*medir*) to measure
tallarines [taʎa'rines] *nmpl* noodles
talle ['taʎe] *nm* (*Anat*) waist; (*fig*) appearance
taller [ta'ʎer] *nm* (*Tec*) workshop; (*de artista*) studio
tallo ['taʎo] *nm* (*de planta*) stem; (*de hierba*) blade; (*brote*) shoot
talón [ta'lon] *nm* (*Anat*) heel; (*Com*) counterfoil; (*cheque*) cheque (BRIT), check (US)
talonario [talo'narjo] *nm* (*de cheques*) chequebook (BRIT), checkbook (US); (*de recibos*) receipt book
tamaño, -a [ta'maɲo, a] *adj* (*tan grande*) such a big; (*tan pequeño*) such a small ▷ *nm* size; **de ~ natural** full-size
tamarindo [tama'rindo] *nm* tamarind
tambalearse [tambale'arse] *vr* (*persona*) to stagger; (*vehículo*) to sway
también [tam'bjen] *adv* (*igualmente*) also, too, as well; (*además*) besides
tambor [tam'bor] *nm* drum; (*Anat*) eardrum; **tambor del freno** brake drum
tamizar [tami'θar] *vt* to sieve
tampoco [tam'poko] *adv* nor, neither; **yo ~ lo compré** I didn't buy it either
tampón [tam'pon] *nm* tampon
tan [tan] *adv* so; **~ es así que ...** so much so that ...
tanda ['tanda] *nf* (*gen*) series; (*turno*) shift
tangente [tan'xente] *nf* tangent
tangerina [tanxe'rina] (LAM) *nf* tangerine
tangible [tan'xiβle] *adj* tangible
tanque ['tanke] *nm* (*cisterna, Mil*) tank; (*Auto*) tanker
tantear [tante'ar] *vt* (*calcular*) to reckon (up); (*medir*) to take the measure of; (*probar*) to test, try out; (*tomar la medida*: *persona*) to take the measurements of; (*situación*) to weigh up; (*persona*: *opinión*) to sound out ▷ *vi* (*Deporte*) to score; **tanteo** *nm* (*cálculo*) (rough) calculation; (*prueba*) test, trial; (*Deporte*) scoring
tanto, -a ['tanto, a] *adj* (*cantidad*) so much, as much ▷ *adv* (*cantidad*) so much, as much; (*tiempo*) so long, as long ▷ *conj*: **en ~ que** while ▷ *nm* (*suma*) certain amount; (*proporción*) so much; (*punto*) point; (*gol*) goal; **un ~ perezoso** somewhat lazy ▷ *pron*: **cado uno paga ~** each one pays so much; **~s** so many, as many; **20 y ~s** 20-odd; **hasta ~ (que)** until such time as; **~ tú como yo** both you and I; **~ como eso** as much as that; **~ más ... cuanto que** all the more ... because; **~ mejor/peor** so much the better/the worse; **~ si viene como si va** whether he comes or whether he goes; **~ es así que** so much so that; **por (lo) ~** therefore; **entre ~** meanwhile; **estar al ~** to be up to date; **me he vuelto ronco de** *o* **con ~ hablar** I have become hoarse with so much talking; **a ~s de agosto** on such and such a day in August
tapa ['tapa] *nf* (*de caja, olla*) lid; (*de botella*) top; (*de libro*) cover; (*comida*) snack
tapadera [tapa'ðera] *nf* lid, cover
tapar [ta'par] *vt* (*cubrir*) to cover; (*envolver*) to wrap *o* cover up; (*la vista*) to obstruct; (*persona, falta*) to conceal; (MÉX, CAM: *diente*) to fill; **taparse** *vr* to wrap o.s. up
taparrabo [tapa'rraβo] *nm* loincloth
tapete [ta'pete] *nm* table cover
tapia ['tapja] *nf* (garden) wall
tapicería [tapiθe'ria] *nf* tapestry; (*para muebles*) upholstery; (*tienda*) upholsterer's (shop)
tapiz [ta'piθ] *nm* (*alfombra*) carpet; (*tela tejida*) tapestry; **tapizar** *vt* (*muebles*) to upholster
tapón [ta'pon] *nm* (*de botella*) top; (*de lavabo*) plug; **tapón de rosca** screw-top
taquigrafía [takiɣra'fia] *nf* shorthand; **taquígrafo, -a** *nm/f* shorthand writer, stenographer

taquilla [ta'kiʎa] *nf* (*donde se compra*) booking office; (*suma recogida*) takings *pl*
tarántula [ta'rantula] *nf* tarantula
tararear [tarare'ar] *vi* to hum
tardar [tar'ðar] *vi* (*tomar tiempo*) to take a long time; (*llegar tarde*) to be late; (*demorar*) to delay; **¿tarda mucho el tren?** does the train take (very) long?; **a más ~** at the latest; **no tardes en venir** come soon
tarde ['tarðe] *adv* late ▷ *nf* (*de día*) afternoon; (*al anochecer*) evening; **de ~ en ~** from time to time; **¡buenas ~s!** good afternoon!; **a** *o* **por la ~** in the afternoon; in the evening
tardío, -a [tar'ðio, a] *adj* (*retrasado*) late; (*lento*) slow (to arrive)
tarea [ta'rea] *nf* task; (*faena*) chore; (*Escol*) homework
tarifa [ta'rifa] *nf* (*lista de precios*) price list; (*precio*) tariff
tarima [ta'rima] *nf* (*plataforma*) platform
tarjeta [tar'xeta] *nf* card; **tarjeta de crédito/de Navidad/postal/telefónica** credit card/Christmas card/postcard/phonecard; **tarjeta de embarque** boarding pass; **tarjeta de memoria** memory card; **tarjeta prepago** top-up card; **tarjeta SIM** SIM card
tarro ['tarro] *nm* jar, pot
tarta ['tarta] *nf* (*pastel*) cake; (*de base dura*) tart
tartamudear [tartamuðe'ar] *vi* to stammer; **tartamudo, -a** *adj* stammering ▷ *nm/f* stammerer
tártaro, -a ['tartaro, a] *adj*: **salsa tártara** tartar(e) sauce
tasa ['tasa] *nf* (*precio*) (fixed) price, rate; (*valoración*) valuation; (*medida, norma*) measure, standard; **tasa de cambio/interés** exchange/interest rate; **tasas de aeropuerto** airport tax; **tasas universitarias** university fees
tasar [ta'sar] *vt* (*arreglar el precio*) to fix a price for; (*valorar*) to value, assess
tasca ['taska] (*fam*) *nf* pub
tatarabuelo, -a [tatara'βwelo, a] *nm/f* great-great-grandfather/mother
tatuaje [ta'twaxe] *nm* (*dibujo*) tattoo; (*acto*) tattooing
tatuar [ta'twar] *vt* to tattoo
taurino, -a [tau'rino, a] *adj* bullfighting *cpd*
Tauro ['tauro] *nm* Taurus
tauromaquia [tauro'makja] *nf* tauromachy, (art of) bullfighting
taxi ['taksi] *nm* taxi; **taxista** [tak'sista] *nmf* taxi driver
taza ['taθa] *nf* cup; (*de retrete*) bowl; **~ para café** coffee cup; **taza de café** cup of coffee; **tazón** *nm* (*taza grande*) mug, large cup; (*de fuente*) basin
te [te] *pron* (*complemento de objeto*) you; (*complemento indirecto*) (to) you; (*reflexivo*) (to) yourself; **¿~ duele mucho el brazo?** does your arm hurt a lot?; **~ equivocas** you're wrong; **¡cálma~!** calm down!
té [te] *nm* tea
teatral [tea'tral] *adj* theatre *cpd*; (*fig*) theatrical
teatro [te'atro] *nm* theatre; (*Literatura*) plays *pl*, drama
tebeo [te'βeo] *nm* comic
techo ['tetʃo] *nm* (*externo*) roof; (*interno*) ceiling; **techo corredizo** sunroof
tecla ['tekla] *nf* key; **teclado** *nm* keyboard; **teclear** *vi* (*Mús*) to strum; (*con los dedos*) to tap ▷ *vt* (*Inform*) to key in
técnica ['teknika] *nf* technique; (*tecnología*) technology; *V tb* **técnico**
técnico, -a ['tekniko, a] *adj* technical ▷ *nm/f* technician; (*experto*) expert
tecnología [teknolo'xia] *nf* technology; **tecnológico, -a** *adj* technological
tecolote [teko'lote] (*MÉX*) *nm* owl
tedioso, -a [te'ðjoso, a] *adj* boring, tedious
teja ['texa] *nf* tile; (*Bot*) lime (tree);

tejado *nm* (tiled) roof
tejemaneje [texema'nexe] *nm* (*lío*) fuss; (*intriga*) intrigue
tejer [te'xer] *vt* to weave; (*hacer punto*) to knit; (*fig*) to fabricate; **tejido** *nm* (*tela*) material, fabric; (*telaraña*) web; (*Anat*) tissue
tel [tel] *abr* (= *teléfono*) tel
tela ['tela] *nf* (*tejido*) material; (*telaraña*) web; (*en líquido*) skin; **telar** *nm* (*máquina*) loom
telaraña [tela'raɲa] *nf* cobweb
tele ['tele] (*fam*) *nf* telly (BRIT), tube (US)
tele... ['tele] *prefijo* tele...; **telebasura** *nf* trash TV; **telecomunicación** *nf* telecommunication; **telediario** *nm* television news; **teledirigido, -a** *adj* remote-controlled
teleférico [tele'feriko] *nm* (*de esquí*) ski-lift
telefonear [telefone'ar] *vi* to telephone
telefónico, -a [tele'foniko, a] *adj* telephone *cpd*
telefonillo [telefo'niʎo] *nm* (*de puerta*) intercom
telefonista [telefo'nista] *nmf* telephonist
teléfono [te'lefono] *nm* (tele)phone; **estar hablando al ~** to be on the phone; **llamar a algn por ~** to ring sb (up) *o* phone sb (up); **teléfono celular** (LAM) mobile phone; **teléfono con cámara** camera phone; **teléfono inalámbrico** cordless phone; **teléfono móvil** (ESP) mobile phone
telégrafo [te'leɣrafo] *nm* telegraph
telegrama [tele'ɣrama] *nm* telegram
tele: telenovela *nf* soap (opera); **teleobjetivo** *nm* telephoto lens; **telepatía** *nf* telepathy; **telepático, -a** *adj* telepathic; **telerrealidad** *nf* reality TV; **telescopio** *nm* telescope; **telesilla** *nm* chairlift; **telespectador, a** *nm/f* viewer; **telesquí** *nm* ski-lift; **teletarjeta** *nf* phonecard; **teletipo** *nm* teletype; **teletrabajador, a** *nm/f* teleworker; **teletrabajo** *nm* teleworking; **televentas** *nfpl* telesales
televidente [teleβi'ðente] *nmf* viewer
televisar [teleβi'sar] *vt* to televise
televisión [teleβi'sjon] *nf* television; **televisión digital** digital television
televisor [teleβi'sor] *nm* television set
télex ['teleks] *nm inv* telex
telón [te'lon] *nm* curtain; **telón de acero** (*Pol*) iron curtain; **telón de fondo** backcloth, background
tema ['tema] *nm* (*asunto*) subject, topic; (*Mús*) theme; **temático, -a** *adj* thematic
temblar [tem'blar] *vi* to shake, tremble; (*por frío*) to shiver; **temblor** *nm* trembling; (*de tierra*) earthquake; **tembloroso, -a** *adj* trembling
temer [te'mer] *vt* to fear ▷ *vi* to be afraid; **temo que llegue tarde** I am afraid he may be late
temible [te'miβle] *adj* fearsome
temor [te'mor] *nm* (*miedo*) fear; (*duda*) suspicion
témpano ['tempano] *nm* (*tb*: **~ de hielo**) ice-floe
temperamento [tempera'mento] *nm* temperament
temperatura [tempera'tura] *nf* temperature
tempestad [tempes'tað] *nf* storm
templado, -a [tem'plaðo, a] *adj* (*moderado*) moderate; (*frugal*) frugal; (*agua*) lukewarm; (*clima*) mild; (*Mús*) well-tuned; **templanza** *nf* moderation; mildness
templar [tem'plar] *vt* (*moderar*) to moderate; (*furia*) to restrain; (*calor*) to reduce; (*afinar*) to tune (up); (*acero*) to temper; (*tuerca*) to tighten up; **temple** *nm* (*ajuste*) tempering; (*afinación*) tuning; (*pintura*) tempera
templo ['templo] *nm* (*iglesia*) church; (*pagano etc*) temple

temporada [tempo'raða] *nf* time, period; (*estación*) season
temporal [tempo'ral] *adj* (*no permanente*) temporary ▷*nm* storm
temprano, -a [tem'prano, a] *adj* early; (*demasiado pronto*) too soon, too early
ten *vb V* **tener**
tenaces [te'naθes] *adj pl V* **tenaz**
tenaz [te'naθ] *adj* (*material*) tough; (*persona*) tenacious; (*creencia, resistencia*) stubborn
tenaza(s) [te'naθa(s)] *nf(pl)* (*Med*) forceps; (*Tec*) pliers; (*Zool*) pincers
tendedero [tende'ðero] *nm* (*para ropa*) drying place; (*cuerda*) clothes line
tendencia [ten'denθja] *nf* tendency; **tener ~ a** to tend to, have a tendency to
tender [ten'der] *vt* (*extender*) to spread out; (*colgar*) to hang out; (*vía férrea, cable*) to lay; (*estirar*) to stretch ▷*vi*: **~ a** to tend to, have a tendency towards; **tenderse** *vr* to lie down; **~ la cama/mesa** (LAM) to make the bed/lay (BRIT) *o* set (US) the table
tenderete [tende'rete] *nm* (*puesto*) stall; (*exposición*) display of goods
tendero, -a [ten'dero, a] *nm/f* shopkeeper
tendón [ten'don] *nm* tendon
tendré *etc vb V* **tener**
tenebroso, -a [tene'βroso, a] *adj* (*oscuro*) dark; (*fig*) gloomy
tenedor [tene'ðor] *nm* (*Culin*) fork
tenencia [te'nenθja] *nf* (*de casa*) tenancy; (*de oficio*) tenure; (*de propiedad*) possession

PALABRA CLAVE

tener [te'ner] *vt* **1** (*poseer, gen*) to have; (*en la mano*) to hold; **¿tienes un boli?** have you got a pen?; **va a tener un niño** she's going to have a baby; **¡ten (*o* tenga)!, ¡aquí tienes (*o* tiene)!** here you are!
2 (*edad, medidas*) to be; **tiene 7 años** she's 7 (years old); **tiene 15 cm de largo** it's 15 cm long; *V* **calor; hambre etc**
3 (*considerar*): **lo tengo por brillante** I consider him to be brilliant; **tener en mucho a algn** to think very highly of sb
4 (+ *pp*: = *pretérito*): **tengo terminada ya la mitad del trabajo** I've done half the work already
5: **tener que hacer algo** to have to do sth; **tengo que acabar este trabajo hoy** I have to finish this job today
6: **¿qué tienes, estás enfermo?** what's the matter with you, are you ill?
tenerse *vr* **1** **tenerse en pie** to stand up
2 **tenerse por** to think o.s.

tengo *etc vb V* **tener**
tenia ['tenja] *nf* tapeworm
teniente [te'njente] *nm* (*rango*) lieutenant; (*ayudante*) deputy
tenis ['tenis] *nm* tennis; **tenis de mesa** table tennis; **tenista** *nmf* tennis player
tenor [te'nor] *nm* (*sentido*) meaning; (*Mús*) tenor; **a ~ de** on the lines of
tensar [ten'sar] *vt* to tighten; (*arco*) to draw
tensión [ten'sjon] *nf* tension; (*Tec*) stress; **tener la ~ alta** to have high blood pressure; **tensión arterial** blood pressure
tenso, -a ['tenso, a] *adj* tense
tentación [tenta'θjon] *nf* temptation
tentáculo [ten'takulo] *nm* tentacle
tentador, a [tenta'ðor, a] *adj* tempting
tentar [ten'tar] *vt* (*seducir*) to tempt; (*atraer*) to attract
tentempié [tentem'pje] *nm* snack
tenue ['tenwe] *adj* (*delgado*) thin, slender; (*neblina*) light; (*lazo, vínculo*) slight
teñir [te'ɲir] *vt* to dye; (*fig*) to tinge; **teñirse** *vr* to dye; **~se el pelo** to dye one's hair
teología [teolo'xia] *nf* theology
teoría [teo'ria] *nf* theory; **en ~** in

theory; **teórico, -a** *adj* theoretic(al) ▹*nm/f* theoretician, theorist; **teorizar** *vi* to theorize

terapéutico, -a [tera'peutiko, a] *adj* therapeutic

terapia [te'rapja] *nf* therapy

tercer *adj* V **tercero**

tercermundista [terθermun'dista] *adj* Third World *cpd*

tercero, -a [ter'θero, a] (*delante de nmsg*: **tercer**) *adj* third ▹*nm* (*Jur*) third party

terceto [ter'θeto] *nm* trio

terciar [ter'θjar] *vi* (*participar*) to take part; (*hacer de árbitro*) to mediate; **terciario, -a** *adj* tertiary

tercio ['terθjo] *nm* third

terciopelo [terθjo'pelo] *nm* velvet

terco, -a ['terko, a] *adj* obstinate

tergal® [ter'ɣal] *nm type of polyester*

tergiversar [terxiβer'sar] *vt* to distort

termal [ter'mal] *adj* thermal

termas ['termas] *nfpl* hot springs

térmico, -a ['termiko, a] *adj* thermal

terminal [termi'nal] *adj, nm, nf* terminal

terminante [termi'nante] *adj* (*final*) final, definitive; (*tajante*) categorical; **terminantemente** *adv*: **terminantemente prohibido** strictly forbidden

terminar [termi'nar] *vt* (*completar*) to complete, finish; (*concluir*) to end ▹*vi* (*llegar a su fin*) to end; (*parar*) to stop; (*acabar*) to finish; **terminarse** *vr* to come to an end; **~ por hacer algo** to end up (by) doing sth

término ['termino] *nm* end, conclusion; (*parada*) terminus; (*límite*) boundary; **en último ~** (*a fin de cuentas*) in the last analysis; (*como último recurso*) as a last resort; **término medio** average; (*fig*) middle way

termómetro [ter'mometro] *nm* thermometer

termo(s)® ['termo(s)] *nm* Thermos®

termostato [termo'stato] *nm* thermostat

ternero, -a [ter'nero, a] *nm/f* (*animal*) calf ▹*nf* (*carne*) veal

ternura [ter'nura] *nf* (*trato*) tenderness; (*palabra*) endearment; (*cariño*) fondness

terrado [te'rraðo] *nm* terrace

terraplén [terra'plen] *nm* embankment

terrateniente [terrate'njente] *nmf* landowner

terraza [te'rraθa] *nf* (*balcón*) balcony; (*tejado*) (flat) roof; (*Agr*) terrace

terremoto [terre'moto] *nm* earthquake

terrenal [terre'nal] *adj* earthly

terreno [te'rreno] *nm* (*tierra*) land; (*parcela*) plot; (*suelo*) soil; (*fig*) field; **un ~** a piece of land

terrestre [te'rrestre] *adj* terrestrial; (*ruta*) land *cpd*

terrible [te'rriβle] *adj* terrible, awful

territorio [terri'torjo] *nm* territory

terrón [te'rron] *nm* (*de azúcar*) lump; (*de tierra*) clod, lump

terror [te'rror] *nm* terror; **terrorífico, -a** *adj* terrifying; **terrorista** *adj, nmf* terrorist; **terrorista suicida** suicide bomber

terso, -a ['terso, a] *adj* (*liso*) smooth; (*pulido*) polished

tertulia [ter'tulja] *nf* (*reunión informal*) social gathering; (*grupo*) group, circle

tesis ['tesis] *nf inv* thesis

tesón [te'son] *nm* (*firmeza*) firmness; (*tenacidad*) tenacity

tesorero, -a [teso'rero, a] *nm/f* treasurer

tesoro [te'soro] *nm* treasure; (*Com, Pol*) treasury

testamento [testa'mento] *nm* will

testarudo, -a [testa'ruðo, a] *adj* stubborn

testículo [tes'tikulo] *nm* testicle

testificar [testifi'kar] *vt* to testify; (*fig*) to attest ▹*vi* to give evidence

testigo [tes'tiɣo] *nmf* witness; **testigo de cargo/descargo** witness for the prosecution/defence; **testigo ocular** eye witness

testimonio [testi'monjo] *nm* testimony

teta ['teta] *nf* (*de biberón*) teat; (*Anat: fam*) breast

tétanos ['tetanos] *nm* tetanus

tetera [te'tera] *nf* teapot

tétrico, -a ['tetriko, a] *adj* gloomy, dismal

textil [teks'til] *adj* textile

texto ['teksto] *nm* text; **textual** *adj* textual

textura [teks'tura] *nf* (*de tejido*) texture

tez [teθ] *nf* (*cutis*) complexion

ti [ti] *pron* you; (*reflexivo*) yourself

tía ['tia] *nf* (*pariente*) aunt; (*fam*) chick, bird

tibio, -a ['tiβjo, a] *adj* lukewarm

tiburón [tiβu'ron] *nm* shark

tic [tik] *nm* (*ruido*) click; (*de reloj*) tick; (*Med*): **~ nervioso** nervous tic

tictac [tik'tak] *nm* (*de reloj*) tick tock

tiempo ['tjempo] *nm* time; (*época, período*) age, period; (*Meteorología*) weather; (*Ling*) tense; (*Deporte*) half; **a ~** in time; **a un** *o* **al mismo ~** at the same time; **al poco ~** very soon (after); **se quedó poco ~** he didn't stay very long; **hace poco ~** not long ago; **mucho ~** a long time; **de ~ en ~** from time to time; **hace buen/mal ~** the weather is fine/bad; **estar a ~** to be in time; **hace ~** some time ago; **hacer ~** to while away the time; **motor de 2 ~s** two-stroke engine; **primer ~** first half

tienda ['tjenda] *nf* shop, store; **tienda de abarrotes** (*MÉX, CAM*) grocer's (*BRIT*), grocery store (*US*); **tienda de alimentación** *o* **comestibles** grocer's (*BRIT*), grocery store (*US*); **tienda de campaña** tent

tienes *etc vb V* **tener**

tienta *etc* ['tjenta] *vb V* **tentar** ▷ *nf*: **andar a ~s** to grope one's way along

tiento *etc* ['tjento] *vb V* **tentar** ▷ *nm* (*tacto*) touch; (*precaución*) wariness

tierno, -a ['tjerno, a] *adj* (*blando*) tender; (*fresco*) fresh; (*amable*) sweet

tierra ['tjerra] *nf* earth; (*suelo*) soil; (*mundo*) earth, world; (*país*) country, land; **~ adentro** inland

tieso, -a ['tjeso, a] *adj* (*rígido*) rigid; (*duro*) stiff; (*fam: orgulloso*) conceited

tiesto ['tjesto] *nm* flowerpot

tifón [ti'fon] *nm* typhoon

tifus ['tifus] *nm* typhus

tigre ['tiɣre] *nm* tiger

tijera [ti'xera] *nf* scissors *pl*; (*Zool*) claw; **tijeras** *nfpl* scissors; (*para plantas*) shears

tila ['tila] *nf* lime blossom tea

tildar [til'dar] *vt*: **~ de** to brand as

tilde ['tilde] *nf* (*Tip*) tilde

tilín [ti'lin] *nm* tinkle

timar [ti'mar] *vt* (*estafar*) to swindle

timbal [tim'bal] *nm* small drum

timbre ['timbre] *nm* (*sello*) stamp; (*campanilla*) bell; (*tono*) timbre; (*Com*) stamp duty

timidez [timi'ðeθ] *nf* shyness; **tímido, -a** *adj* shy

timo ['timo] *nm* swindle

timón [ti'mon] *nm* helm, rudder; **timonel** *nm* helmsman

tímpano ['timpano] *nm* (*Anat*) eardrum; (*Mús*) small drum

tina ['tina] *nf* tub; (*baño*) bath(tub); **tinaja** *nf* large jar

tinieblas [ti'njeβlas] *nfpl* darkness *sg*; (*sombras*) shadows

tino ['tino] *nm* (*habilidad*) skill; (*juicio*) insight

tinta ['tinta] *nf* ink; (*Tec*) dye; (*Arte*) colour

tinte ['tinte] *nm* dye

tintero [tin'tero] *nm* inkwell

tinto ['tinto] *nm* red wine

tintorería [tintore'ria] *nf* dry cleaner's

tío ['tio] *nm* (*pariente*) uncle; (*fam: individuo*) bloke (*BRIT*), guy

tiovivo [tio'βiβo] *nm* merry-go-round
típico, -a ['tipiko, a] *adj* typical
tipo ['tipo] *nm* (*clase*) type, kind; (*hombre*) fellow; (*Anat*: *de hombre*) build; (: *de mujer*) figure; (*Imprenta*) type; **tipo bancario/de descuento/de interés/de cambio** bank/discount/interest/exchange rate
tipografía [tipoɣra'fia] *nf* printing *cpd*
tíquet ['tiket] (*pl* **~s**) *nm* ticket; (*en tienda*) cash slip
tiquismiquis [tikis'mikis] *nm inv* fussy person ▷ *nmpl* (*querellas*) squabbling *sg*; (*escrúpulos*) silly scruples
tira ['tira] *nf* strip; (*fig*) abundance; **tira y afloja** give and take
tirabuzón [tiraβu'θon] *nm* (*rizo*) curl
tirachinas [tira'tʃinas] *nm inv* catapult
tirada [ti'raða] *nf* (*acto*) cast, throw; (*serie*) series; (*Tip*) printing, edition; **de una ~** at one go
tirado, -a [ti'raðo, a] *adj* (*barato*) dirt-cheap; (*fam*: *fácil*) very easy
tirador [tira'ðor] *nm* (*mango*) handle
tirano, -a [ti'rano, a] *adj* tyrannical ▷ *nm/f* tyrant
tirante [ti'rante] *adj* (*cuerda etc*) tight, taut; (*relaciónes*) strained ▷ *nm* (*Arq*) brace; (*Tec*) stay; **tirantes** *nmpl* (*de pantalón*) braces (BRIT), suspenders (US); **tirantez** *nf* tightness; (*fig*) tension
tirar [ti'rar] *vt* to throw; (*dejar caer*) to drop; (*volcar*) to upset; (*derribar*) to knock down *o* over; (*desechar*) to throw out *o* away; (*dinero*) to squander; (*imprimir*) to print ▷ *vi* (*disparar*) to shoot; (*de la puerta etc*) to pull; (*fam*: *andar*) to go; (*tender a, buscar realizar*) to tend to; (*Deporte*) to shoot; **tirarse** *vr* to throw o.s.; **~ abajo** to bring down, destroy; **tira más a su padre** he takes more after his father; **ir tirando** to manage
tirita [ti'rita] *nf* (sticking) plaster (BRIT), Bandaid® (US)
tiritar [tiri'tar] *vi* to shiver
tiro ['tiro] *nm* (*lanzamiento*) throw; (*disparo*) shot; (*Deporte*) shot; (*Golf, Tenis*) drive; (*alcance*) range; **caballo de ~** cart-horse; **tiro al blanco** target practice
tirón [ti'ron] *nm* (*sacudida*) pull, tug; **de un ~** in one go, all at once
tiroteo [tiro'teo] *nm* exchange of shots, shooting
tisis ['tisis] *nf inv* consumption, tuberculosis
títere ['titere] *nm* puppet
titubear [tituβe'ar] *vi* to stagger; to stammer; (*fig*) to hesitate; **titubeo** *nm* staggering; stammering; hesitation
titulado, -a [titu'laðo, a] *adj* (*libro*) entitled; (*persona*) titled
titular [titu'lar] *adj* titular ▷ *nmf* holder ▷ *nm* headline ▷ *vt* to title; **titularse** *vr* to be entitled; **título** *nm* title; (*de diario*) headline; (*certificado*) professional qualification; (*universitario*) (university) degree; **a título de** in the capacity of
tiza ['tiθa] *nf* chalk
toalla [to'aʎa] *nf* towel
tobillo [to'βiʎo] *nm* ankle
tobogán [toβo'ɣan] *nm* (*montaña rusa*) roller-coaster; (*de niños*) chute, slide
tocadiscos [toka'ðiskos] *nm inv* record player
tocado, -a [to'kaðo, a] *adj* (*fam*) touched ▷ *nm* headdress
tocador [toka'ðor] *nm* (*mueble*) dressing table; (*cuarto*) boudoir; (*fam*) ladies' toilet (BRIT) *o* room (US)
tocar [to'kar] *vt* to touch; (*Mús*) to play; (*referirse a*) to allude to; (*timbre*) to ring ▷ *vi* (*a la puerta*) to knock (on *o* at the door); (*ser de turno*) to fall to, be the turn of; (*ser hora*) to be due; **tocarse** *vr* (*cubrirse la cabeza*) to cover one's head; (*tener contacto*) to touch (each other); **por lo que a mí me toca** as far as I am concerned; **te toca a ti** it's your turn

tocayo, -a [to'kajo, a] *nm/f* namesake
tocino [to'θino] *nm* bacon
todavía [toða'βia] *adv* (*aun*) even; (*aún*) still, yet; **~ más** yet more; **~ no** not yet

PALABRA CLAVE

todo, -a ['toðo, a] *adj* **1** (*con artículo sg*) all; **toda la carne** all the meat; **toda la noche** all night, the whole night; **todo el libro** the whole book; **toda una botella** a whole bottle; **todo lo contrario** quite the opposite; **está toda sucia** she's all dirty; **por todo el país** throughout the whole country
2 (*con artículo pl*) all; every; **todos los libros** all the books; **todas las noches** every night; **todos los que quieran salir** all those who want to leave
▷ *pron* **1** everything, all; **todos** everyone, everybody; **lo sabemos todo** we know everything; **todos querían más tiempo** everybody *o* everyone wanted more time; **nos marchamos todos** all of us left
2: **con todo: con todo él me sigue gustando** even so I still like him
▷ *adv* all; **vaya todo seguido** keep straight on *o* ahead
▷ *nm*: **como un todo** as a whole; **del todo: no me agrada del todo** I don't entirely like it

todopoderoso, -a [toðopoðe'roso, a] *adj* all powerful; (*Rel*) almighty
todoterreno [toðote'rreno] *sm inv* four-wheel drive, SUV (ESP US)
toga ['toɣa] *nf* toga; (*Escol*) gown
Tokio ['tokjo] *n* Tokyo
toldo ['toldo] *nm* (*para el sol*) sunshade (BRIT), parasol; (*tienda*) marquee
tolerancia [tole'ranθja] *nf* tolerance; **tolerante** *adj* (*sociedad*) liberal; (*persona*) open-minded
tolerar [tole'rar] *vt* to tolerate; (*resistir*) to endure
toma ['toma] *nf* (*acto*) taking; (*Med*) dose; **toma de corriente** socket; **toma de tierra** earth (wire); **tomacorriente** (LAM) *nm* socket
tomar [to'mar] *vt* to take; (*aspecto*) to take on; (*beber*) to drink ▷ *vi* to take; (LAM: *beber*) to drink; **tomarse** *vr* to take; **~se por** to consider o.s. to be; **~ a bien/mal** to take well/badly; **~ en serio** to take seriously; **~ el pelo a algn** to pull sb's leg; **~la con algn** to pick a quarrel with sb; **¡tome!** here you are!; **~ el sol** to sunbathe
tomate [to'mate] *nm* tomato
tomillo [to'miʎo] *nm* thyme
tomo ['tomo] *nm* (*libro*) volume
ton [ton] *abr* = **tonelada** ▷ *nm*: **sin ~ ni son** without rhyme or reason
tonalidad [tonali'ðað] *nf* tone
tonel [to'nel] *nm* barrel
tonelada [tone'laða] *nf* ton; **tonelaje** *nm* tonnage
tónica ['tonika] *nf* (*Mús*) tonic; (*fig*) keynote
tónico, -a ['toniko, a] *adj* tonic ▷ *nm* (*Med*) tonic
tono ['tono] *nm* tone; **fuera de ~** inappropriate
tontería [tonte'ria] *nf* (*estupidez*) foolishness; (*cosa*) stupid thing; (*acto*) foolish act; **tonterías** *nfpl* (*disparates*) rubbish *sg*, nonsense *sg*
tonto, -a ['tonto, a] *adj* stupid, silly ▷ *nm/f* fool
topar [to'par] *vi*: **~ contra** *o* **en** to run into; **~ con** to run up against
tope ['tope] *adj* maximum ▷ *nm* (*fin*) end; (*límite*) limit; (*Ferro*) buffer; (*Auto*) bumper; **al ~** end to end
tópico, -a ['topiko, a] *adj* topical ▷ *nm* platitude
topo ['topo] *nm* (*Zool*) mole; (*fig*) blunderer
toque *etc* ['toke] *vb V* **tocar** ▷ *nm* touch; (*Mús*) beat; (*de campana*) peal; **dar un ~ a** to warn; **toque de queda**

curfew
toqué *etc vb V* **tocar**
toquetear [tokete'ar] *vt* to finger
toquilla [to'kiʎa] *nf* (*pañuelo*) headscarf; (*chal*) shawl
tórax ['toraks] *nm* thorax
torbellino [torbe'ʎino] *nm* whirlwind; (*fig*) whirl
torcedura [torθe'ðura] *nf* twist; (*Med*) sprain
torcer [tor'θer] *vt* to twist; (*la esquina*) to turn; (*Med*) to sprain ▷ *vi* (*desviar*) to turn off; **torcerse** *vr* (*ladearse*) to bend; (*desviarse*) to go astray; (*fracasar*) to go wrong; **torcido, -a** *adj* twisted; (*fig*) crooked ▷ *nm* curl
tordo, -a ['torðo, a] *adj* dappled ▷ *nm* thrush
torear [tore'ar] *vt* (*fig: evadir*) to avoid; (*jugar con*) to tease ▷ *vi* to fight bulls; **toreo** *nm* bullfighting; **torero, -a** *nm/f* bullfighter
tormenta [tor'menta] *nf* storm; (*fig: confusión*) turmoil
tormento [tor'mento] *nm* torture; (*fig*) anguish
tornar [tor'nar] *vt* (*devolver*) to return, give back; (*transformar*) to transform ▷ *vi* to go back
tornasolado, -a [tornaso'laðo, a] *adj* (*brillante*) iridescent; (*reluciente*) shimmering
torneo [tor'neo] *nm* tournament
tornillo [tor'niʎo] *nm* screw
torniquete [torni'kete] *nm* (*Med*) tourniquet
torno ['torno] *nm* (*Tec*) winch; (*tambor*) drum; **en ~ (a)** round, about
toro ['toro] *nm* bull; (*fam*) he-man; **los ~s** bullfighting
toronja [to'ronxa] *nf* grapefruit
torpe ['torpe] *adj* (*poco hábil*) clumsy, awkward; (*necio*) dim; (*lento*) slow
torpedo [tor'peðo] *nm* torpedo
torpeza [tor'peθa] *nf* (*falta de agilidad*) clumsiness; (*lentitud*) slowness; (*error*) mistake
torre ['torre] *nf* tower; (*de petróleo*) derrick
torrefacto, -a [torre'facto, a] *adj* roasted
torrente [to'rrente] *nm* torrent
torrija [to'rrixa] *nf* French toast
torsión [tor'sjon] *nf* twisting
torso ['torso] *nm* torso
torta ['torta] *nf* cake; (*fam*) slap
tortícolis [tor'tikolis] *nm inv* stiff neck
tortilla [tor'tiʎa] *nf* omelette; (LAM: *de maíz*) maize pancake; **tortilla de papas** (LAM) potato omelette; **tortilla de patatas** (ESP) potato omelette; **tortilla francesa** (ESP) plain omelette
tórtola ['tortola] *nf* turtledove
tortuga [tor'tuɣa] *nf* tortoise
tortuoso, -a [tor'twoso, a] *adj* winding
tortura [tor'tura] *nf* torture; **torturar** *vt* to torture
tos [tos] *nf* cough; **tos ferina** whooping cough
toser [to'ser] *vi* to cough
tostada [tos'taða] *nf* piece of toast; **tostado, -a** *adj* toasted; (*por el sol*) dark brown; (*piel*) tanned
tostador [tosta'ðor] (ESP) *nm* toaster; **tostadora** (LAM) *nf* = **tostador**
tostar [tos'tar] *vt* to toast; (*café*) to roast; (*persona*) to tan; **tostarse** *vr* to get brown
total [to'tal] *adj* total ▷ *adv* in short; (*al fin y al cabo*) when all is said and done ▷ *nm* total; **en ~** in all; **~ que ...** to cut (BRIT) *o* make (US) a long story short ...
totalidad [totali'ðað] *nf* whole
totalitario, -a [totali'tarjo, a] *adj* totalitarian
tóxico, -a ['toksiko, a] *adj* toxic ▷ *nm* poison; **toxicómano, -a** *nm/f* drug addict
toxina [to'ksina] *nf* toxin
tozudo, -a [to'θuðo, a] *adj* obstinate
trabajador, a [traβaxa'ðor, a] *adj* hard-working ▷ *nm/f* worker;

trabajador autónomo *o* **por cuenta propia** self-employed person
trabajar [traβa'xar] *vt* to work; (*Agr*) to till; (*empeñarse en*) to work at; (*convencer*) to persuade ▷*vi* to work; (*esforzarse*) to strive; **trabajo** *nm* work; (*tarea*) task; (*Pol*) labour; (*fig*) effort; **tomarse el trabajo de** to take the trouble to; **trabajo a destajo** piecework; **trabajo en equipo** teamwork; **trabajo por turnos** shift work; **trabajos forzados** hard labour *sg*
trabalenguas [traβa'lengwas] *nm inv* tongue twister
tracción [trak'θjon] *nf* traction; **tracción delantera/trasera** front-wheel/rear-wheel drive
tractor [trak'tor] *nm* tractor
tradición [traði'θjon] *nf* tradition; **tradicional** *adj* traditional
traducción [traðuk'θjon] *nf* translation
traducir [traðu'θir] *vt* to translate; **traductor, a** *nm/f* translator
traer [tra'er] *vt* to bring; (*llevar*) to carry; (*llevar puesto*) to wear; (*incluir*) to carry; (*causar*) to cause; **traerse** *vr*: **~se algo** to be up to sth
traficar [trafi'kar] *vi* to trade
tráfico ['trafiko] *nm* (*Com*) trade; (*Auto*) traffic
tragaluz [traɣa'luθ] *nm* skylight
tragamonedas [traɣamo'neðas] (*LAM*) *nf inv* slot machine
tragaperras [traɣa'perras] (*ESP*) *nf inv* slot machine
tragar [tra'ɣar] *vt* to swallow; (*devorar*) to devour, bolt down; **tragarse** *vr* to swallow
tragedia [tra'xeðja] *nf* tragedy; **trágico, -a** *adj* tragic
trago ['traɣo] *nm* (*líquido*) drink; (*bocado*) gulp; (*fam: de bebida*) swig; (*desgracia*) blow; **echar un ~** to have a drink
traición [trai'θjon] *nf* treachery; (*Jur*) treason; (*una traición*) act of treachery; **traicionar** *vt* to betray
traidor, a [trai'ðor, a] *adj* treacherous ▷*nm/f* traitor
traigo *etc vb V* **traer**
traje ['traxe] *vb V* **traer** ▷*nm* (*de hombre*) suit; (*de mujer*) dress; (*vestido típico*) costume; **traje de baño/chaqueta** swimsuit/suit; **traje de etiqueta** dress suit; **traje de luces** bullfighter's costume
trajera *etc vb V* **traer**
trajín [tra'xin] *nm* (*fam: movimiento*) bustle; **trajinar** *vi* (*moverse*) to bustle about
trama ['trama] *nf* (*intriga*) plot; (*de tejido*) weft (*BRIT*), woof (*US*); **tramar** *vt* to plot; (*Tec*) to weave
tramitar [trami'tar] *vt* (*asunto*) to transact; (*negociar*) to negotiate
trámite ['tramite] *nm* (*paso*) step; (*Jur*) transaction; **trámites** *nmpl* (*burocracia*) procedure *sg*; (*Jur*) proceedings
tramo ['tramo] *nm* (*de tierra*) plot; (*de escalera*) flight; (*de vía*) section
trampa ['trampa] *nf* trap; (*en el suelo*) trapdoor; (*truco*) trick; (*engaño*) fiddle; **trampear** *vt, vi* to cheat
trampolín [trampo'lin] *nm* (*de piscina etc*) diving board
tramposo, -a [tram'poso, a] *adj* crooked, cheating ▷*nm/f* crook, cheat
tranca ['tranka] *nf* (*palo*) stick; (*de puerta, ventana*) bar; **trancar** *vt* to bar
trance ['tranθe] *nm* (*momento difícil*) difficult moment *o* juncture; (*estado hipnotizado*) trance
tranquilidad [trankili'ðað] *nf* (*calma*) calmness, stillness; (*paz*) peacefulness
tranquilizar [trankili'θar] *vt* (*calmar*) to calm (down); (*asegurar*) to reassure; **tranquilizarse** *vr* to calm down; **tranquilo, -a** *adj* (*calmado*) calm; (*apacible*) peaceful; (*mar*) calm; (*mente*) untroubled
transacción [transak'θjon] *nf* transaction

transbordador [transβorða'ðor] *nm* ferry

transbordo [trans'βorðo] *nm* transfer; **hacer ~** to change (trains *etc*)

transcurrir [transku'rrir] *vi* (*tiempo*) to pass; (*hecho*) to take place

transcurso [trans'kurso] *nm*: **~ del tiempo** lapse (of time)

transeúnte [transe'unte] *nmf* passer-by

transferencia [transfe'renθja] *nf* transference; (*Com*) transfer

transferir [transfe'rir] *vt* to transfer

transformador [transforma'ðor] *nm* (*Elec*) transformer

transformar [transfor'mar] *vt* to transform; (*convertir*) to convert

transfusión [transfu'sjon] *nf* transfusion

transgénico, -a [trans'xeniko, a] *adj* genetically modified, GM

transición [transi'θjon] *nf* transition

transigir [transi'xir] *vi* to compromise, make concessions

transitar [transi'tar] *vi* to go (from place to place); **tránsito** *nm* transit; (*Auto*) traffic; **transitorio, -a** *adj* transitory

transmisión [transmi'sjon] *nf* (*Tec*) transmission; (*transferencia*) transfer; **transmisión exterior/en directo** outside/live broadcast

transmitir [transmi'tir] *vt* to transmit; (*Radio, TV*) to broadcast

transparencia [transpa'renθja] *nf* transparency; (*claridad*) clearness, clarity; (*foto*) slide

transparentar [transparen'tar] *vt* to reveal ▷ *vi* to be transparent; **transparente** *adj* transparent; (*claro*) clear

transpirar [transpi'rar] *vi* to perspire

transportar [transpor'tar] *vt* to transport; (*llevar*) to carry; **transporte** *nm* transport; (*Com*) haulage

transversal [transβer'sal] *adj* transverse, cross

tranvía [tram'bia] *nm* tram

trapeador [trapea'ðor] (*LAM*) *nm* mop; **trapear** (*LAM*) *vt* to mop

trapecio [tra'peθjo] *nm* trapeze; **trapecista** *nmf* trapeze artist

trapero, -a [tra'pero, a] *nm/f* ragman

trapicheo [trapi'tʃeo] (*fam*) *nm* scheme, fiddle

trapo ['trapo] *nm* (*tela*) rag; (*de cocina*) cloth

tráquea ['trakea] *nf* windpipe

traqueteo [trake'teo] *nm* rattling

tras [tras] *prep* (*detrás*) behind; (*después*) after

trasatlántico [trasat'lantiko] *nm* (*barco*) (cabin) cruiser

trascendencia [trasθen'denθja] *nf* (*importancia*) importance; (*Filosofía*) transcendence

trascendental [trasθenden'tal] *adj* important; (*Filosofía*) transcendental

trasero, -a [tra'sero, a] *adj* back, rear ▷ *nm* (*Anat*) bottom

trasfondo [tras'fondo] *nm* background

trasgredir [trasɣre'ðir] *vt* to contravene

trashumante [trasu'mante] *adj* (*animales*) migrating

trasladar [trasla'ðar] *vt* to move; (*persona*) to transfer; (*postergar*) to postpone; (*copiar*) to copy; **trasladarse** *vr* (*mudarse*) to move; **traslado** *nm* move; (*mudanza*) move, removal

traslucir [traslu'θir] *vt* to show

trasluz [tras'luθ] *nm* reflected light; **al ~** against *o* up to the light

trasnochador, a [trasnotʃa'ðor, a] *nm/f* night owl

trasnochar [trasno'tʃar] *vi* (*acostarse tarde*) to stay up late

traspapelar [traspape'lar] *vt* (*documento, carta*) to mislay, misplace

traspasar [traspa'sar] *vt* (*suj: bala etc*) to pierce, go through; (*propiedad*) to sell, transfer; (*calle*) to cross over; (*límites*) to go beyond; (*ley*) to break; **traspaso** *nm* (*venta*) transfer, sale

traspatio [tras'patjo] (LAM) *nm* backyard
traspié [tras'pje] *nm* (*tropezón*) trip; (*error*) blunder
trasplantar [trasplan'tar] *vt* to transplant
traste ['traste] *nm* (*Mús*) fret; **dar al ~ con algo** to ruin sth
trastero [tras'tero] *nm* storage room
trastienda [tras'tjenda] *nf* back of shop
trasto ['trasto] (*pey*) *nm* (*cosa*) piece of junk; (*persona*) dead loss
trastornado, -a [trastor'naðo, a] *adj* (*loco*) mad, crazy
trastornar [trastor'nar] *vt* (*fig: planes*) to disrupt; (*: nervios*) to shatter; (*: persona*) to drive crazy; **trastornarse** *vr* (*volverse loco*) to go mad *o* crazy; **trastorno** *nm* (*acto*) overturning; (*confusión*) confusion
tratable [tra'taβle] *adj* friendly
tratado [tra'taðo] *nm* (*Pol*) treaty; (*Com*) agreement
tratamiento [trata'mjento] *nm* treatment; **tratamiento de textos** (*Inform*) word processing *cpd*
tratar [tra'tar] *vt* (*ocuparse de*) to treat; (*manejar, Tec*) to handle; (*Med*) to treat; (*dirigirse a: persona*) to address ▷ *vi*: **~ de** (*hablar sobre*) to deal with, be about; (*intentar*) to try to; **tratarse** *vr* to treat each other; **~ con** (*Com*) to trade in; (*negociar*) to negotiate with; (*tener contactos*) to have dealings with; **¿de qué se trata?** what's it about?; **trato** *nm* dealings *pl*; (*relaciónes*) relationship; (*comportamiento*) manner; (*Com*) agreement
trauma ['trauma] *nm* trauma
través [tra'βes] *nm* (*fig*) reverse; **al ~** across, crossways; **a ~ de** across; (*sobre*) over; (*por*) through
travesaño [traβe'saɲo] *nm* (*Arq*) crossbeam; (*Deporte*) crossbar
travesía [traβe'sia] *nf* (*calle*) cross-street; (*Náut*) crossing
travesura [traβe'sura] *nf* (*broma*) prank; (*ingenio*) wit
travieso, -a [tra'βjeso, a] *adj* (*niño*) naughty
trayecto [tra'jekto] *nm* (*ruta*) road, way; (*viaje*) journey; (*tramo*) stretch; **trayectoria** *nf* trajectory; (*fig*) path
traza ['traθa] *nf* (*aspecto*) looks *pl*; (*señal*) sign; **trazado, -a** *adj*: **bien trazado** shapely, well-formed ▷ *nm* (*Arq*) plan, design; (*fig*) outline
trazar [tra'θar] *vt* (*Arq*) to plan; (*Arte*) to sketch; (*fig*) to trace; (*plan*) to draw up; **trazo** *nm* (*línea*) line; (*bosquejo*) sketch
trébol ['treβol] *nm* (*Bot*) clover
trece ['treθe] *num* thirteen
trecho ['tretʃo] *nm* (*distancia*) distance; (*tiempo*) while
tregua ['treɣwa] *nf* (*Mil*) truce; (*fig*) respite
treinta ['treinta] *num* thirty
tremendo, -a [tre'mendo, a] *adj* (*terrible*) terrible; (*imponente: cosa*) imposing; (*fam: fabuloso*) tremendous
tren [tren] *nm* train; **tren de aterrizaje** undercarriage; **tren de cercanías** suburban train
trenca ['trenka] *nf* duffel coat
trenza ['trenθa] *nf* (*de pelo*) plait (BRIT), braid (US)
trepadora [trepa'ðora] *nf* (*Bot*) climber
trepar [tre'par] *vt, vi* to climb
tres [tres] *num* three
tresillo [tre'siʎo] *nm* three-piece suite; (*Mús*) triplet
treta ['treta] *nf* trick
triángulo ['trjangulo] *nm* triangle
tribu ['triβu] *nf* tribe
tribuna [tri'βuna] *nf* (*plataforma*) platform; (*Deporte*) (grand)stand
tribunal [triβu'nal] *nm* (*Jur*) court; (*comisión, fig*) tribunal; **~ popular** jury
tributo [tri'βuto] *nm* (*Com*) tax
trigal [tri'ɣal] *nm* wheat field
trigo ['triɣo] *nm* wheat
trigueño, -a [tri'ɣeɲo, a] *adj* (*pelo*) corn-coloured

trillar [tri'ʎar] *vt* (*Agr*) to thresh
trimestral [trimes'tral] *adj* quarterly; (*Escol*) termly
trimestre [tri'mestre] *nm* (*Escol*) term
trinar [tri'nar] *vi* (*pájaros*) to sing; (*rabiar*) to fume, be angry
trinchar [trin'tʃar] *vt* to carve
trinchera [trin'tʃera] *nf* (*fosa*) trench
trineo [tri'neo] *nm* sledge
trinidad [trini'ðað] *nf* trio; (*Rel*): **la T~** the Trinity
tripa ['tripa] *nf* (*Anat*) intestine; (*fam*: *tb*: **~s**) insides *pl*
triple ['triple] *adj* triple
triplicado, -a [tripli'kaðo, a] *adj*: **por ~** in triplicate
tripulación [tripula'θjon] *nf* crew
tripulante [tripu'lante] *nmf* crewman/woman
tripular [tripu'lar] *vt* (*barco*) to man; (*Auto*) to drive
triquiñuela [triki'ɲwela] *nf* trick
tris [tris] *nm inv* crack
triste ['triste] *adj* sad; (*lamentable*) sorry, miserable; **tristeza** *nf* (*aflicción*) sadness; (*melancolía*) melancholy
triturar [tritu'rar] *vt* (*moler*) to grind; (*mascar*) to chew
triunfar [trjun'far] *vi* (*tener éxito*) to triumph; (*ganar*) to win; **triunfo** *nm* triumph
trivial [tri'βjal] *adj* trivial
triza ['triθa] *nf*: **hacer ~s** to smash to bits; (*papel*) to tear to shreds
trocear [troθe'ar] *vt* (*carne, manzana*) to cut up, cut into pieces
trocha ['trotʃa] *nf* short cut
trofeo [tro'feo] *nm* (*premio*) trophy; (*éxito*) success
tromba ['tromba] *nf* downpour
trombón [trom'bon] *nm* trombone
trombosis [trom'bosis] *nf inv* thrombosis
trompa ['trompa] *nf* horn; (*trompo*) humming top; (*hocico*) snout; (*fam*): **cogerse una ~** to get tight
trompazo [trom'paθo] *nm* bump, bang
trompeta [trom'peta] *nf* trumpet; (*clarín*) bugle
trompicón [trompi'kon]: **a trompicones** *adv* in fits and starts
trompo ['trompo] *nm* spinning top
trompón [trom'pon] *nm* bump
tronar [tro'nar] *vt* (*MÉX, CAM*: *fusilar*) to shoot; (*MÉX*: *examen*) to flunk ▷ *vi* to thunder; (*fig*) to rage
tronchar [tron'tʃar] *vt* (*árbol*) to chop down; (*fig*: *vida*) to cut short; (: *esperanza*) to shatter; (*persona*) to tire out; **troncharse** *vr* to fall down
tronco ['tronko] *nm* (*de árbol, Anat*) trunk
trono ['trono] *nm* throne
tropa ['tropa] *nf* (*Mil*) troop; (*soldados*) soldiers *pl*
tropezar [trope'θar] *vi* to trip, stumble; (*errar*) to slip up; **~ con** to run into; (*topar con*) to bump into; **tropezón** *nm* trip; (*fig*) blunder
tropical [tropi'kal] *adj* tropical
trópico ['tropiko] *nm* tropic
tropiezo [tro'pjeθo] *vb V* **tropezar** ▷ *nm* (*error*) slip, blunder; (*desgracia*) misfortune; (*obstáculo*) snag
trotamundos [trota'mundos] *nm inv* globetrotter
trotar [tro'tar] *vi* to trot; **trote** *nm* trot; (*fam*) travelling; **de mucho trote** hard-wearing
trozar [tro'θar] (*LAM*) *vt* to cut up, cut into pieces
trozo ['troθo] *nm* bit, piece
trucha ['trutʃa] *nf* trout
truco ['truko] *nm* (*habilidad*) knack; (*engaño*) trick
trueno ['trweno] *nm* thunder; (*estampido*) bang
trueque *etc* ['trweke] *vb V* **trocar** ▷ *nm* exchange; (*Com*) barter
trufa ['trufa] *nf* (*Bot*) truffle
truhán, -ana [tru'an, ana] *nm/f* rogue
truncar [trun'kar] *vt* (*cortar*) to truncate; (*fig*: *la vida etc*) to cut short; (: *el desarrollo*) to stunt

tu [tu] *adj* your
tú [tu] *pron* you
tubérculo [tu'βerkulo] *nm* (*Bot*) tuber
tuberculosis [tuβerku'losis] *nf inv* tuberculosis
tubería [tuβe'ria] *nf* pipes *pl*; (*conducto*) pipeline
tubo ['tuβo] *nm* tube, pipe; **tubo de ensayo** test tube; **tubo de escape** exhaust (pipe)
tuerca ['twerka] *nf* nut
tuerto, -a ['twerto, a] *adj* blind in one eye ▷ *nm/f* one-eyed person
tuerza *etc vb V* **torcer**
tuétano ['twetano] *nm* marrow; (*Bot*) pith
tufo ['tufo] *nm* (*hedor*) stench
tul [tul] *nm* tulle
tulipán [tuli'pan] *nm* tulip
tullido, -a [tu'ʎiðo, a] *adj* crippled
tumba ['tumba] *nf* (*sepultura*) tomb
tumbar [tum'bar] *vt* to knock down; **tumbarse** *vr* (*echarse*) to lie down; (*extenderse*) to stretch out
tumbo ['tumbo] *nm*: **dar ~s** to stagger
tumbona [tum'bona] *nf* (*butaca*) easy chair; (*de playa*) deckchair (BRIT), beach chair (US)
tumor [tu'mor] *nm* tumour
tumulto [tu'multo] *nm* turmoil
tuna ['tuna] *nf* (*Mús*) *student music group*; *V tb* **tuno**

TUNA

A **tuna** is a musical group made up of university students or former students who dress up in costumes from the "Edad de Oro", the Spanish Golden Age. These groups go through the town playing their guitars, lutes and tambourines and serenade the young ladies in the halls of residence or make impromptu appearances at weddings or parties singing traditional Spanish songs for a few coins.

tunante [tu'nante] *nmf* rascal
tunear [tune'ar] *vt* (*Auto*) to style, mod (*inf*)
túnel ['tunel] *nm* tunnel
tuning ['tunin] *nm* (*Auto*) car styling, modding (*inf*)
tuno, -a ['tuno, a] *nm/f* (*fam*) rogue ▷ *nm member of student music group*
tupido, -a [tu'piðo, a] *adj* (*denso*) dense; (*tela*) close-woven
turbante [tur'βante] *nm* turban
turbar [tur'βar] *vt* (*molestar*) to disturb; (*incomodar*) to upset
turbina [tur'βina] *nf* turbine
turbio, -a ['turβjo, a] *adj* cloudy; (*tema etc*) confused
turbulencia [turβu'lenθja] *nf* turbulence; (*fig*) restlessness; **turbulento, -a** *adj* turbulent; (*fig: intranquilo*) restless; (*: ruidoso*) noisy
turco, -a ['turko, a] *adj* Turkish ▷ *nm/f* Turk
turismo [tu'rismo] *nm* tourism; (*coche*) car; **turista** *nmf* tourist; **turístico, -a** *adj* tourist *cpd*
turnar [tur'nar] *vi* to take (it in) turns; **turnarse** *vr* to take (it in) turns; **turno** *nm* (*de trabajo*) shift; (*en juegos etc*) turn
turquesa [tur'kesa] *nf* turquoise
Turquía [tur'kia] *nf* Turkey
turrón [tu'rron] *nm* (*dulce*) nougat
tutear [tute'ar] *vt* to address as familiar "tú"; **tutearse** *vr* to be on familiar terms
tutela [tu'tela] *nf* (*legal*) guardianship; **tutelar** *adj* tutelary ▷ *vt* to protect
tutor, a [tu'tor, a] *nm/f* (*legal*) guardian; (*Escol*) tutor
tuve *etc vb V* **tener**
tuviera *etc vb V* **tener**
tuyo, -a ['tujo, a] *adj* yours, of yours ▷ *pron* yours; **un amigo ~** a friend of yours; **los ~s** (*fam*) your relations *o* family
TV *nf abr* (= *televisión*) TV
TVE *nf abr* = **Televisión Española**

u [u] *conj* or
ubicar [uβi'kar] *vt* to place, situate; (*LAM*: *encontrar*) to find; **ubicarse** *vr* (*LAM*: *encontrarse*) to lie, be located
ubre ['uβre] *nf* udder
UCI *nf abr* (= *Unidad de Cuidados Intensivos*) ICU
Ud(s) *abr* = **usted(es)**
UE *nf abr* (= *Unión Europea*) EU
ufanarse [ufa'narse] *vr* to boast; **ufano, -a** *adj* (*arrogante*) arrogant; (*presumido*) conceited
UGT (*ESP*) *nf abr* = **Unión General de Trabajadores**
úlcera ['ulθera] *nf* ulcer
ulterior [ulte'rjor] *adj* (*más allá*) farther, further; (*subsecuente, siguiente*) subsequent
últimamente ['ultimamente] *adv* (*recientemente*) lately, recently
ultimar [ulti'mar] *vt* to finish; (*finalizar*) to finalize; (*LAM*: *matar*) to kill
ultimátum [ulti'matum] (*pl* **~s**) *nm* ultimatum
último, -a ['ultimo, a] *adj* last; (*más reciente*) latest, most recent; (*más bajo*) bottom; (*más alto*) top; **en las últimas** on one's last legs; **por ~** finally
ultra ['ultra] *adj* ultra ▷ *nmf* extreme right-winger
ultraje [ul'traxe] *nm* outrage; insult
ultramar [ultra'mar] *nm*: **de** *o* **en ~** abroad, overseas
ultramarinos [ultrama'rinos] *nmpl* groceries; **tienda de ~** grocer's (shop)
ultranza [ul'tranθa]: **a ~** *adv* (*a todo trance*) at all costs; (*completo*) outright
umbral [um'bral] *nm* (*gen*) threshold

PALABRA CLAVE

un, una [un, 'una] *art indef* a; (*antes de vocal*) an; **una mujer/naranja** a woman/an orange
▷ *adj*: **unos (***o* **unas): hay unos regalos para ti** there are some presents for you; **hay unas cervezas en la nevera** there are some beers in the fridge

unánime [u'nanime] *adj* unanimous; **unanimidad** *nf* unanimity
undécimo, -a [un'deθimo, a] *adj* eleventh
ungir [un'xir] *vt* to anoint
ungüento [un'gwento] *nm* ointment
único, -a ['uniko, a] *adj* only, sole; (*sin par*) unique
unidad [uni'ðað] *nf* unity; (*Com, Tec etc*) unit
unido, -a [u'niðo, a] *adj* joined, linked; (*fig*) united
unificar [unifi'kar] *vt* to unite, unify
uniformar [unifor'mar] *vt* to make uniform, level up; (*persona*) to put into uniform
uniforme [uni'forme] *adj* uniform, equal; (*superficie*) even ▷ *nm* uniform
unilateral [unilate'ral] *adj* unilateral
unión [u'njon] *nf* union; (*acto*) uniting, joining; (*unidad*) unity; (*Tec*) joint; **Unión Europea** European Union
unir [u'nir] *vt* (*juntar*) to join, unite;

(*atar*) to tie, fasten; (*combinar*) to combine; **unirse** *vr* to join together, unite; (*empresas*) to merge
unísono [u'nisono] *nm*: **al ~** in unison
universal [uniβer'sal] *adj* universal; (*mundial*) world *cpd*
universidad [uniβersi'ðað] *nf* university
universitario, -a [uniβersi'tarjo, a] *adj* university *cpd* ▷ *nm/f* (*profesor*) lecturer; (*estudiante*) (university) student; (*graduado*) graduate
universo [uni'βerso] *nm* universe

PALABRA CLAVE

uno, -a ['uno, a] *adj* one; **unos pocos** a few; **unos cien** about a hundred
▷ *pron* **1** one; **quiero sólo uno** I only want one; **uno de ellos** one of them
2 (*alguien*) somebody, someone; **conozco a uno que se te parece** I know somebody *o* someone who looks like you; **uno mismo** oneself; **unos querían quedarse** some (people) wanted to stay
3 (los) unos ... (los) otros ... some ... others
▷ *nf* one; **es la una** it's one o'clock
▷ *nm* (number) one

untar [un'tar] *vt* (*mantequilla*) to spread; (*engrasar*) to grease, oil
uña ['uɲa] *nf* (*Anat*) nail; (*garra*) claw; (*casco*) hoof; (*arrancaclavos*) claw
uranio [u'ranjo] *nm* uranium
urbanización [urβaniθa'θjon] *nf* (*barrio, colonia*) housing estate
urbanizar [urβani'θar] *vt* (*zona*) to develop, urbanize
urbano, -a [ur'βano, a] *adj* (*de ciudad*) urban; (*cortés*) courteous, polite
urbe ['urβe] *nf* large city
urdir [ur'ðir] *vt* to warp; (*complot*) to plot, contrive
urgencia [ur'xenθja] *nf* urgency; (*prisa*) haste, rush; (*emergencia*) emergency; **servicios de ~** emergency services; **"U~s"** "Casualty"; **urgente** *adj* urgent
urgir [ur'xir] *vi* to be urgent; **me urge** I'm in a hurry for it
urinario, -a [uri'narjo, a] *adj* urinary ▷ *nm* urinal
urna ['urna] *nf* urn; (*Pol*) ballot box
urraca [u'rraka] *nf* magpie
URSS [urs] *nf* (*Hist*): **la URSS** the USSR
Uruguay [uru'ɣwai] *nm* (*tb*: **el ~**) Uruguay; **uruguayo, -a** *adj, nm/f* Uruguayan
usado, -a [u'saðo, a] *adj* used; (*de segunda mano*) secondhand
usar [u'sar] *vt* to use; (*ropa*) to wear; (*tener costumbre*) to be in the habit of; **usarse** *vr* to be used; **uso** *nm* use; wear; (*costumbre*) usage, custom; (*moda*) fashion; **al uso** in keeping with custom; **al uso de** in the style of; **de uso externo** (*Med*) for external use
usted [us'teð] *pron* (*sg*) you *sg*; (*pl*): **~es** you *pl*
usual [u'swal] *adj* usual
usuario, -a [usu'arjo, a] *nm/f* user
usura [u'sura] *nf* usury; **usurero, -a** *nm/f* usurer
usurpar [usur'par] *vt* to usurp
utensilio [uten'siljo] *nm* tool; (*Culin*) utensil
útero ['utero] *nm* uterus, womb
útil ['util] *adj* useful ▷ *nm* tool; **utilidad** *nf* usefulness; (*Com*) profit; **utilizar** *vt* to use, utilize
utopía [uto'pia] *nf* Utopia; **utópico, -a** *adj* Utopian
uva ['uβa] *nf* grape

LAS UVAS

In Spain **Las uvas** play a big part on New Year's Eve (**Nochevieja**), when on the stroke of midnight people gather at home, in restaurants or in the **plaza mayor** and eat a grape for each stroke of the clock of the **Puerta del Sol** in Madrid. It is said to bring luck for the following year.

v *abr* (=*voltio*) v
va *vb V* **ir**
vaca ['baka] *nf* (*animal*) cow; **carne de ~** beef
vacaciones [baka'θjones] *nfpl* holidays
vacante [ba'kante] *adj* vacant, empty ▷ *nf* vacancy
vaciar [ba'θjar] *vt* to empty out; (*ahuecar*) to hollow out; (*moldear*) to cast; **vaciarse** *vr* to empty
vacilar [baθi'lar] *vi* to be unsteady; (*al hablar*) to falter; (*dudar*) to hesitate, waver; (*memoria*) to fail
vacío, -a [ba'θio, a] *adj* empty; (*puesto*) vacant; (*desocupado*) idle; (*vano*) vain ▷ *nm* emptiness; (*Física*) vacuum; (*un vacío*) (empty) space
vacuna [ba'kuna] *nf* vaccine; **vacunar** *vt* to vaccinate
vacuno, -a [ba'kuno, a] *adj* cow *cpd*; **ganado ~** cattle
vadear [baðe'ar] *vt* (*río*) to ford; **vado** *nm* ford
vagabundo, -a [baɣa'βundo, a] *adj* wandering ▷ *nm* tramp
vagancia [ba'ɣanθja] *nf* (*pereza*) idleness, laziness
vagar [ba'ɣar] *vi* to wander; (*no hacer nada*) to idle
vagina [ba'xina] *nf* vagina
vago, -a ['baɣo, a] *adj* vague; (*perezoso*) lazy ▷ *nm/f* (*vagabundo*) tramp; (*flojo*) lazybones *sg*, idler
vagón [ba'ɣon] *nm* (*Ferro: de pasajeros*) carriage; (*: de mercancías*) wagon
vaho ['bao] *nm* (*vapor*) vapour, steam; (*respiración*) breath
vaina ['baina] *nf* sheath
vainilla [bai'niʎa] *nf* vanilla
vais *vb V* **ir**
vaivén [bai'βen] *nm* to-and-fro movement; (*de tránsito*) coming and going; **vaivenes** *nmpl* (*fig*) ups and downs
vajilla [ba'xiʎa] *nf* crockery, dishes *pl*; (*juego*) service, set
valdré *etc vb V* **valer**
vale ['bale] *nm* voucher; (*recibo*) receipt; (*pagaré*) IOU
valedero, -a [bale'ðero, a] *adj* valid
valenciano, -a [balen'θjano, a] *adj* Valencian
valentía [balen'tia] *nf* courage, bravery
valer [ba'ler] *vt* to be worth; (*Mat*) to equal; (*costar*) to cost ▷ *vi* (*ser útil*) to be useful; (*ser válido*) to be valid; **valerse** *vr* to take care of oneself; **~se de** to make use of, take advantage of; **~ la pena** to be worthwhile; **¿vale?** (ESP) OK?; **más vale que nos vayamos** we'd better go; **¡eso a mí no me vale!** (MÉX: *fam: no importar*) I couldn't care less about that
valeroso, -a [bale'roso, a] *adj* brave, valiant
valgo *etc vb V* **valer**
valía [ba'lia] *nf* worth, value
validar [bali'ðar] *vt* to validate; **validez** *nf* validity; **válido, -a** *adj* valid
valiente [ba'ljente] *adj* brave, valiant

▷ *nm* hero
valija [ba'lixa] (cs) *nf* (suit)case
valioso, -a [ba'ljoso, a] *adj* valuable
valla ['baʎa] *nf* fence; (*Deporte*) hurdle; **valla publicitaria** hoarding; **vallar** *vt* to fence in
valle ['baʎe] *nm* valley
valor [ba'lor] *nm* value, worth; (*precio*) price; (*valentía*) valour, courage; (*importancia*) importance; **valores** *nmpl* (*Com*) securities; **valorar** *vt* to value
vals [bals] *nm inv* waltz
válvula ['balβula] *nf* valve
vamos *vb V* **ir**
vampiro, -resa [bam'piro, 'resa] *nm/f* vampire
van *vb V* **ir**
vanguardia [ban'gwardja] *nf* vanguard; (*Arte etc*) avant-garde
vanidad [bani'ðað] *nf* vanity; **vanidoso, -a** *adj* vain, conceited
vano, -a ['bano, a] *adj* vain
vapor [ba'por] *nm* vapour; (*vaho*) steam; **al ~** (*Culin*) steamed; **vapor de agua** water vapour; **vaporizador** *nm* atomizer; **vaporizar** *vt* to vaporize; **vaporoso, -a** *adj* vaporous
vaquero, -a [ba'kero, a] *adj* cattle *cpd* ▷ *nm* cowboy; **vaqueros** *nmpl* (*pantalones*) jeans
vaquilla [ba'kiʎa] *nf* (*Zool*) heifer
vara ['bara] *nf* stick; (*Tec*) rod
variable [ba'rjaβle] *adj, nf* variable
variación [baria'θjon] *nf* variation
variar [bar'jar] *vt* to vary; (*modificar*) to modify; (*cambiar de posición*) to switch around ▷ *vi* to vary
varicela [bari'θela] *nf* chickenpox
varices [ba'riθes] *nfpl* varicose veins
variedad [barje'ðað] *nf* variety
varilla [ba'riʎa] *nf* stick; (*Bot*) twig; (*Tec*) rod; (*de rueda*) spoke
vario, -a ['barjo, a] *adj* varied; **~s** various, several
varita [ba'rita] *nf* (*tb*: **~ mágica**) magic wand
varón [ba'ron] *nm* male, man; **varonil** *adj* manly, virile
Varsovia [bar'soβja] *n* Warsaw
vas *vb V* **ir**
vasco, -a ['basko, a] *adj, nm/f* Basque; **vascongado, -a** [baskon'gaðo, a] *adj* Basque; **las Vascongadas** the Basque Country
vaselina [base'lina] *nf* Vaseline®
vasija [ba'sixa] *nf* container, vessel
vaso ['baso] *nm* glass, tumbler; (*Anat*) vessel

> No confundir **vaso** con la palabra inglesa *vase*.

vástago ['bastaɣo] *nm* (*Bot*) shoot; (*Tec*) rod; (*fig*) offspring
vasto, -a ['basto, a] *adj* vast, huge
Vaticano [bati'kano] *nm*: **el ~** the Vatican
vatio ['batjo] *nm* (*Elec*) watt
vaya *etc vb V* **ir**
Vd(s) *abr* = **usted(es)**
ve [be] *vb V* **ir; ver**
vecindad [beθin'dað] *nf* neighbourhood; (*habitantes*) residents *pl*
vecindario [beθin'darjo] *nm* neighbourhood; residents *pl*
vecino, -a [be'θino, a] *adj* neighbouring ▷ *nm/f* neighbour; (*residente*) resident
veda ['beða] *nf* prohibition; **vedar** [be'ðar] *vt* (*prohibir*) to ban, prohibit; (*impedir*) to stop, prevent
vegetación [bexeta'θjon] *nf* vegetation
vegetal [bexe'tal] *adj, nm* vegetable
vegetariano, -a [bexeta'rjano, a] *adj, nm/f* vegetarian
vehículo [be'ikulo] *nm* vehicle; (*Med*) carrier
veía *etc vb V* **ver**
veinte ['beinte] *num* twenty
vejar [be'xar] *vt* (*irritar*) to annoy, vex; (*humillar*) to humiliate
vejez [be'xeθ] *nf* old age
vejiga [be'xiɣa] *nf* (*Anat*) bladder
vela ['bela] *nf* (*de cera*) candle; (*Náut*) sail; (*insomnio*) sleeplessness; (*vigilia*)

vigil; (*Mil*) sentry duty; **estar a dos ~s** (*fam: sin dinero*) to be skint

velado, -a [be'laðo, a] *adj* veiled; (*sonido*) muffled; (*Foto*) blurred ▷ *nf* soirée

velar [be'lar] *vt* (*vigilar*) to keep watch over ▷ *vi* to stay awake; **~ por** to watch over, look after

velatorio [bela'torjo] *nm* (funeral) wake

velero [be'lero] *nm* (*Náut*) sailing ship; (*Aviac*) glider

veleta [be'leta] *nf* weather vane

veliz [be'lis] (MÉX) *nm* (suit)case

vello ['beʎo] *nm* down, fuzz

velo ['belo] *nm* veil

velocidad [beloθi'ðað] *nf* speed; (*Tec, Auto*) gear

velocímetro [belo'θimetro] *nm* speedometer

velorio [be'lorjo] (LAM) *nm* (funeral) wake

veloz [be'loθ] *adj* fast

ven *vb V* **venir**

vena ['bena] *nf* vein

venado [be'naðo] *nm* deer

vencedor, a [benθe'ðor, a] *adj* victorious ▷ *nm/f* victor, winner

vencer [ben'θer] *vt* (*dominar*) to defeat, beat; (*derrotar*) to vanquish; (*superar, controlar*) to overcome, master ▷ *vi* (*triunfar*) to win (through), triumph; (*plazo*) to expire; **vencido, -a** *adj* (*derrotado*) defeated, beaten; (*Com*) due ▷ *adv*: **pagar vencido** to pay in arrears

venda ['benda] *nf* bandage; **vendaje** *nm* bandage, dressing; **vendar** *vt* to bandage; **vendar los ojos** to blindfold

vendaval [benda'βal] *nm* (*viento*) gale

vendedor, a [bende'ðor, a] *nm/f* seller

vender [ben'der] *vt* to sell; **venderse** *vr* (*estar a la venta*) to be on sale; **~ al contado/al por mayor/al por menor** to sell for cash/wholesale/retail; **"se vende"** "for sale"

vendimia [ben'dimja] *nf* grape harvest

vendré *etc vb V* **venir**

veneno [be'neno] *nm* poison; (*de serpiente*) venom; **venenoso, -a** *adj* poisonous; venomous

venerable [bene'raβle] *adj* venerable; **venerar** *vt* (*respetar*) to revere; (*adorar*) to worship

venéreo, -a [be'nereo, a] *adj*: **enfermedad venérea** venereal disease

venezolano, -a [beneθo'lano, a] *adj* Venezuelan

Venezuela [bene'θwela] *nf* Venezuela

venganza [ben'ganθa] *nf* vengeance, revenge; **vengar** *vt* to avenge; **vengarse** *vr* to take revenge; **vengativo, -a** *adj* (*persona*) vindictive

vengo *etc vb V* **venir**

venia ['benja] *nf* (*perdón*) pardon; (*permiso*) consent

venial [be'njal] *adj* venial

venida [be'niða] *nf* (*llegada*) arrival; (*regreso*) return

venidero, -a [beni'ðero, a] *adj* coming, future

venir [be'nir] *vi* to come; (*llegar*) to arrive; (*ocurrir*) to happen; (*fig*): **~ de** to stem from; **~ bien/mal** to be suitable/unsuitable; **el año que viene** next year; **~se abajo** to collapse

venta ['benta] *nf* (*Com*) sale; **"en ~"** "for sale"; **estar a la** *o* **en ~** to be (up) for sale *o* on the market; **venta a domicilio** door-to-door selling; **venta a plazos** hire purchase; **venta al contado/al por mayor/al por menor** cash sale/wholesale/retail

ventaja [ben'taxa] *nf* advantage; **ventajoso, -a** *adj* advantageous

ventana [ben'tana] *nf* window; **ventanilla** *nf* (*de taquilla*) window (*of booking office etc*)

ventilación [bentila'θjon] *nf* ventilation; (*corriente*) draught

ventilador [bentila'ðor] *nm* fan

ventilar [benti'lar] *vt* to ventilate; (*para secar*) to put out to dry; (*asunto*) to air, discuss
ventisca [ben'tiska] *nf* blizzard
ventrílocuo, -a [ben'trilokwo, a] *nm/f* ventriloquist
ventura [ben'tura] *nf* (*felicidad*) happiness; (*buena suerte*) luck; (*destino*) fortune; **a la (buena) ~** at random; **venturoso, -a** *adj* happy; (*afortunado*) lucky, fortunate
veo *etc vb V* **ver**
ver [ber] *vt* to see; (*mirar*) to look at, watch; (*entender*) to understand; (*investigar*) to look into ▷ *vi* to see; to understand; **verse** *vr* (*encontrarse*) to meet; (*dejarse ver*) to be seen; (*hallarse: en un apuro*) to find o.s., be; **(vamos) a ~** let's see; **no tener nada que ~ con** to have nothing to do with; **a mi modo de ~** as I see it; **ya ~emos** we'll see
vera ['bera] *nf* edge, verge; (*de río*) bank
veranear [berane'ar] *vi* to spend the summer; **veraneo** *nm* summer holiday; **veraniego, -a** *adj* summer *cpd*
verano [be'rano] *nm* summer
veras ['beras] *nfpl* truth *sg*; **de ~** really, truly
verbal [ber'βal] *adj* verbal
verbena [ber'βena] *nf* (*baile*) open-air dance
verbo ['berβo] *nm* verb
verdad [ber'ðað] *nf* truth; (*fiabilidad*) reliability; **de ~** real, proper; **a decir ~** to tell the truth; **verdadero, -a** *adj* (*veraz*) true, truthful; (*fiable*) reliable; (*fig*) real
verde ['berðe] *adj* green; (*chiste*) blue, dirty ▷ *nm* green; **viejo ~** dirty old man; **verdear** *vi* to turn green; **verdor** *nm* greenness
verdugo [ber'ðuɣo] *nm* executioner
verdulero, -a [berðu'lero, a] *nm/f* greengrocer
verduras [ber'ðuras] *nfpl* (*Culin*) greens
vereda [be'reða] *nf* path; (*cs: acera*) pavement (*BRIT*), sidewalk (*US*)
veredicto [bere'ðikto] *nm* verdict
vergonzoso, -a [berɣon'θoso, a] *adj* shameful; (*tímido*) timid, bashful
vergüenza [ber'ɣwenθa] *nf* shame, sense of shame; (*timidez*) bashfulness; (*pudor*) modesty; **me da ~** I'm ashamed
verídico, -a [be'riðiko, a] *adj* true, truthful
verificar [berifi'kar] *vt* to check; (*corroborar*) to verify; (*llevar a cabo*) to carry out; **verificarse** *vr* (*predicción*) to prove to be true
verja ['berxa] *nf* (*cancela*) iron gate; (*valla*) iron railings *pl*; (*de ventana*) grille
vermut [ber'mut] (*pl* **~s**) *nm* vermouth
verosímil [bero'simil] *adj* likely, probable; (*relato*) credible
verruga [be'rruɣa] *nf* wart
versátil [ber'satil] *adj* versatile
versión [ber'sjon] *nf* version
verso ['berso] *nm* verse; **un ~** a line of poetry
vértebra ['berteβra] *nf* vertebra
verter [ber'ter] *vt* (*líquido: adrede*) to empty, pour (out); (*: sin querer*) to spill; (*basura*) to dump ▷ *vi* to flow
vertical [berti'kal] *adj* vertical
vértice ['bertiθe] *nm* vertex, apex
vertidos [ber'tiðos] *nmpl* waste *sg*
vertiente [ber'tjente] *nf* slope; (*fig*) aspect
vértigo ['bertiɣo] *nm* vertigo; (*mareo*) dizziness
vesícula [be'sikula] *nf* blister
vespino® [bes'pino] *nm o nf* moped
vestíbulo [bes'tiβulo] *nm* hall; (*de teatro*) foyer
vestido [bes'tiðo] *nm* (*ropa*) clothes *pl*, clothing; (*de mujer*) dress, frock ▷ *pp de* **vestir**; **~ de azul/marinero** dressed in blue/as a sailor
vestidor [besti'ðor] (*MÉX*) *nm* (*Deporte*) changing (*BRIT*) *o* locker (*US*) room

vestimenta [besti'menta] *nf* clothing
vestir [bes'tir] *vt* (*poner: ropa*) to put on; (*llevar: ropa*) to wear; (*proveer de ropa a*) to clothe; (*sastre*) to make clothes for ▷ *vi* to dress; (*verse bien*) to look good; **vestirse** *vr* to get dressed, dress o.s.
vestuario [bes'twarjo] *nm* clothes *pl*, wardrobe; (*Teatro: cuarto*) dressing room; (*Deporte*) changing (BRIT) *o* locker (US) room
vetar [be'tar] *vt* to veto
veterano, -a [bete'rano, a] *adj, nm* veteran
veterinaria [beteri'narja] *nf* veterinary science; *V tb* **veterinario**
veterinario, -a [beteri'narjo, a] *nm/f* vet(erinary surgeon)
veto ['beto] *nm* veto
vez [beθ] *nf* time; (*turno*) turn; **a la ~ que** at the same time as; **a su ~** in its turn; **otra ~** again; **una ~** once; **de una ~** in one go; **de una ~ para siempre** once and for all; **en ~ de** instead of; **a** *o* **algunas veces** sometimes; **una y otra ~** repeatedly; **de ~ en cuando** from time to time; **7 veces 9** 7 times 9; **hacer las veces de** to stand in for; **tal ~** perhaps
vía ['bia] *nf* track, route; (*Ferro*) line; (*fig*) way; (*Anat*) passage, tube ▷ *prep* via, by way of; **por ~ judicial** by legal means; **en ~s de** in the process of; **vía aérea** airway; **Vía Láctea** Milky Way; **vía pública** public road *o* thoroughfare
viable ['bjaβle] *adj* (*solución, plan, alternativa*) feasible
viaducto [bja'ðukto] *nm* viaduct
viajante [bja'xante] *nm* commercial traveller
viajar [bja'xar] *vi* to travel; **viaje** *nm* journey; (*gira*) tour; (*Náut*) voyage; **estar de viaje** to be on a trip; **viaje de ida y vuelta** round trip; **viaje de novios** honeymoon; **viajero, -a** *adj* travelling; (*Zool*) migratory ▷ *nm/f* (*quien viaja*) traveller; (*pasajero*) passenger
víbora ['biβora] *nf* (*Zool*) viper; (: (MÉX: *venenoso*) poisonous snake
vibración [biβra'θjon] *nf* vibration
vibrar [bi'βrar] *vt, vi* to vibrate
vicepresidente [biθepresi'ðente] *nmf* vice-president
viceversa [biθe'βersa] *adv* vice versa
vicio ['biθjo] *nm* vice; (*mala costumbre*) bad habit; **vicioso, -a** *adj* (*muy malo*) vicious; (*corrompido*) depraved ▷ *nm/f* depraved person
víctima ['biktima] *nf* victim
victoria [bik'torja] *nf* victory; **victorioso, -a** *adj* victorious
vid [bið] *nf* vine
vida ['biða] *nf* (*gen*) life; (*duración*) lifetime; **de por ~** for life; **en la** *o* **mi ~** never; **estar con ~** to be still alive; **ganarse la ~** to earn one's living
vídeo ['biðeo] *nm* video ▷ *adj inv*: **película de ~** video film; **videocámara** *nf* camcorder; **videocasete** *nm* video cassette, videotape; **videoclub** *nm* video club; **videojuego** *nm* video game; **videollamada** *nf* video call; **videoteléfono** *nf* videophone
vidrio ['biðrjo] *nm* glass
vieira ['bjeira] *nf* scallop
viejo, -a ['bjexo, a] *adj* old ▷ *nm/f* old man/woman; **hacerse ~** to get old
Viena ['bjena] *n* Vienna
vienes *etc vb V* **venir**
vienés, -esa [bje'nes, esa] *adj* Viennese
viento ['bjento] *nm* wind; **hacer ~** to be windy
vientre ['bjentre] *nm* belly; (*matriz*) womb
viernes ['bjernes] *nm inv* Friday; **Viernes Santo** Good Friday
Vietnam [bjet'nam] *nm* Vietnam; **vietnamita** *adj* Vietnamese
viga ['biɣa] *nf* beam, rafter; (*de metal*) girder
vigencia [bi'xenθja] *nf* validity; **estar en ~** to be in force; **vigente** *adj* valid, in force; (*imperante*) prevailing

vigésimo, -a [bi'xesimo, a] *adj* twentieth
vigía [bi'xia] *nm* look-out
vigilancia [bixi'lanθja] *nf*: **tener a algn bajo ~** to keep watch on sb
vigilar [bixi'lar] *vt* to watch over ▷ *vi* (*gen*) to be vigilant; (*hacer guardia*) to keep watch; **~ por** to take care of
vigilia [vi'xilja] *nf* wakefulness, being awake; (*Rel*) fast
vigor [bi'ɣor] *nm* vigour, vitality; **en ~** in force; **entrar/poner en ~** to come/put into effect; **vigoroso, -a** *adj* vigorous
VIH *nm abr* (= *virus de la inmunodeficiencia humana*) HIV; **VIH negativo/positivo** HIV-negative/-positive
vil [bil] *adj* vile, low
villa ['biʎa] *nf* (*casa*) villa; (*pueblo*) small town; (*municipalidad*) municipality
villancico [biʎan'θiko] *nm* (Christmas) carol
vilo ['bilo]: **en ~** *adv* in the air, suspended; (*fig*) on tenterhooks, in suspense
vinagre [bi'naɣre] *nm* vinegar
vinagreta [bina'ɣreta] *nf* vinaigrette, French dressing
vinculación [binkula'θjon] *nf* (*lazo*) link, bond; (*acción*) linking
vincular [binku'lar] *vt* to link, bind; **vínculo** *nm* link, bond
vine *etc vb V* **venir**
vinicultura [binikul'tura] *nf* wine growing
viniera *etc vb V* **venir**
vino ['bino] *vb V* **venir** ▷ *nm* wine; **vino blanco/tinto** white/red wine
viña ['biɲa] *nf* vineyard; **viñedo** *nm* vineyard
viola ['bjola] *nf* viola
violación [bjola'θjon] *nf* violation; (*sexual*) rape
violar [bjo'lar] *vt* to violate; (*sexualmente*) to rape
violencia [bjo'lenθja] *nf* violence, force; (*incomodidad*) embarrassment; (*acto injusto*) unjust act; **violentar** *vt* to force; (*casa*) to break into; (*agredir*) to assault; (*violar*) to violate; **violento, -a** *adj* violent; (*furioso*) furious; (*situación*) embarrassing; (*acto*) forced, unnatural
violeta [bjo'leta] *nf* violet
violín [bjo'lin] *nm* violin
violón [bjo'lon] *nm* double bass
virar [bi'rar] *vi* to change direction
virgen ['birxen] *adj, nf* virgin
Virgo ['birɣo] *nm* Virgo
viril [bi'ril] *adj* virile; **virilidad** *nf* virility
virtud [bir'tuð] *nf* virtue; **en ~ de** by virtue of; **virtuoso, -a** *adj* virtuous ▷ *nm/f* virtuoso
viruela [bi'rwela] *nf* smallpox
virulento, -a [biru'lento, a] *adj* virulent
virus ['birus] *nm inv* virus
visa ['bisa] (LAM) *nf* = **visado**
visado [bi'saðo] (ESP) *nm* visa
víscera ['bisθera] *nf* (*Anat, Zool*) gut, bowel; **vísceras** *nfpl* entrails
visceral [bisθe'ral] *adj* (*odio*) intense; **reacción ~** gut reaction
visera [bi'sera] *nf* visor
visibilidad [bisiβili'ðað] *nf* visibility; **visible** *adj* visible; (*fig*) obvious
visillos [bi'siʎos] *nmpl* lace curtains
visión [bi'sjon] *nf* (*Anat*) vision, (eye)sight; (*fantasía*) vision, fantasy
visita [bi'sita] *nf* call, visit; (*persona*) visitor; **hacer una ~** to pay a visit; **visitar** [bisi'tar] *vt* to visit, call on
visón [bi'son] *nm* mink
visor [bi'sor] *nm* (*Foto*) viewfinder
víspera ['bispera] *nf*: **la ~ de ...** the day before ...
vista ['bista] *nf* sight, vision; (*capacidad de ver*) (eye)sight; (*mirada*) look(s) (*pl*); **a primera ~** at first glance; **hacer la ~ gorda** to turn a blind eye; **volver la ~** to look back; **está a la ~ que** it's obvious that; **en ~ de** in view of; **en ~ de que** in view of the fact that; **¡hasta la ~!** so long!, see you!; **con ~s**

a with a view to; **vistazo** *nm* glance; **dar** *o* **echar un vistazo a** to glance at

visto, -a ['bisto, a] *pp de* **ver** ▷ *vb V tb* **vestir** ▷ *adj* seen; (*considerado*) considered ▷ *nm*: **~ bueno** approval; **por lo ~** apparently; **está ~ que** it's clear that; **está bien/mal ~** it's acceptable/unacceptable; **~ que** since, considering that

vistoso, -a [bis'toso, a] *adj* colourful

visual [bi'swal] *adj* visual

vital [bi'tal] *adj* life *cpd*, living *cpd*; (*fig*) vital; (*persona*) lively, vivacious; **vitalicio, -a** *adj* for life; **vitalidad** *nf* (*de persona, negocio*) energy; (*de ciudad*) liveliness

vitamina [bita'mina] *nf* vitamin

vitorear [bitore'ar] *vt* to cheer, acclaim

vitrina [bi'trina] *nf* show case; (LAM: *escaparate*) shop window

viudo, -a ['bjuðo, a] *nm/f* widower/widow

viva ['biβa] *excl* hurrah!; **¡~ el rey!** long live the king!

vivaracho, -a [biβa'ratʃo, a] *adj* jaunty, lively; (*ojos*) bright, twinkling

vivaz [bi'βaθ] *adj* lively

víveres ['biβeres] *nmpl* provisions

vivero [bi'βero] *nm* (*para plantas*) nursery; (*para peces*) fish farm; (*fig*) hotbed

viveza [bi'βeθa] *nf* liveliness; (*agudeza: mental*) sharpness

vivienda [bi'βjenda] *nf* housing; (*una vivienda*) house; (*piso*) flat (BRIT), apartment (US)

viviente [bi'βjente] *adj* living

vivir [bi'βir] *vt, vi* to live ▷ *nm* life, living

vivo, -a ['biβo, a] *adj* living, alive; (*fig: descripción*) vivid; (*persona: astuto*) smart, clever; **en ~** (*transmisión etc*) live

vocablo [bo'kaβlo] *nm* (*palabra*) word; (*término*) term

vocabulario [bokaβu'larjo] *nm* vocabulary

vocación [boka'θjon] *nf* vocation; **vocacional** (LAM) *nf* ≈ technical college

vocal [bo'kal] *adj* vocal ▷ *nf* vowel; **vocalizar** *vt* to vocalize

vocero [bo'θero] (LAM) *nmf* spokesman/woman

voces ['boθes] *pl de* **voz**

vodka ['boðka] *nm o f* vodka

vol *abr* = **volumen**

volado [bo'laðo] (MÉX) *adv* in a rush, hastily

volador, a [bola'ðor, a] *adj* flying

volandas [bo'landas]: **en ~** *adv* in the air

volante [bo'lante] *adj* flying ▷ *nm* (*de coche*) steering wheel; (*de reloj*) balance

volar [bo'lar] *vt* (*edificio*) to blow up ▷ *vi* to fly

volátil [bo'latil] *adj* volatile

volcán [bol'kan] *nm* volcano; **volcánico, -a** *adj* volcanic

volcar [bol'kar] *vt* to upset, overturn; (*tumbar, derribar*) to knock over; (*vaciar*) to empty out ▷ *vi* to overturn; **volcarse** *vr* to tip over

voleibol [bolei'βol] *nm* volleyball

volqué *etc vb V* **volcar**

voltaje [bol'taxe] *nm* voltage

voltear [bolte'ar] *vt* to turn over; (*volcar*) to turn upside down

voltereta [bolte'reta] *nf* somersault

voltio ['boltjo] *nm* volt

voluble [bo'luβle] *adj* fickle

volumen [bo'lumen] (*pl* **volúmenes**) *nm* volume; **voluminoso, -a** *adj* voluminous; (*enorme*) massive

voluntad [bolun'tað] *nf* will; (*resolución*) willpower; (*deseo*) desire, wish

voluntario, -a [bolun'tarjo, a] *adj* voluntary ▷ *nm/f* volunteer

volver [bol'βer] *vt* (*gen*) to turn; (*dar vuelta a*) to turn (over); (*voltear*) to turn round, turn upside down; (*poner al revés*) to turn inside out; (*devolver*) to return ▷ *vi* to return, go back, come back; **volverse** *vr* to turn round; **~ la**

espalda to turn one's back; **~ triste** *etc* **a algn** to make sb sad *etc*; **~ a hacer** to do again; **~ en sí** to come to; **~se insoportable/muy caro** to get *o* become unbearable/very expensive; **~se loco** to go mad
vomitar [bomi'tar] *vt, vi* to vomit; **vómito** *nm* vomit
voraz [bo'raθ] *adj* voracious
vos [bos] (LAM) *pron* you
vosotros, -as [bo'sotros, as] (ESP) *pron* you; (*reflexivo*): **entre/para ~** among/for yourselves
votación [bota'θjon] *nf* (*acto*) voting; (*voto*) vote
votar [bo'tar] *vi* to vote; **voto** *nm* vote; (*promesa*) vow; **votos** *nmpl* (good) wishes
voy *vb V* **ir**
voz [boθ] *nf* voice; (*grito*) shout; (*rumor*) rumour; (*Ling*) word; **dar voces** to shout, yell; **de viva ~** verbally; **en ~ alta** aloud; **en ~ baja** in a low voice, in a whisper; **voz de mando** command
vuelco ['bwelko] *vb V* **volcar** ▷ *nm* spill, overturning
vuelo ['bwelo] *vb V* **volar** ▷ *nm* flight; (*encaje*) lace, frill; **coger al ~** to catch in flight; **vuelo chárter/regular** charter/scheduled flight; **vuelo libre** (*Deporte*) hang-gliding
vuelque *etc vb V* **volcar**
vuelta ['bwelta] *nf* (*gen*) turn; (*curva*) bend, curve; (*regreso*) return; (*revolución*) revolution; (*de circuito*) lap; (*de papel, tela*) reverse; (*cambio*) change; **a la ~** on one's return; **a la ~ (de la esquina)** round the corner; **a ~ de correo** by return of post; **dar ~s** (*cabeza*) to spin; **dar(se) la ~** (*volverse*) to turn round; **dar ~s a una idea** to turn over an idea (in one's head); **estar de ~** to be back; **dar una ~** to go for a walk; (*en coche*) to go for a drive; **vuelta ciclista** (*Deporte*) (cycle) tour
vuelto ['bwelto] *pp de* **volver**
vuelvo *etc vb V* **volver**
vuestro, -a ['bwestro, a] *adj pos* your; **un amigo ~** a friend of yours ▷ *pron*: **el ~/la vuestra, los ~s/las vuestras** yours
vulgar [bul'ɣar] *adj* (*ordinario*) vulgar; (*común*) common; **vulgaridad** *nf* commonness; (*acto*) vulgarity; (*expresión*) coarse expression
vulnerable [bulne'raβle] *adj* vulnerable
vulnerar [bulne'rar] *vt* (*ley, acuerdo*) to violate, breach; (*derechos, intimidad*) to violate; (*reputación*) to damage

W X

walkie-talkie [walki-'talki] (*pl* **~s**) *nm* walkie-talkie
Walkman® ['walkman] *nm* Walkman®
wáter ['bater] *nm* (*taza*) toilet; (*LAM*: *lugar*) toilet (*BRIT*), rest room (*US*)
web [web] *nm o f* (*página*) website; (*red*) (World Wide) Web; **webcam** *nf* webcam; **webmaster** *nmf* webmaster; **website** *nm* website
western ['western] (*pl* **~s**) *nm* western
whisky ['wiski] *nm* whisky, whiskey
windsurf ['winsurf] *nm* windsurfing; **hacer ~** to go windsurfing

xenofobia [kseno'foβja] *nf* xenophobia
xilófono [ksi'lofono] *nm* xylophone
xocoyote, -a [ksoko'yote, a] (*MÉX*) *nm/f* baby of the family, youngest child

y [i] *conj* and
ya [ja] *adv* (*gen*) already; (*ahora*) now; (*en seguida*) at once; (*pronto*) soon ▷ *excl* all right! ▷ *conj* (*ahora que*) now that; **~ lo sé** I know; **~ que ...** since; **¡~ está bien!** that's (quite) enough!; **¡~ voy!** coming!
yacaré [jaka're] (CS) *nm* cayman
yacer [ja'θer] *vi* to lie
yacimiento [jaθi'mjento] *nm* (*de mineral*) deposit; (*arqueológico*) site
yanqui ['janki] *adj, nmf* Yankee
yate ['jate] *nm* yacht
yazco *etc vb V* **yacer**
yedra ['jeðra] *nf* ivy
yegua ['jeɣwa] *nf* mare
yema ['jema] *nf* (*del huevo*) yolk; (*Bot*) leaf bud; (*fig*) best part; **yema del dedo** fingertip
yerno ['jerno] *nm* son-in-law
yeso ['jeso] *nm* plaster
yo [jo] *pron* I; **soy ~** it's me
yodo ['joðo] *nm* iodine
yoga ['joɣa] *nm* yoga
yogur(t) [jo'ɣur(t)] *nm* yoghurt
yuca ['juka] *nf* (*alimento*) cassava, manioc root
Yugoslavia [juɣos'laβja] *nf* (*Hist*) Yugoslavia
yugular [juɣu'lar] *adj* jugular
yunque ['junke] *nm* anvil
yuyo ['jujo] (RPL) *nm* (*mala hierba*) weed

Z

zafar [θa'far] *vt* (*soltar*) to untie; (*superficie*) to clear; **zafarse** *vr* (*escaparse*) to escape; (*Tec*) to slip off
zafiro [θa'firo] *nm* sapphire
zaga ['θaɤa] *nf*: **a la ~** behind
zaguán [θa'ɤwan] *nm* hallway
zalamero, -a [θala'mero, a] *adj* flattering; (*cobista*) suave
zamarra [θa'marra] *nf* (*chaqueta*) sheepskin jacket
zambullirse [θambu'ʎirse] *vr* to dive
zampar [θam'par] *vt* to gobble down
zanahoria [θana'orja] *nf* carrot
zancadilla [θanka'ðiʎa] *nf* trip
zanco ['θanko] *nm* stilt
zanja ['θanxa] *nf* ditch; **zanjar** *vt* (*resolver*) to resolve
zapata [θa'pata] *nf* (*Mecánica*) shoe
zapatería [θapate'ria] *nf* (*oficio*) shoemaking; (*tienda*) shoe shop; (*fábrica*) shoe factory; **zapatero, -a** *nm/f* shoemaker
zapatilla [θapa'tiʎa] *nf* slipper; **zapatilla de deporte** training shoe
zapato [θa'pato] *nm* shoe
zapping ['θapin] *nm* channel-hopping; **hacer ~** to channel-hop
zar [θar] *nm* tsar, czar
zarandear [θaranðe'ar] (*fam*) *vt* to shake vigorously
zarpa ['θarpa] *nf* (*garra*) claw
zarpar [θar'par] *vi* to weigh anchor
zarza ['θarθa] *nf* (*Bot*) bramble; **zarzamora** *nf* blackberry
zarzuela [θar'θwela] *nf* *Spanish light opera*
zigzag [θiɤ'θaɤ] *nm* zigzag
zinc [θink] *nm* zinc
zíper ['θiper] (*MÉX, CAM*) *nm* zip (fastener) (*BRIT*), zipper (*US*)
zócalo ['θokalo] *nm* (*Arq*) plinth, base; (*de pared*) skirting board (*BRIT*), baseboard (*US*); (*MÉX*: *plaza*) main *o* public square
zoclo ['θoklo] (*MÉX*) *nm* skirting board (*BRIT*), baseboard (*US*)
zodíaco [θo'ðiako] *nm* zodiac
zona ['θona] *nf* zone; **zona fronteriza** border area; **zona roja** (*LAM*) red-light district
zonzo, -a (*LAM*: *fam*) ['θonθo, a] *adj* silly ▷ *nm/f* fool
zoo ['θoo] *nm* zoo
zoología [θoolo'xia] *nf* zoology; **zoológico, -a** *adj* zoological ▷ *nm* (*tb*: **parque zoológico**) zoo; **zoólogo, -a** *nm/f* zoologist
zoom [θum] *nm* zoom lens
zopilote [θopi'lote] (*MÉX, CAM*) *nm* buzzard
zoquete [θo'kete] *nm* (*fam*) blockhead
zorro, -a ['θorro, a] *adj* crafty ▷ *nm/f* fox/vixen
zozobrar [θoθo'βrar] *vi* (*hundirse*) to capsize; (*fig*) to fail
zueco ['θweko] *nm* clog
zumbar [θum'bar] *vt* (*golpear*) to hit ▷ *vi* to buzz; **zumbido** *nm* buzzing
zumo ['θumo] *nm* juice
zurcir [θur'θir] *vt* (*coser*) to darn
zurdo, -a ['θurðo, a] *adj* left-handed
zurrar [θu'rrar] (*fam*) *vt* to wallop

Introduction

The **Verb Tables** in the following section contain 31 tables of the most common Spanish verbs (some regular, some irregular and some which change their stems) in alphabetical order. Each table shows you the following tenses and forms: **Present**, **Preterite**, **Future**, **Present Subjunctive**, **Imperfect**, **Conditional**, **Imperative**, **Past Participle** and **Gerund**.

In order to help you use the verbs shown in the Verb Tables correctly, there are also a number of example phrases at the bottom of each page to show the verb as it is used in context.

In Spanish there are **regular** verbs (their forms follow the normal rules); **irregular** verbs (their forms do not follow the normal rules); and verbs which change a vowel in their stem (the part that is left when you take off the ending) in fairly predictable ways. The regular verbs in these tables are:

hablar (regular **-ar** verb, Verb Table 12)
comer (regular **-er** verb, Verb Table 3)
vivir (regular **-ir** verb, Verb Table 31)
lavarse (regular **-ar** reflexive verb, Verb Table 15)

For a list of other Spanish irregular and stem-changing verb forms see pages 33–34.

The key at the top of page 33 explains which verb tenses or forms are shown on pages 33-34. For instance, **7** refers to the past participle. So, when you see abrir **7** abierto, you know that abrir has the irregular past participle *abierto*. Only irregular forms are listed. So, **4** busqué, at buscar, means that although *busqué* is irregular (the spelling changes to keep the [k] sound before the letter 'e'), the rest of the preterite tense behaves like any regular **-ar** verb: *busqué, buscaste, buscó, buscamos, buscasteis, buscaron*.

▶ coger (to take, to catch)

PRESENT

(yo)	cojo
(tú)	coges
(él/ella/usted)	coge
(nosotros/as)	cogemos
(vosotros/as)	cogéis
(ellos/ellas/ustedes)	cogen

PRESENT SUBJUNCTIVE

(yo)	coja
(tú)	cojas
(él/ella/usted)	coja
(nosotros/as)	cojamos
(vosotros/as)	cojáis
(ellos/ellas/ustedes)	cojan

PRETERITE

(yo)	cogí
(tú)	cogiste
(él/ella/usted)	cogió
(nosotros/as)	cogimos
(vosotros/as)	cogisteis
(ellos/ellas/ustedes)	cogieron

IMPERFECT

(yo)	cogía
(tú)	cogías
(él/ella/usted)	cogía
(nosotros/as)	cogíamos
(vosotros/as)	cogíais
(ellos/ellas/ustedes)	cogían

FUTURE

(yo)	cogeré
(tú)	cogerás
(él/ella/usted)	cogerá
(nosotros/as)	cogeremos
(vosotros/as)	cogeréis
(ellos/ellas/ustedes)	cogerán

CONDITIONAL

(yo)	cogería
(tú)	cogerías
(él/ella/usted)	cogería
(nosotros/as)	cogeríamos
(vosotros/as)	cogeríais
(ellos/ellas/ustedes)	cogerían

IMPERATIVE

coge / coged

PAST PARTICIPLE

cogido

GERUND

cogiendo

EXAMPLE PHRASES

La ***cogí*** *entre mis brazos.* I took her in my arms.
Estuvimos cogiendo *setas.* We were picking mushrooms.
¿Por qué no ***coges*** *el tren de las seis?* Why don't you get the six o'clock train?

Remember that subject pronouns are not used very often in Spanish.

▶ comer (to eat)

PRESENT

(yo)	como
(tú)	comes
(él/ella/usted)	come
(nosotros/as)	comemos
(vosotros/as)	coméis
(ellos/ellas/ustedes)	comen

PRESENT SUBJUNCTIVE

(yo)	coma
(tú)	comas
(él/ella/usted)	coma
(nosotros/as)	comamos
(vosotros/as)	comáis
(ellos/ellas/ustedes)	coman

PRETERITE

(yo)	comí
(tú)	comiste
(él/ella/usted)	comió
(nosotros/as)	comimos
(vosotros/as)	comisteis
(ellos/ellas/ustedes)	comieron

IMPERFECT

(yo)	comía
(tú)	comías
(él/ella/usted)	comía
(nosotros/as)	comíamos
(vosotros/as)	comíais
(ellos/ellas/ustedes)	comían

FUTURE

(yo)	comeré
(tú)	comerás
(él/ella/usted)	comerá
(nosotros/as)	comeremos
(vosotros/as)	comeréis
(ellos/ellas/ustedes)	comerán

CONDITIONAL

(yo)	comería
(tú)	comerías
(él/ella/usted)	comería
(nosotros/as)	comeríamos
(vosotros/as)	comeríais
(ellos/ellas/ustedes)	comerían

IMPERATIVE

come / comed

PAST PARTICIPLE

comido

GERUND

comiendo

EXAMPLE PHRASES

*No **come** carne.* He doesn't eat meat.
*No **comas** tan deprisa.* Don't eat so fast.
***Se ha comido** todo.* He's eaten it all.

Remember that subject pronouns are not used very often in Spanish.

dar (to give)

PRESENT

(yo)	doy
(tú)	das
(él/ella/usted)	da
(nosotros/as)	damos
(vosotros/as)	dais
(ellos/ellas/ustedes)	dan

PRESENT SUBJUNCTIVE

(yo)	dé
(tú)	des
(él/ella/usted)	dé
(nosotros/as)	demos
(vosotros/as)	deis
(ellos/ellas/ustedes)	den

PRETERITE

(yo)	di
(tú)	diste
(él/ella/usted)	dio
(nosotros/as)	dimos
(vosotros/as)	disteis
(ellos/ellas/ustedes)	dieron

IMPERFECT

(yo)	daba
(tú)	dabas
(él/ella/usted)	daba
(nosotros/as)	dábamos
(vosotros/as)	dabais
(ellos/ellas/ustedes)	daban

FUTURE

(yo)	daré
(tú)	darás
(él/ella/usted)	dará
(nosotros/as)	daremos
(vosotros/as)	daréis
(ellos/ellas/ustedes)	darán

CONDITIONAL

(yo)	daría
(tú)	darías
(él/ella/usted)	daría
(nosotros/as)	daríamos
(vosotros/as)	daríais
(ellos/ellas/ustedes)	darían

IMPERATIVE

da / dad

PAST PARTICIPLE

dado

GERUND

dando

EXAMPLE PHRASES

*Me **da** miedo la oscuridad*. I'm scared of the dark.
*Nos **dieron** un par de entradas gratis*. They gave us a couple of free tickets.
*Te **daré** el número de mi móvil*. I'll give you my mobile-phone number.

Remember that subject pronouns are not used very often in Spanish.

▶ decir (to say, to tell)

PRESENT

(yo)	digo
(tú)	dices
(él/ella/usted)	dice
(nosotros/as)	decimos
(vosotros/as)	decís
(ellos/ellas/ustedes)	dicen

PRESENT SUBJUNCTIVE

(yo)	diga
(tú)	digas
(él/ella/usted)	diga
(nosotros/as)	digamos
(vosotros/as)	digáis
(ellos/ellas/ustedes)	digan

PRETERITE

(yo)	dije
(tú)	dijiste
(él/ella/usted)	dijo
(nosotros/as)	dijimos
(vosotros/as)	dijisteis
(ellos/ellas/ustedes)	dijeron

IMPERFECT

(yo)	decía
(tú)	decías
(él/ella/usted)	decía
(nosotros/as)	decíamos
(vosotros/as)	decíais
(ellos/ellas/ustedes)	decían

FUTURE

(yo)	diré
(tú)	dirás
(él/ella/usted)	dirá
(nosotros/as)	diremos
(vosotros/as)	diréis
(ellos/ellas/ustedes)	dirán

CONDITIONAL

(yo)	diría
(tú)	dirías
(él/ella/usted)	diría
(nosotros/as)	diríamos
(vosotros/as)	diríais
(ellos/ellas/ustedes)	dirían

IMPERATIVE

di / decid

PAST PARTICIPLE

dicho

GERUND

diciendo

EXAMPLE PHRASES

*¿Qué **dices**?* What are you saying?
*Me lo **dijo** ayer.* He told me yesterday.
*¿Te **ha dicho** lo de la boda?* Has he told you about the wedding?

Remember that subject pronouns are not used very often in Spanish.

▶ dormir (to sleep)

PRESENT

(yo)	duermo
(tú)	duermes
(él/ella/usted)	duerme
(nosotros/as)	dormimos
(vosotros/as)	dormís
(ellos/ellas/ustedes)	duermen

PRESENT SUBJUNCTIVE

(yo)	duerma
(tú)	duermas
(él/ella/usted)	duerma
(nosotros/as)	durmamos
(vosotros/as)	durmáis
(ellos/ellas/ustedes)	duerman

PRETERITE

(yo)	dormí
(tú)	dormiste
(él/ella/usted)	durmió
(nosotros/as)	dormimos
(vosotros/as)	dormisteis
(ellos/ellas/ustedes)	durmieron

IMPERFECT

(yo)	dormía
(tú)	dormías
(él/ella/usted)	dormía
(nosotros/as)	dormíamos
(vosotros/as)	dormíais
(ellos/ellas/ustedes)	dormían

FUTURE

(yo)	dormiré
(tú)	dormirás
(él/ella/usted)	dormirá
(nosotros/as)	dormiremos
(vosotros/as)	dormiréis
(ellos/ellas/ustedes)	dormirán

CONDITIONAL

(yo)	dormiría
(tú)	dormirías
(él/ella/usted)	dormiría
(nosotros/as)	dormiríamos
(vosotros/as)	dormiríais
(ellos/ellas/ustedes)	dormirían

IMPERATIVE

duerme / dormid

PAST PARTICIPLE

dormido

GERUND

durmiendo

EXAMPLE PHRASES

*No **duermo** muy bien.* I don't sleep very well.
***Nos dormimos** en el cine.* We fell asleep at the cinema.
***Durmió** durante doce horas.* He slept for twelve hours.

Remember that subject pronouns are not used very often in Spanish.

▶ empezar (to begin, to start)

PRESENT

(yo)	empiezo
(tú)	empiezas
(él/ella/usted)	empieza
(nosotros/as)	empezamos
(vosotros/as)	empezáis
(ellos/ellas/ustedes)	empiezan

PRESENT SUBJUNCTIVE

(yo)	empiece
(tú)	empieces
(él/ella/usted)	empiece
(nosotros/as)	empecemos
(vosotros/as)	empecéis
(ellos/ellas/ustedes)	empiecen

PRETERITE

(yo)	empecé
(tú)	empezaste
(él/ella/usted)	empezó
(nosotros/as)	empezamos
(vosotros/as)	empezasteis
(ellos/ellas/ustedes)	empezaron

IMPERFECT

(yo)	empezaba
(tú)	empezabas
(él/ella/usted)	empezaba
(nosotros/as)	empezábamos
(vosotros/as)	empezabais
(ellos/ellas/ustedes)	empezaban

FUTURE

(yo)	empezaré
(tú)	empezarás
(él/ella/usted)	empezará
(nosotros/as)	empezaremos
(vosotros/as)	empezaréis
(ellos/ellas/ustedes)	empezarán

CONDITIONAL

(yo)	empezaría
(tú)	empezarías
(él/ella/usted)	empezaría
(nosotros/as)	empezaríamos
(vosotros/as)	empezaríais
(ellos/ellas/ustedes)	empezarían

IMPERATIVE

empieza / empezad

PAST PARTICIPLE

empezado

GERUND

empezando

EXAMPLE PHRASES

***Empieza** por aquí.* Start here.
*¿Cuándo **empiezas** a trabajar en el sitio nuevo?* When do you start work at the new place?
*La semana que viene **empezaremos** un curso nuevo.* We'll start a new course next week.

Remember that subject pronouns are not used very often in Spanish.

▶ entender (to understand)

PRESENT		PRESENT SUBJUNCTIVE	
(yo)	entiendo	(yo)	entienda
(tú)	entiendes	(tú)	entiendas
(él/ella/usted)	entiende	(él/ella/usted)	entienda
(nosotros/as)	entendemos	(nosotros/as)	entendamos
(vosotros/as)	entendéis	(vosotros/as)	entendáis
(ellos/ellas/ustedes)	entienden	(ellos/ellas/ustedes)	entiendan

PRETERITE		IMPERFECT	
(yo)	entendí	(yo)	entendía
(tú)	entendiste	(tú)	entendías
(él/ella/usted)	entendió	(él/ella/usted)	entendía
(nosotros/as)	entendimos	(nosotros/as)	entendíamos
(vosotros/as)	entendisteis	(vosotros/as)	entendíais
(ellos/ellas/ustedes)	entendieron	(ellos/ellas/ustedes)	entendían

FUTURE		CONDITIONAL	
(yo)	entenderé	(yo)	entendería
(tú)	entenderás	(tú)	entenderías
(él/ella/usted)	entenderá	(él/ella/usted)	entendería
(nosotros/as)	entenderemos	(nosotros/as)	entenderíamos
(vosotros/as)	entenderéis	(vosotros/as)	entenderíais
(ellos/ellas/ustedes)	entenderán	(ellos/ellas/ustedes)	entenderían

IMPERATIVE

entiende / entended

PAST PARTICIPLE

entendido

GERUND

entendiendo

EXAMPLE PHRASES

*No lo **entiendo**.* I don't understand.
*¿**Entendiste** lo que dijo?* Did you understand what she said?
*Con el tiempo lo **entenderás**.* You'll understand one day.

Remember that subject pronouns are not used very often in Spanish.

▶ enviar (to send)

PRESENT

(yo)	envío
(tú)	envías
(él/ella/usted)	envía
(nosotros/as)	enviamos
(vosotros/as)	enviáis
(ellos/ellas/ustedes)	envían

PRESENT SUBJUNCTIVE

(yo)	envíe
(tú)	envíes
(él/ella/usted)	envíe
(nosotros/as)	enviemos
(vosotros/as)	enviéis
(ellos/ellas/ustedes)	envíen

PRETERITE

(yo)	envié
(tú)	enviaste
(él/ella/usted)	envió
(nosotros/as)	enviamos
(vosotros/as)	enviasteis
(ellos/ellas/ustedes)	enviaron

IMPERFECT

(yo)	enviaba
(tú)	enviabas
(él/ella/usted)	enviaba
(nosotros/as)	enviábamos
(vosotros/as)	enviabais
(ellos/ellas/ustedes)	enviaban

FUTURE

(yo)	enviaré
(tú)	enviarás
(él/ella/usted)	enviará
(nosotros/as)	enviaremos
(vosotros/as)	enviaréis
(ellos/ellas/ustedes)	enviarán

CONDITIONAL

(yo)	enviaría
(tú)	enviarías
(él/ella/usted)	enviaría
(nosotros/as)	enviaríamos
(vosotros/as)	enviaríais
(ellos/ellas/ustedes)	enviarían

IMPERATIVE

envía / enviad

PAST PARTICIPLE

enviado

GERUND

enviando

EXAMPLE PHRASES

Envíe *todos sus datos personales.* Send all your personal details.
La han ***enviado*** *a Guatemala.* They've sent her to Guatemala.
Nos ***enviarán*** *más información.* They'll send us further information.

Remember that subject pronouns are not used very often in Spanish.

▶ estar (to be)

PRESENT

(yo)	estoy
(tú)	estás
(él/ella/usted)	está
(nosotros/as)	estamos
(vosotros/as)	estáis
(ellos/ellas/ustedes)	están

PRESENT SUBJUNCTIVE

(yo)	esté
(tú)	estés
(él/ella/usted)	esté
(nosotros/as)	estemos
(vosotros/as)	estéis
(ellos/ellas/ustedes)	estén

PRETERITE

(yo)	estuve
(tú)	estuviste
(él/ella/usted)	estuvo
(nosotros/as)	estuvimos
(vosotros/as)	estuvisteis
(ellos/ellas/ustedes)	estuvieron

IMPERFECT

(yo)	estaba
(tú)	estabas
(él/ella/usted)	estaba
(nosotros/as)	estábamos
(vosotros/as)	estabais
(ellos/ellas/ustedes)	estaban

FUTURE

(yo)	estaré
(tú)	estarás
(él/ella/usted)	estará
(nosotros/as)	estaremos
(vosotros/as)	estaréis
(ellos/ellas/ustedes)	estarán

CONDITIONAL

(yo)	estaría
(tú)	estarías
(él/ella/usted)	estaría
(nosotros/as)	estaríamos
(vosotros/as)	estaríais
(ellos/ellas/ustedes)	estarían

IMPERATIVE

está / estad

PAST PARTICIPLE

estado

GERUND

estando

EXAMPLE PHRASES

Estoy *cansado.* I'm tired.
Estuvimos *en casa de mis padres.* We were at my parents' place.
¿A qué hora ***estarás*** *en casa?* What time will you be home?

Remember that subject pronouns are not used very often in Spanish.

▶ haber (to have (auxiliary))

PRESENT

(yo)	he
(tú)	has
(él/ella/usted)	ha
(nosotros/as)	hemos
(vosotros/as)	habéis
(ellos/ellas/ustedes)	han

PRESENT SUBJUNCTIVE

(yo)	haya
(tú)	hayas
(él/ella/usted)	haya
(nosotros/as)	hayamos
(vosotros/as)	hayáis
(ellos/ellas/ustedes)	hayan

PRETERITE

(yo)	hube
(tú)	hubiste
(él/ella/usted)	hubo
(nosotros/as)	hubimos
(vosotros/as)	hubisteis
(ellos/ellas/ustedes)	hubieron

IMPERFECT

(yo)	había
(tú)	habías
(él/ella/usted)	había
(nosotros/as)	habíamos
(vosotros/as)	habíais
(ellos/ellas/ustedes)	habían

FUTURE

(yo)	habré
(tú)	habrás
(él/ella/usted)	habrá
(nosotros/as)	habremos
(vosotros/as)	habréis
(ellos/ellas/ustedes)	habrán

CONDITIONAL

(yo)	habría
(tú)	habrías
(él/ella/usted)	habría
(nosotros/as)	habríamos
(vosotros/as)	habríais
(ellos/ellas/ustedes)	habrían

IMPERATIVE

not used

PAST PARTICIPLE

habido

GERUND

habiendo

EXAMPLE PHRASES

*¿**Has visto** eso?* Did you see that?
*Ya **hemos ido** a ver esa película.* We've already been to see that film.
*Eso nunca **había pasado** antes.* That had never happened before.

Remember that subject pronouns are not used very often in Spanish.

▶ hablar (to speak, to talk)

PRESENT

(yo)	hablo
(tú)	hablas
(él/ella/usted)	habla
(nosotros/as)	hablamos
(vosotros/as)	habláis
(ellos/ellas/ustedes)	hablan

PRESENT SUBJUNCTIVE

(yo)	hable
(tú)	hables
(él/ella/usted)	hable
(nosotros/as)	hablemos
(vosotros/as)	habléis
(ellos/ellas/ustedes)	hablen

PRETERITE

(yo)	hablé
(tú)	hablaste
(él/ella/usted)	habló
(nosotros/as)	hablamos
(vosotros/as)	hablasteis
(ellos/ellas/ustedes)	hablaron

IMPERFECT

(yo)	hablaba
(tú)	hablabas
(él/ella/usted)	hablaba
(nosotros/as)	hablábamos
(vosotros/as)	hablabais
(ellos/ellas/ustedes)	hablaban

FUTURE

(yo)	hablaré
(tú)	hablarás
(él/ella/usted)	hablará
(nosotros/as)	hablaremos
(vosotros/as)	hablaréis
(ellos/ellas/ustedes)	hablarán

CONDITIONAL

(yo)	hablaría
(tú)	hablarías
(él/ella/usted)	hablaría
(nosotros/as)	hablaríamos
(vosotros/as)	hablaríais
(ellos/ellas/ustedes)	hablarían

IMPERATIVE

habla / hablad

PAST PARTICIPLE

hablado

GERUND

hablando

EXAMPLE PHRASES

*Hoy **he hablado** con mi hermana.* I've spoken to my sister today.
*No **hables** tan alto.* Don't talk so loud.
*No **se hablan**.* They don't talk to each other.

Remember that subject pronouns are not used very often in Spanish.

▶ hacer (to do, to make)

PRESENT

(yo)	hago
(tú)	haces
(él/ella/usted)	hace
(nosotros/as)	hacemos
(vosotros/as)	hacéis
(ellos/ellas/ustedes)	hacen

PRESENT SUBJUNCTIVE

(yo)	haga
(tú)	hagas
(él/ella/usted)	haga
(nosotros/as)	hagamos
(vosotros/as)	hagáis
(ellos/ellas/ustedes)	hagan

PRETERITE

(yo)	hice
(tú)	hiciste
(él/ella/usted)	hizo
(nosotros/as)	hicimos
(vosotros/as)	hicisteis
(ellos/ellas/ustedes)	hicieron

IMPERFECT

(yo)	hacía
(tú)	hacías
(él/ella/usted)	hacía
(nosotros/as)	hacíamos
(vosotros/as)	hacíais
(ellos/ellas/ustedes)	hacían

FUTURE

(yo)	haré
(tú)	harás
(él/ella/usted)	hará
(nosotros/as)	haremos
(vosotros/as)	haréis
(ellos/ellas/ustedes)	harán

CONDITIONAL

(yo)	haría
(tú)	harías
(él/ella/usted)	haría
(nosotros/as)	haríamos
(vosotros/as)	haríais
(ellos/ellas/ustedes)	harían

IMPERATIVE

haz / haced

PAST PARTICIPLE

hecho

GERUND

haciendo

EXAMPLE PHRASES

*Lo **haré** yo mismo. I'll do it myself.*
*¿Quién **hizo** eso?* Who did that?
*Quieres que **haga** las camas?* Do you want me to make the beds?

Remember that subject pronouns are not used very often in Spanish.

▶ ir (to go)

PRESENT

(yo)	voy
(tú)	vas
(él/ella/usted)	va
(nosotros/as)	vamos
(vosotros/as)	vais
(ellos/ellas/ustedes)	van

PRESENT SUBJUNCTIVE

(yo)	vaya
(tú)	vayas
(él/ella/usted)	vaya
(nosotros/as)	vayamos
(vosotros/as)	vayáis
(ellos/ellas/ustedes)	vayan

PRETERITE

(yo)	fui
(tú)	fuiste
(él/ella/usted)	fue
(nosotros/as)	fuimos
(vosotros/as)	fuisteis
(ellos/ellas/ustedes)	fueron

IMPERFECT

(yo)	iba
(tú)	ibas
(él/ella/usted)	iba
(nosotros/as)	íbamos
(vosotros/as)	ibais
(ellos/ellas/ustedes)	iban

FUTURE

(yo)	iré
(tú)	irás
(él/ella/usted)	irá
(nosotros/as)	iremos
(vosotros/as)	iréis
(ellos/ellas/ustedes)	irán

CONDITIONAL

(yo)	iría
(tú)	irías
(él/ella/usted)	iría
(nosotros/as)	iríamos
(vosotros/as)	iríais
(ellos/ellas/ustedes)	irían

IMPERATIVE

ve / id

PAST PARTICIPLE

ido

GERUND

yendo

EXAMPLE PHRASES

*¿**Vamos** a comer al campo?* Shall we have a picnic in the country?
*El domingo **iré** a Edimburgo.* I'll go to Edinburgh on Sunday.
*Yo no **voy** con ellos.* I'm not going with them.

Remember that subject pronouns are not used very often in Spanish.

▶ lavarse (to wash oneself)

PRESENT

(yo)	me lavo
(tú)	te lavas
(él/ella/usted)	se lava
(nosotros/as)	nos lavamos
(vosotros/as)	os laváis
(ellos/ellas/ustedes)	se lavan

PRESENT SUBJUNCTIVE

(yo)	me lave
(tú)	te laves
(él/ella/usted)	se lave
(nosotros/as)	nos lavemos
(vosotros/as)	os lavéis
(ellos/ellas/ustedes)	se laven

PRETERITE

(yo)	me lavé
(tú)	te lavaste
(él/ella/usted)	se lavó
(nosotros/as)	nos lavamos
(vosotros/as)	os lavasteis
(ellos/ellas/ustedes)	se lavaron

IMPERFECT

(yo)	me lavaba
(tú)	te lavabas
(él/ella/usted)	se lavaba
(nosotros/as)	nos lavábamos
(vosotros/as)	os lavabais
(ellos/ellas/ustedes)	se lavaban

FUTURE

(yo)	me lavaré
(tú)	te lavarás
(él/ella/usted)	se lavará
(nosotros/as)	nos lavaremos
(vosotros/as)	os lavaréis
(ellos/ellas/ustedes)	se lavarán

CONDITIONAL

(yo)	me lavaría
(tú)	te lavarías
(él/ella/usted)	se lavaría
(nosotros/as)	nos lavaríamos
(vosotros/as)	os lavaríais
(ellos/ellas/ustedes)	se lavarían

IMPERATIVE

lávate / lavaos

PAST PARTICIPLE

lavado

GERUND

lavándose

EXAMPLE PHRASES

***Se lava** todos los días.* He washes every day.
*Ayer **me lavé** el pelo.* I washed my hair yesterday.
***Nos lavaremos** con agua fría.* We'll wash in cold water.

Remember that subject pronouns are not used very often in Spanish.

▶ leer (to read)

PRESENT

(yo)	leo
(tú)	lees
(él/ella/usted)	lee
(nosotros/as)	leemos
(vosotros/as)	leéis
(ellos/ellas/ustedes)	leen

PRESENT SUBJUNCTIVE

(yo)	lea
(tú)	leas
(él/ella/usted)	lea
(nosotros/as)	leamos
(vosotros/as)	leáis
(ellos/ellas/ustedes)	lean

PRETERITE

(yo)	leí
(tú)	leíste
(él/ella/usted)	leyó
(nosotros/as)	leímos
(vosotros/as)	leísteis
(ellos/ellas/ustedes)	leyeron

IMPERFECT

(yo)	leía
(tú)	leías
(él/ella/usted)	leía
(nosotros/as)	leíamos
(vosotros/as)	leíais
(ellos/ellas/ustedes)	leían

FUTURE

(yo)	leeré
(tú)	leerás
(él/ella/usted)	leerá
(nosotros/as)	leeremos
(vosotros/as)	leeréis
(ellos/ellas/ustedes)	leerán

CONDITIONAL

(yo)	leería
(tú)	leerías
(él/ella/usted)	leería
(nosotros/as)	leeríamos
(vosotros/as)	leeríais
(ellos/ellas/ustedes)	leerían

IMPERATIVE

lee / leed

PAST PARTICIPLE

leído

GERUND

leyendo

EXAMPLE PHRASES

Hace mucho tiempo que no ***leo***. I haven't read anything for ages.
*¿**Has leído** esta novela?* Have you read this novel?
Lo ***leí*** *hace tiempo.* I read it a while ago.

Remember that subject pronouns are not used very often in Spanish.

▶ oír (to hear)

PRESENT

(yo)	oigo
(tú)	oyes
(él/ella/usted)	oye
(nosotros/as)	oímos
(vosotros/as)	oís
(ellos/ellas/ustedes)	oyen

PRESENT SUBJUNCTIVE

(yo)	oiga
(tú)	oigas
(él/ella/usted)	oiga
(nosotros/as)	oigamos
(vosotros/as)	oigáis
(ellos/ellas/ustedes)	oigan

PRETERITE

(yo)	oí
(tú)	oíste
(él/ella/usted)	oyó
(nosotros/as)	oímos
(vosotros/as)	oísteis
(ellos/ellas/ustedes)	oyeron

IMPERFECT

(yo)	oía
(tú)	oías
(él/ella/usted)	oía
(nosotros/as)	oíamos
(vosotros/as)	oíais
(ellos/ellas/ustedes)	oían

FUTURE

(yo)	oiré
(tú)	oirás
(él/ella/usted)	oirá
(nosotros/as)	oiremos
(vosotros/as)	oiréis
(ellos/ellas/ustedes)	oirán

CONDITIONAL

(yo)	oiría
(tú)	oirías
(él/ella/usted)	oiría
(nosotros/as)	oiríamos
(vosotros/as)	oiríais
(ellos/ellas/ustedes)	oirían

IMPERATIVE

oye / oíd

PAST PARTICIPLE

oído

GERUND

oyendo

EXAMPLE PHRASES

*No **oigo** nada.* I can't hear anything.
*Si no **oyes** bien, ve al médico.* If you can't hear properly, go and see the doctor.
*¿**Has oído** eso?* Did you hear that?

Remember that subject pronouns are not used very often in Spanish.

▶ pedir (to ask for)

PRESENT

(yo)	pido
(tú)	pides
(él/ella/usted)	pide
(nosotros/as)	pedimos
(vosotros/as)	pedís
(ellos/ellas/ustedes)	piden

PRESENT SUBJUNCTIVE

(yo)	pida
(tú)	pidas
(él/ella/usted)	pida
(nosotros/as)	pidamos
(vosotros/as)	pidáis
(ellos/ellas/ustedes)	pidan

PRETERITE

(yo)	pedí
(tú)	pediste
(él/ella/usted)	pidió
(nosotros/as)	pedimos
(vosotros/as)	pedisteis
(ellos/ellas/ustedes)	pidieron

IMPERFECT

(yo)	pedía
(tú)	pedías
(él/ella/usted)	pedía
(nosotros/as)	pedíamos
(vosotros/as)	pedíais
(ellos/ellas/ustedes)	pedían

FUTURE

(yo)	pediré
(tú)	pedirás
(él/ella/usted)	pedirá
(nosotros/as)	pediremos
(vosotros/as)	pediréis
(ellos/ellas/ustedes)	pedirán

CONDITIONAL

(yo)	pediría
(tú)	pedirías
(él/ella/usted)	pediría
(nosotros/as)	pediríamos
(vosotros/as)	pediríais
(ellos/ellas/ustedes)	pedirían

IMPERATIVE

pide / pedid

PAST PARTICIPLE

pedido

GERUND

pidiendo

EXAMPLE PHRASES

*No nos **pidieron** el pasaporte.* They didn't ask us for our passports.
***Hemos pedido** dos cervezas.* We've ordered two beers.
***Pídele** el teléfono.* Ask her for her telephone number.

Remember that subject pronouns are not used very often in Spanish.

▶ pensar (to think)

PRESENT

(yo)	pienso
(tú)	piensas
(él/ella/usted)	piensa
(nosotros/as)	pensamos
(vosotros/as)	pensáis
(ellos/ellas/ustedes)	piensan

PRESENT SUBJUNCTIVE

(yo)	piense
(tú)	pienses
(él/ella/usted)	piense
(nosotros/as)	pensemos
(vosotros/as)	penséis
(ellos/ellas/ustedes)	piensen

PRETERITE

(yo)	pensé
(tú)	pensaste
(él/ella/usted)	pensó
(nosotros/as)	pensamos
(vosotros/as)	pensasteis
(ellos/ellas/ustedes)	pensaron

IMPERFECT

(yo)	pensaba
(tú)	pensabas
(él/ella/usted)	pensaba
(nosotros/as)	pensábamos
(vosotros/as)	pensabais
(ellos/ellas/ustedes)	pensaban

FUTURE

(yo)	pensaré
(tú)	pensarás
(él/ella/usted)	pensará
(nosotros/as)	pensaremos
(vosotros/as)	pensaréis
(ellos/ellas/ustedes)	pensarán

CONDITIONAL

(yo)	pensaría
(tú)	pensarías
(él/ella/usted)	pensaría
(nosotros/as)	pensaríamos
(vosotros/as)	pensaríais
(ellos/ellas/ustedes)	pensarían

IMPERATIVE

piensa / pensad

PAST PARTICIPLE

pensado

GERUND

pensando

EXAMPLE PHRASES

No lo ***pienses*** *más.* Don't think any more about it.
Está pensando *en comprarse un piso.* He's thinking of buying a flat.
Pensaba *que vendrías.* I thought you'd come.

Remember that subject pronouns are not used very often in Spanish.

▶ poder (to be able to)

PRESENT

(yo)	puedo
(tú)	puedes
(él/ella/usted)	puede
(nosotros/as)	podemos
(vosotros/as)	podéis
(ellos/ellas/ustedes)	pueden

PRESENT SUBJUNCTIVE

(yo)	pueda
(tú)	puedas
(él/ella/usted)	pueda
(nosotros/as)	podamos
(vosotros/as)	podáis
(ellos/ellas/ustedes)	puedan

PRETERITE

(yo)	pude
(tú)	pudiste
(él/ella/usted)	pudo
(nosotros/as)	pudimos
(vosotros/as)	pudisteis
(ellos/ellas/ustedes)	pudieron

IMPERFECT

(yo)	podía
(tú)	podías
(él/ella/usted)	podía
(nosotros/as)	podíamos
(vosotros/as)	podíais
(ellos/ellas/ustedes)	podían

FUTURE

(yo)	podré
(tú)	podrás
(él/ella/usted)	podrá
(nosotros/as)	podremos
(vosotros/as)	podréis
(ellos/ellas/ustedes)	podrán

CONDITIONAL

(yo)	podría
(tú)	podrías
(él/ella/usted)	podría
(nosotros/as)	podríamos
(vosotros/as)	podríais
(ellos/ellas/ustedes)	podrían

IMPERATIVE

puede / poded

PAST PARTICIPLE

podido

GERUND

pudiendo

EXAMPLE PHRASES

¿***Puedo*** *entrar?* Can I come in?
Puedes *venir cuando quieras.* You can come when you like.
¿***Podrías*** *ayudarme?* Could you help me?

Remember that subject pronouns are not used very often in Spanish.

▶ poner (to put)

PRESENT

(yo)	pongo
(tú)	pones
(él/ella/usted)	pone
(nosotros/as)	ponemos
(vosotros/as)	ponéis
(ellos/ellas/ustedes)	ponen

PRESENT SUBJUNCTIVE

(yo)	ponga
(tú)	pongas
(él/ella/usted)	ponga
(nosotros/as)	pongamos
(vosotros/as)	pongáis
(ellos/ellas/ustedes)	pongan

PRETERITE

(yo)	puse
(tú)	pusiste
(él/ella/usted)	puso
(nosotros/as)	pusimos
(vosotros/as)	pusisteis
(ellos/ellas/ustedes)	pusieron

IMPERFECT

(yo)	ponía
(tú)	ponías
(él/ella/usted)	ponía
(nosotros/as)	poníamos
(vosotros/as)	poníais
(ellos/ellas/ustedes)	ponían

FUTURE

(yo)	pondré
(tú)	pondrás
(él/ella/usted)	pondrá
(nosotros/as)	pondremos
(vosotros/as)	pondréis
(ellos/ellas/ustedes)	pondrán

CONDITIONAL

(yo)	pondría
(tú)	pondrías
(él/ella/usted)	pondría
(nosotros/as)	pondríamos
(vosotros/as)	pondríais
(ellos/ellas/ustedes)	pondrían

IMPERATIVE

pon / poned

PAST PARTICIPLE

puesto

GERUND

poniendo

EXAMPLE PHRASES

Ponlo *ahí encima*. Put it on there.
Lo ***pondré*** *aquí*. I'll put it here.
Todos ***nos pusimos*** *de acuerdo*. We all agreed.

Remember that subject pronouns are not used very often in Spanish.

▸ querer (to want, to love)

PRESENT

(yo)	quiero
(tú)	quieres
(él/ella/usted)	quiere
(nosotros/as)	queremos
(vosotros/as)	queréis
(ellos/ellas/ustedes)	quieren

PRESENT SUBJUNCTIVE

(yo)	quiera
(tú)	quieras
(él/ella/usted)	quiera
(nosotros/as)	queramos
(vosotros/as)	queráis
(ellos/ellas/ustedes)	quieran

PRETERITE

(yo)	quise
(tú)	quisiste
(él/ella/usted)	quiso
(nosotros/as)	quisimos
(vosotros/as)	quisisteis
(ellos/ellas/ustedes)	quisieron

IMPERFECT

(yo)	quería
(tú)	querías
(él/ella/usted)	quería
(nosotros/as)	queríamos
(vosotros/as)	queríais
(ellos/ellas/ustedes)	querían

FUTURE

(yo)	querré
(tú)	querrás
(él/ella/usted)	querrá
(nosotros/as)	querremos
(vosotros/as)	querréis
(ellos/ellas/ustedes)	querrán

CONDITIONAL

(yo)	querría
(tú)	querrías
(él/ella/usted)	querría
(nosotros/as)	querríamos
(vosotros/as)	querríais
(ellos/ellas/ustedes)	querrían

IMPERATIVE

quiere / quered

PAST PARTICIPLE

querido

GERUND

queriendo

EXAMPLE PHRASES

*Te **quiero**.* I love you.
***Quisiera** preguntar una cosa.* I'd like to ask something.
*No **quería** decírmelo.* She didn't want to tell me.

Remember that subject pronouns are not used very often in Spanish.

▶ saber (to know)

PRESENT

(yo)	sé
(tú)	sabes
(él/ella/usted)	sabe
(nosotros/as)	sabemos
(vosotros/as)	sabéis
(ellos/ellas/ustedes)	saben

PRESENT SUBJUNCTIVE

(yo)	sepa
(tú)	sepas
(él/ella/usted)	sepa
(nosotros/as)	sepamos
(vosotros/as)	sepáis
(ellos/ellas/ustedes)	sepan

PRETERITE

(yo)	supe
(tú)	supiste
(él/ella/usted)	supo
(nosotros/as)	supimos
(vosotros/as)	supisteis
(ellos/ellas/ustedes)	supieron

IMPERFECT

(yo)	sabía
(tú)	sabías
(él/ella/usted)	sabía
(nosotros/as)	sabíamos
(vosotros/as)	sabíais
(ellos/ellas/ustedes)	sabían

FUTURE

(yo)	sabré
(tú)	sabrás
(él/ella/usted)	sabrá
(nosotros/as)	sabremos
(vosotros/as)	sabréis
(ellos/ellas/ustedes)	sabrán

CONDITIONAL

(yo)	sabría
(tú)	sabrías
(él/ella/usted)	sabría
(nosotros/as)	sabríamos
(vosotros/as)	sabríais
(ellos/ellas/ustedes)	sabrían

IMPERATIVE

sabe / sabed

PAST PARTICIPLE

sabido

GERUND

sabiendo

EXAMPLE PHRASES

No lo ***sé***. I don't know.
*¿**Sabes** una cosa?* Do you know what?
*Pensaba que lo **sabías***. I thought you knew.

Remember that subject pronouns are not used very often in Spanish.

▶ seguir (to follow)

PRESENT

(yo)	sigo
(tú)	sigues
(él/ella/usted)	sigue
(nosotros/as)	seguimos
(vosotros/as)	seguís
(ellos/ellas/ustedes)	siguen

PRESENT SUBJUNCTIVE

(yo)	siga
(tú)	sigas
(él/ella/usted)	siga
(nosotros/as)	sigamos
(vosotros/as)	sigáis
(ellos/ellas/ustedes)	sigan

PRETERITE

(yo)	seguí
(tú)	seguiste
(él/ella/usted)	siguió
(nosotros/as)	seguimos
(vosotros/as)	seguisteis
(ellos/ellas/ustedes)	siguieron

IMPERFECT

(yo)	seguía
(tú)	seguías
(él/ella/usted)	seguía
(nosotros/as)	seguíamos
(vosotros/as)	seguíais
(ellos/ellas/ustedes)	seguían

FUTURE

(yo)	seguiré
(tú)	seguirás
(él/ella/usted)	seguirá
(nosotros/as)	seguiremos
(vosotros/as)	seguiréis
(ellos/ellas/ustedes)	seguirán

CONDITIONAL

(yo)	seguiría
(tú)	seguirías
(él/ella/usted)	seguiría
(nosotros/as)	seguiríamos
(vosotros/as)	seguiríais
(ellos/ellas/ustedes)	seguirían

IMPERATIVE

sigue / seguid

PAST PARTICIPLE

seguido

GERUND

siguiendo

EXAMPLE PHRASES

***Siga** por esta calle hasta el final*. Go on till you get to the end of the street.
***Nos seguiremos** viendo*. We will go on seeing each other.
*Nos **siguió** todo el camino*. He followed us all the way.

Remember that subject pronouns are not used very often in Spanish.

▶ sentir (to feel)

PRESENT

(yo)	siento
(tú)	sientes
(él/ella/usted)	siente
(nosotros/as)	sentimos
(vosotros/as)	sentís
(ellos/ellas/ustedes)	sienten

PRESENT SUBJUNCTIVE

(yo)	sienta
(tú)	sientas
(él/ella/usted)	sienta
(nosotros/as)	sintamos
(vosotros/as)	sintáis
(ellos/ellas/ustedes)	sientan

PRETERITE

(yo)	sentí
(tú)	sentiste
(él/ella/usted)	sintió
(nosotros/as)	sentimos
(vosotros/as)	sentisteis
(ellos/ellas/ustedes)	sintieron

IMPERFECT

(yo)	sentía
(tú)	sentías
(él/ella/usted)	sentía
(nosotros/as)	sentíamos
(vosotros/as)	sentíais
(ellos/ellas/ustedes)	sentían

FUTURE

(yo)	sentiré
(tú)	sentirás
(él/ella/usted)	sentirá
(nosotros/as)	sentiremos
(vosotros/as)	sentiréis
(ellos/ellas/ustedes)	sentirán

CONDITIONAL

(yo)	sentiría
(tú)	sentirías
(él/ella/usted)	sentiría
(nosotros/as)	sentiríamos
(vosotros/as)	sentiríais
(ellos/ellas/ustedes)	sentirían

IMPERATIVE

siente / sentid

PAST PARTICIPLE

sentido

GERUND

sintiendo

EXAMPLE PHRASES

***Siento** mucho lo que pasó.* I'm really sorry about what happened.
***Sentí** un pinchazo en la pierna.* I felt a sharp pain in my leg.
*No creo que lo **sienta**.* I don't think she's sorry.

Remember that subject pronouns are not used very often in Spanish.

▶ ser (to be)

PRESENT

(yo)	soy
(tú)	eres
(él/ella/usted)	es
(nosotros/as)	somos
(vosotros/as)	sois
(ellos/ellas/ustedes)	son

PRESENT SUBJUNCTIVE

(yo)	sea
(tú)	seas
(él/ella/usted)	sea
(nosotros/as)	seamos
(vosotros/as)	seáis
(ellos/ellas/ustedes)	sean

PRETERITE

(yo)	fui
(tú)	fuiste
(él/ella/usted)	fue
(nosotros/as)	fuimos
(vosotros/as)	fuisteis
(ellos/ellas/ustedes)	fueron

IMPERFECT

(yo)	era
(tú)	eras
(él/ella/usted)	era
(nosotros/as)	éramos
(vosotros/as)	erais
(ellos/ellas/ustedes)	eran

FUTURE

(yo)	seré
(tú)	serás
(él/ella/usted)	será
(nosotros/as)	seremos
(vosotros/as)	seréis
(ellos/ellas/ustedes)	serán

CONDITIONAL

(yo)	sería
(tú)	serías
(él/ella/usted)	sería
(nosotros/as)	seríamos
(vosotros/as)	seríais
(ellos/ellas/ustedes)	serían

IMPERATIVE

sé / sed

PAST PARTICIPLE

sido

GERUND

siendo

EXAMPLE PHRASES

***Soy** español.* I'm Spanish.
*¿**Fuiste** tú el que llamó?* Was it you who phoned?
***Era** de noche.* It was dark.

Remember that subject pronouns are not used very often in Spanish.

▶ tener (to have)

PRESENT

(yo)	tengo
(tú)	tienes
(él/ella/usted)	tiene
(nosotros/as)	tenemos
(vosotros/as)	tenéis
(ellos/ellas/ustedes)	tienen

PRESENT SUBJUNCTIVE

(yo)	tenga
(tú)	tengas
(él/ella/usted)	tenga
(nosotros/as)	tengamos
(vosotros/as)	tengáis
(ellos/ellas/ustedes)	tengan

PRETERITE

(yo)	tuve
(tú)	tuviste
(él/ella/usted)	tuvo
(nosotros/as)	tuvimos
(vosotros/as)	tuvisteis
(ellos/ellas/ustedes)	tuvieron

IMPERFECT

(yo)	tenía
(tú)	tenías
(él/ella/usted)	tenía
(nosotros/as)	teníamos
(vosotros/as)	teníais
(ellos/ellas/ustedes)	tenían

FUTURE

(yo)	tendré
(tú)	tendrás
(él/ella/usted)	tendrá
(nosotros/as)	tendremos
(vosotros/as)	tendréis
(ellos/ellas/ustedes)	tendrán

CONDITIONAL

(yo)	tendría
(tú)	tendrías
(él/ella/usted)	tendría
(nosotros/as)	tendríamos
(vosotros/as)	tendríais
(ellos/ellas/ustedes)	tendrían

IMPERATIVE

ten / tened

PAST PARTICIPLE

tenido

GERUND

teniendo

EXAMPLE PHRASES

***Tengo** sed.* I'm thirsty.
*No **tenía** suficiente dinero.* She didn't have enough money.
***Tuvimos** que irnos.* We had to leave.

Remember that subject pronouns are not used very often in Spanish.

▶ traer (to bring)

PRESENT

(yo)	traigo
(tú)	traes
(él/ella/usted)	trae
(nosotros/as)	traemos
(vosotros/as)	traéis
(ellos/ellas/ustedes)	traen

PRESENT SUBJUNCTIVE

(yo)	traiga
(tú)	traigas
(él/ella/usted)	traiga
(nosotros/as)	traigamos
(vosotros/as)	traigáis
(ellos/ellas/ustedes)	traigan

PRETERITE

(yo)	traje
(tú)	trajiste
(él/ella/usted)	trajo
(nosotros/as)	trajimos
(vosotros/as)	trajisteis
(ellos/ellas/ustedes)	trajeron

IMPERFECT

(yo)	traía
(tú)	traías
(él/ella/usted)	traía
(nosotros/as)	traíamos
(vosotros/as)	traíais
(ellos/ellas/ustedes)	traían

FUTURE

(yo)	traeré
(tú)	traerás
(él/ella/usted)	traerá
(nosotros/as)	traeremos
(vosotros/as)	traeréis
(ellos/ellas/ustedes)	traerán

CONDITIONAL

(yo)	traería
(tú)	traerías
(él/ella/usted)	traería
(nosotros/as)	traeríamos
(vosotros/as)	traeríais
(ellos/ellas/ustedes)	traerían

IMPERATIVE

trae / traed

PAST PARTICIPLE

traído

GERUND

trayendo

EXAMPLE PHRASES

*¿**Has traído** lo que te pedí?* Did you bring what I asked you to?
*No **trajo** el dinero.* He didn't bring the money.
***Trae** eso.* Give that here.

Remember that subject pronouns are not used very often in Spanish.

▶ venir (to come)

PRESENT

(yo)	vengo
(tú)	vienes
(él/ella/usted)	viene
(nosotros/as)	venimos
(vosotros/as)	venís
(ellos/ellas/ustedes)	vienen

PRESENT SUBJUNCTIVE

(yo)	venga
(tú)	vengas
(él/ella/usted)	venga
(nosotros/as)	vengamos
(vosotros/as)	vengáis
(ellos/ellas/ustedes)	vengan

PRETERITE

(yo)	vine
(tú)	viniste
(él/ella/usted)	vino
(nosotros/as)	vinimos
(vosotros/as)	vinisteis
(ellos/ellas/ustedes)	vinieron

IMPERFECT

(yo)	venía
(tú)	venías
(él/ella/usted)	venía
(nosotros/as)	veníamos
(vosotros/as)	veníais
(ellos/ellas/ustedes)	venían

FUTURE

(yo)	vendré
(tú)	vendrás
(él/ella/usted)	vendrá
(nosotros/as)	vendremos
(vosotros/as)	vendréis
(ellos/ellas/ustedes)	vendrán

CONDITIONAL

(yo)	vendría
(tú)	vendrías
(él/ella/usted)	vendría
(nosotros/as)	vendríamos
(vosotros/as)	vendríais
(ellos/ellas/ustedes)	vendrían

IMPERATIVE

ven / venid

PAST PARTICIPLE

venido

GERUND

viniendo

EXAMPLE PHRASES

***Vengo** andando desde la playa.* I've walked all the way from the beach.
*¿**Vendrás** conmigo al cine?* Will you come to the cinema with me?
*Prefiero que no **venga**.* I'd rather he didn't come.

Remember that subject pronouns are not used very often in Spanish.

▶ ver (to see)

PRESENT

(yo)	veo
(tú)	ves
(él/ella/usted)	ve
(nosotros/as)	vemos
(vosotros/as)	veis
(ellos/ellas/ustedes)	ven

PRESENT SUBJUNCTIVE

(yo)	vea
(tú)	veas
(él/ella/usted)	vea
(nosotros/as)	veamos
(vosotros/as)	veáis
(ellos/ellas/ustedes)	vean

PRETERITE

(yo)	vi
(tú)	viste
(él/ella/usted)	vio
(nosotros/as)	vimos
(vosotros/as)	visteis
(ellos/ellas/ustedes)	vieron

IMPERFECT

(yo)	veía
(tú)	veías
(él/ella/usted)	veía
(nosotros/as)	veíamos
(vosotros/as)	veíais
(ellos/ellas/ustedes)	veían

FUTURE

(yo)	veré
(tú)	verás
(él/ella/usted)	verá
(nosotros/as)	veremos
(vosotros/as)	veréis
(ellos/ellas/ustedes)	verán

CONDITIONAL

(yo)	vería
(tú)	verías
(él/ella/usted)	vería
(nosotros/as)	veríamos
(vosotros/as)	veríais
(ellos/ellas/ustedes)	verían

IMPERATIVE

ve / ved

PAST PARTICIPLE

visto

GERUND

viendo

EXAMPLE PHRASES

No ***veo*** *muy bien*. I can't see very well.
Los ***veía*** *a todos desde la ventana*. I could see them all from the window.
*¿****Viste*** *lo que pasó?* Did you see what happened?

Remember that subject pronouns are not used very often in Spanish.

▶ vivir (to live)

PRESENT

(yo)	vivo
(tú)	vives
(él/ella/usted)	vive
(nosotros/as)	vivimos
(vosotros/as)	vivís
(ellos/ellas/ustedes)	viven

PRESENT SUBJUNCTIVE

(yo)	viva
(tú)	vivas
(él/ella/usted)	viva
(nosotros/as)	vivamos
(vosotros/as)	viváis
(ellos/ellas/ustedes)	vivan

PRETERITE

(yo)	viví
(tú)	viviste
(él/ella/usted)	vivió
(nosotros/as)	vivimos
(vosotros/as)	vivisteis
(ellos/ellas/ustedes)	vivieron

IMPERFECT

(yo)	vivía
(tú)	vivías
(él/ella/usted)	vivía
(nosotros/as)	vivíamos
(vosotros/as)	vivíais
(ellos/ellas/ustedes)	vivían

FUTURE

(yo)	viviré
(tú)	vivirás
(él/ella/usted)	vivirá
(nosotros/as)	viviremos
(vosotros/as)	viviréis
(ellos/ellas/ustedes)	vivirán

CONDITIONAL

(yo)	viviría
(tú)	vivirías
(él/ella/usted)	viviría
(nosotros/as)	viviríamos
(vosotros/as)	viviríais
(ellos/ellas/ustedes)	vivirían

IMPERATIVE

vive / vivid

PAST PARTICIPLE

vivido

GERUND

viviendo

EXAMPLE PHRASES

Vivo *en Valencia*. I live in Valencia.
Vivieron *juntos dos años*. They lived together for two years.
Hemos vivido *momentos difíciles*. We've had some difficult times.

Remember that subject pronouns are not used very often in Spanish.

▶ volver (to return)

PRESENT

(yo)	vuelvo
(tú)	vuelves
(él/ella/usted)	vuelve
(nosotros/as)	volvemos
(vosotros/as)	volvéis
(ellos/ellas/ustedes)	vuelven

PRESENT SUBJUNCTIVE

(yo)	vuelva
(tú)	vuelvas
(él/ella/usted)	vuelva
(nosotros/as)	volvamos
(vosotros/as)	volváis
(ellos/ellas/ustedes)	vuelvan

PRETERITE

(yo)	volví
(tú)	volviste
(él/ella/usted)	volvió
(nosotros/as)	volvimos
(vosotros/as)	volvisteis
(ellos/ellas/ustedes)	volvieron

IMPERFECT

(yo)	volvía
(tú)	volvías
(él/ella/usted)	volvía
(nosotros/as)	volvíamos
(vosotros/as)	volvíais
(ellos/ellas/ustedes)	volvían

FUTURE

(yo)	volveré
(tú)	volverás
(él/ella/usted)	volverá
(nosotros/as)	volveremos
(vosotros/as)	volveréis
(ellos/ellas/ustedes)	volverán

CONDITIONAL

(yo)	volvería
(tú)	volverías
(él/ella/usted)	volvería
(nosotros/as)	volveríamos
(vosotros/as)	volveríais
(ellos/ellas/ustedes)	volverían

IMPERATIVE

vuelve / volved

PAST PARTICIPLE

vuelto

GERUND

volviendo

EXAMPLE PHRASES

Mi padre ***vuelve*** *mañana*. My father's coming back tomorrow.
No ***vuelvas*** *por aquí*. Don't come back here.
Ha vuelto *a casa*. He's gone back home.

Remember that subject pronouns are not used very often in Spanish.

1 Gerund **2** Imperative **3** Present **4** Preterite **5** Future **6** Present subjunctive **7** Past participle **8** Imperfect

Etc indicates that the irregular root is used for all persons of the tense, e.g. oír: **6** oiga, oigas, oiga, oigamos, oigáis, oigan

abrir 7 abierto
agradecer 3 agradezco **6** agradezca *etc*
almorzar 2 almuerza **3** almuerzo, almuerzas, almuerza, almuerzan **4** almorcé **6** almuerce, almuerces, almuerce, almorcemos, almorcéis, almuercen
andar 4 anduve, anduviste, anduvo, anduvimos, anduvisteis, anduvieron
aprobar 2 aprueba **3** apruebo, apruebas, aprueba, aprueban **6** apruebe, apruebes, apruebe, aprueben
atravesar 2 atraviesa **3** atravieso, atraviesas, atraviesa, atraviesan **6** atraviese, atravieses, atraviese, atraviesen
buscar 4 busqué **6** busque *etc*
caber 3 quepo **4** cupe, cupiste, cupo, cupimos, cupisteis, cupieron **5** cabré *etc* **6** quepa *etc*
caer 1 cayendo **3** caigo **4** caí, caíste, cayó, caímos, caísteis, cayeron **6** caiga *etc* **7** caído
cerrar 2 cierra **3** cierro, cierras, cierra, cierran **6** cierre, cierres, cierre, cierren
coger *see* Verb Table 2
colgar 2 cuelga **3** cuelgo, cuelgas, cuelga, cuelgan **4** colgué **6** cuelgue, cuelgues, cuelgue, colguemos, colguéis, cuelguen
comer (regular **-er** verb) *see* Verb Table 3
conducir 3 conduzco **4** conduje, condujiste condujo, condujimos, condujisteis, condujeron **6** conduzca *etc*
conocer 3 conozco **6** conozca *etc*
construir 1 construyendo **2** construye **3** construyo, construyes, construye, construyen **4** construyó, construyeron **6** construya *etc*
contar 2 cuenta **3** cuento, cuentas, cuenta, cuentan **6** cuente, cuentes, cuente, cuenten
continuar 2 continúa **3** continúo, continúas, continúa, continúan **6** continúe, continúes, continúe, continúen
corregir 3 corrijo, corriges, corrige, corrigen **4** corrigió, corrigieron, **6** corrija *etc*
creer 1 creyendo **4** creí, creíste, creyó, creímos, creísteis, creyeron **7** creído
cubrir 7 cubierto
dar *see* Verb Table 4
decir *see* Verb Table 5
descubrir 7 descubierto
despertar 2 despierta **3** despierto, despiertas, despierta, despiertan **6** despierte, despiertes, despierte, despierten
dirigir 3 dirijo **6** dirija, dirijas, dirija, dirijamos, dirijáis, dirijan
divertir 1 divirtiendo **2** divierte **3** divierto, diviertes, divierte, divierten **4** divirtió, divirtieron **6** divierta, diviertas, divierta, divirtamos, divirtáis, diviertan
dormir *see* Verb Table 6
empezar *see* Verb Table 7
encontrar 2 encuentra **3** encuentro, encuentras, encuentra, encuentran **6** encuentre, encuentres, encuentre, encuentren
entender *see* Verb Table 8
enviar *see* Verb Table 9
escribir 7 escrito
estar *see* Verb Table 10
freír 1 friendo **2** fríe, freíd **3** frío, fríes, fríe, freímos, freís, fríen **4** freí, freíste, frio, freímos, freísteis, frieron **5** freiré *etc* **6** fría, frías, fría, friamos, friais, frían **7** frito

haber *see* Verb Table 11
hablar (regular **-ar** verb) *see* Verb Table 12
hacer *see* Verb Table 13
imprimir **7** impreso
instruir **1** instruyendo **2** instruye **3** instruyo, instruyes, instruye, instruyen **4** instruyó, instruyeron **6** instruya *etc*
ir *see* Verb Table 14
jugar **2** juega **3** juego, juegas, juega, juegan **4** jugué **6** juegue *etc*
lavarse (regular **-ar** reflexive verb) *see* Verb Table 15
leer *see* Verb Table 16
marcar **4** marqué **6** marque *etc*
morir **1** muriendo **2** muere **3** muero, mueres, muere, mueren **4** murió, murieron **6** muera, mueras, muera, muramos, muráis, mueran **7** muerto
mover **2** mueve **3** muevo, mueves,mueve,mueven **6** mueva, muevas, mueva, muevan
negar **2** niega **3** niego, niegas, niega, niegan **4** negué **6** niegue, niegues, niegue, neguemos, neguéis, nieguen
oír *see* Verb Table 17
ofrecer **3** ofrezco **6** ofrezca *etc*
oler **2** huele **3** huelo, hueles, huele, huelen **6** huela, huelas, huela, huelan
pagar **4** pagué **6** pague *etc*
parecer **3** parezco **6** parezca *etc*
pedir *see* Verb Table 18
pensar *see* Verb Table 19
perder **2** pierde **3** pierdo, pierdes, pierde, pierden **6** pierda, pierdas, pierda, pierdan
poder *see* Verb Table 20
poner *see* Verb Table 21
preferir **1** prefiriendo **2** prefiere **3** prefiero, prefieres, prefiere, prefieren **4** prefirió, prefirieron **6** prefiera, prefieras, prefiera, prefiramos, prefiráis, prefieran
producir **3** produzco **4** produje, produjiste produjo, produjimos, produjisteis, produjeron **6** produzca *etc*
prohibir **2** prohíbe **3** prohíbo, prohíbes, prohíbe, prohíben **6** prohíba, prohíbas, prohíba, prohíban
querer *see* Verb Table 22
reír **2** ríe **3** río, ríes, ríe, reímos, reís, ríen **4** reí, reíste, rio, reímos, reísteis, rieron **6** ría, rías, ría, riamos, riais, rían
repetir **1** repitiendo **2** repite **3** repito, repites, repite, repiten **4** repitió, repitieron **6** repita etc
reunir **2** reúne **3** reúno, reúnes, reúne, reúnen, **6** reúna, reúnas, reúna, reúnan
rogar **2** ruega **3** ruego, ruegas, ruega, ruegan **4** rogué **6** ruegue, ruegues, ruegue, roguemos, roguéis, rueguen
romper **7** roto
saber *see* Verb Table 23
sacar **4** saqué **6** saque *etc*
salir **2** sal **3** salgo **5** saldré etc **6** salga *etc*
seguir *see* Verb Table 24
sentar **2** sienta **3** siento, sientas, sienta, sientan **6** siente, sientes, siente, sienten
sentir *see* Verb Table 25
ser *see* Verb Table 26
servir **1** sirviendo **2** sirve **3** sirvo, sirves, sirve, sirven **4** sirvió, sirvieron **6** sirva *etc*
soñar **2** sueña **3** sueño, sueñas, sueña, sueñan **6** sueñe, sueñes, sueñe, sueñen
tener *see* Verb Table 27
torcer **2** tuerce **3** tuerzo, tuerces, tuerce, tuercen **6** tuerza, tuerzas, tuerza, torzamos, torzáis, tuerzan
traer *see* Verb Table 28
valer **2** vale **3** valgo **5** valdré etc **6** valga *etc*
vencer **3** venzo **6** venza *etc*
venir *see* Verb Table 29
ver *see* Verb Table 30
vestir **1** vistiendo **2** viste **3** visto, vistes, viste, visten **4** vistió, vistieron **6** vista *etc*
vivir (regular **-ir** verb) *see* Verb Table 31
volver *see* Verb Table 32

A [eɪ] *n* (*Mus*) la *m*

KEYWORD

a [ə] (*before vowel or silent h: an*) *indef art*
1 un(a); **a book** un libro; **an apple** una manzana; **she's a doctor** (ella) es médica
2 (*instead of the number "one"*) un(a); **a year ago** hace un año; **a hundred/ thousand** *etc* **pounds** cien/mil *etc* libras
3 (*in expressing ratios, prices etc*): **3 a day/week** 3 al día/a la semana; **10 km an hour** 10 km por hora; **£5 a person** £5 por persona; **30p a kilo** 30p el kilo

A2 (BRIT: *Scol*) *n segunda parte de los "A levels"*
A.A. *n abbr* (BRIT: =*Automobile Association*) ≈ RACE *m* (SP); (=*Alcoholics Anonymous*) Alcohólicos Anónimos
A.A.A. (US) *n abbr* (=*American Automobile Association*) ≈ RACE *m* (SP)
aback [ə'bæk] *adv*: **to be taken ~** quedar desconcertado
abandon [ə'bændən] *vt* abandonar; (*give up*) renunciar a
abattoir ['æbətwɑː*] (BRIT) *n* matadero
abbey ['æbɪ] *n* abadía
abbreviation [əbriːvɪ'eɪʃən] *n* (*short form*) abreviatura
abdomen ['æbdəmən] *n* abdomen *m*
abduct [æb'dʌkt] *vt* raptar, secuestrar
abide [ə'baɪd] *vt*: **I can't ~ it/him** no lo/le puedo ver; **abide by** *vt fus* atenerse a
ability [ə'bɪlɪtɪ] *n* habilidad *f*, capacidad *f*; (*talent*) talento
able ['eɪbl] *adj* capaz; (*skilled*) hábil; **to be ~ to do sth** poder hacer algo
abnormal [æb'nɔːməl] *adj* anormal
aboard [ə'bɔːd] *adv* a bordo ▷ *prep* a bordo de
abolish [ə'bɔlɪʃ] *vt* suprimir, abolir
abolition [æbəu'lɪʃən] *n* supresión *f*, abolición *f*
abort [ə'bɔːt] *vt, vi* abortar; **abortion** [ə'bɔːʃən] *n* aborto; **to have an abortion** abortar, hacerse abortar

KEYWORD

about [ə'baut] *adv* 1 (*approximately*) más o menos, aproximadamente; **about a hundred/thousand** *etc* unos(unas) cien/mil *etc*; **it takes about 10 hours** se tarda unas *or* más o menos 10 horas; **at about 2 o'clock** sobre las dos; **I've just about finished** casi he terminado
2 (*referring to place*) por todas partes; **to leave things lying about** dejar las cosas (tiradas) por ahí; **to run about** correr por todas partes; **to walk about** pasearse, ir y venir
3: **to be about to do sth** estar a punto de hacer algo
▷ *prep* 1 (*relating to*) de, sobre, acerca de; **a book about London** un libro sobre *or* acerca de Londres; **what is it**

about? ¿de qué se trata?; **we talked about it** hablamos de eso *or* ello; **what** *or* **how about doing this?** ¿qué tal si hacemos esto?
2 (*referring to place*) por; **to walk about the town** caminar por la ciudad

above [ə'bʌv] *adv* encima, por encima, arriba ▷ *prep* encima de; (*greater than: in number*) más de; (*: in rank*) superior a; **mentioned ~** susodicho; **~ all** sobre todo
abroad [ə'brɔːd] *adv* (*to be*) en el extranjero; (*to go*) al extranjero
abrupt [ə'brʌpt] *adj* (*sudden*) brusco; (*curt*) áspero
abscess ['æbsɪs] *n* absceso
absence ['æbsəns] *n* ausencia
absent ['æbsənt] *adj* ausente; **absent-minded** *adj* distraído
absolute ['æbsəluːt] *adj* absoluto; **absolutely** [-'luːtlɪ] *adv* (*totally*) totalmente; (*certainly!*) ¡por supuesto (que sí)!
absorb [əb'zɔːb] *vt* absorber; **to be ~ed in a book** estar absorto en un libro; **absorbent cotton** (US) *n* algodón *m* hidrófilo; **absorbing** *adj* absorbente
abstain [əb'steɪn] *vi*: **to ~ (from)** abstenerse (de)
abstract ['æbstrækt] *adj* abstracto
absurd [əb'səːd] *adj* absurdo
abundance [ə'bʌndəns] *n* abundancia
abundant [ə'bʌndənt] *adj* abundante
abuse [*n* ə'bjuːs, *vb* ə'bjuːz] *n* (*insults*) insultos *mpl*, injurias *fpl*; (*ill-treatment*) malos tratos *mpl*; (*misuse*) abuso ▷ *vt* insultar; maltratar; abusar de; **abusive** *adj* ofensivo
abysmal [ə'bɪzməl] *adj* pésimo; (*failure*) garrafal; (*ignorance*) supino
academic [ækə'dɛmɪk] *adj* académico, universitario; (*pej: issue*) puramente teórico ▷ *n* estudioso/a, profesor(a) *m/f* universitario/a; **academic year** *n* (*Univ*) año *m* académico; (*Scol*) año *m* escolar
academy [ə'kædəmɪ] *n* (*learned body*) academia; (*school*) instituto, colegio; **~ of music** conservatorio
accelerate [æk'sɛləreɪt] *vt, vi* acelerar; **acceleration** [æksɛlə'reɪʃən] *n* aceleración *f*; **accelerator** (BRIT) *n* acelerador *m*
accent ['æksɛnt] *n* acento; (*fig*) énfasis *m*
accept [ək'sɛpt] *vt* aceptar; (*responsibility, blame*) admitir; **acceptable** *adj* aceptable; **acceptance** *n* aceptación *f*
access ['æksɛs] *n* acceso; **to have ~ to** tener libre acceso a; **accessible** [-'sɛsəbl] *adj* (*place, person*) accesible; (*knowledge etc*) asequible
accessory [æk'sɛsərɪ] *n* accesorio; (*Law*): **~ to** cómplice de
accident ['æksɪdənt] *n* accidente *m*; (*chance event*) casualidad *f*; **by ~** (*unintentionally*) sin querer; (*by chance*) por casualidad; **accidental** [-'dɛntl] *adj* accidental, fortuito; **accidentally** [-'dɛntəlɪ] *adv* sin querer; por casualidad; **Accident and Emergency Department** *n* (BRIT) Urgencias *fpl*; **accident insurance** *n* seguro contra accidentes
acclaim [ə'kleɪm] *vt* aclamar, aplaudir ▷ *n* aclamación *f*, aplausos *mpl*
accommodate [ə'kɔmədeɪt] *vt* (*person*) alojar, hospedar; (*: car, hotel etc*) tener cabida para; (*oblige, help*) complacer
accommodation [əkɔmə'deɪʃən] (US **accommodations**) *n* alojamiento
accompaniment [ə'kʌmpənɪmənt] *n* acompañamiento
accompany [ə'kʌmpənɪ] *vt* acompañar
accomplice [ə'kʌmplɪs] *n* cómplice *mf*
accomplish [ə'kʌmplɪʃ] *vt* (*finish*) concluir; (*achieve*) lograr; **accomplishment** *n* (*skill: gen pl*)

talento; (*completion*) realización *f*

accord [əˈkɔːd] *n* acuerdo ▷*vt* conceder; **of his own ~** espontáneamente; **accordance** *n*: **in accordance with** de acuerdo con; **according** ▷ **according to** *prep* según; (*in accordance with*) conforme a; **accordingly** *adv* (*appropriately*) de acuerdo con esto; (*as a result*) en consecuencia

account [əˈkaunt] *n* (*Comm*) cuenta; (*report*) informe *m*; **accounts** *npl* (*Comm*) cuentas *fpl*; **of no ~** de ninguna importancia; **on ~** a cuenta; **on no ~** bajo ningún concepto; **on ~ of** a causa de, por motivo de; **to take into ~, take ~ of** tener en cuenta; **account for** *vt fus* (*explain*) explicar; (*represent*) representar; **accountable** *adj*: **accountable (to)** responsable (ante); **accountant** *n* contable *mf*, contador(a) *m/f*; **account number** *n* (*at bank etc*) número de cuenta

accumulate [əˈkjuːmjuleɪt] *vt* acumular ▷*vi* acumularse

accuracy [ˈækjurəsɪ] *n* (*of total*) exactitud *f*; (*of description etc*) precisión *f*

accurate [ˈækjurɪt] *adj* (*total*) exacto; (*description*) preciso; (*person*) cuidadoso; (*device*) de precisión; **accurately** *adv* con precisión

accusation [ækjuˈzeɪʃən] *n* acusación *f*

accuse [əˈkjuːz] *vt*: **to ~ sb (of sth)** acusar a algn (de algo); **accused** *n* (*Law*) acusado/a

accustomed [əˈkʌstəmd] *adj*: **~ to** acostumbrado a

ace [eɪs] *n* as *m*

ache [eɪk] *n* dolor *m* ▷*vi* doler; **my head ~s** me duele la cabeza

achieve [əˈtʃiːv] *vt* (*aim, result*) alcanzar; (*success*) lograr, conseguir; **achievement** *n* (*completion*) realización *f*; (*success*) éxito

acid [ˈæsɪd] *adj* ácido; (*taste*) agrio ▷*n* (*Chem, inf: LSD*) ácido

acknowledge [əkˈnɔlɪdʒ] *vt* (*letter: also*: **~ receipt of**) acusar recibo de; (*fact, situation, person*) reconocer; **acknowledgement** *n* acuse *m* de recibo

acne [ˈæknɪ] *n* acné *m*

acorn [ˈeɪkɔːn] *n* bellota

acoustic [əˈkuːstɪk] *adj* acústico

acquaintance [əˈkweɪntəns] *n* (*person*) conocido/a; (*with person, subject*) conocimiento

acquire [əˈkwaɪə*] *vt* adquirir; **acquisition** [ækwɪˈzɪʃən] *n* adquisición *f*

acquit [əˈkwɪt] *vt* absolver, exculpar; **to ~ o.s. well** salir con éxito

acre [ˈeɪkə*] *n* acre *m*

acronym [ˈækrənɪm] *n* siglas *fpl*

across [əˈkrɔs] *prep* (*on the other side of*) al otro lado de, del otro lado de; (*crosswise*) a través de ▷*adv* de un lado a otro, de una parte a otra; a través, al través; (*measurement*): **the road is 10m ~** la carretera tiene 10m de ancho; **to run/swim ~** atravesar corriendo/ nadando; **~ from** enfrente de

acrylic [əˈkrɪlɪk] *adj* acrílico ▷*n* acrílica

act [ækt] *n* acto, acción *f*; (*of play*) acto; (*in music hall etc*) número; (*Law*) decreto, ley *f* ▷*vi* (*behave*) comportarse; (*have effect: drug, chemical*) hacer efecto; (*Theatre*) actuar; (*pretend*) fingir; (*take action*) obrar ▷*vt* (*part*) hacer el papel de; **in the ~ of: to catch sb in the ~ of ...** pillar a algn en el momento en que ...; **to ~ as** actuar *or* hacer de; **act up** (*inf*) *vi* (*person*) portarse mal; **acting** *adj* suplente ▷*n* (*activity*) actuación *f*; (*profession*) profesión *f* de actor

action [ˈækʃən] *n* acción *f*, acto; (*Mil*) acción *f*, batalla; (*Law*) proceso, demanda; **out of ~** (*person*) fuera de combate; (*thing*) estropeado; **to take ~** tomar medidas; **action replay** *n* (*TV*) repetición *f*

activate [ˈæktɪveɪt] *vt* activar

active ['æktɪv] *adj* activo, enérgico; (*volcano*) en actividad; **actively** *adv* (*participate*) activamente; (*discourage, dislike*) enérgicamente
activist ['æktɪvɪst] *n* activista *m/f*
activity [-'tɪvɪtɪ] *n* actividad *f*; **activity holiday** *n vacaciones con actividades organizadas*
actor ['æktə*] *n* actor *m*, actriz *f*
actress ['aektrɪs] *n* actriz *f*
actual ['æktjuəl] *adj* verdadero, real; (*emphatic use*) propiamente dicho
Be careful not to translate **actual** by the Spanish word *actual*.
actually ['æktjuəlɪ] *adv* realmente, en realidad; (*even*) incluso
Be careful not to translate **actually** by the Spanish word *actualmente*.
acupuncture ['ækjupʌŋktʃə*] *n* acupuntura
acute [ə'kju:t] *adj* agudo
ad [æd] *n abbr* = **advertisement**
A.D. *adv abbr* (= *anno Domini*) DC
adamant ['ædəmənt] *adj* firme, inflexible
adapt [ə'dæpt] *vt* adaptar ▷ *vi*: **to ~ (to)** adaptarse (a), ajustarse (a); **adapter** (US **adaptor**) *n* (*Elec*) adaptador *m*; (*for several plugs*) ladrón *m*
add [æd] *vt* añadir, agregar; **add up** *vt* (*figures*) sumar ▷ *vi* (*fig*): **it doesn't add up** no tiene sentido; **add up to** *vt fus* (*Math*) sumar, ascender a; (*fig: mean*) querer decir, venir a ser
addict ['ædɪkt] *n* adicto/a; (*enthusiast*) entusiasta *mf*; **addicted** [ə'dɪktɪd] *adj*: **to be addicted to** ser adicto a, ser fanático de; **addiction** [ə'dɪkʃən] *n* (*to drugs etc*) adicción *f*; **addictive** [ə'dɪktɪv] *adj* que causa adicción
addition [ə'dɪʃən] *n* (*adding up*) adición *f*; (*thing added*) añadidura, añadido; **in ~** además, por añadidura; **in ~ to** además de; **additional** *adj* adicional
additive ['ædɪtɪv] *n* aditivo
address [ə'drɛs] *n* dirección *f*, señas *fpl*; (*speech*) discurso ▷ *vt* (*letter*) dirigir; (*speak to*) dirigirse a, dirigir la palabra a; (*problem*) tratar; **address book** *n* agenda (de direcciones)
adequate ['ædɪkwɪt] *adj* (*satisfactory*) adecuado; (*enough*) suficiente
adhere [əd'hɪə*] *vi*: **to ~ to** (*stick to*) pegarse a; (*fig: abide by*) observar; (*: belief etc*) ser partidario de
adhesive [əd'hi:zɪv] *n* adhesivo; **adhesive tape** *n* (BRIT) cinta adhesiva; (US *Med*) esparadrapo
adjacent [ə'dʒeɪsənt] *adj*: **~ to** contiguo a, inmediato a
adjective ['ædʒɛktɪv] *n* adjetivo
adjoining [ə'dʒɔɪnɪŋ] *adj* contiguo, vecino
adjourn [ə'dʒə:n] *vt* aplazar ▷ *vi* suspenderse
adjust [ə'dʒʌst] *vt* (*change*) modificar; (*clothing*) arreglar; (*machine*) ajustar ▷ *vi*: **to ~ (to)** adaptarse (a); **adjustable** *adj* ajustable; **adjustment** *n* adaptación *f*; (*to machine, prices*) ajuste *m*
administer [əd'mɪnɪstə*] *vt* administrar; **administration** [-'treɪʃən] *n* (*management*) administración *f*; (*government*) gobierno; **administrative** [-trətɪv] *adj* administrativo
administrator [əd'mɪnɪstreɪtə*] *n* administrador(a) *m/f*
admiral ['ædmərəl] *n* almirante *m*
admiration [ædmə'reɪʃən] *n* admiración *f*
admire [əd'maɪə*] *vt* admirar; **admirer** *n* (*fan*) admirador(a) *m/f*
admission [əd'mɪʃən] *n* (*to university, club*) ingreso; (*entry fee*) entrada; (*confession*) confesión *f*
admit [əd'mɪt] *vt* (*confess*) confesar; (*permit to enter*) dejar entrar, dar entrada a; (*to club, organization*) admitir; (*accept: defeat*) reconocer; **to be ~ted to hospital** ingresar en el hospital; **admit to** *vt fus* confesarse

culpable de; **admittance** *n* entrada; **admittedly** *adv* es cierto *or* verdad que

adolescent [ædəu'lɛsnt] *adj, n* adolescente *mf*

adopt [ə'dɔpt] *vt* adoptar; **adopted** *adj* adoptivo; **adoption** [ə'dɔpʃən] *n* adopción *f*

adore [ə'dɔː*] *vt* adorar

adorn [ə'dɔːn] *vt* adornar

Adriatic [eɪdrɪ'ætɪk] *n*: **the ~ (Sea)** el (Mar) Adriático

adrift [ə'drɪft] *adv* a la deriva

adult ['ædʌlt] *n* adulto/a ▷ *adj* (*grown-up*) adulto; (*for adults*) para adultos; **adult education** *n* educación *f* para adultos

adultery [ə'dʌltərɪ] *n* adulterio

advance [əd'vɑːns] *n* (*progress*) adelanto, progreso; (*money*) anticipo, préstamo; (*Mil*) avance *m* ▷ *adj*: **~ booking** venta anticipada; **~ notice, ~ warning** previo aviso ▷ *vt* (*money*) anticipar; (*theory, idea*) proponer (para la discusión) ▷ *vi* avanzar, adelantarse; **to make ~s (to sb)** hacer proposiciones (a algn); **in ~** por adelantado; **advanced** *adj* avanzado; (*Scol*: *studies*) adelantado

advantage [əd'vɑːntɪdʒ] *n* (*also Tennis*) ventaja; **to take ~ of** (*person*) aprovecharse de; (*opportunity*) aprovechar

advent ['ædvənt] *n* advenimiento; **A~** Adviento

adventure [əd'vɛntʃə*] *n* aventura; **adventurous** [-tʃərəs] *adj* atrevido; aventurero

adverb ['ædvəːb] *n* adverbio

adversary ['ædvəsərɪ] *n* adversario, contrario

adverse ['ædvəːs] *adj* adverso, contrario

advert ['ædvəːt] (BRIT) *n abbr* = **advertisement**

advertise ['ædvətaɪz] *vi* (*in newspaper etc*) anunciar, hacer publicidad; **to ~ for** (*staff, accommodation etc*) buscar por medio de anuncios ▷ *vt* anunciar; **advertisement** [əd'vəːtɪsmənt] *n* (*Comm*) anuncio; **advertiser** *n* anunciante *mf*; **advertising** *n* publicidad *f*, anuncios *mpl*; (*industry*) industria publicitaria

advice [əd'vaɪs] *n* consejo, consejos *mpl*; (*notification*) aviso; **a piece of ~** un consejo; **to take legal ~** consultar con un abogado

advisable [əd'vaɪzəbl] *adj* aconsejable, conveniente

advise [əd'vaɪz] *vt* aconsejar; (*inform*): **to ~ sb of sth** informar a algn de algo; **to ~ sb against sth/doing sth** desaconsejar algo a algn/aconsejar a algn que no haga algo; **adviser, advisor** *n* consejero/a; (*consultant*) asesor(a) *m/f*; **advisory** *adj* consultivo

advocate [*vb* 'ædvəkeɪt, *n* -kɪt] *vt* abogar por ▷ *n* (*lawyer*) abogado/a; (*supporter*): **~ of** defensor(a) *m/f* de

Aegean [iː'dʒiːən] *n*: **the ~ (Sea)** el (Mar) Egeo

aerial ['ɛərɪəl] *n* antena ▷ *adj* aéreo

aerobics [ɛə'rəubɪks] *n* aerobic *m*

aeroplane ['ɛərəpleɪn] (BRIT) *n* avión *m*

aerosol ['ɛərəsɔl] *n* aerosol *m*

affair [ə'fɛə*] *n* asunto; (*also*: **love ~**) aventura (amorosa)

affect [ə'fɛkt] *vt* (*influence*) afectar, influir en; (*afflict, concern*) afectar; (*move*) conmover; **affected** *adj* afectado; **affection** *n* afecto, cariño; **affectionate** *adj* afectuoso, cariñoso

afflict [ə'flɪkt] *vt* afligir

affluent ['aefluənt] *adj* (*wealthy*) acomodado; **the ~ society** la sociedad opulenta

afford [ə'fɔːd] *vt* (*provide*) proporcionar; **can we ~ (to buy) it?** ¿tenemos bastante dinero para comprarlo?; **affordable** *adj* asequible

Afghanistan [æf'gænɪstæn] *n* Afganistán *m*

afraid [ə'freɪd] *adj*: **to be ~ of** (*person*) tener miedo a; (*thing*) tener miedo de;

to be ~ to tener miedo de, temer; **I am ~ that** me temo que; **I am ~ not/so** lo siento, pero no/es así

Africa ['æfrɪkə] *n* África; **African** *adj, n* africano/a *m/f*; **African-American** *adj, n* afroamericano/a

after ['ɑːftə*] *prep* (*time*) después de; (*place, order*) detrás de, tras ▷ *adv* después ▷ *conj* después (de) que; **what/who are you ~?** ¿qué/a quién busca usted?; **~ having done/he left** después de haber hecho/después de que se marchó; **to name sb ~ sb** llamar a algn por algn; **it's twenty ~ eight** (*US*) son las ocho y veinte; **to ask ~ sb** preguntar por algn; **~ all** después de todo, al fin y al cabo; **~ you!** ¡pase usted!; **after-effects** *npl* consecuencias *fpl*, efectos *mpl*; **aftermath** *n* consecuencias *fpl*, resultados *mpl*; **afternoon** *n* tarde *f*; **after-shave (lotion)** *n* aftershave *m*; **aftersun (lotion/cream)** *n* loción *f*/crema para después del sol, aftersun *m*; **afterwards** (*US* **afterward**) *adv* después, más tarde

again [ə'gɛn] *adv* otra vez, de nuevo; **to do sth ~** volver a hacer algo; **~ and ~** una y otra vez

against [ə'gɛnst] *prep* (*in opposition to*) en contra de; (*leaning on, touching*) contra, junto a

age [eɪdʒ] *n* edad *f*; (*period*) época ▷ *vi* envejecer(se) ▷ *vt* envejecer; **she is 20 years of ~** tiene 20 años; **to come of ~** llegar a la mayoría de edad; **it's been ~s since I saw you** hace siglos que no te veo; **~d 10** de 10 años de edad; **age group** *n*: **to be in the same age group** tener la misma edad; **age limit** *n* edad *f* mínima (*or* máxima)

agency ['eɪdʒənsɪ] *n* agencia

agenda [ə'dʒɛndə] *n* orden *m* del día

> Be careful not to translate **agenda** by the Spanish word *agenda*.

agent ['eɪdʒənt] *n* agente *mf*; (*Comm: holding concession*) representante *mf*, delegado/a; (*Chem, fig*) agente *m*

aggravate ['ægrəveɪt] *vt* (*situation*) agravar; (*person*) irritar

aggression [ə'grɛʃən] *n* agresión *f*

aggressive [ə'grɛsɪv] *adj* (*belligerent*) agresivo; (*assertive*) enérgico

agile ['ædʒaɪl] *adj* ágil

agitated ['ædʒɪteɪtɪd] *adj* agitado

AGM *n abbr* (= *annual general meeting*) asamblea anual

ago [ə'gəu] *adv*: **2 days ~** hace 2 días; **not long ~** hace poco; **how long ~?** ¿hace cuánto tiempo?

agony ['ægənɪ] *n* (*pain*) dolor *m* agudo; (*distress*) angustia; **to be in ~** retorcerse de dolor

agree [ə'griː] *vt* (*price, date*) acordar, quedar en ▷ *vi* (*have same opinion*): **to ~ (with/that)** estar de acuerdo (con/que); (*correspond*) coincidir, concordar; (*consent*) acceder; **to ~ with** (*person*) estar de acuerdo con, ponerse de acuerdo con; (*: food*) sentar bien a; (*Ling*) concordar con; **to ~ to sth/to do sth** consentir en algo/aceptar hacer algo; **to ~ that** (*admit*) estar de acuerdo en que; **agreeable** *adj* (*sensation*) agradable; (*person*) simpático; (*willing*) de acuerdo, conforme; **agreed** *adj* (*time, place*) convenido; **agreement** *n* acuerdo; (*contract*) contrato; **in agreement** de acuerdo, conforme

agricultural [ægrɪ'kʌltʃərəl] *adj* agrícola

agriculture ['ægrɪkʌltʃə*] *n* agricultura

ahead [ə'hɛd] *adv* (*in front*) delante; (*into the future*): **she had no time to think ~** no tenía tiempo de hacer planes para el futuro; **~ of** delante de; (*in advance of*) antes de; **~ of time** antes de la hora; **go right** *or* **straight ~** (*direction*) siga adelante; (*permission*) hazlo (*or* hágalo)

aid [eɪd] *n* ayuda, auxilio; (*device*) aparato ▷ *vt* ayudar, auxiliar; **in ~ of** a beneficio de

aide [eɪd] *n* (*person, also Mil*) ayudante

mf

AIDS [eɪdz] *n abbr* (= *acquired immune deficiency syndrome*) SIDA *m*

ailing ['eɪlɪŋ] *adj* (*person, economy*) enfermizo

ailment ['eɪlmənt] *n* enfermedad *f*, achaque *m*

aim [eɪm] *vt* (*gun, camera*) apuntar; (*missile, remark*) dirigir; (*blow*) asestar ▷ *vi* (*also*: **take ~**) apuntar ▷ *n* (*in shooting*: *skill*) puntería; (*objective*) propósito, meta; **to ~ at** (*with weapon*) apuntar a; (*objective*) aspirar a, pretender; **to ~ to do** tener la intención de hacer

ain't [eɪnt] (*inf*) = **am not; aren't; isn't**

air [ɛə*] *n* aire *m*; (*appearance*) aspecto ▷ *vt* (*room*) ventilar; (*clothes, ideas*) airear ▷ *cpd* aéreo; **to throw sth into the ~** (*ball etc*) lanzar algo al aire; **by ~** (*travel*) en avión; **to be on the ~** (*Radio, TV*) estar en antena; **airbag** *n* airbag *m inv*; **airbed** (BRIT) *n* colchón *m* neumático; **airborne** *adj* (*in the air*) en el aire; **as soon as the plane was airborne** tan pronto como el avión estuvo en el aire; **air-conditioned** *adj* climatizado; **air conditioning** *n* aire acondicionado; **aircraft** *n inv* avión *m*; **airfield** *n* campo de aviación; **Air Force** *n* fuerzas *fpl* aéreas, aviación *f*; **air hostess** (BRIT) *n* azafata; **airing cupboard** *n* (BRIT) armario *m* para oreo; **airlift** *n* puente *m* aéreo; **airline** *n* línea aérea; **airliner** *n* avión *m* de pasajeros; **airmail** *n*: **by airmail** por avión; **airplane** (US) *n* avión *m*; **airport** *n* aeropuerto; **air raid** *n* ataque *m* aéreo; **airsick** *adj*: **to be airsick** marearse (en avión); **airspace** *n* espacio aéreo; **airstrip** *n* pista de aterrizaje; **air terminal** *n* terminal *f*; **airtight** *adj* hermético; **air-traffic controller** *n* controlador(a) *m/f* aéreo/a; **airy** *adj* (*room*) bien ventilado; (*fig*: *manner*) desenfadado

aisle [aɪl] *n* (*of church*) nave *f*; (*of theatre, supermarket*) pasillo; **aisle seat** *n* (*on plane*) asiento de pasillo

ajar [ə'dʒɑː*] *adj* entreabierto

à la carte [ælæ'kɑːt] *adv* a la carta

alarm [ə'lɑːm] *n* (*in shop, bank*) alarma; (*anxiety*) inquietud *f* ▷ *vt* asustar, inquietar; **alarm call** *n* (*in hotel etc*) alarma; **alarm clock** *n* despertador *m*; **alarmed** *adj* (*person*) alarmado, asustado; (*house, car etc*) con alarma; **alarming** *adj* alarmante

Albania [æl'beɪnɪə] *n* Albania

albeit [ɔːl'biːɪt] *conj* aunque

album ['ælbəm] *n* álbum *m*; (*L.P.*) elepé *m*

alcohol ['ælkəhɔl] *n* alcohol *m*; **alcohol-free** *adj* sin alcohol; **alcoholic** [-'hɔlɪk] *adj, n* alcohólico/a *m/f*

alcove ['ælkəuv] *n* nicho, hueco

ale [eɪl] *n* cerveza

alert [ə'ləːt] *adj* (*attentive*) atento; (*to danger, opportunity*) alerta ▷ *n* alerta *m*, alarma ▷ *vt* poner sobre aviso; **to be on the ~** (*also Mil*) estar alerta *or* sobre aviso

algebra ['ældʒɪbrə] *n* álgebra

Algeria [æl'dʒɪərɪə] *n* Argelia

alias ['eɪlɪəs] *adv* alias, conocido por ▷ *n* (*of criminal*) apodo; (*of writer*) seudónimo

alibi ['ælɪbaɪ] *n* coartada

alien ['eɪlɪən] *n* (*foreigner*) extranjero/a; (*extraterrestrial*) extraterrestre *mf* ▷ *adj*: **~ to** ajeno a; **alienate** *vt* enajenar, alejar

alight [ə'laɪt] *adj* ardiendo; (*eyes*) brillante ▷ *vi* (*person*) apearse, bajar; (*bird*) posarse

align [ə'laɪn] *vt* alinear

alike [ə'laɪk] *adj* semejantes, iguales ▷ *adv* igualmente, del mismo modo; **to look ~** parecerse

alive [ə'laɪv] *adj* vivo; (*lively*) alegre

KEYWORD

all [ɔːl] *adj* (*sg*) todo/a; (*pl*) todos/as; **all day** todo el día; **all night** toda la noche; **all men** todos los hombres;

all five came vinieron los cinco; **all the books** todos los libros; **all his life** toda su vida
▷ *pron* **1** todo; **I ate it all, I ate all of it** me lo comí todo; **all of us went** fuimos todos; **all the boys went** fueron todos los chicos; **is that all?** ¿eso es todo?, ¿algo más?; (*in shop*) ¿algo más?, ¿alguna cosa más?
2 (*in phrases*): **above all** sobre todo; por encima de todo; **after all** después de todo; **at all: not at all** (*in answer to question*) en absoluto; (*in answer to thanks*) ¡de nada!, ¡no hay de qué!; **I'm not at all tired** no estoy nada cansado/a; **anything at all will do** cualquier cosa viene bien; **all in all** a fin de cuentas
▷ *adv*: **all alone** completamente solo/a; **it's not as hard as all that** no es tan difícil como lo pintas; **all the more/the better** tanto más/mejor; **all but** casi; **the score is 2 all** están empatados a 2

Allah ['ælə] *n* Alá *m*
allegation [ælɪ'geɪʃən] *n* alegato
alleged [ə'lɛdʒd] *adj* supuesto, presunto; **allegedly** *adv* supuestamente, según se afirma
allegiance [ə'li:dʒəns] *n* lealtad *f*
allergic [ə'lə:dʒɪk] *adj*: **~ to** alérgico a
allergy ['ælədʒɪ] *n* alergia
alleviate [ə'li:vɪeɪt] *vt* aliviar
alley ['ælɪ] *n* callejuela
alliance [ə'laɪəns] *n* alianza
allied ['ælaɪd] *adj* aliado
alligator ['ælɪgeɪtə*] *n* (*Zool*) caimán *m*
all-in (BRIT) ['ɔ:lɪn] *adj, adv* (*charge*) todo incluido
allocate ['æləkeɪt] *vt* (*money etc*) asignar
allot [ə'lɔt] *vt* asignar
all-out ['ɔ:laut] *adj* (*effort etc*) supremo
allow [ə'lau] *vt* permitir, dejar; (*a claim*) admitir; (*sum, time etc*) dar, conceder; (*concede*): **to ~ that** reconocer que; **to ~ sb to do** permitir a algn hacer; **he is ~ed to ...** se le permite ...; **allow for** *vt fus* tener en cuenta; **allowance** *n* subvención *f*; (*welfare payment*) subsidio, pensión *f*; (*pocket money*) dinero de bolsillo; (*tax allowance*) desgravación *f*; **to make allowances for** (*person*) disculpar a; (*thing*) tener en cuenta
all right *adv* bien; (*as answer*) ¡conforme!, ¡está bien!
ally ['ælaɪ] *n* aliado/a ▷ *vt*: **to ~ o.s. with** aliarse con
almighty [ɔ:l'maɪtɪ] *adj* todopoderoso; (*row etc*) imponente
almond ['ɑ:mənd] *n* almendra
almost ['ɔ:lməust] *adv* casi
alone [ə'ləun] *adj, adv* solo; **to leave sb ~** dejar a algn en paz; **to leave sth ~** no tocar algo, dejar algo sin tocar; **let ~ ...** y mucho menos ...
along [ə'lɔŋ] *prep* a lo largo de, por ▷ *adv*: **is he coming ~ with us?** ¿viene con nosotros?; **he was limping ~** iba cojeando; **~ with** junto con; **all ~** (*all the time*) desde el principio; **alongside** *prep* al lado de ▷ *adv* al lado
aloof [ə'lu:f] *adj* reservado ▷ *adv*: **to stand ~** mantenerse apartado
aloud [ə'laud] *adv* en voz alta
alphabet ['ælfəbɛt] *n* alfabeto
Alps [ælps] *npl*: **the ~** los Alpes
already [ɔ:l'rɛdɪ] *adv* ya
alright ['ɔ:l'raɪt] (BRIT) *adv* = **all right**
also ['ɔ:lsəu] *adv* también, además
altar ['ɔltə*] *n* altar *m*
alter ['ɔltə*] *vt* cambiar, modificar ▷ *vi* cambiar; **alteration** [ɔltə'reɪʃən] *n* cambio; (*to clothes*) arreglo; (*to building*) arreglos *mpl*
alternate [*adj* ɔl'tə:nɪt, *vb* 'ɔltə:neɪt] *adj* (*actions etc*) alternativo; (*events*) alterno; (US) = **alternative** ▷ *vi*: **to ~ (with)** alternar (con); **on ~ days** un día sí y otro no
alternative [ɔl'tə:nətɪv] *adj* alternativo ▷ *n* alternativa; **~**

medicine medicina alternativa; **alternatively** *adv*: **alternatively one could ...** por otra parte se podría ...
although [ɔːl'ðəu] *conj* aunque
altitude ['æltɪtjuːd] *n* altura
altogether [ɔːltə'gɛðə*] *adv* completamente, del todo; (*on the whole*) en total, en conjunto
aluminium [ælju'mɪnɪəm] (BRIT), **aluminum** [ə'luːmɪnəm] (US) *n* aluminio
always ['ɔːlweɪz] *adv* siempre
Alzheimer's (disease) ['æltshaɪməz-] *n* enfermedad *f* de Alzheimer
am [æm] *vb see* **be**
amalgamate [ə'mælgəmeɪt] *vi* amalgamarse ▷*vt* amalgamar, unir
amass [ə'mæs] *vt* amontonar, acumular
amateur ['æmətə*] *n* aficionado/a, amateur *mf*
amaze [ə'meɪz] *vt* asombrar, pasmar; **to be ~d (at)** quedar pasmado (de); **amazed** *adj* asombrado; **amazement** *n* asombro, sorpresa; **amazing** *adj* extraordinario; (*fantastic*) increíble
Amazon ['æməzən] *n* (*Geo*) Amazonas *m*
ambassador [æm'bæsədə*] *n* embajador(a) *m/f*
amber ['æmbə*] *n* ámbar *m*; **at ~** (BRIT *Aut*) en el amarillo
ambiguous [æm'bɪgjuəs] *adj* ambiguo
ambition [æm'bɪʃən] *n* ambición *f*; **ambitious** [-ʃəs] *adj* ambicioso
ambulance ['æmbjuləns] *n* ambulancia
ambush ['æmbuʃ] *n* emboscada ▷*vt* tender una emboscada a
amen [ɑː'mɛn] *excl* amén
amend [ə'mɛnd] *vt* enmendar; **to make ~s** dar cumplida satisfacción; **amendment** *n* enmienda
amenities [ə'miːnɪtɪz] *npl* comodidades *fpl*
America [ə'mɛrɪkə] *n* (*USA*) Estados *mpl* Unidos; **American** *adj*, *n* norteamericano/a; estadounidense *mf*; **American football** *n* (BRIT) fútbol *m* americano
amicable ['æmɪkəbl] *adj* amistoso, amigable
amid(st) [ə'mɪd(st)] *prep* entre, en medio de
ammunition [æmju'nɪʃən] *n* municiones *fpl*
amnesty ['æmnɪstɪ] *n* amnistía
among(st) [ə'mʌŋ(st)] *prep* entre, en medio de
amount [ə'maunt] *n* (*gen*) cantidad *f*; (*of bill etc*) suma, importe *m* ▷*vi*: **to ~ to** sumar; (*be same as*) equivaler a, significar
amp(ère) ['æmp(ɛə*)] *n* amperio
ample ['æmpl] *adj* (*large*) grande; (*abundant*) abundante; (*enough*) bastante, suficiente
amplifier ['æmplɪfaɪə*] *n* amplificador *m*
amputate ['æmpjuteɪt] *vt* amputar
Amtrak ['æmtræk] (US) *n empresa nacional de ferrocarriles de los EEUU*
amuse [ə'mjuːz] *vt* divertir; (*distract*) distraer, entretener; **amusement** *n* diversión *f*; (*pastime*) pasatiempo; (*laughter*) risa; **amusement arcade** *n* salón *m* de juegos; **amusement park** *n* parque *m* de atracciones
amusing [ə'mjuːzɪŋ] *adj* divertido
an [æn] *indef art see* **a**
anaemia [ə'niːmɪə] (US **anemia**) *n* anemia
anaemic [ə'niːmɪk] (US **anemic**) *adj* anémico; (*fig*) soso, insípido
anaesthetic [ænɪs'θɛtɪk] (US **anesthetic**) *n* anestesia
analog(ue) ['ænəlɔg] *adj* (*computer, watch*) analógico
analogy [ə'nælədʒɪ] *n* analogía
analyse ['ænəlaɪz] (US **analyze**) *vt* analizar; **analysis** [ə'næləsɪs] (*pl* **analyses**) *n* análisis *m inv*; **analyst** [-lɪst] *n* (*political analyst, psychoanalyst*) analista *mf*

analyze ['ænəlaɪz] (US) *vt* = **analyse**
anarchy ['ænəkɪ] *n* anarquía, desorden *m*
anatomy [ə'nætəmɪ] *n* anatomía
ancestor ['ænsɪstə*] *n* antepasado
anchor ['æŋkə*] *n* ancla, áncora ▷ *vi* (*also*: **to drop ~**) anclar ▷ *vt* anclar; **to weigh ~** levar anclas
anchovy ['æntʃəvɪ] *n* anchoa
ancient ['eɪnʃənt] *adj* antiguo
and [ænd] *conj* y; (*before i-, hi- + consonant*) e; **men ~ women** hombres y mujeres; **father ~ son** padre e hijo; **trees ~ grass** árboles y hierba; **~ so on** etcétera, y así sucesivamente; **try ~ come** procura venir; **he talked ~ talked** habló sin parar; **better ~ better** cada vez mejor
Andes ['ændi:z] *npl*: **the ~** los Andes
Andorra [æn'dɔ:rə] *n* Andorra
anemia *etc* [ə'ni:mɪə] (US) = **anaemia** *etc*
anesthetic [ænɪs'θɛtɪk] (US) = **anaesthetic**
angel ['eɪndʒəl] *n* ángel *m*
anger ['æŋgə*] *n* cólera
angina [æn'dʒaɪnə] *n* angina (del pecho)
angle ['æŋgl] *n* ángulo; **from their ~** desde su punto de vista
angler ['æŋglə*] *n* pescador(a) *m/f* (de caña)
Anglican ['æŋglɪkən] *adj, n* anglicano/a *m/f*
angling ['æŋglɪŋ] *n* pesca con caña
angrily ['æŋgrɪlɪ] *adv* coléricamente, airadamente
angry ['æŋgrɪ] *adj* enfadado, airado; (*wound*) inflamado; **to be ~ with sb/at sth** estar enfadado con algn/por algo; **to get ~** enfadarse, enojarse
anguish ['æŋgwɪʃ] *n* (*physical*) tormentos *mpl*; (*mental*) angustia
animal ['ænɪməl] *n* animal *m*; (*pej: person*) bestia ▷ *adj* animal
animated [-meɪtɪd] *adj* animado
animation [ænɪ'meɪʃən] *n* animación *f*
aniseed ['ænɪsi:d] *n* anís *m*
ankle ['æŋkl] *n* tobillo
annex [*n* 'ænɛks, *vb* æ'nɛks] *n* (BRIT: *also*: **~e**: *building*) edificio anexo ▷ *vt* (*territory*) anexionar
anniversary [ænɪ'və:sərɪ] *n* aniversario
announce [ə'nauns] *vt* anunciar; **announcement** *n* anuncio; (*official*) declaración *f*; **announcer** *n* (*Radio*) locutor(a) *m/f*; (*TV*) presentador(a) *m/f*
annoy [ə'nɔɪ] *vt* molestar, fastidiar; **don't get ~ed!** ¡no se enfade!; **annoying** *adj* molesto, fastidioso; (*person*) pesado
annual ['ænjuəl] *adj* anual ▷ *n* (*Bot*) anual *m*; (*book*) anuario; **annually** *adv* anualmente, cada año
annum ['ænəm] *n see* **per**
anonymous [ə'nɔnɪməs] *adj* anónimo
anorak ['ænəræk] *n* anorak *m*
anorexia [ænə'rɛksɪə] *n* (*Med*: *also*: **~ nervosa**) anorexia
anorexic [ænə'rɛksɪk] *adj, n* anoréxico/a *m/f*
another [ə'nʌðə*] *adj* (*one more, a different one*) otro ▷ *pron* otro; *see* **one**
answer ['ɑ:nsə*] *n* contestación *f*, respuesta; (*to problem*) solución *f* ▷ *vi* contestar, responder ▷ *vt* (*reply to*) contestar a, responder a; (*problem*) resolver; (*prayer*) escuchar; **in ~ to your letter** contestando *or* en contestación a su carta; **to ~ the phone** contestar *or* coger el teléfono; **to ~ the bell** *or* **the door** acudir a la puerta; **answer back** *vi* replicar, ser respondón/ona; **answerphone** *n* (*esp* BRIT) contestador *m* (automático)
ant [ænt] *n* hormiga
Antarctic [ænt'ɑ:ktɪk] *n*: **the ~** el Antártico
antelope ['æntɪləup] *n* antílope *m*
antenatal ['æntɪ'neɪtl] *adj* antenatal, prenatal
antenna [æn'tɛnə, *pl* -ni:] (*pl* **antennae**) *n* antena

anthem ['ænθəm] *n*: **national ~** himno nacional
anthology [æn'θɔlədʒɪ] *n* antología
anthrax ['ænθræks] *n* ántrax *m*
anthropology [ænθrə'pɔlədʒɪ] *n* antropología
anti [æntɪ] *prefix* anti; **antibiotic** [-baɪ'ɔtɪk] *n* antibiótico; **antibody** ['æntɪbɔdɪ] *n* anticuerpo
anticipate [æn'tɪsɪpeɪt] *vt* prever; (*expect*) esperar, contar con; (*look forward to*) esperar con ilusión; (*do first*) anticiparse a, adelantarse a; **anticipation** [-'peɪʃən] *n* (*expectation*) previsión *f*; (*eagerness*) ilusión *f*, expectación *f*
anticlimax [æntɪ'klaɪmæks] *n* decepción *f*
anticlockwise [æntɪ'klɔkwaɪz] (BRIT) *adv* en dirección contraria a la de las agujas del reloj
antics ['æntɪks] *npl* gracias *fpl*
anti: antidote ['æntɪdəut] *n* antídoto; **antifreeze** ['æntɪfri:z] *n* anticongelante *m*; **antihistamine** [-'hɪstəmi:n] *n* antihistamínico; **antiperspirant** ['æntɪpə:spɪrənt] *n* antitranspirante *m*
antique [æn'ti:k] *n* antigüedad *f* ▷ *adj* antiguo; **antique shop** *n* tienda de antigüedades
antiseptic [æntɪ'sɛptɪk] *adj*, *n* antiséptico
antisocial [æntɪ'səuʃəl] *adj* antisocial
antivirus [æntɪ'vaɪərəs] *adj* (*program*, *software*) antivirus *inv*
antlers ['æntləz] *npl* cuernas *fpl*, cornamenta *sg*
anxiety [æŋ'zaɪətɪ] *n* inquietud *f*; (*Med*) ansiedad *f*; **~ to do** deseo de hacer
anxious ['æŋkʃəs] *adj* inquieto, preocupado; (*worrying*) preocupante; (*keen*): **to be ~ to do** tener muchas ganas de hacer

KEYWORD

any ['ɛnɪ] *adj* **1** (*in questions etc*) algún/alguna; **have you any butter/children?** ¿tienes mantequilla/hijos?; **if there are any tickets left** si quedan billetes, si queda algún billete
2 (*with negative*): **I haven't any money/books** no tengo dinero/libros
3 (*no matter which*) cualquier; **any excuse will do** valdrá *or* servirá cualquier excusa; **choose any book you like** escoge el libro que quieras
4 (*in phrases*): **in any case** de todas formas, en cualquier caso; **any day now** cualquier día (de estos); **at any moment** en cualquier momento, de un momento a otro; **at any rate** en todo caso; **any time: come (at) any time** ven cuando quieras; **he might come (at) any time** podría llegar de un momento a otro
▷ *pron* **1** (*in questions etc*): **have you got any?** ¿tienes alguno(s)/a(s)?; **can any of you sing?** ¿sabe cantar alguno de vosotros/ustedes?
2 (*with negative*): **I haven't any (of them)** no tengo ninguno
3 (*no matter which one(s)*): **take any of those books (you like)** toma el libro que quieras de ésos
▷ *adv* **1** (*in questions etc*): **do you want any more soup/sandwiches?** ¿quieres más sopa/bocadillos?; **are you feeling any better?** ¿te sientes algo mejor?
2 (*with negative*): **I can't hear him any more** ya no le oigo; **don't wait any longer** no esperes más

any: anybody *pron* cualquiera; (*in interrogative sentences*) alguien; (*in negative sentences*): **I don't see anybody** no veo a nadie; **if anybody should phone ...** si llama alguien

...; **anyhow** *adv* (*at any rate*) de todos modos, de todas formas; (*haphazard*): **do it anyhow you like** hazlo como quieras; **she leaves things just anyhow** deja las cosas como quiera *or* de cualquier modo; **I shall go anyhow** de todos modos iré; **anyone** *pron* = **anybody**; **anything** *pron* (*in questions etc*) algo, alguna cosa; (*with negative*) nada; **can you see anything?** ¿ves algo?; **if anything happens to me ...** si algo me ocurre ...; (*no matter what*): **you can say anything you like** puedes decir lo que quieras; **anything will do** vale todo *or* cualquier cosa; **he'll eat anything** come de todo *or* lo que sea; **anytime** *adv* (*at any moment*) en cualquier momento, de un momento a otro; (*whenever*) no importa cuándo, cuando quiera; **anyway** *adv* (*at any rate*) de todos modos, de todas formas; **I shall go anyway** iré de todos modos; (*besides*): **anyway, I couldn't come even if I wanted to** además, no podría venir aunque quisiera; **why are you phoning, anyway?** ¿entonces, por qué llamas?, ¿por qué llamas, pues?; **anywhere** *adv* (*in questions etc*): **can you see him anywhere?** ¿le ves por algún lado?; **are you going anywhere?** ¿vas a algún sitio?; (*with negative*): **I can't see him anywhere** no le veo por ninguna parte; **anywhere in the world** (*no matter where*) en cualquier parte (del mundo); **put the books down anywhere** deja los libros donde quieras

apart [ə'pɑːt] *adv* (*aside*) aparte; (*situation*): **~ (from)** separado (de); (*movement*): **to pull ~** separar; **10 miles ~** separados por 10 millas; **to take ~** desmontar; **~ from** *prep* aparte de

apartment [ə'pɑːtmənt] *n* (US) piso (SP), departamento (LAM), apartamento; (*room*) cuarto; **apartment building** (US) *n* edificio de apartamentos

apathy ['æpəθɪ] *n* apatía, indiferencia

ape [eɪp] *n* mono ▷ *vt* imitar, remedar

aperitif [ə'pɛrɪtɪf] *n* aperitivo

aperture ['æpətʃjuə*] *n* rendija, resquicio; (*Phot*) abertura

APEX ['eɪpɛks] *n abbr* (= *Advanced Purchase Excursion Fare*) tarifa *f* APEX

apologize [ə'pɔlədʒaɪz] *vi*: **to ~ (for sth to sb)** disculparse (con algn de algo)

apology [ə'pɔlədʒɪ] *n* disculpa, excusa

Be careful not to translate **apology** by the Spanish word *apología*.

apostrophe [ə'pɔstrəfɪ] *n* apóstrofo

appal [ə'pɔːl] (US **appall**) *vt* horrorizar, espantar; **appalling** *adj* espantoso; (*awful*) pésimo

apparatus [æpə'reɪtəs] *n* (*equipment*) equipo; (*organization*) aparato; (*in gymnasium*) aparatos *mpl*

apparent [ə'pærənt] *adj* aparente; (*obvious*) evidente; **apparently** *adv* por lo visto, al parecer

appeal [ə'piːl] *vi* (*Law*) apelar ▷ *n* (*Law*) apelación *f*; (*request*) llamamiento; (*plea*) petición *f*; (*charm*) atractivo; **to ~ for** reclamar; **to ~ to** (*be attractive to*) atraer; **it doesn't ~ to me** no me atrae, no me llama la atención; **appealing** *adj* (*attractive*) atractivo

appear [ə'pɪə*] *vi* aparecer, presentarse; (*Law*) comparecer; (*publication*) salir (a luz), publicarse; (*seem*) parecer; **to ~ on TV/in "Hamlet"** salir por la tele/hacer un papel en "Hamlet"; **it would ~ that** parecería que; **appearance** *n* aparición *f*; (*look*) apariencia, aspecto

appendices [ə'pɛndɪsiːz] *npl of* **appendix**

appendicitis [əpɛndɪ'saɪtɪs] *n* apendicitis *f*

appendix [ə'pɛndɪks] (*pl* **appendices**) *n* apéndice *m*

appetite ['æpɪtaɪt] *n* apetito; (*fig*) deseo, anhelo

appetizer ['æpıtaızə*] *n* (*drink*) aperitivo; (*food*) tapas *fpl* (SP)
applaud [ə'plɔ:d] *vt, vi* aplaudir
applause [ə'plɔ:z] *n* aplausos *mpl*
apple ['æpl] *n* manzana; **apple pie** *n* pastel *m* de manzana, pay *m* de manzana (LAM)
appliance [ə'plaıəns] *n* aparato
applicable [ə'plıkəbl] *adj* (*relevant*): **to be ~ (to)** referirse (a)
applicant ['æplıkənt] *n* candidato/a; solicitante *mf*
application [æplı'keıʃən] *n* aplicación *f*; (*for a job etc*) solicitud *f*, petición *f*; **application form** *n* solicitud *f*
apply [ə'plaı] *vt* (*paint etc*) poner; (*law etc: put into practice*) poner en vigor ▷ *vi*: **to ~ to** (*ask*) dirigirse a; (*be applicable*) ser aplicable a; **to ~ for** (*permit, grant, job*) solicitar; **to ~ o.s. to** aplicarse a, dedicarse a
appoint [ə'pɔınt] *vt* (*to post*) nombrar a

> Be careful not to translate **appoint** by the Spanish word *apuntar*.

appointment *n* (*with client*) cita; (*act*) nombramiento; (*post*) puesto; (*at hairdresser etc*): **to have an appointment** tener hora; **to make an appointment (with sb)** citarse (con algn)
appraisal [ə'preızl] *n* valoración *f*
appreciate [ə'pri:ʃıeıt] *vt* apreciar, tener en mucho; (*be grateful for*) agradecer; (*be aware*) comprender ▷ *vi* (*Comm*) aumentar(se) en valor; **appreciation** [-'eıʃən] *n* apreciación *f*; (*gratitude*) reconocimiento, agradecimiento; (*Comm*) aumento en valor
apprehension [æprı'hɛnʃən] *n* (*fear*) aprensión *f*
apprehensive [æprı'hɛnsıv] *adj* aprensivo
apprentice [ə'prɛntıs] *n* aprendiz(a) *m/f*
approach [ə'prəutʃ] *vi* acercarse ▷ *vt* acercarse a; (*ask, apply to*) dirigirse a; (*situation, problem*) abordar ▷ *n* acercamiento; (*access*) acceso; (*to problem, situation*): **~ (to)** actitud *f* (ante)
appropriate [*adj* ə'prəuprııt, *vb* ə'prəuprıeıt] *adj* apropiado, conveniente ▷ *vt* (*take*) apropiarse de
approval [ə'pru:vəl] *n* aprobación *f*, visto bueno; (*permission*) consentimiento; **on ~** (*Comm*) a prueba
approve [ə'pru:v] *vt* aprobar; **approve of** *vt fus* (*thing*) aprobar; (*person*): **they don't approve of her** (ella) no les parece bien
approximate [ə'prɔksımıt] *adj* aproximado; **approximately** *adv* aproximadamente, más o menos
Apr. *abbr* (= *April*) abr
apricot ['eıprıkɔt] *n* albaricoque *m*, chabacano (MEX), damasco (RPL)
April ['eıprəl] *n* abril *m*; **April Fools' Day** *n* el primero de abril, ≈ día *m* de los Inocentes (*28 December*)
apron ['eıprən] *n* delantal *m*
apt [æpt] *adj* acertado, apropiado; (*likely*): **~ to do** propenso a hacer
aquarium [ə'kwɛərıəm] *n* acuario
Aquarius [ə'kwɛərıəs] *n* Acuario
Arab ['ærəb] *adj, n* árabe *mf*
Arabia [ə'reıbıə] *n* Arabia; **Arabian** *adj* árabe; **Arabic** ['ærəbık] *adj* árabe; (*numerals*) arábigo ▷ *n* árabe *m*
arbitrary ['ɑ:bıtrərı] *adj* arbitrario
arbitration [ɑ:bı'treıʃən] *n* arbitraje *m*
arc [ɑ:k] *n* arco
arcade [ɑ:'keıd] *n* (*round a square*) soportales *mpl*; (*shopping mall*) galería comercial
arch [ɑ:tʃ] *n* arco; (*of foot*) arco del pie ▷ *vt* arquear
archaeology [ɑ:kı'ɔlədʒı] (US **archeology**) *n* arqueología
archbishop [ɑ:tʃ'bıʃəp] *n* arzobispo
archeology [ɑ:kı'ɔlədʒı] (US) = **archaeology**
architect ['ɑ:kıtɛkt] *n* arquitecto/a;

architectural [ɑːkɪ'tɛktʃərəl] *adj* arquitectónico; **architecture** *n* arquitectura

archive ['ɑːkaɪv] *n* (*often pl: also Comput*) archivo

Arctic ['ɑːktɪk] *adj* ártico ▷ *n*: **the ~** el Ártico

are [ɑː*] *vb see* **be**

area ['ɛərɪə] *n* área, región *f*; (*part of place*) zona; (*Math etc*) área, superficie *f*; (*in room: e.g. dining area*) parte *f*; (*of knowledge, experience*) campo; **area code** (US) *n* (*Tel*) prefijo

arena [ə'riːnə] *n* estadio; (*of circus*) pista

aren't [ɑːnt] = **are not**

Argentina [ɑːdʒən'tiːnə] *n* Argentina; **Argentinian** [-'tɪnɪən] *adj, n* argentino/a *m/f*

arguably ['ɑːgjuəblɪ] *adv* posiblemente

argue ['ɑːgjuː] *vi* (*quarrel*) discutir, pelearse; (*reason*) razonar, argumentar; **to ~ that** sostener que

argument ['ɑːgjumənt] *n* discusión *f*, pelea; (*reasons*) argumento

Aries ['ɛərɪz] *n* Aries *m*

arise [ə'raɪz] (*pt* **arose**, *pp* **arisen**) *vi* surgir, presentarse

arithmetic [ə'rɪθmətɪk] *n* aritmética

arm [ɑːm] *n* brazo ▷ *vt* armar; **arms** *npl* armas *fpl*; **~ in ~** cogidos del brazo; **armchair** ['ɑːmtʃɛə*] *n* sillón *m*, butaca

armed [ɑːmd] *adj* armado; **armed robbery** *n* robo a mano armada

armour ['ɑːmə*] (US **armor**) *n* armadura; (*Mil: tanks*) blindaje *m*

armpit ['ɑːmpɪt] *n* sobaco, axila

armrest ['ɑːmrɛst] *n* apoyabrazos *m inv*

army ['ɑːmɪ] *n* ejército; (*fig*) multitud *f*

A road *n* (BRIT) ≈ carretera *f* nacional

aroma [ə'rəumə] *n* aroma *m*, fragancia; **aromatherapy** *n* aromaterapia

arose [ə'rəuz] *pt of* **arise**

around [ə'raund] *adv* alrededor; (*in the area*): **there is no one else ~** no hay nadie más por aquí ▷ *prep* alrededor de

arouse [ə'rauz] *vt* despertar; (*anger*) provocar

arrange [ə'reɪndʒ] *vt* arreglar, ordenar; (*organize*) organizar; **to ~ to do sth** quedar en hacer algo; **arrangement** *n* arreglo; (*agreement*) acuerdo; **arrangements** *npl* (*preparations*) preparativos *mpl*

array [ə'reɪ] *n*: **~ of** (*things*) serie *f* de; (*people*) conjunto de

arrears [ə'rɪəz] *npl* atrasos *mpl*; **to be in ~ with one's rent** estar retrasado en el pago del alquiler

arrest [ə'rɛst] *vt* detener; (*sb's attention*) llamar ▷ *n* detención *f*; **under ~** detenido

arrival [ə'raɪvəl] *n* llegada; **new ~** recién llegado/a; (*baby*) recién nacido

arrive [ə'raɪv] *vi* llegar; (*baby*) nacer; **arrive at** *vt fus* (*decision, solution*) llegar a

arrogance ['ærəgəns] *n* arrogancia, prepotencia (LAM)

arrogant ['ærəgənt] *adj* arrogante

arrow ['ærəu] *n* flecha

arse [ɑːs] (BRIT: *inf!*) *n* culo, trasero

arson ['ɑːsn] *n* incendio premeditado

art [ɑːt] *n* arte *m*; (*skill*) destreza; **art college** *n* escuela *f* de Bellas Artes

artery ['ɑːtərɪ] *n* arteria

art gallery *n* pinacoteca; (*saleroom*) galería de arte

arthritis [ɑː'θraɪtɪs] *n* artritis *f*

artichoke ['ɑːtɪtʃəuk] *n* alcachofa; **Jerusalem ~** aguaturma

article ['ɑːtɪkl] *n* artículo

articulate [*adj* ɑː'tɪkjulɪt, *vb* ɑː'tɪkjuleɪt] *adj* claro, bien expresado ▷ *vt* expresar

artificial [ɑːtɪ'fɪʃəl] *adj* artificial; (*affected*) afectado

artist ['ɑːtɪst] *n* artista *mf*; (*Mus*) intérprete *mf*; **artistic** [ɑː'tɪstɪk] *adj*

artístico
art school *n* escuela de bellas artes

KEYWORD

as [æz] *conj* **1** (*referring to time*) cuando, mientras; a medida que; **as the years went by** con el paso de los años; **he came in as I was leaving** entró cuando me marchaba; **as from tomorrow** desde *or* a partir de mañana
2 (*in comparisons*): **as big as** tan grande como; **twice as big as** el doble de grande que; **as much money/many books as** tanto dinero/tantos libros como; **as soon as** en cuanto
3 (*since, because*) como, ya que; **he left early as he had to be home by 10** se fue temprano ya que tenía que estar en casa a las 10
4 (*referring to manner, way*): **do as you wish** haz lo que quieras; **as she said** como dijo; **he gave it to me as a present** me lo dio de regalo
5 (*in the capacity of*): **he works as a barman** trabaja de barman; **as chairman of the company, he ...** como presidente de la compañía ...
6 (*concerning*): **as for** *or* **to that** por *or* en lo que respecta a eso
7: **as if** *or* **though** como si; **he looked as if he was ill** parecía como si estuviera enfermo, tenía aspecto de enfermo; *see also* **long; such; well**

a.s.a.p. *abbr* (= *as soon as possible*) cuanto antes
asbestos [æzˈbɛstəs] *n* asbesto, amianto
ascent [əˈsɛnt] *n* subida; (*slope*) cuesta, pendiente *f*
ash [æʃ] *n* ceniza; (*tree*) fresno
ashamed [əˈʃeɪmd] *adj* avergonzado, apenado (LAM); **to be ~ of** avergonzarse de
ashore [əˈʃɔː*] *adv* en tierra; (*swim etc*) a tierra
ashtray [ˈæʃtreɪ] *n* cenicero
Ash Wednesday *n* miércoles *m* de Ceniza
Asia [ˈeɪʃə] *n* Asia; **Asian** *adj, n* asiático/a *m/f*
aside [əˈsaɪd] *adv* a un lado ▷ *n* aparte *m*
ask [ɑːsk] *vt* (*question*) preguntar; (*invite*) invitar; **to ~ sb sth/to do sth** preguntar algo a algn/pedir a algn que haga algo; **to ~ sb about sth** preguntar algo a algn; **to ~ (sb) a question** hacer una pregunta (a algn); **to ~ sb out to dinner** invitar a cenar a algn; **ask for** *vt fus* pedir; (*trouble*) buscar
asleep [əˈsliːp] *adj* dormido; **to fall ~** dormirse, quedarse dormido
asparagus [əsˈpærəgəs] *n* (*plant*) espárrago; (*food*) espárragos *mpl*
aspect [ˈæspɛkt] *n* aspecto, apariencia; (*direction in which a building etc faces*) orientación *f*
aspirations [æspəˈreɪʃənz] *npl* aspiraciones *fpl*; (*ambition*) ambición *f*
aspire [əsˈpaɪə*] *vi*: **to ~ to** aspirar a, ambicionar
aspirin [ˈæsprɪn] *n* aspirina
ass [æs] *n* asno, burro; (*inf: idiot*) imbécil *mf*; (*US: inf!*) culo, trasero
assassin [əˈsæsɪn] *n* asesino/a; **assassinate** *vt* asesinar
assault [əˈsɔːlt] *n* asalto; (*Law*) agresión *f* ▷ *vt* asaltar, atacar; (*sexually*) violar
assemble [əˈsɛmbl] *vt* reunir, juntar; (*Tech*) montar ▷ *vi* reunirse, juntarse
assembly [əˈsɛmblɪ] *n* reunión *f*, asamblea; (*parliament*) parlamento; (*construction*) montaje *m*
assert [əˈsəːt] *vt* afirmar; (*authority*) hacer valer; **assertion** [-ʃən] *n* afirmación *f*
assess [əˈsɛs] *vt* valorar, calcular; (*tax, damages*) fijar; (*for tax*) gravar; **assessment** *n* valoración *f*; (*for tax*) gravamen *m*
asset [ˈæsɛt] *n* ventaja; **assets** *npl* (*Comm*) activo; (*property, funds*)

fondos *mpl*
assign [ə'saɪn] *vt*: **to ~ (to)** (*date*) fijar (para); (*task*) asignar (a); (*resources*) destinar (a); **assignment** *n* tarea
assist [ə'sɪst] *vt* ayudar; **assistance** *n* ayuda, auxilio; **assistant** *n* ayudante *mf*; (BRIT: *also*: **shop assistant**) dependiente/a *m/f*
associate [*adj*, *n* ə'səuʃɪɪt, *vb* ə'səuʃɪeɪt] *adj* asociado ▷ *n* (*at work*) colega *mf* ▷ *vt* asociar; (*ideas*) relacionar ▷ *vi*: **to ~ with sb** tratar con algn
association [əsəusɪ'eɪʃən] *n* asociación *f*
assorted [ə'sɔːtɪd] *adj* surtido, variado
assortment [ə'sɔːtmənt] *n* (*of shapes, colours*) surtido; (*of books*) colección *f*; (*of people*) mezcla
assume [ə'sjuːm] *vt* suponer; (*responsibilities*) asumir; (*attitude*) adoptar, tomar
assumption [ə'sʌmpʃən] *n* suposición *f*, presunción *f*; (*of power etc*) toma
assurance [ə'ʃuərəns] *n* garantía, promesa; (*confidence*) confianza, aplomo; (*insurance*) seguro
assure [ə'ʃuə*] *vt* asegurar
asterisk ['æstərɪsk] *n* asterisco
asthma ['æsmə] *n* asma
astonish [ə'stɔnɪʃ] *vt* asombrar, pasmar; **astonished** *adj* estupefacto, pasmado; **to be astonished (at)** asombrarse (de); **astonishing** *adj* asombroso, pasmoso; **I find it astonishing that ...** me asombra *or* pasma que ...; **astonishment** *n* asombro, sorpresa
astound [ə'staund] *vt* asombrar, pasmar
astray [ə'streɪ] *adv*: **to go ~** extraviarse; **to lead ~** (*morally*) llevar por mal camino
astrology [æs'trɔlədʒɪ] *n* astrología
astronaut ['æstrənɔːt] *n* astronauta *mf*
astronomer [əs'trɔnəmə*] *n* astrónomo/a
astronomical [æstrə'nɔmɪkəl] *adj* astronómico
astronomy [æs'trɔnəmɪ] *n* astronomía
astute [əs'tjuːt] *adj* astuto
asylum [ə'saɪləm] *n* (*refuge*) asilo; (*mental hospital*) manicomio

KEYWORD

at [æt] *prep* **1** (*referring to position*) en; (*direction*) a; **at the top** en lo alto; **at home/school** en casa/la escuela; **to look at sth/sb** mirar algo/a algn
2 (*referring to time*): **at 4 o'clock** a las 4; **at night** por la noche; **at Christmas** en Navidad; **at times** a veces
3 (*referring to rates, speed etc*): **at £1 a kilo** a una libra el kilo; **two at a time** de dos en dos; **at 50 km/h** a 50 km/h
4 (*referring to manner*): **at a stroke** de un golpe; **at peace** en paz
5 (*referring to activity*): **to be at work** estar trabajando; (*in the office etc*) estar en el trabajo; **to play at cowboys** jugar a los vaqueros; **to be good at sth** ser bueno en algo
6 (*referring to cause*): **shocked/surprised/annoyed at sth** asombrado/sorprendido/fastidiado por algo; **I went at his suggestion** fui a instancias suyas
7 (*symbol*) arroba

ate [eɪt] *pt of* **eat**
atheist ['eɪθɪɪst] *n* ateo/a
Athens ['æθɪnz] *n* Atenas
athlete ['æθliːt] *n* atleta *mf*
athletic [æθ'lɛtɪk] *adj* atlético; **athletics** *n* atletismo
Atlantic [ət'læntɪk] *adj* atlántico ▷ *n*: **the ~ (Ocean)** el (Océano) Atlántico
atlas ['ætləs] *n* atlas *m inv*
A.T.M. *n abbr* (= *automated telling*

machine) cajero automático
atmosphere ['ætməsfɪə*] *n* atmósfera; (*of place*) ambiente *m*
atom ['ætəm] *n* átomo; **atomic** [ə'tɔmɪk] *adj* atómico; **atom(ic) bomb** *n* bomba atómica
A to Z® *n* (*map*) callejero
atrocity [ə'trɔsɪtɪ] *n* atrocidad *f*
attach [ə'tætʃ] *vt* (*fasten*) atar; (*join*) unir, sujetar; (*document, letter*) adjuntar; (*importance etc*) dar, conceder; **to be ~ed to sb/sth** (*to like*) tener cariño a algn/algo; **attachment** *n* (*tool*) accesorio; (*Comput*) archivo, documento adjunto; (*love*): **attachment (to)** apego (a)
attack [ə'tæk] *vt* (*Mil*) atacar; (*criminal*) agredir, asaltar; (*criticize*) criticar; (*task*) emprender ▷ *n* ataque *m*, asalto; (*on sb's life*) atentado; (*fig: criticism*) crítica; (*of illness*) ataque *m*; **heart ~** infarto (de miocardio); **attacker** *n* agresor(a) *m/f*, asaltante *mf*
attain [ə'teɪn] *vt* (*also*: **~ to**) alcanzar; (*achieve*) lograr, conseguir
attempt [ə'tɛmpt] *n* tentativa, intento; (*attack*) atentado ▷ *vt* intentar
attend [ə'tɛnd] *vt* asistir a; (*patient*) atender; **attend to** *vt fus* ocuparse de; (*customer, patient*) atender a; **attendance** *n* asistencia, presencia; (*people present*) concurrencia; **attendant** *n* ayudante *mf*; (*in garage etc*) encargado/a ▷ *adj* (*dangers*) concomitante
attention [ə'tɛnʃən] *n* atención *f*; (*care*) atenciones *fpl* ▷ *excl* (*Mil*) ¡firme(s)!; **for the ~ of ...** (*Admin*) atención ...
attic ['ætɪk] *n* desván *m*
attitude ['ætɪtju:d] *n* actitud *f*; (*disposition*) disposición *f*
attorney [ə'tə:nɪ] *n* (*lawyer*) abogado/a; **Attorney General** *n* (BRIT) ≈ Presidente *m* del Consejo del Poder Judicial (SP); (US) ≈ ministro de Justicia
attract [ə'trækt] *vt* atraer; (*sb's attention*) llamar; **attraction** [ə'trækʃən] *n* encanto; (*gen pl: amusements*) diversiones *fpl*; (*Physics*) atracción *f*; (*fig: towards sb, sth*) atractivo; **attractive** *adj* guapo; (*interesting*) atrayente
attribute [*n* 'ætrɪbju:t, *vb* ə'trɪbju:t] *n* atributo ▷ *vt*: **to ~ sth to** atribuir algo a
aubergine ['əubəʒi:n] (BRIT) *n* berenjena; (*colour*) morado
auburn ['ɔ:bən] *adj* color castaño rojizo
auction ['ɔ:kʃən] *n* (*also*: **sale by ~**) subasta ▷ *vt* subastar
audible ['ɔ:dɪbl] *adj* audible, que se puede oír
audience ['ɔ:dɪəns] *n* público; (*Radio*) radioescuchas *mpl*; (*TV*) telespectadores *mpl*; (*interview*) audiencia
audit ['ɔ:dɪt] *vt* revisar, intervenir
audition [ɔ:'dɪʃən] *n* audición *f*
auditor ['ɔ:dɪtə*] *n* interventor(a) *m/f*, censor(a) *m/f* de cuentas
auditorium [ɔ:dɪ'tɔ:rɪəm] *n* auditorio
Aug. *abbr* (= *August*) ag
August ['ɔ:gəst] *n* agosto
aunt [ɑ:nt] *n* tía; **auntie** *n diminutive of* **aunt**; **aunty** *n diminutive of* **aunt**
au pair ['əu'pɛə*] *n* (*also*: **~ girl**) (chica) au pair *f*
aura ['ɔ:rə] *n* aura; (*atmosphere*) ambiente *m*
austerity [ɔ'stɛrɪtɪ] *n* austeridad *f*
Australia [ɔs'treɪlɪə] *n* Australia; **Australian** *adj, n* australiano/a *m/f*
Austria ['ɔstrɪə] *n* Austria; **Austrian** *adj, n* austríaco/a *m/f*
authentic [ɔ:'θɛntɪk] *adj* auténtico
author ['ɔ:θə*] *n* autor(a) *m/f*
authority [ɔ:'θɔrɪtɪ] *n* autoridad *f*; (*official permission*) autorización *f*; **the authorities** *npl* las autoridades
authorize ['ɔ:θəraɪz] *vt* autorizar

auto ['ɔːtəu] (US) *n* coche *m* (SP), carro (LAM), automóvil *m*
auto: autobiography [ɔːtəbaɪ'ɔgrəfɪ] *n* autobiografía; **autograph** ['ɔːtəgrɑːf] *n* autógrafo ▷ *vt* (*photo etc*) dedicar; (*programme*) firmar; **automatic** [ɔːtə'mætɪk] *adj* automático ▷ *n* (*gun*) pistola automática; (*car*) coche *m* automático; **automatically** *adv* automáticamente; **automobile** ['ɔːtəməbiːl] (US) *n* coche *m* (SP), carro (LAM), automóvil *m*; **autonomous** [ɔː'tɔnəməs] *adj* autónomo; **autonomy** [ɔː'tɔnəmɪ] *n* autonomía
autumn ['ɔːtəm] *n* otoño
auxiliary [ɔːg'zɪlɪərɪ] *adj, n* auxiliar *mf*
avail [ə'veɪl] *vt*: **to ~ o.s. of** aprovechar(se) de ▷ *n*: **to no ~** en vano, sin resultado
availability [əveɪlə'bɪlɪtɪ] *n* disponibilidad *f*
available [ə'veɪləbl] *adj* disponible; (*unoccupied*) libre; (*person*: *unattached*) soltero y sin compromiso
avalanche ['ævəlɑːnʃ] *n* alud *m*, avalancha
Ave. *abbr* = **avenue**
avenue ['ævənjuː] *n* avenida; (*fig*) camino
average ['ævərɪdʒ] *n* promedio, término medio ▷ *adj* medio, de término medio; (*ordinary*) regular, corriente ▷ *vt* sacar un promedio de; **on ~** por regla general
avert [ə'vəːt] *vt* prevenir; (*blow*) desviar; (*one's eyes*) apartar
avid ['ævɪd] *adj* ávido
avocado [ævə'kɑːdəu] *n* (*also* BRIT: **~ pear**) aguacate *m*, palta (SC)
avoid [ə'vɔɪd] *vt* evitar, eludir
await [ə'weɪt] *vt* esperar, aguardar
awake [ə'weɪk] (*pt* **awoke**, *pp* **awoken** *or* **awaked**) *adj* despierto ▷ *vt* despertar ▷ *vi* despertarse; **to be ~** estar despierto
award [ə'wɔːd] *n* premio; (*Law*: *damages*) indemnización *f* ▷ *vt* otorgar, conceder; (*Law*: *damages*) adjudicar
aware [ə'wɛə*] *adj*: **~ (of)** consciente (de); **to become ~ of/that** (*realize*) darse cuenta de/de que; (*learn*) enterarse de/de que; **awareness** *n* conciencia; (*knowledge*) conocimiento
away [ə'weɪ] *adv* fuera; (*movement*): **she went ~** se marchó; **far ~** lejos; **two kilometres ~** a dos kilómetros de distancia; **two hours ~ by car** a dos horas en coche; **the holiday was two weeks ~** faltaban dos semanas para las vacaciones; **he's ~ for a week** estará ausente una semana; **to take ~ (from)** quitar (a); (*subtract*) substraer (de); **to work/pedal ~** seguir trabajando/pedaleando; **to fade ~** (*colour*) desvanecerse; (*sound*) apagarse
awe [ɔː] *n* admiración *f* respetuosa; **awesome** ['ɔːsəm] (US) *adj* (*excellent*) formidable
awful ['ɔːfəl] *adj* horroroso; (*quantity*): **an ~ lot (of)** cantidad (de); **awfully** *adv* (*very*) terriblemente
awkward ['ɔːkwəd] *adj* desmañado, torpe; (*shape*) incómodo; (*embarrassing*) delicado, difícil
awoke [ə'wəuk] *pt of* **awake**
awoken [ə'wəukən] *pp of* **awake**
axe [æks] (US **ax**) *n* hacha ▷ *vt* (*project*) cortar; (*jobs*) reducir
axle ['æksl] *n* eje *m*, árbol *m*
ay(e) [aɪ] *excl* sí
azalea [ə'zeɪlɪə] *n* azalea

b

B [biː] *n* (*Mus*) si *m*
B.A. *abbr* = **Bachelor of Arts**
baby ['beɪbɪ] *n* bebé *mf*; (US: *inf*: *darling*) mi amor; **baby carriage** (US) *n* cochecito; **baby-sit** *vi* hacer de canguro; **baby-sitter** *n* canguro/a; **baby wipe** *n* toallita húmeda (*para bebés*)
bachelor ['bætʃələ*] *n* soltero; **B~ of Arts/Science** licenciado/a en Filosofía y Letras/Ciencias
back [bæk] *n* (*of person*) espalda; (*of animal*) lomo; (*of hand*) dorso; (*as opposed to front*) parte *f* de atrás; (*of chair*) respaldo; (*of page*) reverso; (*of book*) final *m*; (*Football*) defensa *m*; (*of crowd*): **the ones at the ~** los del fondo ▷ *vt* (*candidate*: *also*: **~ up**) respaldar, apoyar; (*horse*: *at races*) apostar a; (*car*) dar marcha atrás a *or* con ▷ *vi* (*car etc*) ir (*or* salir *or* entrar) marcha atrás ▷ *adj* (*payment, rent*) atrasado; (*seats, wheels*) de atrás ▷ *adv* (*not forward*) (hacia) atrás; (*returned*): **he's ~** está de vuelta, ha vuelto; **he ran ~** volvió corriendo; (*restitution*): **throw the ball ~** devuelve la pelota; **can I have it ~?** ¿me lo devuelve?; (*again*): **he called ~** llamó de nuevo; **back down** *vi* echarse atrás; **back out** *vi* (*of promise*) volverse atrás; **back up** *vt* (*person*) apoyar, respaldar; (*theory*) defender; (*Comput*) hacer una copia preventiva *or* de reserva; **backache** *n* dolor *m* de espalda; **backbencher** (BRIT) *n* *miembro del parlamento sin cargo relevante*; **backbone** *n* columna vertebral; **back door** *n* puerta *f* trasera; **backfire** *vi* (*Aut*) petardear; (*plans*) fallar, salir mal; **backgammon** *n* backgammon *m*; **background** *n* fondo; (*of events*) antecedentes *mpl*; (*basic knowledge*) bases *fpl*; (*experience*) conocimientos *mpl*, educación *f*; **family background** origen *m*, antecedentes *mpl*; **backing** *n* (*fig*) apoyo, respaldo; **backlog** *n*: **backlog of work** trabajo atrasado; **backpack** *n* mochila; **backpacker** *n* mochilero/a; **backslash** *n* pleca, barra inversa; **backstage** *adv* entre bastidores; **backstroke** *n* espalda; **backup** *adj* suplementario; (*Comput*) de reserva ▷ *n* (*support*) apoyo; (*also*: **backup file**) copia preventiva *or* de reserva; **backward** *adj* (*person, country*) atrasado; **backwards** *adv* hacia atrás; (*read a list*) al revés; (*fall*) de espaldas; **backyard** *n* traspatio
bacon ['beɪkən] *n* tocino, beicon *m*
bacteria [bæk'tɪərɪə] *npl* bacterias *fpl*
bad [bæd] *adj* malo; (*mistake, accident*) grave; (*food*) podrido, pasado; **his ~ leg** su pierna lisiada; **to go ~** (*food*) pasarse
badge [bædʒ] *n* insignia; (*policeman's*) chapa, placa
badger ['bædʒə*] *n* tejón *m*
badly ['bædlɪ] *adv* mal; **to reflect ~ on sb** influir negativamente en la reputación de algn; **~ wounded** gravemente herido; **he needs it ~** le hace gran falta; **to be ~ off (for money)** andar mal de dinero
bad-mannered ['bæd'mænəd] *adj*

mal educado

badminton ['bædmɪntən] *n* bádminton *m*

bad-tempered ['bæd'tɛmpəd] *adj* de mal genio *or* carácter; (*temporarily*) de mal humor

bag [bæg] *n* bolsa; (*handbag*) bolso; (*satchel*) mochila; (*case*) maleta; **~s of** (*inf*) un montón de; **baggage** *n* equipaje *m*; **baggage allowance** *n* límite *m* de equipaje; **baggage reclaim** *n* recogida de equipajes; **baggy** *adj* amplio; **bagpipes** *npl* gaita

bail [beɪl] *n* fianza ▷ *vt* (*prisoner*: *gen*: *grant bail to*) poner en libertad bajo fianza; (*boat*: *also*: **~ out**) achicar; **on ~** (*prisoner*) bajo fianza; **to ~ sb out** obtener la libertad de algn bajo fianza

bait [beɪt] *n* cebo ▷ *vt* poner cebo en; (*tease*) tomar el pelo a

bake [beɪk] *vt* cocer (al horno) ▷ *vi* cocerse; **baked beans** *npl* judías *fpl* en salsa de tomate; **baked potato** *n* patata al horno; **baker** *n* panadero; **bakery** *n* panadería; (*for cakes*) pastelería; **baking** *n* (*act*) amasar *m*; (*batch*) hornada; **baking powder** *n* levadura (en polvo)

balance ['bæləns] *n* equilibrio; (*Comm*: *sum*) balance *m*; (*remainder*) resto; (*scales*) balanza ▷ *vt* equilibrar; (*budget*) nivelar; (*account*) saldar; (*make equal*) equilibrar; **~ of trade/payments** balanza de comercio/pagos; **balanced** *adj* (*personality*, *diet*) equilibrado; (*report*) objetivo; **balance sheet** *n* balance *m*

balcony ['bælkənɪ] *n* (*open*) balcón *m*; (*closed*) galería; (*in theatre*) anfiteatro

bald [bɔːld] *adj* calvo; (*tyre*) liso

Balearics [bælɪ'ærɪks] *npl*: **the ~** las Baleares

ball [bɔːl] *n* pelota; (*football*) balón *m*; (*of wool*, *string*) ovillo; (*dance*) baile *m*; **to play ~** (*fig*) cooperar

ballerina [bælə'riːnə] *n* bailarina

ballet ['bæleɪ] *n* ballet *m*; **ballet dancer** *n* bailarín/ina *m/f*

balloon [bə'luːn] *n* globo

ballot ['bælət] *n* votación *f*

ballpoint (pen) ['bɔːlpɔɪnt-] *n* bolígrafo

ballroom ['bɔːlrum] *n* salón *m* de baile

Baltic ['bɔːltɪk] *n*: **the ~ (Sea)** el (Mar) Báltico

bamboo [bæm'buː] *n* bambú *m*

ban [bæn] *n* prohibición *f*, proscripción *f* ▷ *vt* prohibir, proscribir

banana [bə'nɑːnə] *n* plátano, banana (LAM), banano (CAM)

band [bænd] *n* grupo; (*strip*) faja, tira; (*stripe*) lista; (*Mus*: *jazz*) orquesta; (: *rock*) grupo; (*Mil*) banda

bandage ['bændɪdʒ] *n* venda, vendaje *m* ▷ *vt* vendar

Band-Aid® ['bændeɪd] (US) *n* tirita

bandit ['bændɪt] *n* bandido

bang [bæŋ] *n* (*of gun*, *exhaust*) estallido, detonación *f*; (*of door*) portazo; (*blow*) golpe *m* ▷ *vt* (*door*) cerrar de golpe; (*one's head*) golpear ▷ *vi* estallar; (*door*) cerrar de golpe

Bangladesh [bɑːŋglə'dɛʃ] *n* Bangladesh *m*

bangle ['bæŋgl] *n* brazalete *m*, ajorca

bangs [bæŋz] (US) *npl* flequillo

banish ['bænɪʃ] *vt* desterrar

banister(s) ['bænɪstə(z)] *n(pl)* barandilla, pasamanos *m inv*

banjo ['bændʒəu] (*pl* **~es** *or* **~s**) *n* banjo

bank [bæŋk] *n* (*Comm*) banco; (*of river*, *lake*) ribera, orilla; (*of earth*) terraplén *m* ▷ *vi* (*Aviat*) ladearse; **bank on** *vt fus* contar con; **bank account** *n* cuenta de banco; **bank balance** *n* saldo; **bank card** *n* tarjeta bancaria; **bank charges** *npl* comisión *fsg*; **banker** *n* banquero; **bank holiday** *n* (BRIT) día *m* festivo *or* de fiesta; **banking** *n* banca; **bank manager** *n* director(a) *m/f* (de sucursal) de banco; **banknote** *n* billete *m* de banco

BANK HOLIDAY

El término **bank holiday** se aplica en el Reino Unido a todo día festivo oficial en el que cierran bancos y comercios. Los más importantes son en Navidad, Semana Santa, finales de mayo y finales de agosto y, al contrario que en los países de tradición católica, no coinciden necesariamente con una celebración religiosa.

bankrupt ['bæŋkrʌpt] *adj* quebrado, insolvente; **to go ~** hacer bancarrota; **to be ~** estar en quiebra; **bankruptcy** *n* quiebra
bank statement *n* balance *m* *or* detalle *m* de cuenta
banner ['bænə*] *n* pancarta
bannister(s) ['bænɪstə(z)] *n(pl)* = **banister(s)**
banquet ['bæŋkwɪt] *n* banquete *m*
baptism ['bæptɪzəm] *n* bautismo; (*act*) bautizo
baptize [bæp'taɪz] *vt* bautizar
bar [bɑː*] *n* (*pub*) bar *m*; (*counter*) mostrador *m*; (*rod*) barra; (*of window, cage*) reja; (*of soap*) pastilla; (*of chocolate*) tableta; (*fig: hindrance*) obstáculo; (*prohibition*) proscripción *f*; (*Mus*) barra ▷ *vt* (*road*) obstruir; (*person*) excluir; (*activity*) prohibir; **the B~** (*Law*) la abogacía; **behind ~s** entre rejas; **~ none** sin excepción
barbaric [bɑː'bærɪk] *adj* bárbaro
barbecue ['bɑːbɪkjuː] *n* barbacoa
barbed wire ['bɑːbd-] *n* alambre *m* de púas
barber ['bɑːbə*] *n* peluquero, barbero; **barber's (shop)** (*US* **barber (shop)**) *n* peluquería
bar code *n* código de barras
bare [bɛə*] *adj* desnudo; (*trees*) sin hojas; (*necessities etc*) básico ▷ *vt* desnudar; (*teeth*) enseñar; **barefoot** *adj, adv* descalzo; **barely** *adv* apenas
bargain ['bɑːgɪn] *n* pacto, negocio; (*good buy*) ganga ▷ *vi* negociar; (*haggle*) regatear; **into the ~** además, por añadidura; **bargain for** *vt fus*: **he got more than he bargained for** le resultó peor de lo que esperaba
barge [bɑːdʒ] *n* barcaza; **barge in** *vi* irrumpir; (*interrupt: conversation*) interrumpir
bark [bɑːk] *n* (*of tree*) corteza; (*of dog*) ladrido ▷ *vi* ladrar
barley ['bɑːlɪ] *n* cebada
barmaid ['bɑːmeɪd] *n* camarera
barman ['bɑːmən] (*irreg*) *n* camarero, barman *m*
barn [bɑːn] *n* granero
barometer [bə'rɔmɪtə*] *n* barómetro
baron ['bærən] *n* barón *m*; (*press baron etc*) magnate *m*; **baroness** *n* baronesa
barracks ['bærəks] *npl* cuartel *m*
barrage ['bærɑːʒ] *n* (*Mil*) descarga, bombardeo; (*dam*) presa; (*of criticism*) lluvia, aluvión *m*
barrel ['bærəl] *n* barril *m*; (*of gun*) cañón *m*
barren ['bærən] *adj* estéril
barrette [bə'rɛt] (*US*) *n* pasador *m* (*LAM, SP*), broche *m* (*MEX*)
barricade [bærɪ'keɪd] *n* barricada
barrier ['bærɪə*] *n* barrera
barring ['bɑːrɪŋ] *prep* excepto, salvo
barrister ['bærɪstə*] (*BRIT*) *n* abogado/a
barrow ['bærəu] *n* (*cart*) carretilla (de mano)
bartender ['bɑːtɛndə*] (*US*) *n* camarero, barman *m*
base [beɪs] *n* base *f* ▷ *vt*: **to ~ sth on** basar *or* fundar algo en ▷ *adj* bajo, infame
baseball ['beɪsbɔːl] *n* béisbol *m*; **baseball cap** *n* gorra *f* de béisbol
basement ['beɪsmənt] *n* sótano
bases¹ ['beɪsiːz] *npl of* **basis**
bases² ['beɪsɪz] *npl of* **base**
bash [bæʃ] (*inf*) *vt* golpear

basic ['beɪsɪk] *adj* básico; **basically** *adv* fundamentalmente, en el fondo; (*simply*) sencillamente; **basics** *npl*: **the basics** los fundamentos
basil ['bæzl] *n* albahaca
basin ['beɪsn] *n* cuenco, tazón *m*; (*Geo*) cuenca; (*also*: **wash~**) lavabo
basis ['beɪsɪs] (*pl* **bases**) *n* base *f*; **on a part-time/trial ~** a tiempo parcial/a prueba
basket ['bɑːskɪt] *n* cesta, cesto; canasta; **basketball** *n* baloncesto
bass [beɪs] *n* (*Mus: instrument*) bajo; (*double bass*) contrabajo; (*singer*) bajo
bastard ['bɑːstəd] *n* bastardo; (*inf!*) hijo de puta (*!*)
bat [bæt] *n* (*Zool*) murciélago; (*for ball games*) palo; (BRIT: *for table tennis*) pala ▷ *vt*: **he didn't ~ an eyelid** ni pestañeó
batch [bætʃ] *n* (*of bread*) hornada; (*of letters etc*) lote *m*
bath [bɑːθ, *pl* bɑːðz] *n* (*action*) baño; (*bathtub*) bañera (SP), tina (LAM), bañadera (RPL) ▷ *vt* bañar; **to have a ~** bañarse, tomar un baño; *see also* **baths**
bathe [beɪð] *vi* bañarse ▷ *vt* (*wound*) lavar
bathing ['beɪðɪŋ] *n* el bañarse; **bathing costume** (US **bathing suit**) *n* traje *m* de baño
bath: bathrobe *n* (*man's*) batín *m*; (*woman's*) bata; **bathroom** *n* (cuarto de) baño; **baths** [bɑːðz] *npl* (*also*: **swimming baths**) piscina; **bath towel** *n* toalla de baño; **bathtub** *n* bañera
baton ['bætən] *n* (*Mus*) batuta; (*Athletics*) testigo; (*weapon*) porra
batter ['bætə*] *vt* maltratar; (*rain etc*) azotar ▷ *n* masa (para rebozar); **battered** *adj* (*hat, pan*) estropeado
battery ['bætərɪ] *n* (*Aut*) batería; (*of torch*) pila; **battery farming** *n* cría intensiva
battle ['bætl] *n* batalla; (*fig*) lucha ▷ *vi* luchar; **battlefield** *n* campo *m* de batalla
bay [beɪ] *n* (*Geo*) bahía; **B~ of Biscay** ≈ mar Cantábrico; **to hold sb at ~** mantener a algn a raya
bazaar [bə'zɑː*] *n* bazar *m*; (*fete*) *venta con fines benéficos*
B. & B. *n abbr* = **bed and breakfast**; (*place*) pensión *f*; (*terms*) cama y desayuno
BBC *n abbr* (= *British Broadcasting Corporation*) *cadena de radio y televisión estatal británica*
B.C. *adv abbr* (= *before Christ*) a. de C.

KEYWORD

be [biː] (*pt* **was, were**, *pp* **been**) *aux vb* **1** (*with present participle: forming continuous tenses*): **what are you doing?** ¿qué estás haciendo?, ¿qué haces?; **they're coming tomorrow** vienen mañana; **I've been waiting for you for hours** llevo horas esperándote
2 (*with pp: forming passives*) ser (*but often replaced by active or reflexive constructions*); **to be murdered** ser asesinado; **the box had been opened** habían abierto la caja; **the thief was nowhere to be seen** no se veía al ladrón por ninguna parte
3 (*in tag questions*): **it was fun, wasn't it?** fue divertido, ¿no? *or* ¿verdad?; **he's good-looking, isn't he?** es guapo, ¿no te parece?; **she's back again, is she?** entonces, ¿ha vuelto?
4 (*+to +infin*): **the house is to be sold** (*necessity*) hay que vender la casa; (*future*) van a vender la casa; **he's not to open it** no tiene que abrirlo
▷ *vb +complement* **1** (*with n or num complement, but see also* 3, 4, 5 *and impers vb below*) ser; **he's a doctor** es médico; **2 and 2 are 4** 2 y 2 son 4
2 (*with adj complement: expressing permanent or inherent quality*) ser; (*: expressing state seen as temporary or reversible*) estar; **I'm English** soy inglés/esa; **she's tall/pretty** es alta/bonita; **he's young** es joven; **be careful/good/quiet** ten cuidado/

pórtate bien/cállate; **I'm tired** estoy cansado/a; **it's dirty** está sucio/a
3 (*of health*) estar; **how are you?** ¿cómo estás?; **he's very ill** está muy enfermo; **I'm better now** ya estoy mejor
4 (*of age*) tener; **how old are you?** ¿cuántos años tienes?; **I'm sixteen (years old)** tengo dieciséis años
5 (*cost*) costar; ser; **how much was the meal?** ¿cuánto fue *or* costó la comida?; **that'll be £5.75, please** son £5.75, por favor; **this shirt is £17** esta camisa cuesta £17
▷ *vi* **1** (*exist, occur etc*) existir, haber; **the best singer that ever was** el mejor cantante que existió jamás; **is there a God?** ¿hay un Dios?, ¿existe Dios?; **be that as it may** sea como sea; **so be it** así sea
2 (*referring to place*) estar; **I won't be here tomorrow** no estaré aquí mañana
3 (*referring to movement*): **where have you been?** ¿dónde has estado?
▷ *impers vb* **1** (*referring to time*): **it's 5 o'clock** son las 5; **it's the 28th of April** estamos a 28 de abril
2 (*referring to distance*): **it's 10 km to the village** el pueblo está a 10 km
3 (*referring to the weather*): **it's too hot/cold** hace demasiado calor/frío; **it's windy today** hace viento hoy
4 (*emphatic*): **it's me** soy yo; **it was Maria who paid the bill** fue María la que pagó la cuenta

beach [bi:tʃ] *n* playa ▷ *vt* varar
beacon ['bi:kən] *n* (*lighthouse*) faro; (*marker*) guía
bead [bi:d] *n* cuenta; (*of sweat etc*) gota; **beads** *npl* (*necklace*) collar *m*
beak [bi:k] *n* pico
beam [bi:m] *n* (*Arch*) viga, travesaño; (*of light*) rayo, haz *m* de luz ▷ *vi* brillar; (*smile*) sonreír
bean [bi:n] *n* judía; **runner/broad ~** habichuela/haba; **coffee ~** grano de café; **beansprouts** *npl* brotes *mpl* de soja
bear [bɛə*] (*pt* **bore**, *pp* **borne**) *n* oso ▷ *vt* (*weight etc*) llevar; (*cost*) pagar; (*responsibility*) tener; (*endure*) soportar, aguantar; (*children*) parir, tener; (*fruit*) dar ▷ *vi*: **to ~ right/left** torcer a la derecha/izquierda
beard [bɪəd] *n* barba
bearer ['bɛərə*] *n* portador(a) *m/f*
bearing ['bɛərɪŋ] *n* porte *m*, comportamiento; (*connection*) relación *f*
beast [bi:st] *n* bestia; (*inf*) bruto, salvaje *m*
beat [bi:t] (*pt* **~**, *pp* **beaten**) *n* (*of heart*) latido; (*Mus*) ritmo, compás *m*; (*of policeman*) ronda ▷ *vt* pegar, golpear; (*eggs*) batir; (*defeat*: *opponent*) vencer, derrotar; (: *record*) sobrepasar ▷ *vi* (*heart*) latir; (*drum*) redoblar; (*rain, wind*) azotar; **off the ~en track** aislado; **to ~ it** (*inf*) largarse; **beat up** *vt* (*attack*) dar una paliza a; **beating** *n* paliza
beautiful ['bju:tɪful] *adj* precioso, hermoso, bello; **beautifully** *adv* maravillosamente
beauty ['bju:tɪ] *n* belleza; **beauty parlour** (*US* **beauty parlor**) *n* salón *m* de belleza; **beauty salon** *n* salón *m* de belleza; **beauty spot** *n* (*Tourism*) lugar *m* pintoresco
beaver ['bi:və*] *n* castor *m*
became [bɪ'keɪm] *pt of* **become**
because [bɪ'kɔz] *conj* porque; **~ of** debido a, a causa de
beckon ['bɛkən] *vt* (*also*: **~ to**) llamar con señas
become [bɪ'kʌm] (*pt* **became**, *pp* **~**) *vt* (*suit*) favorecer, sentar bien a ▷ *vi* (+ *n*) hacerse, llegar a ser; (+ *adj*) ponerse, volverse; **to ~ fat** engordar
bed [bɛd] *n* cama; (*of flowers*) macizo; (*of coal, clay*) capa; (*of river*) lecho; (*of sea*) fondo; **to go to ~** acostarse; **bed and breakfast** *n* (*place*) pensión *f*; (*terms*) cama y desayuno; **bedclothes** *npl* ropa de cama; **bedding** *n* ropa de cama; **bed linen** *n* (BRIT) ropa *f*

de cama

BED AND BREAKFAST

Se llama **bed and breakfast** a una forma de alojamiento, en el campo o la ciudad, que ofrece cama y desayuno a precios inferiores a los de un hotel. El servicio se suele anunciar con carteles en los que a menudo se usa únicamente la abreviatura **B. & B.**

bed: bedroom *n* dormitorio; **bedside** *n*: **at the bedside of** a la cabecera de; **bedside lamp** *n* lámpara de noche; **bedside table** *n* mesilla de noche; **bedsit(ter)** (BRIT) *n* cuarto de alquiler; **bedspread** *n* cubrecama *m*, colcha; **bedtime** *n* hora de acostarse

bee [biː] *n* abeja

beech [biːtʃ] *n* haya

beef [biːf] *n* carne *f* de vaca; **roast ~** rosbif *m*; **beefburger** *n* hamburguesa; **Beefeater** *n alabardero de la Torre de Londres*

been [biːn] *pp of* **be**

beer [bɪə*] *n* cerveza; **beer garden** *n* (BRIT) terraza *f* de verano, jardín *m* (de un bar)

beet [biːt] (US) *n* (*also*: **red ~**) remolacha

beetle ['biːtl] *n* escarabajo

beetroot ['biːtruːt] (BRIT) *n* remolacha

before [bɪ'fɔː*] *prep* (*of time*) antes de; (*of space*) delante de ▷ *conj* antes (de) que ▷ *adv* antes, anteriormente; delante, adelante; **~ going** antes de marcharse; **~ she goes** antes de que se vaya; **the week ~** la semana anterior; **I've never seen it ~** no lo he visto nunca; **beforehand** *adv* de antemano, con anticipación

beg [bɛg] *vi* pedir limosna ▷ *vt* pedir, rogar; (*entreat*) suplicar; **to ~ sb to do sth** rogar a algn que haga algo; *see also* **pardon**

began [bɪ'gæn] *pt of* **begin**

beggar ['bɛgə*] *n* mendigo/a

begin [bɪ'gɪn] (*pt* **began**, *pp* **begun**) *vt, vi* empezar, comenzar; **to ~ doing** *or* **to do sth** empezar a hacer algo; **beginner** *n* principiante *mf*; **beginning** *n* principio, comienzo

begun [bɪ'gʌn] *pp of* **begin**

behalf [bɪ'hɑːf] *n*: **on ~ of** en nombre de, por; (*for benefit of*) en beneficio de; **on my/his ~** por mí/él

behave [bɪ'heɪv] *vi* (*person*) portarse, comportarse; (*well*: *also*: **~ o.s.**) portarse bien; **behaviour** (US **behavior**) *n* comportamiento, conducta

behind [bɪ'haɪnd] *prep* detrás de; (*supporting*): **to be ~ sb** apoyar a algn ▷ *adv* detrás, por detrás, atrás ▷ *n* trasero; **to be ~ (schedule)** ir retrasado; **~ the scenes** (*fig*) entre bastidores

beige [beɪʒ] *adj* color beige

Beijing ['beɪ'dʒɪŋ] *n* Pekín *m*

being ['biːɪŋ] *n* ser *m*; (*existence*): **in ~** existente; **to come into ~** aparecer

belated [bɪ'leɪtɪd] *adj* atrasado, tardío

belch [bɛltʃ] *vi* eructar ▷ *vt* (*gen*: *belch out*: *smoke etc*) arrojar

Belgian ['bɛldʒən] *adj, n* belga *mf*

Belgium ['bɛldʒəm] *n* Bélgica

belief [bɪ'liːf] *n* opinión *f*; (*faith*) fe *f*

believe [bɪ'liːv] *vt, vi* creer; **to ~ in** creer en; **believer** *n* partidario/a; (*Rel*) creyente *mf*, fiel *mf*

bell [bɛl] *n* campana; (*small*) campanilla; (*on door*) timbre *m*

bellboy ['bɛlbɔɪ] (BRIT) *n* botones *m inv*

bellhop ['bɛlhɔp] (US) *n* = **bellboy**

bellow ['bɛləu] *vi* bramar; (*person*) rugir

bell pepper *n* (*esp* US) pimiento, pimentón *m* (LAM)

belly ['bɛlɪ] *n* barriga, panza; **belly button** (*inf*) *n* ombligo

belong [bɪ'lɔŋ] *vi*: **to ~ to** pertenecer

a; (*club etc*) ser socio de; **this book ~s here** este libro va aquí; **belongings** *npl* pertenencias *fpl*

beloved [bɪ'lʌvɪd] *adj* querido/a

below [bɪ'ləu] *prep* bajo, debajo de; (*less than*) inferior a ▷ *adv* abajo, (por) debajo; **see ~** véase más abajo

belt [bɛlt] *n* cinturón *m*; (*Tech*) correa, cinta ▷ *vt* (*thrash*) pegar con correa; **beltway** (US) *n* (*Aut*) carretera de circunvalación

bemused [bɪ'mju:zd] *adj* perplejo

bench [bɛntʃ] *n* banco; (BRIT *Pol*): **the Government/Opposition ~es** (los asientos de) los miembros del Gobierno/de la Oposición; **the B~** (*Law: judges*) magistratura

bend [bɛnd] (*pt, pp* **bent**) *vt* doblar ▷ *vi* inclinarse ▷ *n* (BRIT: *in road, river*) curva; (*in pipe*) codo; **bend down** *vi* inclinarse, doblarse; **bend over** *vi* inclinarse

beneath [bɪ'ni:θ] *prep* bajo, debajo de; (*unworthy*) indigno de ▷ *adv* abajo, (por) debajo

beneficial [bɛnɪ'fɪʃəl] *adj* beneficioso

benefit ['bɛnɪfɪt] *n* beneficio; (*allowance of money*) subsidio ▷ *vt* beneficiar ▷ *vi*: **he'll ~ from it** le sacará provecho

benign [bɪ'naɪn] *adj* benigno; (*smile*) afable

bent [bɛnt] *pt, pp of* **bend** ▷ *n* inclinación *f* ▷ *adj*: **to be ~ on** estar empeñado en

bereaved [bɪ'ri:vd] *npl*: **the ~** *los íntimos de una persona afligidos por su muerte*

beret ['bɛreɪ] *n* boina

Berlin [bə:'lɪn] *n* Berlín

Bermuda [bə:'mju:də] *n* las Bermudas

berry ['bɛrɪ] *n* baya

berth [bə:θ] *n* (*bed*) litera; (*cabin*) camarote *m*; (*for ship*) amarradero ▷ *vi* atracar, amarrar

beside [bɪ'saɪd] *prep* junto a, al lado de; **to be ~ o.s. with anger** estar fuera de sí; **that's ~ the point** eso no tiene nada que ver; **besides** *adv* además ▷ *prep* además de

best [bɛst] *adj* (el/la) mejor ▷ *adv* (lo) mejor; **the ~ part of** (*quantity*) la mayor parte de; **at ~** en el mejor de los casos; **to make the ~ of sth** sacar el mejor partido de algo; **to do one's ~** hacer todo lo posible; **to the ~ of my knowledge** que yo sepa; **to the ~ of my ability** como mejor puedo; **best-before date** *n* fecha de consumo preferente; **best man** (*irreg*) *n* padrino de boda; **bestseller** *n* éxito de librería, bestseller *m*

bet [bɛt] (*pt, pp* **~** *or* **~ted**) *n* apuesta ▷ *vt*: **to ~ money on** apostar dinero por ▷ *vi* apostar; **to ~ sb sth** apostar algo a algn

betray [bɪ'treɪ] *vt* traicionar; (*trust*) faltar a

better ['bɛtə*] *adj, adv* mejor ▷ *vt* superar ▷ *n*: **to get the ~ of sb** quedar por encima de algn; **you had ~ do it** más vale que lo hagas; **he thought ~ of it** cambió de parecer; **to get ~** (*Med*) mejorar(se)

betting ['bɛtɪŋ] *n* juego, el apostar; **betting shop** (BRIT) *n* agencia de apuestas

between [bɪ'twi:n] *prep* entre ▷ *adv* (*time*) mientras tanto; (*place*) en medio

beverage ['bɛvərɪdʒ] *n* bebida

beware [bɪ'wɛə*] *vi*: **to ~ (of)** tener cuidado (con); **"~ of the dog"** "perro peligroso"

bewildered [bɪ'wɪldəd] *adj* aturdido, perplejo

beyond [bɪ'jɔnd] *prep* más allá de; (*past: understanding*) fuera de; (*after: date*) después de, más allá de; (*above*) superior a ▷ *adv* (*in space*) más allá; (*in time*) posteriormente; **~ doubt** fuera de toda duda; **~ repair** irreparable

bias ['baɪəs] *n* (*prejudice*) prejuicio, pasión *f*; (*preference*) predisposición *f*; **bias(s)ed** *adj* parcial

bib [bɪb] *n* babero
Bible ['baɪbl] *n* Biblia
bicarbonate of soda [baɪ'kɑːbənɪt-] *n* bicarbonato sódico
biceps ['baɪsɛps] *n* bíceps *m*
bicycle ['baɪsɪkl] *n* bicicleta; **bicycle pump** *n* bomba de bicicleta
bid [bɪd] (*pt* **bade** *or* **~**, *pp* **bidden** *or* **~**) *n* oferta, postura; (*in tender*) licitación *f*; (*attempt*) tentativa, conato ▷ *vi* hacer una oferta ▷ *vt* (*offer*) ofrecer; **to ~ sb good day** dar a algn los buenos días; **bidder** *n*: **the highest bidder** el mejor postor
bidet ['biːdeɪ] *n* bidet *m*
big [bɪg] *adj* grande; (*brother, sister*) mayor; **bigheaded** *adj* engreído; **big toe** *n* dedo gordo (del pie)
bike [baɪk] *n* bici *f*; **bike lane** *n* carril-bici *m*
bikini [bɪ'kiːnɪ] *n* bikini *m*
bilateral [baɪ'lætərl] *adj* (*agreement*) bilateral
bilingual [baɪ'lɪŋgwəl] *adj* bilingüe
bill [bɪl] *n* cuenta; (*invoice*) factura; (*Pol*) proyecto de ley; (US: *banknote*) billete *m*; (*of bird*) pico; (*of show*) programa *m*; **"post no ~s"** "prohibido fijar carteles"; **to fit** *or* **fill the ~** (*fig*) cumplir con los requisitos; **billboard** (US) *n* cartelera; **billfold** ['bɪlfəuld] (US) *n* cartera
billiards ['bɪljədz] *n* billar *m*
billion ['bɪljən] *n* (BRIT) billón *m* (*millón de millones*); (US) mil millones *mpl*
bin [bɪn] *n* (*for rubbish*) cubo *or* bote *m* (MEX) *or* tacho (SC) de la basura; (*container*) recipiente *m*
bind [baɪnd] (*pt, pp* **bound**) *vt* atar; (*book*) encuadernar; (*oblige*) obligar ▷ *n* (*inf: nuisance*) lata
binge [bɪndʒ] (*inf*) *n*: **to go on a ~** ir de juerga
bingo ['bɪŋgəu] *n* bingo *m*
binoculars [bɪ'nɔkjuləz] *npl* prismáticos *mpl*
bio... [baɪə'] *prefix*: **biochemistry** *n* bioquímica; **biodegradable** [baɪəudɪ'greɪdəbl] *adj* biodegradable; **biography** [baɪ'ɔgrəfɪ] *n* biografía; **biological** *adj* biológico; **biology** [baɪ'ɔlədʒɪ] *n* biología; **biometric** [baɪə'mɛtrɪk] *adj* biométrico
birch [bəːtʃ] *n* (*tree*) abedul *m*
bird [bəːd] *n* ave *f*, pájaro; (BRIT: *inf: girl*) chica; **bird flu** *n* gripe *f* aviar; **bird of prey** *n* ave *f* de presa; **birdwatching** *n*: **he likes to go birdwatching on Sundays** los domingos le gusta ir a ver pájaros
Biro® ['baɪrəu] *n* boli
birth [bəːθ] *n* nacimiento; **to give ~ to** parir, dar a luz; **birth certificate** *n* partida de nacimiento; **birth control** *n* (*policy*) control *m* de natalidad; (*methods*) métodos *mpl* anticonceptivos; **birthday** *n* cumpleaños *m inv* ▷ *cpd* (*cake, card etc*) de cumpleaños; **birthmark** *n* antojo, marca de nacimiento; **birthplace** *n* lugar *m* de nacimiento
biscuit ['bɪskɪt] (BRIT) *n* galleta
bishop ['bɪʃəp] *n* obispo; (*Chess*) alfil *m*
bistro ['biːstrəu] *n* café-bar *m*
bit [bɪt] *pt of* **bite** ▷ *n* trozo, pedazo, pedacito; (*Comput*) bit *m*, bitio; (*for horse*) freno, bocado; **a ~ of** un poco de; **a ~ mad** un poco loco; **~ by ~** poco a poco
bitch [bɪtʃ] *n* perra; (*inf!: woman*) zorra (*!*)
bite [baɪt] (*pt* **bit**, *pp* **bitten**) *vt, vi* morder; (*insect etc*) picar ▷ *n* (*insect bite*) picadura; (*mouthful*) bocado; **to ~ one's nails** comerse las uñas; **let's have a ~ (to eat)** (*inf*) vamos a comer algo
bitten ['bɪtn] *pp of* **bite**
bitter ['bɪtə*] *adj* amargo; (*wind*) cortante, penetrante; (*battle*) encarnizado ▷ *n* (BRIT: *beer*) *cerveza típica británica a base de lúpulos*
bizarre [bɪ'zɑː*] *adj* raro, extraño
black [blæk] *adj* negro; (*tea, coffee*) solo ▷ *n* color *m* negro; (*person*): **B~**

negro/a ▷ *vt* (BRIT *Industry*) boicotear; **to give sb a ~ eye** ponerle a algn el ojo morado; **~ and blue** (*bruised*) amoratado; **to be in the ~** (*bank account*) estar en números negros; **black out** *vi* (*faint*) desmayarse; **blackberry** *n* zarzamora; **blackbird** *n* mirlo; **blackboard** *n* pizarra; **black coffee** *n* café *m* solo; **blackcurrant** *n* grosella negra; **black ice** *n* hielo invisible en la carretera; **blackmail** *n* chantaje *m* ▷ *vt* chantajear; **black market** *n* mercado negro; **blackout** *n* (*Mil*) oscurecimiento; (*power cut*) apagón *m*; (*TV, Radio*) interrupción *f* de programas; (*fainting*) desvanecimiento; **black pepper** *n* pimienta *f* negra; **black pudding** *n* morcilla; **Black Sea** *n*: **the Black Sea** el Mar Negro

bladder ['blædə*] *n* vejiga

blade [bleɪd] *n* hoja; (*of propeller*) paleta; **a ~ of grass** una brizna de hierba

blame [bleɪm] *n* culpa ▷ *vt*: **to ~ sb for sth** echar a algn la culpa de algo; **to be to ~ (for)** tener la culpa (de)

bland [blænd] *adj* (*music, taste*) soso

blank [blæŋk] *adj* en blanco; (*look*) sin expresión ▷ *n* (*of memory*): **my mind is a ~** no puedo recordar nada; (*on form*) blanco, espacio en blanco; (*cartridge*) cartucho sin bala *or* de fogueo

blanket ['blæŋkɪt] *n* manta (SP), cobija (LAM); (*of snow*) capa; (*of fog*) manto

blast [blɑːst] *n* (*of wind*) ráfaga, soplo; (*of explosive*) explosión *f* ▷ *vt* (*blow up*) volar

blatant ['bleɪtənt] *adj* descarado

blaze [bleɪz] *n* (*fire*) fuego; (*fig: of colour*) despliegue *m*; (*: of glory*) esplendor *m* ▷ *vi* arder en llamas; (*fig*) brillar ▷ *vt*: **to ~ a trail** (*fig*) abrir (un) camino; **in a ~ of publicity** con gran publicidad

blazer ['bleɪzə*] *n chaqueta de uniforme de colegial o de socio de club*

bleach [bliːtʃ] *n* (*also*: **household ~**) lejía ▷ *vt* blanquear; **bleachers** (US) *npl* (*Sport*) gradas *fpl* al sol

bleak [bliːk] *adj* (*countryside*) desierto; (*prospect*) poco prometedor(a); (*weather*) crudo; (*smile*) triste

bled [bled] *pt, pp of* **bleed**

bleed [bliːd] (*pt, pp* **bled**) *vt, vi* sangrar; **my nose is ~ing** me está sangrando la nariz

blemish ['blɛmɪʃ] *n* marca, mancha; (*on reputation*) tacha

blend [blɛnd] *n* mezcla ▷ *vt* mezclar; (*colours etc*) combinar, mezclar ▷ *vi* (*colours etc: also*: **~ in**) combinarse, mezclarse; **blender** *n* (*Culin*) batidora

bless [blɛs] (*pt, pp* **~ed** *or* **blest**) *vt* bendecir; **~ you!** (*after sneeze*) ¡Jesús!; **blessing** *n* (*approval*) aprobación *f*; (*godsend*) don *m* del cielo, bendición *f*; (*advantage*) beneficio, ventaja

blew [bluː] *pt of* **blow**

blight [blaɪt] *vt* (*hopes etc*) frustrar, arruinar

blind [blaɪnd] *adj* ciego; (*fig*): **~ (to)** ciego (a) ▷ *n* (*for window*) persiana ▷ *vt* cegar; (*dazzle*) deslumbrar; (*deceive*): **to ~ sb to ...** cegar a algn a ... ; **the blind** *npl* los ciegos; **blind alley** *n* callejón *m* sin salida; **blindfold** *n* venda ▷ *adv* con los ojos vendados ▷ *vt* vendar los ojos a

blink [blɪŋk] *vi* parpadear, pestañear; (*light*) oscilar

bliss [blɪs] *n* felicidad *f*

blister ['blɪstə*] *n* ampolla ▷ *vi* (*paint*) ampollarse

blizzard ['blɪzəd] *n* ventisca

bloated ['bləutɪd] *adj* hinchado; (*person: full*) ahíto

blob [blɔb] *n* (*drop*) gota; (*indistinct object*) bulto

block [blɔk] *n* bloque *m*; (*in pipes*) obstáculo; (*of buildings*) manzana (SP), cuadra (LAM) ▷ *vt* obstruir, cerrar; (*progress*) estorbar; **~ of flats** (BRIT) bloque *m* de pisos; **mental ~** bloqueo mental; **block up** *vt* tapar, obstruir; (*pipe*) atascar; **blockade**

[-'keɪd] *n* bloqueo ▷ *vt* bloquear; **blockage** *n* estorbo, obstrucción *f*; **blockbuster** *n* (*book*) bestseller *m*; (*film*) éxito de público; **block capitals** *npl* mayúsculas *fpl*; **block letters** *npl* mayúsculas *fpl*

blog [blɔg] *n* blog *m*

bloke [bləuk] (BRIT: *inf*) *n* tipo, tío

blond(e) [blɔnd] *adj*, *n* rubio/a *m/f*

blood [blʌd] *n* sangre *f*; **blood donor** *n* donante *mf* de sangre; **blood group** *n* grupo sanguíneo; **blood poisoning** *n* envenenamiento de la sangre; **blood pressure** *n* presión *f* sanguínea; **bloodshed** *n* derramamiento de sangre; **bloodshot** *adj* inyectado en sangre; **bloodstream** *n* corriente *f* sanguínea; **blood test** *n* análisis *m inv* de sangre; **blood transfusion** *n* transfusión *f* de sangre; **blood type** *n* grupo sanguíneo; **blood vessel** *n* vaso sanguíneo; **bloody** *adj* sangriento; (*nose etc*) lleno de sangre; (BRIT: *inf!*): **this bloody ...** este condenado *o* puñetero ... (!) ▷ *adv*: **bloody strong/good** (BRIT: *inf!*) terriblemente fuerte/bueno

bloom [blu:m] *n* flor *f* ▷ *vi* florecer

blossom ['blɔsəm] *n* flor *f* ▷ *vi* florecer

blot [blɔt] *n* borrón *m*; (*fig*) mancha ▷ *vt* (*stain*) manchar

blouse [blauz] *n* blusa

blow [bləu] (*pt* **blew**, *pp* **blown**) *n* golpe *m*; (*with sword*) espadazo ▷ *vi* soplar; (*dust, sand etc*) volar; (*fuse*) fundirse ▷ *vt* (*wind*) llevarse; (*fuse*) quemar; (*instrument*) tocar; **to ~ one's nose** sonarse; **blow away** *vt* llevarse, arrancar; **blow out** *vi* apagarse; **blow up** *vi* estallar ▷ *vt* volar; (*tyre*) inflar; (*Phot*) ampliar; **blow-dry** *n* moldeado (con secador)

blown [bləun] *pp of* **blow**

blue [blu:] *adj* azul; (*depressed*) deprimido; **~ film/joke** película/chiste *m* verde; **out of the ~** (*fig*) de repente; **bluebell** *n* campanilla, campánula azul; **blueberry** *n* arándano; **blue cheese** *n* queso azul; **blues** *npl*: **the blues** (*Mus*) el blues; **to have the blues** estar triste; **bluetit** *n* herrerillo *m* (común)

bluff [blʌf] *vi* tirarse un farol, farolear ▷ *n* farol *m*; **to call sb's ~** coger a algn la palabra

blunder ['blʌndə*] *n* patinazo, metedura de pata ▷ *vi* cometer un error, meter la pata

blunt [blʌnt] *adj* (*pencil*) despuntado; (*knife*) desafilado, romo; (*person*) franco, directo

blur [blə:*] *n* (*shape*): **to become a ~** hacerse borroso ▷ *vt* (*vision*) enturbiar; (*distinction*) borrar; **blurred** *adj* borroso

blush [blʌʃ] *vi* ruborizarse, ponerse colorado ▷ *n* rubor *m*; **blusher** *n* colorete *m*

board [bɔ:d] *n* (*cardboard*) cartón *m*; (*wooden*) tabla, tablero; (*on wall*) tablón *m*; (*for chess etc*) tablero; (*committee*) junta, consejo; (*in firm*) mesa *or* junta directiva; (*Naut, Aviat*): **on ~** a bordo ▷ *vt* (*ship*) embarcarse en; (*train*) subir a; **full ~** (BRIT) pensión completa; **half ~** (BRIT) media pensión; **to go by the ~** (*fig*) ser abandonado *or* olvidado; **board game** *n* juego de tablero; **boarding card** (BRIT) *n* tarjeta de embarque; **boarding pass** (US) *n* = **boarding card**; **boarding school** *n* internado; **board room** *n* sala de juntas

boast [bəust] *vi*: **to ~ (about** *or* **of)** alardear (de)

boat [bəut] *n* barco, buque *m*; (*small*) barca, bote *m*

bob [bɔb] *vi* (*also*: **~ up and down**) menearse, balancearse

bobby pin ['bɔbɪ-] (US) *n* horquilla

body ['bɔdɪ] *n* cuerpo; (*corpse*) cadáver *m*; (*of car*) caja, carrocería; (*fig*: *group*) grupo; (: *organization*) organismo; **body-building** *n* culturismo; **bodyguard** *n* guardaespaldas *m inv*; **bodywork** *n* carrocería

bog [bɔg] *n* pantano, ciénaga ▷ *vt*: **to get ~ged down** (*fig*) empantanarse, atascarse

bogus ['bəugəs] *adj* falso, fraudulento

boil [bɔɪl] *vt* (*water*) hervir; (*eggs*) pasar por agua, cocer ▷ *vi* hervir; (*fig*: *with anger*) estar furioso; (: *with heat*) asfixiarse ▷ *n* (*Med*) furúnculo, divieso; **to come to the ~, to come to a ~** (US) comenzar a hervir; **to ~ down to** (*fig*) reducirse a; **boil over** *vi* salirse, rebosar; (*anger etc*) llegar al colmo; **boiled egg** *n* (*soft*) huevo tibio (MEX) *or* pasado por agua *or* a la copa (SC); (*hard*) huevo duro; **boiled potatoes** *npl* patatas *fpl* (SP) *or* papas *fpl* (LAM) cocidas; **boiler** *n* caldera; **boiling** ['bɔɪlɪŋ] *adj*: **I'm boiling (hot)** (*inf*) estoy asado; **boiling point** *n* punto de ebullición

bold [bəuld] *adj* valiente, audaz; (*pej*) descarado; (*colour*) llamativo

Bolivia [bə'lɪvɪə] *n* Bolivia; **Bolivian** *adj*, *n* boliviano/a *m/f*

bollard ['bɔləd] (BRIT) *n* (*Aut*) poste *m*

bolt [bəult] *n* (*lock*) cerrojo; (*with nut*) perno, tornillo ▷ *adv*: **~ upright** rígido, erguido ▷ *vt* (*door*) echar el cerrojo a; (*also*: **~ together**) sujetar con tornillos; (*food*) engullir ▷ *vi* fugarse; (*horse*) desbocarse

bomb [bɔm] *n* bomba ▷ *vt* bombardear; **bombard** [bɔm'bɑːd] *vt* bombardear; (*fig*) asediar; **bomber** *n* (*Aviat*) bombardero; **bomb scare** *n* amenaza de bomba

bond [bɔnd] *n* (*promise*) fianza; (*Finance*) bono; (*link*) vínculo, lazo; (*Comm*): **in ~** en depósito bajo fianza; **bonds** *npl* (*chains*) cadenas *fpl*

bone [bəun] *n* hueso; (*of fish*) espina ▷ *vt* deshuesar; quitar las espinas a

bonfire ['bɔnfaɪə*] *n* hoguera, fogata

bonnet ['bɔnɪt] *n* gorra; (BRIT: *of car*) capó *m*

bonus ['bəunəs] *n* (*payment*) paga extraordinaria, plus *m*; (*fig*) bendición *f*

boo [buː] *excl* ¡uh! ▷ *vt* abuchear, rechiflar

book [buk] *n* libro; (*of tickets*) taco; (*of stamps etc*) librito ▷ *vt* (*ticket*) sacar; (*seat, room*) reservar; **books** *npl* (*Comm*) cuentas *fpl*, contabilidad *f*; **book in** *vi* (*at hotel*) registrarse; **book up** *vt*: **to be booked up** (*hotel*) estar completo; **bookcase** *n* librería, estante *m* para libros; **booking** *n* reserva; **booking office** *n* (BRIT *Rail*) despacho de billetes (SP) *or* boletos (LAM); (*Theatre*) taquilla (SP), boletería (LAM); **book-keeping** *n* contabilidad *f*; **booklet** *n* folleto; **bookmaker** *n* corredor *m* de apuestas; **bookmark** *n* (*also Comput*) marcador; **bookseller** *n* librero; **bookshelf** *n* estante *m* (para libros); **bookshop, book store** *n* librería

boom [buːm] *n* (*noise*) trueno, estampido; (*in prices etc*) alza rápida; (*Econ, in population*) boom *m* ▷ *vi* (*cannon*) hacer gran estruendo, retumbar; (*Econ*) estar en alza

boost [buːst] *n* estímulo, empuje *m* ▷ *vt* estimular, empujar

boot [buːt] *n* bota; (BRIT: *of car*) maleta, maletero ▷ *vt* (*Comput*) arrancar; **to ~** (*in addition*) además, por añadidura

booth [buːð] *n* (*telephone booth, voting booth*) cabina

booze [buːz] (*inf*) *n* bebida

border ['bɔːdə*] *n* borde *m*, margen *m*; (*of a country*) frontera; (*for flowers*) arriate *m* ▷ *vt* (*road*) bordear; (*another country*: *also*: **~ on**) lindar con; **borderline** *n*: **on the borderline** en el límite

bore [bɔː*] *pt of* **bear** ▷ *vt* (*hole*) hacer un agujero en; (*well*) perforar; (*person*) aburrir ▷ *n* (*person*) pelmazo, pesado; (*of gun*) calibre *m*; **bored** *adj* aburrido; **he's bored to tears** *or* **to death** *or* **stiff** está aburrido como una ostra, está muerto de aburrimiento; **boredom** *n* aburrimiento

boring ['bɔːrɪŋ] *adj* aburrido

born [bɔːn] *adj*: **to be ~** nacer; **I was ~**

in 1960 nací en 1960

borne [bɔːn] *pp of* **bear**

borough ['bʌrə] *n* municipio

borrow ['bɔrəu] *vt*: **to ~ sth (from sb)** tomar algo prestado (a algn)

Bosnia(-Herzegovina) ['bɔːsnɪə(hɛrzə'gəuviːnə)] *n* Bosnia(-Herzegovina); **Bosnian** ['bɔznɪən] *adj, n* bosnio/a

bosom ['buzəm] *n* pecho

boss [bɔs] *n* jefe *m* ▷ *vt* (*also*: **~ about or around**) mangonear; **bossy** *adj* mandón/ona

both [bəuθ] *adj, pron* ambos/as, los dos(las dos); **~ of us went, we ~ went** fuimos los dos, ambos fuimos ▷ *adv*: **~ A and B** tanto A como B

bother ['bɔðə*] *vt* (*worry*) preocupar; (*disturb*) molestar, fastidiar ▷ *vi* (*also*: **~ o.s.**) molestarse ▷ *n* (*trouble*) dificultad *f*; (*nuisance*) molestia, lata; **to ~ doing** tomarse la molestia de hacer

bottle ['bɔtl] *n* botella; (*small*) frasco; (*baby's*) biberón *m* ▷ *vt* embotellar; **bottle bank** *n* contenedor *m* de vidrio; **bottle-opener** *n* abrebotellas *m inv*

bottom ['bɔtəm] *n* (*of box, sea*) fondo; (*buttocks*) trasero, culo; (*of page*) pie *m*; (*of list*) final *m*; (*of class*) último/a ▷ *adj* (*lowest*) más bajo; (*last*) último

bought [bɔːt] *pt, pp of* **buy**

boulder ['bəuldə*] *n* canto rodado

bounce [bauns] *vi* (*ball*) (re)botar; (*cheque*) ser rechazado ▷ *vt* hacer (re)botar ▷ *n* (*rebound*) (re)bote *m*; **bouncer** (*inf*) *n* gorila *m* (*que echa a los alborotadores de un bar, club etc*)

bound [baund] *pt, pp of* **bind** ▷ *n* (*leap*) salto; (*gen pl*: *limit*) límite *m* ▷ *vi* (*leap*) saltar ▷ *vt* (*border*) rodear ▷ *adj*: **~ by** rodeado de; **to be ~ to do sth** (*obliged*) tener el deber de hacer algo; **he's ~ to come** es seguro que vendrá; **out of ~s** prohibido el paso; **~ for** con destino a

boundary ['baundrɪ] *n* límite *m*

bouquet ['bukeɪ] *n* (*of flowers*) ramo

bourbon ['buəbən] (US) *n* (*also*: **~ whiskey**) whisky *m* americano, bourbon *m*

bout [baut] *n* (*of malaria etc*) ataque *m*; (*of activity*) período; (*Boxing etc*) combate *m*, encuentro

boutique [buː'tiːk] *n* boutique *f*, tienda de ropa

bow¹ [bəu] *n* (*knot*) lazo; (*weapon, Mus*) arco

bow² [bau] *n* (*of the head*) reverencia; (*Naut*: *also*: **~s**) proa ▷ *vi* inclinarse, hacer una reverencia

bowels [bauəlz] *npl* intestinos *mpl*, vientre *m*; (*fig*) entrañas *fpl*

bowl [bəul] *n* tazón *m*, cuenco; (*ball*) bola ▷ *vi* (*Cricket*) arrojar la pelota; *see also* **bowls**; **bowler** *n* (*Cricket*) lanzador *m* (de la pelota); (BRIT: *also*: **bowler hat**) hongo, bombín *m*; **bowling** *n* (*game*) bochas *fpl*, bolos *mpl*; **bowling alley** *n* bolera; **bowling green** *n* pista para bochas; **bowls** *n* juego de las bochas, bolos *mpl*

bow tie ['bəu-] *n* corbata de lazo, pajarita

box [bɔks] *n* (*also*: **cardboard ~**) caja, cajón *m*; (*Theatre*) palco ▷ *vt* encajonar ▷ *vi* (*Sport*) boxear; **boxer** ['bɔksə*] *n* (*person*) boxeador *m*; **boxer shorts** ['bɔksəʃɔːts] *pl n* bóxers; **a pair of boxer shorts** unos bóxers; **boxing** ['bɔksɪŋ] *n* (*Sport*) boxeo; **Boxing Day** (BRIT) *n* *día en que se dan los aguinaldos, 26 de diciembre*; **boxing gloves** *npl* guantes *mpl* de boxeo; **boxing ring** *n* ring *m*, cuadrilátero; **box office** *n* taquilla (SP), boletería (LAM)

boy [bɔɪ] *n* (*young*) niño; (*older*) muchacho, chico; (*son*) hijo; **boy band** *n* boy band *m* (*grupo musical de chicos*)

boycott ['bɔɪkɔt] *n* boicot *m* ▷ *vt* boicotear

boyfriend ['bɔɪfrɛnd] *n* novio

bra [brɑː] *n* sostén *m*, sujetador *m*

brace [breɪs] *n* (BRIT: *also*: **~s**: *on teeth*) corrector *m*, aparato; (*tool*) berbiquí *m* ▷ *vt* (*knees, shoulders*) tensionar; **braces** *npl* (BRIT) tirantes *mpl*; **to ~ o.s.** (*fig*)

preparase
bracelet ['breɪslɪt] *n* pulsera, brazalete *m*
bracket ['brækɪt] *n* (*Tech*) soporte *m*, puntal *m*; (*group*) clase *f*, categoría; (*also*: **brace ~**) soporte *m*, abrazadera; (*also*: **round ~**) paréntesis *m inv*; (*also*: **square ~**) corchete *m* ▷ *vt* (*word etc*) poner entre paréntesis
brag [bræg] *vi* jactarse
braid [breɪd] *n* (*trimming*) galón *m*; (*of hair*) trenza
brain [breɪn] *n* cerebro; **brains** *npl* sesos *mpl*; **she's got ~s** es muy lista
braise [breɪz] *vt* cocer a fuego lento
brake [breɪk] *n* (*on vehicle*) freno ▷ *vi* frenar; **brake light** *n* luz *f* de frenado
bran [bræn] *n* salvado
branch [brɑːntʃ] *n* rama; (*Comm*) sucursal *f*; **branch off** *vi*: **a small road branches off to the right** hay una carretera pequeña que sale hacia la derecha; **branch out** *vi* (*fig*) extenderse
brand [brænd] *n* marca; (*fig*: *type*) tipo ▷ *vt* (*cattle*) marcar con hierro candente; **brand name** *n* marca; **brand-new** *adj* flamante, completamente nuevo
brandy ['brændɪ] *n* coñac *m*
brash [bræʃ] *adj* (*forward*) descarado
brass [brɑːs] *n* latón *m*; **the ~** (*Mus*) los cobres; **brass band** *n* banda de metal
brat [bræt] (*pej*) *n* mocoso/a
brave [breɪv] *adj* valiente, valeroso ▷ *vt* (*face up to*) desafiar; **bravery** *n* valor *m*, valentía
brawl [brɔːl] *n* pelea, reyerta
Brazil [brə'zɪl] *n* (el) Brasil; **Brazilian** *adj, n* brasileño/a *m/f*
breach [briːtʃ] *vt* abrir brecha en ▷ *n* (*gap*) brecha; (*breaking*): **~ of contract** infracción *f* de contrato; **~ of the peace** perturbación *f* del órden público
bread [brɛd] *n* pan *m*; **breadbin** *n* panera; **breadbox** (*US*) *n* panera; **breadcrumbs** *npl* migajas *fpl*; (*Culin*) pan rallado
breadth [brɛtθ] *n* anchura; (*fig*) amplitud *f*
break [breɪk] (*pt* **broke**, *pp* **broken**) *vt* romper; (*promise*) faltar a; (*law*) violar, infringir; (*record*) batir ▷ *vi* romperse, quebrarse; (*storm*) estallar; (*weather*) cambiar; (*dawn*) despuntar; (*news etc*) darse a conocer ▷ *n* (*gap*) abertura; (*fracture*) fractura; (*time*) intervalo; (*: at school*) (período de) recreo; (*chance*) oportunidad *f*; **to ~ the news to sb** comunicar la noticia a algn; **break down** *vt* (*figures, data*) analizar, descomponer ▷ *vi* (*machine*) estropearse; (*Aut*) averiarse; (*person*) romper a llorar; (*talks*) fracasar; **break in** *vt* (*horse etc*) domar ▷ *vi* (*burglar*) forzar una entrada; (*interrupt*) interrumpir; **break into** *vt fus* (*house*) forzar; **break off** *vi* (*speaker*) pararse, detenerse; (*branch*) partir; **break out** *vi* estallar; (*prisoner*) escaparse; **to break out in spots** salirle a algn granos; **break up** *vi* (*ship*) hacerse pedazos; (*crowd, meeting*) disolverse; (*marriage*) deshacerse; (*Scol*) terminar (el curso); (*line*) cortarse ▷ *vt* (*rocks etc*) partir; (*journey*) partir; (*fight etc*) acabar con; **the line's** *or* **you're breaking up** se corta; **breakdown** *n* (*Aut*) avería; (*in communications*) interrupción *f*; (*Med*: *also*: **nervous breakdown**) colapso, crisis *f* nerviosa; (*of marriage, talks*) fracaso; (*of statistics*) análisis *m inv*; **breakdown truck, breakdown van** *n* (camión *m*) grúa
breakfast ['brɛkfəst] *n* desayuno
break: break-in *n* robo con allanamiento de morada; **breakthrough** *n* (*also fig*) avance *m*
breast [brɛst] *n* (*of woman*) pecho, seno; (*chest*) pecho; (*of bird*) pechuga; **breast-feed** (*pt, pp* **breast-fed**) *vt, vi* amamantar, criar a los pechos; **breast-stroke** *n* braza (de pecho)
breath [brɛθ] *n* aliento, respiración *f*; **to take a deep ~** respirar hondo; **out of ~** sin aliento, sofocado

Breathalyser® ['brɛθəlaɪzə*] (BRIT) *n* alcoholímetro

breathe [bri:ð] *vt, vi* respirar; **breathe in** *vt, vi* aspirar; **breathe out** *vt, vi* espirar; **breathing** *n* respiración *f*

breath: breathless *adj* sin aliento, jadeante; **breathtaking** *adj* imponente, pasmoso; **breath test** *n* prueba de la alcoholemia

bred [brɛd] *pt, pp of* **breed**

breed [bri:d] (*pt, pp* **bred**) *vt* criar ▷ *vi* reproducirse, procrear ▷ *n* (*Zool*) raza, casta; (*type*) tipo

breeze [bri:z] *n* brisa

breezy ['bri:zɪ] *adj* de mucho viento, ventoso; (*person*) despreocupado

brew [bru:] *vt* (*tea*) hacer; (*beer*) elaborar ▷ *vi* (*fig: trouble*) prepararse; (*storm*) amenazar; **brewery** *n* fábrica de cerveza, cervecería

bribe [braɪb] *n* soborno ▷ *vt* sobornar, cohechar; **bribery** *n* soborno, cohecho

bric-a-brac ['brɪkabræk] *n inv* baratijas *fpl*

brick [brɪk] *n* ladrillo; **bricklayer** *n* albañil *m*

bride [braɪd] *n* novia; **bridegroom** *n* novio; **bridesmaid** *n* dama de honor

bridge [brɪdʒ] *n* puente *m*; (*Naut*) puente *m* de mando; (*of nose*) caballete *m*; (*Cards*) bridge *m* ▷ *vt* (*fig*): **to ~ a gap** llenar un vacío

bridle ['braɪdl] *n* brida, freno

brief [bri:f] *adj* breve, corto ▷ *n* (*Law*) escrito; (*task*) cometido, encargo ▷ *vt* informar; **briefs** *npl* (*for men*) calzoncillos *mpl*; (*for women*) bragas *fpl*; **briefcase** *n* cartera (SP), portafolio (LAM); **briefing** *n* (*Press*) informe *m*; **briefly** *adv* (*glance*) fugazmente; (*say*) en pocas palabras

brigadier [brɪgə'dɪə*] *n* general *m* de brigada

bright [braɪt] *adj* brillante; (*room*) luminoso; (*day*) de sol; (*person: clever*) listo, inteligente; (*: lively*) alegre; (*colour*) vivo; (*future*) prometedor(a)

brilliant ['brɪljənt] *adj* brillante; (*inf*) fenomenal

brim [brɪm] *n* borde *m*; (*of hat*) ala

brine [braɪn] *n* (*Culin*) salmuera

bring [brɪŋ] (*pt, pp* **brought**) *vt* (*thing, person: with you*) traer; (*: to sb*) llevar, conducir; (*trouble, satisfaction*) causar; **bring about** *vt* ocasionar, producir; **bring back** *vt* volver a traer; (*return*) devolver; **bring down** *vt* (*government, plane*) derribar; (*price*) rebajar; **bring in** *vt* (*harvest*) recoger; (*person*) hacer entrar *or* pasar; (*object*) traer; (*Pol: bill, law*) presentar; (*produce: income*) producir, rendir; **bring on** *vt* (*illness, attack*) producir, causar; (*player, substitute*) sacar (de la reserva), hacer salir; **bring out** *vt* sacar; (*book etc*) publicar; (*meaning*) subrayar; **bring up** *vt* subir; (*person*) educar, criar; (*question*) sacar a colación; (*food: vomit*) devolver, vomitar

brink [brɪŋk] *n* borde *m*

brisk [brɪsk] *adj* (*abrupt: tone*) brusco; (*person*) enérgico, vigoroso; (*pace*) rápido; (*trade*) activo

bristle ['brɪsl] *n* cerda ▷ *vi*: **to ~ in anger** temblar de rabia

Brit [brɪt] *n abbr* (*inf: = British person*) británico/a

Britain ['brɪtən] *n* (*also*: **Great ~**) Gran Bretaña

British ['brɪtɪʃ] *adj* británico ▷ *npl*: **the ~** los británicos; **British Isles** *npl*: **the British Isles** las Islas Británicas

Briton ['brɪtən] *n* británico/a

brittle ['brɪtl] *adj* quebradizo, frágil

broad [brɔ:d] *adj* ancho; (*range*) amplio; (*smile*) abierto; (*general: outlines etc*) general; (*accent*) cerrado; **in ~ daylight** en pleno día; **broadband** *n* banda ancha; **broad bean** *n* haba; **broadcast** (*pt, pp* **~**) *n* emisión *f* ▷ *vt* (*Radio*) emitir; (*TV*) transmitir ▷ *vi* emitir; transmitir; **broaden** *vt* ampliar ▷ *vi* ensancharse; **to broaden one's mind** hacer más tolerante a

algn; **broadly** *adv* en general; **broad-minded** *adj* tolerante, liberal
broccoli ['brɔkəlɪ] *n* brécol *m*
brochure ['brəuʃjuə*] *n* folleto
broil [brɔɪl] *vt* (*Culin*) asar a la parrilla
broiler ['brɔɪlə*] *n* (*grill*) parrilla
broke [brəuk] *pt of* **break** ▷ *adj* (*inf*) pelado, sin blanca
broken ['brəukən] *pp of* **break** ▷ *adj* roto; (*machine: also:* **~ down**) averiado; **~ leg** pierna rota; **in ~ English** en un inglés imperfecto
broker ['brəukə*] *n* agente *mf*, bolsista *mf*; (*insurance broker*) agente de seguros
bronchitis [brɔŋ'kaɪtɪs] *n* bronquitis *f*
bronze [brɔnz] *n* bronce *m*
brooch [brəutʃ] *n* prendedor *m*, broche *m*
brood [bru:d] *n* camada, cría ▷ *vi* (*person*) dejarse obsesionar
broom [brum] *n* escoba; (*Bot*) retama
Bros. *abbr* (= *Brothers*) Hnos
broth [brɔθ] *n* caldo
brothel ['brɔθl] *n* burdel *m*
brother ['brʌðə*] *n* hermano; **brother-in-law** *n* cuñado
brought [brɔ:t] *pt, pp of* **bring**
brow [brau] *n* (*forehead*) frente *m*; (*eyebrow*) ceja; (*of hill*) cumbre *f*
brown [braun] *adj* (*colour*) marrón; (*hair*) castaño; (*tanned*) bronceado, moreno ▷ *n* (*colour*) color *m* marrón *or* pardo ▷ *vt* (*Culin*) dorar; **brown bread** *n* pan integral
Brownie ['braunɪ] *n* niña exploradora
brown rice *n* arroz *m* integral
brown sugar *n* azúcar *m* terciado
browse [brauz] *vi* (*through book*) hojear; (*in shop*) mirar; **browser** *n* (*Comput*) navegador *m*
bruise [bru:z] *n* cardenal *m* (SP), moretón *m* ▷ *vt* magullar
brunette [bru:'nɛt] *n* morena
brush [brʌʃ] *n* cepillo; (*for painting, shaving etc*) brocha; (*artist's*) pincel *m*; (*with police etc*) roce *m* ▷ *vt* (*sweep*) barrer; (*groom*) cepillar; (*also:* **~ against**) rozar al pasar
Brussels ['brʌslz] *n* Bruselas
Brussels sprout *n* col *f* de Bruselas
brutal ['bru:tl] *adj* brutal
B.Sc. *abbr* (= *Bachelor of Science*) *licenciado en Ciencias*
BSE *n abbr* (= *bovine spongiform encephalopathy*) encefalopatía espongiforme bovina
bubble ['bʌbl] *n* burbuja ▷ *vi* burbujear, borbotar; **bubble bath** *n* espuma para el baño; **bubble gum** *n* chicle *m* de globo; **bubblejet printer** ['bʌbldʒɛt-] *n* impresora de injección por burbujas
buck [bʌk] *n* (*rabbit*) conejo macho; (*deer*) gamo; (US: *inf*) dólar *m* ▷ *vi* corcovear; **to pass the ~ (to sb)** echar (a algn) el muerto
bucket ['bʌkɪt] *n* cubo, balde *m*
buckle ['bʌkl] *n* hebilla ▷ *vt* abrochar con hebilla ▷ *vi* combarse
bud [bʌd] *n* (*of plant*) brote *m*, yema; (*of flower*) capullo ▷ *vi* brotar, echar brotes
Buddhism ['budɪzm] *n* Budismo
Buddhist ['budɪst] *adj, n* budista *m/f*
buddy ['bʌdɪ] (US) *n* compañero, compinche *m*
budge [bʌdʒ] *vt* mover; (*fig*) hacer ceder ▷ *vi* moverse, ceder
budgerigar ['bʌdʒərɪgɑ:*] *n* periquito
budget ['bʌdʒɪt] *n* presupuesto ▷ *vi*: **to ~ for sth** presupuestar algo
budgie ['bʌdʒɪ] *n* = **budgerigar**
buff [bʌf] *adj* (*colour*) color de ante ▷ *n* (*inf: enthusiast*) entusiasta *mf*
buffalo ['bʌfələu] (*pl* **~** *or* **~es**) *n* (BRIT) búfalo; (US: *bison*) bisonte *m*
buffer ['bʌfə*] *n* (*Comput*) memoria intermedia; (*Rail*) tope *m*
buffet¹ ['bʌfɪt] *vt* golpear
buffet² ['bufeɪ] *n* (BRIT: *in station*) bar *m*, cafetería; (*food*) buffet *m*; **buffet car** (BRIT) *n* (*Rail*) coche-comedor *m*

bug [bʌg] *n* (*esp* US: *insect*) bicho, sabandija; (*Comput*) error *m*; (*germ*) microbio, bacilo; (*spy device*) micrófono oculto ▷ *vt* (*inf*: *annoy*) fastidiar; (*room*) poner micrófono oculto en

buggy ['bʌgɪ] *n* cochecito de niño

build [bɪld] (*pt*, *pp* **built**) *n* (*of person*) tipo ▷ *vt* construir, edificar; **build up** *vt* (*morale*, *forces*, *production*) acrecentar; (*stocks*) acumular; **builder** *n* (*contractor*) contratista *mf*; **building** *n* construcción *f*; (*structure*) edificio; **building site** *n* obra; **building society** (BRIT) *n* sociedad *f* inmobiliaria

built [bɪlt] *pt*, *pp of* **build**; **built-in** *adj* (*cupboard*) empotrado; (*device*) interior, incorporado; **built-up** *adj* (*area*) urbanizado

bulb [bʌlb] *n* (*Bot*) bulbo; (*Elec*) bombilla, foco (MEX), bujía (CAM), bombita (RPL)

Bulgaria [bʌl'gɛərɪə] *n* Bulgaria; **Bulgarian** *adj*, *n* búlgaro/a *m/f*

bulge [bʌldʒ] *n* bulto, protuberancia ▷ *vi* bombearse, pandearse; (*pocket etc*): **to ~ (with)** rebosar (de)

bulimia [bə'lɪmɪə] *n* bulimia

bulimic [bjuː'lɪmɪk] *adj*, *n* bulímico/a *m/f*

bulk [bʌlk] *n* masa, mole *f*; **in ~** (*Comm*) a granel; **the ~ of** la mayor parte de; **bulky** *adj* voluminoso, abultado

bull [bul] *n* toro; (*male elephant*, *whale*) macho

bulldozer ['buldəuzə*] *n* bulldozer *m*

bullet ['bulɪt] *n* bala

bulletin ['bulɪtɪn] *n* anuncio, parte *m*; (*journal*) boletín *m*; **bulletin board** *n* (US) tablón *m* de anuncios; (*Comput*) tablero de noticias

bullfight ['bulfaɪt] *n* corrida de toros; **bullfighter** *n* torero; **bullfighting** *n* los toros, el toreo

bully ['bulɪ] *n* valentón *m*, matón *m* ▷ *vt* intimidar, tiranizar

bum [bʌm] *n* (*inf*: *backside*) culo; (*esp* US: *tramp*) vagabundo

bumblebee ['bʌmblbiː] *n* abejorro

bump [bʌmp] *n* (*blow*) tope *m*, choque *m*; (*jolt*) sacudida; (*on road etc*) bache *m*; (*on head etc*) chichón *m* ▷ *vt* (*strike*) chocar contra; **bump into** *vt fus* chocar contra, tropezar con; (*person*) topar con; **bumper** *n* (*Aut*) parachoques *m inv* ▷ *adj*: **bumper crop** *or* **harvest** cosecha abundante; **bumpy** *adj* (*road*) lleno de baches

bun [bʌn] *n* (BRIT: *cake*) pastel *m*; (US: *bread*) bollo; (*of hair*) moño

bunch [bʌntʃ] *n* (*of flowers*) ramo; (*of keys*) manojo; (*of bananas*) piña; (*of people*) grupo; (*pej*) pandilla; **bunches** *npl* (*in hair*) coletas *fpl*

bundle ['bʌndl] *n* bulto, fardo; (*of sticks*) haz *m*; (*of papers*) legajo ▷ *vt* (*also*: **~ up**) atar, envolver; **to ~ sth/sb into** meter algo/a algn precipitadamente en

bungalow ['bʌŋgələu] *n* bungalow *m*, chalé *m*

bungee jumping ['bʌndʒiː'dʒʌmpɪŋ] *n* puenting *m*, banyi *m*

bunion ['bʌnjən] *n* juanete *m*

bunk [bʌŋk] *n* litera; **bunk beds** *npl* literas *fpl*

bunker ['bʌŋkə*] *n* (*coal store*) carbonera; (*Mil*) refugio; (*Golf*) bunker *m*

bunny ['bʌnɪ] *n* (*inf*: *also*: **~ rabbit**) conejito

buoy [bɔɪ] *n* boya; **buoyant** *adj* (*ship*) capaz de flotar; (*economy*) boyante; (*person*) optimista

burden ['bəːdn] *n* carga ▷ *vt* cargar

bureau [bjuə'rəu] (*pl* **~x**) *n* (BRIT: *writing desk*) escritorio, buró *m*; (US: *chest of drawers*) cómoda; (*office*) oficina, agencia

bureaucracy [bjuə'rɔkrəsɪ] *n* burocracia

bureaucrat ['bjuərəkræt] *n* burócrata *m/f*

bureau de change [-də'ʃɑ̃ʒ] (*pl* **bureaux de change**) *n* caja *f* de cambio

bureaux ['bjuərəuz] *npl of* **bureau**

burger ['bəːgə*] *n* hamburguesa
burglar ['bəːglə*] *n* ladrón/ona *m/f*; **burglar alarm** *n* alarma *f* antirrobo; **burglary** *n* robo con allanamiento, robo de una casa
burial ['bɛrɪəl] *n* entierro
burn [bəːn] (*pt, pp* **~ed** *or* **~t**) *vt* quemar; (*house*) incendiar ▷ *vi* quemarse, arder; incendiarse; (*sting*) escocer ▷ *n* quemadura; **burn down** *vt* incendiar; **burn out** *vt* (*writer etc*): **to burn o.s. out** agotarse; **burning** *adj* (*building etc*) en llamas; (*hot*: *sand etc*) abrasador(a); (*ambition*) ardiente
Burns' Night [bəːnz-] *n* ver recuadro

BURNS' NIGHT

Cada veinticinco de enero los escoceses celebran la llamada **Burns' Night** (noche de Burns), en honor al poeta escocés Robert Burns (1759–1796). Es tradición hacer una cena en la que, al son de la música de la gaita escocesa, se sirve "haggis", plato tradicional de asadura de cordero cocida en el estómago del animal, acompañado de nabos y puré de patatas. Durante la misma se recitan poemas del autor y varios discursos conmemorativos de carácter festivo.

burnt [bəːnt] *pt, pp of* **burn**
burp [bəːp] (*inf*) *n* eructo ▷ *vi* eructar
burrow ['bʌrəu] *n* madriguera ▷ *vi* hacer una madriguera; (*rummage*) hurgar
burst [bəːst] (*pt, pp* **~**) *vt* reventar; (*river*: *banks etc*) romper ▷ *vi* reventarse; (*tyre*) pincharse ▷ *n* (*of gunfire*) ráfaga; (*also*: **~ pipe**) reventón *m*; **a ~ of energy/speed/enthusiasm** una explosión de energía/un ímpetu de velocidad/un arranque deentusiasmo; **to ~ into flames** estallar en llamas; **to ~ into tears** deshacerse en lágrimas; **to ~ out laughing** soltar la carcajada; **to ~ open** abrirse de golpe; **to be ~ing with** (*container*) estar lleno a rebosar de; (: *person*) reventar por *or* de; **burst into** *vt fus* (*room etc*) irrumpir en
bury ['bɛrɪ] *vt* enterrar; (*body*) enterrar, sepultar
bus [bʌs] (*pl* **~es**) *n* autobús *m*; **bus conductor** *n* cobrador(a) *m/f*
bush [buʃ] *n* arbusto; (*scrub land*) monte *m*; **to beat about the ~** andar(se) con rodeos
business ['bɪznɪs] *n* (*matter*) asunto; (*trading*) comercio, negocios *mpl*; (*firm*) empresa, casa; (*occupation*) oficio; **to be away on ~** estar en viaje de negocios; **it's my ~ to ...** me toca *or* corresponde ...; **it's none of my ~** yo no tengo nada que ver; **he means ~** habla en serio; **business class** *n* (*Aer*) clase *f* preferente; **businesslike** *adj* eficiente; **businessman** (*irreg*) *n* hombre *m* de negocios; **business trip** *n* viaje *m* de negocios; **businesswoman** (*irreg*) *n* mujer *f* de negocios
busker ['bʌskə*] (BRIT) *n* músico/a ambulante
bus: bus pass *n* bonobús; **bus shelter** *n* parada cubierta; **bus station** *n* estación *f* de autobuses; **bus-stop** *n* parada de autobús
bust [bʌst] *n* (*Anat*) pecho; (*sculpture*) busto ▷ *adj* (*inf*: *broken*) roto, estropeado; **to go ~** quebrar
bustling ['bʌslɪŋ] *adj* (*town*) animado, bullicioso
busy ['bɪzɪ] *adj* ocupado, atareado; (*shop, street*) concurrido, animado; (*Tel*: *line*) comunicando ▷ *vt*: **to ~ o.s. with** ocuparse en; **busy signal** (US) *n* (*Tel*) señal *f* de comunicando

KEYWORD

but [bʌt] *conj* **1** pero; **he's not very bright, but he's hard-working** no es

muy inteligente, pero es trabajador
2 (*in direct contradiction*) sino; **he's not English but French** no es inglés sino francés; **he didn't sing but he shouted** no cantó sino que gritó
3 (*showing disagreement, surprise etc*): **but that's far too expensive!** ¡pero eso es carísimo!; **but it does work!** ¡(pero) sí que funciona!
▷ *prep* (*apart from, except*) menos, salvo; **we've had nothing but trouble** no hemos tenido más que problemas; **no-one but him can do it** nadie más que él puede hacerlo; **who but a lunatic would do such a thing?** ¡sólo un loco haría una cosa así!; **but for you/your help** si no fuera por ti/tu ayuda; **anything but that** cualquier cosa menos eso
▷ *adv* (*just, only*): **she's but a child** no es más que una niña; **had I but known** si lo hubiera sabido; **I can but try** al menos lo puedo intentar; **it's all but finished** está casi acabado

butcher ['butʃə*] *n* carnicero ▷ *vt* hacer una carnicería con; (*cattle etc*) matar; **butcher's (shop)** *n* carnicería
butler ['bʌtlə*] *n* mayordomo
butt [bʌt] *n* (*barrel*) tonel *m*; (*of gun*) culata; (*of cigarette*) colilla; (BRIT: *fig*: *target*) blanco ▷ *vt* dar cabezadas contra, top(et)ar
butter ['bʌtə*] *n* mantequilla ▷ *vt* untar con mantequilla; **buttercup** *n* botón *m* de oro
butterfly ['bʌtəflaɪ] *n* mariposa; (*Swimming*: *also*: **~ stroke**) braza de mariposa
buttocks ['bʌtəks] *npl* nalgas *fpl*
button ['bʌtn] *n* botón *m*; (US) placa, chapa ▷ *vt* (*also*: **~ up**) abotonar, abrochar ▷ *vi* abrocharse
buy [baɪ] (*pt, pp* **bought**) *vt* comprar ▷ *n* compra; **to ~ sb sth/sth from sb** comprarle algo a algn; **to ~ sb a drink** invitar a algn a tomar algo; **buy out** *vt* (*partner*) comprar la parte de; **buy up** *vt* (*property*) acaparar; (*stock*) comprar todas las existencias de; **buyer** *n* comprador(a) *m/f*
buzz [bʌz] *n* zumbido; (*inf*: *phone call*) llamada (por teléfono) ▷ *vi* zumbar; **buzzer** *n* timbre *m*

KEYWORD

by [baɪ] *prep* 1 (*referring to cause, agent*) por; de; **killed by lightning** muerto por un relámpago; **a painting by Picasso** un cuadro de Picasso
2 (*referring to method, manner, means*): **by bus/car/train** en autobús/coche/tren; **to pay by cheque** pagar con un cheque; **by moonlight/candlelight** a la luz de la luna/una vela; **by saving hard he ...** ahorrando ...
3 (*via, through*) por; **we came by Dover** vinimos por Dover
4 (*close to, past*): **the house by the river** la casa junto al río; **she rushed by me** pasó a mi lado como una exhalación; **I go by the post office every day** paso por delante de Correos todos los días
5 (*time*: *not later than*) para; (: *during*): **by daylight** de día; **by 4 o'clock** para las cuatro; **by this time tomorrow** mañana a estas horas; **by the time I got here it was too late** cuando llegué ya era demasiado tarde
6 (*amount*): **by the metre/kilo** por metro/kilo; **paid by the hour** pagado por hora
7 (*Math, measure*): **to divide/multiply by 3** dividir/multiplicar por 3; **a room 3 metres by 4** una habitación de 3 metros por 4; **it's broader by a metre** es un metro más ancho
8 (*according to*) según, de acuerdo con; **it's 3 o'clock by my watch** según mi reloj, son las tres; **it's all right by me** por mí, está bien
9: **(all) by oneself** *etc* todo solo; **he did it (all) by himself** lo hizo él solo;

he was standing (all) by himself in a corner estaba de pie solo en un rincón
10: **by the way** a propósito, por cierto; **this wasn't my idea, by the way** pues, no fue idea mía
▷ *adv* **1** *see* **go; pass** *etc*
2: **by and by** finalmente; **they'll come back by and by** acabarán volviendo; **by and large** en líneas generales, en general

bye(-bye) ['baɪ('baɪ)] *excl* adiós, hasta luego
by-election (BRIT) *n* elección *f* parcial
bypass ['baɪpɑːs] *n* carretera de circunvalación; (*Med*) (operación *f* de) by-pass *f* ▷ *vt* evitar
byte [baɪt] *n* (*Comput*) byte *m*, octeto

C [siː] *n* (*Mus*) do *m*
cab [kæb] *n* taxi *m*; (*of truck*) cabina
cabaret ['kæbəreɪ] *n* cabaret *m*
cabbage ['kæbɪdʒ] *n* col *f*, berza
cabin ['kæbɪn] *n* cabaña; (*on ship*) camarote *m*; (*on plane*) cabina; **cabin crew** *n* tripulación *f* de cabina
cabinet ['kæbɪnɪt] *n* (*Pol*) consejo de ministros; (*furniture*) armario; (*also*: **display ~**) vitrina; **cabinet minister** *n* ministro/a (del gabinete)
cable ['keɪbl] *n* cable *m* ▷ *vt* cablegrafiar; **cable car** *n* teleférico; **cable television** *n* televisión *f* por cable
cactus ['kæktəs] (*pl* **cacti**) *n* cacto
café ['kæfeɪ] *n* café *m*
cafeteria [kæfɪ'tɪərɪə] *n* cafetería
caffein(e) ['kæfiːn] *n* cafeína
cage [keɪdʒ] *n* jaula
cagoule [kə'guːl] *n* chubasquero
cake [keɪk] *n* (*Culin*: *large*) tarta; (: *small*) pastel *m*; (*of soap*) pastilla
calcium ['kælsɪəm] *n* calcio
calculate ['kælkjuleɪt] *vt* calcular;

calculation [-'leɪʃən] *n* cálculo, cómputo; **calculator** *n* calculadora
calendar ['kæləndə*] *n* calendario
calf [kɑːf] (*pl* **calves**) *n* (*of cow*) ternero, becerro; (*of other animals*) cría; (*also*: **~skin**) piel *f* de becerro; (*Anat*) pantorrilla
calibre ['kælɪbə*] (*US* **caliber**) *n* calibre *m*
call [kɔːl] *vt* llamar; (*meeting*) convocar ▷ *vi* (*shout*) llamar; (*Tel*) llamar (por teléfono); (*visit*: *also*: **~ in, ~ round**) hacer una visita ▷ *n* llamada; (*of bird*) canto; **to be ~ed** llamarse; **on ~** (*on duty*) de guardia; **call back** *vi* (*return*) volver; (*Tel*) volver a llamar; **call for** *vt fus* (*demand*) pedir, exigir; (*fetch*) pasar a recoger; **call in** *vt* (*doctor, expert, police*) llamar; **call off** *vt* (*cancel*: *meeting, race*) cancelar; (: *deal*) anular; (: *strike*) desconvocar; **call on** *vt fus* (*visit*) visitar; (*turn to*) acudir a; **call out** *vi* gritar; **call up** *vt* (*Mil*) llamar al servicio militar; (*Tel*) llamar; **callbox** (*BRIT*) *n* cabina telefónica; **call centre** (*US* **call center**) *n* centro de atención al cliente; **caller** *n* visita; (*Tel*) usuario/a
callous ['kæləs] *adj* insensible, cruel
calm [kɑːm] *adj* tranquilo; (*sea*) liso, en calma ▷ *n* calma, tranquilidad *f* ▷ *vt* calmar, tranquilizar; **calm down** *vi* calmarse, tranquilizarse ▷ *vt* calmar, tranquilizar; **calmly** ['kɑːmlɪ] *adv* tranquilamente, con calma
Calor gas® ['kælə*-] *n* butano
calorie ['kælərɪ] *n* caloría
calves [kɑːvz] *npl of* **calf**
camcorder ['kæmkɔːdə*] *n* videocámara
came [keɪm] *pt of* **come**
camel ['kæməl] *n* camello
camera ['kæmərə] *n* máquina fotográfica; (*Cinema, TV*) cámara; **in ~** (*Law*) a puerta cerrada; **cameraman** (*irreg*) *n* cámara *m*; **camera phone** *n* teléfono con cámara
camouflage ['kæməflɑːʒ] *n* camuflaje *m* ▷ *vt* camuflar
camp [kæmp] *n* campamento, camping *m*; (*Mil*) campamento; (*for prisoners*) campo; (*fig*: *faction*) bando ▷ *vi* acampar ▷ *adj* afectado, afeminado
campaign [kæm'peɪn] *n* (*Mil, Pol etc*) campaña ▷ *vi* hacer campaña; **campaigner** *n*: **campaigner for** defensor(a) *m/f* de
camp: campbed (*BRIT*) *n* cama de campaña; **camper** *n* campista *mf*; (*vehicle*) caravana; **campground** (*US*) *n* camping *m*, campamento; **camping** *n* camping *m*; **to go camping** hacer camping; **campsite** *n* camping *m*
campus ['kæmpəs] *n* ciudad *f* universitaria
can[1] [kæn] *n* (*of oil, water*) bidón *m*; (*tin*) lata, bote *m* ▷ *vt* enlatar

KEYWORD

can[2] [kæn] (*negative* **cannot, can't**, *conditional and pt* **could**) *aux vb* **1** (*be able to*) poder; **you can do it if you try** puedes hacerlo si lo intentas; **I can't see you** no te veo
2 (*know how to*) saber; **I can swim/play tennis/drive** sé nadar/jugar al tenis/conducir; **can you speak French?** ¿hablas *or* sabes hablar francés?
3 (*may*) poder; **can I use your phone?** ¿me dejas *or* puedo usar tu teléfono?
4 (*expressing disbelief, puzzlement etc*): **it can't be true!** ¡no puede ser (verdad)!; **what CAN he want?** ¿qué querrá?
5 (*expressing possibility, suggestion etc*): **he could be in the library** podría estar en la biblioteca; **she could have been delayed** pudo haberse retrasado

Canada ['kænədə] *n* (el) Canadá; **Canadian** [kə'neɪdɪən] *adj, n* canadiense *mf*
canal [kə'næl] *n* canal *m*
canary [kə'nɛərɪ] *n* canario
Canary Islands [kə'nɛərɪ'aɪləndz]

npl: **the ~** las (Islas) Canarias

cancel ['kænsəl] *vt* cancelar; (*train*) suprimir; (*cross out*) tachar, borrar; **cancellation** [-'leɪʃən] *n* cancelación *f*; supresión *f*

Cancer ['kænsə*] *n* (*Astrology*) Cáncer *m*

cancer ['kænsə*] *n* cáncer *m*

candidate ['kændɪdeɪt] *n* candidato/a

candle ['kændl] *n* vela; (*in church*) cirio; **candlestick** *n* (*single*) candelero; (*low*) palmatoria; (*bigger, ornate*) candelabro

candy ['kændɪ] *n* azúcar *m* cande; (US) caramelo; **candy bar** (US) *n* barrita (*dulce*); **candyfloss** (BRIT) *n* algodón *m* (azucarado)

cane [keɪn] *n* (*Bot*) caña; (*stick*) vara, palmeta; (*for furniture*) mimbre *f* ▷ *vt* (BRIT: *Scol*) castigar (con vara)

canister ['kænɪstə*] *n* bote *m*, lata; (*of gas*) bombona

cannabis ['kænəbɪs] *n* marijuana

canned [kænd] *adj* en lata, de lata

cannon ['kænən] (*pl* **~** *or* **~s**) *n* cañón *m*

cannot ['kænɔt] = **can not**

canoe [kə'nu:] *n* canoa; (*Sport*) piragua; **canoeing** *n* piragüismo

canon ['kænən] *n* (*clergyman*) canónigo; (*standard*) canon *m*

can-opener ['kænəupnə*] *n* abrelatas *m inv*

can't [kænt] = **can not**

canteen [kæn'ti:n] *n* (*eating place*) cantina; (BRIT: *of cutlery*) juego

canter ['kæntə*] *vi* ir a medio galope

canvas ['kænvəs] *n* (*material*) lona; (*painting*) lienzo; (*Naut*) velas *fpl*

canvass ['kænvəs] *vi* (*Pol*): **to ~ for** solicitar votos por ▷ *vt* (*Comm*) sondear

canyon ['kænjən] *n* cañón *m*

cap [kæp] *n* (*hat*) gorra; (*of pen*) capuchón *m*; (*of bottle*) tapa, tapón *m*; (*contraceptive*) diafragma *m*; (*for toy gun*) cápsula ▷ *vt* (*outdo*) superar; (*limit*) recortar

capability [keɪpə'bɪlɪtɪ] *n* capacidad *f*

capable ['keɪpəbl] *adj* capaz

capacity [kə'pæsɪtɪ] *n* capacidad *f*; (*position*) calidad *f*

cape [keɪp] *n* capa; (*Geo*) cabo

caper ['keɪpə*] *n* (*Culin*: *gen pl*) alcaparra; (*prank*) broma

capital ['kæpɪtl] *n* (*also*: **~ city**) capital *f*; (*money*) capital *m*; (*also*: **~ letter**) mayúscula; **capitalism** *n* capitalismo; **capitalist** *adj*, *n* capitalista *mf*; **capital punishment** *n* pena de muerte

Capitol ['kæpɪtl] *n* *ver recuadro*

CAPITOL

El Capitolio **(Capitol)** es el edificio del Congreso **(Congress)** de los Estados Unidos, situado en la ciudad de Washington. Por extensión, también se suele llamar así al edificio en el que tienen lugar las sesiones parlamentarias de la cámara de representantes de muchos de los estados.

Capricorn ['kæprɪkɔ:n] *n* Capricornio

capsize [kæp'saɪz] *vt* volcar, hacer zozobrar ▷ *vi* volcarse, zozobrar

capsule ['kæpsju:l] *n* cápsula

captain ['kæptɪn] *n* capitán *m*

caption ['kæpʃən] *n* (*heading*) título; (*to picture*) leyenda

captivity [kæp'tɪvɪtɪ] *n* cautiverio

capture ['kæptʃə*] *vt* prender, apresar; (*animal, Comput*) capturar; (*place*) tomar; (*attention*) captar, llamar ▷ *n* apresamiento; captura; toma; (*data capture*) formulación *f* de datos

car [kɑ:*] *n* coche *m*, carro (LAM), automóvil *m*; (US *Rail*) vagón *m*

carafe [kə'ræf] *n* jarra

caramel ['kærəməl] *n* caramelo

carat ['kærət] *n* quilate *m*

caravan ['kærəvæn] *n* (BRIT) caravana, ruló *f*; (*in desert*) caravana; **caravan site** (BRIT) *n* camping *m* para caravanas
carbohydrate [kɑ:bəu'haɪdreɪt] *n* hidrato de carbono; (*food*) fécula
carbon ['kɑ:bən] *n* carbono; **carbon dioxide** *n* dióxido de carbono, anhídrido carbónico; **carbon monoxide** *n* monóxido de carbono
car boot sale *n* *mercadillo organizado en un aparcamiento, en el que se exponenlas mercancías en el maletero del coche*
carburettor [kɑ:bju'rɛtə*] (US **carburetor**) *n* carburador *m*
card [kɑ:d] *n* (*material*) cartulina; (*index card etc*) ficha; (*playing card*) carta, naipe *m*; (*visiting card, greetings card etc*) tarjeta; **cardboard** *n* cartón *m*; **card game** *n* juego de naipes *or* cartas
cardigan ['kɑ:dɪgən] *n* rebeca
cardinal ['kɑ:dɪnl] *adj* cardinal; (*importance, principal*) esencial ▷ *n* cardenal *m*
cardphone ['kɑ:dfəun] *n* *cabina que funciona con tarjetas telefónicas*
care [kɛə*] *n* cuidado; (*worry*) inquietud *f*; (*charge*) cargo, custodia ▷ *vi*: **to ~ about** (*person, animal*) tener cariño a; (*thing, idea*) preocuparse por; **~ of** en casa de, al cuidado de; **in sb's ~** a cargo de algn; **to take ~ to** cuidarse de, tener cuidado de; **to take ~ of** cuidar; (*problem etc*) ocuparse de; **I don't ~** no me importa; **I couldn't ~ less** eso me trae sin cuidado; **care for** *vt fus* cuidar a; (*like*) querer
career [kə'rɪə*] *n* profesión *f*; (*in work, school*) carrera ▷ *vi* (*also*: **~ along**) correr a toda velocidad
care: carefree *adj* despreocupado; **careful** *adj* cuidadoso; (*cautious*) cauteloso; **(be) careful!** ¡tenga cuidado!; **carefully** *adv* con cuidado, cuidadosamente; con cautela; **caregiver** (US) *n* (*professional*) enfermero/a *m/f*; (*unpaid*) *persona que cuida a un pariente o vecino*; **careless** *adj* descuidado; (*heedless*) poco atento; **carelessness** *n* descuido, falta de atención; **carer** ['kɛərə*] *n* (*professional*) enfermero/a *m/f*; (*unpaid*) *persona que cuida a un pariente o vecino*; **caretaker** *n* portero/a, conserje *mf*
car-ferry ['kɑ:fɛrɪ] *n* transbordador *m* para coches
cargo ['kɑ:gəu] (*pl* **~es**) *n* cargamento, carga
car hire *n* alquiler *m* de automóviles
Caribbean [kærɪ'bi:ən] *n*: **the ~ (Sea)** el (Mar) Caribe
caring ['kɛərɪŋ] *adj* humanitario; (*behaviour*) afectuoso
carnation [kɑ:'neɪʃən] *n* clavel *m*
carnival ['kɑ:nɪvəl] *n* carnaval *m*; (US: *funfair*) parque *m* de atracciones
carol ['kærəl] *n*: **(Christmas) ~** villancico
carousel [kærə'sɛl] (US) *n* tiovivo, caballitos *mpl*
car park (BRIT) *n* aparcamiento, parking *m*
carpenter ['kɑ:pɪntə*] *n* carpintero/a
carpet ['kɑ:pɪt] *n* alfombra; (*fitted*) moqueta ▷ *vt* alfombrar
car rental (US) *n* alquiler *m* de coches
carriage ['kærɪdʒ] *n* (BRIT *Rail*) vagón *m*; (*horse-drawn*) coche *m*; (*of goods*) transporte *m*; (: *cost*) porte *m*, flete *m*; **carriageway** (BRIT) *n* (*part of road*) calzada
carrier ['kærɪə*] *n* (*transport company*) transportista, empresa de transportes; (*Med*) portador(a) *m/f*; **carrier bag** (BRIT) *n* bolsa de papel *or* plástico
carrot ['kærət] *n* zanahoria
carry ['kærɪ] *vt* (*person*) llevar; (*transport*) transportar; (*involve*: *responsibilities etc*) entrañar, implicar; (*Med*) ser portador de ▷ *vi* (*sound*) oírse; **to get carried away** (*fig*) entusiasmarse; **carry on** *vi* (*continue*) seguir (adelante), continuar ▷ *vt* proseguir, continuar; **carry out** *vt*

(*orders*) cumplir; (*investigation*) llevar a cabo, realizar
cart [kɑːt] *n* carro, carreta ▷ *vt* (*inf: transport*) acarrear
carton ['kɑːtən] *n* (*box*) caja (de cartón); (*of milk etc*) bote *m*; (*of yogurt*) tarrina
cartoon [kɑː'tuːn] *n* (*Press*) caricatura; (*comic strip*) tira cómica; (*film*) dibujos *mpl* animados
cartridge ['kɑːtrɪdʒ] *n* cartucho; (*of pen*) recambio
carve [kɑːv] *vt* (*meat*) trinchar; (*wood, stone*) cincelar, esculpir; (*initials etc*) grabar; **carving** *n* (*object*) escultura; (*design*) talla; (*art*) tallado
car wash *n* lavado de coches
case [keɪs] *n* (*container*) caja; (*Med*) caso; (*for jewels etc*) estuche *m*; (*Law*) causa, proceso; (BRIT: *also*: **suit~**) maleta; **in ~ of** en caso de; **in any ~** en todo caso; **just in ~** por si acaso
cash [kæʃ] *n* dinero en efectivo, dinero contante ▷ *vt* cobrar, hacer efectivo; **to pay (in) ~** pagar al contado; **~ on delivery** cóbrese al entregar; **cashback** *n* (*discount*) devolución *f*; (*at supermarket etc*) *retirada de dinero en efectivo de un establecimiento donde se ha pagado con tarjeta; también dinero retirado*; **cash card** *n* tarjeta *f* dinero; **cash desk** (BRIT) *n* caja; **cash dispenser** *n* cajero automático
cashew [kæ'ʃuː] *n* (*also*: **~ nut**) anacardo
cashier [kæ'ʃɪə*] *n* cajero/a
cashmere ['kæʃmɪə*] *n* cachemira
cash point *n* cajero automático
cash register *n* caja
casino [kə'siːnəu] *n* casino
casket ['kɑːskɪt] *n* cofre *m*, estuche *m*; (US: *coffin*) ataúd *m*
casserole ['kæsərəul] *n* (*food, pot*) cazuela
cassette [kæ'sɛt] *n* casete *f*; **cassette player, cassette recorder** *n* casete *m*
cast [kɑːst] (*pt, pp* **~**) *vt* (*throw*) echar, arrojar, lanzar; (*glance, eyes*) dirigir; (*Theatre*): **to ~ sb as Othello** dar a algn el papel de Otelo ▷ *vi* (*Fishing*) lanzar ▷ *n* (*Theatre*) reparto; (*also*: **plaster ~**) vaciado; **to ~ one's vote** votar; **to ~ doubt on** suscitar dudas acerca de; **cast off** *vi* (*Naut*) desamarrar; (*Knitting*) cerrar (los puntos)
castanets [kæstə'nɛts] *npl* castañuelas *fpl*
caster sugar ['kɑːstə*-] (BRIT) *n* azúcar *m* extrafino
Castile [kæs'tiːl] *n* Castilla; **Castilian** *adj, n* castellano/a *m/f*
cast-iron ['kɑːstaɪən] *adj* (*lit*) (hecho) de hierro fundido; (*fig: case*) irrebatible
castle ['kɑːsl] *n* castillo; (*Chess*) torre *f*
casual ['kæʒjul] *adj* fortuito; (*irregular: work etc*) eventual, temporero; (*unconcerned*) despreocupado; (*clothes*) informal

> Be careful not to translate **casual** by the Spanish word *casual*.

casualty ['kæʒjultɪ] *n* víctima, herido/a; (*dead*) muerto/a; (*Med: department*) urgencias *fpl*
cat [kæt] *n* gato; (*big cat*) felino
Catalan ['kætəlæn] *adj, n* catalán/ana *m/f*
catalogue ['kætəlɔg] (US **catalog**) *n* catálogo ▷ *vt* catalogar
Catalonia [kætə'ləunɪə] *n* Cataluña
catalytic converter [kætə'lɪtɪkkən'vəːtə*] *n* catalizador *m*
cataract ['kætərækt] *n* (*Med*) cataratas *fpl*
catarrh [kə'tɑː*] *n* catarro
catastrophe [kə'tæstrəfɪ] *n* catástrofe *f*
catch [kætʃ] (*pt, pp* **caught**) *vt* coger (SP), agarrar (LAM); (*arrest*) detener; (*grasp*) asir; (*breath*) contener; (*surprise: person*) sorprender; (*attract: attention*) captar; (*hear*) oír; (*Med*) contagiarse de, coger; (*also*: **~ up**) alcanzar ▷ *vi* (*fire*) encenderse; (*in branches etc*) enredarse ▷ *n* (*fish etc*) pesca; (*act of catching*) cogida; (*hidden problem*) dificultad *f*; (*game*)

pilla-pilla; (*of lock*) pestillo, cerradura; **to ~ fire** encenderse; **to ~ sight of** divisar; **catch up** *vi* (*fig*) ponerse al día; **catching** ['kætʃɪŋ] *adj* (*Med*) contagioso

category ['kætɪgərɪ] *n* categoría, clase *f*

cater ['keɪtə*] *vi*: **to ~ for** (BRIT) abastecer a; (*needs*) atender a; (*Comm*: *parties etc*) proveer comida a

caterpillar ['kætəpɪlə*] *n* oruga, gusano

cathedral [kə'θi:drəl] *n* catedral *f*

Catholic ['kæθəlɪk] *adj*, *n* (*Rel*) católico/a *m/f*

Catseye® ['kæts'aɪ] (BRIT) *n* (*Aut*) catafoto

cattle ['kætl] *npl* ganado

catwalk ['kætwɔ:k] *n* pasarela

caught [kɔ:t] *pt*, *pp of* **catch**

cauliflower ['kɔlɪflauə*] *n* coliflor *f*

cause [kɔ:z] *n* causa, motivo, razón *f*; (*principle*: *also Pol*) causa ▷ *vt* causar

caution ['kɔ:ʃən] *n* cautela, prudencia; (*warning*) advertencia, amonestación *f* ▷ *vt* amonestar; **cautious** *adj* cauteloso, prudente, precavido

cave [keɪv] *n* cueva, caverna; **cave in** *vi* (*roof etc*) derrumbarse, hundirse

caviar(e) ['kævɪɑ:*] *n* caviar *m*

cavity ['kævɪtɪ] *n* hueco, cavidad *f*

cc *abbr* (= *cubic centimetres*) c.c.; (= *carbon copy*) copia hecha con papel del carbón

CCTV *n abbr* (= *closed-circuit television*) circuito cerrado de televisión

CD *n abbr* (= *compact disc*) CD *m*; (*player*) (reproductor *m* de) CD; **CD player** *n* reproductor *m* de CD; **CD-ROM** [si:di:'rɔm] *n abbr* CD-ROM *m*; **CD writer** *n* grabadora de CD

cease [si:s] *vt*, *vi* cesar; **ceasefire** *n* alto *m* el fuego

cedar ['si:də*] *n* cedro

ceilidh ['keɪlɪ] *n baile con música y danzas tradicionales escocesas o irlandesas*

ceiling ['si:lɪŋ] *n* techo; (*fig*) límite *m*

celebrate ['sɛlɪbreɪt] *vt* celebrar ▷ *vi* divertirse; **celebration** [-'breɪʃən] *n* fiesta, celebración *f*

celebrity [sɪ'lɛbrɪtɪ] *n* celebridad *f*

celery ['sɛlərɪ] *n* apio

cell [sɛl] *n* celda; (*Biol*) célula; (*Elec*) elemento

cellar ['sɛlə*] *n* sótano; (*for wine*) bodega

cello ['tʃɛləu] *n* violoncelo

Cellophane® ['sɛləfeɪn] *n* celofán *m*

cellphone ['sɛlfəʊn] *n* teléfono celular

Celsius ['sɛlsɪəs] *adj* centígrado

Celtic ['kɛltɪk] *adj* celta

cement [sə'mɛnt] *n* cemento

cemetery ['sɛmɪtrɪ] *n* cementerio

censor ['sɛnsə*] *n* censor *m* ▷ *vt* (*cut*) censurar; **censorship** *n* censura

census ['sɛnsəs] *n* censo

cent [sɛnt] *n* (*unit of dollar*) centavo, céntimo; (*unit of euro*) céntimo; *see also* **per**

centenary [sɛn'ti:nərɪ] *n* centenario

centennial [sɛn'tɛnɪəl] (US) *n* centenario

center ['sentə*] (US) = **centre**

centi... [sɛntɪ] *prefix*: **centigrade** *adj* centígrado; **centimetre** (US **centimeter**) *n* centímetro; **centipede** ['sɛntɪpi:d] *n* ciempiés *m inv*

central ['sɛntrəl] *adj* central; (*of house etc*) céntrico; **Central America** *n* Centroamérica; **central heating** *n* calefacción *f* central; **central reservation** *n* (BRIT *Aut*) mediana

centre ['sɛntə*] (US **center**) *n* centro; (*fig*) núcleo ▷ *vt* centrar; **centre-forward** *n* (*Sport*) delantero centro; **centre-half** *n* (*Sport*) medio centro

century ['sɛntjurɪ] *n* siglo; **20th ~** siglo veinte

CEO *n abbr* = **chief executive officer**

ceramic [sɪ'ræmɪk] *adj* cerámico

cereal ['si:rɪəl] *n* cereal *m*

ceremony ['sɛrɪmənɪ] *n* ceremonia; **to stand on ~** hacer ceremonias, estar de cumplido

certain ['sə:tən] *adj* seguro;

(*person*): **a ~ Mr Smith** un tal Sr. Smith; (*particular, some*) cierto; **for ~** a ciencia cierta; **certainly** *adv* (*undoubtedly*) ciertamente; (*of course*) desde luego, por supuesto; **certainty** *n* certeza, certidumbre *f*, seguridad *f*; (*inevitability*) certeza

certificate [sə'tɪfɪkɪt] *n* certificado

certify ['sə:tɪfaɪ] *vt* certificar; (*award diploma to*) conceder un diploma a; (*declare insane*) declarar loco

cf. *abbr* (= *compare*) cfr

CFC *n abbr* (= *chlorofluorocarbon*) CFC *m*

chain [tʃeɪn] *n* cadena; (*of mountains*) cordillera; (*of events*) sucesión *f* ▷ *vt* (*also*: **~ up**) encadenar; **chain-smoke** *vi* fumar un cigarrillo tras otro

chair [tʃɛə*] *n* silla; (*armchair*) sillón *m*, butaca; (*of university*) cátedra; (*of meeting etc*) presidencia ▷ *vt* (*meeting*) presidir; **chairlift** *n* telesilla; **chairman** (*irreg*) *n* presidente *m*; **chairperson** *n* presidente/a *m/f*; **chairwoman** (*irreg*) *n* presidenta

chalet ['ʃæleɪ] *n* chalet *m* (de madera)

chalk [tʃɔ:k] *n* (*Geo*) creta; (*for writing*) tiza, gis *m* (MEX); **chalkboard** (US) *n* pizarrón (LAM), pizarra (SP)

challenge ['tʃælɪndʒ] *n* desafío, reto ▷ *vt* desafiar, retar; (*statement, right*) poner en duda; **to ~ sb to do sth** retar a algn a que haga algo; **challenging** *adj* exigente; (*tone*) de desafío

chamber ['tʃeɪmbə*] *n* cámara, sala; (*Pol*) cámara; (BRIT *Law*: *gen pl*) despacho; **~ of commerce** cámara de comercio; **chambermaid** *n* camarera

champagne [ʃæm'peɪn] *n* champaña *m*, champán *m*

champion ['tʃæmpɪən] *n* campeón/ona *m/f*; (*of cause*) defensor(a) *m/f*; **championship** *n* campeonato

chance [tʃɑ:ns] *n* (*opportunity*) ocasión *f*, oportunidad *f*; (*likelihood*) posibilidad *f*; (*risk*) riesgo ▷ *vt* arriesgar, probar ▷ *adj* fortuito, casual; **to ~ it** arriesgarse, intentarlo; **to take a ~** arriesgarse; **by ~** por casualidad

chancellor ['tʃɑ:nsələ*] *n* canciller *m*; **Chancellor of the Exchequer** (BRIT) *n* Ministro de Hacienda

chandelier [ʃændə'lɪə*] *n* araña (de luces)

change [tʃeɪndʒ] *vt* cambiar; (*replace*) cambiar, reemplazar; (*gear, clothes, job*) cambiar de; (*transform*) transformar ▷ *vi* cambiar(se); (*change trains*) hacer transbordo; (*traffic lights*) cambiar de color; (*be transformed*): **to ~ into** transformarse en ▷ *n* cambio; (*alteration*) modificación *f*; (*transformation*) transformación *f*; (*of clothes*) muda; (*coins*) suelto, sencillo; (*money returned*) vuelta; **to ~ gear** (*Aut*) cambiar de marcha; **to ~ one's mind** cambiar de opinión *or* idea; **for a ~** para variar; **change over** *vi* (*from sth to sth*) cambiar; (*players etc*) cambiar(se) ▷ *vt* cambiar; **changeable** *adj* (*weather*) cambiable; **change machine** *n* máquina de cambio; **changing room** (BRIT) *n* vestuario

channel ['tʃænl] *n* (*TV*) canal *m*; (*of river*) cauce *m*; (*groove*) conducto; (*fig*: *medium*) medio ▷ *vt* (*river etc*) encauzar; **the (English) C~** el Canal (de la Mancha); **the C~ Islands** las Islas Normandas; **Channel Tunnel** *n*: **the Channel Tunnel** el túnel del Canal de la Mancha, el Eurotúnel

chant [tʃɑ:nt] *n* (*of crowd*) gritos *mpl*; (*Rel*) canto ▷ *vt* (*slogan, word*) repetir a gritos

chaos ['keɪɔs] *n* caos *m*

chaotic [keɪ'ɔtɪk] *adj* caótico

chap [tʃæp] (BRIT: *inf*) *n* (*man*) tío, tipo

chapel ['tʃæpəl] *n* capilla

chapped [tʃæpt] *adj* agrietado

chapter ['tʃæptə*] *n* capítulo

character ['kærɪktə*] *n* carácter *m*, naturaleza, índole *f*; (*moral strength, personality*) carácter; (*in novel, film*) personaje *m*; **characteristic** [-'rɪstɪk] *adj* característico ▷ *n* característica; **characterize** ['kærɪktəraɪz] *vt*

caracterizar
charcoal ['tʃɑːkəul] *n* carbón *m* vegetal; (*Art*) carboncillo
charge [tʃɑːdʒ] *n* (*Law*) cargo, acusación *f*; (*cost*) precio, coste *m*; (*responsibility*) cargo ▷ *vt* (*Law*): **to ~ (with)** acusar (de); (*battery*) cargar; (*price*) pedir; (*customer*) cobrar ▷ *vi* precipitarse; (*Mil*) cargar, atacar; **charge card** *n* tarjeta de cuenta; **charger** *n* (*also*: **battery charger**) cargador *m* (de baterías)
charismatic [kærɪz'mætɪk] *adj* carismático
charity ['tʃærɪtɪ] *n* caridad *f*; (*organization*) sociedad *f* benéfica; (*money, gifts*) limosnas *fpl*; **charity shop** *n* (BRIT) *tienda de artículos de segunda mano que dedica su recaudación a causas benéficas*
charm [tʃɑːm] *n* encanto, atractivo; (*talisman*) hechizo; (*on bracelet*) dije *m* ▷ *vt* encantar; **charming** *adj* encantador(a)
chart [tʃɑːt] *n* (*diagram*) cuadro; (*graph*) gráfica; (*map*) carta de navegación ▷ *vt* (*course*) trazar; (*progress*) seguir; **charts** *npl* (*Top 40*): **the ~s** ≈ los 40 principales (SP)
charter ['tʃɑːtə*] *vt* (*plane*) alquilar; (*ship*) fletar ▷ *n* (*document*) carta; (*of university, company*) estatutos *mpl*; **chartered accountant** (BRIT) *n* contable *m/f* diplomado/a; **charter flight** *n* vuelo chárter
chase [tʃeɪs] *vt* (*pursue*) perseguir; (*also*: **~ away**) ahuyentar ▷ *n* persecución *f*
chat [tʃæt] *vi* (*also*: **have a ~**) charlar; (*on Internet*) chatear ▷ *n* charla; **chat up** *vt* (*inf*: *girl*) ligar con, enrollarse con; **chat room** *n* (*Internet*) chat *m*, canal *m* de charla; **chat show** (BRIT) *n* programa *m* de entrevistas
chatter ['tʃætə*] *vi* (*person*) charlar; (*teeth*) castañetear ▷ *n* (*of birds*) parloteo; (*of people*) charla, cháchara
chauffeur ['ʃəufə*] *n* chófer *m*
chauvinist ['ʃəuvɪnɪst] *n* (*male chauvinist*) machista *m*; (*nationalist*) chovinista *mf*
cheap [tʃiːp] *adj* barato; (*joke*) de mal gusto; (*poor quality*) de mala calidad ▷ *adv* barato; **cheap day return** *n billete de ida y vuelta el mismo día*; **cheaply** *adv* barato, a bajo precio
cheat [tʃiːt] *vi* hacer trampa ▷ *vt*: **to ~ sb (out of sth)** estafar (algo) a algn ▷ *n* (*person*) tramposo/a; **cheat on** *vt fus* engañar
Chechnya [tʃɪtʃ'njɑː] *n* Chechenia
check [tʃɛk] *vt* (*examine*) controlar; (*facts*) comprobar; (*halt*) parar, detener; (*restrain*) refrenar, restringir ▷ *n* (*inspection*) control *m*, inspección *f*; (*curb*) freno; (US: *bill*) nota, cuenta; (US) = **cheque**; (*pattern*: *gen pl*) cuadro; **check in** *vi* (*at hotel*) firmar el registro; (*at airport*) facturar el equipaje ▷ *vt* (*luggage*) facturar; **check off** *vt* (*esp* US: *check*) comprobar; (*cross off*) tachar; **check out** *vi* (*of hotel*) marcharse; **check up** *vi*: **to check up on sth** comprobar algo; **to check up on sb** investigar a algn; **checkbook** (US) = **chequebook**; **checked** *adj* a cuadros; **checkers** (US) *n* juego de damas; **check-in** *n* (*also*: **check-in desk**: *at airport*) mostrador *m* de facturación; **checking account** (US) *n* cuenta corriente; **checklist** *n* lista (de control); **checkmate** *n* jaque *m* mate; **checkout** *n* caja; **checkpoint** *n* (punto de) control *m*; **checkroom** (US) *n* consigna; **checkup** *n* (*Med*) reconocimiento general
cheddar ['tʃedə*] *n* (*also*: **~ cheese**) queso *m* cheddar
cheek [tʃiːk] *n* mejilla; (*impudence*) descaro; **what a ~!** ¡qué cara!; **cheekbone** *n* pómulo; **cheeky** *adj* fresco, descarado
cheer [tʃɪə*] *vt* vitorear, aplaudir; (*gladden*) alegrar, animar ▷ *vi* dar vivas ▷ *n* viva *m*; **cheer up** *vi* animarse ▷ *vt* alegrar, animar; **cheerful** *adj* alegre

cheerio [tʃɪərɪ'əu] (BRIT) *excl* ¡hasta luego!
cheerleader ['tʃɪəli:də*] *n* animador(a) *m/f*
cheese [tʃi:z] *n* queso; **cheeseburger** *n* hamburguesa con queso; **cheesecake** *n* pastel *m* de queso
chef [ʃɛf] *n* jefe/a *m/f* de cocina
chemical ['kɛmɪkəl] *adj* químico ▷*n* producto químico
chemist ['kɛmɪst] *n* (BRIT: *pharmacist*) farmacéutico/a; (*scientist*) químico/a; **chemistry** *n* química; **chemist's (shop)**(BRIT) *n* farmacia
cheque [tʃɛk] (US **check**) *n* cheque *m*; **chequebook** *n* talonario de cheques (SP), chequera (LAM); **cheque card** *n* tarjeta de cheque
cherry ['tʃɛrɪ] *n* cereza; (*also*: **~ tree**) cerezo
chess [tʃɛs] *n* ajedrez *m*
chest [tʃɛst] *n* (*Anat*) pecho; (*box*) cofre *m*, cajón *m*
chestnut ['tʃɛsnʌt] *n* castaña; (*also*: **~ tree**) castaño
chest of drawers *n* cómoda
chew [tʃu:] *vt* mascar, masticar; **chewing gum** *n* chicle *m*
chic [ʃi:k] *adj* elegante
chick [tʃɪk] *n* pollito, polluelo; (*inf*: *girl*) chica
chicken ['tʃɪkɪn] *n* gallina, pollo; (*food*) pollo; (*inf*: *coward*) gallina *mf*; **chicken out**(*inf*) *vi* rajarse; **chickenpox** *n* varicela
chickpea ['tʃɪkpi:] *n* garbanzo
chief [tʃi:f] *n* jefe/a *m/f* ▷*adj* principal; **chief executive (officer)** *n* director(a) *m/f* general; **chiefly** *adv* principalmente
child [tʃaɪld] (*pl* **~ren**) *n* niño/a; (*offspring*) hijo/a; **child abuse** *n* (*with violence*) malos tratos *mpl* a niños; (*sexual*) abuso *m* sexual de niños; **child benefit** *n* (BRIT) *subsidio por cada hijo pequeño*; **childbirth** *n* parto; **child-care** *n* cuidado de los niños; **childhood** *n* niñez *f*, infancia; **childish** *adj* pueril, aniñado; **child minder** (BRIT) *n* madre *f* de día; **children** ['tʃɪldrən] *npl of* **child**
Chile ['tʃɪlɪ] *n* Chile *m*; **Chilean** *adj*, *n* chileno/a *m/f*
chill [tʃɪl] *n* frío; (*Med*) resfriado ▷*vt* enfriar; (*Culin*) congelar; **chill out** *vi* (*esp US*: *inf*) tranquilizarse
chil(l)i ['tʃɪlɪ] (BRIT) *n* chile *m*, ají *m* (SC)
chilly ['tʃɪlɪ] *adj* frío
chimney ['tʃɪmnɪ] *n* chimenea
chimpanzee [tʃɪmpæn'zi:] *n* chimpancé *m*
chin [tʃɪn] *n* mentón *m*, barbilla
China ['tʃaɪnə] *n* China
china ['tʃaɪnə] *n* porcelana; (*crockery*) loza
Chinese [tʃaɪ'ni:z] *adj* chino ▷*n inv* chino/a *m/f*; (*Ling*) chino
chip [tʃɪp] *n* (*gen pl*: *Culin*: BRIT) patata (SP) *or* papa (LAM) frita; (: US: *also*: **potato ~**) patata *or* papa frita; (*of wood*) astilla; (*of glass, stone*) lasca; (*at poker*) ficha; (*Comput*) chip *m* ▷*vt* (*cup, plate*) desconchar; **chip shop** pescadería (*donde se vende principalmente pescado rebozado y patatas fritas*)
chiropodist [kɪ'rɔpədɪst] (BRIT) *n* pedicuro/a, callista *m/f*
chisel ['tʃɪzl] *n* (*for wood*) escoplo; (*for stone*) cincel *m*
chives [tʃaɪvz] *npl* cebollinos *mpl*
chlorine ['klɔ:ri:n] *n* cloro
choc-ice ['tʃɔkaɪs] *n* (BRIT) helado *m* cubierto de chocolate
chocolate ['tʃɔklɪt] *n* chocolate *m*; (*sweet*) bombón *m*
choice [tʃɔɪs] *n* elección *f*, selección *f*; (*option*) opción *f*; (*preference*) preferencia ▷*adj* escogido
choir ['kwaɪə*] *n* coro
choke [tʃəuk] *vi* ahogarse; (*on food*) atragantarse ▷*vt* estrangular, ahogar; (*block*): **to be ~d with** estar atascado de ▷*n* (*Aut*) estárter *m*
cholesterol [kə'lɛstərul] *n* colesterol *m*
choose [tʃu:z] (*pt* **chose**, *pp* **chosen**)

vt escoger, elegir; (*team*) seleccionar; **to ~ to do sth** optar por hacer algo

chop [tʃɔp] *vt* (*wood*) cortar, tajar; (*Culin*: *also*: **~ up**) picar ▷ *n* (*Culin*) chuleta; **chop down** *vt* (*tree*) talar; **chop off** *vt* cortar (de un tajo); **chopsticks** ['tʃɔpstɪks] *npl* palillos *mpl*

chord [kɔ:d] *n* (*Mus*) acorde *m*

chore [tʃɔ:*] *n* faena, tarea; (*routine task*) trabajo rutinario

chorus ['kɔ:rəs] *n* coro; (*repeated part of song*) estribillo

chose [tʃəuz] *pt of* **choose**

chosen ['tʃəuzn] *pp of* **choose**

Christ [kraɪst] *n* Cristo

christen ['krɪsn] *vt* bautizar; **christening** *n* bautizo

Christian ['krɪstɪən] *adj*, *n* cristiano/a *m/f*; **Christianity** [-'ænɪtɪ] *n* cristianismo; **Christian name** *n* nombre *m* de pila

Christmas ['krɪsməs] *n* Navidad *f*; **Merry ~!** ¡Felices Pascuas!; **Christmas card** *n* crismas *m inv*, tarjeta de Navidad; **Christmas carol** *n* villancico *m*; **Christmas Day** *n* día *m* de Navidad; **Christmas Eve** *n* Nochebuena; **Christmas pudding** *n* (*esp* BRIT) pudin *m* de Navidad; **Christmas tree** *n* árbol *m* de Navidad

chrome [krəum] *n* cromo

chronic ['krɔnɪk] *adj* crónico

chrysanthemum [krɪ'sænθəməm] *n* crisantemo

chubby ['tʃʌbɪ] *adj* regordete

chuck [tʃʌk] (*inf*) *vt* lanzar, arrojar; (BRIT: *also*: **~ up**) abandonar; **chuck out** *vt* (*person*) echar (fuera); (*rubbish etc*) tirar

chuckle ['tʃʌkl] *vi* reírse entre dientes

chum [tʃʌm] *n* compañero/a

chunk [tʃʌŋk] *n* pedazo, trozo

church [tʃə:tʃ] *n* iglesia; **churchyard** *n* cementerio

churn [tʃə:n] *n* (*for butter*) mantequera; (*for milk*) lechera

chute [ʃu:t] *n* (*also*: **rubbish ~**) vertedero; (*for coal etc*) rampa de caída

chutney ['tʃʌtnɪ] *n* *condimento a base de frutas de la India*

CIA (US) *n abbr* (= *Central Intelligence Agency*) CIA *f*

CID (BRIT) *n abbr* (= *Criminal Investigation Department*) ≈ B.I.C. *f* (SP)

cider ['saɪdə*] *n* sidra

cigar [sɪ'gɑ:*] *n* puro

cigarette [sɪgə'rɛt] *n* cigarrillo; **cigarette lighter** *n* mechero

cinema ['sɪnəmə] *n* cine *m*

cinnamon ['sɪnəmən] *n* canela

circle ['sə:kl] *n* círculo; (*in theatre*) anfiteatro ▷ *vi* dar vueltas ▷ *vt* (*surround*) rodear, cercar; (*move round*) dar la vuelta a

circuit ['sə:kɪt] *n* circuito; (*tour*) gira; (*track*) pista; (*lap*) vuelta

circular ['sə:kjulə*] *adj* circular ▷ *n* circular *f*

circulate ['sə:kjuleɪt] *vi* circular; (*person: at party etc*) hablar con los invitados ▷ *vt* poner en circulación; **circulation** [-'leɪʃən] *n* circulación *f*; (*of newspaper*) tirada

circumstances ['sə:kəmstənsɪz] *npl* circunstancias *fpl*; (*financial condition*) situación *f* económica

circus ['sə:kəs] *n* circo

cite [saɪt] *vt* citar

citizen ['sɪtɪzn] *n* (*Pol*) ciudadano/a; (*of city*) vecino/a, habitante *mf*; **citizenship** *n* ciudadanía; (BRIT: *Scol*) civismo

citrus fruits ['sɪtrəs-] *npl* agrios *mpl*

city ['sɪtɪ] *n* ciudad *f*; **the C~** *centro financiero de Londres*; **city centre** (BRIT) *n* centro de la ciudad; **city technology college** *n* centro de formación profesional (*centro de enseñanza secundaria que da especial importancia a la ciencia y tecnología.*)

civic ['sɪvɪk] *adj* cívico; (*authorities*) municipal

civil ['sɪvɪl] *adj* civil; (*polite*) atento, cortés; **civilian** [sɪ'vɪlɪən] *adj* civil (*no militar*) ▷ *n* civil *mf*, paisano/a

civilization [sɪvɪlaɪ'zeɪʃən] *n* civilización *f*
civilized ['sɪvɪlaɪzd] *adj* civilizado
civil: civil law *n* derecho civil; **civil rights** *npl* derechos *mpl* civiles; **civil servant** *n* funcionario/a del Estado; **Civil Service** *n* administración *f* pública; **civil war** *n* guerra civil
CJD *n abbr* (= *Creutzfeldt-Jakob disease*) *enfermedad de Creutzfeldt-Jakob*
claim [kleɪm] *vt* exigir, reclamar; (*rights etc*) reivindicar; (*assert*) pretender ▷ *vi* (*for insurance*) reclamar ▷ *n* reclamación *f*; pretensión *f*; **claim form** *n* solicitud *f*
clam [klæm] *n* almeja
clamp [klæmp] *n* abrazadera, grapa ▷ *vt* (*two things together*) cerrar fuertemente; (*one thing on another*) afianzar (con abrazadera); (*Aut: wheel*) poner el cepo a
clan [klæn] *n* clan *m*
clap [klæp] *vi* aplaudir
claret ['klærət] *n* burdeos *m inv*
clarify ['klærɪfaɪ] *vt* aclarar
clarinet [klærɪ'nɛt] *n* clarinete *m*
clarity ['klærɪtɪ] *n* claridad *f*
clash [klæʃ] *n* enfrentamiento; choque *m*; desacuerdo; estruendo ▷ *vi* (*fight*) enfrentarse; (*beliefs*) chocar; (*disagree*) estar en desacuerdo; (*colours*) desentonar; (*two events*) coincidir
clasp [klɑːsp] *n* (*hold*) apretón *m*; (*of necklace, bag*) cierre *m* ▷ *vt* apretar; abrazar
class [klɑːs] *n* clase *f* ▷ *vt* clasificar
classic ['klæsɪk] *adj, n* clásico; **classical** *adj* clásico
classification [klæsɪfɪ'keɪʃən] *n* clasificación *f*
classify ['klæsɪfaɪ] *vt* clasificar
classmate ['klɑːsmeɪt] *n* compañero/a de clase
classroom ['klɑːsrum] *n* aula; **classroom assistant** *n* profesor(a) *m/f* de apoyo
classy ['klɑːsɪ] *adj* (*inf*) elegante, con estilo
clatter ['klætə*] *n* estrépito ▷ *vi* hacer ruido *or* estrépito
clause [klɔːz] *n* cláusula; (*Ling*) oración *f*
claustrophobic [klɔːstrə'fəubɪk] *adj* claustrofóbico; **I feel ~** me entra claustrofobia
claw [klɔː] *n* (*of cat*) uña; (*of bird of prey*) garra; (*of lobster*) pinza
clay [kleɪ] *n* arcilla
clean [kliːn] *adj* limpio; (*record, reputation*) bueno, intachable; (*joke*) decente ▷ *vt* limpiar; (*hands etc*) lavar; **clean up** *vt* limpiar, asear; **cleaner** *n* (*person*) asistenta; (*substance*) producto para la limpieza; **cleaner's** *n* tintorería; **cleaning** *n* limpieza
cleanser ['klɛnzə*] *n* (*for face*) crema limpiadora
clear [klɪə*] *adj* claro; (*road, way*) libre; (*conscience*) limpio, tranquilo; (*skin*) terso; (*sky*) despejado ▷ *vt* (*space*) despejar, limpiar; (*Law: suspect*) absolver; (*obstacle*) salvar, saltar por encima de; (*cheque*) aceptar ▷ *vi* (*fog etc*) despejarse ▷ *adv*: **~ of** a distancia de; **to ~ the table** recoger *or* levantar la mesa; **clear away** *vt* (*things, clothes etc*) quitar (de en medio); (*dishes*) retirar; **clear up** *vt* limpiar; (*mystery*) aclarar, resolver; **clearance** *n* (*removal*) despeje *m*; (*permission*) acreditación *f*; **clear-cut** *adj* bien definido, nítido; **clearing** *n* (*in wood*) claro; **clearly** *adv* claramente; (*evidently*) sin duda; **clearway** (BRIT) *n carretera donde no se puede parar*
clench [klɛntʃ] *vt* apretar, cerrar
clergy ['kləːdʒɪ] *n* clero
clerk [klɑːk, (US) kləːrk] *n* (BRIT) oficinista *mf*; (US) dependiente/a *m/f*
clever ['klɛvə*] *adj* (*intelligent*) inteligente, listo; (*skilful*) hábil; (*device, arrangement*) ingenioso
cliché ['kliːʃeɪ] *n* cliché *m*, frase *f* hecha
click [klɪk] *vt* (*tongue*) chasquear; (*heels*) taconear ▷ *vi* (*Comput*) hacer

clic; **to ~ on an icon** hacer clic en un icono

client ['klaɪənt] *n* cliente *m/f*

cliff [klɪf] *n* acantilado

climate ['klaɪmɪt] *n* clima *m*; **climate change** *n* cambio climático

climax ['klaɪmæks] *n* (*of battle, career*) apogeo; (*of film, book*) punto culminante; (*sexual*) orgasmo

climb [klaɪm] *vi* subir; (*plant*) trepar; (*move with effort*): **to ~ over a wall/into a car** trepar a una tapia/subir a un coche ▷ *vt* (*stairs*) subir; (*tree*) trepar a; (*mountain*) escalar ▷ *n* subida; **climb down** *vi* (*fig*) volverse atrás; **climber** *n* alpinista *mf* (SP, MEX), andinista *mf* (LAM); **climbing** *n* alpinismo (SP, MEX), andinismo (LAM)

clinch [klɪntʃ] *vt* (*deal*) cerrar; (*argument*) remachar

cling [klɪŋ] (*pt, pp* **clung**) *vi*: **to ~ to** agarrarse a; (*clothes*) pegarse a

Clingfilm® ['klɪŋfɪlm] *n* plástico adherente

clinic ['klɪnɪk] *n* clínica

clip [klɪp] *n* (*for hair*) horquilla; (*also*: **paper ~**) sujetapapeles *m inv*, clip *m*; (*TV, Cinema*) fragmento ▷ *vt* (*cut*) cortar; (*also*: **~ together**) unir; **clipping** *n* (*newspaper*) recorte *m*

cloak [kləuk] *n* capa, manto ▷ *vt* (*fig*) encubrir, disimular; **cloakroom** *n* guardarropa; (BRIT: *WC*) lavabo (SP), aseos *mpl* (SP), baño (LAM)

clock [klɔk] *n* reloj *m*; **clock in** *or* **on** *vi* (*with card*) fichar, picar; (*start work*) entrar a trabajar; **clock off** *or* **out** *vi* (*with card*) fichar *or* picar la salida; (*leave work*) salir del trabajar; **clockwise** *adv* en el sentido de las agujas del reloj; **clockwork** *n* aparato de relojería ▷ *adj* (*toy*) de cuerda

clog [klɔg] *n* zueco, chanclo ▷ *vt* atascar ▷ *vi* (*also*: **~ up**) atascarse

clone [kləun] *n* clon *m* ▷ *vt* clonar

close¹ [kləus] *adj* (*near*): **~ (to)** cerca (de); (*friend*) íntimo; (*connection*) estrecho; (*examination*) detallado, minucioso; (*weather*) bochornoso ▷ *adv* cerca; **~ by, ~ at hand** muy cerca; **to have a ~ shave** (*fig*) escaparse por un pelo

close² [kləuz] *vt* (*shut*) cerrar; (*end*) concluir, terminar ▷ *vi* (*shop etc*) cerrarse; (*end*) concluirse, terminarse ▷ *n* (*end*) fin *m*, final *m*, conclusión *f*; **close down** *vi* cerrarse definitivamente; **closed** *adj* (*shop etc*) cerrado

closely ['kləuslɪ] *adv* (*study*) con detalle; (*watch*) de cerca; (*resemble*) estrechamente

closet ['klɔzɪt] *n* armario

close-up ['kləusʌp] *n* primer plano

closing time *n* hora de cierre

closure ['kləuʒə*] *n* cierre *m*

clot [klɔt] *n* (*gen*) coágulo; (*inf: idiot*) imbécil *m/f* ▷ *vi* (*blood*) coagularse

cloth [klɔθ] *n* (*material*) tela, paño; (*rag*) trapo

clothes [kləuðz] *npl* ropa; **clothes line** *n* cuerda (para tender la ropa); **clothes peg** (US **clothes pin**) *n* pinza

clothing ['kləuðɪŋ] *n* = **clothes**

cloud [klaud] *n* nube *f*; **cloud over** *vi* (*also fig*) nublarse; **cloudy** *adj* nublado, nubloso; (*liquid*) turbio

clove [kləuv] *n* clavo; **~ of garlic** diente *m* de ajo

clown [klaun] *n* payaso ▷ *vi* (*also*: **~ about, ~ around**) hacer el payaso

club [klʌb] *n* (*society*) club *m*; (*weapon*) porra, cachiporra; (*also*: **golf ~**) palo ▷ *vt* aporrear ▷ *vi*: **to ~ together** (*for gift*) comprar entre todos; **clubs** *npl* (*Cards*) tréboles *mpl*; **club class** *n* (*Aviat*) clase *f* preferente

clue [klu:] *n* pista; (*in crosswords*) indicación *f*; **I haven't a ~** no tengo ni idea

clump [klʌmp] *n* (*of trees*) grupo

clumsy ['klʌmzɪ] *adj* (*person*) torpe, desmañado; (*tool*) difícil de manejar; (*movement*) desgarbado

clung [klʌŋ] *pt, pp of* **cling**

cluster ['klʌstə*] *n* grupo ▷ *vi*

agruparse, apiñarse
clutch [klʌtʃ] *n* (*Aut*) embrague *m*; (*grasp*): **~es** garras *fpl* ▷ *vt* asir; agarrar
cm *abbr* (= *centimetre*) cm
Co. *abbr* = **county; company**
c/o *abbr* (= *care of*) c/a, a/c
coach [kəutʃ] *n* autocar *m* (SP), coche *m* de línea; (*horse-drawn*) coche *m*; (*of train*) vagón *m*, coche *m*; (*Sport*) entrenador(a) *m/f*, instructor(a) *m/f*; (*tutor*) profesor(a) *m/f* particular ▷ *vt* (*Sport*) entrenar; (*student*) preparar, enseñar; **coach station** *n* (BRIT) estación *f* de autobuses *etc*; **coach trip** *n* excursión *f* en autocar
coal [kəul] *n* carbón *m*
coalition [kəuə'lɪʃən] *n* coalición *f*
coarse [kɔːs] *adj* basto, burdo; (*vulgar*) grosero, ordinario
coast [kəust] *n* costa, litoral *m* ▷ *vi* (*Aut*) ir en punto muerto; **coastal** *adj* costero, costanero; **coastguard** *n* guardacostas *m inv*; **coastline** *n* litoral *m*
coat [kəut] *n* abrigo; (*of animal*) pelaje *m*, lana; (*of paint*) mano *f*, capa ▷ *vt* cubrir, revestir; **coat hanger** *n* percha (SP), gancho (LAM); **coating** *n* capa, baño
coax [kəuks] *vt* engatusar
cob [kɔb] *n see* **corn**
cobbled ['kɔbld] *adj*: **~ street** calle *f* empedrada, calle *f* adoquinada
cobweb ['kɔbwɛb] *n* telaraña
cocaine [kə'keɪn] *n* cocaína
cock [kɔk] *n* (*rooster*) gallo; (*male bird*) macho ▷ *vt* (*gun*) amartillar; **cockerel** *n* gallito
cockney ['kɔknɪ] *n habitante de ciertos barrios de Londres*
cockpit ['kɔkpɪt] *n* cabina
cockroach ['kɔkrəutʃ] *n* cucaracha
cocktail ['kɔkteɪl] *n* coctel *m*, cóctel *m*
cocoa ['kəukəu] *n* cacao; (*drink*) chocolate *m*
coconut ['kəukənʌt] *n* coco
cod [kɔd] *n* bacalao
C.O.D. *abbr* (= *cash on delivery*) C.A.E.
code [kəud] *n* código; (*cipher*) clave *f*; (*dialling code*) prefijo; (*post code*) código postal
coeducational [kəuɛdju'keɪʃənl] *adj* mixto
coffee ['kɔfɪ] *n* café *m*; **coffee bar** (BRIT) *n* cafetería; **coffee bean** *n* grano de café; **coffee break** *n* descanso (para tomar café); **coffee maker** *n* máquina de hacer café, cafetera; **coffeepot** *n* cafetera; **coffee shop** *n* café *m*; **coffee table** *n* mesita (para servir el café)
coffin ['kɔfɪn] *n* ataúd *m*
cog [kɔg] *n* (*wheel*) rueda dentada; (*tooth*) diente *m*
cognac ['kɔnjæk] *n* coñac *m*
coherent [kəu'hɪərənt] *adj* coherente
coil [kɔɪl] *n* rollo; (*Elec*) bobina, carrete *m*; (*contraceptive*) espiral *f* ▷ *vt* enrollar
coin [kɔɪn] *n* moneda ▷ *vt* (*word*) inventar, idear
coincide [kəuɪn'saɪd] *vi* coincidir; (*agree*) estar de acuerdo; **coincidence** [kəu'ɪnsɪdəns] *n* casualidad *f*
Coke® [kəuk] *n* Coca-Cola®
coke [kəuk] *n* (*coal*) coque *m*
colander ['kɔləndə*] *n* colador *m*, escurridor *m*
cold [kəuld] *adj* frío ▷ *n* frío; (*Med*) resfriado; **it's ~** hace frío; **to be ~** (*person*) tener frío; **to catch (a) ~** resfriarse; **in ~ blood** a sangre fría; **cold sore** *n* herpes *mpl or fpl*
coleslaw ['kəulslɔː] *n especie de ensalada de col*
colic ['kɔlɪk] *n* cólico
collaborate [kə'læbəreɪt] *vi* colaborar
collapse [kə'læps] *vi* hundirse, derrumbarse; (*Med*) sufrir un colapso ▷ *n* hundimiento, derrumbamiento; (*Med*) colapso
collar ['kɔlə*] *n* (*of coat, shirt*) cuello; (*of dog etc*) collar; **collarbone** *n* clavícula

colleague ['kɔliːg] *n* colega *mf*; (*at work*) compañero/a

collect [kə'lɛkt] *vt* (*litter, mail etc*) recoger; (*as a hobby*) coleccionar; (BRIT: *call and pick up*) recoger; (*debts, subscriptions etc*) recaudar ▷ *vi* reunirse; (*dust*) acumularse; **to call ~** (US *Tel*) llamar a cobro revertido; **collection** [kə'lɛkʃən] *n* colección *f*; (*of mail, for charity*) recogida; **collective** [kə'lɛktɪv] *adj* colectivo; **collector** *n* coleccionista *mf*

college ['kɔlɪdʒ] *n* colegio mayor; (*of agriculture, technology*) escuela universitaria

collide [kə'laɪd] *vi* chocar

collision [kə'lɪʒən] *n* choque *m*

cologne [kə'ləun] *n* (*also*: **eau de ~**) (agua de) colonia

Colombia [kə'lɔmbɪə] *n* Colombia; **Colombian** *adj, n* colombiano/a

colon ['kəulən] *n* (*sign*) dos puntos; (*Med*) colon *m*

colonel ['kəːnl] *n* coronel *m*

colonial [kə'ləunɪəl] *adj* colonial

colony ['kɔlənɪ] *n* colonia

colour *etc* ['kʌlə*] (US **color** *etc*) *n* color *m* ▷ *vt* color(e)ar; (*dye*) teñir; (*fig: account*) adornar; (*: judgement*) distorsionar ▷ *vi* (*blush*) sonrojarse; **colour in** *vt* colorear; **colour-blind** *adj* daltónico; **coloured** *adj* de color; (*photo*) en color; **colour film** *n* película en color; **colourful** *adj* lleno de color; (*story*) fantástico; (*person*) excéntrico; **colouring** *n* (*complexion*) tez *f*; (*in food*) colorante *m*; **colour television** *n* televisión *f* en color

column ['kɔləm] *n* columna

coma ['kəumə] *n* coma *m*

comb [kəum] *n* peine *m*; (*ornamental*) peineta ▷ *vt* (*hair*) peinar; (*area*) registrar a fondo

combat ['kɔmbæt] *n* combate *m* ▷ *vt* combatir

combination [kɔmbɪ'neɪʃən] *n* combinación *f*

combine [*vb* kəm'baɪn, *n* 'kɔmbaɪn] *vt* combinar; (*qualities*) reunir ▷ *vi* combinarse ▷ *n* (*Econ*) cartel *m*

KEYWORD

come [kʌm] (*pt* **came**, *pp* **come**) *vi*
1 (*movement towards*) venir; **to come running** venir corriendo
2 (*arrive*) llegar; **he's come here to work** ha venido aquí para trabajar; **to come home** volver a casa
3 (*reach*): **to come to** llegar a; **the bill came to £40** la cuenta ascendía a cuarenta libras
4 (*occur*): **an idea came to me** se me ocurrió una idea
5 (*be, become*): **to come loose/undone** *etc* aflojarse/desabrocharse/desatarse *etc*; **I've come to like him** por fin ha llegado a gustarme

come across *vt fus* (*person*) topar con; (*thing*) dar con
come along *vi* (BRIT: *progress*) ir
come back *vi* (*return*) volver
come down *vi* (*price*) bajar; (*tree, building*) ser derribado
come from *vt fus* (*place, source*) ser de
come in *vi* (*visitor*) entrar; (*train, report*) llegar; (*fashion*) ponerse de moda; (*on deal etc*) entrar
come off *vi* (*button*) soltarse, desprenderse; (*attempt*) salir bien
come on *vi* (*pupil*) progresar; (*work, project*) desarrollarse; (*lights*) encenderse; (*electricity*) volver; **come on!** ¡vamos!
come out *vi* (*fact*) salir a la luz; (*book, sun*) salir; (*stain*) quitarse
come round *vi* (*after faint, operation*) volver en sí
come to *vi* (*wake*) volver en sí
come up *vi* (*sun*) salir; (*problem*) surgir; (*event*) aproximarse; (*in conversation*) mencionarse
come up with *vt fus* (*idea*) sugerir; (*money*) conseguir

comeback ['kʌmbæk] *n*: **to make a ~**

(*Theatre*) volver a las tablas
comedian [kə'mi:dɪən] *n* humorista *mf*
comedy ['kɔmɪdɪ] *n* comedia; (*humour*) comicidad *f*
comet ['kɔmɪt] *n* cometa *m*
comfort ['kʌmfət] *n* bienestar *m*; (*relief*) alivio ▷ *vt* consolar; **comfortable** *adj* cómodo; (*financially*) acomodado; (*easy*) fácil; **comfort station** (US) *n* servicios *mpl*
comic ['kɔmɪk] *adj* (*also*: **~al**) cómico ▷ *n* (*comedian*) cómico; (BRIT: *for children*) tebeo; (BRIT: *for adults*) comic *m*; **comic book** (US) *n* libro *m* de cómics; **comic strip** *n* tira cómica
comma ['kɔmə] *n* coma
command [kə'mɑ:nd] *n* orden *f*, mandato; (*Mil*: *authority*) mando; (*mastery*) dominio ▷ *vt* (*troops*) mandar; (*give orders to*): **to ~ sb to do** mandar *or* ordenar a algn hacer; **commander** *n* (*Mil*) comandante *mf*, jefe/a *m/f*
commemorate [kə'mɛməreɪt] *vt* conmemorar
commence [kə'mɛns] *vt*, *vi* comenzar, empezar; **commencement** (US) *n* (*Univ*) (ceremonia de) graduación *f*
commend [kə'mɛnd] *vt* elogiar, alabar; (*recommend*) recomendar
comment ['kɔmɛnt] *n* comentario ▷ *vi*: **to ~ on** hacer comentarios sobre; **"no ~"** (*written*) "sin comentarios"; (*spoken*) "no tengo nada que decir"; **commentary** ['kɔməntərɪ] *n* comentario; **commentator** ['kɔmənteɪtə*] *n* comentarista *mf*
commerce ['kɔmə:s] *n* comercio
commercial [kə'mə:ʃəl] *adj* comercial ▷ *n* (*TV*, *Radio*) anuncio; **commercial break** *n* intermedio para publicidad
commission [kə'mɪʃən] *n* (*committee*, *fee*) comisión *f* ▷ *vt* (*work of art*) encargar; **out of ~** fuera de servicio; **commissioner** *n* (*Police*) comisario de policía
commit [kə'mɪt] *vt* (*act*) cometer; (*resources*) dedicar; (*to sb's care*) entregar; **to ~ o.s. (to do)** comprometerse (a hacer); **to ~ suicide** suicidarse; **commitment** *n* compromiso; (*to ideology etc*) entrega
committee [kə'mɪtɪ] *n* comité *m*
commodity [kə'mɔdɪtɪ] *n* mercancía
common ['kɔmən] *adj* común; (*pej*) ordinario ▷ *n* campo común; **commonly** *adv* comúnmente; **commonplace** *adj* de lo más común; **Commons** (BRIT) *npl* (*Pol*): **the Commons** (la Cámara de) los Comunes; **common sense** *n* sentido común; **Commonwealth** *n*: **the Commonwealth** la Commonwealth
communal ['kɔmju:nl] *adj* (*property*) comunal; (*kitchen*) común
commune [*n* 'kɔmju:n, *vb* kə'mju:n] *n* (*group*) comuna ▷ *vi*: **to ~ with** comulgar *or* conversar con
communicate [kə'mju:nɪkeɪt] *vt* comunicar ▷ *vi*: **to ~ (with)** comunicarse (con); (*in writing*) estar en contacto (con)
communication [kəmju:nɪ'keɪʃən] *n* comunicación *f*
communion [kə'mju:nɪən] *n* (*also*: **Holy ~**) comunión *f*
communism ['kɔmjunɪzəm] *n* comunismo; **communist** *adj*, *n* comunista *mf*
community [kə'mju:nɪtɪ] *n* comunidad *f*; (*large group*) colectividad *f*; **community centre** (US **community center**) *n* centro social; **community service** *n* trabajo *m* comunitario (*prestado en lugar de cumplir una pena de prisión*)
commute [kə'mju:t] *vi* *viajar a diario de la casa al trabajo* ▷ *vt* conmutar; **commuter** *n* *persona que viaja a diario de la casa al trabajo*
compact [*adj* kəm'pækt, *n* 'kɔmpækt] *adj* compacto ▷ *n* (*also*: **powder ~**)

polvera; **compact disc** *n* compact disc *m*; **compact disc player** *n* reproductor *m* de disco compacto, compact disc *m*

companion [kəm'pænıən] *n* compañero/a

company ['kʌmpənı] *n* compañía; (*Comm*) sociedad *f*, compañía; **to keep sb ~** acompañar a algn; **company car** *n* coche *m* de la empresa; **company director** *n* director(a) *m/f* de empresa

comparable ['kɔmpərəbl] *adj* comparable

comparative [kəm'pærətıv] *adj* relativo; (*study*) comparativo; **comparatively** *adv* (*relatively*) relativamente

compare [kəm'pɛə*] *vt*: **to ~ sth/sb with** *or* **to** comparar algo/a algn con ▷ *vi*: **to ~ (with)** compararse (con); **comparison** [-'pærısn] *n* comparación *f*

compartment [kəm'pɑ:tmənt] *n* (*also*: *Rail*) compartim(i)ento

compass ['kʌmpəs] *n* brújula; **compasses** *npl* (*Math*) compás *m*

compassion [kəm'pæʃən] *n* compasión *f*

compatible [kəm'pætıbl] *adj* compatible

compel [kəm'pɛl] *vt* obligar; **compelling** *adj* (*fig*: *argument*) convincente

compensate ['kɔmpənseıt] *vt* compensar ▷ *vi*: **to ~ for** compensar; **compensation** [-'seıʃən] *n* (*for loss*) indemnización *f*

compete [kəm'pi:t] *vi* (*take part*) tomar parte, concurrir; (*vie with*): **to ~ with** competir con, hacer competencia a

competent ['kɔmpıtənt] *adj* competente, capaz

competition [kɔmpı'tıʃən] *n* (*contest*) concurso; (*rivalry*) competencia

competitive [kəm'pɛtıtıv] *adj* (*Econ*, *Sport*) competitivo

competitor [kəm'pɛtıtə*] *n* (*rival*) competidor(a) *m/f*; (*participant*) concursante *mf*

complacent [kəm'pleısənt] *adj* autocomplaciente

complain [kəm'pleın] *vi* quejarse; (*Comm*) reclamar; **complaint** *n* queja; reclamación *f*; (*Med*) enfermedad *f*

complement [*n* 'kɔmplımənt, *vb* 'kɔmplımɛnt] *n* complemento; (*esp of ship's crew*) dotación *f* ▷ *vt* (*enhance*) complementar; **complementary** [kɔmplı'mɛntərı] *adj* complementario

complete [kəm'pli:t] *adj* (*full*) completo; (*finished*) acabado ▷ *vt* (*fulfil*) completar; (*finish*) acabar; (*a form*) llenar; **completely** *adv* completamente; **completion** [-'pli:ʃən] *n* terminación *f*; (*of contract*) realización *f*

complex ['kɔmplɛks] *adj*, *n* complejo

complexion [kəm'plɛkʃən] *n* (*of face*) tez *f*, cutis *m*

compliance [kəm'plaıəns] *n* (*submission*) sumisión *f*; (*agreement*) conformidad *f*; **in ~ with** de acuerdo con

complicate ['kɔmplıkeıt] *vt* complicar; **complicated** *adj* complicado; **complication** [-'keıʃən] *n* complicación *f*

compliment ['kɔmplımənt] *n* (*formal*) cumplido ▷ *vt* felicitar; **complimentary** [-'mɛntərı] *adj* lisonjero; (*free*) de favor

comply [kəm'plaı] *vi*: **to ~ with** cumplir con

component [kəm'pəunənt] *adj* componente ▷ *n* (*Tech*) pieza

compose [kəm'pəuz] *vt*: **to be ~d of** componerse de; (*music etc*) componer; **to ~ o.s.** tranquilizarse; **composer** *n* (*Mus*) compositor(a) *m/f*; **composition** [kɔmpə'zıʃən] *n* composición *f*

composure [kəm'pəuʒə*] *n* serenidad *f*, calma

compound ['kɔmpaund] *n* (*Chem*)

compuesto; (*Ling*) palabra compuesta; (*enclosure*) recinto ▷ *adj* compuesto; (*fracture*) complicado

comprehension [-'hɛnʃən] *n* comprensión *f*

comprehensive [kɔmprɪ'hɛnsɪv] *adj* exhaustivo; (*Insurance*) contra todo riesgo; **comprehensive (school)** *n* *centro estatal de enseñanza secundaria* ≈ Instituto Nacional de Bachillerato (SP)

compress [*vb* kəm'prɛs, *n* 'kɔmprɛs] *vt* comprimir; (*information*) condensar ▷ *n* (*Med*) compresa

comprise [kəm'praɪz] *vt* (*also*: **be ~d of**) comprender, constar de; (*constitute*) constituir

compromise ['kɔmprəmaɪz] *n* (*agreement*) arreglo ▷ *vt* comprometer ▷ *vi* transigir

compulsive [kəm'pʌlsɪv] *adj* compulsivo; (*viewing, reading*) obligado

compulsory [kəm'pʌlsərɪ] *adj* obligatorio

computer [kəm'pju:tə*] *n* ordenador *m*, computador *m*, computadora; **computer game** *n* juego para ordenador; **computer-generated** *adj* realizado por ordenador, creado por ordenador; **computerize** *vt* (*data*) computerizar; (*system*) informatizar; **we're computerized now** ya nos hemos informatizado; **computer programmer** *n* programador(a) *m/f*; **computer programming** *n* programación *f*; **computer science** *n* informática; **computer studies** *npl* informática *fsg*, computación *fsg* (LAM); **computing** [kəm'pju:tɪŋ] *n* (*activity, science*) informática

con [kɔn] *vt* (*deceive*) engañar; (*cheat*) estafar ▷ *n* estafa

conceal [kən'si:l] *vt* ocultar

concede [kən'si:d] *vt* (*point, argument*) reconocer; (*territory*) ceder; **to ~ (defeat)** darse por vencido; **to ~ that** admitir que

conceited [kən'si:tɪd] *adj* presumido

conceive [kən'si:v] *vt, vi* concebir

concentrate ['kɔnsəntreɪt] *vi* concentrarse ▷ *vt* concentrar

concentration [kɔnsən'treɪʃən] *n* concentración *f*

concept ['kɔnsɛpt] *n* concepto

concern [kən'sə:n] *n* (*matter*) asunto; (*Comm*) empresa; (*anxiety*) preocupación *f* ▷ *vt* (*worry*) preocupar; (*involve*) afectar; (*relate to*) tener que ver con; **to be ~ed (about)** interesarse (por), preocuparse (por); **concerning** *prep* sobre, acerca de

concert ['kɔnsət] *n* concierto; **concert hall** *n* sala de conciertos

concerto [kən'tʃə:təu] *n* concierto

concession [kən'sɛʃən] *n* concesión *f*; **tax ~** privilegio fiscal

concise [kən'saɪs] *adj* conciso

conclude [kən'klu:d] *vt* concluir; (*treaty etc*) firmar; (*agreement*) llegar a; (*decide*) llegar a la conclusión de; **conclusion** [-'klu:ʒən] *n* conclusión *f*; firma

concrete ['kɔnkri:t] *n* hormigón *m* ▷ *adj* de hormigón; (*fig*) concreto

concussion [kən'kʌʃən] *n* conmoción *f* cerebral

condemn [kən'dɛm] *vt* condenar; (*building*) declarar en ruina

condensation [kɔndɛn'seɪʃən] *n* condensación *f*

condense [kən'dɛns] *vi* condensarse ▷ *vt* condensar, abreviar

condition [kən'dɪʃən] *n* condición *f*, estado; (*requirement*) condición *f* ▷ *vt* condicionar; **on ~ that** a condición (de) que; **conditional** [kən'dɪʃənl] *adj* condicional; **conditioner** *n* suavizante

condo ['kɔndəu] (US) *n* (*inf*) = **condominium**

condom ['kɔndəm] *n* condón *m*

condominium [kɔndə'mɪnɪəm] (US) *n* (*building*) bloque *m* de pisos *or* apartamentos (*propiedad de quienes lo habitan*), condominio (LAM); (*apartment*) piso *or* apartamento (en propiedad),

condominio (LAM)
condone [kən'dəun] *vt* condonar
conduct [*n* 'kɔndʌkt, *vb* kən'dʌkt] *n* conducta, comportamiento ▷ *vt* (*lead*) conducir; (*manage*) llevar a cabo, dirigir; (*Mus*) dirigir; **to ~ o.s.** comportarse; **conducted tour** (BRIT) *n* visita acompañada; **conductor** *n* (*of orchestra*) director *m*; (US: *on train*) revisor(a) *m/f*; (*on bus*) cobrador *m*; (*Elec*) conductor *m*
cone [kəun] *n* cono; (*pine cone*) piña; (*on road*) pivote *m*; (*for ice-cream*) cucurucho
confectionery [kən'fɛkʃənrɪ] *n* dulces *mpl*
confer [kən'fəː*] *vt*: **to ~ sth on** otorgar algo a ▷ *vi* conferenciar
conference ['kɔnfərns] *n* (*meeting*) reunión *f*; (*convention*) congreso
confess [kən'fɛs] *vt* confesar ▷ *vi* admitir; **confession** [-'fɛʃən] *n* confesión *f*
confide [kən'faɪd] *vi*: **to ~ in** confiar en
confidence ['kɔnfɪdns] *n* (*also*: **self-~**) confianza; (*secret*) confidencia; **in ~** (*speak, write*) en confianza; **confident** *adj* seguro de sí mismo; (*certain*) seguro; **confidential** [kɔnfɪ'dɛnʃəl] *adj* confidencial
confine [kən'faɪn] *vt* (*limit*) limitar; (*shut up*) encerrar; **confined** *adj* (*space*) reducido
confirm [kən'fəːm] *vt* confirmar; **confirmation** [kɔnfə'meɪʃən] *n* confirmación *f*
confiscate ['kɔnfɪskeɪt] *vt* confiscar
conflict [*n* 'kɔnflɪkt, *vb* kən'flɪkt] *n* conflicto ▷ *vi* (*opinions*) chocar
conform [kən'fɔːm] *vi* conformarse; **to ~ to** ajustarse a
confront [kən'frʌnt] *vt* (*problems*) hacer frente a; (*enemy, danger*) enfrentarse con; **confrontation** [kɔnfrən'teɪʃən] *n* enfrentamiento
confuse [kən'fjuːz] *vt* (*perplex*) aturdir, desconcertar; (*mix up*) confundir; (*complicate*) complicar; **confused** *adj* confuso; (*person*) perplejo; **confusing** *adj* confuso; **confusion** [-'fjuːʒən] *n* confusión *f*
congestion [kən'dʒɛstʃən] *n* congestión *f*
congratulate [kən'grætjuleɪt] *vt*: **to ~ sb (on)** felicitar a algn (por); **congratulations** [-'leɪʃənz] *npl* felicitaciones *fpl*; **congratulations!** ¡enhorabuena!
congregation [-'geɪʃən] *n* (*of a church*) feligreses *mpl*
congress ['kɔŋgrɛs] *n* congreso; (US): **C~** Congreso; **congressman** (*irreg*: US) *n* miembro del Congreso; **congresswoman** (*irreg*: US) *n* diputada, miembro *f* del Congreso
conifer ['kɔnɪfə*] *n* conífera
conjugate ['kɔndʒugeɪt] *vt* conjugar
conjugation [kɔndʒə'geɪʃən] *n* conjugación *f*
conjunction [kən'dʒʌŋkʃən] *n* conjunción *f*; **in ~ with** junto con
conjure ['kʌndʒə*] *vi* hacer juegos de manos
connect [kə'nɛkt] *vt* juntar, unir; (*Elec*) conectar; (*Tel*: *subscriber*) poner; (*: caller*) poner al habla; (*fig*) relacionar, asociar ▷ *vi*: **to ~ with** (*train*) enlazar con; **to be ~ed with** (*associated*) estar relacionado con; **connecting flight** *n* vuelo *m* de enlace; **connection** [-ʃən] *n* juntura, unión *f*; (*Elec*) conexión *f*; (*Rail*) enlace *m*; (*Tel*) comunicación *f*; (*fig*) relación *f*
conquer ['kɔŋkə*] *vt* (*territory*) conquistar; (*enemy, feelings*) vencer
conquest ['kɔŋkwɛst] *n* conquista
cons [kɔnz] *npl* *see* **convenience; pro; mod**
conscience ['kɔnʃəns] *n* conciencia
conscientious [kɔnʃɪ'ɛnʃəs] *adj* concienzudo; (*objection*) de conciencia
conscious ['kɔnʃəs] *adj* (*deliberate*) deliberado; (*awake, aware*) consciente; **consciousness** *n* conciencia; (*Med*) conocimiento

consecutive [kən'sɛkjutɪv] *adj* consecutivo; **on 3 ~ occasions** en 3 ocasiones consecutivas
consensus [kən'sɛnsəs] *n* consenso
consent [kən'sɛnt] *n* consentimiento ▷ *vi*: **to ~ (to)** consentir (en)
consequence ['kɔnsɪkwəns] *n* consecuencia; (*significance*) importancia
consequently ['kɔnsɪkwəntlɪ] *adv* por consiguiente
conservation [kɔnsə'veɪʃən] *n* conservación *f*
conservative [kən'səːvətɪv] *adj* conservador(a); (*estimate etc*) cauteloso; **Conservative** (BRIT) *adj, n* (*Pol*) conservador(a) *m/f*
conservatory [kən'səːvətrɪ] *n* invernadero; (*Mus*) conservatorio
consider [kən'sɪdə*] *vt* considerar; (*take into account*) tener en cuenta; (*study*) estudiar, examinar; **to ~ doing sth** pensar en (la posibilidad de) hacer algo; **considerable** *adj* considerable; **considerably** *adv* notablemente; **considerate** *adj* considerado; **consideration** [-'reɪʃən] *n* consideración *f*; (*factor*) factor *m*; **to give sth further consideration** estudiar algo más a fondo; **considering** *prep* teniendo en cuenta
consignment [kən'saɪnmənt] *n* envío
consist [kən'sɪst] *vi*: **to ~ of** consistir en
consistency [kən'sɪstənsɪ] *n* (*of argument etc*) coherencia; consecuencia; (*thickness*) consistencia
consistent [kən'sɪstənt] *adj* (*person*) consecuente; (*argument etc*) coherente
consolation [kɔnsə'leɪʃən] *n* consuelo
console[1] [kən'səul] *vt* consolar
console[2] ['kɔnsəul] *n* consola
consonant ['kɔnsənənt] *n* consonante *f*
conspicuous [kən'spɪkjuəs] *adj* (*visible*) visible
conspiracy [kən'spɪrəsɪ] *n* conjura, complot *m*
constable ['kʌnstəbl] (BRIT) *n* policía *mf*; **chief ~** ≈ jefe *m* de policía
constant ['kɔnstənt] *adj* constante; **constantly** *adv* constantemente
constipated ['kɔnstɪpeɪtəd] *adj* estreñido

> Be careful not to translate **constipated** by the Spanish word *constipado*.

constipation [kɔnstɪ'peɪʃən] *n* estreñimiento
constituency [kən'stɪtjuənsɪ] *n* (*Pol*: *area*) distrito electoral; (: *electors*) electorado
constitute ['kɔnstɪtjuːt] *vt* constituir
constitution [kɔnstɪ'tjuːʃən] *n* constitución *f*
constraint [kən'streɪnt] *n* obligación *f*; (*limit*) restricción *f*
construct [kən'strʌkt] *vt* construir; **construction** [-ʃən] *n* construcción *f*; **constructive** *adj* constructivo
consul ['kɔnsl] *n* cónsul *mf*; **consulate** ['kɔnsjulɪt] *n* consulado
consult [kən'sʌlt] *vt* consultar; **consultant** *n* (BRIT *Med*) especialista *mf*; (*other specialist*) asesor(a) *m/f*; **consultation** [kɔnsəl'teɪʃən] *n* consulta; **consulting room** (BRIT) *n* consultorio
consume [kən'sjuːm] *vt* (*eat*) comerse; (*drink*) beberse; (*fire etc, Comm*) consumir; **consumer** *n* consumidor(a) *m/f*
consumption [kən'sʌmpʃən] *n* consumo
cont. *abbr* (= *continued*) sigue
contact ['kɔntækt] *n* contacto; (*person*) contacto; (: *pej*) enchufe *m* ▷ *vt* ponerse en contacto con; **contact lenses** *npl* lentes *fpl* de contacto
contagious [kən'teɪdʒəs] *adj* contagioso
contain [kən'teɪn] *vt* contener;

to ~ o.s. contenerse; **container** *n* recipiente *m*; (*for shipping etc*) contenedor *m*

contaminate [kən'tæmɪneɪt] *vt* contaminar

cont'd *abbr* (= *continued*) sigue

contemplate ['kɔntəmpleɪt] *vt* contemplar; (*reflect upon*) considerar

contemporary [kən'tɛmpərərɪ] *adj, n* contemporáneo/a *m/f*

contempt [kən'tɛmpt] *n* desprecio; **~ of court** (*Law*) desacato (a los tribunales)

contend [kən'tɛnd] *vt* (*argue*) afirmar ▷ *vi*: **to ~ with/for** luchar contra/por

content [*adj, vb* kən'tɛnt, *n* 'kɔntɛnt] *adj* (*happy*) contento; (*satisfied*) satisfecho ▷ *vt* contentar; satisfacer ▷ *n* contenido; **contents** *npl* contenido; **(table of) ~s** índice *m* de materias; **contented** *adj* contento; satisfecho

contest [*n* 'kɔntɛst, *vb* kən'tɛst] *n* lucha; (*competition*) concurso ▷ *vt* (*dispute*) impugnar; (*Pol*) presentarse como candidato/a en

Be careful not to translate **contest** by the Spanish word *contestar*.

contestant [kən'tɛstənt] *n* concursante *mf*; (*in fight*) contendiente *mf*

context ['kɔntɛkst] *n* contexto

continent ['kɔntɪnənt] *n* continente *m*; **the C~** (BRIT) el continente europeo; **continental** [-'nɛntl] *adj* continental; **continental breakfast** *n* desayuno estilo europeo; **continental quilt** (BRIT) *n* edredón *m*

continual [kən'tɪnjuəl] *adj* continuo; **continually** *adv* constantemente

continue [kən'tɪnju:] *vi, vt* seguir, continuar

continuity [kɔntɪ'njuɪtɪ] *n* (*also Cine*) continuidad *f*

continuous [kən'tɪnjuəs] *adj* continuo; **continuous assessment** *n* (BRIT) evaluación *f* continua; **continuously** *adv* continuamente

contour ['kɔntuə*] *n* contorno; (*also*: **~ line**) curva de nivel

contraception [kɔntrə'sɛpʃən] *n* contracepción *f*

contraceptive [kɔntrə'sɛptɪv] *adj, n* anticonceptivo

contract [*n* 'kɔntrækt, *vb* kən'trækt] *n* contrato ▷ *vi* (*Comm*): **to ~ to do sth** comprometerse por contrato a hacer algo; (*become smaller*) contraerse, encogerse ▷ *vt* contraer; **contractor** *n* contratista *mf*

contradict [kɔntrə'dɪkt] *vt* contradecir; **contradiction** [-ʃən] *n* contradicción *f*

contrary¹ ['kɔntrərɪ] *adj* contrario ▷ *n* lo contrario; **on the ~** al contrario; **unless you hear to the ~** a no ser que le digan lo contrario

contrary² [kən'trɛərɪ] *adj* (*perverse*) terco

contrast [*n* 'kɔntrɑ:st, *vt* kən'trɑ:st] *n* contraste *m* ▷ *vt* comparar; **in ~ to** en contraste con

contribute [kən'trɪbju:t] *vi* contribuir ▷ *vt*: **to ~ £10/an article to** contribuir con 10 libras/un artículo a; **to ~ to** (*charity*) donar a; (*newspaper*) escribir para; (*discussion*) intervenir en; **contribution** [kɔntrɪ'bju:ʃən] *n* (*donation*) donativo; (BRIT: *for social security*) cotización *f*; (*to debate*) intervención *f*; (*to journal*) colaboración *f*; **contributor** *n* contribuyente *mf*; (*to newspaper*) colaborador(a) *m/f*

control [kən'trəul] *vt* controlar; (*process etc*) dirigir; (*machinery*) manejar; (*temper*) dominar; (*disease*) contener ▷ *n* control *m*; **controls** *npl* (*of vehicle*) instrumentos *mpl* de mando; (*of radio*) controles *mpl*; (*governmental*) medidas *fpl* de control; **under ~** bajo control; **to be in ~ of** tener el mando de; **the car went out of ~** se perdió el control del coche; **control tower** *n* (*Aviat*) torre *f* de control

controversial [kɔntrə'və:ʃl] *adj*

polémico
controversy ['kɔntrəvə:sɪ] *n* polémica
convenience [kən'vi:nɪəns] *n* (*easiness*) comodidad *f*; (*suitability*) idoneidad *f*; (*advantage*) ventaja; **at your ~** cuando le sea conveniente; **all modern ~s, all mod cons** (BRIT) todo confort
convenient [kən'vi:nɪənt] *adj* (*useful*) útil; (*place, time*) conveniente
convent ['kɔnvənt] *n* convento
convention [kən'vɛnʃən] *n* convención *f*; (*meeting*) asamblea; (*agreement*) convenio; **conventional** *adj* convencional
conversation [kɔnvə'seɪʃən] *n* conversación *f*
conversely [-'və:slɪ] *adv* a la inversa
conversion [kən'və:ʃən] *n* conversión *f*
convert [*vb* kən'və:t, *n* 'kɔnvə:t] *vt* (*Rel, Comm*) convertir; (*alter*): **to ~ sth into/to** transformar algo en/convertir algo a ▷ *n* converso/a; **convertible** *adj* convertible ▷ *n* descapotable *m*
convey [kən'veɪ] *vt* llevar; (*thanks*) comunicar; (*idea*) expresar; **conveyor belt** *n* cinta transportadora
convict [*vb* kən'vɪkt, *n* 'kɔnvɪkt] *vt* (*find guilty*) declarar culpable a ▷ *n* presidiario/a; **conviction** [-ʃən] *n* condena; (*belief, certainty*) convicción *f*
convince [kən'vɪns] *vt* convencer; **convinced** *adj*: **convinced of/that** convencido de/de que; **convincing** *adj* convincente
convoy ['kɔnvɔɪ] *n* convoy *m*
cook [kuk] *vt* (*stew etc*) guisar; (*meal*) preparar ▷ *vi* cocer; (*person*) cocinar ▷ *n* cocinero/a; **cook book** *n* libro de cocina; **cooker** *n* cocina; **cookery** *n* cocina; **cookery book** (BRIT) *n* = **cook book**; **cookie** (US) *n* galleta; **cooking** *n* cocina
cool [ku:l] *adj* fresco; (*not afraid*) tranquilo; (*unfriendly*) frío ▷ *vt* enfriar ▷ *vi* enfriarse; **cool down** *vi* enfriarse; (*fig: person, situation*) calmarse; **cool off** *vi* (*become calmer*) calmarse, apaciguarse; (*lose enthusiasm*) perder (el) interés, enfriarse
cop [kɔp] (*inf*) *n* poli *mf* (SP), tira *mf* (MEX)
cope [kəup] *vi*: **to ~ with** (*problem*) hacer frente a
copper ['kɔpə*] *n* (*metal*) cobre *m*; (BRIT: *inf*) poli *mf*, tira *mf* (MEX)
copy ['kɔpɪ] *n* copia; (*of book etc*) ejemplar *m* ▷ *vt* copiar; **copyright** *n* derechos *mpl* de autor
coral ['kɔrəl] *n* coral *m*
cord [kɔ:d] *n* cuerda; (*Elec*) cable *m*; (*fabric*) pana; **cords** *npl* (*trousers*) pantalones *mpl* de pana; **cordless** *adj* sin hilos
corduroy ['kɔ:dərɔɪ] *n* pana
core [kɔ:*] *n* centro, núcleo; (*of fruit*) corazón *m*; (*of problem*) meollo ▷ *vt* quitar el corazón de
coriander [kɔrɪ'ændə*] *n* culantro
cork [kɔ:k] *n* corcho; (*tree*) alcornoque *m*; **corkscrew** *n* sacacorchos *m inv*
corn [kɔ:n] *n* (BRIT: *cereal crop*) trigo; (US: *maize*) maíz *m*; (*on foot*) callo; **~ on the cob** (*Culin*) mazorca, elote *m* (MEX), choclo (SC)
corned beef ['kɔ:nd-] *n* carne *f* acecinada (en lata)
corner ['kɔ:nə*] *n* (*outside*) esquina; (*inside*) rincón *m*; (*in road*) curva; (*Football*) córner *m*; (*Boxing*) esquina ▷ *vt* (*trap*) arrinconar; (*Comm*) acaparar ▷ *vi* (*in car*) tomar las curvas; **corner shop** (BRIT) tienda de la esquina
cornflakes ['kɔ:nfleɪks] *npl* copos *mpl* de maíz, cornflakes *mpl*
cornflour ['kɔ:nflauə*] (BRIT) *n* harina de maíz
cornstarch ['kɔ:nstɑ:tʃ] (US) *n* = **cornflour**
Cornwall ['kɔ:nwəl] *n* Cornualles *m*
coronary ['kɔrənərɪ] *n* (*also*: **~ thrombosis**) infarto
coronation [kɔrə'neɪʃən] *n* coronación *f*

coroner ['kɔrənə*] *n* juez *mf* de instrucción

corporal ['kɔːpərl] *n* cabo ▷ *adj*: **~ punishment** castigo corporal

corporate ['kɔːpərɪt] *adj* (*action, ownership*) colectivo; (*finance, image*) corporativo

corporation [kɔːpə'reɪʃən] *n* (*of town*) ayuntamiento; (*Comm*) corporación *f*

corps [kɔː*, *pl* kɔːz] *n inv* cuerpo; **diplomatic ~** cuerpo diplomático; **press ~** gabinete *m* de prensa

corpse [kɔːps] *n* cadáver *m*

correct [kə'rɛkt] *adj* justo, exacto; (*proper*) correcto ▷ *vt* corregir; (*exam*) corregir, calificar; **correction** [-ʃən] *n* (*act*) corrección *f*; (*instance*) rectificación *f*

correspond [kɔrɪs'pɔnd] *vi* (*write*): **to ~ (with)** escribirse (con); (*be equivalent to*): **to ~ (to)** corresponder (a); (*be in accordance*): **to ~ (with)** corresponder (con); **correspondence** *n* correspondencia; **correspondent** *n* corresponsal *mf*; **corresponding** *adj* correspondiente

corridor ['kɔrɪdɔː*] *n* pasillo

corrode [kə'rəud] *vt* corroer ▷ *vi* corroerse

corrupt [kə'rʌpt] *adj* (*person*) corrupto; (*Comput*) corrompido ▷ *vt* corromper; (*Comput*) degradar; **corruption** *n* corrupción *f*; (*of data*) alteración *f*

Corsica ['kɔːsɪkə] *n* Córcega

cosmetic [kɔz'mɛtɪk] *adj, n* cosmético; **cosmetic surgery** *n* cirugía *f* estética

cosmopolitan [kɔzmə'pɔlɪtn] *adj* cosmopolita

cost [kɔst] (*pt, pp* **~**) *n* (*price*) precio ▷ *vi* costar, valer ▷ *vt* preparar el presupuesto de; **how much does it ~?** ¿cuánto cuesta?; **to ~ sb time/effort** costarle a algn tiempo/esfuerzo; **it ~ him his life** le costó la vida; **at all ~s** cueste lo que cueste; **costs** *npl* (*Comm*) costes *mpl*; (*Law*) costas *fpl*

co-star ['kəustɑː*] *n* coprotagonista *mf*

Costa Rica ['kɔstə'riːkə] *n* Costa Rica; **Costa Rican** *adj, n* costarriqueño/a

costly ['kɔstlɪ] *adj* costoso

cost of living *n* costo *or* coste *m* (*Sp*) de la vida

costume ['kɔstjuːm] *n* traje *m*; (BRIT: *also*: **swimming ~**) traje de baño

cosy ['kəuzɪ] (US **cozy**) *adj* (*person*) cómodo; (*room*) acogedor(a)

cot [kɔt] *n* (BRIT: *child's*) cuna; (US: *campbed*) cama de campaña

cottage ['kɔtɪdʒ] *n* casita de campo; (*rustic*) barraca; **cottage cheese** *n* requesón *m*

cotton ['kɔtn] *n* algodón *m*; (*thread*) hilo; **cotton on** *vi* (*inf*): **to cotton on (to sth)** caer en la cuenta (de algo); **cotton bud** *n* (BRIT) bastoncillo *m* de algodón; **cotton candy** (US) *n* algodón *m* (azucarado); **cotton wool** (BRIT) *n* algodón *m* (hidrófilo)

couch [kautʃ] *n* sofá *m*; (*doctor's etc*) diván *m*

cough [kɔf] *vi* toser ▷ *n* tos *f*; **cough mixture** *n* jarabe *m* para la tos

could [kud] *pt of* **can²**; **couldn't** = **could not**

council ['kaunsl] *n* consejo; **city** *or* **town ~** consejo municipal; **council estate** (BRIT) *n* *urbanización de viviendas municipales de alquiler*; **council house** (BRIT) *n* *vivienda municipal de alquiler*; **councillor** (US **councilor**) *n* concejal(a) *m/f*; **council tax** *n* (BRIT) contribución *f* municipal (*dependiente del valor de la vivienda*)

counsel ['kaunsl] *n* (*advice*) consejo; (*lawyer*) abogado/a ▷ *vt* aconsejar; **counselling** (US **counseling**) *n* (*Psych*) asistencia *f* psicológica; **counsellor** (US **counselor**) *n* consejero/a, abogado/a

count [kaunt] *vt* contar; (*include*) incluir ▷ *vi* contar ▷ *n* cuenta; (*of votes*) escrutinio; (*level*) nivel *m*;

(*nobleman*) conde *m*; **count in** (*inf*) *vt*: **to count sb in on sth** contar con algn para algo; **count on** *vt fus* contar con; **countdown** *n* cuenta atrás

counter ['kauntə*] *n* (*in shop*) mostrador *m*; (*in games*) ficha ▷ *vt* contrarrestar ▷ *adv*: **to run ~ to** ser contrario a, ir en contra de; **counter clockwise** (US) *adv* en sentido contrario al de las agujas del reloj

counterfeit ['kauntəfɪt] *n* falsificación *f*, simulación *f* ▷ *vt* falsificar ▷ *adj* falso, falsificado

counterpart ['kauntəpɑːt] *n* homólogo/a

countess ['kauntɪs] *n* condesa

countless ['kauntlɪs] *adj* innumerable

country ['kʌntrɪ] *n* país *m*; (*native land*) patria; (*as opposed to town*) campo; (*region*) región *f*, tierra; **country and western (music)** *n* música country; **country house** *n* casa de campo; **countryside** *n* campo

county ['kauntɪ] *n* condado

coup [kuː] (*pl* **~s**) *n* (*also*: **~ d'état**) golpe *m* (de estado); (*achievement*) éxito

couple ['kʌpl] *n* (*of things*) par *m*; (*of people*) pareja; (*married couple*) matrimonio; **a ~ of** un par de

coupon ['kuːpɔn] *n* cupón *m*; (*voucher*) valé *m*

courage ['kʌrɪdʒ] *n* valor *m*, valentía; **courageous** [kə'reɪdʒəs] *adj* valiente

courgette [kuə'ʒɛt] (BRIT) *n* calabacín *m*, calabacita (MEX)

courier ['kurɪə*] *n* mensajero/a; (*for tourists*) guía *mf* (de turismo)

course [kɔːs] *n* (*direction*) dirección *f*; (*of river, Scol*) curso; (*process*) transcurso; (*Med*): **~ of treatment** tratamiento; (*of ship*) rumbo; (*part of meal*) plato; (*Golf*) campo; **of ~** desde luego, naturalmente; **of ~!** ¡claro!

court [kɔːt] *n* (*royal*) corte *f*; (*Law*) tribunal *m*, juzgado; (*Tennis etc*) pista, cancha ▷ *vt* (*woman*) cortejar a; **to take to ~** demandar

courtesy ['kəːtəsɪ] *n* cortesía; **(by) ~ of** por cortesía de; **courtesy bus, courtesy coach** *n* autobús *m* gratuito

court: court-house ['kɔːthaus] (US) *n* palacio de justicia; **courtroom** ['kɔːtrum] *n* sala de justicia; **courtyard** ['kɔːtjɑːd] *n* patio

cousin ['kʌzn] *n* primo/a; **first ~** primo/a carnal, primo/a hermano/a

cover ['kʌvə*] *vt* cubrir; (*feelings, mistake*) ocultar; (*with lid*) tapar; (*book etc*) forrar; (*distance*) recorrer; (*include*) abarcar; (*protect*: *also*: *Insurance*) cubrir; (*Press*) investigar; (*discuss*) tratar ▷ *n* cubierta; (*lid*) tapa; (*for chair etc*) funda; (*envelope*) sobre *m*; (*for book*) forro; (*of magazine*) portada; (*shelter*) abrigo; (*Insurance*) cobertura; (*of spy*) cobertura; **covers** *npl* (*on bed*) sábanas; mantas; **to take ~** (*shelter*) protegerse, resguardarse; **under ~** (*indoors*) bajo techo; **under ~ of darkness** al amparo de la oscuridad; **under separate ~** (*Comm*) por separado; **cover up** *vi*: **to cover up for sb** encubrir a algn; **coverage** *n* (*TV, Press*) cobertura; **cover charge** *n* precio del cubierto; **cover-up** *n* encubrimiento

cow [kau] *n* vaca; (*inf!*: *woman*) bruja ▷ *vt* intimidar

coward ['kauəd] *n* cobarde *mf*; **cowardly** *adj* cobarde

cowboy ['kaubɔɪ] *n* vaquero

cozy ['kəuzɪ] (US) *adj* = **cosy**

crab [kræb] *n* cangrejo

crack [kræk] *n* grieta; (*noise*) crujido; (*drug*) crack *m* ▷ *vt* agrietar, romper; (*nut*) cascar; (*solve*: *problem*) resolver; (: *code*) descifrar; (*whip etc*) chasquear; (*knuckles*) crujir; (*joke*) contar ▷ *adj* (*expert*) de primera; **crack down on** *vt fus* adoptar fuertes medidas contra; **cracked** *adj* (*cup, window*) rajado; (*wall*) resquebrajado; **cracker** *n* (*biscuit*) cráker *m*; (*Christmas cracker*) petardo sorpresa

crackle ['krækl] *vi* crepitar

cradle ['kreɪdl] *n* cuna

craft [krɑːft] *n* (*skill*) arte *m*; (*trade*) oficio; (*cunning*) astucia; (*boat*: *pl inv*) barco; (*plane*: *pl inv*) avión *m*; **craftsman** (*irreg*) *n* artesano; **craftsmanship** *n* (*quality*) destreza

cram [kræm] *vt* (*fill*): **to ~ sth with** llenar algo (a reventar) de; (*put*): **to ~ sth into** meter algo a la fuerza en ▷ *vi* (*for exams*) empollar

cramp [kræmp] *n* (*Med*) calambre *m*; **cramped** *adj* apretado, estrecho

cranberry ['krænbərɪ] *n* arándano agrio

crane [kreɪn] *n* (*Tech*) grúa; (*bird*) grulla

crap [kræp] *n* (*inf!*) mierda (*!*)

crash [kræʃ] *n* (*noise*) estrépito; (*of cars etc*) choque *m*; (*of plane*) accidente *m* de aviación; (*Comm*) quiebra ▷ *vt* (*car, plane*) estrellar ▷ *vi* (*car, plane*) estrellarse; (*two cars*) chocar; (*Comm*) quebrar; **crash course** *n* curso acelerado; **crash helmet** *n* casco (protector)

crate [kreɪt] *n* cajón *m* de embalaje; (*for bottles*) caja

crave [kreɪv] *vt, vi*: **to ~ (for)** ansiar, anhelar

crawl [krɔːl] *vi* (*drag o.s.*) arrastrarse; (*child*) andar a gatas, gatear; (*vehicle*) avanzar (lentamente) ▷ *n* (*Swimming*) crol *m*

crayfish ['kreɪfɪʃ] *n inv* (*freshwater*) cangrejo de río; (*saltwater*) cigala

crayon ['kreɪən] *n* lápiz *m* de color

craze [kreɪz] *n* (*fashion*) moda

crazy ['kreɪzɪ] *adj* (*person*) loco; (*idea*) disparatado; (*inf*: *keen*): **~ about sb/sth** loco por algn/algo

creak [kriːk] *vi* (*floorboard*) crujir; (*hinge etc*) chirriar, rechinar

cream [kriːm] *n* (*of milk*) nata, crema; (*lotion*) crema; (*fig*) flor *f* y nata ▷ *adj* (*colour*) color crema; **cream cheese** *n* queso blanco; **creamy** *adj* cremoso; (*colour*) color crema

crease [kriːs] *n* (*fold*) pliegue *m*; (*in trousers*) raya; (*wrinkle*) arruga ▷ *vt* (*wrinkle*) arrugar ▷ *vi* (*wrinkle up*) arrugarse

create [kriː'eɪt] *vt* crear; **creation** [-ʃən] *n* creación *f*; **creative** *adj* creativo; **creator** *n* creador(a) *m/f*

creature ['kriːtʃə*] *n* (*animal*) animal *m*, bicho; (*person*) criatura

crèche [krɛʃ] *n* guardería (infantil)

credentials [krɪ'dɛnʃlz] *npl* (*references*) referencias *fpl*; (*identity papers*) documentos *mpl* de identidad

credibility [krɛdɪ'bɪlɪtɪ] *n* credibilidad *f*

credible ['krɛdɪbl] *adj* creíble; (*trustworthy*) digno de confianza

credit ['krɛdɪt] *n* crédito; (*merit*) honor *m*, mérito ▷ *vt* (*Comm*) abonar; (*believe*: *also*: **give ~ to**) creer, prestar fe a ▷ *adj* crediticio; **credits** *npl* (*Cinema*) fichas *fpl* técnicas; **to be in ~** (*person*) tener saldo a favor; **to ~ sb with** (*fig*) reconocer a algn el mérito de; **credit card** *n* tarjeta de crédito

creek [kriːk] *n* cala, ensenada; (*US*) riachuelo

creep [kriːp] (*pt, pp* **crept**) *vi* arrastrarse

cremate [krɪ'meɪt] *vt* incinerar

crematorium [krɛmə'tɔːrɪəm] (*pl* **crematoria**) *n* crematorio

crept [krɛpt] *pt, pp of* **creep**

crescent ['krɛsnt] *n* media luna; (*street*) calle *f* (*en forma de semicírculo*)

cress [krɛs] *n* berro

crest [krɛst] *n* (*of bird*) cresta; (*of hill*) cima, cumbre *f*; (*of coat of arms*) blasón *m*

crew [kruː] *n* (*of ship etc*) tripulación *f*; (*TV, Cinema*) equipo; **crew-neck** *n* cuello a la caja

crib [krɪb] *n* cuna ▷ *vt* (*inf*) plagiar

cricket ['krɪkɪt] *n* (*insect*) grillo; (*game*) críquet *m*; **cricketer** *n* jugador(a) *m/f* de críquet

crime [kraɪm] *n* (*no pl*: *illegal activities*) crimen *m*; (*illegal action*) delito; **criminal** ['krɪmɪnl] *n* criminal *mf*, delincuente *mf* ▷ *adj* criminal; (*illegal*)

delictivo; (*law*) penal
crimson ['krɪmzn] *adj* carmesí
cringe [krɪndʒ] *vi* agacharse, encogerse
cripple ['krɪpl] *n* lisiado/a, cojo/a ▷*vt* lisiar, mutilar
crisis ['kraɪsɪs] (*pl* **crises**) *n* crisis *f inv*
crisp [krɪsp] *adj* fresco; (*vegetables etc*) crujiente; (*manner*) seco; **crispy** *adj* crujiente
criterion [kraɪ'tɪərɪən] (*pl* **criteria**) *n* criterio
critic ['krɪtɪk] *n* crítico/a; **critical** *adj* crítico; (*illness*) grave; **criticism** ['krɪtɪsɪzm] *n* crítica; **criticize** ['krɪtɪsaɪz] *vt* criticar
Croat ['krəuæt] *adj, n* = **Croatian**
Croatia [krəu'eɪʃə] *n* Croacia; **Croatian** *adj, n* croata *m/f* ▷*n* (*Ling*) croata *m*
crockery ['krɔkərɪ] *n* loza, vajilla
crocodile ['krɔkədaɪl] *n* cocodrilo
crocus ['krəukəs] *n* croco, crocus *m*
croissant ['krwasŋ] *n* croissant *m*, medialuna (*esp* LAM)
crook [kruk] *n* ladrón/ona *m/f*; (*of shepherd*) cayado; **crooked** ['krukɪd] *adj* torcido; (*dishonest*) nada honrado
crop [krɔp] *n* (*produce*) cultivo; (*amount produced*) cosecha; (*riding crop*) látigo de montar ▷*vt* cortar, recortar; **crop up** *vi* surgir, presentarse
cross [krɔs] *n* cruz *f*; (*hybrid*) cruce *m* ▷*vt* (*street etc*) cruzar, atravesar ▷*adj* de mal humor, enojado; **cross off** *vt* tachar; **cross out** *vt* tachar; **cross over** *vi* cruzar; **cross-Channel ferry** ['krɔs'tʃænl-] *n* transbordador *m* que cruza el Canal de la Mancha; **crosscountry (race)** *n* carrera a campo traviesa, cross *m*; **crossing** *n* (*sea passage*) travesía; (*also*: **pedestrian crossing**) paso para peatones; **crossing guard** (US) *n* *persona encargada de ayudar a los niños a cruzar la calle*; **crossroads** *n* cruce *m*, encrucijada; **crosswalk** (US) *n* paso de peatones; **crossword** *n* crucigrama *m*
crotch [krɔtʃ] *n* (*Anat, of garment*) entrepierna
crouch [krautʃ] *vi* agacharse, acurrucarse
crouton ['kru:tɔn] *n* cubito de pan frito
crow [krəu] *n* (*bird*) cuervo; (*of cock*) canto, cacareo ▷*vi* (*cock*) cantar
crowd [kraud] *n* muchedumbre *f*, multitud *f* ▷*vt* (*fill*) llenar ▷*vi* (*gather*): **to ~ round** reunirse en torno a; (*cram*): **to ~ in** entrar en tropel; **crowded** *adj* (*full*) atestado; (*densely populated*) superpoblado
crown [kraun] *n* corona; (*of head*) coronilla; (*for tooth*) funda; (*of hill*) cumbre *f* ▷*vt* coronar; (*fig*) completar, rematar; **crown jewels** *npl* joyas *fpl* reales
crucial ['kru:ʃl] *adj* decisivo
crucifix ['kru:sɪfɪks] *n* crucifijo
crude [kru:d] *adj* (*materials*) bruto; (*fig*: *basic*) tosco; (: *vulgar*) ordinario; **crude (oil)** *n* (petróleo) crudo
cruel ['kruəl] *adj* cruel; **cruelty** *n* crueldad *f*
cruise [kru:z] *n* crucero ▷*vi* (*ship*) hacer un crucero; (*car*) ir a velocidad de crucero
crumb [krʌm] *n* miga, migaja
crumble ['krʌmbl] *vt* desmenuzar ▷*vi* (*building, also fig*) desmoronarse
crumpet ['krʌmpɪt] *n* ≈ bollo para tostar
crumple ['krʌmpl] *vt* (*paper*) estrujar; (*material*) arrugar
crunch [krʌntʃ] *vt* (*with teeth*) mascar; (*underfoot*) hacer crujir ▷*n* (*fig*) hora *or* momento de la verdad; **crunchy** *adj* crujiente
crush [krʌʃ] *n* (*crowd*) aglomeración *f*; (*infatuation*): **to have a ~ on sb** estar loco por algn; (*drink*): **lemon ~** limonada ▷*vt* aplastar; (*paper*) estrujar; (*cloth*) arrugar; (*fruit*) exprimir; (*opposition*) aplastar; (*hopes*) destruir
crust [krʌst] *n* corteza; (*of snow, ice*) costra; **crusty** *adj* (*bread*) crujiente;

(*person*) de mal carácter
crutch [krʌtʃ] *n* muleta
cry [kraɪ] *vi* llorar ▷*n* (*shriek*) chillido; (*shout*) grito; **cry out** *vi* (*call out, shout*) lanzar un grito, echar un grito ▷*vt* gritar
crystal ['krɪstl] *n* cristal *m*
cub [kʌb] *n* cachorro; (*also*: **~ scout**) niño explorador
Cuba ['kju:bə] *n* Cuba; **Cuban** *adj, n* cubano/a *m/f*
cube [kju:b] *n* cubo ▷*vt* (*Math*) cubicar
cubicle ['kju:bɪkl] *n* (*at pool*) caseta; (*for bed*) cubículo
cuckoo ['kuku:] *n* cuco
cucumber ['kju:kʌmbə*] *n* pepino
cuddle ['kʌdl] *vt* abrazar ▷*vi* abrazarse
cue [kju:] *n* (*snooker cue*) taco; (*Theatre etc*) señal *f*
cuff [kʌf] *n* (*of sleeve*) puño; (US: *of trousers*) vuelta; (*blow*) bofetada ▷**off the ~** *adv* de improviso; **cufflinks** *npl* gemelos *mpl*
cuisine [kwɪ'zi:n] *n* cocina
cul-de-sac ['kʌldəsæk] *n* callejón *m* sin salida
cull [kʌl] *vt* (*idea*) sacar ▷*n* (*of animals*) matanza selectiva
culminate ['kʌlmɪneɪt] *vi*: **to ~ in** terminar en
culprit ['kʌlprɪt] *n* culpable *mf*
cult [kʌlt] *n* culto
cultivate ['kʌltɪveɪt] *vt* cultivar
cultural ['kʌltʃərəl] *adj* cultural
culture ['kʌltʃə*] *n* (*also fig*) cultura; (*Biol*) cultivo
cumin ['kʌmɪn] *n* (*spice*) comino
cunning ['kʌnɪŋ] *n* astucia ▷*adj* astuto
cup [kʌp] *n* taza; (*as prize*) copa
cupboard ['kʌbəd] *n* armario; (*in kitchen*) alacena
cup final *n* (*Football*) final *f* de copa
curator [kjuə'reɪtə*] *n* director(a) *m/f*
curb [kə:b] *vt* refrenar; (*person*) reprimir ▷*n* freno; (US) bordillo
curdle ['kə:dl] *vi* cuajarse
cure [kjuə*] *vt* curar ▷*n* cura, curación *f*; (*fig*: *solution*) remedio
curfew ['kə:fju:] *n* toque *m* de queda
curiosity [kjuərɪ'ɔsɪtɪ] *n* curiosidad *f*
curious ['kjuərɪəs] *adj* curioso; (*person*: *interested*): **to be ~** sentir curiosidad
curl [kə:l] *n* rizo ▷*vt* (*hair*) rizar ▷*vi* rizarse; **curl up** *vi* (*person*) hacerse un ovillo; **curler** *n* rulo; **curly** *adj* rizado
currant ['kʌrnt] *n* pasa (de Corinto); (*blackcurrant, redcurrant*) grosella
currency ['kʌrnsɪ] *n* moneda; **to gain ~** (*fig*) difundirse
current ['kʌrnt] *n* corriente *f* ▷*adj* (*accepted*) corriente; (*present*) actual; **current account** (BRIT) *n* cuenta corriente; **current affairs** *npl* noticias *fpl* de actualidad; **currently** *adv* actualmente
curriculum [kə'rɪkjuləm] (*pl* **~s** *or* **curricula**) *n* plan *m* de estudios; **curriculum vitae** *n* currículum *m*
curry ['kʌrɪ] *n* curry *m* ▷*vt*: **to ~ favour with** buscar favores con; **curry powder** *n* curry *m* en polvo
curse [kə:s] *vi* soltar tacos ▷*vt* maldecir ▷*n* maldición *f*; (*swearword*) palabrota, taco
cursor ['kə:sə*] *n* (*Comput*) cursor *m*
curt [kə:t] *adj* corto, seco
curtain ['kə:tn] *n* cortina; (*Theatre*) telón *m*
curve [kə:v] *n* curva ▷*vi* (*road*) hacer una curva; (*line etc*) curvarse; **curved** *adj* curvo
cushion ['kuʃən] *n* cojín *m*; (*of air*) colchón *m* ▷*vt* (*shock*) amortiguar
custard ['kʌstəd] *n* natillas *fpl*
custody ['kʌstədɪ] *n* custodia; **to take into ~** detener
custom ['kʌstəm] *n* costumbre *f*; (*Comm*) clientela
customer ['kʌstəmə*] *n* cliente *m/f*
customized ['kʌstəmaɪzd] *adj* (*car etc*) hecho a encargo

customs ['kʌstəmz] *npl* aduana; **customs officer** *n* aduanero/a

cut [kʌt] (*pt, pp* ~) *vt* cortar; (*price*) rebajar; (*text, programme*) acortar; (*reduce*) reducir ▷ *vi* cortar ▷ *n* (*of garment*) corte *m*; (*in skin*) cortadura; (*in salary etc*) rebaja; (*in spending*) reducción *f*, recorte *m*; (*slice of meat*) tajada; **to ~ a tooth** echar un diente; **to ~ and paste** (*Comput*) cortar y pegar; **cut back** *vt* (*plants*) podar; (*production, expenditure*) reducir; **cut down** *vt* (*tree*) derribar; (*reduce*) reducir; **cut off** *vt* cortar; (*person, place*) aislar; (*Tel*) desconectar; **cut out** *vt* (*shape*) recortar; (*stop: activity etc*) dejar; (*remove*) quitar; **cut up** *vt* cortar (en pedazos); **cutback** *n* reducción *f*

cute [kju:t] *adj* mono

cutlery ['kʌtlərɪ] *n* cubiertos *mpl*

cutlet ['kʌtlɪt] *n* chuleta; (*nut etc cutlet*) *plato vegetariano hecho con nueces y verdura en forma de chuleta*

cut-price ['kʌt'praɪs] (BRIT) *adj* a precio reducido

cut-rate ['kʌt'reɪt] (US) *adj* = **cut-price**

cutting ['kʌtɪŋ] *adj* (*remark*) mordaz ▷ *n* (BRIT: *from newspaper*) recorte *m*; (*from plant*) esqueje *m*

CV *n abbr* = **curriculum vitae**

cwt *abbr* = **hundredweight(s)**

cybercafé ['saɪbəkæfeɪ] *n* cibercafé *m*

cyberspace ['saɪbəspeɪs] *n* ciberespacio

cycle ['saɪkl] *n* ciclo; (*bicycle*) bicicleta ▷ *vi* ir en bicicleta; **cycle hire** *n* alquiler *m* de bicicletas; **cycle lane** *n* carril-bici *m*; **cycle path** *n* carril-bici *m*; **cycling** *n* ciclismo; **cyclist** *n* ciclista *mf*

cyclone ['saɪkləun] *n* ciclón *m*

cylinder ['sɪlɪndə*] *n* cilindro; (*of gas*) bombona

cymbal ['sɪmbl] *n* címbalo, platillo

cynical ['sɪnɪkl] *adj* cínico

Cypriot ['sɪprɪət] *adj, n* chipriota *m/f*

Cyprus ['saɪprəs] *n* Chipre *f*

cyst [sɪst] *n* quiste *m*; **cystitis** [-'taɪtɪs] *n* cistitis *f*

czar [zɑ:*] *n* zar *m*

Czech [tʃɛk] *adj, n* checo/a *m/f*; **Czech Republic** *n*: **the Czech Republic** la República Checa

D [di:] *n* (*Mus*) re *m*
dab [dæb] *vt* (*eyes*, *wound*) tocar (ligeramente); (*paint*, *cream*) poner un poco de
dad [dæd] *n* = **daddy**
daddy ['dædɪ] *n* papá *m*
daffodil ['dæfədɪl] *n* narciso
daft [dɑ:ft] *adj* tonto
dagger ['dægə*] *n* puñal *m*, daga
daily ['deɪlɪ] *adj* diario, cotidiano ▷ *adv* todos los días, cada día
dairy ['dɛərɪ] *n* (*shop*) lechería; (*on farm*) vaquería; **dairy produce** *n* productos *mpl* lácteos
daisy ['deɪzɪ] *n* margarita
dam [dæm] *n* presa ▷ *vt* construir una presa sobre, represar
damage ['dæmɪdʒ] *n* lesión *f*; daño; (*dents etc*) desperfectos *mpl*; (*fig*) perjuicio ▷ *vt* dañar, perjudicar; (*spoil*, *break*) estropear; **damages** *npl* (*Law*) daños *mpl* y perjuicios
damn [dæm] *vt* condenar; (*curse*) maldecir ▷ *n* (*inf*): **I don't give a ~** me importa un pito ▷ *adj* (*inf*: *also*: **~ed**) maldito; **~ (it)!** ¡maldito sea!
damp [dæmp] *adj* húmedo, mojado ▷ *n* humedad *f* ▷ *vt* (*also*: **~en**: *cloth*, *rag*) mojar; (: *enthusiasm*) enfriar
dance [dɑ:ns] *n* baile *m* ▷ *vi* bailar; **dance floor** *n* pista *f* de baile; **dancer** *n* bailador(a) *m/f*; (*professional*) bailarín/ina *m/f*; **dancing** *n* baile *m*
dandelion ['dændɪlaɪən] *n* diente *m* de león
dandruff ['dændrəf] *n* caspa
Dane [deɪn] *n* danés/esa *m/f*
danger ['deɪndʒə*] *n* peligro; (*risk*) riesgo; **~!** (*on sign*) ¡peligro de muerte!; **to be in ~ of** correr riesgo de; **dangerous** *adj* peligroso
dangle ['dæŋgl] *vt* colgar ▷ *vi* pender, colgar
Danish ['deɪnɪʃ] *adj* danés/esa ▷ *n* (*Ling*) danés *m*
dare [dɛə*] *vt*: **to ~ sb to do** desafiar a algn a hacer ▷ *vi*: **to ~ (to) do sth** atreverse a hacer algo; **I ~ say** (*I suppose*) puede ser (que); **daring** *adj* atrevido, osado ▷ *n* atrevimiento, osadía
dark [dɑ:k] *adj* oscuro; (*hair*, *complexion*) moreno ▷ *n*: **in the ~** a oscuras; **to be in the ~ about** (*fig*) no saber nada de; **after ~** después del anochecer; **darken** *vt* (*colour*) hacer más oscuro ▷ *vi* oscurecerse; **darkness** *n* oscuridad *f*; **darkroom** *n* cuarto oscuro
darling ['dɑ:lɪŋ] *adj*, *n* querido/a *m/f*
dart [dɑ:t] *n* dardo; (*in sewing*) sisa ▷ *vi* precipitarse; **dartboard** *n* diana; **darts** *n* (*game*) dardos *mpl*
dash [dæʃ] *n* (*small quantity*: *of liquid*) gota, chorrito; (*sign*) raya ▷ *vt* (*throw*) tirar; (*hopes*) defraudar ▷ *vi* precipitarse, ir de prisa
dashboard ['dæʃbɔ:d] *n* (*Aut*) salpicadero
data ['deɪtə] *npl* datos *mpl*; **database** *n* base *f* de datos; **data processing** *n* proceso de datos
date [deɪt] *n* (*day*) fecha; (*with*

friend) cita; (*fruit*) dátil *m* ▷ *vt* fechar; (*person*) salir con; **~ of birth** fecha de nacimiento; **to ~** *adv* hasta la fecha; **dated** *adj* anticuado

daughter ['dɔːtə*] *n* hija; **daughter-in-law** *n* nuera, hija política

daunting ['dɔːntɪŋ] *adj* desalentador(a)

dawn [dɔːn] *n* alba, amanecer *m*; (*fig*) nacimiento ▷ *vi* (*day*) amanecer; (*fig*): **it ~ed on him that ...** cayó en la cuenta de que ...

day [deɪ] *n* día *m*; (*working day*) jornada; (*heyday*) tiempos *mpl*, días *mpl*; **the ~ before/after** el día anterior/siguiente; **the ~ after tomorrow** pasado mañana; **the ~ before yesterday** anteayer; **the following ~** el día siguiente; **by ~** de día; **day-care centre** ['deɪkɛə-] *n* centro de día; (*for children*) guardería infantil; **daydream** *vi* soñar despierto; **daylight** *n* luz *f* (del día); **day return** (BRIT) *n* billete *m* de ida y vuelta (en un día); **daytime** *n* día *m*; **day-to-day** *adj* cotidiano; **day trip** *n* excursión *f* (de un día)

dazed [deɪzd] *adj* aturdido

dazzle ['dæzl] *vt* deslumbrar; **dazzling** *adj* (*light, smile*) deslumbrante; (*colour*) fuerte

DC *abbr* (= *direct current*) corriente *f* continua

dead [dɛd] *adj* muerto; (*limb*) dormido; (*telephone*) cortado; (*battery*) agotado ▷ *adv* (*completely*) totalmente; (*exactly*) exactamente; **to shoot sb ~** matar a algn a tiros; **~ tired** muerto (de cansancio); **to stop ~** parar en seco; **dead end** *n* callejón *m* sin salida; **deadline** *n* fecha (*or* hora) tope; **deadly** *adj* mortal, fatal; **Dead Sea** *n*: **the Dead Sea** el Mar Muerto

deaf [dɛf] *adj* sordo; **deafen** *vt* ensordecer; **deafening** *adj* ensordecedor/a

deal [diːl] (*pt, pp* **~t**) *n* (*agreement*) pacto, convenio; (*business deal*) trato ▷ *vt* dar; (*card*) repartir; **a great ~ (of)** bastante, mucho; **deal with** *vt fus* (*people*) tratar con; (*problem*) ocuparse de; (*subject*) tratar de; **dealer** *n* comerciante *m/f*; (*Cards*) mano *f*; **dealings** *npl* (*Comm*) transacciones *fpl*; (*relations*) relaciones *fpl*

dealt [dɛlt] *pt, pp of* **deal**

dean [diːn] *n* (*Rel*) deán *m*; (*Scol*: BRIT) decano; (: US) decano; rector *m*

dear [dɪə*] *adj* querido; (*expensive*) caro ▷ *n*: **my ~** mi querido/a ▷ *excl*: **~ me!** ¡Dios mío!; **D~ Sir/Madam** (*in letter*) Muy Señor Mío, Estimado Señor/Estimada Señora; **D~ Mr/Mrs X** Estimado/a Señor(a) X; **dearly** *adv* (*love*) mucho; (*pay*) caro

death [dɛθ] *n* muerte *f*; **death penalty** *n* pena de muerte; **death sentence** *n* condena a muerte

debate [dɪ'beɪt] *n* debate *m* ▷ *vt* discutir

debit ['dɛbɪt] *n* debe *m* ▷ *vt*: **to ~ a sum to sb** *or* **to sb's account** cargar una suma en cuenta a algn; **debit card** *n* tarjeta *f* de débito

debris ['dɛbriː] *n* escombros *mpl*

debt [dɛt] *n* deuda; **to be in ~** tener deudas

debut [deɪ'bjuː] *n* presentación *f*

Dec. *abbr* (= *December*) dic

decade ['dɛkeɪd] *n* decenio, década

decaffeinated [dɪ'kæfɪneɪtɪd] *adj* descafeinado

decay [dɪ'keɪ] *n* (*of building*) desmoronamiento; (*of tooth*) caries *f inv* ▷ *vi* (*rot*) pudrirse

deceased [dɪ'siːst] *n*: **the ~** el(la) difunto/a

deceit [dɪ'siːt] *n* engaño; **deceive** [dɪ'siːv] *vt* engañar

December [dɪ'sɛmbə*] *n* diciembre *m*

decency ['diːsənsɪ] *n* decencia

decent ['diːsənt] *adj* (*proper*) decente; (*person*: *kind*) amable, bueno

deception [dɪ'sɛpʃən] *n* engaño

deceptive [dɪ'sɛptɪv] *adj* engañoso

> Be careful not to translate **deception** by the Spanish word *decepción*.

decide [dɪ'saɪd] *vt* (*person*) decidir; (*question, argument*) resolver ▷ *vi* decidir; **to ~ to do/that** decidir hacer/que; **to ~ on sth** decidirse por algo
decimal ['dɛsɪməl] *adj* decimal ▷ *n* decimal *m*
decision [dɪ'sɪʒən] *n* decisión *f*
decisive [dɪ'saɪsɪv] *adj* decisivo; (*person*) decidido
deck [dɛk] *n* (*Naut*) cubierta; (*of bus*) piso; (*record deck*) platina; (*of cards*) baraja; **deckchair** *n* tumbona
declaration [dɛklə'reɪʃən] *n* declaración *f*
declare [dɪ'klɛə*] *vt* declarar
decline [dɪ'klaɪn] *n* disminución *f*, descenso ▷ *vt* rehusar ▷ *vi* (*person, business*) decaer; (*strength*) disminuir
decorate ['dɛkəreɪt] *vt* (*adorn*): **to ~ (with)** adornar (de), decorar (de); (*paint*) pintar; (*paper*) empapelar; **decoration** [-'reɪʃən] *n* adorno; (*act*) decoración *f*; (*medal*) condecoración *f*; **decorator** *n* (*workman*) pintor *m* (decorador)
decrease [*n* 'di:kri:s, *vb* dɪ'kri:s] *n*: **~ (in)** disminución *f* (de) ▷ *vt* disminuir, reducir ▷ *vi* reducirse
decree [dɪ'kri:] *n* decreto
dedicate ['dɛdɪkeɪt] *vt* dedicar; **dedicated** *adj* dedicado; (*Comput*) especializado; **dedicated word processor** procesador *m* de textos especializado *or* dedicado; **dedication** [-'keɪʃən] *n* (*devotion*) dedicación *f*; (*in book*) dedicatoria
deduce [dɪ'dju:s] *vt* deducir
deduct [dɪ'dʌkt] *vt* restar; descontar; **deduction** [dɪ'dʌkʃən] *n* (*amount deducted*) descuento; (*conclusion*) deducción *f*, conclusión *f*
deed [di:d] *n* hecho, acto; (*feat*) hazaña; (*Law*) escritura
deem [di:m] *vt* (*formal*) juzgar, considerar
deep [di:p] *adj* profundo; (*expressing measurements*) de profundidad; (*voice*) bajo; (*breath*) profundo; (*colour*) intenso ▷ *adv*: **the spectators stood 20 ~** los espectadores se formaron de 20 en fondo; **to be 4 metres ~** tener 4 metros de profundidad; **deep-fry** *vt* freír en aceite abundante; **deeply** *adv* (*breathe*) a pleno pulmón; (*interested, moved, grateful*) profundamente, hondamente
deer [dɪə*] *n inv* ciervo
default [dɪ'fɔ:lt] *n*: **by ~** (*win*) por incomparecencia ▷ *adj* (*Comput*) por defecto
defeat [dɪ'fi:t] *n* derrota ▷ *vt* derrotar, vencer
defect [*n* 'di:fɛkt, *vb* dɪ'fɛkt] *n* defecto ▷ *vi*: **to ~ to the enemy** pasarse al enemigo; **defective** [dɪ'fɛktɪv] *adj* defectuoso
defence [dɪ'fɛns] (*US* **defense**) *n* defensa
defend [dɪ'fɛnd] *vt* defender; **defendant** *n* acusado/a; (*in civil case*) demandado/a; **defender** *n* defensor(a) *m/f*; (*Sport*) defensa *mf*
defense [dɪ'fɛns] (*US*) = **defence**
defensive [dɪ'fɛnsɪv] *adj* defensivo ▷ *n*: **on the ~** a la defensiva
defer [dɪ'fə:*] *vt* aplazar
defiance [dɪ'faɪəns] *n* desafío; **in ~ of** en contra de; **defiant** [dɪ'faɪənt] *adj* (*challenging*) desafiante, retador(a)
deficiency [dɪ'fɪʃənsɪ] *n* (*lack*) falta; (*defect*) defecto; **deficient** [dɪ'fɪʃənt] *adj* deficiente
deficit ['dɛfɪsɪt] *n* déficit *m*
define [dɪ'faɪn] *vt* (*word etc*) definir; (*limits etc*) determinar
definite ['dɛfɪnɪt] *adj* (*fixed*) determinado; (*obvious*) claro; (*certain*) indudable; **he was ~ about it** no dejó lugar a dudas (sobre ello); **definitely** *adv* desde luego, por supuesto
definition [dɛfɪ'nɪʃən] *n* definición *f*; (*clearness*) nitidez *f*
deflate [di:'fleɪt] *vt* desinflar
deflect [dɪ'flɛkt] *vt* desviar
defraud [dɪ'frɔ:d] *vt*: **to ~ sb of sth** estafar algo a algn

defrost [diː'frɔst] *vt* descongelar
defuse [diː'fjuːz] *vt* desactivar; (*situation*) calmar
defy [dɪ'faɪ] *vt* (*resist*) oponerse a; (*challenge*) desafiar; (*fig*): **it defies description** resulta imposible describirlo
degree [dɪ'griː] *n* grado; (*Scol*) título; **to have a ~ in maths** tener una licenciatura en matemáticas; **by ~s** (*gradually*) poco a poco, por etapas; **to some ~** hasta cierto punto
dehydrated [diːhaɪ'dreɪtɪd] *adj* deshidratado; (*milk*) en polvo
de-icer [diː'aɪsə*] *n* descongelador *m*
delay [dɪ'leɪ] *vt* demorar, aplazar; (*person*) entretener; (*train*) retrasar ▷ *vi* tardar ▷ *n* demora, retraso; **to be ~ed** retrasarse; **without ~** en seguida, sin tardar
delegate [*n* 'dɛlɪgɪt, *vb* 'dɛlɪgeɪt] *n* delegado/a ▷ *vt* (*person*) delegar en; (*task*) delegar
delete [dɪ'liːt] *vt* suprimir, tachar
deli ['dɛlɪ] *n* = **delicatessen**
deliberate [*adj* dɪ'lɪbərɪt, *vb* dɪ'lɪbəreɪt] *adj* (*intentional*) intencionado; (*slow*) pausado, lento ▷ *vi* deliberar; **deliberately** *adv* (*on purpose*) a propósito
delicacy ['dɛlɪkəsɪ] *n* delicadeza; (*choice food*) manjar *m*
delicate ['dɛlɪkɪt] *adj* delicado; (*fragile*) frágil
delicatessen [dɛlɪkə'tɛsn] *n* ultramarinos *mpl* finos
delicious [dɪ'lɪʃəs] *adj* delicioso
delight [dɪ'laɪt] *n* (*feeling*) placer *m*, deleite *m*; (*person, experience etc*) encanto, delicia ▷ *vt* encantar, deleitar; **to take ~ in** deleitarse en; **delighted** *adj*: **delighted (at** *or* **with/to do)** encantado (con/de hacer); **delightful** *adj* encantador(a), delicioso
delinquent [dɪ'lɪŋkwənt] *adj, n* delincuente *mf*
deliver [dɪ'lɪvə*] *vt* (*distribute*) repartir; (*hand over*) entregar; (*message*) comunicar; (*speech*) pronunciar; (*Med*) asistir al parto de; **delivery** *n* reparto; entrega; (*of speaker*) modo de expresarse; (*Med*) parto, alumbramiento; **to take delivery of** recibir
delusion [dɪ'luːʒən] *n* ilusión *f*, engaño
de luxe [də'lʌks] *adj* de lujo
delve [dɛlv] *vi*: **to ~ into** hurgar en
demand [dɪ'mɑːnd] *vt* (*gen*) exigir; (*rights*) reclamar ▷ *n* exigencia; (*claim*) reclamación *f*; (*Econ*) demanda; **to be in ~** ser muy solicitado; **on ~** a solicitud; **demanding** *adj* (*boss*) exigente; (*work*) absorbente
demise [dɪ'maɪz] *n* (*death*) fallecimiento
demo ['dɛməu] (*inf*) *n abbr* (= *demonstration*) manifestación *f*
democracy [dɪ'mɔkrəsɪ] *n* democracia; **democrat** ['dɛməkræt] *n* demócrata *mf*; **democratic** [dɛmə'krætɪk] *adj* democrático; (*US*) demócrata
demolish [dɪ'mɔlɪʃ] *vt* derribar, demoler; (*fig: argument*) destruir
demolition [dɛmə'lɪʃən] *n* derribo, demolición *f*
demon ['diːmən] *n* (*evil spirit*) demonio
demonstrate ['dɛmənstreɪt] *vt* demostrar; (*skill, appliance*) mostrar ▷ *vi* manifestarse; **demonstration** [-'streɪʃən] *n* (*Pol*) manifestación *f*; (*proof, exhibition*) demostración *f*; **demonstrator** *n* (*Pol*) manifestante *mf*; (*Comm*) demostrador(a) *m/f*; vendedor(a) *m/f*
demote [dɪ'məut] *vt* degradar
den [dɛn] *n* (*of animal*) guarida; (*room*) habitación *f*
denial [dɪ'naɪəl] *n* (*refusal*) negativa; (*of report etc*) negación *f*
denim ['dɛnɪm] *n* tela vaquera; **denims** *npl* vaqueros *mpl*
Denmark ['dɛnmɑːk] *n* Dinamarca

denomination [dɪnɔmɪ'neɪʃən] *n* valor *m*; (*Rel*) confesión *f*
denounce [dɪ'nauns] *vt* denunciar
dense [dɛns] *adj* (*crowd*) denso; (*thick*) espeso; (: *foliage etc*) tupido; (*inf*: *stupid*) torpe
density ['dɛnsɪtɪ] *n* densidad *f* ▷ **single/double-~ disk** *n* (*Comput*) disco de densidad sencilla/de doble densidad
dent [dɛnt] *n* abolladura ▷ *vt* (*also*: **make a ~ in**) abollar
dental ['dɛntl] *adj* dental; **dental floss** [-flɔs] *n* seda dental; **dental surgery** *n* clínica *f* dental, consultorio *m* dental
dentist ['dɛntɪst] *n* dentista *mf*
dentures ['dɛntʃəz] *npl* dentadura (postiza)
deny [dɪ'naɪ] *vt* negar; (*charge*) rechazar
deodorant [diː'əudərənt] *n* desodorante *m*
depart [dɪ'pɑːt] *vi* irse, marcharse; (*train*) salir; **to ~ from** (*fig*: *differ from*) apartarse de
department [dɪ'pɑːtmənt] *n* (*Comm*) sección *f*; (*Scol*) departamento; (*Pol*) ministerio; **department store** *n* gran almacén *m*
departure [dɪ'pɑːtʃə*] *n* partida, ida; (*of train*) salida; (*of employee*) marcha; **a new ~** un nuevo rumbo; **departure lounge** *n* (*at airport*) sala de embarque
depend [dɪ'pɛnd] *vi*: **to ~ on** depender de; (*rely on*) contar con; **it ~s** depende, según; **~ing on the result** según el resultado; **dependant** *n* dependiente *mf*; **dependent** *adj*: **to be dependent on** depender de ▷ *n* = **dependant**
depict [dɪ'pɪkt] *vt* (*in picture*) pintar; (*describe*) representar
deport [dɪ'pɔːt] *vt* deportar
deposit [dɪ'pɔzɪt] *n* depósito; (*Chem*) sedimento; (*of ore, oil*) yacimiento ▷ *vt* (*gen*) depositar; **deposit account** (BRIT) *n* cuenta de ahorros
depot ['dɛpəu] *n* (*storehouse*) depósito; (*for vehicles*) parque *m*; (US) estación *f*
depreciate [dɪ'priːʃɪeɪt] *vi* depreciarse, perder valor
depress [dɪ'prɛs] *vt* deprimir; (*wages etc*) hacer bajar; (*press down*) apretar; **depressed** *adj* deprimido; **depressing** *adj* deprimente; **depression** [dɪ'prɛʃən] *n* depresión *f*
deprive [dɪ'praɪv] *vt*: **to ~ sb of** privar a algn de; **deprived** *adj* necesitado
dept. *abbr* (= *department*) dto
depth [dɛpθ] *n* profundidad *f*; (*of cupboard*) fondo; **to be in the ~s of despair** sentir la mayor desesperación; **to be out of one's ~** (*in water*) no hacer pie; (*fig*) sentirse totalmente perdido
deputy ['dɛpjutɪ] *adj*: **~ head** subdirector(a) *m/f* ▷ *n* sustituto/a, suplente *mf*; (US *Pol*) diputado/a; (US: *also*: **~ sheriff**) agente *m* del sheriff
derail [dɪ'reɪl] *vt*: **to be ~ed** descarrilarse
derelict ['dɛrɪlɪkt] *adj* abandonado
derive [dɪ'raɪv] *vt* (*benefit etc*) obtener ▷ *vi*: **to ~ from** derivarse de
descend [dɪ'sɛnd] *vt, vi* descender, bajar; **to ~ from** descender de; **to ~ to** rebajarse a; **descendant** *n* descendiente *mf*
descent [dɪ'sɛnt] *n* descenso; (*origin*) descendencia
describe [dɪs'kraɪb] *vt* describir; **description** [-'krɪpʃən] *n* descripción *f*; (*sort*) clase *f*, género
desert [*n* 'dɛzət, *vb* dɪ'zəːt] *n* desierto ▷ *vt* abandonar ▷ *vi* (*Mil*) desertar; **deserted** [dɪ'zəːtɪd] *adj* desierto
deserve [dɪ'zəːv] *vt* merecer, ser digno de
design [dɪ'zaɪn] *n* (*sketch*) bosquejo; (*layout, shape*) diseño; (*pattern*) dibujo; (*intention*) intención *f* ▷ *vt* diseñar; **design and technology** (BRIT: *Scol*) *n* ≈ dibujo y tecnología
designate [*vb* 'dɛzɪgneɪt, *adj* 'dɛzɪgnɪt] *vt* (*appoint*) nombrar; (*destine*) designar ▷ *adj* designado

designer [dɪ'zaɪnə*] *n* diseñador(a) *m/f*; (*fashion designer*) modisto/a, diseñador(a) *m/f* de moda
desirable [dɪ'zaɪərəbl] *adj* (*proper*) deseable; (*attractive*) atractivo
desire [dɪ'zaɪə*] *n* deseo ▷ *vt* desear
desk [dɛsk] *n* (*in office*) escritorio; (*for pupil*) pupitre *m*; (*in hotel, at airport*) recepción *f*; (BRIT: *in shop, restaurant*) caja; **desk-top publishing** ['dɛsktɔp-] *n* autoedición *f*
despair [dɪs'pɛə*] *n* desesperación *f* ▷ *vi*: **to ~ of** perder la esperanza de
despatch [dɪs'pætʃ] *n, vt* = **dispatch**
desperate ['dɛspərɪt] *adj* desesperado; (*fugitive*) peligroso; **to be ~ for sth/to do** necesitar urgentemente algo/hacer; **desperately** *adv* desesperadamente; (*very*) terriblemente, gravemente
desperation [dɛspə'reɪʃən] *n* desesperación *f*; **in (sheer) ~** (absolutamente) desesperado
despise [dɪs'paɪz] *vt* despreciar
despite [dɪs'paɪt] *prep* a pesar de, pese a
dessert [dɪ'zəːt] *n* postre *m*; **dessertspoon** *n* cuchara (de postre)
destination [dɛstɪ'neɪʃən] *n* destino
destined ['dɛstɪnd] *adj*: **~ for London** con destino a Londres
destiny ['dɛstɪnɪ] *n* destino
destroy [dɪs'trɔɪ] *vt* destruir; (*animal*) sacrificar
destruction [dɪs'trʌkʃən] *n* destrucción *f*
destructive [dɪs'trʌktɪv] *adj* destructivo, destructor(a)
detach [dɪ'tætʃ] *vt* separar; (*unstick*) despegar; **detached** *adj* (*attitude*) objetivo, imparcial; **detached house** *n* ≈ chalé *m*, ≈ chalet *m*
detail ['diːteɪl] *n* detalle *m*; (*no pl*; (: *in picture etc*) detalles *mpl*; (*trifle*) pequeñez *f* ▷ *vt* detallar; (*Mil*) destacar; **in ~** detalladamente; **detailed** *adj* detallado
detain [dɪ'teɪn] *vt* retener; (*in captivity*) detener
detect [dɪ'tɛkt] *vt* descubrir; (*Med, Police*) identificar; (*Mil, Radar, Tech*) detectar; **detection** [dɪ'tɛkʃən] *n* descubrimiento; identificación *f*; **detective** *n* detective *mf*; **detective story** *n* novela policíaca
detention [dɪ'tɛnʃən] *n* detención *f*, arresto; (*Scol*) castigo
deter [dɪ'təː*] *vt* (*dissuade*) disuadir
detergent [dɪ'təːdʒənt] *n* detergente *m*
deteriorate [dɪ'tɪərɪəreɪt] *vi* deteriorarse
determination [dɪtəːmɪ'neɪʃən] *n* resolución *f*
determine [dɪ'təːmɪn] *vt* determinar; **determined** *adj* (*person*) resuelto, decidido; **determined to do** resuelto a hacer
deterrent [dɪ'tɛrənt] *n* (*Mil*) fuerza de disuasión
detest [dɪ'tɛst] *vt* aborrecer
detour ['diːtuə*] *n* (*gen*, US *Aut*) desviación *f*
detract [dɪ'trækt] *vt*: **to ~ from** quitar mérito a, desvirtuar
detrimental [dɛtrɪ'mɛntl] *adj*: **~ (to)** perjudicial (a)
devastating ['dɛvəsteɪtɪŋ] *adj* devastador(a); (*fig*) arrollador(a)
develop [dɪ'vɛləp] *vt* desarrollar; (*Phot*) revelar; (*disease*) coger; (*habit*) adquirir; (*fault*) empezar a tener ▷ *vi* desarrollarse; (*advance*) progresar; (*facts, symptoms*) aparecer; **developing country** *n* país *m* en (vías de) desarrollo; **development** *n* desarrollo; (*advance*) progreso; (*of affair, case*) desenvolvimiento; (*of land*) urbanización *f*
device [dɪ'vaɪs] *n* (*apparatus*) aparato, mecanismo
devil ['dɛvl] *n* diablo, demonio
devious ['diːvɪəs] *adj* taimado
devise [dɪ'vaɪz] *vt* idear, inventar
devote [dɪ'vəut] *vt*: **to ~ sth to** dedicar algo a; **devoted** *adj* (*loyal*)

leal, fiel; **to be devoted to sb** querer con devoción a algn; **the book is devoted to politics** el libro trata de la política; **devotion** *n* dedicación *f*; (*Rel*) devoción *f*
devour [dɪ'vauə*] *vt* devorar
devout [dɪ'vaut] *adj* devoto
dew [dju:] *n* rocío
diabetes [daɪə'bi:ti:z] *n* diabetes *f*
diabetic [daɪə'bɛtɪk] *adj*, *n* diabético/a *m/f*
diagnose ['daɪəgnəuz] *vt* diagnosticar
diagnosis [daɪəg'nəusɪs] (*pl* **-ses**) *n* diagnóstico
diagonal [daɪ'ægənl] *adj*, *n* diagonal *f*
diagram ['daɪəgræm] *n* diagrama *m*, esquema *m*
dial ['daɪəl] *n* esfera (SP), cara (LAM); (*on radio etc*) dial *m*; (*of phone*) disco ▷ *vt* (*number*) marcar
dialect ['daɪəlɛkt] *n* dialecto
dialling code ['daɪəlɪŋ-] *n* prefijo
dialling tone (US **dial tone**) *n* (BRIT) señal *f* or tono de marcar
dialogue ['daɪəlɔg] (US **dialog**) *n* diálogo
diameter [daɪ'æmɪtə*] *n* diámetro
diamond ['daɪəmənd] *n* diamante *m*; (*shape*) rombo; **diamonds** *npl* (*Cards*) diamantes *mpl*
diaper ['daɪəpə*] (US) *n* pañal *m*
diarrhoea [daɪə'ri:ə] (US **diarrhea**) *n* diarrea
diary ['daɪərɪ] *n* (*daily account*) diario; (*book*) agenda
dice [daɪs] *n inv* dados *mpl* ▷ *vt* (*Culin*) cortar en cuadritos
dictate [dɪk'teɪt] *vt* dictar; (*conditions*) imponer; **dictation** [-'teɪʃən] *n* dictado; (*giving of orders*) órdenes *fpl*
dictator [dɪk'teɪtə*] *n* dictador *m*
dictionary ['dɪkʃənrɪ] *n* diccionario
did [dɪd] *pt of* **do**
didn't ['dɪdənt] = **did not**
die [daɪ] *vi* morir; (*fig*: *fade*) desvanecerse, desaparecer; **to be dying for sth/to do sth** morirse por algo/de ganas de hacer algo; **die down** *vi* apagarse; (*wind*) amainar; **die out** *vi* desaparecer
diesel ['di:zəl] *n* vehículo con motor Diesel
diet ['daɪət] *n* dieta; (*restricted food*) régimen *m* ▷ *vi* (*also*: **be on a ~**) estar a dieta, hacer régimen
differ ['dɪfə*] *vi*: **to ~ (from)** (*be different*) ser distinto (a), diferenciarse (de); (*disagree*) discrepar (de); **difference** *n* diferencia; (*disagreement*) desacuerdo; **different** *adj* diferente, distinto; **differentiate** [-'rɛnʃɪeɪt] *vi*: **to differentiate (between)** distinguir (entre); **differently** *adv* de otro modo, en forma distinta
difficult ['dɪfɪkəlt] *adj* difícil; **difficulty** *n* dificultad *f*
dig [dɪg] (*pt*, *pp* **dug**) *vt* (*hole*, *ground*) cavar ▷ *n* (*prod*) empujón *m*; (*archaeological*) excavación *f*; (*remark*) indirecta; **to ~ one's nails into** clavar las uñas en; **dig up** *vt* (*information*) desenterrar; (*plant*) desarraigar
digest [*vb* daɪ'dʒɛst, *n* 'daɪdʒɛst] *vt* (*food*) digerir; (*facts*) asimilar ▷ *n* resumen *m*; **digestion** [dɪ'dʒɛstʃən] *n* digestión *f*
digit ['dɪdʒɪt] *n* (*number*) dígito; (*finger*) dedo; **digital** *adj* digital; **digital camera** *n* cámara digital; **digital TV** *n* televisión *f* digital
dignified ['dɪgnɪfaɪd] *adj* grave, solemne
dignity ['dɪgnɪtɪ] *n* dignidad *f*
digs [dɪgz] (BRIT: *inf*) *npl* pensión *f*, alojamiento
dilemma [daɪ'lɛmə] *n* dilema *m*
dill [dɪl] *n* eneldo
dilute [daɪ'lu:t] *vt* diluir
dim [dɪm] *adj* (*light*) débil; (*outline*) indistinto; (*room*) oscuro; (*inf*: *stupid*) lerdo ▷ *vt* (*light*) bajar
dime [daɪm] (US) *n* *moneda de diez centavos*

dimension [dɪ'mɛnʃən] *n* dimensión *f*
diminish [dɪ'mɪnɪʃ] *vt, vi* disminuir
din [dɪn] *n* estruendo, estrépito
dine [daɪn] *vi* cenar; **diner** *n* (*person*) comensal *mf*
dinghy ['dɪŋgɪ] *n* bote *m*; (*also*: **rubber ~**) lancha (neumática)
dingy ['dɪndʒɪ] *adj* (*room*) sombrío; (*colour*) sucio
dining car ['daɪnɪŋ-] (BRIT) *n* (*Rail*) coche-comedor *m*
dining room ['daɪnɪŋ-] *n* comedor *m*
dining table *n* mesa *f* de comedor
dinner ['dɪnə*] *n* (*evening meal*) cena; (*lunch*) comida; (*public*) cena, banquete *m*; **dinner jacket** *n* smoking *m*; **dinner party** *n* cena; **dinner time** *n* (*evening*) hora de cenar; (*midday*) hora de comer
dinosaur ['daɪnəsɔː*] *n* dinosaurio
dip [dɪp] *n* (*slope*) pendiente *m*; (*in sea*) baño; (*Culin*) salsa ▷ *vt* (*in water*) mojar; (*ladle etc*) meter; (BRIT *Aut*): **to ~ one's lights** poner luces de cruce ▷ *vi* (*road etc*) descender, bajar
diploma [dɪ'pləumə] *n* diploma *m*
diplomacy [dɪ'pləuməsɪ] *n* diplomacia
diplomat ['dɪpləmæt] *n* diplomático/a; **diplomatic** [dɪplə'mætɪk] *adj* diplomático
dipstick ['dɪpstɪk] (BRIT) *n* (*Aut*) varilla de nivel (del aceite)
dire [daɪə*] *adj* calamitoso
direct [daɪ'rɛkt] *adj* directo; (*challenge*) claro; (*person*) franco ▷ *vt* dirigir; (*order*): **to ~ sb to do sth** mandar a algn hacer algo ▷ *adv* derecho; **can you ~ me to ...?** ¿puede indicarme dónde está ...?; **direct debit** (BRIT) *n* domiciliación *f* bancaria de recibos
direction [dɪ'rɛkʃən] *n* dirección *f*; **sense of ~** sentido de la dirección; **directions** *npl* (*instructions*) instrucciones *fpl*; **~s for use** modo de empleo
directly [dɪ'rɛktlɪ] *adv* (*in straight line*) directamente; (*at once*) en seguida
director [dɪ'rɛktə*] *n* director(a) *m/f*
directory [dɪ'rɛktərɪ] *n* (*Tel*) guía (telefónica); (*Comput*) directorio; **directory enquiries** (US **directory assistance**) *n* (servicio de) información *f*
dirt [dəːt] *n* suciedad *f*; (*earth*) tierra; **dirty** *adj* sucio; (*joke*) verde, colorado (MEX) ▷ *vt* ensuciar; (*stain*) manchar
disability [dɪsə'bɪlɪtɪ] *n* incapacidad *f*
disabled [dɪs'eɪbld] *adj*: **to be physically ~** ser minusválido/a; **to be mentally ~** ser deficiente mental
disadvantage [dɪsəd'vɑːntɪdʒ] *n* desventaja, inconveniente *m*
disagree [dɪsə'griː] *vi* (*differ*) discrepar; **to ~ (with)** no estar de acuerdo (con); **disagreeable** *adj* desagradable; (*person*) antipático; **disagreement** *n* desacuerdo
disappear [dɪsə'pɪə*] *vi* desaparecer; **disappearance** *n* desaparición *f*
disappoint [dɪsə'pɔɪnt] *vt* decepcionar, defraudar; **disappointed** *adj* decepcionado; **disappointing** *adj* decepcionante; **disappointment** *n* decepción *f*
disapproval [dɪsə'pruːvəl] *n* desaprobación *f*
disapprove [dɪsə'pruːv] *vi*: **to ~ of** ver mal
disarm [dɪs'ɑːm] *vt* desarmar; **disarmament** [dɪs'ɑːməmənt] *n* desarme *m*
disaster [dɪ'zɑːstə*] *n* desastre *m*
disastrous [dɪ'zɑːstrəs] *adj* desastroso
disbelief [dɪsbə'liːf] *n* incredulidad *f*
disc [dɪsk] *n* disco; (*Comput*) = **disk**
discard [dɪs'kɑːd] *vt* (*old things*) tirar; (*fig*) descartar
discharge [*vb* dɪs'tʃɑːdʒ, *n* 'dɪstʃɑːdʒ] *vt* (*task, duty*) cumplir; (*waste*) verter; (*patient*) dar de alta; (*employee*) despedir; (*soldier*) licenciar; (*defendant*) poner en libertad ▷ *n* (*Elec*)

descarga; (*Med*) supuración *f*; (*dismissal*) despedida; (*of duty*) desempeño; (*of debt*) pago, descargo

discipline ['dɪsɪplɪn] *n* disciplina ▷ *vt* disciplinar; (*punish*) castigar

disc jockey *n* pinchadiscos *mf inv*

disclose [dɪs'kləuz] *vt* revelar

disco ['dɪskəu] *n abbr* discoteca

discoloured [dɪs'kʌləd] (*US* **discolored**) *adj* descolorido

discomfort [dɪs'kʌmfət] *n* incomodidad *f*; (*unease*) inquietud *f*; (*physical*) malestar *m*

disconnect [dɪskə'nɛkt] *vt* separar; (*Elec etc*) desconectar

discontent [dɪskən'tɛnt] *n* descontento

discontinue [dɪskən'tɪnju:] *vt* interrumpir; (*payments*) suspender; **"~d"** (*Comm*) "ya no se fabrica"

discount [*n* 'dɪskaunt, *vb* dɪs'kaunt] *n* descuento ▷ *vt* descontar

discourage [dɪs'kʌrɪdʒ] *vt* desalentar; (*advise against*): **to ~ sb from doing** disuadir a algn de hacer

discover [dɪs'kʌvə*] *vt* descubrir; (*error*) darse cuenta de; **discovery** *n* descubrimiento

discredit [dɪs'krɛdɪt] *vt* desacreditar

discreet [dɪ'skri:t] *adj* (*tactful*) discreto; (*careful*) prudente

discrepancy [dɪ'skrɛpənsɪ] *n* diferencia

discretion [dɪ'skrɛʃən] *n* (*tact*) discreción *f*; **at the ~ of** a criterio de

discriminate [dɪ'skrɪmɪneɪt] *vi*: **to ~ between** distinguir entre; **to ~ against** discriminar contra; **discrimination** [-'neɪʃən] *n* (*discernment*) perspicacia; (*bias*) discriminación *f*

discuss [dɪ'skʌs] *vt* discutir; (*a theme*) tratar; **discussion** [dɪ'skʌʃən] *n* discusión *f*

disease [dɪ'zi:z] *n* enfermedad *f*

disembark [dɪsɪm'bɑ:k] *vt, vi* desembarcar

disgrace [dɪs'greɪs] *n* ignominia; (*shame*) vergüenza, escándalo ▷ *vt* deshonrar; **disgraceful** *adj* vergonzoso

disgruntled [dɪs'grʌntld] *adj* disgustado, descontento

disguise [dɪs'gaɪz] *n* disfraz *m* ▷ *vt* disfrazar; **in ~** disfrazado

disgust [dɪs'gʌst] *n* repugnancia ▷ *vt* repugnar, dar asco a

> Be careful not to translate **disgust** by the Spanish word *disgustar*.

disgusted [dɪs'gʌstɪd] *adj* indignado

> Be careful not to translate **disgusted** by the Spanish word *disgustado*.

disgusting [dɪs'gʌstɪŋ] *adj* repugnante, asqueroso; (*behaviour etc*) vergonzoso

dish [dɪʃ] *n* (*gen*) plato; **to do** *or* **wash the ~es** fregar los platos; **dishcloth** *n* estropajo

dishonest [dɪs'ɔnɪst] *adj* (*person*) poco honrado, tramposo; (*means*) fraudulento

dishtowel ['dɪʃtauəl] (*US*) *n* estropajo

dishwasher ['dɪʃwɔʃə*] *n* lavaplatos *m inv*

disillusion [dɪsɪ'lu:ʒən] *vt* desilusionar

disinfectant [dɪsɪn'fɛktənt] *n* desinfectante *m*

disintegrate [dɪs'ɪntɪgreɪt] *vi* disgregarse, desintegrarse

disk [dɪsk] *n* (*esp US*) = **disc**; (*Comput*) disco, disquete *m*; **single-/double-sided ~** disco de una cara/dos caras; **disk drive** *n* disc drive *m*; **diskette** *n* = **disk**

dislike [dɪs'laɪk] *n* antipatía, aversión *f* ▷ *vt* tener antipatía a

dislocate ['dɪsləkeɪt] *vt* dislocar

disloyal [dɪs'lɔɪəl] *adj* desleal

dismal ['dɪzml] *adj* (*gloomy*) deprimente, triste; (*very bad*) malísimo, fatal

dismantle [dɪs'mæntl] *vt* desmontar, desarmar

dismay [dɪs'meɪ] *n* consternación *f* ▷ *vt* consternar
dismiss [dɪs'mɪs] *vt* (*worker*) despedir; (*pupils*) dejar marchar; (*soldiers*) dar permiso para irse; (*idea, Law*) rechazar; (*possibility*) descartar; **dismissal** *n* despido
disobedient [dɪsə'bi:dɪənt] *adj* desobediente
disobey [dɪsə'beɪ] *vt* desobedecer
disorder [dɪs'ɔ:də*] *n* desorden *m*; (*rioting*) disturbios *mpl*; (*Med*) trastorno
disorganized [dɪs'ɔ:gənaɪzd] *adj* desorganizado
disown [dɪs'əun] *vt* (*action*) renegar de; (*person*) negar cualquier tipo de relación con
dispatch [dɪs'pætʃ] *vt* enviar ▷ *n* (*sending*) envío; (*Press*) informe *m*; (*Mil*) parte *m*
dispel [dɪs'pɛl] *vt* disipar
dispense [dɪs'pɛns] *vt* (*medicines*) preparar; **dispense with** *vt fus* prescindir de; **dispenser** *n* (*container*) distribuidor *m* automático
disperse [dɪs'pə:s] *vt* dispersar ▷ *vi* dispersarse
display [dɪs'pleɪ] *n* (*in shop window*) escaparate *m*; (*exhibition*) exposición *f*; (*Comput*) visualización *f*; (*of feeling*) manifestación *f* ▷ *vt* exponer; manifestar; (*ostentatiously*) lucir
displease [dɪs'pli:z] *vt* (*offend*) ofender; (*annoy*) fastidiar
disposable [dɪs'pəuzəbl] *adj* desechable; (*income*) disponible
disposal [dɪs'pəuzl] *n* (*of rubbish*) destrucción *f*; **at one's ~** a su disposición
dispose [dɪs'pəuz] *vi*: **to ~ of** (*unwanted goods*) deshacerse de; (*problem etc*) resolver; **disposition** [dɪspə'zɪʃən] *n* (*nature*) temperamento; (*inclination*) propensión *f*
disproportionate [dɪsprə'pɔ:ʃənət] *adj* desproporcionado
dispute [dɪs'pju:t] *n* disputa; (*also*: **industrial ~**) conflicto (laboral) ▷ *vt* (*argue*) disputar, discutir; (*question*) cuestionar
disqualify [dɪs'kwɔlɪfaɪ] *vt* (*Sport*) desclasificar; **to ~ sb for sth/from doing sth** incapacitar a algn para algo/hacer algo
disregard [dɪsrɪ'gɑ:d] *vt* (*ignore*) no hacer caso de
disrupt [dɪs'rʌpt] *vt* (*plans*) desbaratar, trastornar; (*conversation*) interrumpir; **disruption** [dɪs'rʌpʃən] *n* trastorno, desbaratamiento; interrupción *f*
dissatisfaction [dɪssætɪs'fækʃən] *n* disgusto, descontento
dissatisfied [dɪs'sætɪsfaɪd] *adj* insatisfecho
dissect [dɪ'sɛkt] *vt* disecar
dissent [dɪ'sɛnt] *n* disensión *f*
dissertation [dɪsə'teɪʃən] *n* tesina
dissolve [dɪ'zɔlv] *vt* disolver ▷ *vi* disolverse; **to ~ in(to) tears** deshacerse en lágrimas
distance ['dɪstəns] *n* distancia; **in the ~** a lo lejos
distant ['dɪstənt] *adj* lejano; (*manner*) reservado, frío
distil [dɪs'tɪl] (*US* **distill**) *vt* destilar; **distillery** *n* destilería
distinct [dɪs'tɪŋkt] *adj* (*different*) distinto; (*clear*) claro; (*unmistakeable*) inequívoco; **as ~ from** a diferencia de; **distinction** [dɪs'tɪŋkʃən] *n* distinción *f*; (*honour*) honor *m*; (*in exam*) sobresaliente *m*; **distinctive** *adj* distintivo
distinguish [dɪs'tɪŋgwɪʃ] *vt* distinguir; **to ~ o.s.** destacarse; **distinguished** *adj* (*eminent*) distinguido
distort [dɪs'tɔ:t] *vt* distorsionar; (*shape, image*) deformar
distract [dɪs'trækt] *vt* distraer; **distracted** *adj* distraído; **distraction** [dɪs'trækʃən] *n* distracción *f*; (*confusion*) aturdimiento
distraught [dɪs'trɔ:t] *adj* loco de

inquietud

distress [dɪs'trɛs] *n* (*anguish*) angustia, aflicción *f* ▷ *vt* afligir; **distressing** *adj* angustioso; doloroso

distribute [dɪs'trɪbju:t] *vt* distribuir; (*share out*) repartir; **distribution** [-'bju:ʃən] *n* distribución *f*, reparto; **distributor** *n* (*Aut*) distribuidor *m*; (*Comm*) distribuidora

district ['dɪstrɪkt] *n* (*of country*) zona, región *f*; (*of town*) barrio; (*Admin*) distrito; **district attorney** (US) *n* fiscal *mf*

distrust [dɪs'trʌst] *n* desconfianza ▷ *vt* desconfiar de

disturb [dɪs'tə:b] *vt* (*person: bother, interrupt*) molestar; (*: upset*) perturbar, inquietar; (*disorganize*) alterar; **disturbance** *n* (*upheaval*) perturbación *f*; (*political etc: gen pl*) disturbio; (*of mind*) trastorno; **disturbed** *adj* (*worried, upset*) preocupado, angustiado; **emotionally disturbed** trastornado; (*childhood*) inseguro; **disturbing** *adj* inquietante, perturbador(a)

ditch [dɪtʃ] *n* zanja; (*irrigation ditch*) acequia ▷ *vt* (*inf: partner*) deshacerse de; (*: plan, car etc*) abandonar

ditto ['dɪtəu] *adv* ídem, lo mismo

dive [daɪv] *n* (*from board*) salto; (*underwater*) buceo; (*of submarine*) sumersión *f* ▷ *vi* (*swimmer: into water*) saltar; (*: under water*) zambullirse, bucear; (*fish, submarine*) sumergirse; (*bird*) lanzarse en picado; **to ~ into** (*bag etc*) meter la mano en; (*place*) meterse de prisa en; **diver** *n* (*underwater*) buzo

diverse [daɪ'və:s] *adj* diversos/as, varios/as

diversion [daɪ'və:ʃən] *n* (BRIT *Aut*) desviación *f*; (*distraction, Mil*) diversión *f*; (*of funds*) distracción *f*

diversity [daɪ'və:sɪtɪ] *n* diversidad *f*

divert [daɪ'və:t] *vt* (*turn aside*) desviar

divide [dɪ'vaɪd] *vt* dividir; (*separate*) separar ▷ *vi* dividirse; (*road*) bifurcarse; **divided highway** (US) *n* carretera de doble calzada

divine [dɪ'vaɪn] *adj* (*also fig*) divino

diving ['daɪvɪŋ] *n* (*Sport*) salto; (*underwater*) buceo; **diving board** *n* trampolín *m*

division [dɪ'vɪʒən] *n* división *f*; (*sharing out*) reparto; (*disagreement*) diferencias *fpl*; (*Comm*) sección *f*

divorce [dɪ'vɔ:s] *n* divorcio ▷ *vt* divorciarse de; **divorced** *adj* divorciado; **divorcee** [-'si:] *n* divorciado/a

D.I.Y. (BRIT) *adj, n abbr* = **do-it-yourself**

dizzy ['dɪzɪ] *adj* (*spell*) de mareo; **to feel ~** marearse

DJ *n abbr* = **disc jockey**

DNA *n abbr* (= *deoxyribonucleic acid*) ADN *m*

KEYWORD

do [du:] (*pt* **did**, *pp* **done**) *n* (*inf: party etc*): **we're having a little do on Saturday** damos una fiestecita el sábado; **it was rather a grand do** fue un acontecimiento a lo grande

▷ *aux vb* **1** (*in negative constructions: not translated*): **I don't understand** no entiendo

2 (*to form questions: not translated*): **didn't you know?** ¿no lo sabías?; **what do you think?** ¿qué opinas?

3 (*for emphasis, in polite expressions*): **people do make mistakes sometimes** sí que se cometen errores a veces; **she does seem rather late** a mí también me parece que se ha retrasado; **do sit down/help yourself** siéntate/sírvete por favor; **do take care!** ¡ten cuidado(, te pido)!

4 (*used to avoid repeating vb*): **she sings better than I do** canta mejor que yo; **do you agree? – yes, I do/no, I don't** ¿estás de acuerdo? – sí (lo estoy)/no (lo estoy); **she lives in Glasgow – so do I** vive en Glasgow – yo también; **he didn't like it and neither did we** no

le gustó y a nosotros tampoco; **who made this mess? – I did** ¿quién hizo esta chapuza? – yo; **he asked me to help him and I did** me pidió que le ayudara y lo hice
5 (*in question tags*): **you like him, don't you?** te gusta, ¿verdad? *or* ¿no?; **I don't know him, do I?** creo que no le conozco
▷ *vt* 1 (*gen, carry out, perform etc*): **what are you doing tonight?** ¿qué haces esta noche?; **what can I do for you?** ¿en qué puedo servirle?; **to do the washing-up/cooking** fregar los platos/cocinar; **to do one's teeth/hair/nails** lavarse los dientes/ arreglarse el pelo/arreglarse las uñas
2 (*Aut etc*): **the car was doing 100** el coche iba a 100; **we've done 200 km already** ya hemos hecho 200 km; **he can do 100 in that car** puede ir a 100 en ese coche
▷ *vi* 1 (*act, behave*) hacer; **do as I do** haz como yo
2 (*get on, fare*): **he's doing well/badly at school** va bien/mal en la escuela; **the firm is doing well** la empresa anda *or* va bien; **how do you do?** mucho gusto; (*less formal*) ¿qué tal?
3 (*suit*): **will it do?** ¿sirve?, ¿está *or* va bien?
4 (*be sufficient*) bastar; **will £10 do?** ¿será bastante con £10?; **that'll do** así está bien; **that'll do!** (*in annoyance*) ¡ya está bien!, ¡basta ya!; **to make do (with)** arreglárselas (con)
do up *vt* (*laces*) atar; (*zip, dress, shirt*) abrochar; (*renovate: room, house*) renovar
do with *vt fus* (*need*): **I could do with a drink/some help** no me vendría mal un trago/un poco de ayuda; (*be connected*) tener que ver con; **what has it got to do with you?** ¿qué tiene que ver contigo?
do without *vi* pasar sin; **if you're late for tea then you'll do without** si llegas tarde tendrás que quedarte sin cenar
▷ *vt fus* pasar sin; **I can do without a car** puedo pasar sin coche

dock [dɔk] *n* (*Naut*) muelle *m*; (*Law*) banquillo (de los acusados) ▷ *vi* (*enter dock*) atracar (la) muelle; (*Space*) acoplarse; **docks** *npl* (*Naut*) muelles *mpl*, puerto *sg*
doctor ['dɔktə*] *n* médico/a; (*Ph. D. etc*) doctor(a) *m/f* ▷ *vt* (*drink etc*) adulterar; **Doctor of Philosophy** *n* Doctor en Filosofía y Letras
document ['dɔkjumənt] *n* documento; **documentary** [-'mɛntərɪ] *adj* documental ▷ *n* documental *m*; **documentation** [-mɛn'teɪʃən] *n* documentación *f*
dodge [dɔdʒ] *n* (*fig*) truco ▷ *vt* evadir; (*blow*) esquivar
dodgy ['dɔdʒɪ] *adj* (*inf: uncertain*) dudoso; (*suspicious*) sospechoso; (*risky*) arriesgado
does [dʌz] *vb see* **do**
doesn't ['dʌznt] = **does not**
dog [dɔg] *n* perro ▷ *vt* seguir los pasos de; (*bad luck*) perseguir; **doggy bag** ['dɔgɪ-] *n* *bolsa para llevarse las sobras de la comida*
do-it-yourself ['du:ɪtjɔ:'sɛlf] *n* bricolaje *m*
dole [dəul] (BRIT) *n* (*payment*) subsidio de paro; **on the ~** parado
doll [dɔl] *n* muñeca; (US: *inf: woman*) muñeca, gachí *f*
dollar ['dɔlə*] *n* dólar *m*
dolphin ['dɔlfɪn] *n* delfín *m*
dome [dəum] *n* (*Arch*) cúpula
domestic [də'mɛstɪk] *adj* (*animal, duty*) doméstico; (*flight, policy*) nacional; **domestic appliance** *n* aparato *m* doméstico, aparato *m* de uso doméstico
dominant ['dɔmɪnənt] *adj* dominante
dominate ['dɔmɪneɪt] *vt* dominar
domino ['dɔmɪnəu] (*pl* **~es**) *n* ficha de dominó; **dominoes** *n* (*game*)

dominó

donate [də'neɪt] *vt* donar; **donation** [də'neɪʃən] *n* donativo

done [dʌn] *pp of* **do**

donkey ['dɔŋkɪ] *n* burro

donor ['dəunə*] *n* donante *mf*; **donor card** *n* carnet *m* de donante

don't [dəunt] = **do not**

donut ['dəunʌt] (US) *n* = **doughnut**

doodle ['du:dl] *vi* hacer dibujitos *or* garabatos

doom [du:m] *n* (*fate*) suerte *f* ▷ *vt*: **to be ~ed to failure** estar condenado al fracaso

door [dɔ:*] *n* puerta; **doorbell** *n* timbre *m*; **door handle** *n* tirador *m*; (*of car*) manija; **doorknob** *n* pomo *m* de la puerta, manilla *f* (LAM); **doorstep** *n* peldaño; **doorway** *n* entrada, puerta

dope [dəup] *n* (*inf: illegal drug*) droga; (*: person*) imbécil *mf* ▷ *vt* (*horse etc*) drogar

dormitory ['dɔ:mɪtrɪ] *n* (BRIT) dormitorio; (US) colegio mayor

DOS *n abbr* (= *disk operating system*) DOS *m*

dosage ['dəusɪdʒ] *n* dosis *f inv*

dose [dəus] *n* dosis *f inv*

dot [dɔt] *n* punto ▷ *vi*: **~ted with** salpicado de; **on the ~** en punto; **dotcom** [dɔt'kɔm] *n* puntocom *f inv*; **dotted line** ['dɔtɪd-] *n*: **to sign on the dotted line** firmar

double ['dʌbl] *adj* doble ▷ *adv* (*twice*): **to cost ~** costar el doble ▷ *n* doble *m* ▷ *vt* doblar ▷ *vi* doblarse; **on the ~, at the ~** (BRIT) corriendo; **double back** *vi* (*person*) volver sobre sus pasos; **double bass** *n* contrabajo; **double bed** *n* cama de matrimonio; **double-check** *vt* volver a revisar ▷ *vi*: **I'll double-check** voy a revisarlo otra vez; **double-click** *vi* (*Comput*) hacer doble clic; **double-cross** *vt* (*trick*) engañar; (*betray*) traicionar; **doubledecker** *n* autobús *m* de dos pisos; **double glazing** (BRIT) *n* doble acristalamiento; **double room** *n* habitación *f* doble; **doubles** *n* (*Tennis*) juego de dobles; **double yellow lines** *npl* (BRIT: *Aut*) *línea doble amarilla de prohibido aparcar*, ≈ línea *fsg* amarilla continua

doubt [daut] *n* duda ▷ *vt* dudar; (*suspect*) dudar de; **to ~ that** dudar que; **doubtful** *adj* dudoso; (*person*): **to be doubtful about sth** tener dudas sobre algo; **doubtless** *adv* sin duda

dough [dəu] *n* masa, pasta; **doughnut** (US **donut**) *n* ≈ rosquilla

dove [dʌv] *n* paloma

down [daun] *n* (*feathers*) plumón *m*, flojel *m* ▷ *adv* (*downwards*) abajo, hacia abajo; (*on the ground*) por *or* en tierra ▷ *prep* abajo ▷ *vt* (*inf: drink*) beberse; **~ with X!** ¡abajo X!; **down-and-out** *n* vagabundo/a; **downfall** *n* caída, ruina; **downhill** *adv*: **to go downhill** (*also fig*) ir cuesta abajo

Downing Street ['daunɪŋ-] *n* (BRIT) Downing Street *f*

down: download *vt* (*Comput*) bajar; **downright** *adj* (*nonsense, lie*) manifiesto; (*refusal*) terminante

Down's syndrome ['daunz-] *n* síndrome *m* de Down

down: downstairs *adv* (*below*) (en el piso de) abajo; (*downwards*) escaleras abajo; **down-to-earth** *adj* práctico; **downtown** *adv* en el centro de la ciudad; **down under** *adv* en Australia (*or* Nueva Zelanda); **downward** [-wəd] *adj, adv* hacia abajo; **downwards** [-wədz] *adv* hacia abajo

doz. *abbr* = **dozen**

doze [dəuz] *vi* dormitar

dozen ['dʌzn] *n* docena; **a ~ books** una docena de libros; **~s of** cantidad de

Dr. *abbr* = **doctor; drive**

drab [dræb] *adj* gris, monótono

draft [drɑ:ft] *n* (*first copy*) borrador *m*; (*Pol: of bill*) anteproyecto; (US: *call-up*) quinta ▷ *vt* (*plan*) preparar; (*write roughly*) hacer un borrador de; *see also* **draught**

drag [dræg] *vt* arrastrar; (*river*) dragar,

rastrear ▷vi (*time*) pasar despacio; (*play, film etc*) hacerse pesado ▷n (*inf*) lata; (*women's clothing*): **in ~** vestido de travesti; **to ~ and drop** (*Comput*) arrastrar y soltar

dragon ['drægən] n dragón m

dragonfly ['drægənflaɪ] n libélula

drain [dreɪn] n desaguadero; (*in street*) sumidero; (*source of loss*): **to be a ~ on** consumir, agotar ▷vt (*land, marshes*) desaguar; (*reservoir*) desecar; (*vegetables*) escurrir ▷vi escurrirse; **drainage** n (*act*) desagüe m; (*Med, Agr*) drenaje m; (*sewage*) alcantarillado; **drainpipe** n tubo de desagüe

drama ['drɑːmə] n (*art*) teatro; (*play*) drama m; (*excitement*) emoción f; **dramatic** [drə'mætɪk] adj dramático; (*sudden, marked*) espectacular

drank [dræŋk] pt of **drink**

drape [dreɪp] vt (*cloth*) colocar; (*flag*) colgar; **drapes** npl (US) cortinas fpl

drastic ['dræstɪk] adj (*measure*) severo; (*change*) radical, drástico

draught [drɑːft] (US **draft**) n (*of air*) corriente f de aire; (*Naut*) calado; **on ~** (*beer*) de barril; **draught beer** n cerveza de barril; **draughts** (BRIT) n (*game*) juego de damas

draw [drɔː] (*pt* **drew**, *pp* **drawn**) vt (*picture*) dibujar; (*cart*) tirar de; (*curtain*) correr; (*take out*) sacar; (*attract*) atraer; (*money*) retirar; (*wages*) cobrar ▷vi (*Sport*) empatar ▷n (*Sport*) empate m; (*lottery*) sorteo; **draw out** vi (*lengthen*) alargarse ▷vt sacar; **draw up** vi (*stop*) pararse ▷vt (*chair*) acercar; (*document*) redactar; **drawback** n inconveniente m, desventaja

drawer [drɔː*] n cajón m

drawing ['drɔːɪŋ] n dibujo; **drawing pin** (BRIT) n chincheta; **drawing room** n salón m

drawn [drɔːn] pp of **draw**

dread [drɛd] n pavor m, terror m ▷vt temer, tener miedo *or* pavor a; **dreadful** adj horroroso

dream [driːm] (*pt, pp* **~ed** *or* **~t**) n sueño ▷vt, vi soñar; **dreamer** n soñador(a) m/f

dreamt [drɛmt] pt, pp of **dream**

dreary ['drɪərɪ] adj monótono

drench [drɛntʃ] vt empapar

dress [drɛs] n vestido; (*clothing*) ropa ▷vt vestir; (*wound*) vendar ▷vi vestirse; **to get ~ed** vestirse; **dress up** vi vestirse de etiqueta; (*in fancy dress*) disfrazarse; **dress circle** (BRIT) n principal m; **dresser** n (*furniture*) aparador m; (: US) cómoda (con espejo); **dressing** n (*Med*) vendaje m; (*Culin*) aliño; **dressing gown** (BRIT) n bata; **dressing room** n (*Theatre*) camarín m; (*Sport*) vestuario; **dressing table** n tocador m; **dressmaker** n modista, costurera

drew [druː] pt of **draw**

dribble ['drɪbl] vi (*baby*) babear ▷vt (*ball*) regatear

dried [draɪd] adj (*fruit*) seco; (*milk*) en polvo

drier ['draɪə*] n = **dryer**

drift [drɪft] n (*of current etc*) flujo; (*of snow*) ventisquero; (*meaning*) significado ▷vi (*boat*) ir a la deriva; (*sand, snow*) amontonarse

drill [drɪl] n (*drill bit*) broca; (*tool for DIY etc*) taladro; (*of dentist*) fresa; (*for mining etc*) perforadora, barrena; (*Mil*) instrucción f ▷vt perforar, taladrar; (*troops*) enseñar la instrucción a ▷vi (*for oil*) perforar

drink [drɪŋk] (*pt* **drank**, *pp* **drunk**) n bebida; (*sip*) trago ▷vt, vi beber; **to have a ~** tomar algo; tomar una copa *or* un trago; **a ~ of water** un trago de agua; **drink-driving** n: **to be charged with drink-driving** ser acusado de conducir borracho *or* en estado de embriaguez; **drinker** n bebedor(a) m/f; **drinking water** n agua potable

drip [drɪp] n (*act*) goteo; (*one drip*) gota; (*Med*) gota a gota m ▷vi gotear

drive [draɪv] (*pt* **drove**, *pp* **driven**) n (*journey*) viaje m (en coche); (*also:* **~way**) entrada; (*energy*) energía, vigor *m*; (*Comput*: *also*: **disk ~**) drive *m* ▷ *vt* (*car*) conducir (SP), manejar (LAM); (*nail*) clavar; (*push*) empujar; (*Tech*: *motor*) impulsar ▷ *vi* (*Aut*: *at controls*) conducir; (: *travel*) pasearse en coche; **left-/right-hand ~** conducción *f* a la izquierda/derecha; **to ~ sb mad** volverle loco a algn; **drive out** *vt* (*force out*) expulsar, echar; **drive-in** *adj* (*esp* US): **drive-in cinema** autocine *m*

driven ['drɪvn] *pp of* **drive**

driver ['draɪvə*] *n* conductor(a) *m/f* (SP), chofer *mf* (LAM); (*of taxi, bus*) chófer *mf* (SP), chofer *mf* (LAM); **driver's license** (US) *n* carnet *m* de conducir

driveway ['draɪvweɪ] *n* entrada

driving ['draɪvɪŋ] *n* el conducir (SP), el manejar (LAM); **driving instructor** *n* profesor(a) *m/f* de autoescuela (SP), instructor(a) *m/f* de manejo (LAM); **driving lesson** *n* clase *f* de conducir (SP) *or* manejar (LAM); **driving licence** (BRIT) *n* licencia de manejo (LAM), carnet *m* de conducir (SP); **driving test** *n* examen *m* de conducir (SP) *or* manejar (LAM)

drizzle ['drɪzl] *n* llovizna

droop [dru:p] *vi* (*flower*) marchitarse; (*shoulders*) encorvarse; (*head*) inclinarse

drop [drɔp] *n* (*of water*) gota; (*lessening*) baja; (*fall*) caída ▷ *vt* dejar caer; (*voice, eyes, price*) bajar; (*passenger*) dejar; (*omit*) omitir ▷ *vi* (*object*) caer; (*wind*) amainar; **drop in** *vi* (*inf*: *visit*): **to drop in (on)** pasar por casa (de); **drop off** *vi* (*sleep*) dormirse ▷ *vt* (*passenger*) dejar; **drop out** *vi* (*withdraw*) retirarse

drought [draut] *n* sequía

drove [drəuv] *pt of* **drive**

drown [draun] *vt* ahogar ▷ *vi* ahogarse

drowsy ['drauzɪ] *adj* soñoliento; **to be ~** tener sueño

drug [drʌg] *n* medicamento; (*narcotic*) droga ▷ *vt* drogar; **to be on ~s** drogarse; **drug addict** *n* drogadicto/a; **drug dealer** *n* traficante *mf* de drogas; **druggist** (US) *n* farmacéutico; **drugstore** (US) *n* farmacia

drum [drʌm] *n* tambor *m*; (*for oil, petrol*) bidón *m*; **drums** *npl* batería; **drummer** *n* tambor *m*

drunk [drʌŋk] *pp of* **drink** ▷ *adj* borracho ▷ *n* (*also*: **~ard**) borracho/a; **drunken** *adj* borracho; (*laughter, party*) de borrachos

dry [draɪ] *adj* seco; (*day*) sin lluvia; (*climate*) árido, seco ▷ *vt* secar; (*tears*) enjugarse ▷ *vi* secarse; **dry off** *vi* secarse ▷ *vt* secar; **dry up** *vi* (*river*) secarse; **dry-cleaner's** *n* tintorería; **dry-cleaning** *n* lavado en seco; **dryer** *n* (*for hair*) secador *m*; (US: *for clothes*) secadora

DSS *n abbr* = **Department of Social Security**

D&T (BRIT: *Scol*) *n abbr* (= *design and technology*) ≈ dibujo y tecnología

DTP *n abbr* (= *desk-top publishing*) autoedición *f*

dual ['djuəl] *adj* doble; **dual carriageway** (BRIT) *n* carretera de doble calzada

dubious ['dju:bɪəs] *adj* indeciso; (*reputation, company*) sospechoso

duck [dʌk] *n* pato ▷ *vi* agacharse

due [dju:] *adj* (*owed*): **he is ~ £10** se le deben 10 libras; (*expected*: *event*): **the meeting is ~ on Wednesday** la reunión tendrá lugar el miércoles; (: *arrival*): **the train is ~ at 8am** el tren tiene su llegada para las 8; (*proper*) debido ▷ *n*: **to give sb his (***or* **her) ~** ser justo con algn ▷ *adv*: **~ north** derecho al norte

duel ['djuəl] *n* duelo

duet [dju:'ɛt] *n* dúo

dug [dʌg] *pt, pp of* **dig**

duke [dju:k] *n* duque *m*

dull [dʌl] *adj* (*light*) débil; (*stupid*) torpe; (*boring*) pesado; (*sound, pain*) sordo; (*weather, day*) gris ▷ *vt* (*pain, grief*) aliviar; (*mind, senses*) entorpecer

dumb [dʌm] *adj* mudo; (*pej*: *stupid*) estúpido

dummy ['dʌmɪ] *n* (*tailor's dummy*)

maniquí *m*; (*mock-up*) maqueta; (BRIT: *for baby*) chupete *m* ▷ *adj* falso, postizo
dump [dʌmp] *n* (*also*: **rubbish ~**) basurero, vertedero; (*inf*: *place*) cuchitril *m* ▷ *vt* (*put down*) dejar; (*get rid of*) deshacerse de; (*Comput*: *data*) transferir
dumpling ['dʌmplɪŋ] *n* *bola de masa hervida*
dune [dju:n] *n* duna
dungarees [dʌŋgə'ri:z] *npl* mono
dungeon ['dʌndʒən] *n* calabozo
duplex ['dju:plɛks] *n* dúplex *m*
duplicate [*n* 'dju:plɪkət, *vb* 'dju:plɪkeɪt] *n* duplicado ▷ *vt* duplicar; (*photocopy*) fotocopiar; (*repeat*) repetir; **in ~** por duplicado
durable ['djuərəbl] *adj* duradero
duration [djuə'reɪʃən] *n* duración *f*
during ['djuərɪŋ] *prep* durante
dusk [dʌsk] *n* crepúsculo, anochecer *m*
dust [dʌst] *n* polvo ▷ *vt* quitar el polvo a, desempolvar; (*cake etc*): **to ~ with** espolvorear de; **dustbin** (BRIT) *n* cubo *or* bote *m* (MEX) *or* tacho (SC) de la basura; **duster** *n* paño, trapo; **dustman** (BRIT: *irreg*) *n* basurero; **dustpan** *n* cogedor *m*; **dusty** *adj* polvoriento
Dutch [dʌtʃ] *adj* holandés/esa ▷ *n* (*Ling*) holandés *m*; **the Dutch** *npl* los holandeses; **to go ~** (*inf*) pagar cada uno lo suyo; **Dutchman** (*irreg*) *n* holandés *m*; **Dutchwoman** (*irreg*) *n* holandésa
duty ['dju:tɪ] *n* deber *m*; (*tax*) derechos *mpl* de aduana; **on ~** de servicio; (*at night etc*) de guardia; **off ~** libre (de servicio); **duty-free** *adj* libre de impuestos
duvet ['du:veɪ] (BRIT) *n* edredón *m*
DVD *n abbr* (= *digital versatile or video disc*) DVD *m*; **DVD player** *n* lector *m* de DVD; **DVD writer** *n* grabadora de DVD
dwarf [dwɔ:f] (*pl* **dwarves**) *n* enano/a ▷ *vt* empequeñecer
dwell [dwɛl] (*pt, pp* **dwelt**) *vi* morar; **dwell on** *vt fus* explayarse en
dwelt [dwɛlt] *pt, pp of* **dwell**
dwindle ['dwɪndl] *vi* disminuir
dye [daɪ] *n* tinte *m* ▷ *vt* teñir
dying ['daɪɪŋ] *adj* moribundo
dynamic [daɪ'næmɪk] *adj* dinámico
dynamite ['daɪnəmaɪt] *n* dinamita
dyslexia [dɪs'lɛksɪə] *n* dislexia
dyslexic [dɪs'lɛksɪk] *adj, n* disléxico/a *m/f*

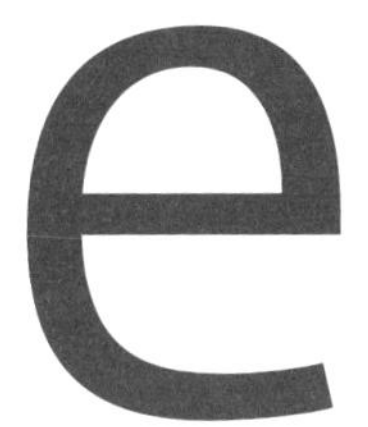

E [iː] *n* (*Mus*) mi *m*
E111 *n abbr* (= *form E111*) impreso E111
each [iːtʃ] *adj* cada *inv* ▷ *pron* cada uno; **~ other** el uno al otro; **they hate ~ other** se odian (entre ellos *or* mutuamente); **they have 2 books ~** tienen 2 libros por persona
eager ['iːgə*] *adj* (*keen*) entusiasmado; **to be ~ to do sth** tener muchas ganas de hacer algo, impacientarse por hacer algo; **to be ~ for** tener muchas ganas de
eagle ['iːgl] *n* águila
ear [ɪə*] *n* oreja; oído; (*of corn*) espiga; **earache** *n* dolor *m* de oídos; **eardrum** *n* tímpano
earl [əːl] *n* conde *m*
earlier ['əːlɪə*] *adj* anterior ▷ *adv* antes
early ['əːlɪ] *adv* temprano; (*before time*) con tiempo, con anticipación ▷ *adj* temprano; (*settlers etc*) primitivo; (*death, departure*) prematuro; (*reply*) pronto; **to have an ~ night** acostarse temprano; **in the ~** *or* **~ in the spring/19th century** a principios de primavera/del siglo diecinueve; **early retirement** *n* jubilación *f* anticipada
earmark ['ɪəmɑːk] *vt*: **to ~ (for)** reservar (para), destinar (a)
earn [əːn] *vt* (*salary*) percibir; (*interest*) devengar; (*praise*) merecerse
earnest ['əːnɪst] *adj* (*wish*) fervoroso; (*person*) serio, formal; **in ~** en serio
earnings ['əːnɪŋz] *npl* (*personal*) sueldo, ingresos *mpl*; (*company*) ganancias *fpl*
ear: earphones *npl* auriculares *mpl*; **earplugs** *npl* tapones *mpl* para los oídos; **earring** *n* pendiente *m*, arete *m*
earth [əːθ] *n* tierra; (BRIT *Elec*) cable *m* de toma de tierra ▷ *vt* (BRIT *Elec*) conectar a tierra; **earthquake** *n* terremoto
ease [iːz] *n* facilidad *f*; (*comfort*) comodidad *f* ▷ *vt* (*lessen: problem*) mitigar; (*: pain*) aliviar; (*: tension*) reducir; **to ~ sth in/out** meter/sacar algo con cuidado; **at ~!** (*Mil*) ¡descansen!
easily ['iːzɪlɪ] *adv* fácilmente
east [iːst] *n* este *m* ▷ *adj* del este, oriental; (*wind*) este ▷ *adv* al este, hacia el este; **the E~** el Oriente; (*Pol*) los países del Este; **eastbound** *adj* en dirección este
Easter ['iːstə*] *n* Pascua (de Resurrección); **Easter egg** *n* huevo de Pascua
eastern ['iːstən] *adj* del este, oriental; (*oriental*) oriental
Easter Sunday *n* Domingo de Resurrección
easy ['iːzɪ] *adj* fácil; (*simple*) sencillo; (*comfortable*) holgado, cómodo; (*relaxed*) tranquilo ▷ *adv*: **to take it** *or* **things ~** (*not worry*) tomarlo con calma; (*rest*) descansar; **easy-going** *adj* acomodadizo
eat [iːt] (*pt* **ate**, *pp* **eaten**) *vt* comer; **eat out** *vi* comer fuera
eavesdrop ['iːvzdrɔp] *vi*: **to ~ (on)** escuchar a escondidas

e-book ['i:buk] *n* libro electrónico
e-business ['i:bɪznɪs] *n* (*company*) negocio electrónico; (*commerce*) comercio electrónico
EC *n abbr* (= *European Community*) CE *f*
eccentric [ɪk'sɛntrɪk] *adj, n* excéntrico/a *m/f*
echo ['ɛkəu] (*pl* **~es**) *n* eco ▷ *vt* (*sound*) repetir ▷ *vi* resonar, hacer eco
eclipse [ɪ'klɪps] *n* eclipse *m*
eco-friendly ['i:kəufrɛndlɪ] *adj* ecológico
ecological [i:kə'lɔdʒɪkl] *adj* ecológico
ecology [ɪ'kɔlədʒɪ] *n* ecología
e-commerce *n abbr* comercio electrónico
economic [i:kə'nɔmɪk] *adj* económico; (*business etc*) rentable; **economical** *adj* económico; **economics** *n* (*Scol*) economía ▷ *npl* (*of project etc*) rentabilidad *f*
economist [ɪ'kɔnəmɪst] *n* economista *m/f*
economize [ɪ'kɔnəmaɪz] *vi* economizar, ahorrar
economy [ɪ'kɔnəmɪ] *n* economía; **economy class** *n* (*Aviat*) clase *f* económica; **economy class syndrome** *n* síndrome *m* de la clase turista
ecstasy ['ɛkstəsɪ] *n* éxtasis *m inv*; (*drug*) éxtasis *m inv*; **ecstatic** [ɛks'tætɪk] *adj* extático
eczema ['ɛksɪmə] *n* eczema *m*
edge [ɛdʒ] *n* (*of knife*) filo; (*of object*) borde *m*; (*of lake*) orilla ▷ *vt* (*Sewing*) ribetear; **on ~** (*fig*) = **edgy**; **to ~ away from** alejarse poco a poco de
edgy ['ɛdʒɪ] *adj* nervioso, inquieto
edible ['ɛdɪbl] *adj* comestible
Edinburgh ['ɛdɪnbərə] *n* Edimburgo
edit ['ɛdɪt] *vt* (*be editor of*) dirigir; (*text, report*) corregir, preparar; **edition** [ɪ'dɪʃən] *n* edición *f*; **editor** *n* (*of newspaper*) director(a) *m/f*; (*of column*): **foreign/political editor** encargado de la sección de extranjero/política; (*of book*) redactor(a) *m/f*; **editorial** [-'tɔ:rɪəl] *adj* editorial ▷ *n* editorial *m*
educate ['ɛdjukeɪt] *vt* (*gen*) educar; (*instruct*) instruir; **educated** ['ɛdjukeɪtɪd] *adj* culto
education [ɛdju'keɪʃən] *n* educación *f*; (*schooling*) enseñanza; (*Scol*) pedagogía; **educational** *adj* (*policy etc*) educacional; (*experience*) docente; (*toy*) educativo
eel [i:l] *n* anguila
eerie ['ɪərɪ] *adj* misterioso
effect [ɪ'fɛkt] *n* efecto ▷ *vt* efectuar, llevar a cabo; **to take ~** (*law*) entrar en vigor *or* vigencia; (*drug*) surtir efecto; **in ~** en realidad; **effects** *npl* (*property*) efectos *mpl*; **effective** *adj* eficaz; (*actual*) verdadero; **effectively** *adv* eficazmente; (*in reality*) efectivamente
efficiency [ɪ'fɪʃənsɪ] *n* eficiencia; rendimiento
efficient [ɪ'fɪʃənt] *adj* eficiente; (*machine*) de buen rendimiento; **efficiently** *adv* eficientemente, de manera eficiente
effort ['ɛfət] *n* esfuerzo; **effortless** *adj* sin ningún esfuerzo; (*style*) natural
e.g. *adv abbr* (= *exempli gratia*) p. ej.
egg [ɛg] *n* huevo; **hard-boiled/soft-boiled ~** huevo duro/pasado por agua; **eggcup** *n* huevera; **eggplant** (*esp US*) *n* berenjena; **eggshell** *n* cáscara de huevo; **egg white** *n* clara de huevo; **egg yolk** *n* yema de huevo
ego ['i:gəu] *n* ego
Egypt ['i:dʒɪpt] *n* Egipto; **Egyptian** [ɪ'dʒɪpʃən] *adj, n* egipcio/a *m/f*
eight [eɪt] *num* ocho; **eighteen** *num* diez y ocho, dieciocho; **eighteenth** *adj* decimoctavo; **the eighteenth floor** la planta dieciocho; **the eighteenth of August** el dieciocho de agosto; **eighth** *num* octavo; **eightieth** ['eɪtɪɪθ] *adj* octogésimo
eighty ['eɪtɪ] *num* ochenta
Eire ['ɛərə] *n* Eire *m*
either ['aɪðə*] *adj* cualquiera de los dos; (*both, each*) cada ▷ *pron*: **~ (of**

them) cualquiera (de los dos) ▷ *adv* tampoco ▷ *conj*: **~ yes or no** o sí o no; **on ~ side** en ambos lados; **I don't like ~** no me gusta ninguno/a de los(las) dos; **no, I don't ~** no, yo tampoco

eject [ɪ'dʒɛkt] *vt* echar, expulsar; (*tenant*) desahuciar

elaborate [*adj* ɪ'læbərɪt, *vb* ɪ'læbəreɪt] *adj* (*complex*) complejo ▷ *vt* (*expand*) ampliar; (*refine*) refinar ▷ *vi* explicar con más detalles

elastic [ɪ'læstɪk] *n* elástico ▷ *adj* elástico; (*fig*) flexible; **elastic band** (BRIT) *n* gomita

elbow ['ɛlbəu] *n* codo

elder ['ɛldə*] *adj* mayor ▷ *n* (*tree*) saúco; (*person*) mayor; **elderly** *adj* de edad, mayor ▷ *npl*: **the elderly** los mayores

eldest ['ɛldɪst] *adj, n* el/la mayor

elect [ɪ'lɛkt] *vt* elegir ▷ *adj*: **the president ~** el presidente electo; **to ~ to do** optar por hacer; **election** *n* elección *f*; **electoral** *adj* electoral; **electorate** *n* electorado

electric [ɪ'lɛktrɪk] *adj* eléctrico; **electrical** *adj* eléctrico; **electric blanket** *n* manta eléctrica; **electric fire** *n* estufa eléctrica; **electrician** [ɪlɛk'trɪʃən] *n* electricista *mf*; **electricity** [ɪlɛk'trɪsɪtɪ] *n* electricidad *f*; **electric shock** *n* electrochoque *m*; **electrify** [ɪ'lɛktrɪfaɪ] *vt* (*Rail*) electrificar; (*fig*: *audience*) electrizar

electronic [ɪlɛk'trɔnɪk] *adj* electrónico; **electronic mail** *n* correo electrónico; **electronics** *n* electrónica

elegance ['ɛlɪgəns] *n* elegancia

elegant ['ɛlɪgənt] *adj* elegante

element ['ɛlɪmənt] *n* elemento; (*of kettle etc*) resistencia

elementary [ɛlɪ'mɛntərɪ] *adj* elemental; (*primitive*) rudimentario; **elementary school** (US) *n* escuela de enseñanza primaria

elephant ['ɛlɪfənt] *n* elefante *m*

elevate ['ɛlɪveɪt] *vt* (*gen*) elevar; (*in rank*) ascender

elevator ['ɛlɪveɪtə*] (US) *n* ascensor *m*; (*in warehouse etc*) montacargas *m inv*

eleven [ɪ'lɛvn] *num* once; **eleventh** *num* undécimo

eligible ['ɛlɪdʒəbl] *adj*: **an ~ young man/woman** un buen partido; **to be ~ for sth** llenar los requisitos para algo

eliminate [ɪ'lɪmɪneɪt] *vt* (*suspect, possibility*) descartar

elm [ɛlm] *n* olmo

eloquent ['ɛləkwənt] *adj* elocuente

else [ɛls] *adv*: **something ~** otra cosa; **somewhere ~** en otra parte; **everywhere ~** en todas partes menos aquí; **where ~?** ¿dónde más?, ¿en qué otra parte?; **there was little ~ to do** apenas quedaba otra cosa que hacer; **nobody ~ spoke** no habló nadie más; **elsewhere** *adv* (*be*) en otra parte; (*go*) a otra parte

elusive [ɪ'lu:sɪv] *adj* esquivo; (*quality*) difícil de encontrar

e-mail ['i:meɪl] *n abbr* (= *electronic mail*) correo electrónico, e-mail *m*; **e-mail address** *n* dirección *f* electrónica, email *m*

embankment [ɪm'bæŋkmənt] *n* terraplén *m*

embargo [ɪm'bɑ:gəu] (*pl* **~es**) *n* (*Comm, Naut*) embargo; (*prohibition*) prohibición *f*; **to put an ~ on sth** poner un embargo en algo

embark [ɪm'bɑ:k] *vi* embarcarse ▷ *vt* embarcar; **to ~ on** (*journey*) emprender; (*course of action*) lanzarse a

embarrass [ɪm'bærəs] *vt* avergonzar; (*government etc*) dejar en mal lugar; **embarrassed** *adj* (*laugh, silence*) embarazoso

> Be careful not to translate **embarrassed** by the Spanish word *embarazada*.

embarrassing *adj* (*situation*) violento; (*question*) embarazoso; **embarrassment** *n* (*shame*) vergüenza; (*problem*): **to be an embarrassment for sb** poner en un aprieto a algn

embassy ['ɛmbəsɪ] *n* embajada
embrace [ɪm'breɪs] *vt* abrazar, dar un abrazo a; (*include*) abarcar ▷*vi* abrazarse ▷*n* abrazo
embroider [ɪm'brɔɪdə*] *vt* bordar; **embroidery** *n* bordado
embryo ['ɛmbrɪəu] *n* embrión *m*
emerald ['ɛmərəld] *n* esmeralda
emerge [ɪ'mə:dʒ] *vi* salir; (*arise*) surgir
emergency [ɪ'mə:dʒənsɪ] *n* crisis *f inv*; **in an ~** en caso de urgencia; **state of ~** estado de emergencia; **emergency brake** (*US*) *n* freno de mano; **emergency exit** *n* salida de emergencia; **emergency landing** *n* aterrizaje *m* forzoso; **emergency room** (*US*: *Med*) *n* sala *f* de urgencias; **emergency services** *npl* (*fire, police, ambulance*) servicios *mpl* de urgencia *or* emergencia
emigrate ['ɛmɪgreɪt] *vi* emigrar; **emigration** [ɛmɪ'greɪʃən] *n* emigración *f*
eminent ['ɛmɪnənt] *adj* eminente
emissions [ɪ'mɪʃənz] *npl* emisión *f*
emit [ɪ'mɪt] *vt* emitir; (*smoke*) arrojar; (*smell*) despedir; (*sound*) producir
emotion [ɪ'məuʃən] *n* emoción *f*; **emotional** *adj* (*needs*) emocional; (*person*) sentimental; (*scene*) conmovedor(a), emocionante; (*speech*) emocionado
emperor ['ɛmpərə*] *n* emperador *m*
emphasis ['ɛmfəsɪs] (*pl* **-ses**) *n* énfasis *m inv*
emphasize ['ɛmfəsaɪz] *vt* (*word, point*) subrayar, recalcar; (*feature*) hacer resaltar
empire ['ɛmpaɪə*] *n* imperio
employ [ɪm'plɔɪ] *vt* emplear; **employee** [-'i:] *n* empleado/a; **employer** *n* patrón/ona *m/f*; empresario; **employment** *n* (*work*) trabajo; **employment agency** *n* agencia de colocaciones
empower [ɪm'pauə*] *vt*: **to ~ sb to do sth** autorizar a algn para hacer algo
empress ['ɛmprɪs] *n* emperatriz *f*
emptiness ['ɛmptɪnɪs] *n* vacío; (*of life etc*) vaciedad *f*
empty ['ɛmptɪ] *adj* vacío; (*place*) desierto; (*house*) desocupado; (*threat*) vano ▷*vt* vaciar; (*place*) dejar vacío ▷*vi* vaciarse; (*house etc*) quedar desocupado; **empty-handed** *adj* con las manos vacías
EMU *n abbr* (= *European Monetary Union*) UME *f*
emulsion [ɪ'mʌlʃən] *n* emulsión *f*; (*also*: **~ paint**) pintura emulsión
enable [ɪ'neɪbl] *vt*: **to ~ sb to do sth** permitir a algn hacer algo
enamel [ɪ'næməl] *n* esmalte *m*; (*also*: **~ paint**) pintura esmaltada
enchanting [ɪn'tʃɑ:ntɪŋ] *adj* encantador(a)
encl. *abbr* (= *enclosed*) adj
enclose [ɪn'kləuz] *vt* (*land*) cercar; (*letter etc*) adjuntar; **please find ~d** le mandamos adjunto
enclosure [ɪn'kləuʒə*] *n* cercado, recinto
encore [ɔŋ'kɔ:*] *excl* ¡otra!, ¡bis! ▷*n* bis *m*
encounter [ɪn'kauntə*] *n* encuentro ▷*vt* encontrar, encontrarse con; (*difficulty*) tropezar con
encourage [ɪn'kʌrɪdʒ] *vt* alentar, animar; (*activity*) fomentar; (*growth*) estimular; **encouragement** *n* estímulo; (*of industry*) fomento
encouraging [ɪn'kʌrɪdʒɪŋ] *adj* alentador(a)
encyclop(a)edia [ɛnsaɪkləu'pi:dɪə] *n* enciclopedia
end [ɛnd] *n* fin *m*; (*of table*) extremo; (*of street*) final *m*; (*Sport*) lado ▷*vt* terminar, acabar; (*also*: **bring to an ~, put an ~ to**) acabar con ▷*vi* terminar, acabar; **in the ~** al fin; **on ~** (*object*) de punta, de cabeza; **to stand on ~** (*hair*) erizarse; **for hours on ~** hora tras hora; **end up** *vi*: **to end up in** terminar en; (*place*) ir a parar en
endanger [ɪn'deɪndʒə*] *vt* poner en peligro; **an ~ed species** una especie en

peligro de extinción

endearing [ɪn'dɪərɪŋ] *adj* simpático, atractivo

endeavour [ɪn'dɛvə*] (US **endeavor**) *n* esfuerzo; (*attempt*) tentativa ▷ *vi*: **to ~ to do** esforzarse por hacer; (*try*) procurar hacer

ending ['ɛndɪŋ] *n* (*of book*) desenlace *m*; (*Ling*) terminación *f*

endless ['ɛndlɪs] *adj* interminable, inacabable

endorse [ɪn'dɔːs] *vt* (*cheque*) endosar; (*approve*) aprobar; **endorsement** *n* (*on driving licence*) nota de inhabilitación

endurance [ɪn'djuərəns] *n* resistencia

endure [ɪn'djuə*] *vt* (*bear*) aguantar, soportar ▷ *vi* (*last*) durar

enemy ['ɛnəmɪ] *adj, n* enemigo/a *m/f*

energetic [ɛnə'dʒɛtɪk] *adj* enérgico

energy ['ɛnədʒɪ] *n* energía

enforce [ɪn'fɔːs] *vt* (*Law*) hacer cumplir

engaged [ɪn'geɪdʒd] *adj* (BRIT: *busy, in use*) ocupado; (*betrothed*) prometido; **to get ~** prometerse; **engaged tone** (BRIT) *n* (*Tel*) señal *f* de comunicando

engagement [ɪn'geɪdʒmənt] *n* (*appointment*) compromiso, cita; (*booking*) contratación *f*; (*to marry*) compromiso; (*period*) noviazgo; **engagement ring** *n* anillo de prometida

engaging [ɪn'geɪdʒɪŋ] *adj* atractivo

engine ['ɛndʒɪn] *n* (*Aut*) motor *m*; (*Rail*) locomotora

engineer [ɛndʒɪ'nɪə*] *n* ingeniero; (BRIT: *for repairs*) mecánico; (*on ship, US Rail*) maquinista *m*; **engineering** *n* ingeniería

England ['ɪŋglənd] *n* Inglaterra

English ['ɪŋglɪʃ] *adj* inglés/esa ▷ *n* (*Ling*) inglés *m*; **the English** *npl* los ingleses *mpl*; **English Channel** *n*: **the English Channel** (el Canal de) la Mancha; **Englishman** (*irreg*) *n* inglés *m*; **Englishwoman** (*irreg*) *n* inglésa

engrave [ɪn'greɪv] *vt* grabar

engraving [ɪn'greɪvɪŋ] *n* grabado

enhance [ɪn'hɑːns] *vt* (*gen*) aumentar; (*beauty*) realzar

enjoy [ɪn'dʒɔɪ] *vt* (*health, fortune*) disfrutar de, gozar de; (*like*) gustarle a algn; **to ~ o.s.** divertirse; **enjoyable** *adj* agradable; (*amusing*) divertido; **enjoyment** *n* (*joy*) placer *m*; (*activity*) diversión *f*

enlarge [ɪn'lɑːdʒ] *vt* aumentar; (*broaden*) extender; (*Phot*) ampliar ▷ *vi*: **to ~ on** (*subject*) tratar con más detalles; **enlargement** *n* (*Phot*) ampliación *f*

enlist [ɪn'lɪst] *vt* alistar; (*support*) conseguir ▷ *vi* alistarse

enormous [ɪ'nɔːməs] *adj* enorme

enough [ɪ'nʌf] *adj*: **~ time/books** bastante tiempo/bastantes libros ▷ *pron* bastante(s) ▷ *adv*: **big ~** bastante grande; **he has not worked ~** no ha trabajado bastante; **have you got ~?** ¿tiene usted bastante(s)?; **~ to eat** (lo) suficiente *or* (lo) bastante para comer; **~!** ¡basta ya!; **that's ~, thanks** con eso basta, gracias; **I've had ~ of him** estoy harto de él; **... which, funnily** *or* **oddly ~ ...** ... lo que, por extraño que parezca ...

enquire [ɪn'kwaɪə*] *vt, vi* = **inquire**

enquiry [ɪn'kwaɪərɪ] *n* (*official investigation*) investigación

enrage [ɪn'reɪdʒ] *vt* enfurecer

enrich [ɪn'rɪtʃ] *vt* enriquecer

enrol [ɪn'rəul] (US **enroll**) *vt* (*members*) inscribir; (*Scol*) matricular ▷ *vi* inscribirse; matricularse; **enrolment** (US **enrollment**) *n* inscripción *f*; matriculación *f*

en route [ɔn'ruːt] *adv* durante el viaje

en suite [ɔn'swiːt] *adj*: **with ~ bathroom** con baño

ensure [ɪn'ʃuə*] *vt* asegurar

entail [ɪn'teɪl] *vt* suponer

enter ['ɛntə*] *vt* (*room*) entrar en; (*club*) hacerse socio de; (*army*) alistarse en; (*sb for a competition*) inscribir; (*write* *down*) anotar, apuntar; (*Comput*) meter ▷*vi* entrar

enterprise ['ɛntəpraɪz] *n* empresa; (*spirit*) iniciativa; **free ~** la libre empresa; **private ~** la iniciativa privada; **enterprising** *adj* emprendedor(a)

entertain [ɛntə'teɪn] *vt* (*amuse*) divertir; (*invite: guest*) invitar (a casa); (*idea*) abrigar; **entertainer** *n* artista *mf*; **entertaining** *adj* divertido, entretenido; **entertainment** *n* (*amusement*) diversión *f*; (*show*) espectáculo

enthusiasm [ɪn'θu:zɪæzəm] *n* entusiasmo

enthusiast [ɪn'θu:zɪæst] *n* entusiasta *mf*; **enthusiastic** [-'æstɪk] *adj* entusiasta; **to be enthusiastic about** entusiasmarse por

entire [ɪn'taɪə*] *adj* entero; **entirely** *adv* totalmente

entitle [ɪn'taɪtl] *vt*: **to ~ sb to sth** dar a algn derecho a algo; **entitled** *adj* (*book*) titulado; **to be entitled to do** tener derecho a hacer

entrance [*n* 'ɛntrəns, *vb* ɪn'trɑ:ns] *n* entrada ▷*vt* encantar, hechizar; **to gain ~ to** (*university etc*) ingresar en; **entrance examination** *n* examen *m* de ingreso; **entrance fee** *n* cuota; **entrance ramp** (*US*) *n* (*Aut*) rampa de acceso

entrant ['ɛntrənt] *n* (*in race, competition*) participante *mf*; (*in examination*) candidato/a

entrepreneur [ɔntrəprə'nə:] *n* empresario

entrust [ɪn'trʌst] *vt*: **to ~ sth to sb** confiar algo a algn

entry ['ɛntrɪ] *n* entrada; (*in competition*) participación *f*; (*in register*) apunte *m*; (*in account*) partida; (*in reference book*) artículo; **"no ~"** "prohibido el paso"; (*Aut*) "dirección prohibida"; **entry phone** *n* portero automático

envelope ['ɛnvələup] *n* sobre *m*

envious ['ɛnvɪəs] *adj* envidioso; (*look*) de envidia

environment [ɪn'vaɪərnmənt] *n* (*surroundings*) entorno; (*natural world*): **the ~** el medio ambiente; **environmental** [-'mɛntl] *adj* ambiental; medioambiental; **environmentally** [-'mɛntəlɪ] *adv*: **environmentally sound/friendly** ecológico

envisage [ɪn'vɪzɪdʒ] *vt* prever

envoy ['ɛnvɔɪ] *n* enviado

envy ['ɛnvɪ] *n* envidia ▷*vt* tener envidia a; **to ~ sb sth** envidiar algo a algn

epic ['ɛpɪk] *n* épica ▷*adj* épico

epidemic [ɛpɪ'dɛmɪk] *n* epidemia

epilepsy ['ɛpɪlɛpsɪ] *n* epilepsia

epileptic [ɛpɪ'lɛptɪk] *adj, n* epiléptico/a *m/f*; **epileptic fit** [ɛpɪ'lɛptɪk-] *n* ataque *m* de epilepsia, acceso *m* epiléptico

episode ['ɛpɪsəud] *n* episodio

equal ['i:kwl] *adj* igual; (*treatment*) equitativo ▷*n* igual *mf* ▷*vt* ser igual a; (*fig*) igualar; **to be ~ to** (*task*) estar a la altura de; **equality** [i:'kwɔlɪtɪ] *n* igualdad *f*; **equalize** *vi* (*Sport*) empatar; **equally** *adv* igualmente; (*share etc*) a partes iguales

equation [ɪ'kweɪʒən] *n* (*Math*) ecuación *f*

equator [ɪ'kweɪtə*] *n* ecuador *m*

equip [ɪ'kwɪp] *vt* equipar; (*person*) proveer; **to be well ~ped** estar bien equipado; **equipment** *n* equipo; (*tools*) avíos *mpl*

equivalent [ɪ'kwɪvələnt] *adj*: **~ (to)** equivalente (a) ▷*n* equivalente *m*

ER *abbr* (BRIT: = *Elizabeth Regina*) *la reina Isabel*; (US: *Med*) = **emergency room**

era ['ɪərə] *n* era, época

erase [ɪ'reɪz] *vt* borrar; **eraser** *n* goma de borrar

erect [ɪ'rɛkt] *adj* erguido ▷*vt* erigir, levantar; (*assemble*) montar; **erection** [-ʃən] *n* construcción *f*; (*assembly*) montaje *m*; (*Physiol*) erección *f*

ERM *n abbr* (= *Exchange Rate Mechanism*) *tipo de cambio europeo*
erode [ɪ'rəud] *vt* (*Geo*) erosionar; (*metal*) corroer, desgastar; (*fig*) desgastar
erosion [ɪ'rəuʒən] *n* erosión *f*; desgaste *m*
erotic [ɪ'rɔtɪk] *adj* erótico
errand ['ɛrnd] *n* recado (SP), mandado (LAM)
erratic [ɪ'rætɪk] *adj* desigual, poco uniforme
error ['ɛrə*] *n* error *m*, equivocación *f*
erupt [ɪ'rʌpt] *vi* entrar en erupción; (*fig*) estallar; **eruption** [ɪ'rʌpʃən] *n* erupción *f*; (*of war*) estallido
escalate ['ɛskəleɪt] *vi* extenderse, intensificarse
escalator ['ɛskəleɪtə*] *n* escalera móvil
escape [ɪ'skeɪp] *n* fuga ▷ *vi* escaparse; (*flee*) huir, evadirse; (*leak*) fugarse ▷ *vt* (*responsibility etc*) evitar, eludir; (*consequences*) escapar a; (*elude*): **his name ~s me** no me sale su nombre; **to ~ from** (*place*) escaparse de; (*person*) escaparse a
escort [*n* 'ɛskɔ:t, *vb* ɪ'skɔ:t] *n* acompañante *mf*; (*Mil*) escolta *mf* ▷ *vt* acompañar
especially [ɪ'spɛʃlɪ] *adv* (*above all*) sobre todo; (*particularly*) en particular, especialmente
espionage ['ɛspɪənɑ:ʒ] *n* espionaje *m*
essay ['ɛseɪ] *n* (*Literature*) ensayo; (*Scol: short*) redacción *f*; (*: long*) trabajo
essence ['ɛsns] *n* esencia
essential [ɪ'sɛnʃl] *adj* (*necessary*) imprescindible; (*basic*) esencial; **essentially** *adv* esencialmente; **essentials** *npl* lo imprescindible, lo esencial
establish [ɪ'stæblɪʃ] *vt* establecer; (*prove*) demostrar; (*relations*) entablar; (*reputation*) ganarse; **establishment** *n* establecimiento; **the Establishment** la clase dirigente
estate [ɪ'steɪt] *n* (*land*) finca, hacienda; (*inheritance*) herencia; (BRIT: *also*: **housing ~**) urbanización *f*; **estate agent** (BRIT) *n* agente *mf* inmobiliario/a; **estate car** (BRIT) *n* furgoneta
estimate [*n* 'ɛstɪmət, *vb* 'ɛstɪmeɪt] *n* estimación *f*, apreciación *f*; (*assessment*) tasa, cálculo; (*Comm*) presupuesto ▷ *vt* estimar, tasar; calcular
etc *abbr* (= *et cetera*) etc
eternal [ɪ'tə:nl] *adj* eterno
eternity [ɪ'tə:nɪtɪ] *n* eternidad *f*
ethical ['ɛθɪkl] *adj* ético; **ethics** ['ɛθɪks] *n* ética ▷ *npl* moralidad *f*
Ethiopia [i:θɪ'əupɪə] *n* Etiopia
ethnic ['ɛθnɪk] *adj* étnico; **ethnic minority** *n* minoría étnica
e-ticket ['i:tɪkɪt] *n* billete *m* electrónico (SP), boleto electrónico (LAM)
etiquette ['ɛtɪkɛt] *n* etiqueta
EU *n abbr* (= *European Union*) UE *f*
euro *n* euro
Europe ['juərəp] *n* Europa; **European** [-'pi:ən] *adj*, *n* europeo/a *m/f*; **European Community** *n* Comunidad *f* Europea; **European Union** *n* Unión *f* Europea
Eurostar® ['juərəustɑ:*] *n* Eurostar® *m*
evacuate [ɪ'vækjueɪt] *vt* (*people*) evacuar; (*place*) desocupar
evade [ɪ'veɪd] *vt* evadir, eludir
evaluate [ɪ'væljueɪt] *vt* evaluar; (*value*) tasar; (*evidence*) interpretar
evaporate [ɪ'væpəreɪt] *vi* evaporarse; (*fig*) desvanecerse
eve [i:v] *n*: **on the ~ of** en vísperas de
even ['i:vn] *adj* (*level*) llano; (*smooth*) liso; (*speed, temperature*) uniforme; (*number*) par ▷ *adv* hasta, incluso; (*introducing a comparison*) aún, todavía; **~ if, ~ though** aunque *+subjun*; **~ more** aun más; **~ so** aun así; **not ~** ni siquiera; **~ he was there** hasta él estuvo allí; **~ on Sundays** incluso los

domingos; **to get ~ with sb** ajustar cuentas con algn

evening ['i:vnɪŋ] *n* tarde *f*; (*late*) noche *f*; **in the ~** por la tarde; **evening class** *n* clase *f* nocturna; **evening dress** *n* (*no pl: formal clothes*) traje *m* de etiqueta; (*woman's*) traje *m* de noche

event [ɪ'vɛnt] *n* suceso, acontecimiento; (*Sport*) prueba; **in the ~ of** en caso de; **eventful** *adj* (*life*) activo; (*day*) ajetreado

eventual [ɪ'vɛntʃuəl] *adj* final

> Be careful not to translate **eventual** by the Spanish word *eventual*.

eventually *adv* (*finally*) finalmente; (*in time*) con el tiempo

ever ['ɛvə*] *adv* (*at any time*) nunca, jamás; (*at all times*) siempre; (*in question*): **why ~ not?** ¿y por qué no?; **the best ~** lo nunca visto; **have you ~ seen it?** ¿lo ha visto usted alguna vez?; **better than ~** mejor que nunca; **~ since** *adv* desde entonces ▷ *conj* después de que; **evergreen** *n* árbol *m* de hoja perenne

KEYWORD

every ['ɛvrɪ] *adj* **1** (*each*) cada; **every one of them** (*persons*) todos ellos/as; (*objects*) cada uno de ellos/as; **every shop in the town was closed** todas las tiendas de la ciudad estaban cerradas

2 (*all possible*) todo/a; **I gave you every assistance** te di toda la ayuda posible; **I have every confidence in him** tiene toda mi confianza; **we wish you every success** te deseamos toda suerte de éxitos

3 (*showing recurrence*) todo/a; **every day/week** todos los días/todas las semanas; **every other car had been broken into** habían forzado uno de cada dos coches; **she visits me every other/third day** me visita cada dos/tres días; **every now and then** de vez en cuando

every: everybody *pron* = **everyone**; **everyday** *adj* (*daily*) cotidiano, de todos los días; (*usual*) acostumbrado; **everyone** *pron* todos/as, todo el mundo; **everything** *pron* todo; **this shop sells everything** esta tienda vende de todo; **everywhere** *adv*: **I've been looking for you everywhere** te he estado buscando por todas partes; **everywhere you go you meet ...** en todas partes encuentras ...

evict [ɪ'vɪkt] *vt* desahuciar

evidence ['ɛvɪdəns] *n* (*proof*) prueba; (*of witness*) testimonio; (*sign*) indicios *mpl*; **to give ~** prestar declaración, dar testimonio

evident ['ɛvɪdənt] *adj* evidente, manifiesto; **evidently** *adv* por lo visto

evil ['i:vl] *adj* malo; (*influence*) funesto ▷ *n* mal *m*

evoke [ɪ'vəuk] *vt* evocar

evolution [i:və'lu:ʃən] *n* evolución *f*

evolve [ɪ'vɔlv] *vt* desarrollar ▷ *vi* evolucionar, desarrollarse

ewe [ju:] *n* oveja

ex [eks] (*inf*) *n*: **my ~** mi ex

ex- [ɛks] *prefix* ex

exact [ɪg'zækt] *adj* exacto; (*person*) meticuloso ▷ *vt*: **to ~ sth (from)** exigir algo (de); **exactly** *adv* exactamente; (*indicating agreement*) exacto

exaggerate [ɪg'zædʒəreɪt] *vt, vi* exagerar; **exaggeration** [-'reɪʃən] *n* exageración *f*

exam [ɪg'zæm] *n abbr* (*Scol*) = **examination**

examination [ɪgzæmɪ'neɪʃən] *n* examen *m*; (*Med*) reconocimiento

examine [ɪg'zæmɪn] *vt* examinar; (*inspect*) inspeccionar, escudriñar; (*Med*) reconocer; **examiner** *n* examinador(a) *m/f*

example [ɪg'za:mpl] *n* ejemplo; **for ~** por ejemplo

exasperated [ɪg'za:spəreɪtɪd] *adj* exasperado

excavate ['ɛkskəveɪt] *vt* excavar

exceed [ɪk'si:d] *vt* (*amount*) exceder;

(*number*) pasar de; (*speed limit*) sobrepasar; (*powers*) excederse en; (*hopes*) superar; **exceedingly** *adv* sumamente, sobremanera

excel [ɪk'sɛl] *vi* sobresalir; **to ~ o.s** lucirse

excellence ['ɛksələns] *n* excelencia

excellent ['ɛksələnt] *adj* excelente

except [ɪk'sɛpt] *prep* (*also*: **~ for, ~ing**) excepto, salvo ▷ *vt* exceptuar, excluir; **~ if/when** excepto si/cuando; **~ that** salvo que; **exception** [ɪk'sɛpʃən] *n* excepción *f*; **to take exception to** ofenderse por; **exceptional** [ɪk'sɛpʃənl] *adj* excepcional; **exceptionally** [ɪk'sepʃənəlɪ] *adv* excepcionalmente, extraordinariamente

excerpt ['ɛksəːpt] *n* extracto

excess [ɪk'sɛs] *n* exceso; **excess baggage** *n* exceso de equipaje; **excessive** *adj* excesivo

exchange [ɪks'tʃeɪndʒ] *n* intercambio; (*conversation*) diálogo; (*also*: **telephone ~**) central *f* (telefónica) ▷ *vt*: **to ~ (for)** cambiar (por); **exchange rate** *n* tipo de cambio

excite [ɪk'saɪt] *vt* (*stimulate*) estimular; (*arouse*) excitar; **excited** *adj*: **to get excited** emocionarse; **excitement** *n* (*agitation*) excitación *f*; (*exhilaration*) emoción *f*; **exciting** *adj* emocionante

exclaim [ɪk'skleɪm] *vi* exclamar; **exclamation** [ɛksklə'meɪʃən] *n* exclamación *f*; **exclamation mark** *n* punto de admiración; **exclamation point** (US) = **exclamation mark**

exclude [ɪk'skluːd] *vt* excluir; exceptuar

excluding [ɪks'kluːdɪŋ] *prep*: **~ VAT** IVA no incluido

exclusion [ɪk'skluːʒən] *n* exclusión *f*; **to the ~ of** con exclusión de

exclusive [ɪk'skluːsɪv] *adj* exclusivo; (*club, district*) selecto; **~ of tax** excluyendo impuestos; **exclusively** *adv* únicamente

excruciating [ɪk'skruːʃɪeɪtɪŋ] *adj* (*pain*) agudísimo, atroz; (*noise, embarrassment*) horrible

excursion [ɪk'skəːʃən] *n* (*tourist excursion*) excursión *f*

excuse [*n* ɪk'skjuːs, *vb* ɪk'skjuːz] *n* disculpa, excusa; (*pretext*) pretexto ▷ *vt* (*justify*) justificar; (*forgive*) disculpar, perdonar; **to ~ sb from doing sth** dispensar a algn de hacer algo; **~ me!** (*attracting attention*) ¡por favor!; (*apologizing*) ¡perdón!; **if you will ~ me** con su permiso

ex-directory ['ɛksdɪ'rɛktərɪ] (BRIT) *adj* que no consta en la guía

execute ['ɛksɪkjuːt] *vt* (*plan*) realizar; (*order*) cumplir; (*person*) ajusticiar, ejecutar; **execution** [-'kjuːʃən] *n* realización *f*; cumplimiento; ejecución *f*

executive [ɪg'zɛkjutɪv] *n* (*person, committee*) ejecutivo; (*Pol*: *committee*) poder *m* ejecutivo ▷ *adj* ejecutivo

exempt [ɪg'zɛmpt] *adj*: **~ from** exento de ▷ *vt*: **to ~ sb from** eximir a algn de

exercise ['ɛksəsaɪz] *n* ejercicio ▷ *vt* (*patience*) usar de; (*right*) valerse de; (*dog*) llevar de paseo; (*mind*) preocupar ▷ *vi* (*also*: **to take ~**) hacer ejercicio(s); **exercise book** *n* cuaderno

exert [ɪg'zəːt] *vt* ejercer; **to ~ o.s.** esforzarse; **exertion** [-ʃən] *n* esfuerzo

exhale [eks'heɪl] *vt* despedir ▷ *vi* exhalar

exhaust [ɪg'zɔːst] *n* (*Aut*: *also*: **~ pipe**) escape *m*; (: *fumes*) gases *mpl* de escape ▷ *vt* agotar; **exhausted** *adj* agotado; **exhaustion** [ɪg'zɔːstʃən] *n* agotamiento; **nervous exhaustion** postración *f* nerviosa

exhibit [ɪg'zɪbɪt] *n* (*Art*) obra expuesta; (*Law*) objeto expuesto ▷ *vt* (*show*: *emotions*) manifestar; (: *courage, skill*) demostrar; (*paintings*) exponer; **exhibition** [ɛksɪ'bɪʃən] *n* exposición *f*; (*of talent etc*) demostración *f*

exhilarating [ɪg'zɪləreɪtɪŋ] *adj* estimulante, tónico

exile ['ɛksaɪl] *n* exilio; (*person*) exiliado/a ▷ *vt* desterrar, exiliar
exist [ɪg'zɪst] *vi* existir; (*live*) vivir; **existence** *n* existencia; **existing** *adj* existente, actual
exit ['ɛksɪt] *n* salida ▷ *vi* (*Theatre*) hacer mutis; (*Comput*) salir (del sistema)

Be careful not to translate **exit** by the Spanish word *éxito*.

exit ramp (US) *n* (*Aut*) vía de acceso
exotic [ɪg'zɔtɪk] *adj* exótico
expand [ɪk'spænd] *vt* ampliar; (*number*) aumentar ▷ *vi* (*population*) aumentar; (*trade etc*) expandirse; (*gas, metal*) dilatarse
expansion [ɪk'spænʃən] *n* (*of population*) aumento; (*of trade*) expansión *f*
expect [ɪk'spɛkt] *vt* esperar; (*require*) contar con; (*suppose*) suponer ▷ *vi*: **to be ~ing** (*pregnant woman*) estar embarazada; **expectation** [ɛkspɛk'teɪʃən] *n* (*hope*) esperanza; (*belief*) expectativa
expedition [ɛkspə'dɪʃən] *n* expedición *f*
expel [ɪk'spɛl] *vt* arrojar; (*from place*) expulsar
expenditure [ɪks'pɛndɪtʃə*] *n* gastos *mpl*, desembolso; consumo
expense [ɪk'spɛns] *n* gasto, gastos *mpl*; (*high cost*) costa; **expenses** *npl* (*Comm*) gastos *mpl*; **at the ~ of** a costa de; **expense account** *n* cuenta de gastos
expensive [ɪk'spɛnsɪv] *adj* caro, costoso
experience [ɪk'spɪərɪəns] *n* experiencia ▷ *vt* experimentar; (*suffer*) sufrir; **experienced** *adj* experimentado
experiment [ɪk'spɛrɪmənt] *n* experimento ▷ *vi* hacer experimentos; **experimental** [-'mɛntl] *adj* experimental; **the process is still at the experimental stage** el proceso está todavía en prueba
expert ['ɛkspə:t] *adj* experto, perito ▷ *n* experto/a, perito/a; (*specialist*) especialista *mf*; **expertise** [-'ti:z] *n* pericia
expire [ɪk'spaɪə*] *vi* caducar, vencer; **expiry** *n* vencimiento; **expiry date** *n* (*of medicine, food item*) fecha de caducidad
explain [ɪk'spleɪn] *vt* explicar; **explanation** [ɛksplə'neɪʃən] *n* explicación *f*
explicit [ɪk'splɪsɪt] *adj* explícito
explode [ɪk'spləud] *vi* estallar, explotar; (*population*) crecer rápidamente; (*with anger*) reventar
exploit [*n* 'ɛksplɔɪt, *vb* ɪk'splɔɪt] *n* hazaña ▷ *vt* explotar; **exploitation** [-'teɪʃən] *n* explotación *f*
explore [ɪk'splɔ:*] *vt* explorar; (*fig*) examinar; investigar; **explorer** *n* explorador(a) *m/f*
explosion [ɪk'spləuʒən] *n* explosión *f*; **explosive** [ɪks'pləusɪv] *adj, n* explosivo
export [*vb* ɛk'spɔ:t, *n, cpd* 'ɛkspɔ:t] *vt* exportar ▷ *n* (*process*) exportación *f*; (*product*) producto de exportación ▷ *cpd* de exportación; **exporter** *n* exportador *m*
expose [ɪk'spəuz] *vt* exponer; (*unmask*) desenmascarar; **exposed** *adj* expuesto
exposure [ɪk'spəuʒə*] *n* exposición *f*; (*publicity*) publicidad *f*; (*Phot: speed*) velocidad *f* de obturación; (*: shot*) fotografía; **to die from ~** (*Med*) morir de frío
express [ɪk'sprɛs] *adj* (*definite*) expreso, explícito; (BRIT: *letter etc*) urgente ▷ *n* (*train*) rápido ▷ *vt* expresar; **expression** [ɪk'sprɛʃən] *n* expresión *f*; (*of actor etc*) sentimiento; **expressway** (US) *n* (*urban motorway*) autopista
exquisite [ɛk'skwɪzɪt] *adj* exquisito
extend [ɪk'stɛnd] *vt* (*visit, street*) prolongar; (*building*) ampliar; (*invitation*) ofrecer ▷ *vi* (*land*)

extenderse; (*period of time*) prolongarse
extension [ɪk'stɛnʃən] *n* extensión *f*; (*building*) ampliación *f*; (*of time*) prolongación *f*; (*Tel: in private house*) línea derivada; (*: in office*) extensión *f*; **extension lead** *n* alargador *m*, alargadera
extensive [ɪk'stɛnsɪv] *adj* extenso; (*damage*) importante; (*knowledge*) amplio
extent [ɪk'stɛnt] *n* (*breadth*) extensión *f*; (*scope*) alcance *m*; **to some ~** hasta cierto punto; **to the ~ of ...** hasta el punto de ...; **to such an ~ that ...** hasta tal punto que ...; **to what ~?** ¿hasta qué punto?
exterior [ɛk'stɪərɪə*] *adj* exterior, externo ▷ *n* exterior *m*
external [ɛk'stə:nl] *adj* externo
extinct [ɪk'stɪŋkt] *adj* (*volcano*) extinguido; (*race*) extinto; **extinction** *n* extinción *f*
extinguish [ɪk'stɪŋgwɪʃ] *vt* extinguir, apagar
extra ['ɛkstrə] *adj* adicional ▷ *adv* (*in addition*) de más ▷ *n* (*luxury, addition*) extra *m*; (*Cinema, Theatre*) extra *mf*, comparsa *mf*
extract [*vb* ɪk'strækt, *n* 'ɛkstrækt] *vt* sacar; (*tooth*) extraer; (*money, promise*) obtener ▷ *n* extracto
extradite ['ɛkstrədaɪt] *vt* extraditar
extraordinary [ɪk'strɔ:dnrɪ] *adj* extraordinario; (*odd*) raro
extravagance [ɪk'strævəgəns] *n* derroche *m*, despilfarro; (*thing bought*) extravagancia
extravagant [ɪk'strævəgənt] *adj* (*lavish: person*) pródigo; (*: gift*) (demasiado) caro; (*wasteful*) despilfarrador(a)
extreme [ɪk'stri:m] *adj* extremo, extremado ▷ *n* extremo; **extremely** *adv* sumamente, extremadamente
extremist [ɪk'stri:mɪst] *adj, n* extremista *m/f*
extrovert ['ɛkstrəvə:t] *n* extrovertido/a
eye [aɪ] *n* ojo ▷ *vt* mirar de soslayo, ojear; **to keep an ~ on** vigilar; **eyeball** *n* globo ocular; **eyebrow** *n* ceja; **eyedrops** *npl* gotas *fpl* para los ojos, colino; **eyelash** *n* pestaña; **eyelid** *n* párpado; **eyeliner** *n* delineador *m* (de ojos); **eyeshadow** *n* sombreador *m* de ojos; **eyesight** *n* vista; **eye witness** *n* testigo *mf* presencial

F [ɛf] *n* (*Mus*) fa *m*
fabric ['fæbrɪk] *n* tejido, tela
Be careful not to translate **fabric** by the Spanish word *fábrica*.
fabulous ['fæbjuləs] *adj* fabuloso
face [feɪs] *n* (*Anat*) cara, rostro; (*of clock*) esfera (SP), cara (LAM); (*of mountain*) cara, ladera; (*of building*) fachada ▷ *vt* (*direction*) estar de cara a; (*situation*) hacer frente a; (*facts*) aceptar; **~ down** (*person, card*) boca abajo; **to lose ~** desprestigiarse; **to make** *or* **pull a ~** hacer muecas; **in the ~ of** (*difficulties etc*) ante; **on the ~ of it** a primera vista; **~ to ~** cara a cara; **face up to** *vt fus* hacer frente a, arrostrar; **face cloth** (BRIT) *n* manopla; **face pack** *n* (BRIT) mascarilla
facial ['feɪʃəl] *adj* de la cara ▷ *n* (*also*: **beauty ~**) tratamiento facial, limpieza
facilitate [fə'sɪlɪteɪt] *vt* facilitar
facilities [fə'sɪlɪtɪz] *npl* (*buildings*) instalaciones *fpl*; (*equipment*) servicios *mpl*; **credit ~** facilidades *fpl* de crédito
fact [fækt] *n* hecho; **in ~** en realidad
faction ['fækʃən] *n* facción *f*
factor ['fæktə*] *n* factor *m*
factory ['fæktərɪ] *n* fábrica
factual ['fæktjuəl] *adj* basado en los hechos
faculty ['fækəltɪ] *n* facultad *f*; (US: *teaching staff*) personal *m* docente
fad [fæd] *n* novedad *f*, moda
fade [feɪd] *vi* desteñirse; (*sound, smile*) desvanecerse; (*light*) apagarse; (*flower*) marchitarse; (*hope, memory*) perderse; **fade away** *vi* (*sound*) apagarse
fag [fæg] (BRIT: *inf*) *n* (*cigarette*) pitillo (SP), cigarro
Fahrenheit ['fɑːrənhaɪt] *n* Fahrenheit *m*
fail [feɪl] *vt* (*candidate, test*) suspender (SP), reprobar (LAM); (*memory etc*) fallar a ▷ *vi* suspender (SP), reprobar (LAM); (*be unsuccessful*) fracasar; (*strength, brakes*) fallar; (*light*) acabarse; **to ~ to do sth** (*neglect*) dejar de hacer algo; (*be unable*) no poder hacer algo; **without ~** sin falta; **failing** *n* falta, defecto ▷ *prep* a falta de; **failure** ['feɪljə*] *n* fracaso; (*person*) fracasado/a; (*mechanical etc*) fallo
faint [feɪnt] *adj* débil; (*recollection*) vago; (*mark*) apenas visible ▷ *n* desmayo ▷ *vi* desmayarse; **to feel ~** estar mareado, marearse; **faintest** *adj*: **I haven't the faintest idea** no tengo la más remota idea; **faintly** *adv* débilmente; (*vaguely*) vagamente
fair [fɛə*] *adj* justo; (*hair, person*) rubio; (*weather*) bueno; (*good enough*) regular; (*considerable*) considerable ▷ *adv* (*play*) limpio ▷ *n* feria; (BRIT: *funfair*) parque *m* de atracciones; **fairground** *n* recinto ferial; **fair-haired** *adj* (*person*) rubio; **fairly** *adv* (*justly*) con justicia; (*quite*) bastante; **fair trade** *n* comercio justo; **fairway** *n* (*Golf*) calle *f*
fairy ['fɛərɪ] *n* hada; **fairy tale** *n* cuento de hadas
faith [feɪθ] *n* fe *f*; (*trust*) confianza; (*sect*) religión *f*; **faithful** *adj*

(*loyal: troops etc*) leal; (*spouse*) fiel; (*account*) exacto; **faithfully** *adv* fielmente; **yours faithfully** (BRIT: *in letters*) le saluda atentamente

fake [feɪk] *n* (*painting etc*) falsificación *f*; (*person*) impostor(a) *m/f* ▷ *adj* falso ▷ *vt* fingir; (*painting etc*) falsificar

falcon [ˈfɔːlkən] *n* halcón *m*

fall [fɔːl] (*pt* **fell**, *pp* **fallen**) *n* caída; (*in price etc*) descenso; (US) otoño ▷ *vi* caer(se); (*price*) bajar, descender; **falls** *npl* (*waterfall*) cascada, salto de agua; **to ~ flat** (*on one's face*) caerse (boca abajo); (*plan*) fracasar; (*joke, story*) no hacer gracia; **fall apart** *vi* deshacerse; **fall down** *vi* (*person*) caerse; (*building, hopes*) derrumbarse; **fall for** *vt fus* (*trick*) dejarse engañar por; (*person*) enamorarse de; **fall off** *vi* caerse; (*diminish*) disminuir; **fall out** *vi* (*friends etc*) reñir; (*hair, teeth*) caerse; **fall over** *vi* caer(se); **fall through** *vi* (*plan, project*) fracasar

fallen [ˈfɔːlən] *pp of* **fall**

fallout [ˈfɔːlaut] *n* lluvia radioactiva

false [fɔːls] *adj* falso; **under ~ pretences** con engaños; **false alarm** *n* falsa alarma; **false teeth** (BRIT) *npl* dentadura postiza

fame [feɪm] *n* fama

familiar [fəˈmɪlɪə*] *adj* conocido, familiar; (*tone*) de confianza; **to be ~ with** (*subject*) conocer (bien); **familiarize** [fəˈmɪlɪəraɪz] *vt*: **to familiarize o.s. with** familiarizarse con

family [ˈfæmɪlɪ] *n* familia; **family doctor** *n* médico/a de cabecera; **family planning** *n* planificación *f* familiar

famine [ˈfæmɪn] *n* hambre *f*, hambruna

famous [ˈfeɪməs] *adj* famoso, célebre

fan [fæn] *n* abanico; (*Elec*) ventilador *m*; (*of pop star*) fan *mf*; (*Sport*) hincha *mf* ▷ *vt* abanicar; (*fire, quarrel*) atizar

fanatic [fəˈnætɪk] *n* fanático/a

fan belt *n* correa del ventilador

fan club *n* club *m* de fans

fancy [ˈfænsɪ] *n* (*whim*) capricho, antojo; (*imagination*) imaginación *f* ▷ *adj* (*luxury*) lujoso, de lujo ▷ *vt* (*feel like, want*) tener ganas de; (*imagine*) imaginarse; (*think*) creer; **to take a ~ to sb** tomar cariño a algn; **he fancies her** (*inf*) le gusta (ella) mucho; **fancy dress** *n* disfraz *m*

fan heater *n* calefactor *m* de aire

fantasize [ˈfæntəsaɪz] *vi* fantasear, hacerse ilusiones

fantastic [fænˈtæstɪk] *adj* (*enormous*) enorme; (*strange, wonderful*) fantástico

fantasy [ˈfæntəzɪ] *n* (*dream*) sueño; (*unreality*) fantasía

fanzine [ˈfænziːn] *n* fanzine *m*

FAQs *abbr* (= *frequently asked questions*) preguntas frecuentes

far [fɑː*] *adj* (*distant*) lejano ▷ *adv* lejos; (*much, greatly*) mucho; **~ away, ~ off** (a lo) lejos; **~ better** mucho mejor; **~ from** lejos de; **by ~** con mucho; **go as ~ as the farm** vaya hasta la granja; **as ~ as I know** que yo sepa; **how ~?** ¿hasta dónde?; (*fig*) ¿hasta qué punto?

farce [fɑːs] *n* farsa

fare [fɛə*] *n* (*on trains, buses*) precio (del billete); (*in taxi: cost*) tarifa; (*food*) comida; **half ~** medio pasaje *m*; **full ~** pasaje completo

Far East *n*: **the ~** el Extremo Oriente

farewell [fɛəˈwɛl] *excl, n* adiós *m*

farm [fɑːm] *n* cortijo (SP), hacienda (LAM), rancho (MEX), estancia (RPL) ▷ *vt* cultivar; **farmer** *n* granjero, hacendado (LAM), ranchero (MEX), estanciero (RPL); **farmhouse** *n* granja, casa del hacendado (LAM), rancho (MEX), casco de la estancia (RPL); **farming** *n* agricultura; (*of crops*) cultivo; (*of animals*) cría; **farmyard** *n* corral *m*

far-reaching [fɑːˈriːtʃɪŋ] *adj* (*reform, effect*) de gran alcance

fart [fɑːt] (*inf!*) *vi* tirarse un pedo (*!*)

farther [ˈfɑːðə*] *adv* más lejos, más allá ▷ *adj* más lejano

farthest ['fɑ:ðɪst] *superlative of* **far**
fascinate ['fæsɪneɪt] *vt* fascinar; **fascinated** *adj* fascinado
fascinating ['fæsɪneɪtɪŋ] *adj* fascinante
fascination [-'neɪʃən] *n* fascinación *f*
fascist ['fæʃɪst] *adj, n* fascista *m/f*
fashion ['fæʃən] *n* moda; (*fashion industry*) industria de la moda; (*manner*) manera ▷ *vt* formar; **in ~** a la moda; **out of ~** pasado de moda; **fashionable** *adj* de moda; **fashion show** *n* desfile *m* de modelos
fast [fɑ:st] *adj* rápido; (*dye, colour*) resistente; (*clock*): **to be ~** estar adelantado ▷ *adv* rápidamente, de prisa; (*stuck, held*) firmemente ▷ *n* ayuno ▷ *vi* ayunar; **~ asleep** profundamente dormido
fasten ['fɑ:sn] *vt* atar, sujetar; (*coat, belt*) abrochar ▷ *vi* atarse; abrocharse
fast food *n* comida rápida, platos *mpl* preparados
fat [fæt] *adj* gordo; (*book*) grueso; (*profit*) grande, pingüe ▷ *n* grasa; (*on person*) carnes *fpl*; (*lard*) manteca
fatal ['feɪtl] *adj* (*mistake*) fatal; (*injury*) mortal; **fatality** [fə'tælɪtɪ] *n* (*road death etc*) víctima; **fatally** *adv* fatalmente; mortalmente
fate [feɪt] *n* destino; (*of person*) suerte *f*
father ['fɑ:ðə*] *n* padre *m*; **Father Christmas** *n* Papá *m* Noel; **father-in-law** *n* suegro
fatigue [fə'ti:g] *n* fatiga, cansancio
fattening ['fætnɪŋ] *adj* (*food*) que hace engordar
fatty ['fætɪ] *adj* (*food*) graso ▷ *n* (*inf*) gordito/a, gordinflón/ona *m/f*
faucet ['fɔ:sɪt] (US) *n* grifo (SP), llave *f*, canilla (RPL)
fault [fɔ:lt] *n* (*blame*) culpa; (*defect*: *in person, machine*) defecto; (*Geo*) falla ▷ *vt* criticar; **it's my ~** es culpa mía; **to find ~ with** criticar, poner peros a; **at ~** culpable; **faulty** *adj* defectuoso
fauna ['fɔ:nə] *n* fauna
favour *etc* ['feɪvə*] (US **favor** *etc*) *n* favor *m*; (*approval*) aprobación *f* ▷ *vt* (*proposition*) estar a favor de, aprobar; (*assist*) ser propicio a; **to do sb a ~** hacer un favor a algn; **to find ~ with sb** caer en gracia a algn; **in ~ of** a favor de; **favourable** *adj* favorable; **favourite** ['feɪvrɪt] *adj, n* favorito, preferido
fawn [fɔ:n] *n* cervato ▷ *adj* (*also*: **~-coloured**) color de cervato, leonado ▷ *vi*: **to ~ (up)on** adular
fax [fæks] *n* (*document*) fax *m*; (*machine*) telefax *m* ▷ *vt* mandar por telefax
FBI (US) *n abbr* (= *Federal Bureau of Investigation*) ≈ BIC *f* (SP)
fear [fɪə*] *n* miedo, temor *m* ▷ *vt* tener miedo de, temer; **for ~ of** por si; **fearful** *adj* temeroso, miedoso; (*awful*) terrible; **fearless** *adj* audaz
feasible ['fi:zəbl] *adj* factible
feast [fi:st] *n* banquete *m*; (*Rel*: *also*: **~ day**) fiesta ▷ *vi* festejar
feat [fi:t] *n* hazaña
feather ['fɛðə*] *n* pluma
feature ['fi:tʃə*] *n* característica; (*article*) artículo de fondo ▷ *vt* (*film*) presentar ▷ *vi*: **to ~ in** tener un papel destacado en; **features** *npl* (*of face*) facciones *fpl*; **feature film** *n* largometraje *m*
Feb. *abbr* (= *February*) feb
February ['fɛbruərɪ] *n* febrero
fed [fɛd] *pt, pp of* **feed**
federal ['fɛdərəl] *adj* federal
federation [fɛdə'reɪʃən] *n* federación *f*
fed up [fɛd'ʌp] *adj*: **to be ~ (with)** estar harto (de)
fee [fi:] *n* pago; (*professional*) derechos *mpl*, honorarios *mpl*; (*of club*) cuota; **school ~s** matrícula
feeble ['fi:bl] *adj* débil; (*joke*) flojo
feed [fi:d] (*pt, pp* **fed**) *n* comida; (*of animal*) pienso; (*on printer*) dispositivo de alimentación ▷ *vt* alimentar; (BRIT: *baby*: *breastfeed*) dar el pecho a; (*animal*) dar de comer a; (*data,*

information): **to ~ into** meter en; **feedback** *n* reacción *f*, feedback *m*

feel [fiːl] (*pt, pp* **felt**) *n* (*sensation*) sensación *f*; (*sense of touch*) tacto; (*impression*): **to have the ~ of** parecerse a ▷*vt* tocar; (*pain etc*) sentir; (*think, believe*) creer; **to ~ hungry/cold** tener hambre/frío; **to ~ lonely/better** sentirse solo/mejor; **I don't ~ well** no me siento bien; **it ~s soft** es suave al tacto; **to ~ like** (*want*) tener ganas de; **feeling** *n* (*physical*) sensación *f*; (*foreboding*) presentimiento; (*emotion*) sentimiento

feet [fiːt] *npl of* **foot**

fell [fɛl] *pt of* **fall** ▷*vt* (*tree*) talar

fellow ['fɛləu] *n* tipo, tío (SP); (*comrade*) compañero; (*of learned society*) socio/a; **fellow citizen** *n* conciudadano/a; **fellow countryman** (*irreg*) *n* compatriota *m*; **fellow men** *npl* semejantes *mpl*; **fellowship** *n* compañerismo; (*grant*) beca

felony ['fɛlənɪ] *n* crimen *m*

felt [fɛlt] *pt, pp of* **feel** ▷*n* fieltro; **felt-tip** *n* (*also*: **felt-tip pen**) rotulador *m*

female ['fiːmeɪl] *n* (*pej*: *woman*) mujer *f*, tía; (*Zool*) hembra ▷*adj* femenino; hembra

feminine ['fɛmɪnɪn] *adj* femenino

feminist ['fɛmɪnɪst] *n* feminista

fence [fɛns] *n* valla, cerca ▷*vt* (*also*: **~ in**) cercar ▷*vi* (*Sport*) hacer esgrima; **fencing** *n* esgrima

fend [fɛnd] *vi*: **to ~ for o.s.** valerse por sí mismo; **fend off** *vt* (*attack*) rechazar; (*questions*) evadir

fender ['fɛndə*] (US) *n* guardafuego; (*Aut*) parachoques *m inv*

fennel ['fɛnl] *n* hinojo

ferment [*vb* fə'mɛnt, *n* 'fəːmɛnt] *vi* fermentar ▷*n* (*fig*) agitación *f*

fern [fəːn] *n* helecho

ferocious [fə'rəuʃəs] *adj* feroz

ferret ['fɛrɪt] *n* hurón *m*

ferry ['fɛrɪ] *n* (*small*) barca (de pasaje), balsa; (*large*: *also*: **~boat**) transbordador *m*, ferry *m* ▷*vt* transportar

fertile ['fəːtaɪl] *adj* fértil; (*Biol*) fecundo; **fertilize** ['fəːtɪlaɪz] *vt* (*Biol*) fecundar; (*Agr*) abonar; **fertilizer** *n* abono

festival ['fɛstɪvəl] *n* (*Rel*) fiesta; (*Art, Mus*) festival *m*

festive ['fɛstɪv] *adj* festivo; **the ~ season** (BRIT: *Christmas*) las Navidades

fetch [fɛtʃ] *vt* ir a buscar; (*sell for*) venderse por

fête [feɪt] *n* fiesta

fetus ['fiːtəs] (US) *n* = **foetus**

feud [fjuːd] *n* (*hostility*) enemistad *f*; (*quarrel*) disputa

fever ['fiːvə*] *n* fiebre *f*; **feverish** *adj* febril

few [fjuː] *adj* (*not many*) pocos ▷*pron* pocos; algunos; **a ~** *adj* unos pocos, algunos; **fewer** *adj* menos; **fewest** *adj* los(las) menos

fiancé [fɪ'ɑ̃ːŋseɪ] *n* novio, prometido; **fiancée** *n* novia, prometida

fiasco [fɪ'æskəu] *n* fiasco

fib [fɪb] *n* mentirilla

fibre ['faɪbə*] (US **fiber**) *n* fibra; **fibreglass** (US **Fiberglass**®) *n* fibra de vidrio

fickle ['fɪkl] *adj* inconstante

fiction ['fɪkʃən] *n* ficción *f*; **fictional** *adj* novelesco

fiddle ['fɪdl] *n* (*Mus*) violín *m*; (*cheating*) trampa ▷*vt* (BRIT: *accounts*) falsificar; **fiddle with** *vt fus* juguetear con

fidelity [fɪ'dɛlɪtɪ] *n* fidelidad *f*

field [fiːld] *n* campo; (*fig*) campo, esfera; (*Sport*) campo (SP), cancha (LAM); **field marshal** *n* mariscal *m*

fierce [fɪəs] *adj* feroz; (*wind, heat*) fuerte; (*fighting, enemy*) encarnizado

fifteen [fɪf'tiːn] *num* quince; **fifteenth** *adj* decimoquinto; **the fifteenth floor** la planta quince; **the fifteenth of August** el quince de agosto

fifth [fɪfθ] *num* quinto

fiftieth ['fɪftɪɪθ] *adj* quincuagésimo

fifty ['fɪftɪ] *num* cincuenta; **fifty-fifty** *adj* (*deal, split*) a medias ▷ *adv* a medias, mitad por mitad

fig [fɪg] *n* higo

fight [faɪt] (*pt, pp* **fought**) *n* (*gen*) pelea; (*Mil*) combate *m*; (*struggle*) lucha ▷ *vt* luchar contra; (*cancer, alcoholism*) combatir; (*election*) intentar ganar; (*emotion*) resistir ▷ *vi* pelear, luchar; **fight back** *vi* defenderse; (*after illness*) recuperarse ▷ *vt* (*tears*) contener; **fight off** *vt* (*attack, attacker*) rechazar; (*disease, sleep, urge*) luchar contra; **fighting** *n* combate *m*, pelea

figure ['fɪgə*] *n* (*Drawing, Geom*) figura, dibujo; (*number, cipher*) cifra; (*body, outline*) tipo; (*personality*) figura ▷ *vt* (*esp US*) imaginar ▷ *vi* (*appear*) figurar; **figure out** *vt* (*work out*) resolver

file [faɪl] *n* (*tool*) lima; (*dossier*) expediente *m*; (*folder*) carpeta; (*Comput*) fichero; (*row*) fila ▷ *vt* limar; (*Law: claim*) presentar; (*store*) archivar; **filing cabinet** *n* fichero, archivador *m*

Filipino [fɪlɪ'pi:nəu] *adj* filipino ▷ *n* (*person*) filipino/a *m/f*; (*Ling*) tagalo

fill [fɪl] *vt* (*space*): **to ~ (with)** llenar (de); (*vacancy, need*) cubrir ▷ *n*: **to eat one's ~** llenarse; **fill in** *vt* rellenar; **fill out** *vt* (*form, receipt*) rellenar; **fill up** *vt* llenar (hasta el borde) ▷ *vi* (*Aut*) poner gasolina

fillet ['fɪlɪt] *n* filete *m*; **fillet steak** *n* filete *m* de ternera

filling ['fɪlɪŋ] *n* (*Culin*) relleno; (*for tooth*) empaste *m*; **filling station** *n* estación *f* de servicio

film [fɪlm] *n* película ▷ *vt* (*scene*) filmar ▷ *vi* rodar (una película); **film star** *n* astro, estrella de cine

filter ['fɪltə*] *n* filtro ▷ *vt* filtrar; **filter lane** (BRIT) *n* carril *m* de selección

filth [fɪlθ] *n* suciedad *f*; **filthy** *adj* sucio; (*language*) obsceno

fin [fɪn] *n* (*gen*) aleta

final ['faɪnl] *adj* (*last*) final, último; (*definitive*) definitivo, terminante ▷ *n* (BRIT *Sport*) final *f*; **finals** *npl* (*Scol*) examen *m* final; (*US Sport*) final *f*

finale [fɪ'nɑ:lɪ] *n* final *m*

final: finalist *n* (*Sport*) finalista *mf*; **finalize** *vt* concluir, completar; **finally** *adv* (*lastly*) por último, finalmente; (*eventually*) por fin

finance [faɪ'næns] *n* (*money*) fondos *mpl* ▷ *vt* financiar; **finances** *npl* finanzas *fpl*; (*personal finances*) situación *f* económica; **financial** [-'nænʃəl] *adj* financiero; **financial year** *n* ejercicio (financiero)

find [faɪnd] (*pt, pp* **found**) *vt* encontrar, hallar; (*come upon*) descubrir ▷ *n* hallazgo; descubrimiento; **to ~ sb guilty** (*Law*) declarar culpable a algn; **find out** *vt* averiguar; (*truth, secret*) descubrir; **to find out about** (*subject*) informarse sobre; (*by chance*) enterarse de; **findings** *npl* (*Law*) veredicto, fallo; (*of report*) recomendaciones *fpl*

fine [faɪn] *adj* excelente; (*thin*) fino ▷ *adv* (*well*) bien ▷ *n* (*Law*) multa ▷ *vt* (*Law*) multar; **to be ~** (*person*) estar bien; (*weather*) hacer buen tiempo; **fine arts** *npl* bellas artes *fpl*

finger ['fɪŋgə*] *n* dedo ▷ *vt* (*touch*) manosear; **little/index ~** (dedo) meñique *m*/índice *m*; **fingernail** *n* uña; **fingerprint** *n* huella dactilar; **fingertip** *n* yema del dedo

finish ['fɪnɪʃ] *n* (*end*) fin *m*; (*Sport*) meta; (*polish etc*) acabado ▷ *vt, vi* terminar; **to ~ doing sth** acabar de hacer algo; **to ~ third** llegar el tercero; **finish off** *vt* acabar, terminar; (*kill*) acabar con; **finish up** *vt* acabar, terminar ▷ *vi* ir a parar, terminar

Finland ['fɪnlənd] *n* Finlandia

Finn [fɪn] *n* finlandés/esa *m/f*; **Finnish** *adj* finlandés/esa ▷ *n* (*Ling*) finlandés *m*

fir [fə:*] *n* abeto

fire ['faɪə*] *n* fuego; (*in hearth*) lumbre *f*; (*accidental*) incendio; (*heater*) estufa ▷ *vt* (*gun*) disparar; (*interest*) despertar; (*inf: dismiss*) despedir ▷ *vi* (*shoot*) disparar; **on ~** ardiendo, en llamas; **fire alarm** *n* alarma de incendios; **firearm** *n* arma de fuego; **fire brigade** (US **fire department**) *n* (cuerpo de) bomberos *mpl*; **fire engine** (BRIT) *n* coche *m* de bomberos; **fire escape** *n* escalera de incendios; **fire exit** *n* salida de incendios; **fire extinguisher** *n* extintor *m* (de incendios); **fireman** (*irreg*) *n* bombero; **fireplace** *n* chimenea; **fire station** *n* parque *m* de bomberos; **firetruck** (US) *n* = **fire engine**; **firewall** *n* (*Internet*) firewall *m*; **firewood** *n* leña; **fireworks** *npl* fuegos *mpl* artificiales

firm [fə:m] *adj* firme; (*look, voice*) resuelto ▷ *n* firma, empresa; **firmly** *adv* firmemente; resueltamente

first [fə:st] *adj* primero ▷ *adv* (*before others*) primero; (*when listing reasons etc*) en primer lugar, primeramente ▷ *n* (*person: in race*) primero/a; (*Aut*) primera; (BRIT *Scol*) *título de licenciado con calificación de sobresaliente*; **at ~** al principio; **~ of all** ante todo; **first aid** *n* primera ayuda, primeros auxilios *mpl*; **first-aid kit** *n* botiquín *m*; **first-class** *adj* (*excellent*) de primera (categoría); (*ticket etc*) de primera clase; **first-hand** *adj* de primera mano; **first lady** *n* (*esp* US) primera dama; **firstly** *adv* en primer lugar; **first name** *n* nombre *m* (de pila); **first-rate** *adj* estupendo

fiscal ['fɪskəl] *adj* fiscal; **fiscal year** *n* año fiscal, ejercicio

fish [fɪʃ] *n inv* pez *m*; (*food*) pescado ▷ *vt, vi* pescar; **to go ~ing** ir de pesca; **~ and chips** pescado frito con patatas fritas; **fisherman** (*irreg*) *n* pescador *m*; **fish fingers** (BRIT) *npl* croquetas *fpl* de pescado; **fishing** *n* pesca; **fishing boat** *n* barca de pesca; **fishing line** *n* sedal *m*; **fishmonger** *n* (BRIT) pescadero/a; **fishmonger's (shop)** (BRIT) *n* pescadería; **fish sticks** (US) *npl* = **fish fingers**; **fishy** (*inf*) *adj* sospechoso

fist [fɪst] *n* puño

fit [fɪt] *adj* (*healthy*) en (buena) forma; (*proper*) adecuado, apropiado ▷ *vt* (*clothes*) estar *or* sentar bien a; (*instal*) poner; (*equip*) proveer, dotar; (*facts*) cuadrar *or* corresponder con ▷ *vi* (*clothes*) sentar bien; (*in space, gap*) caber; (*facts*) coincidir ▷ *n* (*Med*) ataque *m*; **~ to** (*ready*) a punto de; **~ for** apropiado para; **a ~ of anger/pride** un arranque de cólera/orgullo; **this dress is a good ~** este vestido me sienta bien; **by ~s and starts** a rachas; **fit in** *vi* (*fig: person*) llevarse bien (con todos); **fitness** *n* (*Med*) salud *f*; **fitted** *adj* (*jacket, shirt*) entallado; (*sheet*) de cuatro picos; **fitted carpet** *n* moqueta; **fitted kitchen** *n* cocina amueblada; **fitting** *adj* apropiado ▷ *n* (*of dress*) prueba; (*of piece of equipment*) instalación *f*; **fitting room** *n* probador *m*; **fittings** *npl* instalaciones *fpl*

five [faɪv] *num* cinco; **fiver** (*inf*) *n* (BRIT) billete *m* de cinco libras; (US) billete *m* de cinco dólares

fix [fɪks] *vt* (*secure*) fijar, asegurar; (*mend*) arreglar; (*prepare*) preparar ▷ *n*: **to be in a ~** estar en un aprieto; **fix up** *vt* (*meeting*) arreglar; **to fix sb up with sth** proveer a algn de algo; **fixed** *adj* (*prices etc*) fijo; **fixture** *n* (*Sport*) encuentro

fizzy ['fɪzɪ] *adj* (*drink*) gaseoso

flag [flæg] *n* bandera; (*stone*) losa ▷ *vi* decaer ▷ *vt*: **to ~ sb down** hacer señas a algn para que se pare; **flagpole** *n* asta de bandera

flair [flɛə*] *n* aptitud *f* especial

flak [flæk] *n* (*Mil*) fuego antiaéreo; (*inf: criticism*) lluvia de críticas

flake [fleɪk] *n* (*of rust, paint*) escama; (*of snow, soap powder*) copo ▷ *vi* (*also*: **~ off**) desconcharse

flamboyant [flæm'bɔɪənt] *adj* (*dress*) vistoso; (*person*) extravagante

flame [fleɪm] *n* llama

flamingo [flə'mɪŋgəu] *n* flamenco

flammable ['flæməbl] *adj*

inflamable

flan [flæn] (BRIT) *n* tarta

> Be careful not to translate **flan** by the Spanish word *flan*.

flank [flæŋk] *n* (*of animal*) ijar *m*; (*of army*) flanco ▷ *vt* flanquear

flannel ['flænl] *n* (BRIT: *also*: **face ~**) manopla; (*fabric*) franela

flap [flæp] *n* (*of pocket, envelope*) solapa ▷ *vt* (*wings, arms*) agitar ▷ *vi* (*sail, flag*) ondear

flare [flɛə*] *n* llamarada; (*Mil*) bengala; (*in skirt etc*) vuelo; **flares** *npl* (*trousers*) pantalones *mpl* de campana; **flare up** *vi* encenderse; (*fig*: *person*) encolerizarse; (*: revolt*) estallar

flash [flæʃ] *n* relámpago; (*also*: **news ~**) noticias *fpl* de última hora; (*Phot*) flash *m* ▷ *vt* (*light, headlights*) lanzar un destello con; (*news, message*) transmitir; (*smile*) lanzar ▷ *vi* brillar; (*hazard light etc*) lanzar destellos; **in a ~** en un instante; **he ~ed by** *or* **past** pasó como un rayo; **flashback** *n* (*Cinema*) flashback *m*; **flashbulb** *n* bombilla fusible; **flashlight** *n* linterna

flask [flɑ:sk] *n* frasco; (*also*: **vacuum ~**) termo

flat [flæt] *adj* llano; (*smooth*) liso; (*tyre*) desinflado; (*battery*) descargado; (*beer*) muerto; (*refusal etc*) rotundo; (*Mus*) desafinado; (*rate*) fijo ▷ *n* (BRIT: *apartment*) piso (SP), departamento (LAM), apartamento; (*Aut*) pinchazo; (*Mus*) bemol *m*; **to work ~ out** trabajar a toda mecha; **flatten** *vt* (*also*: **flatten out**) allanar; (*smooth out*) alisar; (*building, plants*) arrasar

flatter ['flætə*] *vt* adular, halagar; **flattering** *adj* halagüeño; (*dress*) que favorece

flaunt [flɔ:nt] *vt* ostentar, lucir

flavour *etc* ['fleɪvə*] (US **flavor** *etc*) *n* sabor *m*, gusto ▷ *vt* sazonar, condimentar; **strawberry-flavoured** con sabor a fresa; **flavouring** *n* (*in product*) aromatizante *m*

flaw [flɔ:] *n* defecto; **flawless** *adj* impecable

flea [fli:] *n* pulga; **flea market** *n* rastro, mercadillo

flee [fli:] (*pt, pp* **fled**) *vt* huir de ▷ *vi* huir, fugarse

fleece [fli:s] *n* vellón *m*; (*wool*) lana; (*top*) forro polar ▷ *vt* (*inf*) desplumar

fleet [fli:t] *n* flota; (*of lorries etc*) escuadra

fleeting ['fli:tɪŋ] *adj* fugaz

Flemish ['flɛmɪʃ] *adj* flamenco

flesh [flɛʃ] *n* carne *f*; (*skin*) piel *f*; (*of fruit*) pulpa

flew [flu:] *pt of* **fly**

flex [flɛks] *n* cordón *m* ▷ *vt* (*muscles*) tensar; **flexibility** *n* flexibilidad *f*; **flexible** *adj* flexible; **flexitime** (US **flextime**) *n* horario flexible

flick [flɪk] *n* capirotazo; chasquido ▷ *vt* (*with hand*) dar un capirotazo a; (*whip etc*) chasquear; (*switch*) accionar; **flick through** *vt fus* hojear

flicker ['flɪkə*] *vi* (*light*) parpadear; (*flame*) vacilar

flies [flaɪz] *npl of* **fly**

flight [flaɪt] *n* vuelo; (*escape*) huida, fuga; (*also*: **~ of steps**) tramo (de escaleras); **flight attendant** *n* auxiliar *mf* de vuelo

flimsy ['flɪmzɪ] *adj* (*thin*) muy ligero; (*building*) endeble; (*excuse*) flojo

flinch [flɪntʃ] *vi* encogerse; **to ~ from** retroceder ante

fling [flɪŋ] (*pt, pp* **flung**) *vt* arrojar

flint [flɪnt] *n* pedernal *m*; (*in lighter*) piedra

flip [flɪp] *vt* dar la vuelta a; (*switch*: *turn on*) encender; (*turn*) apagar; (*coin*) echar a cara o cruz

flip-flops ['flɪpflɔps] *npl* (*esp* BRIT chancletas *fpl*

flipper ['flɪpə*] *n* aleta

flirt [flə:t] *vi* coquetear, flirtear ▷ *n* coqueta

float [fləut] *n* flotador *m*; (*in procession*) carroza; (*money*) reserva ▷ *vi* flotar; (*swimmer*) hacer la plancha

flock [flɔk] *n* (*of sheep*) rebaño; (*of

birds) bandada ▷ *vi*: **to ~ to** acudir en tropel a

flood [flʌd] *n* inundación *f*; (*of letters, imports etc*) avalancha ▷ *vt* inundar ▷ *vi* (*place*) inundarse; (*people*): **to ~ into** inundar; **flooding** *n* inundaciones *fpl*; **floodlight** *n* foco

floor [flɔː*] *n* suelo; (*storey*) piso; (*of sea*) fondo ▷ *vt* (*question*) dejar sin respuesta; (: *blow*) derribar; **ground ~, first ~** (*US*) planta baja; **first ~, second ~** (*US*) primer piso; **floorboard** *n* tabla; **flooring** *n* suelo; (*material*) solería; **floor show** *n* cabaret *m*

flop [flɔp] *n* fracaso ▷ *vi* (*fail*) fracasar; (*fall*) derrumbarse; **floppy** *adj* flojo ▷ *n* (*Comput*: *also*: **floppy disk**) floppy *m*

flora ['flɔːrə] *n* flora

floral ['flɔːrl] *adj* (*pattern*) floreado

florist ['flɔrɪst] *n* florista *mf*; **florist's (shop)** *n* floristería

flotation [fləu'teɪʃən] *n* (*of shares*) emisión *f*; (*of company*) lanzamiento

flour ['flauə*] *n* harina

flourish ['flʌrɪʃ] *vi* florecer ▷ *n* ademán *m*, movimiento (ostentoso)

flow [fləu] *n* (*movement*) flujo; (*of traffic*) circulación *f*; (*tide*) corriente *f* ▷ *vi* (*river, blood*) fluir; (*traffic*) circular

flower ['flauə*] *n* flor *f* ▷ *vi* florecer; **flower bed** *n* macizo; **flowerpot** *n* tiesto

flown [fləun] *pp of* **fly**

fl. oz. *abbr* (= *fluid ounce*)

flu [fluː] *n*: **to have ~** tener la gripe

fluctuate ['flʌktjueɪt] *vi* fluctuar

fluent ['fluːənt] *adj* (*linguist*) que habla perfectamente; (*speech*) elocuente; **he speaks ~ French, he's ~ in French** domina el francés

fluff [flʌf] *n* pelusa; **fluffy** *adj* de pelo suave

fluid ['fluːɪd] *adj* (*movement*) fluido, líquido; (*situation*) inestable ▷ *n* fluido, líquido; **fluid ounce** *n* onza *f* líquida

fluke [fluːk] (*inf*) *n* chiripa

flung [flʌŋ] *pt, pp of* **fling**

fluorescent [fluə'rɛsnt] *adj* fluorescente

fluoride ['fluəraɪd] *n* fluoruro

flurry ['flʌrɪ] *n* (*of snow*) temporal *m*; **~ of activity** frenesí *m* de actividad

flush [flʌʃ] *n* rubor *m*; (*fig*: *of youth etc*) resplandor *m* ▷ *vt* limpiar con agua ▷ *vi* ruborizarse ▷ *adj*: **~ with** a ras de; **to ~ the toilet** hacer funcionar la cisterna

flute [fluːt] *n* flauta

flutter ['flʌtə*] *n* (*of wings*) revoloteo, aleteo; (*fig*): **a ~ of panic/excitement** una oleada de pánico/excitación ▷ *vi* revolotear

fly [flaɪ] (*pt* **flew**, *pp* **flown**) *n* mosca; (*on trousers*: *also*: **flies**) bragueta ▷ *vt* (*plane*) pilot(e)ar; (*cargo*) transportar (en avión); (*distances*) recorrer (en avión) ▷ *vi* volar; (*passengers*) ir en avión; (*escape*) evadirse; (*flag*) ondear; **fly away, fly off** *vi* emprender el vuelo; **fly-drive** *n*: **fly-drive holiday** *vacaciones que incluyen vuelo y alquiler de coche*; **flying** *n* (*activity*) (el) volar; (*action*) vuelo ▷ *adj*: **flying visit** visita relámpago; **with flying colours** con lucimiento; **flying saucer** *n* platillo volante; **flyover** (*BRIT*) *n* paso a desnivel *or* superior

FM *abbr* (*Radio*) (= *frequency modulation*) FM

foal [fəul] *n* potro

foam [fəum] *n* espuma ▷ *vi* hacer espuma

focus ['fəukəs] (*pl* **~es**) *n* foco; (*centre*) centro ▷ *vt* (*field glasses etc*) enfocar ▷ *vi*: **to ~ (on)** enfocar (a); (*issue etc*) centrarse en; **in/out of ~** enfocado/desenfocado

foetus ['fiːtəs] (*US* **fetus**) *n* feto

fog [fɔg] *n* niebla; **foggy** *adj*: **it's foggy** hay niebla, está brumoso; **fog lamp** (*US* **fog light**) *n* (*Aut*) faro de niebla

foil [fɔɪl] *vt* frustrar ▷ *n* hoja; (*kitchen foil*) papel *m* (de) aluminio; (*complement*) complemento; (*Fencing*) florete *m*

fold [fəuld] *n* (*bend, crease*) pliegue *m*; (*Agr*) redil *m* ▷ *vt* doblar; (*arms*) cruzar; **fold up** *vi* plegarse, doblarse; (*business*) quebrar ▷ *vt* (*map etc*) plegar; **folder** *n* (*for papers*) carpeta; (*Comput*) directorio; **folding** *adj* (*chair, bed*) plegable

foliage ['fəulɪɪdʒ] *n* follaje *m*

folk [fəuk] *npl* gente *f* ▷ *adj* popular, folklórico; **folks** *npl* (*family*) familia *sg*, parientes *mpl*; **folklore** ['fəuklɔː*] *n* folklore *m*; **folk music** *n* música folk; **folk song** *n* canción *f* popular

follow ['fɔləu] *vt* seguir ▷ *vi* seguir; (*result*) resultar; **to ~ suit** hacer lo mismo; **follow up** *vt* (*letter, offer*) responder a; (*case*) investigar; **follower** *n* (*of person, belief*) partidario/a; **following** *adj* siguiente ▷ *n* afición *f*, partidarios *mpl*; **follow-up** *n* continuación *f*

fond [fɔnd] *adj* (*memory, smile etc*) cariñoso; (*hopes*) ilusorio; **to be ~ of** tener cariño a; (*pastime, food*) ser aficionado a

food [fuːd] *n* comida; **food mixer** *n* batidora; **food poisoning** *n* intoxicación *f* alimenticia; **food processor** *n* robot *m* de cocina; **food stamp** (US) *n* vale *m* para comida

fool [fuːl] *n* tonto/a; (*Culin*) puré *m* de frutas con nata ▷ *vt* engañar ▷ *vi* (*gen*) bromear; **fool about, fool around** *vi* hacer el tonto; **foolish** *adj* tonto; (*careless*) imprudente; **foolproof** *adj* (*plan etc*) infalible

foot [fut] (*pl* **feet**) *n* pie *m*; (*measure*) pie *m* (= 304 *mm*); (*of animal*) pata ▷ *vt* (*bill*) pagar; **on ~** a pie; **footage** *n* (*Cinema*) imágenes *fpl*; **foot-and-mouth (disease)** [futənd'mauθ-] *n* fiebre *f* aftosa; **football** *n* balón *m*; (*game*: BRIT) fútbol *m*; (: US) fútbol *m* americano; **footballer** *n* (BRIT) = **football player**; **football match** *n* partido de fútbol; **football player** *n* (BRIT) futbolista *mf*; (US) jugador *m* de fútbol americano; **footbridge** *n* puente *m* para peatones; **foothills** *npl* estribaciones *fpl*; **foothold** *n* pie *m* firme; **footing** *n* (*fig*) posición *f*; **to lose one's footing** perder el pie; **footnote** *n* nota (al pie de la página); **footpath** *n* sendero; **footprint** *n* huella, pisada; **footstep** *n* paso; **footwear** *n* calzado

KEYWORD

for [fɔː] *prep* **1** (*indicating destination, intention*) para; **the train for London** el tren con destino a *or* de Londres; **he left for Rome** marchó para Roma; **he went for the paper** fue por el periódico; **is this for me?** ¿es esto para mí?; **it's time for lunch** es la hora de comer

2 (*indicating purpose*) para; **what('s it) for?** ¿para qué (es)?; **to pray for peace** rezar por la paz

3 (*on behalf of, representing*): **the MP for Hove** el diputado por Hove; **he works for the government/a local firm** trabaja para el gobierno/en una empresa local; **I'll ask him for you** se lo pediré por ti; **G for George** G de Gerona

4 (*because of*) por esta razón; **for fear of being criticized** por temor a ser criticado

5 (*with regard to*) para; **it's cold for July** hace frío para julio; **he has a gift for languages** tiene don de lenguas

6 (*in exchange for*) por; **I sold it for £5** lo vendí por £5; **to pay 50 pence for a ticket** pagar 50 peniques por un billete

7 (*in favour of*): **are you for or against us?** ¿estás con nosotros o contra nosotros?; **I'm all for it** estoy totalmente a favor; **vote for X** vote (a) X

8 (*referring to distance*): **there are roadworks for 5 km** hay obras en 5 km; **we walked for miles** caminamos kilómetros y kilómetros

9 (*referring to time*): **he was away for two years** estuvo fuera (durante) dos

años; **it hasn't rained for 3 weeks** no ha llovido durante *or* en 3 semanas; **I have known her for years** la conozco desde hace años; **can you do it for tomorrow?** ¿lo podrás hacer para mañana?
10 (*with infinitive clauses*): **it is not for me to decide** la decisión no es cosa mía; **it would be best for you to leave** sería mejor que te fueras; **there is still time for you to do it** todavía te queda tiempo para hacerlo; **for this to be possible ...** para que esto sea posible ...
11 (*in spite of*) a pesar de; **for all his complaints** a pesar de sus quejas
▷ *conj* (*since, as: rather formal*) puesto que

forbid [fə'bɪd] (*pt* **forbad(e)**, *pp* **forbidden**) *vt* prohibir; **to ~ sb to do sth** prohibir a algn hacer algo; **forbidden** *pt of* **forbid** ▷ *adj* (*food, area*) prohibido; (*word, subject*) tabú
force [fɔːs] *n* fuerza ▷ *vt* forzar; (*push*) meter a la fuerza; **to ~ o.s. to do** hacer un esfuerzo por hacer; **forced** *adj* forzado; **forceful** *adj* enérgico
ford [fɔːd] *n* vado
fore [fɔː*] *n*: **to come to the ~** empezar a destacar; **forearm** *n* antebrazo; **forecast** (*pt, pp* **forecast**) *n* pronóstico ▷ *vt* pronosticar; **forecourt** *n* patio; **forefinger** *n* (dedo) índice *m*; **forefront** *n*: **in the forefront of** en la vanguardia de; **foreground** *n* primer plano; **forehead** ['fɔrɪd] *n* frente *f*
foreign ['fɔrɪn] *adj* extranjero; (*trade*) exterior; (*object*) extraño; **foreign currency** *n* divisas *fpl*; **foreigner** *n* extranjero/a; **foreign exchange** *n* divisas *fpl*; **Foreign Office** (BRIT) *n* Ministerio de Asuntos Exteriores; **Foreign Secretary** (BRIT) *n* Ministro de Asuntos Exteriores
fore: foreman (*irreg*) *n* capataz *m*; (*in construction*) maestro de obras; **foremost** *adj* principal ▷ *adv*: **first and foremost** ante todo; **forename** *n* nombre *m* (de pila)
forensic [fə'rɛnsɪk] *adj* forense
foresee [fɔː'siː] (*pt* **foresaw**, *pp* **foreseen**) *vt* prever; **foreseeable** *adj* previsible
forest ['fɔrɪst] *n* bosque *m*; **forestry** *n* silvicultura
forever [fə'rɛvə*] *adv* para siempre; (*endlessly*) constantemente
foreword ['fɔːwəːd] *n* prefacio
forfeit ['fɔːfɪt] *vt* perder
forgave [fə'geɪv] *pt of* **forgive**
forge [fɔːdʒ] *n* herrería ▷ *vt* (*signature, money*) falsificar; (*metal*) forjar; **forger** *n* falsificador(a) *m/f*; **forgery** *n* falsificación *f*
forget [fə'gɛt] (*pt* **forgot**, *pp* **forgotten**) *vt* olvidar ▷ *vi* olvidarse; **forgetful** *adj* despistado
forgive [fə'gɪv] (*pt* **forgave**, *pp* **forgiven**) *vt* perdonar; **to ~ sb for sth** perdonar algo a algn
forgot [fə'gɔt] *pt of* **forget**
forgotten [fə'gɔtn] *pp of* **forget**
fork [fɔːk] *n* (*for eating*) tenedor *m*; (*for gardening*) horca; (*of roads*) bifurcación *f* ▷ *vi* (*road*) bifurcarse
forlorn [fə'lɔːn] *adj* (*person*) triste, melancólico; (*place*) abandonado; (*attempt, hope*) desesperado
form [fɔːm] *n* forma; (BRIT *Scol*) clase *f*; (*document*) formulario ▷ *vt* formar; (*idea*) concebir; (*habit*) adquirir; **in top ~** en plena forma; **to ~ a queue** hacer cola
formal ['fɔːməl] *adj* (*offer, receipt*) por escrito; (*person etc*) correcto; (*occasion, dinner*) de etiqueta; (*dress*) correcto; (*garden*) (de estilo) clásico; **formality** [-'mælɪtɪ] *n* (*procedure*) trámite *m*; corrección *f*; etiqueta
format ['fɔːmæt] *n* formato ▷ *vt* (*Comput*) formatear
formation [fɔː'meɪʃən] *n* formación *f*
former ['fɔːmə*] *adj* anterior; (*earlier*) antiguo; (*ex*) ex; **the ~ ... the latter ...** aquél ... éste ...; **formerly** *adv* antes

formidable ['fɔːmɪdəbl] *adj* formidable
formula ['fɔːmjulə] *n* fórmula
fort [fɔːt] *n* fuerte *m*
forthcoming [fɔːθ'kʌmɪŋ] *adj* próximo, venidero; (*help, information*) disponible; (*character*) comunicativo
fortieth ['fɔːtɪɪθ] *adj* cuadragésimo
fortify ['fɔːtɪfaɪ] *vt* (*city*) fortificar; (*person*) fortalecer
fortnight ['fɔːtnaɪt] (BRIT) *n* quince días *mpl*; quincena; **fortnightly** *adj* de cada quince días, quincenal ▷ *adv* cada quince días, quincenalmente
fortress ['fɔːtrɪs] *n* fortaleza
fortunate ['fɔːtʃənɪt] *adj* afortunado; **it is ~ that ...** (es una) suerte que ...; **fortunately** *adv* afortunadamente
fortune ['fɔːtʃən] *n* suerte *f*; (*wealth*) fortuna; **fortune-teller** *n* adivino/a
forty ['fɔːtɪ] *num* cuarenta
forum ['fɔːrəm] *n* foro
forward ['fɔːwəd] *adj* (*movement, position*) avanzado; (*front*) delantero; (*in time*) adelantado; (*not shy*) atrevido ▷ *n* (*Sport*) delantero ▷ *vt* (*letter*) remitir; (*career*) promocionar; **to move ~** avanzar; **forwarding address** *n* destinatario; **forward(s)** *adv* (hacia) adelante; **forward slash** *n* barra diagonal
fossil ['fɔsl] *n* fósil *m*
foster ['fɔstə*] *vt* (*child*) acoger en una familia; fomentar; **foster child** *n* hijo/a adoptivo/a; **foster mother** *n* madre *f* adoptiva
fought [fɔːt] *pt, pp of* **fight**
foul [faul] *adj* sucio, puerco; (*weather, smell etc*) asqueroso; (*language*) grosero; (*temper*) malísimo ▷ *n* (*Sport*) falta ▷ *vt* (*dirty*) ensuciar; **foul play** *n* (*Law*) muerte *f* violenta
found [faund] *pt, pp of* **find** ▷ *vt* fundar; **foundation** [-'deɪʃən] *n* (*act*) fundación *f*; (*basis*) base *f*; (*also*: **foundation cream**) crema base; **foundations** *npl* (*of building*) cimientos *mpl*
founder ['faundə*] *n* fundador(a) *m/f* ▷ *vi* hundirse
fountain ['fauntɪn] *n* fuente *f*; **fountain pen** *n* (pluma) estilográfica (SP), pluma-fuente *f* (LAM)
four [fɔː*] *num* cuatro; **on all ~s** a gatas; **four-letter word** *n* taco; **four-poster** *n* (*also*: **four-poster bed**) cama de columnas; **fourteen** *num* catorce; **fourteenth** *adj* decimocuarto; **fourth** *num* cuarto; **four-wheel drive** *n* tracción *f* a las cuatro ruedas
fowl [faul] *n* ave *f* (de corral)
fox [fɔks] *n* zorro ▷ *vt* confundir
foyer ['fɔɪeɪ] *n* vestíbulo
fraction ['frækʃən] *n* fracción *f*
fracture ['fræktʃə*] *n* fractura
fragile ['frædʒaɪl] *adj* frágil
fragment ['frægmənt] *n* fragmento
fragrance ['freɪgrəns] *n* fragancia
frail [freɪl] *adj* frágil; (*person*) débil
frame [freɪm] *n* (*Tech*) armazón *m*; (*of person*) cuerpo; (*of picture, door etc*) marco; (*of spectacles*: *also*: **~s**) montura ▷ *vt* enmarcar; **framework** *n* marco
France [frɑːns] *n* Francia
franchise ['fræntʃaɪz] *n* (*Pol*) derecho de votar, sufragio; (*Comm*) licencia, concesión *f*
frank [fræŋk] *adj* franco ▷ *vt* (*letter*) franquear; **frankly** *adv* francamente
frantic ['fræntɪk] *adj* (*distraught*) desesperado; (*hectic*) frenético
fraud [frɔːd] *n* fraude *m*; (*person*) impostor(a) *m/f*
fraught [frɔːt] *adj*: **~ with** lleno de
fray [freɪ] *vi* deshilacharse
freak [friːk] *n* (*person*) fenómeno; (*event*) suceso anormal
freckle ['frɛkl] *n* peca
free [friː] *adj* libre; (*gratis*) gratuito ▷ *vt* (*prisoner etc*) poner en libertad; (*jammed object*) soltar; **~ (of charge), for ~** gratis; **freedom** *n* libertad *f*; **Freefone®** *n* número gratuito; **free gift** *n* prima; **free kick** *n* tiro libre; **freelance** *adj* independiente

▷ *adv* por cuenta propia; **freely** *adv* libremente; (*liberally*) generosamente; **Freepost®** *n* porte *m* pagado; **free-range** *adj* (*hen, eggs*) de granja; **freeway** (*US*) *n* autopista; **free will** *n* libre albedrío; **of one's own free will** por su propia voluntad

freeze [fri:z] (*pt* **froze**, *pp* **frozen**) *vi* (*weather*) helar; (*liquid, pipe, person*) helarse, congelarse ▷ *vt* helar; (*food, prices, salaries*) congelar ▷ *n* helada; (*on arms, wages*) congelación *f*; **freezer** *n* congelador *m*, freezer *m* (*SC*)

freezing ['fri:zɪŋ] *adj* helado; **three degrees below ~** tres grados bajo cero; **freezing point** *n* punto de congelación

freight [freɪt] *n* (*goods*) carga; (*money charged*) flete *m*; **freight train** (*US*) *n* tren *m* de mercancías

French [frɛntʃ] *adj* francés/esa ▷ *n* (*Ling*) francés *m*; **the French** *npl* los franceses; **French bean** *n* judía verde; **French bread** *n* pan *m* francés; **French dressing** *n* (*Culin*) vinagreta; **French fried potatoes, French fries** (*US*) *npl* patatas *fpl* (*SP*) *or* papas *fpl* (*LAM*) fritas; **Frenchman** (*irreg*) *n* francés *m*; **Frenchwoman** (*irreg*) *n* francésa; **French stick** *n* barra de pan; **French window** *n* puerta de cristal

frenzy ['frɛnzɪ] *n* frenesí *m*

frequency ['fri:kwənsɪ] *n* frecuencia

frequent [*adj* 'fri:kwənt, *vb* frɪ'kwɛnt] *adj* frecuente ▷ *vt* frecuentar; **frequently** [-əntlɪ] *adv* frecuentemente, a menudo

fresh [frɛʃ] *adj* fresco; (*bread*) tierno; (*new*) nuevo; **freshen** *vi* (*wind, air*) soplar más recio; **freshen up** *vi* (*person*) arreglarse, lavarse; **fresher** (*BRIT: inf*) *n* (*Univ*) estudiante *mf* de primer año; **freshly** *adv* (*made, painted etc*) recién; **freshman** (*US: irreg*) *n* = **fresher**; **freshwater** *adj* (*fish*) de agua dulce

fret [frɛt] *vi* inquietarse

Fri *abbr* (= *Friday*) vier

friction ['frɪkʃən] *n* fricción *f*

Friday ['fraɪdɪ] *n* viernes *m inv*

fridge [frɪdʒ] (*BRIT*) *n* frigorífico (*SP*), nevera (*SP*), refrigerador *m* (*LAM*), heladera (*RPL*)

fried [fraɪd] *adj* frito

friend [frɛnd] *n* amigo/a; **friendly** *adj* simpático; (*government*) amigo; (*place*) acogedor(a); (*match*) amistoso; **friendship** *n* amistad *f*

fries [fraɪz] (*esp US*) *npl* = **French fried potatoes**

frigate ['frɪgɪt] *n* fragata

fright [fraɪt] *n* (*terror*) terror *m*; (*scare*) susto; **to take ~** asustarse; **frighten** *vt* asustar; **frightened** *adj* asustado; **frightening** *adj* espantoso; **frightful** *adj* espantoso, horrible

frill [frɪl] *n* volante *m*

fringe [frɪndʒ] *n* (*BRIT: of hair*) flequillo; (*on lampshade etc*) flecos *mpl*; (*of forest etc*) borde *m*, margen *m*

Frisbee® ['frɪzbɪ] *n* frisbee® *m*

fritter ['frɪtə*] *n* buñuelo

frivolous ['frɪvələs] *adj* frívolo

fro [frəu] *see* **to**

frock [frɔk] *n* vestido

frog [frɔg] *n* rana; **frogman** (*irreg*) *n* hombre-rana *m*

KEYWORD

from [frɔm] *prep* **1** (*indicating starting place*) de, desde; **where do you come from?** ¿de dónde eres?; **from London to Glasgow** de Londres a Glasgow; **to escape from sth/sb** escaparse de algo/algn

2 (*indicating origin etc*) de; **a letter/telephone call from my sister** una carta/llamada de mi hermana; **tell him from me that ...** dígale de mi parte que ...

3 (*indicating time*): **from one o'clock to** *or* **until** *or* **till two** de(sde) la una a *or* hasta las dos; **from January (on)** a partir de enero

4 (*indicating distance*) de; **the hotel is**

1 km from the beach el hotel está a 1 km de la playa
5 (*indicating price, number etc*) de; **prices range from £10 to £50** los precios van desde £10 a *or* hasta £50; **the interest rate was increased from 9% to 10%** el tipo de interés fue incrementado de un 9% a un 10%
6 (*indicating difference*) de; **he can't tell red from green** no sabe distinguir el rojo del verde; **to be different from sb/sth** ser diferente a algn/algo
7 (*because of, on the basis of*): **from what he says** por lo que dice; **weak from hunger** debilitado por el hambre

front [frʌnt] *n* (*foremost part*) parte *f* delantera; (*of house*) fachada; (*of dress*) delantero; (*promenade*: *also*: **sea ~**) paseo marítimo; (*Mil, Pol, Meteorology*) frente *m*; (*fig*: *appearances*) apariencias *fpl* ▷ *adj* (*wheel, leg*) delantero; (*row, line*) primero; **in ~ (of)** delante (de); **front door** *n* puerta principal; **frontier** ['frʌntɪə*] *n* frontera; **front page** *n* primera plana; **front-wheel drive** *n* tracción *f* delantera
frost [frɔst] *n* helada; (*also*: **hoar~**) escarcha; **frostbite** *n* congelación *f*; **frosting** *n* (*esp* US: *icing*) glaseado; **frosty** *adj* (*weather*) de helada; (*welcome etc*) glacial
froth [frɔθ] *n* espuma
frown [fraun] *vi* fruncir el ceño
froze [frəuz] *pt of* **freeze**
frozen ['frəuzn] *pp of* **freeze**
fruit [fru:t] *n inv* fruta; fruto; (*fig*) fruto; resultados *mpl*; **fruit juice** *n* zumo (SP) *or* jugo (LAM) de fruta; **fruit machine** (BRIT) *n* máquina *f* tragaperras; **fruit salad** *n* macedonia (SP) *or* ensalada (LAM) de frutas
frustrate [frʌs'treɪt] *vt* frustrar; **frustrated** *adj* frustrado
fry [fraɪ] (*pt, pp* **fried**) *vt* freír; **small ~** gente *f* menuda; **frying pan** *n* sartén *f*
ft. *abbr* = **foot; feet**
fudge [fʌdʒ] *n* (*Culin*) *caramelo blando*
fuel [fjuəl] *n* (*for heating*) combustible *m*; (*coal*) carbón *m*; (*wood*) leña; (*for engine*) carburante *m*; **fuel tank** *n* depósito (de combustible)
fulfil [ful'fɪl] *vt* (*function*) cumplir con; (*condition*) satisfacer; (*wish, desire*) realizar
full [ful] *adj* lleno; (*fig*) pleno; (*complete*) completo; (*maximum*) máximo; (*information*) detallado; (*price*) íntegro; (*skirt*) amplio ▷ *adv*: **to know ~ well that** saber perfectamente que; **I'm ~ (up)** no puedo más; **~ employment** pleno empleo; **a ~ two hours** dos horas completas; **at ~ speed** a máxima velocidad; **in ~** (*reproduce, quote*) íntegramente; **full-length** *adj* (*novel etc*) entero; (*coat*) largo; (*portrait*) de cuerpo entero; **full moon** *n* luna llena; **full-scale** *adj* (*attack, war*) en gran escala; (*model*) de tamaño natural; **full stop** *n* punto; **full-time** *adj* (*work*) de tiempo completo ▷ *adv*: **to work full-time** trabajar a tiempo completo; **fully** *adv* completamente; (*at least*) por lo menos
fumble ['fʌmbl] *vi*: **to ~ with** manejar torpemente
fume [fju:m] *vi* (*rage*) estar furioso; **fumes** *npl* humo, gases *mpl*
fun [fʌn] *n* (*amusement*) diversión *f*; **to have ~** divertirse; **for ~** en broma; **to make ~ of** burlarse de
function ['fʌŋkʃən] *n* función *f* ▷ *vi* funcionar
fund [fʌnd] *n* fondo; (*reserve*) reserva; **funds** *npl* (*money*) fondos *mpl*
fundamental [fʌndə'mɛntl] *adj* fundamental
funeral ['fju:nərəl] *n* (*burial*) entierro; (*ceremony*) funerales *mpl*; **funeral director** *n* director(a) *m/f* de pompas fúnebres; **funeral parlour** (BRIT) *n* funeraria
funfair ['fʌnfɛə*] (BRIT) *n* parque *m* de atracciones
fungus ['fʌŋgəs] (*pl* **fungi**) *n* hongo; (*mould*) moho

funnel ['fʌnl] *n* embudo; (*of ship*) chimenea
funny ['fʌnɪ] *adj* gracioso, divertido; (*strange*) curioso, raro
fur [fəː*] *n* piel *f*; (BRIT: *in kettle etc*) sarro; **fur coat** *n* abrigo de pieles
furious ['fjuərɪəs] *adj* furioso; (*effort*) violento
furnish ['fəːnɪʃ] *vt* amueblar; (*supply*) suministrar; (*information*) facilitar; **furnishings** *npl* muebles *mpl*
furniture ['fəːnɪtʃə*] *n* muebles *mpl*; **piece of ~** mueble *m*
furry ['fəːrɪ] *adj* peludo
further ['fəːðə*] *adj* (*new*) nuevo, adicional ▷ *adv* más lejos; (*more*) más; (*moreover*) además ▷ *vt* promover, adelantar; **further education** *n* educación *f* superior; **furthermore** *adv* además
furthest ['fəːðɪst] *superlative of* **far**
fury ['fjuərɪ] *n* furia
fuse [fjuːz] (US **fuze**) *n* fusible *m*; (*for bomb etc*) mecha ▷ *vt* (*metal*) fundir; (*fig*) fusionar ▷ *vi* fundirse; fusionarse; (BRIT *Elec*): **to ~ the lights** fundir los plomos; **fuse box** *n* caja de fusibles
fusion ['fjuːʒən] *n* fusión *f*
fuss [fʌs] *n* (*excitement*) conmoción *f*; (*trouble*) alboroto; **to make a ~** armar un lío *or* jaleo; **to make a ~ of sb** mimar a algn; **fussy** *adj* (*person*) exigente; (*too ornate*) recargado
future ['fjuːtʃə*] *adj* futuro; (*coming*) venidero ▷ *n* futuro; (*prospects*) porvenir *m*; **in ~** de ahora en adelante; **futures** *npl* (*Comm*) operaciones *fpl* a término, futuros *mpl*
fuze [fjuːz] (US) = **fuse**
fuzzy ['fʌzɪ] *adj* (*Phot*) borroso; (*hair*) muy rizado

G [dʒiː] *n* (*Mus*) sol *m*
g. *abbr* (= *gram(s)*) gr.
gadget ['gædʒɪt] *n* aparato
Gaelic ['geɪlɪk] *adj, n* (*Ling*) gaélico
gag [gæg] *n* (*on mouth*) mordaza; (*joke*) chiste *m* ▷ *vt* amordazar
gain [geɪn] *n*: **~ (in)** aumento (de); (*profit*) ganancia ▷ *vt* ganar ▷ *vi* (*watch*) adelantarse; **to ~ from/by sth** sacar provecho de algo; **to ~ on sb** ganar terreno a algn; **to ~ 3 lbs (in weight)** engordar 3 libras
gal. *abbr* = **gallon**
gala ['gɑːlə] *n* fiesta
galaxy ['gæləksɪ] *n* galaxia
gale [geɪl] *n* (*wind*) vendaval *m*
gall bladder ['gɔːl-] *n* vesícula biliar
gallery ['gælərɪ] *n* (*also*: **art ~**: *public*) pinacoteca; (: *private*) galería de arte; (*for spectators*) tribuna
gallon ['gæln] *n* galón *m* (*BRIT* = 4,546 *litros*, *US* = 3,785 *litros*)
gallop ['gæləp] *n* galope *m* ▷ *vi* galopar
gallstone ['gɔːlstəun] *n* cálculo

biliario
gamble ['gæmbl] *n* (*risk*) riesgo ▷ *vt* jugar, apostar ▷ *vi* (*take a risk*) jugárselas; (*bet*) apostar; **to ~ on** apostar a; (*success etc*) contar con; **gambler** *n* jugador(a) *m/f*; **gambling** *n* juego
game [geɪm] *n* juego; (*match*) partido; (*of cards*) partida; (*Hunting*) caza ▷ *adj* (*willing*): **to be ~ for anything** atreverse a todo; **big ~** caza mayor (*contest*) juegos; (BRIT: *Scol*) deportes *mpl*; **games console** [geɪmz-] *n* consola de juegos; **game show** *n* programa *m* concurso *m*, concurso
gammon ['gæmən] *n* (*bacon*) tocino ahumado; (*ham*) jamón *m* ahumado
gang [gæŋ] *n* (*of criminals*) pandilla; (*of friends etc*) grupo; (*of workmen*) brigada
gangster ['gæŋstə*] *n* gángster *m*
gap [gæp] *n* vacío (SP), hueco (LAM); (*in trees, traffic*) claro; (*in time*) intervalo; (*difference*): **~ (between)** diferencia (entre)
gape [geɪp] *vi* mirar boquiabierto; (*shirt etc*) abrirse (completamente)
gap year *n* año sabático (antes de empezar a estudiar en la universidad)
garage ['gærɑːʒ] *n* garaje *m*; (*for repairs*) taller *m*; **garage sale** *n* venta de objetos usados (*en el jardín de una casa particular*)
garbage ['gɑːbɪdʒ] (US) *n* basura; (*inf: nonsense*) tonterías *fpl*; **garbage can** *n* cubo *or* bote *m* (MEX) *or* tacho (SC) de la basura; **garbage collector** (US) *n* basurero/a
garden ['gɑːdn] *n* jardín *m*; **gardens** *npl* (*park*) parque *m*; **garden centre** (BRIT) *n* centro de jardinería; **gardener** *n* jardinero/a; **gardening** *n* jardinería
garlic ['gɑːlɪk] *n* ajo
garment ['gɑːmənt] *n* prenda (de vestir)
garnish ['gɑːnɪʃ] *vt* (*Culin*) aderezar
garrison ['gærɪsn] *n* guarnición *f*
gas [gæs] *n* gas *m*; (*fuel*) combustible *m*; (US: *gasoline*) gasolina ▷ *vt* asfixiar con gas; **gas cooker** (BRIT) *n* cocina de gas; **gas cylinder** *n* bombona de gas; **gas fire** *n* estufa de gas
gasket ['gæskɪt] *n* (*Aut*) junta de culata
gasoline ['gæsəliːn] (US) *n* gasolina
gasp [gɑːsp] *n* boqueada; (*of shock etc*) grito sofocado ▷ *vi* (*pant*) jadear
gas: gas pedal *n* (*esp* US) acelerador *m*; **gas station** (US) *n* gasolinera; **gas tank** (US) *n* (*Aut*) depósito (de gasolina)
gate [geɪt] *n* puerta; (*iron gate*) verja
gateau ['gætəu] (*pl* **~x**) *n* tarta
gatecrash ['geɪtkræʃ] (BRIT) *vt* colarse en
gateway ['geɪtweɪ] *n* puerta
gather ['gæðə*] *vt* (*flowers, fruit*) coger (SP), recoger; (*assemble*) reunir; (*pick up*) recoger; (*Sewing*) fruncir; (*understand*) entender ▷ *vi* (*assemble*) reunirse; **to ~ speed** ganar velocidad; **gathering** *n* reunión *f*, asamblea
gauge [geɪdʒ] *n* (*instrument*) indicador *m* ▷ *vt* medir; (*fig*) juzgar
gave [geɪv] *pt of* **give**
gay [geɪ] *adj* (*homosexual*) gay; (*joyful*) alegre; (*colour*) vivo
gaze [geɪz] *n* mirada fija ▷ *vi*: **to ~ at sth** mirar algo fijamente
GB *abbr* = **Great Britain**
GCSE (BRIT) *n abbr* (= *General Certificate of Secondary Education*) *examen de reválida que se hace a los 16 años*
gear [gɪə*] *n* equipo, herramientas *fpl*; (*Tech*) engranaje *m*; (*Aut*) velocidad *f*, marcha ▷ *vt* (*fig: adapt*): **to ~ sth to** adaptar *or* ajustar algo a; **top** *or* **high** (US)**/low ~** cuarta/primera velocidad; **in ~** en marcha; **gear up** *vi* prepararse; **gear box** *n* caja de cambios; **gear lever** *n* palanca de cambio; **gear shift** (US) *n* = **gear lever**; **gear stick** *n* (BRIT) palanca de cambios
geese [giːs] *npl of* **goose**

gel [dʒɛl] *n* gel *m*
gem [dʒɛm] *n* piedra preciosa
Gemini ['dʒɛmɪnaɪ] *n* Géminis *m*, Gemelos *mpl*
gender ['dʒɛndə*] *n* género
gene [dʒiːn] *n* gen(e) *m*
general ['dʒɛnərl] *n* general *m* ▷ *adj* general; **in ~** en general; **general anaesthetic** (*US* **general anesthetic**) *n* anestesia general; **general election** *n* elecciones *fpl* generales; **generalize** *vi* generalizar; **generally** *adv* generalmente, en general; **general practitioner** *n* médico general; **general store** *n* tienda (*que vende de todo*) (*LAM, SP*), almacén *m* (*SC, SP*)
generate ['dʒɛnəreɪt] *vt* (*Elec*) generar; (*jobs, profits*) producir
generation [dʒɛnə'reɪʃən] *n* generación *f*
generator ['dʒɛnəreɪtə*] *n* generador *m*
generosity [dʒɛnə'rɔsɪtɪ] *n* generosidad *f*
generous ['dʒɛnərəs] *adj* generoso
genetic [dʒɪ'nɛtɪk] *adj*: **~ engineering** ingeniería genética; **~ fingerprinting** identificación *f* genética; **genetically modified** *adj* transgénico; **genetics** *n* genética
genitals ['dʒɛnɪtlz] *npl* (órganos *mpl*) genitales *mpl*
genius ['dʒiːnɪəs] *n* genio
genome ['giːnəum] *n* genoma *m*
gent [dʒɛnt] *n abbr* (*BRIT inf*) = **gentleman**
gentle ['dʒɛntl] *adj* apacible, dulce; (*animal*) manso; (*breeze, curve etc*) suave
Be careful not to translate **gentle** by the Spanish word *gentil*.
gentleman ['dʒɛntlmən] (*irreg*) *n* señor *m*; (*well-bred man*) caballero
gently ['dʒɛntlɪ] *adv* dulcemente; suavemente
gents [dʒɛnts] *n* aseos *mpl* (de caballeros)
genuine ['dʒɛnjuɪn] *adj* auténtico; (*person*) sincero; **genuinely** *adv* sinceramente
geographic(al) [dʒɪə'græfɪk(l)] *adj* geográfico
geography [dʒɪ'ɔgrəfɪ] *n* geografía
geology [dʒɪ'ɔlədʒɪ] *n* geología
geometry [dʒɪ'ɔmətrɪ] *n* geometría
geranium [dʒɪ'reɪnjəm] *n* geranio
geriatric [dʒɛrɪ'ætrɪk] *adj, n* geriátrico/a *m/f*
germ [dʒəːm] *n* (*microbe*) microbio, bacteria; (*seed, fig*) germen *m*
German ['dʒəːmən] *adj* alemán/ana ▷ *n* alemán/ana *m/f*; (*Ling*) alemán *m*; **German measles** *n* rubéola
Germany ['dʒəːmənɪ] *n* Alemania
gesture ['dʒɛstjə*] *n* gesto; (*symbol*) muestra

KEYWORD

get [gɛt] (*pt, pp* **got**, *pp* **gotten** (*US*)) *vi*
1 (*become, be*) ponerse, volverse; **to get old/tired** envejecer/cansarse; **to get drunk** emborracharse; **to get dirty** ensuciarse; **to get married** casarse; **when do I get paid?** ¿cuándo me pagan *or* se me paga?; **it's getting late** se está haciendo tarde
2 (*go*): **to get to/from** llegar a/de; **to get home** llegar a casa
3 (*begin*) empezar a; **to get to know sb** (llegar a) conocer a algn; **I'm getting to like him** me está empezando a gustar; **let's get going** *or* **started** ¡vamos (a empezar)!
4 (*modal aux vb*): **you've got to do it** tienes que hacerlo
▷ *vt* **1**: **to get sth done** (*finish*) terminar algo; (*have done*) mandar hacer algo; **to get one's hair cut** cortarse el pelo; **to get the car going** *or* **to go** arrancar el coche; **to get sb to do sth** conseguir *or* hacer que algn haga algo; **to get sth/sb ready** preparar algo/a algn
2 (*obtain*: *money, permission, results*) conseguir; (*find*: *job, flat*) encontrar; (*fetch*: *person, doctor*) buscar; (*object*) ir a buscar, traer; **to get sth for sb**

conseguir algo para algn; **get me Mr Jones, please** (*Tel*) póngame (*SP*) *or* comuníqueme (*LAM*) con el Sr. Jones, por favor; **can I get you a drink?** ¿quieres algo de beber?
3 (*receive*: *present*, *letter*) recibir; (*acquire*: *reputation*) alcanzar; (: *prize*) ganar; **what did you get for your birthday?** ¿qué te regalaron por tu cumpleaños?; **how much did you get for the painting?** ¿cuánto sacaste por el cuadro?
4 (*catch*) coger (*SP*), agarrar (*LAM*); (*hit*: *target etc*) dar en; **to get sb by the arm/throat** coger *or* agarrar a algn por el brazo/cuello; **get him!** ¡cógelo! (*SP*), ¡atrápalo! (*LAM*); **the bullet got him in the leg** la bala le dio en la pierna
5 (*take*, *move*) llevar; **to get sth to sb** hacer llegar algo a algn; **do you think we'll get it through the door?** ¿crees que lo podremos meter por la puerta?
6 (*catch*, *take*: *plane*, *bus etc*) coger (*SP*), tomar (*LAM*); **where do I get the train for Birmingham?** ¿dónde se coge *or* se toma el tren para Birmingham?
7 (*understand*) entender; (*hear*) oír; **I've got it!** ¡ya lo tengo!, ¡eureka!; **I don't get your meaning** no te entiendo; **I'm sorry, I didn't get your name** lo siento, no cogí tu nombre
8 (*have*, *possess*): **to have got** tener
get away *vi* marcharse; (*escape*) escaparse
get away with *vt fus* hacer impunemente
get back *vi* (*return*) volver ▷ *vt* recobrar
get in *vi* entrar; (*train*) llegar; (*arrive home*) volver a casa, regresar
get into *vt fus* entrar en; (*vehicle*) subir a; **to get into a rage** enfadarse
get off *vi* (*from train etc*) bajar; (*depart*: *person*, *car*) marcharse ▷ *vt* (*remove*) quitar ▷ *vt fus* (*train*, *bus*) bajar de
get on *vi* (*at exam etc*): **how are you getting on?** ¿cómo te va?; (*agree*): **to get on (with)** llevarse bien (con) ▷ *vt fus* subir a
get out *vi* salir; (*of vehicle*) bajar ▷ *vt* sacar
get out of *vt fus* salir de; (*duty etc*) escaparse de
get over *vt fus* (*illness*) recobrarse de
get through *vi* (*Tel*) (lograr) comunicarse
get up *vi* (*rise*) levantarse ▷ *vt fus* subir

getaway ['gɛtəweɪ] *n* fuga
Ghana ['gɑːnə] *n* Ghana
ghastly ['gɑːstlɪ] *adj* horrible
ghetto ['gɛtəu] *n* gueto
ghost [gəust] *n* fantasma *m*
giant ['dʒaɪənt] *n* gigante *mf* ▷ *adj* gigantesco, gigante
gift [gɪft] *n* regalo; (*ability*) talento; **gifted** *adj* dotado; **gift shop** (*US* **gift store**) *n* tienda de regalos; **gift token, gift voucher** *n* vale *m* canjeable por un regalo
gig [gɪg] *n* (*inf*: *concert*) actuación *f*
gigabyte ['dʒɪgəbaɪt] *n* gigabyte *m*
gigantic [dʒaɪ'gæntɪk] *adj* gigantesco
giggle ['gɪgl] *vi* reírse tontamente
gills [gɪlz] *npl* (*of fish*) branquias *fpl*, agallas *fpl*
gilt [gɪlt] *adj*, *n* dorado
gimmick ['gɪmɪk] *n* truco
gin [dʒɪn] *n* ginebra
ginger ['dʒɪndʒə*] *n* jengibre *m*
gipsy ['dʒɪpsɪ] *n* = **gypsy**
giraffe [dʒɪ'rɑːf] *n* jirafa
girl [gəːl] *n* (*small*) niña; (*young woman*) chica, joven *f*, muchacha; (*daughter*) hija; **an English ~** una (chica) inglesa; **girl band** *n* girl band *m* (*grupo musical de chicas*); **girlfriend** *n* (*of girl*) amiga; (*of boy*) novia; **Girl Scout** (*US*) *n* = **Girl Guide**
gist [dʒɪst] *n* lo esencial
give [gɪv] (*pt* **gave**, *pp* **given**) *vt* dar; (*deliver*) entregar; (*as gift*) regalar ▷ *vi* (*break*) romperse; (*stretch*: *fabric*) dar

de sí; **to ~ sb sth, ~ sth to sb** dar algo a algn; **give away** *vt* (*give free*) regalar; (*betray*) traicionar; (*disclose*) revelar; **give back** *vt* devolver; **give in** *vi* ceder ▷ *vt* entregar; **give out** *vt* distribuir; **give up** *vi* rendirse, darse por vencido ▷ *vt* renunciar a; **to give up smoking** dejar de fumar; **to give o.s. up** entregarse

given ['gɪvn] *pp of* **give** ▷ *adj* (*fixed*: *time, amount*) determinado ▷ *conj*: **~ (that) ...** dado (que) ...; **~ the circumstances ...** dadas las circunstancias ...

glacier ['glæsɪə*] *n* glaciar *m*

glad [glæd] *adj* contento; **gladly** ['-lɪ] *adv* con mucho gusto

glamour ['glæmər] (*US* **glamor**) *n* encanto, atractivo; **glamorous** *adj* encantador(a), atractivo

glance [glɑːns] *n* ojeada, mirada ▷ *vi*: **to ~ at** echar una ojeada a

gland [glænd] *n* glándula

glare [glɛə*] *n* (*of anger*) mirada feroz; (*of light*) deslumbramiento, brillo; **to be in the ~ of publicity** ser el foco de la atención pública ▷ *vi* deslumbrar; **to ~ at** mirar con odio a; **glaring** *adj* (*mistake*) manifiesto

glass [glɑːs] *n* vidrio, cristal *m*; (*for drinking*) vaso; (*: with stem*) copa; **glasses** *npl* (*spectacles*) gafas *fpl*

glaze [gleɪz] *vt* (*window*) poner cristales a; (*pottery*) vidriar ▷ *n* vidriado

gleam [gliːm] *vi* brillar

glen [glɛn] *n* cañada

glide [glaɪd] *vi* deslizarse; (*Aviat*: *birds*) planear; **glider** *n* (*Aviat*) planeador *m*

glimmer ['glɪmə*] *n* luz *f* tenue; (*of interest*) muestra; (*of hope*) rayo

glimpse [glɪmps] *n* vislumbre *m* ▷ *vt* vislumbrar, entrever

glint [glɪnt] *vi* centellear

glisten ['glɪsn] *vi* relucir, brillar

glitter ['glɪtə*] *vi* relucir, brillar

global ['gləubl] *adj* mundial; **globalization** *n* globalización *f*; **global warming** *n* (re)calentamiento global *or* de la tierra

globe [gləub] *n* globo; (*model*) globo terráqueo

gloom [gluːm] *n* oscuridad *f*; (*sadness*) tristeza; **gloomy** *adj* (*dark*) oscuro; (*sad*) triste; (*pessimistic*) pesimista

glorious ['glɔːrɪəs] *adj* glorioso; (*weather etc*) magnífico

glory ['glɔːrɪ] *n* gloria

gloss [glɔs] *n* (*shine*) brillo; (*paint*) pintura de aceite

glossary ['glɔsərɪ] *n* glosario

glossy ['glɔsɪ] *adj* lustroso; (*magazine*) de lujo

glove [glʌv] *n* guante *m*; **glove compartment** *n* (*Aut*) guantera

glow [gləu] *vi* brillar

glucose ['gluːkəus] *n* glucosa

glue [gluː] *n* goma (de pegar), cemento ▷ *vt* pegar

GM *adj abbr* (= *genetically modified*) transgénico

gm *abbr* (= *gram*) g

GMO *n abbr* (= *genetically modified organism*) organismo transgénico

GMT *abbr* (= *Greenwich Mean Time*) GMT

gnaw [nɔː] *vt* roer

go [gəu] (*pt* **went**, *pp* **gone**, *pl* **~es**) *vi* ir; (*travel*) viajar; (*depart*) irse, marcharse; (*work*) funcionar, marchar; (*be sold*) venderse; (*time*) pasar; (*fit, suit*): **to ~ with** hacer juego con; (*become*) ponerse; (*break etc*) estropearse, romperse ▷ *n*: **to have a ~ (at)** probar suerte (con); **to be on the ~** no parar; **whose ~ is it?** ¿a quién le toca?; **he's ~ing to do it** va a hacerlo; **to ~ for a walk** ir de paseo; **to ~ dancing** ir a bailar; **how did it ~?** ¿qué tal salió *or* resultó?, ¿cómo ha ido?; **to ~ round the back** pasar por detrás; **go ahead** *vi* seguir adelante; **go away** *vi* irse, marcharse; **go back** *vi* volver; **go by** *vi* (*time*) pasar ▷ *vt fus* guiarse por; **go down** *vi* bajar; (*ship*) hundirse; (*sun*) ponerse ▷ *vt fus* bajar; **go for** *vt fus* (*fetch*) ir por; (*like*) gustar; (*attack*) atacar; **go in** *vi* entrar; **go into** *vt fus* entrar en; (*investigate*) investigar; (*embark on*) dedicarse a; **go off** *vi* irse, marcharse; (*food*) pasarse; (*explode*) estallar; (*event*) realizarse ▷ *vt fus* dejar de gustar; **I'm going off him/the idea** ya no me gusta tanto él/la idea; **go on** *vi* (*continue*) seguir, continuar; (*happen*) pasar, ocurrir; **to go on doing sth** seguir haciendo algo; **go out** *vi* salir; (*fire, light*) apagarse; **go over** *vi* (*ship*) zozobrar ▷ *vt fus* (*check*) revisar; **go past** *vi, vt fus* pasar; **go round** *vi* (*circulate: news, rumour*) correr; (*suffice*) alcanzar, bastar; (*revolve*) girar, dar vueltas; (*visit*): **to go round (to sb's)** pasar a ver (a algn); **to go round (by)** (*make a detour*) dar la vuelta (por); **go through** *vt fus* (*town etc*) atravesar; **go up** *vi, vt fus* subir; **go with** *vt fus* (*accompany*) ir con, acompañar a; **go without** *vt fus* pasarse sin

go-ahead ['gəuəhɛd] *adj* (*person*) dinámico; (*firm*) innovador(a) ▷ *n* luz *f* verde

goal [gəul] *n* meta; (*score*) gol *m*; **goalkeeper** *n* portero; **goal-post** *n* poste *m* (de la portería)

goat [gəut] *n* cabra

gobble ['gɔbl] *vt* (*also*: **~ down, ~ up**) tragarse, engullir

God [gɔd] *n* Dios *m*; **godchild** *n* ahijado/a; **goddaughter** *n* ahijada; **goddess** *n* diosa; **godfather** *n* padrino; **godmother** *n* madrina; **godson** *n* ahijado

goggles ['gɔglz] *npl* gafas *fpl*

going ['gəuɪŋ] *n* (*conditions*) estado del terreno ▷ *adj*: **the ~ rate** la tarifa corriente *or* en vigor

gold [gəuld] *n* oro ▷ *adj* de oro; **golden** *adj* (*made of gold*) de oro; (*gold in colour*) dorado; **goldfish** *n* pez *m* de colores; **goldmine** *n* (*also fig*) mina de oro; **gold-plated** *adj* chapado en oro

golf [gɔlf] *n* golf *m*; **golf ball** *n* (*for game*) pelota de golf; (*on typewriter*) esfera; **golf club** *n* club *m* de golf; (*stick*) palo (de golf); **golf course** *n* campo de golf; **golfer** *n* golfista *mf*

gone [gɔn] *pp of* **go**

gong [gɔŋ] *n* gong *m*

good [gud] *adj* bueno; (*pleasant*) agradable; (*kind*) bueno, amable; (*well-behaved*) educado ▷ *n* bien *m*, provecho; **goods** *npl* (*Comm*) mercancías *fpl*; **~!** ¡qué bien!; **to be ~ at** tener aptitud para; **to be ~ for** servir para; **it's ~ for you** te hace bien; **would you be ~ enough to ...?** ¿podría hacerme el favor de ...?, ¿sería tan amable de ...?; **a ~ deal (of)** mucho; **a ~ many** muchos; **to make ~** reparar; **it's no ~ complaining** no vale la pena (de) quejarse; **for ~** para siempre, definitivamente; **~ morning/afternoon!** ¡buenos días/buenas tardes!; **~ evening!** ¡buenas noches!; **~ night!** ¡buenas noches!

goodbye [gud'baɪ] *excl* ¡adiós!; **to say ~ (to)** (*person*) despedirse (de)

good: Good Friday *n* Viernes *m* Santo; **good-looking** *adj* guapo; **good-natured** *adj* amable, simpático; **goodness** *n* (*of person*) bondad *f*; **for goodness sake!** ¡por Dios!; **goodness gracious!** ¡Dios mío!; **goods train** (BRIT) *n* tren *m* de mercancías; **goodwill** *n* buena voluntad *f*

Google® ['gu:gəl] *n* Google® *m* ▷ *vi* hacer búsquedas en Internet ▷ *vt* buscar información en Internet sobre

goose [gu:s] (*pl* **geese**) *n* ganso, oca

gooseberry ['guzbərɪ] *n* grosella espinosa; **to play ~** hacer de carabina

goose bumps, goose pimples *npl* carne *f* de gallina

gorge [gɔ:dʒ] *n* barranco ▷ *vr*: **to ~ o.s. (on)** atracarse (de)

gorgeous ['gɔ:dʒəs] *adj* (*thing*) precioso; (*weather*) espléndido; (*person*) guapísimo

gorilla [gə'rɪlə] *n* gorila *m*

gosh [gɔʃ] (*inf*) *excl* ¡cielos!

gospel ['gɔspl] *n* evangelio

gossip ['gɔsɪp] *n* (*scandal*)

cotilleo, chismes *mpl*; (*chat*) charla; (*scandalmonger*) cotilla *m/f*, chismoso/a ▷ *vi* cotillear; **gossip column** *n* ecos *mpl* de sociedad

got [gɔt] *pt, pp of* **get**

gotten (US) ['gɔtn] *pp of* **get**

gourmet ['guəmeɪ] *n* gastrónomo/a *m/f*

govern ['gʌvən] *vt* gobernar; (*influence*) dominar; **government** *n* gobierno; **governor** *n* gobernador(a) *m/f*; (*of school etc*) miembro del consejo; (*of jail*) director(a) *m/f*

gown [gaun] *n* traje *m*; (*of teacher*, BRIT: *of judge*) toga

G.P. *n abbr* = **general practitioner**

grab [græb] *vt* coger (SP), agarrar (LAM), arrebatar ▷ *vi*: **to ~ at** intentar agarrar

grace [greɪs] *n* gracia ▷ *vt* honrar; (*adorn*) adornar; **5 days' ~** un plazo de 5 días; **graceful** *adj* grácil, ágil; (*style, shape*) elegante, gracioso; **gracious** ['greɪʃəs] *adj* amable

grade [greɪd] *n* (*quality*) clase *f*, calidad *f*; (*in hierarchy*) grado; (*Scol*: *mark*) nota; (US: *school class*) curso ▷ *vt* clasificar; **grade crossing** (US) *n* paso a nivel; **grade school** (US) *n* escuela primaria

gradient ['greɪdɪənt] *n* pendiente *f*

gradual ['grædjuəl] *adj* paulatino; **gradually** *adv* paulatinamente

graduate [*n* 'grædjuɪt, *vb* 'grædjueɪt] *n* (US: *of high school*) graduado/a; (*of university*) licenciado/a ▷ *vi* graduarse; licenciarse; **graduation** [-'eɪʃən] *n* (*ceremony*) entrega del título

graffiti [grə'fi:tɪ] *n* pintadas *fpl*

graft [grɑ:ft] *n* (*Agr, Med*) injerto; (BRIT: *inf*) trabajo duro; (*bribery*) corrupción *f* ▷ *vt* injertar

grain [greɪn] *n* (*single particle*) grano; (*corn*) granos *mpl*, cereales *mpl*; (*of wood*) fibra

gram [græm] *n* gramo

grammar ['græmə*] *n* gramática; **grammar school** (BRIT) *n* ≈ instituto de segunda enseñanza, liceo (SP)

gramme [græm] *n* = **gram**

gran [græn] (*inf*) *n* (BRIT) abuelita

grand [grænd] *adj* magnífico, imponente; (*wonderful*) estupendo; (*gesture etc*) grandioso; **grandad** (*inf*) *n* = **granddad**; **grandchild** (*pl* **grandchildren**) *n* nieto/a *m/f*; **granddad** (*inf*) *n* yayo, abuelito; **granddaughter** *n* nieta; **grandfather** *n* abuelo; **grandma** (*inf*) *n* yaya, abuelita; **grandmother** *n* abuela; **grandpa** (*inf*) *n* = **granddad**; **grandparents** *npl* abuelos *mpl*; **grand piano** *n* piano de cola; **Grand Prix** ['grɑ̃:'pri:] *n* (*Aut*) gran premio, Grand Prix *m*; **grandson** *n* nieto

granite ['grænɪt] *n* granito

granny ['grænɪ] (*inf*) *n* abuelita, yaya

grant [grɑ:nt] *vt* (*concede*) conceder; (*admit*) reconocer ▷ *n* (*Scol*) beca; (*Admin*) subvención *f*; **to take sth/sb for ~ed** dar algo por sentado/no hacer ningún caso a algn

grape [greɪp] *n* uva

grapefruit ['greɪpfru:t] *n* pomelo (SP, SC), toronja (LAM)

graph [grɑ:f] *n* gráfica; **graphic** ['græfɪk] *adj* gráfico; **graphics** *n* artes *fpl* gráficas ▷ *npl* (*drawings*) dibujos *mpl*

grasp [grɑ:sp] *vt* agarrar, asir; (*understand*) comprender ▷ *n* (*grip*) asimiento; (*understanding*) comprensión *f*

grass [grɑ:s] *n* hierba; (*lawn*) césped *m*; **grasshopper** *n* saltamontes *m inv*

grate [greɪt] *n* parrilla de chimenea ▷ *vi*: **to ~ (on)** chirriar (sobre) ▷ *vt* (*Culin*) rallar

grateful ['greɪtful] *adj* agradecido

grater ['greɪtə*] *n* rallador *m*

gratitude ['grætɪtju:d] *n* agradecimiento

grave [greɪv] *n* tumba ▷ *adj* serio, grave

gravel ['grævl] *n* grava

gravestone ['greɪvstəun] *n* lápida

graveyard ['greɪvjɑ:d] *n* cementerio
gravity ['grævɪtɪ] *n* gravedad *f*
gravy ['greɪvɪ] *n* salsa de carne
gray [greɪ] *adj* = **grey**
graze [greɪz] *vi* pacer ▷ *vt* (*touch lightly*) rozar; (*scrape*) raspar ▷ *n* (*Med*) abrasión *f*
grease [gri:s] *n* (*fat*) grasa; (*lubricant*) lubricante *m* ▷ *vt* engrasar; lubrificar; **greasy** *adj* grasiento
great [greɪt] *adj* grande; (*inf*) magnífico, estupendo; **Great Britain** *n* Gran Bretaña; **great-grandfather** *n* bisabuelo; **great-grandmother** *n* bisabuela; **greatly** *adv* muy; (*with verb*) mucho
Greece [gri:s] *n* Grecia
greed [gri:d] *n* (*also*: **~iness**) codicia, avaricia; (*for food*) gula; (*for power etc*) avidez *f*; **greedy** *adj* avaro; (*for food*) glotón/ona
Greek [gri:k] *adj* griego ▷ *n* griego/a; (*Ling*) griego
green [gri:n] *adj* (*also Pol*) verde; (*inexperienced*) novato ▷ *n* verde *m*; (*stretch of grass*) césped *m*; (*Golf*) green; *m* **greens** *npl* (*vegetables*) verduras *fpl*; **green card** *n* (*Aut*) carta verde; (US: *work permit*) *permiso de trabajo para los extranjeros en EE. UU.*; **greengage** *n* (ciruela) claudia; **greengrocer** (BRIT) *n* verdulero/a; **greenhouse** *n* invernadero; **greenhouse effect** *n* efecto invernadero
Greenland ['gri:nlənd] *n* Groenlandia
green salad *n* ensalada *f* (*de lechuga, pepino, pimiento verde, etc*)
greet [gri:t] *vt* (*welcome*) dar la bienvenida a; (*receive*: *news*) recibir; **greeting** *n* (*welcome*) bienvenida; **greeting(s) card** *n* tarjeta de felicitación
grew [gru:] *pt of* **grow**
grey [greɪ] (US **gray**) *adj* gris; (*weather*) sombrío; **grey-haired** *adj* canoso; **greyhound** *n* galgo
grid [grɪd] *n* reja; (*Elec*) red *f*; **gridlock** *n* (*traffic jam*) retención *f*
grief [gri:f] *n* dolor *m*, pena
grievance ['gri:vəns] *n* motivo de queja, agravio
grieve [gri:v] *vi* afligirse, acongojarse ▷ *vt* dar pena a; **to ~ for** llorar por
grill [grɪl] *n* (*on cooker*) parrilla; (*also*: **mixed ~**) parillada ▷ *vt* (BRIT) asar a la parrilla; (*inf*: *question*) interrogar
grille [grɪl] *n* reja; (*Aut*) rejilla
grim [grɪm] *adj* (*place*) sombrío; (*situation*) triste; (*person*) ceñudo
grime [graɪm] *n* mugre *f*, suciedad *f*
grin [grɪn] *n* sonrisa abierta ▷ *vi* sonreír abiertamente
grind [graɪnd] (*pt, pp* **ground**) *vt* (*coffee, pepper etc*) moler; (US: *meat*) picar; (*make sharp*) afilar ▷ *n* (*work*) rutina
grip [grɪp] *n* (*hold*) asimiento; (*control*) control *m*, dominio; (*of tyre etc*): **to have a good/bad ~** agarrarse bien/mal; (*handle*) asidero; (*holdall*) maletín *m* ▷ *vt* agarrar; (*viewer, reader*) fascinar; **to get to ~s with** enfrentarse con; **gripping** *adj* absorbente
grit [grɪt] *n* gravilla; (*courage*) valor *m* ▷ *vt* (*road*) poner gravilla en; **to ~ one's teeth** apretar los dientes
grits [grɪts] (US) *npl* maíz *msg* a medio moler
groan [grəun] *n* gemido; quejido ▷ *vi* gemir; quejarse
grocer ['grəusə*] *n* tendero (de ultramarinos (SP)); **groceries** *npl* comestibles *mpl*; **grocer's (shop)** *n* tienda de comestibles *or* (MEX, CAM) abarrotes, almacén (SC); **grocery** *n* (*shop*) tienda de ultramarinos
groin [grɔɪn] *n* ingle *f*
groom [gru:m] *n* mozo/a de cuadra; (*also*: **bride~**) novio ▷ *vt* (*horse*) almohazar; (*fig*): **to ~ sb for** preparar a algn para; **well-~ed** de buena presencia
groove [gru:v] *n* ranura, surco
grope [grəup] *vi*: **to ~ for** buscar a tientas
gross [grəus] *adj* (*neglect, injustice*) grave; (*vulgar*: *behaviour*) grosero;

(*: appearance*) de mal gusto; (*Comm*) bruto; **grossly** *adv* (*greatly*) enormemente
grotesque [grə'tɛsk] *adj* grotesco
ground [graund] *pt, pp of* **grind** ▷ *n* suelo, tierra; (*Sport*) campo, terreno; (*reason: gen pl*) causa, razón *f*; (*US: also:* **~ wire**) tierra ▷ *vt* (*plane*) mantener en tierra; (*US Elec*) conectar con tierra; **grounds** *npl* (*of coffee etc*) poso; (*gardens etc*) jardines *mpl*, parque *m*; **on the ~** en el suelo; **to the ~** al suelo; **to gain/lose ~** ganar/perder terreno; **ground floor** *n* (*BRIT*) planta baja; **groundsheet** (*BRIT*) *n* tela impermeable; suelo; **groundwork** *n* preparación *f*
group [gru:p] *n* grupo; (*musical*) conjunto ▷ *vt* (*also:* **~ together**) agrupar ▷ *vi* (*also:* **~ together**) agruparse
grouse [graus] *n inv* (*bird*) urogallo ▷ *vi* (*complain*) quejarse
grovel ['grɔvl] *vi* (*fig*): **to ~ before** humillarse ante
grow [grəu] (*pt* **grew**, *pp* **grown**) *vi* crecer; (*increase*) aumentar; (*expand*) desarrollarse; (*become*) volverse; **to ~ rich/weak** enriquecerse/debilitarse ▷ *vt* cultivar; (*hair, beard*) dejar crecer; **grow on** *vt fus*: **that painting is growing on me** ese cuadro me gusta cada vez más; **grow up** *vi* crecer, hacerse hombre/mujer
growl [graul] *vi* gruñir
grown [grəun] *pp of* **grow**; **grown-up** *n* adulto/a, mayor *mf*
growth [grəuθ] *n* crecimiento, desarrollo; (*what has grown*) brote *m*; (*Med*) tumor *m*
grub [grʌb] *n* larva, gusano; (*inf: food*) comida
grubby ['grʌbɪ] *adj* sucio, mugriento
grudge [grʌdʒ] *n* (motivo de) rencor *m* ▷ *vt*: **to ~ sb sth** dar algo a algn de mala gana; **to bear sb a ~** guardar rencor a algn
gruelling ['gruəlɪŋ] (*US* **grueling**) *adj* penoso, duro
gruesome ['gru:səm] *adj* horrible
grumble ['grʌmbl] *vi* refunfuñar, quejarse
grumpy ['grʌmpɪ] *adj* gruñón/ona
grunt [grʌnt] *vi* gruñir
guarantee [gærən'ti:] *n* garantía ▷ *vt* garantizar
guard [gɑ:d] *n* (*squad*) guardia; (*one man*) guardia *mf*; (*BRIT Rail*) jefe *m* de tren; (*on machine*) dispositivo de seguridad; (*also:* **fire~**) rejilla de protección ▷ *vt* guardar; (*prisoner*) vigilar; **to be on one's ~** estar alerta; **guardian** *n* guardián/ana *m/f*; (*of minor*) tutor(a) *m/f*
guerrilla [gə'rɪlə] *n* guerrillero/a
guess [gɛs] *vi* adivinar; (*US*) suponer ▷ *vt* adivinar; suponer ▷ *n* suposición *f*, conjetura; **to take** *or* **have a ~** tratar de adivinar
guest [gɛst] *n* invitado/a; (*in hotel*) huésped *mf*; **guest house** *n* casa de huéspedes, pensión *f*; **guest room** *n* cuarto de huéspedes
guidance ['gaɪdəns] *n* (*advice*) consejos *mpl*
guide [gaɪd] *n* (*person*) guía *mf*; (*book, fig*) guía; (*also:* **Girl ~**) guía ▷ *vt* (*round museum etc*) guiar; (*lead*) conducir; (*direct*) orientar; **guidebook** *n* guía; **guide dog** *n* perro *m* guía; **guided tour** *n* visita *f* con guía; **guidelines** *npl* (*advice*) directrices *fpl*
guild [gɪld] *n* gremio
guilt [gɪlt] *n* culpabilidad *f*; **guilty** *adj* culpable
guinea pig ['gɪnɪ-] *n* cobaya; (*fig*) conejillo de Indias
guitar [gɪ'tɑ:*] *n* guitarra; **guitarist** *n* guitarrista *m/f*
gulf [gʌlf] *n* golfo; (*abyss*) abismo
gull [gʌl] *n* gaviota
gulp [gʌlp] *vi* tragar saliva ▷ *vt* (*also:* **~ down**) tragarse
gum [gʌm] *n* (*Anat*) encía; (*glue*) goma, cemento; (*sweet*) caramelo de goma; (*also:* **chewing-~**) chicle *m* ▷ *vt*

pegar con goma

gun [gʌn] *n* (*small*) pistola, revólver *m*; (*shotgun*) escopeta; (*rifle*) fusil *m*; (*cannon*) cañón *m*; **gunfire** *n* disparos *mpl*; **gunman** (*irreg*) *n* pistolero; **gunpoint** *n*: **at gunpoint** a mano armada; **gunpowder** *n* pólvora; **gunshot** *n* escopetazo

gush [gʌʃ] *vi* salir a raudales; (*person*) deshacerse en efusiones

gust [gʌst] *n* (*of wind*) ráfaga

gut [gʌt] *n* intestino; **guts** *npl* (*Anat*) tripas *fpl*; (*courage*) valor *m*

gutter ['gʌtə*] *n* (*of roof*) canalón *m*; (*in street*) cuneta

guy [gaɪ] *n* (*also*: **~rope**) cuerda; (*inf*: *man*) tío (SP), tipo; (*figure*) monigote *m*

Guy Fawkes' Night [gaɪ'fɔːks-] *n* *ver recuadro*

GUY FAWKES' NIGHT

La noche del cinco de noviembre, **Guy Fawkes' Night**, se celebra en el Reino Unido el fracaso de la conspiración de la pólvora ("Gunpowder Plot"), un intento fallido de volar el parlamento de Jaime I en 1605. Esa noche se lanzan fuegos artificiales y se hacen hogueras en las que se queman unos muñecos de trapo que representan a **Guy Fawkes**, uno de los cabecillas de la revuelta. Días antes, los niños tienen por costumbre pedir a los transeúntes "a penny for the guy", dinero que emplean en comprar cohetes y petardos.

gym [dʒɪm] *n* gimnasio; **gymnasium** *n* gimnasio *mf*; **gymnast** *n* gimnasta *mf*; **gymnastics** *n* gimnasia; **gym shoes** *npl* zapatillas *fpl* (de deporte)

gynaecologist [gaɪnɪ'kɔlədʒɪst] (US **gynecologist**) *n* ginecólogo/a

gypsy ['dʒɪpsɪ] *n* gitano/a

haberdashery [hæbə'dæʃərɪ] (BRIT) *n* mercería

habit ['hæbɪt] *n* hábito, costumbre *f*; (*drug habit*) adicción *f*; (*costume*) hábito

habitat ['hæbɪtæt] *n* hábitat *m*

hack [hæk] *vt* (*cut*) cortar; (*slice*) tajar ▷ *n* (*pej*: *writer*) escritor(a) *m/f* a sueldo; **hacker** *n* (*Comput*) pirata *mf* informático/a

had [hæd] *pt, pp of* **have**

haddock ['hædək] (*pl* **~** *or* **~s**) *n* *especie de merluza*

hadn't ['hædnt] = **had not**

haemorrhage ['hɛmərɪdʒ] (US **hemorrhage**) *n* hemorragia

haemorrhoids ['hɛmərɔɪdz] (US **hemorrhoids**) *npl* hemorroides *fpl*

haggle ['hægl] *vi* regatear

Hague [heɪg] *n*: **The ~** La Haya

hail [heɪl] *n* granizo; (*fig*) lluvia ▷ *vt* saludar; (*taxi*) llamar a; (*acclaim*) aclamar ▷ *vi* granizar; **hailstone** *n* (piedra de) granizo

hair [hɛə*] *n* pelo, cabellos *mpl*; (*one hair*) pelo, cabello; (*on legs etc*) vello;

to do one's ~ arreglarse el pelo; **to have grey ~** tener canas *fpl*; **hairband** *n* cinta; **hairbrush** *n* cepillo (para el pelo); **haircut** *n* corte *m* (de pelo); **hairdo** *n* peinado; **hairdresser** *n* peluquero/a; **hairdresser's** *n* peluquería; **hair dryer** *n* secador *m* de pelo; **hair gel** *n* fijador; **hair spray** *n* laca; **hairstyle** *n* peinado; **hairy** *adj* peludo; velludo; (*inf: frightening*) espeluznante

hake [heɪk] (*pl* **~** *or* **~s**) *n* merluza

half [hɑːf] (*pl* **halves**) *n* mitad *f*; (*of beer*) ≈ caña (SP), media pinta; (*Rail, Bus*) billete *m* de niño ▷ *adj* medio ▷ *adv* medio, a medias; **two and a ~** dos y media; **~ a dozen** media docena; **~ a pound** media libra; **to cut sth in ~** cortar algo por la mitad; **half board** *n* (BRIT: *in hotel*) media pensión; **half-brother** *n* hermanastro; **half day** *n* medio día *m*, media jornada; **half fare** *n* medio pasaje *m*; **half-hearted** *adj* indiferente, poco entusiasta; **half-hour** *n* media hora; **half-price** *adj, adv* a mitad de precio; **half term** (BRIT) *n* (*Scol*) *vacaciones de mediados del trimestre*; **half-time** *n* descanso; **halfway** *adv* a medio camino; **halfway through** a mitad de

hall [hɔːl] *n* (*for concerts*) sala; (*entrance way*) hall *m*; vestíbulo

hallmark [ˈhɔːlmɑːk] *n* sello

hallo [həˈləu] *excl* = **hello**

hall of residence (BRIT) *n* residencia

Hallowe'en [hæləuˈiːn] *n* víspera de Todos los Santos

HALLOWE'EN

La tradición anglosajona dice que en la noche del 31 de octubre, **Hallowe'en**, víspera de Todos los Santos, es posible ver a brujas y fantasmas. En este día los niños se disfrazan y van de puerta en puerta llevando un farol hecho con una calabaza en forma de cabeza humana. Cuando se les abre la puerta gritan "trick or treat", amenazando con gastar una broma a quien no les dé golosinas o algo de calderilla.

hallucination [həluːsɪˈneɪʃən] *n* alucinación *f*

hallway [ˈhɔːlweɪ] *n* vestíbulo

halo [ˈheɪləu] *n* (*of saint*) halo, aureola

halt [hɔːlt] *n* (*stop*) alto, parada ▷ *vt* parar; interrumpir ▷ *vi* pararse

halve [hɑːv] *vt* partir por la mitad

halves [hɑːvz] *npl of* **half**

ham [hæm] *n* jamón *m* (cocido)

hamburger [ˈhæmbəːgə*] *n* hamburguesa

hamlet [ˈhæmlɪt] *n* aldea

hammer [ˈhæmə*] *n* martillo ▷ *vt* (*nail*) clavar; (*force*): **to ~ an idea into sb/a message home** meter una idea en la cabeza a algn/machacar una idea ▷ *vi* dar golpes

hammock [ˈhæmək] *n* hamaca

hamper [ˈhæmpə*] *vt* estorbar ▷ *n* cesto

hamster [ˈhæmstə*] *n* hámster *m*

hamstring [ˈhæmstrɪŋ] *n* (*Anat*) tendón *m* de la corva

hand [hænd] *n* mano *f*; (*of clock*) aguja; (*writing*) letra; (*worker*) obrero ▷ *vt* dar, pasar; **to give** *or* **lend sb a ~** echar una mano a algn, ayudar a algn; **at ~** a mano; **in ~** (*time*) libre; (*job etc*) entre manos; **on ~** (*person, services*) a mano, al alcance; **to ~** (*information etc*) a mano; **on the one ~ ..., on the other ~ ...** por una parte ... por otra (parte) ...; **hand down** *vt* pasar, bajar; (*tradition*) transmitir; (*heirloom*) dejar en herencia; (US: *sentence, verdict*) imponer; **hand in** *vt* entregar; **hand out** *vt* distribuir; **hand over** *vt* (*deliver*) entregar; **handbag** *n* bolso (SP), cartera (LAM), bolsa (MEX); **hand baggage** *n* = **hand luggage**; **handbook** *n* manual *m*; **handbrake** *n* freno de mano; **handcuffs** *npl* esposas *fpl*; **handful**

n puñado

handicap ['hændɪkæp] *n* minusvalía; (*disadvantage*) desventaja; (*Sport*) handicap *m* ▷ *vt* estorbar; **to be mentally ~ped** ser mentalmente *m/f* discapacitado; **to be physically ~ped** ser minusválido/a

handkerchief ['hæŋkətʃɪf] *n* pañuelo

handle ['hændl] *n* (*of door etc*) tirador *m*; (*of cup etc*) asa; (*of knife etc*) mango; (*for winding*) manivela ▷ *vt* (*touch*) tocar; (*deal with*) encargarse de; (*treat*: *people*) manejar; **"~ with care"** "(manéjese) con cuidado"; **to fly off the ~** perder los estribos; **handlebar(s)** *n(pl)* manillar *m*

hand: hand luggage *n* equipaje *m* de mano; **handmade** *adj* hecho a mano; **handout** *n* (*money etc*) limosna; (*leaflet*) folleto; **hands-free** *adj* (*phone*) manos libres *inv*; **hands-free kit** *n* manos libres *m inv*

handsome ['hænsəm] *adj* guapo; (*building*) bello; (*fig*: *profit*) considerable

handwriting ['hændraɪtɪŋ] *n* letra

handy ['hændɪ] *adj* (*close at hand*) a la mano; (*tool etc*) práctico; (*skilful*) hábil, diestro

hang [hæŋ] (*pt, pp* **hung**) *vt* colgar; (*criminal*: *pt, pp hanged*) ahorcar ▷ *vi* (*painting, coat etc*) colgar; (*hair, drapery*) caer; **to get the ~ of sth** (*inf*) lograr dominar algo; **hang about** *or* **around** *vi* haraganear; **hang down** *vi* colgar, pender; **hang on** *vi* (*wait*) esperar; **hang out** *vt* (*washing*) tender, colgar ▷ *vi* (*inf*: *live*) vivir; (*spend time*) pasar el rato; **to hang out of sth** colgar fuera de algo; **hang round** *vi* = **hang around**; **hang up** *vi* (*Tel*) colgar ▷ *vt* colgar

hanger ['hæŋə*] *n* percha

hang-gliding ['-glaɪdɪŋ] *n* vuelo libre

hangover ['hæŋəuvə*] *n* (*after drinking*) resaca

hankie, hanky ['hæŋkɪ] *n abbr* = **handkerchief**

happen ['hæpən] *vi* suceder, ocurrir; (*chance*): **he ~ed to hear/see** dió la casualidad de que oyó/vió; **as it ~s** da la casualidad de que

happily ['hæpɪlɪ] *adv* (*luckily*) afortunadamente; (*cheerfully*) alegremente

happiness ['hæpɪnɪs] *n* felicidad *f*; (*cheerfulness*) alegría

happy ['hæpɪ] *adj* feliz; (*cheerful*) alegre; **to be ~ (with)** estar contento (con); **to be ~ to do** estar encantado de hacer; **~ birthday!** ¡feliz cumpleaños!

harass ['hærəs] *vt* acosar, hostigar; **harassment** *n* persecución *f*

harbour ['hɑːbə*] (US **harbor**) *n* puerto ▷ *vt* (*fugitive*) dar abrigo a; (*hope etc*) abrigar

hard [hɑːd] *adj* duro; (*difficult*) difícil; (*work*) arduo; (*person*) severo; (*fact*) innegable ▷ *adv* (*work*) mucho, duro; (*think*) profundamente; **to look ~ at** clavar los ojos en; **to try ~** esforzarse; **no ~ feelings!** ¡sin rencor(es)!; **to be ~ of hearing** ser duro de oído; **to be ~ done by** ser tratado injustamente; **hardback** *n* libro en cartoné; **hardboard** *n* aglomerado *m* (*de madera*); **hard disk** *n* (*Comput*) disco duro *or* rígido; **harden** *vt* endurecer; (*fig*) curtir ▷ *vi* endurecerse; curtirse

hardly ['hɑːdlɪ] *adv* apenas; **~ ever** casi nunca

hard: hardship *n* privación *f*; **hard shoulder** (BRIT) *n* (*Aut*) arcén *m*; **hard-up** (*inf*) *adj* sin un duro (SP), pelado, sin un centavo (MEX), pato (SC); **hardware** *n* ferretería; (*Comput*) hardware *m*; (*Mil*) armamento; **hardware shop** (US **hardware store**) ferretería; **hard-working** *adj* trabajador(a)

hardy ['hɑːdɪ] *adj* fuerte; (*plant*) resistente

hare [hɛə*] *n* liebre *f*

harm [hɑːm] *n* daño, mal *m* ▷ *vt* (*person*) hacer daño a; (*health, interests*) perjudicar; (*thing*) dañar; **out of ~'s**

way a salvo; **harmful** *adj* dañino; **harmless** *adj* (*person*) inofensivo; (*joke etc*) inocente

harmony ['hɑːmənɪ] *n* armonía

harness ['hɑːnɪs] *n* arreos *mpl*; (*for child*) arnés *m*; (*safety harness*) arneses *mpl* ▷ *vt* (*horse*) enjaezar; (*resources*) aprovechar

harp [hɑːp] *n* arpa ▷ *vi*: **to ~ on (about)** machacar (con)

harsh [hɑːʃ] *adj* (*cruel*) duro, cruel; (*severe*) severo; (*sound*) áspero; (*light*) deslumbrador(a)

harvest ['hɑːvɪst] *n* (*harvest time*) siega; (*of cereals etc*) cosecha; (*of grapes*) vendimia ▷ *vt* cosechar

has [hæz] *vb see* **have**

hasn't ['hæznt] = **has not**

hassle ['hæsl] (*inf*) *n* lata

haste [heɪst] *n* prisa; **hasten** ['heɪsn] *vt* acelerar ▷ *vi* darse prisa; **hastily** *adv* de prisa; precipitadamente; **hasty** *adj* apresurado; (*rash*) precipitado

hat [hæt] *n* sombrero

hatch [hætʃ] *n* (*Naut*: *also*: **~way**) escotilla; (*also*: **service ~**) ventanilla ▷ *vi* (*bird*) salir del cascarón ▷ *vt* incubar; (*plot*) tramar; **5 eggs have ~ed** han salido 5 pollos

hatchback ['hætʃbæk] *n* (*Aut*) tres *or* cinco puertas *m*

hate [heɪt] *vt* odiar, aborrecer ▷ *n* odio; **hatred** ['heɪtrɪd] *n* odio

haul [hɔːl] *vt* tirar ▷ *n* (*of fish*) redada; (*of stolen goods etc*) botín *m*

haunt [hɔːnt] *vt* (*ghost*) aparecerse en; (*obsess*) obsesionar ▷ *n* guarida; **haunted** *adj* (*castle etc*) embrujado; (*look*) de angustia

KEYWORD

have [haev] (*pt, pp* **had**) *aux vb* **1** (*gen*) haber; **to have arrived/eaten** haber llegado/comido; **having finished** *or* **when he had finished, he left** cuando hubo acabado, se fue

2 (*in tag questions*): **you've done it, haven't you?** lo has hecho, ¿verdad? *or* ¿no?

3 (*in short answers and questions*): **I haven't** no; **so I have** pues, es verdad; **we haven't paid – yes we have!** no hemos pagado – ¡sí que hemos pagado!; **I've been there before, have you?** he estado allí antes, ¿y tú?

▷ *modal aux vb* (*be obliged*): **to have (got) to do sth** tener que hacer algo; **you haven't to tell her** no hay que *or* no debes decírselo

▷ *vt* **1** (*possess*): **he has (got) blue eyes/dark hair** tiene los ojos azules/el pelo negro

2 (*referring to meals etc*): **to have breakfast/lunch/dinner** desayunar/comer/cenar; **to have a drink/a cigarette** tomar algo/fumar un cigarrillo

3 (*receive*) recibir; (*obtain*) obtener; **may I have your address?** ¿puedes darme tu dirección?; **you can have it for £5** te lo puedes quedar por £5; **I must have it by tomorrow** lo necesito para mañana; **to have a baby** tener un niño *or* bebé

4 (*maintain, allow*): **I won't have it/this nonsense!** ¡no lo permitiré!/¡no permitiré estas tonterías!; **we can't have that** no podemos permitir eso

5 **to have sth done** hacer *or* mandar hacer algo; **to have one's hair cut** cortarse el pelo; **to have sb do sth** hacer que algn haga algo

6 (*experience, suffer*): **to have a cold/flu** tener un resfriado/la gripe; **she had her bag stolen/her arm broken** le robaron el bolso/se rompió un brazo; **to have an operation** operarse

7 (+ *noun*): **to have a swim/walk/bath/rest** nadar/dar un paseo/darse un baño/descansar; **let's have a look** vamos a ver; **to have a meeting/party** celebrar una reunión/una fiesta; **let me have a try** déjame intentarlo

haven ['heɪvn] *n* puerto; (*fig*) refugio

haven't ['hævnt] = **have not**
havoc ['hævək] *n* estragos *mpl*
Hawaii [hə'waiː] *n* (Islas *fpl*) Hawai *fpl*
hawk [hɔːk] *n* halcón *m*
hawthorn ['hɔːθɔːn] *n* espino
hay [heɪ] *n* heno; **hay fever** *n* fiebre *f* del heno; **haystack** *n* almiar *m*
hazard ['hæzəd] *n* peligro ▷ *vt* aventurar; **hazardous** *adj* peligroso; **hazard warning lights** *npl* (*Aut*) señales *fpl* de emergencia
haze [heɪz] *n* neblina
hazel ['heɪzl] *n* (*tree*) avellano ▷ *adj* (*eyes*) color *m* de avellano; **hazelnut** *n* avellana
hazy ['heɪzɪ] *adj* brumoso; (*idea*) vago
he [hiː] *pron* él; **~ who ...** él que ..., quien ...
head [hɛd] *n* cabeza; (*leader*) jefe/a *m/f*; (*of school*) director(a) *m/f* ▷ *vt* (*list*) encabezar; (*group*) capitanear; (*company*) dirigir; **~s (or tails)** cara (o cruz); **~ first** de cabeza; **~ over heels** (*in love*) perdidamente; **to ~ the ball** cabecear (la pelota); **head for** *vt fus* dirigirse a; (*disaster*) ir camino de; **head off** *vt* (*threat, danger*) evitar; **headache** *n* dolor *m* de cabeza; **heading** *n* título; **headlamp** (BRIT) *n* = **headlight**; **headlight** *n* faro; **headline** *n* titular *m*; **head office** *n* oficina central, central *f*; **headphones** *npl* auriculares *mpl*; **headquarters** *npl* sede *f* central; (*Mil*) cuartel *m* general; **headroom** *n* (*in car*) altura interior; (*under bridge*) (límite *m* de) altura; **headscarf** *n* pañuelo; **headset** *n* cascos *mpl*; **headteacher** *n* director(directora); **head waiter** *n* maître *m*
heal [hiːl] *vt* curar ▷ *vi* cicatrizarse
health [hɛlθ] *n* salud *f*; **health care** *n* asistencia sanitaria; **health centre** (BRIT) *n* ambulatorio, centro médico; **health food** *n* alimentos *mpl* orgánicos; **Health Service** (BRIT) *n* el servicio de salud pública, ≈ el Insalud (SP); **healthy** *adj* sano, saludable
heap [hiːp] *n* montón *m* ▷ *vt*: **to ~ (up)** amontonar; **to ~ sth with** llenar algo hasta arriba de; **~s of** un montón de
hear [hɪə*] (*pt, pp* **~d**) *vt* (*also Law*) oír; (*news*) saber ▷ *vi* oír; **to ~ about** oír hablar de; **to ~ from sb** tener noticias de algn
heard [həːd] *pt, pp of* **hear**
hearing [hɪərɪŋ] *n* (*sense*) oído; (*Law*) vista; **hearing aid** *n* audífono
hearse [həːs] *n* coche *m* fúnebre
heart [hɑːt] *n* corazón *m*; (*fig*) valor *m*; (*of lettuce*) cogollo; **hearts** *npl* (*Cards*) corazones *mpl*; **to lose/take ~** descorazonarse/cobrar ánimo; **at ~** en el fondo; **by ~** (*learn, know*) de memoria; **heart attack** *n* infarto (de miocardio); **heartbeat** *n* latido (del corazón); **heartbroken** *adj*: **she was heartbroken about it** esto le partió el corazón; **heartburn** *n* acedía; **heart disease** *n* enfermedad *f* cardíaca
hearth [hɑːθ] *n* (*fireplace*) chimenea
heartless ['hɑːtlɪs] *adj* despiadado
hearty ['hɑːtɪ] *adj* (*person*) campechano; (*laugh*) sano; (*dislike, support*) absoluto
heat [hiːt] *n* calor *m*; (*Sport*: *also*: **qualifying ~**) prueba eliminatoria ▷ *vt* calentar; **heat up** *vi* calentarse ▷ *vt* calentar; **heated** *adj* caliente; (*fig*) acalorado; **heater** *n* estufa; (*in car*) calefacción *f*
heather ['hɛðə*] *n* brezo
heating ['hiːtɪŋ] *n* calefacción *f*
heatwave ['hiːtweɪv] *n* ola de calor
heaven ['hɛvn] *n* cielo; (*fig*) una maravilla; **heavenly** *adj* celestial; (*fig*) maravilloso
heavily ['hɛvɪlɪ] *adv* pesadamente; (*drink, smoke*) con exceso; (*sleep, sigh*) profundamente; (*depend*) mucho
heavy ['hɛvɪ] *adj* pesado; (*work, blow*) duro; (*sea, rain, meal*) fuerte; (*drinker, smoker*) grande; (*responsibility*) grave; (*schedule*) ocupado; (*weather*) bochornoso

Hebrew ['hi:bru:] *adj, n* (*Ling*) hebreo
hectare ['hɛktɑ:*] *n* (BRIT) hectárea
hectic ['hɛktɪk] *adj* agitado
he'd [hi:d] = **he would; he had**
hedge [hɛdʒ] *n* seto ▷ *vi* contestar con evasivas; **to ~ one's bets** (*fig*) cubrirse
hedgehog ['hɛdʒhɔg] *n* erizo
heed [hi:d] *vt* (*also*: **take ~**: *pay attention to*) hacer caso de
heel [hi:l] *n* talón *m*; (*of shoe*) tacón *m* ▷ *vt* (*shoe*) poner tacón a
hefty ['hɛftɪ] *adj* (*person*) fornido; (*parcel, profit*) gordo
height [haɪt] *n* (*of person*) estatura; (*of building*) altura; (*high ground*) cerro; (*altitude*) altitud *f*; (*fig*: *of season*): **at the ~ of summer** en los días más calurosos del verano; (: *of power etc*) cúspide *f*; (: *of stupidity etc*) colmo; **heighten** *vt* elevar; (*fig*) aumentar
heir [ɛə*] *n* heredero; **heiress** *n* heredera
held [hɛld] *pt, pp of* **hold**
helicopter ['hɛlɪkɔptə*] *n* helicóptero
hell [hɛl] *n* infierno; **~!** (*inf*) ¡demonios!
he'll [hi:l] = **he will; he shall**
hello [hə'ləu] *excl* ¡hola!; (*to attract attention*) ¡oiga!; (*surprise*) ¡caramba!
helmet ['hɛlmɪt] *n* casco
help [hɛlp] *n* ayuda; (*cleaner etc*) criada, asistenta ▷ *vt* ayudar; **~!** ¡socorro!; **~ yourself** sírvete; **he can't ~ it** no es culpa suya; **help out** *vi* ayudar, echar una mano ▷ *vt*: **to help sb out** ayudar a algn, echar una mano a algn; **helper** *n* ayudante *mf*; **helpful** *adj* útil; (*person*) servicial; (*advice*) útil; **helping** *n* ración *f*; **helpless** *adj* (*incapable*) incapaz; (*defenceless*) indefenso; **helpline** *n* teléfono de asistencia al público
hem [hɛm] *n* dobladillo ▷ *vt* poner *or* coser el dobladillo de
hemisphere ['hɛmɪsfɪə*] *n* hemisferio
hemorrhage ['hɛmərɪdʒ] (US) *n* = **haemorrhage**
hemorrhoids ['hɛmərɔɪdz] (US) *npl* = **haemorrhoids**
hen [hɛn] *n* gallina; (*female bird*) hembra
hence [hɛns] *adv* (*therefore*) por lo tanto; **2 years ~** de aquí a 2 años
hen night, hen party *n* (*inf*) despedida de soltera
hepatitis [hɛpə'taɪtɪs] *n* hepatitis *f*
her [hə:*] *pron* (*direct*) la; (*indirect*) le; (*stressed, after prep*) ella ▷ *adj* su; *see also* **me; my**
herb [hə:b] *n* hierba; **herbal** *adj* de hierbas; **herbal tea** *n* infusión *f* de hierbas
herd [hə:d] *n* rebaño
here [hɪə*] *adv* aquí; (*at this point*) en este punto; **~!** (*present*) ¡presente!; **~ is/are** aquí está/están; **~ she is** aquí está
hereditary [hɪ'rɛdɪtrɪ] *adj* hereditario
heritage ['hɛrɪtɪdʒ] *n* patrimonio
hernia ['hə:nɪə] *n* hernia
hero ['hɪərəu] (*pl* **~es**) *n* héroe *m*; (*in book, film*) protagonista *m*; **heroic** [hɪ'rəuɪk] *adj* heroico
heroin ['hɛrəuɪn] *n* heroína
heroine ['hɛrəuɪn] *n* heroína; (*in book, film*) protagonista
heron ['hɛrən] *n* garza
herring ['hɛrɪŋ] *n* arenque *m*
hers [hə:z] *pron* (el) suyo((la) suya) *etc*; *see also* **mine**[1]
herself [hə:'sɛlf] *pron* (*reflexive*) se; (*emphatic*) ella misma; (*after prep*) sí (misma); *see also* **oneself**
he's [hi:z] = **he is; he has**
hesitant ['hɛzɪtənt] *adj* vacilante
hesitate ['hɛzɪteɪt] *vi* vacilar; (*in speech*) titubear; (*be unwilling*) resistirse a; **hesitation** ['-teɪʃən] *n* indecisión *f*; titubeo; dudas *fpl*
heterosexual [hɛtərəu'sɛksjuəl] *adj* heterosexual
hexagon ['hɛksəgən] *n* hexágono

hey [heɪ] *excl* ¡oye!, ¡oiga!
heyday ['heɪdeɪ] *n*: **the ~ of** el apogeo de
HGV *n abbr* (= *heavy goods vehicle*) vehículo pesado
hi [haɪ] *excl* ¡hola!; (*to attract attention*) ¡oiga!
hibernate ['haɪbəneɪt] *vi* invernar
hiccough ['hɪkʌp] = **hiccup**
hiccup ['hɪkʌp] *vi* hipar
hid [hɪd] *pt of* **hide**
hidden ['hɪdn] *pp of* **hide** ▷ *adj*: **~ agenda** plan *m* encubierto
hide [haɪd] (*pt* **hid**, *pp* **hidden**) *n* (*skin*) piel *f* ▷ *vt* esconder, ocultar ▷ *vi*: **to ~ (from sb)** esconderse *or* ocultarse (de algn)
hideous ['hɪdɪəs] *adj* horrible
hiding ['haɪdɪŋ] *n* (*beating*) paliza; **to be in ~** (*concealed*) estar escondido
hi-fi ['haɪfaɪ] *n* estéreo, hifi *m* ▷ *adj* de alta fidelidad
high [haɪ] *adj* alto; (*speed, number*) grande; (*price*) elevado; (*wind*) fuerte; (*voice*) agudo ▷ *adv* alto, a gran altura; **it is 20 m ~** tiene 20 m de altura; **~ in the air** en las alturas; **highchair** *n* silla alta; **high-class** *adj* (*hotel*) de lujo; (*person*) distinguido, de categoría; (*food*) de alta categoría; **higher education** *n* educación *f or* enseñanza superior; **high heels** *npl* (*heels*) tacones *mpl* altos; (*shoes*) zapatos *mpl* de tacón; **high jump** *n* (*Sport*) salto de altura; **highlands** ['haɪləndz] *npl* tierras *fpl* altas; **the Highlands** (*in Scotland*) las Tierras Altas de Escocia; **highlight** *n* (*fig*: *of event*) punto culminante ▷ *vt* subrayar; **highlights** *npl* (*in hair*) reflejos *mpl*; **highlighter** *n* rotulador; **highly** *adv* (*paid*) muy bien; (*critical, confidential*) sumamente; (*a lot*): **to speak/think highly of** hablar muy bien de/tener en mucho a; **highness** *n* altura; **Her/His Highness** Su Alteza; **high-rise** *n* (*also*: **high-rise block, high-rise building**) torre *f* de pisos; **high school** *n* ≈ Instituto Nacional de Bachillerato (SP); **high season** (BRIT) *n* temporada alta; **high street** (BRIT) *n* calle *f* mayor; **high-tech** (*inf*) *adj* al-tec (*inf*), de alta tecnología; **highway** *n* carretera; (US) carretera nacional; autopista; **Highway Code** (BRIT) *n* código de la circulación
hijack ['haɪdʒæk] *vt* secuestrar; **hijacker** *n* secuestrador(a) *m/f*
hike [haɪk] *vi* (*go walking*) ir de excursión (a pie) ▷ *n* caminata; **hiker** *n* excursionista *mf*; **hiking** *n* senderismo
hilarious [hɪ'lɛərɪəs] *adj* divertidísimo
hill [hɪl] *n* colina; (*high*) montaña; (*slope*) cuesta; **hillside** *n* ladera; **hill walking** *n* senderismo (de montaña); **hilly** *adj* montañoso
him [hɪm] *pron* (*direct*) le, lo; (*indirect*) le; (*stressed, after prep*) él; *see also* **me**; **himself** *pron* (*reflexive*) se; (*emphatic*) él mismo; (*after prep*) sí (mismo); *see also* **oneself**
hind [haɪnd] *adj* posterior
hinder ['hɪndə*] *vt* estorbar, impedir
hindsight ['haɪndsaɪt] *n*: **with ~** en retrospectiva
Hindu ['hɪndu:] *n* hindú *mf*; **Hinduism** *n* (*Rel*) hinduismo
hinge [hɪndʒ] *n* bisagra, gozne *m* ▷ *vi* (*fig*): **to ~ on** depender de
hint [hɪnt] *n* indirecta; (*advice*) consejo; (*sign*) dejo ▷ *vt*: **to ~ that** insinuar que ▷ *vi*: **to ~ at** hacer alusión a
hip [hɪp] *n* cadera
hippie ['hɪpɪ] *n* hippie *m/f*, jipi *m/f*
hippo ['hɪpəu] (*pl* **~s**) *n* hipopótamo
hippopotamus [hɪpə'pɔtəməs] (*pl* **~es** *or* **hippopotami**) *n* hipopótamo
hippy ['hɪpɪ] *n* = **hippie**
hire ['haɪə*] *vt* (BRIT: *car, equipment*) alquilar; (*worker*) contratar ▷ *n* alquiler *m*; **for ~** se alquila; (*taxi*) libre; **hire(d) car** (BRIT) *n* coche *m* de alquiler; **hire purchase** (BRIT) *n* compra a plazos

his [hɪz] *pron* (el) suyo((la) suya) *etc* ▷ *adj* su; *see also* **mine**[1]**; my**
Hispanic [hɪs'pænɪk] *adj* hispánico
hiss [hɪs] *vi* silbar
historian [hɪ'stɔːrɪən] *n* historiador(a) *m/f*
historic(al) [hɪ'stɔrɪk(l)] *adj* histórico
history ['hɪstərɪ] *n* historia
hit [hɪt] (*pt, pp* **~**) *vt* (*strike*) golpear, pegar; (*reach*: *target*) alcanzar; (*collide with*: *car*) chocar contra; (*fig*: *affect*) afectar ▷ *n* golpe *m*; (*success*) éxito; (*on website*) visita; (*in web search*) correspondencia; **to ~ it off with sb** llevarse bien con algn; **hit back** *vi* defenderse; (*fig*) devolver golpe por golpe
hitch [hɪtʃ] *vt* (*fasten*) atar, amarrar; (*also*: **~ up**) remangar ▷ *n* (*difficulty*) dificultad *f*; **to ~ a lift** hacer autostop
hitch-hike ['hɪtʃhaɪk] *vi* hacer autostop; **hitch-hiker** *n* autostopista *m/f*; **hitch-hiking** *n* autostop *m*
hi-tech [haɪ'tɛk] *adj* de alta tecnología
hitman ['hɪtmæn] (*irreg*) *n* asesino a sueldo
HIV *n abbr* (= *human immunodeficiency virus*) VIH *m*; **~-negative/positive** VIH negativo/positivo
hive [haɪv] *n* colmena
hoard [hɔːd] *n* (*treasure*) tesoro; (*stockpile*) provisión *f* ▷ *vt* acumular; (*goods in short supply*) acaparar
hoarse [hɔːs] *adj* ronco
hoax [həuks] *n* trampa
hob [hɔb] *n* quemador *m*
hobble ['hɔbl] *vi* cojear
hobby ['hɔbɪ] *n* pasatiempo, afición *f*
hobo ['həubəu] (*US*) *n* vagabundo
hockey ['hɔkɪ] *n* hockey *m*; **hockey stick** *n* palo *m* de hockey
hog [hɔg] *n* cerdo, puerco ▷ *vt* (*fig*) acaparar; **to go the whole ~** poner toda la carne en el asador
Hogmanay [hɔgmə'neɪ] *n ver recuadro*

HOGMANAY

La Nochevieja o "New Year's Eve" se conoce como "Hogmanay" en Escocia, donde se festeje de forma especial. La familia y los amigos se suelen juntar para oír las campanadas del reloj y luego se hace el "first-footing", costumbre que consiste en visitar a los amigos y vecinos llevando algo de beber (generalmente whisky) y un trozo de carbón que se supone que traerá buena suerte para el año entrante.

hoist [hɔɪst] *n* (*crane*) grúa ▷ *vt* levantar, alzar; (*flag, sail*) izar
hold [həuld] (*pt, pp* **held**) *vt* sostener; (*contain*) contener; (*have*: *power, qualification*) tener; (*keep back*) retener; (*believe*) sostener; (*consider*) considerar; (*keep in position*): **to ~ one's head up** mantener la cabeza alta; (*meeting*) celebrar ▷ *vi* (*withstand pressure*) resistir; (*be valid*) valer ▷ *n* (*grasp*) asimiento; (*fig*) dominio; **~ the line!** (*Tel*) ¡no cuelgue!; **to ~ one's own** (*fig*) defenderse; **to catch** *or* **get (a) ~ of** agarrarse *or* asirse de; **hold back** *vt* retener; (*secret*) ocultar; **hold on** *vi* agarrarse bien; (*wait*) esperar; **hold on!** (*Tel*) ¡(espere) un momento!; **hold out** *vt* ofrecer ▷ *vi* (*resist*) resistir; **hold up** *vt* (*raise*) levantar; (*support*) apoyar; (*delay*) retrasar; (*rob*) asaltar; **holdall** (*BRIT*) *n* bolsa; **holder** *n* (*container*) receptáculo; (*of ticket, record*) poseedor(a) *m/f*; (*of office, title etc*) titular *mf*
hole [həul] *n* agujero
holiday ['hɔlədɪ] *n* vacaciones *fpl*; (*public holiday*) (día *m* de) fiesta, día *m* feriado; **on ~** de vacaciones; **holiday camp** *n* (*BRIT*: *also*: **holiday centre**) centro de vacaciones; **holiday**

job *n* (BRIT) trabajillo extra para las vacaciones; **holiday-maker** (BRIT) *n* turista *mf*; **holiday resort** *n* centro turístico

Holland ['hɔlənd] *n* Holanda

hollow ['hɔləu] *adj* hueco; (*claim*) vacío; (*eyes*) hundido; (*sound*) sordo ▷ *n* hueco; (*in ground*) hoyo ▷ *vt*: **to ~ out** excavar

holly ['hɔlɪ] *n* acebo

Hollywood ['hɔlɪwud] *n* Hollywood *m*

holocaust ['hɔləkɔːst] *n* holocausto

holy ['həulɪ] *adj* santo, sagrado; (*water*) bendito

home [həum] *n* casa; (*country*) patria; (*institution*) asilo ▷ *cpd* (*domestic*) casero, de casa; (*Econ, Pol*) nacional ▷ *adv* (*direction*) a casa; (*right in: nail etc*) a fondo; **at ~** en casa; (*in country*) en el país; (*fig*) como pez en el agua; **to go/come ~** ir/volver a casa; **make yourself at ~** ¡estás en tu casa!; **home address** *n* domicilio; **homeland** *n* tierra natal; **homeless** *adj* sin hogar, sin casa; **homely** *adj* (*simple*) sencillo; **home-made** *adj* casero; **home match** *n* partido en casa; **Home Office** (BRIT) *n* Ministerio del Interior; **home owner** *n* propietario/a *m/f* de una casa; **home page** *n* página de inicio; **Home Secretary** (BRIT) *n* Ministro del Interior; **homesick** *adj*: **to be homesick** tener morriña, sentir nostalgia; **home town** *n* ciudad *f* natal; **homework** *n* deberes *mpl*

homicide ['hɔmɪsaɪd] (US) *n* homicidio

homoeopathic [həumɪɔ'pəθɪk] (US **homeopathic**) *adj* homeopático

homoeopathy [həumɪ'ɔpəθɪ] (US **homeopathy**) *n* homeopatía

homosexual [hɔməu'sɛksjuəl] *adj, n* homosexual *mf*

honest ['ɔnɪst] *adj* honrado; (*sincere*) franco, sincero; **honestly** *adv* honradamente; francamente; **honesty** *n* honradez *f*

honey ['hʌnɪ] *n* miel *f*; **honeymoon** *n* luna de miel; **honeysuckle** *n* madreselva

Hong Kong ['hɔŋ'kɔŋ] *n* Hong-Kong *m*

honorary ['ɔnərərɪ] *adj* (*member, president*) de honor; (*title*) honorífico; **~ degree** doctorado honoris causa

honour ['ɔnə*] (US **honor**) *vt* honrar; (*commitment, promise*) cumplir con ▷ *n* honor *m*, honra; **to graduate with ~s** ≈ licenciarse con matrícula (de honor); **honourable** (US **honorable**) *adj* honorable; **honours degree** *n* (*Scol*) *título de licenciado con calificación alta*

hood [hud] *n* capucha; (BRIT *Aut*) capota; (US *Aut*) capó *m*; (*of cooker*) campana de humos; **hoodie** *n* (*top*) jersey *m* con capucha

hoof [huːf] (*pl* **hooves**) *n* pezuña

hook [huk] *n* gancho; (*on dress*) corchete *m*, broche *m*; (*for fishing*) anzuelo ▷ *vt* enganchar; (*fish*) pescar

hooligan ['huːlɪgən] *n* gamberro

hoop [huːp] *n* aro

hooray [huː'reɪ] *excl* = **hurray**

hoot [huːt] (BRIT) *vi* (*Aut*) tocar el pito, pitar; (*siren*) (hacer) sonar; (*owl*) ulular

Hoover® ['huːvə*] (BRIT) *n* aspiradora ▷ *vt*: **to hoover** pasar la aspiradora por

hooves [huːvz] *npl of* **hoof**

hop [hɔp] *vi* saltar, brincar; (*on one foot*) saltar con un pie

hope [həup] *vt, vi* esperar ▷ *n* esperanza; **I ~ so/not** espero que sí/no; **hopeful** *adj* (*person*) optimista; (*situation*) prometedor(a); **hopefully** *adv* con esperanza; (*one hopes*): **hopefully he will recover** esperamos que se recupere; **hopeless** *adj* desesperado; (*person*): **to be hopeless** ser un desastre

hops [hɔps] *npl* lúpulo

horizon [hə'raɪzn] *n* horizonte *m*; **horizontal** [hɔrɪ'zɔntl] *adj* horizontal

hormone ['hɔːməun] *n* hormona

horn [hɔːn] *n* cuerno; (*Mus*: *also*:

French ~) trompa; (*Aut*) pito, claxon *m*
horoscope ['hɔrəskəup] *n* horóscopo
horrendous [hɔ'rɛndəs] *adj* horrendo
horrible ['hɔrɪbl] *adj* horrible
horrid ['hɔrɪd] *adj* horrible, horroroso
horrific [hɔ'rɪfɪk] *adj* (*accident*) horroroso; (*film*) horripilante
horrifying ['hɔrɪfaɪɪŋ] *adj* horroroso
horror ['hɔrə*] *n* horror *m*; **horror film** *n* película de horror
hors d'œuvre [ɔ:'də:vrə] *n* entremeses *mpl*
horse [hɔ:s] *n* caballo; **horseback** *n*: **on horseback** a caballo; **horse chestnut** *n* (*tree*) castaño de Indias; (*nut*) castaña de Indias; **horsepower** *n* caballo (de fuerza); **horse-racing** *n* carreras *fpl* de caballos; **horseradish** *n* rábano picante; **horse riding** *n* (BRIT) equitación *f*
hose [həuz] *n* manguera; **hosepipe** *n* manguera
hospital ['hɔspɪtl] *n* hospital *m*
hospitality [hɔspɪ'tælɪtɪ] *n* hospitalidad *f*
host [həust] *n* anfitrión *m*; (*TV*, *Radio*) presentador *m*; (*Rel*) hostia; (*large number*): **a ~ of** multitud de
hostage ['hɔstɪdʒ] *n* rehén *m*
hostel ['hɔstl] *n* hostal *m*; **(youth) ~** albergue *m* juvenil
hostess ['həustɪs] *n* anfitriona; (BRIT: *air hostess*) azafata; (*TV*, *Radio*) presentadora
hostile ['hɔstaɪl] *adj* hostil
hostility [hɔ'stɪlɪtɪ] *n* hostilidad *f*
hot [hɔt] *adj* caliente; (*weather*) caluroso, de calor; (*as opposed to warm*) muy caliente; (*spicy*) picante; **to be ~** (*person*) tener calor; (*object*) estar caliente; (*weather*) hacer calor; **hot dog** *n* perro caliente
hotel [həu'tɛl] *n* hotel *m*
hot-water bottle [hɔt'wɔ:tə*-] *n* bolsa de agua caliente
hound [haund] *vt* acosar ▷ *n* perro (de caza)
hour ['auə*] *n* hora; **hourly** *adj* (de) cada hora
house [*n* haus, *pl* 'hauzɪz, *vb* hauz] *n* (*gen*, *firm*) casa; (*Pol*) cámara; (*Theatre*) sala ▷ *vt* (*person*) alojar; (*collection*) albergar; **on the ~** (*fig*) la casa invita; **household** *n* familia; (*home*) casa; **householder** *n* propietario/a; (*head of house*) cabeza de familia; **housekeeper** *n* ama de llaves; **housekeeping** *n* (*work*) trabajos *mpl* domésticos; **housewife** (*irreg*) *n* ama de casa; **house wine** *n* vino *m* de la casa; **housework** *n* faenas *fpl* (de la casa)
housing ['hauzɪŋ] *n* (*act*) alojamiento; (*houses*) viviendas *fpl*; **housing development, housing estate** (BRIT) *n* urbanización *f*
hover ['hɔvə*] *vi* flotar (en el aire); **hovercraft** *n* aerodeslizador *m*
how [hau] *adv* (*in what way*) cómo; **~ are you?** ¿cómo estás?; **~ much milk/many people?** ¿cuánta leche/gente?; **~ much does it cost?** ¿cuánto cuesta?; **~ long have you been here?** ¿cuánto hace que estás aquí?; **~ old are you?** ¿cuántos años tienes?; **~ tall is he?** ¿cómo es de alto?; **~ is school?** ¿cómo (te) va (en) la escuela?; **~ was the film?** ¿qué tal la película?; **~ lovely/awful!** ¡qué bonito/horror!
however [hau'ɛvə*] *adv*: **~ I do it** lo haga como lo haga; **~ cold it is** por mucho frío que haga; **~ fast he runs** por muy rápido que corra; **~ did you do it?** ¿cómo lo hiciste? ▷ *conj* sin embargo, no obstante
howl [haul] *n* aullido ▷ *vi* aullar; (*person*) dar alaridos; (*wind*) ulular
H.P. *n abbr* = **hire purchase**
h.p. *abbr* = **horsepower**
HQ *n abbr* = **headquarters**
hr(s) *abbr* (= *hour(s)*) h
HTML *n abbr* (= *hypertext markup language*) lenguaje *m* de hipertexto
hubcap ['hʌbkæp] *n* tapacubos *m inv*
huddle ['hʌdl] *vi*: **to ~ together**

acurrucarse
huff [hʌf] *n*: **in a ~** enojado
hug [hʌg] *vt* abrazar; (*thing*) apretar con los brazos
huge [hjuːdʒ] *adj* enorme
hull [hʌl] *n* (*of ship*) casco
hum [hʌm] *vt* tararear, canturrear ▷ *vi* tararear, canturrear; (*insect*) zumbar
human ['hjuːmən] *adj, n* humano
humane [hjuː'meɪn] *adj* humano, humanitario
humanitarian [hjuːmænɪ'tɛərɪən] *adj* humanitario
humanity [hjuː'mænɪtɪ] *n* humanidad *f*
human rights *npl* derechos *mpl* humanos
humble ['hʌmbl] *adj* humilde
humid ['hjuːmɪd] *adj* húmedo; **humidity** [-'mɪdɪtɪ] *n* humedad *f*
humiliate [hjuː'mɪlɪeɪt] *vt* humillar
humiliating [hjuː'mɪlɪeɪtɪŋ] *adj* humillante, vergonzoso
humiliation [hjuːmɪlɪ'eɪʃən] *n* humillación *f*
hummus ['huməs] *n paté de garbanzos*
humorous ['hjuːmərəs] *adj* gracioso, divertido
humour ['hjuːmə*] (US **humor**) *n* humorismo, sentido del humor; (*mood*) humor *m* ▷ *vt* (*person*) complacer
hump [hʌmp] *n* (*in ground*) montículo; (*camel's*) giba
hunch [hʌntʃ] *n* (*premonition*) presentimiento
hundred ['hʌndrəd] *num* ciento; (*before n*) cien; **~s of** centenares de; **hundredth** [-ɪdθ] *adj* centésimo
hung [hʌŋ] *pt, pp of* **hang**
Hungarian [hʌŋ'gɛərɪən] *adj, n* húngaro/a *m/f*
Hungary ['hʌŋgərɪ] *n* Hungría
hunger ['hʌŋgə*] *n* hambre *f* ▷ *vi*: **to ~ for** (*fig*) tener hambre de, anhelar
hungry ['hʌŋgrɪ] *adj*: **~ (for)** hambriento (de); **to be ~** tener hambre
hunt [hʌnt] *vt* (*seek*) buscar; (*Sport*) cazar ▷ *vi* (*search*): **to ~ (for)** buscar; (*Sport*) cazar ▷ *n* búsqueda; caza, cacería; **hunter** *n* cazador(a) *m/f*; **hunting** *n* caza
hurdle ['həːdl] *n* (*Sport*) valla; (*fig*) obstáculo
hurl [həːl] *vt* lanzar, arrojar
hurrah [huː'rɑː] *excl* = **hurray**
hurray [hu'reɪ] *excl* ¡viva!
hurricane ['hʌrɪkən] *n* huracán *m*
hurry ['hʌrɪ] *n* prisa ▷ *vt* (*also*: **~ up**: *person*) dar prisa a; (: *work*) apresurar, hacer de prisa; **to be in a ~** tener prisa; **hurry up** *vi* darse prisa, apurarse (LAM)
hurt [həːt] (*pt, pp* **~**) *vt* hacer daño a ▷ *vi* doler ▷ *adj* lastimado
husband ['hʌzbənd] *n* marido
hush [hʌʃ] *n* silencio ▷ *vt* hacer callar; **~!** ¡chitón!, ¡cállate!
husky ['hʌskɪ] *adj* ronco ▷ *n* perro esquimal
hut [hʌt] *n* cabaña; (*shed*) cobertizo
hyacinth ['haɪəsɪnθ] *n* jacinto
hydrangea [haɪ'dreɪnʒə] *n* hortensia
hydrofoil ['haɪdrəfɔɪl] *n* aerodeslizador *m*
hydrogen ['haɪdrədʒən] *n* hidrógeno
hygiene ['haɪdʒiːn] *n* higiene *f*; **hygienic** [-'dʒiːnɪk] *adj* higiénico
hymn [hɪm] *n* himno
hype [haɪp] (*inf*) *n* bombardeo publicitario
hyphen ['haɪfn] *n* guión *m*
hypnotize ['hɪpnətaɪz] *vt* hipnotizar
hypocrite ['hɪpəkrɪt] *n* hipócrita *mf*
hypocritical [hɪpə'krɪtɪkl] *adj* hipócrita
hypothesis [haɪ'pɔθɪsɪs] (*pl* **hypotheses**) *n* hipótesis *f inv*
hysterical [hɪ'stɛrɪkl] *adj* histérico; (*funny*) para morirse de risa
hysterics [hɪ'stɛrɪks] *npl* histeria; **to be in ~** (*fig*) morirse de risa

I [aɪ] *pron* yo
ice [aɪs] *n* hielo; (*ice cream*) helado ▷ *vt* (*cake*) alcorzar ▷ *vi* (*also*: **~ over, ~ up**) helarse; **iceberg** *n* iceberg *m*; **ice cream** *n* helado; **ice cube** *n* cubito de hielo; **ice hockey** *n* hockey *m* sobre hielo
Iceland ['aɪslənd] *n* Islandia; **Icelander** *n* islandés/esa *m/f*; **Icelandic** [aɪs'lændɪk] *adj* islandés/esa ▷ *n* (*Ling*) islandés *m*
ice: ice lolly (BRIT) *n* polo; **ice rink** *n* pista de hielo; **ice skating** *n* patinaje *m* sobre hielo
icing ['aɪsɪŋ] *n* (*Culin*) alcorza; **icing sugar** (BRIT) *n* azúcar *m* glas(eado)
icon ['aɪkɔn] *n* icono
ICT (BRIT: *Scol*) *n abbr* (= *information and communications technology*) informática
icy ['aɪsɪ] *adj* helado
I'd [aɪd] = **I would; I had**
ID card *n* (*identity card*) DNI *m*
idea [aɪ'dɪə] *n* idea
ideal [aɪ'dɪəl] *n* ideal *m* ▷ *adj* ideal; **ideally** [-dɪəlɪ] *adv* idealmente; **they're ideally suited** hacen una pareja ideal
identical [aɪ'dɛntɪkl] *adj* idéntico
identification [aɪdɛntɪfɪ'keɪʃən] *n* identificación *f*; **(means of) ~** documentos *mpl* personales
identify [aɪ'dɛntɪfaɪ] *vt* identificar
identity [aɪ'dɛntɪtɪ] *n* identidad *f*; **identity card** *n* carnet *m* de identidad; **identity theft** *n* robo de identidad
ideology [aɪdɪ'ɔlədʒɪ] *n* ideología
idiom ['ɪdɪəm] *n* modismo; (*style of speaking*) lenguaje *m*

> Be careful not to translate **idiom** by the Spanish word *idioma*.

idiot ['ɪdɪət] *n* idiota *mf*
idle ['aɪdl] *adj* (*inactive*) ocioso; (*lazy*) holgazán/ana; (*unemployed*) parado, desocupado; (*machinery etc*) parado; (*talk etc*) frívolo ▷ *vi* (*machine*) marchar en vacío
idol ['aɪdl] *n* ídolo
idyllic [ɪ'dɪlɪk] *adj* idílico
i.e. *abbr* (= *that is*) esto es
if [ɪf] *conj* si; **~ necessary** si fuera necesario, si hiciese falta; **~ I were you** yo en tu lugar; **~ so/not** de ser así/si no; **~ only I could!** ¡ojalá pudiera!; *see also* **as; even**
ignite [ɪg'naɪt] *vt* (*set fire to*) encender ▷ *vi* encenderse
ignition [ɪg'nɪʃən] *n* (*Aut*: *process*) ignición *f*; (: *mechanism*) encendido; **to switch on/off the ~** arrancar/apagar el motor
ignorance ['ɪgnərəns] *n* ignorancia
ignorant ['ɪgnərənt] *adj* ignorante; **to be ~ of** ignorar
ignore [ɪg'nɔ:*] *vt* (*person, advice*) no hacer caso de; (*fact*) pasar por alto
I'll [aɪl] = **I will; I shall**
ill [ɪl] *adj* enfermo, malo ▷ *n* mal *m* ▷ *adv* mal; **to be taken ~** ponerse enfermo
illegal [ɪ'li:gl] *adj* ilegal
illegible [ɪ'lɛdʒɪbl] *adj* ilegible
illegitimate [ɪlɪ'dʒɪtɪmət] *adj*

ilegítimo
ill health *n* mala salud *f*; **to be in ~** estar mal de salud
illiterate [ɪ'lɪtərət] *adj* analfabeto
illness ['ɪlnɪs] *n* enfermedad *f*
illuminate [ɪ'lu:mɪneɪt] *vt* (*room, street*) iluminar, alumbrar
illusion [ɪ'lu:ʒən] *n* ilusión *f*; (*trick*) truco
illustrate ['ɪləstreɪt] *vt* ilustrar
illustration [ɪlə'streɪʃən] *n* (*act of illustrating*) ilustración *f*; (*example*) ejemplo, ilustración *f*; (*in book*) lámina
I'm [aɪm] = **I am**
image ['ɪmɪdʒ] *n* imagen *f*
imaginary [ɪ'mædʒɪnərɪ] *adj* imaginario
imagination [ɪmædʒɪ'neɪʃən] *n* imaginación *f*; (*inventiveness*) inventiva
imaginative [ɪ'mædʒɪnətɪv] *adj* imaginativo
imagine [ɪ'mædʒɪn] *vt* imaginarse
imbalance [ɪm'bæləns] *n* desequilibrio
imitate ['ɪmɪteɪt] *vt* imitar; **imitation** [ɪmɪ'teɪʃən] *n* imitación *f*; (*copy*) copia
immaculate [ɪ'mækjulət] *adj* inmaculado
immature [ɪmə'tjuə*] *adj* (*person*) inmaduro
immediate [ɪ'mi:dɪət] *adj* inmediato; (*pressing*) urgente, apremiante; (*nearest: family*) próximo; (*: neighbourhood*) inmediato; **immediately** *adv* (*at once*) en seguida; (*directly*) inmediatamente; **immediately next to** muy junto a
immense [ɪ'mɛns] *adj* inmenso, enorme; (*importance*) enorme; **immensely** *adv* enormemente
immerse [ɪ'mə:s] *vt* (*submerge*) sumergir; **to be ~d in** (*fig*) estar absorto en
immigrant ['ɪmɪgrənt] *n* inmigrante *mf*; **immigration** [ɪmɪ'greɪʃən] *n* inmigración *f*
imminent ['ɪmɪnənt] *adj* inminente
immoral [ɪ'mɔrl] *adj* inmoral
immortal [ɪ'mɔ:tl] *adj* inmortal
immune [ɪ'mju:n] *adj*: **~ (to)** inmune (a); **immune system** *n* sistema *m* inmunitario
immunize ['ɪmjunaɪz] *vt* inmunizar
impact ['ɪmpækt] *n* impacto
impair [ɪm'pɛə*] *vt* perjudicar
impartial [ɪm'pɑ:ʃl] *adj* imparcial
impatience [ɪm'peɪʃəns] *n* impaciencia
impatient [ɪm'peɪʃənt] *adj* impaciente; **to get** *or* **grow ~** impacientarse
impeccable [ɪm'pɛkəbl] *adj* impecable
impending [ɪm'pɛndɪŋ] *adj* inminente
imperative [ɪm'pɛrətɪv] *adj* (*tone*) imperioso; (*need*) imprescindible
imperfect [ɪm'pə:fɪkt] *adj* (*goods etc*) defectuoso ▷ *n* (*Ling: also:* **~ tense**) imperfecto
imperial [ɪm'pɪərɪəl] *adj* imperial
impersonal [ɪm'pə:sənl] *adj* impersonal
impersonate [ɪm'pə:səneɪt] *vt* hacerse pasar por; (*Theatre*) imitar
impetus ['ɪmpətəs] *n* ímpetu *m*; (*fig*) impulso
implant [ɪm'plɑ:nt] *vt* (*Med*) injertar, implantar; (*fig: idea, principle*) inculcar
implement [*n* 'ɪmplɪmənt, *vb* 'ɪmplɪmɛnt] *n* herramienta; (*for cooking*) utensilio ▷ *vt* (*regulation*) hacer efectivo; (*plan*) realizar
implicate ['ɪmplɪkeɪt] *vt* (*compromise*) comprometer; **to ~ sb in sth** comprometer a algn en algo
implication [ɪmplɪ'keɪʃən] *n* consecuencia; **by ~** indirectamente
implicit [ɪm'plɪsɪt] *adj* implícito; (*belief, trust*) absoluto
imply [ɪm'plaɪ] *vt* (*involve*) suponer; (*hint*) dar a entender que
impolite [ɪmpə'laɪt] *adj* mal educado

import [*vb* ɪm'pɔːt, *n* 'ɪmpɔːt] *vt* importar ▷ *n* (*Comm*) importación *f*; (: *article*) producto importado; (*meaning*) significado, sentido
importance [ɪm'pɔːtəns] *n* importancia
important [ɪm'pɔːtənt] *adj* importante; **it's not ~** no importa, no tiene importancia
importer [ɪm'pɔːtə*] *n* importador(a) *m/f*
impose [ɪm'pəuz] *vt* imponer ▷ *vi*: **to ~ on sb** abusar de algn; **imposing** *adj* imponente, impresionante
impossible [ɪm'pɔsɪbl] *adj* imposible; (*person*) insoportable
impotent ['ɪmpətənt] *adj* impotente
impoverished [ɪm'pɔvərɪʃt] *adj* necesitado
impractical [ɪm'præktɪkl] *adj* (*person, plan*) poco práctico
impress [ɪm'prɛs] *vt* impresionar; (*mark*) estampar; **to ~ sth on sb** hacer entender algo a algn
impression [ɪm'prɛʃən] *n* impresión *f*; (*imitation*) imitación *f*; **to be under the ~ that** tener la impresión de que
impressive [ɪm'prɛsɪv] *adj* impresionante
imprison [ɪm'prɪzn] *vt* encarcelar; **imprisonment** *n* encarcelamiento; (*term of imprisonment*) cárcel *f*
improbable [ɪm'prɔbəbl] *adj* improbable, inverosímil
improper [ɪm'prɔpə*] *adj* (*unsuitable: conduct etc*) incorrecto; (: *activities*) deshonesto
improve [ɪm'pruːv] *vt* mejorar; (*foreign language*) perfeccionar ▷ *vi* mejorarse; **improvement** *n* mejoramiento; perfección *f*; progreso
improvise ['ɪmprəvaɪz] *vt, vi* improvisar
impulse ['ɪmpʌls] *n* impulso; **to act on ~** obrar sin reflexión; **impulsive** [ɪm'pʌlsɪv] *adj* irreflexivo

KEYWORD

in [ɪn] *prep* **1** (*indicating place, position, with place names*) en; **in the house/garden** en (la) casa/el jardín; **in here/there** aquí/ahí *or* allí dentro; **in London/England** en Londres/Inglaterra
2 (*indicating time*) en; **in spring** en (la) primavera; **in the afternoon** por la tarde; **at 4 o'clock in the afternoon** a las 4 de la tarde; **I did it in 3 hours/days** lo hice en 3 horas/días; **I'll see you in 2 weeks** *or* **in 2 weeks' time** te veré dentro de 2 semanas
3 (*indicating manner etc*) en; **in a loud/soft voice** en voz alta/baja; **in pencil/ink** a lápiz/bolígrafo; **the boy in the blue shirt** el chico de la camisa azul
4 (*indicating circumstances*): **in the sun/shade/rain** al sol/a la sombra/bajo la lluvia; **a change in policy** un cambio de política
5 (*indicating mood, state*): **in tears** en lágrimas, llorando; **in anger/despair** enfadado/desesperado; **to live in luxury** vivir lujosamente
6 (*with ratios, numbers*): **1 in 10 households, 1 household in 10** una de cada 10 familias; **20 pence in the pound** 20 peniques por libra; **they lined up in twos** se alinearon de dos en dos
7 (*referring to people, works*) en; entre; **the disease is common in children** la enfermedad es común entre los niños; **in (the works of) Dickens** en (las obras de) Dickens
8 (*indicating profession etc*): **to be in teaching** estar en la enseñanza
9 (*after superlative*) de; **the best pupil in the class** el(la) mejor alumno/a de la clase
10 (*with present participle*): **in saying this** al decir esto
▷ *adv*: **to be in** (*person: at home*) estar en

casa; (*at work*) estar; (*train, ship, plane*) haber llegado; (*in fashion*) estar de moda; **she'll be in later today** llegará más tarde hoy; **to ask sb in** hacer pasar a algn; **to run/limp** *etc* **in** entrar corriendo/cojeando *etc*
▷ *n*: **the ins and outs** (*of proposal, situation etc*) los detalles

inability [ɪnə'bɪlɪtɪ] *n*: **~ (to do)** incapacidad *f* (de hacer)
inaccurate [ɪn'ækjurət] *adj* inexacto, incorrecto
inadequate [ɪn'ædɪkwət] *adj* (*income, reply etc*) insuficiente; (*person*) incapaz
inadvertently [ɪnəd'vəːtntlɪ] *adv* por descuido
inappropriate [ɪnə'prəuprɪət] *adj* inadecuado; (*improper*) poco oportuno
inaugurate [ɪ'nɔːgjureɪt] *vt* inaugurar; (*president, official*) investir
Inc. (US) *abbr* (= *incorporated*) S.A.
incapable [ɪn'keɪpəbl] *adj* incapaz
incense [*n* 'ɪnsɛns, *vb* ɪn'sɛns] *n* incienso ▷ *vt* (*anger*) indignar, encolerizar
incentive [ɪn'sɛntɪv] *n* incentivo, estímulo
inch [ɪntʃ] *n* pulgada; **to be within an ~ of** estar a dos dedos de; **he didn't give an ~** no dio concesión alguna
incidence ['ɪnsɪdns] *n* (*of crime, disease*) incidencia
incident ['ɪnsɪdnt] *n* incidente *m*
incidentally [ɪnsɪ'dɛntəlɪ] *adv* (*by the way*) a propósito
inclination [ɪnklɪ'neɪʃən] *n* (*tendency*) tendencia, inclinación *f*; (*desire*) deseo; (*disposition*) propensión *f*
incline [*n* 'ɪnklaɪn, *vb* ɪn'klaɪn] *n* pendiente *m*, cuesta ▷ *vt* (*head*) poner de lado ▷ *vi* inclinarse; **to be ~d to** (*tend*) tener tendencia a hacer algo
include [ɪn'kluːd] *vt* (*incorporate*) incluir; (*in letter*) adjuntar; **including** *prep* incluso, inclusive
inclusion [ɪn'kluːʒən] *n* inclusión *f*
inclusive [ɪn'klusɪv] *adj* inclusivo; **~ of tax** incluidos los impuestos
income ['ɪŋkʌm] *n* (*earned*) ingresos *mpl*; (*from property etc*) renta; (*from investment etc*) rédito; **income support** *n* (BRIT) ≈ ayuda familiar; **income tax** *n* impuesto sobre la renta
incoming ['ɪnkʌmɪŋ] *adj* (*flight, government etc*) entrante
incompatible [ɪnkəm'pætɪbl] *adj* incompatible
incompetence [ɪn'kɔmpɪtəns] *n* incompetencia
incompetent [ɪn'kɔmpɪtənt] *adj* incompetente
incomplete [ɪnkəm'pliːt] *adj* (*partial: achievement etc*) incompleto; (*unfinished: painting etc*) inacabado
inconsistent [ɪnkən'sɪstənt] *adj* inconsecuente; (*contradictory*) incongruente; **~ with** (que) no concuerda con
inconvenience [ɪnkən'viːnjəns] *n* inconvenientes *mpl*; (*trouble*) molestia, incomodidad *f* ▷ *vt* incomodar
inconvenient [ɪnkən'viːnjənt] *adj* incómodo, poco práctico; (*time, place, visitor*) inoportuno
incorporate [ɪn'kɔːpəreɪt] *vt* incorporar; (*contain*) comprender; (*add*) agregar
incorrect [ɪnkə'rɛkt] *adj* incorrecto
increase [*n* 'ɪnkriːs, *vb* ɪn'kriːs] *n* aumento ▷ *vi* aumentar; (*grow*) crecer; (*price*) subir ▷ *vt* aumentar; (*price*) subir; **increasingly** *adv* cada vez más, más y más
incredible [ɪn'krɛdɪbl] *adj* increíble; **incredibly** *adv* increíblemente
incur [ɪn'kəː*] *vt* (*expenditure*) incurrir; (*loss*) sufrir; (*anger, disapproval*) provocar
indecent [ɪn'diːsnt] *adj* indecente
indeed [ɪn'diːd] *adv* efectivamente, en realidad; (*in fact*) en efecto; (*furthermore*) es más; **yes ~!** ¡claro

que sí!

indefinitely [ɪn'dɛfɪnɪtlɪ] *adv* (*wait*) indefinidamente

independence [ɪndɪ'pɛndns] *n* independencia; **Independence Day** (US) *n* Día *m* de la Independencia

INDEPENDENCE DAY

El cuatro de julio es **Independence Day**, la fiesta nacional de Estados Unidos, que se celebra en conmemoración de la Declaración de Independencia, escrita por Thomas Jefferson y aprobada en 1776. En ella se proclamaba la independencia total de Gran Bretaña de las trece colonias americanas que serían el origen de los Estados Unidos de América.

independent [ɪndɪ'pɛndənt] *adj* independiente; **independent school** *n* (BRIT) escuela *f* privada, colegio *m* privado

index ['ɪndɛks] (*pl* **~es**) *n* (*in book*) índice *m*; (*: in library etc*) catálogo; (*pl* **indices**: *ratio, sign*) exponente *m*

India ['ɪndɪə] *n* la India; **Indian** *adj, n* indio/a; **Red Indian** piel roja *mf*

indicate ['ɪndɪkeɪt] *vt* indicar; **indication** [-'keɪʃən] *n* indicio, señal *f*; **indicative** [ɪn'dɪkətɪv] *adj*: **to be indicative of** indicar; **indicator** *n* indicador *m*; (*Aut*) intermitente *m*

indices ['ɪndɪsiːz] *npl of* **index**

indict [ɪn'daɪt] *vt* acusar; **indictment** *n* acusación *f*

indifference [ɪn'dɪfrəns] *n* indiferencia

indifferent [ɪn'dɪfrənt] *adj* indiferente; (*mediocre*) regular

indigenous [ɪn'dɪdʒɪnəs] *adj* indígena

indigestion [ɪndɪ'dʒɛstʃən] *n* indigestión *f*

indignant [ɪn'dɪgnənt] *adj*: **to be ~ at sth/with sb** indignarse por algo/con algn

indirect [ɪndɪ'rɛkt] *adj* indirecto

indispensable [ɪndɪ'spɛnsəbl] *adj* indispensable, imprescindible

individual [ɪndɪ'vɪdjuəl] *n* individuo ▷ *adj* individual; (*personal*) personal; (*particular*) particular; **individually** *adv* (*singly*) individualmente

Indonesia [ɪndə'niːzɪə] *n* Indonesia

indoor ['ɪndɔː*] *adj* (*swimming pool*) cubierto; (*plant*) de interior; (*sport*) bajo cubierta; **indoors** [ɪn'dɔːz] *adv* dentro

induce [ɪn'djuːs] *vt* inducir, persuadir; (*bring about*) producir; (*labour*) provocar

indulge [ɪn'dʌldʒ] *vt* (*whim*) satisfacer; (*person*) complacer; (*child*) mimar ▷ *vi*: **to ~ in** darse el gusto de; **indulgent** *adj* indulgente

industrial [ɪn'dʌstrɪəl] *adj* industrial; **industrial estate** (BRIT) *n* polígono (SP) *or* zona (LAM) industrial; **industrialist** *n* industrial *mf*; **industrial park** (US) *n* = **industrial estate**

industry ['ɪndəstrɪ] *n* industria; (*diligence*) aplicación *f*

inefficient [ɪnɪ'fɪʃənt] *adj* ineficaz, ineficiente

inequality [ɪnɪ'kwɔlɪtɪ] *n* desigualdad *f*

inevitable [ɪn'ɛvɪtəbl] *adj* inevitable; **inevitably** *adv* inevitablemente

inexpensive [ɪnɪk'spɛnsɪv] *adj* económico

inexperienced [ɪnɪk'spɪərɪənst] *adj* inexperto

inexplicable [ɪnɪk'splɪkəbl] *adj* inexplicable

infamous ['ɪnfəməs] *adj* infame

infant ['ɪnfənt] *n* niño/a; (*baby*) niño/a pequeño/a, bebé *mf*; (*pej*) aniñado

infantry ['ɪnfəntrɪ] *n* infantería

infant school (BRIT) *n* parvulario

infect [ɪn'fɛkt] *vt* (*wound*) infectar; (*food*) contaminar; (*person, animal*) contagiar; **infection** [ɪn'fɛkʃən] *n* infección *f*; (*fig*) contagio; **infectious**

[ɪn'fɛkʃəs] *adj* (*also fig*) contagioso
infer [ɪn'fəː*] *vt* deducir, inferir
inferior [ɪn'fɪərɪə*] *adj, n* inferior *mf*
infertile [ɪn'fəːtaɪl] *adj* estéril; (*person*) infecundo
infertility [ɪnfəː'tɪlɪtɪ] *n* esterilidad *f*; infecundidad *f*
infested [ɪn'fɛstɪd] *adj*: **~ with** plagado de
infinite ['ɪnfɪnɪt] *adj* infinito; **infinitely** *adv* infinitamente
infirmary [ɪn'fəːmərɪ] *n* hospital *m*
inflamed [ɪn'fleɪmd] *adj*: **to become ~** inflamarse
inflammation [ɪnflə'meɪʃən] *n* inflamación *f*
inflatable [ɪn'fleɪtəbl] *adj* (*ball, boat*) inflable
inflate [ɪn'fleɪt] *vt* (*tyre, price etc*) inflar; (*fig*) hinchar; **inflation** [ɪn'fleɪʃən] *n* (*Econ*) inflación *f*
inflexible [ɪn'flɛksəbl] *adj* (*rule*) rígido; (*person*) inflexible
inflict [ɪn'flɪkt] *vt*: **to ~ sth on sb** infligir algo en algn
influence ['ɪnfluəns] *n* influencia ▷ *vt* influir en, influenciar; **under the ~ of alcohol** en estado de embriaguez; **influential** [-'ɛnʃl] *adj* influyente
influx ['ɪnflʌks] *n* afluencia
info (*inf*) ['ɪnfəu] *n* = **information**
inform [ɪn'fɔːm] *vt*: **to ~ sb of sth** informar a algn sobre *or* de algo ▷ *vi*: **to ~ on sb** delatar a algn
informal [ɪn'fɔːməl] *adj* (*manner, tone*) familiar; (*dress, interview, occasion*) informal; (*visit, meeting*) extraoficial
information [ɪnfə'meɪʃən] *n* información *f*; (*knowledge*) conocimientos *mpl*; **a piece of ~** un dato; **information office** *n* información *f*; **information technology** *n* informática
informative [ɪn'fɔːmətɪv] *adj* informativo
infra-red [ɪnfrə'rɛd] *adj* infrarrojo
infrastructure ['ɪnfrəstrʌktʃə*] *n* (*of system etc*) infraestructura

infrequent [ɪn'friːkwənt] *adj* infrecuente
infuriate [ɪn'fjuərɪeɪt] *vt*: **to become ~d** ponerse furioso
infuriating [ɪn'fjuərɪeɪtɪŋ] *adj* (*habit, noise*) enloquecedor(a)
ingenious [ɪn'dʒiːnjəs] *adj* ingenioso
ingredient [ɪn'griːdɪənt] *n* ingrediente *m*
inhabit [ɪn'hæbɪt] *vt* vivir en; **inhabitant** *n* habitante *mf*
inhale [ɪn'heɪl] *vt* inhalar ▷ *vi* (*breathe in*) aspirar; (*in smoking*) tragar; **inhaler** *n* inhalador *m*
inherent [ɪn'hɪərənt] *adj*: **~ in** *or* **to** inherente a
inherit [ɪn'hɛrɪt] *vt* heredar; **inheritance** *n* herencia; (*fig*) patrimonio
inhibit [ɪn'hɪbɪt] *vt* inhibir, impedir; **inhibition** [-'bɪʃən] *n* cohibición *f*
initial [ɪ'nɪʃl] *adj* primero ▷ *n* inicial *f* ▷ *vt* firmar con las iniciales; **initials** *npl* (*as signature*) iniciales *fpl*; (*abbreviation*) siglas *fpl*; **initially** *adv* al principio
initiate [ɪ'nɪʃɪeɪt] *vt* iniciar; **to ~ proceedings against sb** (*Law*) entablar proceso contra algn
initiative [ɪ'nɪʃətɪv] *n* iniciativa
inject [ɪn'dʒɛkt] *vt* inyectar; **to ~ sb with sth** inyectar algo a algn; **injection** [ɪn'dʒɛkʃən] *n* inyección *f*
injure ['ɪndʒə*] *vt* (*hurt*) herir, lastimar; (*fig: reputation etc*) perjudicar; **injured** *adj* (*person, arm*) herido, lastimado; **injury** *n* herida, lesión *f*; (*wrong*) perjuicio, daño

> Be careful not to translate **injury** by the Spanish word *injuria*.

injustice [ɪn'dʒʌstɪs] *n* injusticia
ink [ɪŋk] *n* tinta; **ink-jet printer** ['ɪŋkdʒɛt-] *n* impresora de chorro de tinta
inland [*adj* 'ɪnlənd, *adv* ɪn'lænd] *adj* (*waterway, port etc*) interior ▷ *adv* tierra adentro; **Inland Revenue** (BRIT) *n* departamento de impuestos ≈

Hacienda (SP)

in-laws ['ɪnlɔ:z] *npl* suegros *mpl*

inmate ['ɪnmeɪt] *n* (*in prison*) preso/a, presidiario/a; (*in asylum*) internado/a

inn [ɪn] *n* posada, mesón *m*

inner ['ɪnə*] *adj* (*courtyard, calm*) interior; (*feelings*) íntimo; **inner-city** *adj* (*schools, problems*) de las zonas céntricas pobres, de los barrios céntricos pobres

inning ['ɪnɪŋ] *n* (US: *Baseball*) inning *m*, entrada; **~s** (*Cricket*) entrada, turno

innocence ['ɪnəsns] *n* inocencia

innocent ['ɪnəsnt] *adj* inocente

innovation [ɪnəu'veɪʃən] *n* novedad *f*

innovative ['ɪnəu'veɪtɪv] *adj* innovador

in-patient ['ɪnpeɪʃənt] *n* paciente *m/f* interno/a

input ['ɪnput] *n* entrada; (*of resources*) inversión *f*; (*Comput*) entrada de datos

inquest ['ɪnkwɛst] *n* (*coroner's*) encuesta judicial

inquire [ɪn'kwaɪə*] *vi* preguntar ▷ *vt*: **to ~ whether** preguntar si; **to ~ about** (*person*) preguntar por; (*fact*) informarse de; **inquiry** *n* pregunta; (*investigation*) investigación *f*, pesquisa; **"Inquiries"** "Información"

ins. *abbr* = **inches**

insane [ɪn'seɪn] *adj* loco; (*Med*) demente

insanity [ɪn'sænɪtɪ] *n* demencia, locura

insect ['ɪnsɛkt] *n* insecto; **insect repellent** *n* loción *f* contra insectos

insecure [ɪnsɪ'kjuə*] *adj* inseguro

insecurity [ɪnsɪ'kjuərɪtɪ] *n* inseguridad *f*

insensitive [ɪn'sɛnsɪtɪv] *adj* insensible

insert [*vb* ɪn'sə:t, *n* 'ɪnsə:t] *vt* (*into sth*) introducir ▷ *n* encarte *m*

inside ['ɪn'saɪd] *n* interior *m* ▷ *adj* interior, interno ▷ *adv* (*be*) (por) dentro; (*go*) hacia dentro ▷ *prep* dentro de; (*of time*): **~ 10 minutes** en menos de 10 minutos; **inside lane** *n* (*Aut: in Britain*) carril *m* izquierdo; (: *in US, Europe etc*) carril *m* derecho; **inside out** *adv* (*turn*) al revés; (*know*) a fondo

insight ['ɪnsaɪt] *n* perspicacia

insignificant [ɪnsɪg'nɪfɪknt] *adj* insignificante

insincere [ɪnsɪn'sɪə*] *adj* poco sincero

insist [ɪn'sɪst] *vi* insistir; **to ~ on** insistir en; **to ~ that** insistir en que; (*claim*) exigir que; **insistent** *adj* insistente; (*noise, action*) persistente

insomnia [ɪn'sɔmnɪə] *n* insomnio

inspect [ɪn'spɛkt] *vt* inspeccionar, examinar; (*troops*) pasar revista a; **inspection** [ɪn'spɛkʃən] *n* inspección *f*, examen *m*; (*of troops*) revista; **inspector** *n* inspector(a) *m/f*; (BRIT: *on buses, trains*) revisor(a) *m/f*

inspiration [ɪnspə'reɪʃən] *n* inspiración *f*; **inspire** [ɪn'spaɪə*] *vt* inspirar; **inspiring** *adj* inspirador(a)

instability [ɪnstə'bɪlɪtɪ] *n* inestabilidad *f*

install [ɪn'stɔ:l] (US **instal**) *vt* instalar; (*official*) nombrar; **installation** [ɪnstə'leɪʃən] *n* instalación *f*

instalment [ɪn'stɔ:lmənt] (US **installment**) *n* plazo; (*of story*) entrega; (*of TV serial etc*) capítulo; **in ~s** (*pay, receive*) a plazos

instance ['ɪnstəns] *n* ejemplo, caso; **for ~** por ejemplo; **in the first ~** en primer lugar

instant ['ɪnstənt] *n* instante *m*, momento ▷ *adj* inmediato; (*coffee etc*) instantáneo; **instantly** *adv* en seguida; **instant messaging** *n* mensajería instantánea

instead [ɪn'stɛd] *adv* en cambio; **~ of** en lugar de, en vez de

instinct ['ɪnstɪŋkt] *n* instinto; **instinctive** *adj* instintivo

institute ['ɪnstɪtju:t] *n* instituto; (*professional body*) colegio ▷ *vt* (*begin*) iniciar, empezar; (*proceedings*) entablar; (*system, rule*) establecer

institution [ɪnstɪ'tjuːʃən] *n* institución *f*; (*Med: home*) asilo; (*: asylum*) manicomio; (*of system etc*) establecimiento; (*of custom*) iniciación *f*

instruct [ɪn'strʌkt] *vt*: **to ~ sb in sth** instruir a algn en *or* sobre algo; **to ~ sb to do sth** dar instrucciones a algn de hacer algo; **instruction** [ɪn'strʌkʃən] *n* (*teaching*) instrucción *f*; **instructions** *npl* (*orders*) órdenes *fpl*; **instructions (for use)** modo de empleo; **instructor** *n* instructor(a) *m/f*

instrument ['ɪnstrəmənt] *n* instrumento; **instrumental** [-'mɛntl] *adj* (*Mus*) instrumental; **to be instrumental in** ser (el) artífice de

insufficient [ɪnsə'fɪʃənt] *adj* insuficiente

insulate ['ɪnsjuleɪt] *vt* aislar; **insulation** [-'leɪʃən] *n* aislamiento

insulin ['ɪnsjulɪn] *n* insulina

insult [*n* 'ɪnsʌlt, *vb* ɪn'sʌlt] *n* insulto ▷ *vt* insultar; **insulting** *adj* insultante

insurance [ɪn'ʃuərəns] *n* seguro; **fire/life ~** seguro contra incendios/ sobre la vida; **insurance company** *n* compañía *f* de seguros; **insurance policy** *n* póliza (de seguros)

insure [ɪn'ʃuə*] *vt* asegurar

intact [ɪn'tækt] *adj* íntegro; (*unharmed*) intacto

intake ['ɪnteɪk] *n* (*of food*) ingestión *f*; (*of air*) consumo; (BRIT *Scol*): **an ~ of 200 a year** 200 matriculados al año

integral ['ɪntɪgrəl] *adj* (*whole*) íntegro; (*part*) integrante

integrate ['ɪntɪgreɪt] *vt* integrar ▷ *vi* integrarse

integrity [ɪn'tɛgrɪtɪ] *n* honradez *f*, rectitud *f*

intellect ['ɪntəlɛkt] *n* intelecto; **intellectual** [-'lɛktjuəl] *adj, n* intelectual *mf*

intelligence [ɪn'tɛlɪdʒəns] *n* inteligencia

intelligent [ɪn'tɛlɪdʒənt] *adj* inteligente

intend [ɪn'tɛnd] *vt* (*gift etc*): **to ~ sth for** destinar algo a; **to ~ to do sth** tener intención de *or* pensar hacer algo

intense [ɪn'tɛns] *adj* intenso

intensify [ɪn'tɛnsɪfaɪ] *vt* intensificar; (*increase*) aumentar

intensity [ɪn'tɛnsɪtɪ] *n* (*gen*) intensidad *f*

intensive [ɪn'tɛnsɪv] *adj* intensivo; **intensive care** *n*: **to be in intensive care** estar bajo cuidados intensivos; **intensive care unit** *n* unidad *f* de vigilancia intensiva

intent [ɪn'tɛnt] *n* propósito; (*Law*) premeditación *f* ▷ *adj* (*absorbed*) absorto; (*attentive*) atento; **to all ~s and purposes** prácticamente; **to be ~ on doing sth** estar resuelto a hacer algo

intention [ɪn'tɛnʃən] *n* intención *f*, propósito; **intentional** *adj* deliberado

interact [ɪntər'ækt] *vi* influirse mutuamente; **interaction** [ɪntər'ækʃən] *n* interacción *f*, acción *f* recíproca; **interactive** *adj* (*Comput*) interactivo

intercept [ɪntə'sɛpt] *vt* interceptar; (*stop*) detener

interchange ['ɪntətʃeɪndʒ] *n* intercambio; (*on motorway*) intersección *f*

intercourse ['ɪntəkɔːs] *n* (*sexual*) relaciones *fpl* sexuales

interest ['ɪntrɪst] *n* (*also Comm*) interés *m* ▷ *vt* interesar; **interested** *adj* interesado; **to be interested in** interesarse por; **interesting** *adj* interesante; **interest rate** *n* tipo *or* tasa de interés

interface ['ɪntəfeɪs] *n* (*Comput*) junción *f*

interfere [ɪntə'fɪə*] *vi*: **to ~ in** entrometerse en; **to ~ with** (*hinder*) estorbar; (*damage*) estropear

interference [ɪntə'fɪərəns] *n* intromisión *f*; (*Radio, TV*) interferencia

interim ['ɪntərɪm] *n*: **in the ~** en el ínterin ▷ *adj* provisional

interior [ɪn'tɪərɪə*] *n* interior *m* ▷ *adj* interior; **interior design** *n* interiorismo, decoración *f* de interiores
intermediate [ɪntə'mi:dɪət] *adj* intermedio
intermission [ɪntə'mɪʃən] *n* intermisión *f*; (*Theatre*) descanso
intern [*vb* ɪn'tə:n, *n* 'ɪntə:n] (*US*) *vt* internar ▷ *n* interno/a
internal [ɪn'tə:nl] *adj* (*layout, pipes, security*) interior; (*injury, structure, memo*) internal; **Internal Revenue Service** (*US*) *n* departamento de impuestos, ≈ Hacienda (*SP*)
international [ɪntə'næʃənl] *adj* internacional ▷ *n* (*BRIT*: *match*) partido internacional
Internet ['ɪntənɛt] *n*: **the ~** Internet *m or f*; **Internet café** *n* cibercafé *m*; **Internet Service Provider** *n* proveedor *m* de (acceso a) Internet; **Internet user** *n* internauta *mf*
interpret [ɪn'tə:prɪt] *vt* interpretar; (*translate*) traducir; (*understand*) entender ▷ *vi* hacer de intérprete; **interpretation** [ɪntə:prɪ'teɪʃən] *n* interpretación *f*; traducción *f*; **interpreter** *n* intérprete *mf*
interrogate [ɪn'tɛrəugeɪt] *vt* interrogar; **interrogation** [-'geɪʃən] *n* interrogatorio
interrogative [ɪntə'rɔgətɪv] *adj* interrogativo
interrupt [ɪntə'rʌpt] *vt, vi* interrumpir; **interruption** [-'rʌpʃən] *n* interrupción *f*
intersection [ɪntə'sɛkʃən] *n* (*of roads*) cruce *m*
interstate ['ɪntərsteɪt] (*US*) *n* carretera interestatal
interval ['ɪntəvl] *n* intervalo; (*BRIT Theatre, Sport*) descanso; (*Scol*) recreo; **at ~s** a ratos, de vez en cuando
intervene [ɪntə'vi:n] *vi* intervenir; (*event*) interponerse; (*time*) transcurrir
interview ['ɪntəvju:] *n* entrevista ▷ *vt* entrevistarse con; **interviewer** *n* entrevistador(a) *m/f*
intimate [*adj* 'ɪntɪmət, *vb* 'ɪntɪmeɪt] *adj* íntimo; (*friendship*) estrecho; (*knowledge*) profundo ▷ *vt* dar a entender
intimidate [ɪn'tɪmɪdeɪt] *vt* intimidar, amedrentar
intimidating [ɪn'tɪmɪdeɪtɪŋ] *adj* amedrentador, intimidante
into ['ɪntu:] *prep* en; (*towards*) a; (*inside*) hacia el interior de; **~ 3 pieces/ French** en 3 pedazos/al francés
intolerant [ɪn'tɔlərənt] *adj*: **~ (of)** intolerante (con *or* para)
intranet ['ɪntrənet] *n* intranet *f*
intransitive [ɪn'trænsɪtɪv] *adj* intransitivo
intricate ['ɪntrɪkət] *adj* (*design, pattern*) intrincado
intrigue [ɪn'tri:g] *n* intriga ▷ *vt* fascinar; **intriguing** *adj* fascinante
introduce [ɪntrə'dju:s] *vt* introducir, meter; (*speaker, TV show etc*) presentar; **to ~ sb (to sb)** presentar a algn (a algn); **to ~ sb to** (*pastime, technique*) introducir a algn a; **introduction** [-'dʌkʃən] *n* introducción *f*; (*of person*) presentación *f*; **introductory** [-'dʌktərɪ] *adj* introductorio; (*lesson, offer*) de introducción
intrude [ɪn'tru:d] *vi* (*person*) entrometerse; **to ~ on** estorbar; **intruder** *n* intruso/a
intuition [ɪntju:'ɪʃən] *n* intuición *f*
inundate ['ɪnʌndeɪt] *vt*: **to ~ with** inundar de
invade [ɪn'veɪd] *vt* invadir
invalid [*n* 'ɪnvəlɪd, *adj* ɪn'vælɪd] *n* (*Med*) minusválido/a ▷ *adj* (*not valid*) inválido, nulo
invaluable [ɪn'væljuəbl] *adj* inestimable
invariably [ɪn'vɛərɪəblɪ] *adv* sin excepción, siempre; **she is ~ late** siempre llega tarde
invasion [ɪn'veɪʒən] *n* invasión *f*
invent [ɪn'vɛnt] *vt* inventar; **invention** [ɪn'vɛnʃən] *n* invento;

(*lie*) ficción *f*, mentira; **inventor** *n* inventor(a) *m/f*
inventory ['ɪnvəntrɪ] *n* inventario
inverted commas [ɪn'və:tɪd-] (BRIT) *npl* comillas *fpl*
invest [ɪn'vɛst] *vt* invertir ▷ *vi*: **to ~ in** (*company etc*) invertir dinero en; (*fig: sth useful*) comprar
investigate [ɪn'vɛstɪgeɪt] *vt* investigar; **investigation** [-'geɪʃən] *n* investigación *f*, pesquisa
investigator [ɪn'vɛstɪgeɪtə*] *n* investigador(a) *m/f*; **private ~** investigador(a) *m/f* privado/a
investment [ɪn'vɛstmənt] *n* inversión *f*
investor [ɪn'vɛstə*] *n* inversionista *mf*
invisible [ɪn'vɪzɪbl] *adj* invisible
invitation [ɪnvɪ'teɪʃən] *n* invitación *f*
invite [ɪn'vaɪt] *vt* invitar; (*opinions etc*) solicitar, pedir; **inviting** *adj* atractivo; (*food*) apetitoso
invoice ['ɪnvɔɪs] *n* factura ▷ *vt* facturar
involve [ɪn'vɔlv] *vt* suponer, implicar; tener que ver con; (*concern, affect*) corresponder; **to ~ sb (in sth)** comprometer a algn (con algo); **involved** *adj* complicado; **to be involved in** (*take part*) tomar parte en; (*be engrossed*) estar muy metido en; **involvement** *n* participación *f*; dedicación *f*
inward ['ɪnwəd] *adj* (*movement*) interior, interno; (*thought, feeling*) íntimo; **inward(s)** *adv* hacia dentro
iPod ® ['aɪpɔd] *n* iPod ® *m*
IQ *n abbr* (= *intelligence quotient*) cociente *m* intelectual
IRA *n abbr* (= *Irish Republican Army*) IRA *m*
Iran [ɪ'rɑ:n] *n* Irán *m*; **Iranian** [ɪ'reɪnɪən] *adj, n* iraní *mf*
Iraq [ɪ'rɑ:k] *n* Iraq; **Iraqi** *adj, n* iraquí *mf*
Ireland ['aɪələnd] *n* Irlanda
iris ['aɪrɪs] (*pl* **~es**) *n* (*Anat*) iris *m*; (*Bot*) lirio
Irish ['aɪrɪʃ] *adj* irlandés/esa ▷ *npl*: **the ~** los irlandeses; **Irishman** (*irreg*) *n* irlandés *m*; **Irishwoman** (*irreg*) *n* irlandésa
iron ['aɪən] *n* hierro; (*for clothes*) plancha ▷ *cpd* de hierro ▷ *vt* (*clothes*) planchar
ironic(al) [aɪ'rɔnɪk(l)] *adj* irónico; **ironically** *adv* irónicamente
ironing ['aɪənɪŋ] *n* (*activity*) planchado; (*clothes: ironed*) ropa planchada; (*: to be ironed*) ropa por planchar; **ironing board** *n* tabla de planchar
irony ['aɪrənɪ] *n* ironía
irrational [ɪ'ræʃənl] *adj* irracional
irregular [ɪ'rɛgjulə*] *adj* irregular; (*surface*) desigual; (*action, event*) anómalo; (*behaviour*) poco ortodoxo
irrelevant [ɪ'rɛləvənt] *adj* fuera de lugar, inoportuno
irresistible [ɪrɪ'zɪstɪbl] *adj* irresistible
irresponsible [ɪrɪ'spɔnsɪbl] *adj* (*act*) irresponsable; (*person*) poco serio
irrigation [ɪrɪ'geɪʃən] *n* riego
irritable ['ɪrɪtəbl] *adj* (*person*) de mal humor
irritate ['ɪrɪteɪt] *vt* fastidiar; (*Med*) picar; **irritating** *adj* fastidioso; **irritation** [-'teɪʃən] *n* fastidio; enfado; picazón *f*
IRS (US) *n abbr* = **Internal Revenue Service**
is [ɪz] *vb see* **be**
ISDN *n abbr* (= *Integrated Services Digital Network*) RDSI *f*
Islam ['ɪzlɑ:m] *n* Islam *m*; **Islamic** [ɪz'læmɪk] *adj* islámico
island ['aɪlənd] *n* isla; **islander** *n* isleño/a
isle [aɪl] *n* isla
isn't ['ɪznt] = **is not**
isolated ['aɪsəleɪtɪd] *adj* aislado
isolation [aɪsə'leɪʃən] *n* aislamiento
ISP *n abbr* = **Internet Service Provider**
Israel ['ɪzreɪl] *n* Israel *m*; **Israeli**

[ɪz'reɪlɪ] *adj, n* israelí *mf*

issue ['ɪsjuː] *n* (*problem, subject*) cuestión *f*; (*outcome*) resultado; (*of banknotes etc*) emisión *f*; (*of newspaper etc*) edición *f* ▷ *vt* (*rations, equipment*) distribuir, repartir; (*orders*) dar; (*certificate, passport*) expedir; (*decree*) promulgar; (*magazine*) publicar; (*cheques*) extender; (*banknotes, stamps*) emitir; **at ~** en cuestión; **to take ~ with sb (over)** estar en desacuerdo con algn (sobre); **to make an ~ of sth** hacer una cuestión de algo

IT *n abbr* = **information technology**

KEYWORD

it [ɪt] *pron* **1** (*specific subject: not generally translated*) él (ella); (*: direct object*) lo, la; (*: indirect object*) le; (*after prep*) él (ella); (*abstract concept*) ello; **it's on the table** está en la mesa; **I can't find it** no lo (*or* la) encuentro; **give it to me** dámelo (*or* dámela); **I spoke to him about it** le hablé del asunto; **what did you learn from it?** ¿qué aprendiste de él (*or* ella)?; **did you go to it?** (*party, concert etc*) ¿fuiste?
2 (*impersonal*): **it's raining** llueve, está lloviendo; **it's 6 o'clock/the 10th of August** son las 6/es el 10 de agosto; **how far is it? - it's 10 miles/2 hours on the train** ¿a qué distancia está? - a 10 millas/2 horas en tren; **who is it? - it's me** ¿quién es? - soy yo

Italian [ɪ'tæljən] *adj* italiano ▷ *n* italiano/a; (*Ling*) italiano

italics [ɪ'tælɪks] *npl* cursiva

Italy ['ɪtəlɪ] *n* Italia

itch [ɪtʃ] *n* picazón *f* ▷ *vi* (*part of body*) picar; **to ~ to do sth** rabiar por hacer algo; **itchy** *adj*: **my hand is itchy** me pica la mano

it'd ['ɪtd] = **it would; it had**

item ['aɪtəm] *n* artículo; (*on agenda*) asunto (a tratar); (*also*: **news ~**) noticia

itinerary [aɪ'tɪnərərɪ] *n* itinerario

it'll ['ɪtl] = **it will; it shall**

its [ɪts] *adj* su; sus *pl*

it's [ɪts] = **it is; it has**

itself [ɪt'sɛlf] *pron* (*reflexive*) sí mismo/a; (*emphatic*) él mismo(ella misma)

ITV *n abbr* (BRIT: = *Independent Television*) *cadena de televisión comercial independiente del Estado*

I've [aɪv] = **I have**

ivory ['aɪvərɪ] *n* marfil *m*

ivy ['aɪvɪ] *n* (*Bot*) hiedra

jab [dʒæb] *vt*: **to ~ sth into sth** clavar algo en algo ▷ *n* (*inf: Med*) pinchazo
jack [dʒæk] *n* (*Aut*) gato; (*Cards*) sota
jacket ['dʒækɪt] *n* chaqueta, americana (*SP*), saco (*LAM*); (*of book*) sobrecubierta; **jacket potato** *n* patata asada (con piel)
jackpot ['dʒækpɔt] *n* premio gordo
Jacuzzi® [dʒə'ku:zɪ] *n* jacuzzi® *m*
jagged ['dʒægɪd] *adj* dentado
jail [dʒeɪl] *n* cárcel *f* ▷ *vt* encarcelar; **jail sentence** *n* pena *f* de cárcel
jam [dʒæm] *n* mermelada; (*also*: **traffic ~**) embotellamiento; (*inf: difficulty*) apuro ▷ *vt* (*passage etc*) obstruir; (*mechanism, drawer etc*) atascar; (*Radio*) interferir ▷ *vi* atascarse, trabarse; **to ~ sth into sth** meter algo a la fuerza en algo
Jamaica [dʒə'meɪkə] *n* Jamaica
jammed [dʒæmd] *adj* atascado
Jan *abbr* (= *January*) ene
janitor ['dʒænɪtə*] *n* (*caretaker*) portero, conserje *m*
January ['dʒænjuərɪ] *n* enero
Japan [dʒə'pæn] *n* (el) Japón; **Japanese** [dʒæpə'ni:z] *adj* japonés/esa ▷ *n inv* japonés/esa *m/f*; (*Ling*) japonés *m*
jar [dʒɑ:*] *n* tarro, bote *m* ▷ *vi* (*sound*) chirriar; (*colours*) desentonar
jargon ['dʒɑ:gən] *n* jerga
javelin ['dʒævlɪn] *n* jabalina
jaw [dʒɔ:] *n* mandíbula
jazz [dʒæz] *n* jazz *m*
jealous ['dʒɛləs] *adj* celoso; (*envious*) envidioso; **jealousy** *n* celos *mpl*; envidia
jeans [dʒi:nz] *npl* vaqueros *mpl*, tejanos *mpl*
Jello® ['dʒɛləu] (*US*) *n* gelatina
jelly ['dʒɛlɪ] *n* (*jam*) jalea; (*dessert etc*) gelatina; **jellyfish** *n inv* medusa, aguaviva (*RPL*)
jeopardize ['dʒɛpədaɪz] *vt* arriesgar, poner en peligro
jerk [dʒə:k] *n* (*jolt*) sacudida; (*wrench*) tirón *m*; (*inf*) imbécil *mf* ▷ *vt* tirar bruscamente de ▷ *vi* (*vehicle*) traquetear
Jersey ['dʒə:zɪ] *n* Jersey *m*
jersey ['dʒə:zɪ] *n* jersey *m*; (*fabric*) (tejido de) punto
Jesus ['dʒi:zəs] *n* Jesús *m*
jet [dʒɛt] *n* (*of gas, liquid*) chorro; (*Aviat*) avión *m* a reacción; **jet lag** *n* desorientación *f* después de un largo vuelo; **jet-ski** *vi* practicar el motociclismo acuático
jetty ['dʒɛtɪ] *n* muelle *m*, embarcadero
Jew [dʒu:] *n* judío/a
jewel ['dʒu:əl] *n* joya; (*in watch*) rubí *m*; **jeweller** (*US* **jeweler**) *n* joyero/a; **jeweller's (shop)** (*US* **jewelry store**) *n* joyería; **jewellery** (*US* **jewelry**) *n* joyas *fpl*, alhajas *fpl*
Jewish ['dʒu:ɪʃ] *adj* judío
jigsaw ['dʒɪgsɔ:] *n* (*also*: **~ puzzle**) rompecabezas *m inv*, puzle *m*
job [dʒɔb] *n* (*task*) tarea; (*post*) empleo; **it's not my ~** no me incumbe a mí; **it's a good ~ that ...** menos mal que

...; **just the ~!** ¡estupendo!; **job centre** (BRIT) *n oficina estatal de colocaciones*; **jobless** *adj* sin trabajo

jockey ['dʒɔkɪ] *n* jockey *mf* ▷ *vi*: **to ~ for position** maniobrar para conseguir una posición

jog [dʒɔg] *vt* empujar (ligeramente) ▷ *vi* (*run*) hacer footing; **to ~ sb's memory** refrescar la memoria a algn; **jogging** *n* footing *m*

join [dʒɔɪn] *vt* (*things*) juntar, unir; (*club*) hacerse socio de; (*Pol*: *party*) afiliarse a; (*queue*) ponerse en; (*meet*: *people*) reunirse con ▷ *vi* (*roads*) juntarse; (*rivers*) confluir ▷ *n* juntura; **join in** *vi* tomar parte, participar ▷ *vt fus* tomar parte *or* participar en; **join up** *vi* reunirse; (*Mil*) alistarse

joiner ['dʒɔɪnə*] (BRIT) *n* carpintero/a

joint [dʒɔɪnt] *n* (*Tech*) junta, unión *f*; (*Anat*) articulación *f*; (BRIT *Culin*) pieza de carne (para asar); (*inf*: *place*) tugurio; (: *of cannabis*) porro ▷ *adj* (*common*) común; (*combined*) combinado; **joint account** *n* (*with bank etc*) cuenta común; **jointly** *adv* (*gen*) en común; (*together*) conjuntamente

joke [dʒəuk] *n* chiste *m*; (*also*: **practical ~**) broma ▷ *vi* bromear; **to play a ~ on** gastar una broma a; **joker** *n* (*Cards*) comodín *m*

jolly ['dʒɔlɪ] *adj* (*merry*) alegre; (*enjoyable*) divertido ▷ *adv* (BRIT: *inf*) muy, terriblemente

jolt [dʒəult] *n* (*jerk*) sacudida; (*shock*) susto ▷ *vt* (*physically*) sacudir; (*emotionally*) asustar

Jordan ['dʒɔːdən] *n* (*country*) Jordania; (*river*) Jordán *m*

journal ['dʒəːnl] *n* (*magazine*) revista; (*diary*) periódico, diario; **journalism** *n* periodismo; **journalist** *n* periodista *mf*, reportero/a

journey ['dʒəːnɪ] *n* viaje *m*; (*distance covered*) trayecto

joy [dʒɔɪ] *n* alegría; **joyrider** *n gamberro que roba un coche para dar una vuelta y luego abandonarlo*; **joy stick** *n* (*Aviat*) palanca de mando; (*Comput*) palanca de control

Jr *abbr* = **junior**

judge [dʒʌdʒ] *n* juez *mf*; (*fig*: *expert*) perito ▷ *vt* juzgar; (*consider*) considerar

judo ['dʒuːdəu] *n* judo

jug [dʒʌg] *n* jarra

juggle ['dʒʌgl] *vi* hacer juegos malabares; **juggler** *n* malabarista *mf*

juice [dʒuːs] *n* zumo (SP), jugo (LAM); **juicy** *adj* jugoso

Jul *abbr* (= *July*) jul

July [dʒuː'laɪ] *n* julio

jumble ['dʒʌmbl] *n* revoltijo ▷ *vt* (*also*: **~ up**) revolver; **jumble sale** (BRIT) *n venta de objetos usados con fines benéficos*

JUMBLE SALE

Los **jumble sales** son unos mercadillos que se organizan con fines benéficos en los locales de un colegio, iglesia u otro centro público. En ellos puede comprarse todo tipo de artículos baratos de segunda mano, sobre todo ropa, juguetes, libros, vajillas o muebles.

jumbo ['dʒʌmbəu] *n* (*also*: **~ jet**) jumbo

jump [dʒʌmp] *vi* saltar, dar saltos; (*with fear etc*) pegar un bote; (*increase*) aumentar ▷ *vt* saltar ▷ *n* salto; aumento; **to ~ the queue** (BRIT) colarse

jumper ['dʒʌmpə*] *n* (BRIT: *pullover*) suéter *m*, jersey *m*; (US: *dress*) mandil *m*

jumper cables (US) *npl* = **jump leads**

jump leads (BRIT) *npl* cables *mpl* puente de batería

Jun. *abbr* = **junior**

junction ['dʒʌŋkʃən] *n* (BRIT: *of roads*) cruce *m*; (*Rail*) empalme *m*

June [dʒuːn] *n* junio

jungle ['dʒʌŋgl] *n* selva, jungla

junior ['dʒuːnɪə*] *adj* (*in age*) menor, más joven; (*brother/sister etc*): **seven**

years her ~ siete años menor que ella; (*position*) subalterno ▷ *n* menor *mf*, joven *mf*; **junior high school** (US) *n* *centro de educación secundaria*; *see also* **high school**; **junior school** (BRIT) *n* escuela primaria

junk [dʒʌŋk] *n* (*cheap goods*) baratijas *fpl*; (*rubbish*) basura; **junk food** *n* *alimentos preparados y envasados de escaso valor nutritivo*

junkie ['dʒʌŋkɪ] (*inf*) *n* drogadicto/a, yonqui *mf*

junk mail *n* propaganda de buzón

Jupiter ['dʒu:pɪtə*] *n* (*Mythology, Astrology*) Júpiter *m*

jurisdiction [dʒuərɪs'dɪkʃən] *n* jurisdicción *f*; **it falls** *or* **comes within/outside our ~** es/no es de nuestra competencia

jury ['dʒuərɪ] *n* jurado

just [dʒʌst] *adj* justo ▷ *adv* (*exactly*) exactamente; (*only*) sólo, solamente; **he's ~ done it/left** acaba de hacerlo/irse; **~ right** perfecto; **~ two o'clock** las dos en punto; **she's ~ as clever as you** (ella) es tan lista como tú; **~ as well that ...** menos mal que ...; **~ as he was leaving** en el momento en que se marchaba; **~ before/enough** justo antes/lo suficiente; **~ here** aquí mismo; **he ~ missed** ha fallado por poco; **~ listen to this** escucha esto un momento

justice ['dʒʌstɪs] *n* justicia; (US: *judge*) juez *mf*; **to do ~ to** (*fig*) hacer justicia a

justification [dʒʌstɪfɪ'keɪʃən] *n* justificación *f*

justify ['dʒʌstɪfaɪ] *vt* justificar; (*text*) alinear

jut [dʒʌt] *vi* (*also*: **~ out**) sobresalir

juvenile ['dʒu:vənaɪl] *adj* (*court*) de menores; (*humour, mentality*) infantil ▷ *n* menor *m* de edad

K *abbr* (= *one thousand*) mil; (= *kilobyte*) kilobyte *m*, kiloocteto

kangaroo [kæŋgə'ru:] *n* canguro

karaoke [kɑ:rə'əukɪ] *n* karaoke

karate [kə'rɑ:tɪ] *n* karate *m*

kebab [kə'bæb] *n* pincho moruno

keel [ki:l] *n* quilla; **on an even ~** (*fig*) en equilibrio

keen [ki:n] *adj* (*interest, desire*) grande, vivo; (*eye, intelligence*) agudo; (*competition*) reñido; (*edge*) afilado; (*eager*) entusiasta; **to be ~ to do** *or* **on doing sth** tener muchas ganas de hacer algo; **to be ~ on sth/sb** interesarse por algo/algn

keep [ki:p] (*pt, pp* **kept**) *vt* (*preserve, store*) guardar; (*hold back*) quedarse con; (*maintain*) mantener; (*detain*) detener; (*shop*) ser propietario de; (*feed*: *family etc*) mantener; (*promise*) cumplir; (*chickens, bees etc*) criar; (*accounts*) llevar; (*diary*) escribir; (*prevent*): **to ~ sb from doing sth** impedir a algn hacer algo ▷ *vi* (*food*) conservarse; (*remain*) seguir, continuar ▷ *n* (*of* *castle*) torreón *m*; (*food etc*) comida, subsistencia; (*inf*): **for ~s** para siempre; **to ~ doing sth** seguir haciendo algo; **to ~ sb happy** tener a algn contento; **to ~ a place tidy** mantener un lugar limpio; **to ~ sth to o.s.** guardar algo para sí mismo; **to ~ sth (back) from sb** ocultar algo a algn; **to ~ time** (*clock*) mantener la hora exacta; **keep away** *vt*: **to keep sth/sb away from sb** mantener algo/a algn apartado de algn ▷ *vi*: **to keep away (from)** mantenerse apartado (de); **keep back** *vt* (*crowd, tears*) contener; (*money*) quedarse con; (*conceal: information*): **to keep sth back from sb** ocultar algo a algn ▷ *vi* hacerse a un lado; **keep off** *vt* (*dog, person*) mantener a distancia ▷ *vi*: **if the rain keeps off** so no lleuve; **keep your hands off!** ¡no toques!; **"keep off the grass"** "prohibido pisar el césped"; **keep on** *vi*: **to keep on doing** seguir *or* continuar haciendo; **to keep on (about sth)** no parar de hablar (de algo); **keep out** *vi* (*stay out*) permanecer fuera; **"keep out"** "prohibida la entrada"; **keep up** *vt* mantener, conservar ▷ *vi* no retrasarse; **to keep up with** (*pace*) ir al paso de; (*level*) mantenerse a la altura de; **keeper** *n* guardián/ana *m/f*; **keeping** *n* (*care*) cuidado; **in keeping with** de acuerdo con

kennel ['kɛnl] *n* perrera; **kennels** *npl* residencia canina

Kenya ['kɛnjə] *n* Kenia

kept [kɛpt] *pt, pp of* **keep**

kerb [kəːb] (BRIT) *n* bordillo

kerosene ['kɛrəsiːn] *n* keroseno

ketchup ['kɛtʃəp] *n* salsa de tomate, catsup *m*

kettle ['kɛtl] *n* hervidor *m* de agua

key [kiː] *n* llave *f*; (*Mus*) tono; (*of piano, typewriter*) tecla ▷ *adj* (*issue etc*) clave *inv* ▷ *vt* (*also*: **~ in**) teclear; **keyboard** *n* teclado; **keyhole** *n* ojo (de la cerradura); **keyring** *n* llavero

kg *abbr* (= *kilogram*) kg

khaki ['kɑːkɪ] *n* caqui

kick [kɪk] *vt* dar una patada *or* un puntapié a; (*inf: habit*) quitarse de ▷ *vi* (*horse*) dar coces ▷ *n* patada; puntapié *m*; (*of animal*) coz *f*; (*thrill*): **he does it for ~s** lo hace por pura diversión; **kick off** *vi* (*Sport*) hacer el saque inicial; **kick-off** *n* saque inicial; **the kick-off is at 10 o'clock** el partido empieza a las diez

kid [kɪd] *n* (*inf: child*) chiquillo/a; (*animal*) cabrito; (*leather*) cabritilla ▷ *vi* (*inf*) bromear

kidnap ['kɪdnæp] *vt* secuestrar; **kidnapping** *n* secuestro

kidney ['kɪdnɪ] *n* riñón *m*; **kidney bean** *n* judía, alubia

kill [kɪl] *vt* matar; (*murder*) asesinar ▷ *n* matanza; **to ~ time** matar el tiempo; **killer** *n* asesino/a; **killing** *n* (*one*) asesinato; (*several*) matanza; **to make a killing** (*fig*) hacer su agosto

kiln [kɪln] *n* horno

kilo ['kiːləu] *n* kilo; **kilobyte** *n* (*Comput*) kilobyte *m*, kiloocteto; **kilogram(me)** *n* kilo, kilogramo; **kilometre** ['kɪləmiːtə*] (US **kilometer**) *n* kilómetro; **kilowatt** *n* kilovatio

kilt [kɪlt] *n* falda escocesa

kin [kɪn] *n* *see* **next-of-kin**

kind [kaɪnd] *adj* amable, atento ▷ *n* clase *f*, especie *f*; (*species*) género; **in ~** (*Comm*) en especie; **a ~ of** una especie de; **to be two of a ~** ser tal para cual

kindergarten ['kɪndəgɑːtn] *n* jardín *m* de la infancia

kindly ['kaɪndlɪ] *adj* bondadoso; cariñoso ▷ *adv* bondadosamente, amablemente; **will you ~ ...** sea usted tan amable de ...

kindness ['kaɪndnɪs] *n* (*quality*) bondad *f*, amabilidad *f*; (*act*) favor *m*

king [kɪŋ] *n* rey *m*; **kingdom** *n* reino; **kingfisher** *n* martín *m* pescador; **king-size(d) bed** *n* cama de matrimonio extragrande

kiosk ['kiːɔsk] *n* quiosco; (BRIT *Tel*) cabina

kipper ['kɪpə*] *n* arenque *m* ahumado

kiss [kɪs] *n* beso ▷*vt* besar; **to ~ (each other)** besarse; **kiss of life** *n* respiración *f* boca a boca
kit [kɪt] *n* (*equipment*) equipo; (*tools etc*) (caja de) herramientas *fpl*; (*assembly kit*) juego de armar
kitchen ['kɪtʃɪn] *n* cocina
kite [kaɪt] *n* (*toy*) cometa
kitten ['kɪtn] *n* gatito/a
kiwi ['ki:wi:-] *n* (*also*: **~ fruit**) kiwi *m*
km *abbr* (= *kilometre*) km
km/h *abbr* (= *kilometres per hour*) km/h
knack [næk] *n*: **to have the ~ of doing sth** tener el don de hacer algo
knee [ni:] *n* rodilla; **kneecap** *n* rótula
kneel [ni:l] (*pt, pp* **knelt**) *vi* (*also*: **~ down**) arrodillarse
knelt [nɛlt] *pt, pp of* **kneel**
knew [nju:] *pt of* **know**
knickers ['nɪkəz] (BRIT) *npl* bragas *fpl*
knife [naɪf] (*pl* **knives**) *n* cuchillo ▷*vt* acuchillar
knight [naɪt] *n* caballero; (*Chess*) caballo
knit [nɪt] *vt* tejer, tricotar ▷*vi* hacer punto, tricotar; (*bones*) soldarse; **to ~ one's brows** fruncir el ceño; **knitting** *n* labor *f* de punto; **knitting needle** *n* aguja de hacer punto; **knitwear** *n* prendas *fpl* de punto
knives [naɪvz] *npl of* **knife**
knob [nɔb] *n* (*of door*) tirador *m*; (*of stick*) puño; (*on radio, TV*) botón *m*
knock [nɔk] *vt* (*strike*) golpear; (*bump into*) chocar contra; (*inf*) criticar ▷*vi* (*at door etc*): **to ~ at/on** llamar a ▷*n* golpe *m*; (*on door*) llamada; **knock down** *vt* atropellar; **knock off** (*inf*) *vi* (*finish*) salir del trabajo ▷*vt* (*from price*) descontar; (*inf: steal*) birlar; **knock out** *vt* dejar sin sentido; (*Boxing*) poner fuera de combate, dejar K.O.; (*in competition*) eliminar; **knock over** *vt* (*object*) tirar; (*person*) atropellar; **knockout** *n* (*Boxing*) K.O. *m*, knockout *m* ▷*cpd* (*competition etc*) eliminatorio
knot [nɔt] *n* nudo ▷*vt* anudar
know [nəu] (*pt* **knew**, *pp* **known**) *vt* (*facts*) saber; (*be acquainted with*) conocer; (*recognize*) reconocer, conocer; **to ~ how to swim** saber nadar; **to ~ about** *or* **of sb/sth** saber de algn/algo; **know-all** *n* sabelotodo *mf*; **know-how** *n* conocimientos *mpl*; **knowing** *adj* (*look*) de complicidad; **knowingly** *adv* (*purposely*) adrede; (*smile, look*) con complicidad; **know-it-all** (US) *n* = **know-all**
knowledge ['nɔlɪdʒ] *n* conocimiento; (*learning*) saber *m*, conocimientos *mpl*; **knowledgeable** *adj* entendido
known [nəun] *pp of* **know** ▷*adj* (*thief, facts*) conocido; (*expert*) reconocido
knuckle ['nʌkl] *n* nudillo
koala [kəu'ɑ:lə] *n* (*also*: **~ bear**) koala *m*
Koran [kɔ'rɑ:n] *n* Corán *m*
Korea [kə'rɪə] *n* Corea; **Korean** *adj, n* coreano/a *m/f*
kosher ['kəuʃə*] *adj* autorizado por la ley judía
Kosovar ['kɔsəvɑ*], **Kosovan** ['kɔ:səvən] *adj* kosovar
Kosovo ['kɔsəvəu] *n* Kosovo
Kremlin ['kremlɪn] *n*: **the ~** el Kremlin
Kuwait [ku'weɪt] *n* Kuwait *m*

l

L (BRIT) *abbr* = **learner driver**
l. *abbr* (= *litre*) l
lab [læb] *n abbr* = **laboratory**
label ['leɪbl] *n* etiqueta ▷ *vt* poner etiqueta a
labor *etc* ['leɪbə*] (US) = **labour** *etc*
laboratory [lə'bɔrətərɪ] *n* laboratorio
Labor Day (US) *n* día *m* de los trabajadores (*primer lunes de septiembre*)
labor union (US) *n* sindicato
labour ['leɪbə*] (US **labor**) *n* (*hard work*) trabajo; (*labour force*) mano *f* de obra; (*Med*): **to be in ~** estar de parto ▷ *vi*: **to ~ (at sth)** trabajar (en algo) ▷ *vt*: **to ~ a point** insistir en un punto; **L~, the L~ party** (BRIT) el partido laborista, los laboristas *mpl*; **labourer** *n* peón *m*; **farm labourer** peón *m*; (*day labourer*) jornalero
lace [leɪs] *n* encaje *m*; (*of shoe etc*) cordón *m* ▷ *vt* (*shoes*: *also*: **~ up**) atarse (los zapatos)
lack [læk] *n* (*absence*) falta ▷ *vt* faltarle a algn, carecer de; **through** *or* **for ~ of** por falta de; **to be ~ing** faltar, no haber; **to be ~ing in sth** faltarle a algn algo
lacquer ['lækə*] *n* laca
lacy ['leɪsɪ] *adj* (*of lace*) de encaje; (*like lace*) como de encaje
lad [læd] *n* muchacho, chico
ladder ['lædə*] *n* escalera (de mano); (BRIT: *in tights*) carrera
ladle ['leɪdl] *n* cucharón *m*
lady ['leɪdɪ] *n* señora; (*dignified, graceful*) dama; **"ladies and gentlemen ..."** "señoras y caballeros ..."; **young ~** señorita; **the ladies' (room)** los servicios de señoras; **ladybird** (US **ladybug**) *n* mariquita
lag [læg] *n* retraso ▷ *vi* (*also*: **~ behind**) retrasarse, quedarse atrás ▷ *vt* (*pipes*) revestir
lager ['lɑːgə*] *n* cerveza (rubia)
lagoon [lə'guːn] *n* laguna
laid [leɪd] *pt, pp of* **lay**; **laid back** (*inf*) *adj* relajado
lain [leɪn] *pp of* **lie**
lake [leɪk] *n* lago
lamb [læm] *n* cordero; (*meat*) (carne *f* de) cordero
lame [leɪm] *adj* cojo; (*excuse*) poco convincente
lament [lə'mɛnt] *n* quejo ▷ *vt* lamentarse de
lamp [læmp] *n* lámpara; **lamppost** (BRIT) *n* (poste *m* de) farol *m*; **lampshade** *n* pantalla
land [lænd] *n* tierra; (*country*) país *m*; (*piece of land*) terreno; (*estate*) tierras *fpl*, finca ▷ *vi* (*from ship*) desembarcar; (*Aviat*) aterrizar; (*fig*: *fall*) caer, terminar ▷ *vt* (*passengers, goods*) desembarcar; **to ~ sb with sth** (*inf*) hacer cargar a algn con algo; **landing** *n* aterrizaje *m*; (*of staircase*) rellano; **landing card** *n* tarjeta de desembarque; **landlady** *n* (*of rented house, pub etc*) dueña; **landlord** *n* propietario; (*of pub etc*) patrón *m*; **landmark** *n* lugar *m* conocido; **to be a landmark** (*fig*) marcar un hito histórico; **landowner** *n*

terrateniente *mf*; **landscape** *n* paisaje *m*; **landslide** *n* (*Geo*) corrimiento de tierras; (*fig*: *Pol*) victoria arrolladora

lane [leɪn] *n* (*in country*) camino; (*Aut*) carril *m*; (*in race*) calle *f*

language ['læŋgwɪdʒ] *n* lenguaje *m*; (*national tongue*) idioma *m*, lengua; **bad ~** palabrotas *fpl*; **language laboratory** *n* laboratorio de idiomas; **language school** *n* academia de idiomas

lantern ['læntn] *n* linterna, farol *m*

lap [læp] *n* (*of track*) vuelta; (*of body*) regazo ▷ *vt* (*also*: **~ up**) beber a lengüetadas ▷ *vi* (*waves*) chapotear; **to sit on sb's ~** sentarse en las rodillas de algn

lapel [lə'pɛl] *n* solapa

lapse [læps] *n* fallo; (*moral*) desliz *m*; (*of time*) intervalo ▷ *vi* (*expire*) caducar; (*time*) pasar, transcurrir; **to ~ into bad habits** caer en malos hábitos

laptop (computer) ['læptɔp-] *n* (ordenador *m*) portátil *m*

lard [lɑːd] *n* manteca (de cerdo)

larder ['lɑːdə*] *n* despensa

large [lɑːdʒ] *adj* grande; **at ~** (*free*) en libertad; (*generally*) en general

> Be careful not to translate **large** by the Spanish word *largo*.

largely *adv* (*mostly*) en su mayor parte; (*introducing reason*) en gran parte; **large-scale** *adj* (*map*) en gran escala; (*fig*) importante

lark [lɑːk] *n* (*bird*) alondra; (*joke*) broma

laryngitis [lærɪn'dʒaɪtɪs] *n* laringitis *f*

lasagne [lə'zænjə] *n* lasaña

laser ['leɪzə*] *n* láser *m*; **laser printer** *n* impresora (por) láser

lash [læʃ] *n* latigazo; (*also*: **eye~**) pestaña ▷ *vt* azotar; (*tie*): **to ~ to/together** atar a/atar; **lash out** *vi*: **to lash out (at sb)** (*hit*) arremeter (contra algn); **to lash out against sb** lanzar invectivas contra algn

lass [læs] (BRIT) *n* chica

last [lɑːst] *adj* último; (*end*: *of series etc*) final ▷ *adv* (*most recently*) la última vez; (*finally*) por último ▷ *vi* durar; (*continue*) continuar, seguir; **~ night** anoche; **~ week** la semana pasada; **at ~** por fin; **~ but one** penúltimo; **lastly** *adv* por último, finalmente; **last-minute** *adj* de última hora

latch [lætʃ] *n* pestillo; **latch onto** *vt fus* (*person, group*) pegarse a; (*idea*) agarrarse a

late [leɪt] *adj* (*far on*: *in time, process etc*) al final de; (*not on time*) tarde, atrasado; (*dead*) fallecido ▷ *adv* tarde; (*behind time, schedule*) con retraso; **of ~** últimamente; **~ at night** a última hora de la noche; **in ~ May** hacia fines de mayo; **the ~ Mr X** el difunto Sr X; **latecomer** *n* recién llegado/a; **lately** *adv* últimamente; **later** *adj* (*date etc*) posterior; (*version etc*) más reciente ▷ *adv* más tarde, después; **latest** ['leɪtɪst] *adj* último; **at the latest** a más tardar

lather ['lɑːðə*] *n* espuma (de jabón) ▷ *vt* enjabonar

Latin ['lætɪn] *n* latín *m* ▷ *adj* latino; **Latin America** *n* América latina; **Latin American** *adj, n* latinoamericano/a *m/f*

latitude ['lætɪtjuːd] *n* latitud *f*; (*fig*) libertad *f*

latter ['lætə*] *adj* último; (*of two*) segundo ▷ *n*: **the ~** el último, éste

laugh [lɑːf] *n* risa ▷ *vi* reír(se); **(to do sth) for a ~** (hacer algo) en broma; **laugh at** *vt fus* reírse de; **laughter** *n* risa

launch [lɔːntʃ] *n* lanzamiento; (*boat*) lancha ▷ *vt* (*ship*) botar; (*rocket etc*) lanzar; (*fig*) comenzar; **launch into** *vt fus* lanzarse a

launder ['lɔːndə*] *vt* lavar

Launderette® [lɔːn'drɛt] (BRIT) *n* lavandería (automática)

Laundromat® ['lɔːndrəmæt] (US) *n* = **Launderette**

laundry ['lɔːndrɪ] *n* (*dirty*) ropa sucia; (*clean*) colada; (*room*) lavadero

lava ['lɑːvə] *n* lava
lavatory ['lævətərɪ] *n* wáter *m*
lavender ['lævəndə*] *n* lavanda
lavish ['lævɪʃ] *adj* (*amount*) abundante; (*person*): **~ with** pródigo en ▷*vt*: **to ~ sth on sb** colmar a algn de algo
law [lɔː] *n* ley *f*; (*Scol*) derecho; (*a rule*) regla; (*professions connected with law*) jurisprudencia; **lawful** *adj* legítimo, lícito; **lawless** *adj* (*action*) criminal
lawn [lɔːn] *n* césped *m*; **lawnmower** *n* cortacésped *m*
lawsuit ['lɔːsuːt] *n* pleito
lawyer ['lɔːjə*] *n* abogado/a; (*for sales, wills etc*) notario/a
lax [læks] *adj* laxo
laxative ['læksətɪv] *n* laxante *m*
lay [leɪ] (*pt, pp* **laid**) *pt of* **lie** ▷*adj* laico; (*not expert*) lego ▷*vt* (*place*) colocar; (*eggs, table*) poner; (*cable*) tender; (*carpet*) extender; **lay down** *vt* (*pen etc*) dejar; (*rules etc*) establecer; **to lay down the law** (*pej*) imponer las normas; **lay off** *vt* (*workers*) despedir; **lay on** *vt* (*meal, facilities*) proveer; **lay out** *vt* (*spread out*) disponer, exponer; **lay-by** *n* (BRIT *Aut*) área de aparcamiento
layer ['leɪə*] *n* capa
layman ['leɪmən] (*irreg*) *n* lego
layout ['leɪaut] *n* (*design*) plan *m*, trazado; (*Press*) composición *f*
lazy ['leɪzɪ] *adj* perezoso, vago; (*movement*) lento
lb. *abbr* = **pound** (*weight*)
lead¹ [liːd] (*pt, pp* **led**) *n* (*front position*) delantera; (*clue*) pista; (*Elec*) cable *m*; (*for dog*) correa; (*Theatre*) papel *m* principal ▷*vt* (*walk etc in front*) ir a la cabeza de; (*guide*): **to ~ sb somewhere** conducir a algn a algún sitio; (*be leader*) dirigir; (*start, guide: activity*) protagonizar ▷*vi* (*road, pipe etc*) conducir a; (*Sport*) ir primero; **to be in the ~** (*Sport*) llevar la delantera; (*fig*) ir a la cabeza; **to ~ the way** llevar la delantera; **lead up to** *vt fus* (*events*) conducir a; (*in conversation*) preparar el terreno para
lead² [lɛd] *n* (*metal*) plomo; (*in pencil*) mina
leader ['liːdə*] *n* jefe/a *m/f*, líder *mf*; (*Sport*) líder *mf*; **leadership** *n* dirección *f*; (*position*) mando; (*quality*) iniciativa
lead-free ['lɛdfriː] *adj* sin plomo
leading ['liːdɪŋ] *adj* (*main*) principal; (*first*) primero; (*front*) delantero
lead singer [liːd-] *n* cantante *mf*
leaf [liːf] (*pl* **leaves**) *n* hoja ▷*vi*: **to ~ through** hojear; **to turn over a new ~** reformarse
leaflet ['liːflɪt] *n* folleto
league [liːg] *n* sociedad *f*; (*Football*) liga; **to be in ~ with** haberse confabulado con
leak [liːk] *n* (*of liquid, gas*) escape *m*, fuga; (*in pipe*) agujero; (*in roof*) gotera; (*in security*) filtración *f* ▷*vi* (*shoes, ship*) hacer agua; (*pipe*) tener (un) escape; (*roof*) gotear; (*liquid, gas*) escaparse, fugarse; (*fig*) divulgarse ▷*vt* (*fig*) filtrar
lean [liːn] (*pt, pp* **~ed** *or* **~t**) *adj* (*thin*) flaco; (*meat*) magro ▷*vt*: **to ~ sth on sth** apoyar algo en algo ▷*vi* (*slope*) inclinarse; **to ~ against** apoyarse contra; **to ~ on** apoyarse en; **lean forward** *vi* inclinarse hacia adelante; **lean over** *vi* inclinarse; **leaning** *n*: **leaning (towards)** inclinación *f* (hacia)
leant [lɛnt] *pt, pp of* **lean**
leap [liːp] (*pt, pp* **~ed** *or* **~t**) *n* salto ▷*vi* saltar
leapt [lɛpt] *pt, pp of* **leap**
leap year *n* año bisiesto
learn [ləːn] (*pt, pp* **~ed** *or* **~t**) *vt* aprender ▷*vi* aprender; **to ~ about sth** enterarse de algo; **to ~ to do sth** aprender a hacer algo; **learner** *n* (BRIT: *also*: **learner driver**) principiante *mf*; **learning** *n* el saber *m*, conocimientos *mpl*
learnt [ləːnt] *pp of* **learn**
lease [liːs] *n* arriendo ▷*vt* arrendar
leash [liːʃ] *n* correa

least [liːst] *adj*: **the ~** (*slightest*) el menor, el más pequeño; (*smallest amount of*) mínimo ▷ *adv* (+ *vb*) menos; (+ *adj*): **the ~ expensive** el (la) menos costoso/a; **the ~ possible effort** el menor esfuerzo posible; **at ~** por lo menos, al menos; **you could at ~ have written** por lo menos podías haber escrito; **not in the ~** en absoluto

leather [ˈlɛðə*] *n* cuero

leave [liːv] (*pt, pp* **left**) *vt* dejar; (*go away from*) abandonar; (*place etc: permanently*) salir de ▷ *vi* irse; (*train etc*) salir ▷ *n* permiso; **to ~ sth to sb** (*money etc*) legar algo a algn; (*responsibility etc*) encargar a algn de algo; **to be left** quedar, sobrar; **there's some milk left over** sobra *or* queda algo de leche; **on ~** de permiso; **leave behind** *vt* (*on purpose*) dejar; (*accidentally*) dejarse; **leave out** *vt* omitir

leaves [liːvz] *npl of* **leaf**

Lebanon [ˈlɛbənən] *n*: **the ~** el Líbano

lecture [ˈlɛktʃə*] *n* conferencia; (*Scol*) clase *f* ▷ *vi* dar una clase ▷ *vt* (*scold*): **to ~ sb on** *or* **about sth** echar una reprimenda a algn por algo; **to give a ~ on** dar una conferencia sobre; **lecture hall** *n* sala de conferencias; (*Univ*) aula; **lecturer** *n* conferenciante *mf*; (BRIT: *at university*) profesor(a) *m/f*; **lecture theatre** *n* = **lecture hall**

led [lɛd] *pt, pp of* **lead[1]**

ledge [lɛdʒ] *n* repisa; (*of window*) alféizar *m*; (*of mountain*) saliente *m*

leek [liːk] *n* puerro

left [lɛft] *pt, pp of* **leave** ▷ *adj* izquierdo; (*remaining*): **there are two ~** quedan dos ▷ *n* izquierda ▷ *adv* a la izquierda; **on** *or* **to the ~** a la izquierda; **the L~** (*Pol*) la izquierda; **left-hand** *adj*: **the left-hand side** la izquierda; **left-hand drive** *adj*: **a left-hand drive car** un coche con el volante a la izquierda; **left-handed** *adj* zurdo; **left-luggage locker** *n* (BRIT) consigna *f* automática; **left-luggage (office)** (BRIT) *n* consigna; **left-overs** *npl* sobras *fpl*; **left-wing** *adj* (*Pol*) de izquierdas, izquierdista

leg [lɛg] *n* pierna; (*of animal, chair*) pata; (*trouser leg*) pernera; (*Culin: of lamb*) pierna; (*: of chicken*) pata; (*of journey*) etapa

legacy [ˈlɛgəsɪ] *n* herencia

legal [ˈliːgl] *adj* (*permitted by law*) lícito; (*of law*) legal; **legal holiday** (US) *n* fiesta oficial; **legalize** *vt* legalizar; **legally** *adv* legalmente

legend [ˈlɛdʒənd] *n* (*also fig: person*) leyenda; **legendary** [-ərɪ] *adj* legendario

leggings [ˈlegɪŋz] *npl* mallas *fpl*, leggins *mpl*

legible [ˈlɛdʒəbl] *adj* legible

legislation [lɛdʒɪsˈleɪʃən] *n* legislación *f*

legislative [ˈlɛdʒɪslətɪv] *adj* legislativo

legitimate [lɪˈdʒɪtɪmət] *adj* legítimo

leisure [ˈlɛʒə*] *n* ocio, tiempo libre; **at ~** con tranquilidad; **leisure centre** (BRIT) *n* centro de recreo; **leisurely** *adj* sin prisa; lento

lemon [ˈlɛmən] *n* limón *m*; **lemonade** *n* (*fizzy*) gaseosa; **lemon tea** *n* té *m* con limón

lend [lɛnd] (*pt, pp* **lent**) *vt*: **to ~ sth to sb** prestar algo a algn

length [lɛŋθ] *n* (*size*) largo, longitud *f*; (*distance*): **the ~ of** todo lo largo de; (*of swimming pool, cloth*) largo; (*of wood, string*) trozo; (*amount of time*) duración *f*; **at ~** (*at last*) por fin, finalmente; (*lengthily*) largamente; **lengthen** *vt* alargar ▷ *vi* alargarse; **lengthways** *adv* a lo largo; **lengthy** *adj* largo, extenso

lens [lɛnz] *n* (*of spectacles*) lente *f*; (*of camera*) objetivo

Lent [lɛnt] *n* Cuaresma

lent [lɛnt] *pt, pp of* **lend**

lentil [ˈlɛntl] *n* lenteja

Leo [ˈliːəu] *n* Leo

leopard [ˈlɛpəd] *n* leopardo

leotard ['li:ətɑ:d] *n* mallas *fpl*
leprosy ['lɛprəsɪ] *n* lepra
lesbian ['lɛzbɪən] *n* lesbiana
less [lɛs] *adj* (*in size, degree etc*) menor; (*in quality*) menos ▷ *pron, adv* menos ▷ *prep*: **~ tax/10% discount** menos impuestos/el 10 por ciento de descuento; **~ than half** menos de la mitad; **~ than ever** menos que nunca; **~ and ~** cada vez menos; **the ~ he works ...** cuanto menos trabaja ...; **lessen** *vi* disminuir, reducirse ▷ *vt* disminuir, reducir; **lesser** ['lɛsə*] *adj* menor; **to a lesser extent** en menor grado
lesson ['lɛsn] *n* clase *f*; (*warning*) lección *f*
let [lɛt] (*pt, pp* **~**) *vt* (*allow*) dejar, permitir; (BRIT: *lease*) alquilar; **to ~ sb do sth** dejar que algn haga algo; **to ~ sb know sth** comunicar algo a algn; **~'s go** ¡vamos!; **~ him come** que venga; **"to ~"** "se alquila"; **let down** *vt* (*tyre*) desinflar; (*disappoint*) defraudar; **let in** *vt* dejar entrar; (*visitor etc*) hacer pasar; **let off** *vt* (*culprit*) dejar escapar; (*gun*) disparar; (*bomb*) accionar; (*firework*) hacer estallar; **let out** *vt* dejar salir; (*sound*) soltar
lethal ['li:θl] *adj* (*weapon*) mortífero; (*poison, wound*) mortal
letter ['lɛtə*] *n* (*of alphabet*) letra; (*correspondence*) carta; **letterbox** (BRIT) *n* buzón *m*
lettuce ['lɛtɪs] *n* lechuga
leukaemia [lu:'ki:mɪə] (US **leukemia**) *n* leucemia
level ['lɛvl] *adj* (*flat*) llano ▷ *adv*: **to draw ~ with** llegar a la altura de ▷ *n* nivel *m*; (*height*) altura ▷ *vt* nivelar; allanar; (*destroy*: *building*) derribar; (: *forest*) arrasar; **to be ~ with** estar a nivel de; **A ~s** (BRIT) ≈ exámenes *mpl* de bachillerato superior, B.U.P.; **AS ~** (BRIT) *asignatura aprobada entre los "GCSEs" y los "A levels"*; **on the ~** (*fig*: *honest*) serio; **level crossing** (BRIT) *n* paso a nivel
lever ['li:və*] *n* (*also fig*) palanca ▷ *vt*: **to ~ up** levantar con palanca; **leverage** *n* (*using bar etc*) apalancamiento; (*fig*: *influence*) influencia
levy ['lɛvɪ] *n* impuesto ▷ *vt* exigir, recaudar
liability [laɪə'bɪlətɪ] *n* (*pej*: *person, thing*) estorbo, lastre *m*; (*Jur*: *responsibility*) responsabilidad *f*
liable ['laɪəbl] *adj* (*subject*): **~ to** sujeto a; (*responsible*): **~ for** responsable de; (*likely*): **~ to do** propenso a hacer
liaise [lɪ'eɪz] *vi*: **to ~ with** enlazar con
liar ['laɪə*] *n* mentiroso/a
liberal ['lɪbərəl] *adj* liberal; (*offer, amount etc*) generoso; **Liberal Democrat** *n* (BRIT) demócrata *m/f* liberal
liberate ['lɪbəreɪt] *vt* (*people*: *from poverty etc*) librar; (*prisoner*) libertar; (*country*) liberar
liberation [lɪbə'reɪʃən] *n* liberación *f*
liberty ['lɪbətɪ] *n* libertad *f*; **to be at ~** (*criminal*) estar en libertad; **to be at ~ to do** estar libre para hacer; **to take the ~ of doing sth** tomarse la libertad de hacer algo
Libra ['li:brə] *n* Libra
librarian [laɪ'brɛərɪən] *n* bibliotecario/a
library ['laɪbrərɪ] *n* biblioteca

> Be careful not to translate **library** by the Spanish word *librería*.

Libya ['lɪbɪə] *n* Libia
lice [laɪs] *npl of* **louse**
licence ['laɪsəns] (US **license**) *n* licencia; (*permit*) permiso; (*also*: **driving ~**) carnet *m* de conducir (SP), licencia de manejo (LAM)
license ['laɪsəns] *n* (US) = **licence** ▷ *vt* autorizar, dar permiso a; **licensed** *adj* (*for alcohol*) autorizado para vender bebidas alcohólicas; (*car*) matriculado; **license plate** (US) *n* placa (de matrícula); **licensing hours** (BRIT) *npl horas durante las cuales se permite la venta y consumo de alcohol (en un bar etc)*

lick [lɪk] *vt* lamer; (*inf*: *defeat*) dar una paliza a; **to ~ one's lips** relamerse
lid [lɪd] *n* (*of box, case*) tapa; (*of pan*) tapadera
lie [laɪ] (*pt* **lay**, *pp* **lain**) *vi* (*rest*) estar echado, estar acostado; (*of object*: *be situated*) estar, encontrarse; (*tell lies*: *pt, pp* **lied**) mentir ▷ *n* mentira; **to ~ low** (*fig*) mantenerse a escondidas; **lie about** *or* **around** *vi* (*things*) estar tirado; (BRIT: *people*) estar tumbado; **lie down** *vi* echarse, tumbarse
Liechtenstein ['lɪktənstaɪn] *n* Liechtenstein *m*
lie-in ['laɪɪn] (BRIT) *n*: **to have a ~** quedarse en la cama
lieutenant [lɛf'tɛnənt, US luː'tɛnənt] *n* (*Mil*) teniente *mf*
life [laɪf] (*pl* **lives**) *n* vida; **to come to ~** animarse; **life assurance** (BRIT) *n* seguro de vida; **lifeboat** *n* lancha de socorro; **lifeguard** *n* vigilante *mf*, socorrista *mf*; **life insurance** *n* = **life assurance**; **life jacket** *n* chaleco salvavidas; **lifelike** *adj* (*model etc*) que parece vivo; (*realistic*) realista; **life preserver** (US) *n* cinturón *m*/chaleco salvavidas; **life sentence** *n* cadena perpetua; **lifestyle** *n* estilo de vida; **lifetime** *n* (*of person*) vida; (*of thing*) período de vida
lift [lɪft] *vt* levantar; (*end*: *ban, rule*) levantar, suprimir ▷ *vi* (*fog*) disiparse ▷ *n* (BRIT: *machine*) ascensor *m*; **to give sb a ~** (BRIT) llevar a algn en el coche; **lift up** *vt* levantar; **lift-off** *n* despegue *m*
light [laɪt] (*pt, pp* **~ed** *or* **lit**) *n* luz *f*; (*lamp*) luz *f*, lámpara; (*Aut*) faro; (*for cigarette etc*): **have you got a ~?** ¿tienes fuego? ▷ *vt* (*candle, cigarette, fire*) encender (SP), prender (LAM); (*room*) alumbrar ▷ *adj* (*colour*) claro; (*not heavy, also fig*) ligero; (*room*) con mucha luz; (*gentle, graceful*) ágil; **lights** *npl* (*traffic lights*) semáforos *mpl*; **to come to ~** salir a luz; **in the ~ of** (*new evidence etc*) a la luz de; **light up** *vi* (*smoke*) encender un cigarrillo; (*face*) iluminarse ▷ *vt* (*illuminate*) iluminar, alumbrar; (*set fire to*) encender; **light bulb** *n* bombilla (SP), foco (MEX), bujía (CAM), bombita (RPL); **lighten** *vt* (*make less heavy*) aligerar; **lighter** *n* (*also*: **cigarette lighter**) encendedor *m*, mechero; **light-hearted** *adj* (*person*) alegre; (*remark etc*) divertido; **lighthouse** *n* faro; **lighting** *n* (*system*) alumbrado; **lightly** *adv* ligeramente; (*not seriously*) con poca seriedad; **to get off lightly** ser castigado con poca severidad
lightning ['laɪtnɪŋ] *n* relámpago, rayo
lightweight ['laɪtweɪt] *adj* (*suit*) ligero ▷ *n* (*Boxing*) peso ligero
like [laɪk] *vt* gustarle a algn ▷ *prep* como ▷ *adj* parecido, semejante ▷ *n*: **and the ~** y otros por el estilo; **his ~s and dislikes** sus gustos y aversiones; **I would ~, I'd ~** me gustaría; (*for purchase*) quisiera; **would you ~ a coffee?** ¿te apetece un café?; **I ~ swimming** me gusta nadar; **she ~s apples** le gustan las manzanas; **to be** *or* **look ~ sb/sth** parecerse a algn/algo; **what does it look/taste/sound ~?** ¿cómo es/a qué sabe/cómo suena?; **that's just ~ him** es muy de él, es característico de él; **do it ~ this** hazlo así; **it is nothing ~ ...** no tiene parecido alguno con ...; **likeable** *adj* simpático, agradable
likelihood ['laɪklɪhud] *n* probabilidad *f*
likely ['laɪklɪ] *adj* probable; **he's ~ to leave** es probable que se vaya; **not ~!** ¡ni hablar!
likewise ['laɪkwaɪz] *adv* igualmente; **to do ~** hacer lo mismo
liking ['laɪkɪŋ] *n*: **~ (for)** (*person*) cariño (a); (*thing*) afición (a); **to be to sb's ~** ser del gusto de algn
lilac ['laɪlək] *n* (*tree*) lilo; (*flower*) lila
Lilo® ['laɪləu] *n* colchoneta inflable
lily ['lɪlɪ] *n* lirio, azucena; **~ of the**

valley lirio de los valles
limb [lɪm] *n* miembro
limbo ['lɪmbəu] *n*: **to be in ~** (*fig*) quedar a la expectativa
lime [laɪm] *n* (*tree*) limero; (*fruit*) lima; (*Geo*) cal *f*
limelight ['laɪmlaɪt] *n*: **to be in the ~** (*fig*) ser el centro de atención
limestone ['laɪmstəun] *n* piedra caliza
limit ['lɪmɪt] *n* límite *m* ▷ *vt* limitar; **limited** *adj* limitado; **to be limited to** limitarse a
limousine ['lɪməzi:n] *n* limusina
limp [lɪmp] *n*: **to have a ~** tener cojera ▷ *vi* cojear ▷ *adj* flojo; (*material*) fláccido
line [laɪn] *n* línea; (*rope*) cuerda; (*for fishing*) sedal *m*; (*wire*) hilo; (*row, series*) fila, hilera; (*of writing*) renglón *m*, línea; (*of song*) verso; (*on face*) arruga; (*Rail*) vía ▷ *vt* (*road etc*) llenar; (*Sewing*) forrar; **to ~ the streets** llenar las aceras; **in ~ with** alineado con; (*according to*) de acuerdo con; **line up** *vi* hacer cola ▷ *vt* alinear; (*prepare*) preparar; organizar
linear ['lɪnɪə*] *adj* lineal
linen ['lɪnɪn] *n* ropa blanca; (*cloth*) lino
liner ['laɪnə*] *n* vapor *m* de línea, transatlántico; (*for bin*) bolsa (de basura)
line-up ['laɪnʌp] *n* (*US*: *queue*) cola; (*Sport*) alineación *f*
linger ['lɪŋgə*] *vi* retrasarse, tardar en marcharse; (*smell, tradition*) persistir
lingerie ['lænʒəri:] *n* lencería
linguist ['lɪŋgwɪst] *n* lingüista *mf*; **linguistic** *adj* lingüístico
lining ['laɪnɪŋ] *n* forro; (*Anat*) (membrana) mucosa
link [lɪŋk] *n* (*of a chain*) eslabón *m*; (*relationship*) relación *f*, vínculo; (*Internet*) link *m*, enlace *m* ▷ *vt* vincular, unir; (*associate*): **to ~ with** *or* **to** relacionar con; **links** *npl* (*Golf*) campo de golf; **link up** *vt* acoplar ▷ *vi* unirse
lion ['laɪən] *n* león *m*; **lioness** *n* leona
lip [lɪp] *n* labio; **lipread** *vi* leer los labios; **lip salve** *n* crema protectora para labios; **lipstick** *n* lápiz *m* de labios, carmín *m*
liqueur [lɪ'kjuə*] *n* licor *m*
liquid ['lɪkwɪd] *adj*, *n* líquido; **liquidizer** [-aɪzə*] *n* licuadora
liquor ['lɪkə*] *n* licor *m*, bebidas *fpl* alcohólicas; **liquor store** (*US*) *n* bodega, *tienda de vinos y bebidas alcohólicas*
Lisbon ['lɪzbən] *n* Lisboa
lisp [lɪsp] *n* ceceo ▷ *vi* cecear
list [lɪst] *n* lista ▷ *vt* (*mention*) enumerar; (*put on a list*) poner en una lista
listen ['lɪsn] *vi* escuchar, oír; **to ~ to sb/sth** escuchar a algn/algo; **listener** *n* oyente *mf*; (*Radio*) radioyente *mf*
lit [lɪt] *pt*, *pp* *of* **light**
liter ['li:tə*] (*US*) *n* = **litre**
literacy ['lɪtərəsɪ] *n* capacidad *f* de leer y escribir
literal ['lɪtərl] *adj* literal; **literally** *adv* literalmente
literary ['lɪtərərɪ] *adj* literario
literate ['lɪtərət] *adj* que sabe leer y escribir; (*educated*) culto
literature ['lɪtərɪtʃə*] *n* literatura; (*brochures etc*) folletos *mpl*
litre ['li:tə*] (*US* **liter**) *n* litro
litter ['lɪtə*] *n* (*rubbish*) basura; (*young animals*) camada, cría; **litter bin** (*BRIT*) *n* papelera; **littered** *adj*: **littered with** (*scattered*) lleno de
little ['lɪtl] *adj* (*small*) pequeño; (*not much*) poco ▷ *adv* poco; **a ~** un poco (de); **~ house/bird** casita/pajarito; **a ~ bit** un poquito; **~ by ~** poco a poco; **little finger** *n* dedo meñique
live[1] [laɪv] *adj* (*animal*) vivo; (*wire*) conectado; (*broadcast*) en directo; (*shell*) cargado
live[2] [lɪv] *vi* vivir; **live together** *vi* vivir juntos; **live up to** *vt fus* (*fulfil*) cumplir con
livelihood ['laɪvlɪhud] *n* sustento
lively ['laɪvlɪ] *adj* vivo;

(*interesting*: *place, book etc*) animado
liven up ['laɪvn-] *vt* animar ▷ *vi* animarse
liver ['lɪvə*] *n* hígado
lives [laɪvz] *npl of* **life**
livestock ['laɪvstɔk] *n* ganado
living ['lɪvɪŋ] *adj* (*alive*) vivo ▷ *n*: **to earn** *or* **make a ~** ganarse la vida; **living room** *n* sala (de estar)
lizard ['lɪzəd] *n* lagarto; (*small*) lagartija
load [ləud] *n* carga; (*weight*) peso ▷ *vt* (*Comput*) cargar; (*also*: **~ up**): **to ~ (with)** cargar (con *or* de); **a ~ of rubbish** (*inf*) tonterías *fpl*; **a ~ of, ~s of** (*fig*) (gran) cantidad de, montones de; **loaded** *adj* (*vehicle*): **to be loaded with** estar cargado de
loaf [ləuf] (*pl* **loaves**) *n* (barra de) pan *m*
loan [ləun] *n* préstamo ▷ *vt* prestar; **on ~** prestado
loathe [ləuð] *vt* aborrecer; (*person*) odiar
loaves [ləuvz] *npl of* **loaf**
lobby ['lɔbɪ] *n* vestíbulo, sala de espera; (*Pol*: *pressure group*) grupo de presión ▷ *vt* presionar
lobster ['lɔbstə*] *n* langosta
local ['ləukl] *adj* local ▷ *n* (*pub*) bar *m*; **the locals** *npl* los vecinos, los del lugar; **local anaesthetic** *n* (*Med*) anestesia local; **local authority** *n* municipio, ayuntamiento (SP); **local government** *n* gobierno municipal; **locally** [-kəlɪ] *adv* en la vecindad; por aquí
locate [ləu'keɪt] *vt* (*find*) localizar; (*situate*): **to be ~d in** estar situado en
location [ləu'keɪʃən] *n* situación *f*; **on ~** (*Cinema*) en exteriores
loch [lɔx] *n* lago
lock [lɔk] *n* (*of door, box*) cerradura; (*of canal*) esclusa; (*of hair*) mechón *m* ▷ *vt* (*with key*) cerrar (con llave) ▷ *vi* (*door etc*) cerrarse (con llave); (*wheels*) trabarse; **lock in** *vt* encerrar; **lock out** *vt* (*person*) cerrar la puerta a; **lock up** *vt* (*criminal*) meter en la cárcel; (*mental patient*) encerrar; (*house*) cerrar (con llave) ▷ *vi* echar la llave
locker ['lɔkə*] *n* casillero; **locker-room** (US) *n* (*Sport*) vestuario
locksmith ['lɔksmɪθ] *n* cerrajero/a
locomotive [ləukə'məutɪv] *n* locomotora
lodge [lɔdʒ] *n* casita (del guarda) ▷ *vi* (*person*): **to ~ (with)** alojarse (en casa de); (*bullet, bone*) incrustarse ▷ *vt* presentar; **lodger** *n* huésped *mf*
lodging ['lɔdʒɪŋ] *n* alojamiento, hospedaje *m*
loft [lɔft] *n* desván *m*
log [lɔg] *n* (*of wood*) leño, tronco; (*written account*) diario ▷ *vt* anotar; **log in, log on** *vi* (*Comput*) entrar en el sistema; **log off, log out** *vi* (*Comput*) salir del sistema
logic ['lɔdʒɪk] *n* lógica; **logical** *adj* lógico
logo ['ləugəu] *n* logotipo
lollipop ['lɔlɪpɔp] *n* pirulí *m*; **lollipop man/lady** (BRIT: *irreg*) *n* *persona encargada de ayudar a los niños a cruzar la calle*
lolly ['lɔlɪ] *n* (*inf*: *ice cream*) polo; (: *lollipop*) piruleta; (: *money*) guita
London ['lʌndən] *n* Londres; **Londoner** *n* londinense *mf*
lone [ləun] *adj* solitario
loneliness ['ləunlɪnɪs] *n* soledad *f*; aislamiento
lonely ['ləunlɪ] *adj* (*situation*) solitario; (*person*) solo; (*place*) aislado
long [lɔŋ] *adj* largo ▷ *adv* mucho tiempo, largamente ▷ *vi*: **to ~ for sth** anhelar algo; **so** *or* **as ~ as** mientras, con tal que; **don't be ~!** ¡no tardes!, ¡vuelve pronto!; **how ~ is the street?** ¿cuánto tiene la calle de largo?; **how ~ is the lesson?** ¿cuánto dura la clase?; **6 metres ~** que mide 6 metros, de 6 metros de largo; **6 months ~** que dura 6 meses, de 6 meses de duración; **all night ~** toda la noche; **he no ~er comes** ya no viene; **I can't stand it any ~er** ya no lo aguanto más; **~ before**

mucho antes; **before ~** (+ *future*) dentro de poco; (+ *past*) poco tiempo después; **at ~ last** al fin, por fin; **long-distance** *adj* (*race*) de larga distancia; (*call*) interurbano; **long-haul** *adj* (*flight*) de larga distancia; **longing** *n* anhelo, ansia; (*nostalgia*) nostalgia ▷ *adj* anhelante

longitude ['lɔŋgɪtjuːd] *n* longitud *f*

long: long jump *n* salto de longitud; **long-life** *adj* (*batteries*) de larga duración; (*milk*) uperizado; **long-sighted** (BRIT) *adj* présbita; **long-standing** *adj* de mucho tiempo; **long-term** *adj* a largo plazo

loo [luː] (BRIT: *inf*) *n* wáter *m*

look [luk] *vi* mirar; (*seem*) parecer; (*building etc*): **to ~ south/on to the sea** dar al sur/al mar ▷ *n* (*gen*): **to have a ~** mirar; (*glance*) mirada; (*appearance*) aire *m*, aspecto; **looks** *npl* (*good looks*) belleza; **~ (here)!** (*expressing annoyance etc*) ¡oye!; **~!** (*expressing surprise*) ¡mira!; **look after** *vt fus* (*care for*) cuidar a; (*deal with*) encargarse de; **look around** *vi* echar una mirada alrededor; **look at** *vt fus* mirar; (*read quickly*) echar un vistazo a; **look back** *vi* mirar hacia atrás; **look down on** *vt fus* (*fig*) despreciar, mirar con desprecio; **look for** *vt fus* buscar; **look forward to** *vt fus* esperar con ilusión; (*in letters*): **we look forward to hearing from you** quedamos a la espera de sus gratas noticias; **look into** *vt* investigar; **look out** *vi* (*beware*): **to look out (for)** tener cuidado (de); **look out for** *vt fus* (*seek*) buscar; (*await*) esperar; **look round** *vi* volver la cabeza; **look through** *vt fus* (*examine*) examinar; **look up** *vi* mirar hacia arriba; (*improve*) mejorar ▷ *vt* (*word*) buscar; **look up to** *vt fus* admirar; **lookout** *n* (*tower etc*) puesto de observación; (*person*) vigía *mf*; **to be on the lookout for sth** estar al acecho de algo

loom [luːm] *vi*: **~ (up)** (*threaten*) surgir, amenazar; (*event: approach*) aproximarse

loony ['luːnɪ] (*inf*) *n, adj* loco/a *m/f*

loop [luːp] *n* lazo ▷ *vt*: **to ~ sth round sth** pasar algo alrededor de algo; **loophole** *n* escapatoria

loose [luːs] *adj* suelto; (*clothes*) ancho; (*morals, discipline*) relajado; **to be on the ~** estar en libertad; **to be at a ~ end** *or* **at ~ ends** (US) no saber qué hacer; **loosely** *adv* libremente, aproximadamente; **loosen** *vt* aflojar

loot [luːt] *n* botín *m* ▷ *vt* saquear

lop-sided ['lɔp'saɪdɪd] *adj* torcido

lord [lɔːd] *n* señor *m*; **L~ Smith** Lord Smith; **the L~** el Señor; **my ~** (*to bishop*) Ilustrísima; (*to noble etc*) Señor; **good L~!** ¡Dios mío!; **Lords** *npl* (BRIT: *Pol*): **the (House of) Lords** la Cámara de los Lores

lorry ['lɔrɪ] (BRIT) *n* camión *m*; **lorry driver** (BRIT) *n* camionero/a

lose [luːz] (*pt, pp* **lost**) *vt* perder ▷ *vi* perder, ser vencido; **to ~ (time)** (*clock*) atrasarse; **lose out** *vi* salir perdiendo; **loser** *n* perdedor(a) *m/f*

loss [lɔs] *n* pérdida; **heavy ~es** (*Mil*) grandes pérdidas; **to be at a ~** no saber qué hacer; **to make a ~** sufrir pérdidas

lost [lɔst] *pt, pp of* **lose** ▷ *adj* perdido; **lost property** (US **lost and found**) *n* objetos *mpl* perdidos

lot [lɔt] *n* (*group: of things*) grupo; (*at auctions*) lote *m*; **the ~** el todo, todos; **a ~** (*large number: of books etc*) muchos; (*a great deal*) mucho, bastante; **a ~ of, ~s of** mucho(s) (*pl*); **I read a ~** leo bastante; **to draw ~s (for sth)** echar suertes (para decidir algo)

lotion ['ləuʃən] *n* loción *f*

lottery ['lɔtərɪ] *n* lotería

loud [laud] *adj* (*voice, sound*) fuerte; (*laugh, shout*) estrepitoso; (*condemnation etc*) enérgico; (*gaudy*) chillón/ona ▷ *adv* (*speak etc*) fuerte; **out ~** en voz alta; **loudly** *adv* (*noisily*) fuerte; (*aloud*) en voz alta; **loudspeaker** *n* altavoz *m*

lounge [laundʒ] *n* salón *m*, sala (de

estar); (*at airport etc*) sala; (BRIT: *also*: **~-bar**) salón-bar *m* ▷ *vi* (*also*: **~ about** *or* **around**) reposar, holgazanear
louse [laus] (*pl* **lice**) *n* piojo
lousy ['lauzɪ] (*inf*) *adj* (*bad quality*) malísimo, asqueroso; (*ill*) fatal
love [lʌv] *n* (*romantic, sexual*) amor *m*; (*kind, caring*) cariño ▷ *vt* amar, querer; (*thing, activity*) encantarle a algn; **"~ from Anne"** (*on letter*) "un abrazo (de) Anne"; **to ~ to do** encantarle a algn hacer; **to be/fall in ~ with** estar enamorado/enamorarse de; **to make ~** hacer el amor; **for the ~ of** por amor de; **"15 ~"** (*Tennis*) "15 a cero"; **I ~ you** te quiero; **I ~ paella** me encanta la paella; **love affair** *n* aventura sentimental; **love life** *n* vida sentimental
lovely ['lʌvlɪ] *adj* (*delightful*) encantador(a); (*beautiful*) precioso
lover ['lʌvə*] *n* amante *mf*; (*person in love*) enamorado; (*amateur*): **a ~ of** un(a) aficionado/a *or* un(a) amante de
loving ['lʌvɪŋ] *adj* amoroso, cariñoso; (*action*) tierno
low [ləu] *adj, adv* bajo ▷ *n* (*Meteorology*) área de baja presión; **to be ~ on** (*supplies etc*) andar mal de; **to feel ~** sentirse deprimido; **to turn (down) ~** bajar; **low-alcohol** *adj* de bajo contenido en alcohol; **low-calorie** *adj* bajo en calorías
lower ['ləuə*] *adj* más bajo; (*less important*) menos importante ▷ *vt* bajar; (*reduce*) reducir ▷ *vr*: **to ~ o.s. to** (*fig*) rebajarse a
low-fat *adj* (*milk, yoghurt*) desnatado; (*diet*) bajo en calorías
loyal ['lɔɪəl] *adj* leal; **loyalty** *n* lealtad *f*; **loyalty card** *n* tarjeta cliente
L.P. *n abbr* (= *long-playing record*) elepé *m*
L-plates ['ɛl-] (BRIT) *npl* placas *fpl* de aprendiz de conductor

L-PLATES

En el Reino Unido las personas que están aprendiendo a conducir deben llevar en la parte delantera y trasera de su vehículo unas placas blancas con una L en rojo conocidas como **L-Plates** (de **learner**). No es necesario que asistan a clases teóricas sino que, desde el principio, se les entrega un carnet de conducir provisional ("provisional driving licence") para que realicen sus prácticas, aunque no pueden circular por las autopistas y deben ir siempre acompañadas por un conductor con carnet definitivo ("full driving licence").

Lt *abbr* (= *lieutenant*) Tte.
Ltd *abbr* (= *limited company*) S.A.
luck [lʌk] *n* suerte *f*; **bad ~** mala suerte; **good ~!** ¡que tengas suerte!, ¡suerte!; **bad** *or* **hard** *or* **tough ~!** ¡qué pena!; **luckily** *adv* afortunadamente; **lucky** *adj* afortunado; (*at cards etc*) con suerte; (*object*) que trae suerte
lucrative ['lu:krətɪv] *adj* lucrativo
ludicrous ['lu:dɪkrəs] *adj* absurdo
luggage ['lʌgɪdʒ] *n* equipaje *m*; **luggage rack** *n* (*on car*) baca, portaequipajes *m inv*
lukewarm ['lu:kwɔ:m] *adj* tibio
lull [lʌl] *n* tregua ▷ *vt*: **to ~ sb to sleep** arrullar a algn; **to ~ sb into a false sense of security** dar a algn una falsa sensación de seguridad
lullaby ['lʌləbaɪ] *n* nana
lumber ['lʌmbə*] *n* (*junk*) trastos *mpl* viejos; (*wood*) maderos *mpl*
luminous ['lu:mɪnəs] *adj* luminoso
lump [lʌmp] *n* terrón *m*; (*fragment*) trozo; (*swelling*) bulto ▷ *vt* (*also*: **~ together**) juntar; **lump sum** *n* suma global; **lumpy** *adj* (*sauce*) lleno de grumos; (*mattress*) lleno de bultos
lunatic ['lu:nətɪk] *adj* loco
lunch [lʌntʃ] *n* almuerzo, comida ▷ *vi* almorzar; **lunch break, lunch hour** *n* hora del almuerzo; **lunch time** *n* hora de comer

lung [lʌŋ] *n* pulmón *m*
lure [luə*] *n* (*attraction*) atracción *f* ▷ *vt* tentar
lurk [lə:k] *vi* (*person, animal*) estar al acecho; (*fig*) acechar
lush [lʌʃ] *adj* exuberante
lust [lʌst] *n* lujuria; (*greed*) codicia
Luxembourg ['lʌksəmbə:g] *n* Luxemburgo
luxurious [lʌg'zjuərıəs] *adj* lujoso
luxury ['lʌkʃərı] *n* lujo ▷ *cpd* de lujo
Lycra® ['laıkrə] *n* licra®
lying ['laııŋ] *n* mentiras *fpl* ▷ *adj* mentiroso
lyrics ['lırıks] *npl* (*of song*) letra

m. *abbr* = **metre; mile; million**
M.A. *abbr* = **Master of Arts**
ma (*inf*) [mɑ:] *n* mamá
mac [mæk] (BRIT) *n* impermeable *m*
macaroni [mækə'rəunı] *n* macarrones *mpl*
Macedonia [mæsı'dəunıə] *n* Macedonia; **Macedonian** [-'dəunıən] *adj* macedonio ▷ *n* macedonio/a; (*Ling*) macedonio
machine [mə'ʃi:n] *n* máquina ▷ *vt* (*dress etc*) coser a máquina; (*Tech*) hacer a máquina; **machine gun** *n* ametralladora; **machinery** *n* maquinaria; (*fig*) mecanismo; **machine washable** *adj* lavable a máquina
macho ['mætʃəu] *adj* machista
mackerel ['mækrl] *n inv* caballa
mackintosh ['mækıntɔʃ] (BRIT) *n* impermeable *m*
mad [mæd] *adj* loco; (*idea*) disparatado; (*angry*) furioso; (*keen*): **to be ~ about sth** volverle loco a algn algo
Madagascar [mædə'gæskə*] *n*

Madagascar *m*
madam ['mædəm] *n* señora
mad cow disease *n* encefalopatía espongiforme bovina
made [meɪd] *pt, pp of* **make**; **made-to-measure** (BRIT) *adj* hecho a la medida; **made-up** ['meɪdʌp] *adj* (*story*) ficticio
madly ['mædlɪ] *adv* locamente
madman ['mædmən] (*irreg*) *n* loco
madness ['mædnɪs] *n* locura
Madrid [mə'drɪd] *n* Madrid
Mafia ['mæfɪə] *n* Mafia
mag [mæg] *n abbr* (BRIT *inf*) = **magazine**
magazine [mægə'ziːn] *n* revista; (*Radio, TV*) programa *m* magazina
maggot ['mægət] *n* gusano
magic ['mædʒɪk] *n* magia ▷ *adj* mágico; **magical** *adj* mágico; **magician** [mə'dʒɪʃən] *n* mago/a; (*conjurer*) prestidigitador(a) *m/f*
magistrate ['mædʒɪstreɪt] *n* juez *mf* (municipal)
magnet ['mægnɪt] *n* imán *m*; **magnetic** [-'nɛtɪk] *adj* magnético; (*personality*) atrayente
magnificent [mæg'nɪfɪsənt] *adj* magnífico
magnify ['mægnɪfaɪ] *vt* (*object*) ampliar; (*sound*) aumentar; **magnifying glass** *n* lupa
magpie ['mægpaɪ] *n* urraca
mahogany [mə'hɔgənɪ] *n* caoba
maid [meɪd] *n* criada; **old ~** (*pej*) solterona
maiden name *n* nombre *m* de soltera
mail [meɪl] *n* correo; (*letters*) cartas *fpl* ▷ *vt* echar al correo; **mailbox** (US) *n* buzón *m*; **mailing list** *n* lista de direcciones; **mailman** (US: *irreg*) *n* cartero; **mail-order** *n* pedido postal
main [meɪn] *adj* principal, mayor ▷ *n* (*pipe*) cañería maestra; (US) red *f* eléctrica ▷ **the ~s** *npl* (BRIT *Elec*) la red eléctrica; **in the ~** en general; **main course** *n* (*Culin*) plato principal; **mainland** *n* tierra firme; **mainly** *adv* principalmente; **main road** *n* carretera; **mainstream** *n* corriente *f* principal; **main street** *n* calle *f* mayor
maintain [meɪn'teɪn] *vt* mantener; **maintenance** ['meɪntənəns] *n* mantenimiento; (*Law*) manutención *f*
maisonette [meɪzə'nɛt] *n* dúplex *m*
maize [meɪz] (BRIT) *n* maíz *m*, choclo (SC)
majesty ['mædʒɪstɪ] *n* majestad *f*; (*title*): **Your M~** Su Majestad
major ['meɪdʒə*] *n* (*Mil*) comandante *mf* ▷ *adj* principal; (*Mus*) mayor
Majorca [mə'jɔːkə] *n* Mallorca
majority [mə'dʒɔrɪtɪ] *n* mayoría
make [meɪk] (*pt, pp* **made**) *vt* hacer; (*manufacture*) fabricar; (*mistake*) cometer; (*speech*) pronunciar; (*cause to be*): **to ~ sb sad** poner triste a algn; (*force*): **to ~ sb do sth** obligar a algn a hacer algo; (*earn*) ganar; (*equal*): **2 and 2 ~ 4** 2 y 2 son 4 ▷ *n* marca; **to ~ the bed** hacer la cama; **to ~ a fool of sb** poner a algn en ridículo; **to ~ a profit/loss** obtener ganancias/sufrir pérdidas; **to ~ it** (*arrive*) llegar; (*achieve sth*) tener éxito; **what time do you ~ it?** ¿qué hora tienes?; **to ~ do with** contentarse con; **make off** *vi* largarse; **make out** *vt* (*decipher*) descifrar; (*understand*) entender; (*see*) distinguir; (*cheque*) extender; **make up** *vt* (*invent*) inventar; (*prepare*) hacer; (*constitute*) constituir ▷ *vi* reconciliarse; (*with cosmetics*) maquillarse; **make up for** *vt fus* compensar; **makeover** ['meɪkəuvə*] *n* (*by beautician*) sesión *f* de maquillaje y peluquería; (*change of image*) lavado de cara; **maker** *n* fabricante *mf*; (*of film, programme*) autor(a) *m/f*; **makeshift** *adj* improvisado; **make-up** *n* maquillaje *m*
making ['meɪkɪŋ] *n* (*fig*): **in the ~** en vías de formación; **to have the ~s of** (*person*) tener madera de
malaria [mə'lɛərɪə] *n* malaria
Malaysia [mə'leɪzɪə] *n* Malasia,

Malaysia

male [meɪl] *n* (*Biol*) macho ▷ *adj* (*sex, attitude*) masculino; (*child etc*) varón

malicious [mə'lɪʃəs] *adj* malicioso; rencoroso

malignant [mə'lɪgnənt] *adj* (*Med*) maligno

mall [mɔːl] (*US*) *n* (*also*: **shopping ~**) centro comercial

mallet ['mælɪt] *n* mazo

malnutrition [mælnjuː'trɪʃən] *n* desnutrición *f*

malpractice [mæl'præktɪs] *n* negligencia profesional

malt [mɔːlt] *n* malta; (*whisky*) whisky *m* de malta

Malta ['mɔːltə] *n* Malta; **Maltese** [-'tiːz] *adj, n inv* maltés/esa *m/f*

mammal ['mæml] *n* mamífero

mammoth ['mæməθ] *n* mamut *m* ▷ *adj* gigantesco

man [mæn] (*pl* **men**) *n* hombre *m*; (*mankind*) el hombre ▷ *vt* (*Naut*) tripular; (*Mil*) guarnecer; (*operate*: *machine*) manejar; **an old ~** un viejo; **~ and wife** marido y mujer

manage ['mænɪdʒ] *vi* arreglárselas, ir tirando ▷ *vt* (*be in charge of*) dirigir; (*control*: *person*) manejar; (: *ship*) gobernar; **manageable** *adj* manejable; **management** *n* dirección *f*; **manager** *n* director(a) *m/f*; (*of pop star*) mánager *mf*; (*Sport*) entrenador(a) *m/f*; **manageress** *n* directora; entrenadora; **managerial** [-ə'dʒɪerɪəl] *adj* directivo; **managing director** *n* director(a) *m/f* general

mandarin ['mændərɪn] *n* (*also*: **~ orange**) mandarina; (*person*) mandarín *m*

mandate ['mændeɪt] *n* mandato

mandatory ['mændətərɪ] *adj* obligatorio

mane [meɪn] *n* (*of horse*) crin *f*; (*of lion*) melena

maneuver [mə'nuːvə*] (*US*) = **manoeuvre**

mangetout [mɔnʒ'tuː] *n* tirabeque *m*

mango ['mæŋgəu] (*pl* **~es**) *n* mango

man: manhole *n* agujero de acceso; **manhood** *n* edad *f* viril; (*state*) virilidad *f*

mania ['meɪnɪə] *n* manía; **maniac** ['meɪnɪæk] *n* maníaco/a; (*fig*) maniático

manic ['mænɪk] *adj* frenético

manicure ['mænɪkjuə*] *n* manicura

manifest ['mænɪfɛst] *vt* manifestar, mostrar ▷ *adj* manifiesto

manifesto [mænɪ'fɛstəu] *n* manifiesto

manipulate [mə'nɪpjuleɪt] *vt* manipular

man: mankind [mæn'kaɪnd] *n* humanidad *f*, género humano; **manly** *adj* varonil; **man-made** *adj* artificial

manner ['mænə*] *n* manera, modo; (*behaviour*) conducta, manera de ser; (*type*): **all ~ of things** toda clase de cosas; **manners** *npl* (*behaviour*) modales *mpl*; **bad ~s** mala educación

manoeuvre [mə'nuːvə*] (*US* **maneuver**) *vt, vi* maniobrar ▷ *n* maniobra

manpower ['mænpauə*] *n* mano *f* de obra

mansion ['mænʃən] *n* palacio, casa grande

manslaughter ['mænslɔːtə*] *n* homicidio no premeditado

mantelpiece ['mæntlpiːs] *n* repisa, chimenea

manual ['mænjuəl] *adj* manual ▷ *n* manual *m*

manufacture [mænju'fæktʃə*] *vt* fabricar ▷ *n* fabricación *f*; **manufacturer** *n* fabricante *mf*

manure [mə'njuə*] *n* estiércol *m*

manuscript ['mænjuskrɪpt] *n* manuscrito

many ['mɛnɪ] *adj, pron* muchos/as; **a great ~** muchísimos, un buen número de; **~ a time** muchas veces

map [mæp] *n* mapa *m* ▷ **to ~ out** *vt* proyectar

maple ['meɪpl] *n* arce *m*, maple *m* (LAM)
Mar *abbr* (=*March*) mar
mar [mɑː*] *vt* estropear
marathon ['mærəθən] *n* maratón *m*
marble ['mɑːbl] *n* mármol *m*; (*toy*) canica
March [mɑːtʃ] *n* marzo
march [mɑːtʃ] *vi* (*Mil*) marchar; (*demonstrators*) manifestarse ▷ *n* marcha; (*demonstration*) manifestación *f*
mare [mɛə*] *n* yegua
margarine [mɑːdʒə'riːn] *n* margarina
margin ['mɑːdʒɪn] *n* margen *m*; (*Comm*: *profit margin*) margen *m* de beneficios; **marginal** *adj* marginal; **marginally** *adv* ligeramente
marigold ['mærɪgəuld] *n* caléndula
marijuana [mærɪ'wɑːnə] *n* marijuana
marina [mə'riːnə] *n* puerto deportivo
marinade [mærɪ'neɪd] *n* adobo
marinate ['mærɪneɪt] *vt* marinar
marine [mə'riːn] *adj* marino ▷ *n* soldado de marina
marital ['mærɪtl] *adj* matrimonial; **marital status** *n* estado *m* civil
maritime ['mærɪtaɪm] *adj* marítimo
marjoram ['mɑːdʒərəm] *n* mejorana
mark [mɑːk] *n* marca, señal *f*; (*in snow, mud etc*) huella; (*stain*) mancha; (BRIT *Scol*) nota ▷ *vt* marcar; manchar; (*damage*: *furniture*) rayar; (*indicate*: *place etc*) señalar; (BRIT *Scol*) calificar, corregir; **to ~ time** marcar el paso; (*fig*) marcar(se) un ritmo; **marked** *adj* (*obvious*) marcado, acusado; **marker** *n* (*sign*) marcador *m*; (*bookmark*) señal *f* (de libro)
market ['mɑːkɪt] *n* mercado ▷ *vt* (*Comm*) comercializar; **marketing** *n* márketing *m*; **marketplace** *n* mercado; **market research** *n* análisis *m inv* de mercados
marmalade ['mɑːməleɪd] *n* mermelada de naranja
maroon [mə'ruːn] *vt*: **to be ~ed** quedar aislado; (*fig*) quedar abandonado ▷ *n* (*colour*) granate *m*
marquee [mɑː'kiː] *n* entoldado
marriage ['mærɪdʒ] *n* (*relationship, institution*) matrimonio; (*wedding*) boda; (*act*) casamiento; **marriage certificate** *n* partida de casamiento
married ['mærɪd] *adj* casado; (*life, love*) conyugal
marrow ['mærəu] *n* médula; (*vegetable*) calabacín *m*
marry ['mærɪ] *vt* casarse con; (*father, priest etc*) casar ▷ *vi* (*also*: **get married**) casarse
Mars [mɑːz] *n* Marte *m*
marsh [mɑːʃ] *n* pantano; (*salt marsh*) marisma
marshal ['mɑːʃl] *n* (*Mil*) mariscal *m*; (*at sports meeting etc*) oficial *m*; (US: *of police, fire department*) jefe/a *m/f* ▷ *vt* (*thoughts etc*) ordenar; (*soldiers*) formar
martyr ['mɑːtə*] *n* mártir *mf*
marvel ['mɑːvl] *n* maravilla, prodigio ▷ *vi*: **to ~ (at)** maravillarse (de); **marvellous** (US **marvelous**) *adj* maravilloso
Marxism ['mɑːksɪzəm] *n* marxismo
Marxist ['mɑːksɪst] *adj, n* marxista *mf*
marzipan ['mɑːzɪpæn] *n* mazapán *m*
mascara [mæs'kɑːrə] *n* rímel *m*
mascot ['mæskət] *n* mascota
masculine ['mæskjulɪn] *adj* masculino
mash [mæʃ] *vt* machacar; **mashed potato(es)** *n(pl)* puré *m* de patatas (SP) *or* papas (LAM)
mask [mɑːsk] *n* máscara ▷ *vt* (*cover*): **to ~ one's face** ocultarse la cara; (*hide*: *feelings*) esconder
mason ['meɪsn] *n* (*also*: **stone~**) albañil *m*; (*also*: **free~**) masón *m*; **masonry** *n* (*in building*) mampostería
mass [mæs] *n* (*people*) muchedumbre *f*; (*of air, liquid etc*) masa; (*of detail, hair etc*) gran cantidad *f*; (*Rel*) misa ▷ *cpd*

masivo ▷ *vi* reunirse; concentrarse; **the masses** *npl* las masas; **~es of** (*inf*) montones de

massacre ['mæsəkə*] *n* masacre *f*

massage ['mæsɑːʒ] *n* masaje *m* ▷ *vt* dar masaje en

massive ['mæsɪv] *adj* enorme; (*support, changes*) masivo

mass media *npl* medios *mpl* de comunicación

mass-produce ['mæsprə'djuːs] *vt* fabricar en serie

mast [mɑːst] *n* (*Naut*) mástil *m*; (*Radio etc*) torre *f*

master ['mɑːstə*] *n* (*of servant*) amo; (*of situation*) dueño, maestro; (*in primary school*) maestro; (*in secondary school*) profesor *m*; (*title for boys*): **M~ X** Señorito X ▷ *vt* dominar; **mastermind** *n* inteligencia superior ▷ *vt* dirigir, planear; **Master of Arts/Science** *n* licenciatura superior en Letras/Ciencias; **masterpiece** *n* obra maestra

masturbate ['mæstəbeɪt] *vi* masturbarse

mat [mæt] *n* estera; (*also*: **door~**) felpudo; (*also*: **table ~**) salvamanteles *m inv*, posavasos *m inv* ▷ *adj* = **matt**

match [mætʃ] *n* cerilla, fósforo; (*game*) partido; (*equal*) igual *m/f* ▷ *vt* (*go well with*) hacer juego con; (*equal*) igualar; (*correspond to*) corresponderse con; (*pair*: *also*: **~ up**) casar con ▷ *vi* hacer juego; **to be a good ~** hacer juego; **matchbox** *n* caja de cerillas; **matching** *adj* que hace juego

mate [meɪt] *n* (*workmate*) colega *mf*; (*inf*: *friend*) amigo/a; (*animal*) macho/hembra; (*in merchant navy*) segundo de a bordo ▷ *vi* acoplarse, aparearse ▷ *vt* aparear

material [mə'tɪərɪəl] *n* (*substance*) materia; (*information*) material *m*; (*cloth*) tela, tejido ▷ *adj* material; (*important*) esencial; **materials** *npl* materiales *mpl*

materialize [mə'tɪərɪəlaɪz] *vi* materializarse

maternal [mə'təːnl] *adj* maternal

maternity [mə'təːnɪtɪ] *n* maternidad *f*; **maternity hospital** *n* hospital *m* de maternidad; **maternity leave** *n* baja por maternidad

math [mæθ] (*US*) *n* = **mathematics**

mathematical [mæθə'mætɪkl] *adj* matemático

mathematician [mæθəmə'tɪʃən] *n* matemático/a

mathematics [mæθə'mætɪks] *n* matemáticas *fpl*

maths [mæθs] (*BRIT*) *n* = **mathematics**

matinée ['mætɪneɪ] *n* sesión *f* de tarde

matron ['meɪtrən] *n* enfermera *f* jefe; (*in school*) ama de llaves

matt [mæt] *adj* mate

matter ['mætə*] *n* cuestión *f*, asunto; (*Physics*) sustancia, materia; (*reading matter*) material *m*; (*Med*: *pus*) pus *m* ▷ *vi* importar; **matters** *npl* (*affairs*) asuntos *mpl*, temas *mpl*; **it doesn't ~** no importa; **what's the ~?** ¿qué pasa?; **no ~ what** pase lo que pase; **as a ~ of course** por rutina; **as a ~ of fact** de hecho

mattress ['mætrɪs] *n* colchón *m*

mature [mə'tjuə*] *adj* maduro ▷ *vi* madurar; **mature student** *n* *estudiante de más de 21 años*; **maturity** *n* madurez *f*

maul [mɔːl] *vt* magullar

mauve [məuv] *adj* de color malva (*SP*) *or* guinda (*LAM*)

max *abbr* = **maximum**

maximize ['mæksɪmaɪz] *vt* (*profits etc*) llevar al máximo; (*chances*) maximizar

maximum ['mæksɪməm] (*pl* **maxima**) *adj* máximo ▷ *n* máximo

May [meɪ] *n* mayo

may [meɪ] (*conditional* **might**) *vi* (*indicating possibility*): **he ~ come** puede que venga; (*be allowed to*): **~ I smoke?** ¿puedo fumar?; (*wishes*): **~ God bless**

you! ¡que Dios le bendiga!; **you ~ as well go** bien puedes irte
maybe ['meɪbiː] *adv* quizá(s)
May Day *n* el primero de Mayo
mayhem ['meɪhɛm] *n* caos *m* total
mayonnaise [meɪə'neɪz] *n* mayonesa
mayor [mɛə*] *n* alcalde *m*; **mayoress** *n* alcaldesa
maze [meɪz] *n* laberinto
MD *n abbr* = **managing director**
me [miː] *pron* (*direct*) me; (*stressed, after pron*) mí; **can you hear ~?** ¿me oyes?; **he heard ME** ¡me oyó a mí!; **it's ~** soy yo; **give them to ~** dámelos/las; **with/without ~** conmigo/sin mí
meadow ['mɛdəu] *n* prado, pradera
meagre ['miːgə*] (*US* **meager**) *adj* escaso, pobre
meal [miːl] *n* comida; (*flour*) harina; **mealtime** *n* hora de comer
mean [miːn] (*pt, pp* **~t**) *adj* (*with money*) tacaño; (*unkind*) mezquino, malo; (*shabby*) humilde; (*average*) medio ▷ *vt* (*signify*) querer decir, significar; (*refer to*) referirse a; (*intend*): **to ~ to do sth** pensar *or* pretender hacer algo ▷ *n* medio, término medio; **means** *npl* (*way*) medio, manera; (*money*) recursos *mpl*, medios *mpl*; **by ~s of** mediante, por medio de; **by all ~s!** ¡naturalmente!, ¡claro que sí!; **do you ~ it?** ¿lo dices en serio?; **what do you ~?** ¿qué quiere decir?; **to be ~t for sb/sth** ser para algn/algo
meaning ['miːnɪŋ] *n* significado, sentido; (*purpose*) sentido, propósito; **meaningful** *adj* significativo; **meaningless** *adj* sin sentido
meant [mɛnt] *pt, pp of* **mean**
meantime ['miːntaɪm] *adv* (*also*: **in the ~**) mientras tanto
meanwhile ['miːnwaɪl] *adv* = **meantime**
measles ['miːzlz] *n* sarampión *m*
measure ['mɛʒə*] *vt, vi* medir ▷ *n* medida; (*ruler*) regla; **measurement** ['mɛʒəmənt] *n* (*measure*) medida; (*act*) medición *f*; **to take sb's measurements** tomar las medidas a algn
meat [miːt] *n* carne *f*; **cold ~** fiambre *m*; **meatball** *n* albóndiga
Mecca ['mɛkə] *n* La Meca
mechanic [mɪ'kænɪk] *n* mecánico/a; **mechanical** *adj* mecánico
mechanism ['mɛkənɪzəm] *n* mecanismo
medal ['mɛdl] *n* medalla; **medallist** (*US* **medalist**) *n* (*Sport*) medallista *mf*
meddle ['mɛdl] *vi*: **to ~ in** entrometerse en; **to ~ with sth** manosear algo
media ['miːdɪə] *npl* medios *mpl* de comunicación ▷ *npl of* **medium**
mediaeval [mɛdɪ'iːvl] *adj* = **medieval**
mediate ['miːdɪeɪt] *vi* mediar
medical ['mɛdɪkl] *adj* médico ▷ *n* reconocimiento médico; **medical certificate** *n* certificado *m* médico
medicated ['mɛdɪkeɪtɪd] *adj* medicinal
medication [mɛdɪ'keɪʃən] *n* medicación *f*
medicine ['mɛdsɪn] *n* medicina; (*drug*) medicamento
medieval [mɛdɪ'iːvl] *adj* medieval
mediocre [miːdɪ'əukə*] *adj* mediocre
meditate ['mɛdɪteɪt] *vi* meditar
meditation [mɛdɪ'teɪʃən] *n* meditación *f*
Mediterranean [mɛdɪtə'reɪnɪən] *adj* mediterráneo; **the ~ (Sea)** el (Mar) Mediterráneo
medium ['miːdɪəm] (*pl* **media**) *adj* mediano, regular ▷ *n* (*means*) medio; (*pl mediums: person*) médium *mf*; **medium-sized** *adj* de tamaño mediano; (*clothes*) de (la) talla mediana; **medium wave** *n* onda media
meek [miːk] *adj* manso, sumiso
meet [miːt] (*pt, pp* **met**) *vt* encontrar; (*accidentally*) encontrarse con, tropezar con; (*by arrangement*) reunirse

con; (*for the first time*) conocer; (*go and fetch*) ir a buscar; (*opponent*) enfrentarse con; (*obligations*) cumplir; (*encounter: problem*) hacer frente a; (*need*) satisfacer ▷ *vi* encontrarse; (*in session*) reunirse; (*join: objects*) unirse; (*for the first time*) conocerse; **meet up** *vi*: **to meet up with sb** reunirse con algn; **meet with** *vt fus* (*difficulty*) tropezar con; **to meet with success** tener éxito; **meeting** *n* encuentro; (*arranged*) cita, compromiso; (*business meeting*) reunión *f*; (*Pol*) mítin *m*; **meeting place** *n* lugar *m* de reunión *or* encuentro

megabyte ['mɛgəbaɪt] *n* (*Comput*) megabyte *m*, megaocteto

megaphone ['mɛgəfəun] *n* megáfono

megapixel ['mɛgəpɪksl] *n* megapíxel *m*

melancholy ['mɛlənkəlɪ] *n* melancolía ▷ *adj* melancólico

melody ['mɛlədɪ] *n* melodía

melon ['mɛlən] *n* melón *m*

melt [mɛlt] *vi* (*metal*) fundirse; (*snow*) derretirse ▷ *vt* fundir

member ['mɛmbə*] *n* (*gen, Anat*) miembro; (*of club*) socio/a; **Member of Congress** (US) *n* miembro *mf* del Congreso; **Member of Parliament** *n* (BRIT) diputado/a *m/f*, parlamentario/a *m/f*; **Member of the European Parliament** *n* diputado/a *m/f* del Parlamento Europeo, eurodiputado/a *m/f*; **Member of the Scottish Parliament** (BRIT) diputado/a del Parlamento escocés; **membership** *n* (*members*) número de miembros; (*state*) filiación *f*; **membership card** *n* carnet *m* de socio

memento [mə'mɛntəu] *n* recuerdo

memo ['mɛməu] *n* apunte *m*, nota

memorable ['mɛmərəbl] *adj* memorable

memorandum [mɛmə'rændəm] (*pl* **memoranda**) *n* apunte *m*, nota; (*official note*) acta

memorial [mɪ'mɔːrɪəl] *n* monumento conmemorativo ▷ *adj* conmemorativo

memorize ['mɛməraɪz] *vt* aprender de memoria

memory ['mɛmərɪ] *n* (*also: Comput*) memoria; (*instance*) recuerdo; (*of dead person*): **in ~ of** a la memoria de; **memory card** *n* (*for digital camera*) tarjeta de memoria

men [mɛn] *npl of* **man**

menace ['mɛnəs] *n* amenaza ▷ *vt* amenazar

mend [mɛnd] *vt* reparar, arreglar; (*darn*) zurcir ▷ *vi* reponerse ▷ *n* arreglo, reparación *f* zurcido ▷ *n*: **to be on the ~** ir mejorando; **to ~ one's ways** enmendarse

meningitis [mɛnɪn'dʒaɪtɪs] *n* meningitis *f*

menopause ['mɛnəupɔːz] *n* menopausia

men's room (US) *n*: **the ~** el servicio de caballeros

menstruation [mɛnstru'eɪʃən] *n* menstruación *f*

menswear ['mɛnzwɛə*] *n* confección *f* de caballero

mental ['mɛntl] *adj* mental; **mental hospital** *n* (hospital *m*) psiquiátrico; **mentality** [mɛn'tælɪtɪ] *n* mentalidad *f*; **mentally** *adv*: **to be mentally ill** tener una enfermedad mental

menthol ['mɛnθɔl] *n* mentol *m*

mention ['mɛnʃən] *n* mención *f* ▷ *vt* mencionar; (*speak*) hablar de; **don't ~ it!** ¡de nada!

menu ['mɛnjuː] *n* (*set menu*) menú *m*; (*printed*) carta; (*Comput*) menú *m*

MEP *n abbr* = **Member of the European Parliament**

mercenary ['məːsɪnərɪ] *adj, n* mercenario/a

merchandise ['məːtʃəndaɪz] *n* mercancías *fpl*

merchant ['məːtʃənt] *n* comerciante *mf*; **merchant navy** (US), **merchant marine** *n* marina mercante

merciless ['mə:sɪlɪs] *adj* despiadado

mercury ['mə:kjurɪ] *n* mercurio

mercy ['mə:sɪ] *n* compasión *f*; (*Rel*) misericordia; **at the ~ of** a la merced de

mere [mɪə*] *adj* simple, mero; **merely** *adv* simplemente, sólo

merge [mə:dʒ] *vt* (*join*) unir ▷ *vi* unirse; (*Comm*) fusionarse; (*colours etc*) fundirse; **merger** *n* (*Comm*) fusión *f*

meringue [mə'ræŋ] *n* merengue *m*

merit ['mɛrɪt] *n* mérito ▷ *vt* merecer

mermaid ['mə:meɪd] *n* sirena

merry ['mɛrɪ] *adj* alegre; **M~ Christmas!** ¡Felices Pascuas!; **merry-go-round** *n* tiovivo

mesh [mɛʃ] *n* malla

mess [mɛs] *n* (*muddle: of situation*) confusión *f*; (*: of room*) revoltijo; (*dirt*) porquería; (*Mil*) comedor *m*; **mess about** *or* **around** (*inf*) *vi* perder el tiempo; (*pass the time*) entretenerse; **mess up** *vt* (*spoil*) estropear; (*dirty*) ensuciar; **mess with** (*inf*) *vt fus* (*challenge, confront*) meterse con (*inf*); (*interfere with*) interferir con

message ['mɛsɪdʒ] *n* recado, mensaje *m*

messenger ['mɛsɪndʒə*] *n* mensajero/a

Messrs *abbr* (*on letters*) (= *Messieurs*) Sres

messy ['mɛsɪ] *adj* (*dirty*) sucio; (*untidy*) desordenado

met [mɛt] *pt, pp of* **meet**

metabolism [mɛ'tæbəlɪzəm] *n* metabolismo

metal ['mɛtl] *n* metal *m*; **metallic** [-'tælɪk] *adj* metálico

metaphor ['mɛtəfə*] *n* metáfora

meteor ['mi:tɪə*] *n* meteoro; **meteorite** [-aɪt] *n* meteorito

meteorology [mi:tɪɔ'rɔlədʒɪ] *n* meteorología

meter ['mi:tə*] *n* (*instrument*) contador *m*; (*US: unit*) = **metre** ▷ *vt* (*US Post*) franquear

method ['mɛθəd] *n* método; **methodical** [mɪ'θɔdɪkl] *adj* metódico

meths [mɛθs] *n* (*BRIT*) alcohol *m* metilado *or* desnaturalizado

meticulous [mɛ'tɪkjuləs] *adj* meticuloso

metre ['mi:tə*] (*US* **meter**) *n* metro

metric ['mɛtrɪk] *adj* métrico

metro ['metrəu] *n* metro

metropolitan [mɛtrə'pɔlɪtən] *adj* metropolitano; **the M~ Police** (*BRIT*) la policía londinense

Mexican ['mɛksɪkən] *adj, n* mexicano/a , mejicano/a

Mexico ['mɛksɪkəu] *n* México, Méjico (*SP*)

mg *abbr* (= *milligram*) mg

mice [maɪs] *npl of* **mouse**

micro... [maɪkrəu] *prefix* micro...; **microchip** *n* microplaqueta; **microphone** *n* micrófono; **microscope** *n* microscopio; **microwave** *n* (*also*: **microwave oven**) horno microondas

mid [mɪd] *adj*: **in ~ May** a mediados de mayo; **in ~ afternoon** a media tarde; **in ~ air** en el aire; **midday** *n* mediodía *m*

middle ['mɪdl] *n* centro; (*half-way point*) medio; (*waist*) cintura ▷ *adj* de en medio; (*course, way*) intermedio; **in the ~ of the night** en plena noche; **middle-aged** *adj* de mediana edad; **Middle Ages** *npl*: **the Middle Ages** la Edad Media; **middle-class** *adj* de clase media; **the middle class(es)** la clase media; **Middle East** *n* Oriente *m* Medio; **middle name** *n* segundo nombre; **middle school** *n* (*US*) *colegio para niños de doce a catorce años*; (*BRIT*) *colegio para niños de ocho o nueve a doce o trece años*

midge [mɪdʒ] *n* mosquito

midget ['mɪdʒɪt] *n* enano/a

midnight ['mɪdnaɪt] *n* medianoche *f*

midst [mɪdst] *n*: **in the ~ of** (*crowd*) en medio de; (*situation, action*) en mitad de

midsummer [mɪd'sʌmə*] *n*: **in ~** en pleno verano

midway [mɪd'weɪ] *adj, adv*: **~ (between)** a medio camino (entre); **~**

through a la mitad (de)
midweek [mɪd'wi:k] *adv* entre semana
midwife ['mɪdwaɪf] (*irreg*) *n* comadrona, partera
midwinter [mɪd'wɪntə*] *n*: **in ~** en pleno invierno
might [maɪt] *vb see* **may** ▷ *n* fuerza, poder *m*; **mighty** *adj* fuerte, poderoso
migraine ['mi:greɪn] *n* jaqueca
migrant ['maɪgrənt] *n, adj* (*bird*) migratorio; (*worker*) emigrante
migrate [maɪ'greɪt] *vi* emigrar
migration [maɪ'greɪʃən] *n* emigración *f*
mike [maɪk] *n abbr* (= *microphone*) micro
mild [maɪld] *adj* (*person*) apacible; (*climate*) templado; (*slight*) ligero; (*taste*) suave; (*illness*) leve; **mildly** ['-lɪ] *adv* ligeramente; suavemente; **to put it mildly** para no decir más
mile [maɪl] *n* milla; **mileage** *n* número de millas ≈ kilometraje *m*; **mileometer** [maɪ'lɔmɪtə] *n* ≈ cuentakilómetros *m inv*; **milestone** *n* mojón *m*
military ['mɪlɪtərɪ] *adj* militar
militia [mɪ'lɪʃə] *n* milicia
milk [mɪlk] *n* leche *f* ▷ *vt* (*cow*) ordeñar; (*fig*) chupar; **milk chocolate** *n* chocolate *m* con leche; **milkman** (*irreg*) *n* lechero; **milky** *adj* lechoso
mill [mɪl] *n* (*windmill etc*) molino; (*coffee mill*) molinillo; (*factory*) fábrica ▷ *vt* moler ▷ *vi* (*also*: **~ about**) arremolinarse
millennium [mɪ'lɛnɪəm] (*pl* **~s** *or* **millennia**) *n* milenio, milenario
milli... ['mɪlɪ] *prefix*: **milligram(me)** *n* miligramo; **millilitre** (*US* **milliliter**) ['mɪlɪli:tə*] *n* mililitro; **millimetre** (*US* **millimeter**) *n* milímetro
million ['mɪljən] *n* millón *m*; **a ~ times** un millón de veces; **millionaire** [-jə'nɛə*] *n* millonario/a; **millionth** [-θ] *adj* millonésimo
milometer [maɪ'lɔmɪtə*] (BRIT) *n* = **mileometer**
mime [maɪm] *n* mímica; (*actor*) mimo/a ▷ *vt* remedar ▷ *vi* actuar de mimo
mimic ['mɪmɪk] *n* imitador(a) *m/f* ▷ *adj* mímico ▷ *vt* remedar, imitar
min. *abbr* = **minimum; minute(s)**
mince [mɪns] *vt* picar ▷ *n* (BRIT *Culin*) carne *f* picada; **mincemeat** *n conserva de fruta picada*; (*US*: *meat*) carne *f* picada; **mince pie** *n empanadilla rellena de fruta picada*
mind [maɪnd] *n* mente *f*; (*intellect*) intelecto; (*contrasted with matter*) espíritu *m* ▷ *vt* (*attend to, look after*) ocuparse de, cuidar; (*be careful*) tener cuidado con; (*object to*): **I don't ~ the noise** no me molesta el ruido; **it is on my ~** me preocupa; **to bear sth in ~** tomar *or* tener algo en cuenta; **to make up one's ~** decidirse; **I don't ~** me es igual; **~ you ...** te advierto que ...; **never ~!** ¡es igual!, ¡no importa!; (*don't worry*) ¡no te preocupes!; **"~ the step"** "cuidado con el escalón"; **mindless** *adj* (*crime*) sin motivo; (*work*) de autómata
mine[1] [maɪn] *pron* el mío/la mía *etc*; **a friend of ~** un(a) amigo/a mío/mía ▷ *adj*: **this book is ~** este libro es mío
mine[2] [maɪn] *n* mina ▷ *vt* (*coal*) extraer; (*bomb*: *beach etc*) minar; **minefield** *n* campo de minas; **miner** *n* minero/a
mineral ['mɪnərəl] *adj* mineral ▷ *n* mineral *m*; **mineral water** *n* agua mineral
mingle ['mɪŋgl] *vi*: **to ~ with** mezclarse con
miniature ['mɪnətʃə*] *adj* (en) miniatura ▷ *n* miniatura
minibar ['mɪnɪbɑ:*] *n* minibar *m*
minibus ['mɪnɪbʌs] *n* microbús *m*
minicab ['mɪnɪkæb] *n* taxi *m* (*que sólo puede pedirse por teléfono*)
minimal ['mɪnɪml] *adj* mínimo
minimize ['mɪnɪmaɪz] *vt* minimizar; (*play down*) empequeñecer
minimum ['mɪnɪməm] (*pl* **minima**)

n, adj mínimo
mining ['maɪnɪŋ] *n* explotación *f* minera
miniskirt ['mɪnɪskəːt] *n* minifalda
minister ['mɪnɪstə*] *n* (BRIT *Pol*) ministro/a (SP), secretario/a (LAM); (*Rel*) pastor *m* ▷ *vi*: **to ~ to** atender a
ministry ['mɪnɪstrɪ] *n* (BRIT *Pol*) ministerio, secretaría (MEX); (*Rel*) sacerdocio
minor ['maɪnə*] *adj* (*repairs, injuries*) leve; (*poet, planet*) menor; (*Mus*) menor ▷ *n* (*Law*) menor *m* de edad
Minorca [mɪ'nɔːkə] *n* Menorca
minority [maɪ'nɔrɪtɪ] *n* minoría
mint [mɪnt] *n* (*plant*) menta, hierbabuena; (*sweet*) caramelo de menta ▷ *vt* (*coins*) acuñar; **the (Royal) M~, the (US) M~** la Casa de la Moneda; **in ~ condition** en perfecto estado
minus ['maɪnəs] *n* (*also*: **~ sign**) signo de menos ▷ *prep* menos; **12 ~ 6 equals 6** 12 menos 6 son 6; **~ 24 °C** menos 24 grados
minute[1] ['mɪnɪt] *n* minuto; (*fig*) momento; **minutes** *npl* (*of meeting*) actas *fpl*; **at the last ~** a última hora
minute[2] [maɪ'njuːt] *adj* diminuto; (*search*) minucioso
miracle ['mɪrəkl] *n* milagro
miraculous [mɪ'rækjuləs] *adj* milagroso
mirage ['mɪrɑːʒ] *n* espejismo
mirror ['mɪrə*] *n* espejo; (*in car*) retrovisor *m*
misbehave [mɪsbɪ'heɪv] *vi* portarse mal
misc. *abbr* = **miscellaneous**
miscarriage ['mɪskærɪdʒ] *n* (*Med*) aborto; **~ of justice** error *m* judicial
miscellaneous [mɪsɪ'leɪnɪəs] *adj* varios/as, diversos/as
mischief ['mɪstʃɪf] *n* travesuras *fpl*, diabluras *fpl*; (*maliciousness*) malicia; **mischievous** [-ʃɪvəs] *adj* travieso
misconception [mɪskən'sɛpʃən] *n* idea equivocada; equivocación *f*
misconduct [mɪs'kɔndʌkt] *n* mala conducta; **professional ~** falta profesional
miser ['maɪzə*] *n* avaro/a
miserable ['mɪzərəbl] *adj* (*unhappy*) triste, desgraciado; (*unpleasant, contemptible*) miserable
misery ['mɪzərɪ] *n* tristeza; (*wretchedness*) miseria, desdicha
misfortune [mɪs'fɔːtʃən] *n* desgracia
misgiving [mɪs'gɪvɪŋ] *n* (*apprehension*) presentimiento; **to have ~s about sth** tener dudas acerca de algo
misguided [mɪs'gaɪdɪd] *adj* equivocado
mishap ['mɪshæp] *n* desgracia, contratiempo
misinterpret [mɪsɪn'təːprɪt] *vt* interpretar mal
misjudge [mɪs'dʒʌdʒ] *vt* juzgar mal
mislay [mɪs'leɪ] *vt* extraviar, perder
mislead [mɪs'liːd] *vt* llevar a conclusiones erróneas; **misleading** *adj* engañoso
misplace [mɪs'pleɪs] *vt* extraviar
misprint ['mɪsprɪnt] *n* errata, error *m* de imprenta
misrepresent [mɪsrɛprɪ'zɛnt] *vt* falsificar
Miss [mɪs] *n* Señorita
miss [mɪs] *vt* (*train etc*) perder; (*fail to hit: target*) errar; (*regret the absence of*): **I ~ him** (yo) le echo de menos *or* a faltar; (*fail to see*): **you can't ~ it** no tiene pérdida ▷ *vi* fallar ▷ *n* (*shot*) tiro fallido *or* perdido; **miss out** (BRIT) *vt* omitir; **miss out on** *vt fus* (*fun, party, opportunity*) perderse
missile ['mɪsaɪl] *n* (*Aviat*) mísil *m*; (*object thrown*) proyectil *m*
missing ['mɪsɪŋ] *adj* (*pupil*) ausente; (*thing*) perdido; (*Mil*): **~ in action** desaparecido en combate
mission ['mɪʃən] *n* misión *f*; (*official representation*) delegación *f*; **missionary** *n* misionero/a

misspell [mɪs'spɛl] (*pt, pp* **misspelt** (BRIT) *or* **~ed**) *vt* escribir mal
mist [mɪst] *n* (*light*) neblina; (*heavy*) niebla; (*at sea*) bruma ▷ *vi* (*eyes: also:* **~ over, ~ up**) llenarse de lágrimas; (BRIT: *windows: also:* **~ over, ~ up**) empañarse
mistake [mɪs'teɪk] (*vt: irreg*) *n* error *m* ▷ *vt* entender mal; **by ~** por equivocación; **to make a ~** equivocarse; **to ~ A for B** confundir A con B; **mistaken** *pp of* **mistake** ▷ *adj* equivocado; **to be mistaken** equivocarse, engañarse
mister ['mɪstə*] (*inf*) *n* señor *m*; *see* **Mr**
mistletoe ['mɪsltəu] *n* muérdago
mistook [mɪs'tuk] *pt of* **mistake**
mistress ['mɪstrɪs] *n* (*lover*) amante *f*; (*of house*) señora (de la casa); (BRIT: *in primary school*) maestra; (*in secondary school*) profesora; (*of situation*) dueña
mistrust [mɪs'trʌst] *vt* desconfiar de
misty ['mɪstɪ] *adj* (*day*) de niebla; (*glasses etc*) empañado
misunderstand [mɪsʌndə'stænd] (*irreg*) *vt, vi* entender mal; **misunderstanding** *n* malentendido
misunderstood [mɪsʌndə'stud] *pt, pp of* **misunderstand** ▷ *adj* (*person*) incomprendido
misuse [*n* mɪs'ju:s, *vb* mɪs'ju:z] *n* mal uso; (*of power*) abuso; (*of funds*) malversación *f* ▷ *vt* abusar de; malversar
mitt(en) ['mɪt(n)] *n* manopla
mix [mɪks] *vt* mezclar; (*combine*) unir ▷ *vi* mezclarse; (*people*) llevarse bien ▷ *n* mezcla; **mix up** *vt* mezclar; (*confuse*) confundir; **mixed** *adj* mixto; (*feelings etc*) encontrado; **mixed grill** *n* (BRIT) parrillada mixta; **mixed salad** *n* ensalada mixta; **mixed-up** *adj* (*confused*) confuso, revuelto; **mixer** *n* (*for food*) licuadora; (*for drinks*) coctelera; (*person*): **he's a good mixer** tiene don de gentes; **mixture** *n* mezcla; (*also:* **cough mixture**) jarabe *m*; **mix-up** *n* confusión *f*
ml *abbr* (= *millilitre(s)*) ml
mm *abbr* (= *millimetre*) mm
moan [məun] *n* gemido ▷ *vi* gemir; (*inf: complain*): **to ~ (about)** quejarse (de)
moat [məut] *n* foso
mob [mɔb] *n* multitud *f* ▷ *vt* acosar
mobile ['məubaɪl] *adj* móvil ▷ *n* móvil *m*; **mobile home** *n* caravana; **mobile phone** *n* teléfono móvil
mobility [məu'bɪlɪtɪ] *n* movilidad *f*
mobilize ['məubɪlaɪz] *vt* movilizar
mock [mɔk] *vt* (*ridicule*) ridiculizar; (*laugh at*) burlarse de ▷ *adj* fingido; **~ exam** *examen preparatorio antes de los exámenes oficiales** (BRIT: *Scol: inf*) exámenes *mpl* de prueba; **mockery** *n* burla
mod cons ['mɔd'kɔnz] *npl abbr* (= *modern conveniences*) *see* **convenience**
mode [məud] *n* modo
model ['mɔdl] *n* modelo; (*fashion model, artist's model*) modelo *mf* ▷ *adj* modelo ▷ *vt* (*with clay etc*) modelar; (*copy*): **to ~ o.s. on** tomar como modelo a ▷ *vi* ser modelo; **to ~ clothes** pasar modelos, ser modelo
modem ['məudəm] *n* modem *m*
moderate [*adj* 'mɔdərət, *vb* 'mɔdəreɪt] *adj* moderado/a ▷ *vi* moderarse, calmarse ▷ *vt* moderar
moderation [mɔdə'reɪʃən] *n* moderación *f*; **in ~** con moderación
modern ['mɔdən] *adj* moderno; **modernize** *vt* modernizar; **modern languages** *npl* lenguas *fpl* modernas
modest ['mɔdɪst] *adj* modesto; (*small*) módico; **modesty** *n* modestia
modification [mɔdɪfɪ'keɪʃən] *n* modificación *f*
modify ['mɔdɪfaɪ] *vt* modificar
module ['mɔdju:l] *n* (*unit, component, Space*) módulo
mohair ['məuhɛə*] *n* mohair *m*
Mohammed [mə'hæmɛd] *n* Mahoma *m*

moist [mɔɪst] *adj* húmedo; **moisture** ['mɔɪstʃə*] *n* humedad *f*; **moisturizer** ['mɔɪstʃəraɪzə*] *n* crema hidratante
mold *etc* [məuld] (*US*) = **mould** *etc*
mole [məul] *n* (*animal, spy*) topo; (*spot*) lunar *m*
molecule ['mɔlɪkjuːl] *n* molécula
molest [məu'lɛst] *vt* importunar; (*assault sexually*) abusar sexualmente de

> Be careful not to translate **molest** by the Spanish word *molestar*.

molten ['məultən] *adj* fundido; (*lava*) líquido
mom [mɔm] (*US*) *n* = **mum**
moment ['məumənt] *n* momento; **at the ~** de momento, por ahora; **momentarily** ['məuməntrɪlɪ] *adv* momentáneamente; (*US: very soon*) de un momento a otro; **momentary** *adj* momentáneo; **momentous** [-'mɛntəs] *adj* trascendental, importante
momentum [məu'mɛntəm] *n* momento; (*fig*) ímpetu *m*; **to gather ~** cobrar velocidad; (*fig*) ganar fuerza
mommy ['mɔmɪ] (*US*) *n* = **mummy**
Mon *abbr* (= *Monday*) lun
Monaco ['mɔnəkəu] *n* Mónaco
monarch ['mɔnək] *n* monarca *mf*; **monarchy** *n* monarquía
monastery ['mɔnəstərɪ] *n* monasterio
Monday ['mʌndɪ] *n* lunes *m inv*
monetary ['mʌnɪtərɪ] *adj* monetario
money ['mʌnɪ] *n* dinero; (*currency*) moneda; **to make ~** ganar dinero; **money belt** *n* riñonera; **money order** *n* giro
mongrel ['mʌŋgrəl] *n* (*dog*) perro mestizo
monitor ['mɔnɪtə*] *n* (*Scol*) monitor *m*; (*also*: **television ~**) receptor *m* de control; (*of computer*) monitor *m* ▷ *vt* controlar
monk [mʌŋk] *n* monje *m*
monkey ['mʌŋkɪ] *n* mono
monologue ['mɔnəlɔg] *n* monólogo
monopoly [mə'nɔpəlɪ] *n* monopolio
monosodium glutamate [mɔnə'səudɪəm'gluːtəmeɪt] *n* glutamato monosódico
monotonous [mə'nɔtənəs] *adj* monótono
monsoon [mɔn'suːn] *n* monzón *m*
monster ['mɔnstə*] *n* monstruo
month [mʌnθ] *n* mes *m*; **monthly** *adj* mensual ▷ *adv* mensualmente
monument ['mɔnjumənt] *n* monumento
mood [muːd] *n* humor *m*; (*of crowd, group*) clima *m*; **to be in a good/bad ~** estar de buen/mal humor; **moody** *adj* (*changeable*) de humor variable; (*sullen*) malhumorado
moon [muːn] *n* luna; **moonlight** *n* luz *f* de la luna
moor [muə*] *n* páramo ▷ *vt* (*ship*) amarrar ▷ *vi* echar las amarras
moose [muːs] *n inv* alce *m*
mop [mɔp] *n* fregona; (*of hair*) greña, melena ▷ *vt* fregar; **mop up** *vt* limpiar
mope [məup] *vi* estar *or* andar deprimido
moped ['məupɛd] *n* ciclomotor *m*
moral ['mɔrl] *adj* moral ▷ *n* moraleja; **morals** *npl* moralidad *f*, moral *f*
morale [mɔ'rɑːl] *n* moral *f*
morality [mə'rælɪtɪ] *n* moralidad *f*
morbid ['mɔːbɪd] *adj* (*interest*) morboso; (*Med*) mórbido

KEYWORD

more [mɔː*] *adj* **1** (*greater in number etc*) más; **more people/work than before** más gente/trabajo que antes
2 (*additional*) más; **do you want (some) more tea?** ¿quieres más té?; **is there any more wine?** ¿queda vino?; **it'll take a few more weeks** tardará unas semanas más; **it's 2 kms more to the house** faltan 2 kms para la casa; **more time/letters than we expected**

más tiempo del que/más cartas de las que esperábamos
▷ *pron* (*greater amount, additional amount*) más; **more than 10** más de 10; **it cost more than the other one/than we expected** costó más que el otro/más de lo que esperábamos; **is there any more?** ¿hay más?; **many/much more** muchos(as)/ mucho(a) más
▷ *adv* más; **more dangerous/easily (than)** más peligroso/fácilmente (que); **more and more expensive** cada vez más caro; **more or less** más o menos; **more than ever** más que nunca

moreover [mɔːˈrəuvə*] *adv* además, por otra parte
morgue [mɔːg] *n* depósito de cadáveres
morning [ˈmɔːnɪŋ] *n* mañana; (*early morning*) madrugada ▷ *cpd* matutino, de la mañana; **in the ~** por la mañana; **7 o'clock in the ~** las 7 de la mañana; **morning sickness** *n* náuseas *fpl* matutinas
Moroccan [məˈrɔkən] *adj, n* marroquí *m/f*
Morocco [məˈrɔkəu] *n* Marruecos *m*
moron [ˈmɔːrɔn] (*inf*) *n* imbécil *mf*
morphine [ˈmɔːfiːn] *n* morfina
Morse [mɔːs] *n* (*also*: **~ code**) (código) Morse
mortal [ˈmɔːtl] *adj, n* mortal *m*
mortar [ˈmɔːtə*] *n* argamasa
mortgage [ˈmɔːgɪdʒ] *n* hipoteca ▷ *vt* hipotecar
mortician [mɔːˈtɪʃən] (US) *n* director/a *m/f* de pompas fúnebres
mortified [ˈmɔːtɪfaɪd] *adj*: **I was ~** me dio muchísima vergüenza
mortuary [ˈmɔːtjuərɪ] *n* depósito de cadáveres
mosaic [məuˈzeɪɪk] *n* mosaico
Moslem [ˈmɔzləm] *adj, n* = **Muslim**
mosque [mɔsk] *n* mezquita
mosquito [mɔsˈkiːtəu] (*pl* **~es**) *n* mosquito (SP), zancudo (LAM)
moss [mɔs] *n* musgo
most [məust] *adj* la mayor parte de, la mayoría de ▷ *pron* la mayor parte, la mayoría ▷ *adv* el más; (*very*) muy; **the ~** (*also*: + *adj*) el más; **~ of them** la mayor parte de ellos; **I saw the ~** yo vi el que más; **at the (very) ~** a lo sumo, todo lo más; **to make the ~ of** aprovechar (al máximo); **a ~ interesting book** un libro interesantísimo; **mostly** *adv* en su mayor parte, principalmente
MOT (BRIT) *n abbr* = **Ministry of Transport**; **the ~ (test)** *inspección (anual) obligatoria de coches y camiones*
motel [məuˈtɛl] *n* motel *m*
moth [mɔθ] *n* mariposa nocturna; (*clothes moth*) polilla
mother [ˈmʌðə*] *n* madre *f* ▷ *adj* materno ▷ *vt* (*care for*) cuidar (como una madre); **motherhood** *n* maternidad *f*; **mother-in-law** *n* suegra; **mother-of-pearl** *n* nácar *m*; **Mother's Day** *n* Día *m* de la Madre; **mother-to-be** *n* futura madre *f*; **mother tongue** *n* lengua materna
motif [məuˈtiːf] *n* motivo
motion [ˈməuʃən] *n* movimiento; (*gesture*) ademán *m*, señal *f*; (*at meeting*) moción *f* ▷ *vt, vi*: **to ~ (to) sb to do sth** hacer señas a algn para que haga algo; **motionless** *adj* inmóvil; **motion picture** *n* película
motivate [ˈməutɪveɪt] *vt* motivar
motivation [məutɪˈveɪʃən] *n* motivación *f*
motive [ˈməutɪv] *n* motivo
motor [ˈməutə*] *n* motor *m*; (BRIT: *inf*: *vehicle*) coche *m* (SP), carro (LAM), automóvil *m* ▷ *adj* motor (*f*: *motora or motriz*); **motorbike** *n* moto *f*; **motorboat** *n* lancha motora; **motorcar** (BRIT) *n* coche *m*, carro, automóvil *m*; **motorcycle** *n* motocicleta; **motorcyclist** *n* motociclista *mf*; **motoring** (BRIT) *n* automovilismo; **motorist** *n* conductor(a) *m/f*, automovilista *mf*;

motor racing (BRIT) *n* carreras *fpl* de coches, automovilismo; **motorway** (BRIT) *n* autopista
motto ['mɔtəu] (*pl* **~es**) *n* lema *m*; (*watchword*) consigna
mould [məuld] (*US* **mold**) *n* molde *m*; (*mildew*) moho ▷ *vt* moldear; (*fig*) formar; **mouldy** *adj* enmohecido
mound [maund] *n* montón *m*, montículo
mount [maunt] *n* monte *m* ▷ *vt* montar, subir a; (*jewel*) engarzar; (*picture*) enmarcar; (*exhibition etc*) organizar ▷ *vi* (*increase*) aumentar; **mount up** *vi* aumentar
mountain ['mauntɪn] *n* montaña ▷ *cpd* de montaña; **mountain bike** *n* bicicleta de montaña; **mountaineer** *n* alpinista *mf* (SP, MEX), andinista *mf* (LAM); **mountaineering** *n* alpinismo (SP, MEX), andinismo (LAM); **mountainous** *adj* montañoso; **mountain range** *n* sierra
mourn [mɔːn] *vt* llorar, lamentar ▷ *vi*: **to ~ for** llorar la muerte de; **mourner** *n* doliente *mf*; dolorido/a; **mourning** *n* luto; **in mourning** de luto
mouse [maus] (*pl* **mice**) *n* (*Zool, Comput*) ratón *m*; **mouse mat** *n* (*Comput*) alfombrilla
moussaka [mu'sɑːkə] *n* musaca
mousse [muːs] *n* (*Culin*) crema batida; (*for hair*) espuma (moldeadora)
moustache [məs'tɑːʃ] (*US* **mustache**) *n* bigote *m*
mouth [mauð, *pl* mauðz] *n* boca; (*of river*) desembocadura; **mouthful** *n* bocado; **mouth organ** *n* armónica; **mouthpiece** *n* (*of musical instrument*) boquilla; (*spokesman*) portavoz *mf*; **mouthwash** *n* enjuague *m*
move [muːv] *n* (*movement*) movimiento; (*in game*) jugada; (*: turn to play*) turno; (*change: of house*) mudanza; (*: of job*) cambio de trabajo ▷ *vt* mover; (*emotionally*) conmover; (*Pol: resolution etc*) proponer ▷ *vi* moverse; (*traffic*) circular; (*also*: **~ house**) trasladarse, mudarse; **to ~ sb to do sth** mover a algn a hacer algo; **to get a ~ on** darse prisa; **move back** *vi* retroceder; **move in** *vi* (*to a house*) instalarse; (*police, soldiers*) intervenir; **move off** *vi* ponerse en camino; **move on** *vi* ponerse en camino; **move out** *vi* (*of house*) mudarse; **move over** *vi* apartarse, hacer sitio; **move up** *vi* (*employee*) ser ascendido; **movement** *n* movimiento
movie ['muːvɪ] *n* película; **to go to the ~s** ir al cine; **movie theater** (US) *n* cine *m*
moving ['muːvɪŋ] *adj* (*emotional*) conmovedor(a); (*that moves*) móvil
mow [məu] (*pt* **~ed**, *pp* **mowed** *or* **mown**) *vt* (*grass, corn*) cortar, segar; **mower** *n* (*also*: **lawnmower**) cortacéspedes *m inv*
Mozambique [məuzæm'biːk] *n* Mozambique *m*
MP *n abbr* = **Member of Parliament**
MP3 *n* MP3; **MP3 player** *n* reproductor *m* (de) MP3
mpg *n abbr* = **miles per gallon**
m.p.h. *abbr* = **miles per hour** (60 *m.p.h.* = 96 *k.p.h.*)
Mr ['mɪstə*] (*US* **Mr.**) *n*: **~ Smith** (el) Sr. Smith
Mrs ['mɪsɪz] (*US* **Mrs.**) *n*: **~ Smith** (la) Sra. Smith
Ms [mɪz] (*US* **Ms.**) *n* = **Miss** *or* **Mrs**; **~ Smith** (la) Sr(t)a. Smith
MSP *n abbr* = **Member of the Scottish Parliament**
Mt *abbr* (*Geo*) (= *mount*) m
much [mʌtʃ] *adj* mucho ▷ *adv* mucho; (*before pp*) muy ▷ *n or pron* mucho; **how ~ is it?** ¿cuánto es?, ¿cuánto cuesta?; **too ~** demasiado; **it's not ~** no es mucho; **as ~ as** tanto como; **however ~ he tries** por mucho que se esfuerce
muck [mʌk] *n* suciedad *f*; **muck up** (*inf*) *vt* arruinar, estropear; **mucky** *adj* (*dirty*) sucio

mucus ['mju:kəs] *n* mucosidad *f*, moco
mud [mʌd] *n* barro, lodo
muddle ['mʌdl] *n* desorden *m*, confusión *f*; (*mix-up*) embrollo, lío ▷ *vt* (*also*: **~ up**) embrollar, confundir
muddy ['mʌdɪ] *adj* fangoso, cubierto de lodo
mudguard ['mʌdgɑ:d] *n* guardabarros *m inv*
muesli ['mju:zlɪ] *n* muesli *m*
muffin ['mʌfɪn] *n* panecillo dulce
muffled ['mʌfld] *adj* (*noise etc*) amortiguado, apagado
muffler (US) ['mʌflə*] *n* (*Aut*) silenciador *m*
mug [mʌg] *n* taza grande (*sin platillo*); (*for beer*) jarra; (*inf*: *face*) jeta ▷ *vt* (*assault*) asaltar; **mugger** ['mʌgə*] *n* atracador(a) *m/f*; **mugging** *n* asalto
muggy ['mʌgɪ] *adj* bochornoso
mule [mju:l] *n* mula
multicoloured ['mʌltɪkʌləd] (US), **multicolored** *adj* multicolor
multimedia ['mʌltɪ'mi:dɪə] *adj* multimedia
multinational [mʌltɪ'næʃənl] *n* multinacional *f* ▷ *adj* multinacional
multiple ['mʌltɪpl] *adj* múltiple ▷ *n* múltiplo; **multiple choice (test)** *n* examen *m* de tipo test; **multiple sclerosis** *n* esclerosis *f* múltiple
multiplex cinema ['mʌltɪplɛks-] *n* multicines *mpl*
multiplication [mʌltɪplɪ'keɪʃən] *n* multiplicación *f*
multiply ['mʌltɪplaɪ] *vt* multiplicar ▷ *vi* multiplicarse
multistorey [mʌltɪ'stɔ:rɪ] (BRIT) *adj* de muchos pisos
mum [mʌm] (BRIT: *inf*) *n* mamá ▷ *adj*: **to keep ~** mantener la boca cerrada
mumble ['mʌmbl] *vt*, *vi* hablar entre dientes, refunfuñar
mummy ['mʌmɪ] *n* (BRIT: *mother*) mamá; (*embalmed*) momia
mumps [mʌmps] *n* paperas *fpl*
munch [mʌntʃ] *vt*, *vi* mascar
municipal [mju:'nɪsɪpl] *adj* municipal
mural ['mjuərl] *n* (pintura) mural *m*
murder ['mə:də*] *n* asesinato; (*in law*) homicidio ▷ *vt* asesinar, matar; **murderer** *n* asesino
murky ['mə:kɪ] *adj* (*water*) turbio; (*street, night*) lóbrego
murmur ['mə:mə*] *n* murmullo ▷ *vt*, *vi* murmurar
muscle ['mʌsl] *n* músculo; (*fig*: *strength*) garra, fuerza; **muscular** ['mʌskjulə*] *adj* muscular; (*person*) musculoso
museum [mju:'zɪəm] *n* museo
mushroom ['mʌʃrum] *n* seta, hongo; (*Culin*) champiñón *m* ▷ *vi* crecer de la noche a la mañana
music ['mju:zɪk] *n* música; **musical** *adj* musical; (*sound*) melodioso; (*person*) con talento musical ▷ *n* (*show*) comedia musical; **musical instrument** *n* instrumento musical; **musician** [-'zɪʃən] *n* músico/a
Muslim ['mʌzlɪm] *adj*, *n* musulmán/ana *m/f*
muslin ['mʌzlɪn] *n* muselina
mussel ['mʌsl] *n* mejillón *m*
must [mʌst] *aux vb* (*obligation*): **I ~ do it** debo hacerlo, tengo que hacerlo; (*probability*): **he ~ be there by now** ya debe (de) estar allí ▷ *n*: **it's a ~** es imprescindible
mustache ['mʌstæʃ] (US) *n* = **moustache**
mustard ['mʌstəd] *n* mostaza
mustn't ['mʌsnt] = **must not**
mute [mju:t] *adj*, *n* mudo/a *m/f*
mutilate ['mju:tɪleɪt] *vt* mutilar
mutiny ['mju:tɪnɪ] *n* motín *m* ▷ *vi* amotinarse
mutter ['mʌtə*] *vt*, *vi* murmurar
mutton ['mʌtn] *n* carne *f* de cordero
mutual ['mju:tʃuəl] *adj* mutuo; (*interest*) común
muzzle ['mʌzl] *n* hocico; (*for dog*) bozal *m*; (*of gun*) boca ▷ *vt* (*dog*) poner

un bozal a

my [maɪ] *adj* mi(s); **~ house/brother/sisters** mi casa/mi hermano/mis hermanas; **I've washed ~ hair/cut ~ finger** me he lavado el pelo/cortado un dedo; **is this ~ pen or yours?** ¿es este bolígrafo mío o tuyo?

myself [maɪ'sɛlf] *pron* (*reflexive*) me; (*emphatic*) yo mismo; (*after prep*) mí (mismo); *see also* **oneself**

mysterious [mɪs'tɪərɪəs] *adj* misterioso

mystery ['mɪstərɪ] *n* misterio

mystical ['mɪstɪkl] *adj* místico

mystify ['mɪstɪfaɪ] *vt* (*perplex*) dejar perplejo

myth [mɪθ] *n* mito; **mythology** [mɪ'θɔlədʒɪ] *n* mitología

n/a *abbr* (= *not applicable*) no interesa

nag [næg] *vt* (*scold*) regañar

nail [neɪl] *n* (*human*) uña; (*metal*) clavo ▷ *vt* clavar; **to ~ sth to sth** clavar algo en algo; **to ~ sb down to doing sth** comprometer a algn a que haga algo; **nailbrush** *n* cepillo para las uñas; **nailfile** *n* lima para las uñas; **nail polish** *n* esmalte *m or* laca para las uñas; **nail polish remover** *n* quitaesmalte *m*; **nail scissors** *npl* tijeras *fpl* para las uñas; **nail varnish** (BRIT) *n* = **nail polish**

naïve [naɪ'i:v] *adj* ingenuo

naked ['neɪkɪd] *adj* (*nude*) desnudo; (*flame*) expuesto al aire

name [neɪm] *n* nombre *m*; (*surname*) apellido; (*reputation*) fama, renombre *m* ▷ *vt* (*child*) poner nombre a; (*criminal*) identificar; (*price, date etc*) fijar; **what's your ~?** ¿cómo se llama?; **by ~** de nombre; **in the ~ of** en nombre de; **to give one's ~ and address** dar sus señas; **namely** *adv* a saber

nanny ['nænɪ] *n* niñera

nap [næp] *n* (*sleep*) sueñecito, siesta
napkin ['næpkɪn] *n* (*also*: **table ~**) servilleta
nappy ['næpɪ] (BRIT) *n* pañal *m*
narcotics *npl* (*illegal drugs*) estupefacientes *mpl*, narcóticos *mpl*
narrative ['nærətɪv] *n* narrativa ▷ *adj* narrativo
narrator [nə'reɪtə*] *n* narrador(a) *m/f*
narrow ['nærəu] *adj* estrecho, angosto; (*fig*: *majority etc*) corto; (: *ideas etc*) estrecho ▷ *vi* (*road*) estrecharse; (*diminish*) reducirse; **to have a ~ escape** escaparse por los pelos; **narrow down** *vt* (*search, investigation, possibilities*) restringir, limitar; (*list*) reducir; **narrowly** *adv* (*miss*) por poco; **narrow-minded** *adj* de miras estrechas
nasal ['neɪzl] *adj* nasal
nasty ['nɑːstɪ] *adj* (*remark*) feo; (*person*) antipático; (*revolting*: *taste, smell*) asqueroso; (*wound, disease etc*) peligroso, grave
nation ['neɪʃən] *n* nación *f*
national ['næʃənl] *adj, n* nacional *m/f*; **national anthem** *n* himno nacional; **national dress** *n* vestido nacional; **National Health Service** (BRIT) *n* servicio nacional de salud pública ≈ Insalud *m* (SP); **National Insurance** (BRIT) *n* seguro social nacional; **nationalist** *adj, n* nacionalista *mf*; **nationality** [-'nælɪtɪ] *n* nacionalidad *f*; **nationalize** *vt* nacionalizar; **national park** (BRIT) *n* parque *m* nacional; **National Trust** *n* (BRIT) *organización encargada de preservar el patrimonio histórico británico*
nationwide ['neɪʃənwaɪd] *adj* en escala *or* a nivel nacional
native ['neɪtɪv] *n* (*local inhabitant*) natural *mf*, nacional *mf* ▷ *adj* (*indigenous*) indígena; (*country*) natal; (*innate*) natural, innato; **a ~ of Russia** un(a) natural *mf* de Rusia; **Native American** *adj, n* americano/a indígena, amerindio/a; **native speaker** *n* hablante *mf* nativo/a
NATO ['neɪtəu] *n abbr* (= *North Atlantic Treaty Organization*) OTAN *f*
natural ['nætʃrəl] *adj* natural; **natural gas** *n* gas *m* natural; **natural history** *n* historia natural; **naturally** *adv* (*speak etc*) naturalmente; (*of course*) desde luego, por supuesto; **natural resources** *npl* recursos *mpl* naturales
nature ['neɪtʃə*] *n* (*also*: **N~**) naturaleza; (*group, sort*) género, clase *f*; (*character*) carácter *m*, genio; **by ~** por *or* de naturaleza; **nature reserve** *n* reserva natural
naughty ['nɔːtɪ] *adj* (*child*) travieso
nausea ['nɔːsɪə] *n* náuseas *fpl*
naval ['neɪvl] *adj* naval, de marina
navel ['neɪvl] *n* ombligo
navigate ['nævɪgeɪt] *vt* gobernar ▷ *vi* navegar; (*Aut*) ir de copiloto; **navigation** [-'geɪʃən] *n* (*action*) navegación *f*; (*science*) náutica
navy ['neɪvɪ] *n* marina de guerra; (*ships*) armada, flota
Nazi ['nɑːtsɪ] *n* nazi *mf*
NB *abbr* (= *nota bene*) nótese
near [nɪə*] *adj* (*place, relation*) cercano; (*time*) próximo ▷ *adv* cerca ▷ *prep* (*also*: **~ to**: *space*) cerca de, junto a; (: *time*) cerca de ▷ *vt* acercarse a, aproximarse a; **nearby** [nɪə'baɪ] *adj* cercano, próximo ▷ *adv* cerca; **nearly** *adv* casi, por poco; **I nearly fell** por poco me caigo; **near-sighted** *adj* miope, corto de vista
neat [niːt] *adj* (*place*) ordenado, bien cuidado; (*person*) pulcro; (*plan*) ingenioso; (*spirits*) solo; **neatly** *adv* (*tidily*) con esmero; (*skilfully*) ingeniosamente
necessarily ['nɛsɪsrɪlɪ] *adv* necesariamente
necessary ['nɛsɪsrɪ] *adj* necesario, preciso
necessity [nɪ'sɛsɪtɪ] *n* necesidad *f*
neck [nɛk] *n* (*of person, garment, bottle*) cuello; (*of animal*) pescuezo ▷ *vi*

(*inf*) besuquearse; **~ and ~** parejos; **necklace** ['nɛklɪs] *n* collar *m*; **necktie** ['nɛktaɪ] *n* corbata
nectarine ['nɛktərɪn] *n* nectarina
need [ni:d] *n* (*lack*) escasez *f*, falta; (*necessity*) necesidad *f* ▷ *vt* (*require*) necesitar; **I ~ to do it** tengo que *or* debo hacerlo; **you don't ~ to go** no hace falta que (te) vayas
needle ['ni:dl] *n* aguja ▷ *vt* (*fig: inf*) picar, fastidiar
needless ['ni:dlɪs] *adj* innecesario; **~ to say** huelga decir que
needlework ['ni:dlwə:k] *n* (*activity*) costura, labor *f* de aguja
needn't ['ni:dnt] = **need not**
needy ['ni:dɪ] *adj* necesitado
negative ['nɛgətɪv] *n* (*Phot*) negativo; (*Ling*) negación *f* ▷ *adj* negativo
neglect [nɪ'glɛkt] *vt* (*one's duty*) faltar a, no cumplir con; (*child*) descuidar, desatender ▷ *n* (*of house, garden etc*) abandono; (*of child*) desatención *f*; (*of duty*) incumplimiento
negotiate [nɪ'gəuʃɪeɪt] *vt* (*treaty, loan*) negociar; (*obstacle*) franquear; (*bend in road*) tomar ▷ *vi*: **to ~ (with)** negociar (con)
negotiations [nɪgəuʃɪ'eɪʃənz] *pl n* negociaciones
negotiator [nɪ'gəuʃɪeɪtə*] *n* negociador(a) *m/f*
neighbour ['neɪbə*] (*US* **neighbor** *etc*) *n* vecino/a; **neighbourhood** *n* (*place*) vecindad *f*, barrio; (*people*) vecindario; **neighbouring** *adj* vecino
neither ['naɪðə*] *adj* ni ▷ *conj*: **I didn't move and ~ did John** no me he movido, ni Juan tampoco ▷ *pron* ninguno ▷ *adv*: **~ good nor bad** ni bueno ni malo; **~ is true** ninguno/a de los(las) dos es cierto/a
neon ['ni:ɔn] *n* neón *m*
Nepal [nɪ'pɔ:l] *n* Nepal *m*
nephew ['nɛvju:] *n* sobrino
nerve [nə:v] *n* (*Anat*) nervio; (*courage*) valor *m*; (*impudence*) descaro, frescura (*nervousness*) nerviosismo *msg*, nervios *mpl*; **a fit of ~s** un ataque de nervios
nervous ['nə:vəs] *adj* (*anxious, Anat*) nervioso; (*timid*) tímido, miedoso; **nervous breakdown** *n* crisis *f* nerviosa
nest [nɛst] *n* (*of bird*) nido; (*wasps' nest*) avispero ▷ *vi* anidar
net [nɛt] *n* (*gen*) red *f*; (*fabric*) tul *m* ▷ *adj* (*Comm*) neto, líquido ▷ *vt* coger (*SP*) *or* agarrar (*LAM*) con red; (*Sport*) marcar; **netball** *n* básquet *m*
Netherlands ['nɛðələndz] *npl*: **the ~** los Países Bajos
nett [nɛt] *adj* = **net**
nettle ['nɛtl] *n* ortiga
network ['nɛtwə:k] *n* red *f*
neurotic [njuə'rɔtɪk] *adj* neurótico/a
neuter ['nju:tə*] *adj* (*Ling*) neutro ▷ *vt* castrar, capar
neutral ['nju:trəl] *adj* (*person*) neutral; (*colour etc, Elec*) neutro ▷ *n* (*Aut*) punto muerto
never ['nɛvə*] *adv* nunca, jamás; **I ~ went** no fui nunca; **~ in my life** jamás en la vida; *see also* **mind**; **never-ending** *adj* interminable, sin fin; **nevertheless** [nɛvəðə'lɛs] *adv* sin embargo, no obstante
new [nju:] *adj* nuevo; (*brand new*) a estrenar; (*recent*) reciente; **New Age** *n* Nueva Era; **newborn** *adj* recién nacido; **newcomer** ['nju:kʌmə*] *n* recién venido/a *or* llegado/a; **newly** *adv* nuevamente, recién
news [nju:z] *n* noticias *fpl*; **a piece of ~** una noticia; **the ~** (*Radio, TV*) las noticias *fpl*; **news agency** *n* agencia de noticias; **newsagent** (*BRIT*) *n* vendedor(a) *m/f* de periódicos; **newscaster** *n* presentador(a) *m/f*, locutor(a) *m/f*; **news dealer** (*US*) *n* = **newsagent**; **newsletter** *n* hoja informativa, boletín *m*; **newspaper** *n* periódico, diario; **newsreader** *n* = **newscaster**
newt [nju:t] *n* tritón *m*
New Year *n* Año Nuevo; **New Year's**

Day *n* Día *m* de Año Nuevo; **New Year's Eve** *n* Nochevieja
New Zealand [nju:'zi:lənd] *n* Nueva Zelanda; **New Zealander** *n* neozelandés/esa *m/f*
next [nɛkst] *adj* (*house, room*) vecino; (*bus stop, meeting*) próximo; (*following: page etc*) siguiente ▷ *adv* después; **the ~ day** el día siguiente; **~ time** la próxima vez; **~ year** el año próximo *or* que viene; **~ to** junto a, al lado de; **~ to nothing** casi nada; **~ please!** ¡el siguiente!; **next door** *adv* en la casa de al lado ▷ *adj* vecino, de al lado; **next-of-kin** *n* pariente *m* más cercano
NHS *n abbr* = **National Health Service**
nibble ['nɪbl] *vt* mordisquear, mordiscar
nice [naɪs] *adj* (*likeable*) simpático; (*kind*) amable; (*pleasant*) agradable; (*attractive*) bonito, lindo (LAM); **nicely** *adv* amablemente; bien
niche [ni:ʃ] *n* (*Arch*) nicho, hornacina
nick [nɪk] *n* (*wound*) rasguño; (*cut, indentation*) mella, muesca ▷ *vt* (*inf*) birlar, robar; **in the ~ of time** justo a tiempo
nickel ['nɪkl] *n* níquel *m*; (US) *moneda de 5 centavos*
nickname ['nɪkneɪm] *n* apodo, mote *m* ▷ *vt* apodar
nicotine ['nɪkəti:n] *n* nicotina
niece [ni:s] *n* sobrina
Nigeria [naɪ'dʒɪərɪə] *n* Nigeria
night [naɪt] *n* noche *f*; (*evening*) tarde *f*; **the ~ before last** anteanoche; **at ~, by ~** de noche, por la noche; **night club** *n* cabaret *m*; **nightdress** (BRIT) *n* camisón *m*; **nightie** ['naɪtɪ] *n* = **nightdress**; **nightlife** *n* vida nocturna; **nightly** *adj* de todas las noches ▷ *adv* todas las noches, cada noche; **nightmare** *n* pesadilla; **night school** *n* clase(s) *f(pl)* nocturna(s); **night shift** *n* turno nocturno *or* de noche; **night-time** *n* noche *f*
nil [nɪl] (BRIT) *n* (*Sport*) cero, nada
nine [naɪn] *num* nueve; **nineteen** *num* diecinueve, diez y nueve; **nineteenth** [naɪn'ti:nθ] *adj* decimonoveno, decimonono; **ninetieth** ['naɪntɪɪθ] *adj* nonagésimo; **ninety** *num* noventa
ninth [naɪnθ] *adj* noveno
nip [nɪp] *vt* (*pinch*) pellizcar; (*bite*) morder
nipple ['nɪpl] *n* (*Anat*) pezón *m*
nitrogen ['naɪtrədʒən] *n* nitrógeno

KEYWORD

no [nəu] (*pl* **noes**) *adv* (*opposite of "yes"*) no; **are you coming? – no (I'm not)** ¿vienes? – no; **would you like some more? – no thank you** ¿quieres más? – no gracias ▷ *adj* (*not any*): **I have no money/time/books** no tengo dinero/tiempo/libros; **no other man would have done it** ningún otro lo hubiera hecho; **"no entry"** "prohibido el paso"; **"no smoking"** "prohibido fumar" ▷ *n* no *m*

nobility [nəu'bɪlɪtɪ] *n* nobleza
noble ['nəubl] *adj* noble
nobody ['nəubədɪ] *pron* nadie
nod [nɔd] *vi* saludar con la cabeza; (*in agreement*) decir que sí con la cabeza; (*doze*) dar cabezadas ▷ *vt*: **to ~ one's head** inclinar la cabeza ▷ *n* inclinación *f* de cabeza; **nod off** *vi* dar cabezadas
noise [nɔɪz] *n* ruido; (*din*) escándalo, estrépito; **noisy** *adj* ruidoso; (*child*) escandaloso
nominal ['nɔmɪnl] *adj* nominal
nominate ['nɔmɪneɪt] *vt* (*propose*) proponer; (*appoint*) nombrar; **nomination** [nɔmɪ'neɪʃən] *n* propuesta; nombramiento; **nominee** [-'ni:] *n* candidato/a
none [nʌn] *pron* ninguno/a ▷ *adv* de ninguna manera; **~ of you** ninguno de vosotros; **I've ~ left** no me queda ninguno/a; **he's ~ the worse for it** no

le ha hecho ningún mal
nonetheless [nʌnðə'lɛs] *adv* sin embargo, no obstante
non-fiction [nɔn'fɪkʃən] *n* literatura no novelesca
nonsense ['nɔnsəns] *n* tonterías *fpl*, disparates *fpl*; **~!** ¡qué tonterías!
non: non-smoker *n* no fumador(a) *m/f*; **non-smoking** *adj* (de) no fumador; **non-stick** *adj* (*pan, surface*) antiadherente
noodles ['nu:dlz] *npl* tallarines *mpl*
noon [nu:n] *n* mediodía *m*
no-one ['nəuwʌn] *pron* = **nobody**
nor [nɔ:*] *conj* = **neither** ▷ *adv* see **neither**
norm [nɔ:m] *n* norma
normal ['nɔ:ml] *adj* normal; **normally** *adv* normalmente
north [nɔ:θ] *n* norte *m* ▷ *adj* del norte, norteño ▷ *adv* al *or* hacia el norte; **North America** *n* América del Norte; **North American** *adj, n* norteamericano/a *m/f*; **northbound** ['nɔ:θbaund] *adj* (*traffic*) que se dirige al norte; (*carriageway*) de dirección norte; **north-east** *n* nor(d)este *m*; **northeastern** *adj* nor(d)este, del nor(d)este; **northern** ['nɔ:ðən] *adj* norteño, del norte; **Northern Ireland** *n* Irlanda del Norte; **North Korea** *n* Corea del Norte; **North Pole** *n* Polo Norte; **North Sea** *n* Mar *m* del Norte; **north-west** *n* nor(d)oeste *m*; **northwestern** ['nɔ:θ'wɛstən] *adj* noroeste, del noroeste
Norway ['nɔ:weɪ] *n* Noruega; **Norwegian** [-'wi:dʒən] *adj* noruego/a ▷ *n* noruego/a; (*Ling*) noruego
nose [nəuz] *n* (*Anat*) nariz *f*; (*Zool*) hocico; (*sense of smell*) olfato ▷ *vi*: **to ~ about** curiosear; **nosebleed** *n* hemorragia nasal; **nosey** (*inf*) *adj* curioso, fisgón/ona
nostalgia [nɔs'tældʒɪə] *n* nostalgia
nostalgic [nɔs'tældʒɪk] *adj* nostálgico
nostril ['nɔstrɪl] *n* ventana de la nariz
nosy ['nəuzɪ] (*inf*) *adj* = **nosey**
not [nɔt] *adv* no; **~ that ...** no es que ...; **it's too late, isn't it?** es demasiado tarde, ¿verdad *or* no?; **~ yet/now** todavía/ahora no; **why ~?** ¿por qué no?; *see also* **all; only**
notable ['nəutəbl] *adj* notable; **notably** *adv* especialmente
notch [nɔtʃ] *n* muesca, corte *m*
note [nəut] *n* (*Mus, record, letter*) nota; (*banknote*) billete *m*; (*tone*) tono ▷ *vt* (*observe*) notar, observar; (*write down*) apuntar, anotar; **notebook** *n* libreta, cuaderno; **noted** ['nəutɪd] *adj* célebre, conocido; **notepad** *n* bloc *m*; **notepaper** *n* papel *m* para cartas
nothing ['nʌθɪŋ] *n* nada; (*zero*) cero; **he does ~** no hace nada; **~ new** nada nuevo; **~ much** no mucho; **for ~** (*free*) gratis, sin pago; (*in vain*) en balde
notice ['nəutɪs] *n* (*announcement*) anuncio; (*warning*) aviso; (*dismissal*) despido; (*resignation*) dimisión *f*; (*period of time*) plazo ▷ *vt* (*observe*) notar, observar; **to bring sth to sb's ~** (*attention*) llamar la atención de algn sobre algo; **to take ~ of** tomar nota de, prestar atención a; **at short ~** con poca anticipación; **until further ~** hasta nuevo aviso; **to hand in one's ~** dimitir

> Be careful not to translate **notice** by the Spanish word *noticia*.

noticeable *adj* evidente, obvio
notify ['nəutɪfaɪ] *vt*: **to ~ sb (of sth)** comunicar (algo) a algn
notion ['nəuʃən] *n* idea; (*opinion*) opinión *f*; **notions** *npl* (*US*) mercería
notorious [nəu'tɔ:rɪəs] *adj* notorio
notwithstanding [nɔtwɪθ'stændɪŋ] *adv* no obstante, sin embargo; **~ this** a pesar de esto
nought [nɔ:t] *n* cero
noun [naun] *n* nombre *m*, sustantivo
nourish ['nʌrɪʃ] *vt* nutrir; (*fig*) alimentar; **nourishment** *n* alimento, sustento
Nov. *abbr* (= *November*) nov
novel ['nɔvl] *n* novela ▷ *adj* (*new*)

nuevo, original; (*unexpected*) insólito; **novelist** *n* novelista *mf*; **novelty** *n* novedad *f*

November [nəu'vɛmbə*] *n* noviembre *m*

novice ['nɔvɪs] *n* (*Rel*) novicio/a

now [nau] *adv* (*at the present time*) ahora; (*these days*) actualmente, hoy día ▷ *conj*: **~ (that)** ya que, ahora que; **right ~** ahora mismo; **by ~** ya; **just ~** ahora mismo; **~ and then, ~ and again** de vez en cuando; **from ~ on** de ahora en adelante; **nowadays** ['nauə deɪz] *adv* hoy (en) día, actualmente

nowhere ['nəuwɛə*] *adv* (*direction*) a ninguna parte; (*location*) en ninguna parte

nozzle ['nɔzl] *n* boquilla

nr *abbr* (BRIT) = **near**

nuclear ['nju:klɪə*] *adj* nuclear

nucleus ['nju:klɪəs] (*pl* **nuclei**) *n* núcleo

nude [nju:d] *adj, n* desnudo/a *m/f*; **in the ~** desnudo

nudge [nʌdʒ] *vt* dar un codazo a

nudist ['nju:dɪst] *n* nudista *mf*

nudity ['nju:dɪtɪ] *n* desnudez *f*

nuisance ['nju:sns] *n* molestia, fastidio; (*person*) pesado, latoso; **what a ~!** ¡qué lata!

numb [nʌm] *adj*: **~ with cold/fear** entumecido por el frío/paralizado de miedo

number ['nʌmbə*] *n* número; (*quantity*) cantidad *f* ▷ *vt* (*pages etc*) numerar, poner número a; (*amount to*) sumar, ascender a; **to be ~ed among** figurar entre; **a ~ of** varios, algunos; **they were ten in ~** eran diez; **number plate** (BRIT) *n* matrícula, placa; **Number Ten** *n* (BRIT: *10 Downing Street*) *residencia del primer ministro*

numerical [nju:'mɛrɪkl] *adj* numérico

numerous ['nju:mərəs] *adj* numeroso

nun [nʌn] *n* monja, religiosa

nurse [nə:s] *n* enfermero/a; (*also*: **~maid**) niñera ▷ *vt* (*patient*) cuidar, atender

nursery ['nə:sərɪ] *n* (*institution*) guardería infantil; (*room*) cuarto de los niños; (*for plants*) criadero, semillero; **nursery rhyme** *n* canción *f* infantil; **nursery school** *n* parvulario, escuela de párvulos; **nursery slope** (BRIT) *n* (*Ski*) cuesta para principiantes

nursing ['nə:sɪŋ] *n* (*profession*) profesión *f* de enfermera; (*care*) asistencia, cuidado; **nursing home** *n* clínica de reposo

nurture ['nə:tʃə*] *vt* (*child, plant*) alimentar, nutrir

nut [nʌt] *n* (*Tech*) tuerca; (*Bot*) nuez *f*

nutmeg ['nʌtmɛg] *n* nuez *f* moscada

nutrient ['nju:trɪənt] *adj* nutritivo ▷ *n* elemento nutritivo

nutrition [nju:'trɪʃən] *n* nutrición *f*, alimentación *f*

nutritious [nju:'trɪʃəs] *adj* nutritivo, alimenticio

nuts [nʌts] (*inf*) *adj* loco

NVQ *n abbr* (BRIT) = **National Vocational Qualification**

nylon ['naɪlɔn] *n* nilón *m* ▷ *adj* de nilón

oath [əuθ] *n* juramento; (*swear word*) palabrota; **on** (BRIT) *or* **under ~** bajo juramento
oak [əuk] *n* roble *m* ▷ *adj* de roble
O.A.P. (BRIT) *n, abbr* = **old-age pensioner**
oar [ɔː*] *n* remo
oasis [əu'eɪsɪs] (*pl* **oases**) *n* oasis *m inv*
oath [əuθ] *n* juramento; (*swear word*) palabrota; **on** (BRIT) *or* **under ~** bajo juramento
oatmeal ['əutmiːl] *n* harina de avena
oats [əuts] *npl* avena
obedience [ə'biːdɪəns] *n* obediencia
obedient [ə'biːdɪənt] *adj* obediente
obese [əu'biːs] *adj* obeso
obesity [əu'biːsɪtɪ] *n* obesidad *f*
obey [ə'beɪ] *vt* obedecer; (*instructions, regulations*) cumplir
obituary [ə'bɪtjuərɪ] *n* necrología
object [*n* 'ɔbdʒɪkt, *vb* əb'dʒɛkt] *n* objeto; (*purpose*) objeto, propósito; (*Ling*) complemento ▷ *vi*: **to ~ to** estar en contra de; (*proposal*) oponerse a; **to ~ that** objetar que; **expense is no ~** no importa cuánto cuesta; **I ~!** ¡yo protesto!; **objection** [əb'dʒɛkʃən] *n* protesta; **I have no objection to ...** no tengo inconveniente en que ...; **objective** *adj, n* objetivo
obligation [ɔblɪ'geɪʃən] *n* obligación *f*; (*debt*) deber *m*; **without ~** sin compromiso
obligatory [ə'blɪgətərɪ] *adj* obligatorio
oblige [ə'blaɪdʒ] *vt* (*do a favour for*) complacer, hacer un favor a; **to ~ sb to do sth** forzar *or* obligar a algn a hacer algo; **to be ~d to sb for sth** estarle agradecido a algn por algo
oblique [ə'bliːk] *adj* oblicuo; (*allusion*) indirecto
obliterate [ə'blɪtəreɪt] *vt* borrar
oblivious [ə'blɪvɪəs] *adj*: **~ of** inconsciente de
oblong ['ɔblɔŋ] *adj* rectangular ▷ *n* rectángulo
obnoxious [əb'nɔkʃəs] *adj* odioso, detestable; (*smell*) nauseabundo
oboe ['əubəu] *n* oboe *m*
obscene [əb'siːn] *adj* obsceno
obscure [əb'skjuə*] *adj* oscuro ▷ *vt* oscurecer; (*hide: sun*) esconder
observant [əb'zəːvnt] *adj* observador(a)
observation [ɔbzə'veɪʃən] *n* observación *f*; (*Med*) examen *m*
observatory [əb'zəːvətrɪ] *n* observatorio
observe [əb'zəːv] *vt* observar; (*rule*) cumplir; **observer** *n* observador(a) *m/f*
obsess [əb'sɛs] *vt* obsesionar; **obsession** [əb'sɛʃən] *n* obsesión *f*; **obsessive** *adj* obsesivo; obsesionante
obsolete ['ɔbsəliːt] *adj*: **to be ~** estar en desuso
obstacle ['ɔbstəkl] *n* obstáculo; (*nuisance*) estorbo
obstinate ['ɔbstɪnɪt] *adj* terco, porfiado; (*determined*) obstinado
obstruct [əb'strʌkt] *vt* obstruir; (*hinder*) estorbar, obstaculizar; **obstruction** [əb'strʌkʃən] *n* (*action*)

obstrucción *f*; (*object*) estorbo, obstáculo

obtain [əb'teɪn] *vt* obtener; (*achieve*) conseguir

obvious ['ɔbvɪəs] *adj* obvio, evidente; **obviously** *adv* evidentemente, naturalmente; **obviously not** por supuesto que no

occasion [ə'keɪʒən] *n* oportunidad *f*, ocasión *f*; (*event*) acontecimiento; **occasional** *adj* poco frecuente, ocasional; **occasionally** *adv* de vez en cuando

occult [ɔ'kʌlt] *adj* (*gen*) oculto

occupant ['ɔkjupənt] *n* (*of house*) inquilino/a; (*of car*) ocupante *mf*

occupation [ɔkju'peɪʃən] *n* ocupación *f*; (*job*) trabajo; (*pastime*) ocupaciones *fpl*

occupy ['ɔkjupaɪ] *vt* (*seat, post, time*) ocupar; (*house*) habitar; **to ~ o.s. in doing** pasar el tiempo haciendo

occur [ə'kəː*] *vi* pasar, suceder; **to ~ to sb** ocurrírsele a algn; **occurrence** [ə'kʌrəns] *n* acontecimiento; (*existence*) existencia

ocean ['əuʃən] *n* océano

o'clock [ə'klɔk] *adv*: **it is 5 ~** son las 5

Oct. *abbr* (= *October*) oct

October [ɔk'təubə*] *n* octubre *m*

octopus ['ɔktəpəs] *n* pulpo

odd [ɔd] *adj* extraño, raro; (*number*) impar; (*sock, shoe etc*) suelto; **60-~** 60 y pico; **at ~ times** de vez en cuando; **to be the ~ one out** estar de más; **oddly** *adv* curiosamente, extrañamente; *see also* **enough**; **odds** *npl* (*in betting*) puntos *mpl* de ventaja; **it makes no odds** da lo mismo; **at odds** reñidos/as; **odds and ends** minucias *fpl*

odometer [ɔ'dɔmɪtə*] (US) *n* cuentakilómetros *m inv*

odour ['əudə*] (US **odor**) *n* olor *m*; (*unpleasant*) hedor *m*

KEYWORD

of [ɔv, əv] *prep* **1** (*gen*) de; **a friend of ours** un amigo nuestro; **a boy of 10** un chico de 10 años; **that was kind of you** eso fue muy amable por *or* de tu parte

2 (*expressing quantity, amount, dates etc*) de; **a kilo of flour** un kilo de harina; **there were three of them** había tres; **three of us went** tres de nosotros fuimos; **the 5th of July** el 5 de julio

3 (*from, out of*) de; **made of wood** (hecho) de madera

off [ɔf] *adj, adv* (*engine*) desconectado; (*light*) apagado; (*tap*) cerrado; (BRIT: *food: bad*) pasado, malo; (: *milk*) cortado; (*cancelled*) cancelado ▷ *prep* de; **to be ~** (*to leave*) irse, marcharse; **to be ~ sick** estar enfermo *or* de baja; **a day ~** un día libre *or* sin trabajar; **to have an ~ day** tener un día malo; **he had his coat ~** se había quitado el abrigo; **10% ~** (*Comm*) (con el) 10% de descuento; **5 km ~ (the road)** a 5 km (de la carretera); **~ the coast** frente a la costa; **I'm ~ meat** (*no longer eat/like it*) paso de la carne; **on the ~ chance** por si acaso; **~ and on** de vez en cuando

offence [ə'fɛns] (US **offense**) *n* (*crime*) delito; **to take ~ at** ofenderse por

offend [ə'fɛnd] *vt* (*person*) ofender; **offender** *n* delincuente *mf*

offense [ə'fɛns] (US) *n* = **offence**

offensive [ə'fɛnsɪv] *adj* ofensivo; (*smell etc*) repugnante ▷ *n* (*Mil*) ofensiva

offer ['ɔfə*] *n* oferta, ofrecimiento; (*proposal*) propuesta ▷ *vt* ofrecer; (*opportunity*) facilitar; **"on ~"** (*Comm*) "en oferta"

offhand [ɔf'hænd] *adj* informal ▷ *adv* de improviso

office ['ɔfɪs] *n* (*place*) oficina; (*room*) despacho; (*position*) carga, oficio; **doctor's ~** (US) consultorio; **to take ~** entrar en funciones; **office block** (US), **office building** *n* bloque *m* de oficinas; **office hours** *npl* horas *fpl* de oficina; (US *Med*) horas *fpl* de consulta

officer ['ɔfɪsə*] *n* (*Mil etc*) oficial *mf*;

(*also*: **police ~**) agente *mf* de policía; (*of organization*) director(a) *m/f*

office worker *n* oficinista *mf*

official [əˈfɪʃl] *adj* oficial, autorizado ▷ *n* funcionario/a, oficial *mf*

off: off-licence (BRIT) *n* (*shop*) bodega *tienda de vinos y bebidas alcohólicas*; **off-line** *adj, adv* (*Comput*) fuera de línea; **off-peak** *adj* (*electricity*) de banda económica; (*ticket*) *billete de precio reducido por viajar fuera de las horas punta*; **off-putting** (BRIT) *adj* (*person*) asqueroso; (*remark*) desalentador(a); **off-season** *adj, adv* fuera de temporada

OFF-LICENCE

En el Reino Unido la venta de bebidas alcohólicas está estrictamente regulada y se necesita una licencia especial, con la que cuentan los bares, restaurantes y los establecimientos de **off-licence**, los únicos lugares en donde se pueden adquirir bebidas alcohólicas para su consumo fuera del local, de donde viene su nombre. También venden bebidas no alcohólicas, tabaco, chocolatinas, patatas fritas, etc. y a menudo forman parte de una cadena nacional.

offset [ˈɔfsɛt] *vt* contrarrestar, compensar

offshore [ɔfˈʃɔː*] *adj* (*breeze, island*) costera; (*fishing*) de bajura

offside [ˈɔfˈsaɪd] *adj* (*Sport*) fuera de juego; (*Aut*: *in UK*) del lado derecho; (: *in US, Europe etc*) del lado izquierdo

offspring [ˈɔfsprɪŋ] *n inv* descendencia

often [ˈɔfn] *adv* a menudo, con frecuencia; **how ~ do you go?** ¿cada cuánto vas?

oh [əu] *excl* ¡ah!

oil [ɔɪl] *n* aceite *m*; (*petroleum*) petróleo; (*for heating*) aceite *m* combustible ▷ *vt* engrasar; **oil filter** *n* (*Aut*) filtro de aceite; **oil painting** *n* pintura al óleo; **oil refinery** *n* refinería de petróleo; **oil rig** *n* torre *f* de perforación; **oil slick** *n* marea negra; **oil tanker** *n* petrolero; (*truck*) camión *m* cisterna; **oil well** *n* pozo (de petróleo); **oily** *adj* aceitoso; (*food*) grasiento

ointment [ˈɔɪntmənt] *n* ungüento

O.K., okay [ˈəuˈkeɪ] *excl* ¡O.K.!, ¡está bien!, ¡vale! (SP) ▷ *adj* bien ▷ *vt* dar el visto bueno a

old [əuld] *adj* viejo; (*former*) antiguo; **how ~ are you?** ¿cuántos años tienes?, ¿qué edad tienes?; **he's 10 years ~** tiene 10 años; **~er brother** hermano mayor; **old age** *n* vejez *f*; **old-age pension** *n* (BRIT) jubilación *f*, pensión *f*; **old-age pensioner** (BRIT) *n* jubilado/a; **old-fashioned** *adj* anticuado, pasado de moda; **old people's home** *n* (*esp* BRIT) residencia *f* de ancianos

olive [ˈɔlɪv] *n* (*fruit*) aceituna; (*tree*) olivo ▷ *adj* (*also*: **~-green**) verde oliva; **olive oil** *n* aceite *m* de oliva

Olympic [əuˈlɪmpɪk] *adj* olímpico; **the ~ Games, the ~s** las Olimpiadas

omelet(te) [ˈɔmlɪt] *n* tortilla francesa (SP), omelette *f* (LAM)

omen [ˈəumən] *n* presagio

ominous [ˈɔmɪnəs] *adj* de mal agüero, amenazador(a)

omit [əuˈmɪt] *vt* omitir

KEYWORD

on [ɔn] *prep* **1** (*indicating position*) en; sobre; **on the wall** en la pared; **it's on the table** está sobre *or* en la mesa; **on the left** a la izquierda

2 (*indicating means, method, condition etc*): **on foot** a pie; **on the train/**

plane (*go*) en tren/avión; (*be*) en el tren/el avión; **on the radio/ television/telephone** por *or* en la radio/televisión/al teléfono; **to be on drugs** drogarse; (*Med*) estar a tratamiento; **to be on holiday/ business** estar de vacaciones/en viaje de negocios
3(*referring to time*): **on Friday** el viernes; **on Fridays** los viernes; **on June 20th** el 20 de junio; **a week on Friday** del viernes en una semana; **on arrival** al llegar; **on seeing this** al ver esto
4(*about, concerning*) sobre, acerca de; **a book on physics** un libro de *or* sobre física
▷ *adv* **1**(*referring to dress*): **to have one's coat on** tener *or* llevar el abrigo puesto; **she put her gloves on** se puso los guantes
2(*referring to covering*): **"screw the lid on tightly"** "cerrar bien la tapa"
3(*further, continuously*): **to walk** *etc* **on** seguir caminando *etc*
▷ *adj* **1**(*functioning, in operation*: *machine, radio, TV, light*) encendido/a (SP), prendido/a (LAM); (: *tap*) abierto/a; (: *brakes*) echado/a, puesto/a; **is the meeting still on?** (*in progress*) ¿todavía continúa la reunión?; (*not cancelled*) ¿va a haber reunión al fin?; **there's a good film on at the cinema** ponen una buena película en el cine
2 that's not on! (*inf*: *not possible*) ¡eso ni hablar!; (: *not acceptable*) ¡eso no se hace!

once [wʌns] *adv* una vez; (*formerly*) antiguamente ▷ *conj* una vez que; **~ he had left/it was done** una vez que se había marchado/se hizo; **at ~** en seguida, inmediatamente; (*simultaneously*) a la vez; **~ a week** una vez por semana; **~ more** otra vez; **~ and for all** de una vez por todas; **~ upon a time** érase una vez
oncoming [ˈɔnkʌmɪŋ] *adj* (*traffic*) que viene de frente

KEYWORD

one [wʌn] *num* un(o)/una; **one hundred and fifty** ciento cincuenta; **one by one** uno a uno
▷ *adj* **1**(*sole*) único; **the one book which** el único libro que; **the one man who** el único que
2(*same*) mismo/a; **they came in the one car** vinieron en un solo coche
▷ *pron* **1 this one** éste(ésta); **that one** ése(ésa); (*more remote*) aquél(aquella); **I've already got (a red) one** ya tengo uno/a rojo/a; **one by one** uno/a por uno/a
2 one another os (SP), se (+ *el uno al otro, unos a otros etc*); **do you two ever see one another?** ¿vosotros dos os veis alguna vez? (SP), ¿se ven ustedes dos alguna vez?; **the boys didn't dare look at one another** los chicos no se atrevieron a mirarse (el uno al otro); **they all kissed one another** se besaron unos a otros
3(*impers*): **one never knows** nunca se sabe; **to cut one's finger** cortarse el dedo; **one needs to eat** hay que comer
one-off(BRIT: *inf*) *n* (*event*) acontecimiento único

oneself [wʌnˈsɛlf] *pron* (*reflexive*) se; (*after prep*) sí; (*emphatic*) uno/a mismo/a; **to hurt ~** hacerse daño; **to keep sth for ~** guardarse algo; **to talk to ~** hablar solo
one: one-shot [wʌnˈʃɔt] (US) *n* = **one-off**; **one-sided** *adj* (*argument*) parcial; **one-to-one** *adj* (*relationship*) de dos; **one-way** *adj* (*street*) de sentido único
ongoing [ˈɔngəuɪŋ] *adj* continuo
onion [ˈʌnjən] *n* cebolla
on-line [ˈɔnlaɪn] *adj, adv* (*Comput*) en línea
onlooker [ˈɔnlukə*] *n* espectador(a) *m/f*

only ['əunlɪ] *adv* solamente, sólo ▷ *adj* único, solo ▷ *conj* solamente que, pero; **an ~ child** un hijo único; **not ~ ... but also ...** no sólo ... sino también ...
on-screen [ɔn'skri:n] *adj* (*Comput etc*) en pantalla; (*romance, kiss*) cinematográfico
onset ['ɔnsɛt] *n* comienzo
onto ['ɔntu] *prep* = **on to**
onward(s) ['ɔnwəd(z)] *adv* (*move*) (hacia) adelante; **from that time ~** desde entonces en adelante
oops [ups] *excl* (*also*: **~-a-daisy!**) ¡huy!
ooze [u:z] *vi* rezumar
opaque [əu'peɪk] *adj* opaco
open ['əupn] *adj* abierto; (*car*) descubierto; (*road, view*) despejado; (*meeting*) público; (*admiration*) manifiesto ▷ *vt* abrir ▷ *vi* abrirse; (*book etc: commence*) comenzar; **in the ~ (air)** al aire libre; **open up** *vt* abrir; (*blocked road*) despejar ▷ *vi* abrirse, empezar; **open-air** *adj* al aire libre; **opening** *n* abertura; (*start*) comienzo; (*opportunity*) oportunidad *f*; **opening hours** *npl* horario de apertura; **open learning** *n* *enseñanza flexible a tiempo parcial*; **openly** *adv* abiertamente; **open-minded** *adj* imparcial; **open-necked** *adj* (*shirt*) desabrochado; sin corbata; **open-plan** *adj*: **open-plan office** *gran oficina sin particiones*; **Open University** *n* (BRIT) ≈ Universidad *f* Nacional de Enseñanza a Distancia, UNED *f*

OPEN UNIVERSITY

La **Open University**, fundada en 1969, está especializada en impartir cursos a distancia que no exigen una dedicación exclusiva. Cuenta con sus propios materiales de apoyo, entre ellos programas de radio y televisión emitidos por la **BBC** y para conseguir los créditos de la licenciatura es necesaria la presentación de unos trabajos y la asistencia a los cursos de verano.

opera ['ɔpərə] *n* ópera; **opera house** *n* teatro de la ópera; **opera singer** *n* cantante *m/f* de ópera
operate ['ɔpəreɪt] *vt* (*machine*) hacer funcionar; (*company*) dirigir ▷ *vi* funcionar; **to ~ on sb** (*Med*) operar a algn
operating room ['ɔpəreɪtɪŋ-] (US) *n* quirófano, sala de operaciones
operating theatre (BRIT) *n* sala de operaciones
operation [ɔpə'reɪʃən] *n* operación *f*; (*of machine*) funcionamiento; **to be in ~** estar funcionando *or* en funcionamiento; **to have an ~** (*Med*) ser operado; **operational** *adj* operacional, en buen estado
operative ['ɔpərətɪv] *adj* en vigor
operator ['ɔpəreɪtə*] *n* (*of machine*) maquinista *mf*, operario/a; (*Tel*) operador(a) *m/f*, telefonista *mf*
opinion [ə'pɪnɪən] *n* opinión *f*; **in my ~** en mi opinión, a mi juicio; **opinion poll** *n* encuesta, sondeo
opponent [ə'pəunənt] *n* adversario/a, contrincante *mf*
opportunity [ɔpə'tju:nɪtɪ] *n* oportunidad *f*; **to take the ~ of doing** aprovechar la ocasión para hacer
oppose [ə'pəuz] *vt* oponerse a; **to be ~d to sth** oponerse a algo; **as ~d to** a diferencia de
opposite ['ɔpəzɪt] *adj* opuesto, contrario a; (*house etc*) de enfrente ▷ *adv* en frente ▷ *prep* en frente de, frente a ▷ *n* lo contrario
opposition [ɔpə'zɪʃən] *n* oposición *f*
oppress [ə'prɛs] *vt* oprimir
opt [ɔpt] *vi*: **to ~ for** optar por; **to ~ to do** optar por hacer; **opt out** *vi*: **to opt out of** optar por no hacer
optician [ɔp'tɪʃən] *n* óptico *m/f*
optimism ['ɔptɪmɪzəm] *n* optimismo
optimist ['ɔptɪmɪst] *n* optimista *mf*;

optimistic [-'mɪstɪk] *adj* optimista
optimum ['ɔptɪməm] *adj* óptimo
option ['ɔpʃən] *n* opción *f*; **optional** *adj* facultativo, discrecional
or [ɔː*] *conj* o; (*before o, ho*) u; (*with negative*): **he hasn't seen ~ heard anything** no ha visto ni oído nada; **~ else** si no
oral ['ɔːrəl] *adj* oral ▷ *n* examen *m* oral
orange ['ɔrɪndʒ] *n* (*fruit*) naranja ▷ *adj* color naranja; **orange juice** *n* jugo *m* de naranja, zumo *m* de naranja (SP); **orange squash** *n* naranjada
orbit ['ɔːbɪt] *n* órbita ▷ *vt, vi* orbitar
orchard ['ɔːtʃəd] *n* huerto
orchestra ['ɔːkɪstrə] *n* orquesta; (US: *seating*) platea
orchid ['ɔːkɪd] *n* orquídea
ordeal [ɔː'diːl] *n* experiencia horrorosa
order ['ɔːdə*] *n* orden *m*; (*command*) orden *f*; (*good order*) buen estado; (*Comm*) pedido ▷ *vt* (*also*: **put in ~**) arreglar, poner en orden; (*Comm*) pedir; (*command*) mandar, ordenar; **in ~** en orden; (*of document*) en regla; **in (working) ~** en funcionamiento; **in ~ to do/that** para hacer/que; **on ~** (*Comm*) pedido; **to be out of ~** estar desordenado; (*not working*) no funcionar; **to ~ sb to do sth** mandar a algn hacer algo; **order form** *n* hoja de pedido; **orderly** *n* (*Mil*) ordenanza *m*; (*Med*) enfermero/a (auxiliar) ▷ *adj* ordenado
ordinary ['ɔːdnrɪ] *adj* corriente, normal; (*pej*) común y corriente; **out of the ~** fuera de lo común
ore [ɔː*] *n* mineral *m*
oregano [ɔrɪ'gɑːnəu] *n* orégano
organ ['ɔːgən] *n* órgano; **organic** [ɔː'gænɪk] *adj* orgánico; **organism** *n* organismo
organization [ɔːgənaɪ'zeɪʃən] *n* organización *f*
organize ['ɔːgənaɪz] *vt* organizar; **organized** ['ɔːgənaizd] *adj* organizado; **organizer** *n* organizador(a) *m/f*
orgasm ['ɔːgæzəm] *n* orgasmo
orgy ['ɔːdʒɪ] *n* orgía
oriental [ɔːrɪ'ɛntl] *adj* oriental
orientation [ɔːrɪen'teɪʃən] *n* orientación *f*
origin ['ɔrɪdʒɪn] *n* origen *m*
original [ə'rɪdʒɪnl] *adj* original; (*first*) primero; (*earlier*) primitivo ▷ *n* original *m*; **originally** *adv* al principio
originate [ə'rɪdʒɪneɪt] *vi*: **to ~ from, to ~ in** surgir de, tener su origen en
Orkneys ['ɔːknɪz] *npl*: **the ~** (*also*: **the Orkney Islands**) las Orcadas
ornament ['ɔːnəmənt] *n* adorno; (*trinket*) chuchería; **ornamental** [-'mɛntl] *adj* decorativo, de adorno
ornate [ɔː'neɪt] *adj* muy ornado, vistoso
orphan ['ɔːfn] *n* huérfano/a
orthodox ['ɔːθədɔks] *adj* ortodoxo
orthopaedic [ɔːθə'piːdɪk] (US **orthopedic**) *adj* ortopédico
osteopath ['ɔstɪəpæθ] *n* osteópata *mf*
ostrich ['ɔstrɪtʃ] *n* avestruz *m*
other ['ʌðə*] *adj* otro ▷ *pron*: **the ~ (one)** el(la) otro/a ▷ *adv*: **~ than** aparte de; **otherwise** *adv* de otra manera ▷ *conj* (*if not*) si no
otter ['ɔtə*] *n* nutria
ouch [autʃ] *excl* ¡ay!
ought [ɔːt] (*pt* **~**) *aux vb*: **I ~ to do it** debería hacerlo; **this ~ to have been corrected** esto debiera haberse corregido; **he ~ to win** (*probability*) debe *or* debiera ganar
ounce [auns] *n* onza (*28.35g*)
our ['auə*] *adj* nuestro; *see also* **my**; **ours** *pron* (el) nuestro/(la) nuestra *etc*; *see also* **mine**[1]; **ourselves** *pron pl* (*reflexive, after prep*) nosotros; (*emphatic*) nosotros mismos; *see also* **oneself**
oust [aust] *vt* desalojar
out [aut] *adv* fuera, afuera; (*not at home*) fuera (de casa); (*light, fire*) apagado; **~ there** allí (fuera); **he's ~** (*absent*) no está, ha salido; **to be ~ in**

one's calculations equivocarse (en sus cálculos); **to run ~** salir corriendo; **~ loud** en alta voz; **~ of** (*outside*) fuera de; (*because of: anger etc*) por; **~ of petrol** sin gasolina; **"~ of order"** "no funciona"; **outback** *n* interior *m*; **outbound** *adj* (*flight*) de salida; (*flight: not return*) de ida; **outbreak** *n* (*of war*) comienzo; (*of disease*) epidemia; (*of violence etc*) ola; **outburst** *n* explosión *f*, arranque *m*; **outcast** *n* paria *mf*; **outcome** *n* resultado; **outcry** *n* protestas *fpl*; **outdated** *adj* anticuado, fuera de moda; **outdoor** *adj* exterior, de aire libre; (*clothes*) de calle; **outdoors** *adv* al aire libre

outer ['autə*] *adj* exterior, externo; **outer space** *n* espacio exterior

outfit ['autfɪt] *n* (*clothes*) conjunto

out: outgoing *adj* (*character*) extrovertido; (*retiring: president etc*) saliente; **outgoings** (BRIT) *npl* gastos *mpl*; **outhouse** *n* dependencia

outing ['autɪŋ] *n* excursión *f*, paseo

out: outlaw *n* proscrito ▷ *vt* proscribir; **outlay** *n* inversión *f*; **outlet** *n* salida; (*of pipe*) desagüe *m*; (*US Elec*) toma de corriente; (*also:* **retail outlet**) punto de venta; **outline** *n* (*shape*) contorno, perfil *m*; (*sketch, plan*) esbozo ▷ *vt* (*plan etc*) esbozar; **in outline** (*fig*) a grandes rasgos; **outlook** *n* (*fig: prospects*) perspectivas *fpl*; (*: for weather*) pronóstico; **outnumber** *vt* superar en número; **out-of-date** *adj* (*passport*) caducado; (*clothes*) pasado de moda; **out-of-doors** *adv* al aire libre; **out-of-the-way** *adj* apartado; **out-of-town** *adj* (*shopping centre etc*) en las afueras; **outpatient** *n* paciente *mf* externo/a; **outpost** *n* puesto avanzado; **output** *n* (volumen *m* de) producción *m*, rendimiento; (*Comput*) salida

outrage ['autreɪdʒ] *n* escándalo; (*atrocity*) atrocidad *f* ▷ *vt* ultrajar; **outrageous** [-'reɪdʒəs] *adj* monstruoso

outright [*adv* aut'raɪt, *adj* 'autraɪt] *adv* (*ask, deny*) francamente; (*refuse*) rotundamente; (*win*) de manera absoluta; (*be killed*) en el acto ▷ *adj* franco; rotundo

outset ['autsɛt] *n* principio

outside [aut'saɪd] *n* exterior *m* ▷ *adj* exterior, externo ▷ *adv* fuera ▷ *prep* fuera de; (*beyond*) más allá de; **at the ~** (*fig*) a lo sumo; **outside lane** *n* (*Aut: in Britain*) carril *m* de la derecha; (*: in US, Europe etc*) carril *m* de la izquierda; **outside line** *n* (*Tel*) línea (exterior); **outsider** *n* (*stranger*) extraño, forastero

out: outsize *adj* (*clothes*) de talla grande; **outskirts** *npl* alrededores *mpl*, afueras *fpl*; **outspoken** *adj* muy franco; **outstanding** *adj* excepcional, destacado; (*remaining*) pendiente

outward ['autwəd] *adj* externo; (*journey*) de ida; **outwards** *adv* (*esp* BRIT) = **outward**

outweigh [aut'weɪ] *vt* pesar más que

oval ['əuvl] *adj* ovalado ▷ *n* óvalo

ovary ['əuvərɪ] *n* ovario

oven ['ʌvn] *n* horno; **oven glove** *n* guante *m* para el horno, manopla para el horno; **ovenproof** *adj* resistente al horno; **oven-ready** *adj* listo para el horno

over ['əuvə*] *adv* encima, por encima ▷ *adj or adv* (*finished*) terminado; (*surplus*) de sobra ▷ *prep* (por) encima de; (*above*) sobre; (*on the other side of*) al otro lado de; (*more than*) más de; (*during*) durante; **~ here** (por) aquí; **~ there** (por) allí *or* allá; **all ~** (*everywhere*) por todas partes; **~ and ~ (again)** una y otra vez; **~ and above** además de; **to ask sb ~** invitar a algn a casa; **to bend ~** inclinarse

overall [*adj, n* 'əuvərɔːl, *adv* əuvər'ɔːl] *adj* (*length etc*) total; (*study*) de conjunto ▷ *adv* en conjunto ▷ *n* (BRIT) guardapolvo; **overalls** *npl* (*boiler suit*) mono (SP) *or* overol *m* (LAM) (de trabajo)

overboard *adv* (*Naut*) por la borda

overcame [əuvəˈkeɪm] *pt of* **overcome**

overcast [ˈəuvəkɑːst] *adj* encapotado

overcharge [əuvəˈtʃɑːdʒ] *vt*: **to ~ sb** cobrar un precio excesivo a algn

overcoat [ˈəuvəkəut] *n* abrigo, sobretodo

overcome [əuvəˈkʌm] *vt* vencer; (*difficulty*) superar

over: overcrowded *adj* atestado de gente; (*city, country*) superpoblado; **overdo** (*irreg*) *vt* exagerar; (*overcook*) cocer demasiado; **to overdo it** (*work etc*) pasarse; **overdone** [əuvəˈdʌn] *adj* (*vegetables*) recocido; (*steak*) demasiado hecho; **overdose** *n* sobredosis *f inv*; **overdraft** *n* saldo deudor; **overdrawn** *adj* (*account*) en descubierto; **overdue** *adj* retrasado; **overestimate** *vt* sobreestimar

overflow [*vb* əuvəˈfləu, *n* ˈəuvəfləu] *vi* desbordarse ▷ *n* (*also*: **~ pipe**) (cañería de) desagüe *m*

overgrown [əuvəˈgrəun] *adj* (*garden*) invadido por la vegetación

overhaul [*vb* əuvəˈhɔːl, *n* ˈəuvəhɔːl] *vt* revisar, repasar ▷ *n* revisión *f*

overhead [*adv* əuvəˈhɛd, *adj, n* ˈəuvəhɛd] *adv* por arriba *or* encima ▷ *adj* (*cable*) aéreo ▷ *n* (US) = **overheads**; **overhead projector** *n* retroproyector; **overheads** *npl* (*expenses*) gastos *mpl* generales

over: overhear (*irreg*) *vt* oír por casualidad; **overheat** *vi* (*engine*) recalentarse; **overland** *adj, adv* por tierra; **overlap** [əuvəˈlæp] *vi* traslaparse; **overleaf** *adv* al dorso; **overload** *vt* sobrecargar; **overlook** *vt* (*have view of*) dar a, tener vistas a; (*miss: by mistake*) pasar por alto; (*excuse*) perdonar

overnight [əuvəˈnaɪt] *adv* durante la noche; (*fig*) de la noche a la mañana ▷ *adj* de noche; **to stay ~** pasar la noche; **overnight bag** *n* fin *m* de semana, neceser *m* de viaje

overpass (US) [ˈəuvəpɑːs] *n* paso superior

overpower [əuvəˈpauə*] *vt* dominar; (*fig*) embargar; **overpowering** *adj* (*heat*) agobiante; (*smell*) penetrante

over: overreact [əuvərɪˈækt] *vi* reaccionar de manera exagerada; **overrule** *vt* (*decision*) anular; (*claim*) denegar; **overrun** (*irreg*) *vt* (*country*) invadir; (*time limit*) rebasar, exceder

overseas [əuvəˈsiːz] *adv* (*abroad: live*) en el extranjero; (*travel*) al extranjero ▷ *adj* (*trade*) exterior; (*visitor*) extranjero

oversee [əuvəˈsiː] (*irreg*) *vt* supervisar

overshadow [əuvəˈʃædəu] *vt*: **to be ~ed by** estar a la sombra de

oversight [ˈəuvəsaɪt] *n* descuido

oversleep [əuvəˈsliːp] (*irreg*) *vi* quedarse dormido

overspend [əuvəˈspɛnd] (*irreg*) *vi* gastar más de la cuenta; **we have overspent by 5 pounds** hemos excedido el presupuesto en 5 libras

overt [əuˈvəːt] *adj* abierto

overtake [əuvəˈteɪk] (*irreg*) *vt* sobrepasar; (BRIT *Aut*) adelantar

over: overthrow (*irreg*) *vt* (*government*) derrocar; **overtime** *n* horas *fpl* extraordinarias

overtook [əuvəˈtuk] *pt of* **overtake**

over: overturn *vt* volcar; (*fig: plan*) desbaratar; (*: government*) derrocar ▷ *vi* volcar; **overweight** *adj* demasiado gordo *or* pesado; **overwhelm** *vt* aplastar; (*emotion*) sobrecoger; **overwhelming** *adj* (*victory, defeat*) arrollador(a); (*feeling*) irresistible

ow [au] *excl* ¡ay!

owe [əu] *vt*: **to ~ sb sth, to ~ sth to sb** deber algo a algn; **owing to** *prep* debido a, por causa de

owl [aul] *n* búho, lechuza

own [əun] *vt* tener, poseer ▷ *adj* propio; **a room of my ~** una habitación propia; **to get one's ~ back** tomar revancha; **on one's ~** solo, a solas; **own up** *vi* confesar; **owner** *n* dueño/a;

ownership *n* posesión *f*
ox [ɔks] (*pl* **~en**) *n* buey *m*
Oxbridge ['ɔksbrɪdʒ] *n* *universidades de Oxford y Cambridge*
oxen ['ɔksən] *npl of* **ox**
oxygen ['ɔksɪdʒən] *n* oxígeno
oyster ['ɔɪstə*] *n* ostra
oz. *abbr* = **ounce(s)**
ozone ['əuzəun] *n* ozono; **ozone friendly** *adj* que no daña la capa de ozono; **ozone layer** *n* capa *f* de ozono

p [pi:] *abbr* = **penny; pence**
P.A. *n abbr* = **personal assistant; public address system**
p.a. *abbr* = **per annum**
pace [peɪs] *n* paso ▷ *vi*: **to ~ up and down** pasearse de un lado a otro; **to keep ~ with** llevar el mismo paso que; **pacemaker** *n* (*Med*) regulador *m* cardíaco, marcapasos *m inv*; (*Sport*: *also*: **pacesetter**) liebre *f*
Pacific [pə'sɪfɪk] *n*: **the ~ (Ocean)** el (Océano) Pacífico
pacifier ['pæsɪfaɪə*] (US) *n* (*dummy*) chupete *m*
pack [pæk] *n* (*packet*) paquete *m*; (*of hounds*) jauría; (*of people*) manada, bando; (*of cards*) baraja; (*bundle*) fardo; (US: *of cigarettes*) paquete *m*; (*back pack*) mochila ▷ *vt* (*fill*) llenar; (*in suitcase etc*) meter, poner; (*cram*) llenar, atestar; **to ~ (one's bags)** hacerse la maleta; **to ~ sb off** despachar a algn; **pack in** *vi* (*watch, car*) estropearse ▷ *vt* (*inf*) dejar; **pack it in!** ¡para!, ¡basta ya!; **pack up** *vi* (*inf*: *machine*) estropearse; (*person*) irse

▷ *vt* (*belongings, clothes*) recoger; (*goods, presents*) empaquetar, envolver

package ['pækɪdʒ] *n* paquete *m*; (*bulky*) bulto; (*also*: **~ deal**) acuerdo global; **package holiday** *n* vacaciones *fpl* organizadas; **package tour** *n* viaje *m* organizado

packaging ['pækɪdʒɪŋ] *n* envase *m*

packed [pækt] *adj* abarrotado; **packed lunch** *n* almuerzo frío

packet ['pækɪt] *n* paquete *m*

packing ['pækɪŋ] *n* embalaje *m*

pact [pækt] *n* pacto

pad [pæd] *n* (*of paper*) bloc *m*; (*cushion*) cojinete *m*; (*inf: home*) casa ▷ *vt* rellenar; **padded** *adj* (*jacket*) acolchado; (*bra*) reforzado

paddle ['pædl] *n* (*oar*) canalete *m*; (*US: for table tennis*) paleta ▷ *vt* impulsar con canalete ▷ *vi* (*with feet*) chapotear; **paddling pool** (BRIT) *n* estanque *m* de juegos

paddock ['pædək] *n* corral *m*

padlock ['pædlɔk] *n* candado

paedophile ['piːdəufaɪl] (*US* **pedophile**) *adj* de pedófilos ▷ *n* pedófilo/a

page [peɪdʒ] *n* (*of book*) página; (*of newspaper*) plana; (*also*: **~ boy**) paje *m* ▷ *vt* (*in hotel etc*) llamar por altavoz a

pager ['peɪdʒə*] *n* (*Tel*) busca *m*

paid [peɪd] *pt, pp of* **pay** ▷ *adj* (*work*) remunerado; (*holiday*) pagado; (*official etc*) a sueldo; **to put ~ to** (BRIT) acabar con

pain [peɪn] *n* dolor *m*; **to be in ~** sufrir; **to take ~s to do sth** tomarse grandes molestias en hacer algo; **painful** *adj* doloroso; (*difficult*) penoso; (*disagreeable*) desagradable; **painkiller** *n* analgésico; **painstaking** ['peɪnzteɪkɪŋ] *adj* (*person*) concienzudo, esmerado

paint [peɪnt] *n* pintura ▷ *vt* pintar; **to ~ the door blue** pintar la puerta de azul; **paintbrush** *n* (*of artist*) pincel *m*; (*of decorator*) brocha; **painter** *n* pintor(a) *m/f*; **painting** *n* pintura

pair [pɛə*] *n* (*of shoes, gloves etc*) par *m*; (*of people*) pareja; **a ~ of scissors** unas tijeras; **a ~ of trousers** unos pantalones, un pantalón

pajamas [pə'dʒɑːməz] (*US*) *npl* pijama *m*

Pakistan [pɑːkɪ'stɑːn] *n* Paquistán *m*; **Pakistani** *adj, n* paquistaní *mf*

pal [pæl] (*inf*) *n* compinche *mf*, compañero/a

palace ['pæləs] *n* palacio

pale [peɪl] *adj* (*gen*) pálido; (*colour*) claro ▷ *n*: **to be beyond the ~** pasarse de la raya

Palestine ['pælɪstaɪn] *n* Palestina; **Palestinian** [-'tɪnɪən] *adj, n* palestino/a *m/f*

palm [pɑːm] *n* (*Anat*) palma; (*also*: **~ tree**) palmera, palma ▷ *vt*: **to ~ sth off on sb** (*inf*) encajar algo a algn

pamper ['pæmpə*] *vt* mimar

pamphlet ['pæmflət] *n* folleto

pan [pæn] *n* (*also*: **sauce~**) cacerola, cazuela, olla; (*also*: **frying ~**) sartén *f*

pancake ['pænkeɪk] *n* crepe *f*

panda ['pændə] *n* panda *m*

pane [peɪn] *n* cristal *m*

panel ['pænl] *n* (*of wood etc*) panel *m*; (*Radio, TV*) panel *m* de invitados

panhandler ['pænhændlə*] (*US*) *n* (*inf*) mendigo/a

panic ['pænɪk] *n* terror *m* pánico ▷ *vi* dejarse llevar por el pánico

panorama [pænə'rɑːmə] *n* panorama *m*

pansy ['pænzɪ] *n* (*Bot*) pensamiento; (*inf, pej*) maricón *m*

pant [pænt] *vi* jadear

panther ['pænθə*] *n* pantera

panties ['pæntɪz] *npl* bragas *fpl*, pantis *mpl*

pantomime ['pæntəmaɪm] (BRIT) *n* *revista musical representada en Navidad, basada en cuentos dehadas*

PANTOMIME

En época navideña se ponen en

escena en los teatros británicos las llamadas **pantomimes**, que son versiones libres de cuentos tradicionales como Aladino o El gato con botas. En ella nunca faltan personajes como la dama ("dame"), papel que siempre interpreta un actor, el protagonista joven ("principal boy"), normalmente interpretado por una actriz, y el malvado ("villain"). Es un espectáculo familiar en el que se anima al público a participar y aunque va dirigido principalmente a los niños, cuenta con grandes dosis de humor para adultos.

pants [pænts] *n* (BRIT: *underwear*: *woman's*) bragas *fpl*; (: *man's*) calzoncillos *mpl*; (US: *trousers*) pantalones *mpl*
paper ['peɪpə*] *n* papel *m*; (*also*: **news~**) periódico, diario; (*academic essay*) ensayo; (*exam*) examen *m* ▷ *adj* de papel ▷ *vt* empapelar, tapizar (MEX); **papers** *npl* (*also*: **identity ~s**) papeles *mpl*, documentos *mpl*; **paperback** *n* libro en rústica; **paper bag** *n* bolsa de papel; **paper clip** *n* clip *m*; **paper shop** (BRIT) *n* tienda de periódicos; **paperwork** *n* trabajo administrativo
paprika ['pæprɪkə] *n* pimentón *m*
par [pɑː*] *n* par *f*; (*Golf*) par *m*; **to be on a ~ with** estar a la par con
paracetamol [pærə'siːtəmɔl] (BRIT) *n* paracetamol *m*
parachute ['pærəʃuːt] *n* paracaídas *m inv*
parade [pə'reɪd] *n* desfile *m* ▷ *vt* (*show*) hacer alarde de ▷ *vi* desfilar; (*Mil*) pasar revista
paradise ['pærədaɪs] *n* paraíso
paradox ['pærədɔks] *n* paradoja
paraffin ['pærəfɪn] (BRIT) *n* (*also*: **~ oil**) parafina
paragraph ['pærəgrɑːf] *n* párrafo
parallel ['pærəlɛl] *adj* en paralelo; (*fig*) semejante ▷ *n* (*line*) paralela; (*fig*, *Geo*) paralelo
paralysed ['pærəlaɪzd] *adj* paralizado
paralysis [pə'rælɪsɪs] *n* parálisis *f inv*
paramedic [pærə'mɛdɪk] *n* auxiliar *m/f* sanitario/a
paranoid ['pærənɔɪd] *adj* (*person*, *feeling*) paranoico
parasite ['pærəsaɪt] *n* parásito/a
parcel ['pɑːsl] *n* paquete *m* ▷ *vt* (*also*: **~ up**) empaquetar, embalar
pardon ['pɑːdn] *n* (*Law*) indulto ▷ *vt* perdonar; **~ me!**, **I beg your ~!** (*I'm sorry!*) ¡perdone usted!; **(I beg your) ~?**, **~ me?** (US: *what did you say?*) ¿cómo?
parent ['pɛərənt] *n* (*mother*) madre *f*; (*father*) padre *m*; **parents** *npl* padres *mpl*

Be careful not to translate **parent** by the Spanish word *pariente*.

parental [pə'rɛntl] *adj* paternal/maternal
Paris ['pærɪs] *n* París
parish ['pærɪʃ] *n* parroquia
Parisian [pə'rɪzɪən] *adj*, *n* parisiense *mf*
park [pɑːk] *n* parque *m* ▷ *vt* aparcar, estacionar ▷ *vi* aparcar, estacionarse
parking ['pɑːkɪŋ] *n* aparcamiento, estacionamiento; **"no ~"** "prohibido estacionarse"; **parking lot** (US) *n* parking *m*; **parking meter** *n* parquímetro; **parking ticket** *n* multa de aparcamiento
parkway ['pɑːkweɪ] (US) *n* alameda
parliament ['pɑːləmənt] *n* parlamento; (*Spanish*) Cortes *fpl*; **parliamentary** [-'mɛntərɪ] *adj* parlamentario

PARLIAMENT

El Parlamento británico (**Parliament**) tiene como sede el palacio de Westminster, también llamado "Houses of Parliament" y consta de dos cámaras. La Cámara de los Comunes ("House of Commons"), compuesta por 650 diputados (**Members of Parliament**) elegidos por sufragio universal en su respectiva circunscripción electoral (constituency), se reúne 175 días al año y sus sesiones son moderadas por el Presidente de la Cámara (**Speaker**). La cámara alta es la Cámara de los Lores ("House of Lords") y está formada por miembros que han sido nombrados por el monarca o que han heredado su escaño. Su poder es limitado, aunque actúa como tribunal supremo de apelación, excepto en Escocia.

Parmesan [pɑːmɪ'zæn] *n* (*also*: **~ cheese**) queso parmesano
parole [pə'rəul] *n*: **on ~** libre bajo palabra
parrot ['pærət] *n* loro, papagayo
parsley ['pɑːslɪ] *n* perejil *m*
parsnip ['pɑːsnɪp] *n* chirivía
parson ['pɑːsn] *n* cura *m*
part [pɑːt] *n* (*gen, Mus*) parte *f*; (*bit*) trozo; (*of machine*) pieza; (*Theatre etc*) papel *m*; (*of serial*) entrega; (*US*: *in hair*) raya ▷ *adv* = **partly** ▷ *vt* separar ▷ *vi* (*people*) separarse; (*crowd*) apartarse; **to take ~ in** tomar parte *or* participar en; **to take sth in good ~** tomar algo en buena parte; **to take sb's ~** defender a algn; **for my ~** por mi parte; **for the most ~** en su mayor parte; **to ~ one's hair** hacerse la raya; **part with** *vt fus* ceder, entregar; (*money*) pagar; **part of speech** *n* parte *f* de la oración, categoría *f* gramatical
partial ['pɑːʃl] *adj* parcial; **to be ~ to** ser aficionado a
participant [pɑː'tɪsɪpənt] *n* (*in competition*) concursante *mf*; (*in campaign etc*) participante *mf*
participate [pɑː'tɪsɪpeɪt] *vi*: **to ~ in** participar en
particle ['pɑːtɪkl] *n* partícula; (*of dust*) grano
particular [pə'tɪkjulə*] *adj* (*special*) particular; (*concrete*) concreto; (*given*) determinado; (*fussy*) quisquilloso; (*demanding*) exigente; **in ~** en particular; **particularly** *adv* (*in particular*) sobre todo; (*difficult, good etc*) especialmente; **particulars** *npl* (*information*) datos *mpl*; (*details*) pormenores *mpl*
parting ['pɑːtɪŋ] *n* (*act*) separación *f*; (*farewell*) despedida; (BRIT: *in hair*) raya ▷ *adj* de despedida
partition [pɑː'tɪʃən] *n* (*Pol*) división *f*; (*wall*) tabique *m*
partly ['pɑːtlɪ] *adv* en parte
partner ['pɑːtnə*] *n* (*Comm*) socio/a; (*Sport, at dance*) pareja; (*spouse*) cónyuge *mf*; (*lover*) compañero/a; **partnership** *n* asociación *f*; (*Comm*) sociedad *f*
partridge ['pɑːtrɪdʒ] *n* perdiz *f*
part-time ['pɑːt'taɪm] *adj, adv* a tiempo parcial
party ['pɑːtɪ] *n* (*Pol*) partido; (*celebration*) fiesta; (*group*) grupo; (*Law*) parte *f* interesada ▷ *cpd* (*Pol*) de partido
pass [pɑːs] *vt* (*time, object*) pasar; (*place*) pasar por; (*overtake*) rebasar; (*exam*) aprobar; (*approve*) aprobar ▷ *vi* pasar; (*Scol*) aprobar, ser aprobado ▷ *n* (*permit*) permiso; (*membership card*) carnet *m*; (*in mountains*) puerto, desfiladero; (*Sport*) pase *m*; (*Scol*: *also*: **~ mark**): **to get a ~ in** aprobar en; **to ~ sth through sth** pasar algo por algo; **to make a ~ at sb** (*inf*) hacer proposiciones a algn; **pass away** *vi* fallecer; **pass by** *vi* pasar ▷ *vt* (*ignore*) pasar por alto; **pass on** *vt* transmitir; **pass out** *vi* desmayarse; **pass over** *vi, vt* omitir, pasar por alto; **pass up** *vt* (*opportunity*) renunciar a; **passable** *adj* (*road*) transitable; (*tolerable*) pasable
passage ['pæsɪdʒ] *n* (*also*: **~way**) pasillo; (*act of passing*) tránsito; (*fare,*

in book) pasaje *m*; (*by boat*) travesía; (*Anat*) tubo

passenger ['pæsɪndʒə*] *n* pasajero/a, viajero/a

passer-by [pɑːsə'baɪ] *n* transeúnte *mf*

passing place *n* (*Aut*) apartadero

passion ['pæʃən] *n* pasión *f*; **passionate** *adj* apasionado; **passion fruit** *n* fruta de la pasión, granadilla

passive ['pæsɪv] *adj* (*gen, also Ling*) pasivo

passport ['pɑːspɔːt] *n* pasaporte *m*; **passport control** *n* control *m* de pasaporte; **passport office** *n* oficina de pasaportes

password ['pɑːswəːd] *n* contraseña

past [pɑːst] *prep* (*in front of*) por delante de; (*further than*) más allá de; (*later than*) después de ▷ *adj* pasado; (*president etc*) antiguo ▷ *n* (*time*) pasado; (*of person*) antecedentes *mpl*; **he's ~ forty** tiene más de cuarenta años; **ten/quarter ~ eight** las ocho y diez/cuarto; **for the ~ few/3 days** durante los últimos días/últimos 3 días; **to run ~ sb** pasar a algn corriendo

pasta ['pæstə] *n* pasta

paste [peɪst] *n* pasta; (*glue*) engrudo ▷ *vt* pegar

pastel ['pæstl] *adj* pastel; (*painting*) al pastel

pasteurized ['pæstəraɪzd] *adj* pasteurizado

pastime ['pɑːstaɪm] *n* pasatiempo

pastor ['pɑːstə*] *n* pastor *m*

past participle [-'pɑːtɪsɪpl] *n* (*Ling*) participio *m* (de) pasado *or* (de) pretérito *or* pasivo

pastry ['peɪstrɪ] *n* (*dough*) pasta; (*cake*) pastel *m*

pasture ['pɑːstʃə*] *n* pasto

pasty[1] ['pæstɪ] *n* empanada

pasty[2] ['peɪstɪ] *adj* (*complexion*) pálido

pat [pæt] *vt* dar una palmadita a; (*dog etc*) acariciar

patch [pætʃ] *n* (*of material,: eye patch*) parche *m*; (*mended part*) remiendo; (*of land*) terreno ▷ *vt* remendar; **(to go through) a bad ~** (pasar por) una mala racha; **patchy** *adj* desigual

pâté ['pæteɪ] *n* paté *m*

patent ['peɪtnt] *n* patente *f* ▷ *vt* patentar ▷ *adj* patente, evidente

paternal [pə'təːnl] *adj* paternal; (*relation*) paterno

paternity leave [pə'təːnɪtɪ-] *n* permiso *m* por paternidad, licencia por paternidad

path [pɑːθ] *n* camino, sendero; (*trail, track*) pista; (*of missile*) trayectoria

pathetic [pə'θɛtɪk] *adj* patético, lastimoso; (*very bad*) malísimo

pathway ['pɑːθweɪ] *n* sendero, vereda

patience ['peɪʃns] *n* paciencia; (*BRIT Cards*) solitario

patient ['peɪʃnt] *n* paciente *mf* ▷ *adj* paciente, sufrido

patio ['pætɪəu] *n* patio

patriotic [pætrɪ'ɔtɪk] *adj* patriótico

patrol [pə'trəul] *n* patrulla ▷ *vt* patrullar por; **patrol car** *n* coche *m* patrulla

patron ['peɪtrən] *n* (*in shop*) cliente *mf*; (*of charity*) patrocinador(a) *m/f*; **~ of the arts** mecenas *m*

patronizing ['pætrənaɪzɪŋ] *adj* condescendiente

pattern ['pætən] *n* (*Sewing*) patrón *m*; (*design*) dibujo; **patterned** *adj* (*material*) estampado

pause [pɔːz] *n* pausa ▷ *vi* hacer una pausa

pave [peɪv] *vt* pavimentar; **to ~ the way for** preparar el terreno para

pavement ['peɪvmənt] (*BRIT*) *n* acera, banqueta (*MEX*), andén *m* (*CAM*), vereda (*SC*)

pavilion [pə'vɪlɪən] *n* (*Sport*) caseta

paving ['peɪvɪŋ] *n* pavimento, enlosado

paw [pɔː] *n* pata

pawn [pɔːn] *n* (*Chess*) peón *m*; (*fig*) instrumento ▷ *vt* empeñar; **pawn broker** *n* prestamista *mf*

pay [peɪ] (*pt, pp* **paid**) *n* (*wage etc*) sueldo, salario ▷ *vt* pagar ▷ *vi* (*be profitable*) rendir; **to ~ attention (to)** prestar atención (a); **to ~ sb a visit** hacer una visita a algn; **to ~ one's respects to sb** presentar sus respetos a algn; **pay back** *vt* (*money*) reembolsar; (*person*) pagar; **pay for** *vt fus* pagar; **pay in** *vt* ingresar; **pay off** *vt* saldar ▷ *vi* (*scheme, decision*) dar resultado; **pay out** *vt* (*money*) gastar, desembolsar; **pay up** *vt* pagar (de mala gana); **payable** *adj*: **payable to** pagadero a; **pay day** *n* día *m* de paga; **pay envelope** (US) *n* = **pay packet**; **payment** *n* pago; **monthly payment** mensualidad *f*; **payout** *n* pago; (*in competition*) premio en metálico; **pay packet** (BRIT) *n* sobre *m* (de paga); **pay phone** *n* teléfono público; **payroll** *n* nómina; **pay slip** *n* recibo de sueldo; **pay television** *n* televisión *f* de pago

PC *n abbr* = **personal computer**; (BRIT) (= *police constable*) policía *mf* ▷ *adv abbr* = **politically correct**

p.c. *abbr* = **per cent**

PDA *n abbr* (= *personal digital assistant*) agenda electrónica

PE *n abbr* (= *physical education*) ed. física

pea [pi:] *n* guisante *m* (SP), arveja (LAM), chícharo (MEX, CAM)

peace [pi:s] *n* paz *f*; (*calm*) paz *f*, tranquilidad *f*; **peaceful** *adj* (*gentle*) pacífico; (*calm*) tranquilo, sosegado

peach [pi:tʃ] *n* melocotón *m* (SP), durazno (LAM)

peacock ['pi:kɔk] *n* pavo real

peak [pi:k] *n* (*of mountain*) cumbre *f*, cima; (*of cap*) visera; (*fig*) cumbre *f*; **peak hours** *npl* horas *fpl* punta

peanut ['pi:nʌt] *n* cacahuete *m* (SP), maní *m* (LAM), cacahuate *m* (MEX); **peanut butter** *n* manteca de cacahuete *or* maní

pear [pɛə*] *n* pera

pearl [pə:l] *n* perla

peasant ['pɛznt] *n* campesino/a

peat [pi:t] *n* turba

pebble ['pɛbl] *n* guijarro

peck [pɛk] *vt* (*also*: **~ at**) picotear ▷ *n* picotazo; (*kiss*) besito; **peckish** (BRIT: *inf*) *adj*: **I feel peckish** tengo ganas de picar algo

peculiar [pɪ'kju:lɪə*] *adj* (*odd*) extraño, raro; (*typical*) propio, característico; **~ to** propio de

pedal ['pɛdl] *n* pedal *m* ▷ *vi* pedalear

pedalo ['pedələu] *n* patín *m* a pedal

pedestal ['pɛdəstl] *n* pedestal *m*

pedestrian [pɪ'dɛstrɪən] *n* peatón/ona *m/f* ▷ *adj* pedestre; **pedestrian crossing** (BRIT) *n* paso de peatones; **pedestrianized** *adj*: **a pedestrianized street** una calle peatonal; **pedestrian precinct** (US **pedestrian zone**) *n* zona peatonal

pedigree ['pɛdɪgri:] *n* genealogía; (*of animal*) raza, pedigrí *m* ▷ *cpd* (*animal*) de raza, de casta

pedophile ['pi:dəufaɪl] (US) *n* = **paedophile**

pee [pi:] (*inf*) *vi* mear

peek [pi:k] *vi* mirar a hurtadillas

peel [pi:l] *n* piel *f*; (*of orange, lemon*) cáscara; (: *removed*) peladuras *fpl* ▷ *vt* pelar ▷ *vi* (*paint etc*) desconcharse; (*wallpaper*) despegarse, desprenderse; (*skin*) pelar

peep [pi:p] *n* (BRIT: *look*) mirada furtiva; (*sound*) pío ▷ *vi* (BRIT: *look*) mirar furtivamente

peer [pɪə*] *vi*: **to ~ at** esudriñar ▷ *n* (*noble*) par *m*; (*equal*) igual *m*; (*contemporary*) contemporáneo/a

peg [pɛg] *n* (*for coat etc*) gancho, colgadero; (BRIT: *also*: **clothes ~**) pinza

pelican ['pɛlɪkən] *n* pelícano; **pelican crossing** (BRIT) *n* (*Aut*) paso de peatones señalizado

pelt [pɛlt] *vt*: **to ~ sb with sth** arrojarle algo a algn ▷ *vi* (*rain*) llover a cántaros; (*inf*: *run*) correr ▷ *n* pellejo

pelvis ['pɛlvɪs] *n* pelvis *f*

pen [pɛn] *n* (*fountain pen*) pluma; (*ballpoint pen*) bolígrafo; (*for sheep*) redil *m*

penalty ['pɛnltɪ] *n* (*gen*) pena; (*fine*) multa
pence [pɛns] *npl of* **penny**
pencil ['pɛnsl] *n* lápiz *m*; **pencil in** *vt* (*appointment*) apuntar con carácter provisional; **pencil case** *n* estuche *m*; **pencil sharpener** *n* sacapuntas *m inv*
pendant ['pɛndnt] *n* pendiente *m*
pending ['pɛndɪŋ] *prep* antes de ▷ *adj* pendiente
penetrate ['pɛnɪtreɪt] *vt* penetrar
penfriend ['pɛnfrɛnd] (BRIT) *n* amigo/a por carta
penguin ['pɛŋgwɪn] *n* pingüino
penicillin [pɛnɪ'sɪlɪn] *n* penicilina
peninsula [pə'nɪnsjulə] *n* península
penis ['pi:nɪs] *n* pene *m*
penitentiary [pɛnɪ'tɛnʃərɪ] (US) *n* cárcel *f*, presidio
penknife ['pɛnnaɪf] *n* navaja
penniless ['pɛnɪlɪs] *adj* sin dinero
penny ['pɛnɪ] (*pl* **pennies** *or* **pence**) (BRIT) *n* penique *m*; (US) centavo
penpal ['pɛnpæl] *n* amigo/a por carta
pension ['pɛnʃən] *n* (*state benefit*) jubilación *f*; **pensioner** (BRIT) *n* jubilado/a
pentagon ['pɛntəgən] (US) *n*: **the P~** (*Pol*) el Pentágono

PENTAGON

Se conoce como **Pentagon** al edificio de planta pentagonal que acoge las dependencias del Ministerio de Defensa estadounidense ("Department of Defense") en Arlington, Virginia. En lenguaje periodístico se aplica también a la dirección militar del país.

penthouse ['pɛnthaus] *n* ático de lujo
penultimate [pɛ'nʌltɪmət] *adj* penúltimo
people ['pi:pl] *npl* gente *f*; (*citizens*) pueblo, ciudadanos *mpl*; (*Pol*): **the ~** el pueblo ▷ *n* (*nation, race*) pueblo, nación *f*; **several ~ came** vinieron varias personas; **~ say that ...** dice la gente que ...
pepper ['pɛpə*] *n* (*spice*) pimienta; (*vegetable*) pimiento ▷ *vt*: **to ~ with** (*fig*) salpicar de; **peppermint** *n* (*sweet*) pastilla de menta
per [pə:*] *prep* por; **~ day/~son** por día/persona; **~ annum** al año
perceive [pə'si:v] *vt* percibir; (*realize*) darse cuenta de
per cent *n* por ciento
percentage [pə'sɛntɪdʒ] *n* porcentaje *m*
perception [pə'sɛpʃən] *n* percepción *f*; (*insight*) perspicacia; (*opinion etc*) opinión *f*
perch [pə:tʃ] *n* (*fish*) perca; (*for bird*) percha ▷ *vi*: **to ~ (on)** (*bird*) posarse (en); (*person*) encaramarse (en)
percussion [pə'kʌʃən] *n* percusión *f*
perfect [*adj, n* 'pə:fɪkt, *vb* pə'fɛkt] *adj* perfecto ▷ *n* (*also*: **~ tense**) perfecto ▷ *vt* perfeccionar; **perfection** [pə'fɛkʃən] *n* perfección *f*; **perfectly** ['pə:fɪktlɪ] *adv* perfectamente
perform [pə'fɔ:m] *vt* (*carry out*) realizar, llevar a cabo; (*Theatre*) representar; (*piece of music*) interpretar ▷ *vi* (*well, badly*) funcionar; **performance** *n* (*of a play*) representación *f*; (*of actor, athlete etc*) actuación *f*; (*of car, engine, company*) rendimiento; (*of economy*) resultados *mpl*; **performer** *n* (*actor*) actor *m*, actriz *f*
perfume ['pə:fju:m] *n* perfume *m*
perhaps [pə'hæps] *adv* quizá(s), tal vez
perimeter [pə'rɪmɪtə*] *n* perímetro
period ['pɪərɪəd] *n* período; (*Scol*) clase *f*; (*full stop*) punto; (*Med*) regla ▷ *adj* (*costume, furniture*) de época; **periodical** [pɪərɪ'ɔdɪkl] *n* periódico; **periodically** *adv* de vez en cuando, cada cierto tiempo

perish ['pɛrɪʃ] *vi* perecer; (*decay*) echarse a perder
perjury ['pə:dʒərɪ] *n* (*Law*) perjurio
perk [pə:k] *n* extra *m*
perm [pə:m] *n* permanente *f*
permanent ['pə:mənənt] *adj* permanente; **permanently** *adv* (*lastingly*) para siempre, de modo definitivo; (*all the time*) permanentemente
permission [pə'mɪʃən] *n* permiso
permit [*n* 'pə:mɪt, *vt* pə'mɪt] *n* permiso, licencia ▷ *vt* permitir
perplex [pə'plɛks] *vt* dejar perplejo
persecute ['pə:sɪkju:t] *vt* perseguir
persecution [pə:sɪ'kju:ʃən] *n* persecución *f*
persevere [pə:sɪ'vɪə*] *vi* persistir
Persian ['pə:ʃən] *adj, n* persa *mf*; **the ~ Gulf** el Golfo Pérsico
persist [pə'sɪst] *vi*: **to ~ (in doing sth)** persistir (en hacer algo); **persistent** *adj* persistente; (*determined*) porfiado
person ['pə:sn] *n* persona; **in ~** en persona; **personal** *adj* personal; individual; (*visit*) en persona; **personal assistant** *n* ayudante *mf* personal; **personal computer** *n* ordenador *m* personal; **personality** [-'nælɪtɪ] *n* personalidad *f*; **personally** *adv* personalmente; (*in person*) en persona; **to take sth personally** tomarse algo a mal; **personal organizer** *n* agenda; **personal stereo** *n* Walkman® *m*
personnel [pə:sə'nɛl] *n* personal *m*
perspective [pə'spɛktɪv] *n* perspectiva
perspiration [pə:spɪ'reɪʃən] *n* transpiración *f*
persuade [pə'sweɪd] *vt*: **to ~ sb to do sth** persuadir a algn para que haga algo
persuasion [pə'sweɪʒən] *n* persuasión *f*; (*persuasiveness*) persuasiva
persuasive [pə'sweɪsɪv] *adj* persuasivo
perverse [pə'və:s] *adj* perverso; (*wayward*) travieso
pervert [*n* 'pə:və:t, *vb* pə'və:t] *n* pervertido/a ▷ *vt* pervertir; (*truth, sb's words*) tergiversar
pessimism ['pɛsɪmɪzəm] *n* pesimismo
pessimist ['pɛsɪmɪst] *n* pesimista *mf*; **pessimistic** [-'mɪstɪk] *adj* pesimista
pest [pɛst] *n* (*insect*) insecto nocivo; (*fig*) lata, molestia
pester ['pɛstə*] *vt* molestar, acosar
pesticide ['pɛstɪsaɪd] *n* pesticida *m*
pet [pɛt] *n* animal *m* doméstico ▷ *cpd* favorito ▷ *vt* acariciar; **teacher's ~** favorito/a (del profesor); **~ hate** manía
petal ['pɛtl] *n* pétalo
petite [pə'ti:t] *adj* chiquita
petition [pə'tɪʃən] *n* petición *f*
petrified ['pɛtrɪfaɪd] *adj* horrorizado
petrol ['pɛtrəl] (BRIT) *n* gasolina
petroleum [pə'trəulɪəm] *n* petróleo
petrol: petrol pump (BRIT) *n* (*in garage*) surtidor *m* de gasolina; **petrol station** (BRIT) *n* gasolinera; **petrol tank** (BRIT) *n* depósito (de gasolina)
petticoat ['pɛtɪkəut] *n* enaguas *fpl*
petty ['pɛtɪ] *adj* (*mean*) mezquino; (*unimportant*) insignificante
pew [pju:] *n* banco
pewter ['pju:tə*] *n* peltre *m*
phantom ['fæntəm] *n* fantasma *m*
pharmacist ['fɑ:məsɪst] *n* farmacéutico/a
pharmacy ['fɑ:məsɪ] *n* farmacia
phase [feɪz] *n* fase *f*; **phase in** *vt* introducir progresivamente; **phase out** *vt* (*machinery, product*) retirar progresivamente; (*job, subsidy*) eliminar por etapas
Ph.D. *abbr* = **Doctor of Philosophy**
pheasant ['fɛznt] *n* faisán *m*
phenomena [fə'nɔmɪnə] *npl of* **phenomenon**
phenomenal [fɪ'nɔmɪnl] *adj* fenomenal, extraordinario
phenomenon [fə'nɔmɪnən] (*pl* **phenomena**) *n* fenómeno
Philippines ['fɪlɪpi:nz] *npl*: **the ~** las

Filipinas
philosopher [fɪ'lɔsəfə*] *n* filósofo/a
philosophical [fɪlə'sɔfɪkl] *adj* filosófico
philosophy [fɪ'lɔsəfɪ] *n* filosofía
phlegm [flɛm] *n* flema
phobia ['fəubjə] *n* fobia
phone [fəun] *n* teléfono ▷ *vt* telefonear, llamar por teléfono; **to be on the ~** tener teléfono; (*be calling*) estar hablando por teléfono; **phone back** *vt, vi* volver a llamar; **phone up** *vt, vi* llamar por teléfono; **phone book** *n* guía telefónica; **phone booth** *n* cabina telefónica; **phone box** (BRIT) *n* = **phone booth**; **phone call** *n* llamada (telefónica); **phonecard** *n* teletarjeta; **phone number** *n* número de teléfono
phonetics [fə'nɛtɪks] *n* fonética
phoney ['fəunɪ] *adj* falso
photo ['fəutəu] *n* foto *f*; **photo album** *n* álbum *m* de fotos; **photocopier** *n* fotocopiadora; **photocopy** *n* fotocopia ▷ *vt* fotocopiar
photograph ['fəutəgrɑːf] *n* fotografía ▷ *vt* fotografiar; **photographer** [fə'tɔgrəfə*] *n* fotógrafo; **photography** [fə'tɔgrəfɪ] *n* fotografía
phrase [freɪz] *n* frase *f* ▷ *vt* expresar; **phrase book** *n* libro de frases
physical ['fɪzɪkl] *adj* físico; **physical education** *n* educación *f* física; **physically** *adv* físicamente
physician [fɪ'zɪʃən] *n* médico/a
physicist ['fɪzɪsɪst] *n* físico/a
physics ['fɪzɪks] *n* física
physiotherapist [fɪzɪəu'θɛrəpɪst] *n* fisioterapeuta
physiotherapy [fɪzɪəu'θɛrəpɪ] *n* fisioterapia
physique [fɪ'ziːk] *n* físico
pianist ['piːənɪst] *n* pianista *mf*
piano [pɪ'ænəu] *n* piano
pick [pɪk] *n* (*tool*: *also*: **~-axe**) pico, piqueta ▷ *vt* (*select*) elegir, escoger; (*gather*) coger (SP), recoger; (*remove, take out*) sacar, quitar; (*lock*) abrir con ganzúa; **take your ~** escoja lo que quiera; **the ~ of** lo mejor de; **to ~ one's nose/teeth** hurgarse las narices/ limpiarse los dientes; **to ~ a quarrel with sb** meterse con algn; **pick on** *vt fus* (*person*) meterse con; **pick out** *vt* escoger; (*distinguish*) identificar; **pick up** *vi* (*improve*: *sales*) ir mejor; (: *patient*) reponerse; (*Finance*) recobrarse ▷ *vt* recoger; (*learn*) aprender; (*Police*: *arrest*) detener; (*person*: *for sex*) ligar; (*Radio*) captar; **to pick up speed** acelerarse; **to pick o.s. up** levantarse
pickle ['pɪkl] *n* (*also*: **~s**: *as condiment*) escabeche *m*; (*fig*: *mess*) apuro ▷ *vt* encurtir
pickpocket ['pɪkpɔkɪt] *n* carterista *mf*
pick-up ['pɪkʌp] *n* (*also*: **~ truck**) furgoneta, camioneta
picnic ['pɪknɪk] *n* merienda ▷ *vi* ir de merienda; **picnic area** *n* zona de picnic; (*Aut*) área de descanso
picture ['pɪktʃə*] *n* cuadro; (*painting*) pintura; (*photograph*) fotografía; (*TV*) imagen *f*; (*film*) película; (*fig*: *description*) descripción *f*; (: *situation*) situación *f* ▷ *vt* (*imagine*) imaginar; **pictures** *npl*: **the ~s** (BRIT) el cine; **picture frame** *n* marco; **picture messaging** *n* (envío de) mensajes con imágenes
picturesque [pɪktʃə'rɛsk] *adj* pintoresco
pie [paɪ] *n* pastel *m*; (*open*) tarta; (*small*: *of meat*) empanada
piece [piːs] *n* pedazo, trozo; (*of cake*) trozo; (*item*): **a ~ of clothing/ furniture/advice** una prenda (de vestir)/un mueble/un consejo ▷ *vt*: **to ~ together** juntar; (*Tech*) armar; **to take to ~s** desmontar
pie chart *n* gráfico de sectores *or* tarta
pier [pɪə*] *n* muelle *m*, embarcadero
pierce [pɪəs] *vt* perforar; **pierced** *adj*: **I've got pierced ears** tengo los agujeros hechos en las orejas
pig [pɪg] *n* cerdo, chancho (LAM);

(*pej*: *unkind person*) asqueroso; (: *greedy person*) glotón/ona *m/f*
pigeon ['pɪdʒən] *n* paloma; (*as food*) pichón *m*
piggy bank ['pɪgɪ-] *n* hucha (*en forma de cerdito*)
pigsty ['pɪgstaɪ] *n* pocilga
pigtail *n* (*girl's*) trenza
pike [paɪk] *n* (*fish*) lucio
pilchard ['pɪltʃəd] *n* sardina
pile [paɪl] *n* montón *m*; (*of carpet, cloth*) pelo; **pile up** *vi +adv* (*accumulate*: *work*) amontonarse, acumularse ▷ *vt +adv* (*put in a heap*: *books, clothes*) apilar, amontonar; (*accumulate*) acumular; **piles** *npl* (*Med*) almorranas *fpl*, hemorroides *mpl*; **pile-up** *n* (*Aut*) accidente *m* múltiple
pilgrimage ['pɪlgrɪmɪdʒ] *n* peregrinación *f*, romería
pill [pɪl] *n* píldora; **the ~** la píldora
pillar ['pɪlə*] *n* pilar *m*
pillow ['pɪləu] *n* almohada; **pillowcase** *n* funda
pilot ['paɪlət] *n* piloto ▷ *cpd* (*scheme etc*) piloto ▷ *vt* pilotar; **pilot light** *n* piloto
pimple ['pɪmpl] *n* grano
PIN *n abbr* (= *personal identification number*) número personal
pin [pɪn] *n* alfiler *m* ▷ *vt* prender (con alfiler); **~s and needles** hormigueo; **to ~ sb down** (*fig*) hacer que algn concrete; **to ~ sth on sb** (*fig*) colgarle a algn el sambenito de algo
pinafore ['pɪnəfɔː*] *n* delantal *m*
pinch [pɪntʃ] *n* (*of salt etc*) pizca ▷ *vt* pellizcar; (*inf*: *steal*) birlar; **at a ~** en caso de apuro
pine [paɪn] *n* (*also*: **~ tree**) pino ▷ *vi*: **to ~ for** suspirar por
pineapple ['paɪnæpl] *n* piña, ananás *m*
ping [pɪŋ] *n* (*noise*) sonido agudo; **ping-pong**® *n* pingpong® *m*
pink [pɪŋk] *adj* rosado, (color de) rosa ▷ *n* (*colour*) rosa; (*Bot*) clavel *m*, clavellina
pinpoint ['pɪnpɔɪnt] *vt* precisar
pint [paɪnt] *n* pinta (BRIT = *568cc*, US = *473cc*); (BRIT: *inf*: *of beer*) pinta de cerveza ≈ jarra (SP)
pioneer [paɪə'nɪə*] *n* pionero/a
pious ['paɪəs] *adj* piadoso, devoto
pip [pɪp] *n* (*seed*) pepita; **the ~s** (BRIT) la señal
pipe [paɪp] *n* tubo, caño; (*for smoking*) pipa ▷ *vt* conducir en cañerías; **pipeline** *n* (*for oil*) oleoducto; (*for gas*) gasoducto; **piper** *n* gaitero/a
pirate ['paɪərət] *n* pirata *mf* ▷ *vt* (*cassette, book*) piratear
Pisces ['paɪsiːz] *n* Piscis *m*
piss [pɪs] (*inf!*) *vi* mear; **pissed** (*inf!*) *adj* (*drunk*) borracho
pistol ['pɪstl] *n* pistola
piston ['pɪstən] *n* pistón *m*, émbolo
pit [pɪt] *n* hoyo; (*also*: **coal ~**) mina; (*in garage*) foso de inspección; (*also*: **orchestra ~**) platea ▷ *vt*: **to ~ one's wits against sb** medir fuerzas con algn
pitch [pɪtʃ] *n* (*Mus*) tono; (BRIT *Sport*) campo, terreno; (*fig*) punto; (*tar*) brea ▷ *vt* (*throw*) arrojar, lanzar ▷ *vi* (*fall*) caer(se); **to ~ a tent** montar una tienda (de campaña); **pitch-black** *adj* negro como boca de lobo
pitfall ['pɪtfɔːl] *n* riesgo
pith [pɪθ] *n* (*of orange*) médula
pitiful ['pɪtɪful] *adj* (*touching*) lastimoso, conmovedor(a)
pity ['pɪtɪ] *n* compasión *f*, piedad *f* ▷ *vt* compadecer(se de); **what a ~!** ¡qué pena!
pizza ['piːtsə] *n* pizza
placard ['plækɑːd] *n* letrero; (*in march etc*) pancarta
place [pleɪs] *n* lugar *m*, sitio; (*seat*) plaza, asiento; (*post*) puesto; (*home*): **at/to his ~** en/a su casa; (*role*: *in society etc*) papel *m* ▷ *vt* (*object*) poner, colocar; (*identify*) reconocer; **to take ~** tener lugar; **to be ~d** (*in race, exam*) colocarse; **out of ~** (*not suitable*) fuera de lugar; **in the first ~** en primer lugar; **to change ~s with sb** cambiarse de

sitio con algn; **~ of birth** lugar *m* de nacimiento; **place mat** *n* (*wooden etc*) salvamanteles *m inv*; (*linen etc*) mantel *m* individual; **placement** *n* (*positioning*) colocación *f*; (*at work*) emplazamiento

placid ['plæsɪd] *adj* apacible

plague [pleɪg] *n* plaga; (*Med*) peste *f* ▷ *vt* (*fig*) acosar, atormentar

plaice [pleɪs] *n inv* platija

plain [pleɪn] *adj* (*unpatterned*) liso; (*clear*) claro, evidente; (*simple*) sencillo; (*not handsome*) poco atractivo ▷ *adv* claramente ▷ *n* llano, llanura; **plain chocolate** *n* chocolate *m* amargo; **plainly** *adv* claramente

plaintiff ['pleɪntɪf] *n* demandante *mf*

plait [plæt] *n* trenza

plan [plæn] *n* (*drawing*) plano; (*scheme*) plan *m*, proyecto ▷ *vt* proyectar, planificar ▷ *vi* hacer proyectos; **to ~ to do** pensar hacer

plane [pleɪn] *n* (*Aviat*) avión *m*; (*Math, fig*) plano; (*also*: **~ tree**) plátano; (*tool*) cepillo

planet ['plænɪt] *n* planeta *m*

plank [plæŋk] *n* tabla

planning ['plænɪŋ] *n* planificación *f*; **family ~** planificación familiar

plant [plɑːnt] *n* planta; (*machinery*) maquinaria; (*factory*) fábrica ▷ *vt* plantar; (*field*) sembrar; (*bomb*) colocar

plantation [plæn'teɪʃən] *n* plantación *f*; (*estate*) hacienda

plaque [plæk] *n* placa

plaster ['plɑːstə*] *n* (*for walls*) yeso; (*also*: **~ of Paris**) yeso mate, escayola (SP); (BRIT: *also*: **sticking ~**) tirita (SP), curita (LAM) ▷ *vt* enyesar; (*cover*): **to ~ with** llenar *or* cubrir de; **plaster cast** *n* (*Med*) escayola; (*model, statue*) vaciado de yeso

plastic ['plæstɪk] *n* plástico ▷ *adj* de plástico; **plastic bag** *n* bolsa de plástico; **plastic surgery** *n* cirujía plástica

plate [pleɪt] *n* (*dish*) plato; (*metal, in book*) lámina; (*dental plate*) placa de dentadura postiza

plateau ['plætəu] (*pl* **~s** *or* **~x**) *n* meseta, altiplanicie *f*

platform ['plætfɔːm] *n* (*Rail*) andén *m*; (*stage*, BRIT: *on bus*) plataforma; (*at meeting*) tribuna; (*Pol*) programa *m* (electoral)

platinum ['plætɪnəm] *adj, n* platino

platoon [plə'tuːn] *n* pelotón *m*

platter ['plætə*] *n* fuente *f*

plausible ['plɔːzɪbl] *adj* verosímil; (*person*) convincente

play [pleɪ] *n* (*Theatre*) obra, comedia ▷ *vt* (*game*) jugar; (*compete against*) jugar contra; (*instrument*) tocar; (*part*: *in play etc*) hacer el papel de; (*tape, record*) poner ▷ *vi* jugar; (*band*) tocar; (*tape, record*) sonar; **to ~ safe** ir a lo seguro; **play back** *vt* (*tape*) poner; **play up** *vi* (*cause trouble to*) dar guerra; **player** *n* jugador(a) *m/f*; (*Theatre*) actor(actriz) *m/f*; (*Mus*) músico/a; **playful** *adj* juguetón/ona; **playground** *n* (*in school*) patio de recreo; (*in park*) parque *m* infantil; **playgroup** *n* jardín *m* de niños; **playing card** *n* naipe *m*, carta; **playing field** *n* campo de deportes; **playschool** *n* = **playgroup**; **playtime** *n* (*Scol*) recreo; **playwright** *n* dramaturgo/a

plc *abbr* (= *public limited company*) ≈ S.A.

plea [pliː] *n* súplica, petición *f*; (*Law*) alegato, defensa

plead [pliːd] *vt* (*Law*): **to ~ sb's case** defender a algn; (*give as excuse*) poner como pretexto ▷ *vi* (*Law*) declararse; (*beg*): **to ~ with sb** suplicar *or* rogar a algn

pleasant ['plɛznt] *adj* agradable

please [pliːz] *excl* ¡por favor! ▷ *vt* (*give pleasure to*) dar gusto a, agradar ▷ *vi* (*think fit*): **do as you ~** haz lo que quieras; **~ yourself!** (*inf*) ¡haz lo que quieras!, ¡como quieras!; **pleased** *adj* (*happy*) alegre, contento; **pleased (with)** satisfecho (de); **pleased to meet you** ¡encantado!, ¡tanto gusto!

pleasure ['plɛʒə*] *n* placer *m*, gusto;

"it's a ~" "el gusto es mío"

pleat [pli:t] *n* pliegue *m*

pledge [plɛdʒ] *n* (*promise*) promesa, voto ▷ *vt* prometer

plentiful ['plɛntɪful] *adj* copioso, abundante

plenty ['plɛntɪ] *n*: **~ of** mucho(s)/a(s)

pliers ['plaɪəz] *npl* alicates *mpl*, tenazas *fpl*

plight [plaɪt] *n* situación *f* difícil

plod [plɔd] *vi* caminar con paso pesado; (*fig*) trabajar laboriosamente

plonk [plɔŋk] (*inf*) *n* (BRIT: *wine*) vino peleón ▷ *vt*: **to ~ sth down** dejar caer algo

plot [plɔt] *n* (*scheme*) complot *m*, conjura; (*of story, play*) argumento; (*of land*) terreno ▷ *vt* (*mark out*) trazar; (*conspire*) tramar, urdir ▷ *vi* conspirar

plough [plau] (US **plow**) *n* arado ▷ *vt* (*earth*) arar; **to ~ money into** invertir dinero en; **ploughman's lunch** (BRIT) *n almuerzo de pub a base de pan, queso y encurtidos*

plow [plau] (US) = **plough**

ploy [plɔɪ] *n* truco, estratagema

pluck [plʌk] *vt* (*fruit*) coger (SP), recoger (LAM); (*musical instrument*) puntear; (*bird*) desplumar; (*eyebrows*) depilar; **to ~ up courage** hacer de tripas corazón

plug [plʌg] *n* tapón *m*; (*Elec*) enchufe *m*, clavija; (*Aut*: *also*: **spark(ing) ~**) bujía ▷ *vt* (*hole*) tapar; (*inf*: *advertise*) dar publicidad a; **plug in** *vt* (*Elec*) enchufar; **plughole** *n* desagüe *m*

plum [plʌm] *n* (*fruit*) ciruela

plumber ['plʌmə*] *n* fontanero/a (SP, CAM), plomero/a (LAM)

plumbing ['plʌmɪŋ] *n* (*trade*) fontanería, plomería; (*piping*) cañería

plummet ['plʌmɪt] *vi*: **to ~ (down)** caer a plomo

plump [plʌmp] *adj* rechoncho, rollizo ▷ *vi*: **to ~ for** (*inf*: *choose*) optar por

plunge [plʌndʒ] *n* zambullida ▷ *vt* sumergir, hundir ▷ *vi* (*fall*) caer; (*dive*) saltar; (*person*) arrojarse; **to take the ~** lanzarse

plural ['pluərl] *adj* plural ▷ *n* plural *m*

plus [plʌs] *n* (*also*: **~ sign**) signo más ▷ *prep* más, y, además de; **ten/twenty ~** más de diez/veinte

ply [plaɪ] *vt* (*a trade*) ejercer ▷ *vi* (*ship*) ir y venir ▷ *n* (*of wool, rope*) cabo; **to ~ sb with drink** insistir en ofrecer a algn muchas copas; **plywood** *n* madera contrachapada

P.M. *n abbr* = **Prime Minister**

p.m. *adv abbr* (= *post meridiem*) de la tarde *or* noche

PMS *n abbr* (= *premenstrual syndrome*) SPM *m*

PMT *n abbr* (= *premenstrual tension*) SPM *m*

pneumatic drill [nju:'mætɪk-] *n* martillo neumático

pneumonia [nju:'məunɪə] *n* pulmonía

poach [pəutʃ] *vt* (*cook*) escalfar; (*steal*) cazar (*or* pescar) en vedado ▷ *vi* cazar (*or* pescar) en vedado; **poached** *adj* escalfado

P.O. Box *n abbr* (= *Post Office Box*) apdo., aptdo.

pocket ['pɔkɪt] *n* bolsillo; (*fig*: *small area*) bolsa ▷ *vt* meter en el bolsillo; (*steal*) embolsar; **to be out of ~** (BRIT) salir perdiendo; **pocketbook** (US) *n* cartera; **pocket money** *n* asignación *f*

pod [pɔd] *n* vaina

podiatrist [pɔ'di:ətrɪst] (US) *n* pedicuro/a

podium ['pəudɪəm] *n* podio

poem ['pəuɪm] *n* poema *m*

poet ['pəuɪt] *n* poeta *m/f*; **poetic** [-'ɛtɪk] *adj* poético; **poetry** *n* poesía

poignant ['pɔɪnjənt] *adj* conmovedor(a)

point [pɔɪnt] *n* punto; (*tip*) punta; (*purpose*) fin *m*, propósito; (*use*) utilidad *f*; (*significant part*) lo significativo; (*moment*) momento; (*Elec*) toma (de corriente); (*also*: **decimal ~**): **2 ~ 3 (2.3)** dos coma tres (2,3) ▷ *vt* señalar; (*gun etc*): **to ~ sth at sb** apuntar algo a algn ▷ *vi*: **to ~ at** señalar; **points** *npl* (*Aut*) contactos *mpl*; (*Rail*) agujas *fpl*; **to be on the ~ of doing sth** estar a punto de hacer algo; **to make a ~ of** poner empeño en; **to get/miss the ~** comprender/no comprender; **to come to the ~** ir al meollo; **there's no ~ (in doing)** no tiene sentido (hacer); **point out** *vt* señalar; **point-blank** *adv* (*say, refuse*) sin más hablar; (*also*: **at point-blank range**) a quemarropa; **pointed** *adj* (*shape*) puntiagudo, afilado; (*remark*) intencionado; **pointer** *n* (*needle*) aguja, indicador *m*; **pointless** *adj* sin sentido; **point of view** *n* punto de vista

poison ['pɔɪzn] *n* veneno ▷ *vt* envenenar; **poisonous** *adj* venenoso; (*fumes etc*) tóxico

poke [pəuk] *vt* (*jab with finger, stick etc*) empujar; (*put*): **to ~ sth in(to)** introducir algo en; **poke about** *or* **around** *vi* fisgonear; **poke out** *vi* (*stick out*) salir

poker ['pəukə*] *n* atizador *m*; (*Cards*) póker *m*

Poland ['pəulənd] *n* Polonia

polar ['pəulə*] *adj* polar; **polar bear** *n* oso polar

Pole [pəul] *n* polaco/a

pole [pəul] *n* palo; (*fixed*) poste *m*; (*Geo*) polo; **pole bean** (*US*) *n* ≈ judía verde; **pole vault** *n* salto con pértiga

police [pə'li:s] *n* policía ▷ *vt* vigilar; **police car** *n* coche-patrulla *m*; **police constable** (*BRIT*) *n* guardia *m*, policía *m*; **police force** *n* cuerpo de policía; **policeman** (*irreg*) *n* policía *m*, guardia *m*; **police officer** *n* guardia *m*, policía *m*; **police station** *n* comisaría; **policewoman** (*irreg*) *n* mujer *f* policía

policy ['pɔlɪsɪ] *n* política; (*also*: **insurance ~**) póliza

polio ['pəulɪəu] *n* polio *f*

Polish ['pəulɪʃ] *adj* polaco ▷ *n* (*Ling*) polaco

polish ['pɔlɪʃ] *n* (*for shoes*) betún *m*; (*for floor*) cera (de lustrar); (*shine*) brillo, lustre *m*; (*fig*: *refinement*) educación *f* ▷ *vt* (*shoes*) limpiar; (*make shiny*) pulir, sacar brillo a; **polish off** *vt* (*food*) despachar; **polished** *adj* (*fig*: *person*) elegante

polite [pə'laɪt] *adj* cortés, atento; **politeness** *n* cortesía

political [pə'lɪtɪkl] *adj* político; **politically** *adv* políticamente; **politically correct** políticamente correcto

politician [pɔlɪ'tɪʃən] *n* político/a

politics ['pɔlɪtɪks] *n* política

poll [pəul] *n* (*election*) votación *f*; (*also*: **opinion ~**) sondeo, encuesta ▷ *vt* encuestar; (*votes*) obtener

pollen ['pɔlən] *n* polen *m*

polling station ['pəulɪŋ-] *n* centro electoral

pollute [pə'lu:t] *vt* contaminar

pollution [pə'lu:ʃən] *n* polución *f*, contaminación *f* del medio ambiente

polo ['pəuləu] *n* (*sport*) polo; **polo-neck** *adj* de cuello vuelto ▷ *n* (*sweater*) suéter *m* de cuello vuelto; **polo shirt** *n* polo, niqui *m*

polyester [pɔlɪ'ɛstə*] *n* poliéster *m*

polystyrene [pɔlɪ'staɪri:n] *n* poliestireno

polythene ['pɔlɪθi:n] (*BRIT*) *n* politeno; **polythene bag** *n* bolsa de plástico

pomegranate ['pɔmɪgrænɪt] *n* granada

pompous ['pɔmpəs] *adj* pomposo

pond [pɔnd] *n* (*natural*) charca; (*artificial*) estanque *m*

ponder ['pɔndə*] *vt* meditar

pony ['pəunɪ] *n* poni *m*; **ponytail** *n* coleta; **pony trekking** (*BRIT*) *n* excursión *f* a caballo

poodle ['pu:dl] *n* caniche *m*

pool [pu:l] *n* (*natural*) charca; (*also*: **swimming ~**) piscina, alberca (*MEX*), pileta (*RPL*); (*fig*: *of light etc*) charco; (*Sport*) chapolín *m* ▷ *vt* juntar; **pools** *npl* quinielas *fpl*

poor [puə*] *adj* pobre; (*bad*) de mala

calidad ▷ *npl*: **the ~** los pobres; **poorly** *adj* mal, enfermo ▷ *adv* mal

pop [pɔp] *n* (*sound*) ruido seco; (*Mus*) (música) pop *m*; (*inf*: *father*) papá *m*; (*drink*) gaseosa ▷ *vt* (*put quickly*) meter (de prisa) ▷ *vi* reventar; (*cork*) saltar; **pop in** *vi* entrar un momento; **pop out** *vi* salir un momento; **popcorn** *n* palomitas *fpl*

poplar ['pɔplə*] *n* álamo

popper ['pɔpə*] (BRIT) *n* automático

poppy ['pɔpɪ] *n* amapola

Popsicle® ['pɔpsɪkl] (US) *n* polo

pop star *n* estrella del pop

popular ['pɔpjulə*] *adj* popular; **popularity** [pɔpju'lærɪtɪ] *n* popularidad *f*

population [pɔpju'leɪʃən] *n* población *f*

pop-up ['pɔpʌp] (*Comput*) *adj* (*menu, window*) emergente ▷ *n* ventana emergente, (ventana *f*) pop-up *f*

porcelain ['pɔːslɪn] *n* porcelana

porch [pɔːtʃ] *n* pórtico, entrada; (US) veranda

pore [pɔː*] *n* poro ▷ *vi*: **to ~ over** engolfarse en

pork [pɔːk] *n* carne *f* de cerdo *or* (LAM) chancho; **pork chop** *n* chuleta de cerdo; **pork pie** *n* (BRIT: *Culin*) empanada de carne de cerdo

porn [pɔːn] *adj* (*inf*) porno *inv* ▷ *n* porno; **pornographic** [pɔːnə'græfɪk] *adj* pornográfico; **pornography** [pɔː'nɔgrəfɪ] *n* pornografía

porridge ['pɔrɪdʒ] *n* gachas *fpl* de avena

port [pɔːt] *n* puerto; (*Naut*: *left side*) babor *m*; (*wine*) vino de Oporto; **~ of call** puerto de escala

portable ['pɔːtəbl] *adj* portátil

porter ['pɔːtə*] *n* (*for luggage*) maletero; (*doorkeeper*) portero/a, conserje *m/f*

portfolio [pɔːt'fəulɪəu] *n* cartera

portion ['pɔːʃən] *n* porción *f*; (*of food*) ración *f*

portrait ['pɔːtreɪt] *n* retrato

portray [pɔː'treɪ] *vt* retratar; (*actor*) representar

Portugal ['pɔːtjugl] *n* Portugal *m*

Portuguese [pɔːtju'giːz] *adj* portugués/esa ▷ *n inv* portugués/esa *m/f*; (*Ling*) portugués *m*

pose [pəuz] *n* postura, actitud *f* ▷ *vi* (*pretend*): **to ~ as** hacerse pasar por ▷ *vt* (*question*) plantear; **to ~ for** posar para

posh [pɔʃ] (*inf*) *adj* elegante, de lujo

position [pə'zɪʃən] *n* posición *f*; (*job*) puesto; (*situation*) situación *f* ▷ *vt* colocar

positive ['pɔzɪtɪv] *adj* positivo; (*certain*) seguro; (*definite*) definitivo; **positively** *adv* (*affirmatively, enthusiastically*) de forma positiva; (*inf*: *really*) absolutamente

possess [pə'zɛs] *vt* poseer; **possession** [pə'zɛʃən] *n* posesión *f*; **possessions** *npl* (*belongings*) pertenencias *fpl*; **possessive** *adj* posesivo

possibility [pɔsɪ'bɪlɪtɪ] *n* posibilidad *f*

possible ['pɔsɪbl] *adj* posible; **as big as ~** lo más grande posible; **possibly** *adv* posiblemente; **I cannot possibly come** me es imposible venir

post [pəust] *n* (BRIT: *system*) correos *mpl*; (BRIT: *letters, delivery*) correo; (*job, situation*) puesto; (*pole*) poste *m* ▷ *vt* (BRIT: *send by post*) echar al correo; (BRIT: *appoint*): **to ~ to** enviar a; **postage** *n* porte *m*, franqueo; **postal** *adj* postal, de correos; **postal order** *n* giro postal; **postbox** (BRIT) *n* buzón *m*; **postcard** *n* tarjeta postal; **postcode** (BRIT) *n* código postal

poster ['pəustə*] *n* cartel *m*

postgraduate ['pəust'grædjuət] *n* posgraduado/a

postman ['pəustmən] (BRIT: *irreg*) *n* cartero

postmark ['pəustmɑːk] *n* matasellos *m inv*

post-mortem [-'mɔːtəm] *n* autopsia

post office *n* (*building*) (oficina de) correos *m*; (*organization*): **the Post Office** Correos *m inv* (SP), Dirección *f* General de Correos (LAM)
postpone [pəs'pəun] *vt* aplazar
posture ['pɔstʃə*] *n* postura, actitud *f*
postwoman ['pəustwumən] (BRIT: *irreg*) *n* cartera
pot [pɔt] *n* (*for cooking*) olla; (*teapot*) tetera; (*coffeepot*) cafetera; (*for flowers*) maceta; (*for jam*) tarro, pote *m*; (*inf*: *marijuana*) chocolate *m* ▷ *vt* (*plant*) poner en tiesto; **to go to ~** (*inf*) irse al traste
potato [pə'teɪtəu] (*pl* **~es**) *n* patata (SP), papa (LAM); **potato peeler** *n* pelapatatas *m inv*
potent ['pəutnt] *adj* potente, poderoso; (*drink*) fuerte
potential [pə'tɛnʃl] *adj* potencial, posible ▷ *n* potencial *m*
pothole ['pɔthəul] *n* (*in road*) bache *m*; (BRIT: *underground*) gruta
pot plant ['pɔtplɑːnt] *n* planta de interior
potter ['pɔtə*] *n* alfarero/a ▷ *vi*: **to ~ around** *or* **about** (BRIT) hacer trabajitos; **pottery** *n* cerámica; (*factory*) alfarería
potty ['pɔtɪ] *n* orinal *m* de niño
pouch [pautʃ] *n* (*Zool*) bolsa; (*for tobacco*) petaca
poultry ['pəultrɪ] *n* aves *fpl* de corral; (*meat*) pollo
pounce [pauns] *vi*: **to ~ on** precipitarse sobre
pound [paund] *n* libra (*weight = 453g or 16oz; money = 100 pence*) ▷ *vt* (*beat*) golpear; (*crush*) machacar ▷ *vi* (*heart*) latir; **pound sterling** *n* libra esterlina
pour [pɔː*] *vt* echar; (*tea etc*) servir ▷ *vi* correr, fluir; **to ~ sb a drink** servirle a algn una copa; **pour in** *vi* (*people*) entrar en tropel; **pour out** *vi* salir en tropel ▷ *vt* (*drink*) echar, servir; (*fig*): **to pour out one's feelings** desahogarse; **pouring** *adj*: **pouring rain** lluvia torrencial
pout [paut] *vi* hacer pucheros
poverty ['pɔvətɪ] *n* pobreza, miseria
powder ['paudə*] *n* polvo; (*also*: **face ~**) polvos *mpl* ▷ *vt* polvorear; **to ~ one's face** empolvarse la cara; **powdered milk** *n* leche *f* en polvo
power ['pauə*] *n* poder *m*; (*strength*) fuerza; (*nation, Tech*) potencia; (*drive*) empuje *m*; (*Elec*) fuerza, energía ▷ *vt* impulsar; **to be in ~** (*Pol*) estar en el poder; **power cut** (BRIT) *n* apagón *m*; **power failure** *n* = **power cut**; **powerful** *adj* poderoso; (*engine*) potente; (*speech etc*) convincente; **powerless** *adj*: **powerless (to do)** incapaz (de hacer); **power point** (BRIT) *n* enchufe *m*; **power station** *n* central *f* eléctrica
p.p. *abbr* (= *per procurationem*); **p.p. J. Smith** p.p. (por poder de) J. Smith; (= *pages*) págs
PR *n abbr* = **public relations**
practical ['præktɪkl] *adj* práctico; **practical joke** *n* broma pesada; **practically** *adv* (*almost*) casi
practice ['præktɪs] *n* (*habit*) costumbre *f*; (*exercise*) práctica, ejercicio; (*training*) adiestramiento; (*Med*: *of profession*) práctica, ejercicio; (*Med, Law*: *business*) consulta ▷ *vt*, *vi* (US) = **practise**; **in ~** (*in reality*) en la práctica; **out of ~** desentrenado
practise ['præktɪs] (US **practice**) *vt* (*carry out*) practicar; (*profession*) ejercer; (*train at*) practicar ▷ *vi* ejercer; (*train*) practicar; **practising** *adj* (*Christian etc*) practicante; (*lawyer*) en ejercicio
practitioner [præk'tɪʃənə*] *n* (*Med*) médico/a
pragmatic [præg'mætɪk] *adj* pragmático
prairie ['prɛərɪ] *n* pampa
praise [preɪz] *n* alabanza(s) *f(pl)*, elogio(s) *m(pl)* ▷ *vt* alabar, elogiar
pram [præm] (BRIT) *n* cochecito de niño
prank [præŋk] *n* travesura
prawn [prɔːn] *n* gamba; **prawn**

cocktail *n* cóctel *m* de gambas
pray [preɪ] *vi* rezar; **prayer** [prɛə*] *n* oración *f*, rezo; (*entreaty*) ruego, súplica
preach [pri:tʃ] *vi* predicar; **preacher** *n* predicador(a) *m/f*
precarious [prɪ'kɛərɪəs] *adj* precario
precaution [prɪ'kɔ:ʃən] *n* precaución *f*
precede [prɪ'si:d] *vt, vi* preceder; **precedent** ['prɛsɪdənt] *n* precedente *m*; **preceding** [prɪ'si:dɪŋ] *adj* anterior
precinct ['pri:sɪŋkt] *n* recinto
precious ['prɛʃəs] *adj* precioso
precise [prɪ'saɪs] *adj* preciso, exacto; **precisely** *adv* precisamente, exactamente
precision [prɪ'sɪʒən] *n* precisión *f*
predator ['prɛdətə*] *n* depredador *m*
predecessor ['pri:dɪsɛsə*] *n* antecesor(a) *m/f*
predicament [prɪ'dɪkəmənt] *n* apuro
predict [prɪ'dɪkt] *vt* pronosticar; **predictable** *adj* previsible; **prediction** [-'dɪkʃən] *n* predicción *f*
predominantly [prɪ'dɔmɪnəntlɪ] *adv* en su mayoría
preface ['prɛfəs] *n* prefacio
prefect ['pri:fɛkt] (BRIT) *n* (*in school*) monitor(a) *m/f*
prefer [prɪ'fə:*] *vt* preferir; **to ~ doing** *or* **to do** preferir hacer; **preferable** ['prɛfrəbl] *adj* preferible; **preferably** ['prɛfrəblɪ] *adv* de preferencia; **preference** ['prɛfrəns] *n* preferencia; (*priority*) prioridad *f*
prefix ['pri:fɪks] *n* prefijo
pregnancy ['prɛgnənsɪ] *n* (*of woman*) embarazo; (*of animal*) preñez *f*
pregnant ['prɛgnənt] *adj* (*woman*) embarazada; (*animal*) preñada
prehistoric ['pri:hɪs'tɔrɪk] *adj* prehistórico
prejudice ['prɛdʒudɪs] *n* prejuicio; **prejudiced** *adj* (*person*) predispuesto
preliminary [prɪ'lɪmɪnərɪ] *adj* preliminar
prelude ['prɛlju:d] *n* preludio
premature ['prɛmətʃuə*] *adj* prematuro
premier ['prɛmɪə*] *adj* primero, principal ▷ *n* (*Pol*) primer(a) ministro/a
première ['prɛmɪɛə*] *n* estreno
Premier League [prɛmɪə'li:g] *n* primera división
premises ['prɛmɪsɪz] *npl* (*of business etc*) local *m*; **on the ~** en el lugar mismo
premium ['pri:mɪəm] *n* premio; (*insurance*) prima; **to be at a ~** ser muy solicitado
premonition [prɛmə'nɪʃən] *n* presentimiento
preoccupied [pri:'ɔkjupaɪd] *adj* ensimismado
prepaid [pri:'peɪd] *adj* porte pagado
preparation [prɛpə'reɪʃən] *n* preparación *f*; **preparations** *npl* preparativos *mpl*
preparatory school [prɪ'pærətərɪ-] *n* escuela preparatoria
prepare [prɪ'pɛə*] *vt* preparar, disponer; (*Culin*) preparar ▷ *vi*: **to ~ for** (*action*) prepararse *or* disponerse para; (*event*) hacer preparativos para; **~d to** dispuesto a; **~d for** listo para
preposition [prɛpə'zɪʃən] *n* preposición *f*
prep school [prɛp-] *n* = **preparatory school**
prerequisite [pri:'rɛkwɪzɪt] *n* requisito
preschool ['pri:'sku:l] *adj* preescolar
prescribe [prɪ'skraɪb] *vt* (*Med*) recetar
prescription [prɪ'skrɪpʃən] *n* (*Med*) receta
presence ['prɛzns] *n* presencia; **in sb's ~** en presencia de algn; **~ of mind** aplomo
present [*adj, n* 'prɛznt, *vb* prɪ'zɛnt] *adj* (*in attendance*) presente; (*current*) actual ▷ *n* (*gift*) regalo; (*actuality*): **the ~** la actualidad, el presente ▷ *vt* (*introduce, describe*) presentar; (*expound*) exponer; (*give*) presentar, dar, ofrecer; (*Theatre*)

representar; **to give sb a ~** regalar algo a algn; **at ~** actualmente; **presentable** [prɪ'zɛntəbl] *adj*: **to make o.s. presentable** arreglarse; **presentation** [-'teɪʃən] *n* presentación *f*; (*of report etc*) exposición *f*; (*formal ceremony*) entrega de un regalo; **present-day** *adj* actual; **presenter** [prɪ'zɛntə*] *n* (*Radio, TV*) locutor(a) *m/f*; **presently** *adv* (*soon*) dentro de poco; (*now*) ahora; **present participle** *n* participio (de) presente

preservation [prɛzə'veɪʃən] *n* conservación *f*

preservative [prɪ'zəːvətɪv] *n* conservante *m*

preserve [prɪ'zəːv] *vt* (*keep safe*) preservar, proteger; (*maintain*) mantener; (*food*) conservar ▷ *n* (*for game*) coto, vedado; (*often pl: jam*) conserva, confitura

preside [prɪ'zaɪd] *vi* presidir

president ['prɛzɪdənt] *n* presidente *m/f*; **presidential** [-'dɛnʃl] *adj* presidencial

press [prɛs] *n* (*newspapers*): **the P~** la prensa; (*printer's*) imprenta; (*of button*) pulsación *f* ▷ *vt* empujar; (*button etc*) apretar; (*clothes: iron*) planchar; (*put pressure on: person*) presionar; (*insist*): **to ~ sth on sb** insistir en que algn acepte algo ▷ *vi* (*squeeze*) apretar; (*pressurize*): **to ~ for** presionar por; **we are ~ed for time/money** estamos apurados de tiempo/dinero; **press conference** *n* rueda de prensa; **pressing** *adj* apremiante; **press stud** (BRIT) *n* botón *m* de presión; **press-up** (BRIT) *n* plancha

pressure ['prɛʃə*] *n* presión *f*; **to put ~ on sb** presionar a algn; **pressure cooker** *n* olla a presión; **pressure group** *n* grupo de presión

prestige [prɛs'tiːʒ] *n* prestigio

prestigious [prɛs'tɪdʒəs] *adj* prestigioso

presumably [prɪ'zjuːməblɪ] *adv* es de suponer que, cabe presumir que

presume [prɪ'zjuːm] *vt*: **to ~ (that)** presumir (que), suponer (que)

pretence [prɪ'tɛns] (US **pretense**) *n* fingimiento; **under false ~s** con engaños

pretend [prɪ'tɛnd] *vt, vi* (*feign*) fingir

Be careful not to translate **pretend** by the Spanish word *pretender*.

pretense [prɪ'tɛns] (US) *n* = **pretence**

pretentious [prɪ'tɛnʃəs] *adj* presumido; (*ostentatious*) ostentoso, aparatoso

pretext ['priːtɛkst] *n* pretexto

pretty ['prɪtɪ] *adj* bonito, lindo (LAM) ▷ *adv* bastante

prevail [prɪ'veɪl] *vi* (*gain mastery*) prevalecer; (*be current*) predominar; **prevailing** *adj* (*dominant*) predominante

prevalent ['prɛvələnt] *adj* (*widespread*) extendido

prevent [prɪ'vɛnt] *vt*: **to ~ sb from doing sth** impedir a algn hacer algo; **to ~ sth from happening** evitar que ocurra algo; **prevention** [prɪ'vɛnʃən] *n* prevención *f*; **preventive** *adj* preventivo

preview ['priːvjuː] *n* (*of film*) preestreno

previous ['priːvɪəs] *adj* previo, anterior; **previously** *adv* antes

prey [preɪ] *n* presa ▷ *vi*: **to ~ on** (*feed on*) alimentarse de; **it was ~ing on his mind** le preocupaba, le obsesionaba

price [praɪs] *n* precio ▷ *vt* (*goods*) fijar el precio de; **priceless** *adj* que no tiene precio; **price list** *n* tarifa

prick [prɪk] *n* (*sting*) picadura ▷ *vt* pinchar; (*hurt*) picar; **to ~ up one's ears** aguzar el oído

prickly ['prɪklɪ] *adj* espinoso; (*fig: person*) enojadizo

pride [praɪd] *n* orgullo; (*pej*) soberbia ▷ *vt*: **to ~ o.s. on** enorgullecerse de

priest [priːst] *n* sacerdote *m*

primarily ['praɪmərɪlɪ] *adv* ante todo

primary ['praɪmərɪ] *adj* (*first in importance*) principal ▷ *n* (US *Pol*)

elección *f* primaria; **primary school** (*BRIT*) *n* escuela primaria
prime [praɪm] *adj* primero, principal; (*excellent*) selecto, de primera clase ▷ *n*: **in the ~ of life** en la flor de la vida ▷ *vt* (*wood: fig*) preparar; **~ example** ejemplo típico; **Prime Minister** *n* primer(a) ministro/a
primitive ['prɪmɪtɪv] *adj* primitivo; (*crude*) rudimentario
primrose ['prɪmrəuz] *n* primavera, prímula
prince [prɪns] *n* príncipe *m*
princess [prɪn'sɛs] *n* princesa
principal ['prɪnsɪpl] *adj* principal, mayor ▷ *n* director(a) *m/f*; **principally** *adv* principalmente
principle ['prɪnsɪpl] *n* principio; **in ~** en principio; **on ~** por principio
print [prɪnt] *n* (*footprint*) huella; (*fingerprint*) huella dactilar; (*letters*) letra de molde; (*fabric*) estampado; (*Art*) grabado; (*Phot*) impresión *f* ▷ *vt* imprimir; (*cloth*) estampar; (*write in capitals*) escribir en letras de molde; **out of ~** agotado; **print out** *vt* (*Comput*) imprimir; **printer** *n* (*person*) impresor(a) *m/f*; (*machine*) impresora; **printout** *n* (*Comput*) impresión *f*
prior ['praɪə*] *adj* anterior, previo; (*more important*) más importante; **~ to** antes de
priority [praɪ'ɔrɪtɪ] *n* prioridad *f*; **to have ~ (over)** tener prioridad (sobre)
prison ['prɪzn] *n* cárcel *f*, prisión *f* ▷ *cpd* carcelario; **prisoner** *n* (*in prison*) preso/a; (*captured person*) prisionero; **prisoner-of-war** *n* prisionero de guerra
pristine ['prɪsti:n] *adj* pristino
privacy ['prɪvəsɪ] *n* intimidad *f*
private ['praɪvɪt] *adj* (*personal*) particular; (*property, industry, discussion etc*) privado; (*person*) reservado; (*place*) tranquilo ▷ *n* soldado raso; **"~"** (*on envelope*) "confidencial"; (*on door*) "prohibido el paso"; **in ~** en privado; **privately** *adv* en privado; (*in o.s.*) en secreto; **private property** *n* propiedad *f* privada; **private school** *n* colegio particular
privatize ['praɪvɪtaɪz] *vt* privatizar
privilege ['prɪvɪlɪdʒ] *n* privilegio; (*prerogative*) prerrogativa
prize [praɪz] *n* premio ▷ *adj* de primera clase ▷ *vt* apreciar, estimar; **prize-giving** *n* distribución *f* de premios; **prizewinner** *n* premiado/a
pro [prəu] *n* (*Sport*) profesional *mf* ▷ *prep* a favor de; **the ~s and cons** los pros y los contras
probability [prɔbə'bɪlɪtɪ] *n* probabilidad *f*; **in all ~** con toda probabilidad
probable ['prɔbəbl] *adj* probable
probably ['prɔbəblɪ] *adv* probablemente
probation [prə'beɪʃən] *n*: **on ~** (*employee*) a prueba; (*Law*) en libertad condicional
probe [prəub] *n* (*Med, Space*) sonda; (*enquiry*) encuesta, investigación *f* ▷ *vt* sondar; (*investigate*) investigar
problem ['prɔbləm] *n* problema *m*
procedure [prə'si:dʒə*] *n* procedimiento; (*bureaucratic*) trámites *mpl*
proceed [prə'si:d] *vi* (*do afterwards*): **to ~ to do sth** proceder a hacer algo; (*continue*): **to ~ (with)** continuar *or* seguir (con); **proceedings** *npl* acto(s) (*pl*); (*Law*) proceso; **proceeds** ['prəusi:dz] *npl* (*money*) ganancias *fpl*, ingresos *mpl*
process ['prəusɛs] *n* proceso ▷ *vt* tratar, elaborar
procession [prə'sɛʃən] *n* desfile *m*; **funeral ~** cortejo fúnebre
proclaim [prə'kleɪm] *vt* (*announce*) anunciar
prod [prɔd] *vt* empujar ▷ *n* empujón *m*
produce [*n* 'prɔdju:s, *vt* prə'dju:s] *n* (*Agr*) productos *mpl* agrícolas ▷ *vt* producir; (*play, film, programme*) presentar; **producer** *n* productor(a)

m/f; (*of film, programme*) director(a) *m/f*; (*of record*) productor(a) *m/f*

product ['prɔdʌkt] *n* producto; **production** [prə'dʌkʃən] *n* producción *f*; (*Theatre*) presentación *f*; **productive** [prə'dʌktɪv] *adj* productivo; **productivity** [prɔdʌk'tɪvɪtɪ] *n* productividad *f*

Prof. [prɔf] *abbr* (= *professor*) Prof

profession [prə'fɛʃən] *n* profesión *f*; **professional** *adj* profesional ▷ *n* profesional *mf*; (*skilled person*) perito

professor [prə'fɛsə*] *n* (BRIT) catedrático/a; (US, CANADA) profesor(a) *m/f*

profile ['prəufaɪl] *n* perfil *m*

profit ['prɔfɪt] *n* (*Comm*) ganancia ▷ *vi*: **to ~ by** *or* **from** aprovechar *or* sacar provecho de; **profitable** *adj* (*Econ*) rentable

profound [prə'faund] *adj* profundo

programme ['prəugræm] (US **program**) *n* programa *m* ▷ *vt* programar; **programmer** (US **programer**) *n* programador(a) *m/f*; **programming** (US **programing**) *n* programación *f*

progress [*n* 'prəugrɛs, *vi* prə'grɛs] *n* progreso; (*development*) desarrollo ▷ *vi* progresar, avanzar; **in ~** en curso; **progressive** [-'grɛsɪv] *adj* progresivo; (*person*) progresista

prohibit [prə'hɪbɪt] *vt* prohibir; **to ~ sb from doing sth** prohibir a algn hacer algo

project [*n* 'prɔdʒɛkt, *vb* prə'dʒɛkt] *n* proyecto ▷ *vt* proyectar ▷ *vi* (*stick out*) salir, sobresalir; **projection** [prə'dʒɛkʃən] *n* proyección *f*; (*overhang*) saliente *m*; **projector** [prə'dʒɛktə*] *n* proyector *m*

prolific [prə'lɪfɪk] *adj* prolífico

prolong [prə'lɔŋ] *vt* prolongar, extender

prom [prɔm] *n abbr* = **promenade** (US: *ball*) baile *m* de gala; **the P~s** *ver* *recuadro*

PROM

El ciclo de conciertos de música clásica más conocido de Londres es el llamado **the Proms** (promenade concerts), que se celebra anualmente en el Royal Albert Hall. Su nombre se debe a que originalmente el público paseaba durante las actuaciones, costumbre que en la actualidad se mantiene de forma simbólica, permitiendo que parte de los asistentes permanezcan de pie. En Estados Unidos se llama **prom** a un baile de gala en un centro de educación secundaria o universitaria.

promenade [prɔmə'nɑːd] *n* (*by sea*) paseo marítimo

prominent ['prɔmɪnənt] *adj* (*standing out*) saliente; (*important*) eminente, importante

promiscuous [prə'mɪskjuəs] *adj* (*sexually*) promiscuo

promise ['prɔmɪs] *n* promesa ▷ *vt, vi* prometer; **promising** *adj* prometedor(a)

promote [prə'məut] *vt* (*employee*) ascender; (*product, pop star*) hacer propaganda por; (*ideas*) fomentar; **promotion** [-'məuʃən] *n* (*advertising campaign*) campaña *f* de promoción; (*in rank*) ascenso

prompt [prɔmpt] *adj* rápido ▷ *adv*: **at 6 o'clock ~** a las seis en punto ▷ *n* (*Comput*) aviso ▷ *vt* (*urge*) mover, incitar; (*when talking*) instar; (*Theatre*) apuntar; **to ~ sb to do sth** instar a algn a hacer algo; **promptly** *adv* rápidamente; (*exactly*) puntualmente

prone [prəun] *adj* (*lying*) postrado; **~ to** propenso a

prong [prɔŋ] *n* diente *m*, punta

pronoun ['prəunaun] *n* pronombre

m

pronounce [prə'nauns] *vt* pronunciar

pronunciation [prənʌnsɪ'eɪʃən] *n* pronunciación *f*

proof [pru:f] *n* prueba ▷ *adj*: **~ against** a prueba de

prop [prɔp] *n* apoyo; (*fig*) sostén *m* accesorios *mpl*, at(t)rezzo *msg*; **prop up** *vt* (*roof, structure*) apuntalar; (*economy*) respaldar

propaganda [prɔpə'gændə] *n* propaganda

propeller [prə'pɛlə*] *n* hélice *f*

proper ['prɔpə*] *adj* (*suited, right*) propio; (*exact*) justo; (*seemly*) correcto, decente; (*authentic*) verdadero; (*referring to place*): **the village ~** el pueblo mismo; **properly** *adv* (*adequately*) correctamente; (*decently*) decentemente; **proper noun** *n* nombre *m* propio

property ['prɔpətɪ] *n* propiedad *f*; (*personal*) bienes *mpl* muebles

prophecy ['prɔfɪsɪ] *n* profecía

prophet ['prɔfɪt] *n* profeta *m*

proportion [prə'pɔ:ʃən] *n* proporción *f*; (*share*) parte *f*; **proportions** *npl* (*size*) dimensiones *fpl*; **proportional** *adj*: **proportional (to)** en proporción (con)

proposal [prə'pəuzl] *n* (*offer of marriage*) oferta de matrimonio; (*plan*) proyecto

propose [prə'pəuz] *vt* proponer ▷ *vi* declararse; **to ~ to do** tener intención de hacer

proposition [prɔpə'zɪʃən] *n* propuesta

proprietor [prə'praɪətə*] *n* propietario/a, dueño/a

prose [prəuz] *n* prosa

prosecute ['prɔsɪkju:t] *vt* (*Law*) procesar; **prosecution** [-'kju:ʃən] *n* proceso, causa; (*accusing side*) acusación *f*; **prosecutor** *n* acusador(a) *m/f*; (*also*: **public prosecutor**) fiscal *mf*

prospect [*n* 'prɔspɛkt, *vb* prə'spɛkt] *n* (*possibility*) posibilidad *f*; (*outlook*) perspectiva ▷ *vi*: **to ~ for** buscar; **prospects** *npl* (*for work etc*) perspectivas *fpl*; **prospective** [prə'spɛktɪv] *adj* futuro

prospectus [prə'spɛktəs] *n* prospecto

prosper ['prɔspə*] *vi* prosperar; **prosperity** [-'spɛrɪtɪ] *n* prosperidad *f*; **prosperous** *adj* próspero

prostitute ['prɔstɪtju:t] *n* prostituta; (*male*) *hombre que se dedica a la prostitución*

protect [prə'tɛkt] *vt* proteger; **protection** [-'tekʃən] *n* protección *f*; **protective** *adj* protector(a)

protein ['prəuti:n] *n* proteína

protest [*n* 'prəutɛst, *vb* prə'tɛst] *n* protesta ▷ *vi*: **to ~ about** *or* **at/against** protestar de/contra ▷ *vt* (*insist*): **to ~ (that)** insistir en (que)

Protestant ['prɔtɪstənt] *adj*, *n* protestante *mf*

protester [prə'tɛstə*] *n* manifestante *mf*

protractor [prə'træktə*] *n* (*Geom*) transportador *m*

proud [praud] *adj* orgulloso; (*pej*) soberbio, altanero

prove [pru:v] *vt* probar; (*show*) demostrar ▷ *vi*: **to ~ (to be) correct** resultar correcto; **to ~ o.s.** probar su valía

proverb ['prɔvə:b] *n* refrán *m*

provide [prə'vaɪd] *vt* proporcionar, dar; **to ~ sb with sth** proveer a algn de algo; **provide for** *vt fus* (*person*) mantener a; (*problem etc*) tener en cuenta; **provided** *conj*: **provided (that)** con tal de que, a condición de que; **providing** [prə'vaɪdɪŋ] *conj*: **providing (that)** a condición de que, con tal de que

province ['prɔvɪns] *n* provincia; (*fig*) esfera; **provincial** [prə'vɪnʃəl] *adj* provincial; (*pej*) provinciano

provision [prə'vɪʒən] *n* (*supplying*)

suministro, abastecimiento; (*of contract etc*) disposición *f*; **provisions** *npl* (*food*) comestibles *mpl*; **provisional** *adj* provisional
provocative [prə'vɔkətɪv] *adj* provocativo
provoke [prə'vəuk] *vt* (*cause*) provocar, incitar; (*anger*) enojar
prowl [praul] *vi* (*also*: **~ about, ~ around**) merodear ▷ *n*: **on the ~** de merodeo
proximity [prɔk'sɪmɪtɪ] *n* proximidad *f*
proxy ['prɔksɪ] *n*: **by ~** por poderes
prudent ['pru:dənt] *adj* prudente
prune [pru:n] *n* ciruela pasa ▷ *vt* podar
pry [praɪ] *vi*: **to ~ (into)** entrometerse (en)
PS *n abbr* (= *postscript*) P.D.
pseudonym ['sju:dəunɪm] *n* seudónimo
PSHE (BRIT: *Scol*) *n abbr* (= *personal, social and health education*) *formación social y sanitaria*
psychiatric [saɪkɪ'ætrɪk] *adj* psiquiátrico
psychiatrist [saɪ'kaɪətrɪst] *n* psiquiatra *mf*
psychic ['saɪkɪk] *adj* (*also*: **~al**) psíquico
psychoanalysis [saɪkəuə'nælɪsɪs] *n* psicoanálisis *m inv*
psychological [saɪkə'lɔdʒɪkl] *adj* psicológico
psychologist [saɪ'kɔlədʒɪst] *n* psicólogo/a
psychology [saɪ'kɔlədʒɪ] *n* psicología
psychotherapy [saɪkəu'θɛrəpɪ] *n* psicoterapia
pt *abbr* = **pint(s); point(s)**
PTO *abbr* (= *please turn over*) sigue
pub [pʌb] *n abbr* (= *public house*) pub *m*, bar *m*
puberty ['pju:bətɪ] *n* pubertad *f*
public ['pʌblɪk] *adj* público ▷ *n*: **the ~** el público; **in ~** en público; **to make ~** hacer público
publication [pʌblɪ'keɪʃən] *n* publicación *f*
public: public company *n* sociedad *f* anónima; **public convenience** (BRIT) *n* aseos *mpl* públicos (SP), sanitarios *mpl* (LAM); **public holiday** *n* (día *m* de) fiesta (SP), (día *m*) feriado (LAM); **public house** (BRIT) *n* bar *m*, pub *m*
publicity [pʌb'lɪsɪtɪ] *n* publicidad *f*
publicize ['pʌblɪsaɪz] *vt* publicitar
public: public limited company *n* sociedad *f* anónima (S.A.); **publicly** *adv* públicamente, en público; **public opinion** *n* opinión *f* pública; **public relations** *n* relaciones *fpl* públicas; **public school** *n* (BRIT) escuela privada; (US) instituto; **public transport** *n* transporte *m* público
publish ['pʌblɪʃ] *vt* publicar; **publisher** *n* (*person*) editor(a) *m/f*; (*firm*) editorial *f*; **publishing** *n* (*industry*) industria del libro
pub lunch *n almuerzo que se sirve en un pub*; **to go for a ~** almorzar *o* comer en un pub
pudding ['pudɪŋ] *n* pudín *m*; (BRIT: *dessert*) postre *m*; **black ~** morcilla
puddle ['pʌdl] *n* charco
Puerto Rico [pwɛ:təu'ri:kəu] *n* Puerto Rico
puff [pʌf] *n* soplo; (*of smoke, air*) bocanada; (*of breathing*) resoplido ▷ *vt*: **to ~ one's pipe** chupar la pipa ▷ *vi* (*pant*) jadear; **puff pastry** *n* hojaldre *m*
pull [pul] *n* (*tug*): **to give sth a ~** dar un tirón a algo ▷ *vt* tirar de; (*press*: *trigger*) apretar; (*haul*) tirar, arrastrar; (*close*: *curtain*) echar ▷ *vi* tirar; **to ~ to pieces** hacer pedazos; **not to ~ one's punches** no andarse con bromas; **to ~ one's weight** hacer su parte; **to ~ o.s. together** sobreponerse; **to ~ sb's leg** tomar el pelo a algn; **pull apart** *vt* (*break*) romper; **pull away** *vi* (*vehicle*: *move off*) salir, arrancar; (*draw back*) apartarse bruscamente; **pull back** *vt* (*lever etc*)

tirar hacia sí; (*curtains*) descorrer ▷ *vi* (*refrain*) contenerse; (*Mil*: *withdraw*) retirarse; **pull down** *vt* (*building*) derribar; **pull in** *vi* (*car etc*) parar (junto a la acera); (*train*) llegar a la estación; **pull off** *vt* (*deal etc*) cerrar; **pull out** *vi* (*car, train etc*) salir ▷ *vt* sacar, arrancar; **pull over** *vi* (*Aut*) hacerse a un lado; **pull up** *vi* (*stop*) parar ▷ *vt* (*raise*) levantar; (*uproot*) arrancar, desarraigar

pulley ['pulɪ] *n* polea

pullover ['puləuvə*] *n* jersey *m*, suéter *m*

pulp [pʌlp] *n* (*of fruit*) pulpa

pulpit ['pulpɪt] *n* púlpito

pulse [pʌls] *n* (*Anat*) pulso; (*rhythm*) pulsación *f*; (*Bot*) legumbre *f*; **pulses** *pl n* legumbres

puma ['pju:mə] *n* puma *m*

pump [pʌmp] *n* bomba; (*shoe*) zapatilla ▷ *vt* sacar con una bomba; **pump up** *vt* inflar

pumpkin ['pʌmpkɪn] *n* calabaza

pun [pʌn] *n* juego de palabras

punch [pʌntʃ] *n* (*blow*) golpe *m*, puñetazo; (*tool*) punzón *m*; (*drink*) ponche *m* ▷ *vt* (*hit*): **to ~ sb/sth** dar un puñetazo *or* golpear a algn/algo; **punch-up** (BRIT: *inf*) *n* riña

punctual ['pʌŋktjuəl] *adj* puntual

punctuation [pʌŋktju'eɪʃən] *n* puntuación *f*

puncture ['pʌŋktʃə*] (BRIT) *n* pinchazo ▷ *vt* pinchar

punish ['pʌnɪʃ] *vt* castigar; **punishment** *n* castigo

punk [pʌŋk] *n* (*also*: **~ rocker**) punki *mf*; (*also*: **~ rock**) música punk; (US: *inf*: *hoodlum*) rufián *m*

pup [pʌp] *n* cachorro

pupil ['pju:pl] *n* alumno/a; (*of eye*) pupila

puppet ['pʌpɪt] *n* títere *m*

puppy ['pʌpɪ] *n* cachorro, perrito

purchase ['pə:tʃɪs] *n* compra ▷ *vt* comprar

pure [pjuə*] *adj* puro; **purely** *adv* puramente

purify ['pjuərɪfaɪ] *vt* purificar, depurar

purity ['pjuərɪtɪ] *n* pureza

purple ['pə:pl] *adj* purpúreo; morado

purpose ['pə:pəs] *n* propósito; **on ~** a propósito, adrede

purr [pə:*] *vi* ronronear

purse [pə:s] *n* monedero; (US: *handbag*) bolso (SP), cartera (LAM), bolsa (MEX) ▷ *vt* fruncir

pursue [pə'sju:] *vt* seguir

pursuit [pə'sju:t] *n* (*chase*) caza; (*occupation*) actividad *f*

pus [pʌs] *n* pus *m*

push [puʃ] *n* empuje *m*, empujón *m*; (*of button*) presión *f*; (*drive*) empuje *m* ▷ *vt* empujar; (*button*) apretar; (*promote*) promover ▷ *vi* empujar; (*demand*): **to ~ for** luchar por; **push in** *vi* colarse; **push off** (*inf*) *vi* largarse; **push on** *vi* seguir adelante; **push over** *vt* (*cause to fall*) hacer caer, derribar; (*knock over*) volcar; **push through** *vi* (*crowd*) abrirse paso a empujones ▷ *vt* (*measure*) despachar; **pushchair** (BRIT) *n* sillita de ruedas; **pusher** *n* (*drug pusher*) traficante *mf* de drogas; **push-up** (US) *n* plancha

pussy(-cat) ['pusɪ-] (*inf*) *n* minino (*inf*)

put [put] (*pt, pp* **~**) *vt* (*place*) poner, colocar; (*put into*) meter; (*say*) expresar; (*a question*) hacer; (*estimate*) estimar; **put aside** *vt* (*lay down*: *book etc*) dejar *or* poner a un lado; (*save*) ahorrar; (*in shop*) guardar; **put away** *vt* (*store*) guardar; **put back** *vt* (*replace*) devolver a su lugar; (*postpone*) aplazar; **put by** *vt* (*money*) guardar; **put down** *vt* (*on ground*) poner en el suelo; (*animal*) sacrificar; (*in writing*) apuntar; (*revolt etc*) sofocar; (*attribute*): **to put sth down to** atribuir algo a; **put forward** *vt* (*ideas*) presentar, proponer; **put in** *vt* (*complaint*) presentar; (*time*) dedicar; **put off** *vt* (*postpone*) aplazar; (*discourage*) desanimar; **put on** *vt* ponerse; (*light etc*) encender; (*play etc*) presentar; (*gain*): **to put on weight** engordar; (*brake*) echar; (*record, kettle etc*) poner; (*assume*) adoptar; **put out** *vt* (*fire, light*) apagar; (*rubbish etc*) sacar; (*cat etc*) echar; (*one's hand*) alargar; (*inf: person*): **to be put out** alterarse; **put through** *vt* (*Tel*) poner; (*plan etc*) hacer aprobar; **put together** *vt* unir, reunir; (*assemble: furniture*) armar, montar; (*meal*) preparar; **put up** *vt* (*raise*) levantar, alzar; (*hang*) colgar; (*build*) construir; (*increase*) aumentar; (*accommodate*) alojar; **put up with** *vt fus* aguantar

putt [pʌt] *n* putt *m*, golpe *m* corto; **putting green** *n* green *m*; minigolf *m*

puzzle ['pʌzl] *n* rompecabezas *m inv*; (*also*: **crossword ~**) crucigrama *m*; (*mystery*) misterio ▷ *vt* dejar perplejo, confundir ▷ *vi*: **to ~ over sth** devanarse los sesos con algo; **puzzled** *adj* perplejo; **puzzling** *adj* misterioso, extraño

pyjamas [pɪ'dʒɑːməz] (BRIT) *npl* pijama *m*

pylon ['paɪlən] *n* torre *f* de conducción eléctrica

pyramid ['pɪrəmɪd] *n* pirámide *f*

q

quack [kwæk] *n* graznido; (*pej: doctor*) curandero/a

quadruple [kwɔ'drupl] *vt, vi* cuadruplicar

quail [kweɪl] *n* codorniz *f* ▷ *vi*: **to ~ at** *or* **before** amedrentarse ante

quaint [kweɪnt] *adj* extraño; (*picturesque*) pintoresco

quake [kweɪk] *vi* temblar ▷ *n abbr* = **earthquake**

qualification [kwɔlɪfɪ'keɪʃən] *n* (*ability*) capacidad *f*; (*often pl: diploma etc*) título; (*reservation*) salvedad *f*

qualified ['kwɔlɪfaɪd] *adj* capacitado; (*professionally*) titulado; (*limited*) limitado

qualify ['kwɔlɪfaɪ] *vt* (*make competent*) capacitar; (*modify*) modificar ▷ *vi* (*in competition*): **to ~ (for)** calificarse (para); (*pass examination(s)*: **to ~ (as)** calificarse (de), graduarse (en); (*be eligible*): **to ~ (for)** reunir los requisitos (para)

quality ['kwɔlɪtɪ] *n* calidad *f*; (*of person*) cualidad *f*

qualm [kwɑːm] *n* escrúpulo
quantify ['kwɔntɪfaɪ] *vt* cuantificar
quantity ['kwɔntɪtɪ] *n* cantidad *f*; **in ~** en grandes cantidades
quarantine ['kwɔrntiːn] *n* cuarentena
quarrel ['kwɔrl] *n* riña, pelea ▷ *vi* reñir, pelearse
quarry ['kwɔrɪ] *n* cantera
quart [kwɔːt] *n* ≈ litro
quarter ['kwɔːtə*] *n* cuarto, cuarta parte *f*; (*US*: *coin*) *moneda de 25 centavos*; (*of year*) trimestre *m*; (*district*) barrio ▷ *vt* dividir en cuartos; (*Mil*: *lodge*) alojar; **quarters** *npl* (*barracks*) cuartel *m*; (*living quarters*) alojamiento; **a ~ of an hour** un cuarto de hora; **quarter final** *n* cuarto de final; **quarterly** *adj* trimestral ▷ *adv* cada 3 meses, trimestralmente
quartet(te) [kwɔː'tɛt] *n* cuarteto
quartz [kwɔːts] *n* cuarzo
quay [kiː] *n* (*also*: **~side**) muelle *m*
queasy ['kwiːzɪ] *adj*: **to feel ~** tener náuseas
queen [kwiːn] *n* reina; (*Cards etc*) dama
queer [kwɪə*] *adj* raro, extraño ▷ *n* (*inf*: *highly offensive*) maricón *m*
quench [kwɛntʃ] *vt*: **to ~ one's thirst** apagar la sed
query ['kwɪərɪ] *n* (*question*) pregunta ▷ *vt* dudar de
quest [kwɛst] *n* busca, búsqueda
question ['kwɛstʃən] *n* pregunta; (*doubt*) duda; (*matter*) asunto, cuestión *f* ▷ *vt* (*doubt*) dudar de; (*interrogate*) interrogar, hacer preguntas a; **beyond ~** fuera de toda duda; **out of the ~** imposible; ni hablar; **questionable** *adj* dudoso; **question mark** *n* punto de interrogación; **questionnaire** [-'nɛə*] *n* cuestionario
queue [kjuː] (*BRIT*) *n* cola ▷ *vi* (*also*: **~ up**) hacer cola
quiche [kiːʃ] *n* quiche *m*
quick [kwɪk] *adj* rápido; (*agile*) ágil; (*mind*) listo ▷ *n*: **cut to the ~** (*fig*) herido en lo vivo; **be ~!** ¡date prisa!; **quickly** *adv* rápidamente, de prisa
quid [kwɪd] (*BRIT*: *inf*) *n inv* libra
quiet ['kwaɪət] *adj* (*voice, music etc*) bajo; (*person, place*) tranquilo; (*ceremony*) íntimo ▷ *n* silencio; (*calm*) tranquilidad *f* ▷ *vt, vi* (*US*) = **quieten**

Be careful not to translate **quiet** by the Spanish word *quieto*.

quietly *adv* tranquilamente; (*silently*) silenciosamente
quilt [kwɪlt] *n* edredón *m*
quirky ['kwˊːkɪ] *adj* raro, estrafalario
quit [kwɪt] (*pt, pp* **~** *or* **~ted**) *vt* dejar, abandonar; (*premises*) desocupar ▷ *vi* (*give up*) renunciar; (*resign*) dimitir
quite [kwaɪt] *adv* (*rather*) bastante; (*entirely*) completamente; **that's not ~ big enough** no acaba de ser lo bastante grande; **~ a few of them** un buen número de ellos; **~ (so)!** ¡así es!, ¡exactamente!
quits [kwɪts] *adj*: **~ (with)** en paz (con); **let's call it ~** dejémoslo en tablas
quiver ['kwɪvə*] *vi* estremecerse
quiz [kwɪz] *n* concurso ▷ *vt* interrogar
quota ['kwəutə] *n* cuota
quotation [kwəu'teɪʃən] *n* cita; (*estimate*) presupuesto; **quotation marks** *npl* comillas *fpl*
quote [kwəut] *n* cita; (*estimate*) presupuesto ▷ *vt* citar; (*price*) cotizar ▷ *vi*: **to ~ from** citar de; **quotes** *npl* (*inverted commas*) comillas *fpl*

rabbi ['ræbaɪ] *n* rabino
rabbit ['ræbɪt] *n* conejo
rabies ['reɪbi:z] *n* rabia
RAC (BRIT) *n abbr* (= *Royal Automobile Club*) ≈ RACE *m*
rac(c)oon [rə'ku:n] *n* mapache *m*
race [reɪs] *n* carrera; (*species*) raza ▷*vt* (*horse*) hacer correr; (*engine*) acelerar ▷*vi* (*compete*) competir; (*run*) correr; (*pulse*) latir a ritmo acelerado; **race car** (US) *n* = **racing car**; **racecourse** *n* hipódromo; **racehorse** *n* caballo de carreras; **racetrack** *n* pista; (*for cars*) autódromo
racial ['reɪʃl] *adj* racial
racing ['reɪsɪŋ] *n* carreras *fpl*; **racing car** (BRIT) *n* coche *m* de carreras; **racing driver** (BRIT) *n* piloto *mf* de carreras
racism ['reɪsɪzəm] *n* racismo; **racist** [-sɪst] *adj*, *n* racista *mf*
rack [ræk] *n* (*also*: **luggage ~**) rejilla; (*shelf*) estante *m*; (*also*: **roof ~**) baca, portaequipajes *m inv*; (*dish rack*) escurreplatos *m inv*; (*clothes rack*) percha ▷*vt* atormentar; **to ~ one's brains** devanarse los sesos
racket ['rækɪt] *n* (*for tennis*) raqueta; (*noise*) ruido, estrépito; (*swindle*) estafa, timo
racquet ['rækɪt] *n* raqueta
radar ['reɪdɑ:*] *n* radar *m*
radiation [reɪdɪ'eɪʃən] *n* radiación *f*
radiator ['reɪdɪeɪtə*] *n* radiador *m*
radical ['rædɪkl] *adj* radical
radio ['reɪdɪəu] *n* radio *f*; **on the ~** por radio; **radioactive** *adj* radioactivo; **radio station** *n* emisora
radish ['rædɪʃ] *n* rábano
RAF *n abbr* (= *Royal Air Force*) las Fuerzas Aéreas Británicas
raffle ['ræfl] *n* rifa, sorteo
raft [rɑ:ft] *n* balsa; (*also*: **life ~**) balsa salvavidas
rag [ræg] *n* (*piece of cloth*) trapo; (*torn cloth*) harapo; (*pej*: *newspaper*) periodicucho; (*for charity*) *actividades estudiantiles benéficas*; **rags** *npl* (*torn clothes*) harapos *mpl*
rage [reɪdʒ] *n* rabia, furor *m* ▷*vi* (*person*) rabiar, estar furioso; (*storm*) bramar; **it's all the ~** (*very fashionable*) está muy de moda
ragged ['rægɪd] *adj* (*edge*) desigual, mellado; (*appearance*) andrajoso, harapiento
raid [reɪd] *n* (*Mil*) incursión *f*; (*criminal*) asalto; (*by police*) redada ▷*vt* invadir, atacar; asaltar
rail [reɪl] *n* (*on stair*) barandilla, pasamanos *m inv*; (*on bridge, balcony*) pretil *m*; (*of ship*) barandilla; (*also*: **towel ~**) toallero; **railcard** *n* (BRIT) *tarjeta para obtener descuentos en el tren*; **railing(s)** *n(pl)* vallado; **railroad** (US) *n* = **railway**; **railway** (BRIT) *n* ferrocarril *m*, vía férrea; **railway line** (BRIT) *n* línea (de ferrocarril); **railway station** (BRIT) *n* estación *f* de ferrocarril
rain [reɪn] *n* lluvia ▷*vi* llover; **in the ~** bajo la lluvia; **it's ~ing** llueve, está lloviendo; **rainbow** *n* arco iris;

raincoat *n* impermeable *m*; **raindrop** *n* gota de lluvia; **rainfall** *n* lluvia; **rainforest** *n* selvas *fpl* tropicales; **rainy** *adj* lluvioso

raise [reɪz] *n* aumento ▷ *vt* levantar; (*increase*) aumentar; (*improve*: *morale*) subir; (: *standards*) mejorar; (*doubts*) suscitar; (*a question*) plantear; (*cattle, family*) criar; (*crop*) cultivar; (*army*) reclutar; (*loan*) obtener; **to ~ one's voice** alzar la voz

raisin ['reɪzn] *n* pasa de Corinto

rake [reɪk] *n* (*tool*) rastrillo; (*person*) libertino ▷ *vt* (*garden*) rastrillar

rally ['rælɪ] *n* (*Pol etc*) reunión *f*, mitin *m*; (*Aut*) rallye *m*; (*Tennis*) peloteo ▷ *vt* reunir ▷ *vi* recuperarse

RAM [ræm] *n abbr* (= *random access memory*) RAM *f*

ram [ræm] *n* carnero; (*also*: **battering ~**) ariete *m* ▷ *vt* (*crash into*) dar contra, chocar con; (*push*: *fist etc*) empujar con fuerza

Ramadan [ræmə'dæn] *n* ramadán *m*

ramble ['ræmbl] *n* caminata, excursión *f* en el campo ▷ *vi* (*pej*: *also*: **~ on**) divagar; **rambler** *n* excursionista *mf*; (*Bot*) trepadora; **rambling** *adj* (*speech*) inconexo; (*house*) laberíntico; (*Bot*) trepador(a)

ramp [ræmp] *n* rampa; **on/off ~** (*US Aut*) vía de acceso/salida

rampage [ræm'peɪdʒ] *n*: **to be on the ~** desmandarse ▷ *vi*: **they went rampaging through the town** recorrieron la ciudad armando alboroto

ran [ræn] *pt of* **run**

ranch [rɑːntʃ] *n* hacienda, estancia

random ['rændəm] *adj* fortuito, sin orden; (*Comput, Math*) aleatorio ▷ *n*: **at ~** al azar

rang [ræŋ] *pt of* **ring**

range [reɪndʒ] *n* (*of mountains*) cadena de montañas, cordillera; (*of missile*) alcance *m*; (*of voice*) registro; (*series*) serie *f*; (*of products*) surtido; (*Mil*: *also*: **shooting ~**) campo de tiro; (*also*: **kitchen ~**) fogón *m* ▷ *vt* (*place*) colocar; (*arrange*) arreglar ▷ *vi*: **to ~ over** (*extend*) extenderse por; **to ~ from ... to ...** oscilar entre ... y ...

ranger [reɪndʒə*] *n* guardabosques *mf inv*

rank [ræŋk] *n* (*row*) fila; (*Mil*) rango; (*status*) categoría; (BRIT: *also*: **taxi ~**) parada de taxis ▷ *vi*: **to ~ among** figurar entre ▷ *adj* fétido, rancio; **the ~ and file** (*fig*) la base

ransom ['rænsəm] *n* rescate *m*; **to hold to ~** (*fig*) hacer chantaje a

rant [rænt] *vi* divagar, desvariar

rap [ræp] *vt* golpear, dar un golpecito en ▷ *n* (*music*) rap *m*

rape [reɪp] *n* violación *f*; (*Bot*) colza ▷ *vt* violar

rapid ['ræpɪd] *adj* rápido; **rapidly** *adv* rápidamente; **rapids** *npl* (*Geo*) rápidos *mpl*

rapist ['reɪpɪst] *n* violador *m*

rapport [ræ'pɔː*] *n* simpatía

rare [rɛə*] *adj* raro, poco común; (*Culin*: *steak*) poco hecho; **rarely** *adv* pocas veces

rash [ræʃ] *adj* imprudente, precipitado ▷ *n* (*Med*) sarpullido, erupción *f* (cutánea); (*of events*) serie *f*

rasher ['ræʃə*] *n* lonja

raspberry ['rɑːzbərɪ] *n* frambuesa

rat [ræt] *n* rata

rate [reɪt] *n* (*ratio*) razón *f*; (*price*) precio; (: *of hotel etc*) tarifa; (*of interest*) tipo; (*speed*) velocidad *f* ▷ *vt* (*value*) tasar; (*estimate*) estimar; **rates** *npl* (BRIT: *property tax*) impuesto municipal; (*fees*) tarifa; **to ~ sth/sb as** considerar algo/a algn como

rather ['rɑːðə*] *adv*: **it's ~ expensive** es algo caro; (*too much*) es demasiado caro; (*to some extent*) más bien; **there's ~ a lot** hay bastante; **I would** *or* **I'd ~ go** preferiría ir; **or ~** mejor dicho

rating ['reɪtɪŋ] *n* tasación *f*; (*score*) índice *m*; (*of ship*) clase *f*; **ratings** *npl* (*Radio, TV*) niveles *mpl* de audiencia

ratio ['reɪʃɪəu] *n* razón *f*; **in the ~ of**

100 to 1 a razón de 100 a 1
ration ['ræʃən] *n* ración *f* ▷ *vt* racionar; **rations** *npl* víveres *mpl*
rational ['ræʃənl] *adj* (*solution, reasoning*) lógico, razonable; (*person*) cuerdo, sensato
rattle ['rætl] *n* golpeteo; (*of train etc*) traqueteo; (*for baby*) sonaja, sonajero ▷ *vi* castañetear; (*car, bus*): **to ~ along** traquetear ▷ *vt* hacer sonar agitando
rave [reɪv] *vi* (*in anger*) encolerizarse; (*with enthusiasm*) entusiasmarse; (*Med*) delirar, desvariar ▷ *n* (*inf: party*) rave *m*
raven ['reɪvən] *n* cuervo
ravine [rə'vi:n] *n* barranco
raw [rɔ:] *adj* crudo; (*not processed*) bruto; (*sore*) vivo; (*inexperienced*) novato, inexperto; **~ materials** materias primas
ray [reɪ] *n* rayo; **~ of hope** (rayo de) esperanza
razor ['reɪzə*] *n* (*open*) navaja; (*safety razor*) máquina de afeitar; (*electric razor*) máquina (eléctrica) de afeitar; **razor blade** *n* hoja de afeitar
Rd *abbr* = **road**
RE *n abbr* (BRIT) = **religious education**
re [ri:] *prep* con referencia a
reach [ri:tʃ] *n* alcance *m*; (*of river etc*) extensión *f* entre dos recodos ▷ *vt* alcanzar, llegar a; (*achieve*) lograr ▷ *vi* extenderse; **within ~** al alcance (de la mano); **out of ~** fuera del alcance; **reach out** *vt* (*hand*) tender ▷ *vi*: **to reach out for sth** alargar *or* tender la mano para tomar algo
react [ri:'ækt] *vi* reaccionar; **reaction** [-'ækʃən] *n* reacción *f*; **reactor** [ri:'æktə*] *n* (*also*: **nuclear reactor**) reactor *m* (nuclear)
read [ri:d, *pt, pp* rɛd] (*pt, pp* **~**) *vi* leer ▷ *vt* leer; (*understand*) entender; (*study*) estudiar; **read out** *vt* leer en alta voz; **reader** *n* lector(a) *m/f*; (BRIT: *at university*) profesor(a) *m/f* adjunto/a
readily ['rɛdɪlɪ] *adv* (*willingly*) de buena gana; (*easily*) fácilmente; (*quickly*) en seguida
reading ['ri:dɪŋ] *n* lectura; (*on instrument*) indicación *f*
ready ['rɛdɪ] *adj* listo, preparado; (*willing*) dispuesto; (*available*) disponible ▷ *adv*: **~-cooked** listo para comer ▷ *n*: **at the ~** (*Mil*) listo para tirar ▷ **to get ~** *vi* prepararse ▷ **to get ~** *vt* preparar; **ready-made** *adj* confeccionado
real [rɪəl] *adj* verdadero, auténtico; **in ~ terms** en términos reales; **real ale** *n* cerveza elaborada tradicionalmente; **real estate** *n* bienes *mpl* raíces; **realistic** [-'lɪstɪk] *adj* realista; **reality** [ri:'ælɪtɪ] *n* realidad *f*; **reality TV** *n* telerrealidad *f*
realization [rɪəlaɪ'zeɪʃən] *n* comprensión *f*; (*fulfilment, Comm*) realización *f*
realize ['rɪəlaɪz] *vt* (*understand*) darse cuenta de
really ['rɪəlɪ] *adv* realmente; (*for emphasis*) verdaderamente; (*actually*): **what ~ happened** lo que pasó en realidad; **~?** ¿de veras?; **~!** (*annoyance*) ¡vamos!, ¡por favor!
realm [rɛlm] *n* reino; (*fig*) esfera
realtor ['rɪəltɔ:*] (US) *n* agente *mf* inmobiliario/a
reappear [ri:ə'pɪə*] *vi* reaparecer
rear [rɪə*] *adj* trasero ▷ *n* parte *f* trasera ▷ *vt* (*cattle, family*) criar ▷ *vi* (*also*: **~ up**: *animal*) encabritarse
rearrange [ri:ə'reɪndʒ] *vt* ordenar *or* arreglar de nuevo
rear: rear-view mirror *n* (*Aut*) (espejo) retrovisor *m*; **rear-wheel drive** *n* tracción *f* trasera
reason ['ri:zn] *n* razón *f* ▷ *vi*: **to ~ with sb** tratar de que algn entre en razón; **it stands to ~ that ...** es lógico que ...; **reasonable** *adj* razonable; (*sensible*) sensato; **reasonably** *adv* razonablemente; **reasoning** *n* razonamiento, argumentos *mpl*
reassurance [ri:ə'ʃuərəns] *n* consuelo
reassure [ri:ə'ʃuə*] *vt* tranquilizar,

alentar; **to ~ sb that ...** tranquilizar a algn asegurando que ...
rebate ['ri:beɪt] *n* (*on tax etc*) desgravación *f*
rebel [*n* 'rɛbl, *vi* rɪ'bɛl] *n* rebelde *mf* ▷ *vi* rebelarse, sublevarse; **rebellion** [rɪ'bɛljən] *n* rebelión *f*, sublevación *f*; **rebellious** [rɪ'bɛljəs] *adj* rebelde; (*child*) revoltoso
rebuild [ri:'bɪld] *vt* reconstruir
recall [*vb* rɪ'kɔ:l, *n* 'ri:kɔl] *vt* (*remember*) recordar; (*ambassador etc*) retirar ▷ *n* recuerdo; retirada
rec'd *abbr* (= *received*) rbdo
receipt [rɪ'si:t] *n* (*document*) recibo; (*for parcel etc*) acuse *m* de recibo; (*act of receiving*) recepción *f*; **receipts** *npl* (*Comm*) ingresos *mpl*

Be careful not to translate **receipt** by the Spanish word *receta*.

receive [rɪ'si:v] *vt* recibir; (*guest*) acoger; (*wound*) sufrir; **receiver** *n* (*Tel*) auricular *m*; (*Radio*) receptor *m*; (*of stolen goods*) perista *mf*; (*Comm*) administrador *m* jurídico
recent ['ri:snt] *adj* reciente; **recently** *adv* recientemente; **recently arrived** recién llegado
reception [rɪ'sɛpʃən] *n* recepción *f*; (*welcome*) acogida; **reception desk** *n* recepción *f*; **receptionist** *n* recepcionista *mf*
recession [rɪ'sɛʃən] *n* recesión *f*
recharge [ri:'tʃɑ:dʒ] *vt* (*battery*) recargar
recipe ['rɛsɪpɪ] *n* receta; (*for disaster, success*) fórmula
recipient [rɪ'sɪpɪənt] *n* recibidor(a) *m/f*; (*of letter*) destinatario/a
recital [rɪ'saɪtl] *n* recital *m*
recite [rɪ'saɪt] *vt* (*poem*) recitar
reckless ['rɛkləs] *adj* temerario, imprudente; (*driving, driver*) peligroso
reckon ['rɛkən] *vt* calcular; (*consider*) considerar; (*think*): **I ~ that ...** me parece que ...
reclaim [rɪ'kleɪm] *vt* (*land, waste*) recuperar; (*land: from sea*) rescatar; (*demand back*) reclamar
recline [rɪ'klaɪn] *vi* reclinarse
recognition [rɛkəg'nɪʃən] *n* reconocimiento; **transformed beyond ~** irreconocible
recognize ['rɛkəgnaɪz] *vt*: **to ~ (by/as)** reconocer (por/como)
recollection [rɛkə'lɛkʃən] *n* recuerdo
recommend [rɛkə'mɛnd] *vt* recomendar; **recommendation** [rɛkəmɛn'deɪʃən] *n* recomendación *f*
reconcile ['rɛkənsaɪl] *vt* (*two people*) reconciliar; (*two facts*) compaginar; **to ~ o.s. to sth** conformarse a algo
reconsider [ri:kən'sɪdə*] *vt* repensar
reconstruct [ri:kən'strʌkt] *vt* reconstruir
record [*n, adj* 'rɛkɔ:d, *vt* rɪ'kɔ:d] *n* (*Mus*) disco; (*of meeting etc*) acta; (*register*) registro, partida; (*file*) archivo; (*also*: **criminal ~**) antecedentes *mpl*; (*written*) expediente *m*; (*Sport, Comput*) récord *m* ▷ *adj* récord, sin precedentes ▷ *vt* registrar; (*Mus: song etc*) grabar; **in ~ time** en un tiempo récord; **off the ~** *adj* no oficial ▷ *adv* confidencialmente; **recorded delivery** (BRIT) *n* (*Post*) entrega con acuse de recibo; **recorder** *n* (*Mus*) flauta de pico; **recording** *n* (*Mus*) grabación *f*; **record player** *n* tocadiscos *m inv*
recount [rɪ'kaunt] *vt* contar
recover [rɪ'kʌvə*] *vt* recuperar ▷ *vi* (*from illness, shock*) recuperarse; **recovery** *n* recuperación *f*
recreate [ri:krɪ'eɪt] *vt* recrear
recreation [rɛkrɪ'eɪʃən] *n* recreo; **recreational vehicle** (US) *n* caravan *or* rulota pequeña; **recreational drug** droga recreativa
recruit [rɪ'kru:t] *n* recluta *mf* ▷ *vt* reclutar; (*staff*) contratar; **recruitment** *n* reclutamiento
rectangle ['rɛktæŋgl] *n* rectángulo; **rectangular** [-'tæŋgjulə*] *adj* rectangular
rectify ['rɛktɪfaɪ] *vt* rectificar

rector ['rɛktə*] *n* (*Rel*) párroco
recur [rɪ'kə:*] *vi* repetirse; (*pain, illness*) producirse de nuevo; **recurring** *adj* (*problem*) repetido, constante
recyclable [ri:'saɪkləbl] *adj* reciclable
recycle [ri:'saɪkl] *vt* reciclar
recycling [ri:'saɪklɪŋ] *n* reciclaje
red [rɛd] *n* rojo ▷ *adj* rojo; (*hair*) pelirrojo; (*wine*) tinto; **to be in the ~** (*account*) estar en números rojos; (*business*) tener un saldo negativo; **to give sb the ~ carpet treatment** recibir a algn con todos los honores; **Red Cross** *n* Cruz *f* Roja; **redcurrant** *n* grosella roja
redeem [rɪ'di:m] *vt* redimir; (*promises*) cumplir; (*sth in pawn*) desempeñar; (*fig, also Rel*) rescatar
red: red-haired *adj* pelirrojo; **redhead** *n* pelirrojo/a; **red-hot** *adj* candente; **red light** *n*: **to go through a red light** (*Aut*) pasar la luz roja; **red-light district** *n* barrio chino
red meat *n* carne *f* roja
reduce [rɪ'dju:s] *vt* reducir; **to ~ sb to tears** hacer llorar a algn; **"~ speed now"** (*Aut*) "reduzca la velocidad"; **reduced** *adj* (*decreased*) reducido, rebajado; **at a reduced price** con rebaja *or* descuento; **"greatly reduced prices"** "grandes rebajas"; **reduction** [rɪ'dʌkʃən] *n* reducción *f*; (*of price*) rebaja; (*discount*) descuento; (*smaller-scale copy*) copia reducida
redundancy [rɪ'dʌndənsɪ] *n* (*dismissal*) despido; (*unemployment*) desempleo
redundant [rɪ'dʌndnt] *adj* (BRIT: *worker*) parado, sin trabajo; (*detail, object*) superfluo; **to be made ~** quedar(se) sin trabajo
reed [ri:d] *n* (*Bot*) junco, caña; (*Mus*) lengüeta
reef [ri:f] *n* (*at sea*) arrecife *m*
reel [ri:l] *n* carrete *m*, bobina; (*of film*) rollo; (*dance*) *baile escocés* ▷ *vt* (*also*: **~ up**) devanar; (*also*: **~ in**) sacar ▷ *vi* (*sway*) tambalear(se)
ref [rɛf] (*inf*) *n abbr* = **referee**
refectory [rɪ'fɛktərɪ] *n* comedor *m*
refer [rɪ'fə:*] *vt* (*send*: *patient*) referir; (: *matter*) remitir ▷ *vi*: **to ~ to** (*allude to*) referirse a, aludir a; (*apply to*) relacionarse con; (*consult*) consultar
referee [rɛfə'ri:] *n* árbitro; (BRIT: *for job application*): **to be a ~ for sb** proporcionar referencias a algn ▷ *vt* (*match*) arbitrar en
reference ['rɛfrəns] *n* referencia; (*for job application*: *letter*) carta de recomendación; **with ~ to** (*Comm*: *in letter*) me remito a; **reference number** *n* número de referencia
refill [*vt* ri:'fɪl, *n* 'ri:fɪl] *vt* rellenar ▷ *n* repuesto, recambio
refine [rɪ'faɪn] *vt* refinar; **refined** *adj* (*person*) fino; **refinery** *n* refinería
reflect [rɪ'flɛkt] *vt* reflejar ▷ *vi* (*think*) reflexionar, pensar; **it ~s badly/well on him** le perjudica/le hace honor; **reflection** [-'flɛkʃən] *n* (*act*) reflexión *f*; (*image*) reflejo; (*criticism*) crítica; **on reflection** pensándolo bien
reflex ['ri:flɛks] *adj, n* reflejo
reform [rɪ'fɔ:m] *n* reforma ▷ *vt* reformar
refrain [rɪ'freɪn] *vi*: **to ~ from doing** abstenerse de hacer ▷ *n* estribillo
refresh [rɪ'frɛʃ] *vt* refrescar; **refreshing** *adj* refrescante; **refreshments** *npl* refrescos *mpl*
refrigerator [rɪ'frɪdʒəreɪtə*] *n* frigorífico (SP), nevera (SP), refrigerador *m* (LAM), heladera (RPL)
refuel [ri:'fjuəl] *vi* repostar (combustible)
refuge ['rɛfju:dʒ] *n* refugio, asilo; **to take ~ in** refugiarse en; **refugee** [rɛfju'dʒi:] *n* refugiado/a
refund [*n* 'ri:fʌnd, *vb* rɪ'fʌnd] *n* reembolso ▷ *vt* devolver, reembolsar
refurbish [ri:'fə:bɪʃ] *vt* restaurar, renovar
refusal [rɪ'fju:zəl] *n* negativa; **to have first ~ on** tener la primera

opción a
refuse¹ ['rɛfjuːs] *n* basura
refuse² [rɪ'fjuːz] *vt* rechazar; (*invitation*) declinar; (*permission*) denegar ▷ *vi*: **to ~ to do sth** negarse a hacer algo; (*horse*) rehusar
regain [rɪ'geɪn] *vt* recobrar, recuperar
regard [rɪ'gɑːd] *n* mirada; (*esteem*) respeto; (*attention*) consideración *f* ▷ *vt* (*consider*) considerar; **to give one's ~s to** saludar de su parte a; **"with kindest ~s"** "con muchos recuerdos"; **as ~s, with ~ to** con respecto a, en cuanto a; **regarding** *prep* con respecto a, en cuanto a; **regardless** *adv* a pesar de todo; **regardless of** sin reparar en
regenerate [rɪ'dʒɛnəreɪt] *vt* regenerar
reggae ['rɛgeɪ] *n* reggae *m*
regiment ['rɛdʒɪmənt] *n* regimiento
region ['riːdʒən] *n* región *f*; **in the ~ of** (*fig*) alrededor de; **regional** *adj* regional
register ['rɛdʒɪstə*] *n* registro ▷ *vt* registrar; (*birth*) declarar; (*car*) matricular; (*letter*) certificar; (*instrument*) marcar, indicar ▷ *vi* (*at hotel*) registrarse; (*as student*) matricularse; (*make impression*) producir impresión; **registered** *adj* (*letter, parcel*) certificado
registrar ['rɛdʒɪstrɑː*] *n* secretario/a (del registro civil)
registration [rɛdʒɪs'treɪʃən] *n* (*act*) declaración *f*; (*Aut*: *also*: **~ number**) matrícula
registry office ['rɛdʒɪstrɪ-] (BRIT) *n* registro civil; **to get married in a ~** casarse por lo civil
regret [rɪ'grɛt] *n* sentimiento, pesar *m* ▷ *vt* sentir, lamentar; **regrettable** *adj* lamentable
regular ['rɛgjulə*] *adj* regular; (*soldier*) profesional; (*usual*) habitual; (: *doctor*) de cabecera ▷ *n* (*client etc*) cliente/a *m/f* habitual; **regularly** *adv* con regularidad; (*often*) repetidas veces
regulate ['rɛgjuleɪt] *vt* controlar; **regulation** [-'leɪʃən] *n* (*rule*) regla, reglamento
rehabilitation ['riːəbɪlɪ'teɪʃən] *n* rehabilitación *f*
rehearsal [rɪ'həːsəl] *n* ensayo
rehearse [rɪ'həːs] *vt* ensayar
reign [reɪn] *n* reinado; (*fig*) predominio ▷ *vi* reinar; (*fig*) imperar
reimburse [riːɪm'bəːs] *vt* reembolsar
rein [reɪn] *n* (*for horse*) rienda
reincarnation [riːɪnkɑː'neɪʃən] *n* reencarnación *f*
reindeer ['reɪndɪə*] *n inv* reno
reinforce [riːɪn'fɔːs] *vt* reforzar; **reinforcements** *npl* (*Mil*) refuerzos *mpl*
reinstate [riːɪn'steɪt] *vt* reintegrar; (*tax, law*) reinstaurar
reject [*n* 'riːdʒɛkt, *vb* rɪ'dʒɛkt] *n* (*thing*) desecho ▷ *vt* rechazar; (*suggestion*) descartar; (*coin*) expulsar; **rejection** [rɪ'dʒɛkʃən] *n* rechazo
rejoice [rɪ'dʒɔɪs] *vi*: **to ~ at** *or* **over** regocijarse *or* alegrarse de
relate [rɪ'leɪt] *vt* (*tell*) contar, relatar; (*connect*) relacionar ▷ *vi* relacionarse; **related** *adj* afín; (*person*) emparentado; **related to** (*subject*) relacionado con; **relating to** *prep* referente a
relation [rɪ'leɪʃən] *n* (*person*) familiar *mf*, pariente *mf*; (*link*) relación *f*; **relations** *npl* (*relatives*) familiares *mpl*; **relationship** *n* relación *f*; (*personal*) relaciones *fpl*; (*also*: **family relationship**) parentesco
relative ['rɛlətɪv] *n* pariente *mf*, familiar *mf* ▷ *adj* relativo; **relatively** *adv* (*comparatively*) relativamente
relax [rɪ'læks] *vi* descansar; (*unwind*) relajarse ▷ *vt* (*one's grip*) soltar, aflojar; (*control*) relajar; (*mind, person*) descansar; **relaxation** [riːlæk'seɪʃən] *n* descanso; (*of rule, control*) relajamiento; (*entertainment*) diversión *f*; **relaxed** *adj* relajado; (*tranquil*) tranquilo; **relaxing** *adj* relajante
relay ['riːleɪ] *n* (*race*) carrera de relevos

▷ *vt* (*Radio, TV*) retransmitir

release [rɪ'li:s] *n* (*liberation*) liberación *f*; (*from prison*) puesta en libertad; (*of gas etc*) escape *m*; (*of film etc*) estreno; (*of record*) lanzamiento ▷ *vt* (*prisoner*) poner en libertad; (*gas*) despedir, arrojar; (*from wreckage*) soltar; (*catch, spring etc*) desenganchar; (*film*) estrenar; (*book*) publicar; (*news*) difundir

relegate ['rɛləgeɪt] *vt* relegar; (BRIT *Sport*): **to be ~d to** bajar a

relent [rɪ'lɛnt] *vi* ablandarse; **relentless** *adj* implacable

relevant ['rɛləvənt] *adj* (*fact*) pertinente; **~ to** relacionado con

reliable [rɪ'laɪəbl] *adj* (*person, firm*) de confianza, de fiar; (*method, machine*) seguro; (*source*) fidedigno

relic ['rɛlɪk] *n* (*Rel*) reliquia; (*of the past*) vestigio

relief [rɪ'li:f] *n* (*from pain, anxiety*) alivio; (*help, supplies*) socorro, ayuda; (*Art, Geo*) relieve *m*

relieve [rɪ'li:v] *vt* (*pain*) aliviar; (*bring help to*) ayudar, socorrer; (*take over from*) sustituir; (*: guard*) relevar; **to ~ sb of sth** quitar algo a algn; **to ~ o.s.** hacer sus necesidades; **relieved** *adj*: **to be relieved** sentir un gran alivio

religion [rɪ'lɪdʒən] *n* religión *f*

religious [rɪ'lɪdʒəs] *adj* religioso; **religious education** *n* educación *f* religiosa

relish ['rɛlɪʃ] *n* (*Culin*) salsa; (*enjoyment*) entusiasmo ▷ *vt* (*food etc*) saborear; (*enjoy*): **to ~ sth** hacerle mucha ilusión a algn algo

relocate [ri:ləu'keɪt] *vt* cambiar de lugar, mudar ▷ *vi* mudarse

reluctance [rɪ'lʌktəns] *n* renuencia

reluctant [rɪ'lʌktənt] *adj* renuente; **reluctantly** *adv* de mala gana

rely on [rɪ'laɪ-] *vt fus* depender de; (*trust*) contar con

remain [rɪ'meɪn] *vi* (*survive*) quedar; (*be left*) sobrar; (*continue*) quedar(se), permanecer; **remainder** *n* resto; **remaining** *adj* que queda(n); (*surviving*) restante(s); **remains** *npl* restos *mpl*

remand [rɪ'mɑ:nd] *n*: **on ~** detenido (bajo custodia) ▷ *vt*: **to be ~ed in custody** quedar detenido bajo custodia

remark [rɪ'mɑ:k] *n* comentario ▷ *vt* comentar; **remarkable** *adj* (*outstanding*) extraordinario

remarry [ri:'mærɪ] *vi* volver a casarse

remedy ['rɛmədɪ] *n* remedio ▷ *vt* remediar, curar

remember [rɪ'mɛmbə*] *vt* recordar, acordarse de; (*bear in mind*) tener presente; (*send greetings to*): **~ me to him** dale recuerdos de mi parte; **Remembrance Day** *n* ≈ día en el que se recuerda a los caídos en las dos guerrasmundiales

REMEMBRANCE DAY

En el Reino Unido el domingo más próximo al 11 de noviembre se conoce como **Remembrance Sunday** o **Remembrance Day**, aniversario de la firma del armisticio de 1918 que puso fin a la Primera Guerra Mundial. Ese día, a las once de la mañana (hora en que se firmó el armisticio), se recuerda a los que murieron en las dos guerras mundiales con dos minutos de silencio ante los monumentos a los caídos. Allí se colocan coronas de amapolas, flor que también se suele llevar prendida en el pecho tras pagar un donativo destinado a los inválidos de guerra.

remind [rɪ'maɪnd] *vt*: **to ~ sb to do sth** recordar a algn que haga algo; **to ~ sb of sth** (*of fact*) recordar algo a algn; **she ~s me of her mother** me recuerda a su madre; **reminder** *n* notificación *f*; (*memento*) recuerdo

reminiscent [rɛmɪ'nɪsnt] *adj*: **to be ~ of sth** recordar algo
remnant ['rɛmnənt] *n* resto; (*of cloth*) retal *m*
remorse [rɪ'mɔːs] *n* remordimientos *mpl*
remote [rɪ'məut] *adj* (*distant*) lejano; (*person*) distante; **remote control** *n* telecontrol *m*; **remotely** *adv* remotamente; (*slightly*) levemente
removal [rɪ'muːvəl] *n* (*taking away*) el quitar; (BRIT: *from house*) mudanza; (*from office: dismissal*) destitución *f*; (*Med*) extirpación *f*; **removal man** (*irreg*) *n* (BRIT) mozo de mudanzas; **removal van** (BRIT) *n* camión *m* de mudanzas
remove [rɪ'muːv] *vt* quitar; (*employee*) destituir; (*name: from list*) tachar, borrar; (*doubt*) disipar; (*abuse*) suprimir, acabar con; (*Med*) extirpar
Renaissance [rɪ'neɪsɑ̃ns] *n*: **the ~** el Renacimiento
rename [riː'neɪm] *vt* poner nuevo nombre a
render ['rɛndə*] *vt* (*thanks*) dar; (*aid*) proporcionar, prestar; (*make*): **to ~ sth useless** hacer algo inútil
rendezvous ['rɔndɪvuː] *n* cita
renew [rɪ'njuː] *vt* renovar; (*resume*) reanudar; (*loan etc*) prorrogar
renovate ['rɛnəveɪt] *vt* renovar
renowned [rɪ'naund] *adj* renombrado
rent [rɛnt] *n* (*for house*) arriendo, renta ▷ *vt* alquilar; **rental** *n* (*for television, car*) alquiler *m*
reorganize [riː'ɔːgənaɪz] *vt* reorganizar
rep [rɛp] *n abbr* = **representative**
repair [rɪ'pɛə*] *n* reparación *f*, compostura ▷ *vt* reparar, componer; (*shoes*) remendar; **in good/bad ~** en buen/mal estado; **repair kit** *n* caja de herramientas
repay [riː'peɪ] *vt* (*money*) devolver, reembolsar; (*person*) pagar; (*debt*) liquidar; (*sb's efforts*) devolver, corresponder a; **repayment** *n* reembolso, devolución *f*; (*sum of money*) recompensa
repeat [rɪ'piːt] *n* (*Radio, TV*) reposición *f* ▷ *vt* repetir ▷ *vi* repetirse; **repeatedly** *adv* repetidas veces; **repeat prescription** *n* (BRIT) receta renovada
repellent [rɪ'pɛlənt] *adj* repugnante ▷ *n*: **insect ~** crema *or* loción *f* anti-insectos
repercussions [riːpə'kʌʃənz] *npl* consecuencias *fpl*
repetition [rɛpɪ'tɪʃən] *n* repetición *f*
repetitive [rɪ'pɛtɪtɪv] *adj* repetitivo
replace [rɪ'pleɪs] *vt* (*put back*) devolver a su sitio; (*take the place*) reemplazar, sustituir; **replacement** *n* (*act*) reposición *f*; (*thing*) recambio; (*person*) suplente *mf*
replay ['riːpleɪ] *n* (*Sport*) desempate *m*; (*of tape, film*) repetición *f*
replica ['rɛplɪkə] *n* copia, reproducción *f* (exacta)
reply [rɪ'plaɪ] *n* respuesta, contestación *f* ▷ *vi* contestar, responder
report [rɪ'pɔːt] *n* informe *m*; (*Press etc*) reportaje *m*; (BRIT: *also*: **school ~**) boletín *m* escolar; (*of gun*) estallido ▷ *vt* informar de; (*Press etc*) hacer un reportaje sobre; (*notify: accident, culprit*) denunciar ▷ *vi* (*make a report*) presentar un informe; (*present o.s.*): **to ~ (to sb)** presentarse (ante algn); **report card** *n* (US, SCOTTISH) cartilla escolar; **reportedly** *adv* según se dice; **reporter** *n* periodista *mf*
represent [rɛprɪ'zɛnt] *vt* representar; (*Comm*) ser agente de; (*describe*): **to ~ sth as** describir algo como; **representation** [-'teɪʃən] *n* representación *f*; **representative** *n* representante *mf*; (US *Pol*) diputado/a *m/f* ▷ *adj* representativo
repress [rɪ'prɛs] *vt* reprimir; **repression** [-'prɛʃən] *n* represión *f*
reprimand ['rɛprɪmaːnd] *n*

reprimenda ▷ *vt* reprender
reproduce [ri:prə'dju:s] *vt* reproducir ▷ *vi* reproducirse; **reproduction** [-'dʌkʃən] *n* reproducción *f*
reptile ['rɛptaɪl] *n* reptil *m*
republic [rɪ'pʌblɪk] *n* república; **republican** *adj, n* republicano/a *m/f*
reputable ['rɛpjutəbl] *adj* (*make etc*) de renombre
reputation [rɛpju'teɪʃən] *n* reputación *f*
request [rɪ'kwɛst] *n* petición *f*; (*formal*) solicitud *f* ▷ *vt*: **to ~ sth of** *or* **from sb** solicitar algo a algn; **request stop** (BRIT) *n* parada discrecional
require [rɪ'kwaɪə*] *vt* (*need: person*) necesitar, tener necesidad de; (*: thing, situation*) exigir; (*want*) pedir; **to ~ sb to do sth** pedir a algn que haga algo; **requirement** *n* requisito; (*need*) necesidad *f*
resat [ri:'sæt] *pt, pp of* **resit**
rescue ['rɛskju:] *n* rescate *m* ▷ *vt* rescatar
research [rɪ'sə:tʃ] *n* investigaciones *fpl* ▷ *vt* investigar
resemblance [rɪ'zɛmbləns] *n* parecido
resemble [rɪ'zɛmbl] *vt* parecerse a
resent [rɪ'zɛnt] *vt* tomar a mal; **resentful** *adj* resentido; **resentment** *n* resentimiento
reservation [rɛzə'veɪʃən] *n* reserva; **reservation desk** (US) *n* (*in hotel*) recepción *f*
reserve [rɪ'zə:v] *n* reserva; (*Sport*) suplente *mf* ▷ *vt* (*seats etc*) reservar; **reserved** *adj* reservado
reservoir ['rɛzəvwɑ:*] *n* (*artificial lake*) embalse *m*, tank; (*small*) depósito
residence ['rɛzɪdəns] *n* (*formal: home*) domicilio; (*length of stay*) permanencia; **residence permit** (BRIT) *n* permiso de permanencia
resident ['rɛzɪdənt] *n* (*of area*) vecino/a; (*in hotel*) huésped *mf* ▷ *adj* (*population*) permanente; (*doctor*) residente; **residential** [-'dɛnʃəl] *adj* residencial
residue ['rɛzɪdju:] *n* resto
resign [rɪ'zaɪn] *vt* renunciar a ▷ *vi* dimitir; **to ~ o.s. to** (*situation*) resignarse a; **resignation** [rɛzɪg'neɪʃən] *n* dimisión *f*; (*state of mind*) resignación *f*
resin ['rɛzɪn] *n* resina
resist [rɪ'zɪst] *vt* resistir, oponerse a; **resistance** *n* resistencia
resit ['ri:sɪt] (BRIT) (*pt, pp* **resat**) *vt* (*exam*) volver a presentarse a; (*subject*) recuperar, volver a examinarse de (SP)
resolution [rɛzə'lu:ʃən] *n* resolución *f*
resolve [rɪ'zɔlv] *n* resolución *f* ▷ *vt* resolver ▷ *vi*: **to ~ to do** resolver hacer
resort [rɪ'zɔ:t] *n* (*town*) centro turístico; (*recourse*) recurso ▷ *vi*: **to ~ to** recurrir a; **in the last ~** como último recurso
resource [rɪ'sɔ:s] *n* recurso; **resourceful** *adj* despabilado, ingenioso
respect [rɪs'pɛkt] *n* respeto ▷ *vt* respetar; **respectable** *adj* respetable; (*large: amount*) apreciable; (*passable*) tolerable; **respectful** *adj* respetuoso; **respective** *adj* respectivo; **respectively** *adv* respectivamente
respite ['rɛspaɪt] *n* respiro
respond [rɪs'pɔnd] *vi* responder; (*react*) reaccionar; **response** [-'pɔns] *n* respuesta; reacción *f*
responsibility [rɪspɔnsɪ'bɪlɪtɪ] *n* responsabilidad *f*
responsible [rɪs'pɔnsɪbl] *adj* (*character*) serio, formal; (*job*) de confianza; (*liable*): **~ (for)** responsable (de); **responsibly** *adv* con seriedad
responsive [rɪs'pɔnsɪv] *adj* sensible
rest [rɛst] *n* descanso, reposo; (*Mus, pause*) pausa, silencio; (*support*) apoyo; (*remainder*) resto ▷ *vi* descansar; (*be supported*): **to ~ on** descansar sobre ▷ *vt*: **to ~ sth on/against** apoyar algo en *or*

sobre/contra; **the ~ of them** (*people, objects*) los demás; **it ~s with him to ...** depende de él el que ...
restaurant ['rɛstərɔŋ] *n* restaurante *m*; **restaurant car** (BRIT) *n* (*Rail*) coche-comedor *m*
restless ['rɛstlɪs] *adj* inquieto
restoration [rɛstə'reɪʃən] *n* restauración *f*; devolución *f*
restore [rɪ'stɔ:*] *vt* (*building*) restaurar; (*sth stolen*) devolver; (*health*) restablecer; (*to power*) volver a poner a
restrain [rɪs'treɪn] *vt* (*feeling*) contener, refrenar; (*person*): **to ~ (from doing)** disuadir (de hacer); **restraint** *n* (*restriction*) restricción *f*; (*moderation*) moderación *f*; (*of manner*) reserva
restrict [rɪs'trɪkt] *vt* restringir, limitar; **restriction** [-kʃən] *n* restricción *f*, limitación *f*
rest room (US) *n* aseos *mpl*
restructure [ri:'strʌktʃə*] *vt* reestructurar
result [rɪ'zʌlt] *n* resultado ▷ *vi*: **to ~ in** terminar en, tener por resultado; **as a ~ of** a consecuencia de
resume [rɪ'zju:m] *vt* reanudar ▷ *vi* comenzar de nuevo

> Be careful not to translate **resume** by the Spanish word *resumir*.

résumé ['reɪzju:meɪ] *n* resumen *m*; (US) currículum *m*
resuscitate [rɪ'sʌsɪteɪt] *vt* (*Med*) resucitar
retail ['ri:teɪl] *adj, adv* al por menor; **retailer** *n* detallista *mf*
retain [rɪ'teɪn] *vt* (*keep*) retener, conservar
retaliation [rɪtælɪ'eɪʃən] *n* represalias *fpl*
retarded [rɪ'tɑ:dɪd] *adj* retrasado
retire [rɪ'taɪə*] *vi* (*give up work*) jubilarse; (*withdraw*) retirarse; (*go to bed*) acostarse; **retired** *adj* (*person*) jubilado; **retirement** *n* (*giving up work: state*) retiro; (*: act*) jubilación *f*
retort [rɪ'tɔ:t] *vi* contestar
retreat [rɪ'tri:t] *n* (*place*) retiro; (*Mil*) retirada ▷ *vi* retirarse
retrieve [rɪ'tri:v] *vt* recobrar; (*situation, honour*) salvar; (*Comput*) recuperar; (*error*) reparar
retrospect ['rɛtrəspɛkt] *n*: **in ~** retrospectivamente; **retrospective** [-'spɛktɪv] *adj* retrospectivo; (*law*) retroactivo
return [rɪ'tə:n] *n* (*going or coming back*) vuelta, regreso; (*of sth stolen etc*) devolución *f*; (*Finance: from land, shares*) ganancia, ingresos *mpl* ▷ *cpd* (*journey*) de regreso; (BRIT: *ticket*) de ida y vuelta; (*match*) de vuelta ▷ *vi* (*person etc: come or go back*) volver, regresar; (*symptoms etc*) reaparecer; (*regain*): **to ~ to** recuperar ▷ *vt* devolver; (*favour, love etc*) corresponder a; (*verdict*) pronunciar; (*Pol: candidate*) elegir; **returns** *npl* (*Comm*) ingresos *mpl*; **in ~ (for)** a cambio (de); **by ~ of post** a vuelta de correo; **many happy ~s (of the day)!** ¡feliz cumpleaños!; **return ticket** *n* (*esp* BRIT) billete *m* (SP) *or* boleto *m* (LAM) de ida y vuelta, billete *m* redondo (MEX)
reunion [ri:'ju:nɪən] *n* (*of family*) reunión *f*; (*of two people, school*) reencuentro
reunite [ri:ju:'naɪt] *vt* reunir; (*reconcile*) reconciliar
revamp [ri:'væmp] *vt* renovar
reveal [rɪ'vi:l] *vt* revelar; **revealing** *adj* revelador(a)
revel ['rɛvl] *vi*: **to ~ in sth/in doing sth** gozar de algo/con hacer algo
revelation [rɛvə'leɪʃən] *n* revelación *f*
revenge [rɪ'vɛndʒ] *n* venganza; **to take ~ on** vengarse de
revenue ['rɛvənju:] *n* ingresos *mpl*, rentas *fpl*
Reverend ['rɛvərənd] *adj* (*in titles*): **the ~ John Smith** (*Anglican*) el Reverendo John Smith; (*Catholic*) el Padre John Smith; (*Protestant*) el Pastor John Smith
reversal [rɪ'və:sl] *n* (*of order*)

inversión *f*; (*of direction, policy*) cambio; (*of decision*) revocación *f*
reverse [rɪ'vəːs] *n* (*opposite*) contrario; (*back: of cloth*) revés *m*; (*: of coin*) reverso; (*: of paper*) dorso; (*Aut: also:* **~ gear**) marcha atrás, revés *m* ▷ *adj* (*order*) inverso; (*direction*) contrario; (*process*) opuesto ▷ *vt* (*decision, Aut*) dar marcha atrás a; (*position, function*) invertir ▷ *vi* (BRIT *Aut*) dar marcha atrás; **reverse-charge call** (BRIT) *n* llamada a cobro revertido; **reversing lights** (BRIT) *npl* (*Aut*) luces *fpl* de retroceso
revert [rɪ'vəːt] *vi*: **to ~ to** volver a
review [rɪ'vjuː] *n* (*magazine, Mil*) revista; (*of book, film*) reseña; (*US: examination*) repaso, examen *m* ▷ *vt* repasar, examinar; (*Mil*) pasar revista a; (*book, film*) reseñar
revise [rɪ'vaɪz] *vt* (*manuscript*) corregir; (*opinion*) modificar; (*price, procedure*) revisar ▷ *vi* (*study*) repasar; **revision** [rɪ'vɪʒən] *n* corrección *f*; modificación *f*; (*for exam*) repaso
revival [rɪ'vaɪvəl] *n* (*recovery*) reanimación *f*; (*of interest*) renacimiento; (*Theatre*) reestreno; (*of faith*) despertar *m*
revive [rɪ'vaɪv] *vt* resucitar; (*custom*) restablecer; (*hope*) despertar; (*play*) reestrenar ▷ *vi* (*person*) volver en sí; (*business*) reactivarse
revolt [rɪ'vəult] *n* rebelión *f* ▷ *vi* rebelarse, sublevarse ▷ *vt* dar asco a, repugnar; **revolting** *adj* asqueroso, repugnante
revolution [rɛvə'luːʃən] *n* revolución *f*; **revolutionary** *adj, n* revolucionario/a *m/f*
revolve [rɪ'vɔlv] *vi* dar vueltas, girar; (*life, discussion*): **to ~ (a)round** girar en torno a
revolver [rɪ'vɔlvə*] *n* revólver *m*
reward [rɪ'wɔːd] *n* premio, recompensa ▷ *vt*: **to ~ (for)** recompensar *or* premiar (por); **rewarding** *adj* (*fig*) valioso
rewind [riː'waɪnd] *vt* rebobinar
rewritable [riː'raɪtəbl] *adj* (*CD, DVD*) reescribible
rewrite [riː'raɪt] (*pt* **rewrote**, *pp* **rewritten**) *vt* reescribir
rheumatism ['ruːmətɪzəm] *n* reumatismo, reúma *m*
rhinoceros [raɪ'nɔsərəs] *n* rinoceronte *m*
rhubarb ['ruːbɑːb] *n* ruibarbo
rhyme [raɪm] *n* rima; (*verse*) poesía
rhythm ['rɪðm] *n* ritmo
rib [rɪb] *n* (*Anat*) costilla ▷ *vt* (*mock*) tomar el pelo a
ribbon ['rɪbən] *n* cinta; **in ~s** (*torn*) hecho trizas
rice [raɪs] *n* arroz *m*; **rice pudding** *n* arroz *m* con leche
rich [rɪtʃ] *adj* rico; (*soil*) fértil; (*food*) pesado; (*: sweet*) empalagoso; (*abundant*): **~ in** (*minerals etc*) rico en
rid [rɪd] (*pt, pp* **~**) *vt*: **to ~ sb of sth** librar a algn de algo; **to get ~ of** deshacerse *or* desembarazarse de
riddle ['rɪdl] *n* (*puzzle*) acertijo; (*mystery*) enigma *m*, misterio ▷ *vt*: **to be ~d with** ser lleno *or* plagado de
ride [raɪd] (*pt* **rode**, *pp* **ridden**) *n* paseo; (*distance covered*) viaje *m*, recorrido ▷ *vi* (*as sport*) montar; (*go somewhere: on horse, bicycle*) dar un paseo, pasearse; (*travel: on bicycle, motorcycle, bus*) viajar ▷ *vt* (*a horse*) montar a; (*a bicycle, motorcycle*) andar en; (*distance*) recorrer; **to take sb for a ~** (*fig*) engañar a algn; **rider** *n* (*on horse*) jinete *mf*; (*on bicycle*) ciclista *mf*; (*on motorcycle*) motociclista *mf*
ridge [rɪdʒ] *n* (*of hill*) cresta; (*of roof*) caballete *m*; (*wrinkle*) arruga
ridicule ['rɪdɪkjuːl] *n* irrisión *f*, burla ▷ *vt* poner en ridículo, burlarse de; **ridiculous** [-'dɪkjuləs] *adj* ridículo
riding ['raɪdɪŋ] *n* equitación *f*; **I like ~** me gusta montar a caballo; **riding school** *n* escuela de equitación
rife [raɪf] *adj*: **to be ~** ser muy común; **to be ~ with** abundar en

rifle ['raɪfl] *n* rifle *m*, fusil *m* ▷ *vt* saquear

rift [rɪft] *n* (*in clouds*) claro; (*fig: disagreement*) desavenencia

rig [rɪg] *n* (*also*: **oil ~**: *at sea*) plataforma petrolera ▷ *vt* (*election etc*) amañar

right [raɪt] *adj* (*correct*) correcto, exacto; (*suitable*) indicado, debido; (*proper*) apropiado; (*just*) justo; (*morally good*) bueno; (*not left*) derecho ▷ *n* bueno; (*title, claim*) derecho; (*not left*) derecha ▷ *adv* bien, correctamente; (*not left*) a la derecha; (*exactly*): **~ now** ahora mismo ▷ *vt* enderezar; (*correct*) corregir ▷ *excl* ¡bueno!, ¡está bien!; **to be ~** (*person*) tener razón; (*answer*) ser correcto; **is that the ~ time?** (*of clock*) ¿es esa la hora buena?; **by ~s** en justicia; **on the ~** a la derecha; **to be in the ~** tener razón; **~ away** en seguida; **~ in the middle** exactamente en el centro; **right angle** *n* ángulo recto; **rightful** *adj* legítimo; **right-hand** *adj*: **right-hand drive** conducción *f* por la derecha; **the right-hand side** derecha; **right-handed** *adj* diestro; **rightly** *adv* correctamente, debidamente; (*with reason*) con razón; **right of way** *n* (*on path etc*) derecho de paso; (*Aut*) prioridad *f*; **right-wing** *adj* (*Pol*) derechista

rigid ['rɪdʒɪd] *adj* rígido; (*person, ideas*) inflexible

rigorous ['rɪgərəs] *adj* riguroso

rim [rɪm] *n* borde *m*; (*of spectacles*) aro; (*of wheel*) llanta

rind [raɪnd] *n* (*of bacon*) corteza; (*of lemon etc*) cáscara; (*of cheese*) costra

ring [rɪŋ] (*pt* **rang**, *pp* **rung**) *n* (*of metal*) aro; (*on finger*) anillo; (*of people*) corro; (*of objects*) círculo; (*gang*) banda; (*for boxing*) cuadrilátero; (*of circus*) pista; (*bull ring*) ruedo, plaza; (*sound of bell*) toque *m* ▷ *vi* (*on telephone*) llamar por teléfono; (*bell*) repicar; (*doorbell, phone*) sonar; (*also*: **~ out**) sonar; (*ears*) zumbar ▷ *vt* (BRIT *Tel*) llamar, telefonear; (*bell etc*) hacer sonar; (*doorbell*) tocar; **to give sb a ~** (BRIT *Tel*) llamar *or* telefonear a algn; **ring back** (BRIT) *vt, vi* (*Tel*) devolver la llamada; **ring off** (BRIT) *vi* (*Tel*) colgar, cortar la comunicación; **ring up** (BRIT) *vt* (*Tel*) llamar, telefonear; **ringing tone** *n* (*Tel*) tono de llamada; **ringleader** *n* (*of gang*) cabecilla *m*; **ring road** (BRIT) *n* carretera periférica *or* de circunvalación; **ringtone** *n* (*on mobile*) tono de llamada

rink [rɪŋk] *n* (*also*: **ice ~**) pista de hielo

rinse [rɪns] *n* aclarado; (*dye*) tinte *m* ▷ *vt* aclarar; (*mouth*) enjuagar

riot ['raɪət] *n* motín *m*, disturbio ▷ *vi* amotinarse; **to run ~** desmandarse

rip [rɪp] *n* rasgón *m*, rasgadura ▷ *vt* rasgar, desgarrar ▷ *vi* rasgarse, desgarrarse; **rip off** *vt* (*inf: cheat*) estafar; **rip up** *vt* hacer pedazos

ripe [raɪp] *adj* maduro

rip-off ['rɪpɔf] *n* (*inf*): **it's a ~!** ¡es una estafa!, ¡es un timo!

ripple ['rɪpl] *n* onda, rizo; (*sound*) murmullo ▷ *vi* rizarse

rise [raɪz] (*pt* **rose**, *pp* **risen**) *n* (*slope*) cuesta, pendiente *f*; (*hill*) altura; (BRIT: *in wages*) aumento; (*in prices, temperature*) subida; (*fig: to power etc*) ascenso ▷ *vi* subir; (*waters*) crecer; (*sun, moon*) salir; (*person: from bed etc*) levantarse; (*also*: **~ up**: *rebel*) sublevarse; (*in rank*) ascender; **to give ~ to** dar lugar *or* origen a; **to ~ to the occasion** ponerse a la altura de las circunstancias; **risen** ['rɪzn] *pp of* **rise**; **rising** *adj* (*increasing: number*) creciente; (*: prices*) en aumento *or* alza; (*tide*) creciente; (*sun, moon*) naciente

risk [rɪsk] *n* riesgo, peligro ▷ *vt* arriesgar; (*run the risk of*) exponerse a; **to take** *or* **run the ~ of doing** correr el riesgo de hacer; **at ~** en peligro; **at one's own ~** bajo su propia responsabilidad; **risky** *adj* arriesgado, peligroso

rite [raɪt] *n* rito; **last ~s** exequias *fpl*

ritual ['rɪtjuəl] *adj* ritual ▷ *n* ritual

m, rito

rival ['raɪvl] *n* rival *mf*; (*in business*) competidor(a) *m/f* ▷ *adj* rival, opuesto ▷ *vt* competir con; **rivalry** *n* competencia

river ['rɪvə*] *n* río ▷ *cpd* (*port*) de río; (*traffic*) fluvial; **up/down ~** río arriba/ abajo; **riverbank** *n* orilla (del río)

rivet ['rɪvɪt] *n* roblón *m*, remache *m* ▷ *vt* (*fig*) captar

road [rəud] *n* camino; (*motorway etc*) carretera; (*in town*) calle *f* ▷ *cpd* (*accident*) de tráfico; **major/minor ~** carretera principal/secundaria; **roadblock** *n* barricada; **road map** *n* mapa *m* de carreteras; **road rage** *n* *agresividad en la carretera*; **road safety** *n* seguridad *f* vial; **roadside** *n* borde *m* (del camino); **roadsign** *n* señal *f* de tráfico; **road tax** *n* (BRIT) impuesto de rodaje; **roadworks** *npl* obras *fpl*

roam [rəum] *vi* vagar

roar [rɔː*] *n* rugido; (*of vehicle, storm*) estruendo; (*of laughter*) carcajada ▷ *vi* rugir; hacer estruendo; **to ~ with laughter** reírse a carcajadas; **to do a ~ing trade** hacer buen negocio

roast [rəust] *n* carne *f* asada, asado ▷ *vt* asar; (*coffee*) tostar; **roast beef** *n* rosbif *m*

rob [rɔb] *vt* robar; **to ~ sb of sth** robar algo a algn; (*fig: deprive*) quitar algo a algn; **robber** *n* ladrón/ona *m/f*; **robbery** *n* robo

robe [rəub] *n* (*for ceremony etc*) toga; (*also*: **bath~**) albornoz *m*

robin ['rɔbɪn] *n* petirrojo

robot ['rəubɔt] *n* robot *m*

robust [rəu'bʌst] *adj* robusto, fuerte

rock [rɔk] *n* roca; (*boulder*) peña, peñasco; (*US: small stone*) piedrecita; (BRIT: *sweet*) ≈ pirulí ▷ *vt* (*swing gently: cradle*) balancear, mecer; (*: child*) arrullar; (*shake*) sacudir ▷ *vi* mecerse, balancearse; sacudirse; **on the ~s** (*drink*) con hielo; (*marriage etc*) en ruinas; **rock and roll** *n* rocanrol *m*; **rock climbing** *n* (*Sport*) escalada

rocket ['rɔkɪt] *n* cohete *m*; **rocking chair** ['rɔkɪŋ-] *n* mecedora

rocky ['rɔkɪ] *adj* rocoso

rod [rɔd] *n* vara, varilla; (*also*: **fishing ~**) caña

rode [rəud] *pt of* **ride**

rodent ['rəudnt] *n* roedor *m*

rogue [rəug] *n* pícaro, pillo

role [rəul] *n* papel *m*; **role-model** *n* modelo a imitar

roll [rəul] *n* rollo; (*of bank notes*) fajo; (*also*: **bread ~**) panecillo; (*register, list*) lista, nómina; (*sound of drums etc*) redoble *m* ▷ *vt* hacer rodar; (*also*: **~ up**: *string*) enrollar; (*cigarette*) liar; (*also*: **~ out**: *pastry*) aplanar; (*flatten: road, lawn*) apisonar ▷ *vi* rodar; (*drum*) redoblar; (*ship*) balancearse; **roll over** *vi* dar una vuelta; **roll up** *vi* (*inf: arrive*) aparecer ▷ *vt* (*carpet*) arrollar; (*: sleeves*) arremangar; **roller** *n* rodillo; (*wheel*) rueda; (*for road*) apisonadora; (*for hair*) rulo; **Rollerblades®** *npl* patines *mpl* en línea; **roller coaster** *n* montaña rusa; **roller skates** *npl* patines *mpl* de rueda; **roller-skating** *n* patinaje sobre ruedas; **to go roller-skating** ir a patinar (*sobre ruedas*); **rolling pin** *n* rodillo (de cocina)

ROM [rɔm] *n abbr* (*Comput: = read only memory*) ROM *f*

Roman ['rəumən] (*irreg*) *adj* romano/a; **Roman Catholic** (*irreg*) *adj, n* católico/a *m/f* (romano/a)

romance [rə'mæns] *n* (*love affair*) amor *m*; (*charm*) lo romántico; (*novel*) novela de amor

Romania *etc* [ruː'meɪnɪə] *n* = **Rumania** *etc*

Roman numeral *n* número romano

romantic [rə'mæntɪk] *adj* romántico

Rome [rəum] *n* Roma

roof [ruːf] (*pl* **~s**) *n* techo; (*of house*) techo, tejado ▷ *vt* techar, poner techo a; **the ~ of the mouth** el paladar; **roof rack** *n* (*Aut*) baca, portaequipajes *m inv*

rook [ruk] *n* (*bird*) graja; (*Chess*) torre *f*

room [ruːm] *n* cuarto, habitación *f*; (*also*: **bed~**) dormitorio, recámara (MEX), pieza (SC); (*in school etc*) sala; (*space, scope*) sitio, cabida; **roommate** *n* compañero/a de cuarto; **room service** *n* servicio de habitaciones; **roomy** *adj* espacioso; (*garment*) amplio

rooster ['ruːstə*] *n* gallo

root [ruːt] *n* raíz *f* ▷ *vi* arraigarse

rope [rəup] *n* cuerda; (*Naut*) cable *m* ▷ *vt* (*tie*) atar *or* amarrar con (una) cuerda; (*climbers*: *also*: **~ together**) encordarse; (*an area*: *also*: **~ off**) acordonar; **to know the ~s** (*fig*) conocer los trucos (del oficio)

rose [rəuz] *pt of* **rise** ▷ *n* rosa; (*shrub*) rosal *m*; (*on watering can*) roseta

rosé ['rəuzeɪ] *n* vino rosado

rosemary ['rəuzmərɪ] *n* romero

rosy ['rəuzɪ] *adj* rosado, sonrosado; **a ~ future** un futuro prometedor

rot [rɔt] *n* podredumbre *f*; (*fig*: *pej*) tonterías *fpl* ▷ *vt* pudrir ▷ *vi* pudrirse

rota ['rəutə] *n* (sistema *m* de) turnos *m*

rotate [rəu'teɪt] *vt* (*revolve*) hacer girar, dar vueltas a; (*jobs*) alternar ▷ *vi* girar, dar vueltas

rotten ['rɔtn] *adj* podrido; (*dishonest*) corrompido; (*inf*: *bad*) pocho; **to feel ~** (*ill*) sentirse fatal

rough [rʌf] *adj* (*skin, surface*) áspero; (*terrain*) quebrado; (*road*) desigual; (*voice*) bronco; (*person, manner*) tosco, grosero; (*weather*) borrascoso; (*treatment*) brutal; (*sea*) picado; (*town, area*) peligroso; (*cloth*) basto; (*plan*) preliminar; (*guess*) aproximado ▷ *n* (*Golf*): **in the ~** en las hierbas altas; **to ~ it** vivir sin comodidades; **to sleep ~** (BRIT) pasar la noche al raso; **roughly** *adv* (*handle*) torpemente; (*make*) toscamente; (*speak*) groseramente; (*approximately*) aproximadamente

roulette [ruː'lɛt] *n* ruleta

round [raund] *adj* redondo ▷ *n* círculo; (BRIT: *of toast*) rebanada; (*of policeman*) ronda; (*of milkman*) recorrido; (*of doctor*) visitas *fpl*; (*game*: *of cards, in competition*) partida; (*of ammunition*) cartucho; (*Boxing*) asalto; (*of talks*) ronda ▷ *vt* (*corner*) doblar ▷ *prep* alrededor de; (*surrounding*): **~ his neck/the table** en su cuello/alrededor de la mesa; (*in a circular movement*): **to move ~ the room/sail ~ the world** dar una vuelta a la habitación/circumnavigar el mundo; (*in various directions*): **to move ~ a room/house** moverse por toda la habitación/casa; (*approximately*) alrededor de ▷ *adv*: **all ~** por todos lados; **the long way ~** por el camino menos directo; **all (the) year ~** durante todo el año; **it's just ~ the corner** (*fig*) está a la vuelta de la esquina; **~ the clock** *adv* las 24 horas; **to go ~ to sb's (house)** ir a casa de algn; **to go ~ the back** pasar por atrás; **enough to go ~** bastante (para todos); **a ~ of applause** una salva de aplausos; **a ~ of drinks/sandwiches** una ronda de bebidas/bocadillos; **round off** *vt* (*speech etc*) acabar, poner término a; **round up** *vt* (*cattle*) acorralar; (*people*) reunir; (*price*) redondear; **roundabout** (BRIT) *n* (*Aut*) isleta; (*at fair*) tiovivo ▷ *adj* (*route, means*) indirecto; **round trip** *n* viaje *m* de ida y vuelta; **roundup** *n* rodeo; (*of criminals*) redada; (*of news*) resumen *m*

rouse [rauz] *vt* (*wake up*) despertar; (*stir up*) suscitar

route [ruːt] *n* ruta, camino; (*of bus*) recorrido; (*of shipping*) derrota

routine [ruː'tiːn] *adj* rutinario ▷ *n* rutina; (*Theatre*) número

row¹ [rəu] *n* (*line*) fila, hilera; (*Knitting*) pasada ▷ *vi* (*in boat*) remar ▷ *vt* conducir remando; **4 days in a ~** 4 días seguidos

row² [rau] *n* (*racket*) escándalo; (*dispute*) bronca, pelea; (*scolding*) regaño ▷ *vi* pelear(se)

rowboat ['rəubəut] (US) = **rowing boat**

rowing ['rəuɪŋ] *n* remo; **rowing boat** (BRIT) *n* bote *m* de remos
royal ['rɔɪəl] *adj* real; **royalty** *n* (*royal persons*) familia real; (*payment to author*) derechos *mpl* de autor
rpm *abbr* (= *revs per minute*) r.p.m.
R.S.V.P. *abbr* (= *répondez s'il vous plaót*) SRC
Rt. Hon. *abbr* (BRIT) (= *Right Honourable*) *título honorífico de diputado*
rub [rʌb] *vt* frotar; (*scrub*) restregar ▷ *n*: **to give sth a ~** frotar algo; **to ~ sb up** *or* **~ sb** (US) **the wrong way** entrarle algn por mal ojo; **rub in** *vt* (*ointment*) aplicar frotando; **rub off** *vi* borrarse; **rub out** *vt* borrar
rubber ['rʌbə*] *n* caucho, goma; (BRIT: *eraser*) goma de borrar; **rubber band** *n* goma, gomita; **rubber gloves** *npl* guantes *mpl* de goma
rubbish ['rʌbɪʃ] (BRIT) *n* basura; (*waste*) desperdicios *mpl*; (*fig*: *pej*) tonterías *fpl*; (*junk*) pacotilla; **rubbish bin** (BRIT) *n* cubo *or* bote *m* (MEX) *or* tacho (SC) de la basura; **rubbish dump** (BRIT) *n* vertedero, basurero
rubble ['rʌbl] *n* escombros *mpl*
ruby ['ru:bɪ] *n* rubí *m*
rucksack ['rʌksæk] *n* mochila
rudder ['rʌdə*] *n* timón *m*
rude [ru:d] *adj* (*impolite*: *person*) mal educado; (: *word, manners*) grosero; (*crude*) crudo; (*indecent*) indecente
ruffle ['rʌfl] *vt* (*hair*) despeinar; (*clothes*) arrugar; **to get ~d** (*fig*: *person*) alterarse
rug [rʌg] *n* alfombra; (BRIT: *blanket*) manta
rugby ['rʌgbɪ] *n* rugby *m*
rugged ['rʌgɪd] *adj* (*landscape*) accidentado; (*features*) robusto
ruin ['ru:ɪn] *n* ruina ▷ *vt* arruinar; (*spoil*) estropear; **ruins** *npl* ruinas *fpl*, restos *mpl*
rule [ru:l] *n* (*norm*) norma, costumbre *f*; (*regulation, ruler*) regla; (*government*) dominio ▷ *vt* (*country, person*) gobernar ▷ *vi* gobernar; (*Law*) fallar; **as a ~** por regla general; **rule out** *vt* excluir; **ruler** *n* (*sovereign*) soberano; (*for measuring*) regla; **ruling** *adj* (*party*) gobernante; (*class*) dirigente ▷ *n* (*Law*) fallo, decisión *f*
rum [rʌm] *n* ron *m*
Rumania [ru:'meɪnɪə] *n* Rumanía; **Rumanian** *adj* rumano/a ▷ *n* rumano/a *m/f*; (*Ling*) rumano
rumble ['rʌmbl] *n* (*noise*) ruido sordo ▷ *vi* retumbar, hacer un ruido sordo; (*stomach, pipe*) sonar
rumour ['ru:mə*] (US **rumor**) *n* rumor *m* ▷ *vt*: **it is ~ed that ...** se rumorea que ...
rump steak *n* filete *m* de lomo
run [rʌn] (*pt* **ran**, *pp* **run**) *n* (*fast pace*): **at a ~** corriendo; (*Sport, in tights*) carrera; (*outing*) paseo, excursión *f*; (*distance travelled*) trayecto; (*series*) serie *f*; (*Theatre*) temporada; (*Ski*) pista ▷ *vt* correr; (*operate*: *business*) dirigir; (: *competition, course*) organizar; (: *hotel, house*) administrar, llevar; (*Comput*) ejecutar; (*pass*: *hand*) pasar; (*Press*: *feature*) publicar ▷ *vi* correr; (*work*: *machine*) funcionar, marchar; (*bus, train*: *operate*) circular, ir; (: *travel*) ir; (*continue*: *play*) seguir; (*contract*) ser válido; (*flow*: *river*) fluir; (*colours, washing*) desteñirse; (*in election*) ser candidato; **there was a ~ on** (*meat, tickets*) hubo mucha demanda de; **in the long ~** a la larga; **on the ~** en fuga; **I'll ~ you to the station** te llevaré a la estación (en coche); **to ~ a risk** correr un riesgo; **to ~ a bath** llenar la bañera; **run after** *vt fus* (*to catch up*) correr tras; (*chase*) perseguir; **run away** *vi* huir; **run down** *vt* (*production*) ir reduciendo; (*factory*) ir restringiendo la producción en; (*car*) atropellar; (*criticize*) criticar; **to be run down** (*person*: *tired*) estar debilitado; **run into** *vt fus* (*meet*: *person, trouble*) tropezar con; (*collide with*) chocar con; **run off** *vt* (*water*) dejar correr; (*copies*) sacar ▷ *vi* huir corriendo; **run out** *vi* (*person*) salir

corriendo; (*liquid*) irse; (*lease*) caducar, vencer; (*money etc*) acabarse; **run out of** *vt fus* quedar sin; **run over** *vt* (*Aut*) atropellar ▷ *vt fus* (*revise*) repasar; **run through** *vt fus* (*instructions*) repasar; **run up** *vt* (*debt*) contraer; **to run up against** (*difficulties*) tropezar con; **runaway** *adj* (*horse*) desbocado; (*truck*) sin frenos; (*child*) escapado de casa

rung [rʌŋ] *pp of* **ring** ▷ *n* (*of ladder*) escalón *m*, peldaño

runner ['rʌnə*] *n* (*in race: person*) corredor(a) *m/f*; (: *horse*) caballo; (*on sledge*) patín *m*; **runner bean** (BRIT) *n* ≈ judía verde; **runner-up** *n* subcampeón/ona *m/f*

running ['rʌnɪŋ] *n* (*sport*) atletismo; (*of business*) administración *f* ▷ *adj* (*water, costs*) corriente; (*commentary*) continuo; **to be in/out of the ~ for sth** tener/no tener posibilidades de ganar algo; **6 days ~** 6 días seguidos

runny ['rʌnɪ] *adj* fluido; (*nose, eyes*) gastante

run-up ['rʌnʌp] *n*: **~ to** (*election etc*) período previo a

runway ['rʌnweɪ] *n* (*Aviat*) pista de aterrizaje

rupture ['rʌptʃə*] *n* (*Med*) hernia ▷ *vt*: **to ~ o.s** causarse una hernia

rural ['ruərl] *adj* rural

rush [rʌʃ] *n* ímpetu *m*; (*hurry*) prisa; (*Comm*) demanda repentina; (*current*) corriente *f* fuerte; (*of feeling*) torrente *m*; (*Bot*) junco ▷ *vt* apresurar; (*work*) hacer de prisa ▷ *vi* correr, precipitarse; **rush hour** *n* horas *fpl* punta

Russia ['rʌʃə] *n* Rusia; **Russian** *adj* ruso/a ▷ *n* ruso/a *m/f*; (*Ling*) ruso

rust [rʌst] *n* herrumbre *f*, moho ▷ *vi* oxidarse

rusty ['rʌstɪ] *adj* oxidado

ruthless ['ru:θlɪs] *adj* despiadado

RV (US) *n abbr* = **recreational vehicle**

rye [raɪ] *n* centeno

S

Sabbath ['sæbəθ] *n* domingo; (*Jewish*) sábado

sabotage ['sæbətɑ:ʒ] *n* sabotaje *m* ▷ *vt* sabotear

saccharin(e) ['sækərɪn] *n* sacarina

sachet ['sæʃeɪ] *n* sobrecito

sack [sæk] *n* (*bag*) saco, costal *m* ▷ *vt* (*dismiss*) despedir; (*plunder*) saquear; **to get the ~** ser despedido

sacred ['seɪkrɪd] *adj* sagrado, santo

sacrifice ['sækrɪfaɪs] *n* sacrificio ▷ *vt* sacrificar

sad [sæd] *adj* (*unhappy*) triste; (*deplorable*) lamentable

saddle ['sædl] *n* silla (de montar); (*of cycle*) sillín *m* ▷ *vt* (*horse*) ensillar; **to be ~d with sth** (*inf*) quedar cargado con algo

sadistic [sə'dɪstɪk] *adj* sádico

sadly ['sædlɪ] *adv* lamentablemente; **to be ~ lacking in** estar por desgracia carente de

sadness ['sædnɪs] *n* tristeza

s.a.e. *abbr* (= *stamped addressed envelope*) *sobre con las propias señas de* *uno y con sello*

safari [sə'fɑːrɪ] *n* safari *m*

safe [seɪf] *adj* (*out of danger*) fuera de peligro; (*not dangerous, sure*) seguro; (*unharmed*) ileso ▷ *n* caja de caudales, caja fuerte; **~ and sound** sano y salvo; **(just) to be on the ~ side** para mayor seguridad; **safely** *adv* seguramente, con seguridad; **to arrive safely** llegar bien; **safe sex** *n* sexo seguro *or* sin riesgo

safety ['seɪftɪ] *n* seguridad *f*; **safety belt** *n* cinturón *m* (de seguridad); **safety pin** *n* imperdible *m*, seguro (MEX), alfiler *m* de gancho (SC)

saffron ['sæfrən] *n* azafrán *m*

sag [sæg] *vi* aflojarse

sage [seɪdʒ] *n* (*herb*) salvia; (*man*) sabio

Sagittarius [sædʒɪ'tɛərɪəs] *n* Sagitario

Sahara [sə'hɑːrə] *n*: **the ~ (Desert)** el (desierto del) Sáhara

said [sɛd] *pt, pp of* **say**

sail [seɪl] *n* (*on boat*) vela; (*trip*): **to go for a ~** dar un paseo en barco ▷ *vt* (*boat*) gobernar ▷ *vi* (*travel*: *ship*) navegar; (*Sport*) hacer vela; (*begin voyage*) salir; **they ~ed into Copenhagen** arribaron a Copenhague; **sailboat** (US) *n* = **sailing boat**; **sailing** *n* (*Sport*) vela; **to go sailing** hacer vela; **sailing boat** *n* barco de vela; **sailor** *n* marinero, marino

saint [seɪnt] *n* santo

sake [seɪk] *n*: **for the ~ of** por

salad ['sæləd] *n* ensalada; **salad cream** (BRIT) *n* (especie *f* de) mayonesa; **salad dressing** *n* aliño

salami [sə'lɑːmɪ] *n* salami *m*, salchichón *m*

salary ['sælərɪ] *n* sueldo

sale [seɪl] *n* venta; (*at reduced prices*) liquidación *f*, saldo; (*auction*) subasta; **sales** *npl* (*total amount sold*) ventas *fpl*, facturación *f*; **"for ~"** "se vende"; **on ~** en venta; **on ~ or return** (*goods*) venta por reposición; **sales assistant** (US), **sales clerk** *n* dependiente/a *m/f*; **salesman/woman** (*irreg*) *n* (*in shop*) dependiente/a *m/f*; **salesperson** (*irreg*) *n* vendedor(a) *m/f*, dependiente/a *m/f*; **sales rep** *n* representante *mf*, agente *mf* comercial

saline ['seɪlaɪn] *adj* salino

saliva [sə'laɪvə] *n* saliva

salmon ['sæmən] *n inv* salmón *m*

salon ['sælɔn] *n* (*hairdressing salon*) peluquería; (*beauty salon*) salón *m* de belleza

saloon [sə'luːn] *n* (US) bar *m*, taberna; (BRIT *Aut*) coche *m* (de) turismo; (*ship's lounge*) cámara, salón *m*

salt [sɔlt] *n* sal *f* ▷ *vt* salar; (*put salt on*) poner sal en; **saltwater** *adj* de agua salada; **salty** *adj* salado

salute [sə'luːt] *n* saludo; (*of guns*) salva ▷ *vt* saludar

salvage ['sælvɪdʒ] *n* (*saving*) salvamento, recuperación *f*; (*things saved*) objetos *mpl* salvados ▷ *vt* salvar

Salvation Army [sæl'veɪʃən-] *n* Ejército de Salvación

same [seɪm] *adj* mismo ▷ *pron*: **the ~** el(la) mismo/a, los(las) mismos/as; **the ~ book as** el mismo libro que; **at the ~ time** (*at the same moment*) al mismo tiempo; (*yet*) sin embargo; **all** *or* **just the ~** sin embargo, aun así; **to do the ~ (as sb)** hacer lo mismo (que algn); **the ~ to you!** ¡igualmente!

sample ['sɑːmpl] *n* muestra ▷ *vt* (*food*) probar; (*wine*) catar

sanction ['sæŋkʃən] *n* aprobación *f* ▷ *vt* sancionar; aprobar; **sanctions** *npl* (*Pol*) sanciones *fpl*

sanctuary ['sæŋktjuərɪ] *n* santuario; (*refuge*) asilo, refugio; (*for wildlife*) reserva

sand [sænd] *n* arena; (*beach*) playa ▷ *vt* (*also*: **~ down**) lijar

sandal ['sændl] *n* sandalia

sand: sandbox (US) *n* = **sandpit**; **sandcastle** *n* castillo de arena; **sand dune** *n* duna; **sandpaper** *n* papel *m* de lija; **sandpit** *n* (*for children*) cajón *m* de arena; **sands** *npl* playa *sg* de arena; **sandstone** ['sændstəun] *n* piedra arenisca

sandwich ['sændwɪtʃ] *n* sandwich *m* ▷ *vt* intercalar; **~ed between** apretujado entre; **cheese/ham ~** sandwich de queso/jamón

sandy ['sændɪ] *adj* arenoso; (*colour*) rojizo

sane [seɪn] *adj* cuerdo; (*sensible*) sensato

Be careful not to translate **sane** by the Spanish word *sano*.

sang [sæŋ] *pt of* **sing**

sanitary towel (*US* **sanitary napkin**) *n* paño higiénico, compresa

sanity ['sænɪtɪ] *n* cordura; (*of judgment*) sensatez *f*

sank [sæŋk] *pt of* **sink**

Santa Claus [sæntə'klɔːz] *n* San Nicolás, Papá Noel

sap [sæp] *n* (*of plants*) savia ▷ *vt* (*strength*) minar, agotar

sapphire ['sæfaɪə*] *n* zafiro

sarcasm ['sɑːkæzm] *n* sarcasmo

sarcastic [sɑː'kæstɪk] *adj* sarcástico

sardine [sɑː'diːn] *n* sardina

SASE (*US*) *n abbr* (= *self-addressed stamped envelope*) *sobre con las propias señas de uno y con sello*

Sat. *abbr* (= *Saturday*) sáb

sat [sæt] *pt, pp of* **sit**

satchel ['sætʃl] *n* (*child's*) mochila, cartera (*SP*)

satellite ['sætəlaɪt] *n* satélite *m*; **satellite dish** *n* antena de televisión por satélite; **satellite television** *n* televisión *f* vía satélite

satin ['sætɪn] *n* raso ▷ *adj* de raso

satire ['sætaɪə*] *n* sátira

satisfaction [sætɪs'fækʃən] *n* satisfacción *f*

satisfactory [sætɪs'fæktərɪ] *adj* satisfactorio

satisfied ['sætɪsfaɪd] *adj* satisfecho; **to be ~ (with sth)** estar satisfecho (de algo)

satisfy ['sætɪsfaɪ] *vt* satisfacer; (*convince*) convencer

Saturday ['sætədɪ] *n* sábado

sauce [sɔːs] *n* salsa; (*sweet*) crema; jarabe *m*; **saucepan** *n* cacerola, olla

saucer ['sɔːsə*] *n* platillo; **Saudi Arabia** *n* Arabia Saudí *or* Saudita

sauna ['sɔːnə] *n* sauna

sausage ['sɔsɪdʒ] *n* salchicha; **sausage roll** *n* empanadita de salchicha

sautéed ['səuteɪd] *adj* salteado

savage ['sævɪdʒ] *adj* (*cruel, fierce*) feroz, furioso; (*primitive*) salvaje ▷ *n* salvaje *mf* ▷ *vt* (*attack*) embestir

save [seɪv] *vt* (*rescue*) salvar, rescatar; (*money, time*) ahorrar; (*put by, keep: seat*) guardar; (*Comput*) salvar (y guardar); (*avoid: trouble*) evitar; (*Sport*) parar ▷ *vi* (*also:* **~ up**) ahorrar ▷ *n* (*Sport*) parada ▷ *prep* salvo, excepto

savings ['seɪvɪŋz] *npl* ahorros *mpl*; **savings account** *n* cuenta de ahorros; **savings and loan association** (*US*) *n* sociedad *f* de ahorro y préstamo

savoury ['seɪvərɪ] (*US* **savory**) *adj* sabroso; (*dish: not sweet*) salado

saw [sɔː] (*pt* **~ed**, *pp* **~ed** *or* **~n**) *pt of* **see** ▷ *n* (*tool*) sierra ▷ *vt* serrar; **sawdust** *n* (a)serrín *m*

sawn [sɔːn] *pp of* **saw**

saxophone ['sæksəfəun] *n* saxófono

say [seɪ] (*pt, pp* **said**) *n*: **to have one's ~** expresar su opinión ▷ *vt* decir; **to have a** *or* **some ~ in sth** tener voz *or* tener que ver en algo; **to ~ yes/no** decir que sí/no; **could you ~ that again?** ¿podría repetir eso?; **that is to ~** es decir; **that goes without ~ing** ni que decir tiene; **saying** *n* dicho, refrán *m*

scab [skæb] *n* costra; (*pej*) esquirol *m*

scaffolding ['skæfəldɪŋ] *n* andamio, andamiaje *m*

scald [skɔːld] *n* escaldadura ▷ *vt* escaldar

scale [skeɪl] *n* (*gen, Mus*) escala; (*of fish*) escama; (*of salaries, fees etc*) escalafón *m* ▷ *vt* (*mountain*) escalar; (*tree*) trepar; **scales** *npl* (*for* *weighing: small*) balanza; (: *large*) báscula; **on a large ~** en gran escala; **~ of charges** tarifa, lista de precios

scallion ['skæljən] (*US*) *n* cebolleta

scallop ['skɔləp] *n* (*Zool*) venera; (*Sewing*) festón *m*

scalp [skælp] *n* cabellera ▷ *vt* escalpar

scalpel ['skælpl] *n* bisturí *m*

scam [skæm] *n* (*inf*) estafa, timo

scampi ['skæmpɪ] *npl* gambas *fpl*

scan [skæn] *vt* (*examine*) escudriñar; (*glance at quickly*) dar un vistazo a; (*TV, Radar*) explorar, registrar ▷ *n* (*Med*): **to have a ~** pasar por el escáner

scandal ['skændl] *n* escándalo; (*gossip*) chismes *mpl*

Scandinavia [skændɪ'neɪvɪə] *n* Escandinavia; **Scandinavian** *adj, n* escandinavo/a *m/f*

scanner ['skænə*] *n* (*Radar, Med*) escáner *m*

scapegoat ['skeɪpgəut] *n* cabeza de turco, chivo expiatorio

scar [skɑ:] *n* cicatriz *f*; (*fig*) señal *f* ▷ *vt* dejar señales en

scarce [skεəs] *adj* escaso; **to make o.s. ~** (*inf*) esfumarse; **scarcely** *adv* apenas

scare [skεə*] *n* susto, sobresalto; (*panic*) pánico ▷ *vt* asustar, espantar; **to ~ sb stiff** dar a algn un susto de muerte; **bomb ~** amenaza de bomba; **scarecrow** *n* espantapájaros *m inv*; **scared** *adj*: **to be scared** estar asustado

scarf [skɑ:f] (*pl* **~s** *or* **scarves**) *n* (*long*) bufanda; (*square*) pañuelo

scarlet ['skɑ:lɪt] *adj* escarlata

scarves [skɑ:vz] *npl of* **scarf**

scary ['skεərɪ] (*inf*) *adj* espeluznante

scatter ['skætə*] *vt* (*spread*) esparcir, desparramar; (*put to flight*) dispersar ▷ *vi* desparramarse; dispersarse

scenario [sɪ'nɑ:rɪəu] *n* (*Theatre*) argumento; (*Cinema*) guión *m*; (*fig*) escenario

scene [si:n] *n* (*Theatre, fig etc*) escena; (*of crime etc*) escenario; (*view*) panorama *m*; (*fuss*) escándalo; **scenery** *n* (*Theatre*) decorado; (*landscape*) paisaje *m*

> Be careful not to translate **scenery** by the Spanish word *escenario*.

scenic *adj* pintoresco

scent [sεnt] *n* perfume *m*, olor *m*; (*fig: track*) rastro, pista

sceptical ['skεptɪkl] *adj* escéptico

schedule ['ʃεdju:l] (*US*) ['skεdju:l] *n* (*timetable*) horario; (*of events*) programa *m*; (*list*) lista ▷ *vt* (*visit*) fijar la hora de; **to arrive on ~** llegar a la hora debida; **to be ahead of/behind ~** estar adelantado/en retraso; **scheduled flight** *n* vuelo regular

scheme [ski:m] *n* (*plan*) plan *m*, proyecto; (*plot*) intriga; (*arrangement*) disposición *f*; (*pension scheme etc*) sistema *m* ▷ *vi* (*intrigue*) intrigar

schizophrenic [skɪtzə'frεnɪk] *adj* esquizofrénico

scholar ['skɔlə*] *n* (*pupil*) alumno/a; (*learned person*) sabio/a, erudito/a; **scholarship** *n* erudición *f*; (*grant*) beca

school [sku:l] *n* escuela, colegio; (*in university*) facultad *f* ▷ *cpd* escolar; **schoolbook** *n* libro de texto; **schoolboy** *n* alumno; **school children** *npl* alumnos *mpl*; **schoolgirl** *n* alumna; **schooling** *n* enseñanza; **schoolteacher** *n* (*primary*) maestro/a; (*secondary*) profesor(a) *m/f*

science ['saɪəns] *n* ciencia; **science fiction** *n* ciencia-ficción *f*; **scientific** [-'tɪfɪk] *adj* científico; **scientist** *n* científico/a

sci-fi ['saɪfaɪ] *n abbr* (*inf*) = **science fiction**

scissors ['sɪzəz] *npl* tijeras *fpl*; **a pair of ~** unas tijeras

scold [skəuld] *vt* regañar

scone [skɔn] *n* *pastel de pan*

scoop [sku:p] *n* (*for flour etc*) pala; (*Press*) exclusiva

scooter ['sku:tə*] *n* moto *f*; (*toy*) patinete *m*

scope [skəup] *n* (*of plan*) ámbito; (*of person*) competencia; (*opportunity*) libertad *f* (de acción)
scorching [ˈskɔːtʃɪŋ] *adj* (*heat, sun*) abrasador(a)
score [skɔː*] *n* (*points etc*) puntuación *f*; (*Mus*) partitura; (*twenty*) veintena ▷ *vt* (*goal, point*) ganar; (*mark*) rayar; (*achieve*: *success*) conseguir ▷ *vi* marcar un tanto; (*Football*) marcar (un) gol; (*keep score*) llevar el tanteo; **~s of** (*lots of*) decenas de; **on that ~** en lo que se refiere a eso; **to ~ 6 out of 10** obtener una puntuación de 6 sobre 10; **score out** *vt* tachar; **scoreboard** *n* marcador *m*; **scorer** *n* marcador *m*; (*keeping score*) encargado/a del marcador
scorn [skɔːn] *n* desprecio
Scorpio [ˈskɔːpɪəu] *n* Escorpión *m*
scorpion [ˈskɔːpɪən] *n* alacrán *m*
Scot [skɔt] *n* escocés/esa *m/f*
Scotch tape® (*US*) *n* cinta adhesiva, celo, scotch® *m*
Scotland [ˈskɔtlənd] *n* Escocia
Scots [skɔts] *adj* escocés/esa; **Scotsman** (*irreg*) *n* escocés; **Scotswoman** (*irreg*) *n* escocésa; **Scottish** [ˈskɔtɪʃ] *adj* escocés/esa; **Scottish Parliament** *n* Parlamento escocés
scout [skaut] *n* (*Mil*: *also*: **boy ~**) explorador *m*; **girl ~** (*US*) niña exploradora
scowl [skaul] *vi* fruncir el ceño; **to ~ at sb** mirar con ceño a algn
scramble [ˈskræmbl] *n* (*climb*) subida (difícil); (*struggle*) pelea ▷ *vi*: **to ~ through/out** abrirse paso/salir con dificultad; **to ~ for** pelear por; **scrambled eggs** *npl* huevos *mpl* revueltos
scrap [skræp] *n* (*bit*) pedacito; (*fig*) pizca; (*fight*) riña, bronca; (*also*: **~ iron**) chatarra, hierro viejo ▷ *vt* (*discard*) desechar, descartar ▷ *vi* reñir, armar una bronca; **scraps** *npl* (*waste*) sobras *fpl*, desperdicios *mpl*; **scrapbook** *n* álbum *m* de recortes
scrape [skreɪp] *n*: **to get into a ~** meterse en un lío ▷ *vt* raspar; (*skin etc*) rasguñar; (*scrape against*) rozar ▷ *vi*: **to ~ through** (*exam*) aprobar por los pelos; **scrap paper** *n* pedazos *mpl* de papel
scratch [skrætʃ] *n* rasguño; (*from claw*) arañazo ▷ *vt* (*paint, car*) rayar; (*with claw, nail*) rasguñar, arañar; (*rub*: *nose etc*) rascarse ▷ *vi* rascarse; **to start from ~** partir de cero; **to be up to ~** cumplir con los requisitos; **scratch card** *n* (*BRIT*) tarjeta *f* de "rasque y gane"
scream [skriːm] *n* chillido ▷ *vi* chillar
screen [skriːn] *n* (*Cinema, TV*) pantalla; (*movable barrier*) biombo ▷ *vt* (*conceal*) tapar; (*from the wind etc*) proteger; (*film*) proyectar; (*candidates etc*) investigar a; **screening** *n* (*Med*) investigación *f* médica; **screenplay** *n* guión *m*; **screen saver** *n* (*Comput*) protector *m* de pantalla
screw [skruː] *n* tornillo ▷ *vt* (*also*: **~ in**) atornillar; **screw up** *vt* (*paper etc*) arrugar; **to screw up one's eyes** arrugar el entrecejo; **screwdriver** *n* destornillador *m*
scribble [ˈskrɪbl] *n* garabatos *mpl* ▷ *vt, vi* garabatear
script [skrɪpt] *n* (*Cinema etc*) guión *m*; (*writing*) escritura, letra
scroll [skrəul] *n* rollo
scrub [skrʌb] *n* (*land*) maleza ▷ *vt* fregar, restregar; (*inf*: *reject*) cancelar, anular
scruffy [ˈskrʌfɪ] *adj* desaliñado, piojoso
scrum(mage) [ˈskrʌm(mɪdʒ)] *n* (*Rugby*) melée *f*
scrutiny [ˈskruːtɪnɪ] *n* escrutinio, examen *m*
scuba diving [ˈskuːbəˈdaɪvɪŋ] *n* submarinismo
sculptor [ˈskʌlptə*] *n* escultor(a) *m/f*
sculpture [ˈskʌlptʃə*] *n* escultura
scum [skʌm] *n* (*on liquid*) espuma;

(*pej*: *people*) escoria

scurry ['skʌrɪ] *vi* correr; **to ~ off** escabullirse

sea [si:] *n* mar *m* ▷ *cpd* de mar, marítimo; **by ~** (*travel*) en barco; **on the ~** (*boat*) en el mar; (*town*) junto al mar; **to be all at ~** (*fig*) estar despistado; **out to ~**, **at ~** en alta mar; **seafood** *n* mariscos *mpl*; **sea front** *n* paseo marítimo; **seagull** *n* gaviota

seal [si:l] *n* (*animal*) foca; (*stamp*) sello ▷ *vt* (*close*) cerrar; **seal off** *vt* (*area*) acordonar

sea level *n* nivel *m* del mar

seam [si:m] *n* costura; (*of metal*) juntura; (*of coal*) veta, filón *m*

search [sə:tʃ] *n* (*for person, thing*) busca, búsqueda; (*Comput*) búsqueda; (*inspection*: *of sb's home*) registro ▷ *vt* (*look in*) buscar en; (*examine*) examinar; (*person, place*) registrar ▷ *vi*: **to ~ for** buscar; **in ~ of** en busca de; **search engine** *n* (*Comput*) buscador *m*; **search party** *n* pelotón *m* de salvamento

sea: seashore *n* playa, orilla del mar; **seasick** *adj* mareado; **seaside** *n* playa, orilla del mar; **seaside resort** *n* centro turístico costero

season ['si:zn] *n* (*of year*) estación *f*; (*sporting etc*) temporada; (*of films etc*) ciclo ▷ *vt* (*food*) sazonar; **in/out of ~** en sazón/fuera de temporada; **seasonal** *adj* estacional; **seasoning** *n* condimento, aderezo; **season ticket** *n* abono

seat [si:t] *n* (*in bus, train*) asiento; (*chair*) silla; (*Parliament*) escaño; (*buttocks*) culo, trasero; (*of trousers*) culera ▷ *vt* sentar; (*have room for*) tener cabida para; **to be ~ed** sentarse; **seat belt** *n* cinturón *m* de seguridad; **seating** *n* asientos *mpl*

sea: sea water *n* agua del mar; **seaweed** *n* alga marina

sec. *abbr* = **second(s)**

secluded [si'klu:dɪd] *adj* retirado

second ['sɛkənd] *adj* segundo ▷ *adv* en segundo lugar ▷ *n* segundo; (*Aut*: *also*: **~ gear**) segunda; (*Comm*) artículo con algún desperfecto; (BRIT *Scol*: *degree*) *título de licenciado con calificación de notable* ▷ *vt* (*motion*) apoyar; **secondary** *adj* secundario; **secondary school** *n* escuela secundaria; **second-class** *adj* de segunda clase ▷ *adv* (*Rail*) en segunda; **secondhand** *adj* de segunda mano, usado; **secondly** *adv* en segundo lugar; **second-rate** *adj* de segunda categoría; **second thoughts**: **to have second thoughts** cambiar de opinión; **on second thoughts** *or* **thought** (US) pensándolo bien

secrecy ['si:krəsɪ] *n* secreto

secret ['si:krɪt] *adj*, *n* secreto; **in ~** en secreto

secretary ['sɛkrətərɪ] *n* secretario/a; **S~ of State (for)** (BRIT *Pol*) Ministro (de)

secretive ['si:krətɪv] *adj* reservado, sigiloso

secret service *n* servicio secreto

sect [sɛkt] *n* secta

section ['sɛkʃən] *n* sección *f*; (*part*) parte *f*; (*of document*) artículo; (*of opinion*) sector *m*; (*cross-section*) corte *m* transversal

sector ['sɛktə*] *n* sector *m*

secular ['sɛkjulə*] *adj* secular, seglar

secure [sɪ'kjuə*] *adj* seguro; (*firmly fixed*) firme, fijo ▷ *vt* (*fix*) asegurar, afianzar; (*get*) conseguir

security [sɪ'kjuərɪtɪ] *n* seguridad *f*; (*for loan*) fianza; (: *object*) prenda; **securities** *npl* (*Comm*) valores *mpl*, títulos *mpl*; **security guard** *n* guardia *m/f* de seguridad

sedan [sɪ'dæn] (US) *n* (*Aut*) sedán *m*

sedate [sɪ'deɪt] *adj* tranquilo ▷ *vt* tratar con sedantes

sedative ['sɛdɪtɪv] *n* sedante *m*, sedativo

seduce [sɪ'dju:s] *vt* seducir; **seductive** [-'dʌktɪv] *adj* seductor(a)

see [si:] (*pt* **saw**, *pp* **seen**) *vt* ver; (*accompany*): **to ~ sb to the door**

acompañar a algn a la puerta; (*understand*) ver, comprender ▷ *vi* ver ▷ *n* (arz)obispado; **to ~ that** (*ensure*) asegurar que; **~ you soon!** ¡hasta pronto!; **see off** *vt* despedir; **see out** *vt* (*take to the door*) acompañar hasta la puerta; **see through** *vt fus* (*fig*) calar ▷ *vt* (*plan*) llevar a cabo; **see to** *vt fus* atender a, encargarse de

seed [si:d] *n* semilla; (*in fruit*) pepita; (*fig: gen pl*) germen *m*; (*Tennis etc*) preseleccionado/a; **to go to ~** (*plant*) granar; (*fig*) descuidarse

seeing ['si:ɪŋ] *conj*: **~ (that)** visto que, en vista de que

seek [si:k] (*pt, pp* **sought**) *vt* buscar; (*post*) solicitar

seem [si:m] *vi* parecer; **there ~s to be ...** parece que hay ...; **seemingly** *adv* aparentemente, según parece

seen [si:n] *pp of* **see**

seesaw ['si:sɔ:] *n* subibaja

segment ['sɛgmənt] *n* (*part*) sección *f*; (*of orange*) gajo

segregate ['sɛgrɪgeɪt] *vt* segregar

seize [si:z] *vt* (*grasp*) agarrar, asir; (*take possession of*) secuestrar; (*: territory*) apoderarse de; (*opportunity*) aprovecharse de

seizure ['si:ʒə*] *n* (*Med*) ataque *m*; (*Law, of power*) incautación *f*

seldom ['sɛldəm] *adv* rara vez

select [sɪ'lɛkt] *adj* selecto, escogido ▷ *vt* escoger, elegir; (*Sport*) seleccionar; **selection** *n* selección *f*, elección *f*; (*Comm*) surtido; **selective** *adj* selectivo

self [sɛlf] (*pl* **selves**) *n* uno mismo; **the ~** el yo ▷ *prefix* auto...; **self-assured** *adj* seguro de sí mismo; **self-catering** (BRIT) *adj* (*flat etc*) con cocina; **self-centred** (US **self-centered**) *adj* egocéntrico; **self-confidence** *n* confianza en sí mismo; **self-confident** *adj* seguro de sí (mismo), lleno de confianza en sí mismo; **self-conscious** *adj* cohibido; **self-contained** (BRIT) *adj* (*flat*) con entrada particular; **self-control** *n* autodominio; **self-defence** (US **self-defense**) *n* defensa propia; **self-drive** *adj* (BRIT) sin chofer *or* (SP) chófer; **self-employed** *adj* que trabaja por cuenta propia; **self-esteem** *n* amor *m* propio; **self-indulgent** *adj* autocomplaciente; **self-interest** *n* egoísmo; **selfish** *adj* egoísta; **self-pity** *n* lástima de sí mismo; **self-raising** [sɛlf'reɪzɪŋ] (US **self-rising**) *adj*: **self-raising flour** harina con levadura; **self-respect** *n* amor *m* propio; **self-service** *adj* de autoservicio

sell [sɛl] (*pt, pp* **sold**) *vt* vender ▷ *vi* venderse; **to ~ at** *or* **for £10** venderse a 10 libras; **sell off** *vt* liquidar; **sell out** *vi*: **to sell out of tickets/milk** vender todas las entradas/toda la leche; **sell-by date** *n* fecha de caducidad; **seller** *n* vendedor(a) *m/f*

Sellotape® ['sɛləuteɪp] (BRIT) *n* celo (SP), cinta Scotch® (LAM) *or* Dúrex® (MEX, ARG)

selves [sɛlvz] *npl of* **self**

semester [sɪ'mɛstə*] (US) *n* semestre *m*

semi... [sɛmɪ] *prefix* semi..., medio...; **semicircle** *n* semicírculo; **semidetached (house)** *n* (casa) semiseparada; **semi-final** *n* semi-final *m*

seminar ['sɛmɪnɑ:*] *n* seminario

semi-skimmed [sɛmɪ'skɪmd] *adj* semidesnatado; **semi-skimmed (milk)** *n* leche semidesnatada

senate ['sɛnɪt] *n* senado; **the S~** (US) el Senado; **senator** *n* senador(a) *m/f*

send [sɛnd] (*pt, pp* **sent**) *vt* mandar, enviar; (*signal*) transmitir; **send back** *vt* devolver; **send for** *vt fus* mandar traer; **send in** *vt* (*report, application, resignation*) mandar; **send off** *vt* (*goods*) despachar; (BRIT *Sport: player*) expulsar; **send on** *vt* (*letter, luggage*) remitir; (*person*) mandar; **send out** *vt* (*invitation*) mandar; (*signal*) emitir; **send up** *vt* (*person, price*) hacer subir;

(BRIT: *parody*) parodiar; **sender** *n* remitente *mf*; **send-off** *n*: **a good send-off** una buena despedida

senile ['si:naɪl] *adj* senil

senior ['si:nɪə*] *adj* (*older*) mayor, más viejo; (: *on staff*) de más antigüedad; (*of higher rank*) superior; **senior citizen** *n* persona de la tercera edad; **senior high school** (US) *n* ≈ instituto de enseñanza media; *see also* **high school**

sensation [sɛn'seɪʃən] *n* sensación *f*; **sensational** *adj* sensacional

sense [sɛns] *n* (*faculty, meaning*) sentido; (*feeling*) sensación *f*; (*good sense*) sentido común, juicio ▷ *vt* sentir, percibir; **it makes ~** tiene sentido; **senseless** *adj* estúpido, insensato; (*unconscious*) sin conocimiento; **sense of humour** (BRIT) *n* sentido del humor

sensible ['sɛnsɪbl] *adj* sensato; (*reasonable*) razonable, lógico

> Be careful not to translate **sensible** by the Spanish word *sensible*.

sensitive ['sɛnsɪtɪv] *adj* sensible; (*touchy*) susceptible

sensual ['sɛnsjuəl] *adj* sensual

sensuous ['sɛnsjuəs] *adj* sensual

sent [sɛnt] *pt, pp of* **send**

sentence ['sɛntns] *n* (*Ling*) oración *f*; (*Law*) sentencia, fallo ▷ *vt*: **to ~ sb to death/to 5 years (in prison)** condenar a algn a muerte/a 5 años de cárcel

sentiment ['sɛntɪmənt] *n* sentimiento; (*opinion*) opinión *f*; **sentimental** [-'mɛntl] *adj* sentimental

Sep. *abbr* (= *September*) sep., set.

separate [*adj* 'sɛprɪt, *vb* 'sɛpəreɪt] *adj* separado; (*distinct*) distinto ▷ *vt* separar; (*part*) dividir ▷ *vi* separarse; **separately** *adv* por separado; **separates** *npl* (*clothes*) coordinados *mpl*; **separation** [-'reɪʃən] *n* separación *f*

September [sɛp'tɛmbə*] *n* se(p)tiembre *m*

septic ['sɛptɪk] *adj* séptico; **septic tank** *n* fosa séptica

sequel ['si:kwl] *n* consecuencia, resultado; (*of story*) continuación *f*

sequence ['si:kwəns] *n* sucesión *f*, serie *f*; (*Cinema*) secuencia

sequin ['si:kwɪn] *n* lentejuela

Serb [sə:b] *adj, n* = **Serbian**

Serbian ['sə:bɪən] *adj* serbio ▷ *n* serbio/a; (*Ling*) serbio

sergeant ['sɑ:dʒənt] *n* sargento

serial ['sɪərɪəl] *n* (*TV*) telenovela, serie *f* televisiva; (*Book*) serie *f*; **serial killer** *n* asesino/a múltiple; **serial number** *n* número de serie

series ['sɪəri:s] *n inv* serie *f*

serious ['sɪərɪəs] *adj* serio; (*grave*) grave; **seriously** *adv* en serio; (*ill, wounded etc*) gravemente

sermon ['sə:mən] *n* sermón *m*

servant ['sə:vənt] *n* servidor(a) *m/f*; (*house servant*) criado/a

serve [sə:v] *vt* servir; (*customer*) atender; (*train*) pasar por; (*apprenticeship*) hacer; (*prison term*) cumplir ▷ *vi* (*at table*) servir; (*Tennis*) sacar; **to ~ as/for/to do** servir de/para/para hacer ▷ *n* (*Tennis*) saque *m*; **it ~s him right** se lo tiene merecido; **server** *n* (*Comput*) servidor *m*

service ['sə:vɪs] *n* servicio; (*Rel*) misa; (*Aut*) mantenimiento; (*dishes etc*) juego ▷ *vt* (*car etc*) revisar; (: *repair*) reparar; **to be of ~ to sb** ser útil a algn; **~ included/not included** servicio incluido/no incluido (*Econ: tertiary sector*) sector *m* terciario *or* (de) servicios; (BRIT: *on motorway*) área de servicio; (*Mil*): **the S~s** las fuerzas armadas; **service area** *n* (*on motorway*) área de servicio; **service charge** (BRIT) *n* servicio; **serviceman** (*irreg*) *n* militar *m*; **service station** *n* estación *f* de servicio

serviette [sə:vɪ'ɛt] (BRIT) *n* servilleta

session ['sɛʃən] *n* sesión *f*; **to be in ~** estar en sesión

set [sɛt] (*pt, pp* **~**) *n* juego; (*Radio*) aparato; (*TV*) televisor *m*; (*of utensils*) batería; (*of cutlery*) cubierto; (*of books*) colección *f*; (*Tennis*) set *m*; (*group of people*) grupo; (*Cinema*) plató *m*; (*Theatre*) decorado; (*Hairdressing*) marcado ▷ *adj* (*fixed*) fijo; (*ready*) listo ▷ *vt* (*place*) poner, colocar; (*fix*) fijar; (*adjust*) ajustar, arreglar; (*decide: rules etc*) establecer, decidir ▷ *vi* (*sun*) ponerse; (*jam, jelly*) cuajarse; (*concrete*) fraguar; (*bone*) componerse; **to be ~ on doing sth** estar empeñado en hacer algo; **to ~ to music** poner música a; **to ~ on fire** incendiar, poner fuego a; **to ~ free** poner en libertad; **to ~ sth going** poner algo en marcha; **to ~ sail** zarpar, hacerse a la vela; **set aside** *vt* poner aparte, dejar de lado; (*money, time*) reservar; **set down** *vt* (*bus, train*) dejar; **set in** *vi* (*infection*) declararse; (*complications*) comenzar; **the rain has set in for the day** parece que va a llover todo el día; **set off** *vi* partir ▷ *vt* (*bomb*) hacer estallar; (*events*) poner en marcha; (*show up well*) hacer resaltar; **set out** *vi* partir ▷ *vt* (*arrange*) disponer; (*state*) exponer; **to set out to do sth** proponerse hacer algo; **set up** *vt* establecer; **setback** *n* revés *m*, contratiempo; **set menu** *n* menú *m*

settee [sɛ'ti:] *n* sofá *m*

setting ['sɛtɪŋ] *n* (*scenery*) marco; (*position*) disposición *f*; (*of sun*) puesta; (*of jewel*) engaste *m*, montadura

settle ['sɛtl] *vt* (*argument*) resolver; (*accounts*) ajustar, liquidar; (*Med: calm*) calmar, sosegar ▷ *vi* (*dust etc*) depositarse; (*weather*) serenarse; **to ~ for sth** convenir en aceptar algo; **to ~ on sth** decidirse por algo; **settle down** *vi* (*get comfortable*) ponerse cómodo, acomodarse; (*calm down*) calmarse, tranquilizarse; (*live quietly*) echar raíces; **settle in** *vi* instalarse; **settle up** *vi*: **to settle up with sb** ajustar cuentas con algn; **settlement** *n* (*payment*) liquidación *f*; (*agreement*) acuerdo, convenio; (*village etc*) pueblo

setup ['sɛtʌp] *n* sistema *m*; (*situation*) situación *f*

seven ['sɛvn] *num* siete; **seventeen** *num* diez y siete, diecisiete; **seventeenth** [sevn'ti:nθ] *adj* decimoséptimo; **seventh** *num* séptimo; **seventieth** ['sevntɪɪθ] *adj* septuagésimo; **seventy** *num* setenta

sever ['sɛvə*] *vt* cortar; (*relations*) romper

several ['sɛvərl] *adj, pron* varios/as *m/fpl*, algunos/as *m/fpl*; **~ of us** varios de nosotros

severe [sɪ'vɪə*] *adj* severo; (*serious*) grave; (*hard*) duro; (*pain*) intenso

sew [səu] (*pt* **~ed**, *pp* **~n**) *vt, vi* coser

sewage ['su:ɪdʒ] *n* aguas *fpl* residuales

sewer ['su:ə*] *n* alcantarilla, cloaca

sewing ['səuɪŋ] *n* costura; **sewing machine** *n* máquina de coser

sewn [səun] *pp of* **sew**

sex [sɛks] *n* sexo; (*lovemaking*): **to have ~** hacer el amor; **sexism** ['sɛksɪzəm] *n* sexismo; **sexist** *adj, n* sexista *mf*; **sexual** ['sɛksjuəl] *adj* sexual; **sexual intercourse** *n* relaciones *fpl* sexuales; **sexuality** [seksju'ælɪtɪ] *n* sexualidad *f*; **sexy** *adj* sexy

shabby ['ʃæbɪ] *adj* (*person*) desharrapado; (*clothes*) raído, gastado; (*behaviour*) ruin *inv*

shack [ʃæk] *n* choza, chabola

shade [ʃeɪd] *n* sombra; (*for lamp*) pantalla; (*for eyes*) visera; (*of colour*) matiz *m*, tonalidad *f*; (*small quantity*): **a ~ (too big/more)** un poquitín (grande/más) ▷ *vt* dar sombra a; (*eyes*) proteger del sol; **in the ~** en la sombra; **shades** *npl* (*sunglasses*) gafas *fpl* de sol

shadow ['ʃædəu] *n* sombra ▷ *vt* (*follow*) seguir y vigilar; **shadow cabinet** (BRIT) *n* (*Pol*) *gabinete paralelo formado por el partido de oposición*

shady ['ʃeɪdɪ] *adj* sombreado; (*fig: dishonest*) sospechoso; (*: deal*) turbio

shaft [ʃɑ:ft] *n* (*of arrow, spear*) astil *m*; (*Aut, Tech*) eje *m*, árbol *m*; (*of mine*) pozo;

(*of lift*) hueco, caja; (*of light*) rayo
shake [ʃeɪk] (*pt* **shook**, *pp* **shaken**) *vt* sacudir; (*building*) hacer temblar; (*bottle, cocktail*) agitar ▷ *vi* (*tremble*) temblar; **to ~ one's head** (*in refusal*) negar con la cabeza; (*in dismay*) mover *or* menear la cabeza, incrédulo; **to ~ hands with sb** estrechar la mano a algn; **shake off** *vt* sacudirse; (*fig*) deshacerse de; **shake up** *vt* agitar; (*fig*) reorganizar; **shaky** *adj* (*hand, voice*) trémulo; (*building*) inestable
shall [ʃæl] *aux vb*: **~ I help you?** ¿quieres que te ayude?; **I'll buy three, ~ I?** compro tres, ¿no te parece?
shallow ['ʃæləu] *adj* poco profundo; (*fig*) superficial
sham [ʃæm] *n* fraude *m*, engaño
shambles ['ʃæmblz] *n* confusión *f*
shame [ʃeɪm] *n* vergüenza ▷ *vt* avergonzar; **it is a ~ that/to do** es una lástima que/hacer; **what a ~!** ¡qué lástima!; **shameful** *adj* vergonzoso; **shameless** *adj* desvergonzado
shampoo [ʃæm'pu:] *n* champú *m* ▷ *vt* lavar con champú
shandy ['ʃændɪ] *n* *mezcla de cerveza con gaseosa*
shan't [ʃɑ:nt] = **shall not**
shape [ʃeɪp] *n* forma ▷ *vt* formar, dar forma a; (*sb's ideas*) formar; (*sb's life*) determinar; **to take ~** tomar forma
share [ʃɛə*] *n* (*part*) parte *f*, porción *f*; (*contribution*) cuota; (*Comm*) acción *f* ▷ *vt* dividir; (*have in common*) compartir; **to ~ out (among** *or* **between)** repartir (entre); **shareholder** (BRIT) *n* accionista *mf*
shark [ʃɑ:k] *n* tiburón *m*
sharp [ʃɑ:p] *adj* (*blade, nose*) afilado; (*point*) puntiagudo; (*outline*) definido; (*pain*) intenso; (*Mus*) desafinado; (*contrast*) marcado; (*voice*) agudo; (*person: quick-witted*) astuto; (*: dishonest*) poco escrupuloso ▷ *n* (*Mus*) sostenido ▷ *adv*: **at 2 o'clock ~** a las 2 en punto; **sharpen** *vt* afilar; (*pencil*) sacar punta a; (*fig*) agudizar; **sharpener** *n* (*also*: **pencil sharpener**) sacapuntas *m inv*; **sharply** *adv* (*turn, stop*) bruscamente; (*stand out, contrast*) claramente; (*criticize, retort*) severamente
shatter ['ʃætə*] *vt* hacer añicos *or* pedazos; (*fig: ruin*) destruir, acabar con ▷ *vi* hacerse añicos; **shattered** *adj* (*grief-stricken*) destrozado, deshecho; (*exhausted*) agotado, hecho polvo
shave [ʃeɪv] *vt* afeitar, rasurar ▷ *vi* afeitarse, rasurarse ▷ *n*: **to have a ~** afeitarse; **shaver** *n* (*also*: **electric shaver**) máquina de afeitar (eléctrica)
shavings ['ʃeɪvɪŋz] *npl* (*of wood etc*) virutas *fpl*
shaving cream ['ʃeɪvɪŋ-] *n* crema de afeitar
shaving foam *n* espuma de afeitar
shawl [ʃɔ:l] *n* chal *m*
she [ʃi:] *pron* ella
sheath [ʃi:θ] *n* vaina; (*contraceptive*) preservativo
shed [ʃɛd] (*pt, pp* **~**) *n* cobertizo ▷ *vt* (*skin*) mudar; (*tears, blood*) derramar; (*load*) derramar; (*workers*) despedir
she'd [ʃi:d] = **she had; she would**
sheep [ʃi:p] *n inv* oveja; **sheepdog** *n* perro pastor; **sheepskin** *n* piel *f* de carnero
sheer [ʃɪə*] *adj* (*utter*) puro, completo; (*steep*) escarpado; (*material*) diáfano ▷ *adv* verticalmente
sheet [ʃi:t] *n* (*on bed*) sábana; (*of paper*) hoja; (*of glass, metal*) lámina; (*of ice*) capa
sheik(h) [ʃeɪk] *n* jeque *m*
shelf [ʃɛlf] (*pl* **shelves**) *n* estante *m*
shell [ʃɛl] *n* (*on beach*) concha; (*of egg, nut etc*) cáscara; (*explosive*) proyectil *m*, obús *m*; (*of building*) armazón *f* ▷ *vt* (*peas*) desenvainar; (*Mil*) bombardear
she'll [ʃi:l] = **she will; she shall**
shellfish ['ʃɛlfɪʃ] *n inv* crustáceo; (*as food*) mariscos *mpl*
shelter ['ʃɛltə*] *n* abrigo, refugio ▷ *vt* (*aid*) amparar, proteger; (*give lodging to*) abrigar ▷ *vi* abrigarse, refugiarse;

sheltered *adj* (*life*) protegido; (*spot*) abrigado
shelves [ʃɛlvz] *npl of* **shelf**
shelving ['ʃɛlvɪŋ] *n* estantería
shepherd ['ʃɛpəd] *n* pastor *m* ▷ *vt* (*guide*) guiar, conducir; **shepherd's pie** (BRIT) *n pastel de carne y patatas*
sheriff ['ʃɛrɪf] (US) *n* sheriff *m*
sherry ['ʃɛrɪ] *n* jerez *m*
she's [ʃi:z] = **she is; she has**
Shetland ['ʃɛtlənd] *n* (*also*: **the ~s, the ~ Isles**) las Islas de Zetlandia
shield [ʃi:ld] *n* escudo; (*protection*) blindaje *m* ▷ *vt*: **to ~ (from)** proteger (de)
shift [ʃɪft] *n* (*change*) cambio; (*at work*) turno ▷ *vt* trasladar; (*remove*) quitar ▷ *vi* moverse
shin [ʃɪn] *n* espinilla
shine [ʃaɪn] (*pt, pp* **shone**) *n* brillo, lustre *m* ▷ *vi* brillar, relucir ▷ *vt* (*shoes*) lustrar, sacar brillo a; **to ~ a torch on sth** dirigir una linterna hacia algo
shingles ['ʃɪŋglz] *n* (*Med*) herpes *mpl or fpl*
shiny ['ʃaɪnɪ] *adj* brillante, lustroso
ship [ʃɪp] *n* buque *m*, barco ▷ *vt* (*goods*) embarcar; (*send*) transportar *or* enviar por vía marítima; **shipment** *n* (*goods*) envío; **shipping** *n* (*act*) embarque *m*; (*traffic*) buques *mpl*; **shipwreck** *n* naufragio ▷ *vt*: **to be shipwrecked** naufragar; **shipyard** *n* astillero
shirt [ʃə:t] *n* camisa; **in (one's) ~ sleeves** en mangas de camisa
shit [ʃɪt] (*inf!*) *excl* ¡mierda! (*!*)
shiver ['ʃɪvə*] *n* escalofrío ▷ *vi* temblar, estremecerse; (*with cold*) tiritar
shock [ʃɔk] *n* (*impact*) choque *m*; (*Elec*) descarga (eléctrica); (*emotional*) conmoción *f*; (*start*) sobresalto, susto; (*Med*) postración *f* nerviosa ▷ *vt* dar un susto a; (*offend*) escandalizar; **shocking** *adj* (*awful*) espantoso; (*outrageous*) escandaloso
shoe [ʃu:] (*pt, pp* **shod**) *n* zapato; (*for horse*) herradura ▷ *vt* (*horse*) herrar; **shoelace** *n* cordón *m*; **shoe polish** *n* betún *m*; **shoeshop** *n* zapatería
shone [ʃɔn] *pt, pp of* **shine**
shook [ʃuk] *pt of* **shake**
shoot [ʃu:t] (*pt, pp* **shot**) *n* (*on branch, seedling*) retoño, vástago ▷ *vt* disparar; (*kill*) matar a tiros; (*wound*) pegar un tiro; (*execute*) fusilar; (*film*) rodar, filmar ▷ *vi* (*Football*) chutar; **shoot down** *vt* (*plane*) derribar; **shoot up** *vi* (*prices*) dispararse; **shooting** *n* (*shots*) tiros *mpl*; (*Hunting*) caza con escopeta
shop [ʃɔp] *n* tienda; (*workshop*) taller *m* ▷ *vi* (*also*: **go ~ping**) ir de compras; **shop assistant** (BRIT) *n* dependiente/a *m/f*; **shopkeeper** *n* tendero/a; **shoplifting** *n* mechería; **shopping** *n* (*goods*) compras *fpl*; **shopping bag** *n* bolsa (de compras); **shopping centre** (US **shopping center**) *n* centro comercial; **shopping mall** *n* centro comercial; **shopping trolley** *n* (BRIT) carrito de la compra; **shop window** *n* escaparate *m* (SP), vidriera (LAM)
shore [ʃɔ:*] *n* orilla ▷ *vt*: **to ~ (up)** reforzar; **on ~** en tierra
short [ʃɔ:t] *adj* corto; (*in time*) breve, de corta duración; (*person*) bajo; (*curt*) brusco, seco; (*insufficient*) insuficiente; **(a pair of) ~s** (unos) pantalones *mpl* cortos; **to be ~ of sth** estar falto de algo; **in ~** en pocas palabras; **~ of doing ...** fuera de hacer ...; **it is ~ for** es la forma abreviada de; **to cut ~** (*speech, visit*) interrumpir, terminar inesperadamente; **everything ~ of ...** todo menos ...; **to fall ~ of** no alcanzar; **to run ~ of** quedarle a algn poco; **to stop ~** parar en seco; **to stop ~ of** detenerse antes de; **shortage** *n*: **a shortage of** una falta de; **shortbread** *n especie de mantecada*; **shortcoming** *n* defecto, deficiencia; **short(crust) pastry** (BRIT) *n* pasta quebradiza; **shortcut** *n* atajo; **shorten** *vt* acortar; (*visit*) interrumpir; **shortfall** *n* déficit *m*; **shorthand** (BRIT) *n*

taquigrafía; **short-lived** *adj* efímero; **shortly** *adv* en breve, dentro de poco; **shorts** *npl* pantalones *mpl* cortos; (US) calzoncillos *mpl*; **short-sighted** (BRIT) *adj* miope; (*fig*) imprudente; **short-sleeved** *adj* de manga corta; **short story** *n* cuento; **short-tempered** *adj* enojadizo; **short-term** *adj* (*effect*) a corto plazo

shot [ʃɔt] *pt, pp of* **shoot** ▷ *n* (*sound*) tiro, disparo; (*try*) tentativa; (*injection*) inyección *f*; (*Phot*) toma, fotografía; **to be a good/poor ~** (*person*) tener buena/mala puntería; **like a ~** (*without any delay*) como un rayo; **shotgun** *n* escopeta

should [ʃud] *aux vb*: **I ~ go now** debo irme ahora; **he ~ be there now** debe de haber llegado (ya); **I ~ go if I were you** yo en tu lugar me iría; **I ~ like to** me gustaría

shoulder [ˈʃəuldə*] *n* hombro ▷ *vt* (*fig*) cargar con; **shoulder blade** *n* omóplato

shouldn't [ˈʃudnt] = **should not**

shout [ʃaut] *n* grito ▷ *vt* gritar ▷ *vi* gritar, dar voces

shove [ʃʌv] *n* empujón *m* ▷ *vt* empujar; (*inf*: *put*): **to ~ sth in** meter algo a empellones

shovel [ˈʃʌvl] *n* pala; (*mechanical*) excavadora ▷ *vt* mover con pala

show [ʃəu] (*pt* **~ed**, *pp* **~n**) *n* (*of emotion*) demostración *f*; (*semblance*) apariencia; (*exhibition*) exposición *f*; (*Theatre*) función *f*, espectáculo; (*TV*) show *m* ▷ *vt* mostrar, enseñar; (*courage etc*) mostrar, manifestar; (*exhibit*) exponer; (*film*) proyectar ▷ *vi* mostrarse; (*appear*) aparecer; **for ~** para impresionar; **on ~** (*exhibits etc*) expuesto; **show in** *vt* (*person*) hacer pasar; **show off** (*pej*) *vi* presumir ▷ *vt* (*display*) lucir; **show out** *vt*: **to show sb out** acompañar a algn a la puerta; **show up** *vi* (*stand out*) destacar; (*inf*: *turn up*) aparecer ▷ *vt* (*unmask*) desenmascarar; **show business** *n* mundo del espectáculo

shower [ˈʃauə*] *n* (*rain*) chaparrón *m*, chubasco; (*of stones etc*) lluvia; (*for bathing*) ducha, regadera (MEX) ▷ *vi* llover ▷ *vt* (*fig*): **to ~ sb with sth** colmar a algn de algo; **to have a ~** ducharse; **shower cap** *n* gorro de baño; **shower gel** *n* gel *m* de ducha

showing [ˈʃəuɪŋ] *n* (*of film*) proyección *f*

show jumping *n* hípica

shown [ʃəun] *pp of* **show**

show: show-off (*inf*) *n* (*person*) presumido/a; **showroom** *n* sala de muestras

shrank [ʃræŋk] *pt of* **shrink**

shred [ʃrɛd] *n* (*gen pl*) triza, jirón *m* ▷ *vt* hacer trizas; (*Culin*) desmenuzar

shrewd [ʃru:d] *adj* astuto

shriek [ʃri:k] *n* chillido ▷ *vi* chillar

shrimp [ʃrɪmp] *n* camarón *m*

shrine [ʃraɪn] *n* santuario, sepulcro

shrink [ʃrɪŋk] (*pt* **shrank**, *pp* **shrunk**) *vi* encogerse; (*be reduced*) reducirse; (*also*: **~ away**) retroceder ▷ *vt* encoger ▷ *n* (*inf, pej*) loquero/a; **to ~ from (doing) sth** no atreverse a hacer algo

shrivel [ˈʃrɪvl] (*also*: **~ up**) *vt* (*dry*) secar ▷ *vi* secarse

shroud [ʃraud] *n* sudario ▷ *vt*: **~ed in mystery** envuelto en el misterio

Shrove Tuesday [ˈʃrəuv-] *n* martes *m* de carnaval

shrub [ʃrʌb] *n* arbusto

shrug [ʃrʌg] *n* encogimiento de hombros ▷ *vt, vi*: **to ~ (one's shoulders)** encogerse de hombros; **shrug off** *vt* negar importancia a

shrunk [ʃrʌŋk] *pp of* **shrink**

shudder [ˈʃʌdə*] *n* estremecimiento, escalofrío ▷ *vi* estremecerse

shuffle [ˈʃʌfl] *vt* (*cards*) barajar ▷ *vi*: **to ~ (one's feet)** arrastrar los pies

shun [ʃʌn] *vt* rehuir, esquivar

shut [ʃʌt] (*pt, pp* **~**) *vt* cerrar ▷ *vi* cerrarse; **shut down** *vt, vi* cerrar; **shut up** *vi* (*inf*: *keep quiet*) callarse ▷ *vt* (*close*) cerrar; (*silence*) hacer callar;

shutter *n* contraventana; (*Phot*) obturador *m*

shuttle ['ʃʌtl] *n* lanzadera; (*also*: **~ service**) servicio rápido y continuo entre dos puntos; (*Aviat*) puente *m* aéreo; **shuttlecock** *n* volante *m*

shy [ʃaɪ] *adj* tímido

sibling ['sɪblɪŋ] *n* (*formal*) hermano/a

Sicily ['sɪsɪlɪ] *n* Sicilia

sick [sɪk] *adj* (*ill*) enfermo; (*nauseated*) mareado; (*humour*) negro; (*vomiting*): **to be ~** (BRIT) vomitar; **to feel ~** tener náuseas; **to be ~ of** (*fig*) estar harto de; **sickening** *adj* (*fig*) asqueroso; **sick leave** *n* baja por enfermedad; **sickly** *adj* enfermizo; (*smell*) nauseabundo; **sickness** *n* enfermedad *f*, mal *m*; (*vomiting*) náuseas *fpl*

side [saɪd] *n* (*gen*) lado; (*of body*) costado; (*of lake*) orilla; (*of hill*) ladera; (*team*) equipo ▷ *adj* (*door, entrance*) lateral ▷ *vi*: **to ~ with sb** tomar el partido de algn; **by the ~ of** al lado de; **~ by ~** juntos/as; **from ~ to ~** de un lado para otro; **from all ~s** de todos lados; **to take ~s (with)** tomar partido (con); **sideboard** *n* aparador *m*; **sideboards** (BRIT) *npl* = **sideburns**; **sideburns** *npl* patillas *fpl*; **sidelight** *n* (*Aut*) luz *f* lateral; **sideline** *n* (*Sport*) línea de banda; (*fig*) empleo suplementario; **side order** *n* *plato de acompañamiento*; **side road** *n* (BRIT) calle *f* lateral; **side street** *n* calle *f* lateral; **sidetrack** *vt* (*fig*) desviar (de su propósito); **sidewalk** (US) *n* acera; **sideways** *adv* de lado

siege [si:dʒ] *n* cerco, sitio

sieve [sɪv] *n* colador *m* ▷ *vt* cribar

sift [sɪft] *vt* cribar; (*fig*: *information*) escudriñar

sigh [saɪ] *n* suspiro ▷ *vi* suspirar

sight [saɪt] *n* (*faculty*) vista; (*spectacle*) espectáculo; (*on gun*) mira, alza ▷ *vt* divisar; **in ~** a la vista; **out of ~** fuera de (la) vista; **on ~** (*shoot*) sin previo aviso; **sightseeing** *n* excursionismo, turismo; **to go sightseeing** hacer turismo

sign [saɪn] *n* (*with hand*) señal *f*, seña; (*trace*) huella, rastro; (*notice*) letrero; (*written*) signo ▷ *vt* firmar; (*Sport*) fichar; **to ~ sth over to sb** firmar el traspaso de algo a algn; **sign for** *vt fus* (*item*) firmar el recibo de; **sign in** *vi* firmar el registro (al entrar); **sign on** *vi* (BRIT: *as unemployed*) registrarse como desempleado; (*for course*) inscribirse ▷ *vt* (*Mil*) alistar; (*employee*) contratar; **sign up** *vi* (*Mil*) alistarse; (*for course*) inscribirse ▷ *vt* (*player*) fichar

signal ['sɪgnl] *n* señal *f* ▷ *vi* señalizar ▷ *vt* (*person*) hacer señas a; (*message*) comunicar por señales

signature ['sɪgnətʃə*] *n* firma

significance [sɪg'nɪfɪkəns] *n* (*importance*) trascendencia

significant [sɪg'nɪfɪkənt] *adj* significativo; (*important*) trascendente

signify ['sɪgnɪfaɪ] *vt* significar

sign language *n* lenguaje *m* para sordomudos

signpost ['saɪnpəust] *n* indicador *m*

Sikh [si:k] *adj, n* sij *mf*

silence ['saɪlns] *n* silencio ▷ *vt* acallar; (*guns*) reducir al silencio

silent ['saɪlnt] *adj* silencioso; (*not speaking*) callado; (*film*) mudo; **to remain ~** guardar silencio

silhouette [sɪlu:'ɛt] *n* silueta

silicon chip ['sɪlɪkən-] *n* plaqueta de silicio

silk [sɪlk] *n* seda ▷ *adj* de seda

silly ['sɪlɪ] *adj* (*person*) tonto; (*idea*) absurdo

silver ['sɪlvə*] *n* plata; (*money*) moneda suelta ▷ *adj* de plata; (*colour*) plateado; **silver-plated** *adj* plateado

similar ['sɪmɪlə*] *adj*: **~ (to)** parecido *or* semejante (a); **similarity** [-'lærɪtɪ] *n* semejanza; **similarly** *adv* del mismo modo

simmer ['sɪmə*] *vi* hervir a fuego lento

simple ['sɪmpl] *adj* (*easy*) sencillo; (*foolish*, *Comm*: *interest*) simple;

simplicity [-'plɪsɪtɪ] *n* sencillez *f*; **simplify** ['sɪmplɪfaɪ] *vt* simplificar; **simply** *adv* (*live, talk*) sencillamente; (*just, merely*) sólo

simulate ['sɪmju:leɪt] *vt* fingir, simular

simultaneous [sɪməl'teɪnɪəs] *adj* simultáneo; **simultaneously** *adv* simultáneamente

sin [sɪn] *n* pecado ▷ *vi* pecar

since [sɪns] *adv* desde entonces, después ▷ *prep* desde ▷ *conj* (*time*) desde que; (*because*) ya que, puesto que; **~ then, ever ~** desde entonces

sincere [sɪn'sɪə*] *adj* sincero; **sincerely** *adv*: **yours sincerely** (*in letters*) le saluda atentamente

sing [sɪŋ] (*pt* **sang**, *pp* **sung**) *vt, vi* cantar

Singapore [sɪŋə'pɔ:*] *n* Singapur *m*

singer ['sɪŋə*] *n* cantante *mf*

singing ['sɪŋɪŋ] *n* canto

single ['sɪŋgl] *adj* único, solo; (*unmarried*) soltero; (*not double*) simple, sencillo ▷ *n* (BRIT: *also*: **~ ticket**) billete *m* sencillo; (*record*) sencillo, single *m*; **singles** *npl* (*Tennis*) individual *m*; **single out** *vt* (*choose*) escoger; **single bed** *n* cama individual; **single file** *n*: **in single file** en fila de uno; **single-handed** *adv* sin ayuda; **single-minded** *adj* resuelto, firme; **single parent** *n* padre *m* soltero, madre *f* soltera (*o divorciado etc*); **single parent family** familia monoparental; **single room** *n* cuarto individual

singular ['sɪŋgjulə*] *adj* (*odd*) raro, extraño; (*outstanding*) excepcional ▷ *n* (*Ling*) singular *m*

sinister ['sɪnɪstə*] *adj* siniestro

sink [sɪŋk] (*pt* **sank**, *pp* **sunk**) *n* fregadero ▷ *vt* (*ship*) hundir, echar a pique; (*foundations*) excavar ▷ *vi* hundirse; **to ~ sth into** hundir algo en; **sink in** *vi* (*fig*) penetrar, calar

sinus ['saɪnəs] *n* (*Anat*) seno

sip [sɪp] *n* sorbo ▷ *vt* sorber, beber a sorbitos

sir [sə*] *n* señor *m*; **S~ John Smith** Sir John Smith; **yes ~** sí, señor

siren ['saɪərn] *n* sirena

sirloin ['sə:lɔɪn] *n* (*also*: **~ steak**) solomillo

sister ['sɪstə*] *n* hermana; (BRIT: *nurse*) enfermera jefe; **sister-in-law** *n* cuñada

sit [sɪt] (*pt, pp* **sat**) *vi* sentarse; (*be sitting*) estar sentado; (*assembly*) reunirse; (*for painter*) posar ▷ *vt* (*exam*) presentarse a; **sit back** *vi* (*in seat*) recostarse; **sit down** *vi* sentarse; **sit on** *vt fus* (*jury, committee*) ser miembro de, formar parte de; **sit up** *vi* incorporarse; (*not go to bed*) velar

sitcom ['sɪtkɔm] *n abbr* (= *situation comedy*) comedia de situación

site [saɪt] *n* sitio; (*also*: **building ~**) solar *m* ▷ *vt* situar

sitting ['sɪtɪŋ] *n* (*of assembly etc*) sesión *f*; (*in canteen*) turno; **sitting room** *n* sala de estar

situated ['sɪtjueɪtɪd] *adj* situado

situation [sɪtju'eɪʃən] *n* situación *f*; **"~s vacant"** (BRIT) "ofrecen trabajo"

six [sɪks] *num* seis; **sixteen** *num* diez y seis, dieciséis; **sixteenth** [sɪks'ti:nθ] *adj* decimosexto; **sixth** [sɪksθ] *num* sexto; **sixth form** *n* (BRIT) clase *f* de alumnos del sexto año (*de 16 a 18 años de edad*); **sixth-form college** *n* instituto *m* para alumnos de 16 a 18 años; **sixtieth** ['sɪkstɪɪθ] *adj* sexagésimo; **sixty** *num* sesenta

size [saɪz] *n* tamaño; (*extent*) extensión *f*; (*of clothing*) talla; (*of shoes*) número; **sizeable** *adj* importante, considerable

sizzle ['sɪzl] *vi* crepitar

skate [skeɪt] *n* patín *m*; (*fish*: *pl inv*) raya ▷ *vi* patinar; **skateboard** *n* monopatín *m*; **skateboarding** *n* monopatín *m*; **skater** *n* patinador(a) *m/f*; **skating** *n* patinaje *m*; **skating rink** *n* pista de patinaje

skeleton ['skɛlɪtn] *n* esqueleto; (*Tech*) armazón *f*; (*outline*) esquema *m*

skeptical ['skɛptɪkl] (US) = **sceptical**
sketch [skɛtʃ] *n* (*drawing*) dibujo; (*outline*) esbozo, bosquejo; (*Theatre*) sketch *m* ▷ *vt* dibujar; (*plan etc*: *also*: **~ out**) esbozar
skewer ['skju:ə*] *n* broqueta
ski: [ski:] *n* esquí *m* ▷ *vi* esquiar; **ski boot** *n* bota de esquí
skid [skɪd] *n* patinazo ▷ *vi* patinar
ski: skier *n* esquiador(a) *m/f*; **skiing** *n* esquí *m*
skilful ['skɪlful] (US **skillful**) *adj* diestro, experto
ski lift *n* telesilla *m*, telesquí *m*
skill [skɪl] *n* destreza, pericia; técnica; **skilled** *adj* hábil, diestro; (*worker*) cualificado
skim [skɪm] *vt* (*milk*) desnatar; (*glide over*) rozar, rasar ▷ *vi*: **to ~ through** (*book*) hojear; **skimmed milk** (US **skim milk**) *n* leche *f* desnatada
skin [skɪn] *n* piel *f*; (*complexion*) cutis *m* ▷ *vt* (*fruit etc*) pelar; (*animal*) despellejar; **skinhead** *n* cabeza *m/f* rapada, skin(head) *m/f*; **skinny** *adj* flaco
skip [skɪp] *n* brinco, salto; (BRIT: *container*) contenedor *m* ▷ *vi* brincar; (*with rope*) saltar a la comba ▷ *vt* saltarse
ski: ski pass *n* forfait *m* (de esquí); **ski pole** *n* bastón *m* de esquiar
skipper ['skɪpə*] *n* (*Naut, Sport*) capitán *m*
skipping rope ['skɪpɪŋ-] (US **skip rope**) *n* comba
skirt [skə:t] *n* falda, pollera (SC) ▷ *vt* (*go round*) ladear
skirting board ['skə:tɪŋ-] (BRIT) *n* rodapié *m*
ski slope *n* pista de esquí
ski suit *n* traje *m* de esquiar
skull [skʌl] *n* calavera; (*Anat*) cráneo
skunk [skʌŋk] *n* mofeta
sky [skaɪ] *n* cielo; **skyscraper** *n* rascacielos *m inv*
slab [slæb] *n* (*stone*) bloque *m*; (*flat*) losa; (*of cake*) trozo
slack [slæk] *adj* (*loose*) flojo; (*slow*) de poca actividad; (*careless*) descuidado; **slacks** *npl* pantalones *mpl*
slain [sleɪn] *pp of* **slay**
slam [slæm] *vt* (*throw*) arrojar (violentamente); (*criticize*) criticar duramente ▷ *vi* (*door*) cerrarse de golpe; **to ~ the door** dar un portazo
slander ['slɑ:ndə*] *n* calumnia, difamación *f*
slang [slæŋ] *n* argot *m*; (*jargon*) jerga
slant [slɑ:nt] *n* sesgo, inclinación *f*; (*fig*) interpretación *f*
slap [slæp] *n* palmada; (*in face*) bofetada ▷ *vt* dar una palmada *or* bofetada a; (*paint etc*): **to ~ sth on sth** embadurnar algo con algo ▷ *adv* (*directly*) exactamente, directamente
slash [slæʃ] *vt* acuchillar; (*fig*: *prices*) fulminar
slate [sleɪt] *n* pizarra ▷ *vt* (*fig*: *criticize*) criticar duramente
slaughter ['slɔ:tə*] *n* (*of animals*) matanza; (*of people*) carnicería ▷ *vt* matar; **slaughterhouse** *n* matadero
Slav [slɑ:v] *adj* eslavo
slave [sleɪv] *n* esclavo/a ▷ *vi* (*also*: **~ away**) sudar tinta; **slavery** *n* esclavitud *f*
slay [sleɪ] (*pt* **slew**, *pp* **slain**) *vt* matar
sleazy ['sli:zɪ] *adj* de mala fama
sled [slɛd] (US) = **sledge**
sledge [slɛdʒ] *n* trineo
sleek [sli:k] *adj* (*shiny*) lustroso; (*car etc*) elegante
sleep [sli:p] (*pt, pp* **slept**) *n* sueño ▷ *vi* dormir; **to go to ~** quedarse dormido; **sleep in** *vi* (*oversleep*) quedarse dormido; **sleep together** *vi* (*have sex*) acostarse juntos; **sleeper** *n* (*person*) durmiente *mf*; (BRIT *Rail*: *on track*) traviesa; (: *train*) coche-cama *m*; **sleeping bag** *n* saco de dormir; **sleeping car** *n* coche-cama *m*; **sleeping pill** *n* somnífero; **sleepover** *n*: **we're having a sleepover at Jo's** nos vamos a quedar a dormir en casa de Jo; **sleepwalk** *vi* caminar dormido;

(*habitually*) ser sonámbulo; **sleepy** *adj* soñoliento; (*place*) soporífero
sleet [sli:t] *n* aguanieve *f*
sleeve [sli:v] *n* manga; (*Tech*) manguito; (*of record*) portada; **sleeveless** *adj* sin mangas
sleigh [sleɪ] *n* trineo
slender ['slɛndə*] *adj* delgado; (*means*) escaso
slept [slɛpt] *pt, pp of* **sleep**
slew [slu:] *pt of* **slay** ▷ *vi* (BRIT: *veer*) torcerse
slice [slaɪs] *n* (*of meat*) tajada; (*of bread*) rebanada; (*of lemon*) rodaja; (*utensil*) pala ▷ *vt* cortar (en tajos), rebanar
slick [slɪk] *adj* (*skilful*) hábil, diestro; (*clever*) astuto ▷ *n* (*also*: **oil ~**) marea negra
slide [slaɪd] (*pt, pp* **slid**) *n* (*movement*) descenso, desprendimiento; (*in playground*) tobogán *m*; (*Phot*) diapositiva; (BRIT: *also*: **hair ~**) pasador *m* ▷ *vt* correr, deslizar ▷ *vi* (*slip*) resbalarse; (*glide*) deslizarse; **sliding** *adj* (*door*) corredizo
slight [slaɪt] *adj* (*slim*) delgado; (*frail*) delicado; (*pain etc*) leve; (*trivial*) insignificante; (*small*) pequeño ▷ *n* desaire *m* ▷ *vt* (*insult*) ofender, desairar; **not in the ~est** en absoluto; **slightly** *adv* ligeramente, un poco
slim [slɪm] *adj* delgado, esbelto; (*fig*: *chance*) remoto ▷ *vi* adelgazar; **slimming** *n* adelgazamiento
slimy ['slaɪmɪ] *adj* cenagoso
sling [slɪŋ] (*pt, pp* **slung**) *n* (*Med*) cabestrillo; (*weapon*) honda ▷ *vt* tirar, arrojar
slip [slɪp] *n* (*slide*) resbalón *m*; (*mistake*) descuido; (*underskirt*) combinación *f*; (*of paper*) papelito ▷ *vt* (*slide*) deslizar ▷ *vi* deslizarse; (*stumble*) resbalar(se); (*decline*) decaer; (*move smoothly*): **to ~ into/out of** (*room etc*) introducirse en/salirse de; **to give sb the ~** eludir a algn; **a ~ of the tongue** un lapsus; **to ~ sth on/off** ponerse/quitarse algo; **slip up** *vi* (*make mistake*) equivocarse; meter la pata
slipper ['slɪpə*] *n* zapatilla, pantufla
slippery ['slɪpərɪ] *adj* resbaladizo; **slip road** (BRIT) *n* carretera de acceso
slit [slɪt] (*pt, pp* **~**) *n* raja; (*cut*) corte *m* ▷ *vt* rajar; cortar
slog [slɔg] (BRIT) *vi* sudar tinta; **it was a ~** costó trabajo (hacerlo)
slogan ['sləugən] *n* eslogan *m*, lema *m*
slope [sləup] *n* (*up*) cuesta, pendiente *f*; (*down*) declive *m*; (*side of mountain*) falda, vertiente *m* ▷ *vi*: **to ~ down** estar en declive; **to ~ up** inclinarse; **sloping** *adj* en pendiente; en declive; (*writing*) inclinado
sloppy ['slɔpɪ] *adj* (*work*) descuidado; (*appearance*) desaliñado
slot [slɔt] *n* ranura ▷ *vt*: **to ~ into** encajar en; **slot machine** *n* (BRIT: *vending machine*) distribuidor *m* automático; (*for gambling*) tragaperras *m inv*
Slovakia [sləu'vækɪə] *n* Eslovaquia
Slovene [sləu'vi:n] *adj* esloveno ▷ *n* esloveno/a; (*Ling*) esloveno; **Slovenia** [sləu'vi:nɪə] *n* Eslovenia; **Slovenian** *adj, n* = **Slovene**
slow [sləu] *adj* lento; (*not clever*) lerdo; (*watch*): **to be ~** atrasar ▷ *adv* lentamente, despacio ▷ *vt, vi* retardar; **"~"** (*road sign*) "disminuir velocidad"; **slow down** *vi* reducir la marcha; **slowly** *adv* lentamente, despacio; **slow motion** *n*: **in slow motion** a cámara lenta
slug [slʌg] *n* babosa; (*bullet*) posta; **sluggish** *adj* lento; (*person*) perezoso
slum [slʌm] *n* casucha
slump [slʌmp] *n* (*economic*) depresión *f* ▷ *vi* hundirse; (*prices*) caer en picado
slung [slʌŋ] *pt, pp of* **sling**
slur [slə:*] *n*: **to cast a ~ on** insultar ▷ *vt* (*speech*) pronunciar mal
sly [slaɪ] *adj* astuto; (*smile*) taimado
smack [smæk] *n* bofetada ▷ *vt* dar con la mano a; (*child, on face*) abofetear

▷ *vi*: **to ~ of** saber a, oler a

small [smɔːl] *adj* pequeño; **small ads** (BRIT) *npl* anuncios *mpl* por palabras; **small change** *n* suelto, cambio

smart [smɑːt] *adj* elegante; (*clever*) listo, inteligente; (*quick*) rápido, vivo ▷ *vi* escocer, picar; **smartcard** *n* tarjeta inteligente

smash [smæʃ] *n* (*also*: **~-up**) choque *m*; (*Mus*) exitazo ▷ *vt* (*break*) hacer pedazos; (*car etc*) estrellar; (*Sport*: *record*) batir ▷ *vi* hacerse pedazos; (*against wall etc*) estrellarse; **smashing** (*inf*) *adj* estupendo

smear [smɪə*] *n* mancha; (*Med*) frotis *m inv* ▷ *vt* untar; **smear test** *n* (*Med*) citología, frotis *m inv* (cervical)

smell [smɛl] (*pt*, *pp* **smelt** *or* **~ed**) *n* olor *m*; (*sense*) olfato ▷ *vt*, *vi* oler; **smelly** *adj* maloliente

smelt [smɛlt] *pt*, *pp of* **smell**

smile [smaɪl] *n* sonrisa ▷ *vi* sonreír

smirk [sməːk] *n* sonrisa falsa *or* afectada

smog [smɔg] *n* esmog *m*

smoke [smǝuk] *n* humo ▷ *vi* fumar; (*chimney*) echar humo ▷ *vt* (*cigarettes*) fumar; **smoke alarm** *n* detector *m* de humo, alarma contra incendios; **smoked** *adj* (*bacon*, *glass*) ahumado; **smoker** *n* fumador(a) *m/f*; (*Rail*) coche *m* fumador; **smoking** *n*: **"no smoking"** "prohibido fumar"

> Be careful not to translate **smoking** by the Spanish word *smoking*.

smoky *adj* (*room*) lleno de humo; (*taste*) ahumado

smooth [smuːð] *adj* liso; (*sea*) tranquilo; (*flavour*, *movement*) suave; (*sauce*) fino; (*person*: *pej*) meloso ▷ *vt* (*also*: **~ out**) alisar; (*creases*, *difficulties*) allanar

smother ['smʌðə*] *vt* sofocar; (*repress*) contener

SMS *n abbr* (= *short message service*) (servicio) SMS; **SMS message** *n* (mensaje *m*) SMS

smudge [smʌdʒ] *n* mancha ▷ *vt* manchar

smug [smʌg] *adj* presumido; orondo

smuggle ['smʌgl] *vt* pasar de contrabando; **smuggling** *n* contrabando

snack [snæk] *n* bocado; **snack bar** *n* cafetería

snag [snæg] *n* problema *m*

snail [sneɪl] *n* caracol *m*

snake [sneɪk] *n* serpiente *f*

snap [snæp] *n* (*sound*) chasquido; (*photograph*) foto *f* ▷ *adj* (*decision*) instantáneo ▷ *vt* (*break*) quebrar; (*fingers*) castañetear ▷ *vi* quebrarse; (*fig*: *speak sharply*) contestar bruscamente; **to ~ shut** cerrarse de golpe; **snap at** *vt fus* (*dog*) intentar morder; **snap up** *vt* agarrar; **snapshot** *n* foto *f* (instantánea)

snarl [snɑːl] *vi* gruñir

snatch [snætʃ] *n* (*small piece*) fragmento ▷ *vt* (*snatch away*) arrebatar; (*fig*) agarrar; **to ~ some sleep** encontrar tiempo para dormir

sneak [sniːk] (*pt* (US) **snuck**) *vi*: **to ~ in/out** entrar/salir a hurtadillas ▷ *n* (*inf*) soplón/ona *m/f*; **to ~ up on sb** aparecérsele de improviso a algn; **sneakers** *npl* zapatos *mpl* de lona

sneer [snɪə*] *vi* reír con sarcasmo; (*mock*): **to ~ at** burlarse de

sneeze [sniːz] *vi* estornudar

sniff [snɪf] *vi* sollozar ▷ *vt* husmear, oler; (*drugs*) esnifar

snigger ['snɪgə*] *vi* reírse con disimulo

snip [snɪp] *n* tijeretazo; (BRIT: *inf*: *bargain*) ganga ▷ *vt* tijeretear

sniper ['snaɪpə*] *n* francotirador(a) *m/f*

snob [snɔb] *n* (e)snob *mf*

snooker ['snuːkə*] *n* *especie de billar*

snoop [snuːp] *vi*: **to ~ about** fisgonear

snooze [snuːz] *n* siesta ▷ *vi* echar una siesta

snore [snɔː*] *n* ronquido ▷ *vi* roncar

snorkel ['snɔːkl] *n* (tubo) respirador *m*

snort [snɔːt] *n* bufido ▷*vi* bufar
snow [snəu] *n* nieve *f* ▷*vi* nevar; **snowball** *n* bola de nieve ▷*vi* (*fig*) agrandirse, ampliarse; **snowstorm** *n* nevada, nevasca
snub [snʌb] *vt* (*person*) desairar ▷*n* desaire *m*, repulsa
snug [snʌg] *adj* (*cosy*) cómodo; (*fitted*) ajustado

KEYWORD

so [səu] *adv* **1** (*thus, likewise*) así, de este modo; **if so** de ser así; **I like swimming – so do I** a mí me gusta nadar – a mí también; **I've got work to do – so has Paul** tengo trabajo que hacer – Paul también; **it's 5 o'clock – so it is!** son las cinco – ¡pues es verdad!; **I hope/think so** espero/creo que sí; **so far** hasta ahora; (*in past*) hasta este momento
2 (*in comparisons etc*: *to such a degree*) tan; **so quickly (that)** tan rápido (que); **so big (that)** tan grande (que); **she's not so clever as her brother** no es tan lista como su hermano; **we were so worried** estábamos preocupadísimos
3: **so much** *adj, adv* tanto; **so many** tantos/as
4 (*phrases*): **10 or so** unos 10, 10 o así; **so long!** (*inf*: *goodbye*) ¡hasta luego!
▷*conj* **1** (*expressing purpose*): **so as to do** para hacer; **so (that)** para que +*subjun*
2 (*expressing result*) así que; **so you see, I could have gone** así que ya ves, (yo) podría haber ido

soak [səuk] *vt* (*drench*) empapar; (*steep in water*) remojar ▷*vi* remojarse, estar a remojo; **soak up** *vt* absorber; **soaking** *adj* (*also*: **soaking wet**) calado *or* empapado (hasta los huesos *or* el tuétano)
so-and-so ['səuənsəu] *n* (*somebody*) fulano/a de tal
soap [səup] *n* jabón *m*; **soap opera** *n* telenovela; **soap powder** *n* jabón *m* en polvo
soar [sɔː*] *vi* (*on wings*) remontarse; (*rocket*: *prices*) dispararse; (*building etc*) elevarse
sob [sɔb] *n* sollozo ▷*vi* sollozar
sober ['səubə*] *adj* (*serious*) serio; (*not drunk*) sobrio; (*colour, style*) discreto; **sober up** *vt* quitar la borrachera
so-called ['səu'kɔːld] *adj* así llamado
soccer ['sɔkə*] *n* fútbol *m*
sociable ['səuʃəbl] *adj* sociable
social ['səuʃl] *adj* social ▷*n* velada, fiesta; **socialism** *n* socialismo; **socialist** *adj, n* socialista *mf*; **socialize** *vi*: **to socialize (with)** alternar (con); **social life** *n* vida social; **socially** *adv* socialmente; **social security** *n* seguridad *f* social; **social services** *npl* servicios *mpl* sociales; **social work** *n* asistencia social; **social worker** *n* asistente/a *m/f* social
society [sə'saɪətɪ] *n* sociedad *f*; (*club*) asociación *f*; (*also*: **high ~**) alta sociedad
sociology [səusɪ'ɔlədʒi] *n* sociología
sock [sɔk] *n* calcetín *m*
socket ['sɔkɪt] *n* cavidad *f*; (BRIT *Elec*) enchufe *m*
soda ['səudə] *n* (*Chem*) sosa; (*also*: **~ water**) soda; (US: *also*: **~ pop**) gaseosa
sodium ['səudɪəm] *n* sodio
sofa ['səufə] *n* sofá *m*; **sofa bed** *n* sofá-cama *m*
soft [sɔft] *adj* (*lenient, not hard*) blando; (*gentle, not bright*) suave; **soft drink** *n* bebida no alcohólica; **soft drugs** *npl* drogas *fpl* blandas; **soften** ['sɔfn] *vt* ablandar; suavizar; (*effect*) amortiguar ▷*vi* ablandarse; suavizarse; **softly** *adv* suavemente; (*gently*) delicadamente, con delicadeza; **software** *n* (*Comput*) software *m*
soggy ['sɔgɪ] *adj* empapado
soil [sɔɪl] *n* (*earth*) tierra, suelo ▷*vt* ensuciar
solar ['səulə*] *adj* solar; **solar power** *n* energía solar; **solar system** *n* sistema *m* solar

sold [səuld] *pt, pp of* **sell**
soldier ['səuldʒə*] *n* soldado; (*army man*) militar *m*
sold out *adj* (*Comm*) agotado
sole [səul] *n* (*of foot*) planta; (*of shoe*) suela; (*fish: pl inv*) lenguado ▷ *adj* único; **solely** *adv* únicamente, sólo, solamente; **I will hold you solely responsible** le consideraré el único responsable
solemn ['sɔləm] *adj* solemne
solicitor [sə'lɪsɪtə*] (BRIT) *n* (*for wills etc*) ≈ notario/a; (*in court*) ≈ abogado/a
solid ['sɔlɪd] *adj* sólido; (*gold etc*) macizo ▷ *n* sólido
solitary ['sɔlɪtərɪ] *adj* solitario, solo
solitude ['sɔlɪtju:d] *n* soledad *f*
solo ['səuləu] *n* solo ▷ *adv* (*fly*) en solitario; **soloist** *n* solista *m/f*
soluble ['sɔlju:bl] *adj* soluble
solution [sə'lu:ʃən] *n* solución *f*
solve [sɔlv] *vt* resolver, solucionar
solvent ['sɔlvənt] *adj* (*Comm*) solvente ▷ *n* (*Chem*) solvente *m*
sombre ['sɔmbə*] (US **somber**) *adj* sombrío

KEYWORD

some [sʌm] *adj* **1** (*a certain amount or number*): **some tea/water/biscuits** té/agua/(unas) galletas; **there's some milk in the fridge** hay leche en el frigo; **there were some people outside** había algunas personas fuera; **I've got some money, but not much** tengo algo de dinero, pero no mucho
2 (*certain: in contrasts*) algunos/as; **some people say that ...** hay quien dice que ...; **some films were excellent, but most were mediocre** hubo películas excelentes, pero la mayoría fueron mediocres
3 (*unspecified*): **some woman was asking for you** una mujer estuvo preguntando por ti; **he was asking for some book (or other)** pedía un libro; **some day** algún día; **some day next week** un día de la semana que viene
▷ *pron* **1** (*a certain number*): **I've got some** (*books etc*) tengo algunos/as
2 (*a certain amount*) algo; **I've got some** (*money, milk*) tengo algo; **could I have some of that cheese?** ¿me puede dar un poco de ese queso?; **I've read some of the book** he leído parte del libro
▷ *adv*: **some 10 people** unas 10 personas, una decena de personas

some: somebody ['sʌmbədɪ] *pron* = **someone**; **somehow** *adv* de alguna manera; (*for some reason*) por una u otra razón; **someone** *pron* alguien; **someplace** (US) *adv* = **somewhere**; **something** *pron* algo; **would you like something to eat/drink?** ¿te gustaría cenar/tomar algo?; **sometime** *adv* (*in future*) algún día, en algún momento; (*in past*): **sometime last month** durante el mes pasado; **sometimes** *adv* a veces; **somewhat** *adv* algo; **somewhere** *adv* (*be*) en alguna parte; (*go*) a alguna parte; **somewhere else** (*be*) en otra parte; (*go*) a otra parte
son [sʌn] *n* hijo
song [sɔŋ] *n* canción *f*
son-in-law ['sʌnɪnlɔ:] *n* yerno
soon [su:n] *adv* pronto, dentro de poco; **~ afterwards** poco después; *see also* **as**; **sooner** *adv* (*time*) antes, más temprano; (*preference: rather*): **I would sooner do that** preferiría hacer eso; **sooner or later** tarde o temprano
soothe [su:ð] *vt* tranquilizar; (*pain*) aliviar
sophisticated [sə'fɪstɪkeɪtɪd] *adj* sofisticado
sophomore ['sɔfəmɔ:*] (US) *n* estudiante *mf* de segundo año
soprano [sə'prɑ:nəu] *n* soprano *f*
sorbet ['sɔ:beɪ] *n* sorbete *m*
sordid ['sɔ:dɪd] *adj* (*place etc*) sórdido; (*motive etc*) mezquino
sore [sɔ:*] *adj* (*painful*) doloroso, que duele ▷ *n* llaga

sorrow ['sɔrəu] *n* pena, dolor *m*
sorry ['sɔrɪ] *adj* (*regretful*) arrepentido; (*condition, excuse*) lastimoso; **~!** ¡perdón!, ¡perdone!; **~?** ¿cómo?; **to feel ~ for sb** tener lástima a algn; **I feel ~ for him** me da lástima
sort [sɔ:t] *n* clase *f*, género, tipo; **sort out** *vt* (*papers*) clasificar; (*organize*) ordenar, organizar; (*resolve*: *problem, situation etc*) arreglar, solucionar
SOS *n* SOS *m*
so-so ['səusəu] *adv* regular, así así
sought [sɔ:t] *pt, pp of* **seek**
soul [səul] *n* alma
sound [saund] *n* (*noise*) sonido, ruido; (*volume*: *on TV etc*) volumen *m*; (*Geo*) estrecho ▷ *adj* (*healthy*) sano; (*safe, not damaged*) en buen estado; (*reliable*: *person*) digno de confianza; (*sensible*) sensato, razonable; (*secure*: *investment*) seguro ▷ *adv*: **~ asleep** profundamente dormido ▷ *vt* (*alarm*) sonar ▷ *vi* sonar, resonar; (*fig*: *seem*) parecer; **to ~ like** sonar a; **soundtrack** *n* (*of film*) banda sonora
soup [su:p] *n* (*thick*) sopa; (*thin*) caldo
sour ['sauə*] *adj* agrio; (*milk*) cortado; **it's ~ grapes** (*fig*) están verdes
source [sɔ:s] *n* fuente *f*
south [sauθ] *n* sur *m* ▷ *adj* del sur, sureño ▷ *adv* al sur, hacia el sur; **South Africa** *n* África del Sur; **South African** *adj, n* sudafricano/a *m/f*; **South America** *n* América del Sur, Sudamérica; **South American** *adj, n* sudamericano/a *m/f*; **southbound** *adj* (con) rumbo al sur; **southeastern** [sauθ'i:stən] *adj* sureste, del sureste; **southern** ['sʌðən] *adj* del sur, meridional; **South Korea** *n* Corea del Sur; **South Pole** *n* Polo Sur; **southward(s)** *adv* hacia el sur; **south-west** *n* suroeste *m*; **southwestern** [sauθ'westən] *adj* suroeste
souvenir [su:və'nɪə*] *n* recuerdo
sovereign ['sɔvrɪn] *adj, n* soberano/a *m/f*
sow[1] [səu] (*pt* **~ed**, *pp* **sown**) *vt* sembrar
sow[2] [sau] *n* cerda, puerca
soya ['sɔɪə] (BRIT) *n* soja
spa [spɑ:] *n* balneario
space [speɪs] *n* espacio; (*room*) sitio ▷ *cpd* espacial ▷ *vt* (*also*: **~ out**) espaciar; **spacecraft** *n* nave *f* espacial; **spaceship** *n* = **spacecraft**
spacious ['speɪʃəs] *adj* amplio
spade [speɪd] *n* (*tool*) pala, laya; **spades** *npl* (*Cards*: *British*) picas *fpl*; (: *Spanish*) espadas *fpl*
spaghetti [spə'gɛtɪ] *n* espaguetis *mpl*, fideos *mpl*
Spain [speɪn] *n* España
spam [spæm] *n* (*junk e-mail*) spam *m*
span [spæn] *n* (*of bird, plane*) envergadura; (*of arch*) luz *f*; (*in time*) lapso ▷ *vt* extenderse sobre, cruzar; (*fig*) abarcar
Spaniard ['spænjəd] *n* español(a) *m/f*
Spanish ['spænɪʃ] *adj* español(a) ▷ *n* (*Ling*) español *m*, castellano; **the Spanish** *npl* los españoles
spank [spæŋk] *vt* zurrar
spanner ['spænə*] (BRIT) *n* llave *f* (inglesa)
spare [spɛə*] *adj* de reserva; (*surplus*) sobrante, de más ▷ *n* = **spare part** ▷ *vt* (*do without*) pasarse sin; (*refrain from hurting*) perdonar; **to ~** (*surplus*) sobrante, de sobra; **spare part** *n* pieza de repuesto; **spare room** *n* cuarto de los invitados; **spare time** *n* tiempo libre; **spare tyre** (US **spare tire**) *n* (*Aut*) neumático *or* llanta (LAM) de recambio; **spare wheel** *n* (*Aut*) rueda de recambio
spark [spɑ:k] *n* chispa; (*fig*) chispazo; **spark(ing) plug** *n* bujía
sparkle ['spɑ:kl] *n* centelleo, destello ▷ *vi* (*shine*) relucir, brillar
sparrow ['spærəu] *n* gorrión *m*
sparse [spɑ:s] *adj* esparcido, escaso
spasm ['spæzəm] *n* (*Med*) espasmo
spat [spæt] *pt, pp of* **spit**
spate [speɪt] *n* (*fig*): **a ~ of** un

torrente de
spatula ['spætjulə] *n* espátula
speak [spi:k] (*pt* **spoke**, *pp* **spoken**) *vt* (*language*) hablar; (*truth*) decir ▷ *vi* hablar; (*make a speech*) intervenir; **to ~ to sb/of** *or* **about sth** hablar con algn/de *or* sobre algo; **~ up!** ¡habla fuerte!; **speaker** *n* (*in public*) orador(a) *m/f*; (*also*: **loudspeaker**) altavoz *m*; (*for stereo etc*) bafle *m*; (*Pol*): **the Speaker** (BRIT) *el Presidente de la Cámara de los Comunes*; (US) *el Presidente del Congreso*
spear [spɪə*] *n* lanza ▷ *vt* alancear
special ['spɛʃl] *adj* especial; (*edition etc*) extraordinario; (*delivery*) urgente; **special delivery** *n* (*Post*): **by special delivery** por entrega urgente; **special effects** *npl* (*Cine*) efectos *mpl* especiales; **specialist** *n* especialista *mf*; **speciality** [spɛʃɪ'ælɪtɪ] (BRIT) *n* especialidad *f*; **specialize** *vi*: **to specialize (in)** especializarse (en); **specially** *adv* sobre todo, en particular; **special needs** *npl* (BRIT): **children with special needs** niños que requieren una atención diferenciada; **special offer** *n* (*Comm*) oferta especial; **special school** *n* (BRIT) colegio *m* de educación especial; **specialty** (US) *n* = **speciality**
species ['spi:ʃi:z] *n inv* especie *f*
specific [spə'sɪfɪk] *adj* específico; **specifically** *adv* específicamente
specify ['spɛsɪfaɪ] *vt, vi* especificar, precisar
specimen ['spɛsɪmən] *n* ejemplar *m*; (*Med*: *of urine*) espécimen *m*; (: *of blood*) muestra
speck [spɛk] *n* grano, mota
spectacle ['spɛktəkl] *n* espectáculo; **spectacles** *npl* (BRIT: *glasses*) gafas *fpl* (SP), anteojos *mpl*; **spectacular** [-'tækjulə*] *adj* espectacular; (*success*) impresionante
spectator [spɛk'teɪtə*] *n* espectador(a) *m/f*
spectrum ['spɛktrəm] (*pl* **spectra**) *n* espectro
speculate ['spɛkjuleɪt] *vi*: **to ~ (on)** especular (en)
sped [spɛd] *pt, pp of* **speed**
speech [spi:tʃ] *n* (*faculty*) habla; (*formal talk*) discurso; (*spoken language*) lenguaje *m*; **speechless** *adj* mudo, estupefacto
speed [spi:d] *n* velocidad *f*; (*haste*) prisa; (*promptness*) rapidez *f*; **at full** *or* **top ~** a máxima velocidad; **speed up** *vi* acelerarse ▷ *vt* acelerar; **speedboat** *n* lancha motora; **speeding** *n* (*Aut*) exceso de velocidad; **speed limit** *n* límite *m* de velocidad, velocidad *f* máxima; **speedometer** [spɪ'dɔmɪtə*] *n* velocímetro; **speedy** *adj* (*fast*) veloz, rápido; (*prompt*) pronto
spell [spɛl] (*pt, pp* **spelt** (BRIT) *or* **~ed**) *n* (*also*: **magic ~**) encanto, hechizo; (*period of time*) rato, período ▷ *vt* deletrear; (*fig*) anunciar, presagiar; **to cast a ~ on sb** hechizar a algn; **he can't ~** pone faltas de ortografía; **spell out** *vt* (*explain*): **to spell sth out for sb** explicar algo a algn en detalle; **spellchecker** ['speltʃekə*] *n* corrector *m* ortográfico; **spelling** *n* ortografía
spelt [spɛlt] *pt, pp of* **spell**
spend [spɛnd] (*pt, pp* **spent**) *vt* (*money*) gastar; (*time*) pasar; (*life*) dedicar; **spending** *n*: **government spending** gastos *mpl* del gobierno
spent [spɛnt] *pt, pp of* **spend** ▷ *adj* (*cartridge, bullets, match*) usado
sperm [spə:m] *n* esperma
sphere [sfɪə*] *n* esfera
spice [spaɪs] *n* especia ▷ *vt* condimentar
spicy ['spaɪsɪ] *adj* picante
spider ['spaɪdə*] *n* araña
spike [spaɪk] *n* (*point*) punta; (*Bot*) espiga
spill [spɪl] (*pt, pp* **spilt** *or* **~ed**) *vt* derramar, verter ▷ *vi* derramarse; **to ~ over** desbordarse
spin [spɪn] (*pt, pp* **spun**) *n* (*Aviat*) barrena; (*trip in car*) paseo (en coche); (*on ball*) efecto ▷ *vt* (*wool etc*) hilar; (*ball*

etc) hacer girar ▷ *vi* girar, dar vueltas
spinach ['spɪnɪtʃ] *n* espinaca; (*as food*) espinacas *fpl*
spinal ['spaɪnl] *adj* espinal
spin doctor *n informador(a) parcial al servicio de un partido político etc*
spin-dryer (BRIT) *n* secador *m* centrífugo
spine [spaɪn] *n* espinazo, columna vertebral; (*thorn*) espina
spiral ['spaɪərl] *n* espiral *f* ▷ *vi* (*fig*: *prices*) subir desorbitadamente
spire ['spaɪə*] *n* aguja, chapitel *m*
spirit ['spɪrɪt] *n* (*soul*) alma; (*ghost*) fantasma *m*; (*attitude, sense*) espíritu *m*; (*courage*) valor *m*, ánimo; **spirits** *npl* (*drink*) licor(es) *m(pl)*; **in good ~s** alegre, de buen ánimo
spiritual ['spɪrɪtjuəl] *adj* espiritual ▷ *n* espiritual *m*
spit [spɪt] (*pt, pp* **spat**) *n* (*for roasting*) asador *m*, espetón *m*; (*saliva*) saliva ▷ *vi* escupir; (*sound*) chisporrotear; (*rain*) lloviznar
spite [spaɪt] *n* rencor *m*, ojeriza ▷ *vt* causar pena a, mortificar; **in ~ of** a pesar de, pese a; **spiteful** *adj* rencoroso, malévolo
splash [splæʃ] *n* (*sound*) chapoteo; (*of colour*) mancha ▷ *vt* salpicar ▷ *vi* (*also*: **~ about**) chapotear; **splash out** (*inf*) *vi* (BRIT) derrochar dinero
splendid ['splɛndɪd] *adj* espléndido
splinter ['splɪntə*] *n* (*of wood etc*) astilla; (*in finger*) espigón *m* ▷ *vi* astillarse, hacer astillas
split [splɪt] (*pt, pp* **~**) *n* hendedura, raja; (*fig*) división *f*; (*Pol*) escisión *f* ▷ *vt* partir, rajar; (*party*) dividir; (*share*) repartir ▷ *vi* dividirse, escindirse; **split up** *vi* (*couple*) separarse; (*meeting*) acabarse
spoil [spɔɪl] (*pt, pp* **~t** *or* **~ed**) *vt* (*damage*) dañar; (*mar*) estropear; (*child*) mimar, consentir
spoilt [spɔɪlt] *pt, pp of* **spoil** ▷ *adj* (*child*) mimado, consentido; (*ballot paper*) invalidado
spoke [spəuk] *pt of* **speak** ▷ *n* rayo, radio
spoken ['spəukn] *pp of* **speak**
spokesman ['spəuksmən] (*irreg*) *n* portavoz *m*
spokesperson ['spəukspə:sn] (*irreg*) *n* portavoz *m/f*, vocero/a (LAM)
spokeswoman ['spəukswumən] (*irreg*) *n* portavoz *f*
sponge [spʌndʒ] *n* esponja; (*also*: **~ cake**) bizcocho ▷ *vt* (*wash*) lavar con esponja ▷ *vi*: **to ~ off** *or* **on sb** vivir a costa de algn; **sponge bag** (BRIT) *n* esponjera
sponsor ['spɔnsə*] *n* patrocinador(a) *m/f* ▷ *vt* (*applicant, proposal etc*) proponer; **sponsorship** *n* patrocinio
spontaneous [spɔn'teɪnɪəs] *adj* espontáneo
spooky ['spu:kɪ] (*inf*) *adj* espeluznante, horripilante
spoon [spu:n] *n* cuchara; **spoonful** *n* cucharada
sport [spɔ:t] *n* deporte *m*; (*person*): **to be a good ~** ser muy majo ▷ *vt* (*wear*) lucir, ostentar; **sport jacket** (US) *n* = **sports jacket**; **sports car** *n* coche *m* deportivo; **sports centre** (BRIT) *n* polideportivo; **sports jacket** (BRIT) *n* chaqueta deportiva; **sportsman** (*irreg*) *n* deportista *m*; **sports utility vehicle** *n* todoterreno *m inv*; **sportswear** *n* trajes *mpl* de deporte *or* sport; **sportswoman** (*irreg*) *n* deportista; **sporty** *adj* deportista
spot [spɔt] *n* sitio, lugar *m*; (*dot*: *on pattern*) punto, mancha; (*pimple*) grano; (*Radio*) cuña publicitaria; (*TV*) espacio publicitario; (*small amount*): **a ~ of** un poquito de ▷ *vt* (*notice*) notar, observar; **on the ~** allí mismo; **spotless** *adj* perfectamente limpio; **spotlight** *n* foco, reflector *m*; (*Aut*) faro auxiliar
spouse [spauz] *n* cónyuge *mf*
sprain [spreɪn] *n* torcedura ▷ *vt*: **to ~ one's ankle/wrist** torcerse el tobillo/la muñeca
sprang [spræŋ] *pt of* **spring**

sprawl [sprɔ:l] *vi* tumbarse
spray [spreɪ] *n* rociada; (*of sea*) espuma; (*container*) atomizador *m*; (*for paint etc*) pistola rociadora; (*of flowers*) ramita ▷*vt* rociar; (*crops*) regar
spread [sprɛd] (*pt, pp* **~**) *n* extensión *f*; (*for bread etc*) pasta para untar; (*inf: food*) comilona ▷*vt* extender; (*butter*) untar; (*wings, sails*) desplegar; (*work, wealth*) repartir; (*scatter*) esparcir ▷*vi* (*also*: **~ out**: *stain*) extenderse; (*news*) diseminarse; **spread out** *vi* (*move apart*) separarse; **spreadsheet** *n* hoja electrónica *or* de cálculo
spree [spri:] *n*: **to go on a ~** ir de juerga
spring [sprɪŋ] (*pt* **sprang**, *pp* **sprung**) *n* (*season*) primavera; (*leap*) salto, brinco; (*coiled metal*) resorte *m*; (*of water*) fuente *f*, manantial *m* ▷*vi* saltar, brincar; **spring up** *vi* (*thing: appear*) aparecer; (*problem*) surgir; **spring onion** *n* cebolleta
sprinkle ['sprɪŋkl] *vt* (*pour: liquid*) rociar; (*: salt, sugar*) espolvorear; **to ~ water** *etc* **on, ~ with water** *etc* rociar *or* salpicar de agua *etc*
sprint [sprɪnt] *n* esprint *m* ▷*vi* esprintar
sprung [sprʌŋ] *pp of* **spring**
spun [spʌn] *pt, pp of* **spin**
spur [spə:*] *n* espuela; (*fig*) estímulo, aguijón *m* ▷*vt* (*also*: **~ on**) estimular, incitar; **on the ~ of the moment** de improviso
spurt [spə:t] *n* chorro; (*of energy*) arrebato ▷*vi* chorrear
spy [spaɪ] *n* espía *mf* ▷*vi*: **to ~ on** espiar a ▷*vt* (*see*) divisar, lograr ver
sq. *abbr* = **square**
squabble ['skwɔbl] *vi* reñir, pelear
squad [skwɔd] *n* (*Mil*) pelotón *m*; (*Police*) brigada; (*Sport*) equipo
squadron ['skwɔdrn] *n* (*Mil*) escuadrón *m*; (*Aviat, Naut*) escuadra
squander ['skwɔndə*] *vt* (*money*) derrochar, despilfarrar; (*chances*) desperdiciar
square [skwɛə*] *n* cuadro; (*in town*) plaza; (*inf: person*) carca *m/f* ▷*adj* cuadrado; (*inf: ideas, tastes*) trasnochado ▷*vt* (*arrange*) arreglar; (*Math*) cuadrar; (*reconcile*) compaginar; **all ~** igual(es); **to have a ~ meal** comer caliente; **2 metres ~** 2 metros en cuadro; **2 ~ metres** 2 metros cuadrados; **square root** *n* raíz *f* cuadrada
squash [skwɔʃ] *n* (BRIT: *drink*): **lemon/orange ~** zumo (SP) *or* jugo (LAM) de limón/naranja; (*US Bot*) calabacín *m*; (*Sport*) squash *m* ▷*vt* aplastar
squat [skwɔt] *adj* achaparrado ▷*vi* (*also*: **~ down**) agacharse, sentarse en cuclillas; **squatter** *n* okupa *mf* (SP)
squeak [skwi:k] *vi* (*hinge*) chirriar, rechinar; (*mouse*) chillar
squeal [skwi:l] *vi* chillar, dar gritos agudos
squeeze [skwi:z] *n* presión *f*; (*of hand*) apretón *m*; (*Comm*) restricción *f* ▷*vt* (*hand, arm*) apretar
squid [skwɪd] *n inv* calamar *m*; (*Culin*) calamares *mpl*
squint [skwɪnt] *vi* bizquear, ser bizco ▷*n* (*Med*) estrabismo
squirm [skwə:m] *vi* retorcerse, revolverse
squirrel ['skwɪrəl] *n* ardilla
squirt [skwə:t] *vi* salir a chorros ▷*vt* chiscar
Sr *abbr* = **senior**
Sri Lanka [srɪ'læŋkə] *n* Sri Lanka *m*
St *abbr* = **saint; street**
stab [stæb] *n* (*with knife*) puñalada; (*of pain*) pinchazo; (*inf: try*): **to have a ~ at (doing) sth** intentar (hacer) algo ▷*vt* apuñalar
stability [stə'bɪlɪtɪ] *n* estabilidad *f*
stable ['steɪbl] *adj* estable ▷*n* cuadra, caballeriza
stack [stæk] *n* montón *m*, pila ▷*vt* amontonar, apilar
stadium ['steɪdɪəm] *n* estadio
staff [stɑ:f] *n* (*work force*) personal *m*,

plantilla; (BRIT *Scol*) cuerpo docente ▷ *vt* proveer de personal

stag [stæg] *n* ciervo, venado

stage [steɪdʒ] *n* escena; (*point*) etapa; (*platform*) plataforma; (*profession*): **the ~** el teatro ▷ *vt* (*play*) poner en escena, representar; (*organize*) montar, organizar; **in ~s** por etapas

stagger ['stægə*] *vi* tambalearse ▷ *vt* (*amaze*) asombrar; (*hours, holidays*) escalonar; **staggering** *adj* asombroso

stagnant ['stægnənt] *adj* estancado

stag night, stag party *n* despedida de soltero

stain [steɪn] *n* mancha; (*colouring*) tintura ▷ *vt* manchar; (*wood*) teñir; **stained glass** *n* vidrio *m* de color; **stainless steel** *n* acero inoxidable

staircase ['stɛəkeɪs] *n* = **stairway**

stairs [stɛəz] *npl* escaleras *fpl*

stairway ['stɛəweɪ] *n* escalera

stake [steɪk] *n* estaca, poste *m*; (*Comm*) interés *m*; (*Betting*) apuesta ▷ *vt* (*money*) apostar; (*life*) arriesgar; (*reputation*) poner en juego; (*claim*) presentar una reclamación; **to be at ~** estar en juego

stale [steɪl] *adj* (*bread*) duro; (*food*) pasado; (*smell*) rancio; (*beer*) agrio

stalk [stɔːk] *n* tallo, caña ▷ *vt* acechar, cazar al acecho

stall [stɔːl] *n* (*in market*) puesto; (*in stable*) casilla (de establo) ▷ *vt* (*Aut*) calar; (*fig*) dar largas a ▷ *vi* (*Aut*) calarse; (*fig*) andarse con rodeos

stamina ['stæmɪnə] *n* resistencia

stammer ['stæmə*] *n* tartamudeo ▷ *vi* tartamudear

stamp [stæmp] *n* sello (SP), estampilla (LAM), timbre *m* (MEX); (*mark*) marca, huella; (*on document*) timbre *m* ▷ *vi* (*also*: **~ one's foot**) patear ▷ *vt* (*mark*) marcar; (*letter*) franquear; (*with rubber stamp*) sellar; **stamp out** *vt* (*fire*) apagar con el pie; (*crime, opposition*) acabar con; **stamped addressed envelope** *n* (BRIT) sobre *m* sellado con las señas propias

stampede [stæm'piːd] *n* estampida

stance [stæns] *n* postura

stand [stænd] (*pt, pp* **stood**) *n* (*position*) posición *f*, postura; (*for taxis*) parada; (*hall stand*) perchero; (*music stand*) atril *m*; (*Sport*) tribuna; (*at exhibition*) stand *m* ▷ *vi* (*be*) estar, encontrarse; (*be on foot*) estar de pie; (*rise*) levantarse; (*remain*) quedar en pie; (*in election*) presentar candidatura ▷ *vt* (*place*) poner, colocar; (*withstand*) aguantar, soportar; (*invite to*) invitar; **to make a ~** (*fig*) mantener una postura firme; **to ~ for parliament** (BRIT) presentarse (como candidato) a las elecciones; **stand back** *vi* retirarse; **stand by** *vi* (*be ready*) estar listo ▷ *vt fus* (*opinion*) aferrarse a; (*person*) apoyar; **stand down** *vi* (*withdraw*) ceder el puesto; **stand for** *vt fus* (*signify*) significar; (*tolerate*) aguantar, permitir; **stand in for** *vt fus* suplir a; **stand out** *vi* destacarse; **stand up** *vi* levantarse, ponerse de pie; **stand up for** *vt fus* defender; **stand up to** *vt fus* hacer frente a

standard ['stændəd] *n* patrón *m*, norma; (*level*) nivel *m*; (*flag*) estandarte *m* ▷ *adj* (*size etc*) normal, corriente; (*text*) básico; **standards** *npl* (*morals*) valores *mpl* morales; **standard of living** *n* nivel *m* de vida

standing ['stændɪŋ] *adj* (*on foot*) de pie, en pie; (*permanent*) permanente ▷ *n* reputación *f*; **of many years' ~** que lleva muchos años; **standing order** (BRIT) *n* (*at bank*) orden *f* de pago permanente

stand: standpoint *n* punto de vista; **standstill** *n*: **at a standstill** (*industry, traffic*) paralizado; (*car*) parado; **to come to a standstill** quedar paralizado; pararse

stank [stæŋk] *pt of* **stink**

staple ['steɪpl] *n* (*for papers*) grapa ▷ *adj* (*food etc*) básico ▷ *vt* grapar

star [stɑː*] *n* estrella; (*celebrity*) estrella, astro ▷ *vt* (*Theatre, Cinema*) ser el/la protagonista de; **the stars** *npl* (*Astrology*) el horóscopo

starboard ['stɑːbəd] *n* estribor *m*

starch [stɑːtʃ] *n* almidón *m*

stardom ['stɑːdəm] *n* estrellato

stare [stɛə*] *n* mirada fija ▷ *vi*: **to ~ at** mirar fijo

stark [stɑːk] *adj* (*bleak*) severo, escueto ▷ *adv*: **~ naked** en cueros

start [stɑːt] *n* principio, comienzo; (*departure*) salida; (*sudden movement*) salto, sobresalto; (*advantage*) ventaja ▷ *vt* empezar, comenzar; (*cause*) causar; (*found*) fundar; (*engine*) poner en marcha ▷ *vi* comenzar, empezar; (*with fright*) asustarse, sobresaltarse; (*train etc*) salir; **to ~ doing** *or* **to do sth** empezar a hacer algo; **start off** *vi* empezar, comenzar; (*leave*) salir, ponerse en camino; **start out** *vi* (*begin*) empezar; (*set out*) partir, salir; **start up** *vi* comenzar; (*car*) ponerse en marcha ▷ *vt* comenzar; poner en marcha; **starter** *n* (*Aut*) botón *m* de arranque; (*Sport: official*) juez *mf* de salida; (BRIT *Culin*) entrante *m*; **starting point** *n* punto de partida

startle ['stɑːtl] *vt* asustar, sobrecoger; **startling** *adj* alarmante

starvation [stɑː'veɪʃən] *n* hambre *f*

starve [stɑːv] *vi* tener mucha hambre; (*to death*) morir de hambre ▷ *vt* hacer pasar hambre

state [steɪt] *n* estado ▷ *vt* (*say, declare*) afirmar; **the S~s** los Estados Unidos; **to be in a ~** estar agitado; **statement** *n* afirmación *f*; **state school** *n* escuela *or* colegio estatal; **statesman** (*irreg*) *n* estadista *m*

static ['stætɪk] *n* (*Radio*) parásitos *mpl* ▷ *adj* estático

station ['steɪʃən] *n* estación *f*; (*Radio*) emisora; (*rank*) posición *f* social ▷ *vt* colocar, situar; (*Mil*) apostar

stationary ['steɪʃnərɪ] *adj* estacionario, fijo

stationer's (shop) (BRIT) *n* papelería

stationery [-nərɪ] *n* papel *m* de escribir, articulos *mpl* de escritorio

station wagon (US) *n* ranchera

statistic [stə'tɪstɪk] *n* estadística; **statistics** *n* (*science*) estadística

statue ['stætjuː] *n* estatua

stature ['stætʃə*] *n* estatura; (*fig*) talla

status ['steɪtəs] *n* estado; (*reputation*) estatus *m*; **status quo** *n* (e)statu quo *m*

statutory ['stætjutrɪ] *adj* estatutario

staunch [stɔːntʃ] *adj* leal, incondicional

stay [steɪ] *n* estancia ▷ *vi* quedar(se); (*as guest*) hospedarse; **to ~ put** seguir en el mismo sitio; **to ~ the night/5 days** pasar la noche/estar 5 días; **stay away** *vi* (*from person, building*) no acercarse; (*from event*) no acudir; **stay behind** *vi* quedar atrás; **stay in** *vi* quedarse en casa; **stay on** *vi* quedarse; **stay out** *vi* (*of house*) no volver a casa; (*on strike*) permanecer en huelga; **stay up** *vi* (*at night*) velar, no acostarse

steadily ['stɛdɪlɪ] *adv* constantemente; (*firmly*) firmemente; (*work, walk*) sin parar; (*gaze*) fijamente

steady ['stɛdɪ] *adj* (*firm*) firme; (*regular*) regular; (*person, character*) sensato, juicioso; (*boyfriend*) formal; (*look, voice*) tranquilo ▷ *vt* (*stabilize*) estabilizar; (*nerves*) calmar

steak [steɪk] *n* filete *m*; (*beef*) bistec *m*

steal [stiːl] (*pt* **stole**, *pp* **stolen**) *vt* robar ▷ *vi* robar; (*move secretly*) andar a hurtadillas

steam [stiːm] *n* vapor *m*; (*mist*) vaho, humo ▷ *vt* (*Culin*) cocer al vapor ▷ *vi* echar vapor; **steam up** *vi* (*window*) empañarse; **to get steamed up about sth** (*fig*) ponerse negro por algo; **steamy** *adj* (*room*) lleno de vapor; (*window*) empañado; (*heat, atmosphere*) bochornoso

steel [stiːl] *n* acero ▷ *adj* de acero

steep [sti:p] *adj* escarpado, abrupto; (*stair*) empinado; (*price*) exorbitante, excesivo ▷ *vt* empapar, remojar

steeple ['sti:pl] *n* aguja

steer [stɪə*] *vt* (*car*) conducir (SP), manejar (LAM); (*person*) dirigir ▷ *vi* conducir, manejar; **steering** *n* (*Aut*) dirección *f*; **steering wheel** *n* volante *m*

stem [stɛm] *n* (*of plant*) tallo; (*of glass*) pie *m* ▷ *vt* detener; (*blood*) restañar

step [stɛp] *n* paso; (*on stair*) peldaño, escalón *m* ▷ *vi*: **to ~ forward/back** dar un paso adelante/hacia atrás; **steps** *npl* (BRIT) = **stepladder**; **in/out of ~ (with)** acorde/en disonancia (con); **step down** *vi* (*fig*) retirarse; **step in** *vi* entrar; (*fig*) intervenir; **step up** *vt* (*increase*) aumentar; **stepbrother** *n* hermanastro; **stepchild** (*pl* **stepchildren**) *n* hijastro/a *m/f*; **stepdaughter** *n* hijastra; **stepfather** *n* padrastro; **stepladder** *n* escalera doble *or* de tijera; **stepmother** *n* madrastra; **stepsister** *n* hermanastra; **stepson** *n* hijastro

stereo ['stɛrɪəu] *n* estéreo ▷ *adj* (*also*: **~phonic**) estéreo, estereofónico

stereotype ['stɪərɪətaɪp] *n* estereotipo ▷ *vt* estereotipar

sterile ['stɛraɪl] *adj* estéril; **sterilize** ['stɛrɪlaɪz] *vt* esterilizar

sterling ['stə:lɪŋ] *adj* (*silver*) de ley ▷ *n* (*Econ*) libras *fpl* esterlinas *fpl*; **one pound ~** una libra esterlina

stern [stə:n] *adj* severo, austero ▷ *n* (*Naut*) popa

steroid ['stɪərɔɪd] *n* esteroide *m*

stew [stju:] *n* estofado, guiso ▷ *vt* estofar, guisar; (*fruit*) cocer

steward ['stju:əd] *n* camarero; **stewardess** *n* (*esp on plane*) azafata

stick [stɪk] (*pt, pp* **stuck**) *n* palo; (*of dynamite*) barreno; (*as weapon*) porra; (*also*: **walking ~**) bastón *m* ▷ *vt* (*glue*) pegar; (*inf*: *put*) meter; (*: tolerate*) aguantar, soportar; (*thrust*): **to ~ sth into** clavar *or* hincar algo en ▷ *vi* pegarse; (*be unmoveable*) quedarse parado; (*in mind*) quedarse grabado; **stick out** *vi* sobresalir; **stick up** *vi* sobresalir; **stick up for** *vt fus* defender; **sticker** *n* (*label*) etiqueta engomada; (*with slogan*) pegatina; **sticking plaster** *n* esparadrapo; **stick shift** (US) *n* (*Aut*) palanca de cambios

sticky ['stɪkɪ] *adj* pegajoso; (*label*) engomado; (*fig*) difícil

stiff [stɪf] *adj* rígido, tieso; (*hard*) duro; (*manner*) estirado; (*difficult*) difícil; (*person*) inflexible; (*price*) exorbitante ▷ *adv*: **scared/bored ~** muerto de miedo/aburrimiento

stifling ['staɪflɪŋ] *adj* (*heat*) sofocante, bochornoso

stigma ['stɪgmə] *n* (*fig*) estigma *m*

stiletto [stɪ'lɛtəu] (BRIT) *n* (*also*: **~ heel**) tacón *m* de aguja

still [stɪl] *adj* inmóvil, quieto ▷ *adv* todavía; (*even*) aun; (*nonetheless*) sin embargo, aun así

stimulate ['stɪmjuleɪt] *vt* estimular

stimulus ['stɪmjuləs] (*pl* **stimuli**) *n* estímulo, incentivo

sting [stɪŋ] (*pt, pp* **stung**) *n* picadura; (*pain*) escozor *m*, picazón *f*; (*organ*) aguijón *m* ▷ *vt, vi* picar

stink [stɪŋk] (*pt* **stank**, *pp* **stunk**) *n* hedor *m*, tufo ▷ *vi* heder, apestar

stir [stə:*] *n* (*fig*: *agitation*) conmoción *f* ▷ *vt* (*tea etc*) remover; (*fig*: *emotions*) provocar ▷ *vi* moverse; **stir up** *vt* (*trouble*) fomentar; **stir-fry** *vt* sofreír removiendo ▷ *n* *plato preparado sofriendo y removiendo los ingredientes*

stitch [stɪtʃ] *n* (*Sewing*) puntada; (*Knitting*) punto; (*Med*) punto (de sutura); (*pain*) punzada ▷ *vt* coser; (*Med*) suturar

stock [stɔk] *n* (*Comm*: *reserves*) existencias *fpl*, stock *m*; (*: selection*) surtido; (*Agr*) ganado, ganadería; (*Culin*) caldo; (*descent*) raza, estirpe *f*; (*Finance*) capital *m* ▷ *adj* (*fig*: *reply etc*) clásico ▷ *vt* (*have in stock*) tener existencias de; **~s and shares** acciones y valores; **in ~** en existencia *or* almacén; **out of ~** agotado; **to take ~ of** (*fig*) asesorar, examinar; **stockbroker** ['stɔkbrəukə*] *n* agente *mf or* corredor *mf* de bolsa(a); **stock cube** (BRIT) *n* pastilla de caldo; **stock exchange** *n* bolsa; **stockholder** ['stɔkhəuldə*] (US) *n* accionista *m/f*

stocking ['stɔkɪŋ] *n* media

stock market *n* bolsa (de valores)

stole [stəul] *pt of* **steal** ▷ *n* estola

stolen ['stəuln] *pp of* **steal**

stomach ['stʌmək] *n* (*Anat*) estómago; (*belly*) vientre *m* ▷ *vt* tragar, aguantar; **stomachache** *n* dolor *m* de estómago

stone [stəun] *n* piedra; (*in fruit*) hueso (= 6.348 *kg*; 14 *libras*) ▷ *adj* de piedra ▷ *vt* apedrear; (*fruit*) deshuesar

stood [stud] *pt, pp of* **stand**

stool [stu:l] *n* taburete *m*

stoop [stu:p] *vi* (*also*: **~ down**) doblarse, agacharse; (*also*: **have a ~**) ser cargado de espaldas

stop [stɔp] *n* parada; (*in punctuation*) punto ▷ *vt* parar, detener; (*break*) suspender; (*block*: *pay*) suspender; (: *cheque*) invalidar; (*also*: **put a ~ to**) poner término a ▷ *vi* pararse, detenerse; (*end*) acabarse; **to ~ doing sth** dejar de hacer algo; **stop by** *vi* pasar por; **stop off** *vi* interrumpir el viaje; **stopover** *n* parada; (*Aviat*) escala; **stoppage** *n* (*strike*) paro; (*blockage*) obstrucción *f*

storage ['stɔ:rɪdʒ] *n* almacenaje *m*

store [stɔ:*] *n* (*stock*) provisión *f*; (*depot* (BRIT: *large shop*) almacén *m*; (US) tienda; (*reserve*) reserva, repuesto ▷ *vt* almacenar; **stores** *npl* víveres *mpl*; **to be in ~ for sb** (*fig*) esperarle a algn; **storekeeper** (US) *n* tendero/a

storey ['stɔ:rɪ] (US **story**) *n* piso

storm [stɔ:m] *n* tormenta; (*fig*: *of applause*) salva; (: *of criticism*) nube *f* ▷ *vi* (*fig*) rabiar ▷ *vt* tomar por asalto; **stormy** *adj* tempestuoso

story ['stɔ:rɪ] *n* historia; (*lie*) mentira; (US) = **storey**

stout [staut] *adj* (*strong*) sólido; (*fat*) gordo, corpulento; (*resolute*) resuelto ▷ *n* cerveza negra

stove [stəuv] *n* (*for cooking*) cocina; (*for heating*) estufa

straight [streɪt] *adj* recto, derecho; (*frank*) franco, directo; (*simple*) sencillo ▷ *adv* derecho, directamente; (*drink*) sin mezcla; **to put** *or* **get sth ~** dejar algo en claro; **~ away, ~ off** en seguida; **straighten** *vt* (*also*: **straighten out**) enderezar, poner derecho ▷ *vi* (*also*: **straighten up**) enderezarse, ponerse derecho; **straightforward** *adj* (*simple*) sencillo; (*honest*) honrado, franco

strain [streɪn] *n* tensión *f*; (*Tech*) presión *f*; (*Med*) torcedura; (*breed*) tipo, variedad *f* ▷ *vt* (*back etc*) torcerse; (*resources*) agotar; (*stretch*) estirar; (*food, tea*) colar; **strained** *adj* (*muscle*) torcido; (*laugh*) forzado; (*relations*) tenso; **strainer** *n* colador *m*

strait [streɪt] *n* (*Geo*) estrecho (*fig*): **to be in dire ~s** estar en un gran apuro

strand [strænd] *n* (*of thread*) hebra; (*of hair*) trenza; (*of rope*) ramal *m*; **stranded** *adj* (*person*: *without money*) desamparado; (: *without transport*) colgado

strange [streɪndʒ] *adj* (*not known*) desconocido; (*odd*) extraño, raro; **strangely** *adv* de un modo raro; **stranger** *n* desconocido/a; (*from another area*) forastero/a

> Be careful not to translate **stranger** by the Spanish word *extranjero*.

strangle ['stræŋgl] *vt* estrangular

strap [stræp] *n* correa; (*of slip, dress*) tirante *m*

strategic [strə'ti:dʒɪk] *adj* estratégico

strategy ['strætɪdʒɪ] *n* estrategia

straw [strɔ:] *n* paja; (*drinking straw*) caña, pajita; **that's the last ~!** ¡eso es el colmo!

strawberry ['strɔ:bərɪ] *n* fresa,

frutilla (*SC*)

stray [streɪ] *adj* (*animal*) extraviado; (*bullet*) perdido; (*scattered*) disperso ▷ *vi* extraviarse, perderse

streak [stri:k] *n* raya; (*in hair*) raya ▷ *vt* rayar ▷ *vi*: **to ~ past** pasar como un rayo

stream [stri:m] *n* riachuelo, arroyo; (*of people, vehicles*) riada, caravana; (*of smoke, insults etc*) chorro ▷ *vt* (*Scol*) dividir en grupos por habilidad ▷ *vi* correr, fluir; **to ~ in/out** (*people*) entrar/salir en tropel

street [stri:t] *n* calle *f*; **streetcar** (*US*) *n* tranvía *m*; **street light** *n* farol *m* (*LAM*), farola (*SP*); **street map** *n* plano (de la ciudad); **street plan** *n* plano

strength [strɛŋθ] *n* fuerza; (*of girder, knot etc*) resistencia; (*fig: power*) poder *m*; **strengthen** *vt* fortalecer, reforzar

strenuous ['strɛnjuəs] *adj* (*energetic, determined*) enérgico

stress [strɛs] *n* presión *f*; (*mental strain*) estrés *m*; (*accent*) acento ▷ *vt* subrayar, recalcar; (*syllable*) acentuar; **stressed** *adj* (*tense* estresado, agobiado; (*syllable*) acentuado; **stressful** *adj* (*job*) estresante

stretch [strɛtʃ] *n* (*of sand etc*) trecho ▷ *vi* estirarse; (*extend*): **to ~ to** *or* **as far as** extenderse hasta ▷ *vt* extender, estirar; (*make demands*) exigir el máximo esfuerzo a; **stretch out** *vi* tenderse ▷ *vt* (*arm etc*) extender; (*spread*) estirar

stretcher ['strɛtʃə*] *n* camilla

strict [strɪkt] *adj* severo; (*exact*) estricto; **strictly** *adv* severamente; estrictamente

stride [straɪd] (*pt* **strode**, *pp* **stridden**) *n* zancada, tranco ▷ *vi* dar zancadas, andar a trancos

strike [straɪk] (*pt, pp* **struck**) *n* huelga; (*of oil etc*) descubrimiento; (*attack*) ataque *m* ▷ *vt* golpear, pegar; (*oil etc*) descubrir; (*bargain, deal*) cerrar ▷ *vi* declarar la huelga; (*attack*) atacar; (*clock*) dar la hora; **on ~** (*workers*) en huelga; **to ~ a match** encender un fósforo; **striker** *n* huelguista *mf*; (*Sport*) delantero; **striking** *adj* llamativo

string [strɪŋ] (*pt, pp* **strung**) *n* cuerda; (*row*) hilera ▷ *vt*: **to ~ together** ensartar; **to ~ out** extenderse; **the strings** *npl* (*Mus*) los instrumentos de cuerda; **to pull ~s** (*fig*) mover palancas

strip [strɪp] *n* tira; (*of land*) franja; (*of metal*) cinta, lámina ▷ *vt* desnudar; (*paint*) quitar; (*also*: **~ down**: *machine*) desmontar ▷ *vi* desnudarse; **strip off** *vt* (*paint etc*) quitar ▷ *vi* (*person*) desnudarse

stripe [straɪp] *n* raya; (*Mil*) galón *m*; **striped** *adj* a rayas, rayado

stripper ['strɪpə*] *n* artista *mf* de striptease

strip-search ['strɪpsə:tʃ] *vt*: **to ~ sb** desnudar y registrar a algn

strive [straɪv] (*pt* **strove**, *pp* **striven**) *vi*: **to ~ for sth/to do sth** luchar por conseguir/hacer algo

strode [strəud] *pt of* **stride**

stroke [strəuk] *n* (*blow*) golpe *m*; (*Swimming*) brazada; (*Med*) apoplejía; (*of paintbrush*) toque *m* ▷ *vt* acariciar; **at a ~** de un solo golpe

stroll [strəul] *n* paseo, vuelta ▷ *vi* dar un paseo *or* una vuelta; **stroller** (*US*) *n* (*for child*) sillita de ruedas

strong [strɔŋ] *adj* fuerte; **they are 50 ~** son 50; **stronghold** *n* fortaleza; (*fig*) baluarte *m*; **strongly** *adv* fuertemente, con fuerza; (*believe*) firmemente

strove [strəuv] *pt of* **strive**

struck [strʌk] *pt, pp of* **strike**

structure ['strʌktʃə*] *n* estructura; (*building*) construcción *f*

struggle ['strʌgl] *n* lucha ▷ *vi* luchar

strung [strʌŋ] *pt, pp of* **string**

stub [stʌb] *n* (*of ticket etc*) talón *m*; (*of cigarette*) colilla; **to ~ one's toe on sth** dar con el dedo (del pie) contra algo; **stub out** *vt* apagar

stubble ['stʌbl] *n* rastrojo; (*on chin*)

barba (incipiente)
stubborn ['stʌbən] *adj* terco, testarudo
stuck [stʌk] *pt, pp of* **stick** ▷ *adj* (*jammed*) atascado
stud [stʌd] *n* (*shirt stud*) corchete *m*; (*of boot*) taco; (*earring*) pendiente *m* (de bolita); (*also*: **~ farm**) caballeriza; (*also*: **~ horse**) caballo semental ▷ *vt* (*fig*): **~ded with** salpicado de
student ['stju:dənt] *n* estudiante *mf* ▷ *adj* estudiantil; **student driver** (US) *n* conductor(a) *mf* en prácticas; **students' union** *n* (*building*) centro de estudiantes; (BRIT: *association*) federación *f* de estudiantes
studio ['stju:dɪəu] *n* estudio; (*artist's*) taller *m*; **studio flat** *n* estudio
study ['stʌdɪ] *n* estudio ▷ *vt* estudiar; (*examine*) examinar, investigar ▷ *vi* estudiar
stuff [stʌf] *n* materia; (*substance*) material *m*, sustancia; (*things*) cosas *fpl* ▷ *vt* llenar; (*Culin*) rellenar; (*animals*) disecar; (*inf*: *push*) meter; **stuffing** *n* relleno; **stuffy** *adj* (*room*) mal ventilado; (*person*) de miras estrechas
stumble ['stʌmbl] *vi* tropezar, dar un traspié; **to ~ across, ~ on** (*fig*) tropezar con
stump [stʌmp] *n* (*of tree*) tocón *m*; (*of limb*) muñón *m* ▷ *vt*: **to be ~ed for an answer** no saber qué contestar
stun [stʌn] *vt* dejar sin sentido
stung [stʌŋ] *pt, pp of* **sting**
stunk [stʌŋk] *pp of* **stink**
stunned [stʌnd] *adj* (*dazed*) aturdido, atontado; (*amazed*) pasmado; (*shocked*) anonadado
stunning ['stʌnɪŋ] *adj* (*fig*: *news*) pasmoso; (: *outfit etc*) sensacional
stunt [stʌnt] *n* (*in film*) escena peligrosa; (*publicity stunt*) truco publicitario
stupid ['stju:pɪd] *adj* estúpido, tonto; **stupidity** [-'pɪdɪtɪ] *n* estupidez *f*
sturdy ['stə:dɪ] *adj* robusto, fuerte
stutter ['stʌtə*] *n* tartamudeo ▷ *vi* tartamudear
style [staɪl] *n* estilo; **stylish** *adj* elegante, a la moda; **stylist** *n* (*hair stylist*) peluquero/a
sub... [sʌb] *prefix* sub...; **subconscious** *adj* subconsciente
subdued [səb'dju:d] *adj* (*light*) tenue; (*person*) sumiso, manso
subject [*n* 'sʌbdʒɪkt, *vb* səb'dʒɛkt] *n* súbdito; (*Scol*) asignatura; (*matter*) tema *m*; (*Grammar*) sujeto ▷ *vt*: **to ~ sb to sth** someter a algn a algo; **to be ~ to** (*law*) estar sujeto a; (*person*) ser propenso a; **subjective** [-'dʒɛktɪv] *adj* subjetivo; **subject matter** *n* (*content*) contenido
subjunctive [səb'dʒʌŋktɪv] *adj, n* subjuntivo
submarine [sʌbmə'ri:n] *n* submarino
submission [səb'mɪʃən] *n* sumisión *f*
submit [səb'mɪt] *vt* someter ▷ *vi*: **to ~ to sth** someterse a algo
subordinate [sə'bɔ:dɪnət] *adj, n* subordinado/a *m/f*
subscribe [səb'skraɪb] *vi* suscribir; **to ~ to** (*opinion, fund*) suscribir, aprobar; (*newspaper*) suscribirse a
subscription [səb'skrɪpʃən] *n* abono; (*to magazine*) subscripción *f*
subsequent ['sʌbsɪkwənt] *adj* subsiguiente, posterior; **subsequently** *adv* posteriormente, más tarde
subside [səb'saɪd] *vi* hundirse; (*flood*) bajar; (*wind*) amainar
subsidiary [səb'sɪdɪərɪ] *adj* secundario ▷ *n* sucursal *f*, filial *f*
subsidize ['sʌbsɪdaɪz] *vt* subvencionar
subsidy ['sʌbsɪdɪ] *n* subvención *f*
substance ['sʌbstəns] *n* sustancia
substantial [səb'stænʃl] *adj* sustancial, sustancioso; (*fig*) importante
substitute ['sʌbstɪtju:t] *n* (*person*) suplente *mf*; (*thing*) sustituto ▷ *vt*: **to ~ A for B** sustituir A por B, reemplazar B por A; **substitution** *n* sustitución *f*

subtle ['sʌtl] *adj* sutil
subtract [səb'trækt] *vt* restar, sustraer
suburb ['sʌbəːb] *n* barrio residencial; **the ~s** las afueras (de la ciudad); **suburban** [sə'bəːbən] *adj* suburbano; (*train etc*) de cercanías
subway ['sʌbweɪ] *n* (BRIT) paso subterráneo *or* inferior; (US) metro
succeed [sək'siːd] *vi* (*person*) tener éxito; (*plan*) salir bien ▷ *vt* suceder a; **to ~ in doing** lograr hacer
success [sək'sɛs] *n* éxito

Be careful not to translate **success** by the Spanish word *suceso*.

successful *adj* exitoso; (*business*) próspero; **to be successful (in doing)** lograr (hacer); **successfully** *adv* con éxito
succession [sək'sɛʃən] *n* sucesión *f*, serie *f*
successive [sək'sɛsɪv] *adj* sucesivo, consecutivo
successor [sək'sɛsə*] *n* sucesor(a) *m/f*
succumb [sə'kʌm] *vi* sucumbir
such [sʌtʃ] *adj* tal, semejante; (*of that kind*): **~ a book** tal libro; (*so much*): **~ courage** tanto valor ▷ *adv* tan; **~ a long trip** un viaje tan largo; **~ a lot of** tanto(s)/a(s); **~ as** (*like*) tal como; **as ~** como tal; **such-and-such** *adj* tal o cual
suck [sʌk] *vt* chupar; (*bottle*) sorber; (*breast*) mamar
Sudan [su'dæn] *n* Sudán *m*
sudden ['sʌdn] *adj* (*rapid*) repentino, súbito; (*unexpected*) imprevisto; **all of a ~** de repente; **suddenly** *adv* de repente
sue [suː] *vt* demandar
suede [sweɪd] *n* ante *m*, gamuza
suffer ['sʌfə*] *vt* sufrir, padecer; (*tolerate*) aguantar, soportar ▷ *vi* sufrir; **to ~ from** (*illness etc*) padecer; **suffering** *n* sufrimiento
suffice [sə'faɪs] *vi* bastar, ser suficiente
sufficient [sə'fɪʃənt] *adj* suficiente, bastante
suffocate ['sʌfəkeɪt] *vi* ahogarse, asfixiarse
sugar ['ʃugə*] *n* azúcar *m* ▷ *vt* echar azúcar a, azucarar
suggest [sə'dʒɛst] *vt* sugerir; **suggestion** [-'dʒɛstʃən] *n* sugerencia
suicide ['suɪsaɪd] *n* suicidio; (*person*) suicida *mf*; *see also* **commit**; **suicide attack** *n* atentado suicida; **suicide bomber** *n* terrorista *mf* suicida; **suicide bombing** *n* atentado suicida
suit [suːt] *n* (*man's*) traje *m*; (*woman's*) conjunto; (*Law*) pleito; (*Cards*) palo ▷ *vt* convenir; (*clothes*) sentar a, ir bien a; (*adapt*): **to ~ sth to** adaptar *or* ajustar algo a; **well ~ed** (*well matched*: *couple*) hecho el uno para el otro; **suitable** *adj* conveniente; (*apt*) indicado; **suitcase** *n* maleta, valija (RPL)
suite [swiːt] *n* (*of rooms*, *Mus*) suite *f*; (*furniture*): **bedroom/dining room ~** (juego de) dormitorio/comedor; *see also* **three-piece suite**
sulfur ['sʌlfə*] (US) *n* = **sulphur**
sulk [sʌlk] *vi* estar de mal humor
sulphur ['sʌlfə*] (US **sulfur**) *n* azufre *m*
sultana [sʌl'tɑːnə] *n* (*fruit*) pasa de Esmirna
sum [sʌm] *n* suma; (*total*) total *m*; **sum up** *vt* resumir ▷ *vi* hacer un resumen
summarize ['sʌməraɪz] *vt* resumir
summary ['sʌmərɪ] *n* resumen *m* ▷ *adj* (*justice*) sumario
summer ['sʌmə*] *n* verano ▷ *cpd* de verano; **in ~** en verano; **summer holidays** *npl* vacaciones *fpl* de verano; **summertime** *n* (*season*) verano
summit ['sʌmɪt] *n* cima, cumbre *f*; (*also*: **~ conference, ~ meeting**) (conferencia) cumbre *f*
summon ['sʌmən] *vt* (*person*) llamar; (*meeting*) convocar; (*Law*) citar
Sun. *abbr* (= *Sunday*) dom
sun [sʌn] *n* sol *m*; **sunbathe** *vi* tomar el sol; **sunbed** *n* cama solar;

sunblock *n* filtro solar; **sunburn** *n* (*painful*) quemadura; (*tan*) bronceado; **sunburned, sunburnt** *adj* (*painfully*) quemado por el sol; (*tanned*) bronceado
Sunday ['sʌndɪ] *n* domingo
sunflower ['sʌnflauə*] *n* girasol *m*
sung [sʌŋ] *pp of* **sing**
sunglasses ['sʌnglɑ:sɪz] *npl* gafas *fpl* (SP) *or* anteojos *fpl* (LAM) de sol
sunk [sʌŋk] *pp of* **sink**
sun: sunlight *n* luz *f* del sol; **sun lounger** *n* tumbona, perezosa (LAM); **sunny** *adj* soleado; (*day*) de sol; (*fig*) alegre; **sunrise** *n* salida del sol; **sun roof** *n* (*Aut*) techo corredizo; **sunscreen** *n* protector *m* solar; **sunset** *n* puesta del sol; **sunshade** *n* (*over table*) sombrilla; **sunshine** *n* sol *m*; **sunstroke** *n* insolación *f*; **suntan** *n* bronceado; **suntan lotion** *n* bronceador *m*; **suntan oil** *n* aceite *m* bronceador
super ['su:pə*] (*inf*) *adj* genial
superb [su:'pə:b] *adj* magnífico, espléndido
superficial [su:pə'fɪʃəl] *adj* superficial
superintendent [su:pərɪn'tɛndənt] *n* director(a) *m/f*; (*Police*) subjefe/a *m/f*
superior [su'pɪərɪə*] *adj* superior; (*smug*) desdeñoso ▷ *n* superior *m*
superlative [su'pə:lətɪv] *n* superlativo
supermarket ['su:pəmɑ:kɪt] *n* supermercado
supernatural [su:pə'nætʃərəl] *adj* sobrenatural ▷ *n*: **the ~** lo sobrenatural
superpower ['su:pəpauə*] *n* (*Pol*) superpotencia
superstition [su:pə'stɪʃən] *n* superstición *f*
superstitious [su:pə'stɪʃəs] *adj* supersticioso
superstore ['su:pəstɔ:*] *n* (BRIT) hipermercado
supervise ['su:pəvaɪz] *vt* supervisar; **supervision** [-'vɪʒən] *n* supervisión *f*; **supervisor** *n* supervisor(a) *m/f*
supper ['sʌpə*] *n* cena
supple ['sʌpl] *adj* flexible
supplement [*n* 'sʌplɪmənt, *vb* sʌplɪ'mɛnt] *n* suplemento ▷ *vt* suplir
supplier [sə'plaɪə*] *n* (*Comm*) distribuidor(a) *m/f*
supply [sə'plaɪ] *vt* (*provide*) suministrar; (*equip*): **to ~ (with)** proveer (de) ▷ *n* provisión *f*; (*of gas, water etc*) suministro; **supplies** *npl* (*food*) víveres *mpl*; (*Mil*) pertrechos *mpl*
support [sə'pɔ:t] *n* apoyo; (*Tech*) soporte *m* ▷ *vt* apoyar; (*financially*) mantener; (*uphold, Tech*) sostener

> Be careful not to translate **support** by the Spanish word *soportar*.

supporter *n* (*Pol etc*) partidario/a; (*Sport*) aficionado/a
suppose [sə'pəuz] *vt* suponer; (*imagine*) imaginarse; (*duty*): **to be ~d to do sth** deber hacer algo; **supposedly** [sə'pəuzɪdlɪ] *adv* según cabe suponer; **supposing** *conj* en caso de que
suppress [sə'prɛs] *vt* suprimir; (*yawn*) ahogar
supreme [su'pri:m] *adj* supremo
surcharge ['sə:tʃɑ:dʒ] *n* sobretasa, recargo
sure [ʃuə*] *adj* seguro; (*definite, convinced*) cierto; **to make ~ of sth/that** asegurarse de algo/asegurar que; **~!** (*of course*) ¡claro!, ¡por supuesto!; **~ enough** efectivamente; **surely** *adv* (*certainly*) seguramente
surf [sə:f] *n* olas *fpl* ▷ *vt*: **to ~ the Net** navegar por Internet
surface ['sə:fɪs] *n* superficie *f* ▷ *vt* (*road*) revestir ▷ *vi* salir a la superficie; **by ~ mail** por vía terrestre
surfboard ['sə:fbɔ:d] *n* tabla (de surf)
surfer ['sə:fə*] *n* (*in sea*) surfista *mf*; **web** *or* **net ~** internauta *mf*
surfing ['sə:fɪŋ] *n* surf *m*
surge [sə:dʒ] *n* oleada, oleaje *m* ▷ *vi* (*wave*) romper; (*people*) avanzar en tropel
surgeon ['sə:dʒən] *n* cirujano/a

surgery ['səːdʒərɪ] *n* cirugía; (BRIT: *room*) consultorio
surname ['səːneɪm] *n* apellido
surpass [səː'pɑːs] *vt* superar, exceder
surplus ['səːpləs] *n* excedente *m*; (*Comm*) superávit *m* ▷ *adj* excedente, sobrante
surprise [sə'praɪz] *n* sorpresa ▷ *vt* sorprender; **surprised** *adj* (*look, smile*) de sorpresa; **to be surprised** sorprenderse; **surprising** *adj* sorprendente; **surprisingly** *adv*: **it was surprisingly easy** me *etc* sorprendió lo fácil que fue
surrender [sə'rɛndə*] *n* rendición *f*, entrega ▷ *vi* rendirse, entregarse
surround [sə'raund] *vt* rodear, circundar; (*Mil etc*) cercar; **surrounding** *adj* circundante; **surroundings** *npl* alrededores *mpl*, cercanías *fpl*
surveillance [səː'veɪləns] *n* vigilancia
survey [*n* 'səːveɪ, *vb* səː'veɪ] *n* inspección *f*, reconocimiento; (*inquiry*) encuesta ▷ *vt* examinar, inspeccionar; (*look at*) mirar, contemplar; **surveyor** *n* agrimensor(a) *m/f*
survival [sə'vaɪvl] *n* supervivencia
survive [sə'vaɪv] *vi* sobrevivir; (*custom etc*) perdurar ▷ *vt* sobrevivir a; **survivor** *n* superviviente *mf*
suspect [*adj, n* 'sʌspɛkt, *vb* səs'pɛkt] *adj, n* sospechoso/a *m/f* ▷ *vt* (*person*) sospechar de; (*think*) sospechar
suspend [səs'pɛnd] *vt* suspender; **suspended sentence** *n* (*Law*) libertad *f* condicional; **suspenders** *npl* (BRIT) ligas *fpl*; (US) tirantes *mpl*
suspense [səs'pɛns] *n* incertidumbre *f*, duda; (*in film etc*) suspense *m*; **to keep sb in ~** mantener a algn en suspense
suspension [səs'pɛnʃən] *n* (*gen, Aut*) suspensión *f*; (*of driving licence*) privación *f*; **suspension bridge** *n* puente *m* colgante
suspicion [səs'pɪʃən] *n* sospecha; (*distrust*) recelo; **suspicious** *adj* receloso; (*causing suspicion*) sospechoso
sustain [səs'teɪn] *vt* sostener, apoyar; (*suffer*) sufrir, padecer
SUV (*esp* US) *n abbr* (= *sports utility vehicle*) todoterreno *m inv*, 4x4 *m*
swallow ['swɔləu] *n* (*bird*) golondrina ▷ *vt* tragar; (*fig,: pride*) tragarse
swam [swæm] *pt of* **swim**
swamp [swɔmp] *n* pantano, ciénaga ▷ *vt* (*with water etc*) inundar; (*fig*) abrumar, agobiar
swan [swɔn] *n* cisne *m*
swap [swɔp] *n* canje *m*, intercambio ▷ *vt*: **to ~ (for)** cambiar (por)
swarm [swɔːm] *n* (*of bees*) enjambre *m*; (*fig*) multitud *f* ▷ *vi* (*bees*) formar un enjambre; (*people*) pulular; **to be ~ing with** ser un hervidero de
sway [sweɪ] *vi* mecerse, balancearse ▷ *vt* (*influence*) mover, influir en
swear [swɛə*] (*pt* **swore**, *pp* **sworn**) *vi* (*curse*) maldecir; (*promise*) jurar ▷ *vt* jurar; **swear in** *vt*: **to be sworn in** prestar juramento; **swearword** *n* taco, palabrota
sweat [swɛt] *n* sudor *m* ▷ *vi* sudar
sweater ['swɛtə*] *n* suéter *m*
sweatshirt ['swɛtʃəːt] *n* suéter *m*
sweaty ['swɛtɪ] *adj* sudoroso
Swede [swiːd] *n* sueco/a
swede [swiːd] (BRIT) *n* nabo
Sweden ['swiːdn] *n* Suecia; **Swedish** ['swiːdɪʃ] *adj* sueco ▷ *n* (*Ling*) sueco
sweep [swiːp] (*pt, pp* **swept**) *n* (*act*) barrido; (*also*: **chimney ~**) deshollinador(a) *m/f* ▷ *vt* barrer; (*with arm*) empujar; (*current*) arrastrar ▷ *vi* barrer; (*arm etc*) moverse rápidamente; (*wind*) soplar con violencia
sweet [swiːt] *n* (*candy*) dulce *m*, caramelo; (BRIT: *pudding*) postre *m* ▷ *adj* dulce; (*fig: kind*) dulce, amable; (: *attractive*) mono; **sweetcorn** *n* maíz *m*; **sweetener** ['swiːtnə*] *n* (*Culin*) edulcorante *m*; **sweetheart** *n* novio/a; **sweetshop** *n* (BRIT) confitería, bombonería
swell [swɛl] (*pt* **~ed**, *pp* **swollen** *or* **~ed**)

n (*of sea*) marejada, oleaje *m* ▷ *adj* (*US: inf: excellent*) estupendo, fenomenal ▷ *vt* hinchar, inflar ▷ *vi* (*also*: ~ **up**) hincharse; (*numbers*) aumentar; (*sound, feeling*) ir aumentando; **swelling** *n* (*Med*) hinchazón *f*

swept [swɛpt] *pt, pp of* **sweep**

swerve [swəːv] *vi* desviarse bruscamente

swift [swɪft] *n* (*bird*) vencejo ▷ *adj* rápido, veloz

swim [swɪm] (*pt* **swam**, *pp* **swum**) *n*: **to go for a ~** ir a nadar *or* a bañarse ▷ *vi* nadar; (*head, room*) dar vueltas ▷ *vt* nadar; (*the Channel etc*) cruzar a nado; **swimmer** *n* nadador(a) *m/f*; **swimming** *n* natación *f*; **swimming costume** (BRIT) *n* bañador *m*, traje *m* de baño; **swimming pool** *n* piscina, alberca (MEX), pileta (RPL); **swimming trunks** *npl* bañador *m* (de hombre); **swimsuit** *n* = **swimming costume**

swing [swɪŋ] (*pt, pp* **swung**) *n* (*in playground*) columpio; (*movement*) balanceo, vaivén *m*; (*change of direction*) viraje *m*; (*rhythm*) ritmo ▷ *vt* balancear; (*also*: ~ **round**) voltear, girar ▷ *vi* balancearse, columpiarse; (*also*: ~ **round**) dar media vuelta; **to be in full ~** estar en plena marcha

swipe card [swaɪp-] *n* tarjeta magnética deslizante, tarjeta swipe

swirl [swəːl] *vi* arremolinarse

Swiss [swɪs] *adj, n inv* suizo/a *m/f*

switch [swɪtʃ] *n* (*for light etc*) interruptor *m*; (*change*) cambio ▷ *vt* (*change*) cambiar de; **switch off** *vt* apagar; (*engine*) parar; **switch on** *vt* encender (SP), prender (LAM); (*engine, machine*) arrancar; **switchboard** *n* (*Tel*) centralita (SP), conmutador *m* (LAM)

Switzerland ['swɪtsələnd] *n* Suiza

swivel ['swɪvl] *vi* (*also*: ~ **round**) girar

swollen ['swəulən] *pp of* **swell**

swoop [swuːp] *n* (*by police etc*) redada ▷ *vi* (*also*: ~ **down**) calarse

swop [swɔp] = **swap**

sword [sɔːd] *n* espada; **swordfish** *n* pez *m* espada

swore [swɔː*] *pt of* **swear**

sworn [swɔːn] *pp of* **swear** ▷ *adj* (*statement*) bajo juramento; (*enemy*) implacable

swum [swʌm] *pp of* **swim**

swung [swʌŋ] *pt, pp of* **swing**

syllable ['sɪləbl] *n* sílaba

syllabus ['sɪləbəs] *n* programa *m* de estudios

symbol ['sɪmbl] *n* símbolo; **symbolic(al)** [sɪm'bɔlɪk(l)] *adj* simbólico; **to be symbolic(al) of sth** simbolizar algo

symmetrical [sɪ'mɛtrɪkl] *adj* simétrico

symmetry ['sɪmɪtrɪ] *n* simetría

sympathetic [sɪmpə'θɛtɪk] *adj* (*understanding*) comprensivo; (*showing support*): ~ **to(wards)** bien dispuesto hacia

> Be careful not to translate **sympathetic** by the Spanish word *simpático*.

sympathize ['sɪmpəθaɪz] *vi*: **to ~ with** (*person*) compadecerse de; (*feelings*) comprender; (*cause*) apoyar

sympathy ['sɪmpəθɪ] *n* (*pity*) compasión *f*

symphony ['sɪmfənɪ] *n* sinfonía

symptom ['sɪmptəm] *n* síntoma *m*, indicio

synagogue ['sɪnəgɔg] *n* sinagoga

syndicate ['sɪndɪkɪt] *n* sindicato; (*of newspapers*) agencia (de noticias)

syndrome ['sɪndrəum] *n* síndrome *m*

synonym ['sɪnənɪm] *n* sinónimo

synthetic [sɪn'θɛtɪk] *adj* sintético

Syria ['sɪrɪə] *n* Siria

syringe [sɪ'rɪndʒ] *n* jeringa

syrup ['sɪrəp] *n* jarabe *m*; (*also*: **golden ~**) almíbar *m*

system ['sɪstəm] *n* sistema *m*; (*Anat*) organismo; **systematic** [-'mætɪk] *adj* sistemático, metódico; **systems analyst** *n* analista *mf* de sistemas

ta [tɑː] (BRIT: *inf*) *excl* ¡gracias!

tab [tæb] *n* lengüeta; (*label*) etiqueta; **to keep ~s on** (*fig*) vigilar

table ['teɪbl] *n* mesa; (*of statistics etc*) cuadro, tabla ▷ *vt* (BRIT: *motion etc*) presentar; **to lay** *or* **set the ~** poner la mesa; **tablecloth** *n* mantel *m*; **table d'hôte** [tɑːbl'dəut] *adj* del menú; **table lamp** *n* lámpara de mesa; **tablemat** *n* (*for plate*) posaplatos *m inv*; (*for hot dish*) salvamantel *m*; **tablespoon** *n* cuchara de servir; (*also*: **tablespoonful**: *as measurement*) cucharada

tablet ['tæblɪt] *n* (*Med*) pastilla, comprimido; (*of stone*) lápida

table tennis *n* ping-pong *m*, tenis *m* de mesa

tabloid ['tæblɔɪd] *n* periódico popular sensacionalista

TABLOID PRESS

El término **tabloid press** o **tabloids** se usa para referirse a la prensa popular británica, por el tamaño más pequeño de los periódicos. A diferencia de los de la llamada **quality press**, estas publicaciones se caracterizan por un lenguaje sencillo, una presentación llamativa y un contenido sensacionalista, centrado a veces en los escándalos financieros y sexuales de los famosos, por lo que también reciben el nombre peyorativo de "gutter press".

taboo [tə'buː] *adj, n* tabú *m*

tack [tæk] *n* (*nail*) tachuela; (*fig*) rumbo ▷ *vt* (*nail*) clavar con tachuelas; (*stitch*) hilvanar ▷ *vi* virar

tackle ['tækl] *n* (*fishing tackle*) aparejo (de pescar); (*for lifting*) aparejo ▷ *vt* (*difficulty*) enfrentarse con; (*challenge*: *person*) hacer frente a; (*grapple with*) agarrar; (*Football*) cargar; (*Rugby*) placar

tacky ['tækɪ] *adj* pegajoso; (*pej*) cutre

tact [tækt] *n* tacto, discreción *f*; **tactful** *adj* discreto, diplomático

tactics ['tæktɪks] *npl* táctica

tactless ['tæktlɪs] *adj* indiscreto

tadpole ['tædpəul] *n* renacuajo

taffy ['tæfɪ] (US) *n* melcocha

tag [tæg] *n* (*label*) etiqueta

tail [teɪl] *n* cola; (*of shirt, coat*) faldón *m* ▷ *vt* (*follow*) vigilar a; **tails** *npl* (*formal suit*) levita

tailor ['teɪlə*] *n* sastre *m*

Taiwan [taɪ'wɑːn] *n* Taiwán *m*; **Taiwanese** [taɪwə'niːz] *adj, n* taiwanés/esa *m/f*

take [teɪk] (*pt* **took**, *pp* **taken**) *vt* tomar; (*grab*) coger (SP), agarrar (LAM); (*gain*: *prize*) ganar; (*require*: *effort, courage*) exigir; (*tolerate*: *pain etc*) aguantar; (*hold*: *passengers etc*) tener cabida para; (*accompany, bring, carry*) llevar; (*exam*) presentarse a; **to ~ sth from** (*drawer etc*) sacar algo de; (*person*) quitar algo a; **I ~ it that ...** supongo que ...; **take after** *vt fus* parecerse a; **take apart** *vt* desmontar; **take away** *vt* (*remove*) quitar; (*carry*) llevar; (*Math*) restar; **take back** *vt* (*return*) devolver; (*one's words*) retractarse de; **take down** *vt* (*building*) derribar; (*letter etc*) apuntar; **take in** *vt* (*deceive*) engañar; (*understand*) entender; (*include*) abarcar; (*lodger*) acoger, recibir; **take off** *vi* (*Aviat*) despegar ▷ *vt* (*remove*) quitar; **take on** *vt* (*work*) aceptar; (*employee*) contratar; (*opponent*) desafiar; **take out** *vt* sacar; **take over** *vt* (*business*) tomar posesión de; (*country*) tomar el poder ▷ *vi*: **to take over from sb** reemplazar a algn; **take up** *vt* (*a dress*) acortar; (*occupy: time, space*) ocupar; (*engage in: hobby etc*) dedicarse a; (*accept*): **to take sb up on** aceptar algo de algn; **takeaway** (BRIT) *adj* (*food*) para llevar ▷ *n* tienda *or* restaurante *m* de comida para llevar; **taken** *pp of* **take**; **takeoff** *n* (*Aviat*) despegue *m*; **takeout** (US) *n* = **takeaway**; **takeover** *n* (*Comm*) absorción *f*; **takings** *npl* (*Comm*) ingresos *mpl*

talc [tælk] *n* (*also*: **~um powder**) (polvos de) talco

tale [teɪl] *n* (*story*) cuento; (*account*) relación *f*; **to tell ~s** (*fig*) chivarse

talent ['tælnt] *n* talento; **talented** *adj* de talento

talk [tɔːk] *n* charla; (*conversation*) conversación *f*; (*gossip*) habladurías *fpl*, chismes *mpl* ▷ *vi* hablar; **talks** *npl* (*Pol etc*) conversaciones *fpl*; **to ~ about** hablar de; **to ~ sb into doing sth** convencer a algn para que haga algo; **to ~ sb out of doing sth** disuadir a algn de que haga algo; **to ~ shop** hablar del trabajo; **talk over** *vt* discutir; **talk show** *n* programa *m* de entrevistas

tall [tɔːl] *adj* alto; (*object*) grande; **to be 6 feet ~** (*person*) ≈ medir 1 metro 80

tambourine [tæmbə'riːn] *n* pandereta

tame [teɪm] *adj* domesticado; (*fig*) mediocre

tamper ['tæmpə*] *vi*: **to ~ with** tocar, andar con

tampon ['tæmpən] *n* tampón *m*

tan [tæn] *n* (*also*: **sun~**) bronceado ▷ *vi* ponerse moreno ▷ *adj* (*colour*) marrón

tandem ['tændəm] *n* tándem *m*

tangerine [tændʒə'riːn] *n* mandarina

tangle ['tæŋgl] *n* enredo; **to get in(to) a ~** enredarse

tank [tæŋk] *n* (*water tank*) depósito, tanque *m*; (*for fish*) acuario; (*Mil*) tanque *m*

tanker ['tæŋkə*] *n* (*ship*) buque *m*, cisterna; (*truck*) camión *m* cisterna

tanned [tænd] *adj* (*skin*) moreno

tantrum ['tæntrəm] *n* rabieta

Tanzania [tænzə'nɪə] *n* Tanzania

tap [tæp] *n* (BRIT: *on sink etc*) grifo (SP), llave *f*, canilla (RPL); (*gas tap*) llave *f*; (*gentle blow*) golpecito ▷ *vt* (*hit gently*) dar golpecitos en; (*resources*) utilizar, explotar; (*telephone*) intervenir; **on ~** (*fig: resources*) a mano; **tap dancing** *n* claqué *m*

tape [teɪp] *n* (*also*: **magnetic ~**) cinta magnética; (*cassette*) cassette *f*, cinta; (*sticky tape*) cinta adhesiva; (*for tying*) cinta ▷ *vt* (*record*) grabar (en cinta); (*stick with tape*) pegar con cinta adhesiva; **tape measure** *n* cinta métrica, metro; **tape recorder** *n* grabadora

tapestry ['tæpɪstrɪ] *n* (*object*) tapiz *m*; (*art*) tapicería

tar [tɑː] *n* alquitrán *m*, brea

target ['tɑːgɪt] *n* blanco

tariff ['tærɪf] *n* (*on goods*) arancel *m*; (BRIT: *in hotels etc*) tarifa

tarmac ['tɑːmæk] *n* (BRIT: *on road*) asfaltado; (*Aviat*) pista (de aterrizaje)

tarpaulin [tɑː'pɔːlɪn] *n* lona impermeabilizada

tarragon ['tærəgən] *n* estragón *m*

tart [tɑːt] *n* (*Culin*) tarta; (BRIT: *inf: prostitute*) puta ▷ *adj* agrio, ácido

tartan ['tɑːtn] *n* tejido escocés *m*
tartar(e) sauce ['tɑːtə-] *n* salsa tártara
task [tɑːsk] *n* tarea; **to take to ~** reprender
taste [teɪst] *n* (*sense*) gusto; (*flavour*) sabor *m*; (*sample*): **have a ~!** ¡prueba un poquito!; (*fig*) muestra, idea ▷ *vt* probar ▷ *vi*: **to ~ of** *or* **like** (*fish, garlic etc*) saber a; **you can ~ the garlic (in it)** se nota el sabor a ajo; **in good/bad ~** de buen/mal gusto; **tasteful** *adj* de buen gusto; **tasteless** *adj* (*food*) soso; (*remark etc*) de mal gusto; **tasty** *adj* sabroso, rico
tatters ['tætəz] *npl*: **in ~** hecho jirones
tattoo [tə'tuː] *n* tatuaje *m*; (*spectacle*) espectáculo militar ▷ *vt* tatuar
taught [tɔːt] *pt, pp of* **teach**
taunt [tɔːnt] *n* burla ▷ *vt* burlarse de
Taurus ['tɔːrəs] *n* Tauro
taut [tɔːt] *adj* tirante, tenso
tax [tæks] *n* impuesto ▷ *vt* gravar (con un impuesto); (*fig*: *memory*) poner a prueba; (: *patience*) agotar; **tax-free** *adj* libre de impuestos
taxi ['tæksɪ] *n* taxi *m* ▷ *vi* (*Aviat*) rodar por la pista; **taxi driver** *n* taxista *mf*; **taxi rank** (BRIT) *n* = **taxi stand**; **taxi stand** *n* parada de taxis
tax payer *n* contribuyente *mf*
TB *n abbr* = **tuberculosis**
tea [tiː] *n* té *m*; (BRIT: *meal*) ≈ merienda (SP); cena; **high ~** (BRIT) merienda-cena (SP); **tea bag** *n* bolsita de té; **tea break** (BRIT) *n* descanso para el té
teach [tiːtʃ] (*pt, pp* **taught**) *vt*: **to ~ sb sth, ~ sth to sb** enseñar algo a algn ▷ *vi* (*be a teacher*) ser profesor(a), enseñar; **teacher** *n* (*in secondary school*) profesor(a) *m/f*; (*in primary school*) maestro/a, profesor(a) de EGB; **teaching** *n* enseñanza
tea: tea cloth *n* (BRIT) paño de cocina, trapo de cocina (LAM); **teacup** *n* taza para el té
tea leaves *npl* hojas de té
team [tiːm] *n* equipo; (*of horses*) tiro; **team up** *vi* asociarse
teapot ['tiːpɔt] *n* tetera
tear¹ [tɪə*] *n* lágrima; **in ~s** llorando
tear² [tɛə*] (*pt* **tore**, *pp* **torn**) *n* rasgón *m*, desgarrón *m* ▷ *vt* romper, rasgar ▷ *vi* rasgarse; **tear apart** *vt* (*also fig*) hacer pedazos; **tear down** *vt +adv* (*building, statue*) derribar; (*poster, flag*) arrancar; **tear off** *vt* (*sheet of paper etc*) arrancar; (*one's clothes*) quitarse a tirones; **tear up** *vt* (*sheet of paper etc*) romper
tearful ['tɪəfəl] *adj* lloroso
tear gas ['tɪə-] *n* gas *m* lacrimógeno
tearoom ['tiːruːm] *n* salón *m* de té
tease [tiːz] *vt* tomar el pelo a
tea: teaspoon *n* cucharita; (*also*: **teaspoonful**: *as measurement*) cucharadita; **teatime** *n* hora del té; **tea towel** (BRIT) *n* paño de cocina
technical ['tɛknɪkl] *adj* técnico
technician [tɛk'nɪʃn] *n* técnico/a
technique [tɛk'niːk] *n* técnica
technology [tɛk'nɔlədʒɪ] *n* tecnología
teddy (bear) ['tɛdɪ-] *n* osito de felpa
tedious ['tiːdɪəs] *adj* pesado, aburrido
tee [tiː] *n* (*Golf*) tee *m*
teen [tiːn] *adj* = **teenage** ▷ *n* (US) = **teenager**
teenage ['tiːneɪdʒ] *adj* (*fashions etc*) juvenil; (*children*) quinceañero; **teenager** *n* adolescente *mf*
teens [tiːnz] *npl*: **to be in one's ~** ser adolescente
teeth [tiːθ] *npl of* **tooth**
teetotal ['tiː'təutl] *adj* abstemio
telecommunications [tɛlɪkəmjuː-nɪ'keɪʃənz] *n* telecomunicaciones *fpl*
telegram ['tɛlɪgræm] *n* telegrama *m*
telegraph pole ['tɛlɪgrɑːf-] *n* poste *m* telegráfico
telephone ['tɛlɪfəun] *n* teléfono ▷ *vt* llamar por teléfono, telefonear; (*message*) dar por teléfono; **to be on the ~** (*talking*) hablar por teléfono; (*possessing telephone*) tener teléfono;

telephone book *n* guía *f* telefónica; **telephone booth, telephone box** (BRIT) *n* cabina telefónica; **telephone call** *n* llamada (telefónica); **telephone directory** *n* guía (telefónica); **telephone number** *n* número de teléfono

telesales ['tɛlɪseɪlz] *npl* televenta(s) (*f(pl)*

telescope ['tɛlɪskəup] *n* telescopio

televise ['tɛlɪvaɪz] *vt* televisar

television ['tɛlɪvɪʒən] *n* televisión *f*; **on ~** en la televisión; **television programme** *n* programa *m* de televisión

tell [tɛl] (*pt, pp* **told**) *vt* decir; (*relate: story*) contar; (*distinguish*): **to ~ sth from** distinguir algo de ▷ *vi* (*talk*): **to ~ (of)** contar; (*have effect*) tener efecto; **to ~ sb to do sth** mandar a algn hacer algo; **tell off** *vt*: **to tell sb off** regañar a algn; **teller** *n* (*in bank*) cajero/a

telly ['tɛlɪ] (BRIT: *inf*) *n abbr* (= *television*) tele *f*

temp [tɛmp] *n abbr* (BRIT) (= *temporary*) temporero/a

temper ['tɛmpə*] *n* (*nature*) carácter *m*; (*mood*) humor *m*; (*bad temper*) (mal) genio; (*fit of anger*) acceso de ira ▷ *vt* (*moderate*) moderar; **to be in a ~** estar furioso; **to lose one's ~** enfadarse, enojarse

temperament ['tɛmprəmə nt] *n* (*nature*) temperamento; **temperamental** [tɛmprə'mɛntl] *adj* temperamental

temperature ['tɛmprətʃə*] *n* temperatura; **to have** *or* **run a ~** tener fiebre

temple ['tɛmpl] *n* (*building*) templo; (*Anat*) sien *f*

temporary ['tɛmpərərɪ] *adj* provisional; (*passing*) transitorio; (*worker*) temporero; (*job*) temporal

tempt [tɛmpt] *vt* tentar; **to ~ sb into doing sth** tentar *or* inducir a algn a hacer algo; **temptation** *n* tentación *f*; **tempting** *adj* tentador(a); (*food*) apetitoso/a

ten [tɛn] *num* diez

tenant ['tɛnənt] *n* inquilino/a

tend [tɛnd] *vt* cuidar ▷ *vi*: **to ~ to do sth** tener tendencia a hacer algo; **tendency** ['tɛndənsɪ] *n* tendencia

tender ['tɛndə*] *adj* (*person, care*) tierno, cariñoso; (*meat*) tierno; (*sore*) sensible ▷ *n* (*Comm: offer*) oferta; (*money*): **legal ~** moneda de curso legal ▷ *vt* ofrecer

tendon ['tɛndən] *n* tendón *m*

tenner ['tɛnə*] *n* (*inf*) (billete *m* de) diez libras *m*

tennis ['tɛnɪs] *n* tenis *m*; **tennis ball** *n* pelota de tenis; **tennis court** *n* cancha de tenis; **tennis match** *n* partido de tenis; **tennis player** *n* tenista *mf*; **tennis racket** *n* raqueta de tenis

tenor ['tɛnə*] *n* (*Mus*) tenor *m*

tenpin bowling ['tɛnpɪn-] *n* (juego de los) bolos

tense [tɛns] *adj* (*person*) nervioso; (*moment, atmosphere*) tenso; (*muscle*) tenso, en tensión ▷ *n* (*Ling*) tiempo

tension ['tɛnʃən] *n* tensión *f*

tent [tɛnt] *n* tienda (de campaña) (SP), carpa (LAM)

tentative ['tɛntətɪv] *adj* (*person, smile*) indeciso; (*conclusion, plans*) provisional

tenth [tɛnθ] *num* décimo

tent: tent peg *n* clavija, estaca; **tent pole** *n* mástil *m*

tepid ['tɛpɪd] *adj* tibio

term [tə:m] *n* (*word*) término; (*period*) período; (*Scol*) trimestre *m* ▷ *vt* llamar; **terms** *npl* (*conditions, Comm*) condiciones *fpl*; **in the short/long ~** a corto/largo plazo; **to be on good ~s with sb** llevarse bien con algn; **to come to ~s with** (*problem*) aceptar

terminal ['tə:mɪnl] *adj* (*disease*) mortal; (*patient*) terminal ▷ *n* (*Elec*) borne *m*; (*Comput*) terminal *m*; (*also*: **air ~**) terminal *f*; (BRIT: *also*: **coach ~**)

estación *f* terminal *f*
terminate ['tə:mɪneɪt] *vt* terminar
termini ['tə:mɪnaɪ] *npl of* **terminus**
terminology [tə:mɪ'nɔlədʒɪ] *n* terminología
terminus ['tə:mɪnəs] (*pl* **termini**) *n* término, (estación *f*) terminal *f*
terrace ['tɛrəs] *n* terraza; (BRIT: *row of houses*) hilera de casas adosadas; **the ~s** (BRIT *Sport*) las gradas *fpl*; **terraced** *adj* (*garden*) en terrazas; (*house*) adosado
terrain [tɛ'reɪn] *n* terreno
terrestrial [tɪ'restrɪəl] *adj* (*life*) terrestre; (BRIT: *channel*) de transmisión (por) vía terrestre
terrible ['tɛrɪbl] *adj* terrible, horrible; (*inf*) atroz; **terribly** *adv* terriblemente; (*very badly*) malísimamente
terrier ['tɛrɪə*] *n* terrier *m*
terrific [tə'rɪfɪk] *adj* (*very great*) tremendo; (*wonderful*) fantástico, fenomenal
terrified ['tɛrɪfaɪd] *adj* aterrorizado
terrify ['tɛrɪfaɪ] *vt* aterrorizar; **terrifying** *adj* aterrador(a)
territorial [tɛrɪ'tɔ:rɪəl] *adj* territorial
territory ['tɛrɪtərɪ] *n* territorio
terror ['tɛrə*] *n* terror *m*; **terrorism** *n* terrorismo; **terrorist** *n* terrorista *mf*; **terrorist attack** *n* atentado (terrorista)
test [tɛst] *n* (*gen, Chem*) prueba; (*Med*) examen *m*; (*Scol*) examen *m*, test *m*; (*also*: **driving ~**) examen *m* de conducir ▷ *vt* probar, poner a prueba; (*Med, Scol*) examinar
testicle ['tɛstɪkl] *n* testículo
testify ['tɛstɪfaɪ] *vi* (*Law*) prestar declaración; **to ~ to sth** atestiguar algo
testimony ['tɛstɪmənɪ] *n* (*Law*) testimonio
test: test match *n* (*Cricket, Rugby*) partido internacional; **test tube** *n* probeta
tetanus ['tɛtənəs] *n* tétano
text [tɛkst] *n* texto; (*on mobile phone*) mensaje *m* de texto ▷ *vt*: **to ~ sb** (*inf*) enviar un mensaje (de texto) *or* un SMS a algn; **textbook** *n* libro de texto
textile ['tɛkstaɪl] *n* textil *m*, tejido
text message *n* mensaje *m* de texto
text messaging [-'mɛsɪdʒɪŋ] *n* (envío de) mensajes *mpl* de texto
texture ['tɛkstʃə*] *n* textura
Thai [taɪ] *adj, n* tailandés/esa *m/f*
Thailand ['taɪlænd] *n* Tailandia
than [ðaen] *conj* (*in comparisons*): **more ~ 10/once** más de 10/una vez; **I have more/less ~ you/Paul** tengo más/menos que tú/Paul; **she is older ~ you think** es mayor de lo que piensas
thank [θæŋk] *vt* dar las gracias a, agradecer; **~ you (very much)** muchas gracias; **~ God!** ¡gracias a Dios! ▷ *excl* (*also*: **many ~s, ~s a lot**) ¡gracias! ▷ **~s to** *prep* gracias a; **thanks** *npl* gracias *fpl*; **thankfully** *adv* (*fortunately*) afortunadamente; **Thanksgiving (Day)** *n* día *m* de Acción de Gracias

THANKSGIVING (DAY)

En Estados Unidos el cuarto jueves de noviembre es **Thanksgiving Day**, fiesta oficial en la que se recuerda la celebración que hicieron los primeros colonos norteamericanos ("Pilgrims" o "Pilgrim Fathers") tras la estupenda cosecha de 1621, por la que se dan gracias a Dios. En Canadá se celebra una fiesta semejante el segundo lunes de octubre, aunque no está relacionada con dicha fecha histórica.

KEYWORD

that [ðæt] (*pl* **those**) *adj* (*demonstrative*) ese/a; (*pl*) esos/as; (*more remote*) aquel(aquella); (*pl*) aquellos/as; **leave those books on the table** deja

esos libros sobre la mesa; **that one** ése(ésa); (*more remote*) aquél(aquélla); **that one over there** ése(ésa) de ahí; aquél(aquélla) de allí
▷ *pron* **1** (*demonstrative*) ése/a; (*pl*) ésos/as; (*neuter*) eso; (*more remote*) aquél(aquélla); (*pl*) aquéllos/as; (*neuter*) aquello; **what's that?** ¿qué es eso (*or* aquello)?; **who's that?** ¿quién es ése/a (*or* aquél (aquella))?; **is that you?** ¿eres tú?; **will you eat all that?** ¿vas a comer todo eso?; **that's my house** ésa es mi casa; **that's what he said** eso es lo que dijo; **that is (to say)** es decir
2 (*relative*: *subject, object*) que; (*with preposition*) (el (la)) que *etc*, el(la) cual *etc*; **the book (that) I read** el libro que leí; **the books that are in the library** los libros que están en la biblioteca; **all (that) I have** todo lo que tengo; **the box (that) I put it in** la caja en la que *or* donde lo puse; **the people (that) I spoke to** la gente con la que hablé
3 (*relative*: *of time*) que; **the day (that) he came** el día (en) que vino
▷ *conj* que; **he thought that I was ill** creyó que yo estaba enfermo
▷ *adv* (*demonstrative*): **I can't work that much** no puedo trabajar tanto; **I didn't realise it was that bad** no creí que fuera tan malo; **that high** así de alto

thatched [θætʃt] *adj* (*roof*) de paja; (*cottage*) con tejado de paja
thaw [θɔː] *n* deshielo ▷ *vi* (*ice*) derretirse; (*food*) descongelarse ▷ *vt* (*food*) descongelar

KEYWORD

the [ðiː, ðə] *def art* **1** (*gen*) el *f*, la *pl*, los *fpl*, las (*NB 'el' immediately before f n beginning with stressed (h)a; a+ el =al; de + el = del*); **the boy/girl** el chico/la chica; **the books/flowers** los libros/las flores; **to the postman/from the drawer** al cartero/del cajón; **I haven't the time/money** no tengo tiempo/dinero
2 (*+adj to form n*) los; lo; **the rich and the poor** los ricos y los pobres; **to attempt the impossible** intentar lo imposible
3 (*in titles*): **Elizabeth the First** Isabel primera; **Peter the Great** Pedro el Grande
4 (*in comparisons*): **the more he works the more he earns** cuanto más trabaja más gana

theatre ['θɪətə*] (*US* **theater**) *n* teatro; (*also*: **lecture ~**) aula; (*Med*: *also*: **operating ~**) quirófano
theft [θɛft] *n* robo
their [ðɛə*] *adj* su; **theirs** *pron* (el) suyo((la) suya etc); *see also* **my; mine[1]**
them [ðɛm, ðəm] *pron* (*direct*) los/las; (*indirect*) les; (*stressed, after prep*) ellos(ellas); *see also* **me**
theme [θiːm] *n* tema *m*; **theme park** *n* parque de atracciones (*en torno a un tema central*)
themselves [ðəm'sɛlvz] *pl pron* (*subject*) ellos mismos(ellas mismas); (*complement*) se; (*after prep*) sí (mismos(as)); *see also* **oneself**
then [ðɛn] *adv* (*at that time*) entonces; (*next*) después; (*later*) luego, después; (*and also*) además ▷ *conj* (*therefore*) en ese caso, entonces ▷ *adj*: **the ~ president** el entonces presidente; **by ~** para entonces; **from ~ on** desde entonces
theology [θɪ'ɔlədʒɪ] *n* teología
theory ['θɪərɪ] *n* teoría
therapist ['θɛrəpɪst] *n* terapeuta *mf*
therapy ['θɛrəpɪ] *n* terapia

KEYWORD

there ['ðɛə*] *adv* **1** **there is, there are** hay; **there is no-one here/no bread left** no hay nadie aquí/no queda pan; **there has been an accident** ha habido un accidente
2 (*referring to place*) ahí; (*distant*) allí; **it's**

there está ahí; **put it in/on/up/down there** ponlo ahí dentro/encima/arriba/abajo; **I want that book there** quiero ese libro de ahí; **there he is!** ¡ahí está!
3 **there, there** (*esp to child*) ea, ea

there: thereabouts *adv* por ahí; **thereafter** *adv* después; **thereby** *adv* así, de ese modo; **therefore** *adv* por lo tanto; **there's** = **there is; there has**
thermal ['θə:ml] *adj* termal; (*paper*) térmico
thermometer [θə'mɔmɪtə*] *n* termómetro
thermostat ['θə:məustæt] *n* termostato
these [ði:z] *pl adj* estos/as ▷ *pl pron* éstos/as
thesis ['θi:sɪs] (*pl* **theses**) *n* tesis *f inv*
they [ðeɪ] *pl pron* ellos(ellas); (*stressed*) ellos (mismos)(ellas (mismas)); **~ say that ...** (*it is said that*) se dice que ...; **they'd** = **they had; they would**; **they'll** = **they shall; they will**; **they're** = **they are**; **they've** = **they have**
thick [θɪk] *adj* (*in consistency*) espeso; (*in size*) grueso; (*stupid*) torpe ▷ *n*: **in the ~ of the battle** en lo más reñido de la batalla; **it's 20 cm ~** tiene 20 cm de espesor; **thicken** *vi* espesarse ▷ *vt* (*sauce etc*) espesar; **thickness** *n* espesor *m*; grueso
thief [θi:f] (*pl* **thieves**) *n* ladrón/ona *m/f*
thigh [θaɪ] *n* muslo
thin [θɪn] *adj* (*person, animal*) flaco; (*in size*) delgado; (*in consistency*) poco espeso; (*hair, crowd*) escaso ▷ *vt*: **to ~ (down)** diluir
thing [θɪŋ] *n* cosa; (*object*) objeto, artículo; (*matter*) asunto; (*mania*): **to have a ~ about sb/sth** estar obsesionado con algn/algo; **things** *npl* (*belongings*) efectos *mpl* (personales); **the best ~ would be to ...** lo mejor sería ...; **how are ~s?** ¿qué tal?
think [θɪŋk] (*pt, pp* **thought**) *vi* pensar ▷ *vt* pensar, creer; **what did you ~ of them?** ¿qué te parecieron?; **to ~ about sth/sb** pensar en algo/algn; **I'll ~ about it** lo pensaré; **to ~ of doing sth** pensar en hacer algo; **I ~ so/not** creo que sí/no; **to ~ well of sb** tener buen concepto de algn; **think over** *vt* reflexionar sobre, meditar; **think up** *vt* (*plan etc*) idear
third [θə:d] *adj* (*before n*) tercer(a); (*following n*) tercero/a ▷ *n* tercero/a; (*fraction*) tercio; (BRIT *Scol*: *degree*) *título de licenciado con calificación de aprobado*; **thirdly** *adv* en tercer lugar; **third party insurance** (BRIT) *n* seguro contra terceros; **Third World** *n* Tercer Mundo
thirst [θə:st] *n* sed *f*; **thirsty** *adj* (*person, animal*) sediento; (*work*) que da sed; **to be thirsty** tener sed
thirteen ['θə:'ti:n] *num* trece; **thirteenth** [-'ti:nθ] *adj* decimotercero
thirtieth ['θə:tɪəθ] *adj* trigésimo
thirty ['θə:tɪ] *num* treinta

KEYWORD

this [ðɪs] (*pl* **these**) *adj* (*demonstrative*) este/a *pl*; estos/as; (*neuter*) esto; **this man/woman** este hombre(esta mujer); **these children/flowers** estos chicos/estas flores; **this one (here)** éste/a, esto (de aquí)
▷ *pron* (*demonstrative*) éste/a *pl*, éstos/as; (*neuter*) esto; **who is this?** ¿quién es éste/ésta?; **what is this?** ¿qué es esto?; **this is where I live** aquí vivo; **this is what he said** esto es lo que dijo; **this is Mr Brown** (*in introductions*) le presento al Sr. Brown; (*photo*) éste es el Sr. Brown; (*on telephone*) habla el Sr. Brown
▷ *adv* (*demonstrative*): **this high/long** *etc* así de alto/largo *etc*; **this far** hasta aquí

thistle ['θɪsl] *n* cardo

thorn [θɔːn] *n* espina
thorough ['θʌrə] *adj* (*search*) minucioso; (*wash*) a fondo; (*knowledge, research*) profundo; (*person*) meticuloso; **thoroughly** *adv* (*search*) minuciosamente; (*study*) profundamente; (*wash*) a fondo; (*utterly: bad, wet etc*) completamente, totalmente
those [ðəuz] *pl adj* esos(esas); (*more remote*) aquellos/as
though [ðəu] *conj* aunque ▷ *adv* sin embargo
thought [θɔːt] *pt, pp of* **think** ▷ *n* pensamiento; (*opinion*) opinión *f*; **thoughtful** *adj* pensativo; (*serious*) serio; (*considerate*) atento; **thoughtless** *adj* desconsiderado
thousand ['θauzənd] *num* mil; **two ~** dos mil; **~s of** miles de; **thousandth** *num* milésimo
thrash [θræʃ] *vt* azotar; (*defeat*) derrotar
thread [θrɛd] *n* hilo; (*of screw*) rosca ▷ *vt* (*needle*) enhebrar
threat [θrɛt] *n* amenaza; **threaten** *vi* amenazar ▷ *vt*: **to threaten sb with/ to do** amenazar a algn con/con hacer; **threatening** *adj* amenazador(a), amenazante
three [θriː] *num* tres; **three-dimensional** *adj* tridimensional; **three-piece suite** *n* tresillo; **three-quarters** *npl* tres cuartas partes; **three-quarters full** tres cuartas partes lleno
threshold ['θrɛʃhəuld] *n* umbral *m*
threw [θruː] *pt of* **throw**
thrill [θrɪl] *n* (*excitement*) emoción *f*; (*shudder*) estremecimiento ▷ *vt* emocionar; **to be ~ed** (*with gift etc*) estar encantado; **thrilled** *adj*: **I was thrilled** Estaba emocionada; **thriller** *n* novela (*or* obra *or* película) de suspense; **thrilling** *adj* emocionante
thriving ['θraɪvɪŋ] *adj* próspero
throat [θrəut] *n* garganta; **to have a sore ~** tener dolor de garganta
throb [θrɔb] *vi* latir; dar punzadas; vibrar
throne [θrəun] *n* trono
through [θruː] *prep* por, a través de; (*time*) durante; (*by means of*) por medio de, mediante; (*owing to*) gracias a ▷ *adj* (*ticket, train*) directo ▷ *adv* completamente, de parte a parte; de principio a fin; **to put sb ~ to sb** (*Tel*) poner *or* pasar a algn con algn; **to be ~** (*Tel*) tener comunicación; (*have finished*) haber terminado; **"no ~ road"** (BRIT) "calle sin salida"; **throughout** *prep* (*place*) por todas partes de, por todo; (*time*) durante todo ▷ *adv* por *or* en todas partes
throw [θrəu] (*pt* **threw**, *pp* **thrown**) *n* tiro; (*Sport*) lanzamiento ▷ *vt* tirar, echar; (*Sport*) lanzar; (*rider*) derribar; (*fig*) desconcertar; **to ~ a party** dar una fiesta; **throw away** *vt* tirar; (*money*) derrochar; **throw in** *vt* (*Sport: ball*) sacar; (*include*) incluir; **throw off** *vt* deshacerse de; **throw out** *vt* tirar; (*person*) echar; expulsar; **throw up** *vi* vomitar
thru [θruː] (US) = **through**
thrush [θrʌʃ] *n* zorzal *m*, tordo
thrust [θrʌst] (*pt, pp* **~**) *vt* empujar con fuerza
thud [θʌd] *n* golpe *m* sordo
thug [θʌg] *n* gamberro/a
thumb [θʌm] *n* (*Anat*) pulgar *m*; **to ~ a lift** hacer autostop; **thumbtack** (US) *n* chincheta (SP)
thump [θʌmp] *n* golpe *m*; (*sound*) ruido seco *or* sordo ▷ *vt* golpear ▷ *vi* (*heart etc*) palpitar
thunder ['θʌndə*] *n* trueno ▷ *vi* tronar; (*train etc*): **to ~ past** pasar como un trueno; **thunderstorm** *n* tormenta
Thur(s). *abbr* (= *Thursday*) juev
Thursday ['θəːzdɪ] *n* jueves *m inv*
thus [ðʌs] *adv* así, de este modo
thwart [θwɔːt] *vt* frustrar
thyme [taɪm] *n* tomillo
Tibet [tɪ'bɛt] *n* el Tibet
tick [tɪk] *n* (*sound: of clock*) tictac *m*;

(*mark*) palomita; (*Zool*) garrapata; (BRIT: *inf*): **in a ~** en un instante ▷ *vi* hacer tictac ▷ *vt* marcar; **tick off** *vt* marcar; (*person*) reñir

ticket ['tɪkɪt] *n* billete *m* (SP), boleto (LAM); (*for cinema etc*) entrada; (*in shop: on goods*) etiqueta; (*for raffle*) papeleta; (*for library*) tarjeta; (*parking ticket*) multa de aparcamiento (SP) *or* por estacionamiento (indebido) (LAM); **ticket barrier** *n* (BRIT: *Rail*) *barrera más allá de la cual se necesita billete/boleto*; **ticket collector** *n* revisor(a) *m/f*; **ticket inspector** *n* revisor(a) *m/f*, inspector(a) *m/f* de boletos (LAM); **ticket machine** *n* máquina de billetes (SP) *or* boletos (LAM); **ticket office** *n* (*Theatre*) taquilla (SP), boletería (LAM); (*Rail*) mostrador *m* de billetes (SP) *or* boletos (LAM)

tickle ['tɪkl] *vt* hacer cosquillas a ▷ *vi* hacer cosquillas; **ticklish** *adj* (*person*) cosquilloso; (*problem*) delicado

tide [taɪd] *n* marea; (*fig: of events etc*) curso, marcha

tidy ['taɪdɪ] *adj* (*room etc*) ordenado; (*dress, work*) limpio; (*person*) (bien) arreglado ▷ *vt* (*also*: **~ up**) poner en orden

tie [taɪ] *n* (*string etc*) atadura; (BRIT: *also*: **neck~**) corbata; (*fig: link*) vínculo, lazo; (*Sport etc: draw*) empate *m* ▷ *vt* atar ▷ *vi* (*Sport etc*) empatar; **to ~ in a bow** atar con un lazo; **to ~ a knot in sth** hacer un nudo en algo; **tie down** *vt* (*fig: person: restrict*) atar; (*: to price, date etc*) obligar a; **tie up** *vt* (*dog, person*) atar; (*arrangements*) concluir; **to be tied up** (*busy*) estar ocupado

tier [tɪə*] *n* grada; (*of cake*) piso

tiger ['taɪgə*] *n* tigre *m*

tight [taɪt] *adj* (*rope*) tirante; (*money*) escaso; (*clothes*) ajustado; (*bend*) cerrado; (*shoes, schedule*) apretado; (*budget*) ajustado; (*security*) estricto; (*inf: drunk*) borracho ▷ *adv* (*squeeze*) muy fuerte; (*shut*) bien; **tighten** *vt* (*rope*) estirar; (*screw, grip*) apretar; (*security*) reforzar ▷ *vi* estirarse; apretarse; **tightly** *adv* (*grasp*) muy fuerte; **tights** (BRIT) *npl* panti *mpl*

tile [taɪl] *n* (*on roof*) teja; (*on floor*) baldosa; (*on wall*) azulejo

till [tɪl] *n* caja (registradora) ▷ *vt* (*land*) cultivar ▷ *prep, conj* = **until**

tilt [tɪlt] *vt* inclinar ▷ *vi* inclinarse

timber [tɪmbə*] *n* (*material*) madera

time [taɪm] *n* tiempo; (*epoch: often pl*) época; (*by clock*) hora; (*moment*) momento; (*occasion*) vez *f*; (*Mus*) compás *m* ▷ *vt* calcular *or* medir el tiempo de; (*race*) cronometrar; (*remark, visit etc*) elegir el momento para; **a long ~** mucho tiempo; **4 at a ~** de 4 en 4; 4 a la vez; **for the ~ being** de momento, por ahora; **from ~ to ~** de vez en cuando; **at ~s** a veces; **in ~** (*soon enough*) a tiempo; (*after some time*) con el tiempo; (*Mus*) al compás; **in a week's ~** dentro de una semana; **in no ~** en un abrir y cerrar de ojos; **any ~** cuando sea; **on ~** a la hora; **5 ~s 5** 5 por 5; **what ~ is it?** ¿qué hora es?; **to have a good ~** pasarlo bien, divertirse; **time limit** *n* plazo; **timely** *adj* oportuno; **timer** *n* (*in kitchen etc*) programador *m* horario; **time-share** *n* apartamento (*or* casa) a tiempo compartido; **timetable** *n* horario; **time zone** *n* huso horario

timid ['tɪmɪd] *adj* tímido

timing ['taɪmɪŋ] *n* (*Sport*) cronometraje *m*; **the ~ of his resignation** el momento que eligió para dimitir

tin [tɪn] *n* estaño; (*also*: **~ plate**) hojalata; (BRIT: *can*) lata; **tinfoil** *n* papel *m* de estaño

tingle ['tɪŋgl] *vi* (*person*): **to ~ (with)** estremecerse (de); (*hands etc*) hormiguear

tinker ['tɪŋkə*]: **~ with** *vt fus* jugar con, tocar

tinned [tɪnd] (BRIT) *adj* (*food*) en lata, en conserva

tin opener [-əupnə*] (BRIT) *n* abrelatas *m inv*

tint [tɪnt] *n* matiz *m*; (*for hair*) tinte *m*; **tinted** *adj* (*hair*) teñido; (*glass, spectacles*) ahumado

tiny ['taɪnɪ] *adj* minúsculo, pequeñito

tip [tɪp] *n* (*end*) punta; (*gratuity*) propina; (BRIT: *for rubbish*) vertedero; (*advice*) consejo ▷ *vt* (*waiter*) dar una propina a; (*tilt*) inclinar; (*empty: also:* **~ out**) vaciar, echar; (*overturn: also:* **~ over**) volcar; **tip off** *vt* avisar, poner sobreaviso a

tiptoe ['tɪptəu] *n*: **on ~** de puntillas

tire ['taɪə*] *n* (US) = **tyre** ▷ *vt* cansar ▷ *vi* cansarse; (*become bored*) aburrirse; **tired** *adj* cansado; **to be tired of sth** estar harto de algo; **tire pressure** (US) = **tyre pressure**; **tiring** *adj* cansado

tissue ['tɪʃuː] *n* tejido; (*paper handkerchief*) pañuelo de papel, kleenex® *m*; **tissue paper** *n* papel *m* de seda

tit [tɪt] *n* (*bird*) herrerillo común; **to give ~ for tat** dar ojo por ojo

title ['taɪtl] *n* título

T-junction ['tiːdʒʌŋkʃən] *n* cruce *m* en T

TM *abbr* = **trademark**

KEYWORD

to [tuː, tə] *prep* **1** (*direction*) a; **to go to France/London/school/the station** ir a Francia/Londres/al colegio/a la estación; **to go to Claude's/the doctor's** ir a casa de Claude/al médico; **the road to Edinburgh** la carretera de Edimburgo

2 (*as far as*) hasta, a; **from here to London** de aquí a *or* hasta Londres; **to count to 10** contar hasta 10; **from 40 to 50 people** entre 40 y 50 personas

3 (*with expressions of time*): **a quarter/twenty to 5** las 5 menos cuarto/veinte

4 (*for, of*): **the key to the front door** la llave de la puerta principal; **she is secretary to the director** es la secretaría del director; **a letter to his wife** una carta a *or* para su mujer

5 (*expressing indirect object*) a; **to give sth to sb** darle algo a algn; **to talk to sb** hablar con algn; **to be a danger to sb** ser un peligro para algn; **to carry out repairs to sth** hacer reparaciones en algo

6 (*in relation to*): **3 goals to 2** 3 goles a 2; **30 miles to the gallon** ≈ 94 litros a los cien (kms)

7 (*purpose, result*): **to come to sb's aid** venir en auxilio *or* ayuda de algn; **to sentence sb to death** condenar a algn a muerte; **to my great surprise** con gran sorpresa mía

▷ *with vb* **1** (*simple infin*): **to go/eat** ir/comer

2 (*following another vb*): **to want/try/start to do** querer/intentar/empezar a hacer

3 (*with vb omitted*): **I don't want to** no quiero

4 (*purpose, result*) para; **I did it to help you** lo hice para ayudarte; **he came to see you** vino a verte

5 (*equivalent to relative clause*): **I have things to do** tengo cosas que hacer; **the main thing is to try** lo principal es intentarlo

6 (*after adj etc*): **ready to go** listo para irse; **too old to ...** demasiado viejo (como) para ...

▷ *adv*: **pull/push the door to** tirar de/empujar la puerta

toad [təud] *n* sapo; **toadstool** *n* hongo venenoso

toast [təust] *n* (*Culin*) tostada; (*drink, speech*) brindis *m* ▷ *vt* (*Culin*) tostar; (*drink to*) brindar por; **toaster** *n* tostador *m*

tobacco [tə'bækəu] *n* tabaco

toboggan [tə'bɔgən] *n* tobogán *m*

today [tə'deɪ] *adv, n* (*also fig*) hoy *m*

toddler ['tɔdlə*] *n* niño/a (que empieza a andar)

toe [təu] *n* dedo (del pie); (*of shoe*) punta; **to ~ the line** (*fig*) conformarse;

toenail *n* uña del pie
toffee ['tɔfɪ] *n* toffee *m*
together [tə'gɛðə*] *adv* juntos; (*at same time*) al mismo tiempo, a la vez; **~ with** junto con
toilet ['tɔɪlət] *n* inodoro; (BRIT: *room*) (cuarto de) baño, servicio ▷ *cpd* (*soap etc*) de aseo; **toilet bag** *n* neceser *m*, bolsa de aseo; **toilet paper** *n* papel *m* higiénico; **toiletries** *npl* artículos *mpl* de tocador; **toilet roll** *n* rollo de papel higiénico
token ['təukən] *n* (*sign*) señal *f*, muestra; (*souvenir*) recuerdo; (*disc*) ficha ▷ *adj* (*strike, payment etc*) simbólico; **book/record ~** (BRIT) vale *m* para comprar libros/discos; **gift ~** (BRIT) vale-regalo
Tokyo ['təukjəu] *n* Tokio, Tokío
told [təuld] *pt, pp of* **tell**
tolerant ['tɔlərnt] *adj*: **~ of** tolerante con
tolerate ['tɔləreɪt] *vt* tolerar
toll [təul] *n* (*of casualties*) número de víctimas; (*tax, charge*) peaje *m* ▷ *vi* (*bell*) doblar; **toll call** *n* (US *Tel*) conferencia, llamada interurbana; **toll-free** (US) *adj, adv* gratis
tomato [tə'mɑːtəu] (*pl* **~es**) *n* tomate *m*; **tomato sauce** *n* salsa de tomate
tomb [tuːm] *n* tumba; **tombstone** *n* lápida
tomorrow [tə'mɔrəu] *adv, n* (*also*: *fig*) mañana; **the day after ~** pasado mañana; **~ morning** mañana por la mañana
ton [tʌn] *n* tonelada (BRIT = *1016 kg*; US = *907 kg*); (*metric ton*) tonelada métrica; **~s of** (*inf*) montones de
tone [təun] *n* tono ▷ *vi* (*also*: **~ in**) armonizar; **tone down** *vt* (*criticism*) suavizar; (*colour*) atenuar
tongs [tɔŋz] *npl* (*for coal*) tenazas *fpl*; (*curling tongs*) tenacillas *fpl*
tongue [tʌŋ] *n* lengua; **~ in cheek** irónicamente
tonic ['tɔnɪk] *n* (*Med*) tónico; (*also*: **~ water**) (agua) tónica
tonight [tə'naɪt] *adv, n* esta noche; esta tarde
tonne [tʌn] *n* tonelada (métrica) (*1.000kg*)
tonsil ['tɔnsl] *n* amígdala; **tonsillitis** [-'laɪtɪs] *n* amigdalitis *f*
too [tuː] *adv* (*excessively*) demasiado; (*also*) también; **~ much** demasiado; **~ many** demasiados/as
took [tuk] *pt of* **take**
tool [tuːl] *n* herramienta; **tool box** *n* caja de herramientas; **tool kit** *n* juego de herramientas
tooth [tuːθ] (*pl* **teeth**) *n* (*Anat, Tech*) diente *m*; (*molar*) muela; **toothache** *n* dolor *m* de muelas; **toothbrush** *n* cepillo de dientes; **toothpaste** *n* pasta de dientes; **toothpick** *n* palillo
top [tɔp] *n* (*of mountain*) cumbre *f*, cima; (*of tree*) copa; (*of head*) coronilla; (*of ladder, page*) lo alto; (*of table*) superficie *f*; (*of cupboard*) parte *f* de arriba; (*lid*: *of box*) tapa; (: *of bottle, jar*) tapón *m*; (*of list etc*) cabeza; (*toy*) peonza; (*garment*) blusa; camiseta ▷ *adj* de arriba; (*in rank*) principal, primero; (*best*) mejor ▷ *vt* (*exceed*) exceder; (*be first in*) encabezar; **on ~ of** (*above*) sobre, encima de; (*in addition to*) además de; **from ~ to bottom** de pies a cabeza; **top up** *vt* llenar; (*mobile phone*) recargar (el saldo de); **top floor** *n* último piso; **top hat** *n* sombrero de copa
topic ['tɔpɪk] *n* tema *m*; **topical** *adj* actual
topless ['tɔplɪs] *adj* (*bather, bikini*) topless *inv*
topping ['tɔpɪŋ] *n* (*Culin*): **with a ~ of cream** con nata por encima
topple ['tɔpl] *vt* derribar ▷ *vi* caerse
top-up card *n* (*for mobile phone*) tarjeta prepago
torch [tɔːtʃ] *n* antorcha; (BRIT: *electric*) linterna
tore [tɔː*] *pt of* **tear²**
torment [*n* 'tɔːmɛnt, *vt* tɔː'mɛnt] *n* tormento ▷ *vt* atormentar; (*fig*: *annoy*) fastidiar

torn [tɔːn] *pp of* **tear²**
tornado [tɔːˈneɪdəu] (*pl* **~es**) *n* tornado
torpedo [tɔːˈpiːdəu] (*pl* **~es**) *n* torpedo
torrent [ˈtɔrnt] *n* torrente *m*; **torrential** [tɔˈrɛnʃl] *adj* torrencial
tortoise [ˈtɔːtəs] *n* tortuga
torture [ˈtɔːtʃə*] *n* tortura ▷ *vt* torturar; (*fig*) atormentar
Tory [ˈtɔːrɪ] (BRIT) *adj*, *n* (*Pol*) conservador(a) *m/f*
toss [tɔs] *vt* tirar, echar; (*one's head*) sacudir; **to ~ a coin** echar a cara o cruz; **to ~ up for sth** jugar a cara o cruz algo; **to ~ and turn** (*in bed*) dar vueltas
total [ˈtəutl] *adj* total, entero; (*emphatic: failure etc*) completo, total ▷ *n* total *m*, suma ▷ *vt* (*add up*) sumar; (*amount to*) ascender a
totalitarian [təutælɪˈtɛərɪən] *adj* totalitario
totally [ˈtəutəlɪ] *adv* totalmente
touch [tʌtʃ] *n* tacto; (*contact*) contacto ▷ *vt* tocar; (*emotionally*) conmover; **a ~ of** (*fig*) un poquito de; **to get in ~ with sb** ponerse en contacto con algn; **to lose ~** (*friends*) perder contacto; **touch down** *vi* (*on land*) aterrizar; **touchdown** *n* aterrizaje *m*; (*on sea*) amerizaje *m*; (US *Football*) ensayo; **touched** *adj* (*moved*) conmovido; **touching** *adj* (*moving*) conmovedor(a); **touchline** *n* (*Sport*) línea de banda; **touch-sensitive** *adj* sensible al tacto
tough [tʌf] *adj* (*material*) resistente; (*meat*) duro; (*problem etc*) difícil; (*policy, stance*) inflexible; (*person*) fuerte
tour [ˈtuə*] *n* viaje *m*, vuelta; (*also:* **package ~**) viaje *m* todo comprendido; (*of town, museum*) visita; (*by band etc*) gira ▷ *vt* recorrer, visitar; **tour guide** *n* guía *mf* turístico/a
tourism [ˈtuərɪzm] *n* turismo
tourist [ˈtuərɪst] *n* turista *mf* ▷ *cpd* turístico; **tourist office** *n* oficina de turismo
tournament [ˈtuənəmənt] *n* torneo
tour operator *n* touroperador(a) *m/f*, operador(a) *m/f* turístico/a
tow [təu] *vt* remolcar; **"on** *or* **in** (US) **~"** (*Aut*) "a remolque"; **tow away** *vt* llevarse a remolque
toward(s) [təˈwɔːd(z)] *prep* hacia; (*attitude*) respecto a, con; (*purpose*) para
towel [ˈtauəl] *n* toalla; **towelling** *n* (*fabric*) felpa
tower [ˈtauə*] *n* torre *f*; **tower block** (BRIT) *n* torre *f* (de pisos)
town [taun] *n* ciudad *f*; **to go to ~** ir a la ciudad; (*fig*) echar la casa por la ventana; **town centre** (BRIT) *n* centro de la ciudad; **town hall** *n* ayuntamiento
tow truck (US) *n* camión *m* grúa
toxic [ˈtɔksɪk] *adj* tóxico
toy [tɔɪ] *n* juguete *m*; **toy with** *vt fus* jugar con; (*idea*) acariciar; **toyshop** *n* juguetería
trace [treɪs] *n* rastro ▷ *vt* (*draw*) trazar, delinear; (*locate*) encontrar; (*follow*) seguir la pista de
track [træk] *n* (*mark*) huella, pista; (*path: gen*) camino, senda; (*: of bullet etc*) trayectoria; (*: of suspect, animal*) pista, rastro; (*Rail*) vía; (*Sport*) pista; (*on tape, record*) canción *f* ▷ *vt* seguir la pista de; **to keep ~ of** mantenerse al tanto de, seguir; **track down** *vt* (*prey*) seguir el rastro de; (*sth lost*) encontrar; **tracksuit** *n* chandal *m*
tractor [ˈtræktə*] *n* tractor *m*
trade [treɪd] *n* comercio; (*skill, job*) oficio ▷ *vi* negociar, comerciar ▷ *vt* (*exchange*): **to ~ sth (for sth)** cambiar algo (por algo); **trade in** *vt* (*old car etc*) ofrecer como parte del pago; **trademark** *n* marca de fábrica; **trader** *n* comerciante *mf*; **tradesman** (*irreg*) *n* (*shopkeeper*) tendero; **trade union** *n* sindicato
trading [ˈtreɪdɪŋ] *n* comercio
tradition [trəˈdɪʃən] *n* tradición *f*; **traditional** *adj* tradicional
traffic [ˈtræfɪk] *n* (*gen, Aut*) tráfico,

circulación *f* ▷ *vi*: **to ~ in** (*pej*: *liquor, drugs*) traficar en; **traffic circle** (US) *n* isleta; **traffic island** *n* refugio, isleta; **traffic jam** *n* embotellamiento; **traffic lights** *npl* semáforo; **traffic warden** *n* guardia *mf* de tráfico

tragedy ['trædʒədɪ] *n* tragedia

tragic ['trædʒɪk] *adj* trágico

trail [treɪl] *n* (*tracks*) rastro, pista; (*path*) camino, sendero; (*dust, smoke*) estela ▷ *vt* (*drag*) arrastrar; (*follow*) seguir la pista de ▷ *vi* arrastrar; (*in contest etc*) ir perdiendo; **trailer** *n* (*Aut*) remolque *m*; (*caravan*) caravana; (*Cinema*) trailer *m*, avance *m*

train [treɪn] *n* tren *m*; (*of dress*) cola; (*series*) serie *f* ▷ *vt* (*educate, teach skills to*) formar; (*sportsman*) entrenar; (*dog*) adiestrar; (*point*: *gun etc*): **to ~ on** apuntar a ▷ *vi* (*Sport*) entrenarse; (*learn a skill*): **to ~ as a teacher** *etc* estudiar para profesor *etc*; **one's ~ of thought** el razonamiento de algn; **trainee** [treɪ'ni:] *n* aprendiz(a) *m/f*; **trainer** *n* (*Sport*: *coach*) entrenador(a) *m/f*; (*of animals*) domador(a) *m/f*; **trainers** *npl* (*shoes*) zapatillas *fpl* (de deporte); **training** *n* formación *f*; entrenamiento; **to be in training** (*Sport*) estar entrenando; **training course** *n* curso de formación; **training shoes** *npl* zapatillas *fpl* (de deporte)

trait [treɪt] *n* rasgo

traitor ['treɪtə*] *n* traidor(a) *m/f*

tram [træm] (BRIT) *n* (*also*: **~car**) tranvía *m*

tramp [træmp] *n* (*person*) vagabundo/a; (*inf*: *pej*: *woman*) puta

trample ['træmpl] *vt*: **to ~ (underfoot)** pisotear

trampoline ['træmpəli:n] *n* trampolín *m*

tranquil ['træŋkwɪl] *adj* tranquilo; **tranquillizer** (US **tranquilizer**) *n* (*Med*) tranquilizante *m*

transaction [træn'zækʃən] *n* transacción *f*, operación *f*

transatlantic ['trænzət'læntɪk] *adj* transatlántico

transcript ['trænskrɪpt] *n* copia

transfer [*n* 'trænsfə:*, *vb* træns'fə:*] *n* (*of employees*) traslado; (*of money, power*) transferencia; (*Sport*) traspaso; (*picture, design*) calcomanía ▷ *vt* trasladar; transferir; **to ~ the charges** (BRIT *Tel*) llamar a cobro revertido

transform [træns'fɔ:m] *vt* transformar; **transformation** *n* transformación *f*

transfusion [træns'fju:ʒən] *n* transfusión *f*

transit ['trænzɪt] *n*: **in ~** en tránsito

transition [træn'zɪʃən] *n* transición *f*

transitive ['trænzɪtɪv] *adj* (*Ling*) transitivo

translate [trænz'leɪt] *vt* traducir; **translation** [-'leɪʃən] *n* traducción *f*; **translator** *n* traductor(a) *m/f*

transmission [trænz'mɪʃən] *n* transmisión *f*

transmit [trænz'mɪt] *vt* transmitir; **transmitter** *n* transmisor *m*

transparent [træns'pærnt] *adj* transparente

transplant ['trænsplɑ:nt] *n* (*Med*) transplante *m*

transport [*n* 'trænspɔ:t, *vt* træns'pɔ:t] *n* transporte *m*; (*car*) coche *m* (SP), carro (LAM), automóvil *m* ▷ *vt* transportar; **transportation** [-'teɪʃən] *n* transporte *m*

transvestite [trænz'vɛstaɪt] *n* travestí *mf*

trap [træp] *n* (*snare, trick*) trampa; (*carriage*) cabriolé *m* ▷ *vt* coger (SP) *or* agarrar (LAM) (en una trampa); (*trick*) engañar; (*confine*) atrapar

trash [træʃ] *n* (*rubbish*) basura; (*nonsense*) tonterías *fpl*; (*pej*): **the book/film is ~** el libro/la película no vale nada; **trash can** (US) *n* cubo *or* bote *m* (MEX) *or* tacho (SC) de la basura

trauma ['trɔ:mə] *n* trauma *m*; **traumatic** [trɔ:'mætɪk] *adj* traumático

travel ['trævl] *n* el viajar ▷*vi* viajar ▷*vt* (*distance*) recorrer; **travel agency** *n* agencia de viajes; **travel agent** *n* agente *mf* de viajes; **travel insurance** *n* seguro de viaje; **traveller** (*US* **traveler**) *n* viajero/a; **traveller's cheque** (*US* **traveler's check**) *n* cheque *m* de viajero; **travelling** (*US* **traveling**) *n* los viajes, el viajar; **travel-sick** *adj*: **to get travel-sick** marearse al viajar; **travel sickness** *n* mareo

tray [treɪ] *n* bandeja; (*on desk*) cajón *m*

treacherous ['trɛtʃərəs] *adj* traidor, traicionero; (*dangerous*) peligroso

treacle ['tri:kl] (BRIT) *n* melaza

tread [trɛd] (*pt* **trod**, *pp* **trodden**) *n* (*step*) paso, pisada; (*sound*) ruido de pasos; (*of stair*) escalón *m*; (*of tyre*) banda de rodadura ▷*vi* pisar; **tread on** *vt fus* pisar

treasure ['trɛʒə*] *n* tesoro ▷*vt* (*value*: *object*, *friendship*) apreciar; (: *memory*) guardar; **treasurer** *n* tesorero/a

treasury ['trɛʒərɪ] *n*: **the T~** el Ministerio de Hacienda

treat [tri:t] *n* (*present*) regalo ▷*vt* tratar; **to ~ sb to sth** invitar a algn a algo; **treatment** *n* tratamiento

treaty ['tri:tɪ] *n* tratado

treble ['trɛbl] *adj* triple ▷*vt* triplicar ▷*vi* triplicarse

tree [tri:] *n* árbol *m*; **~ trunk** tronco (de árbol)

trek [trɛk] *n* (*long journey*) viaje *m* largo y difícil; (*tiring walk*) caminata

tremble ['trɛmbl] *vi* temblar

tremendous [trɪ'mɛndəs] *adj* tremendo, enorme; (*excellent*) estupendo

trench [trɛntʃ] *n* zanja

trend [trɛnd] *n* (*tendency*) tendencia; (*of events*) curso; (*fashion*) moda; **trendy** *adj* de moda

trespass ['trɛspəs] *vi*: **to ~ on** entrar sin permiso en; **"no ~ing"** "prohibido el paso"

trial ['traɪəl] *n* (*Law*) juicio, proceso; (*test*: *of machine etc*) prueba; **trial period** *n* periodo de prueba

triangle ['traɪæŋgl] *n* (*Math*, *Mus*) triángulo

triangular [traɪ'æŋgjulə*] *adj* triangular

tribe [traɪb] *n* tribu *f*

tribunal [traɪ'bju:nl] *n* tribunal *m*

tribute ['trɪbju:t] *n* homenaje *m*, tributo; **to pay ~ to** rendir homenaje a

trick [trɪk] *n* (*skill*, *knack*) tino, truco; (*conjuring trick*) truco; (*joke*) broma; (*Cards*) baza ▷*vt* engañar; **to play a ~ on sb** gastar una broma a algn; **that should do the ~** a ver si funciona así

trickle ['trɪkl] *n* (*of water etc*) goteo ▷*vi* gotear

tricky ['trɪkɪ] *adj* difícil; delicado

tricycle ['traɪsɪkl] *n* triciclo

trifle ['traɪfl] *n* bagatela; (*Culin*) *dulce de bizcocho borracho, gelatina, fruta y natillas* ▷*adv*: **a ~ long** un poquito largo

trigger ['trɪgə*] *n* (*of gun*) gatillo

trim [trɪm] *adj* (*house*, *garden*) en buen estado; (*person*, *figure*) esbelto ▷*n* (*haircut etc*) recorte *m*; (*on car*) guarnición *f* ▷*vt* (*neaten*) arreglar; (*cut*) recortar; (*decorate*) adornar; (*Naut*: *a sail*) orientar

trio ['tri:əu] *n* trío

trip [trɪp] *n* viaje *m*; (*excursion*) excursión *f*; (*stumble*) traspié *m* ▷*vi* (*stumble*) tropezar; (*go lightly*) andar a paso ligero; **on a ~** de viaje; **trip up** *vi* tropezar, caerse ▷*vt* hacer tropezar *or* caer

triple ['trɪpl] *adj* triple

triplets ['trɪplɪts] *npl* trillizos/as *mpl/fpl*

tripod ['traɪpɔd] *n* trípode *m*

triumph ['traɪʌmf] *n* triunfo ▷*vi*: **to ~ (over)** vencer; **triumphant** [traɪ'ʌmfənt] *adj* (*team etc*) vencedor(a); (*wave*, *return*) triunfal

trivial ['trɪvɪəl] *adj* insignificante; (*commonplace*) banal

trod [trɔd] *pt of* **tread**

trodden ['trɔdn] *pp of* **tread**
trolley ['trɔlɪ] *n* carrito; (*also*: **~ bus**) trolebús *m*
trombone [trɔm'bəun] *n* trombón *m*
troop [tru:p] *n* grupo, banda; **troops** *npl* (*Mil*) tropas *fpl*
trophy ['trəufɪ] *n* trofeo
tropical ['trɔpɪkl] *adj* tropical
trot [trɔt] *n* trote *m* ▷ *vi* trotar; **on the ~** (BRIT: *fig*) seguidos/as
trouble ['trʌbl] *n* problema *m*, dificultad *f*; (*worry*) preocupación *f*; (*bother, effort*) molestia, esfuerzo; (*unrest*) inquietud *f*; (*Med*): **stomach** *etc* **~** problemas *mpl* gástricos *etc* ▷ *vt* (*disturb*) molestar; (*worry*) preocupar, inquietar ▷ *vi*: **to ~ to do sth** molestarse en hacer algo; **troubles** *npl* (*Pol etc*) conflictos *mpl*; (*personal*) problemas *mpl*; **to be in ~** estar en un apuro; **it's no ~!** ¡no es molestia (ninguna)!; **what's the ~?** (*with broken TV etc*) ¿cuál es el problema?; (*doctor to patient*) ¿qué pasa?; **troubled** *adj* (*person*) preocupado; (*country, epoch, life*) agitado; **troublemaker** *n* agitador(a) *m/f*; (*child*) alborotador *m*; **troublesome** *adj* molesto
trough [trɔf] *n* (*also*: **drinking ~**) abrevadero; (*also*: **feeding ~**) comedero; (*depression*) depresión *f*
trousers ['trauzəz] *npl* pantalones *mpl*; **short ~** pantalones *mpl* cortos
trout [traut] *n inv* trucha
trowel ['trauəl] *n* (*of gardener*) palita; (*of builder*) paleta
truant ['truənt] *n*: **to play ~** (BRIT) hacer novillos
truce [tru:s] *n* tregua
truck [trʌk] *n* (*lorry*) camión *m*; (*Rail*) vagón *m*; **truck driver** *n* camionero
true [tru:] *adj* verdadero; (*accurate*) exacto; (*genuine*) auténtico; (*faithful*) fiel; **to come ~** realizarse
truly ['tru:lɪ] *adv* (*really*) realmente; (*truthfully*) verdaderamente; (*faithfully*): **yours ~** (*in letter*) le saluda atentamente
trumpet ['trʌmpɪt] *n* trompeta
trunk [trʌŋk] *n* (*of tree, person*) tronco; (*of elephant*) trompa; (*case*) baúl *m*; (US *Aut*) maletero; **trunks** *npl* (*also*: **swimming ~s**) bañador *m* (de hombre)
trust [trʌst] *n* confianza; (*responsibility*) responsabilidad *f*; (*Law*) fideicomiso ▷ *vt* (*rely on*) tener confianza en; (*hope*) esperar; (*entrust*): **to ~ sth to sb** confiar algo a algn; **to take sth on ~** fiarse de algo; **trusted** *adj* de confianza; **trustworthy** *adj* digno de confianza
truth [tru:θ, *pl* tru:ðz] *n* verdad *f*; **truthful** *adj* veraz
try [traɪ] *n* tentativa, intento; (*Rugby*) ensayo ▷ *vt* (*attempt*) intentar; (*test*: *also*: **~ out**) probar, someter a prueba; (*Law*) juzgar, procesar; (*strain*: *patience*) hacer perder ▷ *vi* probar; **to have a ~** probar suerte; **to ~ to do sth** intentar hacer algo; **~ again!** ¡vuelve a probar!; **~ harder!** ¡esfuérzate más!; **well, I tried** al menos lo intenté; **try on** *vt* (*clothes*) probarse; **trying** *adj* (*experience*) cansado; (*person*) pesado
T-shirt ['ti:ʃə:t] *n* camiseta
tub [tʌb] *n* cubo (SP), cubeta (SP, MEX), balde *m* (LAM); (*bath*) bañera (SP), tina (LAM), bañadera (RPL)
tube [tju:b] *n* tubo; (BRIT: *underground*) metro; (*for tyre*) cámara de aire
tuberculosis [tjubə:kju'ləusɪs] *n* tuberculosis *f inv*
tube station (BRIT) *n* estación *f* de metro
tuck [tʌk] *vt* (*put*) poner; **tuck away** *vt* (*money*) guardar; (*building*): **to be tucked away** esconderse, ocultarse; **tuck in** *vt* meter dentro; (*child*) arropar ▷ *vi* (*eat*) comer con apetito; **tuck shop** *n* (*Scol*) tienda ≈ bar *m* (del colegio) (SP)
Tue(s). *abbr* (= *Tuesday*) mart
Tuesday ['tju:zdɪ] *n* martes *m inv*
tug [tʌg] *n* (*ship*) remolcador *m* ▷ *vt* tirar de
tuition [tju:'ɪʃən] *n* (BRIT) enseñanza;

(: *private tuition*) clases *fpl* particulares; (*US*: *school fees*) matrícula
tulip ['tju:lɪp] *n* tulipán *m*
tumble ['tʌmbl] *n* (*fall*) caída ▷*vi* caer; **to ~ to sth** (*inf*) caer en la cuenta de algo; **tumble dryer** (BRIT) *n* secadora
tumbler ['tʌmblə*] *n* (*glass*) vaso
tummy ['tʌmɪ] (*inf*) *n* barriga, tripa
tumour ['tju:mə*] (US **tumor**) *n* tumor *m*
tuna ['tju:nə] *n inv* (*also*: **~ fish**) atún *m*
tune [tju:n] *n* melodía ▷*vt* (*Mus*) afinar; (*Radio, TV, Aut*) sintonizar; **to be in/out of ~** (*instrument*) estar afinado/desafinado; (*singer*) cantar afinadamente/desafinar; **to be in/out of ~ with** (*fig*) estar de acuerdo/en desacuerdo con; **tune in** *vi*: **to tune in (to)** (*Radio, TV*) sintonizar (con); **tune up** *vi* (*musician*) afinar (su instrumento)
tunic ['tju:nɪk] *n* túnica
Tunisia [tju:'nɪzɪə] *n* Túnez *m*
tunnel ['tʌnl] *n* túnel *m*; (*in mine*) galería ▷*vi* construir un túnel/una galería
turbulence ['tə:bjuləns] *n* (*Aviat*) turbulencia
turf [tə:f] *n* césped *m*; (*clod*) tepe *m* ▷*vt* cubrir con césped
Turk [tə:k] *n* turco/a
Turkey ['tə:kɪ] *n* Turquía
turkey ['tə:kɪ] *n* pavo
Turkish ['tə:kɪʃ] *adj, n* turco; (*Ling*) turco
turmoil ['tə:mɔɪl] *n*: **in ~** revuelto
turn [tə:n] *n* turno; (*in road*) curva; (*of mind, events*) rumbo; (*Theatre*) número; (*Med*) ataque *m* ▷*vt* girar, volver; (*collar, steak*) dar la vuelta a; (*page*) pasar; (*change*): **to ~ sth into** convertir algo en ▷*vi* volver; (*person*: *look back*) volverse; (*reverse direction*) dar la vuelta; (*milk*) cortarse; (*become*): **to ~ nasty/forty** ponerse feo/cumplir los cuarenta; **a good ~** un favor; **it gave me quite a ~** me dio un susto; **"no left ~"** (*Aut*) "prohibido girar a la izquierda"; **it's your ~** te toca a ti; **in ~** por turnos; **to take ~s (at)** turnarse (en); **turn around** *vi* (*person*) volverse, darse la vuelta ▷*vt* (*object*) dar la vuelta a, voltear (LAM); **turn away** *vi* apartar la vista ▷*vi* rechazar; **turn back** *vi* volverse atrás ▷*vt* hacer retroceder; (*clock*) retrasar; **turn down** *vt* (*refuse*) rechazar; (*reduce*) bajar; (*fold*) doblar; **turn in** *vi* (*inf*: *go to bed*) acostarse ▷*vt* (*fold*) doblar hacia dentro; **turn off** *vi* (*from road*) desviarse ▷*vt* (*light, radio etc*) apagar; (*tap*) cerrar; (*engine*) parar; **turn on** *vt* (*light, radio etc*) encender (SP), prender (LAM); (*tap*) abrir; (*engine*) poner en marcha; **turn out** *vt* (*light, gas*) apagar; (*produce*) producir ▷*vi* (*voters*) concurrir; **to turn out to be ...** resultar ser ...; **turn over** *vi* (*person*) volverse ▷*vt* (*object*) dar la vuelta a; (*page*) volver; **turn round** *vi* volverse; (*rotate*) girar; **turn to** *vt fus*: **to turn to sb** acudir a algn; **turn up** *vi* (*person*) llegar, presentarse; (*lost object*) aparecer ▷*vt* (*gen*) subir; **turning** *n* (*in road*) vuelta; **turning point** *n* (*fig*) momento decisivo
turnip ['tə:nɪp] *n* nabo
turn: turnout *n* concurrencia; **turnover** *n* (*Comm*: *amount of money*) volumen *m* de ventas; (: *of goods*) movimiento; **turnstile** *n* torniquete *m*; **turn-up** (BRIT) *n* (*on trousers*) vuelta
turquoise ['tə:kwɔɪz] *n* (*stone*) turquesa ▷*adj* color turquesa
turtle ['tə:tl] *n* galápago; **turtleneck (sweater)** *n* jersey *m* de cuello vuelto
tusk [tʌsk] *n* colmillo
tutor ['tju:tə*] *n* profesor(a) *m/f*; **tutorial** [-'tɔ:rɪəl] *n* (*Scol*) seminario
tuxedo [tʌk'si:dəu] (US) *n* smóking *m*, esmoquin *m*
TV [ti:'vi:] *n abbr* (= *television*) tele *f*
tweed [twi:d] *n* tweed *m*
tweezers ['twi:zəz] *npl* pinzas *fpl* (de depilar)

twelfth [twɛlfθ] *num* duodécimo
twelve [twɛlv] *num* doce; **at ~ o'clock** *(midday)* a mediodía; *(midnight)* a medianoche
twentieth ['twɛntɪɪθ] *adj* vigésimo
twenty ['twɛntɪ] *num* veinte
twice [twaɪs] *adv* dos veces; **~ as much** dos veces más
twig [twɪg] *n* ramita
twilight ['twaɪlaɪt] *n* crepúsculo
twin [twɪn] *adj, n* gemelo/a *m/f* ▷ *vt* hermanar; **twin(-bedded) room** *n* habitación *f* doble; **twin beds** *npl* camas *fpl* gemelas
twinkle ['twɪŋkl] *vi* centellear; *(eyes)* brillar
twist [twɪst] *n* *(action)* torsión *f*; *(in road, coil)* vuelta; *(in wire, flex)* doblez *f*; *(in story)* giro ▷ *vt* torcer; *(weave)* trenzar; *(roll around)* enrollar; *(fig)* deformar ▷ *vi* serpentear
twit [twɪt] *(inf)* *n* tonto
twitch [twɪtʃ] *n* *(pull)* tirón *m*; *(nervous)* tic *m* ▷ *vi* crisparse
two [tuː] *num* dos; **to put ~ and ~ together** *(fig)* atar cabos
type [taɪp] *n* *(category)* tipo, género; *(model)* tipo; *(Typ)* tipo, letra ▷ *vt* *(letter etc)* escribir a máquina; **typewriter** *n* máquina de escribir
typhoid ['taɪfɔɪd] *n* tifoidea
typhoon [taɪ'fuːn] *n* tifón *m*
typical ['tɪpɪkl] *adj* típico; **typically** *adv* típicamente
typing ['taɪpɪŋ] *n* mecanografía
typist ['taɪpɪst] *n* mecanógrafo/a
tyre ['taɪə*] (US **tire**) *n* neumático, llanta (LAM); **tyre pressure** (BRIT) *n* presión *f* de los neumáticos

UFO ['juːfəu] *n abbr* (= *unidentified flying object*) OVNI *m*
Uganda [juː'gændə] *n* Uganda
ugly ['ʌglɪ] *adj* feo; *(dangerous)* peligroso
UHT *abbr* (= *UHT milk*) leche *f* UHT, leche *f* uperizada
UK *n abbr* = **United Kingdom**
ulcer ['ʌlsə*] *n* úlcera; *(mouth ulcer)* llaga
ultimate ['ʌltɪmət] *adj* último, final; *(greatest)* máximo; **ultimately** *adv* *(in the end)* por último, al final; *(fundamentally)* a *or* en fin de cuentas
ultimatum [ʌltɪ'meɪtəm] (*pl* **~s** *or* **ultimata**) *n* ultimátum *m*
ultrasound ['ʌltrəsaund] *n* *(Med)* ultrasonido
ultraviolet ['ʌltrə'vaɪəlɪt] *adj* ultravioleta
umbrella [ʌm'brɛlə] *n* paraguas *m inv*; *(for sun)* sombrilla
umpire ['ʌmpaɪə*] *n* árbitro
UN *n abbr* (= *United Nations*) NN. UU.
unable [ʌn'eɪbl] *adj*: **to be ~ to do sth**

no poder hacer algo

unacceptable [ʌnək'sɛptəbl] *adj* (*proposal, behaviour, price*) inaceptable; **it's ~ that** no se puede aceptar que

unanimous [ju:'nænɪməs] *adj* unánime

unarmed [ʌn'ɑ:md] *adj* (*defenceless*) inerme; (*without weapon*) desarmado

unattended [ʌnə'tɛndɪd] *adj* desatendido

unattractive [ʌnə'træktɪv] *adj* poco atractivo

unavailable [ʌnə'veɪləbl] *adj* (*article, room, book*) no disponible; (*person*) ocupado

unavoidable [ʌnə'vɔɪdəbl] *adj* inevitable

unaware [ʌnə'wɛə*] *adj*: **to be ~ of** ignorar; **unawares** *adv*: **to catch sb unawares** pillar a algn desprevenido

unbearable [ʌn'bɛərəbl] *adj* insoportable

unbeatable [ʌn'bi:təbl] *adj* (*team*) invencible; (*price*) inmejorable; (*quality*) insuperable

unbelievable [ʌnbɪ'li:vəbl] *adj* increíble

unborn [ʌn'bɔ:n] *adj* que va a nacer

unbutton [ʌn'bʌtn] *vt* desabrochar

uncalled-for [ʌn'kɔ:ldfɔ:*] *adj* gratuito, inmerecido

uncanny [ʌn'kænɪ] *adj* extraño

uncertain [ʌn'sə:tn] *adj* incierto; (*indecisive*) indeciso; **uncertainty** *n* incertidumbre *f*

unchanged [ʌn'tʃeɪndʒd] *adj* igual, sin cambios

uncle ['ʌŋkl] *n* tío

unclear [ʌn'klɪə*] *adj* poco claro; **I'm still ~ about what I'm supposed to do** todavía no tengo muy claro lo que tengo que hacer

uncomfortable [ʌn'kʌmfətəbl] *adj* incómodo; (*uneasy*) inquieto

uncommon [ʌn'kɔmən] *adj* poco común, raro

unconditional [ʌnkən'dɪʃənl] *adj* incondicional

unconscious [ʌn'kɔnʃəs] *adj* sin sentido; (*unaware*): **to be ~ of** no darse cuenta de ▷ *n*: **the ~** el inconsciente

uncontrollable [ʌnkən'trəuləbl] *adj* (*child etc*) incontrolable; (*temper*) indomable; (*laughter*) incontenible

unconventional [ʌnkən'vɛnʃənl] *adj* poco convencional

uncover [ʌn'kʌvə*] *vt* descubrir; (*take lid off*) destapar

undecided [ʌndɪ'saɪdɪd] *adj* (*character*) indeciso; (*question*) no resuelto

undeniable [ʌndɪ'naɪəbl] *adj* innegable

under ['ʌndə*] *prep* debajo de; (*less than*) menos de; (*according to*) según, de acuerdo con; (*sb's leadership*) bajo ▷ *adv* debajo, abajo; **~ there** allí abajo; **~ repair** en reparación; **undercover** *adj* clandestino; **underdone** *adj* (*Culin*) poco hecho; **underestimate** *vt* subestimar; **undergo** (*irreg*) *vt* sufrir; (*treatment*) recibir; **undergraduate** *n* estudiante *mf*; **underground** *n* (BRIT: *railway*) metro; (*Pol*) movimiento clandestino ▷ *adj* (*car park*) subterráneo ▷ *adv* (*work*) en la clandestinidad; **undergrowth** *n* maleza; **underline** *vt* subrayar; **undermine** *vt* socavar, minar; **underneath** [ʌndə'ni:θ] *adv* debajo ▷ *prep* debajo de, bajo; **underpants** *npl* calzoncillos *mpl*; **underpass** (BRIT) *n* paso subterráneo; **underprivileged** *adj* desposeído; **underscore** *vt* subrayar; **undershirt** (US) *n* camiseta; **underskirt** (BRIT) *n* enaguas *fpl*

understand [ʌndə'stænd] *vt, vi* entender, comprender; (*assume*) tener entendido; **understandable** *adj* comprensible; **understanding** *adj* comprensivo ▷ *n* comprensión *f*, entendimiento; (*agreement*) acuerdo

understatement ['ʌndəsteɪtmənt] *n* modestia (excesiva); **that's an ~!** ¡eso es decir poco!

understood [ʌndə'stud] *pt, pp of*

understand ▷ *adj* (*agreed*) acordado; (*implied*): **it is ~ that** se sobreentiende que

undertake [ʌndə'teɪk] (*irreg*) *vt* emprender; **to ~ to do sth** comprometerse a hacer algo

undertaker ['ʌndəteɪkə*] *n* director(a) *m/f* de pompas fúnebres

undertaking ['ʌndəteɪkɪŋ] *n* empresa; (*promise*) promesa

under: underwater *adv* bajo el agua ▷ *adj* submarino; **underway** *adj*: **to be underway** (*meeting*) estar en marcha; (*investigation*) estar llevándose a cabo; **underwear** *n* ropa interior; **underwent** *vb see* **undergo**; **underworld** *n* (*of crime*) hampa, inframundo

undesirable [ʌndɪ'zaɪrəbl] *adj* (*person*) indeseable; (*thing*) poco aconsejable

undisputed [ʌndɪ'spju:tɪd] *adj* incontestable

undo [ʌn'du:] (*irreg*) *vt* (*laces*) desatar; (*button etc*) desabrochar; (*spoil*) deshacer

undone [ʌn'dʌn] *pp of* **undo** ▷ *adj*: **to come ~** (*clothes*) desabrocharse; (*parcel*) desatarse

undoubtedly [ʌn'dautɪdlɪ] *adv* indudablemente, sin duda

undress [ʌn'drɛs] *vi* desnudarse

unearth [ʌn'ə:θ] *vt* desenterrar

uneasy [ʌn'i:zɪ] *adj* intranquilo, preocupado; (*feeling*) desagradable; (*peace*) inseguro

unemployed [ʌnɪm'plɔɪd] *adj* parado, sin trabajo ▷ *npl*: **the ~** los parados

unemployment [ʌnɪm'plɔɪmənt] *n* paro, desempleo; **unemployment benefit** *n* (BRIT) subsidio de desempleo *or* paro

unequal [ʌn'i:kwəl] *adj* (*unfair*) desigual; (*size, length*) distinto

uneven [ʌn'i:vn] *adj* desigual; (*road etc*) lleno de baches

unexpected [ʌnɪk'spɛktɪd] *adj* inesperado; **unexpectedly** *adv* inesperadamente

unfair [ʌn'fɛə*] *adj*: **~ (to sb)** injusto (con algn)

unfaithful [ʌn'feɪθful] *adj* infiel

unfamiliar [ʌnfə'mɪlɪə*] *adj* extraño, desconocido; **to be ~ with** desconocer

unfashionable [ʌn'fæʃnəbl] *adj* pasado *or* fuera de moda

unfasten [ʌn'fɑ:sn] *vt* (*knot*) desatar; (*dress*) desabrochar; (*open*) abrir

unfavourable [ʌn'feɪvərəbl] (US **unfavorable**) *adj* desfavorable

unfinished [ʌn'fɪnɪʃt] *adj* inacabado, sin terminar

unfit [ʌn'fɪt] *adj* bajo de forma; (*incompetent*): **~ (for)** incapaz (de); **~ for work** no apto para trabajar

unfold [ʌn'fəuld] *vt* desdoblar ▷ *vi* abrirse

unforgettable [ʌnfə'gɛtəbl] *adj* inolvidable

unfortunate [ʌn'fɔ:tʃnət] *adj* desgraciado; (*event, remark*) inoportuno; **unfortunately** *adv* desgraciadamente

unfriendly [ʌn'frɛndlɪ] *adj* antipático; (*behaviour, remark*) hostil, poco amigable

unfurnished [ʌn'fə:nɪʃt] *adj* sin amueblar

unhappiness [ʌn'hæpɪnɪs] *n* tristeza, desdicha

unhappy [ʌn'haepɪ] *adj* (*sad*) triste; (*unfortunate*) desgraciado; (*childhood*) infeliz; **~ about/with** (*arrangements etc*) poco contento con, descontento de

unhealthy [ʌn'hɛlθɪ] *adj* (*place*) malsano; (*person*) enfermizo; (*fig: interest*) morboso

unheard-of [ʌn'hə:dɔv] *adj* inaudito, sin precedente

unhelpful [ʌn'hɛlpful] *adj* (*person*) poco servicial; (*advice*) inútil

unhurt [ʌn'hə:t] *adj* ileso

unidentified [ʌnaɪ'dɛntɪfaɪd] *adj* no identificado, sin identificar; *see* *also* **UFO**

uniform ['ju:nɪfɔ:m] *n* uniforme *m* ▷ *adj* uniforme

unify ['ju:nɪfaɪ] *vt* unificar, unir

unimportant [ʌnɪm'pɔ:tənt] *adj* sin importancia

uninhabited [ʌnɪn'hæbɪtɪd] *adj* desierto

unintentional [ʌnɪn'tɛnʃənəl] *adj* involuntario

union ['ju:njən] *n* unión *f*; (*also*: **trade ~**) sindicato ▷ *cpd* sindical; **Union Jack** *n* bandera del Reino Unido

unique [ju:'ni:k] *adj* único

unisex ['ju:nɪsɛks] *adj* unisex

unit ['ju:nɪt] *n* unidad *f*; (*section*: *of furniture etc*) elemento; (*team*) grupo; **kitchen ~** módulo de cocina

unite [ju:'naɪt] *vt* unir ▷ *vi* unirse; **united** *adj* unido; (*effort*) conjunto; **United Kingdom** *n* Reino Unido; **United Nations (Organization)** *n* Naciones *fpl* Unidas; **United States (of America)** *n* Estados *mpl* Unidos

unity ['ju:nɪtɪ] *n* unidad *f*

universal [ju:nɪ'və:sl] *adj* universal

universe ['ju:nɪvə:s] *n* universo

university [ju:nɪ'və:sɪtɪ] *n* universidad *f*

unjust [ʌn'dʒʌst] *adj* injusto

unkind [ʌn'kaɪnd] *adj* poco amable; (*behaviour, comment*) cruel

unknown [ʌn'nəun] *adj* desconocido

unlawful [ʌn'lɔ:ful] *adj* ilegal, ilícito

unleaded [ʌn'lɛdɪd] *adj* (*petrol, fuel*) sin plombo

unleash [ʌn'li:ʃ] *vt* desatar

unless [ʌn'lɛs] *conj* a menos que; **~ he comes** a menos que venga; **~ otherwise stated** salvo indicación contraria

unlike [ʌn'laɪk] *adj* (*not alike*) distinto de *or* a; (*not like*) poco propio de ▷ *prep* a diferencia de

unlikely [ʌn'laɪklɪ] *adj* improbable; (*unexpected*) inverosímil

unlimited [ʌn'lɪmɪtɪd] *adj* ilimitado

unlisted [ʌn'lɪstɪd] (*US*) *adj* (*Tel*) que no consta en la guía

unload [ʌn'ləud] *vt* descargar

unlock [ʌn'lɔk] *vt* abrir (con llave)

unlucky [ʌn'lʌkɪ] *adj* desgraciado; (*object, number*) que da mala suerte; **to be ~** tener mala suerte

unmarried [ʌn'mærɪd] *adj* soltero

unmistak(e)able [ʌnmɪs'teɪkəbl] *adj* inconfundible

unnatural [ʌn'nætʃrəl] *adj* (*gen*) antinatural; (*manner*) afectado; (*habit*) perverso

unnecessary [ʌn'nɛsəsərɪ] *adj* innecesario, inútil

UNO ['ju:nəu] *n abbr* (= *United Nations Organization*) ONU *f*

unofficial [ʌnə'fɪʃl] *adj* no oficial; (*news*) sin confirmar

unpack [ʌn'pæk] *vi* deshacer las maletas ▷ *vt* deshacer

unpaid [ʌn'peɪd] *adj* (*bill, debt*) sin pagar, impagado; (*Comm*) pendiente; (*holiday*) sin sueldo; (*work*) sin pago, voluntario

unpleasant [ʌn'plɛznt] *adj* (*disagreeable*) desagradable; (*person, manner*) antipático

unplug [ʌn'plʌg] *vt* desenchufar, desconectar

unpopular [ʌn'pɔpjulə*] *adj* impopular, poco popular

unprecedented [ʌn'prɛsɪdəntɪd] *adj* sin precedentes

unpredictable [ʌnprɪ'dɪktəbl] *adj* imprevisible

unprotected ['ʌnprə'tɛktɪd] *adj* (*sex*) sin protección

unqualified [ʌn'kwɔlɪfaɪd] *adj* sin título, no cualificado; (*success*) total

unravel [ʌn'rævl] *vt* desenmarañar

unreal [ʌn'rɪəl] *adj* irreal; (*extraordinary*) increíble

unrealistic [ʌnrɪə'lɪstɪk] *adj* poco realista

unreasonable [ʌn'ri:znəbl] *adj* irrazonable; (*demand*) excesivo

unrelated [ʌnrɪ'leɪtɪd] *adj* sin

relación; (*family*) no emparentado

unreliable [ʌnrɪ'laɪəbl] *adj* (*person*) informal; (*machine*) poco fiable

unrest [ʌn'rɛst] *n* inquietud *f*, malestar *m*; (*Pol*) disturbios *mpl*

unroll [ʌn'rəul] *vt* desenrollar

unruly [ʌn'ru:lɪ] *adj* indisciplinado

unsafe [ʌn'seɪf] *adj* peligroso

unsatisfactory ['ʌnsætɪs'fæktərɪ] *adj* poco satisfactorio

unscrew [ʌn'skru:] *vt* destornillar

unsettled [ʌn'sɛtld] *adj* inquieto, intranquilo; (*weather*) variable

unsettling [ʌn'sɛtlɪŋ] *adj* perturbador(a), inquietante

unsightly [ʌn'saɪtlɪ] *adj* feo

unskilled [ʌn'skɪld] *adj* (*work*) no especializado; (*worker*) no cualificado

unspoiled ['ʌn'spɔɪld], **unspoilt** ['ʌn'spɔɪlt] *adj* (*place*) que no ha perdido su belleza natural

unstable [ʌn'steɪbl] *adj* inestable

unsteady [ʌn'stɛdɪ] *adj* inestable

unsuccessful [ʌnsək'sɛsful] *adj* (*attempt*) infructuoso; (*writer, proposal*) sin éxito; **to be ~** (*in attempting sth*) no tener éxito, fracasar

unsuitable [ʌn'su:təbl] *adj* inapropiado; (*time*) inoportuno

unsure [ʌn'ʃuə*] *adj* inseguro, poco seguro

untidy [ʌn'taɪdɪ] *adj* (*room*) desordenado; (*appearance*) desaliñado

untie [ʌn'taɪ] *vt* desatar

until [ən'tɪl] *prep* hasta ▷ *conj* hasta que; **~ he comes** hasta que venga; **~ now** hasta ahora; **~ then** hasta entonces

untrue [ʌn'tru:] *adj* (*statement*) falso

unused [ʌn'ju:zd] *adj* sin usar

unusual [ʌn'ju:ʒuəl] *adj* insólito, poco común; (*exceptional*) inusitado; **unusually** *adv* (*exceptionally*) excepcionalmente; **he arrived unusually early** llegó más temprano que de costumbre

unveil [ʌn'veɪl] *vt* (*statue*) descubrir

unwanted [ʌn'wɔntɪd] *adj* (*clothing*) viejo; (*pregnancy*) no deseado

unwell [ʌn'wɛl] *adj*: **to be/feel ~** estar indispuesto/sentirse mal

unwilling [ʌn'wɪlɪŋ] *adj*: **to be ~ to do sth** estar poco dispuesto a hacer algo

unwind [ʌn'waɪnd] (*irreg*) *vt* desenvolver ▷ *vi* (*relax*) relajarse

unwise [ʌn'waɪz] *adj* imprudente

unwittingly [ʌn'wɪtɪŋlɪ] *adv* inconscientemente, sin darse cuenta

unwrap [ʌn'ræp] *vt* desenvolver

unzip [ʌn'zɪp] *vt* abrir la cremallera de; (*Comput*) descomprimir

KEYWORD

up [ʌp] *prep*: **to go/be up sth** subir/estar subido en algo; **he went up the stairs/the hill** subió las escaleras/la colina; **we walked/climbed up the hill** subimos la colina; **they live further up the street** viven más arriba en la calle; **go up that road and turn left** sigue por esa calle y gira a la izquierda

▷ *adv* **1** (*upwards, higher*) más arriba; **up in the mountains** en lo alto (de la montaña); **put it a bit higher up** ponlo un poco más arriba *or* alto; **up there** ahí *or* allí arriba; **up above** en lo alto, por encima, arriba

2: **to be up** (*out of bed*) estar levantado; (*prices, level*) haber subido

3: **up to** (*as far as*) hasta; **up to now** hasta ahora *or* la fecha

4: **to be up to: it's up to you** (*depending on*) depende de ti; **he's not up to it** (*job, task etc*) no es capaz de hacerlo; **his work is not up to the required standard** su trabajo no da la talla; (*inf: be doing*): **what is he up to?** ¿que estará tramando?

▷ *n*: **ups and downs** altibajos *mpl*

up-and-coming [ʌpənd'kʌmɪŋ] *adj* prometedor(a)

upbringing ['ʌpbrɪŋɪŋ] *n* educación

f
update [ʌp'deɪt] *vt* poner al día
upfront [ʌp'frʌnt] *adj* claro, directo ▷ *adv* a las claras; (*pay*) por adelantado; **to be ~ about sth** admitir algo claramente
upgrade [ʌp'greɪd] *vt* (*house*) modernizar; (*employee*) ascender
upheaval [ʌp'hiːvl] *n* trastornos *mpl*; (*Pol*) agitación *f*
uphill [ʌp'hɪl] *adj* cuesta arriba; (*fig: task*) penoso, difícil ▷ *adv*: **to go ~** ir cuesta arriba
upholstery [ʌp'həulstərɪ] *n* tapicería
upmarket [ʌp'mɑːkɪt] *adj* (*product*) de categoría
upon [ə'pɔn] *prep* sobre
upper ['ʌpə*] *adj* superior, de arriba ▷ *n* (*of shoe: also*: **~s**) empeine *m*; **upper-class** *adj* de clase alta
upright ['ʌpraɪt] *adj* derecho; (*vertical*) vertical; (*fig*) honrado
uprising ['ʌpraɪzɪŋ] *n* sublevación *f*
uproar ['ʌprɔː*] *n* escándalo
upset [*n* 'ʌpsɛt, *vb, adj* ʌp'sɛt] *n* (*to plan etc*) revés *m*, contratiempo; (*Med*) trastorno ▷ *vt irreg* (*glass etc*) volcar; (*plan*) alterar; (*person*) molestar, disgustar ▷ *adj* molesto, disgustado; (*stomach*) revuelto
upside-down [ʌpsaɪd'daun] *adv* al revés; **to turn a place ~** (*fig*) revolverlo todo
upstairs [ʌp'stɛəz] *adv* arriba ▷ *adj* (*room*) de arriba ▷ *n* el piso superior
up-to-date ['ʌptə'deɪt] *adj* al día
uptown ['ʌptaun] (*US*) *adv* hacia las afueras ▷ *adj* exterior, de las afueras
upward ['ʌpwəd] *adj* ascendente; **upward(s)** *adv* hacia arriba; (*more than*): **upward(s) of** más de
uranium [juə'reɪnɪəm] *n* uranio
Uranus [juə'reɪnəs] *n* Urano
urban ['əːbən] *adj* urbano
urge [əːdʒ] *n* (*desire*) deseo ▷ *vt*: **to ~ sb to do sth** animar a algn a hacer algo
urgency ['əːdʒənsɪ] *n* urgencia
urgent ['əːdʒənt] *adj* urgente; (*voice*) perentorio
urinal ['juərɪnl] *n* (*building*) urinario; (*vessel*) orinal *m*
urinate ['juərɪneɪt] *vi* orinar
urine ['juərɪn] *n* orina, orines *mpl*
US *n abbr* (= *United States*) EE. UU.
us [ʌs] *pron* nos; (*after prep*) nosotros/as; *see also* **me**
USA *n abbr* (= *United States (of America)*) EE.UU.
use [*n* juːs, *vb* juːz] *n* uso, empleo; (*usefulness*) utilidad *f* ▷ *vt* usar, emplear; **she ~d to do it** (ella) solía *or* acostumbraba hacerlo; **in ~** en uso; **out of ~** en desuso; **to be of ~** servir; **it's no ~** (*pointless*) es inútil; (*not useful*) no sirve; **to be ~d to** estar acostumbrado a, acostumbrar; **use up** *vt* (*food*) consumir; (*money*) gastar; **used** [juːzd] *adj* (*car*) usado; **useful** *adj* útil; **useless** *adj* (*unusable*) inservible; (*pointless*) inútil; (*person*) inepto; **user** *n* usuario/a; **user-friendly** *adj* (*computer*) amistoso
usual ['juːʒuəl] *adj* normal, corriente; **as ~** como de costumbre; **usually** *adv* normalmente
utensil [juː'tɛnsl] *n* utensilio; **kitchen ~s** batería de cocina
utility [juː'tɪlɪtɪ] *n* utilidad *f*; (*public utility*) (empresa de) servicio público
utilize ['juːtɪlaɪz] *vt* utilizar
utmost ['ʌtməust] *adj* mayor ▷ *n*: **to do one's ~** hacer todo lo posible
utter ['ʌtə*] *adj* total, completo ▷ *vt* pronunciar, proferir; **utterly** *adv* completamente, totalmente
U-turn ['juː'təːn] *n* viraje *m* en redondo

v. *abbr* = **verse; versus**; (= *volt*) v; (= *vide*) véase

vacancy ['veɪkənsɪ] *n* (BRIT: *job*) vacante *f*; (*room*) habitación *f* libre; **"no vacancies"** "completo"

vacant ['veɪkənt] *adj* desocupado, libre; (*expression*) distraído

vacate [və'keɪt] *vt* (*house, room*) desocupar; (*job*) dejar (vacante)

vacation [və'keɪʃən] *n* vacaciones *fpl*; **vacationer** (US **vacationist**) *n* turista *m/f*

vaccination [væksɪ'neɪʃən] *n* vacunación *f*

vaccine ['væksi:n] *n* vacuna

vacuum ['vækjum] *n* vacío; **vacuum cleaner** *n* aspiradora

vagina [və'dʒaɪnə] *n* vagina

vague [veɪg] *adj* vago; (*memory*) borroso; (*ambiguous*) impreciso; (*person*: *absent-minded*) distraído; (: *evasive*): **to be ~** no decir las cosas claramente

vain [veɪn] *adj* (*conceited*) presumido; (*useless*) vano, inútil; **in ~** en vano

Valentine's Day ['væləntaɪnzdeɪ] *n* día de los enamorados

valid ['vælɪd] *adj* válido; (*ticket*) valedero; (*law*) vigente

valley ['vælɪ] *n* valle *m*

valuable ['væljuəbl] *adj* (*jewel*) de valor; (*time*) valioso; **valuables** *npl* objetos *mpl* de valor

value ['vælju:] *n* valor *m*; (*importance*) importancia ▷ *vt* (*fix price of*) tasar, valorar; (*esteem*) apreciar; **values** *npl* (*principles*) principios *mpl*

valve [vælv] *n* válvula

vampire ['væmpaɪə*] *n* vampiro

van [væn] *n* (*Aut*) furgoneta, camioneta

vandal ['vændl] *n* vándalo/a; **vandalism** *n* vandalismo; **vandalize** *vt* dañar, destruir

vanilla [və'nɪlə] *n* vainilla

vanish ['vænɪʃ] *vi* desaparecer

vanity ['vænɪtɪ] *n* vanidad *f*

vapour ['veɪpə*] (US **vapor**) *n* vapor *m*; (*on breath, window*) vaho

variable ['vɛərɪəbl] *adj* variable

variant ['vɛərɪənt] *n* variante *f*

variation [vɛərɪ'eɪʃən] *n* variación *f*

varied ['vɛərɪd] *adj* variado

variety [və'raɪətɪ] *n* (*diversity*) diversidad *f*; (*type*) variedad *f*

various ['vɛərɪəs] *adj* (*several*: *people*) varios/as; (*reasons*) diversos/as

varnish ['vɑ:nɪʃ] *n* barniz *m*; (*nail varnish*) esmalte *m* ▷ *vt* barnizar; (*nails*) pintar (con esmalte)

vary ['vɛərɪ] *vt* variar; (*change*) cambiar ▷ *vi* variar

vase [vɑ:z] *n* jarrón *m*

> Be careful not to translate **vase** by the Spanish word *vaso*.

Vaseline® ['væsɪli:n] *n* vaselina®

vast [vɑ:st] *adj* enorme

VAT [væt] (BRIT) *n abbr* (= *value added tax*) IVA *m*

vault [vɔ:lt] *n* (*of roof*) bóveda; (*tomb*) panteón *m*; (*in bank*) cámara acorazada ▷ *vt* (*also*: **~ over**) saltar (por encima de)

VCR *n abbr* = **video cassette recorder**
VDU *n abbr* (= *visual display unit*) UPV *f*
veal [vi:l] *n* ternera
veer [vɪə*] *vi* (*vehicle*) virar; (*wind*) girar
vegan ['vi:gən] *n* vegetariano/a estricto/a, vegetaliano/a
vegetable ['vɛdʒtəbl] *n* (*Bot*) vegetal *m*; (*edible plant*) legumbre *f*, hortaliza ▷ *adj* vegetal
vegetarian [vɛdʒɪ'tɛərɪən] *adj*, *n* vegetariano/a *m/f*
vegetation [vɛdʒɪ'teɪʃən] *n* vegetación *f*
vehicle ['vi:ɪkl] *n* vehículo; (*fig*) medio
veil [veɪl] *n* velo ▷ *vt* velar
vein [veɪn] *n* vena; (*of ore etc*) veta
Velcro® ['vɛlkrəu] *n* velcro® *m*
velvet ['vɛlvɪt] *n* terciopelo
vending machine ['vɛndɪŋ-] *n* distribuidor *m* automático
vendor ['vɛndə*] *n* vendedor(a) *m/f*; **street ~** vendedor(a) *m/f* callejero/a
vengeance ['vɛndʒəns] *n* venganza; **with a ~** (*fig*) con creces
venison ['vɛnɪsn] *n* carne *f* de venado
venom ['vɛnəm] *n* veneno; (*bitterness*) odio
vent [vɛnt] *n* (*in jacket*) respiradero; (*in wall*) rejilla (de ventilación) ▷ *vt* (*fig: feelings*) desahogar
ventilation [vɛntɪ'leɪʃən] *n* ventilación *f*
venture ['vɛntʃə*] *n* empresa ▷ *vt* (*opinion*) ofrecer ▷ *vi* arriesgarse, lanzarse; **business ~** empresa comercial
venue ['vɛnju:] *n* lugar *m*
Venus ['vi:nəs] *n* Venus *m*
verb [və:b] *n* verbo; **verbal** *adj* verbal
verdict ['və:dɪkt] *n* veredicto, fallo; (*fig*) opinión *f*, juicio
verge [və:dʒ] (BRIT) *n* borde *m*; **"soft ~s"** (*Aut*) "arcén *m* no asfaltado"; **to be on the ~ of doing sth** estar a punto de hacer algo
verify ['vɛrɪfaɪ] *vt* comprobar, verificar
versatile ['və:sətaɪl] *adj* (*person*) polifacético; (*machine, tool etc*) versátil
verse [və:s] *n* poesía; (*stanza*) estrofa; (*in bible*) versículo
version ['və:ʃən] *n* versión *f*
versus ['və:səs] *prep* contra
vertical ['və:tɪkl] *adj* vertical
very ['vɛrɪ] *adv* muy ▷ *adj*: **the ~ book which** el mismo libro que; **the ~ last** el último de todos; **at the ~ least** al menos; **~ much** muchísimo
vessel ['vɛsl] *n* (*ship*) barco; (*container*) vasija; *see* **blood**
vest [vɛst] *n* (BRIT) camiseta; (US: *waistcoat*) chaleco
vet [vɛt] *vt* (*candidate*) investigar ▷ *n abbr* (BRIT) = **veterinary surgeon**
veteran ['vɛtərn] *n* excombatiente *mf*, veterano/a
veterinary surgeon ['vɛtrɪnərɪ-] (US **veterinarian**) *n* veterinario/a *m/f*
veto ['vi:təu] (*pl* **~es**) *n* veto ▷ *vt* prohibir, poner el veto a
via ['vaɪə] *prep* por, por medio de
viable ['vaɪəbl] *adj* viable
vibrate [vaɪ'breɪt] *vi* vibrar
vibration [vaɪ'breɪʃən] *n* vibración *f*
vicar ['vɪkə*] *n* párroco (de la Iglesia Anglicana)
vice [vaɪs] *n* (*evil*) vicio; (*Tech*) torno de banco; **vice-chairman** (*irreg*) *n* vicepresidente *m*
vice versa ['vaɪsɪ'və:sə] *adv* viceversa
vicinity [vɪ'sɪnɪtɪ] *n*: **in the ~ (of)** cercano (a)
vicious ['vɪʃəs] *adj* (*attack*) violento; (*words*) cruel; (*horse, dog*) resabido
victim ['vɪktɪm] *n* víctima
victor ['vɪktə*] *n* vencedor(a) *m/f*
Victorian [vɪk'tɔ:rɪən] *adj* victoriano
victorious [vɪk'tɔ:rɪəs] *adj* vencedor(a)
victory ['vɪktərɪ] *n* victoria
video ['vɪdɪəu] *n* vídeo (SP), video (LAM); **video call** *n* videollamada; **video camera** *n* videocámara, cámara de vídeo; **video (cassette) recorder** *n* vídeo (SP), video

(LAM); **video game** *n* videojuego; **videophone** *n* videoteléfono; **video shop** *n* videoclub *m*; **video tape** *n* cinta de vídeo

vie [vaɪ] *vi*: **to ~ (with sb for sth)** competir (con algn por algo)

Vienna [vɪ'ɛnə] *n* Viena

Vietnam [vjɛt'næm] *n* Vietnam *m*; **Vietnamese** [-nə'mi:z] *n inv, adj* vietnamita *mf*

view [vju:] *n* vista; (*outlook*) perspectiva; (*opinion*) opinión *f*, criterio ▷ *vt* (*look at*) mirar; (*fig*) considerar; **on ~** (*in museum etc*) expuesto; **in full ~ (of)** en plena vista (de); **in ~ of the weather/the fact that** en vista del tiempo/del hecho de que; **in my ~** en mi opinión; **viewer** *n* espectador(a) *m/f*; (*TV*) telespectador(a) *m/f*; **viewpoint** *n* (*attitude*) punto de vista; (*place*) mirador *m*

vigilant ['vɪdʒɪlənt] *adj* vigilante

vigorous ['vɪgərəs] *adj* enérgico, vigoroso

vile [vaɪl] *adj* vil, infame; (*smell*) asqueroso; (*temper*) endemoniado

villa ['vɪlə] *n* (*country house*) casa de campo; (*suburban house*) chalet *m*

village ['vɪlɪdʒ] *n* aldea; **villager** *n* aldeano/a

villain ['vɪlən] *n* (*scoundrel*) malvado/a; (*in novel*) malo; (BRIT: *criminal*) maleante *mf*

vinaigrette [vɪneɪ'grɛt] *n* vinagreta

vine [vaɪn] *n* vid *f*

vinegar ['vɪnɪgə*] *n* vinagre *m*

vineyard ['vɪnjɑ:d] *n* viña, viñedo

vintage ['vɪntɪdʒ] *n* (*year*) vendimia, cosecha ▷ *cpd* de época

vinyl ['vaɪnl] *n* vinilo

viola [vɪ'əulə] *n* (*Mus*) viola

violate ['vaɪəleɪt] *vt* violar

violation [vaɪə'leɪʃən] *n* violación *f*; **in ~ of sth** en violación de algo

violence ['vaɪələns] *n* violencia

violent ['vaɪələnt] *adj* violento; (*intense*) intenso

violet ['vaɪələt] *adj* violado, violeta ▷ *n* (*plant*) violeta

violin [vaɪə'lɪn] *n* violín *m*

VIP *n abbr* (= *very important person*) VIP *m*

virgin ['və:dʒɪn] *n* virgen *f*

Virgo ['və:gəu] *n* Virgo

virtual ['və:tjuəl] *adj* virtual; **virtually** *adv* prácticamente; **virtual reality** *n* (*Comput*) mundo *or* realidad *f* virtual

virtue ['və:tju:] *n* virtud *f*; (*advantage*) ventaja; **by ~ of** en virtud de

virus ['vaɪərəs] *n* (*also Comput*) virus *m inv*

visa ['vɪ:zə] *n* visado (SP), visa (LAM)

vise [vaɪs] (US) *n* (*Tech*) = **vice**

visibility [vɪzɪ'bɪlɪtɪ] *n* visibilidad *f*

visible ['vɪzəbl] *adj* visible

vision ['vɪʒən] *n* (*sight*) vista; (*foresight, in dream*) visión *f*

visit ['vɪzɪt] *n* visita ▷ *vt* (*person* (US: *also*: **~ with**) visitar, hacer una visita a; (*place*) ir a, (ir a) conocer; **visiting hours** *npl* (*in hospital etc*) horas *fpl* de visita; **visitor** *n* (*in museum*) visitante *mf*; (*invited to house*) visita; (*tourist*) turista *mf*; **visitor centre** (US **visitor center**) *n* centro *m* de información

visual ['vɪzjuəl] *adj* visual; **visualize** *vt* imaginarse

vital ['vaɪtl] *adj* (*essential*) esencial, imprescindible; (*dynamic*) dinámico; (*organ*) vital

vitality [vaɪ'tælɪtɪ] *n* energía, vitalidad *f*

vitamin ['vɪtəmɪn] *n* vitamina

vivid ['vɪvɪd] *adj* (*account*) gráfico; (*light*) intenso; (*imagination, memory*) vivo

V-neck ['vi:nɛk] *n* cuello de pico

vocabulary [vəu'kæbjulərɪ] *n* vocabulario

vocal ['vəukl] *adj* vocal; (*articulate*) elocuente

vocational [vəu'keɪʃənl] *adj* profesional

vodka ['vɔdkə] *n* vodka *m*

vogue [vəug] *n*: **in ~** en boga

voice [vɔɪs] *n* voz *f* ▷ *vt* expresar; **voice mail** *n* fonobuzón *m*
void [vɔɪd] *n* vacío; (*hole*) hueco ▷ *adj* (*invalid*) nulo, inválido; (*empty*): **~ of** carente *or* desprovisto de
volatile ['vɔlətaɪl] *adj* (*situation*) inestable; (*person*) voluble; (*liquid*) volátil
volcano [vɔl'keɪnəu] (*pl* **~es**) *n* volcán *m*
volleyball ['vɔlɪbɔːl] *n* vol(e)ibol *m*
volt [vəult] *n* voltio; **voltage** *n* voltaje *m*
volume ['vɔljuːm] *n* (*gen*) volumen *m*; (*book*) tomo
voluntarily ['vɔləntrɪlɪ] *adv* libremente, voluntariamente
voluntary ['vɔləntərɪ] *adj* voluntario
volunteer [vɔlən'tɪə*] *n* voluntario/a ▷ *vt* (*information*) ofrecer ▷ *vi* ofrecerse (de voluntario); **to ~ to do** ofrecerse a hacer
vomit ['vɔmɪt] *n* vómito ▷ *vt, vi* vomitar
vote [vəut] *n* voto; (*votes cast*) votación *f*; (*right to vote*) derecho de votar; (*franchise*) sufragio ▷ *vt* (*chairman*) elegir; (*propose*): **to ~ that** proponer que ▷ *vi* votar, ir a votar; **~ of thanks** voto de gracias; **voter** *n* votante *mf*; **voting** *n* votación *f*
voucher ['vautʃə*] *n* (*for meal, petrol*) vale *m*
vow [vau] *n* voto ▷ *vt*: **to ~ to do/that** jurar hacer/que
vowel ['vauəl] *n* vocal *f*
voyage ['vɔɪɪdʒ] *n* viaje *m*
vulgar ['vʌlgə*] *adj* (*rude*) ordinario, grosero; (*in bad taste*) de mal gusto
vulnerable ['vʌlnərəbl] *adj* vulnerable
vulture ['vʌltʃə*] *n* buitre *m*

waddle ['wɔdl] *vi* anadear
wade [weɪd] *vi*: **to ~ through** (*water*) vadear; (*fig: book*) leer con dificultad
wafer ['weɪfə*] *n* galleta, barquillo
waffle ['wɔfl] *n* (*Culin*) gofre *m* ▷ *vi* dar el rollo
wag [wæg] *vt* menear, agitar ▷ *vi* moverse, menearse
wage [weɪdʒ] *n* (*also*: **~s**) sueldo, salario ▷ *vt*: **to ~ war** hacer la guerra
wag(g)on ['wægən] *n* (*horse-drawn*) carro; (BRIT *Rail*) vagón *m*
wail [weɪl] *n* gemido ▷ *vi* gemir
waist [weɪst] *n* cintura, talle *m*; **waistcoat** (BRIT) *n* chaleco
wait [weɪt] *n* (*interval*) pausa ▷ *vi* esperar; **to lie in ~ for** acechar a; **I can't ~ to** (*fig*) estoy deseando; **to ~ for** esperar (a); **wait on** *vt fus* servir a; **waiter** *n* camarero; **waiting list** *n* lista de espera; **waiting room** *n* sala de espera; **waitress** ['weɪtrɪs] *n* camarera
waive [weɪv] *vt* suspender
wake [weɪk] (*pt* **woke** *or* **~d**, *pp* **woken**

or **~d**) *vt* (*also*: **~ up**) despertar ▷ *vi* (*also*: **~ up**) despertarse ▷ *n* (*for dead person*) vela, velatorio; (*Naut*) estela

Wales [weɪlz] *n* País *m* de Gales; **the Prince of ~** el príncipe de Gales

walk [wɔːk] *n* (*stroll*) paseo; (*hike*) excursión *f* a pie, caminata; (*gait*) paso, andar *m*; (*in park etc*) paseo, alameda ▷ *vi* andar, caminar; (*for pleasure, exercise*) pasear ▷ *vt* (*distance*) recorrer a pie, andar; (*dog*) pasear; **10 minutes' ~ from here** a 10 minutos de aquí andando; **people from all ~s of life** gente de todas las esferas; **walk out** *vi* (*audience*) salir; (*workers*) declararse en huelga; **walker** *n* (*person*) paseante *mf*, caminante *mf*; **walkie-talkie** ['wɔːkɪ'tɔːkɪ] *n* walkie-talkie *m*; **walking** *n* el andar; **walking shoes** *npl* zapatos *mpl* para andar; **walking stick** *n* bastón *m*; **Walkman®** *n* Walkman® *m*; **walkway** *n* paseo

wall [wɔːl] *n* pared *f*; (*exterior*) muro; (*city wall etc*) muralla

wallet ['wɔlɪt] *n* cartera, billetera

wallpaper ['wɔːlpeɪpə*] *n* papel *m* pintado ▷ *vt* empapelar

walnut ['wɔːlnʌt] *n* nuez *f*; (*tree*) nogal *m*

walrus ['wɔːlrəs] (*pl* **~** *or* **~es**) *n* morsa

waltz [wɔːlts] *n* vals *m* ▷ *vi* bailar el vals

wand [wɔnd] *n* (*also*: **magic ~**) varita (mágica)

wander ['wɔndə*] *vi* (*person*) vagar; deambular; (*thoughts*) divagar ▷ *vt* recorrer, vagar por

want [wɔnt] *vt* querer, desear; (*need*) necesitar ▷ *n*: **for ~ of** por falta de; **wanted** *adj* (*criminal*) buscado; **"wanted"** (*in advertisements*) "se busca"

war [wɔː*] *n* guerra; **to make ~ (on)** declarar la guerra (a)

ward [wɔːd] *n* (*in hospital*) sala; (*Pol*) distrito electoral; (*Law*: *child*: *also*: **~ of court**) pupilo/a

warden ['wɔːdn] *n* (BRIT: *of institution*) director(a) *m/f*; (*of park, game reserve*) guardián/ana *m/f*; (BRIT: *also*: **traffic ~**) guardia *mf*

wardrobe ['wɔːdrəub] *n* armario, ropero; (*clothes*) vestuario

warehouse ['wɛəhaus] *n* almacén *m*, depósito

warfare ['wɔːfɛə*] *n* guerra

warhead ['wɔːhɛd] *n* cabeza armada

warm [wɔːm] *adj* caliente; (*thanks*) efusivo; (*clothes etc*) abrigado; (*welcome, day*) caluroso; **it's ~** hace calor; **I'm ~** tengo calor; **warm up** *vi* (*room*) calentarse; (*person*) entrar en calor; (*athlete*) hacer ejercicios de calentamiento ▷ *vt* calentar; **warmly** *adv* afectuosamente; **warmth** *n* calor *m*

warn [wɔːn] *vt* avisar, advertir; **warning** *n* aviso, advertencia; **warning light** *n* luz *f* de advertencia

warrant ['wɔrnt] *n* autorización *f*; (*Law*: *to arrest*) orden *f* de detención; (: *to search*) mandamiento de registro

warranty ['wɔrəntɪ] *n* garantía

warrior ['wɔrɪə*] *n* guerrero/a

Warsaw ['wɔːsɔː] *n* Varsovia

warship ['wɔːʃɪp] *n* buque *m* *or* barco de guerra

wart [wɔːt] *n* verruga

wartime ['wɔːtaɪm] *n*: **in ~** en tiempos de guerra, en la guerra

wary ['wɛərɪ] *adj* cauteloso

was [wɔz] *pt of* **be**

wash [wɔʃ] *vt* lavar ▷ *vi* lavarse; (*sea etc*): **to ~ against/over sth** llegar hasta/cubrir algo ▷ *n* (*clothes etc*) lavado; (*of ship*) estela; **to have a ~** lavarse; **wash up** *vi* (BRIT) fregar los platos; (US) lavarse; **washbasin** (US) *n* lavabo; **wash cloth** (US) *n* manopla; **washer** *n* (*Tech*) arandela; **washing** *n* (*dirty*) ropa sucia; (*clean*) colada; **washing line** *n* cuerda de (colgar) la ropa; **washing machine** *n* lavadora; **washing powder** (BRIT) *n* detergente *m* (en polvo)

Washington ['wɔʃɪŋtən] *n* Washington *m*

wash: washing-up (BRIT) *n* fregado, platos *mpl* (para fregar); **washing-up liquid** (BRIT) *n* líquido lavavajillas; **washroom** (US) *n* servicios *mpl*
wasn't ['wɔznt] = **was not**
wasp [wɔsp] *n* avispa
waste [weɪst] *n* derroche *m*, despilfarro; (*of time*) pérdida; (*food*) sobras *fpl*; (*rubbish*) basura, desperdicios *mpl* ▷ *adj* (*material*) de desecho; (*left over*) sobrante; (*land*) baldío, descampado ▷ *vt* malgastar, derrochar; (*time*) perder; (*opportunity*) desperdiciar; **waste ground** (BRIT) *n* terreno baldío; **wastepaper basket** *n* papelera
watch [wɔtʃ] *n* (*also*: **wrist ~**) reloj *m*; (*Mil: group of guards*) centinela *m*; (*act*) vigilancia; (*Naut: spell of duty*) guardia ▷ *vt* (*look at*) mirar, observar; (*: match, programme*) ver; (*spy on, guard*) vigilar; (*be careful of*) cuidarse de, tener cuidado de ▷ *vi* ver, mirar; (*keep guard*) montar guardia; **watch out** *vi* cuidarse, tener cuidado; **watchdog** *n* perro guardián; (*fig*) *persona u organismo encargado de asegurarse de que las empresasactúan dentro de la legalidad*; **watch strap** *n* pulsera (de reloj)
water ['wɔːtə*] *n* agua ▷ *vt* (*plant*) regar ▷ *vi* (*eyes*) llorar; (*mouth*) hacerse la boca agua; **water down** *vt* (*milk etc*) aguar; (*fig: story*) dulcificar, diluir; **watercolour** (US **watercolor**) *n* acuarela; **watercress** *n* berro; **waterfall** *n* cascada, salto de agua; **watering can** *n* regadera; **watermelon** *n* sandía; **waterproof** *adj* impermeable; **water-skiing** *n* esquí *m* acuático
watt [wɔt] *n* vatio
wave [weɪv] *n* (*of hand*) señal *f* con la mano; (*on water*) ola; (*Radio, in hair*) onda; (*fig*) oleada ▷ *vi* agitar la mano; (*flag etc*) ondear ▷ *vt* (*handkerchief, gun*) agitar; **wavelength** *n* longitud *f* de onda
waver ['weɪvə*] *vi* (*voice, love etc*) flaquear; (*person*) vacilar
wavy ['weɪvɪ] *adj* ondulado
wax [wæks] *n* cera ▷ *vt* encerar ▷ *vi* (*moon*) crecer
way [weɪ] *n* camino; (*distance*) trayecto, recorrido; (*direction*) dirección *f*, sentido; (*manner*) modo, manera; (*habit*) costumbre *f*; **which ~? – this ~** ¿por dónde? *or* ¿en qué dirección? – por aquí; **on the ~** (*en route*) en (el) camino; **to be on one's ~** estar en camino; **to be in the ~** bloquear el camino; (*fig*) estorbar; **to go out of one's ~ to do sth** desvivirse por hacer algo; **under ~** en marcha; **to lose one's ~** extraviarse; **in a ~** en cierto modo *or* sentido; **no ~!** (*inf*) ¡de eso nada!; **by the ~ ...** a propósito ...; **"~ in"** (BRIT) "entrada"; **"~ out"** (BRIT) "salida"; **the ~ back** el camino de vuelta; **"give ~"** (BRIT *Aut*) "ceda el paso"
W.C. *n* (BRIT) wáter *m*
we [wiː] *pl pron* nosotros/as
weak [wiːk] *adj* débil, flojo; (*tea etc*) claro; **weaken** *vi* debilitarse; (*give way*) ceder ▷ *vt* debilitar; **weakness** *n* debilidad *f*; (*fault*) punto débil; **to have a weakness for** tener debilidad por
wealth [wɛlθ] *n* riqueza; (*of details*) abundancia; **wealthy** *adj* rico
weapon ['wɛpən] *n* arma; **~s of mass destruction** armas de destrucción masiva
wear [wɛə*] (*pt* **wore**, *pp* **worn**) *n* (*use*) uso; (*deterioration through use*) desgaste *m* ▷ *vt* (*clothes*) llevar; (*shoes*) calzar; (*damage: through use*) gastar, usar ▷ *vi* (*last*) durar; (*rub through etc*) desgastarse; **evening ~** ropa de etiqueta; **sports~/baby~** ropa de deportes/de niños; **wear off** *vi* (*pain etc*) pasar, desaparecer; **wear out** *vt* desgastar; (*person, strength*) agotar
weary ['wɪərɪ] *adj* cansado; (*dispirited*) abatido ▷ *vi*: **to ~ of** cansarse de
weasel ['wiːzl] *n* (*Zool*) comadreja
weather ['wɛðə*] *n* tiempo ▷ *vt* (*storm, crisis*) hacer frente a; **under**

the ~ (*fig: ill*) indispuesto, pachucho; **weather forecast** *n* boletín *m* meteorológico

weave [wi:v] (*pt* **wove**, *pp* **woven**) *vt* (*cloth*) tejer; (*fig*) entretejer

web [wɛb] *n* (*of spider*) telaraña; (*on duck's foot*) membrana; (*network*) red *f*; **the (World Wide) W~** la Red; **web address** *n* dirección *f* de Internet; **webcam** *n* webcam *f*; **web page** *n* (página) web *m or f*; **website** *n* sitio web

Wed. *abbr* (= *Wednesday*) miérc

wed [wɛd] (*pt, pp* **~ded**) *vt* casar ▷ *vi* casarse

we'd [wi:d] = **we had; we would**

wedding ['wɛdɪŋ] *n* boda, casamiento; **silver/golden ~ (anniversary)** bodas *fpl* de plata/de oro; **wedding anniversary** *n* aniversario de boda; **wedding day** *n* día *m* de la boda; **wedding dress** *n* traje *m* de novia; **wedding ring** *n* alianza

wedge [wɛdʒ] *n* (*of wood etc*) cuña; (*of cake*) trozo ▷ *vt* acuñar; (*push*) apretar

Wednesday ['wɛdnzdɪ] *n* miércoles *m inv*

wee [wi:] (SCOTTISH) *adj* pequeñito

weed [wi:d] *n* mala hierba, maleza ▷ *vt* escardar, desherbar; **weedkiller** *n* herbicida *m*

week [wi:k] *n* semana; **a ~ today/on Friday** de hoy/del viernes en ocho días; **weekday** *n* día *m* laborable; **weekend** *n* fin *m* de semana; **weekly** *adv* semanalmente, cada semana ▷ *adj* semanal ▷ *n* semanario

weep [wi:p] (*pt, pp* **wept**) *vi, vt* llorar

weigh [weɪ] *vt, vi* pesar; **to ~ anchor** levar anclas; **weigh up** *vt* sopesar

weight [weɪt] *n* peso; (*metal weight*) pesa; **to lose/put on ~** adelgazar/engordar; **weightlifting** *n* levantamiento de pesas

weir [wɪə*] *n* presa

weird [wɪəd] *adj* raro, extraño

welcome ['wɛlkəm] *adj* bienvenido ▷ *n* bienvenida ▷ *vt* dar la bienvenida a; (*be glad of*) alegrarse de; **thank you – you're ~** gracias – de nada

weld [wɛld] *n* soldadura ▷ *vt* soldar

welfare ['wɛlfɛə*] *n* bienestar *m*; (*social aid*) asistencia social; **welfare state** *n* estado del bienestar

well [wɛl] *n* fuente *f*, pozo ▷ *adv* bien ▷ *adj*: **to be ~** estar bien (de salud) ▷ *excl* ¡vaya!, ¡bueno!; **as ~** también; **as ~ as** además de; **~ done!** ¡bien hecho!; **get ~ soon!** ¡que te mejores pronto!; **to do ~** (*business*) ir bien; (*person*) tener éxito

we'll [wi:l] = **we will; we shall**

well: well-behaved *adj* bueno; **well-built** *adj* (*person*) fornido; **well-dressed** *adj* bien vestido

wellies ['welɪz] (*inf*) *npl* (BRIT) botas de goma

well: well-known *adj* (*person*) conocido; **well-off** *adj* acomodado; **well-paid** [wel'peɪd] *adj* bien pagado, bien retribuido

Welsh [wɛlʃ] *adj* galés/esa ▷ *n* (*Ling*) galés *m*; **Welshman** (*irreg*) *n* galés *m*; **Welshwoman** (*irreg*) *n* galesa

went [wɛnt] *pt of* **go**

wept [wɛpt] *pt, pp of* **weep**

were [wə:*] *pt of* **be**

we're [wɪə*] = **we are**

weren't [wə:nt] = **were not**

west [wɛst] *n* oeste *m* ▷ *adj* occidental, del oeste ▷ *adv* al *or* hacia el oeste; **the W~** el Oeste, el Occidente; **westbound** ['wɛstbaund] *adj* (*traffic, carriageway*) con rumbo al oeste; **western** *adj* occidental ▷ *n* (*Cinema*) película del oeste; **West Indian** *adj, n* antillano/a *m/f*

wet [wɛt] *adj* (*damp*) húmedo; (*soaked*): **~ through** mojado; (*rainy*) lluvioso ▷ *n* (BRIT: *Pol*) conservador(a) *m/f* moderado/a; **to get ~** mojarse; **"~ paint"** "recién pintado"; **wetsuit** *n* traje *m* térmico

we've [wi:v] = **we have**

whack [wæk] *vt* dar un buen golpe a

whale [weɪl] *n* (*Zool*) ballena

wharf [wɔːf] (*pl* **wharves**) *n* muelle *m*

KEYWORD

what [wɔt] *adj* **1** (*in direct/indirect questions*) qué; **what size is he?** ¿qué talla usa?; **what colour/shape is it?** ¿de qué color/forma es?
2 (*in exclamations*): **what a mess!** ¡qué desastre!; **what a fool I am!** ¡qué tonto soy!
▷ *pron* **1** (*interrogative*) qué; **what are you doing?** ¿qué haces *or* estás haciendo?; **what is happening?** ¿qué pasa *or* está pasando?; **what is it called?** ¿cómo se llama?; **what about me?** ¿y yo qué?; **what about doing ...?** ¿qué tal si hacemos ...?
2 (*relative*) lo que; **I saw what you did/was on the table** vi lo que hiciste/había en la mesa
▷ *excl* (*disbelieving*) ¡cómo!; **what, no coffee!** ¡que no hay café!

whatever [wɔt'ɛvə*] *adj*: **~ book you choose** cualquier libro que elijas ▷ *pron*: **do ~ is necessary** haga lo que sea necesario; **~ happens** pase lo que pase; **no reason ~** *or* **whatsoever** ninguna razón sea la que sea; **nothing ~** nada en absoluto
whatsoever [wɔtsəu'ɛvə*] *adj see* **whatever**
wheat [wiːt] *n* trigo
wheel [wiːl] *n* rueda; (*Aut*: *also*: **steering ~**) volante *m*; (*Naut*) timón *m* ▷ *vt* (*pram etc*) empujar ▷ *vi* (*also*: **~ round**) dar la vuelta, girar; **wheelbarrow** *n* carretilla; **wheelchair** *n* silla de ruedas; **wheel clamp** *n* (*Aut*) cepo
wheeze [wiːz] *vi* resollar

KEYWORD

when [wɛn] *adv* cuando; **when did it happen?** ¿cuándo ocurrió?; **I know when it happened** sé cuándo ocurrió
▷ *conj* **1** (*at, during, after the time that*) cuando; **be careful when you cross the road** ten cuidado al cruzar la calle; **that was when I needed you** fue entonces que te necesité
2 (*on, at which*): **on the day when I met him** el día en qué le conocí
3 (*whereas*) cuando

whenever [wɛn'ɛvə*] *conj* cuando; (*every time that*) cada vez que ▷ *adv* cuando sea
where [wɛə*] *adv* dónde ▷ *conj* donde; **this is ~** aquí es donde; **whereabouts** *adv* dónde ▷ *n*: **nobody knows his whereabouts** nadie conoce su paradero; **whereas** *conj* visto que, mientras; **whereby** *pron* por lo cual; **wherever** *conj* dondequiera que; (*interrogative*) dónde
whether ['wɛðə*] *conj* si; **I don't know ~ to accept or not** no sé si aceptar o no; **~ you go or not** vayas o no vayas

KEYWORD

which [wɪtʃ] *adj* **1** (*interrogative*: *direct, indirect*) qué; **which picture(s) do you want?** ¿qué cuadro(s) quieres?; **which one?** ¿cuál?
2 in which case en cuyo caso; **we got there at 8 pm, by which time the cinema was full** llegamos allí a las 8, cuando el cine estaba lleno
▷ *pron* **1** (*interrogative*) cual; **I don't mind which** el/la que sea
2 (*relative*: *replacing noun*) que; (: *replacing clause*) lo que; (: *after preposition*) (el(la)) que *etc* el/la cual *etc*; **the apple which you ate/which is on the table** la manzana que comiste/que está en la mesa; **the chair on which you are sitting** la silla en la que estás sentado; **he said he knew, which is true/I feared** dijo que lo sabía, lo cual *or* lo

que es cierto/me temía

whichever [wɪtʃ'ɛvə*] *adj*: **take ~ book you prefer** coja (*SP*) el libro que prefiera; **~ book you take** cualquier libro que coja
while [waɪl] *n* rato, momento ▷ *conj* mientras; (*although*) aunque; **for a ~** durante algún tiempo
whilst [waɪlst] *conj* = **while**
whim [wɪm] *n* capricho
whine [waɪn] *n* (*of pain*) gemido; (*of engine*) zumbido; (*of siren*) aullido ▷ *vi* gemir; zumbar; (*fig: complain*) gimotear
whip [wɪp] *n* látigo; (*Pol: person*) *encargado de la disciplina partidaria en el parlamento* ▷ *vt* azotar; (*Culin*) batir; (*move quickly*): **to ~ sth out/off** sacar/quitar algo de un tirón; **whipped cream** *n* nata *or* crema montada
whirl [wəːl] *vt* hacer girar, dar vueltas a ▷ *vi* girar, dar vueltas; (*leaves etc*) arremolinarse
whisk [wɪsk] *n* (*Culin*) batidor *m* ▷ *vt* (*Culin*) batir; **to ~ sb away** *or* **off** llevar volando a algn
whiskers ['wɪskəz] *npl* (*of animal*) bigotes *mpl*; (*of man*) patillas *fpl*
whiskey ['wɪskɪ] (*US, IRELAND*) *n* = **whisky**
whisky ['wɪskɪ] *n* whisky *m*
whisper ['wɪspə*] *n* susurro ▷ *vi, vt* susurrar
whistle ['wɪsl] *n* (*sound*) silbido; (*object*) silbato ▷ *vi* silbar
white [waɪt] *adj* blanco; (*pale*) pálido ▷ *n* blanco; (*of egg*) clara; **whiteboard** *n* pizarra blanca; **interactive whiteboard** pizarra interactiva; **White House** (*US*) *n* Casa Blanca; **whitewash** *n* (*paint*) jalbegue *m*, cal *f* ▷ *vt* blanquear
whiting ['waɪtɪŋ] *n inv* (*fish*) pescadilla
Whitsun ['wɪtsn] *n* pentecostés *m*
whittle ['wɪtl] *vt*: **to ~ away, ~ down** ir reduciendo
whizz [wɪz] *vi*: **to ~ past** *or* **by** pasar a toda velocidad

KEYWORD

who [huː] *pron* **1** (*interrogative*) quién; **who is it?, who's there?** ¿quién es?; **who are you looking for?** ¿a quién buscas?; **I told her who I was** le dije quién era yo
2 (*relative*) que; **the man/woman who spoke to me** el hombre/la mujer que habló conmigo; **those who can swim** los que saben *or* sepan nadar

whoever [huː'ɛvə*] *pron*: **~ finds it** cualquiera *or* quienquiera que lo encuentre; **ask ~ you like** pregunta a quien quieras; **~ he marries** no importa con quién se case
whole [həul] *adj* (*entire*) todo, entero; (*not broken*) intacto ▷ *n* todo; (*all*): **the ~ of the town** toda la ciudad, la ciudad entera ▷ *n* (*total*) total *m*; (*sum*) conjunto; **on the ~, as a ~** en general; **wholefood(s)** *n(pl)* alimento(s) *m(pl)* integral(es); **wholeheartedly** [həul'hɑːtɪdlɪ] *adv* con entusiasmo; **wholemeal** *adj* integral; **wholesale** *n* venta al por mayor ▷ *adj* al por mayor; (*fig: destruction*) sistemático; **wholewheat** *adj* = **wholemeal**; **wholly** *adv* totalmente, enteramente

KEYWORD

whom [huːm] *pron* **1** (*interrogative*): **whom did you see?** ¿a quién viste?; **to whom did you give it?** ¿a quién se lo diste?; **tell me from whom you received it** dígame de quién lo recibió
2 (*relative*) que; **to whom** a quien(es); **of whom** de quien(es), del/de la que *etc*; **the man whom I saw/to whom I wrote** el hombre que vi/a quien escribí; **the lady about/with whom I was talking** la señora de (la) que/con

quien *or* (la) que hablaba

whore [hɔː*] (*inf, pej*) *n* puta

KEYWORD

whose [huːz] *adj* **1** (*possessive: interrogative*): **whose book is this?, whose is this book?** ¿de quién es este libro?; **whose pencil have you taken?** ¿de quién es el lápiz que has cogido?; **whose daughter are you?** ¿de quién eres hija?
2 (*possessive: relative*) cuyo/a, *pl* cuyos/as; **the man whose son you rescued** el hombre cuyo hijo rescataste; **those whose passports I have** aquellas personas cuyos pasaportes tengo; **the woman whose car was stolen** la mujer a quien le robaron el coche
▷ *pron* de quién; **whose is this?** ¿de quién es esto?; **I know whose it is** sé de quién es

KEYWORD

why [waɪ] *adv* por qué; **why not?** ¿por qué no?; **why not do it now?** ¿por qué no lo haces (*or* hacemos *etc*) ahora?
▷ *conj*: **I wonder why he said that** me pregunto por qué dijo eso; **that's not why I'm here** no es por eso (por lo) que estoy aquí; **the reason why** la razón por la que
▷ *excl* (*expressing surprise, shock, annoyance*) ¡hombre!, ¡vaya!; (*explaining*): **why, it's you!** ¡hombre, eres tú!; **why, that's impossible** ¡pero sí eso es imposible!

wicked ['wɪkɪd] *adj* malvado, cruel
wicket ['wɪkɪt] *n* (*Cricket: stumps*) palos *mpl*; (*: grass area*) terreno de juego
wide [waɪd] *adj* ancho; (*area, knowledge*) vasto, grande; (*choice*) amplio ▷ *adv*: **to open ~** abrir de par en par; **to shoot ~** errar el tiro; **widely** *adv* (*travelled*) mucho; (*spaced*) muy; **it is widely believed/known that ...** mucha gente piensa/sabe que ...; **widen** *vt* ensanchar; (*experience*) ampliar ▷ *vi* ensancharse; **wide open** *adj* abierto de par en par; **widespread** *adj* extendido, general
widow ['wɪdəu] *n* viuda; **widower** *n* viudo
width [wɪdθ] *n* anchura; (*of cloth*) ancho
wield [wiːld] *vt* (*sword*) blandir; (*power*) ejercer
wife [waɪf] (*pl* **wives**) *n* mujer *f*, esposa
wig [wɪg] *n* peluca
wild [waɪld] *adj* (*animal*) salvaje; (*plant*) silvestre; (*person*) furioso, violento; (*idea*) descabellado; (*rough: sea*) bravo; (*: land*) agreste; (*: weather*) muy revuelto; **wilderness** ['wɪldənɪs] *n* desierto; **wildlife** *n* fauna; **wildly** *adv* (*behave*) locamente; (*lash out*) a diestro y siniestro; (*guess*) a lo loco; (*happy*) a más no poder

KEYWORD

will [wɪl] *aux vb* **1** (*forming future tense*): **I will finish it tomorrow** lo terminaré *or* voy a terminar mañana; **I will have finished it by tomorrow** lo habré terminado para mañana; **will you do it? – yes I will/no I won't** ¿lo harás? – sí/no
2 (*in conjectures, predictions*): **he will** *or* **he'll be there by now** ya habrá *or* debe (de) haber llegado; **that will be the postman** será *or* debe ser el cartero
3 (*in commands, requests, offers*): **will you be quiet!** ¿quieres callarte?; **will you help me?** ¿quieres ayudarme?; **will you have a cup of tea?** ¿te apetece un té?; **I won't put up with it!** ¡no lo soporto!
▷ *vt* (*pt, pp* **willed**): **to will sb to do sth** desear que algn haga algo; **he willed himself to go on** con gran fuerza de voluntad, continuó

▷*n* voluntad *f*; (*testament*) testamento

willing ['wɪlɪŋ] *adj* (*with goodwill*) de buena voluntad; (*enthusiastic*) entusiasta; **he's ~ to do it** está dispuesto a hacerlo; **willingly** *adv* con mucho gusto
willow ['wɪləu] *n* sauce *m*
willpower ['wɪlpauə*] *n* fuerza de voluntad
wilt [wɪlt] *vi* marchitarse
win [wɪn] (*pt, pp* **won**) *n* victoria, triunfo ▷*vt* ganar; (*obtain*) conseguir, lograr ▷*vi* ganar; **win over** *vt* convencer a
wince [wɪns] *vi* encogerse
wind[1] [wɪnd] *n* viento; (*Med*) gases *mpl* ▷*vt* (*take breath away from*) dejar sin aliento a
wind[2] [waɪnd] (*pt, pp* **wound**) *vt* enrollar; (*wrap*) envolver; (*clock, toy*) dar cuerda a ▷*vi* (*road, river*) serpentear; **wind down** *vt* (*car window*) bajar; (*fig: production, business*) disminuir; **wind up** *vt* (*clock*) dar cuerda a; (*debate, meeting*) concluir, terminar
windfall ['wɪndfɔːl] *n* golpe *m* de suerte
winding ['waɪndɪŋ] *adj* (*road*) tortuoso; (*staircase*) de caracol
windmill ['wɪndmɪl] *n* molino de viento
window ['wɪndəu] *n* ventana; (*in car, train*) ventanilla; (*in shop etc*) escaparate *m* (SP), vidriera (LAM); **window box** *n* jardinera de ventana; **window cleaner** *n* (*person*) limpiacristales *mf inv*; **window pane** *n* cristal *m*; **window seat** *n* asiento junto a la ventana; **windowsill** *n* alféizar *m*, repisa
windscreen ['wɪndskriːn] (US **windshield**) *n* parabrisas *m inv*; **windscreen wiper** (US **windshield wiper**) *n* limpiaparabrisas *m inv*
windsurfing ['wɪndsəːfɪŋ] *n* windsurf *m*
windy ['wɪndɪ] *adj* de mucho viento; **it's ~** hace viento
wine [waɪn] *n* vino; **wine bar** *n* enoteca; **wine glass** *n* copa (para vino); **wine list** *n* lista de vinos; **wine tasting** *n* degustación *f* de vinos
wing [wɪŋ] *n* ala; (*Aut*) aleta; **wing mirror** *n* (espejo) retrovisor *m*
wink [wɪŋk] *n* guiño, pestañeo ▷*vi* guiñar, pestañear
winner ['wɪnə*] *n* ganador(a) *m/f*
winning ['wɪnɪŋ] *adj* (*team*) ganador(a); (*goal*) decisivo; (*smile*) encantador(a)
winter ['wɪntə*] *n* invierno ▷*vi* invernar; **winter sports** *npl* deportes *mpl* de invierno; **wintertime** *n* invierno
wipe [waɪp] *n*: **to give sth a ~** pasar un trapo sobre algo ▷*vt* limpiar; (*tape*) borrar; **wipe out** *vt* (*debt*) liquidar; (*memory*) borrar; (*destroy*) destruir; **wipe up** *vt* limpiar
wire ['waɪə*] *n* alambre *m*; (*Elec*) cable *m* (eléctrico); (*Tel*) telegrama *m* ▷*vt* (*house*) poner la instalación eléctrica en; (*also*: **~ up**) conectar; (*person: telegram*) telegrafiar
wiring ['waɪərɪŋ] *n* instalación *f* eléctrica
wisdom ['wɪzdəm] *n* sabiduría, saber *m*; (*good sense*) cordura; **wisdom tooth** *n* muela del juicio
wise [waɪz] *adj* sabio; (*sensible*) juicioso
wish [wɪʃ] *n* deseo ▷*vt* querer; **best ~es** (*on birthday etc*) felicidades *fpl*; **with best ~es** (*in letter*) saludos *mpl*, recuerdos *mpl*; **to ~ sb goodbye** despedirse de algn; **he ~ed me well** me deseó mucha suerte; **to ~ to do/sb to do sth** querer hacer/que algn haga algo; **to ~ for** desear
wistful ['wɪstful] *adj* pensativo
wit [wɪt] *n* ingenio, gracia; (*also*: **~s**) inteligencia; (*person*) chistoso/a
witch [wɪtʃ] *n* bruja

KEYWORD

with [wɪð, wɪθ] *prep* **1** (*accompanying, in the company of*) con (*con +mí, ti, sí =*

conmigo, contigo, consigo); **I was with him** estaba con él; **we stayed with friends** nos quedamos en casa de unos amigos; **I'm (not) with you** (*don't understand*) (no) te entiendo; **to be with it** (*inf*: *person*: *up-to-date*) estar al tanto; (: *alert*) ser despabilado
2 (*descriptive, indicating manner etc*) con; de; **a room with a view** una habitación con vistas; **the man with the grey hat/blue eyes** el hombre del sombrero gris/de los ojos azules; **red with anger** rojo de ira; **to shake with fear** temblar de miedo; **to fill sth with water** llenar algo de agua

withdraw [wɪθ'drɔː] *vt* retirar, sacar ▷ *vi* retirarse; **to ~ money (from the bank)** retirar fondos (del banco); **withdrawal** *n* retirada; (*of money*) reintegro; **withdrawn** *pp of* **withdraw** ▷ *adj* (*person*) reservado, introvertido
withdrew [wɪθ'druː] *pt of* **withdraw**
wither ['wɪðə*] *vi* marchitarse
withhold [wɪθ'həuld] *vt* (*money*) retener; (*decision*) aplazar; (*permission*) negar; (*information*) ocultar
within [wɪð'ɪn] *prep* dentro de ▷ *adv* dentro; **~ reach (of)** al alcance (de); **~ sight (of)** a la vista (de); **~ the week** antes de acabar la semana; **~ a mile (of)** a menos de una milla (de)
without [wɪð'aut] *prep* sin; **to go ~ sth** pasar sin algo
withstand [wɪθ'stænd] *vt* resistir a
witness ['wɪtnɪs] *n* testigo *mf* ▷ *vt* (*event*) presenciar; (*document*) atestiguar la veracidad de; **to bear ~ to** (*fig*) ser testimonio de
witty ['wɪtɪ] *adj* ingenioso
wives [waɪvz] *npl of* **wife**
wizard ['wɪzəd] *n* hechicero
wk *abbr* = **week**
wobble ['wɔbl] *vi* temblar; (*chair*) cojear
woe [wəu] *n* desgracia
woke [wəuk] *pt of* **wake**
woken ['wəukən] *pp of* **wake**
wolf [wulf] *n* lobo
woman ['wumən] (*pl* **women**) *n* mujer *f*
womb [wuːm] *n* matriz *f*, útero
women ['wɪmɪn] *npl of* **woman**
won [wʌn] *pt, pp of* **win**
wonder ['wʌndə*] *n* maravilla, prodigio; (*feeling*) asombro ▷ *vi*: **to ~ whether/why** preguntarse si/por qué; **to ~ at** asombrarse de; **to ~ about** pensar sobre *or* en; **it's no ~ (that)** no es de extrañarse (que *+subjun*); **wonderful** *adj* maravilloso
won't [wəunt] = **will not**
wood [wud] *n* (*timber*) madera; (*forest*) bosque *m*; **wooden** *adj* de madera; (*fig*) inexpresivo; **woodwind** *n* (*Mus*) instrumentos *mpl* de viento de madera; **woodwork** *n* carpintería
wool [wul] *n* lana; **to pull the ~ over sb's eyes** (*fig*) engatusar a algn; **woollen** (US **woolen**) *adj* de lana; **woolly** (US **wooly**) *adj* lanudo, de lana; (*fig*: *ideas*) confuso
word [wəːd] *n* palabra; (*news*) noticia; (*promise*) palabra (de honor) ▷ *vt* redactar; **in other ~s** en otras palabras; **to break/keep one's ~** faltar a la palabra/cumplir la promesa; **to have ~s with sb** reñir con algn; **wording** *n* redacción *f*; **word processing** *n* proceso de textos; **word processor** *n* procesador *m* de textos
wore [wɔː*] *pt of* **wear**
work [wəːk] *n* trabajo; (*job*) empleo, trabajo; (*Art, Literature*) obra ▷ *vi* trabajar; (*mechanism*) funcionar, marchar; (*medicine*) ser eficaz, surtir efecto ▷ *vt* (*shape*) trabajar; (*stone etc*) tallar; (*mine etc*) explotar; (*machine*) manejar, hacer funcionar ▷ *npl* (*of clock, machine*) mecanismo; **to be out of ~** estar parado, no tener trabajo; **to ~ loose** (*part*) desprenderse; (*knot*) aflojarse; **works** *n* (BRIT: *factory*) fábrica; **work out** *vi* (*plans etc*) salir

bien, funcionar; **works** *vt* (*problem*) resolver; (*plan*) elaborar; **it works out at £100** suma 100 libras; **worker** *n* trabajador(a) *m/f*, obrero/a; **work experience** *n*: **I'm going to do my work experience in a factory** voy a hacer las prácticas en una fábrica; **workforce** *n* mano de obra; **working class** *n* clase *f* obrera ▷ *adj*: **working-class** obrero; **working week** *n* semana laboral; **workman** (*irreg*) *n* obrero; **work of art** *n* obra de arte; **workout** *n* (*Sport*) sesión *f* de ejercicios; **work permit** *n* permiso de trabajo; **workplace** *n* lugar *m* de trabajo; **worksheet** *n* (*Scol*) hoja de ejercicios; **workshop** *n* taller *m*; **work station** *n* puesto *or* estación *f* de trabajo; **work surface** *n* encimera; **worktop** *n* encimera

world [wəːld] *n* mundo ▷ *cpd* (*champion*) del mundo; (*power, war*) mundial; **to think the ~ of sb** (*fig*) tener un concepto muy alto de algn; **World Cup** *n* (*Football*): **the World Cup** el Mundial, los Mundiales; **world-wide** *adj* mundial, universal; **World-Wide Web** *n*: **the World-Wide Web** el World Wide Web

worm [wəːm] *n* (*also*: **earth ~**) lombriz *f*

worn [wɔːn] *pp of* **wear** ▷ *adj* usado; **worn-out** *adj* (*object*) gastado; (*person*) rendido, agotado

worried ['wʌrɪd] *adj* preocupado

worry ['wʌrɪ] *n* preocupación *f* ▷ *vt* preocupar, inquietar ▷ *vi* preocuparse; **worrying** *adj* inquietante

worse [wəːs] *adj, adv* peor ▷ *n* lo peor; **a change for the ~** un empeoramiento; **worsen** *vt, vi* empeorar; **worse off** *adj* (*financially*): **to be worse off** tener menos dinero; (*fig*): **you'll be worse off this way** de esta forma estarás peor que nunca

worship ['wəːʃɪp] *n* adoración *f* ▷ *vt* adorar; **Your W~** (BRIT: *to mayor*) señor alcalde; (: *to judge*) señor juez

worst [wəːst] *adj, adv* peor ▷ *n* lo peor; **at ~** en lo peor de los casos

worth [wəːθ] *n* valor *m* ▷ *adj*: **to be ~** valer; **it's ~ it** vale *or* merece la pena; **to be ~ one's while (to do)** merecer la pena (hacer); **worthless** *adj* sin valor; (*useless*) inútil; **worthwhile** *adj* (*activity*) que merece la pena; (*cause*) loable

worthy ['wəːðɪ] *adj* respetable; (*motive*) honesto; **~ of** digno de

KEYWORD

would [wud] *aux vb* **1** (*conditional tense*): **if you asked him he would do it** si se lo pidieras, lo haría; **if you had asked him he would have done it** si se lo hubieras pedido, lo habría *or* hubiera hecho

2 (*in offers, invitations, requests*): **would you like a biscuit?** ¿quieres una galleta?; (*formal*) ¿querría una galleta?; **would you ask him to come in?** ¿quiere hacerle pasar?; **would you open the window please?** ¿quiere *or* podría abrir la ventana, por favor?

3 (*in indirect speech*): **I said I would do it** dije que lo haría

4 (*emphatic*): **it WOULD have to snow today!** ¡tenía que nevar precisamente hoy!

5 (*insistence*): **she wouldn't behave** no quiso comportarse bien

6 (*conjecture*): **it would have been midnight** sería medianoche; **it would seem so** parece ser que sí

7 (*indicating habit*): **he would go there on Mondays** iba allí los lunes

wouldn't ['wudnt] = **would not**

wound[1] [wuːnd] *n* herida ▷ *vt* herir

wound[2] [waund] *pt, pp of* **wind**[2]

wove [wəuv] *pt of* **weave**

woven ['wəuvən] *pp of* **weave**

wrap [ræp] *vt* (*also*: **~ up**) envolver; (*gift*) envolver, abrigar ▷ *vi* (*dress* *warmly*) abrigarse; **wrapper** *n* (*on chocolate*) papel *m*; (BRIT: *of book*) sobrecubierta; **wrapping** *n* envoltura, envase *m*; **wrapping paper** *n* papel *m* de envolver; (*fancy*) papel *m* de regalo

wreath [ri:ð, *pl* ri:ðz] *n* (*funeral wreath*) corona

wreck [rɛk] *n* (*ship: destruction*) naufragio; (*: remains*) restos *mpl* del barco; (*pej: person*) ruina ▷ *vt* (*car etc*) destrozar; (*chances*) arruinar; **wreckage** *n* restos *mpl*; (*of building*) escombros *mpl*

wren [rɛn] *n* (*Zool*) reyezuelo

wrench [rɛntʃ] *n* (*Tech*) llave *f* inglesa; (*tug*) tirón *m*; (*fig*) dolor *m* ▷ *vt* arrancar; **to ~ sth from sb** arrebatar algo violentamente a algn

wrestle ['rɛsl] *vi*: **to ~ (with sb)** luchar (con *or* contra algn); **wrestler** *n* luchador(a) *m/f* (de lucha libre); **wrestling** *n* lucha libre

wretched ['rɛtʃɪd] *adj* miserable

wriggle ['rɪgl] *vi* (*also*: **~ about**) menearse, retorcerse

wring [rɪŋ] (*pt, pp* **wrung**) *vt* retorcer; (*wet clothes*) escurrir; (*fig*): **to ~ sth out of sb** sacar algo por la fuerza a algn

wrinkle ['rɪŋkl] *n* arruga ▷ *vt* arrugar ▷ *vi* arrugarse

wrist [rɪst] *n* muñeca

writable ['raɪtəbl] *adj* (*CD, DVD*) escribible

write [raɪt] (*pt* **wrote**, *pp* **written**) *vt* escribir; (*cheque*) extender ▷ *vi* escribir; **write down** *vt* escribir; (*note*) apuntar; **write off** *vt* (*debt*) borrar (como incobrable); (*fig*) desechar por inútil; **write out** *vt* escribir; **write-off** *n* siniestro total; **writer** *n* escritor(a) *m/f*

writing ['raɪtɪŋ] *n* escritura; (*hand-writing*) letra; (*of author*) obras *fpl*; **in ~** por escrito; **writing paper** *n* papel *m* de escribir

written ['rɪtn] *pp of* **write**

wrong [rɔŋ] *adj* (*wicked*) malo; (*unfair*) injusto; (*incorrect*) equivocado, incorrecto; (*not suitable*) inoportuno, inconveniente; (*reverse*) del revés ▷ *adv* equivocadamente ▷ *n* injusticia ▷ *vt* ser injusto con; **you are ~ to do it** haces mal en hacerlo; **you are ~ about that, you've got it ~** en eso estás equivocado; **to be in the ~** no tener razón, tener la culpa; **what's ~?** ¿qué pasa?; **to go ~** (*person*) equivocarse; (*plan*) salir mal; (*machine*) estropearse; **wrongly** *adv* mal, incorrectamente; (*by mistake*) por error; **wrong number** *n* (*Tel*): **you've got the wrong number** se ha equivocado de número

wrote [rəut] *pt of* **write**

wrung [rʌŋ] *pt, pp of* **wring**

WWW *n abbr* (= *World Wide Web*) WWW *m*

XL *abbr* = **extra large**
Xmas ['ɛksməs] *n abbr* = **Christmas**
X-ray ['ɛksreɪ] *n* radiografía ▷ *vt* radiografiar, sacar radiografías de
xylophone ['zaɪləfəun] *n* xilófono

yacht [jɔt] *n* yate *m*; **yachting** *n* (*sport*) balandrismo
yard [jɑːd] *n* patio; (*measure*) yarda; **yard sale** (US) *n* venta de objetos usados (*en el jardín de una casa particular*)
yarn [jɑːn] *n* hilo; (*tale*) cuento, historia
yawn [jɔːn] *n* bostezo ▷ *vi* bostezar
yd. *abbr* (= *yard*) yda
yeah [jɛə] (*inf*) *adv* sí
year [jɪə*] *n* año; **to be 8 ~s old** tener 8 años; **an eight-~-old child** un niño de ocho años (de edad); **yearly** *adj* anual ▷ *adv* anualmente, cada año
yearn [jəːn] *vi*: **to ~ for sth** añorar algo, suspirar por algo
yeast [jiːst] *n* levadura
yell [jɛl] *n* grito, alarido ▷ *vi* gritar
yellow ['jɛləu] *adj* amarillo; **Yellow Pages®** *npl* páginas *fpl* amarillas
yes [jɛs] *adv* sí ▷ *n* sí *m*; **to say/answer ~** decir/contestar que sí
yesterday ['jɛstədɪ] *adv* ayer ▷ *n* ayer *m*; **~ morning/evening** ayer por la mañana/tarde; **all day ~** todo el

día de ayer

yet [jɛt] *adv* ya; (*negative*) todavía ▷ *conj* sin embargo, a pesar de todo; **it is not finished ~** todavía no está acabado; **the best ~** el/la mejor hasta ahora; **as ~** hasta ahora, todavía

yew [juː] *n* tejo

Yiddish ['jɪdɪʃ] *n* yiddish *m*

yield [jiːld] *n* (*Agr*) cosecha; (*Comm*) rendimiento ▷ *vt* ceder; (*results*) producir, dar; (*profit*) rendir ▷ *vi* rendirse, ceder; (*US Aut*) ceder el paso

yob(bo) ['jɔb(bəu)] *n* (*BRIT inf*) gamberro

yoga ['jəugə] *n* yoga *m*

yog(h)ourt ['jəugət] *n* yogur *m*

yog(h)urt ['jəugət] *n* = **yog(h)ourt**

yolk [jəuk] *n* yema (de huevo)

KEYWORD

you [juː] *pron* **1** (*subject: familiar*) tú; (*pl*) vosotros/as (*SP*), ustedes (*LAM*); (*polite*) usted; (*pl*) ustedes; **you are very kind** eres/es *etc* muy amable; **you Spanish enjoy your food** a vosotros (*or* ustedes) los españoles os (*or* les) gusta la comida; **you and I will go** iremos tú y yo

2 (*object: direct: familiar*) te; (*pl*) os (*SP*), les (*LAM*); (*polite*) le; (*pl*) les; (*f*) la; (*pl*) las; **I know you** te/le etc conozco

3 (*object: indirect: familiar*) te; (*pl*) os (*SP*), les (*LAM*); (*polite*) le; (*pl*) les; **I gave the letter to you yesterday** te/os *etc* di la carta ayer

4 (*stressed*): **I told YOU to do it** te dije a ti que lo hicieras, es a ti a quien dije que lo hicieras; *see also* **3; 5**

5 (*after prep: NB: con +ti = contigo: familiar*) ti; (*pl*) vosotros/as (*SP*), ustedes (*LAM*); (*: polite*) usted; (*pl*) ustedes; **it's for you** es para ti/vosotros *etc*

6 (*comparisons: familiar*) tú; (*pl*) vosotros/as (*SP*), ustedes (*LAM*); (*: polite*) usted; (*pl*) ustedes; **she's younger than you** es más joven que tú/vosotros etc

7 (*impersonal one*): **fresh air does you good** el aire puro (te) hace bien; **you never know** nunca se sabe; **you can't do that!** ¡eso no se hace!

you'd [juːd] = **you had; you would**

you'll [juːl] = **you will; you shall**

young [jʌŋ] *adj* joven ▷ *npl* (*of animal*) cría; (*people*): **the ~** los jóvenes, la juventud; **youngster** *n* joven *mf*

your [jɔː*] *adj* tu; (*pl*) vuestro; (*formal*) su; *see also* **my**

you're [juə*] = **you are**

yours [jɔːz] *pron* tuyo (*pl*), vuestro; (*formal*) suyo; *see also* **faithfully; mine**[1] *see also* **sincerely**

yourself [jɔː'sɛlf] *pron* tú mismo; (*complement*) te; (*after prep*) tí (mismo); (*formal*) usted mismo; (*: complement*) se; (*: after prep*) sí (mismo); **yourselves** *pl pron* vosotros mismos; (*after prep*) vosotros (mismos); (*formal*) ustedes (mismos); (*: complement*) se; (*: after prep*) sí mismos; *see also* **oneself**

youth [*pl* juːðz *n* juventud *f*; (*young man*) joven *m*; **youth club** *n* club *m* juvenil; **youthful** *adj* juvenil; **youth hostel** *n* albergue *m* de juventud

you've [juːv] = **you have**

Z

zeal [zi:l] *n* celo, entusiasmo
zebra ['zi:brə] *n* cebra; **zebra crossing** (BRIT) *n* paso de peatones
zero ['zɪərəu] *n* cero
zest [zɛst] *n* ánimo, vivacidad *f*; (*of orange*) piel *f*
zigzag ['zɪgzæg] *n* zigzag *m* ▷ *vi* zigzaguear, hacer eses
Zimbabwe [zɪm'bɑ:bwɪ] *n* Zimbabwe *m*
zinc [zɪŋk] *n* cinc *m*, zinc *m*
zip [zip] *n* (*also*: **~ fastener,** (US) **~per**) cremallera (SP), cierre (AM) *m*, zíper *m* (MEX, CAM) ▷ *vt* (*also*: **~ up**) cerrar la cremallera de; (*file*) comprimir; **zip code** (US) *n* código postal; **zip file** *n* (*Comput*) archivo comprimido; **zipper** (US) *n* cremallera
zit [zɪt] *n* grano
zodiac ['zəudɪæk] *n* zodíaco
zone [zəun] *n* zona
zoo [zu:] *n* (jardín *m*) zoo *m*
zoology [zu'ɔlədʒɪ] *n* zoología
zoom [zu:m] *vi*: **to ~ past** pasar zumbando; **zoom lens** *n* zoom *m*
zucchini [zu:'ki:nɪ] (US) *n(pl)* calabacín(ines) *m(pl)*